West Academic Publishing's Emeritus Advisory Board

WILLS, TRUSTS AND ESTATES

INCLUDING TAXATION AND FUTURE INTERESTS

Sixth Edition

Sheldon F. Kurtz
David H. Vernon Professor of Law
University of Iowa

David M. English
William Franklin Fratcher Professor of Law
University of Missouri

Thomas P. Gallanis
Allan D. Vestal Chair in Law
University of Iowa

HORNBOOK SERIES®

WEST ACADEMIC PUBLISHING

The publisher is not engaged in rendering legal or other professional advice, and this publication is not a substitute for the advice of an attorney. If you require legal or other expert advice, you should seek the services of a competent attorney or other professional.

444 Cedar Street, Suite 700
St. Paul, MN 55101
1-877-888-1330

Printed in the United States of America

ISBN: 978-1-64708-800-2

Preface

In most law schools today, the formerly separate courses in Wills, Trusts, and Future Interests have been integrated into a single offering. This book reflects this trend. It covers the same ground (roughly) as Atkinson on Wills, Bogert on Trusts, and Simes on Future Interests. It also introduces students to federal transfer taxes. We think there are clear advantages in a unified treatment of these subjects.

Much of the law of wills is statutory, and this is increasingly true of the law of trusts. We emphasize the Uniform Probate Code and the Uniform Trust Code, even though neither has been adopted as widely as the Uniform Commercial Code. We think in most instances these Codes represent the "better view." They have influenced or will influence legislation in many states which have not adopted either completely. However, persons using this book should make sure that the governing law in their respective jurisdictions conforms to the statements in this book.

Many law school courses in trusts and estates and related casebooks cover the various federal tax laws that affect wealth dispositions. Thus, it is appropriate that this edition continue to introduce students to the federal gift, estate, and generation skipping transfer tax laws and grantor trust rules affecting the wealth disposition process (see Chapter 15). In addition, we discuss three other topics which are prominent in the minds of many clients—planning for incapacity, end-of-life care, and anatomical gifts (see Chapter 9). Furthermore, with the increasing use of trusts for the purpose of passing property at death, we devote considerable attention to matters of trust administration (see Chapter 14).

Changes in the Law

The law of estates and trusts is more stable than some other areas of law. Some states still impose the formal requirements for wills which were prescribed by the Wills Act of 1837. In others, statutes based on the Statute of Frauds of 1677 lay down the formal requirements for both wills and trusts.

Nevertheless, the law of trusts and estates has undergone numerous changes in recent years. The popularity of will substitutes, including revocable trusts, has affected the law of wills. Former doubts about whether these devices were valid have disappeared (see Chapter 4), and many states allow surviving spouses and creditors to reach assets transferred outside of probate (see Chapters 8 and 13). The difference between the tax treatment of gifts and transfers at death has been minimized (see Chapter 15).

The conception of who is a child worthy of inheritance has changed markedly. The definition was once limited to children conceived by coitus and born to a married couple. At common law, children born out of wedlock (then called illegitimate children but today more appropriately called nonmarital children) were not entitled to inherit. Today, that is no longer the case (see Section 2.9). Similarly, at common law, adopted children could not inherit from adopting parents; today that is no longer true (see Section 2.10). And increasingly the law has had to confront the rights of blended families and of children born as the result of assisted reproductive technologies, including children conceived posthumously, in order to resolve the question of whether inheritance rights follow biology or nurturing (see Section 2.11).

In 2015, the United States Supreme Court held in *Obergefell v. Hodges* that same-sex couples enjoy a constitutional right to marry, making same-sex marriage legal in every state. Thus, rules applicable to spouses apply whether the spouses are in an opposite-sex or same-sex marriage (see Section 2.12). Parties to an invalid marriage and cohabitants who never participated in a marriage ceremony may today be treated as "spouses" for some purposes.

The differences between separate- and community-property states with respect to tax treatment and property division at divorce have been reduced (see Section 8.8). Significant differences still exist between the elective share in separate property states and the spouse's rights in community property, but the Uniform Probate Code's elective share is modeled on community property concepts (see Section 8.7) Agreements limiting the claims of spouses are becoming common with the increasing incidence of multiple marriages (see Section 8.9).

Many states have reduced the formal requirements for wills. The Uniform Probate Code allows holographic wills and interested witnesses and allows witnesses to sign the will outside of the testator's presence (see Sections 3.1–3.4). Doubts about the validity of pour-over wills have disappeared (see Section 7.2). The old rule that wills cannot be reformed for mistake is increasingly ignored or discarded (see Section 7.1). Many states have permitted a testator's informally expressed wishes to be effectuated by making the drafting attorney liable to the intended beneficiary, despite the "lack of privity" between them (see Section 7.1).

Probate avoidance has affected the law governing estate administration (see Chapter 13). The Uniform Probate Code reflects a widely shared view that the costs of court supervision of personal representatives and trustees outweigh the benefits. In order to expedite the settlement of estates, most states have reduced the period allowed for will contests and for filing claims against estates (see Sections 13.3–13.5). However, simplification of administration, if carried too far, may run afoul of the requirement of due process. The United States Supreme Court held unconstitutional a nonclaim statute which cut off claims of creditors after notice by publication only.

With regard to trust investments, legal lists were long ago replaced by the "prudent person" (or "prudent man") rule, which has in turn been replaced by the "prudent investor" rule. This trend has been extended in many states to other fiduciaries, such as executors and conservators. Commentators have questioned the traditional practice of scrutinizing individual investments, saying that courts should instead examine the performance of the portfolio as a whole. This view is adopted both by the Third Restatement of Trusts and the Uniform Prudent Investor Act (see Section 14.2).

Changes in some of the rules governing principal and income appear in the Uniform Fiduciary Income and Principal Act (see Section 10.6). These rules have become somewhat less important because trusts today increasingly grant the trustee discretion over distributions, whether of principal or income. This has given added importance to rules governing trustees' discretionary decisions. One aspect of this question relates to the eligibility of beneficiaries of discretionary trusts for governmental welfare benefits. Many trusts allow the trustee to accumulate income. Statutory restrictions on accumulations have largely vanished, but their tax advantages have been largely eliminated.

The tax on generation skipping transfers (see Section 15.5) has reduced the estate tax advantages of bypass trusts in large estates. However, the commonest form of trust—one for the life of the settlor's spouse—continues to have tax and other advantages. Despite improvements in the law of guardianship, a trust is usually the best way to manage property for persons who are incompetent to handle it. However, custodianships under the Uniform Transfers to Minors Act and durable powers of attorney have become popular substitutes for the trust in some situations (see Section 9.3).

Spendthrift trusts continue to arouse controversy, although their practical importance is less significant than pension plans because of the large number of people who participate in the latter and because pension plans enjoy protection against creditors under the federal ERISA statute.

The frequent complaint that the Attorney General's supervision of charities is inadequate may have made courts more liberal in conferring standing on private persons to sue trustees for breach of trust. On the other hand, some have urged an expanded use of *cy pres* to remove restrictions imposed by settlors in charitable trusts. Constitutional law, public opinion, and the Internal Revenue Code have done more than trust law to eliminate racially discriminatory terms (see Section 10.10).

Reform of the Rule Against Perpetuities has received much attention in the law reviews and state legislatures, even though litigated cases on the subject are rare. Sophisticated practitioners generally avoid the Rule by a saving clause. The widely adopted Uniform Statutory Rule Against Perpetuities produces in most instances the same result for less competent drafters (see Section 12.4).

The law's traditional preference for early vesting of future interests has been questioned by modern commentators. Sophisticated drafters usually postpone vesting and state expressly that "heirs" should be determined as of the date when their interest becomes possessory. Because most future interests today involve trusts where the trustee has a power of sale, postponement of vesting does not impede alienability. Thus, the Uniform Probate Code makes this the preferred construction. This may make it harder to get the consent of all the beneficiaries to modify a trust, though some states have sought to address this problem by the use of guardians ad litem. The *Claflin* rule continues to predominate in American law, but some authorities have questioned the traditional assumption that a spendthrift provision in a trust shows a purpose which would be frustrated by early termination (see Section 10.9). Sophisticated drafters continue to urge the use of powers of appointment to provide flexibility in trusts, but their effect on tax objectives and creditors must be considered by a careful drafter (see Section 11.5).

Often a testator's circumstances change after the will is executed. Most states now provide that a divorce revokes any devises to the testator's former spouse (see Section 4.4). Antilapse statutes deal with devisees who predecease the testator (see Section 6.5). These statutes traditionally have not applied to will substitutes, but the Uniform Probate Code changes this rule, and also gives a decedent's creditors and spouse rights against nonprobate assets (see Sections 8.7, 13.6). It also rejects the traditional rule (still retained in some states) that the compensation of the personal representative and attorney for an estate should be determined by the size of the probate estate (see Section 14.7). Ademption of specific devises where the devised property is not in the estate when the testator dies is reduced under the Uniform Probate Code, which on this point also has been followed by many states (see Section 6.2).

Choice-of-law problems arise when the law changes. Does the new rule apply to a will previously executed? To a testator already dead? The traditional reluctance to make changes "retroactive" has been questioned, particularly when the old rule is thought to have frustrated the testator's probable intent (see Section 1.3). Choice-of-law problems also arise when two or more states (or foreign countries) are involved in an estate or trust. A tendency to make domicile more important than situs in determining the governing law is noticeable in the Uniform Probate Code, which also seeks to reduce the traditional difficulties of probate and administration in several jurisdictions (see Sections 1.2, 13.1).

Professor John Langbein has described what he calls a "revolution in family wealth transmission." Because of the importance of "human capital" in today's technological society, middle-class parents now devote a large proportion of their resources to their children's education. Much of the rest goes into pension plans which usually take the form of annuities which expire when the parents die. As a result, transfer of wealth on death is no longer the dominant mode of wealth transmission of the middle classes. Nevertheless, wealth transmission at death continues to be an important subject, worthy of a lawyer's attention. Despite the popularity of will substitutes, most persons with substantial wealth want wills and hire lawyers to draft them. Indeed, the only contact which many persons have with the legal system arises from the devolution of property at death.

Many wills and trusts are never scrutinized by a court except for a cursory examination at probate. This book emphasizes the lawyer's role as drafter or "estate planner." All the chapters suggest ways to avoid problems that otherwise might lead to litigation.

In this edition, the authors have cited appropriate cases decided since the last edition, as well as updated references to the relevant Restatements. The authors also have incorporated all of the relevant uniform acts, including the Uniform Electronic Wills Act, the Uniform Directed Trust Act, the Uniform Trust Decanting Act, the Uniform Fiduciary Income and Principal Act, the Revised Uniform Fiduciary Access to Digital Assets Act, the 2017 Uniform Parentage Act, and the 2019 amendments to the Uniform Probate Code.

Professor McGovern, who died in 2018, was an Adviser to the Third Restatement of Trusts and the Third Restatement of Property (Wills and Other Donative Transfers). Professors Kurtz, English, and Gallanis are deeply indebted to him as the "founding father" of this book. Professor Kurtz is a member emeritus of the Joint Editorial Board for Uniform Trusts and Estates Acts (JEB-UTEA) and the author of numerous works in the area of property law. Professor English, who was the Executive Director of the JEB-UTEA until 2013, was the Reporter for the Uniform Trust Code. Professor Gallanis has been since 2013 the Executive Director of the JEB-UTEA and served as Associate Reporter for the Third Restatement of Trusts. Professors Kurtz, English, and Gallanis have served on multiple drafting committees of the Uniform Law Commission in the preparation of uniform statutes affecting the areas of Trusts and Estates. These associations have immeasurably helped them in writing this book.

The authors wish to thank a cadre of research assistants who helped them in the preparation of this edition. Professor Kurtz would like to give a "shout out" to his talented and resourceful research assistants who worked closely with him from this book's inception. He'd also like to give special mention and express profound appreciation to his administrative assistant, Melanie Stutzman. Professor Gallanis would like to express his deep appreciation to his research assistants for academic year 2020–21: Florence Neale, Miles Patton, and Emily Tosoni. Professor English is grateful for the help given by his research assistants in preparing summaries of cases decided under the Uniform Trust Code, much of which has found its way into the book.

SHELDON F. KURTZ
DAVID M. ENGLISH
THOMAS P. GALLANIS

May 2021

Summary of Contents

Page

PREFACE III

CHAPTER 1. TERMINOLOGY AND CHOICE OF LAW 1

CHAPTER 2. INTESTATE SUCCESSION 53

CHAPTER 3. FORMALITIES 127

CHAPTER 4. REVOCATION, GIFTS, AND WILL SUBSTITUTES 189

CHAPTER 5. INCAPACITY AND UNDUE INFLUENCE 219

CHAPTER 6. ADEMPTION, ABATEMENT, AND LAPSE 247

CHAPTER 7. EXTRINSIC EVIDENCE 279

CHAPTER 8. LIMITS ON TESTAMENTARY POWER 315

CHAPTER 9. PLANNING FOR INCAPACITY 381

CHAPTER 10. TRUSTS 401

CHAPTER 11. FUTURE INTERESTS 481

CHAPTER 12. THE RULE AGAINST PERPETUITIES 519

CHAPTER 13. PROBATE ISSUES 565

CHAPTER 14. FIDUCIARY DUTIES AND ADMINISTRATION 597

CHAPTER 15. OVERVIEW OF THE FEDERAL TAX LAWS RELATING TO ESTATES AND TRUSTS 687

TABLE OF CASES 751

TABLE OF UNIFORM PROBATE CODE SECTIONS 789

TABLE OF UNIFORM TRUST CODE SECTIONS 793

TABLE OF RESTATEMENT REFERENCES 797

INDEX 819

Table of Contents

Page

PREFACE III

CHAPTER 1. TERMINOLOGY AND CHOICE OF LAW 1
§ 1.1 Terminology 1
§ 1.2 Conflict of Laws 30
§ 1.3 Change in the Law 42

CHAPTER 2. INTESTATE SUCCESSION 53
§ 2.1 The Surviving Spouse's Share 53
§ 2.2 Relatives 57
§ 2.3 General Aspects of Intestacy; Statutory Wills 68
§ 2.4 Gifts to "Heirs" 71
§ 2.5 Recovery for Wrongful Death 74
§ 2.6 Advancements 78
§ 2.7 Homicide 83
§ 2.8 Disclaimers 92
§ 2.9 Nonmarital Children 101
§ 2.10 Adoption and De Facto Parentage 105
§ 2.11 ART Children 113
§ 2.12 Spouses 117

CHAPTER 3. FORMALITIES 127
§ 3.1 History and Policy 127
§ 3.2 Signature 133
§ 3.3 Witnesses 136
§ 3.4 Holographic and Oral Wills 145
§ 3.5 Formalities for Gifts 150
§ 3.6 Trusts 162
§ 3.7 Payable-on-Death Contracts 172
§ 3.8 Joint Tenancy 174
§ 3.9 Contracts to Make Wills 179

CHAPTER 4. REVOCATION, GIFTS, AND WILL SUBSTITUTES 189
§ 4.1 Subsequent Instrument 189
§ 4.2 Physical Act 192
§ 4.3 Revival and Dependent Relative Revocation 199
§ 4.4 Divorce 202
§ 4.5 Gifts and Will Substitutes 204

CHAPTER 5. INCAPACITY AND UNDUE INFLUENCE 219
§ 5.1 Incapacity 219
§ 5.2 Conservatorship and Durable Powers of Attorney 224
§ 5.3 Undue Influence 231
§ 5.4 Role of Lawyers 238

CHAPTER 6. ADEMPTION, ABATEMENT, AND LAPSE 247
§ 6.1 Classification of Devises 247
§ 6.2 Ademption 248
§ 6.3 Increases 257
§ 6.4 Abatement 258
§ 6.5 Lapse 263

CHAPTER 7. EXTRINSIC EVIDENCE 279
§ 7.1 Wills: Mistake and Ambiguity 279
§ 7.2 Integration, Incorporation by Reference, Facts of Independent Significance, and Pour-Over Wills 292
§ 7.3 Will Substitutes 299
§ 7.4 Deeds of Land: Reformation, Constructive and Resulting Trusts 303

CHAPTER 8. LIMITS ON TESTAMENTARY POWER 315
§ 8.1 Policy Considerations 315
§ 8.2 History and Comparative Law 322
§ 8.3 Survival of Claims for Support 327
§ 8.4 Family Allowance and Homestead 330
§ 8.5 Pretermitted Heirs 335
§ 8.6 Omitted Spouse 340
§ 8.7 Elective Share 343
§ 8.8 Community Property 354
§ 8.9 Waivers 367
§ 8.10 Negative Limitations 374

CHAPTER 9. PLANNING FOR INCAPACITY 381
§ 9.1 Introduction 381
§ 9.2 Guardianship 382
§ 9.3 The Durable Power of Attorney 386
§ 9.4 End-of-Life Decision Making 390
§ 9.5 Advance Health-Care Directives 395
§ 9.6 Family Consent Laws 397
§ 9.7 Anatomical Gifts 398

CHAPTER 10. TRUSTS 401
§ 10.1 Introduction 401
§ 10.2 The Uniform Trust Code 403
§ 10.3 Creation of Trusts 406
§ 10.4 The Revocable Trust 413
§ 10.5 Revocable Trust Alternatives 421
§ 10.6 Principal and Income 427
§ 10.7 Discretionary Trusts 433
§ 10.8 Spendthrift Provisions and Creditor Claims 443
§ 10.9 Modification and Termination of Trusts 454
§ 10.10 Charitable Trusts 467

CHAPTER 11. FUTURE INTERESTS 481
§ 11.1 Conditions of Survival 481

§ 11.2 Rule of Convenience 493
§ 11.3 Gifts to Heirs 497
§ 11.4 Continuing Effect of Old Rules 499
§ 11.5 Powers of Appointment 504

CHAPTER 12. THE RULE AGAINST PERPETUITIES 519
§ 12.1 History and Policy of the Rule 519
§ 12.2 Operation of the Rule 527
§ 12.3 Planning to Avoid the Rule 535
§ 12.4 Modern Reforms 538
§ 12.5 Powers and the Rule 544
§ 12.6 Gifts to Charity; Reversionary Interests 548
§ 12.7 Commercial Transactions 553
§ 12.8 Restraints on Alienation 556
§ 12.9 Accumulations 561

CHAPTER 13. PROBATE ISSUES 565
§ 13.1 Probate Process 565
§ 13.2 Necessity for Administration 570
§ 13.3 Will Contests 575
§ 13.4 Ancillary Administration 583
§ 13.5 Claims Against Estate 586
§ 13.6 Claims Against Nonprobate Assets 592

CHAPTER 14. FIDUCIARY DUTIES AND ADMINISTRATION 597
§ 14.1 Duty of Loyalty 597
§ 14.2 Investments 604
§ 14.3 Duty to Inform and Account 616
§ 14.4 Other Duties 626
§ 14.5 Administrative Powers 632
§ 14.6 Selection of Fiduciary 639
§ 14.7 Compensation 652
§ 14.8 Remedies of Beneficiaries 662
§ 14.9 Relationships with Third Parties 680

CHAPTER 15. OVERVIEW OF THE FEDERAL TAX LAWS RELATING TO ESTATES AND TRUSTS 687
§ 15.1 Introduction 687
§ 15.2 Income Taxation of Gifts and Bequests and Basis of Gifted and Inherited Property 689
§ 15.3 Gift Tax 692
§ 15.4 The Estate Tax 705
§ 15.5 Generation Skipping Transfer Tax 735
§ 15.6 Income Taxation of Estates and Trusts 742
§ 15.7 Income Taxation of Grantor Trusts 746

TABLE OF CASES 751

TABLE OF UNIFORM PROBATE CODE SECTIONS 789

TABLE OF UNIFORM TRUST CODE SECTIONS 793

TABLE OF RESTATEMENT REFERENCES 797

INDEX 819

WILLS, TRUSTS AND ESTATES

INCLUDING TAXATION AND FUTURE INTERESTS

Sixth Edition

Chapter 1

TERMINOLOGY AND CHOICE OF LAW

Analysis

Sec.

1.1 Terminology.

1.2 Conflict of Laws.

1.3 Change in the Law.

---

§ 1.1 Terminology

This section alphabetically lists terms which recur elsewhere in the book. A brief definition of the term is given with a reference to the section in the book where the term is more fully discussed.

abatement

The reduction of devises in a will in order to pay claims against the estate. The rules on abatement are discussed in Section 6.4.

ademption

The failure of a specific devise by pre-death transfer or loss of the property that is the subject matter of the devise after the will is executed, such that the property is not in the decedent's probate estate.[1] *See* Section 6.2. The word is also used for gifts made by a testator while still alive to a devisee designated in the will which are intended to replace, in whole or part, the devisee's right under the will. *See* Section 6.2 and Section 2.6 for the analogous rules for intestacy. When used in the former sense, the phrase "ademption by extinction" is sometimes used; when used in the latter sense, the phrase "ademption by satisfaction" is sometimes used.

administrator

Someone appointed to administer the estate of a decedent who either died intestate or whose will be failed effectively to designate an executor. An administrator who operates under a will is called an administrator "with will annexed." Sometimes the Latin *cum testamento annexo* (or "c.t.a") is used.[2] The rules for choosing administrators are discussed in Section 14.6. Many states

---

[1] In re Estate of Schreiber, 357 P.3d 920 (Mont. 2015).

[2] Cal.Prob.Code § 8440. Although the functions of an administrator and an executor are very similar, courts occasionally draw distinctions between them. In Gager v. Gager and Peterson, LLP, 820 A.2d 1063 (Conn.App. 2003), an administrator c.t.a who had been appointed after the designated executor resigned was held not to have a right given by a contract to the testator's "executor."

today use the phrase "personal representative" rather than administrator but this phrase is also defined to include an executor as well.[3]

advancement

An inter vivos gift made by an individual who later dies intestate that is taken into account in computing the shares of the intestate's heirs. *See* Section 2.6.

ancillary administration

Administration of assets outside the state where a decedent was domiciled at death. *See* Section 13.4.

annuity

A provision for periodic fixed payments (typically payable annually or monthly) to a person, usually for life, but sometimes for a stipulated fixed period. The trustee of a trust may be directed to pay an annuity to a person, although this is less common than a direction that the trustee pay all trust income to a person or persons or as much as the trustee deems appropriate out of the income or principal.

Annuities can also be created by a contract between a company and a person who buys an annuity, either for the benefit of the purchaser or of another. In this situation the annuity performs a function like life insurance; the company by promising to pay the agreed amount for the life of the annuitant assumes the risk that the annuitant will live so long that the aggregate annuity payments total more than the original cost of the annuity contract. Life insurance proceeds are often paid out in the form of an annuity after the death of the insured. The extent to which "spendthrift" provisions can be attached to such contracts is discussed in Section 10.8.

appointment

As to the appointment of executors, administrators, and other fiduciaries, *see* Section 14.6. *See also* **power of appointment**.

attest

Bear witness, especially as to a will. *See* Section 3.3.

attorney, attorney-in-fact

See **power of attorney**.

bequeath, bequest

A somewhat antiquated name for a gift of personal property in a will. It is the Anglo-Saxon equivalent to legacy, a word which is derived from Latin. *See* **devise**.

bypass trust

A trust created for the benefit of the spouse of a settlor or testator. The assets of the trust are excluded from the taxable or probate estate of the spouse.

[3] UPC § 2–201(35).

The trust typically provides that the spouse is entitled to all of the trust's income for life and may empower the spouse to appoint the property to others. *See* Section 15.4.

cestui que trust (use)

Obsolete term for trust beneficiary, derived from Law French.[4]

charity

An entity organized and operated for religious, charitable, scientific, literary, or educational purposes.[5] Charitable trusts are trusts created for the benefit of charities and are subject to certain special rules, discussed in Section 10.10.

child

Many problems arise from this simple word. Does it include an adopted child? A step child? *See* Section 2.10. A child born as the result of assisted reproductive technologies? *See* Section 2.11. A child born out-of-wedlock—a so-called "nonmarital child"? *See* Section 2.9. A grandchild? *See* Section 2.2.

civil law

Used in this book in contradistinction to the common law of England and all of the United States outside Louisiana. *See* Section 8.2, 12.1.

class gifts

A gift to a group, like "children," as distinguished from a gift to individuals, like "John and Mary."[6] The consequence of being a "class gift" can be important, as class gifts are potentially expansive to admit new members to share in the gift. There is much case law defining the term in borderline situations, such as a gift "to my children, John and Mary" which could be interpreted as a class gift or a gift to two individuals not capable of expansion by the birth of an additional child. Typically, class members are related to each other through a common ancestor. *See* Section 6.5.

clear and convincing evidence

A requirement of proof intermediate between a preponderance of the evidence, the ordinary rule in civil cases, and proof beyond a reasonable doubt, which is required to convict in criminal cases.[7] The phrase occurs frequently. For example, the Uniform Probate Code (hereinafter in the text and notes referred to as "UPC") validates wills which fail to meet the formal requirements to be probated if there is "clear and convincing evidence" that the

---

[4] "The beneficiary is described in law french as 'cestui a qui use le feoffment fuit fait,' and from this obtains his curious title 'cestui que use.' The plural of this term is often rendered charmingly as 'cestuis que usent,' an expression calculated to give a grammarian bad dreams." A. Simpson, *An Introduction to the History of the Land Law* 163–64 (1961).

[5] *See*, Int. Rev. Code § 501(c)(3).

[6] *See* Hood v. Todd, 695 S.E.2d 31 (GA 2010) (gift limited in favor of "lawful blood descendants" excludes a nonmarital child.

[7] First Nat. Bank v. King, 635 N.E.2d 755 (Ill.App.Ct.1994). In re Estate of Mecello, 633 N.W.2d 892, 899 (Neb. 2001) ("clear and convincing evidence is evidence which produces in the trier of fact a firm belief or conviction about the existence of the fact to be proved.")

decedent intended the document to be a will.[8] What is *not* clear is (a) what effect this standard has on juries when it appears in an instruction,[9] and (b) in cases tried by the court, whether it is the trial court or the appellate court which must be satisfied that the evidence was clear and convincing.[10] Some courts regard uncorroborated testimony of an interested witness as not "clear and convincing,"[11] but there is no general rule to this effect.

codicil

A document used to modify a will. From the Latin *codicillus,*[12] a diminutive of *codex,* the source for our word "code." Codicils are usually shorter than wills, but they are subject to the same formal execution requirements to be valid.[13] "Republication" by codicil is discussed in Section 7.2.

collateral relatives

Distinguished from ancestors and lineal descendants or issue, they are individuals related to a decedent through a common ancestor such as a parent or grandparent. The term includes brothers, sisters, nieces, nephews, cousins, etc. Derived from the Latin *latus*, meaning side. *See* Section 2.2.

common trust fund

A fund maintained by a professional trustee for investment of the assets of multiple trusts administered by the trustee in order to reduce costs and facilitate diversification of investments. *See* Section 14.2.

community property

The system of property ownership for spouses in eight American states (Arizona, California, Idaho, Louisiana, Nevada, New Mexico, Texas, and Washington)[14] and many foreign countries. It affects both intestate succession and the limitations on one spouse's right to devise or give away property. Community property is discussed in Section 8.8.

---

8 UPC § 2–503. *See also id.* § 6–211(b) (ownership of a joint account is based on contributions unless clear and convincing evidence of a different intent); Cal.Prob.Code §§ 220 (clear and convincing evidence of survival required), 5302 (clear and convincing evidence of right of survivorship in joint account), 6453 (clear and convincing evidence of paternity).

9 In Matter of Estate of Bennett, 865 P.2d 1062, 1067 (Kan. Ct. App. 1993), the court said "we doubt very much that an experienced trial judge is much bothered by euphemisms such as clear and convincing or preponderance of the evidence. . . . it is highly unlikely that the decision in this case would have been any different if the evidence had been weighed by a higher standard." But in Matter of Estate of Mitchell, 623 So.2d 274 (Miss.1993) judgment on a verdict was reversed because a jury had erroneously been instructed that a preponderance of the evidence was sufficient.

10 2 McCormick, Evidence 340 (4th ed. 1992). In Williams v. Estate of Pender, 738 So.2d 453 (Fla. Dist. Ct. App.1999), a trial court's finding which was expressly based on a "preponderance of the evidence" was reversed because the "clear and convincing" standard was appropriate.

11 Kelley v. Yadon, 247 P.3d 199, 201 (Idaho 2011); Ryan v. Ryan, 642 N.E.2d 1028 (Mass. 1994); Hettinga v. Sybrandy, 886 P.2d 772 (Idaho 1994).

12 The word had a somewhat different meaning in Latin, however. "Codicili" were informal instruments which were sometimes used even without a will. W. Buckland and A. McNair, *Roman Law and Common Law* 12 (2d ed. 1965).

13 UPC § 1–201(57) (" 'will' includes codicil").

14 In addition Wisconsin has a form of community property as it is the only state to have adopted the Uniform Marital Property Act.

confidential relationship

This term is used in connection with a presumption that can arise when a will or gift is challenged on the basis of undue influence. *See* Section 5.3. It is also the basis for an exception to the requirement that trusts of land must be in writing.

conservator

Some persons accent the first syllable of the word, others the second. There is also inconsistency as to its meaning. Under the UPC, a conservator is a "person appointed by a court to manage the estate of a protected person."[15] In other words, the conservator only deals with the conservatee's property. A "protected person" may be either an adult who has been judged incompetent to handle property or a minor. This usage, however, is not universal. For example, in some states a protected person is called a "ward;"[16] in some states the person fulfilling the role of conservator may be referred to as the guardian of an estate or guardian of the property.

Both guardians and conservators are fiduciaries, and many of the rules governing trustees also apply to them.[17] The differences between conservatorships (or guardianships) and trusts are discussed in Section 9.2.

constructive trust

A constructive trust arises as a judicial equitable remedy and usually is said to be imposed regardless of intent for the purpose of preventing unjust enrichment, *e.g.*, on a thief, who obviously intends only to benefit himself.[18] However, constructive trusts are also imposed to carry out an intent which was informally expressed, as in oral trusts of land.

contingent remainder

A future interest that may not become possessory, as in a gift "to A for life, then to her children who survive her." While A is alive, one cannot know whether she will have children who survive her. Contingent remainders are contrasted with "vested" remainders, *e.g.*, "To A for life, then to B." Even though B cannot take possession while A is alive, B's remainder is vested; if B dies before A, the property will be part of B's estate. For further discussion, *see* Section 11.1. Proposed Restatement (Third) of Property, § 25.2 would discontinue the distinctions between remainders and executory interests and subsume all remainders, executory interests, reversions, possibilities of reverter, and rights of entry into the phrase "future interests."

corpus

Another term for the principal (or res) of a trust as distinguished from its income. *See* Section 10.6.

---

[15] UPC § 5–102(1). *See also* UTC § 103(5). *See also*, Unif. Adult Guardianship and Protective Proceedings Jurisdiction Act, § 102(2).

[16] Cal.Prob.Code Division 4.

[17] *Id.*

[18] *Restatement (Third) of Trusts* § 1, cmt. e (2003); Underhill & Hayton, *Law Relating to Trusts and Trustees* 26–7 (14th ed. 1987).

curtesy

See **dower**.

custodian

A fiduciary designated to handle property under the Uniform Transfers to Minors Act. *See* Section 10.5.

cy pres

From the French *si pres*, meaning "as near." The term is most often used to describe the modification of charitable trusts the terms of which have become illegal, impossible, or impractical to fulfill. *See* Section 10.10. The term has also been used for modifying a private trust which violates the Rule Against Perpetuities. *See* Section 12.4.

dead man statute

A rule which in some states bars testimony by an interested witness when the opposing party is dead. The rule, with its many variations, has often been criticized. For further discussion *see* 1 McCormick, *Evidence* § 65 (4th ed. 1992).

death taxes

The generic term for taxes occasioned by death. The most common types are the estate tax, imposed by the federal government and several states, and "inheritance" taxes imposed by some states. Inheritance taxes are based on the amount passing to each successor, with different rates for different kinds of successors, *e.g.*, children are taxed at a lower rate than unrelated devisees or not taxed at all. The estate tax, on the other hand, is based on the value of the estate as a whole and is not affected by who takes the property, except for the deductions for gifts to spouses and charities. A survey of the federal estate tax appears in Chapter 15.4. State inheritance taxes vary and the rates are generally much lower than the federal estate tax.

deed

Although in ordinary English, the word can refer to any act, in this area of the law it usually means a written instrument transferring property (usually land). *See* Section 3.5.

descend

Traditionally, land was said to "descend" to the heirs of an individual who died without a will—a so-called "intestate," whereas personal property was "distributed" to the intestate's next of kin.[19] Vestiges of this terminology survive,[20] but the rules governing both types of property are the same nearly everywhere today.

---

[19] 2 W. BLACKSTONE, COMMENTARIES 201 (descent is the title to land acquired by an heir), *515 (rules for distribution of an intestate's goods).

[20] *See* Mass. Gen. Laws ch. 199 § 1 (realty shall *descend* according to the laws of this commonwealth; personalty shall be *distributed* under the laws of the state of which the owner was an inhabitant); Va. Code § 64.1–1 (real estate *descends* . . .), § 64.1–11 (*distribution* of personalty is the same).

Do not confuse "descend" and "descendant." Property may "descend" to a descendant. But it may also descend to an ancestor, a collateral relative, or spouse of the intestate. *See* Section 2.2.

descendant

Synonymous with "issue,"[21] this term includes children, grandchildren, great-grandchildren, etc., but not collateral relatives; the latter are descendants of the decedent's *parents* or other more remote ancestors. *See* Section 2.2. In other words, all children are descendants or issue, but not all descendants or issue are children of the designated ancestor.

devise

Originally this word was used (both as a noun and a verb) to describe a gift of *land* in a will.[22] The proper term for a gift of personal property was "bequest" or "legacy."[23] Today, the UPC uses "devise" to cover both real and personal property.[24] One who receives a devise is a "devisee." In the lexicon of the UPC, this term has displaced the older "legatee."[25]

Wills often use the term "give" to make a devise,[26] but there are tax consequences and other differences between a gift properly speaking and a devise in a will. *See* Section 15.3, 15.4.

disclaimer

A refusal to accept a gift or inheritance. Different consequences attach to disclaimers as distinguished from accepting property and then giving it away. *See* Section 2.8. Renunciation is sometimes used as an equivalent term.[27]

distribute

See **descend**.

domicil, or domicile

Either spelling is acceptable. From the Latin *domus*, meaning home. The term is significant in the choice of law, especially for personal property. *See* Section 1.2. It is also important for venue; under the UPC, for example, administration of an estate may be commenced "where the decedent had his domicile at the time of his death."[28]

---

21 UPC § 1–201(24) (issue means descendant); In re Estate of Goodwin, 739 N.Y.S.2d 239, 245 (Surr.Ct. 2002).

22 2 W. BLACKSTONE, COMMENTARIES 372.

23 *Id.* at *512 ("A legacy is a bequest or gift of goods and chattels by testament; and the person to whom it was given is styled the legatee.") But the distinction was never rigidly followed; the term "bequests" in a will sometimes is construed to cover a devise of land as well. Estate of Lindner, 149 Cal.Rptr. 331 (App.1978).

24 UPC § 1–201(10).

25 *Id.* § 1–201(11). *See also* Cal.Prob.Code § 34.

26 D. Parry & J. Clark, *The Law of Succession* 171 (10th ed. 1996).

27 Cal.Prob.Code § 265: " 'Disclaimer' means any writing which declines, refuses, renounces, or disclaims any interest."

28 UPC § 3–201.

donee

(1) The recipient of a gift, or (2) a person on whom a power of appointment is conferred. *See* **power of appointment**.

dower

The term given by the common law to a widow's rights in her husband's land; the counterpart to the widower's right to "curtesy." *See* Section 8.7.

durable power

A power of attorney which does not terminate when the principal becomes incompetent. It is a modern device to avoid the need for conservatorship. *See* Section 9.3.

entireties, tenancy by

A special form of joint tenancy between spouses, which no longer exists in many states. *See* Section 4.5. Unlike the joint tenancy, generally the spouses cannot easily unilaterally sever this tenancy, and the interest of neither spouse is readily subject to the claims of that spouse's creditors. *See* Section 13.6.

equitable conversion

The term used to describe the fact that when land is sold, the proceeds may be treated as personal property, *e.g.*, for applying the rule that personal property is governed by the law of the domicile of the owner. *See* Section 1.2.

equitable interest

See **legal interest**.

ERISA

Employee Retirement Income Security Act of 1974, ("ERISA") is a federal statute governing most pension plans, which subjects them to many of the rules governing trusts.[29] *See* Section 10.8. ERISA expressly supersedes state laws and yet is silent on many matters for which state law provides detailed rules, *e.g.*, as to the effect of homicide on succession.

escheat

When a person dies without a will and without heirs, the person's property passes to the state by "escheat."[30]

estate

In this book the term is used primarily to describe the property of a decedent. The term sometimes refers only to the "probate" estate, the assets which pass by will or intestacy under the jurisdiction of the probate court. Because of the popularity of will substitutes, much property today passes "outside probate." *See* Section 10.4. Most of this property is subject to the

---

[29] For a good summary of the relationship between ERISA and trust law, *see* Langbein, *What ERISA Means by 'Equitable': The Supreme Court's Trail of Error in Russell, Mertens and Great West*, 103 Colum. L. Rev. 1317, 1321 (2003).

[30] Historically, escheat occurred when land reverted to the lord of the fee, either for lack of qualified heirs or as a forfeiture. 2 W. BLACKSTONE, COMMENTARIES 244.

federal estate tax, which is based on the "gross" estate, not just the probate estate. The gross estate is made up of the probate estate and a number of statutorily described property interests created as the result of a lifetime transfer by the decedent or by lifetime and testamentary transfers by others. *See* Section 15.4.

execute

Doing what is necessary to make an instrument formally valid, typically signing a will or deed. The place where an instrument was executed may be significant for choice of law, and the time of execution may also be important for various purposes. *See* Sections 1.2, 1.3.

executor

A person or persons designated in a will to "execute," *i.e.*, carry out the testator's wishes expressed in the will. The executor may be either an individual or a bank with a trust department. The term "executrix" for female executors was once common but is rarely used today. Executors have no power to act until they are appointed by the court, which usually happens when the will is probated. *See* Section 14.6. Their compensation is one of the costs of probate. *See* Section 14.7. Many modern statutes include an executor within the phrase "personal representative."[31]

executory interest

A type of future interest distinguishable from a remainder on technical grounds. The distinction between remainders and executory interests was once important but is virtually obsolete today.[32] *See* Section 12.1. The Restatement (Third) of Property eliminates executory interests as a special category of future interests. It reduces all future interests to either reversions (future interests retained by a transferor) or remainders (future interests created in a transferee).[33]

expectancy

A hope of acquiring property, *e.g.*, by inheritance or devise from a parent who is still alive. *Property* can be transferred without consideration, but an *expectancy* cannot. The distinction between the two is thin in borderline cases. *See* Section 3.5.

express trust

A term used in contradistinction to resulting and constructive trusts.[34] Typically refers to the case where a settlor gratuitously transfers property in trust (either during life or by will).

---

[31] UPC § 1–201(35).

[32] Still, the term occasionally crops up in modern cases. Cooley v. Williams, 31 S.W.3d 810, 813 (Tex.App.2000) (devise "to Paul and when he dies to Rhobbin" gives Rhobbin an executory interest). Proposed *Restatement (Third) of Property* § 25.2, would discontinue the distinctions between remainders and executory interests and subsume all remainders, executory interests, reversions, possibilities of reverter, and rights of entry into the phrase "future interests."

[33] *See Restatement (Third) of Property* § 25.2.

[34] *Restatement (Third) of Trusts* § 2, cmt. a (2003).

fee simple, fee tail

A fee tail, in contrast to a fee simple, ceased when the holder died without issue. A serious clog on alienation at one time, the fee tail has been abolished or severely restricted today in almost all states. *See* Section 11.4.

fiduciary

Derived from the Latin *fiducia*, meaning "trust or confidence," the term covers a wide spectrum of persons who are entrusted with property belonging to another. The UPC defines the term to include personal representatives, guardians, conservators, and trustees.[35] Custodians and agents are also fiduciaries.[36] The relationship between clients and lawyers often is described as a fiduciary relationship. The term can be misleading because not all "fiduciaries" are treated the same way. "The duties of a trustee are more rigorous than those of most other fiduciaries."[37]

fraud

A knowing misrepresentation, which may be the basis for denying probate to a will. *See* Section 7.1. The term is also used to describe a promise made without intent to perform, which may cause the imposition of a constructive trust even if the promise was oral. *See* Section 7.4. Fraud is also sometimes used to get around various defenses, such as statutes of limitations and res judicata. *See* Section 14.8. For example, under the UPC, "if a will which is known to be a forgery is probated informally, and forgery is not discovered until after the period for [a will] contest has run, the defrauded heirs could still bring a fraud action."[38]

fraudulent conveyance

A gift which is subject to attack by the donor's creditors, *e.g.*, because the donor was insolvent when the gift was made. *See* Sections 10.8.

future interest

An interest in property to which the owner is not currently entitled to present possession or enjoyment but may be entitled to possession or enjoyment in the future; a generic term for remainders, executory interests, reversions, possibility of reverters, and rights of entry. The Restatement (Third) of Property defines a future interest as "an ownership interest in property that does not currently entitle the owner to possession or enjoyment of the property. The owner's right to possession or enjoyment is postponed until some time in the future and may be contingent or vested."[39]

---

35 UPC § 1–201(15). *See also* Cal.Prob.Code § 39.

36 For some of the differences and similarities between trustees, custodians, and agents, *see* McGovern, *Trusts, Custodianships, and Durable Powers of Attorney*, 27 Real Prop., Prob. and Trust J. 1, 4 (1992).

37 *Restatement (Third) of Trusts* § 2, cmt. b (2003).

38 UPC § 1–106, Comment.

39 *Restatement (Third) of Property*, § 25.1.

general devise

Contrasted with both specific and residuary devises for purposes of ademption and abatement. *See* Chapter 6. General devises are typically pecuniary, *e.g.*, "$1,000 to my friend, Mary."

general power

See **power of appointment**.

gift causa mortis

A concept borrowed from Roman law which applied special rules to gifts made by individuals who were contemplating imminent death at the time of the making of the gift, typically from a known illness or life threatening condition. *See* Section 4.5.

grantor

A word often used to describe the person who executes a deed of gift or creates a living trust. For the latter, settlor and trustor are also used.

guardian

A judicially-appointed person to make decisions affecting the care, support, health, education, or welfare of either a minor or an adult who is incapable of making such decisions.[40] *See* **conservator**.

guardian ad litem

A person appointed to represent a minor or other incompetent person in litigation (from the Latin *lis, litis*, meaning suit). Under the UPC, for example, "a court may appoint a guardian ad litem to represent the interest of a minor, an incapacitated, unborn or unascertained person."[41] Appointment of a guardian ad litem is optional, because the person(s) may already be adequately represented by others who have the same interest. *See* Section 14.8. A guardian ad litem's role is generally limited to litigation, unlike other guardians.

Hague Convention

The trust is a creation of the common law and has traditionally been confined to countries like the United States and England whose legal systems derive from the common law. However, some civil law countries have shown an interest in adopting or at least recognizing trusts. The Hague Convention Relative to the Law Applicable to Trusts of 1985 has been ratified by the United Kingdom and a few other countries[42] and provides basic rules for the recognition of, and governing law applicable, to trusts.

---

40 *See, e.g.*, UTC § 103(7).

41 UPC. § 1–403(5). *See also* Cal.Prob.Code § 1003.

42 Australia, 8 of Canada's provinces, China (Hong Kong only), Italy, Luxemburg, Lichtenstein, Malta, Monaco, the Netherlands, San Marino, Switzerland. Also signed, but not ratified by France. See M. Lupoi, *Trusts: A Comparative Study* 5 (2000). As to England, *see* Recognition of Trusts Act, 1987.

heir

From the Latin *heres*, which can be translated as "heir." But a Latin *heres* was often a person designated in the will of a testator to whom the testator was not related, whereas in English such a person is a "devisee" but not an heir.[43] In correct English usage, heirs are the person(s) designated by the law of intestacy to take from an intestate. Thus, when a trust provided that property pass to the "heirs at law" of the settlor's son, it did not pass to a friend of the son whom he had designated as his "heir," but rather to the son's cousins who were his closest blood relatives, because "the term 'heir at law' must be defined with reference to the statute of descent and distribution."[44] However, the term is sometimes used by ill-informed testators to mean devisees or children. *See* Section 2.4.[45]

At common law, the term "heir" did not include a surviving widow or widower. While the surviving spouse may have been entitled to property following the decedent's death in the form of dower or curtesy, this interest was not conceptualized as an entitlement in the intestate's estate. Some states continue to exclude the spouse from the definition of heir even though the spouse is entitled to an intestate share.[46]

When a person dies without issue, the estate passes to ancestors and/or collateral relatives, such as brothers and sisters. *See* Section 2.2. They can be heirs, but "heirs *of the body*" connotes only issue (descendants) and so ancestors and collateral relatives would not qualify as "heirs of the body."

Sometimes the word "heirs" is used as a "word of limitation" as in a deed "to *A* and his heirs." In this case *A's* heirs acquire no interest at all; the word simply means *A* gets a fee simple. *See* Section 11.4.

Historically, "heirs" was used to designate those who took the decedent's land. The persons who inherited personal property were called the "next of kin."[47] However, in modern usage, the term heir generally covers anyone who takes real or personal property by intestacy.[48]

holographic

From the Greek *holos*, meaning "whole" and *graphein*, meaning "write," a holographic will is a will written entirely (or in some states substantially) in the testator's handwriting. In many states they are valid even though the will is unwitnessed. *See* Section 3.4.

---

43 See In re Estate of Picillo, 99 A.3d 975 (R.I. 2014).

44 PNC Bank, Ohio, N.A. v. Stanton, 662 N.E.2d 875 (OhioApp.1995). The German word for "heir"—"Erbe," like the Latin *heres*, includes devisees. BGB (German Civil Code) § 1937 (testator can designate his heirs). But a devise to "*gesetzlichen* Erben" (*legal* heirs), like one to "heirs" in Anglo-American law, incorporates the intestacy rules. *Id.*, § 2066.

45 *See also* Snyder v. Davis, 699 So.2d 999 (Fla. 1997) ("heirs" in a constitutional provision protecting homestead includes devisees); Gallagher v. Evert, 577 S.E.2d 217, 218 (S.C.App.2002) (will "named his son as . . . sole heir"); Hodel v. Irving, 481 U.S. 704, 718 (1987).

46 *See, e.g.*, Iowa Code § 633.3(21).

47 2 W. BLACKSTONE, COMMENTARIES 515.

48 UPC § 1–201(20); Cal.Prob.Code § 44. But *see*, Iowa Code § 633.3(22) (while spouse entitled to intestate share, spouse is not an heir).

homestead

A certain amount of real property, usually a residence, which is exempt from the claims of creditors. There are typically restrictions on an owner's voluntary transfer of the homestead without the consent of the owner's spouse. *See* Section 8.4. Under the UPC, however, "homestead" refers to a pecuniary allowance to which a surviving spouse or, if decedent died without a surviving spouse, surviving minor or dependent children are entitled.[49]

honorary trust

A name sometimes given to trusts for non-charitable purposes without a definite human beneficiary, like a trust for a pet. *See* Section 10.10.

hotchpot

Used to describe a mathematical procedure used to take account of an advancement when distributing an intestate's estate. *See* Section 2.6.

illegitimate

Until recently, this term was used to describe children born out-of-wedlock. Now it is deemed unfairly degrading and is avoided in most legal discussions. *See* Section 2.9. Children born to parents who are not married to each other are more appropriately referred to as "non-marital children."

immoveable property

The distinction between moveable and immoveable property corresponds roughly with that between real and personal property. *See* Section 1.2.

inheritance tax

See **death taxes**.

instrument

A generic term for a document by which an interest in property passes, including wills, deeds, trusts etc.[50]

intangible

From the Latin *tangere*, meaning "touch," intangible refers to property such as securities, bank accounts, patents, which cannot be touched, in contrast to property that can be touched such as furniture, cattle, etc. Even if securities are represented by a certificate, they are considered to be intangibles. Wills often distinguish between intangible property, which is put into a trust, and tangible property, which is devised outright.[51] The formal requirements for lifetime gifts are somewhat different for tangible and intangible property. *See* Section 3.5.

---

[49] UPC § 2–402.

[50] UPC § 1–201(18); Cal.Prob.Code § 45.

[51] *See*, Unif. Stat.Will Act § 5(a)(2).

international will

A will which is subject to special requirements. When these are followed, the will can be probated in any country which signed a 1973 treaty on the subject.[52]

in terrorem

Related to the word "terror," the phrase is often used to refer to a clause in a will designed to deter someone from contesting the will by providing that any devise to a contestant in the will is forfeited by such a contest.[53] *See* Section 13.3. In terrorem clauses in a will are also known as no-contest clauses.

inter-vivos

Latin "between the living," contrasted with a testamentary bequest or trust which is made by a will. "Living" trust is a commonly used synonym for inter-vivos. *See* Section 10.1.

intestate

Without a will, related to the Latin word for will, *testamentum*. The rules governing intestate succession are described in Chapter 2. The word can be used as a verb to describe the status of having died without a will, as Tom died intestate or as a noun describing the status of being a person who died without a will, as under the intestate's will.

issue

See **descendants**.

joint tenancy

A form of co-ownership in which property passes to the surviving owner(s) when a tenant dies. Contrasted with tenancy in common, under which the decedent's interest passes to his/her estate. *See* Section 4.5.

joint will

A will signed by two persons, usually husband and wife, purporting to dispose of the property of both. *See* Section 3.9. The joint will may or may not be viewed as a contract; if viewed as contract, the surviving testator may be limited in the ability to alter the dispositive provisions in the joint will.

laches

An equitable defense to a claim based on delay in asserting it. It is the equitable counterpart to statutes of limitations, but laches is discretionary, whereas statutes of limitations provide fixed limits, like two years. *See* Section 14.8.

---

[52] *See*, Unif. Internat'l Wills Act.

[53] For the changing meanings of the phrase over time, *see* Beyer, et al. *The Fine Art of Intimidating Disgruntled Beneficiaries with In Terrorem Clauses*, 51 S.M.U. L.Rev. 225, 227 n. 1 (1998).

lapse

From the Latin *lapsus*, meaning "to fall." In the context of wills, the word refers to the failure of a devise, usually because the devisee predeceased the testator. Most states have "anti-lapse" statutes to deal with this situation. *See* Section 6.5.

latent ambiguity

From the Latin *latens*, meaning "hidden," an ambiguity in a will or other document which is not apparent from reading the document, as contrasted with a "patent" ambiguity which is apparent. A devise "to my cousin, Mary Jones" does not appear to be ambiguous, but it is if the testator has two cousins with that name. *See* Section 7.1.

laughing heirs

A term used to describe remote relatives who inherit intestate property in the absence of closer relatives. They are so named because they are not sorry about the death of the decedent whom they hardly knew, if at all. *See* Section 2.2.

legacy, legatee

See **devise**.

legal interest, title

An interest historically enforced in the law courts, as distinguished from equitable interests, which were recognized only in the courts of equity. In a trust, the trustee has legal title, while the interests of the beneficiaries are equitable. *See* Section 10.1.

legal list

Refers to lists of the types of investment authorized by a statute in which fiduciaries are allowed to invest. *See* Section 14.2. Today, legal list statutes are generally obsolete as applied to trust investments. They have been supplanted by the Uniform Prudent Investor Act or like statutes.

legitimate

See **illegitimate**. Also used as a verb (with the last syllable accented) to describe a procedure whereby a child born out-of-wedlock (a/k/a "nonmarital child") may be rendered equivalent to one born in wedlock.

letters

An official certification of the appointment of a fiduciary by a court designed to establish the fiduciary's authority to deal with other persons on behalf of an estate. Thus, the UPC provides that any restrictions "on the power of a personal representative which may be ordered by the Court must be endorsed on the *letters of appointment*."[54] The general term "letters" may refer

---

[54] UPC § 3–504. *See also* Cal.Prob.Code § 8405.

to letters testamentary (given to an executor), letters of administration (given to an administrator), letters of guardianship, and letters of conservatorship.[55]

lineal descendants

See **descendant**.

living trust

See **inter-vivos**.

living will

A relatively short instrument stating that a terminally ill individual does not wish to have the individual's life prolonged by the administration of life support systems, such as respiration and food and hydration administered tubally. *See* Section 9.5. Living wills are to be distinguished from durable health care powers of attorney under which an individual designates another to make health care decisions on the individual's behalf when the individual lacks the capacity to make the decision. *See* Chapter 9. Living wills and durable health care powers may be combined in one instrument.

marital deduction

A deduction permitted under the federal estate and gift taxes for transfers from one spouse to another. *See* Section Chapter 15.4.

marital property

Roughly the equivalent of community property. A Uniform Marital Property Act has been adopted only in Wisconsin, but the phrase is used in many other states to categorize property acquired during a marriage, other than by gift or devise, for division upon a divorce. *See* Section 8.8.

Medicaid Trust

A trust meeting the special needs of a beneficiary without disqualifying the beneficiary for Medicaid. *See* Section 10.7.

mistake

The law distinguishes between mistake of fact and mistake in execution. If I sign a "will" not realizing it is a will, it may be denied probate, but if my will disinherits my son because I erroneously think he is a drug addict, the will is valid. *See* Section 7.1.

mobilia sequuntur personam

A Latin maxim saying that moveable goods (mobilia) are governed by the law of the domicile of the owner. *See* Section 1.2.

Model Code of Professional Responsibility, Model Rules of Professional Conduct

Two sets of provisions governing proper conduct by lawyers. Nearly all states have adopted one or the other. Several provisions are particularly relevant to this area of law, *e.g.*, lawyers who draft wills from which they

---

[55] UPC § 1–201(27). *See also* Cal.Prob.Code § 52.

benefit. *See* Section 5.4. "Understanding and complying with the ethical rules is an essential requirement of being a capable estate planner."[56]

mortmain

Statutes that restrict gifts to charity by will. In nearly all states they have been repealed or held unconstitutional. *See* Section 8.10.

mutual wills

Wills executed by two persons, usually spouses, with reciprocal provisions, *e.g.*, H leaves his estate to W if she survives, W leaves her estate to H if he survives. *See* Section 3.9. These are sometimes referred to as "mirror-image" wills.

next of kin

See **heirs**.

no contest clause

See **in terrorem**.

non-claim statutes

Statutes that require claims against a deceased debtor's estate to be filed within a specified period to be enforceable against the debtor's estate. *See* Section 13.5.

notary public

"A person authorized by law to administer oaths, [and] authenticate signatures and documents." Do not confuse the American notary with "the far more significant role and status of notaries public in civil law jurisdictions."[57] *See* Sections 3.3, 3.5.

nuncupative will

An oral will, allowed in some states in limited circumstances. *See* Section 3.4.

patent ambiguity

See **latent ambiguity**.

per capita, per stirpes

Alternative ways to divide property among heirs or devisees, but this dichotomy oversimplifies the possibilities. *See* Section 2.2.

personal property

The distinction between real and personal property is roughly comparable, but not identical to the difference between moveable and immoveable property. The distinction has lost much of its importance today, but it still remains

---

[56] J. Price, *Contemporary Estate Planning* § 1.1 (2d ed. 2000).

[57] MELLINKOFF, DICTIONARY OF AMERICAN LEGAL USAGE 428 (1992).

relevant in the choice of law.[58] *See* Section 1.2. Also, it can be important in construing wills, *e.g.*, a devise of "all my personal estate" did not pass the testator's land.[59]

personal representative

The generic phrase which covers both executors and administrators.[60] *See* Section 14.6.

possibility of reverter

A type of future interest retained by a grantor who conveys away a fee simple determinable. The technical distinctions between these and rights of entry for condition broker (a/k/a power of termination) are discussed in Section 12.6. Section 25.2 of the proposed Restatement (Third) of Property would subsume all possibilities of reverter into the concept of a reversion as they have no functional distinction.

pourover (also pour-over)

A popular name for a will which leaves property to a trust created by another document. *See* Section 7.2.

power

Authority conferred on a fiduciary to act, such as an executor's power to sell property of an estate. It may be conferred by the terms of the instrument or implied by law. *See* Section 14.5.

power of appointment

Authority given to a person (called the donee) to direct where property shall pass. Powers are either testamentary or presently exercisable. The law also distinguishes between general and special powers. All these terms are defined in Section 11.5.

power of attorney

Authority given to a person, known as an "attorney in fact," to perform acts on behalf of the principal who confers the authority. Such attorneys should not be confused with attorneys at law.

> Persons holding powers of attorney have historically not been considered attorneys who can appear in the courts. When a principal . . . designates another to transact some business . . . he appoints an agent to act for him as an "attorney in fact." . . . An "attorney in fact" has been consistently distinguished from an "attorney at law."[61]

---

[58] *But see,* CitiFinancial Inc. v. Balch, 86 A.3d 414 (Vt. 2013) (noting the distinction between real and personal property in the estate of a ward and indicating that judicial approval is necessary to dispose of real property as opposed to personal property within the ward's estate).

[59] Re Cook, [1948] Ch. 212, 216. *Compare* San Antonio Area Foundation v. Lang, 35 S.W.3d 636, 640 (Tex. 2000) (devise of "real estate" does not include notes received when land sold).

[60] UPC § 1–201(35); Cal.Prob.Code § 58.

[61] Disciplinary Counsel v. Coleman, 724 N.E.2d 402 (Ohio 2000).

Do not confuse powers of attorney with powers of appointment, as some persons have done.[62] *See also* **durable power**.

precatory

Directions in an instrument that are construed not to impose any legal obligation, from the Latin *precor*, meaning "to ask." Disputes about whether particular words are mandatory or only precatory are discussed in Section 3.6.

presumption

This "slipperiest of the family of legal terms"[63] is often used in this area of the law. For example, under the California Probate Code if a will is lost, "it is *presumed* that the testator destroyed the will with the intent to revoke it."[64] If the issue is decided by a jury, a presumption means that a verdict must be directed for the party claiming revocation when the basic fact is proved (that the will is lost) unless the other side (the proponents of the will) come up with evidence to the contrary.[65] If such contrary evidence is produced (*e.g.*, indicating that the will was lost by accident), there is disagreement as to whether the presumption should be mentioned to the jury. It is not under the "bursting bubble" view advocated by some[66] but criticized by others.[67]

Under the Uniform Rules of Evidence, Rule 301, "a presumption imposes on the party against whom it is directed the burden of proving that the nonexistence of the presumed fact is more probable than its existence." Under Federal Rule 301, on the other hand, a presumption merely "imposes on the party against whom it is directed the burden of going forward with evidence to rebut or meet the presumption, but does not shift to such party the burden of proof." In close cases this distinction makes a difference.[68]

pretermitted

Used to describe a child or other heir who is omitted from a will by oversight. *See* Section 8.5. The word "omitted" is synonymous and is also used.[69]

---

[62] *See* Matter of Estate of Krokowsky, 896 P.2d 247 (Ariz. 1995) (holographic will conferring a "power of attorney" did not give a power of appointment).

[63] 2 McCormick, Evidence 342 (4th ed. 1992).

[64] Cal.Prob.Code § 6124. A similar presumption exists at common law. *See* Section 4.2.

[65] In this respect a presumption differs from a "permissible inference" which would *allow* the jury to find that the will was revoked, but not compel them to do so. MCCORMICK, *supra* note 10, at 342. When a case is tried by the court, if a presumption is not rebutted, the court must find accordingly. Matter of Estate of Nelson, 274 N.W.2d 584 (S.D.1978).

[66] Matter of Estate of McCoy, 844 P.2d 1131 (Alaska 1993) (error to mention presumption to jury); Matter of Berry, 524 N.E.2d 689, 694 (Ill. App. 1988) (in case regarding undue influence of a testator, once presumption of undue influence is rebutted, the "bubble bursts" and the jury is not informed of the instruction); In re Estate of Kline, 613 N.E.2d 1329, 1338 (Ill. App. 1993) (describing when the presumption has in fact been rebutted and the "bubble has burst").

[67] Fed. R. Evid. 301 Interpretive Notes and Decision, n.2.

[68] Higgs v. Estate of Higgs, 892 S.W.2d 284, 288 (Ark.App.1995).

[69] UPC § 2–302; Cal.Prob.Code § 6570.

principal

There are two different meanings of the word "principal." One is a synonym for the res or corpus of a trust. The distinction between "principal" and "income" of a trust is discussed in Section 10.6.

The second use is for an individual who grants authority to an agent to act on the principal's behalf as under a durable power of attorney or a durable health care power of attorney. The relationship between a "principal" and an agent is discussed at Section 9.3.

Neither word should be confused with "principle" which is like a rule.

private trust

A trust created for the benefit of noncharitable beneficiaries; to be distinguished from a charitable trust. *See* Section 10.10.

probate

From the Latin *probare*, meaning "prove," the term often refers to the process of proving that a will is valid. A will which the court finds valid is "admitted to probate." The court performing this function is usually called the probate court or the probate division of the court of general jurisdiction in the state. *See* Section 13.1.

The court which admits the will to probate also appoints the personal representative to administer the estate and continues to supervise the administration of the estate. For this reason, the term "probate" is often loosely used to include the ongoing administration of the estate, and the property subject to that administration is referred to as the "probate estate."[70] *See* Section 13.1.

Probate courts traditionally had limited jurisdiction, but in recent years there has been a trend to expand their competence. This has tended to reduce disputes about which court has jurisdiction to decide a particular matter.[71]

prudent person rule

Traditionally, in states which did not have a **legal list** of proper investments for fiduciaries, this rule set the standard by which fiduciaries were judged in making investments for a trust. Over time, however, the concept has been applied to other conduct by the fiduciary. For example, under the Uniform Transfers to Minors Act, the custodian "shall observe the standard of care that would be observed by a prudent person dealing with the property of another."[72] And, under the Uniform Trust Code (hereinafter in the text and footnotes referred to as the "UTC"), the trustee is directed to "administer the trust" as a

---

[70] *See, Restatement (Third) of Property (Wills and Other Donative Transfers)* § 1.1.

[71] In re Messer Trust, 579 N.W.2d 73 (Mich.1998) (probate court now has jurisdiction over inter-vivos as well as testamentary trusts); State ex rel. Sladoje v. Belskis, 776 N.E.2d 557 (Ohio App.2002) (same). *See also* Sullivan v. Kodsi, 836 N.E.2d 125 (Ill. App. 2005) (discussing the far-reaching geographical jurisdiction granted through a trust).

[72] Unif. Transfers to Minors Act § 12(b).

prudent person would.[73] As applied to investments, the phrase is now obsolete in light of the nearly uniform adoption of the Uniform Prudent Investor Rule.

publication

An oral statement by the testator that a document is the testator's will, so the witnesses understand that the testator knows what the testator is signing. *See* Section 3.3. The term is also used to refer to a notice published in a newspaper, *e.g.*, to creditors of an estate. *See* Section 13.5.

putative spouse

A person not legally married, but who is treated as a spouse, *e.g.*, for purposes of intestate succession, because the person in good faith thought there was a valid marriage even though the marriage turns out to be invalid (*e.g.*, because the other party was already married to someone else.) *See* Section 2.12.

quasi community property

Property treated as if it were community property even though it is not, because it was acquired by someone while living in a separate property state who later moved to a community property state. *See* Section 8.8.

QTIP trust

A form of trust which qualifies for the federal gift and estate tax marital deduction. *See* Section 15.4.

reformation

Correcting a writing to make it conform to what the signer intended. Traditionally, applied to deeds, arguably the same remedy should be available for wills.[74] *See* Sections 7.1, 7.4. Also used for modifying a trust to avoid a violation of the Rule Against Perpetuities. *See* Section 12.4.

representation

The concept whereby more remote relatives take a share of a decedent's property in place of a parent or other ancestor who would have taken the property had the parent or more remote ancestor survived the decedent. *See* Section 2.2.

The term is also used when holding that a judgment binds someone who was a minor or unborn when it was rendered on the ground that his/her interest was represented by another.

res

From the Latin *res*, meaning "thing." A somewhat antiquated term for the property held in a trust.[75] Trust property is also known as "corpus" or "principal."

---

[73] UTC § 804.

[74] UPC §§ 2–805; 2–806.

[75] *Restatement (Third) of Trusts* § 3, cmt. b (2003).

residue, residuary estate

The property remaining in an estate after the payment of claims and specific and general devises. The classification of devises is important for purposes of abatement and for allocating the income earned during the administration of an estate. Sections 6.1, 6.4. In most estates, the value of the residue is significantly larger than the value of the specific and general devises.

resulting trust

When a trust fails, there is a "resulting trust" for the settlor who presumably did not intend to let the trustee keep the property in this event. The term is used in various situations in which there has been a transfer without an intent that the transferee retain beneficial enjoyment of the property, and there is no beneficiary other than the settlor. It is the equitable counterpart to a reversion.[76] The term is also used for a "purchase money resulting trust" when one person pays for property which is transferred to another. *See* Section 7.4.

Restatement

Two of the many Restatements are particularly important in this area, namely the Restatement of the Law of Property of which there are now three versions and the Restatement of the Law of Trusts of which there are now three versions.

Other restatements of particular, albeit more limited, relevance include the *Restatement (Second) of Conflict of Laws* (1971) and the *Restatements of Contracts, Torts, and Law Governing Lawyers*.

While restatements were once conceived as expressing merely the law as it existed when the restatement was written, increasingly they have taken on a "reform mode" and reflect both existing law and what the reporters believe the law should be.

restraint on alienation

A restriction applied to an interest in property designed to prevent the property from being alienated. It is different from, but associated with, the Rule Against Perpetuities. *See* Section 12.8. Typically, restraints on legal interests are invalid; restraints on equitable interest are permissible.

reversion

A future interest reserved to a grantor, expressly or by implication. When A gives B a life estate and the deed says nothing about what happens when B dies, the land will "revert" to A. The Rule Against Perpetuities does not usually apply to reversions and similar interests like **possibilities of reverter.** *See* Section 12.6. Section 25.2 of the Proposed Restatement (Third) of Property would subsume all remainders, executory interests, reversions, possibilities of reverter, and rights of entry into the phrase "future interests."

---

[76] *E.g.*, Estate of Hull v. Williams, 885 P.2d 1153 (Idaho App.1994). *See also Restatement (Third) of Trusts* §§ 7–8 (2003); Underhill & Hayton, *Law Relating to Trusts and Trustees* 27 (14th ed. 1987).

revival

When a will that revoked a prior will is in turn revoked, this may "revive" the first will. *See* Section 4.3.

Rule Against Perpetuities

A common-law rule designed to prevent property from being tied up by the dead hand for too long. *See* Chapter 12. Many states have also adopted the Uniform Statutory Rule Against Perpetuities; some states have abolished the rule entirely.

Rule in Shelley's Case

A rule dealing with a remainder to the "heirs" of a life tenant. *See* Section 11.4.

separate property

Contrasted with **community property**.

settlor

The term commonly used for a person who creates a trust. "Trustor" and "grantor" are also used occasionally.[77]

sever, severance

The term for turning a joint tenancy into a tenancy in common. *See* Section 4.5.

situs

From the Latin *situs*, meaning "location." The situs of property is often important for choice of law. *See* Section 1.2. It is also important for venue; an estate can be administered "where property of the decedent was located" if the decedent was not domiciled in the state.[78]

special power

See **power of appointment**.

specific devise

A devise of specific property, such as "my house" or "my furniture," contrasted with a general or residuary devise. *See* Section 6.1.

spendthrift trust

A trust which restricts a beneficiary from alienating the beneficiary's interest and prevents creditors of the beneficiary from reaching the interest. *See* Section 10.8.

---

[77] *Restatement (Third) of Trusts* § 3, cmt. a (2003); cf. Matter of Estate of West, 948 P.2d 351, 353 (Utah 1997) (referring to creators of a trust as "trustors").

[78] UPC § 3–201.

Statute of Frauds

Most parts of the original English statute of 1676 have become part of the law in most states. It (a) prescribed formal requirements for wills[79] (later superseded in England by the Wills Act of 1837), (b) required a signed writing to convey land, to create a trust of land, and for certain contracts. *See* Sections 3.1, 3.5, and 3.9.

substituted judgment

The standard employed by courts in authorizing conservators (guardians) to make gifts of the conservatee's (ward's) property. *See* Section 8.2. The standard is also applicable in the context of making end-of-life care decisions for a patient who is incapable of making a health care decision.

testament/testamentary/testator

From the Latin word for will, *testamentum*. In modern English, "will" has largely replaced testament, but the adjective "testamentary" is still current, *e.g.*, a trust created by will is a testamentary trust, in contradistinction to a "living" trust.[80] The person who executes a will is a testator. Testatrix, for a female, is archaic.[81]

Totten trust

Trusts of a bank account, named after a leading case which held them valid.[82] *See* Section 4.5. They are really will substitutes and have little in common with ordinary trusts, because they terminate when the settlor dies. They are functionally the same as pay-on-death bank accounts.

trust

Certain uses of this multi-purpose word have nothing to do with the subject of this book, such as business trusts and "trust deeds" which are a security device much like a mortgage.[83] The primary purposes of trusts covered in this book are described in Section 10.1 and generally relate to the orderly transmission of wealth, typically from one generation to the next.

trustor

A word sometimes used to designate the creator of a trust, although "settlor" is more common.

Uniform Acts

Many Uniform Acts relate to the subject matter of this book. The most important ones are listed below: *Caveat:* The word "uniform" is a misnomer. Almost none of the Uniform acts have been universally adopted. Many states which have adopted one of the "uniform" acts have departed in some

---

[79] The first Statute of Wills in England was enacted in 1540. All states today have their own variation of the Statute of Wills.

[80] *Restatement (Third) of Trusts* § 2, illus. 3, 5 (2003).

[81] UPC § 1–201(51) (" 'Testator' includes an individual of either sex.").

[82] Matter of Totten, 71 N.E. 748 (NY 1904).

[83] See also the disclaimer in *Restatement (Second) of Trusts* § 1, cmt. b (1959); UPC § 1–201(53); Cal.Prob.Code § 82.

particulars from the version as promulgated by the Uniform Law Commission (previously known as the National Conference of Commissioners on Uniform State Laws). Also, many of the Acts have been revised from time to time, and states may have adopted different versions. In one case a court reiterated the principle of interpreting "uniform laws in a uniform manner," but it did not note that the provision of "the UPC" which it was interpreting departed in important ways from the one currently sponsored by the Commission.[84] A Uniform act is not law in any state unless adopted into law by the state. Thus, Uniform acts are essentially legislative recommendations to the states for adoption.

Uniform Adoption Act

A version promulgated in 1994 was adopted in only one state. A 1969 version was adopted in four states but was withdrawn by the Uniform Commissioners in 1986 as obsolete. It is mentioned in Section 2.10.

Uniform Common Trust Fund Act

This act, approved in 1938, has been adopted in 35 jurisdictions.

Uniform Custodial Trust Act

This act, approved in 1987, has been adopted in 19 jurisdictions. It allows standard trust provisions to be incorporated by reference. *See* Section 9.5.

Uniform Directed Trust Act

This act, approved in 2017, addresses the issues arising as a result of granting a person other than the trustee a power over some aspect of the trust's administration. This act has been adopted in 13 jurisdictions.

Uniform Disposition of Community Property Rights at Death Act

This act, approved in 1971, has been adopted in 14 jurisdictions. *See* Section 8.8.

Uniform Electronic Wills Act

This act, approved in 2019, permits a testator to execute a will electronically and authorizes courts to give legal effect to a testator's electronic will. It has been adopted in one state.

Uniform Fiduciary Access to Digital Assets Act

This act, approved in 2017, clarifies the application of federal privacy laws and gives legal effect to the instructions of an account holder respecting the disposition of the holder's digital assets. It has been adopted in one state.

Uniform Fiduciaries Act

This act, approved in 1922, has been adopted in 26 jurisdictions. The act deals with situations "where one person deals with another whom he knows to be a fiduciary . . . The liabilities of the fiduciary himself are not dealt with but only the liabilities of the person dealing with the fiduciary." The parts of the

[84] In re Estate of Gleeson, 655 N.W.2d 69, 72 (N.D.2002).

Act dealing with the transfer of securities have been superseded by the Uniform Commercial Code and by a Uniform Act for the Simplification of Fiduciaries Securities Transfers. *See* Section 14.9.

Uniform Fiduciary Income and Principal Act

This act, approved in 2018, revises the Uniform Principal and Income Act. It provides greater flexibility in the allocation of receipts and disbnursement between income and principal to take account of trustees growing preferences for investing to achieve the greatest total return, with an adjustment between interest and principal to assure all beneficiaries receive a fair result. It has been adopted in one state.

Uniform Guardianship, Conservatorship, and Other Protective Arrangements Act

This act, approved in 2017, is a comprehensive statute dealing with guardianships, conservatorship, and other protective arrangements. It has been enacted in two jurisdictions.

Uniform Management of Institutional Funds Act

This act, approved in 1972, has been superseded by the Uniform Prudent Management of Institutional Funds Act (UPMIFA) which was approved in 2006 and has been adopted in all states but Pennsylvania.

Uniform Marriage and Divorce Act

Promulgated in 1970, revised in 1971 and 1973, the Act has been adopted in eight jurisdictions. It is no longer a uniform act but a model act.

Uniform Parentage Act

This Act exists in a 1973 version which has been adopted by 18 jurisdictions. Another version was promulgated in 2000, revised and amended in 2002 This 2002 act has been adopted in eight states. In 2017 the act was again revised and the 2017 revision had been adopted in 4 states. *See* Section 2.9.

Uniform Powers of Appointment Act

This act, approved in 2013, has been enacted in ten jurisdictions, codifies the common law of powers of appointment. *See* Section 11.5.

Uniform Power of Attorney Act

This act approved in 2006, has been enacted in 28 jurisdictions. This act modernizes the law relating to powers of attorney and sets forth in detail the power held by an attorney-in-fact. *See* Section 9.3.

Uniform Principal and Income Act

The 1997 revision, with amendments in 2000, supplanting two prior versions enacted in 1931 and 1962, respectively, has 47 adoptions. *See* Section 10.6. In 2018, the act was revised, given a new name (Uniform Fiduciary Income and Principal Act), and improved with new provisions to provide greater flexibility to trustees preferring to invest for total return with proper adjustments to assure all beneficiaries are treated fairly.

Uniform Probate Code

Promulgated in 1969 and adopted in 19 jurisdictions. A revised version of Article VI appeared in 1989, of Article II in 1990, 2008, and 2019, and of Article V in 1998. The UPC incorporated certain existing Uniform acts, and parts of it appear in free-standing versions, some of which have been more widely adopted than the Code as a whole. A list of the more important ones follows:

Disclaimer of Property Interests Act[85]

This act, approved in 1978 has been adopted in 21 jurisdictions. A new version was approved in 1999 and has been adopted in 25 jurisdictions. *See* Section 2.8.

Durable Power of Attorney Act

This act, approved in 1979 and amended in 1987, was once adopted in nearly all state but has been replaced by the later Uniform Power of Attorney Act of 2006. *See* Section 9.3. The Uniform Power of Attorney Act of 2006 has been adopted in 28 jurisdictions.

Estate Tax Apportionment Act

This act has been revised many times, most recently in 2003. It has been adopted in numerous jurisdictions in one of its varying forms. The 2003 version has been adopted in twelve jurisdictions. *See* Section 15.4.

Guardianship and Protective Proceedings Act

This act, approved in 1997, has been adopted in five jurisdictions.

Prudent Investor Act

This act, approved in 1994, has been almost universally adopted. *See* Section 14.2.

Simultaneous Death Act

This act, originally promulgated in 1940, has been almost universally adopted. The UPC incorporates the revision made in 1991 as revised in 1993. The 1993 version has been adopted in 19 jurisdictions.[86]

Statutory Rule Against Perpetuities[87]

This act was approved in 1986 and revised in 1990. It has been adopted in 32 jurisdictions. *See* Section 12.4.

---

[85] UPC §§ 2–1101 et seq.

[86] *See also,* UPC §§ 2–104; 2–702.

[87] *See also,* UPC §§ 2–901 et seq.

Testamentary Additions to Trusts Act[88]

This act was first adopted in 1960 and was adopted in 44 jurisdictions. The 1991 version which is part of the UPC has been adopted in 26 jurisdictions. *See* Section 7.2.

Uniform Prudent Management of Institutional Funds Act

This act, approved in 2006, has been adopted in nearly all jurisdictions.

Uniform Statutory Will Act

This act, approved in 1984, has been adopted in two jurisdictions. It was drafted by knowledgeable estate planners as a model for lawyers who are less experienced in the field. It is often cited in this book as an example of what good drafters can do to avoid problems treated in the book. In 1996, this act was withdrawn from recommendation for enactment.

Uniform Supervision of Trustees for Charitable Purposes Act

This act, approved in 1954, has been adopted in four jurisdictions. *See* Section 10.10.

Uniform Transfers to Minors Act

A revision of the Uniform Gifts to Minors Act, this act was approved in 1983 and was amended in 1986. It has been adopted in nearly all jurisdictions. *See* Section 10.5.

Uniform Trust Code

This act was approved in 2000, and has been adopted in 35 jurisdictions. The trust code should not be confused with the Uniform Trusts Act, which is much less comprehensive. This Code "mostly restates familiar principles," its purpose being "to organize and clarify the law, while making interstitial reforms."[89] Mentioned in many places in this book, the Code is intended to replace the Uniform Trustees Powers and Uniform Trusts Acts.[90]

Uniform Trust Decanting Act

This act, approved in 2015 and enacted in three jurisdictions, authorizes a trustee to amend a discretionary trust to create a new trust on different terms. *See* Section 10.9.

Uniform Trustees' Powers Act

This act, approved in 1964, has been adopted in 16 jurisdictions. *See* Chapter 12.

Uniform Trusts Act

This act, approved in 1937, has been adopted in six states. *See* Section 7.4. This act was withdrawn from recommendation for enactment.

---

[88] *See also,* UPC § 2–511.

[89] Langbein, *The Uniform Trust Code: Codification of the Law of Trusts in the United States,* 15 Trust Law International 66 (2001).

[90] UTC § 1105.

vested remainder

See **contingent remainder**.

wait-and-see

A reform of the common-law Rule Against Perpetuities based on waiting to see if a nonvested interest actually vests or fails on time. *See* Section 12.4.

ward

A person for whom a guardian has been appointed.

waste

Misuse or neglect of property by a legal life tenant which may be actionable by the remainderman. *See* Section 10.5.

will

In this book the word normally refers to a document by which a testator disposes of property after death. Although the word is also used as a synonym for "wish" or "intent," those words are generally used when this is meant.[91]

will contest

A proceeding brought to have a will declared invalid, *e.g.*, for incapacity or undue influence. In many states a contest can be instituted even after the will is admitted to probate. *See* Section 13.3.

will substitutes

A general name for various devices whereby property passes at death. These devices are free from the formal requirements for wills, including probate and administration. Common examples are life insurance, certain types of bank accounts, pension plans, and revocable trusts. A recurring question is whether will substitutes should be subject to the rules governing wills themselves.

workers' compensation

Statutes providing benefits to employees and their dependents for accidental injury or death of an employee.

worthier title

An almost obsolete doctrine which held that a gift to the "heirs" of a grantor or testator gave them no interest in the property conveyed. *See* Section 11.4.

wrongful death

Statutes abrogating the common-law rule that death of an injured person abated any claim for the injury. *See* Section 2.5.

---

[91] In Estate of Gillespie, 903 P.2d 590 (Ariz.1995), the court distinguishes between the "Will" and "will" of the testator.

§ 1.2 Conflict of Laws

Importance

The law of wills is largely statutory. Although the laws of the American states agree on most basic points, they differ in many details.[92] For example, in all states, if an individual dies without a will, the surviving spouse gets a share of the estate, but the size of that share differs.[93] When the law of foreign countries is taken into account, the differences may become greater. Nearly all American states reject a "forced share" for children of a person who dies with a will, but most other countries provide for this.[94] Thus, it is often necessary to decide which law applies to a case. A whole Restatement is devoted to the subject of conflict of laws.[95] Various factors have been used to determine the governing law.

Designation by Transferor

A statement in a will that "this will shall be governed by the law of [for example] Virginia" is usually controlling. Section 2–703 of the UPC says that "the meaning and legal effect of a governing instrument is determined by the local law of the state selected in the governing instrument" with certain exceptions. A similar idea appears in other statutes[96] and in the Restatement.[97] Sometimes the choice of law designation is inferred. For example, the will of a testator who died in New York was held to show an intent to apply Massachusetts law to a trust because the will named Massachusetts residents as trustees and provided for approval of successor trustees by a Massachusetts court.[98]

Allowing the transferor to choose the applicable law makes good sense insofar as the law seeks to effectuate intention. The UPC says that the "legal effect" as well as the "meaning" of a will can be controlled by the testator's

---

[92] In "inheritance law ... the intrinsic merits of interjurisdictional consistency are relatively scant. ... [The Uniform Law] Commissioners' uniformity ideal has long proved a chimera; with the notable exception of commercial law, nothing approaching a universal adoption has ever been achieved." Hirsch, *Revisions in Need of Revising: The Uniform Disclaimer Property Interests Act*, 29 Fla.State L.Rev. 109, 181 (2001). In contrast, while Germany has a federal constitution not unlike that of the United States, its rules of inheritance are governed by the federal Civil Code (BGB).

[93] *See* Section 2.1.

[94] *See* Section 8.2, note 37 et seq.

[95] *Restatement (Second) of Conflict of Laws* (1971). Because the conflicts rules of various jurisdictions often differ, the result in some cases may depend on which court hears the matter. H. Flick & D. Piltz, *Der Internationale Erbfall* 3–4 (1999) (result depends on whether case brought in Germany or Belgium). Thus, the rules governing which courts have jurisdiction over a matter may be an important factor in the final result.

[96] Cal.Prob.Code § 21103; N.Y.E.P.T.L. § 3–5.1(h); UTC § 107(1); Hague Convention on Trusts, 1985, art. 6. In some countries the right of the owner to designate governing law is restricted or non-existent. H. Flick & D. Piltz, *supra* note 95, at 65 et seq.

[97] *Restatement (Second) of Conflict of Laws* § 224(1) (construction of conveyance of land), § 264(1) (construction of will of movables), § 268(1) (construction of a trust of movables). *See also* Cantor v. Dep't of Income Maintenance, 531 A.2d 608 (Conn.Super.1985) (applying Maryland law because trust instrument so provided).

[98] Amerige v. Attorney General, 88 N.E.2d 126, 133 (Mass.1949). *See also* Brown v. Ryan, 788 N.E.2d 1183, 1194 (Ill.App.2003) (concurring opinion).

designation.[99] This provision is qualified in order to prevent an individual from avoiding domiciliary laws which limit freedom of choice, such as the elective share of the transferor's surviving spouse.[100] For example, a testator's designation of New York law in a will was held not to bar his spouse from claiming greater rights under the law of Virginia where they s were domiciled at the husband's death.[101] The UPC provision allowing a testator to select the governing law does not apply if this would produce a result contrary to a "public policy of this state."[102]

Can a testator (or other transferor) designate as governing law, the law of a state which has no connection to the testator, the property, or the beneficiaries? One court refused to respect a designation of Georgia law in a trust because Georgia had no such tie.[103] However, this is not a stated requirement in the UPC or the Restatement.[104] The Hague Convention on the Law Applicable to Succession to the Estates of Deceased Persons allows designation only of a state where the designator is or was a "habitual resident."[105] But there is no such limitation in the 1985 Hague Convention on Trusts. Thus, it is possible for Italians, because Italy has ratified the 1985 Convention, to "create trusts governed by English law on assets located in Italy for Italian beneficiaries," even though Italy has no law of trusts as such.[106]

The same problem can arise in a contract. For example, a wife waived her right to a share of her husband's estate by an agreement which recited that it was to be governed by the law of New York, even though the parties were married in Connecticut where the husband later died. A Connecticut court

---

[99] The Restatement, on the other hand, distinguishes between "construction," as to which the testator's designation controls, (see the sections cited in Note 97), and "validity." *See Restatement (Second) of Conflict of Laws* §§ 239 (wills of land), 263 (wills of movables), 269 (testamentary trusts). However, Section 270 allows the designation of the settlor of an inter-vivos trust to control its validity (with qualifications). In Germany, the freedom of a transferor to stipulate the governing law is much greater for inter-vivos transactions than for wills. Flick & Piltz, *supra* note 95, at 53.

[100] UPC § 2–703. *See also* Cal.Prob.Code § 21103.

[101] Estate of Clark, 236 N.E.2d 152 (N.Y.1968). *See also Restatement (Second) of Conflict of Laws* § 270, cmt. b (1971). However, the same court allowed a designation of New York law in a will to defeat a claim by the testator's child to a forced share under the law of France, the testator's domicile. Matter of Estate of Renard, 439 N.E.2d 341 (N.Y.1982). *See also* Dahl v. Dahl, 2015 WL 5098249 (UT 2015) (choice of Nevada law in trust instrument rejected because to do so would violate an important public policy of Utah regarding division of marital property); Matter of Estate of Wright, 637 A.2d 106 (Me.1994) (designation of Maine law bars child's claim under Swiss law). In National Shawmut Bank v. Cumming, 91 N.E.2d 337 (Mass.1950), the settlor of an inter-vivos trust defeated his wife's claim to an elective share by providing that the trust would be governed by Massachusetts law.

[102] UPC § 2–703; cf. UTC § 107(1) ("contrary to a strong public policy of the state having the most significant relationship to the matter at issue").

[103] First National Bank v. Daggett, 497 N.W.2d 358 (Neb.1993). *See also* Morris & Leach, *The Rule Against Perpetuities* 25 (1962); Effland, *Will Construction Under the UPC* 63 Ore.L.Rev. 337, 346 (1984).

[104] *Restatement (Second) of Conflict of Laws* §§ 224, cmt. e, 264, cmt. e, 268, cmt. b. But if the question is the validity of the trust, the designated state must have "a substantial relation to the trust." *Id.* § 270, cmt. b; Russell v. Wachovia Bank, N.A., 578 S.E.2d 329, 336 (S.C.2003) (designation of N.C. law effective because the trustee and trust property located there).

[105] Schoenblum, *Multijurisdictional Estates and Article II of the Uniform Probate Code*, 55 Alb.L.Rev. 1291, 1324 (1992).

[106] Graziadei, *Trust Law*, in J. Lena and U. Mattei, Introduction to Italian Law 338 (2002). This enthusiasm for trusts is not shared in Germany. Flick & Piltz, *supra* note 95 at 257.

gave effect to the choice of New York law, but only after determining that the provision had not been inserted in the contract by fraud or undue influence and that New York had a substantial relationship to the parties (the wife was residing there).[107]

To say "the law of X shall govern" may include X's rules on the choice of law, which may point to another state's substantive rules, a concept commonly known as renvoi.[108] Thus, a trust provision that Massachusetts law should govern was held to include the Massachusetts rule that the legitimacy of a child was governed by the law of the donor's domicile, which in this case was New Hampshire.[109] However, the UPC assumes that a reference to state law means "the local law of the state" named.[110]

Situs

The situs of land often determines the choice of law. For example, when a woman domiciled in Germany died owning land in Florida, the court applied Florida law to determine her heirs as to her land in Florida.[111] Similarly, when an Illinois domiciliary revoked a will disposing of Iowa real property, the Iowa court disregarded the revocation even though it fully complied with Illinois law because the manner of revocation did not comply with Iowa law.[112] Many state statutes and the Restatement are similar.[113]

This rule has been questioned. Scoles and Hay argue that "the law of the situs . . . often defeats the superior interests or policy concerns of nonsitus states."[114] A person who leaves property in several states probably considers the estate "as a unit without regard to where the parts are located," whereas the situs rule may impose different laws on the various parts of the estate.[115]

---

[107] Elgar v. Elgar, 679 A.2d 937 (Conn.1996) (following *Restatement (Second) Conflict of Laws* § 187 (1971)).

[108] *See* Miller, *International Aspects of Succession* 19–24 (2000); Flick & Piltz, *supra* note 95 at 31–32.

[109] Powers v. Steele, 475 N.E.2d 395 (Mass.1985). *See also* Wilmington Trust Co. v. Annan, 531 A.2d 1209 (Del.Ch.1987) (reference to law of Quebec leads to law of domicile); H. Flick & D. Piltz, *supra* note 95 at 66–67 (designation of New York law leads to application of German law as domicile of testator).

[110] UPC § 2–703.

[111] In re Estate of Salathe, 703 So.2d 1167 (Fla.App.1997). *See also* Matter of Estate of Allen, 772 P.2d 297 (Mont.1989); Cohn v. Heymann, 544 So.2d 1242 (La.App.1989) (forced heirship allowed as to Louisiana land); First National Bank v. Daggett, 497 N.W.2d 358 (Neb.1993) (despite designation of Georgia law in trust instrument); In re Estate of Rubert, 651 A.2d 937 (N.H.1994) (right of pretermitted heir); Flick & Piltz, *supra* note 95, at 64 (immovables in Rumania owned by German citizen governed by Rumanian law); French Code Civil art 3 (immovables in France governed by French law).

[112] In re Estate of Barrie, 35 N.W.2d 658 (Iowa 1949).

[113] Cal. Civil Code § 755 (land within California governed by California law); N.Y.E.P.T.L. § 3–5.1(b)(1); Mass.Gen.Laws ch. 199, § 1; *Restatement (Second) of Conflict of Laws* §§ 223 (conveyance of land), 277–78 (trust of land). The reference to the law of the situs may eventually lead somewhere else. However, "in most situations the courts of the state of the situs will apply its local law." *Restatement (Second) of Conflict of Laws* § 278, cmt. a (1971).

[114] Scoles & Hay, *Conflict of Laws* 798 (2d ed. 1992). *See also* Weintraub, *Obstacles to Sensible Choice of Law for Determining Marital Property Rights on Divorce or in Probate*, 25 Houston L.Rev 1113, 1122 (1988).

[115] Scoles & Hay, *supra* note 114, at 796. *See also* Reif v. Reif, 621 N.E.2d 1279, 1281 (Ohio App.1993); Howard v. Reynolds, 283 N.E.2d 629 (Ohio 1972) (looking to the law of the owner's domicile in order to treat the estate as a unit). For a case in which the situs rule produced an

Thus, when a Virginia resident left her estate to the issue of her children, even though in Virginia this language did not include adopted children, a Nebraska court awarded her land in Nebraska to an adopted child applying Nebraska law under the situs rule.[116]

The situs rule can protect legitimate interests. It allows prospective purchasers of land to consult the law with which they are most familiar.[117] In other situations the interest of the situs is more doubtful, for example, a dispute between members of a family who all reside in a state other than the situs state.

In the case of land, the situs rule is easy to apply.[118] The leading alternative is to look to the law of the owner's domicile, which, as we shall see, is often hard to determine. But, situs also can be hard to determine when the concept is applied to personal property.

Generally, the situs rule is confined to land. This raises the question: what is land and what is personal property? If I own a company which owns land, should one focus on the stock which represents my interest (personal property) or the underlying asset, the land?[119] Is a leasehold land or personal property?[120]

Classification of property may be affected by "equitable conversion." For example, a will directed the executor to sell the testator's property and distribute the proceeds to "my heirs at law." The testator owned land in Indiana, but the court determined his heirs under the law of Illinois, the state of his domicile, because "a direction in a will to the executor to sell realty converts such realty into personalty."[121] The result would have been different if the will had simply *authorized,* rather than *directed* a sale of his land.[122]

---

injustice as to an estate which was "spread around the world," *see* Re Collens, [1986] 1 All E.R. 611 (Ch. 1985).

[116] In re Estate of Hannan, 523 N.W.2d 672 (Neb.1994); In re Estate of Rubert, 651 A.2d 937 (N.H.1994) (child awarded share of land in New Hampshire but not personal property because decedent was domiciled in Virginia).

[117] *Restatement (Second) of Conflict of Laws* § 223, cmt. b (1971).

[118] Pfau v. Moseley, 222 N.E.2d 639 (Ohio 1966) (citing the desirability of certainty in applying the law of the situs).

[119] Cohn v. Heymann, 544 So.2d 1242 (La.App.1989) treated the stock as personal property in this situation. *See also* Blood v. Poindexter, 534 N.E.2d 768 (Ind.Tax 1989); Indiana Department of State Revenue v. Estate of Puschel, 582 N.E.2d 923 (Ind.Tax 1991) (interest in trust holding land is personal property); Flick & Piltz, *supra* note 95, at 68–70 (interest of partner in partnership which owns land is not real property for choice of law purposes).

[120] N.Y.E.P.T.L. § 3–5.1(a)(1) defines "real property" to include leaseholds. For a general discussion *see Restatement (Second) of Conflict of Laws* § 278, cmt. e (1971); 1 J. Schoenblum, *Multistate and Multinational Estate Planning* § 10.06 (2d ed.1999).

[121] Moore v. Livingston, 265 N.E.2d 251 (Ind.App.1970). *See also* In re Estate of Janney, 446 A.2d 1265 (Pa.1982) (New Jersey. law not controlling because land in New Jersey had been sold); Cal.Prob. Code § 21107; *Restatement (Second) of Conflict of Laws* § 225 (1971); 1 J. Schoenblum, *supra* note 120 at § 11.04. Cf. Funk v. Funk, 563 N.E.2d 127, 129 (Ind. App. 1990) ("equitable conversion is a legal fiction invented to protect the beneficiaries and to sustain and carry out the intention of the testator, not to defeat it").

[122] 5 *Amer. Law of Prop.* § 22.58. Thus, in In re Estate of Hannan, 523 N.W.2d 672 (Neb.1994), the court applied Nebraska law to the sale proceeds of land in Nebraska even though the testator was domiciled in Virginia.

Although the law of the situs is primarily important for land, in some cases it is held to govern personal property as well. For example, an Illinois resident died intestate without heirs, owning a bank account in Washington. The account escheated to Washington: when "property goes by escheat . . . the country in which the property is located is entitled to the funds rather than the country in which the decedent was domiciled."[123] When a resident of Brazil opened a trust account in a New York bank, a court applied New York law on the theory that the owner had "elected" to have New York law govern when he chose a bank there.[124]

The situs of property may also be relevant for purposes other than the choice of law. A gift of tangible personal property within the United States is subject to federal gift tax law even when owned by a nonresident.[125] A will can generally be probated where the testator had property.[126] But suppose the testator owned stock or a bank account. Where are these located? Under the UPC, claims represented by instruments (like a stock certificate) are located where the instrument is, and other claims are located "where the debtor resides or, if the debtor is a person other than an individual, at the place where it has its principal office."[127] For federal gift tax purposes, debts owed by an American and stock issued by an American corporation are deemed to be situated within the United States even though they are owned by a non-resident.[128] Because the rules are often murky, more than one state may have a reasonable claim to be the situs of some assets, and, as a result, multiple taxation of the same property is not uncommon.[129]

Domicile

The law of the owner's domicile usually governs personal property, or "movables," the term commonly used in conflicts literature.[130] This concept is

---

[123] O'Keefe v. State, Department of Revenue, 488 P.2d 754 (Wash.1971). *But see* Delaware v. New York, 507 U.S. 490, 498 (1993) ("because a debt is property of the creditor . . . the debt should be accorded to the state of the creditor's last known address"). Some states give intangibles (like a bank account) to the state of the intestate's residence if that state would recognize its claim in the converse case. Cal.Prob. Code § 6805(b).

[124] Neto v. Thorner, 718 F.Supp. 1222 (S.D.N.Y. 1989). *See also* De Werthein v. Gotlib, 594 N.Y.S.2d 230 (App.Div.1993); Sanchez v. Sanchez De Davila, 547 So.2d 943 (Fla.App.1989) (applying Florida law on similar facts against children's claim under Venezuela law); Flick & Piltz, *supra* note 95, at 258 (German court recognizes trust of N.Y. bank account created by German because N.Y. law applies).

[125] Int. Rev. Code § 2501.

[126] *Restatement (Second) of Conflict of Laws* § 314 (1971); UPC § 3–201; Cal.Prob.Code §§ 7051–52; Section 12.1, note 12.

[127] UPC § 3–201(d). *But cf.* Delaware v. New York, 507 U.S. 490, 506 (1993) (opting for the state of incorporation rather than the corporation's "main office" as determinative for escheat).

[128] Int. Rev. Code § 2511(b).

[129] Flick & Piltz, *supra* note 95 at 9–11, who point out that such instances are often alleviated by treaties.

[130] *Restatement (Second) of Conflict of Laws* §§ 260 (intestate succession), 263 (validity and effect of will), 264 (construction of will), 265 (spouse's forced share). "It has now long been accepted that for purposes of private international law the civil law classification" between movables and immovable property applies rather than the traditional common law one between "real" and "personal" property. G Miller, *supra* note 108 at 33; note 28.

In some countries the owner's *citizenship* controls the choice of law for *all* property. H. Flick & D. Piltz, *supra* note 95, at 58 (Portuguese law governs property of citizen of Portugal even though he was domiciled and the property was located in Germany); 1 J Schoenblum, *supra* note 121 at

expressed by the Latin maxim *mobilia sequuntur personam*, movables follow the person. Thus, an Ohio court applied Vermont law to determine the inheritance of the assets of a decedent who died domiciled in Vermont.[131] When a man domiciled in New York died owning property in Louisiana, his wife invoked Louisiana law to claim a share as community property. Her claim was allowed as to land but not as to the personal property, because Louisiana was said to have no interest "in protecting and regulating the rights of married persons residing and domiciled in New York."[132]

The UPC uses domicile to determine the elective share of a surviving spouse as to *all* the decedent's property, including land.[133] California subjects even land outside the state acquired by couples domiciled in California to its community property laws.[134] Conversely, if a couple domiciled elsewhere acquires land in California, the spouse's rights to an elective share in the land are governed by the law of the domicile.[135] Domicile is also an important concept in the assessment of taxes. For example, the estate of a citizen or resident of the United States is subject to United States estate tax regardless where the property is situated.[136]

Some courts refer to the law of the testator's domicile when construing a will even when land is involved.[137] When a couple owned a condominium in Florida, their respective liability on the mortgage was determined by the law of their domicile. "Even though the property is located in Florida . . . the

§§ 9.03, 9.07. Citizenship has been less important in English and American law, where "nationality does not as such connect a person with one of the [several] legal systems operative within" the country. G. Miller, *supra* note 108 at 32. However, the nationality of the testator is one possible basis for validating a will under the English Wills Act, 1963 § 1.

[131] Howard v. Reynolds, 283 N.E.2d 629 (Ohio 1972). *See also* Morris v. Cullipher, 816 S.W.2d 878 (Ark.1991) (applying law of domicile, Arkansas, as to CDs issued by Texas bank); In re Estate of Rubert, 651 A.2d 937 (N.H.1994) (personal property governed by law of Virginia because decedent domiciled there at death); Knight v. Knight, 589 N.Y.S.2d 195 (App.Div.1992); Fifth Third Bank v. Crosley, 669 N.E.2d 904, 908 (Ohio Com.Pl.1996) (applying Florida law in construing a will because testator was domiciled there at death). *But cf.* Cal.Civil Code § 946 ("*if there is no law to the contrary, in the place where personal property is situated,* it is deemed to follow the person of its owner, and is governed by the law of his domicile").

[132] Estate of Crichton, 228 N.E.2d 799 (N.Y.1967). *See also Restatement (Second) of Conflict of Laws* § 265 (1971).

[133] UPC § 2–202(d). *See also* Lotz v. Atamaniuk, 304 S.E.2d 20 (W.Va.1983) (applying law of domicile to defeat claim); English Inheritance (Provision for Family and Dependants) Act, 1975, § 1(1) (applicable to persons who die domiciled in England). Professor Schoenblum suggests that non-UPC states in which land is located will not in fact defer to this choice of law. Schoenblum, *supra* note 105, at 1315. Professor Schoenblum also criticizes the UPC using domicile without regard to its duration as the basis for the spouse's elective share. Schoenblum, *supra* note 105, at 1316.

[134] Cal. Family Code § 760.

[135] Cal.Prob.Code § 120. *See also* Estate of Rhoades, 607 N.Y.S.2d 893 (Sup.1994) (refusing to apply N.Y. law because decedent domiciled in Florida).

[136] Internal Revenue Code §§ 2001(a), 2031(a). Section 2014 gives a credit for taxes paid to a foreign country "in respect to any property situated within such foreign country" included in the estate. *See* Share, *Domicile is Key to Determining Transfer Tax of Non-Citizens,* 22 Est.Plan. 31 (1995).

[137] Beauchamp v. Beauchamp, 574 So.2d 18, 20–21 (Miss. 1990); Estate of Buckley, 677 S.W.2d 946 (Mo.App.1984); *Restatement (Second) of Conflict of Laws* § 224, illus. 1 (1971).

settling of debts between District of Columbia domiciliaries appears to us to be of paramount interest to the District of Columbia."[138]

Because many persons own property in more than one jurisdiction but have a single domicile, reference to the law of the domicile has the advantage of treating the owner's property as a unit. It is unlikely that a testator intended words in a will to have different meaning when applied to land as distinguished from personalty.

In construing the terms of the will, a court could apply the law of the testator's domicile at death on the theory that testator is "most familiar with the laws of the state of domicil immediately prior to death"[139] or the law of the place where the will was drafted and executed (particularly if the testator was domiciled there at that time) on a like theory.[140] According to the Restatement, however, courts "usually construe a given word or phrase [in a will] in accordance with the usage prevailing in the state where the testator was domiciled at the time the will was executed, [because] this would presumably be in accord with the expectations of the testator."[141]

Domicile may also be important in questions of status, which in turn may control inheritance. Thus, when a man claimed to inherit a share of his "wife's" estate, the court applied German law to determine the validity of their marriage, because they were domiciled there.[142]

A person can have only one domicile at a time.[143] Domicile is often hard to determine. Although the words "domicile" and "residence" are often used interchangeably,[144] they are not the same. A person may have several residences, but only one domicile.[145] When a man died in a nursing home where he had lived for eight years, the court held he was not domiciled there. "A change of domicile requires 'an actual moving with an intent to go to a given place and remain there.' "[146] Conversely, a residence of only a few days may

---

138 Sarbacher v. McNamara, 564 A.2d 701, 707 (D.C.App.1989).

139 Siegemund v. Shapland, 324 F. Supp. 2d 176, 186 (D.Me. 2004); Gellerstedt v. United Missouri Bank, 865 S.W.2d 707 (Mo.App.1993) (even though the testator was domiciled in Kansas when she executed her will, the court held that if she had moved to Missouri before she died, Missouri law should control).

140 *Id. See also*, Estate of Buckley, 677 S.W.2d 946 (Mo.App. 1984).

141 *Restatement (Second) of Conflict of Laws* § 264, cmt. f (1971). *See also id.* § 268, cmt. f; Estate of Stellwag v. Kennedy, 817 S.W.2d 466 (Mo.App.1990).

142 In re Estate of Salathe, 703 So.2d 1167 (Fla.App.1997).

143 Shim v. Rutgers, 924 A.2d 465, 474 (N.J. 2007).

144 Skiles v. Skiles, 646 N.E.2d 353, 355 (Ind.App.1995). A Hague Convention of 1989 promoted the idea of "habitual residence" as determining factor, being regarded as a compromise between the competing notions of nationality and domicile, but few countries have adopted the Convention. G. Miller, *supra* note 108 at 41.

145 Hager v. Hager, 607 N.E.2d 63 (Ohio App.1992); Matter of Estate of Burshiem, 483 N.W.2d 175 (N.D.1992).

146 Matter of Estate of Brown, 587 N.E.2d 686, 689 (Ind.App.1992); Guardianship of Parker, 189 P.3d 730 (Okla. Civ. App. Div. 2008) (there must be an actual abandonment of the first domicile coupled with an intention not to return). *See also* Nora v. Nora, 494 So.2d 16 (Ala.1986) (decedent who spent the last 36 years of his life in Alabama remained domiciled in Louisiana); Matter of Estate of Marcos, 963 P.2d 1124 (Haw.1998) (Decedent not domiciled in Hawaii although he spent the last 3 1/2 years of his life there); Gellerstedt v. United Missouri Bank, 865 S.W.2d 707 (Mo.App.1993) (move to Missouri nursing home did not necessarily show a change of domicile). The guardian of an incompetent person may be authorized to change her domicile. In re Seyse, 803

constitute a change of domicile when there was an intent to make the new residence home.[147]

Because reasonable minds can often differ as to where a person was domiciled, courts may reach conflicting decisions on the question. A finding in State A that the decedent was domiciled there bars a court in State B from finding otherwise only as to parties over whom the court in State A had jurisdiction.[148] But under the UPC, when conflicting claims of domicile arise in different states, "the determination of domicile in the proceeding first commenced must be accepted as determinative" in all cases on the theory that "the decedent would prefer that his estate be unified under either rule rather than wasted in litigation."[149]

Reference in the will to the law of the domicile usually means the domicile of the decedent at the time of death,[150] but not always. When a testator was domiciled in New York when she executed her will, but moved to New Hampshire before she died at a time when she was mentally incapacitated, the court refused to look to New Hampshire law to determine her heirs. It refused to look to New Hampshire law because the will had been executed with reference to New York law and had specifically referred to New York law as the source for ascertaining her heirs.[151]

In some cases, the court looks to the domicile of the survivors rather than that of the decedent. Thus, when a question arose as to the rights to insurance proceeds on a policy on the life of a man who worked in Arkansas, the court looked to Oklahoma law because all of the claimants lived there.[152]

A.2d 694 (N.J.Super.App.Div.2002); *cf.* 1 J Schoenblum, *supra* note 120 at § 7.06 (general discussion of the domicile of an incompetent).

[147] In re Estate of Elson, 458 N.E.2d 637 (Ill.App.1983). (Intent may be particularly hard to determine when a change of residence is involuntary, as in the case of prisoners or members of the armed services. J Schoenblum, *supra* note 120, at § 7.09[A]. *See also*, The Milton H. Greene Archives, Inc. v. CMG Worldwide, Inc., 568 F. Supp. 2d 1152 (C.D. Ca)(2008) (domicile and residence are distinct concepts; domicile being a residence with an intent that it be permanent).

[148] *Restatement (Second) of Conflict of Laws* § 317 (1971); In re Estate of Rubert, 651 A.2d 937 (N.H.1994) (Virginia court's determination contested by interested parties living there was entitled to full faith and credit); In re Estate of Tolson, 947 P.2d 1242 (Wash.App.1997) (California court's determination that decedent was domiciled there entitled to full faith and credit); Nahar v. Nahar, 656 So.2d 225 (Fla.App.1995) (comity given to Dutch court's determination of decedent's domicile).

[149] UPC § 3–202 and comments thereunder.

[150] *Restatement (Second) of Conflict of Laws* §§ 260, 263, 264 (1971); Atkins v. Atkins, 340 S.E.2d 537 (S.C.1986).

[151] Royce v. Estate of Denby, 379 A.2d 1256 (N.H.1977). In this case, because the testator was incapacitated during her residence in New Hampshire, arguably she never changed her domicile. *See Restatement (Second) of Conflict of Laws* § 23, cmt. b (1971). Cf. In re Estate of Rupert, 651 A.2d 937 (N.H. 1994). In Matter of Estate of Garver, 343 A.2d 817 (N.J.Super.App.Div.1975), the court also refused to apply the law of the domicile at death on the ground that it would defeat the decedent's intent.

[152] Whirlpool Corp. v. Ritter, 929 F.2d 1318, 1321 (8th Cir.1991). *See also* Matter of Estate of Gilmore, 946 P.2d 1130, 1138 (N.M.App.1997) (interest of state of decedent's domicile is "slight" as against the domicile of the potential beneficiaries of a wrongful death claim); Estate of Jones v. Howell, 687 So.2d 1171, 1179 (Miss.1996) (dissent).

Forum

Sometimes the forum simply applies its own law. According to the Restatement, "a court usually applies its own local rules prescribing how litigation shall be conducted."[153] This is justified by the fact that it may be difficult to apply another state's rules, and the parties do not rely on them in entering transactions because they do not anticipate litigation at all.[154] For example, an Oregon court refused to apply a Washington statute that would have barred an insured's widow from testifying even though Washington substantive law governed the case.[155] Similarly, an Arkansas court applied its own law as to burden of proof and presumptions in considering a will executed in Tennessee.[156] But, it is not always clear how a particular question should be characterized for this purpose. When a mother and daughter died in an air raid in 1940, the succession turned on which one survived; in resolving this question the rules in England (the forum) and Germany (the domicile of the decedents) differed.[157] The court treated the question as one of substantive law and so applied German law.[158]

In the absence of satisfactory proof of contrary applicable foreign law, the law of the forum is applied. Thus, even though a decedent was domiciled in Mexico when he died, a New York court applied its own law, because it was "reluctant to take upon itself the burden of determining what the law of Mexico is."[159]

When a choice-of-law rule directs a court to apply the law of another jurisdiction, this may be ignored if the foreign law is deemed inconsistent with a fundamental policy of the forum. This restriction is construed narrowly, because otherwise the forum would never apply a foreign law which differed from its own.[160]

---

[153] *Restatement (Second) of Conflict of Laws* § 122 (1971).

[154] *Id.* at, cmt. a.

[155] Equitable Life Assurance Society v. McKay, 760 P.2d 871 (Or.1988), following *Restatement (Second) of Conflict of Laws* § 138 (1971).

[156] Warner v. Warner, 687 S.W.2d 856 (Ark.App.1985). *See also Restatement (Second) of Conflict of Laws* §§ 133–34 (1971); Beall v. Beall, 577 S.E.2d 356 (N.C.App.2003) (forum applies its own statute of limitations). *But cf.* Matter of Estate of Gilmore, 946 P.2d 1130, 1133 (N.M.App.1997) (the disposition of wrongful death proceeds is not a "procedural" matter governed by the law of the forum).

[157] The problem of simultaneous death is discussed in Section 6.5, note 207 et seq.

[158] In re Cohn, [1945] Ch 5 (1944).

[159] Matter of Estate of Edwards, 452 N.Y.S.2d 293 (Surr.1982). *See also Restatement (Second) of Conflict of Laws* § 136, cmt. f (1971); Razzaghe-Ashrafi v. Razzaghe-Ashrafi, 558 So.2d 1368, 1370 (La.App.1990) (N.Y. assumed to have community property because no evidence to the contrary produced!)

[160] *See* Flick & Piltz, *supra* note 95, at 38–39; In re Portnoy, 201 B.R. 685, 700 (S.D.N.Y.1996) (choice of law provision in a trust disregarded as contrary to public policy disallowing persons from creating a trust for their own benefit that cannot be reached by their creditors); *cf.* Allen v. Storer, 600 N.E.2d 1263 (Ill.App.1992) (error to reject claim of common-law marriage as against public policy of Illinois).

Interests

Professor Schoenblum criticizes the UPC's use of domicile for most choice of law questions, arguing for a "broader interests analysis favored in one form or another by many conflicts scholars."[161]

The Restatement, while restating the traditional rules described above on many issues, says that for inter-vivos trusts where the governing law is not designated by the settlor, the court should look to "the local law of the state with which, as to the matter at issue, the trust has its most significant relationship."[162] This permits consideration of several factors, including the place of execution of the trust, the situs of the assets, and the domicile of the settlor and of the beneficiaries.[163] As to particular questions some factors may be more important than others. For example, a comment to the UTC distinguishes between "dispositive provisions" and "administrative matters;" as to the latter, the "law of the trust's principal place of administration will govern."[164]

This flexible approach has had a mixed reception in the courts. A Louisiana court rejected it because the Louisiana Civil Code required reference to the law of the decedent's domicile, but the court added that "even under the interest analysis" the result would probably be the same.[165] Some other courts have expressly "rejected wooden applications of the traditional conflicts rules" in favor of "choices of law based on the relevant policies and interests at stake in given situations."[166] In a case involving a contract to devise property to the promissor's child, the court applied Massachusetts law, even though the promissor died domiciled in New Hampshire. It applied Massachusetts law because Massachusetts "has the most significant relationship to the transaction," and the contract was negotiated and executed and the beneficiaries resided there.[167]

---

[161] Schoenblum, *supra* note 105, at 1317. However, the same author has conceded that "the unwillingness of many courts to engage in a more flexible interest analysis is likely to persist." 1 J Shoenblum, *supra* note 120, at 682.

[162] *Restatement (Second) of Conflict of Laws* § 270(2) (1971). *See also* UTC § 107(2); Hague Convention on Trusts, 1985, art 7.

[163] *Restatement (Second) of Conflict of Laws* § 270, cmt. c (1971). In Fifth Third Bank v. Crosley, 669 N.E.2d 904, 908 (Ohio Com.Pl.1996), the court applied Ohio law to two living trusts because they were "executed in Ohio and the situs of each trust is Ohio," presumably because the trustee was an Ohio trust company. *See also*, Russell v. Wachovia Bank, NA, 578 S.E.2d 329 (SC 2003).

[164] UTC § 107, comment. *See also Restatement (Second) of Conflict of Laws* § 268(2) (1971); Brown v. Ryan, 788 N.E.2d 1183, 1188 (Ill.App.2003).

[165] Cohn v. Heymann, 544 So.2d 1242 (La.App.1989). The court noted that the children who sought to apply Louisiana law to get a forced share were domiciled in New York. In Lewis v. Steinreich, 652 N.E.2d 981 (Ohio 1995), the court, following the Restatement, looked to the state with "the most significant contacts," but this turned out to be the decedent's domicile. *See also* In re Estate of Delaney, 819 A.2d 968, 989 (D.C.2003) (law of domicile applied because it had "the stronger interest").

[166] Royce v. Estate of Denby, 379 A.2d 1256, 1259 (N.H.1977). *See also* Whirlpool Corp. v. Ritter, 929 F.2d 1318, 1321 (8th Cir.1991).

[167] Nile v. Nile, 734 N.E.2d 1153, 1161 (Mass.2000).

Favoring Validity

A recurring theme in choice of law is fulfilling the expectations of the transferor (testator, settlor, etc.). This underlies a liberal rule as to the formal validity of wills. Under the UPC a will is valid if it complies with the Code *or* with the law of the place where the will was executed *or* where the testator was domiciled, the purpose being "to provide a wide opportunity for validation of expectations of testators."[168] Many states have similar provisions,[169] and courts may reach this result even without a statute "where the requirements of form . . . have been satisfied in substance."[170] Thus, when a will attested by interested witnesses was executed in Florida, which allowed this, it could be probated in Ohio, where the testator was domiciled at death. Furthermore, the interested witnesses did not forfeit their bequests as they would have had the will been executed in Ohio.[171]

The UPC is limited to "written" wills, and so would not validate an oral will even if made by a testator in a jurisdiction which allowed them.[172] Nor can the rule be used to escape limitations on testamentary freedom, such as the spouse's elective share. If a testator executed a will in a state which did not give spouses an elective share, the spouse could claim a share under the law of the testator's domicile.[173]

The choice of law rules on marriage reflect a similar desire to sustain validity. "There is a strong inclination to uphold a marriage because of the hardship that might otherwise be visited upon the parties and their children."[174] Generally a marriage between a man and a woman which satisfies the requirements of the state where it took place will be recognized in other states.[175] But even a marriage invalid where contracted may be valid when "it

---

[168] UPC § 2–506, comment. *See also* UTC § 403; *Restatement (Third) of Property (Wills and Other Donative Transfers)* § 3.1, cmt. e (1998) (favoring rule "as a principle of decisional law" where there was no statute). A similar desire to avoid having wills fail through formal defects underlies a Hague Convention of 1961 which many countries have adopted. *See* Flick & Piltz, *supra* note 95, at 267; 1 J Schoenblum, *supra* note 120, at § 15.04. This was the basis for the English Wills Act, 1963, §§ 1, 2.

[169] Cal.Prob.Code § 6113; *Restatement (Second) of Conflict of Laws* § 263, cmt. c (1971); Scoles & Hay, *supra* note 114, § 20.9. In Matter of Estate of Zelikovitz, 923 P.2d 740 (Wyo.1996), a codicil was probated under such a statute; because it was valid under Wyoming law, it was not necessary to examine its validity under the law of Oklahoma where it was executed. However, Schoenblum notes that many states with similar statutes "do not go as far as the Uniform Probate Code." Schoenblum, *supra* note 105, at 1294.

[170] *Restatement (Second) of Conflict of Laws* § 223, cmt. e (1971). But in Matter of Estate of Campbell, 673 P.2d 645 (Wyo.1983), the court applied the law of the state of execution to invalidate a will which would have been valid by the law of the state of domicile.

[171] Hairelson v. Estate of Franks, 720 N.E.2d 989 (Ohio App.1998). As to interested witnesses, *see* Section 3.3, note 87 et seq.

[172] Professor Schoenblum criticizes the writing requirement in UPC § 2–506, arguing that an oral manifestation of intent may be more reliable than a writing. Schoenblum, *supra* note 105, at 1300. As to oral wills, *see* Section 3.4, note 197 et seq.

[173] UPC § 2–202(d). As to the elective share, *see* Section 8.7.

[174] *Restatement (Second) of Conflict of Laws* § 283, cmt. h (1971). The hardships historically inflicted on children of unmarried parents have been considerably reduced in recent years by the trend to give equivalent rights to children born out of wedlock. *See* Section 2.9. As to the validity of marriage in general, *see*, Section 2.12.

[175] *Id.* at § 283(2); Cal. Family Code § 308; Estate of Loughmiller, 629 P.2d 156 (Kan.1981) (marriage between first cousins valid because it occurred in state which allowed it). This principle is sometimes rejected when the marriage occurred during a brief visit by a couple which was

would be valid under the local law of some other state having a substantial relation to the parties," such as their domicile.[176]

On the question of whether a child is "legitimate," the choice of law may be determinative. According to the Restatement, "the law favors the status of legitimacy" so that a change of domicile may operate in the child's favor, but not against him.[177] Thus, when a child was born out of wedlock in Ohio but died domiciled in Washington, the court applied Washington law which allowed her paternal relatives to inherit. Although "determinations of personal status" were usually governed by the place of birth, the question here was inheritance, and as to this, Washington had the dominant interest.[178] A child who had been declared legitimate under German law, where his father was domiciled at the time, was deemed legitimate under Illinois law where the child died. Thus, the father's relatives could inherit from the child; this result was "consistent with public policy which generally favors the status of legitimacy."[179]

Drafting

One who undertakes to draft a will or trust should be familiar with the foregoing choice of law issues. The client may have property in another jurisdiction either now or later or may die domiciled in another state or country. A provision in the instrument which specifies the governing law may avoid undesirable rules or uncertainty as to the governing law.

Clients should be advised to make their domicile clear, in order to avoid litigation on the issue and possible double taxation.[180] A recital in a will as to

---

domiciled elsewhere. Vaughn v. Hufnagel, 473 S.W.2d 124 (Ky.1971); Matter of Lamb's Estate, 655 P.2d 1001 (N.M.1982); Matter of Marriage of Wharton, 639 P.2d 652 (Or.App.1982). *But see* Mott v. Duncan Petroleum Trans., 414 N.E.2d 657 (N.Y.1980); Estate of Smart v. Smart, 676 P.2d 1379 (Okl.App.1983); Renshaw v. Heckler, 787 F.2d 50 (2d Cir.1986).

As of 2015, same sex marriage is legal in the United States in all states and states cannot refuse to recognize an out-of-state gay marriage. See Obergefell v. Hodges, 576 U.S. 644, 135 S.Ct. 2584 (2015).

[176] *Restatement (Second) of Conflict of Laws* § 283, cmt. i (1971); McPeek v. McCardle, 888 N.E.2d 171, 175–76 (Ind. 2008). *See* In re Estate of Shippy, 678 P.2d 848 (Wash.App.1984) (marriage valid under Washington law where couple resided when husband died, even though invalid in Alaska where marriage contracted); Unif. Marriage and Divorce Act § 210 (marriages valid by place contracted *or* by domicil of the parties are valid); Allen v. Storer, 600 N.E.2d 1263 (Ill.App.1992) (common-law marriage valid because couple was domiciled in Ohio which allowed them).

[177] *Restatement (Second) of Conflict of Laws* § 287, cmt. d (1971). As we shall see in Section 2.9, substantive discussions of this subject today generally avoid the term "illegitimate" to describe a child born out of wedlock. Moreover the rights of children rarely depend on the marital status of their parents today.

[178] Matter of Estate of Cook, 698 P.2d 1076 (Wash.App.1985). *See also* Buchea v. United States, 154 F.3d 1114 (9th Cir.1998) (even though tribal customary adoption did not terminate parental rights, it has that effect under governing Alaska law).

[179] In re Estate of Janussek, 666 N.E.2d 774 (Ill.App.1996). *See also* Powers v. Steele, 475 N.E.2d 395 (Mass.1985). *But see* In re Dumaine, 600 A.2d 127 (N.H.1991) (applying New Hampshire law to bar a child born out of wedlock in New York).

[180] Parks, *Special Estate Planning Strategies to fit the Needs of the Mobile Client*, 18 Est.Plan. 150 (1991). As to double taxation based on inconsistent findings as to domicile, *see* Scoles & Hay, *supra* note 114, at § 4.5; Dorrance Estate, 309 Pa. 151, 163 A. 303 (1932), cert. denied, 287 U.S. 660 (1932); In re Estate of Dorrance, 115 N.J.Eq. 268, 170 A. 601 (1934), cert. denied, 298 U.S. 678, reh'g denied, 298 U.S. 692 (1936).

the testator's domicile is helpful, because domicile is largely a question of intent.[181] However, a recital is not conclusive because the testator may have changed domicile after signing the will.[182]

§ 1.3 Change in the Law

Although the law of property has a reputation for being conservative, it has been subject to many changes over time. A question when a change in the law becomes effective often arises. The answer may depend on whether the change comes about by a judicial decision overruling prior cases or by a statute. Because of the notion that judges "discover" the law but do not make it, they ordinarily do not hesitate to apply their rulings to their prior cases. According to Blackstone, when judges find that an older decision "is most evidently contrary to reason," they "do not pretend to make a new law, but to vindicate the old one from misinterpretation. For if it be found that the former decision is manifestly absurd or unjust, it is declared, not that such a sentence was *bad law*, but that it was *not law*."[183] Despite this comforting rationalization, judges hesitate to overrule precedents on which parties may have relied and may prefer to leave a questionable rule unchanged. Blackstone, for example, citing the common law rule which barred half-blood relatives from inheriting land, says that "though a modern judge . . . might wish [the rule] had been otherwise settled, yet it is not in his power to alter it."[184] Similar reasoning can be found in modern cases.[185]

Judges sometimes overrule precedents prospectively. For example, in 1984 a court announced that "for the future we shall no longer follow the rule announced" in an earlier case, but because "the bar has been entitled reasonably to rely on that rule in advising clients" the new rule would apply only in future cases.[186] Prospective overruling is rather rare, however. One court has said that it "should be limited to a case in which the hardship on a party who has relied on the old rule outweighs the hardship on the party denied the benefit of the new rule; and there are few cases where such rigorous demonstrations can be made."[187] On the other hand, it is not unusual for a precedent-breaking decision in one case not to be applied retroactively in similar cases. In 1988, the United States Supreme Court in *Tulsa Professional Collection Services v. Pope*[188] held unconstitutional a state statute that barred claims against a decedent's estate where a notice to file the claim had not been mailed to a creditor whose name and whereabouts were known to the executor.

---

181 The court relied on a will recital in determining domicile in Matter of Estate of Brown, 587 N.E.2d 686 (Ind.App.1992); Cohn v. Heymann, 544 So.2d 1242 (La.App.1989).

182 Lotz v. Atamaniuk, 304 S.E.2d 20 (W.Va.1983) (finding of Ohio domicile erroneous even though the will recited it). For suggestions, how to document a claim of domicile other than by a will recital, *see* J. Schoenblum, *supra* note 120, at § 8.05.

183 1 Blackstone, *Commentaries* 69–70 (1765).

184 *Id.* at 71. For the modern rules on this question, *see* Section 2.2, note 88 et seq.

185 Wasserman v. Cohen, 606 N.E.2d 901 (Mass.1993) (adhering to the rules of ademption because "stability in the field of trusts and estates requires that we continue the doctrine").

186 Sullivan v. Burkin, 460 N.E.2d 572, 576–77 (Mass.1984). *See also* Jeruzal's Estate v. Jeruzal, 130 N.W.2d 473 (Minn.1964); Rosenberg v. Lipnick, 389 N.E.2d 385 (Mass.1979).

187 Decker v. Meriwether, 708 S.W.2d 390, 394–95 (Tenn.App.1985).

188 485 U.S. 478 (1988). Such "nonclaim" statutes are discussed in Section 13.5, note 201 et seq.

The next year another case arose involving a claim against an estate which had closed in 1987. The relevant state statute "involved the same constitutional infirmities," but the court refused to apply *Tulsa*, because retroactive application "could cause the disturbance of many property rights" which had "created immeasurable reliance" and were "unexpectedly declared invalid."[189]

When change in law comes through legislation, the effective date usually depends on the terms of the statute. In most states, for example, the common-law Rule in Shelley's Case has been abolished by statutes which are expressly limited to instruments executed after the statute was passed.[190] The UTC alters the common law by making trusts presumptively revocable, but this rule is expressly inapplicable to trusts created before the Code became effective.[191] On the other hand, a statute passed in 1997 was applied to a conveyance made in 1996 because the court accepted the legislature's claim that the statute was "intended as a clarification of existing law and not as a new enactment."[192] Some courts even use statutes which by their terms are prospective only as evidence of a state "policy" and, thus, as a justification for the court to apply the same policy retroactively.[193]

Statutes which do not make clear when they become applicable are usually presumed to be prospective. Courts give "retrospective applications to statutes 'only when the mandate of the legislature [to do so] is imperative.' "[194] Even when a statute is clearly stated to apply retrospectively, a court may hold that this is unconstitutional. For example, a wife put title to a house bought with her funds into joint tenancy with her husband who agreed orally that the house was to remain her separate property. The legislature later passed a statute providing that property held in joint tenancy was community property

---

189 Hanesworth v. Johnke, 783 P.2d 173, 176–77 (Wyo.1989). *See also* Farm Credit Bank v. Brown, 577 N.E.2d 906, 911 (Ill.App.1991). *But see* In re Estate of Reynolds, 970 P.2d 537, 543 (Kan.1998) (applying *Tulsa* retroactively).

190 Society Nat. Bank v. Jacobson, 560 N.E.2d 217 (Ohio 1990) (Rule applied even though statute abolished in 1941 because the trust was created in 1931); Toler v. Harbour, 589 S.W.2d 529 (Tex.Civ.App.1979); City Bank & Trust Co. v. Morrissey, 454 N.E.2d 1195 (Ill.App.1983). As to the Rule in Shelley's Case, *see* Section 10.4, note 13. Often such legislation is expressly made prospective because of doubts, not necessarily well founded, about the constitutionality of retroactive legislation. Leach, *Perpetuities Legislation, Massachusetts Style*, 67 Harv.L.Rev. 1349, 1365 (1954).

191 UTC § 602(a).

192 Premier Property Management, Inc. v. Chavez, 728 N.E.2d 476, 480 (Ill.2000). *See also* Noggle v. Bank of America, 82 Cal.Rptr.2d 829, 834 (App.1999); Department of Social Serv. v. Saunders, 724 A.2d 1093 (Conn.1999); Matter of Estate of Thomas, 998 P.2d 560, 562 (Nev.2000) ("amendment is persuasive evidence of what the legislature intended by the prior statute").

193 Warner v. Whitman, 233 N.E.2d 14, 17 (Mass.1968) (perpetuities reform statute); In re Arens' Trust, 197 A.2d 1 (N.J.1964) (Principal and Income Act); Estate of Coe, 201 A.2d 571 (N.J.1964) (inclusion of adopted child in class gift); In re Estate of Hollister, 221 N.E.2d 376, 379 (N.Y.1966) (concurring opinion); re Last Will and Testament of Tamplin, 48 P.3d 471, 474 (Alaska 2002).

194 Connecticut Bank & Trust Co. v. Brody, 392 A.2d 445, 451 (Conn.1978) (perpetuities reform statute). *See also* Levy v. Crawford, 600 N.E.2d 597, 598 (Mass.App.Ct.1992); Estate of Hilton, 52 Cal.Rptr.2d 491 (App.1996) (change in statutory fees of attorney for an estate). However, a statute which said that it was "declaratory of existing law" was applied retroactively in Estate of Ridenour v. Commissioner, 36 F.3d 332 (4th Cir.1994) (scope of a durable power). *See also* Matter of OnBank & Trust Co., 688 N.E.2d 245 (N.Y.1997) (statute dealing with trustee's fees found intended to apply retroactively); In re Estate of Dewitt, 54 P.3d 849, 854 (Colo.2002).

unless there was a written agreement to the contrary. The statute purported to apply to pending proceedings, but the court held this was an unconstitutional impairment of the wife's property rights. If existing law had required the parties to execute a writing to prove their agreement, they would probably have done so. "The parties' legitimate expectations, therefore, are substantially disregarded in favor of needless retroactivity."[195] On the other hand, other constitutional attacks on retroactive legislation have failed. For example, a statute which restricted gifts to lawyers in instruments that they drafted was applied to a revocable trust drafted before the statute was enacted. This did not violate due process because the lawyer "did not have a vested right" under the trust so long as it was revocable.[196] Generally, the law applicable to estates is the law in effect when the testator dies, at least as respects determining the size of the share of an heir or beneficiary.[197]

Today there is less reluctance to make changes in the law retroactive. For example, the first Uniform Principal and Income Act (1931) did not apply to trusts in existence when the Act was adopted, but the second version (1962) did and has been held constitutional.[198] The Uniform Prudent Investor Act was expressly made applicable to trusts existing at the time of its adoption, though only to "actions occurring thereafter."[199] When in 1955, Illinois changed existing law to presume that adopted children were included in class gifts, it did so only as to instruments thereafter executed, but in 1989, it made the new rule applicable to all instruments, regardless of when they were made.[200] Likewise, section 2–707 of the UPC retroactively applies a condition of survivorship to an indefeasibly vested remainder in a trust. And, the UTC applies to all trusts, whenever created, being "intended to have the widest possible effect within constitutional limitations."[201]

There are at least two good arguments in favor of making changes retroactive. First, presumably the new rule is better than the old one or it would not have been made. If the new rule is better, why postpone its

---

[195] In re Marriage of Buol, 705 P.2d 354 (Cal.1985). For other decisions holding retroactive statutes unconstitutional, *see* Whirlpool Corp. v. Ritter, 929 F.2d 1318 (8th Cir.1991); Willcox v. Penn Mutual Life Ins. Co., 55 A.2d 521 (Pa.1947); Board of Education v. Miles, 207 N.E.2d 181 (N.Y.1965).

Some state constitutions prohibit retroactive legislation in general terms. *E.g.*, Colo.Const. art 2, § 11. Query whether this makes any difference. *See* In re Estate of Dewitt, 54 P.3d 849 (Colo.2002) (upholding a "retroactive" statute because not "retrospective").

[196] Bank of America v. Angel View, 85 Cal.Rptr.2d 117, 121 (App.1999). *See also* Evans v. McCoy, 436 A.2d 436 (Md.1981); First Nat. Bank v. King, 651 N.E.2d 127 (Ill.1995); Hiddleston v. Nebraska Jewish Education Society, 186 N.W.2d 904 (Neb.1971); In re Estate of Dewitt, 54 P.3d 849, 856 (Colo.2002) (statute affecting insurance beneficiaries upheld because they have only an expectancy, not a vested interest).

[197] See In re Estate of Myers, 825 N.W.2d 1, 6 (Iowa 2012).

[198] National Geographic Society v. Williams, 497 S.W.2d 908 (Tenn.App.1972) (first UPIA inapplicable to an existing trust); Venables v. Seattle-First Nat. Bank, 808 P.2d 769 (Wash.App.1991) (applying a newer version to an existing trust); Bogert, *The Revised Uniform Principal and Income Act,* 38 N.D.Law 50, 52 (1962). However, one part of the 1962 Act and its counterpart in the 1997 version (§ 411(d)) are made prospective due to "concerns about the constitutionality" of retroactivity. *See* Comment to § 411.

[199] Unif.Prud.Inv.Act § 11 (1994).

[200] Chicago Title and Trust Co. v. Steinitz, 681 N.E.2d 669, 671 (Ill.App.1997).

[201] UTC § 1106, comment.

applicability? Second, having the new rule and the old one operate simultaneously makes the law more complicated. Trustees, for example, would have to keep track of different rules applicable to different trusts depending upon the date of their creation.[202] This problem can be avoided if the new rule applies to *all* trusts.

On the other hand, it may be unfair to parties who have relied on existing law when a change is made retroactive. Sometimes this argument focuses on the transferor (testator, settlor, etc.), sometimes on other persons, such as the transferee, or a fiduciary who has acted in reliance on the old rule. For example, even though Illinois now includes adopted children in class gifts, regardless of when a will was executed, a trustee who made a distribution under the old law which excluded adopted children cannot be held liable therefor.[203]

"Retroactivity" is a general term, and courts do not always use it consistently. In the law applicable to wills and trusts, several points in time may be deemed relevant.

Execution of an Instrument

Before 1981 many testators executed wills that left property "equal to the maximum marital deduction allowable" under the Internal Revenue Code to their spouse. At that time this amounted to 50% of the estate, but in 1981 the maximum marital deduction was increased to 100%. Recognizing that this change "might have an unintended impact on existing wills, Congress provided a transitional rule" whereby such clauses in wills executed before 1981 should be construed to provide the more limited gift allowed by prior law even if the testator died after 1981.[204] Some statutes dealing with other issues by their terms apply only to instruments executed thereafter.[205] However, the more common effective date for laws affecting wills is the date of the testator's death. Thus, when an anti-lapse statute was changed between the time the testator executed his will and his death, the court applied the amended version of the statute. "When laws are changed after a will is executed but before it is probated, the parties' rights are determined in accordance with the law in

---

[202] Levin, *Section 6104(d) of the Pennsylvania Rule against Perpetuities,* 25 Vill.L.Rev. 213, 215 (1980). The Uniform Transfers to Minors Act applies to transfers made under its predecessor because "it will be more orderly to subject gifts . . . under the prior Act to the procedures of this Act, rather than to keep both Acts in force." Uniform Transfers to Minors Act § 22, comment.

[203] 755 ILCS § 5/2–4(g); Chicago Title and Trust Co. v. Steinitz, 681 N.E.2d 669 (Ill.App.1997). As to the rights of adopted children *see* Section 2.10.

[204] In re Estate of Pouser, 975 P.2d 704, 707 (Ariz.1999). As to the potential disadvantages of making a marital deduction gift too large, *see* Section 15.3, note 184. *See also* Reynolds v. Russell, 433 A.2d 699, 702 (Del.Ch.1981); Bank One Ohio Trust Co. v. Hiram College, 684 N.E.2d 1275 (Ohio App.1996) (reference to statutorily authorized investments means statute as it existed when will was executed); Boston Safe Deposit & Trust Co. v. Wilbur, 728 N.E.2d 264, 268 (Mass.2000) (looking to cases decided at the time a will was executed). However, in *Pouser, supra,* and in several other cases courts have decided that the testator actually intended the new rule to apply. Estate of Weeks, 462 A.2d 44 (Me.1983); Matter of Estate of Eversole, 885 P.2d 657 (Okl.1994).

[205] Cal.Prob.Code § 246(b) (construction of the term "per stirpes"); In re Estate of Cruikshank, 746 N.Y.S.2d 769, 772 (Surr.2002) (1986 amendment inapplicable to will executed in 1942).

existence at the testator's death."[206] When a change occurs after a testator has executed a will but before the testator dies, he/she can change the will if the change in the law does not reflect the testator's desires. This is also true for revocable trusts. Thus, a statute restricting donative transfers to attorneys drafting instruments was applied to a revocable trust created prior to the statute's enactment because, by its terms, the statute governed "instruments that become irrevocable" thereafter.[207] However, for *irrevocable* instruments the date of execution is more significant.[208] The UPC applies to "instruments executed before the effective date" of the Code when "executed by decedents dying thereafter."[209] As to wills and revocable trusts, this is the general view, but as to irrevocable instruments it is questionable.[210]

In *Whirlpool Corp. v. Ritter*[211] a man purchased life insurance in 1985 and designated his wife as beneficiary. In 1989, they were later divorced. In 1987, a statute was passed under which a divorce revoked the benefits to a former spouse. Although the statute by its terms applied to anyone dying thereafter, the court held that its application to a prior contract violated the constitution, because "an individual could rely on the pre-existing law and neither know nor expect that the rules governing his policy have changed."[212] This decision was criticized by the Joint Editorial Board of the UPC,[213] and has been rejected in some other cases involving similar facts.[214]

For some purposes, however, the UPC looks to the date of execution of a will. A will is valid if it complies "with the law at the time of execution" even if it does not comply with more stringent formalities imposed thereafter.[215] However, if formal requirements are *relaxed* after the will is executed, this may validate a defectively executed will. The purpose of this rule is "to provide a

---

206 Matter of Estate of Micheel, 577 N.W.2d 407, 410 (Iowa 1998). As to the anti-lapse statutes *see* Section 8.5 at 356.

207 Bank of America v. Angel View, 85 Cal.Rptr.2d 117 (App.1999).

208 Shortridge v. Sherman, 406 N.E.2d 565 (Ill.App.1980) (1912 deed not affected by 1955 change in the law re adoptees); *cf.* UTC § 602(a) (provision making trusts presumptively revocable inapplicable to trusts previously executed). Under Section 602(a) of the UTC trusts created after the effective date in an enacting state are presumptively revocable. This rule is contrary to the rule in most states.

209 UPC § 8–101(b).

210 *Compare* Del.Code tit. 12 § 213 (in construing a will or trust, determine class by law in effect when instrument becomes irrevocable). In Powers v. Wilkinson, 506 N.E.2d 842, 849 (Mass.1987), the court announced a new rule to apply "only to trust instruments executed after the date of this opinion," apparently without distinction between revocable and irrevocable trusts.

211 929 F.2d 1318 (8th Cir.1991).

212 *Id.* at 1323. As to the effect of divorce on prior instruments, *see* Section 5.5, note 72 et seq. In Baker v. Leonard, 843 P.2d 1050 (Wash.1993), the court applied the law in effect when a bank account was opened to determine the depositor's intent, ignoring a change in the law which occurred before she died.

213 Halbach & Waggoner, *The Uniform Probate Code's New Survivorship and Anti-lapse Provisions*, 55 Alb.L.Rev. 1091, 1129 (1992). *See also*, In re Estate of Searl, 811 P.2d 828 (Hawaii 1991) (applying revised elective share statute to estate of person who died testate after the statute was enacted leaving a will executed prior to the enactment of the statute).

214 Buchholz v. Storsve, 740 N.W.2d 107 (S.D. 2007); Matter of Estate of Dobert, 963 P.2d 327 (Ariz.App.1998); Mearns v. Scharbach, 12 P.3d 1048 (Wash.App.2000); In re Estate of Dewitt, 54 P.3d 849 (Colo.2002).

215 UPC § 2–506. *See also* Cal.Prob.Code § 6113; Matter of Estate of Fitzgerald, 738 P.2d 236 (Utah App.1987); H. Flick & D. Piltz, *Der Internationale Erbfall* 271 (1999) (German law).

wide opportunity for validation of the expectations of testators."[216] Similarly a court applied a statute validating non-probate transfers of securities under a contract made prior to the statute's enactment on the ground that it "simply protect[ed] what the parties intended."[217] The Uniform Marriage and Divorce Act validates all marriages which "were valid at the time of the contract or were subsequently validated" by law.[218] On the same principle, statutes imposing formal requirements on contracts to make wills do not apply to contracts previously made.[219]

Date of Death

For most purposes the date of death determines the governing law. When changes in status, such as adoption, marriage, and divorce affect the distribution of property at death, courts generally look to the law as of the date of death rather than the law in effect when the adoption, marriage, or divorce occurred.[220]

Sometimes a change in the law occurs shortly after a decedent's death, before the estate has been distributed. Even here the courts usually apply the law as of the date of death. For example, when a woman was killed in April 1972, the then governing law split the estate between her parents and her husband. In July, the state adopted the UPC which would give a larger share to her husband, but the court held that the new law did not apply.[221] Although by its terms the Code applies to proceedings which are still pending when the Code takes effect,[222] any "accrued right" is protected, and the court held that this included the parents' share under prior law.

---

[216] UPC § 2–506, comment. *See also* Cal.Prob.Code § 6113; Succession of Gresham, 506 So.2d 156 (La.App.1987); Uniform Transfers to Minors Act § 22(a) (validating transfers made prior to the Act).

[217] Bielat v. Bielat, 721 N.E.2d 28, 34 (Ohio 2000). *But see* Bessett v. Huson, 39 P.3d 220, 225 (Or.App.2002) (undelivered renunciation ineffective unless it was executed after a statute abolishing delivery requirement became effective).

[218] Unif. Marriage and Divorce Act § 210. *See also* Matter of Heirship of McLeod, 506 So.2d 289 (Miss.1987); Warren Gen. Hosp. v. Brink, 610 N.E.2d 1128 (Ohio App.1992) (common-law marriage made prior to their abolition is valid). Compare the validation principle applied in the choice of law between states. Section 1.2, note 71 et seq. The validity of marriages is discussed in Section 2.12.

[219] Cal.Prob.Code § 21700(c); Mabry v. McAfee, 783 S.W.2d 356 (Ark.1990); Matter of Estate of Kerr, 918 P.2d 1354, 1357 (N.M.App.1996); Junot v. Estate of Gilliam, 759 S.W.2d 654, 658 (Tenn.1988); In re Estate of Roccamonte, 735 A.2d 614, 618 (N.J.Super.App.Div.1999). As to contracts to make wills, *see* Section 3.9.

[220] As to adoption, *see* In re Estate of Dye, 112 Cal.Rptr.2d 362 (App.2001); Matter of Estate of Ryan, 928 P.2d 735 (Ariz.App.1996); Aldridge v. Mims, 884 P.2d 817 (N.M.App.1994); Matter of Estate of Hinderliter, 882 P.2d 1001 (Kan.App.1994); In re Raymond Estate, 641 A.2d 1342 (Vt.1994). As to divorce, *see* Buehler v. Buehler, 425 N.E.2d 905 (Ohio App.1979); Matter of Will of Reilly, 493 A.2d 32 (N.J.Super.App. 1985) (applying revocation-on-divorce statute enacted between date of will's execution and date of death to gift to a woman where the marriage and its annulment occurred prior to the enactment of the statute). *But see* In re Estate of Crohn, 494 P.2d 258 (Or.App.1972) (applying statute in effect at date of divorce); In re Estate of Ralston, 674 P.2d 1001 (Colo.App.1983) (applying law at the date of a marriage).

[221] Hogan v. Hermann, 623 P.2d 900 (Idaho 1980). As to the spouse's intestate share, *see* Section 2.1. *See also* Pazzi v. Taylor, 342 N.W.2d 481 (Iowa 1984) (refusing to apply a new law passed a few months after an intestate died); Hermanson v. Hermanson, 133 Cal.Rptr.2d 486 (App.2003) (law passed shortly after settlor's death made trust irrevocable did not apply to trust).

[222] UPC § 8–101(b)(2). In Scribner v. Berry, 489 A.2d 8 (Me.1985), this was held to apply only to "procedural rules," because there is an exception for cases where "in the opinion of the

Unconstitutional Laws

If the law in effect at the date of death is unconstitutional it may not control.[223] For example, a father's surviving nonmarital children could not inherit under Texas law. A few months later the United States Supreme Court held a similar statute unconstitutional. The Court said that Texas could not apply its statute to bar inheritance by a nonmarital child because the administration of the father's estate was still in progress, but "after an estate has been finally distributed, the interest in finality may provide [a] . . . valid justification for barring the belated assertion of claims."[224] While the latter statement is only dictum, many cases have refused to upset distributions which have occurred under unconstitutional laws.[225]

The probable reliance of persons who receive distributions is protected, and it is not necessary for them to prove actual reliance.[226] An even stronger claim for protection is presented by bona fide purchasers for value[227] and fiduciaries who have made prior distributions. When a will made a gift of income to the testator's "descendants," a statutory presumption excluding children born out-of-wedlock was held to be unconstitutional, but the court refused to hold that a child born out-of-wedlock was entitled to income from the beginning, because this would "ignore the countervailing interests of the beneficiaries [born in wedlock who had been getting all the income] and the trustee." The child, however, was entitled to receive income that the trustee had held in reserve pending resolution of the dispute.[228] The California Probate Code protects fiduciaries from liability "for any action taken before the operative date that was proper at the time the action was taken."[229]

Court the former procedure should be made applicable in the interests of justice." But in In re Smith's Estate, 651 N.W.2d 153 (Mich.App.2002), the court applied a statute passed after a testator's death in admitting extrinsic evidence of his intent on the ground that the devisees acquired no "accrued right" by the testator's death.

223 So also, if a retroactive statute replaces an unconstitutional one, its retroactive application is likely to be upheld. In re Marriage of Bouquet, 546 P.2d 1371 (Cal.1976) (statute providing equal treatment for wives and husbands could be applied retroactively); Cooper v. Harris, 499 F.Supp. 266 (N.D.Ill.1980) (applying statute passed after father died to allow inheritance by child born out of wedlock).

224 Reed v. Campbell, 476 U.S. 852, 855 (1986).

225 Turner v. Nesby, 848 S.W.2d 872 (Tex.App.1993) (claim by a non-marital child barred by 4 year time limit of review of declarations of heirship); Boan v. Watson, 316 S.E.2d 401 (S.C.1984) (when husband died prior to a case holding a widow's statutory right was unconstitutional, his widow could claim dower); Dooley v. Reimer Farms, Inc., 638 N.E.2d 260 (Ill.App.1994) (because testator died in 1968, a remainder interest did not include illegitimate children); Stallworth v. Hicks, 434 So.2d 229 (Ala.1983); Flick & Piltz, *supra* note 95 at 90–92 (statute fixing marital property rule on basis of husband's citizenship applies to marriage which took place prior to statute's being held unconstitutional).

226 Contrast UPC § 3–909 which allows property which has been improperly distributed to be recovered unless the payment "can no longer be questioned because of adjudication, estoppel, or limitation."

227 Levin, *Section 6104(d) of the Pennsylvania Rule against Perpetuities*, 25 Vill.L.Rev. 213, 218–19 (1980) (describing a case of a purchaser of property distributed under a mortmain statute which was later held unconstitutional).

228 Estate of Dulles, 431 A.2d 208 (Pa.1981).

229 Cal.Prob.Code § 3(f). UPC § 8–101(b)(4) protects any "act done before the effective date."

Future Interests

Suppose a will gives an interest to *A* for life, and, upon A's death, to A's "issue." Under the law in effect when the testator died, neither an adopted child of *A* nor a nonmarital child of A would have taken. After the testator dies but during *A's* life, the law changes. Does the new rule apply? The many decisions on this issue are inconsistent. Many cases hold the new law inapplicable on the theory that the testator relied on the law in effect at the testator's death.[230] The UPC has been held inapplicable to the construction of wills of testators who died prior to its effective date.[231] A Massachusetts decision overruling the presumption that "issue" did not include children born out-of-wedlock was made prospective only because "the Bar has been entitled reasonably to rely on [the old] rule in advising clients."[232] The dissenting justices in this case questioned whether the testator had actually relied on the old rule. "It is likely that the donor did not have any 'intention at all with respect to the question.' "[233] As one court observed, "surely any scrivener who had those previous cases [excluding adopted children] in mind would not have left" the question open to a court's interpretation, but would have made a clear provision in the will on the subject.[234] Some courts, on the other hand, have applied the new rules on the ground that the testator intended to have whatever law was in effect at the time of final distribution of the trust control.[235]

A related question is raised by the use of the word "heirs" in a will. This is normally construed to incorporate the rules of intestate succession, but as of what date? According to the Restatement of Property, "even though the donor knew at the time the dispositive instrument was drafted that the statute governing intestate succession . . . excluded adopted children and children born out of wedlock, a change in the law of such State, before [the person whose 'heirs' are to receive the gift] dies . . . would apply."[236]

---

[230] Calhoun v. Campbell, 763 S.W.2d 744 (Tenn.1988) (adoptee excluded because will took effect in 1939 and drafters rely on existing law); Callan v. Winters, 534 N.E.2d 298 (Mass.1989); Lutz v. Fortune, 758 N.E.2d 77 (Ind.App.2001); Continental Bank, N.A. v. Herguth, 617 N.E.2d 852 (Ill.App.1993); Matter of Estate of Jenkins, 904 P.2d 1316 (Colo.1995) (adopted child excluded because of rule existing when testator died); Ohio Citizens Bank v. Mills, 543 N.E.2d 1206 (Ohio 1989) (adoptee excluded under law in effect when trust executed); Newman v. Wells Fargo Bank, N.A., 59 Cal.Rptr.2d 2, 926 P.2d 969 (1996) (adopted-out child excluded by applying the law in effect when the testator died).

[231] Scribner v. Berry, 489 A.2d 8 (Me.1985).

[232] Powers v. Wilkinson, 506 N.E.2d 842, 849 (Mass.1987).

[233] *Id.* at 851.

[234] Zimmerman v. First Nat. Bank, 348 So.2d 1359, 1366 (Ala.1977). Perhaps this argument is less persuasive when the old rule was embodied in a clear statute. *See* Newman v. Wells Fargo Bank, N.A., 926 P.2d 969 (Cal.1996).

[235] Annan v. Wilmington Trust Co., 559 A.2d 1289 (Del.1989) (inclusion of children born out of wedlock); Brown v. Trust Co., 196 S.E.2d 872 (Ga.1973); In re Sollid, 647 P.2d 1033 (Wash.App.1982) (inclusion of adopted child). Ohio Citizens Bank v. Mills, 543 N.E.2d 1206 (Ohio 1989) construed a statute allowing adopted children to take as prospective only, but the legislature later amended the statute so that it now applies to instruments previously executed. Fifth Third Bank v. Crosley, 669 N.E.2d 904 (Ohio Com.Pl.1996).

[236] *Restatement (Second) of Property (Donative Transfers)* § 29.3, cmt. d (1987). *See also* Conway v. Childress, 896 S.W.2d 15 (Ky.App.1994) (illegitimate child included as "heir"); Matter of Dodge Testamentary Trust, 330 N.W.2d 72 (Mich.App.1982) (inclusion of spouse as heir); Boatmen's Trust Co. v. Conklin, 888 S.W.2d 347, 354 (Mo.App.1994) (even though the court

Sometimes the discussion focuses on the interests of the devisees rather than the testator's intentions. As we have seen, once property has been distributed, it will not be taken back from the distributee on the ground that the law has changed. On the other hand, rights that have not yet irrevocably vested may be defeated by a change in the law. When a man created a joint tenancy in land with his son, a subsequent change in the law giving the man's widow a claim to share in the land was held to apply because the father could have destroyed the son's right of survivorship by severing the joint tenancy.

> Although [the son's] ownership rights in the property vested at the deed of conveyance, his right of survivorship to the whole property was not an 'irrevocable accrued right' until [the father's] death. Therefore the subsequent act of the legislature in creating the spouse's elective share rights did not divest [the son] of an irrevocably accrued right.[237]

Courts often say that "vested" interests are entitled to protection, but this word is variously interpreted. When a will left land to the testator's son for life, remainder to the son's children, this was held to include an adopted child under a statute which by its terms applied to wills whenever executed unless the estate had already "vested." The statute applied because, according to the court, the remainder did not vest until the son died.[238]

Rule Against Perpetuities

The Rule Against Perpetuities has been changed in most states and a number of states have repealed the rule. These changes are of two types. The first validates interests that would under the common law rule have been invalid.[239] It has been persuasively argued that making such changes retroactive promotes rather than defeats the expectations of the testator, because no one would go to the trouble of creating an invalid interest.[240] Although some statutory reforms of the Rule have been by their terms prospective only,[241] a Massachusetts court applied such a statute to an earlier

---

construed the word "issue" in the same will under the law as of the date of execution); Cal.Prob.Code § 21114; UPC § 2–711. As to other questions raised by the use of "heirs" in a will, *see* Sections 2.4, 11.3.

[237] In re Estate of Antonopoulos, 993 P.2d 637, 644 (Kan.1999). As to severing joint tenancies, *see* Section 5.5, note 49 et seq. As to the elective share, *see* Section 8.7.

[238] Thurston v. Thurston, 363 N.W.2d 298 (Mich.App.1985). The court's characterization of the remainder as contingent, not vested, is inconsistent with prevailing law. The court mistakenly concluded that because the son could have more children, his living children's interest was contingent. At common law, their interest would have been characterized as either vested subject to partial divestment or vested subject to open. *See also* Sola v. Clostermann, 679 P.2d 317 (Or.App.1984) (applying new law to include child born out of wedlock because remainder was contingent); Crumpton v. Mitchell, 281 S.E.2d 1, 6 (N.C.1981) (upholding a retroactive statute because due process does not protect contingent interests). *But see* Billings v. Fowler, 279 N.E.2d 906 (Mass.1972). For the ambiguities inherent in the terms "contingent" and "vested" *see* Section 11.1, note 7 et seq.

[239] These reforms are discussed in Section 12.4.

[240] Morris & Leach, *The Rule Against Perpetuities* 32 (1962); Levin, *Section 6104(d) of the Pennsylvania Rule against Perpetuities,* 25 Vill.L.Rev. 213, 229 (1980).

[241] Connecticut Bank & Trust Co. v. Brody, 392 A.2d 445, 451 (Conn.1978); Low v. Spellman, 629 A.2d 57 (Me.1993); Texas Prop. Code § 5.043(d).

will on the ground that it expressed the policy of the state.[242] The Uniform Statutory Rule Against Perpetuities is partially retroactive, and some statutes are fully so.[243] The Iowa Supreme Court upheld the retroactive application of that state's statute.[244]

The second type of reform has subjected to time limits interests that were previously exempt from the Rule, such as possibilities of reverter.[245] In this context the notion that no one expects to create an invalid interest argues *against* retroactive application. The New York Court of Appeals held unconstitutional a 1958 statute limiting possibilities of reverter when applied to an 1854 deed, saying that "retrospective legislation . . . cannot impair vested rights."[246] But even if possibilities of reverter are "vested," their value when a statute is passed is usually slight, and this, in the view of some courts, justifies imposing retroactive limitations on them.[247]

Fiduciary Administration

Many trusts endure for years during which questions of allocations between principal and income arise. The Uniform Principal and Income Act of 1962, unlike its predecessor, applied to trusts created prior to its adoption, but only to "any receipt or expense received or incurred after the effective date" of the Act.[248] A similar approach is taken to investments by trustees. "Whether an investment is proper is determined by the terms of the statute in force at the time when the investment is made" rather than by the rules in force when the trust was created.[249] On the other hand, the Uniform Principal and Income Act of 1997 applies to every trust or estate existing on the effective date of the act "except as otherwise provided in the will or terms of the trust or in this Act."[250]

The Uniform Trustees' Powers Act contains alternate provisions as to its effective date; one version applies to previously established trusts, but this

---

[242] Warner v. Whitman, 233 N.E.2d 14, 17 (Mass.1968). *See also* Juliano & Sons v. Chevron, U.S.A., 593 A.2d 814 (N.J.Super.App.Div.1991); Fleet Nat. Bank v. Colt, 529 A.2d 122 (R.I.1987).

[243] The "wait and see" aspect of the Uniform Statutory Rule applies only to interests created after the effective date, but prior interests, if invalid, can be reformed. Section 12.4. *Compare* Cal.Prob.Code § 21202 (statute applies regardless of when interest created, but not if validity has been determined in a proceeding or settlement). The Pennsylvania statute was originally prospective but later amended to make it retroactive. In re Estate of Weaver, 572 A.2d 1249, 1257 (Pa.Super.1990) (applying 1947 statute to will taking effect in 1935).

[244] Henderson v. Millis, 373 N.W.2d 497, 506 (Iowa 1985).

[245] For a discussion of this exemption *see* Section 12.6, note 231 et seq.

[246] Board of Education v. Miles, 207 N.E.2d 181, 184 (N.Y.1965). *See* Walton v. City of Red Bluff, 3 Cal.Rptr.2d 275 (App.1991) for a more recent discussion of the authorities on this question. *Contra*, Presbytery of Southeast Iowa, 226 N.W.2d 232 (Iowa 1975) (upholding a statute requiring periodic re-registration of an intent to enforce reversion, other reversionary interests, easements and covenants even as to interests created prior to effective date of statute).

[247] Hiddleston v. Nebraska Jewish Education Society, 186 N.W.2d 904 (Neb.1971). *See also* Opinion of the Justices, 151 N.E.2d 475 (Mass.1958) (limitation on dower justified by its slight value).

[248] Unif. Prin. & Inc. Act (1962) § 14. In In re Reznor's Estate, 213 A.2d 791 (Pa.1965), the court refused to apply the Act to stock dividends which had been allocated to principal in 1928 and 1938. Presumably any distributions to an income beneficiary would not be disturbed.

[249] *Restatement (Second) of Trusts* § 227, cmt. p (1959). *See also* Uniform Prudent Investor Act § 11. As to investments by fiduciaries, *see* Section 12.2.

[250] Unif. Prin. & Inc. Act (1997) § 605.

"will not affect the validity of any act of the trustee performed prior to its enactment."[251]

Procedural Changes

It is sometimes said that legislatures are "free to apply changes in rules of evidence or procedure retroactively."[252] For example, a testator died in April; in June of the same year, the period allowed for probating wills was reduced from none to six months from the date of the testator's death. This change was applied to bar an attempt to probate the will in December. "The statute in effect when the petition . . . is filed should apply if there is a reasonable time in which to commence a proceeding before the expiration of the shortened limitation period provided by the amended statute." Here there was three months left to run when the statute was passed and that was enough.[253] The UPC says that in some cases it may be appropriate to defer the effectiveness of procedural changes "in the interest of justice."[254] But when a will contest was pending when the legislature abolished trial by jury in such proceedings, the court applied the new law despite a similar savings clause.[255]

§§ 1.4–2.0 are reserved for supplemental material.

---

[251] Unif. Trustees' Powers Act § 8, and comment. *See also* UTC § 1106(a).

[252] In re Marriage of Buol, 705 P.2d 354, 358 (Cal.1985). This was the rationale for upholding a limitation of possibilities of reverter in Presbytery of Southeast Iowa v. Harris, 226 N.W.2d 232, 242 (Iowa 1975): the statute "does not abolish or alter any vested right. Rather it modifies the procedure for effectuation of the remedy." In Evans v. McCoy, 436 A.2d 436, 448 (Md.1981), the court upheld a retroactive statute creating a presumption of intent to include adoptees because "this is a rule of evidence and not a rule of substantive law." *See also* In re Estate of Pendleton, 753 N.E.2d 237, 240 (Ohio App.2001) (constitutional prohibition against "retroactive laws . . . applies to laws affecting substantive rights, not laws of a remedial or procedural nature".

[253] Matter of Estate of Forrester, 762 P.2d 198, 201 (Kan.App.1988). As to the time limits for probate of wills, *see* Section 13.3, note 97 et seq.

[254] UPC § 8–101(b)(2). *See also* UTC § 1106(a)(3).

[255] Estate of Gardner, 2 Cal.Rptr.2d 664 (App.1991). As to jury trial in will contests, *see* Section 12.1, note 44 et seq. *See also* Matter of Will of Cargill, 420 N.W.2d 268, 271 (Minn.App.1988) (UPC effective in 1976 applied to a testamentary trust created in 1933).

Chapter 2

INTESTATE SUCCESSION

Analysis

Sec.

2.1 The Surviving Spouse's Share.
2.2 Relatives.
2.3 General Aspects of Intestacy; Statutory Wills.
2.4 Gifts to "Heirs".
2.5 Recovery for Wrongful Death.
2.6 Advancements.
2.7 Homicide.
2.8 Disclaimers.
2.9 Nonmarital Children.
2.10 Adoption and De Facto Parentage.
2.11 ART Children.
2.12 Spouses.

§ 2.1 The Surviving Spouse's Share

What happens to the property of a person who dies without a will? In this section we deal with the share that passes to the decedent's surviving spouse, if any,[1] and in the following sections we deal with the share that passes to the decedent's other relatives.

Blackstone in the 18th century devoted considerable discussion to the common law "canons of descent."[2] These applied only to land; succession to personal property was governed by the Statute of Distribution. Today in every U.S. state, intestate succession is controlled by statute,[3] and, with few exceptions, the rules are the same for land and personal property.

History

At common law, the spouse was never an heir to land. Widows and widowers were limited to lifetime enjoyment of the marital estates of dower and curtesy.[4] Dower for a widow was a life estate limited to one third of her husband's land capable of inheritance by issue of the marriage. Curtesy for a widower extended to a life estate in all his wife's land. But curtesy was dependent on issue actually being born of the marriage: "if a cry was heard

---

1 As to who is a "spouse," *see* Section 2.12.

2 *See* 2 W. Blackstone, *Commentaries* Ch. 14 (1766).

3 *Restatement (Third) of Property (Wills and Other Donative Transfers)* Ch. 2, Introductory Note (1999).

4 For the history of dower and curtesy, *see* 3 W. Holdsworth, *History of English Law* 185–197 (5th ed. 1942).

within [the] four walls, as the old writers quaintly put it. It mattered nothing that issue did not survive."[5] Limiting spouses to a life interest stemmed from a fear that if the surviving spouse inherited land in fee it would be permanently removed from the decedent's family, particularly if the couple had no children or if the surviving spouse remarried or had children by another marriage.

The marital life estates in land hindered marketability; land is hard to sell when ownership is divided between a life tenant and a remainderman.[6] Even in the 18th century Blackstone observed "in estates of considerable consequence, tenancy in dower happens very seldom: for the claim of the wife to her dower at the common law . . . became a great clog to alienations" and so was usually eliminated in wealthy families by an premarital agreement.[7]

Personal property was subject to different rules. Under the Statute of Distribution (1670), a widow took one-third of her husband's personalty if he left surviving issue and one-half if he did not.[8] Intestacy provisions for widowers were unnecessary because a husband acquired all his wife's personal property upon marriage on the theory that "husband and wife . . . are one person in law."[9] (This legal fiction inspired the famous remark in Dickens "if the law supposes that . . . then the law is a ass."[10])

Most American jurisdictions today give a surviving spouse (whether a widow or a widower) an outright (fee simple) share of the deceased spouse's property. A few states, however, retain vestiges of the historical distinction between land and personalty and give the surviving spouse only a life interest in the former.[11] The Uniform Probate Code (UPC), however, like most modern statutes, gives spouses the same share in land and personal property.[12] Distinctions between widows and widowers have disappeared and, no doubt, would be unconstitutional today.

In virtually all U.S. states today, surviving spouses receive a larger share by intestacy than was provided by common-law dower and curtesy or the

---

5 A. Simpson, *A History of the Land Law* 69 (2d. ed. 1986). *See also* 2 W. Blackstone, *supra* note 2, at 126, 129 (1766).

6 For the disadvantages of legal life estates *see* Section 10.5.

7 2 W. Blackstone, *supra* note 2, at 136. A premarital agreement is an agreement under which prospective spouses waive property rights they would otherwise acquire in the property of the other because of the marriage. As to the legal issues raised by premarital agreements today *see* Section 8.9.

8 22 & 23 Car. 2, c. 10, § 5.

9 2 W. Blackstone, *Commentaries* 433 (1766).

10 J. Baker, *An Introduction to English Legal History* 522 (5th ed. 2019).

11 West's Ann. Ind. Code 29–1–2–1(c) (if spouse had no children by the decedent who left children by another marriage). *E.g.*, Parson v. Wolfe, 676 S.W.2d 689 (Tex.App.1984) (land contract treated as personalty). In Iowa, distinctions are made between realty and personalty with respect to exemptions from creditor claims and time of ownership. For realty the share attaches to realty owned during the marriage in which the spouse's share is not released; for personalty, its personal property owned at death. *See* Iowa Code § 633.211; 633.212.

In 1890, 69% of the common-law states limited the surviving spouse to a life interest in the decedent's land. By 1982 this had dropped to 11.9%. Shammas, et. al., *Inheritance in America* 165 (1987).

12 Uniform Probate Code [UPC] § 2–102.

Statute of Distribution. Empirical evidence reveals that most people want a larger share to pass to the spouse than the former rules provided.[13]

Division Between Spouse and Descendants

When a decedent is survived by a spouse and one or more children who are also children of the spouse, arguably the entire estate should go to the spouse. This accords with empirical evidence of donative intention. It is also practical. If the children include minors, giving them a share would require a guardianship or other arrangement for managing the property.[14] For these reasons as well as a recognition that a surviving spouse is more likely to have contributed to the accumulation of the decedent's wealth, the UPC gives the entire intestate estate to the surviving spouse "if all the decedent's surviving descendants are also descendants of the surviving spouse and there is no other [surviving] descendant of the surviving spouse."[15] The UPC comment states that this is justified by the fact that "testators in smaller estates (which intestate estates overwhelmingly tend to be) tend to devise their entire estates to their surviving spouses, even when the couple has children."

Because multiple marriages and blended families are common today, decedents often are survived by children who are not children of the decedent's surviving spouse. Or the surviving spouse may have children who survive the decedent but are not the decedent's children. The UPC reduces the spouse's share in these situations, and so do many other (but not all) intestacy statutes.[16]

Arguably the spouse's share ought to depend upon the length of the marriage.[17] The UPC uses the length of the marriage in determining the spouse's elective share when the spouse is claiming against a will[18] but ignores the length of the marriage in fixing the size of the spouse's intestate share. The length of the marriage is an important factor in community property states where the spouse typically receives all the community property and only a fraction of the decedent's separate property upon intestacy.[19] Because

---

[13] *E.g.*, Waggoner, *The Multiple-Marriage Society and Spousal Rights under the Revised Uniform Probate Code*, 76 Iowa L. Rev. 223, 230–31 (1991). The use of surveys to shape intestacy rules is discussed in Section 2.3.

[14] As to the disadvantages of guardianship for managing property *see* Section 9.2.

[15] UPC § 2–102(1)(B). The surviving spouse also takes the entire estate if "no descendant or parent of the decedent survives the decedent." *Id.* at § 2–102(1)(A). In California if the decedent was survived by one child and the surviving spouse was that child's parent, the spouse takes 1/2 of the intestate estate but if the decedent and the spouse had two or more children, the spouse's share is reduced to 1/3 of the estate. Cal.Prob.Code § 6401(c).

[16] UPC § 2–102(3) & (4). *See also* New Hampshire Rev. Stat. Ann. 561:1; Iowa Code § 633.212. These special rules do not cover the case where the spouse remarries and has children by another person after the decedent dies, a fact that usually cannot be known when the prior spouse's estate is distributed. *Cf.* La.Civ.Code art. 890 (spouse gets usufruct of decedent's share of community property *terminable upon remarriage*).

[17] Spitko, *An Accrual/Multi-Factor Approach to Intestate Inheritance Rights for Unmarried Committed Partners*, 81 Or.L.Rev. 255, 290 (2002).

[18] *See* Section 8.7.

[19] Cal.Prob.Code § 6401 says the spouse gets "the one-half of the community property that belongs to the decedent;" the other half already belongs to the spouse. The spouse's share of separate property is 1/2 or 1/3 depending on the number of children. The surviving spouse also gets all the community property under UPC § 2–102A(b). *See also* Rev.Code Wash. § 11.04.015(1).

community property generally is limited to property acquired during the marriage, there usually is little or no community property accumulated during a brief marriage.[20]

The size of the estate also is important in fixing the amount of the spouse's intestate share. Under the UPC, if the decedent is survived by a spouse and by one or more children who are not the spouse's children, the spouse receives $150,000 and one half of the balance of the intestate estate, *i.e.*, all of an intestate estate valued at $150,000 or less, but only a fraction of an intestate estate larger than $150,000.[21] This rule applies even if the decedent is survived by other children who are children of the surviving spouse.

Spouse's Share in the Absence of Descendants

When an intestate decedent was survived by a widow but no descendants, the Statute of Distribution increased the widow's share of personal property from one-third to one-half, but the widow's interest in land remained the same. Even if the husband's only surviving relatives were remote cousins, the widow's dower remained one-third. Modern statutes generally increase the spouse's share if the intestate decedent has no descendants. Some statutes give the entire intestate estate to the surviving spouse if no descendants survive,[22] but under some statutes, the decedent's parents share with the surviving spouse. The UPC gives the spouse the first $300,000 and three-fourths of the balance of the intestate estate when the decedent dies without descendants but survived by one or more parents, with the parent(s) taking the rest.[23] If no parent survives, the surviving spouse takes the entire intestate estate under the UPC, but in some states the spouse must share the estate with the intestate's siblings or their issue.[24]

When the entire intestate estate passes to the surviving spouse, the property of both spouses may pass ultimately to the relatives of the surviving spouse at the surviving spouse's later death. California avoids this result by giving the relatives of the first spouse to die a share of the surviving spouse's estate if the latter dies intestate. Thus, when W survives H and dies intestate a few years later "the portion of [her] estate attributable to" H will pass to H's

---

In Louisiana, the spouse only gets a usufruct (life interest) in the decedent's half of community property. La.Civ.Code art. 890.

20 A more complete discussion of community property appears in Section 8.8.

21 UPC § 2–102(4). *See also* N.Y. EPTL § 4–1.1(a)(1) (spouse gets $50,000 plus one-half the residue). Statutes which give the spouse a lump sum can present a problem when the law of more than one state applies. The Reporter's Note to *Restatement (Third) of Property (Wills and Other Donative Transfers)* § 2.1 argues that the spouse should only get the lump sum provided by the state of domicile.

Unlike some state statutes, the UPC also reduces the surviving spouse's share if the decedent was survived by descendants who are descendants of the surviving spouse but the surviving spouse has other descendants who are not descendants of the decedent. In this case, the surviving spouse takes $225,000, plus one half of the balance of the estate. UPC § 2–102(3).

Under Section 1–109 of the UPC added in 2008, fixed sums set forth in the Code are adjusted to take account of changes in the Consumer Price Index. Numbers used in this text are unadjusted.

22 Ariz.Rev.Stat. § 14–2102(1) (separate property); Iowa Code § 633.211.

23 UPC §§ 2–102(2); 2–103(d).

24 Cal.Prob.Code § 6401 (separate property equally divided between spouse and parents or issue of parents).

relatives rather than to hers.[25] Because of the administrative difficulties of identifying property of the first spouse in the surviving spouse's estate, a time limit is imposed, so that in this hypothetical the statute would not apply if W survived H by more than 5 years.[26] Nor would the statute apply if W was survived by a later spouse or by descendants, or if she had a will devising her estate to others. Thus, if H wishes to make sure that "his" property returns to his family when his widow dies, he should put it into a trust for W for life with remainder to his relatives rather than relying on the statute. Such "bypass" trusts are discussed in Section 10.6.

§ 2.2 Relatives

Normally whatever does not pass to the surviving spouse on intestacy goes to the decedent's other relatives. Spouses of relatives (*e.g.*, sons-in-law, daughters-in-law) receive no share. The descendants of an intestate decedent are the first takers. Descendants (or issue—the two terms are synonymous) include children, grandchildren, great-grandchildren, etc.[27] Only if there are no surviving descendants do collateral relatives (such as brothers, sisters, nieces, nephews, etc.) or ancestors (parents, grandparents, etc.) inherit.[28] This is true in all states.

Representation

One possible way to divide the decedent's intestate estate would be to count the decedent's heirs and then divide the estate in equal shares among them. However, this is not the U.S. approach. Intestacy law in the U.S. is *representational*. This means that members of a lower generation inherit only when the relevant ancestor has failed to survive. A related principle is that only persons who survive the intestate decedent can be heirs. In most states, there is no requirement that the heir survive the intestate decedent for any specific period of time. However, under the UPC and some other statutes, heirs must survive a decedent by 120 hours.[29] If not, they are treated as if they had predeceased the decedent. On the other hand, in no state must an heir survive to the time the decedent's estate is actually distributed. If the heir survives the decedent but dies prior to distribution, the heir's share passes to the heir's estate,[30] to be distributed to the takers of that estate.

Children of a relative who would have been an heir but for the relative's failure to survive the decedent take in place of that relative. For example, if a child of the decedent predeceases but that child's children survive the decedent, they take in lieu of their deceased parent. These children (the

---

[25] Cal.Prob.Code § 6402.5.

[26] The limit is 15 years for real property.

[27] UPC § 1–201(9), (24); *Restatement (Third) of Property (Wills and Other Donative Transfers)* § 2.3, cmt. b (1999).

[28] In re Estate of Peters, 29 P.3d 90 (Wyo.2001) (a parent cannot inherit when decedent had surviving children) The rule may be otherwise with respect to claims for wrongful death. *See* Section 2.5.

[29] UPC § 2–104; Cal.Prob.Code § 6403. For a discussion of simultaneous death, *see* Section 6.5.

[30] Booker v. Lal, 726 N.E.2d 638, 641 (Ill.App.2000); *cf.* Cal.Prob.Code § 11802 (direct distribution to heirs of minor heir who dies before distribution).

decedent's grandchildren) are said to "represent" their parent, but they inherit directly from the decedent; their share is not subject to the deceased parent's will or to claims of the deceased parent's creditors.[31]

All U.S. states today use representation.[32] For the practical implementation of representation, see the discussion below under "Computation of Shares."

The common law governing land allowed representation without limit,[33] but the Statute of Distribution, which governed personal property, did not allow representation among collateral relatives except in the case of brothers' and sisters' children (the decedent's nephews and nieces).[34] Some U.S. statutes today also bar representation among collaterals who are only remotely related to the decedent. For example, under the UPC only collaterals related to the intestate through a common grandparent can inherit; collaterals related through a common great-grandparent and beyond are excluded.[35]

Questions of representation arise not only in intestacy but also in the construction of donative instruments, including wills. A gift to "A's children" is usually held not to include A's grandchildren.[36] Sophisticated drafters usually use the word "descendants" or "issue" rather than "children" in order to include the descendants of deceased children. For example, the Uniform Statutory Will Act leaves the estate (if the testator has no spouse) to "the children of the testator if all of them survive, otherwise to the surviving issue of the testator by representation."[37] A devise to "descendants" or "issue," as in intestate succession, is understood *representationally*: the devise excludes descendants whose parent is living.[38]

Computation of Shares Among Descendants

Suppose that Mary has three children, Alice, Andrew and Arthur. Alice predeceased Mary, but Andrew and Arthur and Alice's three children, Bob, Bill, and Betsy, survive.

---

31 UPC § 2–106; Cal.Prob.Code § 6410.

32 At one time the idea of representation was in doubt. When King Richard I died without issue in the 12th century, he was survived by a brother, John, and a nephew, Arthur, the son of John's deceased older brother. John seized the crown, but under the law as it was ultimately settled, Arthur should have succeeded as his father's representative. 2 F. Pollock & F. Maitland, *History of English Law* 283–86 (2d ed. 1898), T. Plucknett, *Concise History of the Common Law* 717 (5th ed. 1956); J. Baker, *Introduction to English Legal History* 285 (5th ed. 2019).

33 2 W. Blackstone, *Commentaries* 217 (1766).

34 Statute of Distribution, 22 & 23 Car. 2, c. 10, § 7 (1670). The Statute of Distribution was drafted by persons familiar with Roman law which did not allow representation among collaterals. Gaius, *Institutes* 3.15; Justinian, *Institutes* 3.1.6, 3.2.4.

35 UPC § 2–103. In Iowa, collaterals up through common great-grandparents can inherit. *See* Iowa Code § 633.219.

36 *See* Section 11.1. However, such a devise may pass down to remoter issue under an anti-lapse statute if the children predecease the testator. *See* Section 6.5.

37 Uniform Statutory Will Act § 7(a)(1).

38 *Restatement (Third) of Property (Wills and Other Donative Transfers)* § 14.4 (2011); Theopold v. Sears, 258 N.E.2d 559 (Mass.1970); Central Trust Bank v. Stout, 579 S.W.2d 825 (Mo.App.1979). Under UPC § 2–708 a gift to "issue" or "descendants" goes to the persons who would take under the rules of intestacy.

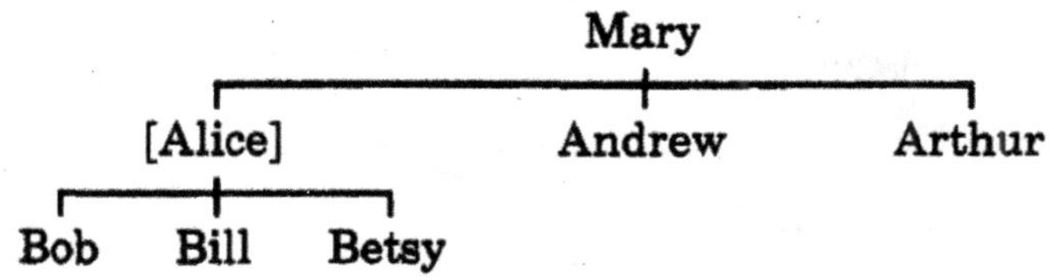

All states agree that Bob, Bill and Betsy (Alice's three children) would split Alice's one-third and so each takes one-ninth of Mary's estate by representation. The other thirds pass equally to Andrew and Arthur.

States differ, however, on the division of property among grandchildren and more remote descendants when none of intestate's children survive. Suppose all of Mary's children predecease her and that she is survived by Alice's three children (Bob, Bill, and Betsy), Andrew's one child (Ben) and Arthur's two children (Burt and Barbara).

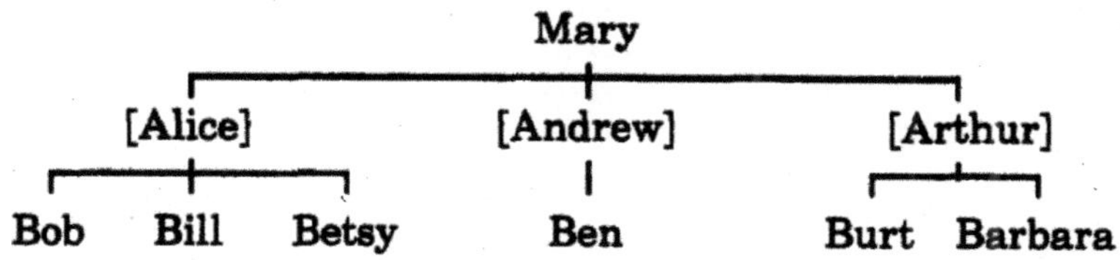

Under the Uniform Probate Code, each of the six grandchildren would take an equal (1/6) share.[39] Bob, Bill, Betsy, Ben, Burt, and Barbara each take 1/6th of Mary's intestate estate. This method of division is called "per capita at each generation."

The common law, on the other hand, adopted a method of division called per stirpes, which means "according to the roots; since all the branches [of a family] inherit the same share that their root, whom they represent, would have done."[40] Under this system, Alice's three children (Bob, Bill, and Betsy) would each take 1/9, Ben would take the whole of his father Andrew's 1/3 share, and Burt and Barbara would divide their father Arthur's 1/3, each getting 1/6. Some states still follow this approach.[41] In these states, grandchildren take the share their parent would have taken had the parent survived.

Suppose instead that there are surviving children as well as grandchildren by two or more deceased children, *e.g.,* Alice and Andrew predeceased Mary, but Arthur survives her.

---

39 *See* UPC § 2–103(c) & UPC § 2–106(b).

40 2 W. Blackstone, *Commentaries* 217 (1766). Perhaps a more appropriate metaphor would treat the decedent's children as trunks, and the recipients as roots growing out of the trunk.

41 755 ILCS § 5/2–1(a); Kentucky Rev. Stat. § 391.040; Iowa Code § 633.219.

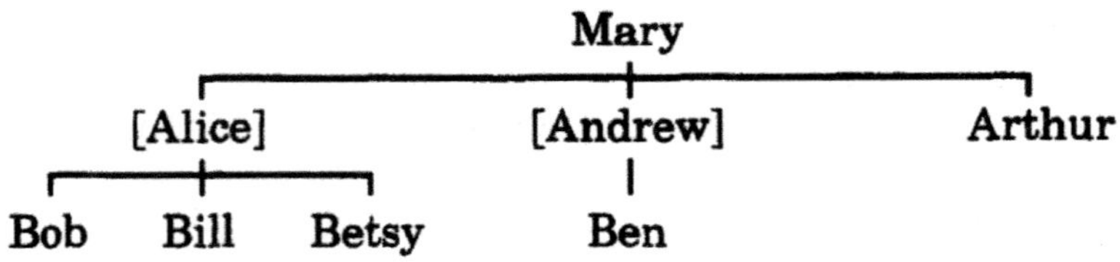

Under the per stirpes method of division, Arthur takes one-third in his own right; by representation, Bob, Bill, and Betsy divide Alice's one-third share, each receiving one-ninth of Mary's intestate estate; and Ben takes Andrew's share of one-third.[42] This causes persons in the same generation (*i.e.*, Bob, Bill, Betsy, and Ben) to get unequal shares. Ben gets more than each of Bob, Bill, and Betsy even though all four are of the same degree of kinship to Mary.

Under the UPC's system of per capita at each generation, which Professor Waggoner has summarized as "equally near, equally dear,"[43] Arthur gets one-third, and the remaining two-thirds (being the shares of Alice and Andrew) drop down to the next generation and are divided equally among all takers in that generation, so the children of Alice and Andrew each receive one-sixth (1/4th of 2/3rds) of Mary's intestate estate.[44]

If there are no surviving children and an estate is to be divided among grandchildren and great-grandchildren (or among nephews and grandnephews), where does the initial division occur? A leading case on this question arose from a trust created by Clinton Hastings, the founder of the Hastings Law School and the only person to be Chief Justice of two states (Iowa and California). When Hastings' trust was distributed, his living descendants were four grandchildren and two great-grandchildren (children of two deceased grandchildren).[45]

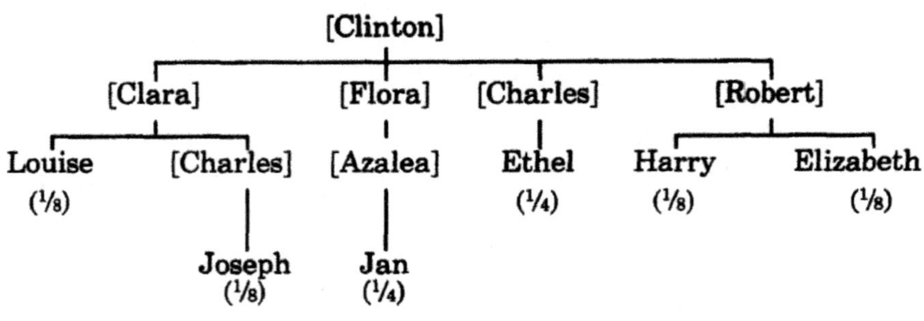

The court divided the estate at the level of Hastings' children even though they were all dead. As a consequence, claimants in the same degree received unequal shares (*e.g.*, Ethel and Harry), and a great-grandchild (Jan) received more than three of the grandchildren. The Restatement calls this method of

---

42 The same result on these facts would have been produced by the pre-1990 UPC.

43 Waggoner, *A Proposed Alternative to the Uniform Probate Code's System for Intestate Distribution Among Descendants,* 66 Nw.U.L.Rev. 626, 628 (1971).

44 UPC §§ 2–103(c), 2–106(b).

45 Maud v. Catherwood, 155 P.2d 111 (Cal.App.1945).

division "strict per stirpes."[46] Under the UPC, on the other hand, the estate would have been divided initially at the closest level to the decedent where there were living claimants; Hastings' children would be ignored because they were all dead.[47] Louise, Ethel, Harry and Elizabeth would get one-sixth, as would Joseph and Jan.

Interpretation of Wills

The question how to compute shares also arises under wills. If a will devises property to a single-generation class such as "my grandchildren" (or "the grandchildren of X"), courts usually require an equal distribution, without regard to the number of children from which the claimants stem.[48] However, if the devisees are described in the will as "the children of my daughter *A* and the children of my son *B*," some courts would first divide the property into two halves, one half for the children of *A* and one half for the children of *B*.[49]

If a devise is to a class that is not, or need not be, single-generational, such as a devise to "descendants" or "heirs." the UPC would follow the rules of intestacy in determining the shares,[50] but additional language may change the result because the testator's intent controls. There has been much litigation about what a testator intended by words like "equally" or "share and share alike." For example, a will left land to the testator's son's "heirs, share and share alike." The son was survived by a daughter and by two children of a deceased son. By the law of intestacy, the son's estate would go half to the daughter and half to the children of the deceased son, but the court held that the words "share and share alike" required that each heir take one third.[51] Another court held that a devise to "the descendants of Jean, share and share alike," gave an equal share to Jean's children, grandchildren and great-grandchildren, even though all of Jean's children were living, contrary to the general rule excluding descendants of a living ancestor.[52] Other courts, however, have held that " 'equally,' referring to a multi-generational class, normally means per stirpes,"[53] *i.e.*, each stirps (root) gets an equal share, but not necessarily each taker.

---

[46] *Restatement (Third) of Property (Wills and Other Donative Transfers)* § 2.3, cmt. d (1999). The same method was followed in Boston Safe Deposit & Trust Co. v. Goodwin, 795 N.E.2d 581 (Mass.App.2003).

[47] UPC § 2–106(b). *See also* Hockman v. Estate of Lowe, 624 S.W.2d 719 (Tex.App.1981) (when intestate had nine nieces and nephews, each living one gets 1/8 and the ninth share divided between the children of a dead nephew); Estate of McCrary, 62 Cal.Rptr.2d 504 (App.1997) (decedent survived by 4 first cousins and 67 descendants of 14 deceased cousins; each surviving first cousin takes 1/18, balance divided among the others).

[48] *Restatement (Third) of Property (Wills and Other Donative Transfers)* § 14.2 (2011).

[49] *Restatement (Third) of Property (Wills and Other Donative Transfers)* § 14.2, cmt. d, e (2011) (distinguishing this from a devise "to the children of A and B").

[50] UPC §§ 2–708, 2–711. *See also Restatement (Third) of Property (Wills and Other Donative Transfers)* § 14.5 (2011).

[51] Black v. Unknown Creditors, 155 N.W.2d 784 (S.D.1968). *See also* Johnson v. Johnson, 468 N.E.2d 945 (Ohio Prob.1984); Old Colony Trust Co. v. Stephens, 190 N.E.2d 110 (Mass.1963).

[52] In re Estate of Goodwin, 739 N.Y.S.2d 239, 245 (Surr.2002).

[53] Dewire v. Haveles, 534 N.E.2d 782, 786 (Mass.1989). *See also* First Illini Bank v. Pritchard, 595 N.E.2d 728 (Ill.App.1992); In re Trust of Woodworth, 492 N.W.2d 818 (Mich.App.1992); Matter of Trust Estate of Dwight, 909 P.2d 561 (Haw.1995) (direction to distribute "equally per stirpes" means each branch of the family gets an equal share).

The phrase "per stirpes" can be ambiguous. In California, if an instrument calls for distribution "per stirpes" or "by representation" to the descendants of X, the division is made at the level of X's children even if they are all dead.[54] This is also the UPC's interpretation of the phrase "per stirpes"[55] when used in a governing instrument, such as a will, but not the interpretation of the phrase "by representation." For the latter, the distribution is per capita at each generation.[56]

After ascertaining the client's wishes, a drafter using a phrase such as "per stirpes" or "by representation" in an instrument should define it, given the uncertainty of the phrases' judicial interpretation. The UPC provides definitions of the alternatives to which drafters can refer to make the testator's preference clear.[57] An example of a possible clause follows:

> When under any provision of this Will, my residuary estate or the principal of any trust created hereunder becomes distributable "by representation" to my descendants or the descendants of any other designated person, my residuary estate or the principal of such trust, as the case may be, shall be distributed to such descendants as follows: The property is divided into as many equal shares as there are (i) surviving descendants in the generation nearest to the designated ancestor which contains one or more surviving descendants and (ii) deceased descendants in the same generation who left surviving descendants, if any. Each surviving descendant in the nearest generation is allocated one share. The remaining shares, if any, are combined and then divided in the same manner among the surviving descendants of the deceased descendants as if the surviving descendants who were allocated a share and their surviving descendants had predeceased the distribution date.[58]

Parents and Their Descendants

If a decedent leaves no surviving descendants, then parents or siblings are next in line to inherit. Historically, ascendants (parents, grandparents, great-grandparents, etc.), never inherited.[59] The reasons for this rule are mysterious.[60] That prohibition was abolished in England in 1833[61] and survives nowhere.

Some U.S. jurisdictions today prefer the decedent's parents (or surviving parent) over brothers and sisters.[62] In other states, however, siblings share

---

[54] Cal.Prob.Code § 246.

[55] *See* UPC § 2–709(c).

[56] *See* UPC § 2–709(b).

[57] *See* UPC § 2–709.

[58] *See* UPC § 2–709(c).

[59] T. Littleton, *Tenures* § 3.

[60] Blackstone attributed it to feudalism: "the decrepit grandsire of a vigorous vassal" would not be able to perform the feudal services. 2 W. Blackstone, *Commentaries* 212 (1765). Maitland rejected this reason but confessed that it was "by no means easy" to explain the rule. 2 F. Pollock & W. Maitland, *The History of English Law* 286–93 (2d ed. 1898).

[61] 3 & 4 Will. 4, c. 106, § 6 (1833).

[62] UPC § 2–103(a)(2) (pre-2019 version); Cal.Prob.Code § 6402(b); Conn.Gen.Stat.Ann. § 45a–439(a)(1).

with parents under a variety of formulas.[63] The UPC's intestacy provisions were revised in 2019 to take blended families into account not only in the share passing to the surviving spouse but also in the share(s) passing to other heirs. Before 2019, if the decedent had one or more surviving parents, the parent(s) took to the exclusion of the decedent's surviving sibling(s). As revised in 2019, the surviving parent(s) take to the exclusion of the surviving sibling(s) only if the family is nonblended. Consider the following two examples. In the first example, the decedent is survived by one parent and two siblings, both of whom are children of the decedent's parents. Under the pre-2019 and current UPC, all of the decedent's intestate estate passes to the surviving parent.[64]

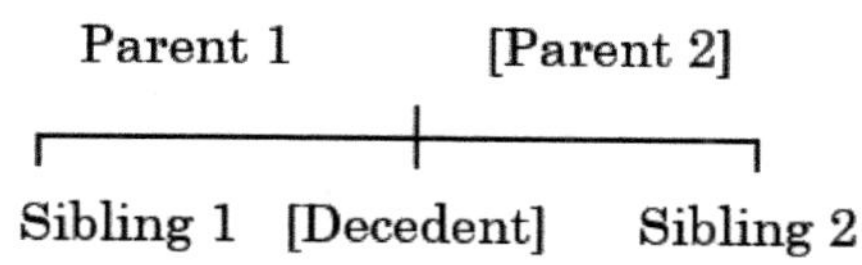

In the second example, the decedent is survived by one parent and two siblings, but the siblings each have only one parent in common with the decedent. Under the pre-2019 UPC, all of the decedent's intestate estate passes to the surviving parent.[65] Under the current UPC, however, the estate is divided between the surviving parent (Parent 1) and the sibling (Sibling 2) who is not the child of the surviving parent.[66] This takes the blended family into account.

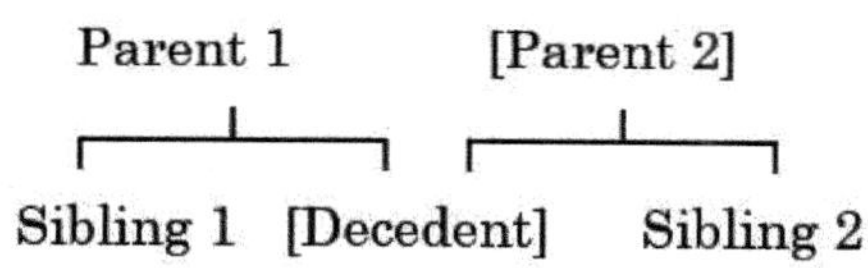

More Remote Relatives

Some intestacy statutes name no specific takers after the descendants of parents; they simply give the inheritance to the decedent's "next of kin."[67] These may be the decedent's more remote ancestors, such as grandparents, or they may be the decedent's collateral relatives, such as aunts and uncles. One way of determining the intestate takers is to favor those relatives having a closer degree of consanguinity (relationship) to the decedent over those with a more remote degree of consanguinity. To compute the degree of kinship between a decedent and a collateral relative, one must add the number of generations up from the decedent to the common ancestor and then down from the common ancestor to the relative. Thus, a brother is in the second degree (one up to parent, one down to brother), a nephew is in the third degree (one up to parent, two down to nephew), the common ancestors being the decedent's

[63] 755 ILCS § 5/2–1(d) (equal division among parents and siblings); Tex. Est. Code § 201.001(d) (West 2015) (all to parents but if one dead 1/2 to siblings).

[64] *See* UPC § 2–103(a)(2) (pre-2019 version); UPC § 2–103(d) & (e)(1) (current version).

[65] *See* UPC § 2–103(a)(2) (pre-2019 version).

[66] *See* UPC § 2–103(d) & (e)(1) (current version).

[67] Conn.Gen.Stat. § 45a–439; 12 Del.Code § 503(4); 14 Vt. Stat. Ann. tit. 14, § 314 (West 2015).

parents. First cousins are related in the fourth degree: two generations from the first cousin to the common ancestors (the grandparents) and two generations from the grandparents down. The degrees of kinship are illustrated in the following chart:[68]

TABLE OF CONSANGUINITY

Showing Degrees of Relationship

Figures show degree of relationship

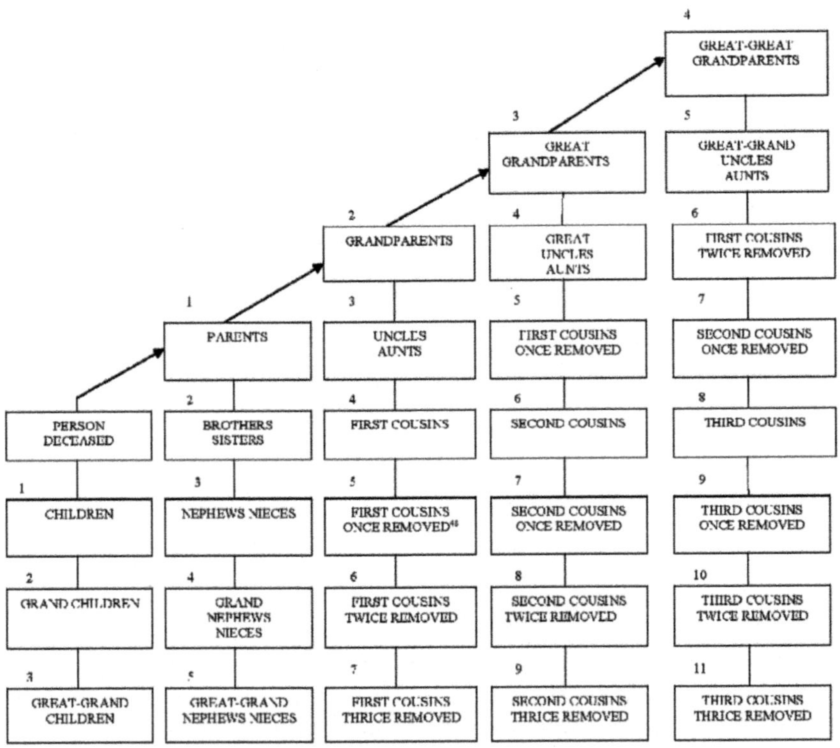

In contradistinction to inheritance among heirs of closer degrees of consanguinity, a different way to determine inheritance is according to the parentelic principle: the descendants of a nearer ancestor are preferred to descendants of a more remote ancestor. The decedent's descendants are in the first parentela; parents and their descendants (the decedent's brothers, sisters, nieces, nephews, etc.) are in the second parentela; grandparents and their descendants (the decedent's uncles, aunts, first cousins, etc.) are in the third parentela; and so forth. A nephew, even though he is in the third degree of kinship, takes ahead of grandparents who are in the second degree because the nephew is issue of a closer ancestor (the decedent's parents).[69]

68 This table of consanguinity is based upon the civil law method.

69 Pollock & Maitland, *supra* note 32, at 296.

Modern intestacy statutes generally follow the parentelic principle.[70] The UPC designates as heirs first the descendants of the decedent (§ 2–103(c), the first parentela), then the decedent's parents and their descendants (§ 2–103(d)–(f), the second parentela), then the grandparents and their descendants (§ 2–103(g)–(i), the third parentela).[71] Inheritance by relatives in a more remote parentela is extinguished.

As revised in 2019, the UPC applies the per capita at each generation method of division consistently. Thus, for example, if the decedent is survived only by three first cousins, one of whom is on one parent of the decedent's side of the family and two of whom are on another parent's side, the three first cousins share equally in the decedent's intestate estate.[72] Equally near, equally dear.

Ancestral Property

Historically, land returned to the branch of the family from which it came.[73] If a woman had inherited land from her paternal grandfather and died without surviving issue of herself or her parents, her paternal collaterals (uncles, aunts, cousins) would take the land to the exclusion of her maternal collaterals. This doctrine never applied to personalty.

The ancestral property idea creates administrative difficulties because it requires tracing the source of land. It has been discarded by most jurisdictions today, but a few states retain vestiges of it.[74]

Half-Blood

Half-blood relatives are related to each other through only one common ancestor in the same generation. If Arthur and Andrew have the same father but different mothers, Arthur being a child of his father's prior marriage, Arthur and Andrew are half-brothers. A son of Andrew would be Arthur's half-nephew.

Historically, half-blood relatives could not inherit land from each other.[75] Blackstone ascribed this to the ancestral property rule. If Arthur could inherit from Andrew, he *might* receive property which Andrew had inherited from his mother, to whom Arthur was not related. Henry Maine rejected Blackstone's

---

[70] The parentelic principle is not always followed among remoter relatives. *Restatement (Third) of Property (Wills and Other Donative Transfers)* § 2.4, illus. 1 (1999) (third cousins share with second cousin twice removed in some states).

[71] *See also* Cal.Prob.Code § 6402, which provides that if there are no relatives in the first three parentelas, the estate goes "to the next of kin in equal degree, but where there are two or more collateral kindred in equal degree who claim through different ancestors, those who claim through the nearest ancestor are preferred to those claiming through an ancestor more remote." There is no comparable provision in the UPC because it does not allow inheritance beyond the descedants of grandparents, other than, as a last resort before escheat, stepchildren (of deceased spouses). *See* UPC § 2–103(j).

[72] *See* UPC § 2–103(i).

[73] 2 W. Blackstone, *Commentaries* 220 (1766).

[74] Ky.Rev.Stat. § 391.020. *See Restatement (Third) of Property (Wills and Other Donative Transfers)* § 2.4, cmt. d (1999).

[75] 2 W. Blackstone, *Commentaries* 224 (1766).

explanation and offered one of his own, which Maitland in turn rejected.[76] Whatever the reasons for the historical rule, it was replaced in 1833 by a statute which allowed half-bloods to inherit land, but only if no siblings of the whole-blood survived.[77] As to personal property, half-bloods always shared equally with whole-blood relatives.[78]

Most modern statutes, including the UPC, make no distinction between whole-bloods and half-bloods.[79] A few states give the half-blood only half as much as a whole-blood of the same degree.[80] Others combine the ancestral property rule with a limited exclusion of the half-blood. For example, in Washington, half-blood and whole-blood kindred receive the same share "unless the inheritance comes to the intestate by descent, devise, or gift from one of his ancestors . . . in which case all who are not of the blood of such ancestors shall be excluded from such inheritance."[81]

A devise of property "to my brothers and sisters" is presumed to include half-brothers and half-sisters.[82]

In the modern era, references to "blood" obscure the many other ways in which parent-child relationships can be created. The UPC was revised in 2019 to state its principle neutrally, without using the language of blood: "An heir inherits without regard to how many common ancestors in the same generation the heir shares with the decedent."[83]

"Laughing Heirs" and Escheat

If a person dies survived by neither spouse nor close relatives, should the decedent's property escheat to the state or be distributed to more remote relatives? The latter are sometimes called "laughing heirs" because they are personally unaffected by the decedent's death and so (supposedly) laugh all the way to the bank. The UPC excludes such remote relatives, limiting inheritance to descendants of grandparents.[84] Second cousins of a decedent who were barred from inheriting under a similar statute challenged it as

---

[76] H. Maine, *Ancient Law* 126 (World Classics ed.); Pollock & Maitland, *supra* note 32, at 305.

[77] 3 & 4 Will. 4, c. 106, § 6 (1833).

[78] 2 W. Blackstone, *Commentaries* 505 (1766).

[79] UPC § 2–107; Cal.Prob.Code § 6406; Conn.Gen.Stat.Ann. § 45a–439(e); Matter of Estate of Seaman, 583 N.E.2d 294 (N.Y.1991). It was so provided in the Northwest Ordinance of 1787, § 2.

[80] Fla.Stat.Ann. § 732.105; Ky.Rev.Stat. § 391.050; Iowa Code § 633.219. *See*, Curry v. Williman, 834 S.W.2d 443 (Tex.App.1992) (full brother gets 20% of estate, 3 half-brothers get 10% each); Sheppard v. Junes, 756 S.E. 2d 409 (Va. 2014) (statute that half-bloods take $1/2$ of whole blood share did not trump the parentelic descent of $1/2$ to the paternal side of the family where there was only one descendant, albeit a half-blood, on that side.

[81] Rev.Code Wash. § 11.04.035. Under this statute more remote whole-blood relatives can be preferred to half-bloods. Matter of Estate of Little, 721 P.2d 950 (Wash.1986).

[82] *Restatement (Third) of Property (Wills and Other Donative Transfers)* § 14.1, cmt. m (2011); UPC § 2–705(b); Cal.Prob.Code § 21115.

[83] UPC § 2–107.

[84] UPC § 2–103(i). As a last resort, before escheat, provision is made for stepchildren (of deceased spouses). *See* UPC § 2–103(j). *See also Restatement (Third) of Property (Wills and Other Donative Transfers)* § 2.4, cmt. i (1999).

unconstitutional. The court upheld the statute, citing the following reasons for limiting inheritance:

> (1) It is restricted to relatives whom the decedent probably knew and had an interest in; (2) it solves problems occasioned by . . . the expense and difficulty in locating more remote relatives, the threat of frivolous litigation in will contests by so-called "laughing heirs," and the administrative problems which may be caused by dividing an estate into too many small portions;[85] and (3) the enumerated relatives and . . . the state are more likely to care for decedent than are the decedent's more remote relatives.[86]

Despite these considerations, some statutes permit inheritance by distant blood relatives before the estate escheats to the state,[87] under the theory that "escheats are not favored by the law and are to be avoided wherever possible."[88]

Some states allow persons related to the decedent's spouse, but not to the decedent, to inherit if the decedent has no other surviving heirs. In California, for example, descendants of a predeceased spouse inherit when the decedent has no relatives closer than descendants of grandparents.[89] In 2008, the UPC was amended to reflect a similar result and even takes into account the possibility that the decedent had stepchildren from multiple deceased spouses.[90]

A person who feels no affection for remote relatives (or close ones) can disinherit them by will; as we shall see in Chapter 8, most American states protect only the decedent's spouse against disinheritance. But heirs can contest a will, *e.g.*, for incapacity or undue influence, and in most states they must be notified when a will is offered for probate.[91] As a result, an heir tracing industry has evolved. Most firms charge the estate a fee based upon the size of the estate or charge the fee to the heirs based upon the amount passing to the heirs. In a large estate these fees can be quite substantial.[92] If heirs cannot be found, property of an intestate estate is held on deposit for a period of years, after which, if no one claims it, the property escheats to the state.[93]

---

[85] Blackstone calculated that "if we suppose each couple of our ancestors to have left . . . two children; and each of those on an average to have left two more, . . . all of us have now subsisting near two hundred and seventy millions of kindred in the fifteenth degree." 2 W. Blackstone, *Commentaries* 205 (1766).

[86] Matter of Estate of Jurek, 428 N.W.2d 774, 777 (Mich.App.1988).

[87] This includes states which otherwise adhere to the UPC scheme of intestate succession. Minn.Stat.Ann. § 524.2–103(5).

[88] Estate of McGuigan, 99 Cal.Rptr.2d 887, 890 (Cal.App.2000).

[89] Cal.Prob.Code § 6402(e). Under paragraph (g) issue of a spouse's parents take if the decedent has no relatives at all. Under Conn.Gen.Stat. Ann. § 45a–439(a)(4) the estate goes to stepchildren if a decedent has no spouse or relatives. *See also* Fla. Stat. Ann. § 732.103(5) (kindred of deceased spouse); Ohio Rev. Code § 2105.06(J) (stepchildren or their descendants).

[90] UPC § 2–103(j). *See also* Iowa Code § 633.219.

[91] As to notice and standing to contest wills *see* Section 13.3. As to incapacity and undue influence *see* Sections 5.1, 5.3.

[92] Rodenbush, *Missing Heirs: Put Yourself in their Shoes*, 130 Trusts & Estates (Dec. 1991) p. 53.

[93] Cal.Prob.Code § 6800–06; N.Y. S.C.P.A. § 2225; UPC § 2–105.

Aliens

Under English common law an alien could not hold land in England. "If the person to whom land would descend according to the common rules of inheritance, be an alien, it misses him and passes to some remoter kinsman of the dead man."[94] This rule has been invoked in modern cases, *e.g.*, to deny Polish relatives of a decedent any share in his real estate. The right to inherit could be conferred on aliens by treaty or statute, but at that time there was no such treaty between Poland and the United States, and a statute conferred rights only on resident aliens.[95] The Third Restatement of Property, however, reverses the presumption: unless a statute otherwise provides, noncitizens can acquire and transmit property.[96]

§ 2.3 General Aspects of Intestacy; Statutory Wills

Empirical Studies

Intestate succession statutes purport to distribute an intestate estate along the lines that the average person would prefer. However, studies of public preferences regarding the disposition of wealth at death suggest that some common statutory provisions are out of line with general attitudes. These studies are of two types. The first examines probate court records of decedents' wills.[97] These studies influenced the UPC.[98] The second type relies on interviews with living persons who say how they would want their property to pass on death in various hypothetical situations.[99] Both types of studies have deficiencies.

---

[94] Pollock & Maitland, *supra* note 32, vol. 1, p. 442. The authors doubt (at p. 460) whether this rule existed before the end of the thirteenth century, because William the Conqueror, "a foreigner at the head of an army recruited from many lands conquered England [and] endowed his followers with English lands."

[95] In re Estate of Constan, 384 A.2d 495 (N.H.1978).

[96] *Restatement (Third) of Property (Wills and Other Donative Transfers)* § 1.3 (1999). A Statutory Note appended to this section lists many relevant statutes.

[97] *See* M. Sussman *et al., The Family and Inheritance* (study of probate court records of estates in Cuyahoga County, Ohio); Browder, *Recent Patterns of Testate Succession,* 67 Mich.L.Rev. 1303 (1969) (study of probate court records of estates in Washtenaw County, Michigan, and London, England); Dunham, *The Method, Process and Frequency of Wealth Transmission at Death,* 30 U.Chi.L.Rev. 241 (1963) (study of probate court records of estates in Cook County, Illinois); Price, *The Transmission of Wealth at Death in a Community Property Jurisdiction,* 50 Wash.L.Rev. 277 (1975) (death certificates, probate records and inheritance tax files of 211 adults who died in King County, Wash. in 1969); Ward & Beucher, *The Inheritance Process in Wisconsin,* 1950 Wis.L.Rev. 393 (study of county court records of estates in Dane County, Wisconsin).

[98] *See* UPC Article II, Part 1, general comment. Professor Hirsch has criticized the UPC for failing to use similar empirical evidence in formulating rules of construction for wills and other instruments. Hirsch, *Revisions in Need of Revising: The Uniform Disclaimer of Property Interests Act,* 29 Fla.State U.L.Rev. 109, 182 (2001).

[99] Note, "A Comparison of Iowans Dispositive Preferences With Selected Provisions of the Iowa and Uniform Probate Codes," 63 Iowa L. Rev. 1041 (1978) (telephone and personal interviews); Fellows *et al., Public Attitudes about Property Distribution,* 1978 Am.B. Found. Research J. 321 (market research organization conducted 750 telephone interviews of respondents in five states); Fellows, Simon, Snapp & Snapp, *An Empirical Study of the Illinois Statutory Estate Plan,* 1976 U.Ill.L.F. 717 (interviews of 182 Illinois residents); *Intestate Succession in New Jersey: Does it Conform to Popular Expectations?,* 12 Colum.J.L. & Soc.Prob. 253 (1976) (telephone survey of randomly selected Morris County residents).

The examination of wills may be misleading as to the average person's desires because "willmakers tend to be wealthier, better educated, and engaged in higher status occupations than those who die without a will."[100] According to one study, 72% of persons with estates under $100,000 have no wills, as compared with 15% of those with estates between $200,000 and $1 million.[101] Also wills can reflect the influence of the lawyers who draft them, and perhaps the law should strive to follow "innate preferences" that are unadulterated by such influences. On the other hand, the lawyer's advice is often sound and brings up factors that the client had not previously considered but which, once mentioned, cause the client to make sensible changes in an initial dispositive plan. Should not the law be modeled on the *informed* wishes of citizens? If so, studies based on interviews with the public may mislead as to what people *really* want.

Why Not Die Intestate?

Attorneys may be asked why a client needs a will. One reason is that state intestacy laws at best only meet the needs of a "typical" family and may not fit the client's situation. A spouse of one year is generally treated the same as the spouse of a long time; a wealthy or unloving child is treated the same as a needy and devoted one.[102] Unrelated persons are excluded even if they have enjoyed the same kind of relationship with the decedent as a child. Remote relatives may take an estate which the owner would prefer to leave to a charity or friends.[103] One who dies intestate gives up the opportunity to tailor the dispositions to the particular family situation.

Some countries have more flexible intestate succession laws, allowing courts in distributing estates to "punish the bad, reward the good, and protect the needy and the caring. . . . The exemplary neighbor or friend may inherit at the expense of those 'closest' to the decedent by blood alone."[104] The policy arguments for and against such a scheme will be treated in Section 3.1. For the present, it suffices to say that in all of the United States, such departures from the statutory norms require a person to use a will (or will substitute).

When a client has minor children, intestacy is particularly undesirable. When property passes directly to a minor, a conservator[105] may have to be appointed to manage the minor's property. Some states impose strict court supervision over a conservator's actions. These restrictions are cumbersome and generally antithetical to the child's interest in earning a fair return on the

---

[100] Beckstrom, *Sociobiology and Intestate Wealth Transfers*, 76 Nw.U.L.Rev. 216, 217–19 (1981).

[101] Waggoner, *Marital Property Rights in Transition*, 59 Mo.L.Rev. 21, 29–30 (1994).

[102] An Illinois statute allowing family members who have devoted themselves to the care of a disabled relative to receive compensation from the relative's estate makes some rather arbitrary distinctions, but was upheld against constitutional challenge in In re Estate of Jolliff, 771 N.E.2d 346 (Ill.2002).

[103] In Estate of Griswold, 24 P.3d 1191 (Cal. 2001) half siblings with whom decedent had had no contact and who were unaware of his existence inherited from him.

[104] Foster, *The Dark Side of Trusts: Challenges to Chinese Inheritance Law*, 2 Wash.U. Global Studies L.Rev. 151, 155, 161 (2003).

[105] In some states conservators are called guardians of the property. Under the UPC, conservators administer a minor's property; a guardian has responsibility for the minor's person. *See* UPC § 5–102(1) & (3).

property and reducing costs.[106] Moreover, conservatorships end when a child ceases to be a minor, and some children who are 18 (or even older) need to have property managed for them. The best method for accomplishing this is a trust. For this reason some states allow wrongful death proceeds awarded to a minor to be placed in a trust, but such provisions do not exist for ordinary intestate succession.[107]

Many testators with minor children avoid conservatorship by leaving everything to the surviving spouse in the expectation that the spouse will take care of the children. This solution may not be satisfactory if the spouse is not the parent of the decedent's children or has other children by a prior marriage. Also, the spouse may remarry and have another family to which the client's property may be diverted. In large estates an "all to spouse" will may result in unnecessarily high estate tax when the spouse dies.[108] Here, too, a trust can provide a better solution than any of the intestacy statutes.[109] Even if the testator's children are adults, their share may pass to their minor descendants by representation or under an antilapse statute if the child predeceases the testator.[110] A well drafted will should provide that any share of the estate which happens to pass to a minor shall be held in trust, at least until the minor comes of age.[111]

Even if a person wants all her property to pass to the heirs designated by the intestacy laws, and if no trust is needed, a will may still be desirable. A will can designate an executor to administer the estate and can give the executor powers beyond those conferred by law. Administration of an estate is more efficient when the executor has such powers.[112] For example, some states may require the administrator of an intestate estate to seek court approval prior to selling real estate, whereas a testator's will can confer a power of sale on an executor exercisable without court approval.

Statutory Wills

Despite the advantages of wills, many persons do not have them. According to one study, only 20% of the decedents in the area studied had a will.[113] To some extent this is due to the availability of nonprobate methods of transfer at death, such as revocable inter vivos trusts and joint tenancy.[114] To

---

[106] For further discussion of alternatives to guardianship *see* Section 10.5.

[107] In Sawyer v. Lebanon Citizens Natl. Bank, 664 N.E.2d 571 (Ohio App.1995), such a trust was created for the decedent's minor children who were to get the funds outright when they reached age 25, whereas in most states a guardianship ends at age 18.

[108] *See* the material on "Marital Deduction Planning" in Section 15.4.

[109] For the advantages of trusts over legal life estates *see* Section 10.5.

[110] *See* Section 6.5.

[111] *See* J. Price & S. Donaldson, *Contemporary Estate Planning* § 4.24 (2019).

[112] For examples of how a will can avoid restrictive administrative procedures *see* Stein & Fierstein, *The Demography of Probate Administration,* 15 U.Balt.L.Rev. 54, 80–81 (1985). A general discussion of administration appears in Chapter 14.

[113] Schoenblum, *Will Contests—An Empirical Study,* 22 Real Prop. Prob. and Trust J. 607 (1987). *See* also Warren, *Advisors Often Fail to Heed Own Advice,* Trusts & Estates Jan. 1995, p. 6 (38% of accountants and 25% of lawyers surveyed had no will). Wills are even less common in civil law countries, presumably because of the restrictions on disinheriting relatives. *See* Section 8.2.

[114] For a discussion of the advantages of avoiding probate, see Section 10.4.

some extent it is based on a reluctance to hire lawyers. No state requires that wills be drafted by lawyers, but wills that are drafted without lawyers often cause problems, and many lay persons are reluctant (perhaps wisely) to draft their own will. A favorite among probate lawyers are jokes about "the Jolly Testator who draws his own will."

Some states have promulgated statutory wills that lay persons can use at a very modest cost. Many of the disadvantages of dying intestate can be avoided by using, for example, the California Statutory Will. It allows a testator to leave all the estate to the spouse by signing the appropriate box.[115] The testator can designate a custodian for his/her children, which avoids many of the disadvantages of a conservatorship.[116] The form allows designation of an executor and confers powers on the executor that are more extensive than those given to an administrator without a will.[117] The Statutory Will does not purport to deal with tax planning appropriate for larger estates and the instructions warn users to consult an attorney if they have property over a specified amount.[118]

The Uniform Statutory Will Act, promulgated in 1984 but since withdrawn by the Uniform Law Commission, is more ambitious; it allows a testator to create a trust for the spouse for life, and a trust for a child who "cannot effectively manage . . . property by reason of mental illness . . . or other cause."[119] Few lay persons are aware of this Act; the drafters primary goal was "to provide attorneys a simple will . . . at minimum cost to the client" rather than one which laypersons would adopt themselves.[120] Lawyers who have little experience or training in probate are well advised to consult the statutory will before drafting a will "from scratch." Although the Act has been adopted in only a few states, a drafter in any state can incorporate it by reference.[121]

§ 2.4 Gifts to "Heirs"

Most lawyers advise clients not to die intestate. Still, some lawyers use the intestacy laws in drafting wills and trusts by including a gift to the "heirs" of the testator, the settlor, or another person. This term is normally interpreted to incorporate by reference the laws of intestate succession.[122]

Equivalent Words

Occasionally an instrument uses the phrase "next of kin" rather than the word "heirs." Historically, the phrase "next of kin" was used to describe persons

---

[115] Cal.Prob.Code § 6240, par. 5, Choice One.

[116] Custodianships are discussed at Section 10.5.

[117] Cal.Prob.Code § 6241. Price & Donaldson, *supra* note 111, at § 4.3, give the California statutory will and others like it a mixed review.

[118] Cal.Prob.Code § 6240(8).

[119] Unif.Stat.Will Act § 6 (trust for spouse), § 9 (trust for disabled individual).

[120] *Id.*, Prefatory Note.

[121] *Id.* § 3. As to incorporation by reference *see* Section 7.2.

[122] *Restatement (Third) of Property (Wills and Other Donative Transfers)* § 16.1 (2011); UPC § 2–711; Cal.Prob.Code § 21114.

who took personal property as distinguished from heirs who inherited land,[123] but the differences between the two have almost universally disappeared. The UPC uses "heirs" for all takers by intestacy[124] and calls for interpreting the phrase "next of kin" in an instrument in the same manner.[125] Arguments that the word "next" excludes more remote relatives who would take by representation on intestacy are usually rejected.[126]

The UPC also construes words of more uncertain import, like "relatives" and "family" to mean the takers under intestacy statutes.[127] Some courts have so construed the word "representatives," so that a bequest to "children and the representatives of any deceased child" referred to the deceased child's heirs.[128]

Other Meanings of Heirs: Devisees

The word "heirs" does not always refer to the intestacy statutes, however. Its Latin root, *heres,* was used in Roman law to mean *either* a person designated by will *or* someone who took upon intestacy.[129] This usage still survives in Louisiana, where a husband's devise of property to his wife's "heirs" allowed her to "will the property to whomever she pleases" because "heirs" included testamentary legatees.[130]

In the common-law tradition, however, heirs ordinarily means only those persons designated by law to take upon intestacy.[131] Thus, a gift to "the heirs at law" of the testator's son passed to the son's relatives and not to a friend whom the son had designated as his "heir."[132] And where a testator left her estate to her heirs at law, mistakenly thinking that her first cousins were her heirs when, under state law, only her aunt was her heir, the first cousins were excluded from taking under the will.[133] But sometimes the context shows that the testator used the word "heirs" to mean devisees. For example, when a will made devises to eight named individuals in paragraph 5, and left the residue of his estate "to the heirs set forth in Item 5," the named individuals, although not heirs of the testator, were awarded the residue.[134]

---

[123] In In re Johnson's Will, 301 N.Y.S.2d 174 (App.Div.1969) the court applied the law governing real estate even though the property to be distributed was personal property because the will devised it to "heirs."

[124] UPC § 1–201(20). *See also* Cal.Prob.Code § 44.

[125] UPC § 2–711. *See also* Cal.Prob.Code § 21114.

[126] *Restatement (Third) of Property (Wills and Other Donative Transfers)* § 16.1, cmt. b (2011); Graves v. Hyer, 626 S.W.2d 661, 668 (Mo.App.1981) ("nearest blood kin"). As to representation, see Section 2.2.

[127] UPC § 2–711. *See also Restatement (Third) of Property (Wills and Other Donative Transfers)* § 16.1, cmt. b (2011). Professor Fratcher questioned this construction in situations where the intestacy statute gives everything to a spouse and nothing to the decedent's blood relatives. Fratcher, *Class Gifts to "Heirs," "Issue," and Like Groups,* 55 Alb.L.Rev. 1205, 1217 (1992).

[128] Boston Safe Deposit & Trust Co. v. Wilbur, 728 N.E.2d 264, 268 (Mass.2000).

[129] Justinian, *Institutes* 2.20.34 (the main purpose of a will is to designate the heir).

[130] Succession of Dinwiddie, 263 So.2d 739 (La.App.1972).

[131] Glanvill, *Tractatus de Legibus* 71 (G. Hall ed. 1965).

[132] PNC Bank, Ohio, N.A. v. Stanton, 662 N.E.2d 875 (Ohio App.1995).

[133] Mahoney v. Grainger, 186 N.E. 86 (1933).

[134] Evans v. Cass, 256 N.E.2d 738 (Ohio Prob.1970). *See also* In re Leake's Estate, 246 N.E.2d 314 (Ill.App.1969); Hancock v. Krause, 757 S.W.2d 117 (Tex.App.1988).

Is the Spouse an "Heir"?

Most courts construe gifts to "heirs" to include a spouse because most modern intestacy statutes give spouses a share of the estate on intestacy.[135] The UPC agrees unless the spouse has remarried when the disposition would become possessory. Thus, in a devise "to A for life, remainder to my heirs," if the testator's widow has remarried before A dies, she would not qualify as an heir of the testator.[136]

Sometimes "heirs" appears in a context which shows that the spouse was not intended to take the devise. A devise to the "heirs per stirpes" of the testator's daughter was interpreted to exclude her husband.[137] Likewise, a devise to "the heirs of Mary's body" would exclude her husband.[138]

Some testators incorrectly use the word "heirs" to mean "children" or "descendants." When a testator left land to his grandson's heirs, "and if he should die without heirs to my other Grandchildren," the court construed "heirs" to mean "descendants," because the "other Grandchildren" would *be* the grandson's heirs if he had no descendants, and a gift to a person's heirs if he dies without heirs is nonsense.[139] An intent to exclude a spouse from the "heir" category may also be found in a direction that "the heirs of a deceased child shall take the share *their parent* would have taken if living."[140]

Choice of Law

A drafter who decides to use a gift to "heirs" in a will should make clear *which* intestacy statute should control, because the intestacy laws in the states can differ. For example, a trust provided that at the death of the settlor's grandson, his widow "shall receive such portion of the corpus of the trust as she would be entitled to had her husband died intestate." This portion was greater under Maryland law, where the trust was created and administered, than under the law of Texas, where the grandson was domiciled at death. The court held that Maryland law governed,[141] but the UPC looks to the "law of the designated individual's domicile," *i.e.*, Texas on these facts.[142] The Third Restatement of Property would have looked to the law of Texas including its choice of law rules, which might in turn look to the situs of any real property involved.[143] A well drafted will can avoid controversy by specifying the relevant law, *e.g.*, the Uniform Statutory Will Act refers to "the individuals who would

---

[135] *Restatement (Third) of Property (Wills and Other Donative Transfers)* § 16.1 (2011); Estate of Calden, 712 A.2d 522 (Me.1998). As to the spouse's share on intestacy, see Section 2.1.

[136] UPC § 2–711. *See also Restatement (Third) of Property (Wills and Other Donative Transfers)* § 16.1, cmt. h (2011). *But see* Iowa Code § 633.3(24) excluding a spouse from being considered an heir.

[137] Varns v. Varns, 610 N.E.2d 440 (Ohio App.1991). *Contra,* Wright v. Brandon, 863 S.W.2d 400 (Tenn.1993).

[138] *Restatement (Second) of Property (Donative Transfers)* § 29.1, cmt. j (1988).

[139] Cheuvront v. Haley, 444 S.W.2d 734 (Ky.1969). *See also* Dickson v. Renfro, 569 S.W.2d 66 (Ark.1978); Estate of Forrest, TC Memo 1990–464.

[140] *Restatement (Second) of Property (Donative Transfers)* § 29.1, cmt. e (1988).

[141] Lansburgh v. Lansburgh, 632 A.2d 221 (Md.App.1993).

[142] UPC § 2–711.

[143] *Restatement (Third) of Property (Wills and Other Donative Transfers)* § 16.1, cmt. g (2011).

be entitled to receive the estate as if the property were located in this state and [the ancestor] had then died intestate domiciled in this state."[144]

The governing intestacy statute may change between the time the testator executes the will and the time the property is distributed. Therefore, the will should also specify the time for applying the controlling law.[145] Some states have different rules for different types of property (real and personal or separate and community), so the will should say which rules apply.

Planning

Objections can be raised to using words like "heirs" in drafting. Most testators do not know what the intestacy statutes provide. Even if the drafter describes them, an oral summary may be misunderstood or forgotten. Some testators whose wills left property to "heirs" apparently understood this to mean something different from what the law provides.[146] Nevertheless, the word "heirs" is useful because the intestacy statutes cover a wide variety of situations. Many wills specify a distribution for the situations most likely to prevail, but then use a devise to "heirs" as an "end limitation" to cover remote contingencies.[147] This is simpler than spelling out all possible contingencies in the will—*e.g.*, to my parents, if living, otherwise to my brothers and sisters, if living, otherwise to their descendants, if living, otherwise etc. However, particularly in a jurisdiction which limits inheritance, like the UPC, a gift to the "heirs" of someone who dies without close relatives or a spouse may produce an unintended escheat.[148] If heirship is *not* limited by the governing law, a gift to "heirs" may require a costly search for remote relatives.[149] To avoid this problem, many testators might prefer a devise to charity, in which case there will be no resulting intestacy if all other devises fail.

§ 2.5 Recovery for Wrongful Death

Decedents who have accumulated little or no property may nevertheless provide their families with a valuable claim against a tortfeasor who was responsible for their death.[150] At common law, tort claims died with the person, but all states now allow wrongful death actions. The original statute was Lord Campbell's Act, an 1846 English statute.[151]

---

[144] Uniform Statutory Will Act § 6(3).

[145] *See* In re Succession of Celestin, 82 So.3d 520, 521 (La. App. 5 Cir. 2011 (applying statute in existence at testator's death, not the statute in effect when the will was executed in determining if son of the decedent was a "forced heir.")

[146] *See* Matter of Taff's Estate, 133 Cal.Rptr. 737 (App.1976); Gustafson v. Svenson, 366 N.E.2d 761 (Mass.1977); Brunson v. Citizens Bank and Trust Co., 752 S.W.2d 316 (Ky.App.1988) (testator apparently thought his "heirs" included his sisters even though he had a daughter).

[147] Uniform Statutory Will Act § 7(a)(2) (devise to heirs if testator dies without issue); *cf.* J. Price & S. Donaldson, *Contemporary Estate Planning* § 4.22.7 (2019) (suggesting clause distributing to heirs of testator and testator's spouse).

[148] UPC § 2–711 expressly allows the state to take under a gift to "heirs." *See also Restatement (Third) of Property (Wills and Other Donative Transfers)* § 16.1, cmt. i (2011).

[149] *See* Section 2.2.

[150] In some states a wrongful death action may be brought on behalf of a fetus. See, e.g., Mack v. Carmack, 79 So.3d 118 (Ala. 2011).

[151] An Act for Compensating the families of Persons killed by Accidents, 9 & 10 Vict. ch. 93 (1846).

The law on this subject is not generally considered part of the law of wills. For example, wrongful death recovery is dealt with in the California Code of Civil Procedure, not the Probate Code.[152] But wrongful death actions typically are brought by the decedent's personal representative, who is appointed by the probate court.[153] The recovery, however, is not an asset of the decedent's estate[154] nor is it subject to the will of the decedent or the claims of the decedent's creditors.[155]

Many statutes refer to the intestacy laws in designating the beneficiaries of wrongful death proceeds. In California, for example, the action is brought on behalf of the "decedent's surviving spouse, domestic partner, children, and issue of deceased children, or . . . the persons . . . who would be entitled to the property of the decedent by intestate succession."[156] As to "children," courts usually look to the intestacy statutes to determine who is included, *e.g.*, in the case of an adopted child.[157] However, the beneficiaries of wrongful death actions are not always the same persons who take on intestacy. For example, a statute which designated "the heir or heirs of the deceased" was interpreted to include only descendants of the decedent and not collateral relatives who might inherit. The statute was interpreted in this manner because the purpose of the statute was "to compensate those who suffer pecuniary loss by reason of the death," and this would not be generally true of collaterals.[158] In Georgia, children of a deceased child of the decedent can inherit but are not entitled to claim for wrongful death.[159] In other states, certain heirs, such as the surviving

---

[152] Cal.Code Civ.Proc. § 377.60 et seq.

[153] Lord Campbell's Act created an action for the "the Executor or Administrator of the Person deceased." 9 & 10 Vict. ch. 93, § 2. *See also* Cal.Code Civ.Proc. § 377.60 (action may be brought by decedent's personal representative); Model Survival and Death Act § 3(a); Utah Code § 78B–3–106 (action brought by heirs or personal representative). In many jurisdictions, the personal representative's right to sue is made exclusive to avoid multiplicity of litigation. Weeks v. Cessna Aircraft Co., 895 P.2d 731 (Okl.App.1994). Some states allow a wrongful death action for a fetus, even a pre-viable fetus. Mack v. Carmack, 79 So. 3d 597, 611–612 (Ala. 2011).

[154] See, e.g., Ex parte Taylor, 93 So. 3d 118 (Ala. 2012).

[155] *Compare* "survival" claims, discussed *infra*. *See also* Ex parte Taylor, 93 So.3d 118,119 (Ala. 2012)(wrongful death proceeds are not subject to administration and do not become part of the decedent's estate.)

[156] Cal.Code Civ.Proc. § 377.60. *See also* Ohio Rev.Code § 2125.02(A) (for spouse, children, parents, and "other next of kin"); Ouellette v. State Farm, 918 P.2d 1363 (Okl.1994) (parents are not "next of kin" and so cannot recover for wrongful death of child who was married and had children); Baugh v. Baugh ex rel. Smith, 973 P.2d 202 (Kan.App.1999); Morris v. William L. Dawson Nursing Center, 702 N.E.2d 345 (Ill.App.1998) (same for siblings); Booker v. Lal, 726 N.E.2d 638 (Ill.App.2000) (children of deceased siblings eligible to take by representation). *See,* however, the cases cited at note 175 *infra*.

[157] Cheyanna M. v. A.C. Nielsen Co., 78 Cal.Rptr.2d 335 (App.1998); Estate of Jones v. Howell, 687 So.2d 1171 (Miss.1996) (adopted away child is heir and wrongful death beneficiary). *But see* Brookbank v. Gray, 658 N.E.2d 724 (Ohio 1996) (child born out of wedlock can recover for wrongful death even though ineligible to inherit). As to adoption, see Section 2.10.

[158] Ablin v. Richard O'Brien Plastering Co., 885 P.2d 289 (Colo.App.1994) (siblings cannot sue even though they are literally "heirs"); Whitenhill v. Kaiser Permanente, 940 P.2d 1129 (Colo.App.1997) (parents). *Compare* Kelson v. Salt Lake County, 784 P.2d 1152 (Utah 1989) (siblings cannot sue because they are not "heirs" if the decedent is survived by parents). *See also* In re Estate of Wolfe, 915 A.2d 1197 (Pa. Super. 2006), appeal granted and pending, 946 A.2d 641 (2008) (distributing award in accordance with intestacy rules but suggesting adult child who suffers no pecuniary loss or lacked a significant relationship to decedent should not share in proceeds).

[159] Tolbert v. Maner, 518 S.E.2d 423 (Ga.1999). *But see* Booker v. Lal, 726 N.E.2d 638 (Ill.App.2000) (children of deceased siblings eligible by representation).

spouse and children, are presumed to have been damaged by the death, whereas others are eligible to claim but must prove that they were damaged.[160] Conversely, dependent relatives of the decedent have been allowed to recover for wrongful death even though they would not have inherited because there was a closer relative.[161] Lord Campbell's Act allowed recovery by stepchildren and stepparents, even though they do not usually inherit.[162] Parents do not inherit if the decedent was survived by descendants; nonetheless dependent parents have been allowed to recover in a wrongful death action even if they were not heirs.[163] Even unrelated dependents who resided with the decedent qualify in some states.[164]

Even if the decedent's heirs and the statutory wrongful death beneficiaries are the same persons, the fixed shares prescribed by the intestacy statutes do not always control the allocation of a wrongful death recovery.[165] Under the typical intestacy statute, parents inherit equally, but they often are awarded unequal amounts for wrongful death based on their relationship with the child.[166]

In California, the court allocates the recovery among the eligible claimants.[167] The statute gives no guidance as to how this discretion is to be exercised. In Ohio, the court makes the allocation "having due regard for the injury and loss to each beneficiary . . . and for the age and condition of the beneficiaries."[168] Under the Model Survival and Death Act, the determination is made by the "trier of fact," whether court or jury. If the claim is settled, the court must approve its terms and can control the allocation.[169]

---

160 Miller v. Allstate Ins. Co., 676 N.E.2d 943 (Ohio App.1996) (sister of decedent can claim but does not benefit from the statutory presumption of damage); Wolf v. Boren, 685 N.E.2d 86 (Ind.App.1997) (no recovery for parents and siblings who were not "dependent" on decedent).

161 Luider v. Skaggs, 693 N.E.2d 593 (Ind.App.1998).

162 9 & 10 Vict. ch. 93, § 5. As to the treatment of stepchildren, see Section 2.10.

163 Butler v. Halstead, 770 P.2d 698 (Wyo.1989) (even though a child was the only heir, decedent's mother could share in the wrongful death recovery); Chavez v. Carpenter, 111 Cal.Rptr.2d 534 (App.2001); Oxendine v. Overturf, 973 P.2d 417 (Utah 1999); Model Survival and Death Act § 1(2) ("survivors" includes ascendants as well as descendants); Ramage v. Central Ohio Emergency Serv. Inc., 592 N.E.2d 828 (Ohio 1992) (grandparents can claim even when there was a surviving parent).

164 Cal.Code Civ.Proc. § 377.60. Under the Model Survival and Death Act § 1(2) the beneficiaries can include dependents who "were members of the decedent's household or related to the decedent by blood or marriage." In Lealaimatafao v. Woodward-Clyde Consl., 867 P.2d 220 (Haw.1994) a woman living with the decedent and her child were allowed to recover under a statute which provided for a spouse, children, parents "or other dependent."

165 In some states, however, the intestacy statutes control the allocation. Estate of Boyd, 606 P.2d 1243 (Wyo.1980) (applying a statute later repealed); Pogue v. Pogue, 434 So.2d 262 (Ala.Civ.App.1983) (recovery equally divided between mother and father who had failed to support the child because intestacy statute controlled).

166 Jones v. Jones, 641 N.E.2d 98 (Ind.App.1994) (proper to award 65% to the mother who had custody of the child); Guy v. Johnson, 448 N.E.2d 1142 (Mass.App.Ct.1983); Matter of Estate of Lande, 567 N.E.2d 668 (Ill.App.1991) (same); In re Estate of Marinelli, 650 N.E.2d 935 (Ohio App.1994) (nothing awarded to father who "failed to maintain any semblance of a father-son relationship" with decedent).

167 Cal.Code Civ.Proc. § 377.61.

168 Ohio Rev. Code § 2125.03(A)(1); *cf.* Booker v. Lal, 726 N.E.2d 638, 641 (Ill.App.2000) (allocation on basis of "percentage of dependency").

169 Model Survival and Death Act § 3(f)(g). Cal.Prob.Code § 9835 requires that the settlement of a wrongful death action by a personal representative be approved by the court.

The flexibility given by most wrongful death statutes in allocating the recovery stands in sharp contrast to the fixed shares provided by the intestacy statutes. Perhaps this difference is due to the fact that if the intestacy statute produces a "bad" result in a given case, *e.g.*, by allowing an undeserving child an equal share with his siblings, this can be avoided by a will. Wrongful death recoveries, on the other hand, are not governed by the decedent's will. Consequently, parents who have accumulated property are free to disinherit their children by will. But parents who are killed before they have accumulated property cannot effectively extinguish their children's rights to recover a wrongful death award.[170]

Survival Claims

Most states allow the decedent's estate to recover for some losses, and this recovery can be controlled by the decedent's will.[171] It is also independent of the wrongful death claim.[172] Survival claims differ from wrongful death claims in that any recovery belongs to the decedent's estate and, therefore, does not necessarily inure to the benefit of decedent's spouse or descendants, unless, of course, they are the beneficiaries of the estate.

Under the Model Act, for example, damages which "accrued to [the decedent] before his death . . . become part of the decedent's estate and are distributable in the same manner as other assets of the estate."[173] These damages usually include medical expenses or an award for pain and suffering by the decedent before death.[174] Arguably they also should include the decedent's prospective earnings,[175] but the Model Act gives to the statutory beneficiaries rather than the decedent's estate as part of their wrongful death claim "the present monetary value of . . . financial contributions they would have received from the decedent had death not ensued."[176] When a decedent was survived by two children who received only half of his estate under his will, damages for loss of prospective inheritance, based on the decedent's anticipated earnings, went to the children under the statute even though they would not have actually received them under their father's will.[177]

---

[170] As to a parent's freedom to disinherit a child in U.S. law, see Section 8.1.

[171] *Restatement (Third) of Property (Wills and Other Donative Transfers)* § 1.1, illus. 20 (1999). Under Alaska Stat. § 09.55.580(a), when a decedent is survived "by no spouse or children or other dependents," the recovery "shall be administered as other personal property of the decedent."

[172] Peters v. Columbus Steel Castings Co., 873 N.E.2d 1258 (Ohio 2007).

[173] Model Survival and Death Act § 2(b). *See also* Cal. Code Civ. Proc. § 377.34; Matter of Estate of Sims, 918 P.2d 132 (Utah App.1996) (widow who collects for personal injuries suffered by her husband must turn over the proceeds to his estate).

[174] In re Thornton, 481 N.W.2d 828 (Mich.App.1992) (pain and suffering).

[175] Smedley, *Some Order out of Chaos in Wrongful Death Law*, 37 Vand.L.Rev. 273, 280 (1984).

[176] Model Survival and Death Act § 3(d)(2). *See also* Ohio Rev. Code 2125.02(B)(4) ("loss of prospective inheritance").

[177] Kulawik v. ERA Jet Alaska, 820 P.2d 627 (Alaska 1991).

Thus, a death may produce two types of recovery, one going to the decedent's estate and the other to the statutory beneficiaries.[178] Both claims usually are enforced by the decedent's personal representative, and the Model Act allows them to be combined in a single action.[179] When the personal representative brings both actions, it may be hard to allocate a recovery between the wrongful death claim and the survivor's action.[180]

§ 2.6 Advancements

If Mary has three children, Alice, Arthur, and Andrew, in all states they would share equally if Mary died intestate. But suppose that while Mary was alive she gave $10,000 to Alice. If this $10,000 is ignored in dividing Mary's estate, Alice will get more of Mary's property than Arthur and Andrew, contrary to the general assumption that parents want their children to share equally. Many states today have statutes dealing with such "advancements" on an inheritance.[181] These statutes differ from each other on several points.

The doctrine of advancements only applies where the decedent's estate passes by intestacy. The theory here is that if the decedent made an advancement and thereafter executed a will, the decedent presumably took the advancement into account when making the will. On the other hand, if after executing a will, the testator gifts property to a beneficiary named in the will, that gift is not an advancement but may be deemed a "satisfaction."

Proof of Intent

Under the UPC, a lifetime gift to a donee who turns out to be an heir is treated as an advancement against the donee's share of the donor's intestate estate only if "the decedent declared in a contemporaneous writing or the heir acknowledged in writing that the gift is an advancement."[182] The fact that a gift is in writing (*e.g.*, a check or a deed) does not suffice unless the writing describes the gift as an advancement. The word "advancement" does not have to be used if the writing makes the intent clear.[183] Under this statute, few advancements will be legally recognized because persons who die intestate do not usually consult lawyers, and nonlawyers are not likely to know about the writing requirement.[184]

---

178 If a wrongful death claim beneficiary dies before bringing suit, the wrongful death claim itself may be asserted under a survival act. Chavez v. Carpenter, 111 Cal.Rptr.2d 534, 542 (App.2001).

179 Model Survival and Death Act § 4. *See also* Cal.Code Civ. Proc. § 377.62.

180 Hooks v. Owen, 719 N.E.2d 581 (Ohio App.1998) (abuse of discretion to allocate part of settlement proceeds to wrongful death beneficiaries).

181 Elbert, *Advancements I,* 51 Mich.L.Rev. 665, 674 (1953) (hereinafter cited as *Advancements I*).

182 UPC § 2–109(a). *See also Restatement (Third) of Property (Wills and Other Donative Transfers)* § 2.6 (1999); Cal.Prob.Code § 6409; N.Y.EPTL § 2–1.5(b); Ohio Rev.Code § 2105.051.

183 *Restatement (Third) of Property (Wills and Other Donative Transfers)* § 2.6, cmt. c (1999). UPC § 2–109 is clearer on this point than its predecessor, Section 2–110 of the pre-1990 Code.

184 Fellows, *Concealing Legislative Reform in the Common-Law Tradition,* 37 Vand.L.Rev. 671, 678 (1984).

Some have praised the UPC because it eliminates "wasteful litigation" about the decedent's intention which is often "either nonexistent or obscure"[185] and might have to be resolved on the basis of untrustworthy testimony.[186] In fact, litigation about advancements is rare, perhaps because intestate estates (to which the concept of advancement is limited) are usually too small to warrant litigation. In any event, the difficulties in determining intent could also be eliminated by a contrary presumption, *i.e.*, treating *all* gifts as advancements absent written evidence of a contrary intent.[187] Professor Fellows has suggested that "the distribution of a decedent's estate [should] take into account all gifts to lineal descendants of substantial sums not given for maintenance or education of the donee . . . without further inquiry into the decedent's intent" in order to further "the decedent's probable intent to treat children or their families equally."[188] The drafters of the UPC, on the other hand, thought that "most inter vivos transfers today are intended to be absolute gifts" rather than advancements.[189] There is no empirical evidence either for this or for the opposite assumption.[190] If all lifetime gifts were treated as advancements, there would undoubtedly be a burdensome and potentially costly accounting problem as well. Thus, on balance, the UPC's position seems to make the most sense.

Many states do not require a writing to prove that a gift was intended as an advancement. In such states, oral evidence may be introduced to establish intent. Absent any evidence, some states presume that gifts are not advancements;[191] some make the opposite presumption.[192]

The intention that a gift be an advancement must have existed when the gift was made. The donor cannot later convert an absolute gift into an advancement; thus, the UPC's requirement of a "contemporaneous writing."[193] However, a change of heart by the donor which is *beneficial* to the recipient is allowed. For example, a provision in a will that loans previously made to a child shall be treated only as advancements was given effect,[194] as doing so would, in all likelihood, be more advantageous to the child. Conversely, the *recipient* can acknowledge that a prior gift be deemed an advancement; the

---

185 Chaffin, *A Reappraisal of the Wealth Transmission Process,* 10 Ga.L.Rev. 447, 497, 499 (1976). *See also* Bratt, *Kentucky's Doctrine of Advancements: A Time For Reform,* 75 Ky.L.J. 341, 388 (1986) (proposing a similar statute).

186 In Matter of Martinez' Estate, 633 P.2d 727 (N.M.App.1981), the court refused to accept the claim of an advancement on the basis of "self-serving testimony in 1980 [by another heir] to a conversation with [the decedent] in 1953 to prove [his] intent in 1941."

187 Such a presumption appears in La.Civ.Code § 1230.

188 *See* Fellows, *supra* note 184 at 704–05.

189 UPC § 2–109, comment.

190 Averill, *An Eclectic History and Analysis of the 1990 Uniform Probate Code,* 55 Alb.L.Rev. 891, 915 (1992).

191 Iowa Code § 633.224.

192 La.Civ.Code § 1230; Elbert, *Advancements II,* 52 Mich.L.Rev. 231, 249 (1953) (hereinafter cited as *Advancements II*).

193 UPC § 2–109(a); *Restatement (Third) of Property (Wills and Other Donative Transfers)* § 2.6, cmt. c (1999).

194 O'Brien v. O'Brien, 526 S.E.2d 1 (Va.2000).

word "contemporaneous" does not apply to such a writing.[195] In states not requiring a writing, later declarations may be accepted as evidence of the donor's intent at the time of the gift.[196]

Circumstantial evidence may show that a gift was not intended to be an advancement. Payments for a child's support or education, such as paying college tuition,[197] are not usually deemed advancements. Neither are sales, but if the consideration was inadequate the difference between price and value may be an advancement.[198] A recital of consideration in a deed can be rebutted by proof that in fact there was none.[199]

Will substitutes such as insurance, joint tenancy, and revocable trusts can be treated as advancements,[200] even though the recipient gets no benefit *in advance* of the decedent's death. Even a bequest in a will which fails to dispose of all the testator's estate operates as an advancement as to the intestate property in some states, but others recognize advancements only in cases of total intestacy.[201]

Computation of Shares

A comment to the UPC illustrates how shares are computed when there is an advancement.[202] Essentially, the advancements are added to the actual value of the probate estate to calculate what the estate would have been worth if the advancements had not been made. This estate is often called a "hotchpot." Then the share of the spouse, if any, and the heirs are computed in the hotchpot. An heir's hypothetical share in the hotchpot is then reduced by the amount of that heir's advancement.

To illustrate, suppose the decedent died intestate survived by three children: *A*, to whom he had advanced $50,000, *B*, to whom he had advanced $10,000, and *C* who received no advancements. The value of the probate estate is $180,000. But when the two advancements totaling $60,000 are added back in, there is a hotchpot of $240,000. Each child would be entitled to $80,000 from that hotchpot. *A*, who already received $50,000, is entitled to $30,000; *B*, who received an advancement of $10,000, is entitled to $70,000; and C, who

---

[195] Some statutes requiring a writing are not specific as to the time. *See* 755 ILCS § 5/2–5(a); Md. Code, Estates and Trusts § 3–106(a).

[196] Matter of Martinez' Estate, 633 P.2d 727 (N.M.App.1981).

[197] La.Civ.Code § 1244 (support, education, and marriage presents); Elbert, *Advancements III*, 52 Mich.L.Rev. 535, 535 (support), p. 538 (education) (1954) (hereinafter cited as *Advancements III*); *Advancements II*, p. 254 (trifling gift). *But cf.* Bratt, *supra* note 185, at 386 (paying for professional school education is an advancement).

[198] La.Civ.Code § 1248; *Advancements I*, p. 678, *Advancements II*, p. 255. *But see* In re Scott's Estate, 642 P.2d 1287 (Wyo.1982); 3 *Amer.Law of Prop.* § 14.10, at 587 (if consideration substantial, even if inadequate, should be no presumption of advancement).

[199] Thomas v. Thomas, 398 S.W.2d 231 (Ky.1965).

[200] Brodrick v. Moore, 226 F.2d 105 (10th Cir.1955); *Restatement (Third) of Property (Wills and Other Donative Transfers)* § 2.6, cmt. f (1999); UPC § 2–109, comment.

[201] *Advancements II*, p. 242; Bratt, *supra* note 185, at 344.

[202] The statute itself "does not specify the method of taking an advancement into account. . . . That process, called the hotchpot method, is provided by the common law." UPC § 2–109, comment. *See also Restatement (Third) of Property (Wills and Other Donative Transfers)* § 2.6, illus. 1 (1999).

received no advancements, is entitled to $80,000. Thus, the actual probate estate of $180,000 is distributed $30,000 to *A*, $70,000 to B, and $80,000 to *C*.

Suppose *A* had received $110,000 in advancements rather than $50,000. In this case the hotchpot would have been $300,000, and *A's* share would have been $100,000. Because *A* received more than his intestate share in this hotchpot, *A* is not entitled to any further share from the intestate estate and is no longer considered in the advancement calculation. *A* is not required to refund anything to the estate. The only heirs considered in calculating the amount of, and who share in, the hotchpot are B and C. The hotchpot is now $190,000 because *A's* share is no longer considered. *B* and *C* each are entitled to $95,000. *B* takes $85,000 from the actual probate estate, and C takes $95,000. In other words, if an advancee receives an advancement greater than the advancee's share in the hotchpot, no refund is required.[203]

What if *B* (who received a $10,000 advancement) predeceases the decedent and *B's* children take by representation? Under the UPC, their share would not be affected by the advancement "unless the decedent's contemporaneous writing provides otherwise,"[204] but some states take advancements into account in computing the shares of descendants of the advancee.[205]

The recipient of an advancement is not charged with interest for the period between the time of the advancement and the donor's death.[206] If the advancement is in the form of property, any subsequent appreciation or depreciation of the property is ignored; the UPC follows the generally accepted principle that the "property advanced is valued as of the time the heir came into possession or enjoyment of the property or as of the time of the death of the decedent, whichever first occurs."[207]

Satisfaction of Devises

The rules on advancements apply only to intestate succession. If a will leaves an estate "to my children equally," no child's share is reduced by any gifts received from the testator before the will was executed; the law assumes that the testator has taken into account any prior gifts.[208] Should a gift by a

---

[203] The calculations are complicated if the intestate was also survived by a spouse. For example, if the intestate spouse was entitled to intestate's entire estate, then the advancement is effectively without consequence because intestate's heirs would have no interest in the hotchpot to which the spouse alone would be entitled. Likewise, because of the no refund rule, she would not benefit from the hotchpot either. *See also* UPC § 2–109, comment.

[204] UPC § 2–109(c). *See also* Cal.Prob.Code § 6409(d); *Restatement (Third) of Property (Wills and Other Donative Transfers)* § 2.6, cmt. h (1999). On the other hand, a gift to a grandchild may be an advancement even though the recipient was not a prospective heir at the time of the gift, if the grandchild later turns out to be an heir.

[205] Md. Estates and Trusts Code § 3–106(c); Iowa Code § 633.226; La.Civ.Code § 1240.

[206] *Advancements III* p. 561; Ga.Code § 53–1–11.

[207] UPC § 2–109(b). *See also* Cal.Prob.Code § 6409(b); Md. Estates and Trusts Code § 3–106(b); *Restatement (Third) of Property (Wills and Other Donative Transfers)* § 2.6, cmt. d (1998). *But see* N.Y. EPTL § 2–1.5(d)(2) (value it would have for estate tax purposes).

[208] 3 *Amer.Law of Prop.* § 14.10, at 586; Bratt, *supra* note 185, at 343; *cf.* O'Brien v. O'Brien, 526 S.E.2d 1 (Va.2000) (provision in a will that prior loan be treated as advancement effective). If a will directs distribution to the testator's "heirs" some cases would take advancements into account in carrying out this direction. *Advancements II*, p. 241; *cf. Restatement of Property* § 316 (1940). In Louisiana, "collation" is required both in testate and intestate succession. La. Civ. Code § 1228.

testator *after* she executed her will be treated as a partial or total satisfaction of a devise?[209] The UPC provision on this issue parallels its rule on advancements; lifetime gifts are not taken into account unless the will (or some other writing) so provides.[210] The writing must be contemporaneous with the gift; a later writing by the donor is too late.[211]

Some states allow oral evidence of intent in all such cases[212] and even presume that any gift by a testator to a child was intended to satisfy an earlier bequest.[213] Similarities between the devise and the gift may show an intent to substitute one for the other, *e.g.*, a will left $5,000 to a home in memory of the testator's wife, and the testator later gave the same amount to the home for the same purpose.[214] There is authority that "a devise of land cannot be satisfied except by a conveyance of the same land," and so a devise of a share of the testator's real estate is not adeemed by a later lifetime gift of a specific parcel to the devisee.[215]

The UPC rules on valuation of gifts in satisfaction of devises are the same as for advancements, but the effect on the descendants of a recipient who predeceases the donor differs: a donor-testator is presumed to have intended that the share of the donee-devisee's descendants be reduced or eliminated in this situation.[216]

Planning

An attorney drafting a will should ask the testator about any prior gifts. The testator may wish to reduce the share of a child or spouse who has already received substantial gifts. The law assumes that testators have taken prior gifts into account, and drafters should make sure that this assumption is correct. If the share of a child is reduced because of a prior gift, a recital in the

[209] N.Y. EPTL § 2–1.5(a) uses the term "advancement" to include gifts to the "beneficiary under an existing will of the donor," but the more common term is "satisfaction" or "ademption by satisfaction" of the prior devise. A specific devise can be adeemed by extinction when the testator gives the devised property to the devisee or someone else. In this case the testator's intent can be effected without a writing. *See* Section 6.2.

[210] UPC § 2–609. *See also Restatement (Third) of Property (Wills and Other Donative Transfers)* § 5.4 (1998); Cal.Prob.Code § 21135; N.Y. EPTL § 2–1.5(b).

[211] In In re Estate of McFayden, 454 N.W.2d 676 (Neb.1990), a written statement by the donor that all gifts were to be treated as advances on a devise was held ineffective both as to prior and later gifts because it was not contemporaneous with them. A statement in the donor's will could have effectuated his intent. *See also* In Estate of Gill ex. rel. Grant v. Clemson University Foundation, 725 S.E.2d 516 (SC Ct. App. 2012)(the written designation of the Foundation as the beneficiary of an IRA was not a contemporaneous writing such that it reduced a testamentary bequest of a like amount made under the decedent's will).

[212] Ky. Rev. Stat. § 394.370.

[213] 3 *Amer.Law of Prop.* § 14.11; Carmichael v. Lathrop, 66 N.W. 350 (Mich.1896); *cf.* Chaffin, *The Time Gap in Wills*, 6 Ga.L.Rev. 649, 668 (1972).

[214] In re Kreitman's Estate, 386 N.E.2d 650 (Ill.App.1979). *See also* Trustees of Baker Univ. v. Trustees of End. Ass'n of Kansas State College of Pittsburg, 564 P.2d 472 (Kan.1977). But see, Grant v. Clemson Univ. Foundation, 725 S.E. 2d 516 (Ct. App. 2012) ($100,000 devise in will not satisfied by designation of legatee as beneficiary of a $100,000 IRA account).

[215] Maestas v. Martinez, 752 P.2d 1107 (N.M.App.1988).

[216] UPC § 2–609. The Comment to this section notes the discrepancy but does not explain it. *Restatement (Third) of Property (Wills and Other Donative Transfers)* § 2.6, cmt. h (1998) purports to explain the rule in intestacy by saying "the heir must have received the advanced property in order to be charged" but in fact the heir is not charged whether or not he inherited the advanced property from the original recipient.

will can explain what might otherwise seem to be an unfair disposition of the estate. A will which seems "unfair" because children are treated unequally is more likely to be upset if contested for incapacity or undue influence.[217]

Should the will say anything about later gifts? A provision which reduces devises if a later gift is made to the devisee would be effective under the UPC, but this would require the executor of the will to determine if the testator had made such gifts and whether the clause was meant to apply to them, *e.g.*, should Christmas presents be counted?[218] It is better to keep a will current by periodic revision so as to reflect the testator's current wishes as to prior gifts or other changes in the testator's circumstances. These will be discussed later.[219]

§ 2.7 Homicide

A person who is otherwise eligible to inherit or take by will or will substitute may be barred because the person killed the decedent.

History

If one spouse murders the other can the surviving spouse inherit? There were no reported decisions on this question before the end of the nineteenth century. The absence of cases may be explained by the fact that, historically, convicted felons forfeited their property, but most states abolished forfeiture for crime long before courts raised the question whether a murderer could inherit. Apparently during this interval American courts allowed murderers to inherit without questioning the result. When the argument that a murderer should not be allowed to inherit began to appear, many courts rejected it, saying that any change in the intestacy statute that would bar inheritance must come from legislation.[220]

In 1897, Dean Ames suggested that courts should impose a constructive trust on the murderer.[221] The Restatement of Restitution and some courts adopted this suggestion[222] because it "avoids the dubious practice of reading implied exceptions into a statute."[223] This reasoning seems questionable. How can a court claim to be applying a statute when it awards property to someone other than the one to whom the statute gives it? Many courts reject the constructive trust approach as "somewhat fictitious."[224]

---

[217] *See* Sections 5.1 and 5.3.

[218] The law relating to advancements has been used to interpret such clauses. *Advancements I*, pp. 679–81.

[219] *See* Sections 8.5 (birth of children), 8.6 (marriage), 4.4 (divorce), 6.5 (death of legatee).

[220] McGovern, *Homicide and Succession to Property*, 68 Mich.L.Rev. 65 (1969).

[221] Ames, *Can a Murderer Acquire Title by His Crime and Keep It?*, 36 Am.Law Reg. (n.s.) 225, 228–29 (1897). [This essay was republished in J. Ames, *Lectures on Legal History* 310 (1913).]

[222] *Restatement of Restitution* § 187 (1937); Angleton v. Estate of Angleton, 671 N.E.2d 921 (Ind.App.1996) (based on statute); Parks v. Dumas, 321 S.W.2d 653 (Tex.Civ.App.1959); Sikora v. Sikora, 499 P.2d 808 (Mont.1972).

[223] G. Bogert, *Trusts* § 478, at 78 (2d ed. 1960). *See also Restatement of Restitution* § 187, comment a at 764 (1937).

[224] In re Duncan's Estates, 246 P.2d 445 (Wash.1952). *See also* Wall v. Pfanschmidt, 106 N.E. 785 (Ill.1914); Fellows, *The Slayer Rule: Not Solely a Matter of Equity*, 71 Iowa L.Rev. 489, 550–51 (1986); McGovern, *supra* note 220, at 68–9; In re Estate of Thomann, 649 N.W.2d 1, 8 (Iowa

In states that still maintain separate courts of law and equity, the constructive trust rationale may require the parties to resort to the court of equity, which traditionally had exclusive jurisdiction over trusts.[225] This requirement may be more theoretical than real as evidenced by the fact that many probate courts have assumed the power not to distribute property to the murderer.[226]

Statutes

Most states now have statutes barring a murderer from inheriting from the victim. Some of these statutes are incomplete. The cases interpreting such incomplete statutes are hard to reconcile. One court allowed a person convicted of manslaughter to inherit because the governing statute only covered "murder."[227] But another court operating under a similar statute barred a person convicted of manslaughter on the theory that the statute did not "completely supplant the common law principle . . . that one should not be allowed to profit by his own wrong."[228] Sometimes a statute which does not literally apply is construed to apply because it evinces "a legislative policy to deny the convicted murderer of the fruits of his crime."[229]

The UPC provision on this subject covers a variety of cases and adds a catchall: "A wrongful acquisition of property or interest by a killer not covered by this section must be treated in accordance with the principle that a killer cannot profit from the killer's wrong."[230] This principle was applied in a case where an individual killed his grandmother. The grandmother's heir was her daughter, the parent of the slayer. A few months after the grandmother was killed, the daughter died, and her son (the slayer) stood to take his mother's estate which included property the daughter inherited from the grandmother's estate. In holding that the slayer could not inherit the portion of his mother's estate the mother inherited from the grandmother, the court stated that "the fact that there is an intervening estate should not . . . thwart the intent of the

---

2002) (court will not "substitute its judgment for that of the legislature by imposing a constructive trust on the murderer's proportional share").

[225] In re Estate of Mahoney, 220 A.2d 475 (Vt.1966) (probate court must follow statute literally; constructive trust only enforceable in equity).

[226] Mitchem v. First Interstate Bank, 802 P.2d 1141 (Colo.App.1990) (suit to impose constructive trust dismissed because probate court has power to handle the issue); Maine Savings Bank v. Bridges, 431 A.2d 633, 637 (Me.1981). In Angleton v. Estate of Angleton, 671 N.E.2d 921 (Ind.App.1996), the probate court itself imposed a constructive trust, and rejected the argument that the proceeds must first be distributed to the slayer before the trust is imposed.

[227] Nable v. Godfrey's Estate, 403 So.2d 1038 (Fla.App.1981). *See also* Estate of Kramme, 573 P.2d 1369 (Cal.1978).

[228] Quick v. United Benefit Life Ins. Co., 213 S.E.2d 563 (N.C.1975). *See also* Harper v. Prudential Ins. Co., 662 P.2d 1264 (Kan.1983); Wright v. Wright, 449 S.W.2d 952 (Ark.1970).

[229] Bailey v. Retirement Board of Policemen's Annuity and Ben. Fund, 366 N.E.2d 966, 969 (Ill.App.1977). *See also* Sundin v. Klein, 269 S.E.2d 787 (Va.1980); New Orleans Elec. Pension Fund v. DeRocha, 779 F.Supp. 845, 850 (E.D.La.1991) (statute dealing with insurance is a "guidepost" to treatment of pensions).

[230] UPC § 2–803(f). The pre-1990 version of this provision simply referred to "the principles of this section" without identifying them. *See* UPC § 2–803(d) (pre-1990). *See also* Cal.Prob.Code § 252. A similar provision appeared in a statute proposed in 1936 which a few states adopted. Wade, *Acquisition of Property by Willfully Killing Another—A Statutory Solution*, 49 Harv.L.Rev. 715, 750–51 (1936). For a summary description of the various statutes as of 2003 *see Restatement (Third) of Property (Wills and Other Donative Transfers)* § 8.4, Reporter's Note (2003).

legislature that the murderer not profit by his wrong."[231] Courts have extended statutes to accessories who did not actually kill the decedent.[232] On the other hand, some courts have refused to apply to wrongful death claims the principle that a slayer cannot profit for a wrong.[233]

The drafters of the UPC feared that the preemption provisions of ERISA which "supersede any and all state laws insofar as they . . . relate to any employee benefit plan"[234] might preclude application of the Code to pension plans,[235] but these fears, at least as to homicide, have so far proved groundless.[236] And, in *Egelhoff v. Egelhoff*,[237] in which the Court held that ERISA preempted a state law barring a divorced spouse from claiming a nonprobate asset of the deceased spouse naming her as a beneficiary, the court suggested that the preemption rule might not apply to a state slayer statute given that the slayer statute bar merely reflects a "well established [rule] in the law and has a long historical pedigree predating ERISA."[238]

Degree of Crime

Georgia and Virginia at one time barred succession only by those who killed in order to obtain the victim's property[239] but later amended their statutes to eliminate any reference to motive.[240] Virtually all courts today hold that a slayer's motives are immaterial.[241]

Some courts have allowed a slayer to take if the killing did not amount to murder,[242] but Louisiana bars an insurance beneficiary from collecting the proceeds if he is "criminally responsible" for the death of the insured; this

---

[231] In re Estate of Vallerius, 629 N.E.2d 1185, 1189 (Ill.App.1994). *See also Restatement (Second) of Property (Donative Transfers)* § 34.8, illus. 2 (1992) (son who kills sibling cannot thereby increase his share of his mother's estate, a principle reaffirmed by *Restatement (Third) of Property (Wills and Other Donative Transfers)* § 8.4, cmt. m (2003)).

[232] In re Estate of Walker, 847 P.2d 162 (Colo.App.1992); Matter of Estate of Gibbs, 490 N.W.2d 504 (S.D.1992); UPC § 2–803, comment (criminal accountability "as an accomplice or co-conspirator" is encompassed).

[233] Aranda v. Camacho, 931 P.2d 757 (N.M.App.1997) (the murderer's bar in the probate code does not apply to wrongful death actions); Marks v. Lyerla, 2 Cal.Rptr.2d 63 (App.1991). After the latter case Cal.Prob.Code § 258 was enacted to change the result.

[234] 29 U.S.C. § 1144(a).

[235] UPC § 2–803, comment. *See also* UPC § 2–804, comment.

[236] Mendez-Bellido v. Board of Trustees, 709 F.Supp. 329 (E.D.N.Y.1989) (spouse barred by killing her husband from taking under pension plan); New Orleans Elec. Pension Fund v. DeRocha, 779 F.Supp. 845 (E.D.La.1991) (same); Metropolitan Life Ins. Co. v. White, 972 F.2d 122 (5th Cir.1992) (federal employees insurance). *See also* Atwater v. Nortel Networks, Inc., 388 F. Supp.2d 610 (M.D.N.C. 2005) (plan administrator had fiduciary duty to ascertain whether murderer had right to victim's pension benefits).

[237] 532 U.S. 141 (2001).

[238] *Id.* at 1330. *See also* Nale v. Ford Motor Co. 703 F.Supp.2d 714, 721–723 (E.D. Mich. 2010) (the language in *Egelhoff* suggests that ERISA would not preempt a state slayer statute.).

[239] *See* Life & Cas. Ins. Co. v. Webb, 145 S.E.2d 63 (Ga.App.1965); Ward v. Ward, 6 S.E.2d 664 (Va.1940).

[240] Ga.Code §§ 33–25–13 (insurance), 53–1–5; Va.Code § 64.2–2501.

[241] Francis v. Marshall, 841 S.W.2d 51 (Tex.App.1992). *See also* Sherman, *Mercy Killing and the Right to Inherit*, 61 U.Cinn.L.Rev. 803 (1993) (mercy slayer should be allowed to inherit); *Restatement (Third) of Property (Wills and Other Donative Transfers)* § 8.4, cmt. n (2003) (raising the question but giving no answer).

[242] Nable v. Godfrey's Estate, 403 So.2d 1038 (Fla.App.1981); Aranda v. Camacho, 931 P.2d 757 (N.M.App.1997).

includes even an unintentional killing.[243] The UPC takes an intermediate position, barring anyone who "feloniously and intentionally" kills the decedent,[244] a formula which encompasses voluntary manslaughter as well as murder, but not involuntary manslaughter. Most modern cases also disqualify a slayer for voluntary manslaughter[245] but not for unintentional homicide even though criminal.[246] Arguably, even a negligent slayer should not be allowed to profit from a wrong, but the existence of profit from the crime is often questionable, because the slayer might have survived and inherited from the decedent anyway.

A slayer who is guilty of no criminal offense at all, *e.g.*, one who kills in self-defense or by accident, is not disqualified.[247] A slayer who was insane is not disqualified in most states[248] but not all[249] and juvenile slayers may be precluded from inheriting even if their act was not subject to the ordinary criminal law.[250]

Proof of Crime

The problem of proof typically arises in three different situations. First, often the alleged slayer has not been tried, either because the slayer committed suicide after the crime or the criminal case is still pending when the decedent's estate is to be distributed.[251] Courts operating under a statute which bars one "convicted" of murder have held that the murder can be established only by a

---

243 In re Hamilton, 446 So.2d 463 (La.App.1984).

244 UPC § 2–803(b).

245 Cook v. Nale, 290 Mich. App. 704 (Mich. Ct. App. 2010). *See also* Davis v. Secretary of Health and Human Services, 867 F.2d 336 (6th Cir.1989) (Social security denied to widow convicted of manslaughter); Sikora v. Sikora, 499 P.2d 808 (Mont.1972). *cf.* In re Estate of Malbrough, 768 N.E.2d 120 (Ill.App.2002) (person who caused death by providing "grossly inadequate care" may be disqualified).

246 Miller v. Kramarczyk, 714 N.E.2d 613 (Ill.App.1999) (negligent slayer not disqualified); Matter of Safran's Estate, 306 N.W.2d 27 (Wis.1981); Hood v. Vandevender, 661 So.2d 198 (Miss.1995).

247 State Farm Life Ins. Co. v. Smith, 363 N.E.2d 785 (Ill.1977); Powell v. Powell, 604 S.W.2d 491 (Tex.Civ.App.1980); Huff v. Union Fidelity Life Ins. Co., 470 N.E.2d 236 (Ohio App.1984) (killing in defense of another).

248 Estate of Kissinger v. Hoge, 173 P.3d 956 (Wash. App. Div. 2007); Estate of Artz v. Artz, 487 A.2d 1294 (N.J.Super.App.Div.1985); Ford v. Ford, 512 A.2d 389 (Md.1986); Turner v. Estate of Turner, 454 N.E.2d 1247 (Ind.App.1983). *Contra* Ind.Code § 29–1–2–12.1. *See also* Osman v. Osman, 737 S.E.2d 876 (Va. 2013)(slayer barred from taking even though found not guilty by reason of insanity). Contra, In re Estate of Armstrong, 170 So.3d 510 (Miss. 2015).

249 Osman v. Osman, 285 Va. 384, 393 (VA 2013)(applying slayer statute to intentionally killings even by the criminally insane); Dougherty v. Cole, 401 Ill. App. 3d 341 (Ill. App. Ct. Dist 2010)(finding that Illinois statute applies to the criminally insane.) *Contra*, Armstrong v. Armstrong, 170 So.3d 510 (Miss. 2015).

250 Huff v. Union Fidelity Life Ins. Co., 470 N.E.2d 236 (Ohio App.1984); Matter of Josephsons' Estates, 297 N.W.2d 444 (N.D.1980); 20 Code Fed.Reg. § 404.305.

251 If an heir is convicted of killing the decedent and appeals, should distribution of the estate be postponed while the appeal is pending? Courts have disagreed on this question. *Compare* In re Estate of Kiejliches, 740 N.Y.S.2d 85 (App.Div.2002) (wife accused of murdering husband enjoined from withdrawing money from joint account and disposing of joint realty) *with* Prudential Ins. Co. v. Tull, 524 F.Supp. 166 (E.D.Va.1981); Angleton v. Estate of Angleton, 671 N.E.2d 921 (Ind.App.1996) (no abuse of discretion to order immediate distribution). As to the recovery of property which has been wrongly distributed, *see* Section 14.3.

criminal conviction,[252] but courts operating under common-law principles conclude, usually without even discussing the point, that the absence of a criminal conviction does not prevent them from determining guilt.[253]

Second, sometimes the accused has been acquitted (or convicted of an offense not serious enough to bar succession). Most courts in this situation admit evidence that the accused was in fact guilty.[254] This can be justified because proof beyond a reasonable doubt is not necessary to establish the existence of a crime in a civil proceeding, and an acquittal may merely mean failure to meet the higher standard of proof required in criminal proceedings. Under the UPC, "in the absence of a conviction, the court . . . must determine whether, under the preponderance of evidence standard, the individual would be found criminally accountable."[255]

Third, if the slayer has been convicted, this proof of guilt beyond a reasonable doubt should *a fortiori* satisfy the preponderance-of-the-evidence test in the civil proceeding. Thus, the UPC makes a conviction conclusive in determining the right to succession,[256] and some courts have so held even without statutory authority,[257] but some statutes simply make the conviction admissible evidence.[258] However, a plea of guilty is not the same as a conviction; thus, the slayer is free to litigate the question of intent in a later civil action regarding the right to inherit.[259]

Avoiding Forfeiture

The law no longer imposes forfeiture of property for crime; indeed, many state constitutions expressly prohibit it.[260] Barring a murderer from inheriting

---

[252] Holliday v. McMullen, 756 P.2d 1179 (Nev.1988); Button by Curio v. Elmhurst Nat. Bank, 522 N.E.2d 1368 (Ill.App.1988); Bird v. Plunkett, 95 A.2d 71 (Conn.1953).

[253] *Restatement of Restitution* § 187, comment f (1937); Bernstein v. Rosenthal, 671 P.2d 979 (Colo.App.1983).

[254] Matter of Congdon's Estate, 309 N.W.2d 261 (Minn.1981); Matter of Eliasen's Estate, 668 P.2d 110 (Idaho 1983); California-Western States Life Ins. Co. v. Sanford, 515 F.Supp. 524 (E.D.La.1981). *But see* Turner v. Estate of Turner, 454 N.E.2d 1247 (Ind.App.1983).

[255] UPC § 2–803(g). *See also* Cal.Prob.Code § 254; Matter of Estates of Young, 831 P.2d 1014 (Okl.App.1992) (acquittal not conclusive because of higher standard of proof in criminal cases); Matter of Estate of Gibbs, 490 N.W.2d 504 (S.D.1992). In Federal Kemper Life Assur. v. Eichwedel, 639 N.E.2d 246 (Ill.App.1994), a confession which was inadmissible in criminal proceedings was used to bar the slayer from collecting insurance.

[256] UPC § 2–803(g). *See also* Cal.Prob.Code § 254(b); Metropolitan Life Ins. Co. v. White, 972 F.2d 122 (5th Cir.1992) (federal employees' insurance). Under the UPC, the conviction is conclusive only "after all right of appeal has been exhausted." But some courts treat a conviction as conclusive even if an appeal is pending. Angleton v. Estate of Angleton, 671 N.E.2d 921 (Ind.App.1996); Matter of Dorsey, 613 N.Y.S.2d 335 (Surr.1994).

[257] Travelers Ins. Co. v. Thompson, 163 N.W.2d 289 (Minn.1968); In re Laspy's Estate, 409 S.W.2d 725 (Mo.App.1966); In re Glenn's Estate, 299 A.2d 203 (Pa.1973).

[258] 20 Pa.Stat. § 8814; Rev.Code Wash. § 11.84.130.

[259] In re Estates of Swanson, 187 P.3d 631 (Mont. 2008).

[260] *E.g.* Ill. Const. art. 1, § 11; *cf.* United States Constitution, art. 3, § 3 ("no Attainder of Treason shall work . . . Forfeiture except during the Life of the Person attainted"); In re Estates of Covert, 761 N.E.2d 571, 575 (N.Y.2001) (statute bars forfeiture of property upon conviction of a crime).

is distinguishable, however, because it does "not deprive the murderer of any property rights, but [only] prevent(s) his acquisition of *additional* rights."[261]

The distinction between depriving someone of what is already owned and barring the "acquisition of additional rights" gets fuzzy in some instances. Suppose *A* and *B* own land in joint tenancy,[262] and *A* murders *B*. Most authorities would allow *A* to keep his share of income from the property because he did not acquire that interest by his crime.[263] When *A* dies, some courts would award all the land to *B*'s estate on the theory that, but for the murder, *B* might have taken as surviving joint tenant.[264] Most courts, however, divide the property equally between the estates of *A* and *B*[265] on the theory that no one knows who would have survived but for the killing. The UPC agrees; it terminates the right of survivorship, but the slayer's half interest is preserved.[266] Courts have reached the same result as to community property; the slayer spouse retains his or her half interest.[267]

Joint bank accounts are treated differently from land held in joint tenancy. Ownership of joint bank accounts under the UPC (and most other states) is proportional to contributions. Thus, if *A* contributed all the money in a joint bank account, the account is *A*'s during *A*'s lifetime, even if *B* is also designated as a party.[268] *A* could therefore keep the account if he killed *B*. On the other hand, if *B* killed *A*, the whole account would be awarded to *A*'s estate.[269] As to land, on the other hand, the source of the funds used to acquire it is irrelevant, because "if one spouse provides all the funds for property conveyed to a married couple jointly, it will be presumed that the provider makes a gift to the other spouse of an undivided one-half interest in the

---

[261] Sundin v. Klein, 269 S.E.2d 787, 789 (Va.1980) (emphasis added). *See also* In re Estate of Fiore, 476 N.E.2d 1093, 1097 (Ohio App.1984) (statute is constitutional because it "only prevented the murderer from inheriting property, rather than divesting him of such property").

[262] A form of ownership in which the property passes at the death of one tenant to the survivor. *See* Section 3.8.

[263] *Restatement of Restitution* § 188, cmt. b (1937); In re Hawkins' Estate, 213 N.Y.S.2d 188 (Surr.1961); *cf.* Homanich v. Miller, 221 S.E.2d 739 (N.C.App.1976). *But see* First Kentucky Trust Co. v. United States, 737 F.2d 557 (6th Cir.1984) (slayer forfeits all interest in joint tenancy).

[264] *Restatement of Restitution* § 188, comment b (1937); Hargrove v. Taylor, 389 P.2d 36 (Or.1964); *cf.* Glass v. Adkins, 436 So.2d 844 (Ala.1983).

[265] Gallimore v. Washington, 666 A.2d 1200 (D.C.App.1995); Estate of Grund v. Grund, 648 N.E.2d 1182 (Ind.App.1995); Hicks v. Boshears, 846 S.W.2d 812 (Tenn.1993); In re Estates of Covert, 761 N.E.2d 571, 576 (N.Y.2001).

[266] UPC § 2–803(c)(2). *See also* Cal.Prob.Code § 251.

[267] Armstrong v. Bray, 826 P.2d 706 (Wash.App.1992); Matter of Estates of Spear, 845 P.2d 491 (Ariz.App.1992).

[268] UPC § 6–211(b). If the parties are married, their contributions are presumed to have been equal. *See also* Cal.Prob.Code §§ 5301(a), 5305 (contributions presumed to be community property).

[269] UPC § 2–803, comment: "any portion of the decedent's contribution to the co-ownership registration running in favor of the killer would be treated as a revocable and revoked disposition." *See also* Estate of Castiglioni, 47 Cal.Rptr.2d 288 (App.1995) (error to award funds in joint account traceable to H's separate property to W who killed him). In In re Estate of Fiore, 476 N.E.2d 1093 (Ohio App.1984), where both parties had contributed but the proportions were unclear, the whole account was awarded to the victim's estate.

property."[270] The donee who murdered the donor would not forfeit the property previously given.

Suppose a trust was created to pay the income to *A* for life, remainder to *B*, and *B* kills *A*. Few statutes cover this case. *B*'s enrichment from accelerating the remainder could be avoided by postponing *B*'s enjoyment for the duration of *A*'s normal life expectancy.[271] If *B*'s remainder was indefeasibly vested, *B* ought not to forfeit it.[272] If it was contingent on surviving *A*, *B* might be deemed to have predeceased on the theory that doubts should be resolved against the slayer;[273] alternatively, the court could wait to see if *B* outlives *A*'s normal life expectancy.[274]

The beneficiary of an insurance policy on *A*'s life who then kills *A* will not collect the proceeds. But if the premiums were paid with community property, some courts would give the slayer half of the proceeds,[275] others would allow only half of the *cash surrender value* of the policy.[276]

In some situations, the insurance company is not bound to pay anyone; for example, if the beneficiary took out the policy with the intent to kill the insured, the policy is voidable for fraud.[277] Even if the intent to kill arose after the policy was taken out, the insurer may escape liability if the slayer owned the policy, as distinguished from being merely a beneficiary.[278]

Alternate Takers

If a slayer is disqualified, who takes the share that would have been the slayer's? In most situations, the victim's property is distributed as if the slayer predeceased the victim.[279] This principle may allow the children of the slayer

---

[270] Sundin v. Klein, 269 S.E.2d 787, 789 (Va.1980). The distinction between land in joint tenancy and joint accounts also arises in connection with attempts to revoke. *See* Section 4.5.

[271] *Restatement of Restitution* § 188, comment c (1937); *cf.* In re Moses' Estate, 300 N.E.2d 473 (Ill.App.1973).

[272] *Restatement of Restitution* § 188, comment c (1936); *cf.* Moore v. Moore, 201 S.E.2d 133 (Ga.1973).

[273] *Restatement of Restitution* § 188, comment c (1937); Fellows, *supra* note 224, at 511.

[274] In re Moses' Estate, 300 N.E.2d 473 (Ill.App.1973). The question whether remainders are contingent on survival is discussed in Section 11.1.

[275] New York Life Ins. Co. v. Cawthorne, 121 Cal.Rptr. 808 (App.1975).

[276] In re Hart's Estate, 185 Cal.Rptr. 544 (App.1982); Aetna Life Ins. Co. v. Primofiore, 145 Cal.Rptr. 922 (App.1978). The present California statute, Cal.Prob.Code § 252, says that the slayer "is not entitled to any benefit under the . . . policy." It is not clear exactly what effect this has. As to community property, see Section 8.8.

[277] Federal Kemper Life Assur. v. Eichwedel, 639 N.E.2d 246 (Ill.App.1994); Flood v. Fidelity & Guar. Life Ins. Co., 394 So.2d 1311 (La.App.1981).

[278] Caliman v. American General Fire & Cas. Co., 641 N.E.2d 261 (Ohio App.1994). The distinction between owning a policy and being a designated beneficiary is also relevant with respect to the right to change beneficiaries. *See* Section 4.5.

[279] *Restatement (Third) of Property (Wills and Other Donative Transfers)* § 8.4, cmts. j & k (2003). UPC § 2–803 uses the expression "as if the killer disclaimed," but this amounts to the same thing, because under § 2–1106(b)(3)(A) property disclaimed normally devolves as if the disclaimant "did not exist.". This provision does not control the disposition of the slayer's own property; the victim's estate takes from the slayer's when both are deceased only if the victim actually survived. For example, if *A* shoots *B* and then shoots himself, but *B* dies 10 minutes after *A*, *A* is deemed to predecease *B* and cannot inherit from *B* but *B* can inherit from *A*'s estate because *B* actually survived *A*. Mothershed v. Schrimsher, 412 S.E.2d 123 (N.C.App.1992); In re Estate of Miller, 840 So.2d 703 (Miss.2003).

to take by representation in case of intestacy or under an antilapse statute in case of a will.[280] Wills and insurance policies often designate alternate beneficiaries if a devisee or primary beneficiary fails to survive. Usually the fiction that the slayer died before the victim is also applied in this situation, and the alternate beneficiary takes.[281] Some courts, however, refuse to allow this when it seems to advantage the slayer. For example, when a husband who was convicted of killing his wife was named beneficiary of his wife's estate and his children from a prior marriage were named the contingent beneficiaries, the children were barred from inheriting because they admitted they planned to use the estate assets to pay for their father's criminal defense.[282] And when a will left property to the testator's wife, with an alternative gift to her children from a prior marriage if she died first, a court refused to allow the children to take when the wife killed the testator[283] even though they had nothing to do with the crime. In another case, where the policy named the slayer's sister as alternate beneficiary, the court remanded the case for a trial as to the decedent's intent, saying that if the insured "had an independent relationship of some kind" with the slayer's sister, he might have wanted her to take despite the crime. A concurring opinion doubted that such a search for the "hypothetical" intent of the decedent would prove fruitful.[284] More recently, an Alabama court held that where the husband killed his wife and then committed suicide, the slayer statute applied only to the wife's estate. As a result, her intestate estate passed as if he predeceased her; his intestate estate passed to his heirs determined on the basis that his wife predeceased him.[285]

Protection of Third Parties

Sometimes a crime is discovered after a person has acted in reliance on the normal devolution of property, *e.g.*, by buying property from the slayer. The UPC does not apply its slayer-disqualification rules to anyone who "purchases property for value and without notice."[286] Another provision protects "payors" (such as insurance companies) from liability for payments made before they

---

[280] Matter of Estate of Van Der Veen, 935 P.2d 1042 (Kan.1997); Estate of Benson, 548 So.2d 775 (Fla.App.1989); Misenheimer v. Misenheimer, 325 S.E.2d 195 (N.C.1985); *cf.* Heinzman v. Mason, 694 N.E.2d 1164 (Ind.App.1998) (children of slayer by another marriage do not take because they were not heirs of the victim-stepmother). Cal.Prob.Code § 250(b)(1) makes the antilapse statute inapplicable in this situation. *See* McGovern, *supra* note 220, at 76–77. As to antilapse statutes, see Section 6.5; as to representation in intestacy, see Section 2.2.

[281] Bradley v. Bradley, 443 S.E.2d 863 (Ga.App.1994); Francis v. Marshall, 841 S.W.2d 51 (Tex.App.1992); Hulett v. First Nat. Bank and Trust Co., 956 P.2d 879 (Okl.1998); In re Estates of Covert, 761 N.E.2d 571, 576 (N.Y.2001). If no alternate beneficiary is designated, insurance proceeds may go to the insured's probate estate. Estate of Chiesi v. First Citizens Bank, 613 N.E.2d 14 (Ind.1993).

[282] Swain v. Estate of Tyre, 57 A.3d 283 (RI 2012).

[283] In re Estate of Mueller, 655 N.E.2d 1040 (Ill.App.1995). *See also* Bennett v. Allstate Ins. Co., 722 A.2d 115 (N.J.Super.App.Div.1998) (proceeds awarded to the common children of slayer and victim rather than to slayer's mother, the alternate beneficiary).

[284] State Farm Life Ins. Co. v. Pearce, 286 Cal.Rptr. 267 (App.1991). Another court suggested that "to visit the consequences of [the slayer's] crime on his brother and sister [the alternate beneficiaries] conjures up the ghosts of corruption of the blood which is prohibited by" the state constitution. Diep v. Rivas, 745 A.2d 1098, 1103 (Md.2000).

[285] Willingham v. Matthews, 163 So.3d 1016 (Ala. 2014).

[286] UPC § 2–803(i)(1). *See also* Cal.Prob.Code § 255; McGovern, *supra* note 220, at 69.

receive "written notice of a claimed forfeiture."[287] Despite the statutory reference to written notice, one court held that this provision did not protect an insurer who was negligent in paying proceeds to a slayer. "If an insurer is on notice of facts suggesting that the primary beneficiary is not entitled to . . . policy proceeds, the insurer has a duty to make a reasonable inquiry and to withhold payment until its suspicion is dispelled."[288]

Other Cases of Misconduct

Courts have refused to make other exceptions to the intestacy statutes to bar persons guilty of misconduct vis à vis the decedent from inheriting. For example, a mother was allowed to inherit from her 15-year-old child although for most of his life she had "failed to provide any financial support to, maintain any interest in, or display any love and affection for" him. The court noted that statutes providing procedures for the termination of parental rights had not been pursued. "If the law is to be changed to make provision for the situation at hand, it is for the legislature to make the change, not the courts."[289]

The UPC, however, bars a parent from inheriting from and through[290] a child if (1) the parent's parental rights were terminated and not later judicially reestablished or (2) if the child died under the age of 18 and there is clear and convincing evidence that "immediately before the child's death the parental rights . . . could have been terminated . . . on the basis of nonsupport, abandonment, abuse, neglect, or other actions or inactions of the parent toward the child."[291] The Third Restatement of Property states a similar principle barring a parent from inheriting from or through a child if the parent refused to acknowledge the child, abandoned the child, or had parental rights terminated.[292] Neither the UPC nor the Restatement applies this so-called "bad parent" rule in reverse by barring, for example, children who abuse their parents from inheriting from the parent.[293]

The approach of the UPC with its "from and through" concept is to bar only inheritance by the parent. Thus, the child and those claiming through the child can claim from the estate of the parent even if that parent failed to support the child.[294]

The UPC states that "the principles of law and equity supplement its provisions."[295] This provision was invoked to bar devisees from receiving a

---

[287] UPC § 2–803(h)(1). *See also* Cal.Prob.Code § 256. As to whether a negligent buyer can be a bona fide purchaser, see Section 14.9.

[288] Lunsford v. Western States Life Ins., 908 P.2d 79, 85 (Colo.1995).

[289] Hotarek v. Benson, 557 A.2d 1259, 1263 (Conn.1989).

[290] The concept of "from and through" is important to an understanding of intestacy law. Inheritance "from" contemplates taking directly from the decedent. For example, if a parent dies survived only by a child, the child inherits from the parent. If, on the other hand, the child's grandparent has died and the child's parent is predeceased, the child inherits from the grandparent through the deceased parent.

[291] UPC § 2–114(a).

[292] *Restatement (Third) of Property (Wills and Other Donative Transfers)* § 2.5(5) (1999).

[293] *Compare* Cal.Prob.Code § 259 (persons guilty of "physical abuse, neglect, or financial abuse" of elderly decedent forfeit right to inherit).

[294] *See* UPC § 2–119(c).

[295] UPC § 1–103.

share of the punitive damages which the estate had recovered from them for converting property of the testator. The court wished to "uphold the public policy of this state that perpetrators of fraud will be deprived of the fruit of their wrongdoing."[296]

The effect of misconduct by one spouse toward the other will be treated in Section 2.12.

§ 2.8 Disclaimers

Disclaimers are typically motivated by two reasons: a desire to obtain a tax advantage while keeping the disclaimed property in the family or a desire to deny one's creditors the opportunity to satisfy their claims from the disclaimed property. Empirically the first probably explains most disclaimers.

Tax Consequences

Suppose that a person dies survived by a spouse and a child who would share the property by intestate succession or by will. The spouse may have ample resources and may prefer that the property pass to the child who has greater need and is in a lower income tax bracket. (The progressive nature of our tax laws often fosters such altruism among family members.) The spouse could give estate property to the child, but this might require payment of a gift tax.[297] The spouse can avoid a gift tax by making a "qualified disclaimer" under the Internal Revenue Code.[298] Alternatively, a disclaimer *by the child* may have advantageous tax consequences for the estate if it increases the size of the allowable marital deduction, because property passing to a spouse qualifies for the marital deduction.[299]

These results occur because in theory a disclaimer "relates back" to the time of the decedent's death, so the share never passes to the disclaimant but rather goes directly to the person who takes because of the disclaimer. Some have attacked this result because the disclaimant could have chosen to accept the share, and normally someone who fails to exercise a power to take property is treated as making a transfer.[300] But Professor Halbach has defended the special tax treatment of disclaimers because they allow "post-mortem estate planning," *e.g.*, correcting a failure to make proper use of the marital deduction. Without recognition of qualified disclaimers there would be "an unwarranted and unrealistic demand for wills to be perfected and updated before a testator's death."[301] Taxpayers who could afford to keep their wills up to date would pay less taxes than those who could not.

---

296 Matter of Estate of O'Keefe, 583 N.W.2d 138, 141 (S.D.1998).

297 For an overview of the gift tax, *see* Section 15.3.

298 Internal Revenue Code § 2518.

299 DePaoli v. C.I.R., 62 F.3d 1259 (10th Cir.1995). As to the marital deduction, see Section 15.3. The estate tax charitable deduction can also under some circumstances be augmented by a disclaimer. Treas.Reg. § 20.2055–2(c).

300 Martin, *Perspectives on Federal Disclaimer Legislation,* 46 U.Chi.L.Rev. 316, 357 (1979). As to the tax consequences of unexercised powers of appointment, see Section 11.5.

301 Halbach, *Curing Deficiencies in Tax and Property Law,* 65 Minn.L.Rev. 89, 120 (1980). For a recent discussion of ways to use disclaimers in estate planning, see J. Price & S. Donaldson, *Contemporary Estate Planning* § 13.26 (2019).

Before 1977, a disclaimer resulted in a taxable gift unless it was "effective under the local law,"[302] and state disclaimer laws varied considerably.[303] Since then, many states have liberalized their rules on disclaimers to maximize the potential for tax savings by their citizens. The Uniform Disclaimer of Property Interests Act along these lines is incorporated into the UPC.[304] However, because most disclaimers are driven by federal tax considerations, a comment to the UPC warns lawyers that "the requirements for a tax qualified disclaimer are set by a different law."[305] The Uniform Act has a catch-all provision designed to assure that all tax-effective disclaimers are also valid for state law purposes.[306]

Congress attempted to avoid unequal treatment of citizens of different states in 1976 by enacting Section 2518 of the Internal Revenue Code which sets forth requirements for a "qualified disclaimer." Even a disclaimer that is not recognized under state law may escape gift tax if it meets the requirements of the Internal Revenue Code.[307] However, there still are instances where a disclaimer which fails to satisfy state law requirements is ineffective for federal tax purposes.[308]

Lawyers who fail to advise clients about the possible tax advantages of disclaimers are subject to suit for malpractice.[309]

Creditors' Rights

Sometimes a person wishes to disclaim inherited property so that the inherited property will not be available to pay the claims of the disclaimant's creditors. Some states treat disclaimers motivated by a desire to avoid creditors' claims as a fraudulent conveyance.[310] Some states bar disclaimers by a person who is insolvent.[311] Most states, however, adopt the "relation-back" idea in this context also, so a disclaimed share passes directly to the new takers free from the claims of the disclaimant's creditors.[312] However, a disclaimer

---

[302] Treas.Reg. § 25.2511–1(c).

[303] Martin, *supra* note 300, at 321–22.

[304] *See* UPC §§ 2–1101 et seq.

[305] General Comment preceding UPC § 2–1101.

[306] UDPIA § 14, incorporated into UPC § 2–1114. Hereafter, references are to the sections of the UPC.

[307] Internal Revenue Code § 2518(c)(3).

[308] Estate of Bennett, 100 T.C. 42 (1993).

[309] Kinney v. Shinholser, 663 So.2d 643 (Fla.App.1995); Linck v. Barokas & Martin, 667 P.2d 171 (Alaska 1983).

[310] Stein v. Brown, 480 N.E.2d 1121 (Ohio 1985); Matter of Reed's Estate, 566 P.2d 587 (Wyo.1977). As to fraudulent conveyances, see Section 10.8. As to the tax consequences when a disclaimer is voided by the disclaimant's creditors, see Treas.Reg. § 2518–1(c)(2).

[311] Mass.Gen.Laws c. 190B, § 2–801(h)(2); Fla. Stat. § 739.402(2)(d).

[312] In re Atchison, 925 F.2d 209 (7th Cir.1991); Frances Slocum Bank and Trust Co. v. Martin, 666 N.E.2d 411 (Ind.App.1996); Dyer v. Eckols, 808 S.W.2d 531 (Tex.App.1991); *cf.* Succession of Neuhauser, 579 So.2d 437 (La.1991) (creditor of disclaimant can bar disclaimer only in case of "fraud"). A disclaimer can bar even creditors who have attempted to reach the property before the disclaimer, Matter of Estate of Opatz, 554 N.W.2d 813 (N.D.1996), but under UPC § 2–1113(b)(3) a judicial sale of the property cuts off the right to disclaim.

A discussion of the policy issues appears in Hirsch, *The Problem of the Insolvent Heir*, 74 Corn.L.Rev 587 (1989). In a later article, Hirsch, *Revisions in Need of Revising: The Uniform*

made by a person who has previously filed for bankruptcy is voidable.[313] Also, disclaimers have been held ineffective to defeat federal tax liens.[314] And several courts have treated disclaimers as an assignment that disqualifies the disclaimant for welfare benefits under need-based programs, such as Medicaid.[315] On the other hand, the Second Restatement of Property takes the position that a disclaimer is effective for an heir to avoid the costs of environmental clean-up that would otherwise be incurred by the heir with respect to real property inherited from a decedent.[316]

Requirements for a Disclaimer

Disclaimers, when properly made, are irrevocable.[317] Unlike the release or assignment of an expectancy which requires consideration,[318] a disclaimer can be gratuitous. In fact, if a disclaimant receives consideration for the disclaimer, it does not qualify for tax purposes.[319]

At common law, oral disclaimers were recognized,[320] but under the UPC a disclaimer must be signed by the disclaimant.[321] Perhaps an unsigned disclaimer could still be valid at common law.[322] The Internal Revenue Code requires disclaimers to be in writing to qualify for tax purposes.

Some statutes require the disclaimer to be filed in court where the estate is being administered, and an unfiled disclaimer has been held to be revocable.[323] Section 2518 of the Internal Revenue Code merely requires that the disclaimer be "received by" the legal representative of the transferor.[324]

Disclaimer of Property Interests Act, 29 Fla.State U.L.Rev. 109, 154–63 (2001), Professor Hirsch criticized the UDPIA for leaving this issue unresolved.

313 In re Cornell, 95 B.R. 219 (Bkrtcy.W.D.Okl.1989); In re Detlefsen, 610 F.2d 512 (8th Cir.1979). A disclaimer made on the eve of bankruptcy, on the other hand, is not voidable unless it constitutes a fraudulent conveyance under state law. Matter of Simpson, 36 F.3d 450 (5th Cir.1994); In re Atchison, 925 F.2d 209 (7th Cir.1991).

314 Drye v. United States, 528 U.S. 49 (1999).

315 Troy v. Hart, 697 A.2d 113 (Md.App.1997); Hoesly v. State, Dept. of Social Services, 498 N.W.2d 571 (Neb.1993); Department of Income Maintenance v. Watts, 558 A.2d 998 (Conn.1989).

316 *Restatement (Second) of Property (Donative Transfers)* § 32.3, cmt. e (1992).

317 *See* UPC § 2–1105(e). *See also* Caffoni, 787 A.2d 971 (Pa.Super.2001) (even though estate had not been distributed when disclaimant sought to revoke his disclaimer). As to revocation of gifts, see Section 4.5.

318 As to expectancies, see Section 3.5.

319 Treas.Reg. § 25.2518–2(d)(1); Estate of Allen, TC Memo 1990–514. But in Estate of Monroe v. C.I.R., 124 F.3d 699 (5th Cir.1997), disclaimers were held to qualify even though the disclaimants received equivalent gifts from the beneficiary of the disclaimers.

320 3 *Amer. Law of Prop.* § 14.15, at 630.

321 UPC § 2–1105(c), defined to include an electronic signature. In Estate of Allen, TC Memo 1989–111, a disclaimer signed by an orally authorized agent was held to be effective. *See also* In re Estate of Weill, 122 So.3d 763, 770 (Miss. Ct. App. 2012) (telephonic disclaimer ineffective).

322 Medlin, *An Examination of Disclaimers Under UPS Section 2–801*, 55 Alb.L.Rev. 1233, 1276 (1992). Cal.Prob.Code § 288 specifically requires that all disclaimers comply with the statute. UPC § 2–1104(b), on the other hand, preserves the right to disclaim under other law.

323 Matter of Estate of Griffin, 812 P.2d 1256 (Mont.1991). See also, Carmichael v. Lively, 762 S.E.2d 283, 287–289 (N.C. Ct. App. 2014) (renunciation of real property inherited under will must be filed with the registry of deeds to be effective).

324 But in Estate of Bennett, 100 T.C. 42 (1993), a disclaimer delivered to executor but not filed in court was ineffective under state law. UPC § 2–1112 offers several options depending on the circumstances.

Once a person has accepted property, it is too late to disclaim it.[325] Mere failure to act for an extended period may constitute an acceptance; at common law, a disclaimer must be made within a "reasonable time."[326] The Internal Revenue Code is more precise: it allow nine months from the date of the decedent's death to disclaim testamentary transfers to adults 21 years or older.[327] This creates problems if probate of a will is delayed or contested. For example, if a will was not discovered for ten months after the testator dies, it would be too late for a devisee over age 21 to disclaim.[328] Similarly, if a will is contested and declared invalid ten months after a testator died, it would be too late for an heir over age 21 to disclaim.

Under the UPC, a disclaimer can be made at any time before the disclaimed interest is accepted.[329] This may occur long after a will which created the disclaimed interest took effect. If a will creates a trust for "Mary for life, and at her death, to her then living descendants," the interest of her descendants would not become possessory until Mary died. Assuming no prior acceptance of the remainder interest, Mary's descendants could disclaim at her death, and their disclaimer could occur more than nine months after the testator's death. While their disclaimer would be valid under the UPC, if they disclaim more than nine months after the testator died, their disclaimer may not be a qualified disclaimer for federal tax law purposes.

Under Section 2518, the time allowed to an individual under age 21 to make a qualified disclaimer does not begin to run until the individual reaches age 21,[330] presumably because an individual under age 21 is not competent to decide whether to disclaim. Most states deal with this problem differently, by allowing a guardian to disclaim on behalf of a minor.

Disclaimers by Fiduciaries

The UPC allows disclaimers by fiduciaries, including the conservator of a disabled person or guardian of a minor.[331] This requires court approval, based "primarily [on] the decision that the protected person would have made, to the extent that the decision can be ascertained."[332] Normally, guardians have a duty to conserve a minor's property. For example, a court refused to allow the

---

[325] Estate of Selby v. United States, 726 F.2d 643 (10th Cir.1984); In re Gardner, 230 Ariz. 329, 331–332 (Ariz. Ct. App. 2012) (beneficiary of life estate in a home could not disclaim upon "learning" that the beneficiary was liable for paying the mortgage on the home after having lived in the home for many years); Internal Revenue Code § 2518(b)(3); Estate of Hall, 456 S.E.2d 439 (S.C.App.1995) (person who had executed a receipt for property cannot thereafter disclaim it).

[326] In re Nunn's Estate, 518 P.2d 1151 (Cal.1974) (nine years is too late); In the Matter of the Estate of Gardner, 283 P.3d 676 (Ariz. Ct. App. 2012) (life tenant could not disclaim after living in the home for several years and upon learning life tenant would be liable for real estate taxes).

[327] Internal Revenue Code § 2518(b); Treas. Reg. § 25.2518–2(c)(3). *Cf.* Cal.Prob.Code § 279 (9 months is conclusively presumed a reasonable time). The UPDIA imposes no time limits on disclaimers. *See* Prefatory Note. For transfers to persons under age 21, the disclaimer must be made within nine months of their 21st birthday.

[328] Estate of Fleming v. Commissioner, 974 F.2d 894 (7th Cir.1992) (rejecting claim that time runs from probate of the will).

[329] UPC § 2–1113.

[330] Internal Revenue Code § 2518(b)(2)(B). Although virtually all states have reduced the age of majority from 21 to 18, the Code does not take this change into account.

[331] UPC §§ 2–1105(b), 1–201(15). *See also* Cal.Prob.Code § 277(a).

[332] UPC § 5–411(c) (1998 rev). *See also* Cal.Prob.Code § 277(f).

guardian of minor children to disclaim their share in their father's estate in order to get the maximum marital deduction for the estate because the children would lose by it. "Where an infant is involved there must be a showing that the renunciation would be directly advantageous to him and not merely to the parent."[333] However, arguably a court acting under the UPC might have approved the disclaimer because the children's mother would benefit from the disclaimer, and she would probably use the funds (augmented by the tax savings) for their support, and so the minor children may well have decided to disclaim if they had the capacity to do so.[334]

The UPC also allows disclaimers by an agent acting under a power of attorney. This can save the expense of court proceedings when a disclaimer for a principal who has been adjudicated incompetent is appropriate.[335] However, if the power of attorney does not authorize disclaimers expressly, some courts hesitate to infer that an attorney is empowered to diminish the principal's estate.[336] In addition the Uniform Power of Attorney Act provides that an agent under a power of attorney does not have the power to disclaim unless the power of attorney "expressly grants the agent the authority and exercise of the authority is not otherwise prohibited by another agreement or instrument to which the authority . . . is subject."[337]

If an heir or devisee dies shortly after the decedent, can that person's executor disclaim the share of the decedent's estate, assuming the allowed time has not run? The UPC allows the personal representative to disclaim on behalf of a decedent,[338] but here, too, fiduciary duties of the personal representative may be an obstacle.[339] In California, the court can approve a disclaimer by a personal representative only if it thinks the decedent would have disclaimed.[340] One court rejected a disclaimer by the executor of a will which had created a trust for the testator's children because the disclaimer would give them the property outright.[341] Another court refused to allow an executor to disclaim over an objection of one of the testator's creditors, saying that executors have duties to creditors.[342] On the other hand, a court allowed a trustee to disclaim on behalf of trust beneficiaries when the decision was "made in good faith with

---

[333] In re Estate of De Domenico, 418 N.Y.S.2d 1012, 1013 (Surr.1979). *See also* Matter of Estate of Horowitz, 531 A.2d 1364 (N.J.Super.Law Div.1987).

[334] Compare the problem of guardians of minors and unborn trust beneficiaries in agreeing to the modification of a trust. *See* Section 10.9.

[335] For the advantages of a durable power of attorney in avoiding the need for conservatorship, see Sections 9.2 & 9.3.

[336] Cal.Prob.Code § 4264(d) (agent cannot disclaim unless expressly authorized without court approval). As to gifts under a power of attorney, see Section 9.3.

[337] Unif. Power of Attorney Act § 201(a)(9).

[338] UPC §§ 2–1102(4); 2–1105(b). In In re Estate of Lamson, 662 A.2d 287 (N.H.1995), the court held that such a power existed even without a statute.

[339] *E.g.* UPC § 3–709: personal representatives must "take possession or control of the decedent's property." UPC § 3–715(11) allows them to abandon property that is "valueless."

[340] Cal.Prob. Code § 277(f).

[341] In re Morgan's Estate, 411 N.E.2d 213 (Ill.1980). In Matter of Estate of Schock, 543 A.2d 488 (N.J.Super.Law Div.1988), on the other hand, the court approved an executor's disclaimer when the persons who benefited thereby agreed to create a trust with the property like the one in the decedent's will.

[342] In re Estate of Heater, 640 N.E.2d 654 (Ill.App.1994). This is hard to reconcile with the general rule that a live debtor can disclaim to defeat his creditors.

the best interests of the trust's beneficiaries in mind."[343] This is possible when the disclaimer reduces taxes, particularly if one looks at the situation from the viewpoint of the family as a unit rather than its individual members.

The UPC expressly allows disclaimers by fiduciaries in general, as well as by trustees. The comment to the latter provision, but not the former, requires that the disclaimer "be compatible with the trustee's fiduciary obligations."[344]

Disclaimable Interests

Historically, heirs taking by intestacy could not disclaim even though devisees under a will could.[345] There was no good reason for this distinction, and most states have abolished it. The UPC expressly allows a disclaimer of "any interest in . . . property."[346]

One can also disclaim an inter vivos gift. To obtain a gift tax benefit from the disclaimer, the time starts to run "when there is a completed gift for Federal gift tax purposes."[347] Thus, if a person creates a revocable living trust, the time within which the beneficiaries must disclaim does not start to run until the settlor's power to revoke expires (normally at the settlor's death). The same rule applies to joint accounts where the depositor usually retains a right of withdrawal until death.[348]

Formalities of Disclaimers

A disclaimer must be written. Although state law variations are possible, typically the disclaimant must declare the disclaimer and describe the power or the interest being disclaimed. The written disclaimer must be signed by the disclaimant and in the case of either an outright bequest or a testamentary or inter vivos trust, delivered[349] to the appropriate fiduciary.[350]

Partial Disclaimers

The UPC expressly allows a person to disclaim property "in whole or part."[351] But a partial disclaimer may not be effective for tax purposes because the Treasury Regulations require that the interest retained be "severable"

---

[343] McClintock v. Scahill, 530 N.E.2d 164 (Mass.1988). *See also* Cleaveland v. United States, 88–1 USTC #13,766, 1988 WL 123836 (C.D.Ill.1988) (trustee disclaims power without objection of adversely affected beneficiaries, thereby saving the marital deduction). *But see* Rev.Rul. 90–110, 1990–2 C.B. 209 (trustee's disclaimer of power to invade corpus for a grandchild is ineffective without grandchild's consent).

[344] UPC §§ 2–1105(b) (fiduciaries), 2–1108 (trustees).

[345] Coomes v. Finegan, 7 N.W.2d 729 (Iowa 1943) (disclaimer by heir ineffective); Hardenbergh v. Commissioner, 198 F.2d 63 (8th Cir.1952) (disclaimer by heir is a taxable gift).

[346] UPC § 2–1105(a). *See also* Md. Estates and Trusts Code § 9–201(a). A right to sue for wrongful death of a relative may not be disclaimed, because such claims may not be assigned and a disclaimer would be "the functional equivalent of an assignment." Mayo v. White, 224 Cal.Rptr. 373, 377 (App.1986).

[347] Treas.Reg. § 25.2518–2(b)(3). As to when a gift is complete for tax purposes, see Section 15.3.

[348] *Id.* § 25.2518–2(c)(4). The rule is otherwise for joint tenancies in land. *Compare* UPC § 2–1107.

[349] UPC § 2–1105(c).

[350] UPC § 2–1112(c)(1) & (d).

[351] UPC § 2–1105(a). *See also* Cal.Prob.Code § 267; Palmer v. White, 784 P.2d 449 (Or.App.1989) (allowing disclaimer of some but not all devises in a will).

from the one disclaimed. Thus, while the regulations would allow for a disclaimer of 50% of a bequeathed interest, they would not allow a person to disclaim property left to her in fee while retaining a life interest.[352]

Effect of Disclaimer

If property is effectively disclaimed, the UPC provides that the "disclaimed interest passes as if the disclaimant had died immediately before the time of distribution."[353] The consequence of deeming the disclaimant to have predeceased depends on the circumstances. In the hypothetical described at the beginning of this section, if the child was the decedent's only descendant and the decedent died intestate and the local intestacy statute gave the surviving spouse everything in the absence of descendants, the child's disclaimer would cause the child's share to go to the spouse. But if the child had children, those children (the decedent's grandchildren) would take the child's share by representation, even though a statute provides that a disclaimer is binding on persons "claiming through" the disclaimant.[354] Thus, the child could not in this situation increase the marital deduction by a disclaimer because the disclaimed share would not pass to the decedent's spouse,[355] unless as the result of an appropriate disclaimer by the child and the child's children, the interest passed to the spouse.[356]

If a decedent had two children, *A* and *B,* and *A* had no descendants, *B* would take *A*'s share as the only surviving "descendant" of the decedent.[357] If *B* was dead, survived by one child, and *A* had three children, what would happen if *A* disclaimed? Section 2–106 of the UPC would call for an equal division among the four grandchildren if both children are dead (constructively in the case of *A* and actually in the case of *B*),[358] but Section 2–1106(b)(3)(C) prevents *A* from swelling *A*'s children's share of the estate by disclaiming.[359] Thus, *A*'s children would each take 1/6 and *B*'s child 1/2 rather than each of the four grandchildren taking 1/4.

---

[352] Treas.Reg. § 25.2518–3. Here, too, state law is sometimes more liberal.

[353] UPC § 2–1106(b)(3)(B); *cf.* Cal.Prob.Code § 282.

[354] Estate of Bryant, 196 Cal.Rptr. 856 (App.1983); Estate of Burmeister, 594 P.2d 226 (Kan.1979). *But see* In re Estate of Rohn, 175 N.W.2d 419 (Iowa 1970) (disclaimer bars takers under an antilapse statute).

[355] Hunt v. United States, 566 F.Supp. 356 (E.D.Ark.1983). *See also* Webb v. Webb, 301 S.E.2d 570 (W.Va.1983) (disclaimant intended to benefit his mother but property goes to his children); Ernst v. Shaw, 783 S.W.2d 400 (Ky.App.1990) (disclaimer causes property to pass to disclaimant's children, not his sister, whom he intended to benefit). In In re Estate of York, 727 N.E.2d 607 (Ohio App.1999) a similar error led to a malpractice claim against the attorney who drafted the documents.

[356] Matter of Guardianship of Kramer, 421 N.Y.S.2d 975 (Surr.1979); *cf.* McInnis v. McInnis, 560 S.E.2d 632 (S.C.App.2002) (disclaimer by children and grandchildren of IRA account owner causes it to pass under will to his widow).

[357] Under Cal.Prob.Code § 6401, the spouse gets a larger share of a decedent's separate property when there is only one child, so the disclaimer might increase the spouse's share too.

[358] *See* Section 2.2.

[359] The idea is expressed more clearly in the Comment, Examples 2(a) & (b) and in Cal.Prob.Code § 282(b). The courts which have dealt with this situation without statutory guidance have reached divergent results. *Compare* Estate of Bryant, 196 Cal.Rptr. 856 (App.1983), *with* Welder v. Hitchcock, 617 S.W.2d 294 (Tex.Civ.App.1981). A similar issue can arise when a child of the intestate is disqualified by homicide. Fellows, *The Slayer Rule: Not Solely a Matter of Equity*, 71 Iowa L.Rev. 489, 525–27 (1986).

Because "time of distribution" under the Code is defined to mean "time when a disclaimed interest would have taken effect in possession or enjoyment" in the case of a disclaimer by the remainderman of a testamentary trust, the disclaimant is deemed to have predeceased the life income beneficiary, not the deceased testator. If decedent creates a testamentary trust to pay the income to *A* for life, remainder to *B*, and *B* disclaims, the takers of *B's* interest are determined at *A's* death, not the testator's death. Assuming *B* had two children living at the testator's death but three children living at *A's* death, *B's* three children take under the UPC,[360] whereas under other disclaimer statutes which treat *B* as predeceasing the testator and not *A*, only *B*'s older two children alive at the testator's death would take.[361]

Estate planners sometimes draft wills in anticipation of a possible disclaimer by a devisee. If a will devises property "to my wife Mary, but if she predeceases me, to Andrew," Andrew would take if Mary survived the testator but disclaimed.[362] Mary may need property for her support for life, but also may wish to reduce her estate taxes at death. The best solution may be to have the property pass to a trust in which Mary gets the income for life without the trust property being taxable in her estate when she dies.[363] A testator, when executing a will, may be uncertain whether the estate at death will be large enough to warrant such a trust and may want to leave it to the surviving spouse outright with the idea that the spouse can disclaim all or part of it if this is appropriate. A will can provide that any property the surviving spouse disclaims shall go into a trust for the spouse for life.[364] This type of provision supersedes the general rule that a disclaimant is deemed to have predeceased the decedent.[365]

Agreements Among Successors

Heirs and devisees can alter the devolution of an estate by agreement as well as by disclaimer. With a disclaimer, the disclaimant cannot direct who receives the property. Conversely, a private agreement among successors to alter the shares they would receive from an estate can provide for whatever distribution the parties desire. For example, a child can agree that the child's

---

360 UPC § 2–707.

361 This assumes that under the applicable antilapse statute, *B*'s children are substituted for *B*.

362 Matter of Estate of Bruce, 877 P.2d 999 (Mont.1994) (secondary beneficiaries of IRA account take when primary beneficiary disclaims). When a life interest under a will is disclaimed, the remainder is accelerated so as to take effect immediately. UPC § 2–1106(b)(4); Pate v. Ford, 376 S.E.2d 775 (S.C.1989). *But cf.* Richey v. Hurst, 798 So.2d 841 (Fla.App.2001) (trust with remainder interests never comes into existence when spouse disclaims, so property passes into residue).

363 On bypass trusts, see Section 15.4. This will work only for the testator's spouse, because Int.Rev.Code § 2518(b)(4) requires that as a result of qualified disclaimer, the property must pass to the testator's spouse or a person other than the disclaimant.

364 Llewellyn, *Estate Planning for the Married Couple,* 28 Vill.L.Rev. 491, 508–09 (1983); J. Price & S. Donaldson, *Contemporary Estate Planning* § 5.23.8 (2019).

365 UPC § 2–1106(b)(2). *See also* Cal.Prob.Code § 282(a). It would also get around the limitation on partial disclaimers.

share should go to the child's parent, even though the child's disclaimer would give the share to the child's children.[366]

Unlike disclaimers, private agreements constitute transfers subject to taxes and to the rights of the parties' creditors. Therefore, Section 3–912 of the UPC, which allows such agreements, is prefaced by the words "subject to the rights of creditors and taxing authorities." When a child who owed his ex-wife money agreed to give his share of his mother's estate to his sibling, the ex-wife had the agreement set aside.[367] When a child, to whom a will left most of the estate, agreed to divide it equally with her siblings, the inheritance tax was based on the shares each received under the will, not under the private agreement.[368] Even when an agreement increases the surviving spouse's share, the marital deduction will not be increased because only property which passes from one spouse to the other qualifies for the marital deduction.[369]

The UPC refers to a "written" agreement, and this has been interpreted by some courts to make an oral agreement among successors unenforceable.[370] But a letter which repudiates an agreement while acknowledging its existence may suffice.[371] In some states no writing is necessary to effectuate a private agreement to redistribute assets.[372]

Some cases speak as if consideration were necessary to make such an agreement enforceable,[373] but it would seem that a person who agrees to take less is making a gift, which requires no consideration.[374] Sometimes an heir makes an agreement with an "heir-hunting" firm which locates the heir and informs the heir of the interest in an undisclosed estate. The firm agrees to tell the heir the name of the estate only if the heir agrees to give the firm a percentage of the heir's share. In California, a court may refuse to distribute a share of an estate to the firm if it finds that the consideration for the assignment was "grossly unreasonable."[375] But in other states, courts have upheld agreements that gave the firm a large percentage of the heir's share.[376]

---

[366] Crowden v. Aldridge, [1993] 1 W.L.R. 433 (Ch.D.) (informal memorandum by all devisees to increase devise to testator's housekeeper).

[367] Matter of Estate of Haggerty, 805 P.2d 1338 (Mont.1990).

[368] Estate of McNicholas v. State, 580 N.E.2d 978 (Ind.App.1991).

[369] Jeschke v. United States, 814 F.2d 568 (10th Cir.1987). The result is different if the agreement is made to settle a bona fide contest. Treas. Reg. § 20.2056(c)–2(d).

[370] Matter of Estate of Leathers, 876 P.2d 619 (Kan.App.1994); Estate of Webster, 920 S.W.2d 600 (Mo.App.1996).

[371] Matter of Estate of Cruse, 710 P.2d 733 (N.M.1985); *Restatement (Second) of Contracts* § 133, cmt. c (1981).

[372] Gregory v. Rice, 678 S.W.2d 603 (Tex.App.1984).

[373] Matter of Estate of Wahby, 758 S.W.2d 440 (Mo.1988) (refusing to enforce agreement because of duress, adding there was "little or no consideration"). But courts do no usually examine the adequacy of consideration. Emberson v. Hartley, 762 P.2d 364 (Wash.App.1988); *cf.* Matter of Estate of Grimm, 784 P.2d 1238 (Utah App.1989) (good faith controversy supplies consideration even if not well founded).

[374] As to the requirements for making a gift, see Section 3.5.

[375] Cal.Prob.Code § 11604. In In re Betlem, 753 N.Y.S.2d 632 (App.Div.2002), an assignee of an interest in the estate of a New York domiciliary unsuccessfully sought to evade a similar New York statute by a forum selection clause.

[376] Nelson v. McGoldrick, 896 P.2d 1258 (Wash.1995) (50% fee was not unconscionable as a matter of law); Matter of Estate of Katze-Miller, 463 N.W.2d 853 (Wis.App.1990) (40% fee upheld).

§ 2.9 Nonmarital Children

At common law, the child of parents not married to each other was *filius nullius*—the child of no one.[377] In modern law, the rule is the contrary. The UPC provides: "A parent-child relationship extends equally to every child and parent, regardless of the marital status of the parent."[378]

What has brought about this great change? What reasons lay behind the historical refusal to allow inheritance by nonmarital children? Four reasons can be suggested, but none of them is entirely satisfactory.

(1) *Feudalism.* The rule barring inheritance by nonmarital children has often been ascribed to feudalism.[379] If a feudal tenant died without heirs, his land escheated to the lord. Barring nonmarital children from inheriting produced an escheat when an intestate left no other heirs.[380] However, the theory that feudal lords promoted the bar on inheritance in order to increase the incidence of escheat is implausible because usually there are other relatives to inherit if nonmarital children are excluded, thus making escheat unlikely.

(2) *Intent.* Intestacy laws are designed to carry out the presumed intent of the average decedent. The bar against inheritance by nonmarital children may have reflected the average decedent's intent, at one time. However, many parents, even in the past, probably loved their nonmarital children.[381] In the 15th century, Fortescue assumed that parents wanted their nonmarital children to inherit; the law frustrated this desire in order to punish the parents for their sin.[382]

(3) *Sin.* In the 19th century Kent echoed Fortescue's explanation: the rule was designed "to discourage illicit commerce between the sexes."[383] Today, sexual "commerce" between unmarried persons no longer appears immoral to many. This change in attitudes has contributed to the change in the law, but even if sex outside marriage was [or is] regarded as wrong, it was [and is] unfair to punish children for the sins of their parents. "No child is responsible for his birth and penalizing the illegitimate child is an ineffectual—as well as an unjust—way of deterring the parent."[384] Blackstone thought it "unjust" to

---

See also Landi v. Arkules, 835 P.2d 458 (Ariz.App.1992) which allowed an heir to rescind a similar contract. Several cases on both sides of this issue are cited in In re Estate of Campbell, 742 A.2d 639, 640 (N.J.Super.Ch.Div.1999).

[377] *See* Glanvill, *Tractatus de Legibus* 88 (G. Hall ed. 1965); 1 W. Blackstone, *Commentaries* 459 (1765).

[378] UPC § 2–117. *See also* Unif. Parentage Act § 202 (2017); *Restatement (Third) of Property (Wills and Other Donative Transfers)* § 2.5 (1998).

[379] Butcher v. Pollard, 288 N.E.2d 204, 207 (Ohio App.1972).

[380] King v. Commonwealth, 269 S.E.2d 793 (Va.1980).

[381] "Our father's love is to the bastard Edmund/As to the legitimate . . . " W. Shakespeare, King Lear, Act I, Scene 2, lines 17–18. *See also* L. Tolstoy, *War and Peace,* part 1, Chapter 18.

[382] J. Fortescue, *De Laudibus Legum Anglie* 94 (S. Chrimes ed. 1949).

[383] J. Kent, *Commentaries on American Law* 175 (1827).

[384] Weber v. Aetna Casualty & Surety Co., 406 U.S. 164, 175 (1972). *See also* Succession of Brown, 388 So.2d 1151, 1153 (La.1980); In re Woodward's Estate, 40 Cal.Rptr. 781, 784 (App.1964).

impose disabilities on an illegitimate "innocent offspring of his parents' crimes."[385]

The "deterring sin" explanation also is hard to reconcile with the fact that even a secret marriage, unblessed by the church, made the children of the marriage legitimate. "Parties sinned by marrying without publications of banns and blessing by a priest," but their marriage was valid and their children were legitimate.[386] Most states do not permit such informal "common-law" marriages[387] but have improved the legal position of children born out of wedlock.

(4) *Problems of Proof.* For Blackstone, the purpose of marriage "taken in a civil light, abstractly from any religious view" was "to ascertain and fix upon some certain person, to whom the care . . . of the children should belong. [To allow nonmarital children to inherit would create] very great uncertainty . . . in the proof that the issue was really begotten by" the alleged father.[388]

The problem of proving paternity clearly influenced the common-law rules on inheritance. When a married woman gave birth to a child, her husband was held to be the child's father despite any evidence to the contrary, because "the privity between a man and his wife cannot be known."[389] This presumption of paternity avoided difficult problems of proof (and also served to legitimate many children who were the fruit of adultery).

Maternity often is more easily proved than paternity. In the 18th century Blackstone pointed out that in the civil law a nonmarital child could inherit from the *mother:* "the mother being sufficiently certain, though the father is not."[390] At that time English inheritance law made no distinction between fathers and mothers on this point, but the first step in protecting inheritance rights generally was to allow nonmarital children to inherit from their mother.

Proof of Parentage

Science has made great progress in enabling accurate parentage determinations.[391] This development has undercut the difficulty-of-proof

---

385 1 W. Blackstone, *Commentaries* 459 (1765).

386 R. Helmholz, *Marriage Litigation in Medieval England* 27 (1974). *See also* 2 F. Pollock & F. Maitland, *The History of English Law* 379–80 (2d ed. 1898).

387 *See* Section 2.12. For a claim by a child to have been born in wedlock on the basis of such an informal marriage, *see* Ruscilli v. Ruscilli, 630 N.E.2d 745 (Ohio App.1993).

388 1 W. Blackstone, *Commentaries* 455 (1765).

389 Y.B. 32 & 33 Edw. 1 (R.S.) 60, 63 (1304) (Hengham J.). For modern vestiges of the idea, see Hess v. Whitsitt, 65 Cal.Rptr. 45 (App.1967) (black child born to a white mother deemed to be the child of her white husband); Rumlin v. Lewis, 381 So.2d 194 (Ala.1980) (child born 4 years after husband and wife separated); Estate of Cornelious, 674 P.2d 245 (Cal.1984) (husband deemed to be father even though this was "biologically impossible"). Modern cases have weakened the presumption considerably. Johnson v. Adams, 479 N.E.2d 866 (Ohio 1985); State ex rel. Munoz v. Bravo, 678 P.2d 974 (Ariz.App.1984); Matter of Marriage of Hodge, 722 P.2d 1235 (Or.1986) (presumption inapplicable if husband and wife not cohabiting).

390 2 W. Blackstone, *Commentaries* 248 (1765).

391 *E.g.* Nwabara v. Willacy, 733 N.E.2d 267, 274 (Ohio App.1999) (DNA test identifies father with 99.95% probability). L.A. Times, Feb. 7, 2001 (paternity claims asserted by alleged children of air crash victim dismissed on the basis of DNA testing).

argument against inheritance by nonmarital children.[392] Proof of parentage may be available even after the parent is dead.[393] Proof of biological parentage is not always determinative of the parent/child relationship, however. If a woman is inseminated artificially with the sperm of a donor, the donor is not the child's parent.[394] Rather, an individual "who consents . . . to assisted reproduction by a woman with the intent to be a parent of a child conceived by the assisted reproduction is a parent of the child."[395] The Third Restatement of Property accords with this approach: children produced by assisted reproductive technologies "should be treated as part of the family of . . . parents who treat the child as their own" even though they "might not be the child's genetic parent."[396] Conversely, "the mere genetic tie of the decedent to any posthumously conceived child" has been held insufficient to make the child the decedent's heir.[397]

Failure to act like a parent may outweigh biological claims. For example, the UPC bars a parent from inheriting from a child if the parent failed to support the child.[398]

Presumptions of Parentage

In many cases the question of parentage may be resolved by a presumption. The Uniform Parentage Act of 2017 creates a number of presumptions.[399]

First, an individual is presumed to be a parent of a child if the individual and the woman who gave birth to the child are married to each other and the child is born during the marriage or not later than 300 days after the marriage is terminated.[400]

Second, an individual is presumed to be a parent of a child if the individual and the woman who gave birth to the child married each other after the child's birth, the individual asserted parentage of the child, and either (1) the assertion is in a record filed with the state agency maintaining birth records or (2) the individual agreed to be and is named as a parent on the child's birth certificate.[401]

---

392 S.M.V. v. Littlepage, 443 N.E.2d 103, 110 (Ind.App.1982) (concurring); Woodward v. Commissioner of Social Security, 760 N.E.2d 257, 267 (Mass.2002). *cf.* Mills v. Habluetzel, 456 U.S. 91, 98n, 104n (1982); Pickett v. Brown, 462 U.S. 1 (1983).

393 Alexander v. Alexander, 537 N.E.2d 1310 (Ohio Prob.1988) (proper to order body exhumed for DNA testing to establish paternity); Batcheldor v. Boyd, 423 S.E.2d 810 (N.C.App.1992) (same). Contra, Estate of Sekanic, 653 N.Y.S.2d 449 (App.Div.1997).

394 Unif. Parentage Act § 702 (2017).

395 Unif. Parentage Act § 703 (2017).

396 *Restatement (Third) of Property (Wills and Other Donative Transfers)* § 2.5, cmt. *l* (1998); *id.* § 14.8 (2011).

397 Woodward v. Commissioner of Social Security, 760 N.E.2d 257, 270 (Mass.2002) (there must have been both the genetic tie and the decedent's consent to the use of his sperm). *See also Restatement (Third) of Property (Wills and Other Donative Transfers)* § 14.8, cmt. n (2011); Unif. Parentage Act § 702 (2017).

398 UPC § 2–114(a)(2). *See also Restatement (Third) of Property (Wills and Other Donative Transfers)* § 2.5(5) (1998).

399 *See* Unif. Parentage Act § 204 (2017).

400 *See* Unif. Parentage Act § 204(a)(1)(A) & (B) (2017).

401 *See* Unif. Parentage Act § 204(a)(1)(C) (2017).

Third, an individual is presumed to be a parent of a child if the individual resided in the same household as the child for the child's first two years and openly held out the child as the individual's child.[402]

All of these presumptions may be overcome by an adjudication under Article 6 of the Uniform Act or a valid denial of parentage under Article 3 of the Uniform Act.[403]

Inheritance by and Through Parents from Child

The common law deemed a nonmarital child to be *filius nullius,* the child of no one, so that a nonmarital child with no surviving spouse or descendants had no heirs.[404] Today, however, most statutes allow parents of a nonmarital child and the relatives of those parents to inherit from or through the child. The UPC, for example, allows inheritance by and through parents of a nonmarital child, unless the parent is otherwise barred from inheritance.[405]

Wills and Other Donative Documents

Claims to take under a will or other donative document turn on the testator's intent. If the will gives no clue to the intent, courts traditionally presumed the testator intended to exclude nonmarital children from a devise to "children" or the like.[406] This traditional presumption was able to be overcome by showing "a contrary intent . . . from additional language or circumstances," such as the fact that the only possible takers under the devise were nonmarital children.[407] Some authorities distinguished between fathers and mothers. If a will left property to the "children" of a woman, all were included because of "the natural affection of a mother for her children, whether legitimate or illegitimate." A devise to a man's "children" was different because of the difficulty of proving paternity and because there was usually no "close association between an illegitimate child and his father."[408]

The law today construes wills and other donative documents more favorably to nonmarital children. Under the UPC, in the absence of a finding of a donor's contrary intention,[409] nonmarital children of the donor are included in a class gift in a governing instrument[410] "in accordance with the rules for intestate succession."[411] Recall the UPC's rule in intestacy that "a parent child-relationship extends equally to every parent and child, regardless of the

---

[402] *See* Unif. Parentage Act § 204(a)(2) (2017).

[403] *See* Unif. Parentage Act § 204(b) (2017).

[404] Glanvill, *supra* note 377, at 88; 1 W. Blackstone, *Commentaries* 459 (1765).

[405] UPC §§ 2–114, 2–117. *See also Restatement (Third) of Property (Wills and Other Donative Transfers)* § 2.5 (1998).

[406] *Restatement of Property* § 286 (1940); Theobald, *Wills* § 851 (12th ed. 1963); Dutra De Amorim v. Norment, 460 A.2d 511 (Del.1983); Tindol v. McCoy, 535 S.W.2d 745 (Tex.Civ.App.1976).

[407] *Restatement of Property* § 286(1)(a) (1940). *See also* Theobald, *Wills* §§ 857–58 (12th ed. 1963).

[408] 5 *Amer. Law of Prop.* § 22.33.

[409] *See* UPC § 2–701.

[410] For the expansive definition of "governing instrument," see UPC § 1–201(18).

[411] UPC § 2–705(b). As to whether such statutes apply to instruments creating future interests which were executed prior to the statute's effective date *see* Section 1.3.

marital status of the parent."[412] Even in states without a similar statute, intestacy statutes often are cited as evidence of probable intent in construction issues,[413] and today's more favorable attitude toward inheritance by nonmarital children has persuaded several courts to presume that class gifts in wills include nonmarital children.[414]

Giving effect to a particular testator's intent to exclude nonmarital children does not violate the Constitution because the exclusion does not involve "state action;"[415] but a statutory presumption that nonmarital children were not included in class gifts was held unconstitutional.[416]

Planning

An attorney who drafts a will or other donative document should ascertain the donor's intent regarding the inclusion or exclusion of nonmarital children and make it clear in the instrument. Some persons would wish nonmarital children to share in their property, and some would not. Even if there are no such children currently in the donor's family, the question cannot be ignored because wills often provide for children who are as yet unborn.

The effect of a provision for "lawful" descendants is not clear. Because most states no longer use the term "illegitimate" to describe nonmarital children, they might be included in a gift to "lawful" children.[417] A restriction to children "born in wedlock" is clearer,[418] but it might bar persons whom the testator wished to include, such as children of an invalid marriage or of a marriage-like relationship.

§ 2.10 Adoption and De Facto Parentage

This section addresses two means by which a parent-child relationship can be created after the child's birth: adoption and de facto parentage.

---

[412] UPC § 2–117.

[413] *Restatement of Property* § 286(2)(c) (1940); *Restatement (Second) of Property (Donative Transfers)* § 25.2, comment a (1988). If the will gives property to "heirs," the intestacy statute is particularly persuasive as to intent. *See Restatement (Second) of Property (Donative Transfers)* § 29.1 (1988); *Restatement (Third) of Property (Wills and Other Donative Transfers)* § 16.1 (2011).

[414] Matter of Estate of Best, 485 N.E.2d 1010 (N.Y.1985); Vincent v. Sutherland, 691 P.2d 85 (Okl.App.1984); Annan v. Wilmington Trust Co., 559 A.2d 1289 (Del.1989); Butcher v. Pollard, 288 N.E.2d 204 (Ohio App.1972) (insurance).

[415] Harris Trust and Sav. Bank v. Donovan, 582 N.E.2d 120 (Ill.1991); In re Dumaine, 600 A.2d 127 (N.H.1991).

[416] Estate of Dulles, 431 A.2d 208 (Pa.1981).

[417] *Restatement (Second) of Property (Donative Transfers)* § 25.2, illus. 1 (1988) ("lawful" includes child born out of wedlock but legitimated). *See also* Bell v. Forti, 584 A.2d 77 (Md.App.1991). *But see* Decker v. Meriwether, 708 S.W.2d 390 (Tenn.App.1985) (same); In re Dumaine, 600 A.2d 127 (N.H.1991) ("legitimate" excludes child born out of wedlock even though parents later married).

[418] *See Restatement (Third) of Property (Wills and Other Donative Transfers)* § 14.7, cmt. e (2011) ("children born in wedlock" indicates intent to exclude nonmarital children).

History of Adoption

The common law did not recognize adoption.[419] England legalized it by statute only in 1926.[420] In the United States, at first child placement involved almost no governmental regulation. Homeless children were simply "put-out" to be raised by a suitable relative.[421] Some families formalized the arrangement through private statutes. In the middle of the 19th century, state legislatures began to enact general adoption legislation.[422] Formal adoption today has evolved from a relative rarity to a common occurrence in the U.S.; Americans adopt approximately 135,000 children annually.[423]

Adoption raises questions both as to intestate succession and the construction of wills and other donative instruments. It may also have tax consequences.[424]

Adoption and Intestate Succession

When *A* adopts *B*, several questions can arise regarding intestate succession. Can *B* inherit from *A* if *A* dies intestate? Can *B* inherit from *A's* relative if *A* has predeceased? Can *B*'s *children* inherit from *A* or *A*'s relatives? Can *A* or *A*'s relatives inherit from *B*? UPC Section 2–118(a) answers yes to all these questions. It states: "A parent-child relationship exists between an adoptee and the adoptee's adoptive parent."[425] This rule applies for all purposes of intestate succession. Most states reach the same result today[426] even though, in the case of relatives of the adopter, they were not parties to the adoption contract. Indeed, in 1996 a court held unconstitutional a state statute that did not allow an adopted child to inherit from a half-sister by adoption.

> The argument that adoptees should not inherit from adoptive relatives who were not parties to the adoption contract "ignore[s] the fact that a child's birth always imposed a potential heir on the relatives of his biological parents, yet no one would suggest that the

---

[419] On the history of adoption *see* Binavince, *Adoption and the Law of Descent and Distribution: A Comparative Study and a Proposal for Modern Legislation*, 51 Cornell L.Q. 152, 154–58 (1966); Kuhlman, *Intestate Succession By and From the Adopted Child*, 28 Wash.U.L.Q. 221, 222–24 (1943); Presser, *The Historical Background of the American Law of Adoption*, 11 Journal of Family Law 443 (1971); Huard, *The Law of Adoption: Ancient and Modern*, 9 Vand.L.Rev. 743 (1956).

[420] Adoption of Children Act, 16 & 17 Geo. 5, ch. 29 (1926).

[421] *See A Social History of the American Family* 124–27 (1917); Witmer, Herzog, et al., *Independent Adoptions* 33–34 (1963).

[422] The first comprehensive adoption act providing for the welfare of adopted children was passed by the Massachusetts legislature in 1851. Mass. Acts of 1851, c. 324. Earlier statutes only required the filing of a deed of adoption. Miss. Laws 1846, c. 60; Tex. Acts of 1849–50, p. 36, c. 39.

[423] *See* https://adoptionnetwork.com/adoption-statistics.

[424] *See* Section 15.5 (generation skipping transfer tax).

[425] UPC § 2–118(a).

[426] *E.g.*, Cal.Prob.Code § 6450; Iowa Code § 633.223; Tenn. Code § 31–2–105(a)(1); In re Estate of Brittin, 664 N.E.2d 687 (Ill.App.1996) (children of adopted child inherit from adopter); McClure v. Noble, 602 So.2d 377 (Ala.1992) (inheritance from relative of adopter); *Restatement (Third) of Property (Wills and Other Donative Transfers)* § 2.5(2) (1998).

child should not inherit from his blood relatives because they had not consented to his conception.[427]

The question of inheritance is more complex with respect to the adopted child and the *prior* parents and relatives. Should an adopted child inherit from the child's prior parents and their relatives, and vice versa?

A traditional answer to this question is "no." The adoption creates a "fresh start" or a "clean slate."[428] The adopted child is the child of the adoptive parents, not of the prior parents.

In many instances, however, the "fresh start" is inappropriate.

In many adoptions, the previous parent(s) or their relatives continue to associate with the child. Over half the adoptions occurring today involve children adopted by step-parents or relatives.[429] In this situation, continued association between the child and the previous family is likely to occur. These realities are taken into account by the UPC.

The UPC maintains the parent-child relationship between an adoptee and a previous parent if the adoption: was by the spouse of a previous parent (*i.e.*, a step-parent adoption); was by a relative or the spouse or surviving spouse of a relative of a previous parent; or occurred after the death of a previous parent.[430]

An adoptee who can inherit from two sets of relatives has an advantage denied to other children. Some courts have even allowed a child adopted by a family member to inherit twice from the same decedent, once as an adopted child and once, by representation, through his genetic parents.[431] The UPC, however, gives the child only a single share in this situation.[432] For example, suppose *F's* child *C-1* dies survived by *C-1*'s child *GC*, whom *F* adopts. *F* later dies intestate survived by *GC* and *C-2*, who is *F's* other child. *GC* could potentially claim a 1/3rd share through *C-1* and a 1/3rd share as an adopted child; thus, taking 2/3rds of the estate. Under the UPC, however, *GC's* share is limited to one half, and *C-2* takes the other half.

De Facto Parentage and Intestate Succession

Most states by statute or case law recognize a doctrine that extends some or all parental rights to an individual who has performed functions customarily

---

[427] MacCallum v. Seymour, 686 A.2d 935 (Vt.1996). However, in Nunnally v. Trust Co. Bank, 261 S.E.2d 621 (Ga.1979), a similar attack on a Georgia statute was rejected. *See also* Lutz v. Fortune, 758 N.E.2d 77, 84 (Ind.App.2001).

[428] Estates of Donnelly, 502 P.2d 1163 (Wash. 1973).

[429] Prefatory Note, Uniform Adoption Act (1994).

[430] UPC § 2–119(b).

[431] In re Estate of Cregar, 333 N.E.2d 540 (Ill.App.1975) (children adopted by an aunt can inherit from another aunt in both capacities).

[432] UPC § 2–113. *See also Restatement (Third) of Property (Wills and Other Donative Transfers)* § 2.5, cmt. i (1998); Cal.Prob.Code § 6413; Unsel v. Meier, 972 S.W.2d 466 (Mo.App.1998) (construing a gift to "bodily heirs" to give an adoptee a double share would violate public policy).

associated with parenting.[433] The Uniform Parentage Act of 2017 treats an adjudication of de facto parentage as a "new means by which an individual can establish a parent-child relationship."[434] Section 609 of the UPA, in an effort to "provide greater clarity to the parties and affected child," sets forth procedures to establish a parent-child relationship based on an adjudication of a claim of de facto parentage.[435] The individual claiming to be a de facto parent must show the following by clear and convincing evidence:

> (1) the individual resided with the child as a regular member of the child's household for a significant period;
>
> (2) the individual engaged in consistent caretaking of the child;
>
> (3) the individual undertook full and permanent responsibilities of a parent of the child without expectation of financial compensation;
>
> (4) the individual held out the child as the individual's child;
>
> (5) the individual established a bonded and dependent relationship with the child which is parental in nature;
>
> (6) another parent of the child fostered or supported the bonded and dependent relationship required under [the previous paragraph]; and
>
> (7) continuing the relationship between the individual and the child is in the best interest of the child.[436]

The UPA provisions on de facto parentage promote the efficient application of succession law by requiring that a proceeding to adjudicate a claim of de facto parentage commence while both the child and the individual who claims to be a de facto parent are alive.[437] The UPA also requires that the proceeding commence "before the child attains 18 years of age."[438]

The UPC incorporates the de facto parentage doctrine into the rules of intestate succession. Section 2–118(b) recognizes a parent-child relationship between an individual and the individual's de facto parent. It states: "A parent-child relationship exists between an individual and the individual's de facto parent."[439] Section 2–119(c) addresses the effect of de facto parentage on parent-child relationships in existence before the adjudication of a claim of de facto parentage. It provides that "an adjudication that an individual is a child

---

[433] *See* Unif. Parentage Act Prefatory Note & § 609, comment (2017) (describing the similarities and differences among the states regarding the equitable doctrines referred to variously as de facto parentage, in loco parentis, or the psychological parent doctrine).

[434] Unif. Parentage Act § 609, comment (2017).

[435] *Id.* Section 613(a) sets forth factors for adjudicating "parentage in the best interest of the child." Alternative B of § 613(c) authorizes a court to "adjudicate a child to have more than two parents . . . if the court finds that failure to recognize more than two parents would be detrimental to the child."

[436] Unif. Parentage Act § 609(d) (2017).

[437] Unif. Parentage Act § 609(a) & (b) (2017).

[438] Unif. Parentage Act § 609(b)(1) (2017). Although state law other than the UPA does not necessarily require that an individual claiming to be a de facto parent must do so before the child of the de facto parent reaches adulthood, the criteria to qualify as a de facto parent appear to presume that the de facto parent has built a parent-child relationship while the child of the de facto parent was a minor. *See, e.g.*, Me. Rev. Stat. tit. 19–A § 1891(3).

[439] UPC § 2–118(b).

of a de facto parent does not affect a parent-child relationship between the child and an individual who was the child's parent before the adjudication."[440] The continuing recognition of parent-child relationships established before an adjudication of de facto parentage reflects the de facto parentage doctrine. De facto parentage adds, rather than replaces, a parent.

Adult Adoptions

Adult adoptions pose special problems. Some states have no provision for adult adoption[441] and others restrict it by requiring a specified age differential or relationship between the adopter and the adoptee.[442] Most states, however, permit such adoptions with few or no limitations.[443]

Procedures for adult adoptions are simpler than for child adoptions. No home investigation is made and consent of the adoptee's parents is not required.[444] Parental support obligations involved in the adoption of a minor do not apply. The adoptee often does not undergo a change of name or live with the adopter. Nevertheless, the legal consequences of the adoption of an adult are generally the same as for the adoption of a minor. This is true for intestate succession under the UPC.[445]

In construing class gifts, however, many courts have refused to allow persons adopted as adults to take as "children" of the adopter. For example, a wife who was adopted by her husband was held not to be one of his "issue" under the terms of his parent's trust.[446] However, in many other cases adult adoptees have been held to qualify under class gifts.[447]

---

[440] UPC § 2–119(c).

[441] Matter of Adoption of Chaney, 887 P.2d 1061 (Idaho 1995) (refusing to allow an 18 year old to be adopted because statutory procedures contemplated only adoption of minors).

[442] N.J.Stat. § 2A:22–2 (adoptee must be at least 10 years younger than adopter, but court may waive this requirement); Ohio Rev.Code § 3107.02 (adult may be adopted only if disabled, mentally retarded, or established a child-parent relationship while still a minor).

[443] E.g., Adoption of Swanson, 623 A.2d 1095 (Del.1993) (allowing adoption of 51-year-old regardless of motive). Under Uniform Adoption Act § 5–101(a)(1) (1994) one cannot adopt one's spouse. In In re Jones, 411 A.2d 910 (R.I.1980), the court refused to allow a married man to adopt his mistress. In Matter of Adoption of Robert Paul, 471 N.E.2d 424 (N.Y.1984), a gay man was not permitted to adopt his lover.

[444] Wadlington, *Adoption of Adults: A Family Law Anomaly,* 54 Cornell L.Rev. 566, 571–73 (1969); Note, 1972 Wash.U.L.Q. 253, 257–58 (1972).

[445] UPC § 2–115(1). *See also* Uniform Adoption Act § 5–102 (1994). *Compare* In re Estate of Brittin, 664 N.E.2d 687 (Ill.App.1996) (children of person adopted at age 46 inherit from adopter) *with* Kummer v. Donak, 715 S.E.2d 7 (VA 2011) (children of adult adoptee can not inherit from their mother's biological relatives).

[446] Matter of Trust Created by Belgard, 829 P.2d 457 (Colo.App.1991). *See also* Matter of Duke, 702 A.2d 1007 (N.J.Super.App.Div.1997); Cox v. Whitten, 704 S.W.2d 628 (Ark.1986) (48 year old adoptee); Cross v. Cross, 532 N.E.2d 486 (Ill.App.1988) (power to appoint to "issue" does not allow appointment to adult adoptee); BGB (German Civil Code) § 1771(1) (adoption of an adult normally has no effect on relatives of the adopter).

[447] Solomon v. Central Trust Co., 584 N.E.2d 1185 (Ohio 1992) (adoptee had lived with adopter from age 9, even though adopted as an adult); Satterfield v. Bonyhady, 446 N.W.2d 214 (Neb.1989) (adopted stepchild); In re Estate of Joslyn, 45 Cal.Rptr.2d 616 (App.1995); Hagaman v. Morgan, 886 S.W.2d 398 (Tex.App.1994) (stepdaughter); Evans v. McCoy, 436 A.2d 436 (Md.1981) (adoption of a 53 year old cousin bars a gift over "on death without issue").

A few courts have questioned the motive for the adoption of an adult, but this is hard to determine and is not even discussed in most opinions.[448]

As noted earlier, under the UPC the rules governing the construction of class gifts differ depending on whether the donor is the parent. An adult adopted by the donor would be presumptively included in a class gift to the donor's "children" or "descendants."[449] But if the class gift is to another person's "children" or "descendants," an adopted adult would be presumptively included in the class only if (1) the parent, a relative of the parent, or the spouse or surviving spouse of the parent or of a relative of the parent performed functions customarily performed by a parent before the adoptee reached the age of 18, or (2) there is clear and convincing evidence that the parent intended to perform such parental functions but was prevented from doing so, for example by death or incapacity.[450]

Because adoptions can affect succession to property, they are sometimes challenged by persons adversely affected by them. For example, when a remainder was devised to the issue of the testator's two sons, Leo and Roy, and Leo adopted his stepchildren, Roy's children challenged the adoption so they would take the entire devise. The court held that they had no standing to challenge the validity of the adoption. Moreover, a statute required any challenge to an adoption to be brought within one year of the decree and this time-period had long expired.[451] Another court, however, set aside an adoption for "fraud" when challenged by the adopter's blood-related heir, despite the running of a six-month statute of limitations, saying that "heirs of a deceased person who adopted an adult have standing to challenge the adoption."[452]

Normally an adoption in one state will be given effect in other jurisdictions.[453] A New Jersey court recognized an adoption of an adult which had taken place in California, even though it would not have been permitted in New Jersey.[454] However, a state may refuse to recognize a foreign adoption as being "repugnant to its policies,"[455] or for fraud on the court because an affected party had no notice of the adoption.[456] The law of the state of adoption does not always control its effect in another state. For example, an adoption in Louisiana was held not to bar inheritance from the birth father under

---

448 The court in In re Trust Created Under Agreement with Lane, 660 N.W.2d 421, 427 (Minn.App.2003) included an adult adoptee, saying the motivation for the adoption was irrelevant.

449 *See* UPC § 2–705(b).

450 *See* UPC § 2–705(d).

451 Hurt v. Noble, 817 P.2d 744 (Okl.App.1991). *See also* Estate of Hart, 209 Cal.Rptr. 272 (App.1984) (one year limit bars adoptee's challenge to an adoption which cut off his right to inherit).

452 In re Estate of Reid, 825 So.2d 1, 7 (Miss.2002).

453 *See Restatement (Second) of Conflict of Laws* § 290 (1971).

454 Matter of Estate of Griswold, 354 A.2d 717 (N.J.Co.Prob.Div.1976). However, the adoptee was not allowed to take as a matter of construction. In Tsilidis v. Pedakis, 132 So.2d 9 (Fla.App.1961) the court refused to recognize a Greek adoption which would not have been allowed in Florida.

455 Kupec v. Cooper, 593 So.2d 1176, 1178 (Fla.App.1992). Also, the state which granted the adoption must have had jurisdiction to do so. 1 J. Schoenblum, *Multistate and Multinational Estate Planning* § 12.05.

456 Bouton v. Labiche, 1994 *NSW LEXIS* 14288 (N.S.W) (court told that whereabouts of child's father was unknown and so he was not notified).

Mississippi law even though it would have had that effect in Louisiana.[457] Forum shopping is deterred to some extent by jurisdictional requirements. Under the Uniform Adoption Act,[458] for example, a petitioner for adoption of an adult must have lived in the state for at least 90 days before the petition is filed.

Equitable Adoption

Some children who have never been formally adopted have been treated as if they had been under the theory of equitable adoption. The usual rationale is that the child is the beneficiary of a promise made to adopt him.

> When there is a valid contract for adoption, although not consummated and given effect by adoption proceedings during the lifetime of the adopting parent, the contract may be enforced to the extent of decreeing that the child occupy the status of an adopted child in equity, entitled to rights of inheritance from the adoptive parent.[459]

Even when a child has been raised by a non-adopting parent during the child's minority, most courts will not find an equitable adoption unless there was a contract to adopt the child,[460] but one court has rejected this requirement,[461] and others have inferred such a contract from conduct.[462]

Although most states recognize equitable adoption in some contexts, courts tend to give it limited effect.[463] Perhaps because of the contract rationale, it does not usually allow the child to take *through* the adoptive parents,[464] allow the adoptive parents to take from the child,[465] cut off inheritance by the child from the child's genetic relatives or their right to inherit from the child,[466] or allow the child to take as a child of an adoptive

---

457 Estate of Jones v. Howell, 687 So.2d 1171, 1177 (Miss.1996).

458 Uniform Adoption Act § 5–104 (1994).

459 Board of Education v. Browning, 635 A.2d 373, 376–77 (Md.1994). *See also* Lankford v. Wright, 489 S.E.2d 604 (N.C.1997); *cf.* Williams v. Estate of Pender, 738 So.2d 453 (Fla.App.1999) (clear and convincing proof required).

460 O'Neal v. Wilkes, 439 S.E.2d 490 (Ga.1994) (contract made by unauthorized relative and so did not create equitable adoption); In re Estate of Castaneda, 687 S.W.2d 465 (Tex.App.1985); In re Estate of Ford, 116 Cal.Rptr.2d 858 (App.2002).

461 Wheeling Dollar Sav. & Trust Co. v. Singer, 250 S.E.2d 369, 374 (W.Va.1978). *See also* Welch v. Wilson, 516 S.E.2d 35 (W.Va.1999) (finding equitable adoption without reference to any contract).

462 *Restatement (Third) of Property (Wills and Other Donative Transfers)* § 2.5, cmt. k (1998); In re Lamfrom's Estate, 368 P.2d 318, 321 (Ariz.1962).

463 McGarvey v. State, 533 A.2d 690 (Md.1987) (equitably adopted child not a "child" entitled to favorable inheritance tax rate); In re Estate of Seader, 76 P.3d 1236 (Wyo.2003) (equitably adopted child not a descendant for purposes of the anti lapse statute).

464 Board of Education v. Browning, 635 A.2d 373 (Md.1994) (claim to inherit from adopter's sister); Matter of Estate of Jenkins, 904 P.2d 1316 (Colo.1995); Estate of Furia, 126 Cal.Rptr.2d 384 (App.2002). But in Wheeling Dollar Sav. & Trust Co. v. Singer, 250 S.E.2d 369 (W.Va.1978), the court allowed an equitably adopted child to take under the will of a relative of the adopter.

465 Reynolds v. City of Los Angeles, 222 Cal.Rptr. 517 (App.1986) (parents of equitably adopted child cannot sue for wrongful death of child); Matter of Estate of Edwards, 435 N.E.2d 1379 (Ill.App.1982); Whitchurch v. Perry, 408 A.2d 627 (Vt.1979). *Contra* Lawson v. Atwood, 536 N.E.2d 1167 (Ohio 1989).

466 Curry v. Williman, 834 S.W.2d 443 (Tex.App.1992); Gardner v. Hancock, 924 S.W.2d 857 (Mo.App.1996) (equitably adopted child can inherit from birth father).

parent under a class gift to the adoptive parent's issue.[467] Some courts refuse to give any effect to an alleged equitable adoption.[468]

While the UPC does not address equitable adoption in any extended way, in Section 2–122 the UPC preserves the opportunity to apply the doctrine in enacting states by providing that the UPC "does not affect the doctrine of equitable adoption."[469]

Stepchildren

Unadopted stepchildren (children of a spouse) are not heirs in many states. The definition of "child" in the UPC expressly excludes them.[470] But under the UPC, certain stepchildren can inherit from a decedent who dies with no surviving spouse, descendants, grandparents, or descendants of grandparents. In such a situation, the UPC provides that "the intestate estate passes by representation to the surviving descendants of the [decedent's] deceased spouse or spouses."[471] California allows a foster child or stepchild to inherit if (1) the relationship began during the child's minority "and continued throughout the joint lifetimes" of the child and parent, and (2) the foster or step parent "would have adopted the [child] but for a legal barrier."[472] This provision also allows the child's descendants to inherit "from or through a foster parent or stepparent" but gives the foster or stepparent no rights. Presumably the "legal barrier" to formal adoption which the statute contemplates is the refusal of a noncustodial parent to consent to the child's adoption. But this refusal ceases to be a barrier when the child reaches majority,[473] so if the stepchild reaches majority before the stepparent dies, the statute does not apply.[474]

A class gift to "children" or "descendants" normally does not include stepchildren or step descendants,[475] but courts sometimes infer from the circumstances that a donor intended otherwise. A will which left property to "my children" was held to include stepchildren whom the testator had raised

---

[467] In re Trust of VanderPoel, 933 A.2d 628 (N.J.Super 2007).

[468] In re Estate of Scherer, 336 P.3d 129 (Wy 2014) (Wyoming does not recognize "equitable adoption"); Matter of Estate of Robbins, 738 P.2d 458 (Kan.1987); Maui Land & Pineapple Co. v. Naiapaakai Heirs of Makeelani, 751 P.2d 1020 (Haw.1988); Lindsey v. Wilcox, 479 N.E.2d 1330 (Ind.App.1985); York v. Nunley, 610 N.E.2d 576 (Ohio App.1992) (limited to wrongful death cases).

[469] Hill v. Nakai, 311 P.3d 1016 (UT 2013) (equitable adoption superseded by statute).

[470] UPC § 1–201(5). *See also Restatement (Third) of Property (Wills and Other Donative Transfers)* § 2.5, cmt. j (1998). This view may not be the view of many step-parents. *See* Fellows et al., *Committed Partners and Inheritance: An Empirical Study*, 16 Law & Inequality 1, 73 (1998) (most persons interviewed would give an intestate share to a child born to or adopted by a partner of the decedent, when the child had lived in the decedent's household).

[471] UPC § 2–103(j). *See also* Iowa Code § 633.219(6), Md. Estates and Trusts Code § 3–104(e); Ohio Stat. § 2105.06(J); Fla.Stat. § 732.103(5) (kindred of deceased spouse).

[472] Cal.Prob.Code § 6454.

[473] Uniform Adoption Act § 5–103 (1994) (adoption of adult requires only consent of adoptee and adopter and the latter's spouse).

[474] Estate of Joseph, 949 P.2d 472 (Cal.1998). Earlier decisions were divided on this point. *Compare* In re Estate of Stevenson, 14 Cal.Rptr.2d 250 (App.1992) (stepchild can inherit) *with* Estate of Cleveland, 22 Cal.Rptr.2d 590 (App.1993) (foster child cannot inherit on similar facts).

[475] *Restatement (Third) of Property (Wills and Other Donative Transfers)* § 14.1, cmt. k (2011); National Home Life Assur. Co. v. Patterson, 746 P.2d 696 (Okl.App.1987) (insurance beneficiary designation).

from infancy and habitually referred to as her children, because she had only one natural child and the will referred to "children" in the plural.[476] Similarly, a trust for the settlor's "nephews and nieces" was construed to refer to her husband's nephews and nieces when she had none of her own.[477] And under the UPC, under certain circumstances stepchildren are included in a class gift to the stepparent's children.[478]

Planning

A lawyer planning a client's estate should find out if an adoption or an adjudication of de facto parentage has occurred in the client's family and, if so, how the client wishes to deal with it. Even if there has been no adoption or adjudication of de facto parentage yet, one may later take place.

Many standard forms used in drafting wills assume that the testator intends to include adopted children in class gifts.[479] Unless qualified, such language includes all adoptees,[480] but some suggested forms expressly exclude persons adopted as adults.[481] This exclusion can be too broad, for example if the testator wishes to include an individual raised from infancy by the adopter and adopted later when the individual has become an adult.[482]

The Uniform Statutory Will has a provision which treats an adoptee as "the child of the adopting parents and not of the natural parents" except when the adopter is a natural parent's spouse.[483] But this language is far more restrictive than the UPC. Many testators would not want an adoption to break the tie to previous parents or their relatives in several other cases, especially if the adoptee lived with previous parents or relatives for a significant period or continued to associate with them.[484]

§ 2.11 ART Children

Introduction

Throughout most of history, children were produced only by coitus. Medical science now has developed to the point that children can be born as the result of any number of assisted reproductive technologies (ART). These technologies range from the relatively simple therapy of artificial insemination

---

[476] In re Gehl's Estate, 159 N.W.2d 72 (Wis.1968). *See also* Transamerica Occidental Life Ins. Co. v. Burke, 368 S.E.2d 301 (W.Va.1988) (stepchildren included as "children" under an insurance policy when insured treated them like his own children); Matter of Estate of Neshem, 574 N.W.2d 883 (N.D.1998) (stepchild described as "our child" elsewhere in will included in devise to "issue").

[477] Clymer v. Mayo, 473 N.E.2d 1084 (Mass.1985). *See also* Estate of Anderson, 359 N.W.2d 479 (Iowa 1984); Martin v. Palmer, 1 S.W.3d 875 (Tex.App.1999) (error on summary judgment to exclude nephews and nieces of spouse in devise to "my nephews and nieces"); *Restatement (Third) of Property* (*Wills and Other Donative Transfers*) § 14.1, illus. 7 (2011) ("children of my wife and me" includes children of each spouse by previous marriages when they had no common children).

[478] *See* UPC § 2–705(c) and comment.

[479] J. Farr & J. Wright, *An Estate Planner's Handbook* 452–53 (4th ed. 1979).

[480] Diemer v. Diemer, 717 S.W.2d 160 (Tex.App.1986).

[481] Martin, *The Draftsman Views Wills for a Young Family,* 54 N.C.L.Rev. 277, 307 (1976).

[482] T. Shaffer, *The Planning and Drafting of Wills and Trusts* 172–73 (2d ed. 1979).

[483] Uniform Statutory Will Act § 1(1).

[484] Halbach, *Issues About Issue: Some Recurrent Class Gift Problems,* 48 Mo.L.Rev. 333, 348 (1983).

to highly sophisticated procedures involving the fertilization of an egg outside of the uterus and the implantation of the resulting embryo into the womb of the intended mother or the womb of another woman. For purposes of inheritance and construction of wills, medical science requires us to answer the question: who are the parents of an ART child?

In 2017, the Uniform Law Commission approved a new Uniform Parentage Act. Article 7 of that Act addresses parent-child relationships by assisted reproduction not involving a surrogate. The following sections of Article 7 are of primary importance.

Section 702 governs the parental status of a donor, meaning an individual who simply provides gametes intended for use in assisted reproduction but who is not an intended parent.[485] This section states: "A donor is not a parent of a child conceived by assisted reproduction."[486]

Section 703 provides the general rule on parentage by assisted reproduction. This section states: "An individual who consents under Section 704 to assisted reproduction by a woman with the intent to be a parent of a child conceived by the assisted reproduction is a parent of the child."[487]

Section 704 describes the means by which an individual may consent to assisted reproduction. Consent may be evidenced by a signed record,[488] by clear and convincing evidence of an express agreement entered into before conception,[489] or by evidence that

> the woman and the individual for the first two years of the child's life, including any period of temporary absence, resided together in the same household with the child and both openly held out the child as the individual's child, unless the individual dies or becomes incapacitated before the child attains two years of age or the child dies before the child attains two years of age, in which case the court may find consent . . . to parentage if a party proves by clear-and-convincing evidence that the woman and the individual intended to reside together in the same household with the child and both intended the individual would openly hold out the child as the individual's child, but the individual was prevented from carrying out that intent by death or incapacity.[490]

Section 708 addresses the parental status of a deceased individual. If the individual dies "between the transfer of a gamete or embryo and the birth of the child, the individual's death does not preclude the establishment of . . . parentage . . . if the individual otherwise would be a parent of the child under" the UPA.[491] If, instead, the individual dies "before a transfer of gametes or

[485] See the definition in Unif. Parentage Act § 102(9) (2017).

[486] Unif. Parentage Act § 702 (2017).

[487] Unif. Parentage Act § 703 (2017).

[488] *See* Unif. Parentage Act § 704(a) (2017).

[489] *See* Unif. Parentage Act § 704(b)(1) (2017).

[490] Unif. Parentage Act § 704(b)(2) (2017).

[491] Unif. Parentage Act § 708(a) (2017).

embryos," the individual is a parent only if the individual "consented in a record" to the assisted reproduction, and

> (1) either: (A) the individual consented in a record that if assisted reproduction were to occur after the death of the individual, the individual would be a parent of the child; or (B) the individual's intent to be a parent . . . is established by clear-and-convincing evidence; and
>
> (2) either: (A) the embryo is in utero not later than 36 months after the individual's death; or (B) the child is born not later than 45 months after the individual's death.[492]

Article 8 of the UPA addresses parent-child relationships by assisted reproduction involving a surrogate. The UPA distinguishes a "genetic surrogate" (meaning "a woman who is not an intended parent and who agrees to become pregnant through assisted reproduction using her own gamete") from a "gestational surrogate" (meaning "a woman who is not an intended parent and who agrees to become pregnant through assisted reproduction using gametes that are not her own").[493] Article 8 is primarily about the validity and effect of surrogacy agreements. For purposes of succession law, the crucial point is that the ART child is the child of the intended parent or parents, not of the surrogate.[494] It also should be noted that Article 8 imposes analogous time-limits as Article 7 does on posthumous parentage; if an intended parent dies before the transfer of the gamete or embryo, the individual is a parent of the child only if, among other requirements, "the transfer of a gamete or embryo occurs not later than 36 months after the death of the intended parent or birth of the child occurs not later than 45 months after the death of the intended parent."[495]

Prior to the approval of the UPA in 2017, the UPC contained extensive provisions on parent-child relationships arising by assisted reproduction. These provisions were in Sections 2–120 and 2–121. The approval of the UPA in 2017 enabled the UPC largely to incorporate the UPA by reference. The UPC was amended accordingly in 2019. Section 2–120 now states: "Except as otherwise provided under Section 2–121, parentage of an individual conceived by assisted reproduction is determined under [cite to Uniform Parentage Act (2017) Article 7 other than Section 708(b)(2)] [cite to equivalent provisions of state's parentage act][applicable state law]."[496] Section 2–121 now states: "Parentage of an individual conceived by assisted reproduction and born to a gestational or genetic surrogate is determined under [cite to Uniform Parentage Act (107) Article 8 other than Sections 810(b)(2) and 817(b)(2)][cite to equivalent provisions of state's parentage act][applicable state law]."[497] The first bracketed option is for states that have enacted the 2017 UPA. The second

---

[492] Unif. Parentage Act § 708(b) (2017).

[493] The definitions are in Unif. Parentage Act § 801(1) & (2) (2017).

[494] *See* Unif. Parentage Act §§ 809 & 815 (2017).

[495] Unif. Parentage Act § 810(b)(2) (2017) (gestational surrogacy). Essentially identical language appears in Unif. Parentage Act § 817(b)(2) (2017) (genetic surrogacy).

[496] UPC § 2–120.

[497] UPC § 2–121.

bracketed option is for states that have enacted a parentage act other than the 2017 UPA governing parent-child relationships by assisted reproduction. The third bracketed option is for states that have neither.

An alert reader will have noticed that the UPC incorporates almost all of the UPA's provisions on parentage by assisted reproduction, but not the UPA's time-limits on posthumous parentage. The reason is that the UPC has its own time-limits on posthumous parentage that are more appropriate for purposes of succession law. For example, UPC Section 2–104 provides in pertinent part:

> If the decedent dies before the start of a pregnancy by assisted reproduction resulting in the birth of an individual . . . that individual is deemed to be living at the decedent's death if . . . (A) the embryo was in utero not later than 36 months after the decedent's death; or (B) the individual was born not later than 45 months after the decedent's death.[498]

Consider the following example. Suppose that *S*, facing impending death, deposited genetic material in a medical facility. Five years later, *S*'s parent *P*, died intestate, survived only by *P*'s grandchild, *X*. Fifteen months after *P*'s death, *S*'s surviving spouse used *S*'s genetic material and the embryo was in utero. Twenty-four months after *P*'s death, *S*'s surviving spouse gave birth to a child, *C*. Assume that all of the requirements in the UPA for *S*'s parentage of *C* are met except the time-limits in UPA Section 708(b)(2). Under the UPC, *P*'s intestate estate is divided equally between *X* and *C*.[499] The reason is that, for purposes of succession law, the relevant time-period is from the death of the decedent whose estate is being administered (*P*), not from the death of the parent (*S*).

The same analysis applies in the context of a class gift in a donative document. UPC Section 2–705 provides in pertinent part:

> (1) If a particular time is during a gestational period that results in the birth of an individual . . . the individual is deemed to be living at that time.
>
> (2) If the start of a pregnancy resulting in the birth of an individual occurs after the death of the individual's parent *and the distribution date is the death of that parent*, the individual is deemed to be living on the distribution date if . . . (A) the embryo was in utero not later than 36 months after the deceased parent's death; or (2) the individual was born not later than 45 months after the deceased parent's death.[500]

These rules, not the time-limits in the UPA, are appropriate in the context of class gifts. Consider the following example. *G* created a revocable trust. The trustee was directed to pay income to *G* for life, then to pay the income to G's spouse, *S*, for life, then to distribute the trust principal by representation to *G*'s "descendants" who survive *S*. When *G* died, *G* and *S* had no children.

[498] UPC § 2–104(b)(3).

[499] *See* UPC § 2–120, comment, example 2.

[500] UPC § 2–705(e)(1) & (2).

Shortly before *G*'s death and after being diagnosed with leukemia, *G* deposited sperm at a medical facility. Assume that the parentage requirements of the 2017 UPA were satisfied other than the time-limits in UPA Section 708(b)(2). After *G*'s death, *S* decided to become inseminated with *G*'s sperm so that *S* could have *G*'s child. The child, *X*, was born five years after *G*'s death. Upon *S*'s death many years later, *X* was a grown adult. Under the UPC, *X* is entitled to receive the trust principal.[501] The reason is that, for purposes of succession and trust law, the relevant date is the date of distribution (*S*'s death), not the death of *G*.

§ 2.12 Spouses

For many purposes, it becomes necessary to determine whether a person was a decedent's "spouse." Under the UPC, the "surviving spouse" receives, among other things, a share of an intestate estate, a right to elect against a will, a family allowance, and priority in appointment as a decedent's personal representative.[502] A will or other instrument frequently designates a spouse as beneficiary.

When a person has been married twice, a reference to his or her spouse may raise a question as to *which* spouse was intended. For example, a trust made a provision for "the surviving spouse" of the settlor's son. The son was married to Amelia when the trust was created, but he later married Bette. The court held that Bette was intended, even though the settlor never knew her.[503]

A number of objections can be raised to a person's claim to be a spouse, but choice of law rules are designed to sustain the validity of a marriage if possible.[504] Also, challenges to a marriage are often not allowed after the death of one of the parties which is the time when the validity of a marriage becomes relevant in probate. For example, under the Model Marriage and Divorce Act, a claim that the purported marriage is void as incestuous[505] can be made only while both spouses are alive.[506]

Because marriage is a contract, it is subject to the standard grounds for avoiding contracts, such as fraud, duress and incapacity.[507] Some states bar

---

501 *See* UPC § 2–705, example 13.

502 UPC §§ 2–102, 2–202, 2–404, 3–203(a).

503 Dillow v. Wagner, 715 So.2d 362 (Fla.App.1998). *See also* Matter of Trust of Killian, 459 N.W.2d 497, 501 (Iowa 1990). "A wealthy man wrote his own will [leaving property] 'to my son John, his beautiful wife and wonderful children.' Of course, by the time the testator died, John had a different beautiful wife and additional wonderful children. Much litigation ensued." Feldman, *Reviewing Wills and Trusts: What Planners Should Look For*, 29 Est.Plan. 299, 301 (2002).

504 *See* Section 1.2.

505 In re Levie's Estate, 123 Cal.Rptr. 445 (App.1975) (claim by spouse rejected because marriage between first cousins is invalid); Estate of Loughmiller, 629 P.2d 156 (Kan.1981) (in similar circumstances marriage held valid under choice of law rules).

506 Model Marriage and Divorce Act § 208(c). This is not true under Alternative B, but the comment suggests disapproval of this alternative. *See also* 1 W. Blackstone, *Commentaries* 422–23 (1765) (incestuous marriages only voidable during life of the parties).

507 In re Marriage of Davis, 576 N.E.2d 972 (Ill.App.1991) (suit by spouse's guardian to avoid marriage for incapacity); Nelson v. Nelson, 878 P.2d 335 (N.M.App.1994) (same); Model Marriage and Divorce Act § 208(a)(1) (marriage can be voided for fraud or incapacity).

such challenges after one of the spouses has died,[508] but others do not. For example, one court declared a marriage invalid after the death of a spouse where there was "fraud of the grossest kind, without apparent opportunity to detect or correct the inequity during the lifetime of the deceased spouse" who had been married while she was incapacitated and terminally ill.[509] Another court reached the same conclusion despite a statute barring attacks on a marriage for incapacity after the death of a spouse: "at the alleged ceremony, [the] decedent did not respond because of his brain tumor," and this made the marriage void rather than voidable.[510]

Two challenges to a marriage are especially common and usually survive death: (1) bigamy and (2) lack of a marriage ceremony.

Bigamy

Suppose John marries Frances, abandons her without a valid divorce, and then marries Sally who is unaware of the prior marriage or who in good faith believes that John's marriage had been legally dissolved. When John dies, who is his spouse?

Sally can invoke a number of theories to support her claim.[511] A presumption that a marriage is valid may lead a court to assume that John had divorced Frances before he married Sally or that his marriage to Frances was invalid and, thus, no bar to his later marriage to Sally.[512] But the presumption of validity may be rebutted if Frances never received notice of any divorce proceedings.[513]

If Frances died or divorced John after his marriage to Sally,[514] Sally could argue that her marriage became valid when she and John continued to cohabit. This argument is particularly persuasive in jurisdictions which allow common-law marriages,[515] but some other states also allow for this result.[516]

---

508 Model Marriage and Divorce Act § 208(b); Cal. Family Code § 2211(b)(2); Matter of Estate of Fuller, 862 P.2d 1037 (Colo.App.1993) (children cannot challenge their father's marriage for incapacity after his death); Riddell v. Edwards, 76 P.3d 847 (Alaska 2003) ("voidable" marriage cannot be challenged after wife dies).

509 Matter of Estate of Lint, 957 P.2d 755 (Wash.1998). *See also* Matter of Estate of Hendrickson, 805 P.2d 20 (Kan.1991); In re Marriage of Goldberg, 27 Cal.Rptr.2d 298 (App.1994) (action to nullify marriage for fraud survives plaintiff's death).

510 In re Estate of Crockett, 728 N.E.2d 765, 766 (Ill.App.2000).

511 An additional theory, which will not be further discussed here, is that the marriage took place in a jurisdiction that recognizes polygamous marriages. Re Sehota, [1978] 3 All ER 385 (Ch.) (claim by one of two spouses, legally married under the law of India.)

512 Chandler v. Central Oil Corp., 853 P.2d 649 (Kan.1993); Matter of Fray, 721 P.2d 1054, 1058 (Wyo.1986); Matter of Estate of Allen, 738 P.2d 142, 145 (Okl.1987) (concurring opinion).

513 Daniels v. Retirement Board, 435 N.E.2d 1276 (Ill.App.1982); Succession of Choyce, 183 So.2d 457 (La.App.1966).

514 If John had obtained an *interlocutory* divorce decree from Frances before he married Sally, a final divorce entered nunc pro tunc may validate his marriage. In re Estate of Shippy, 678 P.2d 848 (Wash.App.1984).

515 Matter of Estate of Alcorn, 868 P.2d 629 (Mont.1994); Brown v. Carr, 402 S.E.2d 296 (Ga.App.1991); Estate of Smart v. Smart, 676 P.2d 1379 (Okl.App.1983).

516 Model Marriage and Divorce Act § 207(b); In re Estate of Banks, 629 N.E.2d 1223 (Ill.App.1994). For a case reaching this result even without a statute *see* Proctor on Behalf of Proctor v. Insurance Co. of North America, 714 P.2d 1156 (Utah 1986). On the other hand, in Batey v. Batey, 933 P.2d 551 (Alaska 1997), the court refused to treat the second "wife" as married

Even if Frances were still living and not divorced, Sally might have rights as a "putative spouse." The Louisiana Civil Code, borrowing from the Napoleonic Code, says that a void marriage "nevertheless produces civil effects in favor of a party who contracted it in good faith."[517] "Good faith" includes reasonable errors of law as well as mistakes of fact.[518] The "civil effects" enjoyed by a putative "spouse" include the right to inherit, sue for wrongful death, and take under an insurance policy payable by its terms to the insured's "widow."[519]

The common law did not recognize "putative" spouses,[520] but the idea is spreading. According to the Third Restatement of Property, "a putative spouse is treated as a legal spouse for purposes of intestacy," unless a statute provides otherwise.[521] California would allow Sally to inherit from John, collect worker's compensation benefits, or bring a wrongful death action as his widow.[522] The Model Marriage and Divorce Act gives putative spouses all the rights of a legal spouse.[523] The Social Security Act gives benefits to applicants who "in good faith went through a marriage ceremony" which "but for a legal impediment not known to the applicant . . . would have been a valid marriage."[524] If the lawful wife is entitled to social security benefits, the putative spouse gets none,[525] but the Model Marriage and Divorce Act authorizes courts to "apportion property . . . among the claimants as appropriate in the circumstances and in the interests of justice," and suggests that "a fair and efficient apportionment standard is likely to be the length of time each spouse cohabited with the common partner."[526] In a case in which a husband had lived

---

because she had no good faith belief in the validity of the marriage when she entered it, even though the husband later divorced his legal wife.

[517] La.Civ.Code, art. 96. Canon law is the ultimate source of the idea. *See* Blakesley, *The Putative Marriage Doctrine*, 60 Tul.L.Rev. 1, 11 (1985).

[518] Jones v. Equitable Life Assur. Soc., 173 So.2d 373 (La.App.1965).

[519] King v. Cancienne, 316 So.2d 366 (La.1975); Succession of Choyce, 183 So.2d 457 (La.App.1966).

[520] Evans, *Property Interests Arising from Quasi-Marital Relations,* 9 Cornell L.Q. 246, 247 (1924); Tatum v. Tatum, 736 P.2d 506 (Okl.1982). However, according to Blakesley, *supra* note 517, at 52, most states give some relief on some theory.

In Batey v. Batey, 933 P.2d 551 (Alaska 1997) the court refused to recognize the claim of a putative spouse who failed to meet a statutory requirement of a good faith belief in the validity of the marriage. A dissenting judge believed the husband who had lived with the claimant for 20 years, should be "estopped" to deny the marriage.

[521] *Restatement (Third) of Property (Wills and Other Donative Transfers)* § 2.2, cmt. e (1999).

[522] Cal.Fam.Code § 2251; Cal.Code Civ.Proc. § 377.60(b). A putative spouse inherits separate as well as community property (*see* Section 2.1), and can administer the decedent's estate, Estate of Leslie, 689 P.2d 133 (Cal.1984), and can claim as an omitted spouse (*see* Section 8.6), In re Estate of Sax, 263 Cal.Rptr. 190 (App.1989), but has been denied a family allowance (*see* Section 8.4), Estate of Hafner, 229 Cal.Rptr. 676 (App.1986), and benefits under a pension plan designed for persons to whom the employee "was married." Allen v. Western Conference of Teamsters Pension Trust Fund, 788 F.2d 648 (9th Cir.1986).

[523] Model Marriage and Divorce Act § 209; Estate of Whyte v. Whyte, 614 N.E.2d 372 (Ill.App.1993); Williams v. Fireman's Fund Ins. Co., 670 P.2d 453 (Colo.App.1983).

[524] 42 U.S.C.A. § 416(h)(1)(B).

[525] Martin v. Harris, 653 F.2d 428 (10th Cir.1981). This is not true if the putative spouse is treated as a spouse by state law. Blakesley, *supra* note 517, at 49–51.

[526] Model Marriage and Divorce Act § 209 & comment. *See also Restatement (Third) of Property (Wills and Other Donative Transfers)* § 2.2, cmt. e (1999); *cf.* Estate of Hafner, 229

with a putative wife for about a year, but his only substantial assets at death were pension benefits from employment during his marriage to his lawful wife, the putative wife was held to have "no equitable interest."[527]

Separation and Divorce

Some states bar even lawful spouses from rights in the other spouse's estate under certain circumstances. In Pennsylvania, a spouse who has "willfully and maliciously" deserted or "willfully neglected or refused" to support the other spouse for a year or more cannot share in the spouse's estate.[528] A Kansas statute barring workers' compensation benefits to a spouse who "for more than six months willfully deserted or abandoned the employee" was extended to cases of "mutual abandonment of the marital relationship" regardless of who instigated it.[529] Modern counterparts appear in some states to the Statute of Westminster of 1285 which barred an adulterous wife from claiming dower.[530] Under the UPC, however, a separation, absent a divorce, does not affect succession rights unless the spouse in a separation agreement waived claims to share in the other's estate.[531] Many spouses have successfully asserted claims to share in a decedent spouse's estate even though divorce proceedings between them were pending when the decedent died.[532] However, some courts have held that a surviving spouse in this situation could only claim an equitable share of the marital property as in a divorce between living spouses.[533]

A legal spouse who contracts a bigamous marriage may be barred from asserting rights under the first marriage "if, under the circumstances, it would be inequitable for him to do so."[534] However a deserted wife who had remarried

---

Cal.Rptr. 676 (App.1986) (equal division between legal and putative spouses). For a discussion of alternative methods of equitable division *see* Blakesley, *supra* note 517, at 38–40.

527 In re Marriage of Himes, 965 P.2d 1087, 1101 (Wash.1998).

528 20 Pa.C.S. § 2106(a). In Estate of Fulton, 619 A.2d 280 (Pa.Super.1992), the court barred a husband from claiming a share of the estate of a wife who had deserted him. His "acquiescence" in this—he began cohabiting with another woman by whom he had a child, was held to fall under the statute.

529 Redditt v. McDonald's Restaurant, 990 P.2d 759 (Kan.App.1999).

530 In Oliver v. Estate of Oliver, 554 N.E.2d 8 (Ind.App.1990), such a statute was used to bar a husband from claiming a devise under his wife's will.

531 UPC § 2–802, comment; In re Estate of Zimmerman, 579 N.W.2d 591, 597 (N.D.1998); In re Estate of Salathe, 703 So.2d 1167 (Fla.App.1997) (husband gets a share of wife's estate despite separation agreement); In re Estate of Carlisle, 653 N.W.2d 368 (Iowa 2002). As to waiver, *see* Section 8.9.

532 McClinton v. Sullivan, 430 S.E.2d 794 (Ga.App.1993); Hamilton v. Hamilton, 879 S.W.2d 416 (Ark.1994); Matter of Estate of Duncan, 525 N.E.2d 1212 (Ill.App.1988).

533 Carr v. Carr, 576 A.2d 872 (N.J.1990). In Estate of Burford v. Burford, 935 P.2d 943 (Colo.1997), divorce proceedings were bifurcated and a decree of dissolution was entered. The husband died before the property division was adjudicated. The court held that the wife was no longer entitled to the rights of a spouse in probate proceedings, and remanded for consideration of the property issues remaining in the dissolution proceedings. *See also* Estate of Lahey, 91 Cal.Rptr.2d 30 (App.1999) (legal separation terminates right to inherit); Magoon v. Magoon, 780 P.2d 80 (Haw.1989).

534 Kosak v. MacKechnie, 505 N.E.2d 579 (Mass.App.Ct.1987). *See also* Matter of Estate of Warner, 687 S.W.2d 686 (Mo.App.1985) (husband estopped to challenge validity of Mexican divorce so as to claim property as tenant by the entirety); Mitchell v. Diangelo, 787 A.2d 715 (Del.Ch.2001) (wife who obtained a fraudulent "quickie" divorce estopped from claiming to inherit from her

was allowed rights as her legal husband's widow when he died.[535] The UPC denies spousal status to persons who have obtained or consented to an invalid divorce, or who have remarried after such a divorce.[536] Of course, a *valid* divorce terminates a marriage without resort to the idea of estoppel. Thus, when spouses are divorced, the survivor is not the decedent's "surviving spouse.".[537] However, in a community property state the survivor may assert rights to community property of the former marriage if they were not disposed of at the time of the divorce.[538]

In some community property states, if spouses separate, their subsequent earnings cease to be community property,[539] but in others this is true only in the event of a formal separation agreement or decree.[540]

No Ceremonial Marriage

Some states do not require a ceremony for a valid marriage. Canon law, which governed the law of marriage throughout the Middle Ages, held that consent alone was necessary for marriage, until the 16th century when the Catholic Church required the presence of a priest for a valid marriage.[541] In England, no marriage ceremony was legally required until a statute of 1753.[542] Today a few U.S. states still permit non-ceremonial "common-law" marriages, but their number is declining.[543] Nevertheless, all states recognize a common-law marriage if it was valid where contracted.[544]

---

husband); In re Estate of Dalton, 647 N.E.2d 581 (Ohio Com.Pl.1995) (remarriage of deserted spouse estops her from claim against husband's estate).

[535] Matter of Estate of Kueber, 390 N.W.2d 22 (Minn.App.1986); *cf.* In re Estate of Anderson, 559 S.E.2d 222, 225 (N.C.App.2002) (estoppel cannot be invoked by a third party against a husband who remarried without divorcing his wife, the decedent).

[536] UPC § 2–802(b). Cal.Prob.Code § 78 is similar, but Estate of Anderson, 70 Cal.Rptr.2d 266 (App.1997), held that a husband who had remarried was estopped to inherit from his legal wife even though there had been no divorce. In Farrell v. Porter, 830 P.2d 299 (Utah App.1992) a wife's obtaining a divorce not knowing that her husband had died was held not to estop her under the Code. In In re Estate of Newton, 583 N.E.2d 1026 (Ohio App.1989), a wife was allowed to claim a Mexican divorce was invalid; the fact that she lived separate from her husband for 25 years thereafter did not estop her.

[537] Parada v. Parada, 999 P.2d 184, 188 (Ariz.2000). This may be true even if the divorce was granted in another jurisdiction. Petition of Brown, 505 N.Y.S.2d 334 (Surr.1986) (Korean divorce bars claim to elective share where husband resided in Korea).

[538] In re Marriage of Moore and Ferrie, 18 Cal.Rptr.2d 543, 547 (App.1993).

[539] Aetna Life Ins. Co. v. Bunt, 754 P.2d 993 (Wash.1988); Cal. Family Code § 771. *But see* In re Marriage of von der Nuell, 28 Cal.Rptr.2d 447 (App.1994) (couple not "separated" when they continued to see each other even though husband had moved out); Seizer v. Sessions, 940 P.2d 261 (Wash.1997) (desertion by one spouse does not constitute separation absent acquiescence by the other).

[540] Forrest v. Forrest, 668 P.2d 275 (Nev.1983); Keller v. Department of Revenue, 642 P.2d 284 (Or.1982) (parties who are living apart are not "separated" for this purpose if the marriage is still intact); Lynch v. Lynch, 791 P.2d 653 (Ariz.App.1990) (wife shares in $2.2 million lottery winnings while couple separated and divorce pending).

[541] Donahue, *The Case of the Man Who Fell into the Tiber: The Roman Law of Marriage at the Time of the Glossators,* 22 American J.Legal History 1, 3, 52 (1978).

[542] 1 W. Blackstone, *Commentaries* 423 (1765); 26 Geo. 2, c. 33 (1753). Even with a ceremony, a marriage may be invalid in some states today if the parties have not obtained a marriage license.

[543] Younger, *Marital Regimes,* 67 Cornell L.Rev. 45, 75 (1981).

[544] Varoz v. Estate of Shepard, 585 N.E.2d 31 (Ind.App.1992) (Indiana must recognize Colorado judgment declaring plaintiff to be decedent's common-law wife); Allen v. Storer, 600

How is a "common-law" marriage proved? Definitions vary from state to state;[545] some require "clear and convincing evidence,"[546] but in others a preponderance of the evidence suffices.[547] Some courts require a specific agreement to be married,[548] but others infer a marriage contract when a couple live together and hold themselves out as man and wife.[549] Even when a contract of marriage exists, some courts hold that cohabitation and reputation as husband and wife are also necessary.[550]

Even if the relevant law does not recognize common-law marriages, the dramatic increase in recent years of cohabitation by unmarried couples and its increasing social acceptability may bring about a change in the law comparable to the expansion of the rights of nonmarital children.[551]

To date protection for unmarried cohabitants has been limited. The Third Restatement of Property calls the right of a "domestic partner" to be treated as a spouse a "developing question," as to which it takes no position.[552]

The equal protection clause in the Constitution which has been invoked to prevent discrimination against nonmarital[553] children does not protect unmarried cohabitants. The Supreme Court upheld a limitation of Social Security benefits to widows and divorcees because:

> Congress could reasonably conclude that a woman who has never been married to the wage earner is far less likely to be dependent

---

N.E.2d 1263 (Ill.App.1992) (error to reject claim of common-law marriage as against public policy of Illinois). In In re Estate of Fajardo, 597 So.2d 362 (Fla.App.1992), the court recognized a Philippine marriage on the basis that "while common law marriages are not recognized in the Philippines, there is a presumption that 'a man and a woman deporting themselves as husband and wife have entered into a lawful contract of marriage.' "

[545] Weyrauch, *Informal and Formal Marriage,* 28 U.Chi.L.Rev. 88, 91 (1960).

[546] In re Estate of Hall, 588 N.E.2d 203 (Ohio App.1990); Mueggenborg v. Walling, 836 P.2d 112 (Okl.1992); *cf.* In re Marriage of Mosher, 612 N.E.2d 838 (Ill.App.1993) (such claims are regarded with suspicion).

[547] East v. East, 536 A.2d 1103 (D.C.App.1988); Hansen v. Hansen, 958 P.2d 931 (Utah App.1998); In re Estate of Antonopoulos, 993 P.2d 637, 648 (Kan.1999) (finding of common law marriage affirmed where supported by "substantial evidence").

[548] Matter of Peltomaa's Estate, 630 P.2d 215 (Mont.1981).

[549] Brown v. Carr, 402 S.E.2d 296 (Ga.App.1991); Mott v. Duncan Petroleum Trans., 414 N.E.2d 657 (N.Y.1980); In re Glasco, 619 S.W.2d 567, 570 (Tex.Civ.App.1981); Estate of Smart v. Smart, 676 P.2d 1379 (Okl.App.1983); In re Marriage of O'Connor-Sherrets, 760 N.W.2d 209 (Ct.App. 2008) (there must be intent and agreement to be married, continuous cohabitation, and public declaration by parties that they are husband and wife). *But see* Estate of Wires, 765 P.2d 618 (Colo.App.1988) (no marriage where couple cohabited for years but chose not to marry so W would not lose her Social Security); Wilkins v. Wilkins, 48 P.3d 644, 650 (Idaho 2002) (similar).

[550] Matter of Estate of Vandenhook, 855 P.2d 518 (Mont.1993) (no marriage if parties do not cohabit or hold selves out as spouses); Hansen v. Hansen, 958 P.2d 931 (Utah App.1998) (claim of marriage fails where "the parties' closest friends did not consider the two married").

[551] Prager, *Sharing Principles and the Future of Marital Property Law,* 25 UCLA L.Rev. 1, 19–21 (1977). *See* Section 2.9.

[552] *Restatement (Third) of Property (Wills and Other Donative Transfers)* § 2.2, cmt. g (1999). A provision for giving a surviving domestic partner a share upon intestacy was advanced by Professors Waggoner and Gallanis (*see* Gallanis, *Inheritance Rights for Domestic Partners,* 79 Tul.L.Rev. 55, 87–90 (2004) (building on a draft statute prepared by Professor Waggoner)), but such a proposal has not found its way into the UPC. Empirical evidence of popular support of limited inheritance rights by a surviving "committed partner" appears in Fellows, *Committed Partners and Inheritance: An Empirical Study,* 16 Law & Inequality 1, 38 (1998).

[553] *See* Section 2.9.

> upon the wage earner at the time of his death . . . General rules are essential if a fund of this magnitude is to be administered with a modicum of efficiency, even though such rules inevitably produce seemingly arbitrary consequences in some individual cases. . . . A process of case-by-case adjudication that would provide a 'perfect fit' in theory would increase administrative expenses to a degree that benefit levels would probably be reduced.[554]

Contract

Unmarried cohabitants sometimes assert rights under a mutual contract. Most of these cases arise while both parties are alive. "Claims arising at death are less common because, if the parties remain devoted to one another, the surviving partner is probably provided for in the decedent's will or other parts of the estate plan."[555] The argument that such contracts violate public policy because they involve illicit sex is generally rejected on the ground that sex plays only an incidental role in the relationship.[556] Occasionally cohabiting couples make an express contract concerning the arrangement,[557] but this is rather unusual. Because of the "enormous disparity of bargaining power" which often exists, any contract is more likely to take the form of the subordinate party waiving all rights.[558] Therefore, the significant issue is whether courts will infer a contract between cohabitants. Professor Waggoner favors giving them an intestate share under some circumstances but says any implied contract is "a fiction" because generally the parties do not share the same expectations about the arrangement.[559]

Some critics contend that recognizing an implied contract between cohabitants conflicts with the legislative decision to abolish common-law marriage,[560] but there are differences between the two. Historically, common-law marriages were often used to invalidate a later formal marriage as bigamous,[561] whereas courts can imply a contract which does not eliminate the rights of a lawful spouse.[562] However, a line must be drawn between casual

[554] Califano v. Boles, 443 U.S. 282, 289 (1979), quoting Califano v. Jobst, 434 U.S. 47, 53 (1977). The protection given by the Social Security Act to putative spouses is limited to those who go through a marriage ceremony. Thomas v. Sullivan, 922 F.2d 132 (2d Cir.1990).

[555] Waggoner, *With Marriage on the Decline and Cohabitation on the Rise, What about Marital Rights for Unmarried Partners?*, 41 ACTEC L.J. 49, 65 (2015).

[556] Marvin v. Marvin, 557 P.2d 106 (Cal.1976); Morone v. Morone, 413 N.E.2d 1154 (N.Y.1980); Salzman v. Bachrach, 996 P.2d 1263 (Colo.2000).

[557] Sullivan v. Rooney, 533 N.E.2d 1372 (Mass.1989) (promise to give cohabitant a half interest in a house enforced); Byrne v. Laura, 60 Cal.Rptr.2d 908 (App.1997) (oral agreement to support cohabitant for life and for her to receive defendant's property at death).

[558] Waggoner, *supra* note 555, at 67–68. As to waiver of spousal rights *see* Section 8.9.

[559] Waggoner, *supra* note 555, at 73.

[560] Clark, *The New Marriage,* 12 Will.L.J. 441, 449 (1976); In re Estate of Alexander, 445 So.2d 836 (Miss.1984).

[561] Richard III claimed the throne of England on the basis of an earlier unsolemnized marriage by his brother which made the brother's children illegitimate. P. Kendall, *Richard the Third* 257 (1955).

[562] "Enforcement of the contract between plaintiff and defendant . . . will not impair any right of" Marvin's wife. Marvin v. Marvin, 557 P.2d 106, 115 (Cal.1976). *See also* Younger, *Marital Regimes, supra* note 543, at 100; Waggoner, *supra* note 555, at 79 (under proposed statute for partners only persons not married to another qualify).

cohabitation and a stable relationship. Commentators have suggested a test based on the birth of children or the length of the relationship.[563]

Assuming a court implies a contract, what will be its terms? One theory would compensate the plaintiff for services performed during the relationship, less any benefits received,[564] but courts often reject such claims because the services were rendered without any expectation of payment.[565] A cohabitant who contributes to the acquisition of property in ways other than performing domestic services has more chance of success.[566] For example, a court rejected a claim for compensation for domestic services, like cooking and laundering. "If two persons live together in the same household concurrently rendering services to each other . . . in the absence of an *express* contract that payment is to be made in addition to the benefit derived from the arrangement . . . the law presumes such benefit to be the full recompense to each for the services rendered." But the same court allowed the claimant compensation for "non-domestic type services she performed for decedent's businesses," and for expenses she had incurred in maintaining a townhouse in which they lived.[567]

Courts sometimes infer an agreement to divide all property acquired during a relationship equally.[568] Washington courts have divided property between separating unmarried cohabitants on principles similar, though not identical, to those which control the division between spouses upon a divorce,[569] but they do not allow unmarried cohabitants to inherit as a spouse.[570]

Professor Blumberg has proposed that the law should "assimilate cohabitants to married persons" for all purposes, because "most cohabitants feel there is no difference between marriage and cohabitation,"[571] but others argue that this would defeat expectations, because cohabitants refrain from marriage because they wish to avoid its legal incidents.[572] Professor

---

563 Younger, *Marital Regimes*, *supra* note 543, at 99 ("substantial duration"); Blumberg, *Cohabitation without Marriage: A Different Perspective*, 28 UCLA L.Rev. 1125, 1143 (1981) (2 years); Wolk, *Federal Tax Consequences of Wealth Transfers between Unmarried Cohabitants*, 27 UCLA L.Rev. 1240, 1268 (1980) (3 years); Waggoner, *supra* note 555, at 79 (duration of relationship a factor in establishing "marriage-like" status, presumed when parties have cohabited for 5 years).

564 Matter of Steffes' Estate, 290 N.W.2d 697 (Wis.1980).

565 Matter of Lamb's Estate, 655 P.2d 1001 (N.M.1982); Osborne v. Boatmen's Nat. Bank, 732 S.W.2d 242 (Mo.App.1987) (disregarding claimant's "self-serving" testimony to the contrary); Neumann v. Rogstad, 757 P.2d 761 (Mont.1988) (rejecting a claim by a husband for compensation for services to his wife).

566 Adams v. Jankouskas, 452 A.2d 148 (Del.1982); Brooks v. Kunz, 637 S.W.2d 135 (Mo.App.1982); Waggoner, *supra* note 555, at 66.

567 Estate of Erickson, 722 S.W.2d 330 (Mo.App.1986). *See also* Suggs v. Norris, 364 S.E.2d 159 (N.C.App.1988).

568 Western States Construction v. Michoff, 840 P.2d 1220 (Nev.1992).

569 Connell v. Francisco, 898 P.2d 831 (Wash.1995). *See also* Shuraleff v. Donnelly, 817 P.2d 764 (Or.App.1991); Matter of Marriage of Thomas, 825 P.2d 1163 (Kan.App.1992).

570 Peffley-Warner v. Bowen, 778 P.2d 1022 (Wash.1989). In In re Marriage of Hilt, 704 P.2d 672 (Wash.App.1985), a couple began cohabiting in 1974 and married in 1978. Property which they acquired in 1974 to which both contributed was treated as community property.

571 Blumberg, *supra* note 563, at 1166–67.

572 Lauper v. Harold, 492 N.E.2d 472, 474 (Ohio App.1985); Connell v. Francisco, 898 P.2d 831, 836 (Wash.1995).

Waggoner's proposed statute would give cohabitants "a substantially smaller intestate share than a spouse would take under the UPC" and no right to an elective share or claim to act as the decedent's personal representative.[573] A legislative note at the beginning of Article II of the UPC states in pertinent part:

> References to spouse or marriage appear throughout Article II. States that recognize civil union, domestic partnerships, or similar relationships between unmarried individuals should add appropriate language whenever such references or similar references appear. States that do not recognize such relationships between unmarried individuals are urged to consider whether to recognize the spousal-type rights that partners acquired under the law of another jurisdiction in which the relationship was formed but who die domiciled in this state.[574]

In summary, the legal position of cohabitants who do not solemnize a marriage is unclear. Recognition of common-law marriage is declining, but the rights of unmarried cohabitants are increasing to some extent. As this edition goes to press, a Uniform Law Commission drafting committee is working on a proposed uniform act on the economic rights of unmarried cohabitants, but the committee's work is far from finished.

Same-Sex Marriage

In 2009 Vermont became the first state to allow same-sex marriage by legislation. Massachusetts[575] and Iowa[576] recognized same-sex marriage because of judicial decisions. Because of the general rule which recognizes marriages as valid if valid in the state where they took place[577] other states might have been forced by these developments to recognize same-sex marriages. In order to avoid this, the 1996 Defense of Marriage Act (DOMA) provided that states were not "required to give effect" to laws of other states "respecting a relationship between persons of the same sex that is treated as a marriage."[578] It also provided that for purposes of federal entitlements marriage was limited to marriages between a man and a woman. This latter provision was held to be unconstitutional in *United States v. Windsor*.[579] Then in 2015 the United States Supreme Court held in *Obergefell v. Hodges*[580] that under both the due process and equal protection clauses of the Constitution same-sex couples could not be deprived of the right to marry. In addition, the Court invalidated DOMA's provision that states need not give full faith and credit to same-sex marriages that occurred in other states.

---

[573] Waggoner, *supra* note 555, at 80.

[574] UPC Prefatory Note to Article II, Legislative Note.

[575] Goodridge v. Department of Public Health, 798 N.E.2d 941 (2003).

[576] Varnum v. Brien, 763 N.W. 862 (Iowa 2009).

[577] *See* Section 1.2.

[578] 28 U.S.C. § 1738C.

[579] 570 U.S. 744 (2013).

[580] 576 U.S. 644 (2015).

Planning

Insofar as the problems discussed in this section involve the construction of a written instrument, they can be solved by careful drafting. The Uniform Statutory Will Act defines the term "surviving spouse" of the testator to exclude a person from whom the testator was separated under a decree of separation or a written separation agreement, or if the marriage was dissolved by a divorce even if the divorce is not recognized in the state. Conversely, a person to whom the testator is not legally married because the termination of a previous marriage was not valid is deemed to be the testator's spouse.[581] In an ordinary will in which the testator's spouse is named, such a definition is unnecessary, because the named devisee may take even if designated as a spouse and the marriage is not valid. If the testator after executing the will divorces the spouse or they are separated, the testator should review the will and make appropriate changes, although, as we shall see, the law makes default provisions to cover this situation.[582]

Some wills provide for the spouse of a child or other relative of the testator. The testator may have a particular spouse in mind, but not always. If the testator wishes to include a future spouse, *e.g.*, of a currently unmarried child, the definitions in the Uniform Statutory Will Act could be expanded to cover "spouses" of persons other than the testator. But the testator may prefer more flexibility by giving the child a broad power of appointment. Powers of appointment are covered in Section 11.4.

Does a class gift—*e.g.* "to my descendants and their spouses"—include a same-sex spouse? Prior to 2019, the UPC offered no answer to this question. As revised in 2019, the answer is yes.[583]

With respect to unmarried partners, although their legal rights are quite limited under current law, a client who wishes to provide for such a partner has options available, such as designating the partner in a will or will substitute. Adoption of the partner *may* even allow the adoptee to benefit under a will of a relative of the adopter.[584] Although the marital deduction is not available to avoid transfer taxes on gifts or devises to the non-spouse partner, other tax-reducing methods can help.[585] One problem that requires careful drafting is what should happen if the relationship is later dissolved.[586]

§§ 2.13–3.0 are reserved for supplemental material.

---

[581] Unif. Statutory Will Act § 1(7).

[582] *See* Section 4.4.

[583] *See* UPC § 2–705(b) and the accompanying comment.

[584] *See* Section 2.10.

[585] Cohen, *Estate Planning Needs of Unmarried Partners*, 30 Est.Plan. 188, 190–91 (2003).

[586] *Id.*, at 189.

Chapter 3

FORMALITIES

Analysis

Sec.

3.1 History and Policy.
3.2 Signature.
3.3 Witnesses.
3.4 Holographic and Oral Wills.
3.5 Formalities for Gifts.
3.6 Trusts.
3.7 Payable-on-Death Contracts.
3.8 Joint Tenancy.
3.9 Contracts to Make Wills.

§ 3.1 History and Policy

Over the course of history wills have been subjected to an increasing number of formal requirements, but in recent years a contrary trend has emerged. In the Middle Ages, the ecclesiastical courts allowed oral wills of personal property,[1] and equity enforced oral devises of uses.[2] The Statute of Wills of 1540 authorized wills of land at law, but required that they be in writing.[3] The writing did not have to be signed by the testator; oral instructions written down before the testator died were sufficient.[4] The Statute of Frauds of 1677, however, required that devises of land be signed by the testator and subscribed by witnesses. Wills of personal property also had to be in writing, but were valid even though neither signed nor witnessed.[5] The Wills Act of 1837 imposed the same requirements for both types of property and added a few new ones, *e.g.*, that the signature must be at the "end" of the will, and that the witnesses must be present at the same time.[6] The Statute of Frauds and the 1837 Wills Act have been the models for many American statutes, but an

1 3 W. Holdsworth, *History of English Law* 537 (5th ed. 1942).

2 K. Digby, *History of the Law of Real Property* 335–36 (4th ed. 1892); Kiralfy, *A Source Book of English Law* 266–67 (1957). As to uses *see* Section 8.2, note 69 et seq.

3 Statute of Wills, 32 Hen. 8, c. 1 (1540).

4 Brown v. Sackville, 73 Eng.Rep. 152 (1552).

5 "Though written in another man's hand, and never signed by the testator . . . it hath been held a good testament of the personal estate . . . I speak not here of devises of land, which are quite of a different nature." 2 W. Blackstone, *Commentaries* 501–2 (1766).

6 Wills Act, 1 Vict. c. 26, § 9 (1837). The present English statute is substantially like the 1837 Act. D. Parry & J. Clark, *The Law of Succession* 77 (10th ed. 1996) (England).

important American development is the authorization of unwitnessed holographic wills,[7] and most recently, notarized wills.[8]

Functions of Formalities

The most obvious function of formal requirements is evidentiary. If wills did not have to be in writing, witnesses might either misremember or deliberately lie about alleged statements of intention by the testator. The weakness of oral testimony is "especially serious" in the case of wills, as distinguished from contracts, because the testator is "unavailable to testify, or to clarify or contradict other evidence" concerning the testator's intention.[9] States that allow oral wills in special situations typically require that the testator's statements be reduced to writing shortly after they are uttered in order to reduce the faulty memory problem.[10]

Even if the testator actually said (or wrote) particular words, they may not have been intended to effectuate a disposition:

> People are often careless in conversation and in informal writings. Even if the witnesses are entirely truthful and accurate, what is a court to conclude from testimony showing only that a father once stated that he wanted to give certain bonds to his son John? Does this remark indicate finality of intention to transfer, or rambling meditation about some future disposition. . . . Possibly, the remark was inadvertent, or made in jest. Or suppose that . . . a writing containing dispositive language was found among papers of the deceased at the time of his death? Does this demonstrate a deliberate transfer, or was it merely a tentative draft of some contemplated instrument, or perhaps random scribbling? . . . Dispositive effect should not be given to statements which were not intended to have that effect. The formalities of transfer therefore generally require the performance of some ceremonial.[11]

The ceremony surrounding the execution of the will—the questions asked of a testator and the testator's statements to the witnesses—also serves an important function. It causes the testator to realize the seriousness of the enterprise and allows courts to determine whether words were uttered or written with testamentary intent. Thus, when an instrument "was executed in full accord with the formalities of the statute of wills," a court had no trouble finding that its author had testamentary intent even though it was not labeled a "Will."[12] That these functions arguably are more important than the evidentiary one is evident from the fact that lost wills, under certain

---

[7] *See* Section 3.4.

[8] UPC § 2–502(a)(3)(B).

[9] Gulliver & Tilson, *Classification of Gratuitous Transfers,* 51 Yale L.J. 1, 4 (1941). This argument also applies to other cases in which a party is dead when the controversy is litigated. It has inspired "dead-man" statutes in some states. *See* Section 1.1.

[10] *See* Section 3.4, note 197 et seq.

[11] Gulliver & Tilson, *supra* note 9, at 3–4.

[12] Matter of Catanio, 703 A.2d 988 (N.J.Super.App.Div.1997). *See also* Langbein, *Substantial Compliance With the Wills Act,* 88 Harv.L.Rev. 489, 494–96 (1975).

circumstances, can be admitted to probate, even though in this situation no writing is extant.[13]

More than one ceremonial might fulfill these functions. Even an oral will might be upheld, if the testator used a certain form of words to show seriousness of intent. Statutes that allow oral wills require that the testator "call on a person to take notice or bear testimony that such is his will."[14] As Blackstone explained, "the testamentary words must be spoken with an intent to bequeath, not any loose idle discourse in his illness; for he must require the bystanders to bear witness of such his intention."[15] Such words are not likely to be used inadvertently or in jest. On the other hand, writings are often so casual in our society that some have questioned whether holographic wills (handwritten and signed by the testator but not witnessed) involve sufficient ceremonial.[16]

Liberalizing Trend

Many today believe that the traditional requirements for wills are too strict; they emanate from a time when most wills were made on the testator's deathbed and are no longer needed because wills today are usually made "in the prime of life and in the presence of attorneys."[17] Also, today when form-free will substitutes like joint tenancy are allowed to pass property at death, to impose more rigorous formalities for wills seems "incongruous and indefensible."[18] The advent of the computer and tape recorder has raised questions about the need for a writing. The Second Restatement of Property would treat "a process that produces words on a screen [or] a recording of spoken words" as equivalent to a writing,[19] but the Uniform Electronic Transactions Act, which says that an electronic record satisfies any writing requirement, expressly excludes wills from its operation.[20]

Some requirements, like the one that witnesses be disinterested,[21] probably do more harm than good; for every attempted fraud which these rules prevent, hundreds of genuine wills may be defeated by them. This hypothesis has not been empirically verified—it is hard to imagine how it could be. Nevertheless, some intelligent observers have concluded that "the remedies

---

[13] As to the probate of lost wills *see* Section 4.2, at note 73 et seq.

[14] Tex.Est.Code § 251.052; Ohio Rev.Code § 2107.60; Miss. Code § 91–5–15. This idea also goes back to the Statute of Frauds.

[15] 2 W. Blackstone, *Commentaries* 501 (1766).

[16] Gulliver & Tilson, *supra* note 9, at 14; Bird, *Sleight of Handwriting: The Holographic Will in California,* 32 Hast.L.J. 605, 610 (1981); Langbein, *supra* note 12, at 494–96.

[17] Langbein, *supra* note 12, at 497. *See* Stein & Fierstein, *The Demography of Probate Distribution,* 15 U.Balt.L.Rev. 54, 86 (1985) (average testator executes a will 5 to 7 years prior to death).

[18] Langbein, *supra* note 12, at 504; Lindgren, *Abolishing the Attestation Requirement for Wills,* 68 N.C.L.Rev. 541, 543 (1990); * * * *of Property (Donative Transfers)* § 33.1, cmt. g (1990). The formal requirements for various will substitutes are discussed in Sections 3.6–3.8; *Restatement (Third) of Property (Wills and Other Donative Transfers)* § 7.1, cmt. 3 (1998) ("joint tenancy . . . need not be executed in compliance with the statutory formalities required for a will").

[19] * * * *of Property (Donative Transfers)* § 32.1, cmt. b (1990). *But see* Matter of Reed's Estate, 672 P.2d 829 (Wyo.1983).

[20] Uniform Electronic Transactions Act §§ 3(b)(1), 7.

[21] *See* Section 3.3, note 87 et seq.

are employed more frequently against innocent parties who have accidentally transgressed the requirement than against deliberate wrongdoers."[22]

Many statutes have reduced the formal requirements for wills. The Uniform Probate Code (hereinafter referred to in the text and footnotes as "UPC"), for example, dropped the requirements that the witnesses sign in the testator's presence or that the testator sign the will at the end.[23] In fact the Code has eliminated the traditional witnessing requirement entirely and now validates wills where the testator's signature is only notarized.[24]

Many states that have not adopted the complete UPC have followed it in liberalizing the formal requirements for wills.[25] The trend away from formalism also appears in judicial opinions. Several recent cases have overruled earlier decisions that had rejected wills due to formal defects.[26]

The most recent liberalization of the law of wills that has been the approved by the Uniform Law Commission is the Uniform Electronic Wills Act in 2019. While it has only been adopted in Utah as of this writing, it would not be surprising to have it more widely adopted over the next few years. This act allows for a will to be created solely on a computer and not reduced to a writing. An electronic will is valid if signed by the testator or another acting at the testator's direction and signed in either the physical or electronic presence of the testator by at least two witnesses in the manner provided in the act. A signature typed onto the electronic document would be sufficient to satisfy the signature requirements for both the testator and the witnesses. The act does not goes as far as authorizing audio or audio-visual recordings of a will.

Substantial Compliance

In 1975, Professor John Langbein proposed a rule of "substantial compliance" whereby a noncomplying document which sufficiently approximated the prescribed formalities to fulfill their underlying purposes should be admitted to probate.[27] The UPC builds upon this concept with a more liberal "harmless error" rule. It provides that "although a document . . . was not executed [with the requisite statutory formalities] . . . the document . . . is treated as if it had been . . . if the proponent . . . establishes by clear and convincing evidence that the decedent intended the document . . . to constitute (i) the decedent's will . . . "[28] The Restatement of Property prescribes a similar

---

[22] Gulliver & Tilson, *supra* note 9, at 12.

[23] UPC § 2–502.

[24] UPC § 2–502(a)(3)(B).

[25] *E.g.*, Cal.Prob.Code § 6110.

[26] Estate of Black v. Rombotis, 641 P.2d 754 (Cal.1982); Waldrep v. Goodwin, 195 S.E.2d 432 (Ga.1973).

[27] Langbein, *supra* note 12, at 489. For earlier expressions of this idea in some judicial opinions *see* Bonfield, *Reforming the Requirements for Due Execution of Wills: Some Guidance from the Past*, 70 Tul.L.Rev. 1893, 1900–01 (1996). *See also*, In re Will of Ferree, 848 A.2d 81, 89 (N.J.Super. Ch. 2003) ("will may be admitted to probate if it substantially, if not, entirely, complies" with statute of wills); In the Matter of Will of Ranney, 589 A.2d 1339, 1345 (N.J. 1991) ("the purpose of the [substantial compliance] doctrine is to remove procedural peccadillos as a bar to probate"); Fischer v. Kinzalow, 198 S.W.3d 555 (Ark. 2004) (will admitted after trial court found substantial compliance with wills act).

[28] UPC § 2–503. Such "clear and convincing evidence" is *not* required in order to probate a formally valid will. In re Estate of Johnson, 60 P.3d 1014, 1016 (Mont. 2002). The "harmless error"

approach for courts "in the absence of a legislative corrective" such as that provided by the UPC.[29] Theoretically, the Code's harmless error rule could allow for the probate of unsigned or unattested typewritten wills although it would not appear from its language that a court could dispense with some writing.

It remains to be seen how far courts will accept this idea. One commentator has suggested that American courts have given the "substantial compliance" idea a "cool reception" despite nearly "uniform support" from academic commentators.[30] The English Court of Chancery traditionally exercised a similar dispensing power for the exercise of powers of appointment that failed to literally comply with formal requirements, but only for the benefit of a person who was "a natural object of the donee's affection."[31] Ordinarily, however, American courts do not (at least expressly) consider who the devisees are in passing upon the formal validity of wills.[32]

One court invoked the substantial compliance notion in upholding a will when the witnesses signed an affidavit attached to the will rather than the will itself.[33] But another court rejected a defectively attested will saying: "substantial compliance" does not mean noncompliance, and the fact that the testator's and witnesses' signatures may be genuine does not obviate other express statutory requirements.[34] And, most recently a court which characterized itself as committed to the substantial compliance doctrine rejected the argument that a will without any signature of the testator could be valid under that doctrine.[35] To apply the substantial compliance doctrine to a will without testator's signature would be to completely disregard the statutory direction that the will be signed.

A comment to the UPC suggests that some statutory requirements are more important than others in assessing substantial compliance. In dealing with similar legislation in Australia and Israel, courts "lightly excuse breaches of the attestation requirements, [but] they have never excused noncompliance

---

rule appears to have been adopted in a number of states, e.g., Colorado, Hawaii, Mississippi, Montana, New Jersey, South Dakota, and Utah. *See also* Section 6 of the Uniform Electronic Wills Act.

29 * * * *of Property (Donative Transfers)* § 33.1, cmt. g (1990); *Restatement (Third) of Property (Wills and Other Donative Transfers)* § 3.3 (1998). However, the English Law Reform Committee rejected a similar proposal. D. Parry & J. Clark, *The Law of Succession* 85–86 (10th ed. 1996).

30 Bonfield, *supra* note 27, at 1906.

31 * * * *of Property (Donative Transfers)* § 18.3 (1984). As to powers of appointment *see* Section 10.5.

32 Chinese courts, however, apparently do so. Foster, *The Dark Side of Trusts: Challenges to Chinese Inheritance Law*, 2 Wash.U. Global Studies L.Rev. 151, 168–69 (2003).

33 Matter of Will of Ranney, 589 A.2d 1339 (N.J.1991). As to this problem *see also* Section 3.2, note 68.

34 Kirkeby v. Covenant House, 970 P.2d 241, 247 (Or.App.1998). *See also* Burns v. Adamson, 854 S.W.2d 723, 724–5 (Ark.1993); Stevens v. Casdorph, 508 S.E.2d 610 (W.Va.1998); Estate of Burton v. Didricksen, 358 P.3d 1222 (Wash. Ct. App. 2015).

35 Brown v. Fluharty, 748 S.E.2d 809, 813 (WV 2013) (the court noted that even though the will was signed by two witnesses, there was no evidence that they signed in the presence of each other or the testator).

with the requirement that a will be in writing."[36] Professor James Lindgren suggests that so long as "attestation is going to be lightly excused," it should be legislatively abolished.[37] However, most courts have refused to treat as valid an unattested document which does not qualify as a holograph.[38] *A fortiori* they are not likely to treat an unsigned will as being in substantial compliance with the requirements.[39]

> Attestation itself, unlike the ceremonies associated with it, has been nearly as fundamental in the statutory schemes as signature and writing. . . . [T]he attestation requirement may seem to set the level of cautionary and evidentiary functions unreasonably high, *but that is the legislature's policy choice.*[40]

Advocates of probating defectively executed wills do not deny that cautionary procedures for wills are desirable, but they argue that the sanction of invalidating noncomplying wills is often inappropriate. Professor Lindgren cites a New York statute which requires witnesses to write their addresses on the will. This is a sensible requirement which helps to locate the witnesses when the will needs to be probated, but noncompliance does not invalidate the will. Along the same line Professor Lindgren contends that "supervising a will execution . . . without using witnesses could subject the lawyer or other professional to a fine" or damages, "but the will itself would not be invalidated by the drafter's ignorance or carelessness."[41]

The Second Restatement of Property recommends eight steps to follow in executing a will. This checklist goes beyond the minimum formalities prescribed by any statute. It includes a colloquy between the lawyer and the testator in which the latter states that the will reflects his or her desires.[42] Such precautionary measures are particularly desirable for wills that may have to be probated in several states, some of which have stricter requirements than others. However, many states have liberal choice of law rules that allow

---

[36] UPC § 2–503, comment. *See also Restatement (Third) of Property (Wills and Other Donative Transfers)* § 3.3, cmt. b (1998).

[37] Lindgren, *The Fall of Formalism*, 55 Alb.L.Rev. 1009, 1025 (1992). *See also* Lindgren, *Abolishing the Attestation Requirement for Wills*, 68 N.C.L.Rev. 541 (1990).

[38] *But see* In re Estate of Hall, 51 P.3d 1134 (Mont.2002) (under a statute based on the UPC 2–503). *See also*, SunMicrosystems, Inc. v. Lema, 2006 WL 278386, 4 (N.D.Cal. 2006) ("[e]ven assuming that the California doctrine of substantial compliance does apply, there is little support for the contention that . . . [an] unwitnessed signature . . . would meet the requirements of that doctrine").

[39] BankAmerica Pension Plan v. McMath, 206 F.3d 821, 831 (9th Cir.2000) (unsigned beneficiary designation "did not substantially comply with" requirements of pension plan); Allen v. Dalk, 826 So.2d 245 (Fla.2002) (court refuses to give effect to an unsigned will via a constructive trust); Malleiro v. Mori, 182 So.3d 5, 10 (Fla. Dist. Ct. 2015) (unsigned notarial will invalid).

[40] Catch v. Phillips, 86 Cal.Rptr.2d 584, 591 (App.1999) (quoting Langbein) (emphasis added). *See also* Norton v. Hinson, 989 S.W.2d 535, 537 (Ark.1999) (no substantial compliance when one of the attesting witnesses was under age).

[41] Lindgren, *The Fall of Formalism*, 55 Alb.L.Rev. 1009, 1026–7 (1992). *Compare* BGB (German Civil Code) § 2247 (will should state time and place of execution, but failure to do so does not necessarily cause invalidity). As to the malpractice liability of lawyers for defective wills, *see* Section 7.1, note 67 et seq.

[42] * * * *of Property (Donative Transfers)* § 33.1, cmt. c (1990). *Compare* the "publication" requirement imposed in some states, discussed at Section 3.3, at note 114 et seq.

wills to be probated if they were executed in compliance with the law at the time and place of execution.[43]

§ 3.2 Signature

The requirement that wills be signed was introduced by the Statute of Frauds in the 17th century. Signing is required in all states today. The signature helps to link the will with the testator. It also serves to show finality; the distinction between tentative scribblings and a consummated product is symbolized by the act of signing. This second function is more significant than the first, as shown by the fact that virtually all statutes allow someone else to sign for the testator. The UPC says that the will must be signed "by the testator or in the testator's name by some other individual."[44] When another person signs the testator's name, the signature does not show that the testator approved the will, but if the signer acted at the testator's request, the testator considered the will to be complete.

A partial signature, even initials, an "X," or a nickname[45] suffices,[46] whereas the typewritten full name of the testator does not.[47] In this situation a court refused to apply by analogy the definition of "signed" in the Uniform Commercial Code ("it may be found . . . in a . . . letterhead"), saying "much more formality has historically been required in the execution of wills than in the execution of day-to-day business and commercial papers."[48] Similarly, the federal Electronic Signatures Act which provides that "an electronic signature satisfies the law" as to contracts is inapplicable to wills.[49]

Place of Signature

Most of the controversy regarding the signature centers on its location on the will. The Statute of Frauds was silent on this point. Courts held that the testator's name at the beginning of a will ("I, John Smith . . . ") was a valid

---

[43] *See* Section 1.2, note 168, and Section 1.3, note 215.

[44] UPC § 2–502. *See also* Tex.Est.Code § 251.051; Ohio Rev.Code § 2107.03; Walker v. Walker, 929 P.2d 316 (Or.App.1996); *Restatement (Third) of Property (Wills and Other Donative Transfers)* § 3.1, cmt. n (1998); *cf.* Muhlbauer v. Muhlbauer, 686 S.W.2d 366 (Tex.App.1985) (will signed by the testator's wife was denied probate for failure to prove she signed "by his direction"); Estate of Leavey, 202 P.3d 99 (Kan. Ct. App. 2009) (initials at the lower corner of each page of will were not a signature).

For international wills (*see* Section 3.3, note 82), another person is allowed to sign for the testator only "when the testator is unable to sign" and a note of this is made on the will. UPC § 2–1003; *cf.* 20 Pa.Stat. § 2502(3).

[45] UPC § 2–502, cmt.

[46] Orozco v. Orozco, 917 S.W.2d 70 (Tex.App.1996); Trim v. Daniels, 862 S.W.2d 8 (Tex.App.1992) (will signed with initials); UPC § 2–502, Comment; cf. Succession of Squires, 640 So.2d 813 (La.App.1994) (initials constitute "substantial compliance" with signature requirement). But placing an "X" on a will is not a signature if the writer does not intend it as such. Williams v. Overton, 709 P.2d 1115 (Or.App.1985).

[47] Allen v. Dalk, 826 So.2d 245, 248 (Fla. 2002) (testator did not intend "the typewritten name below the signature line to serve as her signature"). *Compare*, Matter of Estate of Reed, 693 P.2d 1156 (Kan. 1985) (engraved name of testator on stationery is no substitute for a signature) *with* In re Estate of Williams, 66 Cal.Rptr.3d 34 (Ca. App. 6th Dist. 2007) (testator's name in blocked letters written by him satisfies statutory signature requirement).

[48] Matter of Reed's Estate, 625 P.2d 447, 452 (Kan.1981).

[49] 15 U.S.C. §§ 7001, 7003(a)(1).

signature.[50] This was a dubious rule if the signature is designed to indicate finality, so the 1837 Wills Act required wills to be signed at the end.[51] This gives rise to a host of problems if taken literally, *e.g.*, is a will signed at the end if any blank space appears between the writing and the testator's signature? In 1852 Parliament amended the Wills Act in order to prevent courts from taking the "end" requirement too literally.[52] In 1982, England eliminated the requirement altogether; now it suffices "that the testator intended by his signature to give effect to the will."[53]

Some American statutes still require that wills be signed at the end.[54] A similar requirement has been inferred from the word "subscribe" in other statutes,[55] but many do not specify where the signature must appear.[56] Differences in the governing statutes are not always determinative. Courts have upheld wills that were not literally signed "at the end" even when these words appeared in the controlling statute. When there was no room at the bottom of a will and the signature appeared in the margin, the court upheld the will on the theory that the statute meant "the logical end," not "the point which is farthest removed from the beginning."[57] On the other hand, even under the UPC the testator's putting his or her name on a will does not necessarily constitute a sufficient signature. In rejecting a will a court noted that although the Code:

> does not require the that the signature appear at the end of the instrument . . . [T]he problem of signatory intent is more difficult where, as here, the signature appears somewhere other than at the end . . . The instrument does not have sufficient indicia of completeness to support an inference that Erickson intended his name in the exordium [the beginning of the will] to be his signature. . . . The instrument as we have it before us contains nothing to indicate that Erickson had finished his writing.[58]

Other courts, however, have probated wills that they regarded as complete documents even though the testator's name did not appear at the end.[59] Such

---

[50] 2 W. Blackstone, *Commentaries* 376 (1765). The *Restatement (Third) of Property (Wills and Other Donative Transfers)*, § 3.1, cmt. k (1998) provides that the testator's signature in the exordium of the will (the clause at the beginning of the will, typically in the form, (I, [name of testator], do hereby make . . .) "should not be counted as a signature unless there is evidence that the person adopted the document as his or her will."

[51] Wills Act, 1 Vict. c. 26, § 9 (1837).

[52] Wills Act Amendment, 15 & 16 Vict. c. 24, § 1 (1852).

[53] Administration of Justice Act, 1982, § 17.

[54] 20 Pa.Stat. § 2502; Ohio Rev.Code § 2107.03; N.Y.E.P.T.L. § 3–2.1(a).

[55] Matter of Estate of Rowell, 585 So.2d 731 (Miss.1991); Matter of Reed's Estate, 625 P.2d 447 (Kan.1981); *cf.* Matter of Estate of Wedeberg, 589 N.E.2d 1000 (Ill.App.1992) (will not "signed" when testator's name appeared at the top).

[56] UPC § 2–502; Cal.Prob.Code § 6110; Tex.Est.Code § 251.051.

[57] In re Estate of Stasis, 307 A.2d 241, 244 (Pa.1973). *See also* In re Powell's Will, 395 N.Y.S.2d 334, 336 (Surr.1977) (page following the signature "constructively inserted" above it).

[58] Matter of Estate of Erickson, 806 P.2d 1186, 1189–90 (Utah 1991). *See also* Matter of Estate of Wedeberg, 589 N.E.2d 1000 (Ill.App.1992); Kidd v. Gunter, 551 S.E.2d 646 (Va.2001).

[59] In re Estate of Carroll, 548 N.E.2d 650, 653 (Ill.App.1989) (exordium) ("Any act, sign or gesture will suffice which indicates an acknowledgement of the instrument with unmistakable certainty. It is enough if the testator acknowledges to the witnesses, either by words or acts, that the instrument in question is his act and deed."); Clark v. Studenwalt, 419 S.E.2d 308, 311

a finding is easier if there is extrinsic evidence that the testator viewed the document as finished. The UPC expressly allows extrinsic evidence to be used to show testamentary intent.[60] For example, such intent may be inferred from the testator asking the witnesses to sign.[61]

Many wills contain several pages. For "international wills" the UPC says that "each sheet will be signed," but failure to do so does not invalidate the will.[62] American courts routinely uphold wills that are signed only on the last page, but careful lawyers have the testator sign (or at least initial) each page.[63] At the least, a connection between the signature and the preceding pages should be shown by numbering the pages, attaching them with staples, or run-over sentences.[64] Otherwise unsigned pages may be denied probate.[65]

Most wills contain an attestation clause at the end, designed for the witnesses' signature. If the testator signs below the attestation clause, the signature, though removed from the body of the will proper, is usually held sufficient.[66] There has also been an increasing use of self-proving will affidavits signed by both the testator and the witnesses[67] that can be used to dispense with the need to have the witnesses physically appear before the probate court to attest to the due execution of the will after the testator dies. The UPC expressly provides that a testator's signature to a self-proving will affidavit is considered to be a signature to the will for purpose of proving due execution.[68] However, there are cases to the contrary.[69]

(W.Va.1992) (exordium) (act of securing two witnesses was sufficient evidence to "demonstrate . . . [that testator] did intend the document to be his . . . [will]. Therefore, the placing of testator's name in the opening line of the document . . . constitutes testator's signature); Draper v. Pauley, 480 S.E.2d 495 (Va.1997) (testator signed before will written out).

[60] UPC § 2–502(c). *See also* Cal.Prob.Code § 6111.5.

[61] *Restatement (Third) of Property (Wills and Other Donative Transfers)* § 3.1, illus. 2 (1998).

[62] UPC § 2–1004(a); 1004(d).

[63] *Restatement (Second) of Property (Donative Transfers)* § 33.1, cmt. (1990). See also, *Restatement (Third) of Property (Wills and Other Donative Transfers)* § 3.1, cmt. *l* (1998)

[64] *Restatement (Third) of Property (Wills and Other Donative Transfers)* § 3.5, cmt. b and c (1998). *See also* Castruccio v. Estate of Castruccio, 146 A.3d 1132 (Md. Ct. Spec. App. 2016) (multi-page will valid even though testator and witnesses signed different pages if the pages were connected by "the meaning and coherence of the subject matter" or they may be "identified as one will by their internal sense.").

[65] In Matter of Estate of Rigsby, 843 P.2d 856 (Okl.App.1992), two pages were found folded together after the testator's death. Because they did not refer to each other, only the signed page was probated. *See also* In re Estate of Foreman, 984 P.2d 258 (Okl.App.1999).

[66] In re Estate of Milward, 73 P.3d 155, 159 (Kan.App.2003); Gardner v. Balboni, 588 A.2d 634 (Conn.1991); Hickox v. Wilson, 496 S.E.2d 711 (Ga.1998). *But see* Orrell v. Cochran, 695 S.W.2d 552 (Tex.1985) (signature on self-proving affidavit does not suffice).

[67] *See* § 3.3, *infra* and notes 150–154 and accompanying text. Section 8 of the Uniform Electronics Wills Act allows for an electronic will to be made self-proving.

[68] UPC § 2–504(c).

[69] In re Estate of Chastain, 401 S.W.3d 612 (Tn. 2012) (testator must sign the will, not a wholly separate document. The court noted that its holding was not to be construed as requiring a testator to sign each page of the will that is written "on several detached sheets of paper" or to sign the will at a particular location).

§ 3.3 Witnesses

Number and Competency

The Statute of Frauds required that wills be attested by "three or four credible" witnesses. The Wills Act reduced the number to two,[70] and the UPC, like most American states today, requires only two witnesses for non-holographic-non-notarized wills.[71] Professor Langbein argues that "attestation by two witnesses where the statute calls for three, or by one where it asks for two" should be deemed "substantial compliance,"[72] but most courts would not agree.[73] In any event, if a will is signed by two witnesses, it can be probated even if only one (or none) of them is available to testify when the will is offered for probate.[74] Nevertheless, it is advisable to use as witnesses to a will persons who are likely to survive the testator and be able to testify if the will is contested.

The UPC says that "any person generally competent to be a witness may act as a witness to a will."[75] This is the prevailing rule.[76] A few states have minimum age requirements for witnesses,[77] but most only demand that they can understand the significance of an oath.[78] At common law someone who had been convicted of an infamous crime could not be a witness, but the modern trend is to remove such disabilities. Even a witness who had been convicted of perjury was held to be an acceptable witness.[79]

In Europe, the profession of notary is closely regulated, and wills executed before notaries are difficult to challenge.[80] The notary may be held liable for

---

[70] Statute of Frauds, 29 Car. 2, c. 3, § 5 (1677); Wills Act, 1 Vict. c. 26, § 9 (1837).

[71] *E.g.,* UPC § 2–502; Cal.Prob.Code § 6110. Some cautious drafters nevertheless recommend using three witnesses. * * * *of Property (Donative Transfers)* § 33.1, cmt. c (1990); *Restatement (Third) of Property (Wills and Other Donative Transfers)* § 3.1, cmt. *o* (1998).

[72] Langbein, *Substantial Compliance With the Wills Act,* 88 Harv.L.Rev. 489, 521–22 (1975).

[73] Matter of Estate of Brooks, 927 P.2d 1024 (Mont.1996) (will with one witness denied probate); In re Estate of Carmedy, 642 N.E.2d 1170 (Ohio App.1994) (same); Estate of Whitlatch v. Richardson, 783 P.2d 46 (Or.App.1989). However, in Estate of McNeill, 463 A.2d 782 (Me.1983), a will signed by only two witnesses although the law required three was held effective to exercise a power of appointment. South Australian courts have probated wills attested by one witness. Langbein, *Excusing Harmless Errors in the Execution of Wills,* 87 Colum.L.Rev. 1, 22 (1987).

[74] Estate of Burdette, 97 Cal.Rptr.2d 263 (App.2000); UPC § 3–406(a); In re Will of McCauley, 565 S.E.2d 88, 92 (N.C.2002).

[75] UPC § 2–505(a).

[76] Chaffin, *Execution, Revocation, and Revalidation of Wills,* 11 Ga.L.Rev. 297, 313 (1977). *But cf.* D. Parry & J. Clark, *The Law of Succession* 82 (10th ed. 1996) (questioning whether a blind person can witness a will).

[77] Tex.Est.Code § 251.051 (witness must be over fourteen); Iowa Code § 633.280 (witness must be at least sixteen years old); Norton v. Hinson, 989 S.W.2d 535 (Ark.1999) (will witnessed by a fourteen year old is invalid under a like statute); La.Civ.Code art. 1581 (witness must have attained age sixteen); *cf.* Grossen's Estate v. Vincent, 657 P.2d 1345 (Utah 1983) (will with sixteen year old witness valid, even though after the will was executed minimum age raised to eighteen).

[78] Chaffin, *supra* note 76, at 312–13;

[79] McGarvey v. McGarvey, 405 A.2d 250 (Md.1979); Chaffin, *supra* note 76, at 314.

[80] Bonfield, *Reforming the Requirements for Due Execution of Wills,* 70 Tul.L.Rev. 1893, 1918 (1996) ("by requiring written wills to be drafted by notaries, continental Europeans essentially eliminated the will contest"). *See also* H. Brox, *Erbrecht* 66 (18th Ed. 1999) ("doubt can hardly arise as to the authenticity of a notarial will") Also, the minimum age for testators is reduced for them on the ground that the notary provides advice. *Id.*, at 59. Witnesses other than

failure to fulfill the duties imposed by law of overseeing the execution process.[81] An American counterpart to the notarial will is the "international will," based on the Washington Convention of 1973 which several countries have signed. Such a will requires two witnesses and an "authorized person," which, under the UPC means a lawyer who is "in good standing" as an active practitioner.[82] In 2008, the UPC was amended to allow for notarized wills,[83] and it is expected that this change will spur many states to adopt a similar rule. As noted in the Code's comments, allowing notarized wills to be probated should avoid invalidating a document clearly intended to be a will that was signed and notarized under circumstances where several other estate planning documents not requiring witnessing (such as a revocable trust, a durable power of attorney, and a health care power of attorney) were being signed, but where the will did not receive special witnessing treatment.[84] A court might also uphold a notarized but unwitnessed will under the harmless error rule, although it would not have to do so in states following or adopting the UPC's notarized will provision.[85]

Witnesses to ordinary wills need no special qualifications, but care in the choice of witnesses is advisable, especially if a contest is likely because the testimony of witnesses, even if not medically trained, is often relied on when the testator's capacity is litigated.[86]

Most litigation concerning the legal competency of witnesses involves witnesses who benefit from the will—the so-called "interested witness." The Statute of Frauds said that the witnesses had to be "credible." Courts in the 18th century construed this to mean disinterested. A decision that use of an interested witness rendered the entire will void "threatened to shake most of the titles in the kingdom."[87] So Parliament passed a statute which "declar[ed] void all legacies given to witnesses, thereby removing all possibility of their interest affecting their testimony."[88] Many American jurisdictions today have

---

the notary are not necessary. Liberal choice of law rules may allow a will executed in America to be effective in countries requiring wills to be notarized. H. Flick & D. Piltz, *Der Internationale Erbfall* 266–67 (1999).

[81] Brox, *supra* note 80, at 68. *Compare* the malpractice liability of lawyers in America for errors in wills which they have drafted. *See* Section 7.1, note 67. "The number of notaries in a jurisdiction is severely limited . . . [B]ecause of the near monopoly condition [in] which a notary works, he generally enjoys a high income" even though fees are limited by law. 1 J. Schoenblum, *Multistate and Multinational Estate Planning* § 5.18 (2d ed.1999).

[82] UPC §§ 2–1003, 2–1009; *cf.* (England) Administration of Justice Act, 1982 §§ 27–28 ("authorized person" can be either a solicitor or a notary public). As to the Washington Convention *see* Schoenblum, *supra* note 81, at § 15.05.

[83] UPC § 2–502(a)(3)(B).

[84] *Id.* at comments. *See* Orrell v. Cochran, 695 S.W.2d 552 (Tex. 1985) (holding notarized will invalid).

[85] In re Estate of Hall, 51 P.3d 1134 (Mont. 2002). *See* UPC § 2–502(a).

[86] *See* Section 5.1, note 27.

[87] Holdfast v. Dowsing, 93 Eng.Rep. 1164 (1747).

[88] 2 W. Blackstone, *Commentaries* 377 (1765). The question is now governed in England by a similar provision in Wills Act, 1837 § 15.

similar statutes,[89] even though the general common law bar against interested witnesses in litigation has almost disappeared.

Some interested witness statutes apply to a devisee's spouse as well as the devisee,[90] but other relatives of the devisee are not disqualified.[91] For example, a devise to a church whose minister was a subscribing witness has been upheld.[92]

Persons designated in a will as executor or trustee can act as witnesses on the theory that they earn their fee, unlike devisees who receive an unearned benefit.[93] However, when a will specified a generous compensation for an executor-witness, the compensation was denied.[94]

Many statutes also accept supernumerary (extra) witnesses, *i.e.*, if three persons witness a will which leaves property to one of them and the statute requires only two witnesses, the devise to the interested witness is valid.[95] Similarly, if a will can be probated as a holograph, a devise to a subscribing witness is valid.[96] But if the will makes devises to two witnesses, neither can take by claiming that *he* is a supernumerary witness.[97]

A witness who is both a devisee and an heir of the testator has no interest in having the will probated and so is not disqualified unless the devise exceeds what the witness would take by intestacy. In this case only the excess is void.[98]

---

89 *E.g.*, 755 ILCS § 5/4–6(a); Tex.Est.Code § 254.002; Ohio Rev.Code § 2107.15; Iowa Code § 633.281.

90 Wills Act 1 Vict. c. 26, § 15 (1837); Conn.Gen.Stat. § 45a–258; Matter of Estate of Webster, 574 N.E.2d 245 (Ill.App.1991). However, in Matter of Estate of Harrison, 738 P.2d 964 (Okl.App.1987), the court refused to invalidate a devise to a witness's spouse, because "[n]either husband nor wife has any legal interest in the separate property of the other." *See also* In re Estate of Livingston, 999 S.W.2d 874, 877 (Tex.App.1999); *Restatement (Third) of Property (Wills and Other Donative Transfers)* § 3.1, cmt. *o* (1998).

91 Succession of Harvey, 573 So.2d 1304, 1308 (La.App.1991) (granddaughter of devisee, daughter of the named devisee, can serve as witness because she was not an heir or legatee who was disqualified from witnessing testator's signing of the will); *cf.* In re Estate of Farr, 49 P.3d 415, 425 (Kan.2002) (friends of devisees, even if not disinterested, were competent witnesses). In Dorfman v. Allen, 434 N.E.2d 1012 (Mass.1982), voiding the devise to the witnesses spouse caused the property to pass to the devisee's children.

92 Estate of Tkachuk, 139 Cal.Rptr. 55 (App.1977). *See also* Conn.Stat. § 45a–258; Guidry v. Hardy, 254 So.2d 675 (La.App.1971) (witness represented devisee as attorney).

93 Wills Act, 1 Vict. c. 26, § 17 (1837); Wis.Stat. § 853.07(3)(a); *Restatement (Third) of Trusts* § 32, cmt. a (2001). However, naming the drafter of a will as executor or trustee may raise ethical and other problems. Drosos v. Drosos, 103 N.W.2d 167 (Iowa 1960). *See* Section 5.4, at note 195 et seq.

94 In re Small's Estate, 346 F.Supp. 600 (D.D.C.1972). Under Wis.Stat. § 853.07(3) the exception for designation of the witness as fiduciary is qualified by the requirement of "a provision for compensation at a rate or in an amount not greater than that usual for the services to be performed."

95 N.Y. EPTL § 3–3.2(a)(1); Wis.Stat. § 853.07(2); Brickhouse v. Brickhouse, 407 S.E.2d 607 (N.C.App.1991); *cf.* King v. Smith, 302 A.2d 144 (N.J.Super.Ch.Div.1973) (devise validated when will republished by codicil signed by disinterested witnesses).

96 Maines v. Davis, 227 So.2d 844 (Miss.1969).

97 Matter of Watts' Estate, 384 N.E.2d 589 (Ill.App.1979); In re Lubbe's Estate, 142 So.2d 130 (Fla.App.1962). *But see* Rogers v. Helmes, 432 N.E.2d 186 (Ohio 1982).

98 Wis.Stat. § 853.07(2)(b); Tex.Est.Code § 254.002; Ohio Rev.Code § 2107.15; *But see* Rosenbloom v. Kokofsky, 369 N.E.2d 1142 (Mass.1977).

Thus, the typical interested witness statute voids bequests to witness unless there is either a supernumerary witness or the bequest exceeds the witness's intestate share in which case only the excess is void. For example, if a testator bequeaths $50,000 to Harry, one of only two witnesses to the will, the bequest to Harry is void unless Harry is also the intestate's heir. If Harry is an heir, then the bequest is void only to the extent it exceeds Harry's intestate share. If Harry's intestate share is $40,000, then $10,000 of the bequest is void; if the intestate share is $60,000, then the entire $50,000 bequest is valid.

The statutory bar "looks solely to the time of execution and attestation of the will." Therefore, a subsequent disclaimer of a devise by a witness does not "transform an interested witness into a 'disinterested' one."[99] On the other hand, if a testator's will is witnessed by an interested witness but the testator later executes a codicil republishing the will using two disinterested witnesses, the bequest to the interested witness is no longer invalid as the will is deemed executed when the codicil was executed and at that time no witness was interested.[100]

Many commentators have criticized the statutes that invalidate devises to witnesses as an outmoded vestige of the old rules against interested witnesses. A similar hold-over exists today in the "dead-man" statutes that exclude testimony of interested witnesses in proceedings involving decedents on the theory that the decedent cannot rebut their testimony. "Dead man statutes are widely condemned among commentators and practitioners" on the theory that "cross examination and the other safeguards for truth are a sufficient guaranty" of truth without any such "artificial barriers."[101] Today the law allows interested witnesses to testify in ordinary litigation; indeed, they may provide the only available testimony.[102] Testators can get disinterested persons to witness a will, but most laymen and many lawyers are unaware of the rule, and so there are many "accidental" infringements of the disinterested witness rule. The deterrent effect of the rule is questionable; "in most cases of fraud or undue influence, the wrongdoer would be careful not to sign as a witness" but would find an apparently "disinterested" witness, who might be bribed without this appearing on the face of the will.[103]

The UPC breaks with tradition by providing that "the signing of a will by an interested witness does not invalidate the will or any provision of it."[104] California has replaced the bar against devises to witnesses by a rebuttable "presumption that the witness procured the devise by duress, menace, fraud,

---

99 Estate of Parsons, 163 Cal.Rptr. 70, 72 (App.1980).

100 King v. Smith, 302 A.2d 144 (N.J.Super. Ch. 1973).

101 Langbein, *supra* note 72, at 502.

102 *See, e.g.*, Matter of Succession of Calhoun, 674 So.2d 989 (La.App.1996) (devisees can testify as to the authenticity of a holographic will).

103 Chaffin, *supra* note 76, at 317. *See also* Gulliver & Tilson, *Classification of Gratuitous Transfers*, 51 Yale L.J. 1, 12–13 (1941); Uniform Prob.Code § 2–505, comment; Langbein, *supra* note 72, at 516.

104 UPC § 2–505(b).

or undue influence."[105] Of course, a careful drafter will always use disinterested witnesses, because, if the will is contested, testimony from a disinterested witness will carry more weight. A careless drafter who caused a devise to be invalid by using an interested witness has been held liable to the devisee for negligence.[106]

Must Witnesses See Testator Sign?

Normally the testator signs the will in the presence of the witnesses, but the will may be valid even if the testator signed before the witnesses appeared. The courts interpreted the Statute of Frauds to mean that "the witnesses must all see the testator sign, *or* at least acknowledge the signing, yet they may do it at different times."[107] The 1837 Wills Act, however, required that the testator's signature "shall be made or acknowledged by the Testator in the Presence of Two or more Witnesses *present at the same Time*,"[108] and some American statutes also so provide.[109] The requirement that the witnesses be present together adds to the ceremonial nature of the execution, but it is unlikely to prevent any fraud.

If a witness does not actually see the testator sign, what sort of acknowledgment must a testator make to the witness? Some cases hold that merely telling a witness "this is my will" is insufficient;[110] others require that the testator must acknowledge that the *signature* on the will is his, but the UPC requires only that the witnesses witnessed either the testator's signing "or the testator's acknowledgment of that signature *or* acknowledgment of the will" as a whole.[111] A will witnessed by someone who does not witness the testator sign or hear the testator acknowledge the will is invalid.[112] A testator's acknowledgment of her signature over the telephone does not suffice, because "an 'acknowledgment' made to a witness who cannot perceive what is being 'acknowledged' is meaningless."[113]

Publication and Request

A testator might sign a paper in the presence of witnesses without realizing that it was a will. Roman law at one time required testators to hold the tablets on which the will was written and ask the witnesses to bear witness

---

105 Cal.Prob.Code § 6112. The presumption does not apply when the witness is simply named as a fiduciary, or if there are two other disinterested subscribing witnesses.

106 Ross v. Caunters, [1980] Ch. 297.

107 2 W. Blackstone, *Commentaries* 377 (1765).

108 Wills Act, 1 Vict. c. 26, § 9 (1837).

109 Cal.Prob.Code § 6110; Va.Code § 64.1–49; Iowa Code § 633.279.

110 Matter of McKellar's Estate, 380 So.2d 1273 (Miss.1980); In re Groffman, [1969] 1 W.L.R. 733. *But see* In re Estate of Mowdy, 973 P.2d 345, 350 (Okl.Civ.App.1998).

111 UPC § 2–502(a)(3); Matter of Estate of Lindsay, 957 P.2d 818, 821 (Wash.App.1998); *cf.* Slack v. Truitt, 791 A.2d 129, 138 (Md.2002) (will valid even though one witness did not know it was a will and did not see the testator's signature). In Farrell v. McDonnell, 967 N.E.2d 637 (Mass. Ct. App. 2012), the court held that testator acknowledged her signature to the witness by being physically present when the witness signed after first reading the attestation clause to the witness.

112 Toms v. Davies, 912 P.2d 671 (Idaho App.1995); Matter of Estate of Brooks, 927 P.2d 1024 (Mont.1996); Stevens v. Casdorph, 508 S.E.2d 610 (W.Va.1998).

113 Kirkeby v. Covenant House, 970 P.2d 241, 245 (Or.App.1998). However, the governing statute in this case required the testator to acknowledge the signature "in the presence of each of the witnesses," words which do not appear in UPC § 2–502.

that they contained the will.[114] Some American statutes require a comparable "publication" in order to drive home to the testator that the document being signed is the testator's "will." In New York, the testator must "*declare* to each of the attesting witnesses that the instrument . . . is his will" and *request* them to sign[115] as witnesses. Courts interpret this requirement liberally, so long as it appears that the testator knew she was signing a will.[116] However, lawyers supervising a will execution should ask the testator whether the document "is your will, its terms have been explained to you, and [it] expresses your desires as to the disposition of your property on your death" in order to remove any doubts about testamentary intent.[117]

The law does not generally require wills to be read aloud or be orally explained to the testator,[118] although in some cases this might be desirable in order to assure the testator understood what the will said. But reading the will in the presence of witnesses would reveal its contents, and many testators want their wills kept secret until they die.[119] A lawyer who drafted a will knows what it says, but has a duty not to disclose its contents to others prior to the testator's death.[120]

Signing in Testator's Presence

The Statute of Frauds required wills of land to be "subscribed [by the witnesses] in the presence of" the testator as well as by the testator.[121] Most modern statutes impose a similar requirement for all wills.[122] Even a statute only requiring witnesses to "attest" the will has been construed to require them to sign it too.[123] The requirement is supposed "to prevent a fraud's being

---

[114] Gaius, *Institutes* 2.104. This requirement was later eliminated, *Id.* 149a, but something like it applies in modern German law to notarized wills. BGB (German Civil Code) § 2232; H. Brox, *supra* note 11, at 68 (testator's affirmative answer to notary's question suffices, but not merely nodding). *See also* French Code Civil art. 972, 976; Italian Codice Civile art 603 (testamento pubblico). UPC § 2–1003(b) requires publication for international wills.

[115] N.Y. EPTL § 3–2.1(a)(3), (4) (emphasis added). *See also*, Iowa Code § 633.279(1).

[116] Matter of Estate of Bearbower, 426 N.W.2d 392 (Iowa 1988); Faith v. Singleton, 692 S.W.2d 239 (Ark.1985); Matter of Estate of Burke, 613 P.2d 481 (Okl.App.1979). *See also*, Foster v. Foster, 377 S.W.3d 497 (Ark. Ct. App. 2010).

[117] * * * *of Property(Donative Transfers)* § 33.1, cmt. c (1990).

[118] *Restatement (Third) of Property (Wills and Other Donative Transfers)* § 3.1, cmt. h (1998). *But see* La.Civ.Code art. 1579. *Compare* In re Succession of Graham, 803 So.2d 195 (La.App.2001) (will rejected because not read to illiterate testator) with In re Succession of Lanasa, 948 So.2d 288 (La.App. 5th Cir. 2006) (will needn't have been read aloud to testator under facts of the case). *See also* BGB (German Civil Code) § 2233(2) (illiterate testator must declare will orally to notary); French Code Civil art. 978; Italian Codice Civile art. 604.

[119] In France, wills by "public act" are dictated to the notaries by the testator, but the Code also allows "mystic" wills which the testator delivers under seal to the notary (if the testator is literate). Code Civil art. 972, 976. BGB (German Civil Code) § 2232 is similar. In America when wills are probated after the testator dies, they become public documents. *See* Section 10.4, at note 104 et seq.

[120] Model Rules of Professional Conduct 1.6.

[121] 29 Car. 2, c. 3, § 5 (1676). *See also* Administration of Justice Act 1982 § 17 (witnesses must sign or acknowledge signature in testator's presence).

[122] Ohio Rev.Code § 2107.03; Md.Estates and Trusts Code § 4–102; Matter of Estate of Norton, 410 S.E.2d 484 (N.C.1991) (will rejected because the witnesses did not sign it); In re Succession of Smith, 806 So.2d 909 (La.App.2002) (will rejected because witness signed in another room). A witness' acknowledging to the testator a signature previously made elsewhere has been held sufficient. Brammer v. Taylor, 338 S.E.2d 207 (W.Va.1985).

[123] In re Estate of Lum, 699 N.E.2d 1049 (Ill.App.1998).

perpetrated . . . by substituting another for the true will,"[124] but dishonest witnesses could falsely swear they signed a spurious will in the testator's presence.[125] The rule may allow *honest* witnesses to spot a substitution by someone else for the document they saw the testator sign. However, avoiding this risk does not necessarily require witnesses to sign *in the testator's presence*.

There are two versions of the "presence" requirement—the "line of vision" test and the "conscious presence" test. The "line of vision" test contemplates that the testator "without changing his position, might have seen the will being attested" by the witnesses, even if he did not actually see it.[126] Under the "conscious presence" test, it is sufficient that a person "can sense the presence of another without seeing him or her."[127] Being in the testator's presence, however, is not sufficient to satisfy the witnessing requirement if the witness who saw the testator sign did not also sign the will as a witness.[128]

Many commentators have attacked the "presence" requirement.[129] Professor Langbein argues that it should be ignored under the substantial compliance concept, but most courts have not followed his view.[130] However, a will is not invalid simply because the testator did not see the witnesses sign because of poor vision or because of their positions if they were all in the same room.[131] Even if a witness takes the will into another room to sign, some courts uphold the will if the testator was aware that the witness was signing the will,[132] but not if the only contact between a witness and the testator was over the telephone.[133]

The UPC dispenses with the presence requirement altogether; the witnesses must sign the will, but it does not matter where they are when they sign.[134] Several courts have rejected wills that the witnesses signed only after

---

[124] Glenn v. Mann, 214 S.E.2d 911, 918 (Ga.1975). *See also* Taylor v. Estate of Taylor, 770 P.2d 163, 166 (Utah App.1989).

[125] O'Connell & Effland, *Intestate Succession and Wills,* 14 Ariz.L.Rev. 205, 240 (1972).

[126] Newton v. Palmour, 266 S.E.2d 208, 209–210 (Ga. 1980). *See also,* McCormick v. Jeffers, 637 S.E.2d 666 (Ga. 2006) (will invalidly executed when testator was in bedroom when the witnesses signed in the dining room).

[127] *Restatement (Third) of Property (Wills and Other Donative Transfers),* § 3.1, cmt. p. *See, e.g.,* Whitacre v. Crowe, 972 N.E.2d 659 (Ct. App. Ohio 2012).

[128] Smith v. Smith, 348 S.W.3d 63 (Ct. App. Ky. 2011).

[129] *Id.;* Gulliver & Tilson, *supra* note 103, at 10–11; Chaffin, *supra* note 76, at 318–22.

[130] Langbein, *supra* note 72, at 517. *But see* Flagle v. Martinelli, 360 N.E.2d 1269 (Ind.App.1977); Taylor v. Estate of Taylor, 770 P.2d 163 (Utah App.1989); In re Estate of McDevitt, 755 So.2d 1125 (Miss.App.1999).

[131] In re Lynch's Estate, 431 N.E.2d 734 (Ill.App.1982).

[132] In re Demaris' Estate, 110 P.2d 571 (Or.1941); In re Politowicz' Estate, 304 A.2d 569 (N.J.Super.App.Div.1973). *See also Restatement (Third) of Property (Wills and Other Donative Transfers)* § 3.1, cmt. p (1998).

[133] Matter of Jefferson's Will, 349 So.2d 1032 (Miss.1977); Matter of Estate of McGurrin, 743 P.2d 994 (Idaho App.1987).

[134] UPC § 2–502. However, the Code adopts the "conscious presence" test in the unusual cases where a third party signs on the testator's behalf by requiring the third party to sign "in the testator's conscious presence and by the testator's direction." UPC § 2–502(a)(2). *See also* Cal.Prob.Code § 6110. For an international will the witnesses must sign in the testator's presence. UPC § 2–1003(e).

the testator died,[135] but the present version of the Code would allow this so long as the signing occurs "within a reasonable time" after the witnesses witnessed either the testator's signing or acknowledgement.[136] Thus, in an Idaho case, the court upheld a will where the witness signed after the testator died.[137] If that proves to be the wave of the future, the requirement of the witnesses' signature arguably becomes totally meaningless.

Normally, the witnesses sign after the testator, but if they sign first, most cases uphold the will, at least if the signatures are part of a continuous transaction.[138] Most statutes do not prescribe any particular place for the witnesses' signatures.[139]

"One who signs his name to a will is not an attesting witness unless he signs with that intention and not for some other purpose."[140] However, a notary who signs a will is usually held to qualify as a witness.[141]

Attestation Clauses and Affidavits

Even though the wills acts are based on distrust of oral testimony, wills may stand or fall on the basis of such testimony, because a will which appears regular on its face may be denied probate if the witnesses testify that it was not duly executed.[142] The standard way to deal with this problem is to append an attestation clause reciting that all the formalities were duly performed. For example:

> On October 14, 1999, Mary Jones declared to us that the foregoing instrument, consisting of 14 pages including this one,[143] was her will and she requested us to act as witnesses to it. She then signed the will in our presence, all of us being present at the same

---

[135] Matter of Estate of Royal, 826 P.2d 1236 (Colo.1992); In re Estate of Saueressig, 136 P.3d 201, 205 (Cal. 2006) (witnesses' signatures must be affixed no later than the time of the testator's death). In Disciplinary Counsel v. Bandy, 690 N.E.2d 1280 (Ohio 1998) a lawyer who induced a witness to sign a will after the testator died was suspended from practice.

[136] UPC § 2–502(a)(3), comment ("no requirement that the witnesses sign before the testator's death"); *cf.* In Matter of Estate of McGrew, 906 S.W.2d 53 (Tex.App.1995) (will allowed even though two years elapsed between the testator's death and the witnesses' signing).

[137] In re Estate of Miller, 149 P.3d 840 (Idaho 2006). Accord, In re Estate of Jung, 109 P.3d 97, 101 (Ariz.App. Div. 2005).

[138] Gardner v. Balboni, 588 A.2d 634, 639 (Conn.1991); Waldrep v. Goodwin, 195 S.E.2d 432, 435 (Ga.1973); *Restatement (Third) of Property (Wills and Other Donative Transfers)* § 3.1, cmt. m (1998). *But see* Burns v. Adamson, 854 S.W.2d 723 (Ark.1993); Norwood v. Sellers, 328 S.W.3d 182 (Ark. Ct. App. 2009).

[139] Casson v. Swogell, 500 A.2d 1031 (Md.1985). *But see* 84 Okl.Stat. § 55 (witnesses must sign "at the end").

[140] In re Estate of Alfaro, 703 N.E.2d 620, 626 (Ill.App.1998).

[141] In re Friedman, 6 P.3d 473 (Nev.2000); Brickhouse v. Brickhouse, 407 S.E.2d 607 (N.C.App.1991); Matter of Estate of Zelikovitz, 923 P.2d 740 (Wyo.1996). *Contra,* Estate of Overt, 768 P.2d 378 (Okl.App.1989). *See also,* In re Estate of Gerhardt, 763 A.2d 1289 (N.J. Super Ct. App. Div. 2000).

[142] Young v. Young, 313 N.E.2d 593 (Ill.App.1974); Matter of Mackaben's Estate, 617 P.2d 765 (Ariz.App.1980); Burns v. Adamson, 854 S.W.2d 723 (Ark.1993); Pool v. Estate of Shelby, 821 P.2d 361 (Okl.1991).

[143] This helps to connect the signature page with the preceding unsigned pages. *See* Section 3.2, note 64.

time. We now subscribe our names as witnesses in her presence and in the presence of each other.[144]

Walter Witness

Francis True

John Jones

No state requires that wills contain an attestation clause, but their use is generally recommended by attorneys.[145] The clause is not conclusive; wills have been denied probate on the strength of testimony that the acts described in the attestation clause did not actually take place,[146] but many wills have been sustained on the basis of such a clause even though the witnesses' testimony contradicted it.[147] While an attestation clause creates a presumption of validity,[148] some courts have even upheld a will without an attestation clause on the basis of a general presumption of due execution despite the "inability of a witness to remember the facts surrounding the execution."[149]

If the witnesses sign an affidavit (known as a self-proving will affidavit), in many states the will can be probated without producing the witnesses in court.[150] This streamlines probate proceedings for uncontested wills. In contested cases, "compliance with signature requirements is conclusively presumed" when the witnesses have signed an affidavit.[151] While some courts have held that if the witnesses sign only an affidavit they have not witnessed "the will,"[152] others appropriately reject this hypertechnical interpretation of the wills act[153] and conclude that even though the witnesses signed the affidavit, but not the will, the will is valid.[154]

---

144 Attestation clauses often add a statement that the testator was of sound mind and not under undue influence. *See* Section 5.1, note 31.

145 "No self-respecting draftsman would omit it." Chaffin, *supra* note 7, at 310. Similar clauses appear in the California statutory will, Cal.Prob.Code § 6240, and the Uniform Statutory Will Act, App. 7; *Restatement (Third) of Property (Wills and Other Donative Transfers)* § 3.1, cmt. q (1998).

146 Matter of Estate of Johnson, 780 P.2d 692 (Okl.1989); In re Groffman, [1969] 1 W.L.R. 733; In re Birkeland's Estate, 519 P.2d 154 (Mont.1974).

147 In re Estate of Carroll, 548 N.E.2d 650 (Ill.App.1989); In re Rosen, 737 N.Y.S.2d 656 (App.Div.2002); Fitch v. Maesch, 690 N.E.2d 350 (Ind.App.1998); *Restatement (Third) of Property (Wills and Other Donative Transfers)* § 3.1, cmt. q (1999) (clause raises a "rebuttable presumption of the truth of the recitals"). *See also,* Callaway v. Callaway, 932 N.E.2d 215 (Ind. Ct. App. 2010) (attestation clause showed that will was properly witnessed).

148 In re Will of Halpern, 906 N.Y.S.2d 253 (A.D. 1st Dept. 2010); Scribner v. Gibbs, 953 N.E.2d 475 (Ind. Ct. App. 2011); In re Will of Falk, 845 N.Y.S.2d 287 (A.D. 1st Dept. 2007).

149 Slack v. Truitt, 791 A.2d 129, 138 (Md.2002).

150 UPC § 2–504 which suggests a form of affidavit suitable for this purpose.

151 *Id.* § 3–406(b).

152 Wich v. Fleming, 652 S.W.2d 353 (Tex.1983); In re Estate of Ricketts, 773 P.2d 93 (Wash.App.1989). For a critique of such cases *see* Mann, *Self-proving Affidavits and Formalism in Wills Adjudication*, 63 Wash.U.L.Q. 39 (1985).

153 In re Estate of Livingston, 999 S.W.2d 874 (Tex.App.1999) (based on amended Texas Probate Code § 59(b)); Matter of Will of Ranney, 589 A.2d 1339 (N.J.1991); Estate of Dellinger v. 1st Source Bank, 793 N.E.2d 1041 (Ind.2003); UPC § 2–504(c).

154 In re Estate of Fordonski, 678 N.W.2d 413 (Iowa 2004).

§ 3.4 Holographic and Oral Wills

Holographic wills are wholly handwritten by the testator.[155] The word "holograph" comes from two Greek words meaning "whole" and "written."[156] Because they provide a more generous sample of the testator's handwriting than just a signature, there is less risk of an undetected forgery. Therefore, no witnesses are needed for them.[157] Holographic wills came into America via the Napoleonic Code, the model for Louisiana's Civil Code.[158] The UPC allows them, as do many, but not all states.[159]

Litigation about holographic wills has centered on three points: (1) a requirement in many states that holographic wills be dated; (2) the requirement in many states that they be "entirely" in the testator's handwriting; and (3) testamentary intent.

Date

It may be necessary to ascertain the date of a will (1) to determine which of several inconsistent wills was the testator's last[160] and (2) to establish that the will was made while the testator was competent. In theory, the witnesses to an attested will can establish the date of its execution, but because holographic wills have no witnesses, many states require that they be dated.[161] Holographic wills in such states have been rejected for lack of a date even though the date was irrelevant in the particular case or was otherwise known. The UPC does not require that holographic wills be dated.[162] California has

---

[155] In re Estate of Hand, 684 A.2d 521 (N.J.Super.Ch.Div.1996), the court probated a hand-printed will as a holograph, saying that it was a susceptible to analysis as cursive writing. In Estate of Brenner, 91 Cal.Rptr.2d 149 (App.1999) the court allowed a photocopy of a handwritten will as a holograph on the ground that it would provide "the same assurance of authenticity as original ink."

Proxy signatures or a rubber stamp, though allowed in attested wills, *see* Section 4.2, note 1, are unacceptable in a holograph. Stout, *Handwritten Wills May Be Valid if Certain Requirements Are Met*, 30 Est.Plann. 174, 177 (2003).

[156] Bird, *Sleight of Handwriting: the Holographic Will in California*, 32 Hast.L.J. 605 (1981).

[157] Pennsylvania is unique in allowing unwitnessed wills which are *not* in the testator's handwriting. 20 Pa.Stat. § 2502. American law has not recognized typewritten wills as holographs, although they are so treated in some foreign countries. 1 J. Schoenblum, *Multistate and Multinational Estate Planning* § 15.02.[A] n. 6 (2d ed. 1999); *cf.* Hirsch, *Inheritance and Inconsistency*, 57 Ohio St.L.J. 1057, 1075 (1996) (if formalities are to be relaxed by allowing holographs, the law should give "effect to any signed will, whether handwritten or typed").

[158] Bird, *supra* note 156, at 606. *See also* BGB (German Civil Code) § 2247; Italian Codice Civile art. 602. Holographic wills were not generally accepted in Roman or canon law, but were allowed in the ecclesiastical courts of England (which had jurisdiction over testaments of personal property) beginning around 1600, until they were abolished by the Wills Act of 1837. Helmholz, *The Origin of Holographic Wills in English Law*, 15 J. Leg.Hist. 97 (1994).

[159] UPC § 2–502(b); Cal.Prob.Code § 6111; Tenn.Stat. § 32–1–105. *Compare* In re Estate of Salathe, 703 So.2d 1167 (Fla.App.1997) (holograph has no effect in Florida). They are now allowed in 26 states. Stout, *supra* note 155, at 174. A similar discrepancy exists in foreign countries. H. Flick & D. Piltz, *Der Internationale Erbfall* 268 (1999) (holographic will allowed in Quebec but not in England).

[160] As to the revocation of earlier wills by a later one *see* Section 4.1.

[161] *E.g.*, La.Civ.Code art. 1575; French Code Civil art. 970; Italian Codice Civile art 602.

[162] UPC § 2–502; Matter of Grobman's Estate, 635 P.2d 231 (Colo.App.1981).

also eliminated the requirement but provides that an undated will may be invalid if the date is important and cannot be established by other proof.[163]

If a statute requires that a will be dated, abbreviations are allowed but the date must be complete; the month and year are not enough.[164] Extrinsic evidence can be used to clarify an ambiguous date like "10/4/84"—does this mean October 4 or April 10?[165] A will is not invalidated by the fact that the date is incorrect.[166]

Printed Matter

Often a testator writes out a holographic will on a sheet of paper containing printed or typewritten words, such as preprinted stationery or a will form with filled-in blanks. Sometimes words are added to a holograph by another person with the testator's consent. Even if the governing statute requires that the will be "entirely" in the testator's handwriting, some cases have overlooked other writing on the page as "surplusage."[167] Some courts, however, reject the will if the testator intended the nonholographic material to be part of it.[168]

It is hard to see what purpose is served by rejecting such wills. A substantial sample of the testator's handwriting provides a safeguard against forgery whether or not other words appear on the same page. Moreover, the printed-form wills involved in many of these cases serve the channeling policy especially well,[169] because, unlike handwritten letters, use of a will form shows testamentary intent.

The UPC only requires that the "signature and material portions" of the will be in the testator's handwriting.[170] This may permit a printed will form

---

[163] Cal.Prob.Code § 6111(b). BGB (German Civil Code) § 2247(5) is similar. In Matter of Estate of Harrington, 850 P.2d 158 (Colo.App.1993), an undated holograph was rejected where an attested will revoked all prior wills, but in In re Estate of Kleinman, 970 P.2d 1286 (Utah 1998), the case was remanded to determine whether the holograph was made subsequent to the will.

[164] Bird, *supra* note 156, at 612; Succession of Holloway, 531 So.2d 431 (La.1988). *But see* In re Estate of Wells, 497 N.W.2d 683 (Neb.1993) (accepting a will dated "Oct. 85"). The validity of a will dated "Monday 26, 1978" has been held to depend on whether Monday fell on the 26th in more than one month during that year. *Compare* Estate of Rudolph, 169 Cal.Rptr. 126 (App.1980) *with* Succession of Raiford, 404 So.2d 251 (La.1981).

[165] Succession of Bacot, 502 So.2d 1118 (La.App.1987); *Restatement (Third) of Property (Wills and Other Donative Transfers)* § 3.2, cmt. e (1998).

[166] Bird, *supra* note 156, at 612.

[167] Charleston Nat. Bank v. Thru the Bible, 507 S.E.2d 708, 712 (W.Va.1998); Succession of Burke, 365 So.2d 858 (La.App.1978); *Restatement (Third) of Property (Wills and Other Donative Transfers)* 3.2, cmt. b (1998). The California Supreme Court has adopted this view, overruling earlier cases which rejected wills containing insubstantial printed matter. Estate of Black, 641 P.2d 754 (Cal.1982). *See also* H. Brox, *Erbrecht* 75–76 (18th ed. 1999) (handwritten portions alone are valid unless this would be contrary to testator's intent).

[168] Bird, *supra* note 156, at 621; Matter of Estate of Dobson, 708 P.2d 422 (Wyo.1985); Matter of Estate of Krueger, 529 N.W.2d 151 (N.D.1995) (will invalid when the name of one devisee was not in testator's handwriting).; Berry v. Trible, 626 S.E.2d 440 (Va. 2006) (holographic will with handwritten language on typewritten draft is not valid).

[169] *See* Gulliver & Tilson, *Classification of Gratuitous Transfers*, 51 Yale L. J. 1, 4 (1941).

[170] UPC § 2–502(b). The older version of the UPC used the words "signature and the material provisions." *See also* Cal.Prob.Code § 6111. The change was "to leave no doubt about the validity of a will in which immaterial parts of a dispositive provision—such as 'I give, devise and bequeath'—are not in the testator's handwriting." *Restatement (Third) of Property (Wills and Other Donative Transfers)* § 3.2, cmt. b (1998).

with handwritten insertions to be probated as a holograph.[171] But, even then, if the handwritten provisions of the document are unintelligible as a disposition of property without considering the pre-printed words which must be ignored, the handwritten portions will not suffice to be a valid holograph.[172]

Testamentary Intent

The absence of attestation in holographic wills may create doubt whether a writing was intended to be a will. A paper need not be labeled "will" in order to have that effect,[173] but use of the word "will" helps to show testamentary intent.[174] Some courts regard language of present gift as inconsistent with an intent to make a *will*. For example a hand-written paper which said "I would like Maymie Gilson to have all my personal effects, furniture, and belongings" was denied probate.[175]

A writing which appears to be notes for a contemplated will rather than a will itself, such as a paper listing "names and addresses of those to be named in my will," and a letter to the testator's attorney listing "changes to be made in my will" have been denied probate.[176] In the law of contracts, the fact that the parties contemplated executing a formal contract in the future is evidence that they did not yet regard the deal as complete, but this is not conclusive.[177] So too in the law of wills. For example, a court probated a letter written by the testator to her attorney with instructions regarding the disposal of her estate. She died before a formal will was drafted. The court said that "even if decedent intended that the attorney draft a formal will for execution, she would also have intended that her property pass in accordance with her recorded wishes if she died before execution of a formal will."[178] However, that decision was overturned because there was no evidence that the decedent intended the

---

[171] In re Estate of Gonzalez, 855 A.2d 1146 (Me. 2004); Matter of Estate of Muder, 765 P.2d 997 (Ariz.1988); In re Estate of Cunningham, 487 A.2d 777 (N.J.Super.Law Div.1984); *Restatement (Third) of Property (Wills and Other Donative Transfers)* § 3.2, illus. 4 (1998).

[172] In re Will of Ferree, 848 A.2d 81 (N.J. Super. Ch. 2003).

[173] In re Estate of Kleinman, 970 P.2d 1286, 1289 (Utah 1998). *See also* Succession of Bacot, 502 So.2d 1118 (La.App.1987) ("I leave all to Danny"); Seifert v. Sanders, 358 S.E.2d 775 (W.Va.1987); Matter of Estate of Ramirez, 869 P.2d 263 (Mont.1994) (letter); Trim v. Daniels, 862 S.W.2d 8 (Tex.App.1992) (back of greeting card).

[174] In re Estate of Lambert, 143 P.3d 426 (Mont. 2006); In re Estate of Ehrlich, 47 A.3d 12 (N.J. Super. Ct. App. 2012); Thomas v. Copenhaver, 365 S.E.2d 760 (Va.1988); *cf.* Matter of Rogers, 895 S.W.2d 375 (Tex.App.1994) ("codicil"). "A professional draftsman invariably inserts words describing the document as a will or as a codicil at the beginning" in order to make the maker's intent clear. D. Parry & J. Clark, *The Law of Succession* 2 (10th ed. 1996).

[175] Dahlgren v. First National Bank, 580 P.2d 478 (Nev.1978). *See also* In re Gasparovich's Estate, 487 P.2d 1148 (Mont.1971); In re Estate of Ike, 454 N.E.2d 577 (Ohio App.1982); *cf.* Ayala v. Martinez, 883 S.W.2d 270 (Tex.App.1994) (probating a paper saying property "shall be divided").

[176] Matter of Will of Smith, 528 A.2d 918 (N.J.1987) (instructions to attorney for preparing will); Estate of Southworth, 59 Cal.Rptr.2d 272 (App.1996) (statement that "I am not taking action now but my intent is to leave my estate to . . . "); Matter of Estate of Erickson, 806 P.2d 1186 (Utah 1991) (note cards intended as a draft). *See also* In re Probate of Will and Codicil of Macool, 3 A.3d 1258 (N.J. Super. Ct. App. Div. 2010) (rough draft of document was not intended to be the last will).

[177] * * * *of Contracts* § 27 (1981).

[178] Will of Smith, 507 A.2d 748, 750 (N.J.Super.App.Div.1986), rev'd 528 A.2d 918 (N.J. 1987). *See also* Maines v. Davis, 227 So.2d 844 (Miss.1969) (probating a paper which said "I will finish this later" on the ground that the signature showed finality); In re Estate of Kuralt, 15 P.3d 931 (Mont.2000).

letter itself to be her will.[179] This position reflects the view that the testator must have intended the document she signed to be her will. *Caveat to lawyers:* English solicitors who unreasonably delayed preparing a new will for a client were held liable to the intended devisees when the testator died before it was executed.[180]

Courts are divided on the question of whether testamentary intent can be proved through extrinsic evidence. Many courts, and the UPC,[181] allow proof by extrinsic evidence. For example, a letter was probated as a will in part because it was consistent with the decedent's oral statement that "he was leaving everything to" the person named in the letter.[182] But some courts insist that testamentary intent must be evidenced by the document itself without resort to extrinsic evidence.[183]

The place where the paper is found may be relevant to the validity of a holographic will. A North Carolina statute requires that holographic wills be found among the testator's "valuable papers" or in the custody of someone with whom it was "deposited by him . . . for safekeeping."[184]

The fact that the testator once executed an attested will arguably shows that an unattested paper was not written with testamentary intent,[185] but courts have found testamentary intent in a holograph written after an attested will.[186]

A question as to testamentary intent arises when a will is expressed in conditional terms. For example, a holographic will started with the words "If anything should happen to me on this trip to Rapid City." The testator survived the trip but died later. The court probated the will, in part because of extrinsic evidence.

> The trial court properly concluded that the reference to her Rapid City trip was not a condition but . . . represented the motivation behind the drafting of the will. . . . [The testator's] comments to

---

[179] Matter of Will of Smith, 528 A.2d 918 (N.J. 1987).

[180] White v. Jones, [1995] 2 W.L.R. 187 (H.L.) For American authorities on this question *see* J. Price, *Contemporary Estate Planning* § 1.6.3 (2d ed. 2000).

[181] UPC § 2–502(c). *See also* Cal.Prob.Code § 6111.5; *Restatement (Third) of Property (Wills and Other Donative Transfers)* § 3.2, cmt. c (1998). Therefore, the question of testamentary intent in a formally valid holograph cannot be decided by summary judgment. In re Estate of Johnson, 60 P.3d 1014 (Mont.2002); In re Estate of Smith, 651 N.W.2d 153 (Mich.App.2002).

[182] Blake's Estate v. Benza, 587 P.2d 271, 274 (Ariz.App.1978). *See also* Will of Smith, 507 A.2d 748 (N.J.Super.App.Div.1986); In re Estate of Kuralt, 15 P.3d 931 (Mont.2000); Parry & Clark, *supra* note 174, at 2. *But see* Estate of Southworth, 59 Cal.Rptr.2d 272, 277 (App.1996) (extrinsic evidence overcome by language of instrument showing no present intent to devise). For the converse case of extrinsic evidence used to show *lack* of testamentary intent in an apparent will *see* Section 7.1, note 12 et seq.

[183] Mallory v. Mallory, 862 S.W.2d 879 (Ky.1993); Wolfe v. Wolfe, 448 S.E.2d 408 (Va.1994).

[184] N.C.Gen.Stat. § 31–3.4(a)(3). The statute has been rather liberally interpreted. *E.g.*, Matter of Will of Church, 466 S.E.2d 297 (N.C.App.1996) (will found in pocketbook); Stephens v. McPherson, 362 S.E.2d 826 (N.C.App.1987) (jewelry box).

[185] *Cf.* Williams v. Springfield Marine Bank, 475 N.E.2d 1122 (Ill.App.1985) (fact that decedent executed a will on the same day indicates another paper was written without testamentary intent).

[186] Blake's Estate v. Benza, 587 P.2d 271 (Ariz.App.1978); In re Laurin's Estate, 424 A.2d 1290 (Pa.1981).

several disinterested individuals, before and after she made the will, and in the days immediately preceding her death, demonstrate that [she] intended her writing to be an effective disposition of her property.[187]

Testamentary intent is usually treated as a question of fact, so a trial court's findings are affirmed if not clearly erroneous,[188] but some courts call it a question of law if the issue turns on the writing alone.[189]

Are Holographic Wills Desirable?

Some commentators argue that holographic wills provide no protection against undue influence because of the lack of witnesses.[190] This objection seems weak, because undue influence is usually exerted at times prior to and leading up to the will's execution and outside of the presence of any witnesses.[191] A stronger argument against holographic wills is the difficulty of determining testamentary intent. "If a document has been executed with the usual testamentary formalities, a court can be reasonably certain that . . . it was seriously intended as a will," whereas a holograph leaves this question "open to doubt."[192] However, just because witnesses attested to the signing of a document does not preclude claims that there was no testamentary intent.[193] In any event, cases of holographs where testamentary intent is doubtful are probably rarer than those in which a testator's clear intent to devise property was frustrated because the jurisdiction did not recognize holographs.

Few lawyers would advise clients to write a holographic will, because the costs of attestation are slight compared with reducing the risk of contest by using witnesses. Because holographic wills are primarily the work of lay persons, they are often ill-considered and ambiguous.[194] Indeed, some make so little sense that they fail for "uncertainty" even though they were duly executed.[195] However, because "the public plainly insists on being permitted to use a 'do-it-yourself' approach to will making, as is permitted in virtually every other enterprise," to deny effect to holographic wills appears "to force the public to rely on lawyers," and hurts the image of the profession.[196]

---

187 In re Estate of Martin, 635 N.W.2d 473, 477 (S.D.2001); Cason v. Taylor, 51 S.W.3d 397, 407 (Tex.App.2001).

188 In re Teubert's Estate, 298 S.E.2d 456 (W.Va.1982); Blake's Estate v. Benza, 587 P.2d 271 (Ariz.App.1978); Matter of Martinez' Estate, 664 P.2d 1007 (N.M.App.1983).

189 McDonald v. Petty, 559 S.W.2d 1 (Ark.1977); Wolfe v. Wolfe, 448 S.E.2d 408 (Va.1994).

190 Gulliver & Tilson, *supra* note 169, at 14. *See also* Bird, *supra* note 156, at 609.

191 As to undue influence *see* Section 5.3. The subscribing witnesses are more likely to play an important role when the testator's capacity is at issue. *See* Section 5.1, note 28 et seq.

192 Estate of Brown, 218 Cal.Rptr. 108, 110 (App.1985).

193 In re Estate of Ike, 454 N.E.2d 577 (Ohio App.1982); Williams v. Springfield Marine Bank, 475 N.E.2d 1122 (Ill.App.1985); *cf.* Currier Gallery of Art v. Packard, 504 N.E.2d 368 (Mass.App.1987).

194 Chaffin, *Execution, Revocation, and Revalidation of Wills,* 11 Ga.L.Rev. 297, 325 (1977); Bird, *supra* note 156 at 631–32.

195 In re Estate of Casselman, 364 N.W.2d 27 (Neb.1985); Matter of Estate of Lewis, 738 P.2d 617 (Utah 1987).

196 Wellman, *Arkansas and the Uniform Probate Code,* 2 U.Ark.L.R.L.J. 1, 15 (1979). *See also* In re Teubert's Estate, 298 S.E.2d 456, 460 (W.Va.1982). Holographic wills provide a

Oral Wills

Roman law relaxed the formal requirements for soldiers' wills. Perhaps this was regarded as a reward for military service, or perhaps it was thought that soldiers engaged in active service could not easily comply with the formalities prescribed for ordinary wills.[197] In order to prevent casual statements from being mistaken for wills, informal soldiers' wills were recognized only when the testator used formal language "calling together men to witness his will."[198]

These ideas have found their way into modern law. The Statute of Frauds of 1676 permitted nuncupative (oral) wills when made "in the time of the last sickness of the deceased" when there might be no time to draft and execute a written will. The testator must "bid the persons present . . . bear witness that such was his will."[199] Blackstone says that the requisites for oral wills were "so numerous" that they had "fallen into disuse."[200] The Wills Act of 1837 abolished them but with a proviso that "any Soldier being in actual Military Service, or any Mariner or Seaman being at Sea, may dispose of his Personal Estate" as permitted under prior law.[201]

Many states have provisions for oral wills modeled on the Statute of Frauds.[202] Others have special rules for wills of soldiers and seamen.[203] Neither provision is often used. Courts require the evidence of an oral will to be of the "clearest and most convincing character,"[204] and insist on strict compliance with the statutory limitations.[205] The UPC does not allow oral wills, and its liberal choice-of-law rule only applies to "written" wills.[206]

§ 3.5 Formalities for Gifts

In order to make a valid gift, there must be intent, delivery, and acceptance.[207] The intent must be to "make an irrevocable present transfer of ownership; if the intention is to make a testamentary disposition effective only

---

particularly useful alternative in the civil law because of the rather elaborate requirements for notarial wills. Schoenblum, *supra* note 157 § 15.02[B].

[197] Gaius, *Institutes* 2.109 attributes the rule to the "ignorance" (*imperitiam*) of soldiers. *Compare* the *Nottestament* and *See testament,* oral wills allowed by BGB (German Civil Code) §§ 2250–2 based on inaccessibility of a notary. *See also* French Code Civil art 984.

[198] Justinian, *Institutes* 2.11.1.

[199] Statute of Frauds, 29 Car. 2, c. 3, § 19 (1676).

[200] W. Blackstone, *Commentaries* 501 (1765).

[201] Wills Act, 1 Vict. c. 26, §§ 9, 11 (1837). This privilege was extended to realty in 1918. Parry & Clark, *supra* note 174, at 87.

[202] Ohio Rev.Code § 2107.60; Miss.Code § 91–5–15.

[203] Va.Code § 64.1–53; N.Y. EPTL 3–2.2(b) (holographic and nuncupative will allowed if testator in armed services); Md. Estates and Trusts Code § 4–103.

[204] Dabney v. Thomas, 596 S.W.2d 561, 563 (Tex.Civ.App.1980).

[205] In re McClellan's Estate, 189 A. 315 (Pa.1937) (will rejected because no explicit request to witnesses); Kay v. Sandler, 718 S.W.2d 872 (Tex.App.1986) (will rejected because only one witness heard it).

[206] UPC § 2–506. In the Matter of Buffi's Estate, 564 P.2d 150 (Idaho 1977) the court held that the "common law doctrine of nuncupative wills" was irrelevant when testator died after the adoption of the UPC, even though the will was made prior thereto. *Compare* Section 1.3, note 215.

[207] Typically acceptance is presumed and is rarely discussed in cases. *See* Wasniewski v. Quick and Reilly, Inc., 940 A.2d 811 (Conn. App. 2008).

at death, the gift is invalid unless made by will."[208] The history of the formal requirements for gifts is marked by four stages.

History

(1) First Stage: Delivery of Property Required

Originally, an effective transfer required delivery of the property. A writing purporting to transfer property was ineffective if the transferor stayed in possession of the property, even if the writing was delivered.[209] An actual change of possession was necessary because the legal system depended on juries who originally were expected to know the facts before they were impaneled. If a donor stayed in possession of land, the jury from the neighborhood would not know that the gift had taken place.[210] Secondly, delivery prevented frauds on third parties. A transferor who stayed in possession of property he had given to A might later sell it to *B* who would be unaware of the prior transfer. The delivery requirement protected *B* by invalidating the prior transfer.[211]

(2) Second Stage: Deed as a Substitute for Delivery

In the 15th century, it was suggested that goods could be transferred without delivery; the buyer in a sale of personal property got title even before the goods were delivered, unlike land which would "not pass without livery."[212] A few years later a deed of gift was said to be effective even though the donor kept possession of the goods.[213] These ideas were extended to land in the equity courts. When land was sold, the buyer acquired the use (*i.e.,* became the equitable owner) by virtue of the bargain and sale.[214] Later, any deed supported by "consideration" was sufficient to transfer the use. Consideration was broadly defined to include affection for a relative or spouse.[215] A leading case of the 16th century involved a man who executed a deed purporting to transfer land after he died to his brother. The deed was challenged by an argument which restated the traditional rationale for requiring delivery of land:

> Livery of seisin was first invented [i.e., required] as an act of notoriety, whereby people might have knowledge of estates, and be more able to try them, if they should be empanelled on a jury; and by the like reason when a use shall pass, there ought to be . . . a public

---

[208] Gruen v. Gruen, 496 N.E.2d 869, 872 (N.Y. 1986).

[209] Bracton's Note Book pl. 1971 (1221); 2 H. Bracton, *De Legibus* 124 (1968); T. Littleton *Tenures* § 59; R. Glanville, *Tractatus de Legibus* 69–70 (G. Hall ed. 1965).

[210] *See* Section 8.2, note 65.

[211] 3 W. Holdsworth, *A History of English Law* 224 (5th ed. 1942). Glanville makes this point in discussing mortgages: if the mortgagor remained in possession, the same property could be mortgaged to several creditors. Glanville, *supra* note 209, at 123–24.

[212] Shipton v. Dog, reprinted in A. Kiralfy, *A Source Book of English Law* 192, 196 (1957) (Fortescue, C.J.).

[213] Mich. 7 Edw. 4, f. 20, pl. 21 (1467).

[214] Y.B.Hil. 21 Hen. 7, f. 18, pl. 30 (1505). *See also* Y.B.Pas. 27 Hen. 8, pl. 22, at f. 8 (1535); C. St. Germain, *Doctor & Student* (1530), 91 Sel.Soc. 225.

[215] R. Brooke, *Abridgement,* Feffements and Uses ¶ 54 (1573). Consideration is defined more narrowly today. * * * *of Contracts* § 17 (1971).

and notorious consideration . . . which may cause the country to have knowledge of the use for the better trial thereof. . . . And if uses might be so easily raised by covenants . . . where no act or thing apparent is done whereof the country may have notice it would . . . make it very difficult for the people to know who were the owners of lands.[216]

Nevertheless the court upheld the deed, saying that the donor's affection for his brother was "sufficient consideration" to support it.[217] By the 16th century, juries could be informed by evidence produced in court (like deeds), so the reasons for the law's earlier insistence on delivery of land had disappeared. The expansion of literacy also contributed to the law's recognition of deeds as a means of conveyance. "In the days when few people could write, . . . livery of seisin was necessary to transfer ownership of real estate. As people became more literate and writing became more common, deeds and written instruments . . . were found to be more reliable in demonstrating the intentions of the parties."[218]

(3) Third Stage: Writing Required for All Transfers of Land

By the end of the 16th century land could be transferred *either* by a written deed[219] *or* by livery of seisin without any writing. The Statute of Frauds of 1676, however, provided that livery of seisin of land conveyed only an estate at will absent a signed writing.[220] As a result, a writing, which was originally ineffective to transfer land, became the *only* effective method to transfer land.

Nearly all American states today have legislation based on the Statute of Frauds requiring a signed writing in order to convey land.[221] The writing must be signed by the donor or an authorized agent; in many states an agent must be authorized in writing to act.[222] Because of the signature requirement, when the grantee named in a deed added the name of his wife to the deed, she acquired no interest because he "never signed the altered instrument."[223]

The writing must identify the subject matter of the gift; delivery of a signed blank deed does not suffice unless the donor gives the recipient authority in writing to fill in the blanks.[224] "The owner of an interest in land

---

[216] Sharington v. Strotton, 75 Eng.Rep. 454, 460 (1565).

[217] *Id. at* 471.

[218] Lewis v. Burke, 226 N.E.2d 332, 335 (Ind.1967).

[219] Callard v. Callard, 72 Eng.Rep. 841 (1594) (a use is "not raised upon natural affection without a deed").

[220] Statute of Frauds, 29 Car. 2, c. 3, § 1 (1676). Similar provisions now appear in Law of Property Act, 1925, § 53.

[221] *Restatement (Third) of Property (Wills and Other Donative Transfers)* § 6.3 (2001). *Compare* the requirement in Italian Codice Civile art. 782–3 of a "public act" for gifts except for goods of "modest value" for which delivery suffices.

[222] This does not apply when the signer acted as an "amanuensis" whom the donor requested to sign for him. Estate of Stephens, 122 Cal.Rptr.2d 358, 49 P.3d 1093 (Cal.2002). *Compare* the proxy signature allowed for wills. Section 3.2, note 44.

[223] Julian v. Petersen, 966 P.2d 878, 881 (Utah App.1998).

[224] McCormick v. Brevig, 980 P.2d 603, 616 (Mont.1999); * * * *of Property (Donative Transfers)* § 32.1 (1990); *Restatement (Third) of Property (Wills and Other Donative Transfers)* § 6.3, cmt. c (1998).

cannot make an effective donative transfer thereof . . . by delivering the land to the donee," although short term oral leases are commonly permitted.[225]

These statutes do not apply to personal property, for which an oral statement of donative intent plus delivery still suffices.[226] This leads to some technical distinctions, *e.g.*, the owner of a condominium has an interest in land that must be transferred in writing, whereas an interest in a cooperative apartment is represented by shares of stock that can be transferred orally.[227]

Despite the Statute of Frauds, courts give effect to oral gifts of land if the donee has taken possession of the land and made valuable improvements.[228] Taking possession is not enough unless substantial improvements have been made,[229] and even then, a court may simply require reimbursement for the value of the improvements.[230] An oral gift of land accompanied by delivery of the donor's title deeds has also been held to create a constructive trust for the intended donee.[231]

The Statute of Frauds does not bar giving effect to a lost deed if there is clear proof that it once existed.[232]

(4) Modern Recording Statutes

American states today all have recording statutes under which unrecorded deeds are ineffective against later bona fide purchasers from the transferor,[233] but are still valid between the parties. Thus, when a mother deeded land to her daughter but the deed was not recorded, the daughter had a good title to the land as against the mother's estate.[234] Third-party transferees, are usually not protected if they had notice of the prior unrecorded conveyance.[235] For example, if Andrea conveyed Blackacre to Emily who did not record that deed and later Andrea conveyed Blackacre to Alice who had actual notice of the Andrea to Emily conveyance, Alice would not be protected by the recording act because she would not be a bona fide purchaser.

---

[225] *Id.* § 31.4, cmt. a.

[226] However, many contracts for the *sale* of personal property are also subject to a writing requirement. *See* Uniform Commercial Code § 2–201; * * * *of Contracts* §§ 110, 125 et seq. (1979).

[227] * * * *of Property (Donative Transfers)* § 31.4, cmt. f. An interest under a contract to sell land must be transferred by a writing. *Restatement (Third) of Property (Wills and Other Donative Transfers)* § 6.3, cmt. n (1998). First Nat. Bank v. Gregory, 468 N.E.2d 739 (Ohio App.1983).

[228] Montoya v. New Mexico Human Services Dept., 771 P.2d 196 (N.M.App.1989); Ortmeyer v. Bruemmer, 680 S.W.2d 384 (Mo.App.1984); Conradi v. Perkins, 941 P.2d 1083 (Or.App.1997); * * * *of Contracts* § 129, illus. 4 (1979).

[229] Isaak v. Smith, 848 P.2d 1014 (Mont.1993) *overruled on other grounds.*

[230] * * * *of Property, Donative Transfers,* § 31.4, cmt. e (1990); *cf.* * * * *of Contracts* § 129, illus. 5 (1979).

[231] Sen v. Headley, [1991] 2 All E.R. 636 (C.A.) *Compare* Section 7.4, note 197 et seq.

[232] * * * *of Contracts,* § 137 (1979); Cole v. Guy, 539 N.E.2d 436 (Ill.App.1989).

[233] The statutes differ as to who exactly is protected against an unrecorded deed. *Compare* Cal.Civ.Code § 1214 (unrecorded deed is "void as against any subsequent purchaser or mortgagee . . . in good faith and for a valuable consideration, whose conveyance is first duly recorded, and as against any judgment affecting the title") *with* Siegel Mobile Home Group, Inc. v. Bowen, 757 P.2d 1250 (Idaho App.1988) (unrecorded deed effective against judgment creditor of donor).

[234] Estate of Blettell v. Snider, 834 P.2d 505 (Or.App.1992). *See also* In re Estate of Ault, 609 N.E.2d 568 (Ohio App.1992).

[235] Calhoun v. Higgins, 797 P.2d 404 (Or.App.1990).

Most statutes require special formalities in addition to the transferor's signature in order to have a deed recorded. For example, in California, deeds must be "duly acknowledged" before a notary public or other official before they can be recorded.[236]

Even though personal property is generally not covered by a recording system, if a transfer is "not accompanied by an immediate delivery" it may be deemed "fraudulent and void" against subsequent bona fide purchasers from the transferor.[237]

Personal Property: Tangibles

A person can give away tangible personal property either by delivering the property itself[238] or by executing and delivering a written instrument of gift. A father's letter to his son saying "I wish to give you as a present the oil painting by Gustave Klimt which now hangs in the New York living room" was effective even though the son did not take possession of the painting.[239] Conversely, an oral gift of a horse was held to be effective despite a statute requiring "a written and acknowledged bill of sale from the vendor to the purchaser" for "the transfer of livestock." This did not mean "that the transfer of livestock without a bill of sale is ineffective."[240] In the case of a gift of an automobile, good practice would suggest that the car be registered in the name of the donee, but courts have sustained gifts of automobiles without that registration in light of other facts and circumstances.[241]

Intangibles

Most wealth today is in the form of intangible property, like bank accounts, shares of stock, and bonds. Gifts of such property can be made in several ways. If they are represented by a paper like a stock certificate or a passbook, the donor may simply deliver it to the donee.[242] Even for a registered

---

[236] Cal.Civ.Code §§ 1170, 1181; *cf.* Galloway v. Cinello, 423 S.E.2d 875 (W.Va.1992) (notary should be disinterested, but use of an interested notary does not invalidate the instrument). As to when a notary's certificate precludes proof by handwriting experts that a deed was forged *see* Cazares v. Cosby, 65 P.3d 1184 (Utah 2003).

[237] Cal.Civ.Code § 3440. *See also* * * * *of Property (Donative Transfers)* § 34.9 (1990); Center v. Hampton Affiliates, Inc., 488 N.E.2d 828 (N.Y.1985) (based on Uniform Commercial Code § 8–302).

[238] Barham v. Jones, 647 P.2d 397 (N.M.1982) (diamond rings); In re Estate of Kremer, 546 N.E.2d 1047 (Ill.App.1989) (cameras); * * * *of Property (Donative Transfers)* § 31.1 (1990); *Restatement (Third) of Property (Wills and Other Donative Transfers)* § 6.2 (1998).

[239] Gruen v. Gruen, 496 N.E.2d 869 (N.Y.1986). *See also* Carey v. Jackson, 603 P.2d 868 (Wyo.1979); Lewis v. Burke, 226 N.E.2d 332 (Ind.1967); * * * *of Contracts* § 332, cmt. b (1981); * * * *of Property (Donative Transfers)* §§ 32.1–.2 (1990); *Restatement (Third) of Property (Wills and Other Donative Transfers)* § 6.2, cmt. t (1998) Such a letter may not constitute a gift, however, if the language is more equivocal as to the donor's intent. In re Estate of McIntosh, 773 A.2d 649, 654 (N.H.2001) (letter saying that writer was "willing to divide" property with his siblings was not a gift). *See also* Bader v. Digney, 864 N.Y.S. 2d 606 (N.Y. App. Div. 4th Dept. 2008) (intent element requires irrevocable present transfer of ownership but donor may retain possession of the property for his or her life).

[240] Milner v. Colonial Trust Co., 6 P.3d 329, 332 (Ariz.App.2000). *Compare* In re Estate of Brownlee, 654 N.W.2d 206, 213–14 (S.D.2002) (no effective gift when a bill of sale of the property was not delivered *and* the donee's testimony that a gift was made "lacked credibility").

[241] Howard v. Himmelrick, 2004 WL 1405293 (Ohio App. Dist 10 2004).

[242] Mashburn v. Wright, 420 S.E.2d 379 (Ga.App.1992) (certificate of deposit); Rogers v. Rogers, 319 A.2d 119 (Md.1974) (stock); In re Watson's Estate, 256 N.E.2d 113 (Ill.App.1970)

security, delivery of the certificate by the registered owner without endorsement is effective.[243] However, intangibles usually represent a claim against an institution, and the rules of the institution may require that it receive notice of the transfer. When a woman delivered United States Savings Bonds to her granddaughters, the gift of the bonds was ineffective because she failed to have the bonds reissued in the donees' names as required by Treasury regulations notwithstanding her clear intent to make a gift.[244] Some courts hold that such rules are only designed to protect the institution from liability if it pays without notice of the transfer and should not control who owns the claim,[245] just as an unrecorded deed is effective when no third-party's rights are involved. However, failure to notify the institution of the transfer may cast doubt on donative intent. Thus, a court found that a father who had delivered certificates of deposit to his son did not intend a gift because he had not "bothered to change the names of the payees."[246]

Second, a donor may give intangibles by having them re-registered in the donee's name, even if nothing is delivered, and even if the donee is not aware of the gift. The Uniform Transfers to Minors Act expressly sanctions this method for making gifts.[247]

Third, the donor may sign a writing indicating an intent to give stock (for example), and deliver the writing but retain the stock certificate. Thus, a donor of stock was held to have made an effective gift of it by executing and delivering a deed of gift to the donees; the donor's "failure to deliver the stock certificates did not invalidate her gift."[248]

Signing and delivering a check to a payee-donee, on the other hand, is not effective as an assignment of the drawer-donor's funds in the bank.[249] A payee-donee who cashes the check before the drawer-donor dies can keep the money,

---

(passbook); * * * *of Contracts* § 332, illus. 4 (1981); * * * *of Property (Donative Transfers)* § 31.1, cmt. a (1990); *Restatement (Third) of Property (Wills and Other Donative Transfers)* § 6.2, cmt. h (1998); D. Parry & J. Clark, *The Law of Succession* 26 (10th ed. 1996) (England).

[243] Estate of Novetzke, TC Memo 1988–268; Andrews v. Troy Bank & Trust Co., 529 So.2d 987 (Ala.1988).

[244] United States v. Chandler, 410 U.S. 257 (1973); DeSantis v. Prothero, 916 A.2d 671 (Pa. Super. 2007). *See also* In re Estate of Kenworthy, 377 P.3d 1281 (Okla. Civ. App. 2015).

[245] * * * *of Property (Donative Transfers)* § 31.1, cmt. b (1990); *Restatement (Third) of Property (Wills and Other Donative Transfers)* § 6.2, cmt. h (1998) Abney v. Western Res. Mut. Cas. Co., 602 N.E.2d 348 (Ohio App.1991) (gift of boat effective despite failure to get new title certificate).

[246] Gibson v. Boling, 622 S.W.2d 180 (Ark.1981). *See also* Cassiday v. Cassiday, 259 A.2d 299 (Md.1969) (failure to change designated beneficiary on insurance policy); Matter of Estate of Casey, 507 N.E.2d 962 (Ill.App.1987) (failure to endorse CD indicates no gift intended); *Restatement (Third) of Property (Wills and Other Donative Transfers)* § 6.2, cmt. i (2001).

[247] Uniform Transfers to Minors Act § 9(a)(1)(i). *See also* Barham v. Jones, 647 P.2d 397, 399 (N.M.1982) (trailer registered in donee's name); Parson v. United States, 460 F.2d 228 (5th Cir.1972) (policy taken out in another's name); Matter of Carroll, 474 N.Y.S.2d 340 (App.Div.1984). Sending stock to the issuer for reissue in the donee's name may be treated as delivery to the donee's agent. Kintzinger v. Millin, 117 N.W.2d 68 (Iowa 1962).

[248] Estate of Davenport v. C.I.R., 184 F.3d 1176, 1186 (10th Cir.1999). *See also* * * * *of Property (Donative Transfers)* § 32.2, illus. 4 (1990); *Restatement (Third) of Property (Wills and Other Donative Transfers)* § 6.2 cmt. p (1998); Tanner v. Robinson, 411 So.2d 240, 242 (Fla.App.1982). *But see* * * * *of Contracts* § 332, illus. 3 (1981).

[249] Uniform Commercial Code § 3–408; Hieber v. Uptown Nat. Bank, 557 N.E.2d 408 (Ill.App.1990); Parry & Clark, *supra* note 242 at 27.

but if the drawer-donor dies before the check is paid, the check most likely is not enforceable against the drawer-donor's estate.[250] The bank is protected if it pays the check without knowledge of the drawer-donor's death, but in this case the drawer-donor's estate can recover the funds from the payee-donee.[251]

Delivery

The idea of delivery often recurs in the law of gifts. A person can convey land while retaining possession of it,[252] but the donor must deliver a *deed* to the donee; an undelivered deed is ineffective.[253] Delivery of a deed to the grantee creates a rebuttable presumption that the grantor intended to make a present transfer.[254] If a deed has been recorded, delivery is presumed,[255] but the presumption can be rebutted.[256] Similarly a gift of personal property may fail for lack of delivery. Thus, when the owner of a company endorsed stock certificates intending to give them to certain employees but died before they were delivered, the stock was held to belong to his estate.[257] Parents who had loaned money to their daughter later told her that the loan was forgiven. The intent to forgive the indebtedness was supported by an entry in the mother's diary. However, this entry was insufficient to bar a suit by the father's executor to collect the debt from the daughter, because a release of the debt obligation required "the delivery of some instrument in writing."[258]

Delivery performs a function like the formal requirements for wills.[259] It "forces upon the most thoughtless and hasty donor at least a moment's consideration of the effects of what he is planning to do." It also has evidentiary

---

[250] In re Estate of Bolton, 444 N.W.2d 482 (Iowa 1989); In re Estate of Heyn, 47 P.3d 724 (Colo.App.2002); Creekmore v. Creekmore, 485 S.E.2d 68 (N.C.App.1997); Estate of Dillingham v. C.I.R., 903 F.2d 760 (10th Cir.1990). *But see* Sinclair v. Fleischman, 773 P.2d 101 (Wash.App.1989). *Restatement (Third) of Property (Wills and Other Donative Transfers)* § 6.2, cmt. n (2001) says that delivery of a "certified or cashier's check" can be a gift, and even an ordinary check given to a charity may represent an enforceable promise. In Donahue v. Shughart, Thomson & Kilroy, P.C., 900 S.W.2d 624 (Mo.1995) a law firm's failure to deal promptly with checks sent to it by a client subjected the firm to malpractice liability to the payees when the intended gift failed. *See also* In re Estate of Lamplaugh, 708 N.W.2d 645 (Neb. 2006) (upheld gift of uncashed check because of a state statute).

[251] Uniform Commercial Code § 4–405; * * * *of Contracts* § 332, illus. 9 (1981).

[252] Matter of Estate of Williams, 496 N.E.2d 547 (Ill.App.1986).

[253] Matter of Estate of Dittus, 497 N.W.2d 415 (N.D.1993); Julian v. Petersen, 966 P.2d 878 (Utah App.1998).

[254] Blancett v. Blancett, 102 P.3d 640 (N.M. 2004).

[255] Giefer v. Swenton, 928 P.2d 906 (Kan.App.1996); Matter of Estate of Rohrer, 646 N.E.2d 17 (Ill.App.1995); *Restatement (Third) of Property (Wills and Other Donative Transfers)* § 6.3, cmt. e (2001).

[256] Matter of Estate of Shedrick, 462 N.E.2d 581 (Ill.App.1984); Barlow Soc. v. Commercial Sec. Bank, 723 P.2d 398, 400 (Utah 1986); Johnson v. Ramsey, 817 S.W.2d 200 (Ark.1991); First Sec. Bank v. Geels, 383 S.W.3d 437 (Ark. Ct. App. 2011). However, under Uniform Transfers to Minors Act § 9(a)(5), recording alone is sufficient.

[257] Lauerman v. Destocki, 622 N.E.2d 1122 (Ohio App.1993). *See also* Matter of Estate of Hoyle, 866 P.2d 451 (Okl.App.1993) (alleged intent to forgive loans ineffective because notes retained); Young v. Young, 393 S.E.2d 398 (Va.1990); * * * *of Contracts* § 332(1) (1979).

[258] Gartin v. Taylor, 577 N.W.2d 410, 413 (Iowa 1998). *See also* Bessett v. Huson, 39 P.3d 220 (Or.App.2002). In the latter case, however, the court noted that under a later statute a renunciation by a signed writing would be effective without delivery. *Id.* at. 225. As to disclaimers generally *see* Section 2.8, note 337.

[259] The requirement of delivery "acts as a legal substitute for the execution of a formal will signed in front of competent witnesses." Bessett v. Huson, 39 P.3d 220, 222 (Or.App.2002).

value in that a donee's possession supports the claim of gift.[260] Nevertheless, the delivery requirement has been questioned. The Second Restatement of Property suggests that the law should recognize gifts of personal property "without a delivery by proof of the donor's manifested intention to make a gift."[261] Courts are usually less strict about delivery than about the requirements for validating wills and often uphold gifts on the basis of a "constructive" delivery.[262] Even this fiction is occasionally dispensed with: some cases say there is no reason to insist on delivery when donative intent is clear and no third party is affected.[263]

The same physical facts may or may not constitute delivery depending on intent. A donor who puts a deed in a safe-deposit box has "delivered" it but only if he intended "to relinquish control over it and to effect delivery."[264] In such cases "delivery" seems to describe a result reached on other grounds, *i.e.*, a finding of "no delivery" simply reflects a belief that no gift was intended.[265]

Courts tend to excuse delivery in situations where it was impossible or very difficult. When a woman two days before she died told the donee that he was to have certain securities which were not in her possession, because the donor was "physically incapable of" delivering the property, the "unequivocal evidence" of her intent to give constituted "constructive delivery."[266]

Even if delivery is possible, it may be inconvenient to leave the donee in possession. Sometimes a donor delivers a deed to the donee who returns it to the donor "to hold for her," *e.g.*, because the donee has no safe-deposit box. This is deemed delivery, even though the donee's claim is not corroborated by possession, because the original handing over of the deed shows a serious intent to give,[267] as distinguished from the case in which the donor simply executes a deed and tells the donee that he will hold it for her but never hands it over.[268]

---

[260] Mecham, *The Requirement of Delivery,* 21 Ill.L.Rev. 341, 348–49 (1926). *See also Restatement Third, of Property (Wills and Other Donative Transfers)* § 6.2, cmt. b (2001).

[261] * * * *of Property (Donative Transfers)* § 31.1, cmt. k (1990). *See also Restatement (Third) of Property (Wills and Other Donative Transfers)* § 6.2, cmt. yy (1998).

[262] Whisnant v. Whisnant, 928 P.2d 999 (Or.App.1996) (instructions to broker); Tierce v. Macedonia United Methodist Church, 519 So.2d 451 (Ala.1987) (symbolic delivery in recording); Estate of Davenport v. C.I.R., 184 F.3d 1176, 1185 (10th Cir.1999) (Oklahoma law). * * * *of Property (Donative Transfers)* § 31.1, cmt. b (1990); *Restatement (Third) of Property (Wills and Other Donative Transfers)* § 6.2, cmt. g (1998).

[263] Hengst v. Hengst, 420 A.2d 370 (Pa.1980); Estate of O'Brien v. Robinson, 749 P.2d 154 (Wash.1988).

[264] Bennion v. Hansen, 699 P.2d 757, 759 (Utah 1985). *See also* Lenhart v. Desmond, 705 P.2d 338 (Wyo.1985). *But see* Longstreet v. Decker, 717 S.E.2d 513 (Ga. Ct. App. 2011) (no gift made when testator retained access to safe deposit box and contents could have been reclaimed at any time).

[265] *Cf.* Gulliver & Tilson, *Classification of Gratuitous Transfers,* 51 Yale L.J. 1, 16 (1941).

[266] McCarton v. Estate of Watson, 693 P.2d 192 (Wash.App.1984). *See also* Brown v. Metz, 393 S.E.2d 402 (Va.1990) (terminally ill donor tells donee to take bonds from his safe deposit box).

[267] Barham v. Jones, 647 P.2d 397, 399 (N.M.1982); In re Estate of Kelly, 608 N.E.2d 423 (Ill.App.1992); Fontaine v. Colt's Mfg. Co., Inc., 814 A.2d 433, 436 (Conn.App.2003) (constructive delivery when revolver "presented" but then taken back to make improvements); * * * *of Contracts* § 332, cmt. e (1981); * * * *of Property (Donative Transfers)* § 31.1, illus. 12, § 31.2, illus. 12 (1990).

[268] *Id.*, § 31.2, illus. 10.

If the donee is already in possession of the property when the donor decides to make the gift, *e.g.*, as a custodian or borrower, the law dispenses with delivery.[269] A similar exception is made when donor and donee live in the same household, *e.g.*, a husband gives his wife a piano in their living room.[270]

Delivery can be made to someone other than the donee. When a man executed a deed of land to his wife and her son and handed the deed to his wife, the conveyance to the son was held effective, even though he was unaware of it.[271] The wife was deemed to be acting on behalf of the son. However, because agencies terminate upon the death of the principal or agent, if the third party to whom the deed is delivered is the donor's agent (and not trustee for the intended donee) and the donor dies before the deed is delivered to the intended donee, the gift fails.[272]

Testamentary Transfers

When gifts are challenged after the donor's death, the problems of proof of the decedent's intent resemble those that arise in proving wills. Some gifts are held to be "testamentary" and, thus, subject to the statutory requirements for a will. For example, when a father executed deeds of land to two sons and put them in his safe deposit box, the land was included in the father's estate on the ground that he "intended the deeds to operate as testamentary transfers."[273] On the other hand, deeds have been held valid even though they had the practical effects of a will because the donor reserved a life estate, or a power to revoke.[274] Even a document which was labeled "LAST WILL" was held to be effective as a deed because it said "I hereby grant" the property involved and was delivered to the donee.[275] The question whether a transfer is "testamentary" is often linked with the delivery requirement.

---

[269] Justinian, *Institutes* 2.1.44; * * * *of Contracts* § 332, cmt. e (1981); * * * *of Property (Donative Transfers)* § 31.1, illus. 1 (1990); Little City Foundation v. Capsonic Group, 596 N.E.2d 146 (Ill.App.1992); *Restatement (Third) of Property (Wills and Other Donative Transfers)* § 6.2 cmt. d (1998).

[270] *Restatement (Third) of Property (Wills and Other Donative Transfers)* § 6.2, cmt. e (2001).

[271] Matter of Estate of Ashe, 753 P.2d 281 (Idaho App.1988). *See also* In re Estate of Kremer, 546 N.E.2d 1047 (Ill.App.1989); * * * *of Property (Donative Transfers)* § 31.1 (1990); *Restatement (Third) of Property (Wills and Other Donative Transfers)* § 6.2, cmt. k (1998). When the same person is both donor and one of the donees, as in a joint tenancy, this theory may dispense with delivery altogether. Kresser v. Peterson, 675 P.2d 1193 (Utah 1984). *But see* Wasniewski v. Quick and Reilly, Inc. 971 A.2d 8 (Conn. 2009) (no gift where father deposited funds in brokerage account titled in son's name because son was not notified of the account and father had not instructed brokerage firm to deliver funds to son).

[272] Kesterson v. Cronan, 806 P.2d 134 (Or.App.1991); Albrecht v. Brais, 754 N.E.2d 396 (Ill.App.2001) (revocable transfer in escrow not delivery); Huskins v. Huskins, 517 S.E.2d 146 (N.C.App.1999) (mailing letter to third party, donor dies before letter received). * * * *of Trusts* § 57, cmt. b (1959). *But see* Herron v. Underwood, 503 N.E.2d 1111 (Ill.App.1987); Poling v. Northup, 652 A.2d 1114 (Me.1995) (delivery to donor's lawyer suffices, because intent controls).

[273] Matter of Estate of Dittus, 497 N.W.2d 415 (N.D.1993). *See also* Kesterson v. Cronan, 806 P.2d 134 (Or.App.1991); In re Estate of Clouse, 739 N.Y.S.2d 470 (App.Div.2002); Succession of Young, 563 So.2d 502 (La.App.1990). Under BGB (German Civil Code) § 2301 any gifts which require the donee to outlive the donor are subject to the rules governing wills.

[274] Hamilton v. Caplan, 518 A.2d 1087 (Md.App.1987).

[275] Ex parte Rucker, 702 So.2d 456 (Ala.1997). *See also* Vigil v. Sandoval, 741 P.2d 836 (N.M.App.1987); Black v. Poole, 196 S.E.2d 20 (Ga.1973).

The Restatement of Property, like the UPC, validates documents of transfer, such as joint accounts, POD arrangements and life insurance arrangements that are used as "a substitute for a will in that the donor's current beneficial enjoyment of the gift property is not significantly curtailed during the donor's lifetime."[276] The Restatement eliminates the delivery requirement for gifts evidenced by a document, as distinguished from gifts made without a document.[277]

When a decedent's intention is manifested by a signed writing, this provides almost as much protection against fraud as an attested will. Even more protection is afforded by the formalities prescribed for recorded deeds in many jurisdictions.[278] A comment to the UPC observes:

> the benign experience with such familiar will substitutes as the revocable inter-vivos trust, the multiple party bank account, and United States government bonds payable on death to named beneficiaries all demonstrated that the evils envisioned if the statute of wills were not rigidly enforced simply do not materialize . . . Because these provisions often are part of a business transaction and are evidenced by a writing, the danger of fraud is largely eliminated.[279]

The "business transaction" mentioned in this comment presumably refers to such acts as opening a banking or brokerage account, in which the donor deals with a disinterested person who performs a function analogous to that of the witnesses to a will.

Although the formal requirements for gifts are somewhat less than those for wills, the difference is relatively trivial and is not a major motive for the use of gifts in estate planning. Gifts are often used to reduce a family's income taxes by shifting income producing property to persons in lower income tax brackets.[280] They can also be used to reduce estate taxes, even though gifts are basically taxed at the same rates as probate transfers.[281] Accomplishment of this objective, however, requires that the gift not be testamentary in character. A revocable gift, for example, even if not subject to the formal requirements for a will is subject to tax in the donor's estate at death, and, in many states, to the claims of the donor's creditors or the claim of the donor's spouse to an elective share.[282]

---

[276] * * * *of Property (Donative Transfers)* § 32.4 (1990); UPC Art. 6.

[277] *Compare id.* § 32.3 *with* § 31.1.

[278] *Id.* § 32.3, cmt. *a. See* note 233, *supra.*

[279] UPC § 6–101, Comment. Many non-UPC states have adopted a similar provision. *E.g.*, Cal.Prob.Code § 5000. As to revocable trusts, multiple party and payable on death accounts *see* Sections 3.6–3.7.

[280] J. Price, *Contemporary Estate Planning* § 2.43 (2d ed. 2000).

[281] *Id.*, § 2.44–2.45.

[282] As to the gifts which are includable in the donor's taxable estate *see* Section 15.4, note 160 et seq. As to rights of the creditors of a settlor of a revocable trust, *see* Section 10.4, note 111 et seq. As to the elective share *see* Section 8.7, note 260 et seq.

Clear and Convincing Evidence

The UPC allows probate of defectively executed wills if there is "clear and convincing evidence" that they represent the decedent's intent.[283] Many courts use similar language when examining claims that a decedent had made a gift prior to death. For example, in rejecting such a claim a court said that "the burden of showing [that] an *inter-vivos* gift was made is on the donee by clear and convincing evidence."[284] Sometimes this burden cannot be satisfied because a Dead Man statute bars testimony by the donee,[285] but in some cases gifts have been proved by the donee's own testimony.[286] It is difficult to ascertain what "clear and convincing evidence" really means, because appellate courts usually defer to trial courts' findings. Conflicting evidence does not preclude a finding that a gift was made.[287] Evidence of donative intent need not be contemporaneous with the gift itself.[288]

Distinction Between Gifts and Promises

The need for "consideration" in conveyances by deed has disappeared in modern law, although consideration is customarily recited.[289] Promises, on the other hand, must be supported by consideration. A note given without consideration promising to pay money in the future, even if delivered, is unenforceable by the payee,[290] unless (in some states) the note is under seal, or unless action in reliance makes it enforceable by promissory estoppel.[291] Courts tend to expand the notion of consideration or ignore it when promises to charity are involved. For example, Martin Luther King wrote a letter stating that upon his death papers which he had deposited with Boston University "shall become . . . the absolute property" of the university. The court held that BU's care of the papers amounted to enough "consideration or reliance" to make this promise enforceable against King's estate.[292]

The law normally refuses to enforce donative *promises* because they are "more likely to be uncalculated than deliberative."[293] Delivery and a signed

---

[283] UPC § 2–503.

[284] Smith v. Shafer, 623 N.E.2d 1261, 1263 (Ohio App.1993). *See also* Wright v. Union Nat. Bank, 819 S.W.2d 698 (Ark.1991); Succession of Young, 563 So.2d 502 (La.App.1990); Duggan v. Keto, 554 A.2d 1126 (D.C.App.1989).

[285] Matter of Collier, 381 So.2d 1338 (Miss.1980); Judson Post Estate v. Commonwealth Bank and Trust Co., 456 A.2d 1360 (Pa.1983); Hamilton v. Caplan, 518 A.2d 1087 (Md.App.1987).

[286] Grau v. Dooley, 431 N.E.2d 1164 (Ill.App.1981); Estate of Lennon v. Lennon, 29 P.3d 1258, 1266 (Wash.App.2001).

[287] Rogers v. Rogers, 319 A.2d 119, 121 (Md.1974).

[288] In re Estate of Deahl, 524 N.E.2d 810 (Ind.App.1988).

[289] Rubenstein v. Sela, 672 P.2d 492 (Ariz.App.1983); In re Conservatorship of Moran, 821 So.2d 903, 907 (Miss.App.2002) ("love and affection" sufficient consideration to support a deed); *cf. supra* note 215.

[290] Matter of Wetmore's Estate, 343 N.E.2d 224 (Ill.App.1976); Unthank v. Rippstein, 386 S.W.2d 134 (Tex.1964). *See also* Dementas v. Estate of Tallas, 764 P.2d 628 (Utah App.1988) (promise to leave money at death).

[291] *See* Brown v. Branch, 758 N.E.2d 48 (Ind. 2001). *See * * * of Contracts* §§ 90, 95 (1981).

[292] King v. Trustees of Boston University, 647 N.E.2d 1196 (Mass.1995). *See also * * * of Contracts* § 90(2) (1971).

[293] Eisenberg, *Donative Promises,* 47 U.Chi.L.Rev. 1, 5 (1979).

writing are not *enough* protection against rash promises because persons tend to be less cautious about future commitments.

Whether a transaction is treated as a gift for which no consideration is needed or as a promise may depend on the form of words used. When a woman who owned land subject to a life estate in her mother agreed to convey it "at the expiration of the outstanding life estate," this transfer was held to be ineffective without consideration because "the property was not to be transferred until some future date."[294] On the other hand, a deed purporting to transfer land immediately subject to a life estate is an effective gift of a remainder.[295]

The nature of the interest is also important. A person cannot give property that she expects to inherit even if she uses words indicating a present transfer; such a transfer of an "expectancy" is effective only if supported by adequate consideration.[296] So, also, "a purported assignment of a right expected to arise under a contract not in existence operates only as a promise to assign the right."[297] The restriction on gifts of expectancies guards against improvident transfers, such as when Esau, according to the Bible, sold his inheritance for beans.[298] The line between "expectancies" and "property" is elusive. At one time, contingent remainders were regarded as expectancies, but in modern law they are considered property.[299] The expectation of inheriting from a parent can be less speculative than many contingent remainders, *e.g.*, "to Clara if Alice (who has seven healthy children) dies without issue." Rights under an existing contract may be more uncertain than a contract which the assignor expects to make in the future.[300] Instead of distinguishing between "expectancy" and "property," perhaps the law should weigh how speculative the particular right actually was, or the improvidence of the transfer, but these would be hard tests to apply.[301]

---

[294] Larabee v. Booth, 437 N.E.2d 1010 (Ind.App.1982). *See also* * * * *of Contracts* §§ 330, 332, comment b (1981).

[295] * * * *of Property (Donative Transfers)* § 32.1, illus. 4 (1990).

[296] Johnson By and Through Lackey v. Schick, 882 P.2d 1059 (Okl.1994) (expected inheritance assigned to satisfy assignor's debts); Scott v. First Nat. Bank, 168 A.2d 349 (Md.1961); *Restatement (Third) of Property (Wills and Other Donative Transfers)* § 2.6, cmt. j (1998).

Some countries allow a prospective heir to effectively *disclaim* an expectancy. H. Flick & D. Piltz, *Der Internationale Erbfall* 52, 275 (1999) (son's renunciation of inheritance of his living mother effective under German but not French law). On the other hand, even under German law, a *transfer* of an expectancy to a stranger is null. BGB (German Civil Code) § 312. *See also* French Code Civil art. 791, 943; Italian Codice Civile art. 458. This should not be confused with a disclaimer or transfer after the ancestor has died. *See* Section 2.8.

[297] * * * *of Contracts* § 321(2) (1981).

[298] *Id.* comment b; Genesis 25:29–34.

[299] *Compare* Cal.Civ.Code § 1044 *with* 2 W. Blackstone, *Commentaries* 290 (1766). As to the transfer of reversionary interests *see* Section 12.6, note 245 et seq. As to the right of creditors to reach them *see* Section 10.8, note 341.

[300] The New York Court of Appeals upheld a gratuitous assignment of a contractual right to the profits of "My Fair Lady," made before the musical was even written. Speelman v. Pascal, 178 N.E.2d 723 (N.Y.1961).

[301] Eisenberg, *supra* note 293, at 15. The requirement in Germany of a notarized document in order to disclaim an expectancy may provide some protection against improvidence. BGB (German Civil Code) § 312(2).

§ 3.6 Trusts

The modern trust arose from the medieval use.[302] Like uses, trusts were enforced by the courts of equity when they were separate from the law courts. A maxim of equity says that "equity follows the law," *i.e.*, the rules governing trusts are usually (though not always) the same as those governing legal interests. A person who creates a trust (usually called the settlor, sometimes "grantor" or "trustor"), is simply making a gift of a special type.

A settlor can create a trust in one of two ways.[303] First, she can declare herself trustee of property; in this case the same person is both settlor and trustee.[304] Second, the settlor can transfer the property to another individual or to a corporation (typically a bank or trust company) as trustee. If the settlor does this by a will, the trust is a "testamentary" trust. If the settlor transfers the property to the trustee during life, or declares herself trustee, the trust is an *inter-vivos* or "living" trust. The latter type is often used as a will substitute.[305]

Generally speaking, every trust has one or more beneficiaries[306] as well as a settlor(s) and trustee(s). In older cases the beneficiary was called the *cestui que use,* a word stemming from the medieval use, but this expression is rarely encountered today.

Consideration and Delivery

A declaration of trust, like an outright gift, requires no consideration.[307] Delivery acts as a substitute for consideration in outright gifts, but even delivery is not required for a declaration of trust.[308] Nor does the law require "formal change in ownership records or documents of title," such as recording a deed or re-registration of stock certificates, assuming no rights of third parties are affected.[309]

Delivery was deemed unnecessary for declarations of trust, because courts of equity did not use juries, and the delivery requirement was associated with

---

[302] *See* Section 8.2, note 69 et seq.

[303] *Restatement (Third) of Trusts* § 10 (2001); UTC § 401. Not all trusts are created by a settlor. For example, UPC § 2–212(b) puts the elective share of an incapacitated spouse into a custodial trust for the spouse.

[304] "No trust exists when the same individual is the sole settlor, sole trustee, *and sole beneficiary*." Vittands v. Sudduth, 730 N.E.2d 325, 334 (Mass.App.2000) (italics added). However, this rarely happens because most trusts have several beneficiaries. *Restatement (Third) of Trusts* § 32, cmt. b (2001).

[305] The reasons for using trusts as a will substitute to "avoid probate" are discussed in Section 10.4.

[306] For the exceptional case of trusts for a purpose without a beneficiary *see* Section 10.10.

[307] *Restatement (Third) of Trusts* § 15 (2001); UTC, § 401; Cal.Prob.Code § 15208; cf. Section 3.5, note 289. As to promises to create trusts in the future *see* note 335 et seq. *infra.*

[308] Estate of Heggstad, 20 Cal.Rptr.2d 433 (App.1993); Taliaferro v. Taliaferro, 921 P.2d 803 (Kan.1996).

[309] *Restatement (Third) of Trusts* § 10, cmt. e (2001); Taliaferro v. Taliaferro, 921 P.2d 803 (Kan.1996); Samuel v. King, 64 P.3d 1206 (Or.App.2003) (assets listed in attached schedule effectively put into declared trust). UTC § 401, comment, agrees but *recommends* that assets comprising the trust be reregistered in the settlor's name as trustee. For the significance of how title is registered *see* Section 12.4, note 35 et seq.

a jury trial.[310] Delivery is "an act of notoriety," required for the jury's edification and can be dispensed with in equity where there are no juries. A feeling that juries are less sophisticated fact finders than judges is reflected in other rules such as the parol evidence rule, which does not apply to equitable proceedings. Courts of equity, operating without a jury, are free to reform mistakes in written instruments on the basis of oral testimony.[311]

Gulliver and Tilson suggest that the absence of a delivery requirement for trusts was unimportant because "laymen would not normally think of using a declaration of trust."[312] The words "I declare myself trustee of this property" are unusual in normal discourse, and so they perform a channeling function similar to delivery.[313] But this reasoning supposes that courts actually require the use of special words to create a trust. Two lines of authority on this issue are hard to reconcile. The Restatement of Trusts says that a "property arrangement may constitute a trust . . . even though such terms as 'trust' or 'trustee' are not used."[314] A woman who signed a piece of paper stating that "in the event of my death" certain stock "belongs to Miss Peck" was held to have created a trust.[315] A father who manifested an intent to give stock to his children but retain the power to manage it was also held to have created a trust. "The law will delineate a trust where, in view of a sufficiently manifested purpose or intent, that is the appropriate instrumentality, even though its creator calls it something else, or doesn't call it anything."[316] An English treatise remarks that:

> Where the donor's intentions are unclear then the court, in order to give effect to the general intention of the donor to benefit the donee, may be prepared to apply the maxim 'Verba ita sunt intelligenda ut res magis valeat quam pereat' [words are to be understood so that a transaction is valid rather than fail] particularly when the court is 'dealing with simple people unaware of the subtleties of equity.'[317]

---

310 *See* Section 3.5, note 216.

311 * * * *of Contracts* § 214, cmt. d (1979); Section 7.4, at note 183 et seq.

312 Gulliver & Tilson, *Classification of Gratuitous Transfers*, 51 Yale L.J. 1, 16–17 (1941).

313 The "technical phraseology" required for a *stipulatio* in Roman law was similar in that it prevented "the attention from gliding over a dangerous pledge." H. Maine, *Ancient Law* 272–73 (1861).

314 *Restatement (Third) of Trusts* § 5, cmt. a (2001). *See also* Marshall v. Grauberger, 796 P.2d 34 (Colo.App.1990); Underhill & Hayton, *Law Relating to Trusts and Trustees* 41 (14th ed. 1987).

315 Mahoney v. Leddy, 223 A.2d 456 (Vt.1966). *See also* Underwood v. Bank of Huntsville, 494 So.2d 619 (Ala.1986) (deposit "as custodian" creates a trust); Cohen v. City of Lynn, 598 N.E.2d 682 (Mass.App.1992) (conveyance of land to city "for park purposes" creates a trust); Brotman v. East Lake Creek Ranch, L.L.P., 31 P.3d 886, 893 (Colo.2001) (land granted to state "for the support of common schools").

316 Elyachar v. Gerel Corp., 583 F.Supp. 907, 922 (S.D.N.Y.1984). *See also* Hatton v. Meade, 502 N.E.2d 552 (Mass.App.1987). Of such cases Langbein remarks "we can understand why our law might wish to have a curative device for failure of delivery when a gift was clearly intended, although we may lament that the measure takes the form of a fictional declaration of trust rather than a candid harmless error doctrine." Langbein, *The Contractarian Basis of the Law of Trusts*, 105 Yale L.J. 625, 674 (1995).

317 Underhill & Hayton, *supra* note 314, at 103. The quote about "simple people" comes from Paul v. Constance, [1977] 1 All E.R. 195, 196 (C.A.1976) where a trust was found although the settlor never used the word.

On the other hand, the Restatement also says that an unsuccessful attempt to make an outright gift as distinguished from a trust "will not be given effect by treating it as a declaration of trust." In other words, a gift that fails for want of delivery will not be sustained as a trust. A court refused to impose a trust on a woman who had signed a deed but never delivered it, saying that no trust is created "when a property owner merely intends to give his property to another but the gift is never completed."[318]

An intent to grant to another person authority over property does not necessarily constitute a trust; if powers are given to a person as agent, they can be revoked, whereas trusts are often irrevocable.[319]

Transfer to Trustee

A settlor who wishes to use another person as trustee must effectively transfer the property to the trustee.[320] A person cannot be a trustee against his or her will.[321] A trusteeship must be accepted by an express acceptance or by the receipt of the trust property and the subsequent exercise of trustee responsibilities over the property.[322]

If the settlor does not have power to transfer the property, the trust fails.[323] If "title does not pass to the intended trustee for want of delivery of the property or the deed, no trust is created." For this purpose the rules governing transfer of legal title control.[324] Thus, no enforceable trust was created when a settlor executed a trust agreement with a trustee which provided for the disposition of her condominium because she never transferred the condominium's title to the trustee.[325] And, in one case a trust was held ineffective where the settlor was one of several trustees and failed to deliver a deed to the others.[326] It is not necessary that the title to the property be transferred to the trustee simultaneously with the creation of the trust, although that may be the best practice. In fact, the transfer of title can occur after the trust instrument is executed.[327] Lawyers who draft a trust but fail to

---

[318] French v. French, 606 P.2d 830, 833 (Ariz.App.1980). *See also* Duggan v. Keto, 554 A.2d 1126 (D.C.App.1989) (letter authorizing removal of bonds from box did not show intent to create a trust); Sussman v. Sussman, 392 N.E.2d 881 (N.Y.1979).

[319] Eychaner v. Gross, 779 N.E.2d 1115, 1134 (Ill.2002); *Restatement (Third) of Trusts* § 5, cmt. e (2001). As to the revocation of trusts *see* Section 4.5, note 141 et seq.

[320] UTC § 401(1).

[321] UTC § 701(b) (A trusteeship not accepted within a reasonable time is deemed rejected).

[322] UTC § 701(a).

[323] Jewish Community Ass'n v. Community First Nat. Bank, 6 P.3d 1264 (Wyo.2000) (purported transfer by board of association without the requisite approval of its members).

[324] *Restatement (Third) of Trusts* § 14, cmt. d (2001).

[325] Dahlgren v. First Nat. Bank, 580 P.2d 478 (Nev.1978). *See also* In re Estate of Wittmond, 732 N.E.2d 659, 662 (Ill.App.2000); Ballard v. McCoy, 443 S.E.2d 146 (Va.1994); Papale-Keefe v. Altomare, 647 N.E.2d 722 (Mass.App.1995); McCormick v. Brevig, 980 P.2d 603, 612 (Mont.1999).

[326] Pizel v. Pizel, 643 P.2d 1094 (Kan.App.1982). *But see* Aiello v. Clark, 680 P.2d 1162 (Alaska 1984) (declaration of trust effective despite lack of delivery to co-trustee).

[327] UTC § 401, comment.

see that the property is properly transferred to the trustee may be sued for malpractice.[328]

The delivery requirement has been watered down in this context just as in non-trust cases.[329] When a settlor who wished to convey valuable drawings to a trust earmarked them but kept them in her possession, her "placing labels and stamps on the drawings and sequestering them in special containers" was held to constitute "a form of symbolic delivery" because the evidence of donative intent was strong.[330] Delivery of a deed of land to a trustee is effective even though the settlor retains possession of the land itself.[331]

In a testamentary trust, the trust property is transferred to the trustee by the will; no delivery is necessary but the formal requirements for wills apply.[332] Under the *maxim*, "a trust will not fail for want of a trustee," failure to designate a trustee in a testamentary trust, or the designated trustee's refusal to serve as a trustee, does not cause the trust to fail; normally a new trustee will be appointed to do the job.[333]

Words of Futurity; Expectancies

Present gifts require no consideration, but promises to make a gift in the future do.[334] A similar distinction applies to trusts. A declaration that the settlor "will" create a trust is not sufficient without consideration or some recognized substitute.[335] Thus, a letter stating that "in the event of a sale" of specified land, the writer "will hold the sale proceeds in trust" did not create a trust.[336] A man cannot create a trust of property which he does not yet own, any more than he can make an outright gift of an expectancy. A man who agreed to acquire football tickets for another person did not thereby create an enforceable trust because he had no right to the tickets when the agreement was made and "mere expectancies cannot be held in trust."[337] Also, claims for personal injury are generally held to be not transferable and, thus, cannot be put into a trust.[338]

---

[328] In Pizel v. Whalen, 845 P.2d 37 (Kan.1993), lawyers in such a suit escaped liability because of contributory negligence by the plaintiffs. *Cf.* Poullette v. Silverstein, 767 N.E.2d 477 (Ill.App.2002) (similar claim defeated by statute of limitations).

[329] Section 3.5, note 262 et seq (courts look to intent rather than actual delivery.)

[330] Edinburg v. Edinburg, 492 N.E.2d 1164, 1169 (Mass.App.1986). *See also* Poling v. Northup, 652 A.2d 1114 (Me.1995) (delivery of deed to settlor's lawyer sufficient even though he was settlor's agent); *Restatement (Third) of Trusts* § 16, cmt. b (2001) (delivery may be "constructive or symbolic").

[331] Golleher v. Horton, 715 P.2d 1225 (Ariz.App.1985).

[332] *Restatement (Third) of* Trusts § 17 (2001); Underhill & Hayton, *supra* note 314, at 175.

[333] *Restatement (Third) of Trusts* § 31 (2001); Underhill & Hayton, *supra* note 314, at 41. As to the appointment of trustees *see* Section 14.6, note 362 et seq.

[334] *See* Section 3.5, at note 289 et seq.

[335] *Restatement (Third) of Trusts* § 15, cmt. b (2001); Cal.Prob.Code § 15208; Tierce v. Macedonia United Meth. Church, 519 So.2d 451, 457 (Ala.1987). A seal does not suffice, because "equity gives no assistance to volunteers." Underhill & Hayton, *supra* note 314, at 98.

[336] Kavanaugh v. Dobrowolski's Estate, 407 N.E.2d 856 (Ill.App.1980).

[337] Kully v. Goldman, 305 N.W.2d 800, 802 (Neb.1981); *Restatement (Third) of Trusts* § 41 (2001).

[338] Vittands v. Sudduth, 730 N.E.2d 325, 333 (Mass.App.2000); *Restatement (Third) of Trusts* § 40, cmt. d (2001).

A trust of an expectancy, or a promise to create a trust in the future, is binding if supported by consideration.[339] If Jenna, in consideration of $50,000, promises to create a trust of any inheritance she might receive from her mother, a trust will be imposed upon that inheritance even though she does not receive it until her mother later dies. Even without consideration, the trust becomes effective if it begins to operate with the settlor's tacit consent.[340]

Sometimes the only asset put into a trust is an insurance policy on the settlor's life. The policy may have little present value so long as the settlor is alive, especially if the settlor reserves the right to change the beneficiary or the policy is a term life insurance policy. Nevertheless, courts routinely uphold such "insurance trusts," and many state statutes confirm their validity.[341]

Is the Revocable Trust Testamentary?

Many living trusts are the functional equivalent of wills; the settlor retains the right to control and enjoy the property for life, and the beneficiary's interest becomes meaningful only when the settlor dies. Some older cases and the First Restatement of Trusts held such trusts were testamentary and invalid unless executed with the formalities prescribed for wills.[342] The Second Restatement, however, says that a trust is not testamentary "merely because the settlor reserves a beneficial life interest or because he reserves a power to revoke the trust . . . and a power to control the trustee as to the administration of the trust."[343] A claim that a trust is invalid as "testamentary" is unlikely to succeed today.[344] The UPC reflects the modern attitude in providing that trusts (and other) provisions "for a nonprobate transfer on death" are "nontestamentary."[345]

Why should a transfer which has so many characteristics of a will *not* be treated like one? A common explanation is that a living trust, unlike a will, gives the beneficiaries a "present interest."[346] This argument is unconvincing. Admittedly, a testator has somewhat more freedom to deal with property while alive than the settlor-trustee of a revocable trust, because the latter has some responsibilities to the beneficiaries. But these responsibilities are minimal so

---

339 In re Estate of Chaitlen, 534 N.E.2d 482 (Ill.App.1989) (promise to create trust at death); Bemis v. Estate of Bemis, 967 P.2d 437 (Nev.1998) (promise to create a trust for children in divorce settlement); Bednar v. Bednar, 485 N.E.2d 834 (Ohio App.1984).

340 Estate of Brenner, 547 P.2d 938 (Colo.App.1976); Sundquist v. Sundquist, 639 P.2d 181 (Utah 1981).

341 Huff, *Life Insurance Trusts for Everyman,* 39 U.Colo.L.Rev. 239, 147 (1967); Barrientos v. Nava, 94 S.W.3d 270, 281 (Tex.App.2002); *cf.* Rosenblum v. Gibbons, 685 S.W.2d 924 (Mo.App.1984) (benefits under retirement plan); Ind.Code 27–1–12–16(B); N.Y. EPTL § 13–3.3(a); N.C.Gen.Stat. § 36A–100(a). For the estate planning uses of irrevocable life insurance trusts *see* Section 15.4, note 265 et seq.; J. Price, *Contemporary Estate Planning* §§ 6.23 (2d ed.2000).

342 *Restatement of Trusts* § 57(2) (1935). *See also* Osborn v. Osborn, 226 N.E.2d 814, 822–25 (Ohio Com.Pl.1966).

343 * * * *of Trusts* § 57 (1959). *See also Restatement (Third) of Trusts* § 25 (2001). However, if the trustee or the property "cannot be identified until the transferor's death" the instrument must comply with the wills act. *Id.*, § 17, cmt. a.

344 In re Estate of Zukerman, 578 N.E.2d 248 (Ill.App.1991); Zuckerman v. Alter, 615 So.2d 661 (Fla.1993); Matter of Estate of Groesbeck, 935 P.2d 1255 (Utah 1997).

345 UPC § 6–101. *See also* Cal.Prob.Code § 5000.

346 Farkas v. Williams, 125 N.E.2d 600 (Ill.1955); Blue Valley Federal Savings and Loan Ass'n v. Burrus, 617 S.W.2d 111, 114 (Mo.App.1981).

long as the settlor can revoke the trust.[347] Moreover, any such limitations on the settlor-trustee's freedom to deal with the trust property have little to do with the purposes behind formal requirements for wills.

A more persuasive rationale for the validity of revocable trusts was offered by Gulliver and Tilson. Normally in a living trust "a formal instrument will be prepared and delivered even though it is not doctrinally essential to do so. As a result, the main objectives of the statute of wills seem to be satisfied."[348] This rationale suggests that the law should distinguish between formal and informal trusts. The authorization of nonprobate transfers in Section 6–101 of the UPC is limited to those in a "written instrument," but the Comment says this was not intended to "invalidate other arrangements" such as oral trusts. A trust drafted by an attorney and signed by the settlor and an independent trustee seems to satisfy the purposes of the wills act formalities. More questionable is a declaration of trust like a "Dacey" trust, so called after the author of *How to Avoid Probate,* a phenomenally successful book of the 60s, which contains "simplistic tear-out trust and will forms." Arguably the functions of will formalities are *not* fulfilled when a settlor "sits down in the privacy of his living room, fills in several blanks on a printed form" like Dacey's and signs it with no "active participation of another party to the transaction."[349] Nevertheless, Dacey trusts have been upheld, perhaps because they are hard to distinguish from printed forms that can be probated as holographic wills in many states.[350]

Many persons open bank accounts as "trustee" for another. Such trusts are often called "Totten" trusts after a leading case decided over a century ago.[351] Use of the word "trustee" indicates that the depositor meant to create a trust, but there is often little other evidence of intent. The trustee's duties and the beneficiary's rights are not specified. Nevertheless, courts hold that trusts were intended and are effective to pass the account to the designated beneficiary when the trustee dies.[352] Several state statutes permit banks to pay the money in such accounts to the designated beneficiary after the depositor dies. Although these statutes literally only protect banks, they have been held to support the beneficiary's right to the account.[353] Other statutes make clear that the account belongs to the beneficiary when the trustee dies.[354]

---

[347] Cal.Prob.Code § 16064(c) (trustee has no duty to account to beneficiary of a revocable trust).

[348] Gulliver & Tilson, *supra* note 312 at 24. *See also* Roberts v. Roberts, 646 N.E.2d 1061, 1065 (Mass.1995). No "delivery," however, is customary for a declaration of trust.

[349] Johanson, *Revocable Trusts and Community Property,* 47 Tex.L.Rev. 537, 538 (1969).

[350] Barnette v. McNulty, 516 P.2d 583 (Ariz.App.1973); Wilkerson v. McClary, 647 S.W.2d 79 (Tex.App.1983). As to printed forms as holographic wills *see* Section 3.4, at note 167 et seq.

[351] In re Totten, 71 N.E. 748 (N.Y.1904).

[352] Sanchez v. Sanchez De Davila, 547 So.2d 943 (Fla.App.1989); Estate of Bischof, 770 S.W.2d 474 (Mo.App.1989); Byrd v. Lanahan, 783 P.2d 426 (Nev.1989); *Restatement (Third) of Trusts* § 26 (2001). Langbein quite properly objects that "the nonprobate will effected" by such trusts "should not be confused with the trust . . . The trust label is simply being used to legitimize probate avoidance." Langbein, *supra* note 316, at 673.

[353] Blue Valley Federal Savings and Loan Ass'n v. Burrus, 617 S.W.2d 111 (Mo.App.1981); Matter of Estate of Stokes, 747 P.2d 300 (Okl.1987).

[354] Cal.Prob.Code § 5302(c). The Uniform Probate Code now assimilates Totten Trusts to P.O.D. accounts. UPC § 6–201(8). As to these *see* Section 3.7.

Some cases suggest that this arrangement will also be recognized for forms of property other than bank accounts.[355]

Totten trusts have been called "the poor man's will" (even though substantial amounts occasionally pass under them).[356] They are "widely used as a legitimate means of avoiding the costs and delays typically associated with the processes of administering decedents' estates."[357] Because they are "widely used," the expectations of many settlors would be defeated if courts were to hold such trusts invalid.[358] On the other hand, because Totten trusts are so much like wills, they are treated like wills for purposes other than formal requirements for due execution, such as the rights of the settlor's spouse to claim them as part of an elective share and of creditors to reach them in payment of their claims.[359]

Need for a Writing

A living trust does not have to be executed like a will, but Section 7 of the Statute of Frauds of 1676 required that "all declarations or creations of trust . . . of any lands . . . shall be manifested and proved by some writing signed by the party who is by law enabled to declare such trust." Section 8 made an exception for trusts which "arise or result by the implication or construction of law." The requirement of a signed writing was not limited to trusts; Section 1 of the Statute also required a signed writing to convey a legal interest in land.[360]

Most American states have provisions like Section 7 of the original Statute of Frauds.[361] The writing requirement arises in two contexts. First, a person may declare herself trustee of land for another. Even in states that have not copied Section 7 of the English statute, such oral declarations may be held subject to section 1 as an attempt to convey land orally.[362] They are not enforceable under the exception in section 8 for constructive trusts[363] unless the beneficiary improves the land or otherwise changes his position in reliance on the trust.[364]

---

[355] In re Estate of Zukerman, 578 N.E.2d 248 (Ill.App.1991) (bond); Tomlinson v. Tomlinson, 960 S.W.2d 337 (Tex.App.1997) (pension benefits). *But see* Matter of Estate of Gagliardi, 432 N.E.2d 774 (N.Y.1982) (refusing to extend Totten trust idea to land).

[356] McGovern, *The Payable on Death Account and Other Will Substitutes,* 67 Nw.U.L.Rev. 7, 11–12 (1972).

[357] *Restatement (Third) Trusts* § 25, cmt. a (2001). *See also* Westerfeld v. Huckaby, 474 S.W.2d 189 (Tex.1971). For further discussion of the disadvantages of probate *see* Section 13.4.

[358] Johanson, *supra* note 349, at 557; Gulliver & Tilson, *supra* note 312, at 24.

[359] As to the rights of the settlor's spouse *see* Section 8.7, note 260 et seq. As to rights of creditors *see* Sections 13.5–13.6.

[360] *See* Section 3.5, note 219. These provisions are now combined in England (in slightly revised language) in Law of Property Act, 1925, § 53.

[361] *Restatement (Third) of Trusts* § 20, cmt. a (2001); Cal.Prob.Code § 15206; Fla.Stat. § 689.05. In the relatively few states which have not adopted this section, some courts treat it as part of the common law, Aragon v. Rio Costilla Cooperative Livestock Ass'n, 812 P.2d 1300 (N.M.1991), but others do not. Ellis v. Vespoint, 403 S.E.2d 542 (N.C.App.1991).

[362] Brame v. Read, 118 S.E. 117 (Va.1923).

[363] French v. French, 606 P.2d 830 (Ariz.App.1980). *But see* Section 3.5, note 231.

[364] *Restatement (Third) of Trusts* § 24, cmt. c (2001). *See also* Section 3.5, note 228.

More commonly the settlor conveys land to another by a deed which does not indicate that the grantee named in the deed was intended to hold the land in trust for another. Such a deed, although in writing and signed, does not satisfy the Statute because it does not refer to the trust.[365] But the transferee, if allowed to keep land intended for another, would be unjustly enriched, so courts frequently impose a constructive trust in order to avoid this result.[366]

In order to satisfy Section 7 of the Statute of Frauds, a writing must indicate the terms of the trust. A deed which simply conveys land "to *T* as trustee" is not enough,[367] but a deed "to *T* in trust for *B*" may be sufficient. The designation of a trustee and beneficiaries for death benefits in a pension plan was held sufficient to create a trust because "all necessary details are supplied by" statutory provisions governing trusts.[368]

The writing may be signed[369] by either the settlor or by the trustee, depending upon the circumstances. If *S*'s deed to *T* sets forth the terms of the trust, *T* is bound even though she did not sign it, but *S* cannot impose a trust by signing a writing after title to the land has passed to *T*.[370] *T*, on the other hand, can satisfy the Statute by signing a writing prior to, or subsequent to the transfer to her.[371] The writing need not have created the trust; a later written acknowledgment of the trust is sufficient. The "writing" may be a series of documents; for example, a woman conveyed land by deed "to hold in trust" and a later will directed the trustees how to dispose of the property.[372] (Had she not executed the will, the transferee would have held the land in a resulting trust for the woman.)[373]

The Statute of Frauds applies only to trusts of land.[374] A few states also require a writing for trusts of personal property. In most states oral trusts of personal property are valid,[375] but they are rarely encountered. Even in

---

[365] *Restatement (Third) of Trusts* § 22(1) (2001).

[366] *See* Section 7.4, at note 216 et seq.

[367] Gammarino v. Hamilton Cty. Bd. of Revision, 702 N.E.2d 415, 418 (Ohio 1998); Jordan v. Exxon Corp., 802 S.W.2d 880 (Tex.App.1991); Hickman v. Trust of Heath, House & Boyles, 835 S.W.2d 880 (Ark.1992); *Restatement (Third) of Trusts* § 22 (2001). However, a *devise* to "X, as trustee" may be the basis for imposing a *constructive* trust if there is extrinsic evidence of the trust terms. In Osswald v. Anderson, 57 Cal.Rptr.2d 23 (App.1996), the settlors signed a trust agreement but it failed to adequately describe the land so the statute was not satisfied.

[368] Tomlinson v. Tomlinson, 960 S.W.2d 337 (Tex.App.1997). *See also* Goytizolo v. Moore, 604 A.2d 362 (Conn.App.1992).

[369] For this purpose, initials constitute a "signing." In re Estate of Dotterrer, 579 A.2d 952 (Pa.Super.1990). *See also* Section 3.2, note 45 et seq.

[370] Trustees of Presbytery v. Hammer, 385 P.2d 1013 (Or.1963); *Restatement (Third) of Trusts* § 23(1) (2001).

[371] *Restatement (Third) of Trusts* § 23(2)(b) (2001); McCaffrey v. Laursen, 697 P.2d 103 (Mont.1985); Schaneman v. Wright, 470 N.W.2d 566 (Neb.1991). *Compare* the similar rules for the writing requirement for advancements. Section 2.6, notes 207–209.

[372] Ramage v. Ramage, 322 S.E.2d 22 (S.C.App.1984). *See also* Hall v. World Savings and Loan Ass'n, 943 P.2d 855 (Ariz.App.1997); *Restatement (Third) of Trusts* § 22, cmt. c (2001).

[373] *Id.*, § 7.

[374] However, in some states it also covers the assignment of an interest in any trust. *Id.*, § 53, cmt. a; Law of Property Act, 1925, § 53(1)(c). As to what is "land" for this purpose *see id.*, § 22, cmt. b; Section 3.5, note 227 et seq.

[375] Snuggs v. Snuggs, 571 S.E.2d 800 (Ga.2002) (action to enforce oral trust upheld); In re Trbovich's Estate, 413 A.2d 379 (Pa.1980); Paul v. Constance, [1977] 1 All E.R. 195 (C.A.1976).

informal bank-account trusts the settlor usually signs a card indicating that the account is held in trust. The Uniform Trust Code (hereinafter in the text and footnotes referred to as the "UTC") says that "the creation of an oral trust . . . may only be established by clear and convincing evidence."[376] Many courts use similar language in cases rejecting claims of a trust for insufficient proof.[377]

Precatory Language

The legal effect of wills that contain language suggesting that a devisee should use property for someone can be ambiguous. The language could evidence the testator's intent to impose a trust or other legal obligation upon the devisee for the benefit of another, or the words could be merely precatory, *i.e.*, intended to impose only a moral obligation, or to explain the motive for the devise, *e.g.*, "to enable him to bring up his children."[378] When a will left property to the testator's father "for the reason that I feel confident that any property which . . . my father . . . receive[s] from my estate will be used in the best interests of my said children," the children claimed that this created a trust, but the court disagreed. "This language does not impose any sort of clear directive or obligation (other than perhaps a moral or ethical one) . . . The purported trustee is given no direction as to how the supposed settlor intends his estate to be used to further 'the best interests' of the children."[379] Vagueness as to the beneficiaries and their interests "tends to suggest that the transferor did not intend to create a trust."[380] In contrast, when a will "requested" that the devisees pay the testator's sister-in-law "$208.33 per month as long as she shall live," these "precise and explicit terms" were held to be mandatory.[381]

The words "wish," "hope," and "desire" are usually construed as precatory,[382] but not always; a statement in a will that "it is my desire that Lee Davis . . . be allowed to purchase" property of the testator was held to give him an enforceable option.[383] Courts sometimes compare different parts of the will in construing ambiguous language. The word "request" in a will was held not

---

[376] UTC § 407; *cf.* Cal.Prob.Code § 15207.

[377] Spearman v. Estate of Spearman, 618 So.2d 276 (Fla.App.1993); Kurtz v. Solomon, 656 N.E.2d 184, 189 (Ill.App.1995) (evidence "must be so unequivocal as to lead to only one conclusion").

[378] Underhill & Hayton, *supra* note 314, at 97. Even when a trust clearly was intended, questions may arise as to whether a particular direction in it was intended to be merely precatory. *See, e.g.*, Section 10.3, note 70.

[379] Matter of Estate of Bolinger, 943 P.2d 981, 987 (Mont.1997). *See also* Cickyj v. Skeltinska, 417 N.E.2d 699 (Ill.App.1981); Dwyer v. Allyn, 596 N.E.2d 903 (Ind.App.1992). A similar problem can arise under German law as to whether an expression in a will is only a non-binding "wish" (Wunsch) of the testator. H. Brox, *Erbrecht* 264 (18th ed. 1999).

[380] *Restatement (Third) Trusts* § 13, cmt. d (2001).

[381] Spencer v. Childs, 134 N.E.2d 60 (N.Y.1956). *See also* Levin v. Fisch, 404 S.W.2d 889 (Tex.Civ.App.1966) ("desire" that testator's children pay her sister an annuity of $2,400).

[382] Dwyer v. Allyn, 596 N.E.2d 903 (Ind.App.1992); Chandler v. Chandler, 292 S.E.2d 685 (Ga.1982); Langston v. Hunt, 601 S.W.2d 833 (Ark.1980); *Restatement (Third) of Trusts* § 13, illus. 5–7 (2001).

[383] Gillespie v. Davis, 410 S.E.2d 613 (Va.1991). *See also* Snider v. Wood, 531 So.2d 864 (Ala.1988) ("wish"); Saunders v. Callaway, 708 P.2d 652 (Wash.App.1985). Underhill & Hayton, *supra* note 314, at 90, contrast a "modern rule" finding no trust in words like "wish" and "desire," and a former presumption to the contrary. *See also* Stephens v. McPherson, 362 S.E.2d 826 (N.C.App.1987) (construing "wish" in a holographic will as mandatory).

to create a trust when other provisions in the same will showed that the testator "was aware of how to leave assets in trust."[384]

It may make a difference who drafted the will. In construing a will which used "wish and desire" a court thought it noteworthy "that the testator in his lifetime was a professor of law" who "operated a well known bar review" course in which wills "received an appropriate share of attention" and so must have been "familiar with the leading cases wherein the term 'wish and desire' was held to be precatory."[385] In contrast, the word "want" in a home-drawn will was held to be mandatory because "informal language used by a layman who did not have legal advice in drawing his will" should not be construed "technically."[386]

The financial situation of the affected parties may also be relevant. A devise of the testator's estate to his wife with a "request that she use whatever of it she thinks necessary for the support and care of my brother," imposes a duty upon her "as trustee to make reasonable provision for *B*'s support and care" if he is needy and the wife is independently wealthy. These circumstances "overcome the inference normally drawn from precatory words."[387]

Charge and Condition

Language which creates a legal obligation does not necessarily create a trust. For example, a man left a building to his son "subject to the provision that for two (2) years after my death, . . . the net rental monies . . . shall be divided equally amongst my three (3) children." The son's sister claimed that this created a trust so that the building after the first two years would pass under the residuary clause of the will as a resulting trust. The court, however, held that the son received the property "outright, subject to a charge for two-thirds of the income for two years."[388] The Restatement of Trusts explains the difference between a charge and a trust:

> A transfer subject to an equitable charge is beneficial to the transferee as well as to the person to be benefited by the charge. Although this may also be true in the case of a trust, the intention to confer a beneficial interest . . . upon a trustee is not readily inferred, the usual inference being that a resulting trust arises with respect to the remaining beneficial interest.[389]

Some instruments are construed to impose a condition rather than a trust. When land was conveyed to a town "in trust for" a library, the question arose what should happen to the land when the town later closed the library. Had this been a trust, the property might have been applied to a related purpose

---

[384] Matter of Lowry's Estate, 418 N.E.2d 10, 12 (Ill.App.1981). *See also* Page v. Buchfinck, 275 N.W.2d 826 (Neb.1979).

[385] Matter of Sparacio's Estate, 402 N.Y.S.2d 857 (App.Div.1978). *See also* Dwyer v. Allyn, 596 N.E.2d 903 (Ind.App.1992) ("desire" is precatory in a will drafted by an experienced lawyer).

[386] First United Methodist Church v. Allen, 557 S.W.2d 175 (Tex.Civ.App.1977). *See also* note 384.

[387] *Restatement (Third) of Trusts* § 13, illus. 8 (2001).

[388] In re Estate of Krotz, 522 N.E.2d 790, 793 (Ill.App.1988).

[389] *Restatement (Third) of Trusts* § 5, cmt. h (2001). *See also* Underhill & Hayton, *supra* note 314, at 20–21.

under the *cy pres* doctrine.[390] But the court held that the property should return to the grantors' heirs (the grantors having died in the interim), because the town held "subject to a condition subsequent" rather than in trust. Even though the deed used the word "trust," other language showed "an intent to divest the transferee of its interest if it fails to maintain a library, indicating no trust was intended."[391]

On the other hand, the word "condition" is not always read literally. Even when property is transferred "on condition"

> a trust is created if the transferor manifested an intention (a) that the transferee should be subject to a duty to use the specific property for the transferor's or a third person's benefit rather than (b) that the transferee's interest should be divested upon failure to perform the act specified.[392]

Courts are especially reluctant to read the word "condition" literally when this might frustrate the transferor's intent to benefit a third person. When a testator left his estate to his son Barnard "on the condition" that he support his brother, James, the court refused to construe this as a condition, because that would mean that Barnard's failure to support James would cause the estate to pass by intestacy to the testator's disinherited children. This would "make less of the assets of the estate available for the support of James" contrary to the testator's wishes.[393]

§ 3.7 Payable-on-Death Contracts

A payable-on-death (P.O.D.) account is created when a person deposits money in a bank under an agreement which provides that upon the depositor's death the account will be paid to another. Trust accounts are almost universally held valid,[394] but the validity of P.O.D. accounts has been more doubtful, perhaps because they are more recent.[395] However, the policy reasons discussed in the previous section for upholding Totten trusts—the convenience of avoiding probate, the small amounts usually involved, widespread popular use, and the lack of serious doubt as to the decedent's intent when manifested in a written instrument[396]—apply equally to P.O.D. accounts.

P.O.D. accounts are valid under the UPC and many other state statutes.[397] Some statutes protect banks, permitting but not requiring them to

---

[390] State v. Rand, 366 A.2d 183 (Me.1976); Section 10.10, at note 606.

[391] Walton v. City of Red Bluff, 3 Cal.Rptr.2d 275 (App.1991). *See also* Underhill & Hayton, *supra* note 314, at 21.

[392] *Restatement (Third) of Trusts* § 5, cmt. h (2001).

[393] Whicher v. Abbott, 449 A.2d 353, 355 (Me.1982).

[394] Section 3.6, notes 352 et seq.

[395] Waitman v. Waitman, 505 P.2d 171, 175 (Okl.1972). *See also* Milliken v. First Nat. Bank, 290 A.2d 889 (Me.1972); Matter of Collier, 381 So.2d 1338 (Miss.1980); McGovern, *The Payable on Death Account and other Will Substitutes*, 67 Nw.U.L.Rev. 7, 9 (1972).

[396] But *see* notes 409–412 *infra* as to whether a signed writing is required for a P.O.D. account.

[397] UPC §§ 6–212(b), 6–214; Cal.Prob.Code §§ 5302(b), 5304. The prefatory note to Article VI of the UPC says that this part of the Code "is one of the most broadly accepted, having been adopted . . . by over half the states." In In re Estate of Fields, 46 P.3d 176, 178 (Okl.App.2001), the court noted that *Waitman*, cited in note 2 *supra*, had been altered by a statute like the UPC.

pay the deposit to the designated beneficiary, but such statutes are often interpreted to make P.O.D. accounts "a valid method of transferring property upon death, irrespective of the . . . the Statute of Wills."[398] Some statutes govern only one type of financial institution, banks, for example, but not savings and loan associations.[399] Some courts have interpreted such statutes narrowly; a statute authorizing P.O.D. accounts was held not to apply to an Individual Retirement Account (IRA).[400] However, upholding a P.O.D. designation in an IRA is more typical of recent cases. One court noted that "courts have upheld beneficiary designations in a variety of contractual arrangements analogous to IRA's. For example, the proceeds from an insurance policy are generally payable to the named beneficiary of the policy outside of the insured's probate estate."[401]

Insurance contracts on an insured's life are quite similar to wills in that they only call for payments upon the insured's death and until then they are typically revocable by the insured. Nonetheless, they have long been upheld as nontestamentary devices to which the Statute of Wills does not apply.[402] Their widespread use and "the high probability that they do not present an evil at which the Statute of Wills is aimed" is held to justify this result.[403] In insurance beneficiary designations, as in P.O.D. bank accounts, evidence of the decedent's (insured's) intention appears in the written records of a disinterested institution, the insurer.

Another analog to the P.O.D. account is an installment sale contract or note which provides for a change in payments when the payee dies. Most cases give effect to such provisions.[404] Even though no financial institution acts as an independent witness in this situation, a signed writing is usually involved.

In 1989, the UPC was revised to extend the P.O.D. concept to securities. The drafters noted that any distinction between bank accounts and securities made little sense when banks were "offering certificates of deposit of large value" while brokerage houses were providing "cash management accounts."[405] Nevertheless, the provisions in the Code for securities and bank accounts are

---

[398] Virginia National Bank v. Harris, 257 S.E.2d 867 (Va.1979). *But see* In re Hoffman's Estate, 195 N.E.2d 106 (Ohio 1963) (involving bank account trusts).

[399] McGovern, *supra* note 395, at 10. The Uniform Probate Code, on the other hand covers all accounts at financial institutions. These terms are broadly defined in UPC § 6–201.

[400] McCarty v. State Bank, 795 P.2d 940 (Kan.App.1990). *See also* Powell v. City Nat. Bank & Trust Co., 440 N.E.2d 560 (Ohio App.1981) (church cannot be a P.O.D. beneficiary, because statute authorizes them only for individuals).

[401] E.F. Hutton & Co., Inc. v. Wallace, 863 F.2d 472, 473 (6th Cir.1988). *See also* Matter of Estate of Lahren, 886 P.2d 412 (Mont.1994); D. Parry & J. Clark, *The Law of Succession* 21 (10th ed. 1996) (noting recent English cases upholding designation of beneficiary under pension).

[402] *See* Section 4.5, notes 164 et seq.

[403] Zimmerman v. Mutual Life Ins. Co., 156 F.Supp. 589 (N.D.Ala.1957). For the usefulness of life insurance in estate planning *see* J. Price, *Contemporary Estate Planning* chap. 6 (2d ed. 2000).

[404] Tierce v. Macedonia United Meth. Church, 519 So.2d 451 (Ala.1987); Herman v. Herman, 707 P.2d 1374 (Wash.App.1985); Williams v. Williams, 438 So.2d 735 (Ala.1983) (partnership agreement). *But see* Martinson v. Holso, 424 N.W.2d 664 (S.D.1988) (provision in land sale that on seller's death payments should go to his sister invalid as testamentary).

[405] UPC Art. VI, Prefatory Note.

somewhat different.[406] As to securities the Code uses the term T.O.D. or "transfer on death" rather than P.O.D. in order to avoid the implication that "the investment is to be sold or redeemed at the owner's death so that the sums realized may be 'paid' to the beneficiary."[407]

Legislation in Missouri has gone even further. It authorizes deeds of land and certificates of title to motor vehicles to effect transfers at death without a will.[408] This result might also be reached under the more general terms of Section 6–101 of the UPC which allow nonprobate transfers on death in a "deed of gift . . . or other written instrument of a similar nature."

The Missouri statute allowing nonprobate transfers requires that the beneficiary designation be in writing and subscribed by the owner.[409] An Ohio statute authorizing P.O.D. accounts created by a "written contract" was interpreted to require a signed writing.

> One of the basic requirements of the Statute of Wills cannot be ignored; that is, the requirement of a writing signed by the testator evidencing his intent. Because a P.O.D. account is testamentary in nature, it follows that the term 'written contract' means a writing signed by the owner of the funds.[410]

However, other cases have upheld oral designations of a beneficiary.[411] The UPC by its terms requires a signed writing to *change* an account, but not to establish one.[412]

§ 3.8 Joint Tenancy

Like the trust, joint tenancy has roots in medieval law going back to the 13th century.[413] In the 15th century, Littleton stated rules for joint tenancy substantially in their modern form. "The nature of joint tenancy is that the one who survives will have the whole tenancy." This applied to both land and personal property, but not where two or more persons held as tenants in common.[414] In modern times, joint tenancy has become a popular way to avoid probate, particularly for bank accounts and land.[415]

---

[406] The differences are examined in McGovern, *Nonprobate Transfers under the Revised Uniform Probate Code,* 55 Alb.L.Rev. 1329 (1992).

[407] UPC § 6–305, comment. *See also* Unif. Real Prop. Transfer on Death Act (2009).

[408] Mo.Stat.Ann. §§ 301.681 (motor vehicles), 461.025 (deeds of land). *See also* Cal.Veh.Code § 4150.7.

[409] Mo.Stat. § 461.062. *See also* N.Y. EPTL § 13–3.2(e) (designation of beneficiary of pension or insurance). A bank has been held liable to the intended beneficiary for failure to advise a customer that a writing was necessary to effectuate his intent. Corning Bank v. Rice, 645 S.W.2d 675 (Ark.1983).

[410] Witt v. Ward, 573 N.E.2d 201, 207 (Ohio App.1989). *See also* In re Estate of Waitkevich, 323 N.E.2d 545 (Ill.App.1975) (P.O.D. designation ineffective when added after decedent signed the ledger card for the account).

[411] Union Nat. Bank v. Ornelas-Gutierrez, 772 F.Supp. 962 (S.D.Tex.1991).

[412] UPC § 6–213.

[413] J. Bean, *The Decline of English Feudalism* 87–88 (1968); Spitzer, *Joint Tenancy with Right of Survivorship,* 16 Texas Tech.L.Rev. 629 (1985).

[414] T. Littleton, *Tenures* §§ 280–82.

[415] Hines, *Personal Property Joint Tenancies* 54 Minn.L.Rev. 509, 517, 521 (1970); Hines, *Real Property Joint Tenancies,* 51 Iowa L.Rev. 582, 586–87 (1966). As to the advantages and

Differences Between Historical and Modern Joint Tenancy

There are differences between modern joint tenancy and its medieval antecedent. Historically, if *A* wished to put land into joint tenancy with *B*, he had to deliver it to a third person who would reconvey the property to *A* and *B*.[416] Modern statutes allow persons to create a joint tenancy without any such conveyance to a straw man.[417] Even without a statute, challenges to joint tenancy for lack of delivery usually fail.[418] Some courts say that joint bank accounts are created by a contract between the depositor and the bank so the requirements for gifts do not apply.[419] Even as to deeds of land, delivery has been held unnecessary on the ground that "delivery to one cotenant or reservation of an estate connotes delivery to all cotenants, where the grantor is also the grantee."[420]

A frequently litigated issue in modern cases concerns the language needed to create a joint tenancy. Historically, a joint tenancy was created whenever property was conveyed "to *A* and *B*" without more.[421] Blackstone reaffirmed this rule in the 18th century,[422] but courts had already begun to question it, saying that joint tenancies "are not favoured," because they "do not make provision for posterity," *i.e.,* land passes to the surviving joint tenant(s) and the dead tenant's heirs get nothing, whereas in a tenancy in common, they would inherit the decedent's share (or it would pass under the decedent's will). The common law had favored joint tenancies because feudal lords wanted to keep land undivided, but this reason had ceased with the end of feudalism.[423]

Today, many statutes reverse the common-law presumption in favor of joint tenancy. For example, in Missouri "every interest in real estate granted or devised to two or more persons . . . shall be a tenancy in common unless expressly declared, in such grant or devise, to be in joint tenancy."[424] These statutes differ in their terms and have led to some curious distinctions that probably do not reflect the parties' understanding. This is unfortunate, because

possible disadvantages of using joint tenancy to avoid probate *see* Section 13.6, note 257 et seq. As to the gift and estate tax consequences of putting property into joint tenancy *see* J. Price, *Contemporary Estate Planning* § 3.14 (2d ed. 2000); Section 15.4, note 230 et seq.

416 T. Plucknett, *A Concise History of the Common Law* 577 (5th ed. 1956); McGovern, *The Enforcement of Oral Covenants Prior to Assumpsit,* 65 Nw.U.L.Rev. 576, 589 (1970).

417 Neb.Rev.Stat. § 76–118; Kan.Stat. § 58–501; 33 Me.Rev.Stat. § 901 (stocks and bonds); Helmholz, *Realism and Formalism in the Severance of Joint Tenancies*, 77 Neb.L.Rev. 1, 5 (1998).

418 *But see* Estate of Grove v. Selken, 820 P.2d 895 (Or.App.1991) (attempt to create joint tenancy in books by a signed writing fails for lack of delivery).

419 Malek v. Patten, 678 P.2d 201, 205 (Mont.1984); Vetter v. Hampton, 375 N.E.2d 804, 806 (Ohio 1978). The same reasoning was applied to the creation of a joint tenancy in securities in Matter of Estate of Evanco, 955 P.2d 525, 528 (Alaska 1998).

420 Kresser v. Peterson, 675 P.2d 1193, 1194 (Utah 1984). *See also* Matter of Estate of Rohrer, 646 N.E.2d 17 (Ill.App.1995); Winterton v. Kaufmann, 504 So.2d 439 (Fla.App.1987).

421 On the other hand, a *devise* to A and B did not. It created a tenancy in common between them.

422 2 W. Blackstone, *Commentaries* 180 (1765).

423 Hawes v. Hawes, 95 Eng.Rep. 552 (1747). *See also* Choman v. Epperley, 592 P.2d 714 (Wyo.1979). This explanation, though often repeated, is questionable because joint tenancy deprived lords of their feudal incidents. *See* note 413 *supra.*

424 Mo.Stat. § 442.450. *See also* Kan.Stat. § 58–501; 765 ILCS § 1005/1.

joint tenancy is typically created without the benefit of legal advice.[425] Under some statutes even a statement that property is held "jointly" is not enough, unless a right of survivorship is expressly mentioned.[426] Some statutes distinguish between the words "*A and B*" and "*A or B*."[427] Others presume a joint tenancy was intended only if *A* and *B* are married to each other.[428] Many courts allow an ambiguous registration of title to be clarified by extrinsic evidence of intent,[429] but some do not, *e.g.*, failure to provide for survivorship in a joint bank account "will be conclusive evidence of an intent not to transfer any right of survivorship to the survivor."[430] The most effective way to assure the creation of a joint tenancy with right of survivorship when one is intended is to place the title in the names of "A and B, as joint tenants with right of survivorship and not as tenants in common."

The UPC (relating to multiparty bank accounts) provides that bank accounts which are payable to two or more parties pass to the survivor "whether or not a right of survivorship is mentioned" unless "the terms of the account" negate a right of survivorship.[431] This probably reflects most depositors' intent because it avoids probate and administration for the whole account when one party dies.[432] More questionable is the Code's rule that if there are *two* surviving parties to the bank account, one of whom was the decedent's spouse, the spouse takes the entire account to the extent it is wholly attributable to the deceased's contribution;[433] it seems odd to presume that someone who gives property "to my spouse and *X*" intends that *X* get nothing.[434]

The Code provides model forms, which, if used intelligently, provide better evidence of the parties' wishes than phrases like "joint tenancy," the meaning of which is not clear to many persons. Under the Code's suggested forms, depositors can check boxes labeled, *e.g.*, "MULTIPLE-PARTY ACCOUNT

---

[425] Even lawyers trip up occasionally. In Estate of Hurst v. Hurst, 769 N.E.2d 55 (Ill.App.2002), a note drafted by a lawyer intended to create a joint tenancy in the payees had to be reformed because it was payable to "A or B or either of them."

[426] In re Estate of Hill, 931 P.2d 1320 (Mont.1997); Hoover v. Smith, 444 S.E.2d 546 (Va.1994); Stauffer v. Henderson, 801 S.W.2d 858 (Tex.1990). *But see* Matter of Estate of Epstein, 561 N.W.2d 82, 86 (Iowa App.1996).

[427] Fla.Stat. § 319.22(2)(a). Under Cal.Vehicle Code § 4150.5 both "or" and "and" create a right of survivorship, but "and" requires all living parties to sign when title is transferred.

[428] Mich.Comp.L. § 557.151 (stocks and bonds); Mo.Stat. § 442.450 (real estate); Lutz v. Lemon, 715 N.E.2d 1268 (Ind.App.1999) (household goods acquired during marriage); *cf.* Voss v. Brooks, 907 P.2d 465 (Alaska 1995) (joint tenancy deed creates tenancy in common when parties are not married).

[429] Matter of Estate of Briley, 825 P.2d 1181 (Kan.App.1992); Matter of Estate of Vadney, 634 N.E.2d 976 (N.Y.1994) (deed reformed to show intent to create joint tenancy).

[430] Trust of McManus v. McManus, 18 A.3d 550 (RI. 2011); Robinson v. Delfino, 710 A.2d 154, 161 (R.I.1998). *See also* Starr v. Rousselet, 877 P.2d 525 (Nev.1994); In re Estate of Hill, 931 P.2d 1320 (Mont.1997); State ex rel. Pilard v. Berninger, 571 S.E.2d 836, 844 (N.C.App.2002).

[431] UPC §§ 6–201(5), 6–212. *Compare* In re Estate of Ancell, 741 N.Y.S.2d 397 (Surr.2002) (presumption of right of survivorship in Banking Law inapplicable when survivorship was not indicated on signature card).

[432] For the advantages of avoiding probate *see* Section 13.4.

[433] UPC § 6–212(a).

[434] McGovern, *Nonprobate Transfers under the Revised Uniform Probate Code*, 55 Alb.L.Rev. 1329, 1331 (1992). The presumption applies only to amounts contributed by the decedent; if *X* had contributed to the account, his or her contribution would not pass to the spouse.

WITH RIGHT OF SURVIVORSHIP" or "MULTIPLE-PARTY ACCOUNT WITHOUT RIGHT OF SURVIVORSHIP".[435]

The foregoing provisions apply to accounts at a "financial institution" (including checking and savings accounts and certificates of deposit at banks, savings and loans and credit unions),[436] but not to securities or accounts with a broker. The Code provisions dealing with these provide only for T.O.D. registration which the drafters preferred to the "frequently troublesome joint tenancy form of title."[437] Nor does the Code apply to deeds of land; as to these, the interpretation of the words "to *A* and *B*" may differ from that given to the same words when used to create a bank account. California follows the Code as to bank accounts, but otherwise presumes that two or more persons hold title to property as tenants in common.[438] Perhaps this distinction is justified by the fact that land is usually worth more than a bank account, so the survivor's taking the whole property can have more serious consequences. In this respect, securities are more like land, but there are obviously exceptions both ways; certificates of deposit, which are treated as bank accounts, may be quite large, whereas cash-management accounts administered by brokers can be rather small. And, still another set of rules or presumptions may apply to motor vehicles.

Safe Deposit Boxes

Deposit of articles into a jointly leased safe-deposit box usually has no effect on the ownership of the contents of the box. The joint-tenancy language in the lease is generally construed to apply only to use of the box.[439] However, a contract which provided that "upon the death of either [party, the] . . . entire contents . . . shall belong exclusively to the survivor" was held to pass currency in a box to the survivor.[440] But when $600,000 worth of registered securities was left in such a box, the court refused to award them to the surviving tenant of the box.[441] In California, any contract which purports to create a joint tenancy in the contents of a box is void.[442]

A safe-deposit box differs from a bank account in that it usually contains most of the lessee's title documents. A surviving joint tenant's claim to the

---

[435] UPC § 6–204. The form does not reveal that the decedent's spouse, if one of the "surviving parties," will get the entire account under § 6–212(a).

[436] *Id.* § 6–201 In Raichel v. Raichel, 65 S.W.3d 497 (Ky.2001), a similar provision was held to apply to a cashier's check payable to "Eddie or James," so it passed to the latter when the former died.

[437] UPC, Prefatory Note to Article VI. For a criticism of this omission *see* McGovern, *supra* note 434, at 1332. In In re Estate of Delaney, 819 A.2d 968, 989 (D.C.2003) the court drew a similar distinction between a credit union account and a brokerage account under Virginia law.

[438] Cal.Prob.Code §§ 5130, 5302 (as to bank accounts, like the UPC but without the provision favoring the decedent's spouse); Cal.Civ.Code § 683(a) (presumption of tenancy in common).

[439] In re Estate of Finkelstein, 817 P.2d 617 (Colo.App.1991); Wright v. Union Nat. Bank, 819 S.W.2d 698 (Ark.1991); In re Estate of Silver, 1 P.3d 358, 362 (Mont.2000); Hines, *supra* note 415 at 525.

[440] Matter of Estate of Langley, 546 N.E.2d 1287 (Ind.App.1989). *See also* Steinhauser v. Repko, 285 N.E.2d 55 (Ohio 1972).

[441] Estate of Matelich v. Matelich, 772 P.2d 319 (Nev.1989).

[442] Cal.Civ.Code § 683.1.

contents of a box may conflict with the form of registered securities in the box. If *A* and *B* jointly lease a box and *A* deposits stock certificates registered in the names of "*A* and *C* as joint tenants into the box," the ownership of the stock would be in doubt if joint tenancy in the contents of a box were recognized.

Validity of Joint Tenancy

Attacks on joint tenancy as a testamentary transfer are rare, but courts occasionally hold that if the decedent did not intend to give the other joint tenant a "present interest" in the property there can be no right of survivorship.[443] Most courts, however, accept the fact that joint tenancy is often used as a will substitute. "We see no harm in that. . . . The formal requisites of wills serve . . . to insure that dispositions are carefully and seriously made, and to provide reliable evidence of the disposition. Those purposes are adequately served by the institutional setting and the signed writing normally involved."[444]

Although the *validity* of joint tenancy is rarely challenged today, claims are frequently made that a purported joint tenancy in a bank account was not *intended* to give the other party a beneficial interest, but rather was only intended to allow him or her to make deposits and withdrawals on behalf of the sole depositor who opened the account.[445] When adjudicating that claim, the law of the situs of the account, not the law of the depositor's domicile at death, governs.[446] A person who does not intend to give another a beneficial interest in an account should not use a joint account but should use a power-of-attorney instead. The forms suggested by the UPC call attention to this option.[447]

A few states require a signed writing to create a joint account,[448] but most do not.[449] Even a statute which required "a written instrument" to create a joint tenancy was held to be satisfied by a form filled out by a broker on oral instructions from his clients.[450] The UPC allows joint bank accounts to be opened orally but requires a signed writing to alter the form of the account thereafter.[451]

---

[443] Lewis v. Steinreich, 652 N.E.2d 981 (Ohio 1995). *See also* Matter of Bobeck, 531 N.Y.S.2d 340 (App.Div.1988).

[444] Blanchette v. Blanchette, 287 N.E.2d 459, 463–5 (Mass.1972). *See also* Section 3.6, note 348.

[445] Litigation on this issue is further treated at Section 7.3, at note 143 et seq.

[446] Barboza v. McLeod, 853 N.E.2d 192 (2006); Tyler v. Suburban Trust Co., 231 A.2d 678 (Md. 1967).

[447] UPC § 6–204.

[448] Rynn v. Owens, 536 N.E.2d 959 (Ill.App.1989) (right of survivorship exists only between persons who sign); Tex.Est.Code § 111.001.

[449] Morris v. Cullipher, 816 S.W.2d 878 (Ark.1991) (applying Arkansas law which does not require a writing rather than Texas law which does); Martinson v. Holso, 424 N.W.2d 664 (S.D.1988) (oral agreement that partnership assets will go to survivor enforced); Simmons v. Foster, 622 S.W.2d 838 (Tenn.App.1981) (orally created joint account).

[450] Estate of Tressel v. Tressel, 986 P.2d 72 (Or.App.1999).

[451] UPC § 6–213. *See also* Section 3.7, note 412. For a discussion of cases dealing with this problem *see* McGovern, *supra* note 434, at 1335–1337.

§ 3.9 Contracts to Make Wills

Contracts to devise property appear often in litigation. Sometimes they are made in return for services to be performed by the promisee, but more commonly the contract is for the benefit of a third party, for example, spouses promise each other that the survivor will leave their property to relatives of both spouses. Even jurisdictions that do not ordinarily allow third party beneficiaries to enforce contracts make an exception in this situation.[452]

Joint and Mutual Wills

Some courts infer the existence of a contract when two spouses execute a "joint" will—one will signed by two testators. For example, a husband and wife executed a joint will which said "It is our intention that this Will shall be binding." The husband survived the wife and executed a new will leaving his estate to one of their two children. The other child successfully claimed that the new will was a breach of contract.

> A joint will . . . may by its language evidence an irrevocable agreement between the parties. . . . The [earlier] will evidence a definite, clear and unequivocal intention to establish a binding, irrevocable agreement.[453]

Many courts, however, have refused to infer the existence of a contract from joint wills with somewhat different wording.[454] The UPC provides that: "the execution of a joint will . . . does not create a presumption of a contract not to revoke the will."[455] Even one providing that "we agree that the provisions hereof shall not be changed" was held insufficient to show a contract barring the survivor from changing it because the will left the testators' property to the survivor "absolutely."[456]

More common than joint wills are "mutual" wills, separate wills executed by spouses at the same time with reciprocal provisions (sometimes called "mirror image" wills). Most courts say that whatever inference may be derived from a *joint* will, execution of mutual wills does not indicate a contract.[457] The

---

[452] Bettencourt v. Bettencourt, 284 N.E.2d 238 (Mass.1972); Youdan, *The Mutual Wills Doctrine,* 29 U.Tor.L.J. 390, 401 (1979).

[453] Adkins v. Oppio, 769 P.2d 62, 64 (Nev.1989). *See also* In re Estate of Kaplan, 579 N.E.2d 963 (Ill.App.1991); Wetzel v. Watson, 328 S.E.2d 526 (W.Va.1985). Similarly, under BGB (German Civil Code) § 2271(2) a joint will of spouses with reciprocal provisions cannot be revoked after the first spouse dies unless the surviving spouse renounces benefits under the will. French and Italian law, on the other hand, do not allow joint wills. Code Civil art. 968; Codice Civile art. 589. This disparity raises difficult choice of law questions. H. Flick & D. Piltz, *Der Internationale Erbfall* 25 (1999).

[454] Hodges v. Callaway, 621 S.E.2d 428 (Ga. 2005); King v. Travis, 524 N.E.2d 974 (Ill.App.1988); Matter of Estate of Di Siena, 576 N.Y.S.2d 952 (App.Div.1991); Long v. Waggoner, 558 S.E.2d 380 (Ga.2002).

[455] UPC § 2–514. *See also* Cal.Prob.Code § 21700(b).

[456] In re Estate of Armijo, 31 P.3d 372 (N.M.2001). *See also* Oravec v. Phillips, 785 S.E.2d 295 (G. 2016).

[457] Smith v. Turner, 477 S.E.2d 663 (Ga.App.1996); Junot v. Estate of Gilliam, 759 S.W.2d 654 (Tenn.1988); Pearce v. Meek, 780 S.W.2d 289 (Tex.App.1989).

UPC agrees, but some courts relying on extrinsic evidence, have found that mutual wills were in fact made pursuant to a contract.[458]

Statute of Frauds

The Statute of Frauds may bar oral evidence of such a contract. Contracts to devise land may fall under the provision of the 1676 Statute of Frauds which required contracts to sell land to be in writing.[459] Many states today have provisions that specifically deal with contracts to make wills. The UPC provides that a contract to make or not to revoke a will can be established only by "(i) provisions of a will stating material provisions of the contract, (ii) an express reference in a will to a contract and extrinsic evidence proving the terms of the contract, or (iii) a writing signed by the decedent evidencing the contract."[460]

Simply signing a will does not satisfy the statute unless the will refers to or states the terms of the contract. Even a recital in a joint will that the parties had "heretofore agreed, for valuable consideration . . . to make joint and mutual wills giving to the survivor of us all property" was held insufficient to bind the survivor not to revoke the will after the first party died.[461]

Refusal to enforce a contract after one party has performed it leads to unjust enrichment. Courts sometimes avoid this by granting restitutionary relief.[462] A comment to the UPC says that the writing requirement does "not preclude recovery in quantum meruit for the value of services rendered the testator."[463] In such actions, courts have used the value of the promisor's estate which was promised to the plaintiff as evidence of the value of the services performed, so that the result is nearly equivalent to enforcing the contract. For example, when a father promised to leave his son a share of a company if he continued to work for him and the son proved that the value of the promised share was $463,965, he recovered $443,985 "in quantum meruit for the value of his services in reliance on the unenforceable oral promise."[464] On the other hand, services rendered by one family member to another are presumed to have been intended as gifts and are not compensable unless this presumption is rebutted.[465]

---

458 Todd v. Cartwright, 684 S.W.2d 154 (Tex.App.1984); In re Dale, [1994] Ch. 31 (1993).

459 B Sparks, *Contracts to Make Wills* 41–43 (1956).

460 UPC § 2–514. As to England *see* D. Parry & J. Clark, *The Law of Succession* 12 (10th ed. 1996). *Compare* BGB (German Civil Code) § 2276 (contracts concerning inheritance must be executed before a notary). Hirsch argues that logically the law should require no less formalities for contracts to make wills than for wills themselves. Hirsch, *Inheritance and Inconsistency*, 57 Ohio St.L.J. 1057, 1081 (1996). Such statutes may not apply to contracts made prior to their enactment. Section 1.3, note 219.

461 Matter of Lubins, 673 N.Y.S.2d 204 (App.Div.1998). *See also* Estate of Hearn v. Hearn, 101 S.W.3d 657 (Tex.App.2003).

462 * * * *of Contracts* § 373 (1979).

463 UPC § 2–514, Comment.

464 Slawsby v. Slawsby, 601 N.E.2d 478 (Mass.App.1992). *See also* * * * *of Contracts* § 375 (1979); *cf.* Williams v. Mason, 556 So.2d 1045 (Miss.1990) (error to award promised estate, remand for recovery for value of services).

465 Clark v. Gale, 966 P.2d 431, 439 (Wyo.1998). *See also* In re Estate of Orr, 60 P.3d 962 (Mont.2002); *cf.* In re Estate of White, 31 P.3d 1071 (Okl.Civ.App.2001) (quantum meruit recovery allowed only for work in improving property; other services were part of "shared domestic life").

Many courts hold that a promisee's part performance satisfies or excuses a statutory writing requirement.[466] The UPC contains no part-performance exception, but courts may nevertheless recognize one, just as they did for the original Statute of Frauds without any basis in the statutory language.[467] But some courts have taken the Code's tightened proof requirements seriously, saying that "application of the equitable principle of part performance . . . would nullify the purpose of the statute."[468]

An oral promise which was made without intent to perform it has been held to be actionable as fraud.[469] A lost or destroyed writing has been held to satisfy the statute.[470]

Clear and Convincing Evidence

Even if a statutory writing requirement is not a bar, claims under a contract often fail because the plaintiff's evidence is not clear and convincing. Thus, a daughter's claim that her parents had contracted to leave her a share of their property was rejected because "the proof failed to establish an agreement by clear and convincing evidence . . . [Plaintiff] and the witnesses called in her behalf were all related [to her] by blood or marriage and their testimony did not have that degree of disinterest which would render it obligatory on the fact finder."[471]

Even evidence in writing may not suffice if the terms are vague. "At best, the documents prove that, at one point in time, decedent planned to leave his house to appellant's family, but changed his mind . . . There was no reference to any contract."[472] Testimony of discrepant versions of the contract terms may also persuade a court that the proof is insufficient.[473]

Executory Contracts

Parties who have agreed that a will shall be irrevocable may agree to rescind the contract.[474] Most authorities also allow either party to repudiate

[466] Shepherd v. Mazzetti, 545 A.2d 621 (Del.1988); Estate of Von Wendesse, 618 N.E.2d 1332 (Ind.App.1993); * * * *of Contracts* § 129, illus. 10 (1979).

[467] Estate of Housley, 65 Cal.Rptr.2d 628 (App.1997). California for many years had a statute modeled on the UPC, but it was recently changed to allow an oral agreement to be proved by "clear and convincing evidence." Cal.Prob.Code § 21700(a)(4).

[468] Rieck v. Rieck, 724 P.2d 674, 676 (Colo.App.1986). *See also* Cole v. Rivers, 861 S.W.2d 551 (Ark.App.1993); Estate of Hearn v. Hearn, 101 S.W.3d 657, 660 (Tex.App.2003).

[469] Brody v. Bock, 897 P.2d 769 (Colo.1995). *Cf.* Taylor v. Johnson, 677 S.W.2d 680 (Tex.App.1984) (no fraud absent a finding of intent not to perform when promise was made); Section 7.4, at note 201 et seq.

[470] Murphy v. Glenn, 964 P.2d 581, 585 (Colo.App.1998); Baker v. Mohr, 826 P.2d 111 (Or.App.1992). *Accord,* * * * *of Contracts* § 137 (1979).

[471] Mabry v. McAfee, 783 S.W.2d 356, 358 (Ark.1990). *See also* Smith v. Turner, 477 S.E.2d 663 (Ga.App.1996); In re Estate of White, 31 P.3d 1071 (Okl.Civ.App.2001).

[472] Olesen v. Manty, 438 N.W.2d 404, 407 (Minn.App.1989). *See also* Kahn v. First Nat. Bank, 576 N.E.2d 321, 325 (Ill.App.1991) ("statements of testamentary intent" do not create "a specific contract capable of enforcement").

[473] In re Layton's Estate, 323 N.W.2d 817, 823 (Neb.1982).

[474] Matter of Estate of Cohen, 629 N.E.2d 1356 (N.Y.1994) (wife's accepting appointment as administrator of her husband's estate was a tacit consent to his revocation of a contractual will); *cf.* * * * *of Contracts* § 311 (1979) (limiting ability of parties to a contract to discharge duties to a third party beneficiary in some situations).

the contract *unilaterally* before there has been any performance, meaning the death of either testator. When a couple agreed to leave their property at the death of the survivor to their son, the wife later repudiated the contract, and made a new will. A suit by the son to enforce the contract was dismissed. "While ... the parties to such an agreement are yet alive, any party may recede therefrom, ... on giving proper notice to the other party."[475] The notice requirement allows the other party to change his or her will in light of the knowledge that other party will not abide by the contract. Given that the purpose of the notice requirement is to allow the party receiving the notice to change his or her will, where notice was given to a testator while in a persistent vegetative state, the court held the contractual will was not revoked.[476]

Courts usually enforce contracts even though they have not been partly performed (assuming the Statute of Frauds is no bar), but because contracts to make wills are usually between family members, courts may feel that the parties did not intend them to be enforceable to the same extent as a commercial contract.

Fairness

Contracts to make a will must be supported by consideration.[477] A promise to devise in return for services previously rendered by the promisee is not enforceable.[478] Technical consideration may not suffice. Plaintiffs usually seek what amounts to specific performance,[479] and this brings into play equity's traditional reluctance to enforce unfair contracts.[480] Nevertheless, many contracts have been enforced despite the lack of an equal exchange. The value of a party's performance may be hard to measure in monetary terms, for example, the promisee's "emigration to this country and the consequent disruption this caused to both himself and his family."[481] Moreover, fairness is determined as of the date of the contract; subsequent events that make the exchange unequal in hindsight are not considered.[482] Many contracts are between spouses with estates of very different size. One court refused to enforce such a contract against the husband's estate because the wife had left

---

[475] Boyle v. Schmitt, 602 So.2d 665, 667 (Fla.App.1992). *See also* Matter of Estate of Edington, 489 N.E.2d 612, 615 (Ind.App.1986); BGB (German Civil Code) § 2271(1) (either spouse can revoke mutual will while both are still living by giving notice to the other spouse). *But cf.* Matter of Estate of Lilienthal, 574 N.W.2d 349 (Iowa App.1997) (unilateral rescission not allowed when other party was alive but incompetent); In re Estate of Johnson, 781 S.W.2d 390 (Tex.App.1989) (refusing to allow unilateral rescission).

[476] Matter of Estate of Lilienthal, 574 N.W.2d 349 (Iowa App. 1997).

[477] In the typical contractual will between spouses, adequate consideration exists where each agrees to forebear executing a new will inconsistent with the contract.

[478] In re Estate of Casey, 583 N.E.2d 83 (Ill.App.1991); Rowell v. Plymouth-Home Nat. Bank, 434 N.E.2d 648 (Mass.App.1982); Dementas v. Estate of Tallas, 764 P.2d 628 (Utah App.1988); *cf.* * * * *of Contracts* § 86 (1979) (promises made in recognition of benefit previously received are "binding to the extent necessary to prevent injustice").

[479] This is often called "quasi-specific performance ... since the making of a will cannot be compelled." Walton v. Walton, 36 Cal.Rptr.2d 901, 905 (App.1995).

[480] * * * *of Contracts* § 364 (1979).

[481] In re Beeruk's Estate, 241 A.2d 755, 759 (Pa.1968).

[482] Matter of Marriage of Ellinwood, 651 P.2d 190, 192 (Or.App.1982). But this inequality may persuade a court to find that no contract existed. *See* In re Estate of Trobaugh, 380 N.W.2d 152 (Minn.App.1986) (plaintiff cared for decedent for less than 2 months).

him no property. "Although the mutual promises may have amounted to technical consideration, . . . certainly there was great inequality of consideration moving from the two makers. Thus, the agreement was not sufficiently fair."[483] However, in many cases a great disparity between the consideration received and the value of the promise has not prevented enforcement.[484]

Inter-Vivos Transfers

Sometimes a promisor while still living seeks to undercut the contract by conveying property to others. The beneficiaries of the contract may succeed in setting aside such conveyances on the theory that the contract confined the promisor to a life estate in his or her property with a remainder in the beneficiaries of the contract,[485] or the agreement not to change a will "carried with it an implicit agreement . . . to make no disposition of that estate property inconsistent with that intent."[486] Other courts do not go so far in enforcing the contract. A husband's promise to leave his estate to his children was held to give them no claim to assets he put in joint tenancy, because the contract did not require that he "have property at the time of his demise."[487] Some courts apply a rule of reason. The contract "does not prohibit the [promisor] from using her property for the necessities and comforts of life.[488] . . . from changing the form of the property[489] and . . . from making reasonable gifts of estate property to third parties. Reasonableness of a gift would depend upon the proportion that the value of the gift bears to the value of the estate."[490]

Even changes in a will have been allowed if they are not inconsistent with the spirit of a contract. For example, a couple's contractual will left their estate in trust for their daughters with a remainder to the grandchildren. After the

---

[483] Levis v. Hammond, 100 N.W.2d 638 (Iowa 1960).

[484] Kitchen v. Estate of Blue, 498 N.E.2d 41, 45 (Ind.App.1986) (promisor's receipt of his wife's $300 estate was sufficient consideration for his promise to dispose of $130,000 estate).

[485] Young v. Young, 569 N.E.2d 1, 5 (Ill.App.1991). *See also* Foulds v. First Nat. Bank, 707 P.2d 1171, 1174 (N.M.1985).

[486] Robison v. Graham, 799 P.2d 610, 615 (Okl.1990). *See also* Matter of Estate of Kerr, 918 P.2d 1354 (N.M.App.1996) (putting property into joint tenancy was a breach); In re Estate of Gibson, 893 S.W.2d 749 (Tex.App.1995).

[487] Duran v. Komyatte, 490 N.E.2d 388 (Ind.App.1986). *See also* Blackmon v. Estate of Battcock, 587 N.E.2d 280 (N.Y.1991) (revocable trust); D. Parry & J. Clark, *The Law of Succession* 13 (10th ed. 1996) (only inter-vivos dispositions with "testamentary effect" are barred); *cf.* BGB (German Civil Code) §§ 2286–87 (promisor can make inter-vivos gifts, but beneficiary of contract has a claim against the donee if the promisor made the gift with the intention to injure the beneficiary); Foster, *The Dark Side of Trusts: Challenges to Chinese Inheritance Law*, 2 Wash.U. Global Studies L.Rev. 151, 170–72 (2003) (fearing that China's new Trust Law will allow evasion of contracts to devise).

[488] *See also* Matter of Ciochon's Estate, 609 P.2d 177, 183 (Kan.App.1980); Pyle by Straub v. United States, 766 F.2d 1141, 1144 (7th Cir.1985) ("she may invade corpus only for health, support and comfort"); Westbrook v. Superior Court, 222 Cal.Rptr. 317, 323 (App.1986) ("reasonably necessary living expenses").

[489] The promisor can sell the property if the consideration is adequate. Long v. Buehler, 648 P.2d 270 (Kan.App.1982); *cf.* Pyle by Straub v. United States, 766 F.2d 1141, 1144 (7th Cir.1985) (can exchange for assets "of equal or greater value"). In any event, a bona fide purchaser is protected. *See* note 493 *infra*.

[490] Powell v. American Charter Fed. S. & L., 514 N.W.2d 326, 334 (Neb.1994). *See also* Murphy v. Glenn, 964 P.2d 581, 586 (Colo.App.1998); Peirce v. Peirce, 994 P.2d 193, 200 (Utah 2000); Nile v. Nile, 734 N.E.2d 1153, 1160 (Mass.2000).

wife died, the husband made a new will which left the property to the daughters outright. The court rejected a challenge filed on behalf of the grandchildren on the ground that the later will "substantially complied with the contract." The grandchildren's "expectancy was realized in the form of benefits flowing directly to their mothers and indirectly to them as dependents of their mothers and as the natural heirs of their mother's estates."[491]

Third Parties

The promisor is usually dead when an action to enforce the contract is brought, and the action is brought either against the promisor's estate or against a third party. Two theories are used to protect contract beneficiaries. Under one theory, contract beneficiaries are protected by courts granting them a claim against the estate. Under the other, courts protect them by impressing a constructive trust upon the property in favor of the contract beneficiaries.[492]

Protecting intended beneficiaries by granting them a claim against the estate rather than imposing a constructive trust can have consequences if the claims of the contract beneficiary are not timely filed within the time period for filing claims. If the claim is protected by use of a constructive trust, timely filing under a non-claims statute would not be required. Also, a bona fide purchaser of property prevails over the equitable claims of the contract beneficiaries,[493] but the beneficiaries can recover property in the hands of donees and devisees of the promisor.[494]

Complications arise when spouses execute contractual wills and the survivor of them dies survived by another spouse. Is the survivor's surviving spouse entitled to an elective share in the assets subject to the contract against the interest of the contract's beneficiaries? Some courts reject a surviving spouse's claim to an elective share on the ground that it only applies to the decedent's estate after payment of claims, which includes claims based on the contract.[495] This reasoning would allow the surviving spouse at least a family allowance which is not subject to the decedent's creditors,[496] but not if the decedent-promisor is viewed as only a life tenant or trustee of the property subject to the contract.[497] On the other hand, some courts have allowed the

---

[491] Kerper v. Kerper, 780 P.2d 923, 937 (Wyo.1989). *See also* In re Estate of Milward, 73 P.3d 155, 160 (Kan.App.2003) (survivor could designate a different executor); In re Estate of Espey, 729 S.W.2d 99, 102 (Tenn.App.1986) (survivor could dispose of her estate "in such a manner as befits the circumstances"); H. Brox, *Erbrecht* 94 (18th ed. 1999) (when contract divides estate between relatives of H and W, H can change the provision for his relatives after W dies).

[492] Robison v. Graham, 799 P.2d 610 (Okl.1990); Chapman v. Citizens & Southern Nat. Bank, 395 S.E.2d 446 (S.C.App.1990); In re Dale, [1994] Ch. 31 (1993).

[493] Olive v. Biggs, 173 S.E.2d 301 (N.C.1970). As to the rights of a bona fide purchaser from a trustee *see* Section 12.9, note 23 et seq. In Dickie v. Dickie, 769 P.2d 225 (Or.App.1989), after the promisor sold the property to a bona fide purchaser, the court imposed a constructive trust on the sale proceeds.

[494] Musselman v. Mitchell, 611 P.2d 675 (Or.App.1980); O'Connor v. Immele, 43 N.W.2d 649 (N.D.1950).

[495] Johnson v. Girtman, 542 So.2d 1033 (Fla.App.1989); In re Beeruk's Estate, 241 A.2d 755 (Pa.1968); Schaefer v. Schuhman, [1972] 2 W.L.R. 481 (P.C. 1971); Section 8.7, note 266.

[496] Kinne v. Kinne, 617 P.2d 442 (Wash.App.1980); Matter of Estate of Harper, 486 N.E.2d 295 (Ill.App.1985); Section 8.4, note 151.

[497] Gregory v. Estate of Gregory, 866 S.W.2d 379 (Ark.1993); In re Estate of Stewart, 444 P.2d 337 (Cal.1968); Rubenstein v. Mueller, 225 N.E.2d 540 (N.Y.1967).

surviving spouse to prevail over the contract beneficiaries because of "the public policy surrounding the marriage relationship,"[498] or because even if the survivor had performed the contract, the spouse's elective share would have precedence over the survivor's will.[499] Other courts have reached intermediate solutions.

In determining whether to award specific performance to contract beneficiaries, courts have considered several different factors, including whether the surviving spouse had notice of the contract prior to the marriage, . . . the length of the marriage and . . . whether the surviving spouse would be deprived of the entire estate by enforcement of the contract.[500] Likewise, the contribution of the spouse to the accumulation of the decedent's property may also be relevant to the enforcement of a contract.

If property is located in a community property state, the spouse should get half of any community property of the marriage even though the deceased spouse was a party to an earlier contractual will.[501] Where the promisor (the survivor of the parties to a contractual will) and his second wife had "made substantial financial contributions to the construction of a house and to a joint savings account," the court refused to subject these assets to a constructive trust for the beneficiary of the earlier contractual will, which it enforced only with respect to the husband's "separate estate."[502] Some courts construe the contract as not intended to include *any* property acquired by the promissor after the death of the first spouse.[503]

After-born children of the promisor may also be protected if full enforcement of a contract would deprive them of any share of their father's estate.[504]

Remedies

Because probate courts traditionally had no jurisdiction to enforce contracts, a will executed in breach of a contract is often admitted to probate, and the contract beneficiary's only remedy is in a court of general jurisdiction.[505] Admitting a will to probate in one court and denying it effect in another seems inefficient, and some cases have made a breach of contract the basis for refusing to probate a will made in breach of contract.[506]

---

[498] Via v. Putnam, 656 So.2d 460 (Fla.1995) (allowing widow to claim as an omitted spouse); Shimp v. Huff, 556 A.2d 252, 263 (Md.1989); *cf.* Sheldon v. Sheldon, 987 P.2d 1229 (Or.App.1999). For a critique of *Via, see* Hirsch, *Cognitive Jurisprudence*, 76 So.Cal.L.Rev. 1331, 1356 (2003).

[499] In re Estate of Tensfeldt, 839 So.2d 720, 727 (Fla.App.2003).

[500] Shimp v. Huff, 556 A.2d 252, 259 (Md.1989).

[501] Perl v. Howell, 650 S.W.2d 523, 525 (Tex.App.1983); Porter v. Porter, 726 P.2d 459 (Wash.1986). *But see* Cal.Fam.Code § 910 (community property is liable for a debt incurred by either spouse before or during the marriage).

[502] Kassahn v. Kassahn, 868 P.2d 9 (Or.App.1994).

[503] In re Estate of Gibson, 893 S.W.2d 749 (Tex.App.1995).

[504] Matter of Estate of Sherry, 698 P.2d 94 (Wash.App.1985).

[505] Lewis v. Tanner, 312 S.E.2d 798 (Ga.1984); Perino v. Eldert, 577 N.E.2d 807 (Ill.App.1991); Coffman v. Woods, 696 S.W.2d 386 (Tex.App.1985).

[506] Estate of McKusick, 629 A.2d 41 (Me.1993); In re Estate of Gibson, 893 S.W.2d 749 (Tex.App.1995).

Where law and equity are still separated, actions to enforce contracts to make wills are usually classified as equitable, which means there is no right to a jury trial.[507] The statute of limitations starts to run only when the promisor dies, so cases often come to trial many years after the alleged contract was made.[508] However, claims may be barred shortly after the promissor's death by virtue of a "non-claim" statute which requires that claims against a decedent be filed within a brief period after administration of the estate begins.[509]

Suit is sometimes brought against a promisor who has repudiated the contract while still alive.[510] Courts have enjoined the promisor from transferring the property, vacated conveyances previously made, and even appointed a trustee to take charge of the property.[511] However, a trust is imposed only if the promisor has attempted to dispose of property improperly, because this would curtail the promisor's extensive rights over the property while alive.[512]

Planning

Contracts to make wills are common, but most commentators think they are a bad idea. "The uncertain federal and state tax consequences of contractual wills . . . makes them generally undesirable.[513] . . . [A] trust is almost invariably a better way to provide for survivors" because "a trust may avoid the uncertainty that inheres in contractual arrangements."[514] Many courts share this feeling. As one judge has said:

---

[507] Walton v. Walton, 36 Cal.Rptr.2d 901 (App.1995); In re Layton's Estate, 323 N.W.2d 817 (Neb.1982); Peirce v. Peirce, 994 P.2d 193, 197 (Utah 2000). *But see* Wilkison v. Wiederkehr, 124 Cal.Rptr.2d 631 (App.2002) (equitable relief denied because damages provided an adequate remedy).

[508] Estate of Brenzikofer, 57 Cal.Rptr.2d 401 (App.1996) (agreement made in 1981, promisor died in 1991, action filed in 1994 was timely); Taylor v. Abernethy, 560 S.E.2d 233, 240 (N.C.App.2002) (action filed in 1998 on contract made in 1978 is timely because promisor died in 1998); In re Estate of Tensfeldt, 839 So.2d 720, 725 (Fla.App.2003); *cf.* In re Estate of Blumenthal, 812 A.2d 1279, 1289 (Pa.Super.2002) (when decedent had promised to make *inter-vivos gifts,* statute runs from time gifts should have been made).

[509] Steen and Berg Co., v. Berg, 713 N.W.2d 87 (ND 2006); McEwen v. McEwen, 529 N.E.2d 355, 359 (Ind.App.1988); In re Estate of Leavitt, 733 A.2d 348 (Me.1999); Matter of Estate of Nichols, 544 N.E.2d 430 (Ill.App.1989). However, there is contrary authority. See also Murphy v. Glenn, 964 P.2d 581, 584 (Colo.App.1998). *See* also notes 492–494, *supra* and accompanying text. For a general discussion of non-claim statutes, *see* Section 13.5, at note 201 et seq.

[510] Wyrick v. Wyrick, 349 S.E.2d 705 (Ga.1986); Dickie v. Dickie, 769 P.2d 225 (Or.App.1989); Thompson v. Thompson, 495 A.2d 678 (R.I.1985); * * * *of Contracts* § 253 (1979).

[511] Lawrence v. Ashba, 59 N.E.2d 568 (Ind.App.1945); Turley v. Adams, 484 P.2d 668 (Ariz.App.1971).

[512] In re Marriage of Edwards, 45 Cal.Rptr.2d 138 (App.1995). *See* note 488 *supra.*

[513] Among these uncertainties are (1) whether benefits accruing under the contract are taxable income. Getty v. Commissioner, 913 F.2d 1486 (9th Cir.1990); (2) whether a gift tax is payable when the first party dies, making the will of the other irrevocable. Grimes v. Commissioner, 851 F.2d 1005 (7th Cir.1988). (3) Whether the estate tax marital deduction is allowed when a spouse receives property under a contractual will. Bartlett v. Commissioner, 937 F.2d 316 (7th Cir.1991).

[514] J. Price, *Contemporary Estate Planning* §§ 4.7.1–.2 (2d ed. 2000). *See also* Browder, *Recent Patterns of Testate Succession in the United States and England,* 67 Mich.L.Rev. 1303, 1343 (1969); *cf.* H. Brox, *supra* note 491, at 112 (joint wills by spouses are ambiguous; the UPC allows them only because they are so commonly used).

> If a young husband and wife sign a [contractual] will when they are about twenty-five years of age and then one of them dies, the survivor is bound (even if he or she lives another fifty years) [to] leave all of his or her property exactly as required by the joint will. In other words, the concrete once poured, is permanently set .... The vicissitudes of life are such that ... we ought not to presume such an intent ....[515]

There is no objective sought by a contractual will that could not be better accomplished by a trust. An independent, financially responsible trustee provides more security that the plan desired by the parties will be carried out. Even without an independent trustee, trust law itself provides generally effective remedies against breach of trust.[516] The rights of trust beneficiaries are not subject to claims of the trustee's spouse or creditors[517] as is often true under a contract. A discretionary trust provides flexibility so the plan is not "set in concrete."

Spouses who wish to establish a common plan governing the property of both can create a joint trust, but such a trust should make clear the extent to which either settlor can revoke the trust, particularly after one of them has died. For example, when a husband and wife jointly created a trust, reserving the "right at any time during *our* lifetime to revoke" it, the court held (over a strong dissent) that, after the husband died, the wife could amend the trust to cut out his children by a prior marriage.[518]

It has been suggested that, because of the risk of false claims that mutual wills were made pursuant to a contract, wills that spouses execute at the same time should expressly state that they have not made such a contract.[519]

§§ 3.10–4.0 are reserved for supplemental material.

---

[515] In re Hoeppner's Estate, 145 N.W.2d 754, 760 (Wis.1966) (concurring opinion). *See also* Craddock v. Berryman, 645 P.2d 399 (1982) ("contracts to make wills are looked upon with disfavor"); Moore v. Harvey, 406 N.E.2d 354 (Ind.App.1980).

[516] For remedies against breach of trust, *see* Section 14.8.

[517] Section 10.8, note 335; Bongaards v. Millen, 793 N.E.2d 335 (Mass.2003) (elective share does not extend to a trust created by another in which decedent had a life interest).

[518] Perrenoud v. Harman, 8 P.3d 293 (Utah App.2000). For further discussion of this problem, *see* Section 4.5, note 145 et seq. *See also* UTC § 602, comment: "Joint trusts are often poorly drafted ... Their use can also lead to unintended tax consequences."

[519] T. Shaffer, *The Planning and Drafting of Wills and Trusts* 237 (2d ed. 1979); Martin, *The Draftsman Views Wills for a Young Family,* 54 N.C.L.Rev. 277, 308 (1976).

Chapter 4

REVOCATION, GIFTS, AND WILL SUBSTITUTES

Analysis

Sec.

4.1 Subsequent Instrument.

4.2 Physical Act.

4.3 Revival and Dependent Relative Revocation.

4.4 Divorce.

4.5 Gifts and Will Substitutes.

§ 4.1 Subsequent Instrument

A will can be revoked even if a power of revocation is not expressly reserved in the will,[1] but all states impose formal requirements for revocation. Wills can be revoked (1) by a subsequent will, (2) by a physical act, or (3) by a change of circumstances.[2]

As to the first method, the UPC (hereinafter in the text and footnotes referred to as the "UPC") is typical. "A will or any part thereof is revoked (1) by executing a subsequent will that revokes the previous will or part expressly or by inconsistency."[3] A "will" with an express revocation clause can revoke prior wills even though it contains no dispositive provisions, with the result that the testator's estate is distributed as if the testator died intestate.[4]

In order to revoke a prior will, the subsequent will must itself be valid, *i.e.*, it must be executed with the formalities prescribed for wills by an individual with testamentary capacity and free of fraud and undue influence.

---

1 2 W. Blackstone, *Commentaries* 502 (1765); T. Littleton, *Tenures* § 168. This was also true in Roman law, R. Villers, *Rome et le Droit Privé* 471 (1977), and in modern civil law as well. BGB (German Civil Code) § 2253; French Code Civil art. 1035. However, the power to revoke may be limited by a contract. *See* Section 4.9.

2 Changes of circumstances like marriage and divorce today do not usually cause a total revocation of the will. *See* Sections 4.4 and 8.6.

3 UPC § 2–507(a)(1). *See also* Cal.Prob.Code § 6120. Section 7(b)(1) provides that an electronic will may be revoked, in whole or in part, by a subsequent will expressly or by inconsistency.

4 UPC § 1–201(57) ("will" includes "any testamentary instrument that merely . . . revokes . . . another will"). In Coussee v. Estate of Efston, 633 N.E.2d 815 (Ill.App.1994), a will expressly revoked former wills but failed to dispose of all the testator's property and so a partial intestacy resulted. *But see* In re Estate of Martinez, 985 P.2d 1230 (N.M.App.1999).

Thus, a will which was invalid for lack of publication did not revoke earlier wills.[5] However, a lost will, if duly proved, may revoke an earlier will.[6]

In jurisdictions that allow holographic wills, a holographic will may revoke an attested will,[7] but handwritten changes by the testator on a typewritten will may not necessarily be effective revocations. To be effective, the handwritten changes must amount to a holographic will. When a testator crossed out the name of a deceased devisee in a typewritten will and wrote "her share to be divided between her siblings," the change was held ineffective because the handwritten words had no meaning divorced from the typewritten words and, thus, did not constitute a valid holographic will.[8]

In order to revoke a prior will by the execution of a subsequent will, the subsequently executed document must have been intended to be a will, not something else. Thus, a document entitled "revocation of missing will" which contained no dispositive provisions was ineffective to revoke testator's will as the document was not intended to be a will.[9]

Oral wills, even in states that allow them, have been held ineffective to revoke a written one.[10]

The mere execution of a subsequent will revokes prior will. It is not necessary that the subsequent will be probated. But, if the subsequent will is denied probate for lack of due execution or lack of testamentary capacity, then the will is not a will and, therefore, the prior will is not revoked.[11] Similarly a later will held invalid because of undue influence does not revoke a prior will.[12]

A lawyer who files a will for probate without disclosing to the court the existence of a later will of which the lawyer knows violates the rules of professional conduct.[13]

---

5 Matter of Estate of Beal, 769 P.2d 150 (Okl.1989) (as to publication *see* Section 4.3, note 45). *See also* In re Estate of Laura, 690 A.2d 1011 (N.H.1997); In re Estate of Martinez, 985 P.2d 1230 (N.M.App.1999) (only one witness).

6 In re Will of McCauley, 565 S.E.2d 88, 93 (N.C.2002).

7 Matter of Estate of Custick, 842 P.2d 934 (Utah App.1992); Cason v. Taylor, 51 S.W.3d 397 (Tex.App.2001) (even though statute required revocation by a "subsequent will . . . executed with like formalities").

8 Estate of Sola, 275 Cal.Rptr. 98 (App.1990) (under California law, a holograph must be entirely in the testator's handwriting); In re Estate of Foxley, 575 N.W.2d 150 (Neb.1998).

9 Gushwa v. Hunt, 197 P.3d 1 (N.M. 2008). *But see* In re Estate of Melton, 272 P.3d 668, 671 (Nev. 2012)(will revoked by later document executed in accordance with the statute of wills that contained no dispositive provision was effective to revoke the earlier will because Nevada had a statute allowed this).

10 In re Estate of Mantalis, 671 N.E.2d 1062 (Ohio App.1996); In re Carlton's Estate, 221 So.2d 184 (Fla.App.1969). A contrary decision in the 17th century led to the enactment of the Statute of Frauds. Whitman, *Revocation and Revival: An Analysis of the 1990 Revision of the Uniform Probate Code and Suggestions for the Future*, 55 Alb.L.Rev. 1035, 1038 (1992).

11 White v. Flood, 138 N.W.2d 863 (Iowa 1965).

12 Dauray v. Mee, 109 A.3d 832, 841 (R.I. 2015).

13 In re Conduct of Hedrick, 822 P.2d 1187 (Or.1991) (lawyer suspended for this). The case was decided under the Code of Professional Responsibility, but the same result seems required by Model Rule 1.3 (Candor Toward the Tribunal).

Inconsistency

Most wills contain a clause or phrase expressly revoking prior wills.[14] Even if a will does not have such language, an implied revocation may occur if a later will contains provisions that are inconsistent with an earlier will. Courts are reluctant to find a revocation by inconsistency, however. Thus "a grant of an option to one son to purchase certain real estate at below market price is not inconsistent with a bequest of all the assets to all the testator's children in equal shares," and the provisions in both wills were carried out.[15] On the other hand, where a testator's first will left substantial devises to two children and the residue to his wife and thereafter the testator and his wife divorced, he remarried, and in a later will he left $100 to the two children, the substantial devises in the prior will to the two children were impliedly revoked by inconsistency.[16]

Under the UPC a "testator is presumed to have intended a subsequent will to replace rather than supplement a previous will if the subsequent will makes a complete disposition of the testator's estate."[17] This presumption is reversed when the later document does not purport to dispose of the entire estate.[18] The reluctance to find revocation by inconsistency is particularly strong when the subsequent instrument is called a "codicil," because this word suggests a supplement to a prior will rather than an abrogation of it.[19] When a testator executed four "wills" on the same day, each disposing of only part of his estate but containing a boiler-plate form revoking prior wills, the court ignored the clause and probated all four wills.[20]

The appropriateness of implying a revocation may depend on the nature of the devise. If will #1 gives "my gold watch to Alice" and will #2 leaves the same watch to Joshua, the devise to Alice is impliedly revoked. But if will #1 leaves $30,000 to Alice and will #2 leaves $20,000 to Joshua, the two devises are not inconsistent.[21] However, if will #2 had left $20,000 to *Alice*, the question arises whether the testator wanted her to get a total of $50,000 or just

---

[14] J. Price, *Contemporary Estate Planning* § 4.10 (2d ed.2000); Cal.Prob.Code § 6241 (statutory will clause 1).

[15] Matter of Estate of Hoffman, 375 N.W.2d 231, 235 (Iowa 1985). *See also* In re Succession of White, 961 So.2d 439 (La.App. 1 Cir. 2007); Smith v. United States, 801 F.2d 975 (7th Cir.1986); In re Succession of Lee, 831 So.2d 477, 479 (La.App.2002). In In re Estate of Lowe, 577 S.E.2d 315 (N.C.App.2003), a written statement, executed like a will, which stated that the signer "has not written a will" was held insufficient to revoke a prior will.

[16] Mitchell v. Mitchell, 612 S.E.2d 274 (Ga. 2005).

[17] UPC § 2–507(c). *See also Restatement (Second) of Property (Donative Transfers)* § 33.2, cmt. b (1990); *Restatement (Third) of Property (Wills and Other Donative Transfers)* § 4.1, cmt. d (1998); Blake's Estate v. Benza, 587 P.2d 271 (Ariz.App.1978); Cason v. Taylor, 51 S.W.3d 397, 411 (Tex.App.2001).

[18] UPC § 2–507(d).

[19] Starratt v. Morse, 332 F.Supp. 1038 (D.S.C.1971).

[20] deGraaf v. Owen, 598 So.2d 892 (Ala.1992).

[21] However, if the testator's estate contains less than $50,000, the devises would abate prorata. *See* Section 6.4, note 86.

$20,000?[22] Drafters ought to make the relationship between a codicil and an earlier will clear.

§ 4.2 Physical Act

Nature of Act

The Statute of Frauds allowed devises to be revoked "by burning, cancelling, tearing or obliterating the same."[23] American states today have similar provisions.[24] The UPC uses the phrase: "burning, tearing, canceling, obliterating, or destroying."[25] The slight differences in wording among the statutes are not usually important.[26]

A will can be effectively revoked by physical act even though the words of the will remain legible,[27] but merely throwing a will in the trash is not enough to revoke it.[28] Nor, according to some courts, is it enough to make marks on a will that do not touch any words on the face of the will,[29] although the UPC provides otherwise if the intent to revoke is clear.[30] However, the marks evidencing the intent to revoke must be on the will. Revisions made on an unexecuted copy of a will even when initialed are not sufficient to revoke the will.[31]

The act upon the will must be done "by either (1) the testator or (2) another person in the testator's presence and by the testator's direction."[32] This

---

[22] *Compare* In re Estate of Lund, 110 Cal.Rptr. 183 (App.1973) (devises are cumulative) *with* Anderson v. Dubel, 580 S.W.2d 404 (Tex.Civ.App.1979). UPC § 2–507, comment raises this question but does not answer it.

[23] Statute of Frauds, 29 Car. 2, c. 3, § 6 (1676). The Statute of Wills used the terms "burning, tearing or otherwise destroying." 1 Vict., c. 26, § 20 (1837).

[24] *E.g.*, UPC § 2–507(a)(2); Cal.Prob.Code § 6120. *See also* BGB (German Civil Code) § 2255; Italian Codice Civile art. 684 (limited to holographic wills).

[25] UPC § 2–507(a)(2).

[26] *But see* Estate of Eglee, 383 A.2d 586 (R.I.1978) (drawing a line through every word in a will is insufficient where statute only mentions "burning tearing or otherwise destroying"); D. Parry & J. Clark, *The Law of Succession* 99 (10th ed. 1996) (England). Under Section 7 of the Uniform Electronic Wills Act, an electronic will can also be revoked, in whole or in part, by physical act. What that act could be is not set forth in the act, but comments to the act indicate that a physical act could include the deletion of a file, the physical act of ripping up a printed copy of the electronic will, or typing revoked on the electronic copy of the will. The comments also note that sending an email stating "I revoke my will" is not a physical act revocation of the electronic will. However, such email could be treated as revocation by execution of a subsequent will if the email met the requirements of Section 5(a) for the execution of an electronic will. The comments also note that if there are multiple files of the electronic will, revocation of one is revocation of all.

[27] Matter of Estate of Ausley, 818 P.2d 1226 (Okl.1991) (VOID written over parts of will); In re Estate of Dickson, 590 So.2d 471 (Fla.App.1991); Board of Trustees of University of Alabama v. Calhoun, 514 So.2d 895 (Ala.1987) (signature page removed).

[28] SouthTrust Bank v. Winter, 689 So.2d 69 (Ala.Civ.App.1996). *See also* H. Brox, *Erbrecht* 86 (18th ed. 1999).

[29] Thompson v. Royall, 175 S.E. 748 (Va. 1934); Kronauge v. Stoecklein, 293 N.E.2d 320 (Ohio App.1972).

[30] UPC § 2–507(a)(2) ("a burning, tearing, or canceling is a 'revocatory act on the will,' whether or not the burn, tear, or cancellation touched any of the words on the will."). *See also Restatement (Third) of Property (Wills and Other Donative Transfers)* § 4.1, cmt. g (1998); Kroll v. Nehmer, 705 A.2d 716, 717 (Md.1998) (will revoked by writing VOID on the back).

[31] In re Estate of Sullivan, 868 N.W.2d 750 (Minn. Ct. App. 2015).

[32] Cal.Prob.Code § 6120(b); Ind.Code § 29–1–5–6; S.C.Code § 21–7–210; Estate of DeWald v. Whittenburg, 925 P.2d 903 (Okl.App.1996) (cancellation by a friend of testator at his direction).

limitation may frustrate a testator's clear intent to revoke if the testator's directions to destroy a will are carried out in another place.[33] The UPC requires only the "testator's conscious presence" which, according to the comment "need not be . . . in the testator's line of sight."[34]

Sometimes a testator's directions to destroy a will are not carried out. In one case, a testator's wife pretended to tear up the will according to his instructions, but produced it unharmed after the testator died. The court probated the will but said that a constructive trust might be imposed on the widow.[35] Another court used the constructive trust rationale when the testator, intending to revoke a codicil, tore up a copy instead of the original. "Although this equitable remedy is usually limited to circumstances in which fraud or a breach of confidence has occurred, it is proper in cases in which one party has benefitted by the mistake of another."[36]

If a will is found burned, torn, cancelled, or otherwise destroyed, it is not always clear whether that physical act was the result of a mistake, was done with the intent to cause the will to be revoked, or, in the case of markings on the will, was done for the purpose of providing notes to assist the testator's lawyer in preparing a new will. In fact, it might not be clear whether the physical act was actually done by the testator. Thus, unlike revocations resulting from the execution of a subsequent will, physical act revocations are effective only when there is evidence that the act was done by the testator or another acting at the testator's direction with the intent to revoke the will. If the will was last known to have been in the testator's possession a presumption arises that marks of revocation on the will were made by the testator with the intent to revoke the will. Because of the intent requirement, an accidental destruction of a will does not revoke a will.[37]

If a testator executes a will in duplicate and later physically destroys one copy with the intent to revoke, the question arises whether the revocation of one copy revokes all or only the copy that was actually destroyed. Because physical act revocations require an intent to revoke, the answer to the question depends upon the testator's intent. If the intent was to destroy a duplicate because testator believed he did not need two copies of his will, revocation of the duplicate should not result in the revocation of the will. If it was destroyed with the intent to revoke the will, then the will is revoked.[38] Most of the cases

---

[33] In re Estate of Bancker, 232 So.2d 431 (Fla.App.1970); In re Haugk's Estate, 280 N.W.2d 684 (Wis.1979); Parry & Clark, *supra* note 26, at 100.

[34] UPC § 2–507(a)(2), cmt. Even when the destruction did not occur in the testator's "conscious presence," the intent to revoke may be effectuated under the "harmless error" rule according to *Restatement (Third) of Property (Wills and Other Donative Transfers)* § 4.1, illus. 9 (1998). *See* Section 3.1, at note 27 et seq.

[35] Morris v. Morris, 642 S.W.2d 448 (Tex.1982). *See also Restatement (Third) of Property (Wills and Other Donative Transfers)* § 8.3, cmt. *l* (2001). *But cf.* Robinson v. Benton, 842 So.2d 631(Ala.2002) (lawyer who disregarded testator's instructions to destroy will not liable to testator's heir).

[36] In re Estate of Tolin, 622 So.2d 988, 990–91 (Fla.1993).

[37] UPC § 2–507(a)(2); Evans v. May, 923 S.W.2d 712 (Tex.App.1996); McKenzie v. Francis, 197 S.E.2d 221 (Va.1973).

[38] *See* notes 64–72, *infra*, regarding the effect of having a duplicate on the presumption of intent.

find that the revocation of one copy of a will revokes all copies,[39] but there are cases to the contrary.[40] This problem does not arise if testator writes "revoked" on an unexecuted copy of a will. In this case, because the unexecuted copy is not a will, no will has been revoked.[41]

If testator executes a will, then executes a codicil making minor changes to the will but later revokes the will, the revocation of the will also revokes the codicil at least in those cases where the codicil "is not so complete a testamentary instrument as to stand alone."[42] But, if the codicil can stand independently, revocation of the will does not revoke the codicil.[43]

Partial Revocation

Markings on just a portion of a will may show an intent to revoke the will entirely, even if the will is not totally destroyed or every bequest in the will has marks of cancellation or obliteration on them.[44] But, in cases where only some of the bequests or pages have marks of cancellation on them, the issue arises whether testator intended to revoke the entire will or only the bequests or pages with the marks. These types of cases have given courts much trouble. For example, if the testator writes "VOID" on page one of a two page will and nothing on page two, is only page one revoked or is the entire will revoked? Likewise, if testator marks out one bequest on page one but makes no marks on the other three bequests on page one, is only the marked bequest revoked?

Many states do not permit partial revocations by a physical act. The UPC, on the other hand, allows a will "or any part thereof" to be revoked. Thus, partial revocations are permitted. Where a partial revocation occurs, the issue arises as to what happens to the revoked bequest. The matter is complicated by the fact that, if the revocation is viewed as the equivalent of the making a new will, it is invalid for that purpose unless the manner of revocation comports with the requirements for the making of a new will. In one case, testator left his entire estate to his sons, Michael and Edward. He later crossed out Edward's name, but the court refused to give this effect "because this amounted to an enlargement of the bequest to Michael."[45] Another court reached the same result as to the testator's striking out the name of a residuary legatee, but it gave effect to the cancellation of a pecuniary devise in the same

---

[39] Roberts v. Fisher, 105 N.E.2d 595 (Ind. 1952). *See also Restatement (Third) of Property (Wills and Other Donative Transfers)* § 4.1, cmt. f (1998).

[40] Stiles v. Brown, 380 So.2d 792 (Ala. 1980).

[41] Gushwa v. Hunt, 197 P.3d 1 (N.M. 2008); Morrison v. Morrison, 655 S.E.2d 571 (Ga. 2008).

[42] In re Estate of King, 817 A.2d 297, 300 (N.H. 2003). *But see* In re Estate of Smith, 378 N.W.2d 555 (Mich. App. 1985) (will and codicil are separate documents and destruction of will does not revoke the codicil).

[43] In re Estate of King, *supra* note 42, at 300.

[44] Matter of Brune's Estate, 606 P.2d 647 (Or.App.1980) (where every bequest but one was crossed out, presumption arose that entire will revoked).

[45] In re Estate of Eastman, 812 P.2d 521 (Wash.App.1991). *See also* Hansel v. Head, 706 So.2d 1142 (Ala.1997) (even though the statute, like the UPC, allowed a will "or any part thereof" to be revoked by physical act); Matter of Estate of Malloy, 949 P.2d 804 (Wash.1998); Dodson v. Walton, 597 S.W.2d 814 (Ark. 1980). *Restatement (Third) of Property (Wills and Other Donative Transfers)* § 4.1, cmt. i (1998) disapproves these cases, as drawing "a distinction without a difference."

will, saying that this was only a "minor" change even though the effect was to increase the residuary devise.[46]

Where a partial revocation occurs to a general or specific bequest, courts generally allow the bequest to augment the residuary bequest. When a residuary bequest is partially revoked, however, courts have essentially the following three options, two of which philosophically run afoul of the concerns underlying the Statute of Wills. The three options include: honor the partial revocation but have the revoked share pass under the intestacy rule, honor the partial revocation and have the revoked share inure to the benefit of the other residuary legatees, or not honor the partial revocation and honor the will as originally executed.

While a testator cannot add words to a will without re-executing it,[47] alterations made in a will *prior* to execution are valid. For example, a five-page will was offered for probate. The testator had revised the will before executing it by substituting a new fifth page. All five pages were admitted to probate, on the theory that "there is no requirement in law that each page of a testament must be . . . typed at the same time, only that the document be complete at the time it is signed."[48] Correcting typographical errors in a will by hand is risky, because someone may argue that the change was made after the will was executed in an ineffective attempt to alter it informally.[49] However, some courts have given effect to changes made by a testator in a holographic will after it was signed.[50] Also, unsigned alterations in a will may be effective under the doctrine of incorporation by reference if the will is later republished by a codicil.[51]

Sometimes a testator executes a will, then later executes a codicil to the will, and then destroys the will. Courts are split as to whether the revocation of the will in this situation also revokes the codicils to it.[52]

Presumption of Revocation

Contestants of a will have the burden of proving that a will was revoked,[53] but when a will which was last known to have been in the testator's possession cannot be found, or is found in a mutilated condition after the testator dies, a

---

[46] Patrick v. Patrick, 649 A.2d 1204 (Md.App.1994). *See also* Walpole v. Lewis, 492 S.W.2d 410 (Ark.1973).

[47] Hansel v. Head, 706 So.2d 1142 (Ala.1997).

[48] Succession of Norton, 451 So.2d 1203 (La.App.1984). *See also* Wood v. Smith, [1993] Ch. 90, 112 (C.A.) (words appearing after signature were probated where signing and writing were "one operation").

[49] There is a weak presumption that alterations appearing on a will were made after it was executed. Parry & Clark, *supra* note 26, at 111. If this presumption is not rebutted, the changes are invalid. Re White, [1991] Ch. 1.

[50] Charleston Nat. Bank v. Thru the Bible, 507 S.E.2d 708, 712 (W.Va.1998); *cf.* Section 4.1, note 8.

[51] Parry & Clark, *supra* note 26, at 112; Section 7.2, note 109.

[52] Hirsch, *Inheritance and Inconsistency*, 57 Ohio St.L.J. 1057, 1090 (1996); In re Estate of King, 817 A.2d 297, 301 (N.H.2003) (destruction of will would also revoke codicil which made only minor changes).

[53] UPC § 3–407; Cal.Prob.Code § 8252.

presumption arises that the testator intended to revoke the will.[54] If, on the other hand, the will was last known to have been in the possession of another but cannot be found at testator's death, the presumption is that the will was lost and not revoked.[55]

This presumption of revocation comes from the common law,[56] but California has codified it. The California statute applies only if "the testator was competent until death."[57] Even without such a statute, if a testator became incompetent prior to death, a court may assume that she destroyed the will while she was incompetent and so there was no effective revocation.[58]

If the presumption of revocation applies, and if the proponents of the will produce no contrary evidence, the fact finder must find that the will was revoked.[59] Proponents of the will usually offer evidence to rebut the presumption, and findings of no intent to revoke are often affirmed even though the original will cannot be found.[60] Such evidence may include the fact that persons other than the testator had access to the will.[61] Some courts have inferred from evidence of a testator's sloppy habits that the will was simply lost in the mess.[62] Courts admit into evidence even alleged oral declarations by the testator indicating that the lost will reflected her wishes or that she continued to feel affection for the devisees or hostility toward persons who are disinherited by the will.[63]

The presumption of revocation is sometimes overcome by the preservation of a duplicate.[64] The California statutory presumption does not apply at all if

---

[54] In re Estate of Beauregard, 921 N.E.2d 954 (Mass. 2010); Balboni v. LaRocque, 991 So.2d 993 (Fla. App. Dist. 4 2008); In re Estate of Turner, 265 S.W.3d 709 (Tex. App. Eastland 2008).

[55] Ferris v. Faford, 890 A.2d 602 (Conn. App. 2006).

[56] *Restatement (Third) of Property (Wills and Other Donative Transfers)* § 4.1 (1998). The presumption has been applied under the UPC on the theory that under section 1–103 common law principles may supplement the Code's provisions. In re Estate of Perry, 33 P.3d 1235 (Colo.App.2001).

[57] Cal.Prob.Code § 6124.

[58] In re Fuller's Estate, 399 A.2d 960 (N.H.1979). As to testamentary capacity *see* Section 5.1.

[59] Perez v. Gilbert, 586 N.E.2d 921 (Ind.App.1992). Query, however, if this is true when the mark on the will is "a blemish that could easily have occurred accidentally." *Restatement (Third) of Property (Wills and Other Donative Transfers)* § 4.1, cmt. j (1998).

[60] *E.g.*, McBride v. Jones, 494 S.E.2d 319 (Ga.1998). *See also* In re Estate of Perry, 33 P.3d 1235, 1237 (Colo.App.2001) (where evidence is conflicting, appellate courts generally defer to a trial court's "reasonable inferences drawn from the facts").

[61] Lonergan v. Estate of Budahazi, 669 So.2d 1062 (Fla.App.1996); Matter of Estate of Wiarda, 508 N.W.2d 740 (Iowa App.1993); Thomas v. Thomas, 784 S.W.2d 173 (Ark.App.1990). Destruction of a will without the testator's permission does not, of course, revoke it and may constitute a criminal offense. E.g., 18 Pa.C.S.A. § 4103.

[62] Tucker v. Stacy, 616 S.W.2d 473 (Ark.1981); Hanners v. Sistrunk, 264 S.E.2d 224 (Ga.1980); Matter of Estate of Kasper, 887 P.2d 702 (Kan.App.1994).

[63] Succession of Altazan, 682 So.2d 1320 (La.App.1996); Matter of Estate of Borom, 562 N.E.2d 772 (Ind.App.1990); Matter of Estate of Kasper, 887 P.2d 702 (Kan.App.1994). But in In re Will of Bonner, 214 N.E.2d 154 (N.Y.1966), the court held that declarations of the decedent were inadmissible to show lack of intent to revoke unless they were made in connection with the alleged revocatory act. *See also* Edmonds v. Edmonds, 772 S.E.2d 898 (Va. 2015).

[64] In re Estate of Koester v. First Mid-Illinois Bank & Trust, N.A., 975 N.E.2d 1115, 1127 (Ill. App. 2012); Matter of Estate of Shaw, 572 P.2d 229 (Okl.1977).

"a duplicate original of the will can be found."[65] But some courts have found a will was revoked despite the production of a duplicate, particularly when the duplicate was not in the testator's possession.[66] Conversely, the presumption of revocation applies only when the missing will was once in the testator's possession.[67]

The loss or preservation of an *unexecuted* copy of the will has no significance in determining whether there was a revocation. Presumably this applies also to photocopies of an executed original, although there has been little case law as to them. Many lawyers advise testators to sign only one copy of a will in order to reduce the risk that accidental loss of an executed copy would create a presumption that the will was revoked.[68] The lawyer can keep the executed will in a safe place[69] (giving the client a conformed copy for reference), but this practice raises ethical problems because it may be construed as an attempt to give the drafter an edge in being hired to handle the testator's estate. One court expressly disapproved of attorneys' "safekeeping" wills.

> There is little justification [for this] today because most people do have safekeeping boxes, and if not, [a statute] provides for the deposit of a will with the register in probate for safekeeping during the lifetime of the testator.[70] The correct practice is that the original will should be delivered to the testator and should only be kept by the attorney upon specific unsolicited request of the client.[71]

Professor Johnston would prohibit attorneys from safekeeping wills altogether on the ground that "attempting to determine whether the drafting attorney or the testator requested the safekeeping" is too difficult.[72]

Lost Will Statutes

Normally when a will cannot be found and the fact-finder (court or jury) determines that it was not revoked, a copy of the will is probated or other proof

---

65 Cal.Prob.Code § 6124.

66 Estate of Fowler v. Perry, 681 N.E.2d 739 (Ind.App.1997); Harrison v. Bird, 621 So.2d 972 (Ala.1993); Matter of Estate of Day, 753 P.2d 1296 (Kan.App.1988). *But cf.* In re Estate of King, 817 A.2d 297, 303 (N.H.2003) (overturning finding of revocation in part because of original retained by lawyer).

67 Golini v. Bolton, 482 S.E.2d 784 (S.C.App.1997). In In re Estate of Mecello, 633 N.W.2d 892, 902 (Neb.2001), the court refused to apply the presumption on the theory that the missing will was not in the testator's possession, even though it was in her safe-deposit box. A concurring opinion argued that the presumption arose but had been rebutted, *inter alia* by evidence that an interested person had entered the box after the testator died.

68 Beyer, *The Will Execution Ceremony*, 29 S.Tex.L.Rev. 413, 442–43 (1988).

69 Cal.Prob.Code §§ 701–35 deals with the liability of lawyers who lose wills entrusted to them for safekeeping.

70 *See* UPC § 2–515; Mass. Gen. Laws Ann. Ch. 190B, § 2–515. Court safekeeping of wills seems to be the rule in Germany. BGB (German Civil Code) § 2258a; Brox, *supra* note 28, at 66.

71 State v. Gulbankian, 196 N.W.2d 733 (Wis.1972).

72 Johnston, *An Ethical Analysis of Common Estate Planning Practices*, 45 Ohio St.L.J. 57, 133 (1984). *Compare Developments Regarding the Professional Responsibility of the Estate Planning Lawyer*, 22 Real Prop., Prob. and Trust L.J. 1, 28 (1987) (attorney safekeeping is ethical if he "makes it clear that his safekeeping is only an alternative to safekeeping by the client"). The burden of proof is on the proponent of a lost will to prove it was not revoked, and, if not, to prove its contents. *See* In re Estate of Wayne, 753 N.W.2d 384 (N.D. 2008).

is used to establish its contents.[73] The matter may be complicated, however, by a state statute governing the proof of "lost wills." One state allows lost wills to be probated if they were "destroyed subsequent to the death of the testator, or before the death of the testator if the testator's lack of knowledge of such . . . destruction can be proved." This provision was held to bar the probate of a will which the testator had destroyed under undue influence.

> While a lost will or destroyed will could be admitted to probate if . . . a third party surreptitiously destroyed it, that same will could not be admitted to probate if the third party instead held a gun to the testator's head and instructed her to destroy it. . . . This would certainly seem to reflect a deficiency in the statute. Unfortunately it is a deficiency that the legislature must remedy.[74]

A similar statute was held to bar probate of a will which the testator had accidentally lost.[75]

Some lost wills cannot be probated even though there is no evidence that the testator wished to revoke them, simply because the contents cannot be satisfactorily proved. An alleged lost will of Howard Hughes was denied probate because the statute required proof of lost wills by two witnesses and the proponents produced only one.[76]

In some states partial revocations are not permitted. However, even if a state does not allow partial revocation by physical act, if obliterated words cannot be read, they cannot be given effect.[77]

Because of the problems raised by physical act revocations, one wonders why the law allows it[78] or presumes revocation from circumstances so ambiguous as a missing will. The only explanation is that physical act revocations seem logical to lay persons and, therefore, should be permitted. No lawyer should advise a client to revoke a will by tearing it up because this act, even though legally effective, can be easily misinterpreted. If the testator keeps the will, the lawyer should warn the testator to keep it in a safe place and not to try to change the will without professional assistance. The location of the original should be noted on the copies, one of which should be retained by the drafter.[79]

---

[73] *Restatement (Third) of Property (Wills and Other Donative Transfers)* § 4.1, cmt. k (1998); Cal.Prob.Code § 8223 (probate of lost wills); Cason v. Taylor, 51 S.W.3d 397 (Tex.App.2001) (lost will probated on the basis of oral testimony as to its contents); In re Estate of Mecello, 633 N.W.2d 892 (Neb.2001) (unsigned copy of lost will probated); Tudor v. Bradford, 709 S.E.2d 235 (Ga. 2011).

[74] Sheridan v. Harbison, 655 N.E.2d 256, 258 (Ohio App.1995). As to undue influence *see* Section 5.3.

[75] Matter of Estate of Wheadon, 579 P.2d 930 (Utah 1978).

[76] Howard Hughes Medical Institute v. Gavin, 621 P.2d 489 (Nev.1980). *See also* Matter of Estate of Wilson, 875 P.2d 1154 (Okl.App.1994); In re Parker's Estate, 382 So.2d 652 (Fla.1980). In In re Will of McCauley, 565 S.E.2d 88, 95 (N.C.2002), a single witness' testimony was held sufficient to prove a lost will, but only if the evidence was "clear, strong and convincing." The missing will of a former English Chancellor was probated on the basis of oral evidence of its contents by an interested witness. Sugden v. Lord St. Leonards, (1876) 1 P.D. 154.

[77] Hansel v. Head, 706 So.2d 1142 (Ala.1997).

[78] Roman jurists hesitated on whether to allow revocation by physical act. Gaius, *Institutes* 2.151.

[79] Beyer, *supra* note 68, at 442–43.

§ 4.3 Revival and Dependent Relative Revocation

Dependent Relative Revocation

Destruction of a will revokes the will only if the testator destroys the will "with the intent and for the purpose of revoking" the will.[80] Even an intentional act of destruction may not revoke the will if the circumstances indicate that the testator did not want to revoke the will. For example, if the destruction of a will is coupled with an abortive attempt to make a new will, the destruction may not amount to a revocation under the doctrine of dependent relative revocation. The concept underlying dependent relative revocation is that testator's act of revocation was dependent upon either a subsequent will being effective or a prior will being revived when it turns out that neither is the case.[81] For example, when a will was found marked up in such a manner that it appeared to have been revoked together with an unsigned (and therefore invalid) will of a later date, the court probated the marked-up will under the doctrine of dependent relative revocation.[82] The court concluded that the revocation of the old will was conditioned on the validity of the new. "If it is clear that the cancellation and the making of the new will were parts of one scheme, and the revocation of the old will was so related to the making of the new as to be dependent upon it, then if the new will . . . is invalid, the old will, though canceled, should be given effect."[83] The question is one of intent; here the testator "would have preferred . . . the earlier will over the only other alternative—intestacy."[84] This is a reasonable inference if the dispositive provisions of the two wills are similar,[85] *e.g.,* both wills disinherited the testator's heirs who would take if neither will were probated.

Likewise, when testator executed Will #1 and then Will #2, but later revoked Will #2 mistakenly thinking that the revocation would validate (revive) Will #1, a court ignored the revocation of Will #2 whose terms were very similar to Will #1 believing that testator would prefer Will #2 to intestacy.[86]

But if the two wills are dissimilar, the court may infer that the testator would have preferred to die intestate.[87] Because the question of the testator's

---

80 UPC § 2–507(a)(2); Cal.Prob.Code § 6120. Ind.Code § 29–1–5–6.

81 *See Restatement (Third) of Property (Wills and Other Donative Transfers),* § 4.3 (1998).

82 In England today the less cumbersome phrase "conditional revocation" is preferred. D. Parry & J. Clark, *The Law of Succession* 107 (10th ed. 1996).

83 Carter v. First United Methodist Church, 271 S.E.2d 493, 496 (Ga. 1980).

84 *Id.* at 497. *See also* In re Estate of Glennie, 265 P.3d 654 (MT. 2011); Mincey v. Deckle, 662 S.E.2d 126 (Ga. 2008); Churchill v. Allessio, 719 A.2d 913 (Conn.App.1998).

85 Using the provisions of an unsigned will to show the testator's intent might seem counter to the wills act, but in physical act revocations *any* evidence of the testator's intent is admissible when a will is missing or mutilated. Section 4.2, at notes 59–63.

86 Estate of Auburn, 118 N.W.2d 919 (Wis. 1963).

87 *Restatement (Third) of Property (Wills and Other Donative Transfers)* § 4.3, cmt. c (1998); Estate of DeWald v. Whittenburg, 925 P.2d 903 (Okl.App.1996); Kroll v. Nehmer, 705 A.2d 716, 723 (Md.1998). This test is not always easy to apply. When the beneficiaries of the old and new will were the same but their shares were different, a majority of the court rejected dependent relative revocation but a dissent thought that "this evidence strongly indicates . . . the testator would have preferred the cancelled will over no will." Matter of Estate of Ausley, 818 P.2d 1226 (Okl.1991).

intent is one of fact, it may be decided by a jury. Whether by court or jury, the fact-finder's decision is accorded deference on any appeal.[88]

Dependent relative revocation is sometimes applied to partial revocations. A will devised 12 shares (out of 100) to the testator's mother and 7 each to his sisters and brother. The testator later crossed out the number 12 in the bequest to his mother and put "24" in its place, while reducing his sisters' shares to 3 and his brother's to 1. The court, finding that the cancellations "were made with conditional revocatory intent," admitted the original provisions to probate.[89] Because the testator wanted to double his mother's share, he would have preferred her to get the original devise rather than nothing, but the decision as to the sisters and brother is more doubtful, because he tried to reduce their shares by more than 50%.[90]

Courts have also applied dependent relative revocation when a devise in a revoking will was invalid under the Rule Against Perpetuities. For example, if a testator devises property to a charity in Will #1 and in Will #2 (which expressly revokes Will #1) devises the residuary estate to the same charity but in a way that violates the Rule Against Perpetuities, the devise in Will #1 could be given effect under the doctrine of dependent relative revocation.[91] Similar results could occur if a devise in a valid subsequent will is invalid under a mortmain statute,[92] the rule invalidating devises to a witness of the will,[93] or when a testator revoked a devise under the supposition that the devisee was dead.[94]

Revival

When a testator validly executes two wills and then revokes the second, is the first one revived or does the testator die intestate? This question is typically governed by a statute, in contrast to dependent relative revocation, which is a common law doctrine.[95] For example, a will left the residuary estate to one child. A subsequent will left it to three children equally. The testator later revoked the second will. This was held not to revive the earlier will. It did not

---

[88] Churchill v. Allessio, 719 A.2d 913 (Conn.App.1998); Estate of Lyles, 615 So.2d 1186, 1190 (Miss.1993) (issue on review was whether the trial judge "was clearly and manifestly wrong").

[89] Estate of Uhl, 81 Cal.Rptr. 436 (App.1969). The changes might have been effective if the testator had initialed them, because California allows holographic wills. *See also*, Estate of Carpenter v. Cosby, 34 So.3d 1230 (Miss Ct. App. 2010) (doctrine used to validate portions of a will that a testator had crossed out and changed in an ineffective attempt to amend the will).

[90] *Cf. Restatement (Third) of Property (Wills and Other Donative Transfers)* § 4.3, illus. 7 (1998).

[91] *Cf.*, In re Bernard's Settlement, [1916] 1 Ch. 552; In re Jones' Estate, 352 So.2d 1182 (Fla.App.1977); *Restatement (Third) of Property (Wills and Other Donative Transfers)* § 4.3, illus. 17 (1998).

[92] Linkins v. Protestant Episcopal Cathedral Foundation, 187 F.2d 357 (D.C.Cir.1950); In re Kaufman's Estate, 155 P.2d 831 (Cal.1945); *Restatement (Third) of Property (Wills and Other Donative Transfers)* § 4.3, illus. 14 (1998). *Contra,* Crosby v. Alton Ochsner Medical Foundation, 276 So.2d 661 (Miss.1973). As to mortmain statutes *see* Section 8.10, note 492 et seq.

[93] Re Finnemore, [1991] 1 W.L.R. 793 (Ch.D). As to the invalidation of devises to witnesses *see* Section 3.3, note 87 et seq.

[94] Palmer, *Dependent Relative Revocation and Its Relation to Relief for Mistake*, 69 Mich.L.Rev. 989, 991 (1971). As to mistake generally *see* Section 7.1.

[95] Dependent relative revocation is not mentioned in the text of the UPC, but a comment to section 2–507 says "each court is free to apply its own doctrine of dependent relative revocation."

matter whether by revoking the later will she intended to revive her prior will, because a statute, derived from the English Wills Act of 1837, provided that a "revoked will . . . shall not be revived except by re-execution or by a duly executed codicil expressing an intention to revive it."

> The formalities of the statute were neither observed nor attempted. . . . [The child favored in the first will] argues that that cannot have been his mother's intent. . . . We do not reach that question.[96]

In a similar case another court invoked dependent relative revocation in order to probate the destroyed will when the testator mistakenly thought she was reviving her earlier will.[97] But this conclusion seems warranted only if the two wills are substantially similar.

Revival and dependent relative revocation are sometimes confused. When a trial court found that a testator's physical destruction of a will "was a revocation conditional upon his making a new will" which was not executed before he died, the court held that an anti-revival statute precluded application of dependent relative revocation. As a concurring opinion observed, this reasoning is fallacious because an anti-revival statute "only comes into effect if there has been a revocation. It is to determine precisely that question, *i.e.*, whether there has been a revocation" that the doctrine of dependent relative revocation is applied.[98] Nevertheless, the court probably reached the correct result; because the testator had destroyed his will before the new one was executed, and the new will was to be "quite a bit different" from the old. This suggests he probably intended an unconditional revocation when he destroyed the will.

The UPC allows the testator's intent to revive an earlier will to be given effect: revocation of a second will by physical act revives the first if "it is evident from the circumstances of the revocation of the subsequent will or from testator's contemporary or subsequent declarations that the testator intended" this result.[99] Presumably even testimony by interested witnesses would be admissible, *i.e.*, the beneficiaries of the first will could testify that the testator told them she wished to revive it,[100] but the Third Restatement of Property

---

[96] Matter of Estate of Lagreca, 687 A.2d 783, 785 (N.J.Super.App.Div.1997). *See also* Matter of Estate of Greenwald, 584 N.W.2d 294 (Iowa 1998); In re Will of McCauley, 565 S.E.2d 88, 94 (N.C.2002). This situation is to be distinguished from one in which the later will is ineffective because of faulty execution or incapacity. Here the earlier will is never revoked. *E.g.*, First Union Nat. Bank v. Estate of Mizell, 807 So.2d 78 (Fla.App.2001). Professor Hirsch finds it illogical to admit extrinsic evidence in deciding whether the testator intended to revoke by physical act (*see* Section 4.2, note 63), but not in deciding whether there was an intent to revive. Hirsch, *Inheritance and Inconsistency*, 57 Ohio St.L.J. 1057, 1094 (1996).

[97] In re Alburn's Estate, 118 N.W.2d 919 (Wis.1963). *See also Restatement (Third) of Property (Wills and Other Donative Transfers)* § 4.3, cmt. b (1988) (approves this result, but argues that the intent to revive should be given effect directly); Parry & Clark, *supra* note 82, at 108.

[98] Larrick v. Larrick, 607 S.W.2d 92, 96 (Ark.App.1980). *See also* Matter of Estate of Greenwald, 584 N.W.2d 294 (Iowa 1998).

[99] UPC § 2–509(a). *See also* Cal.Prob.Code § 6123(a). When a will is revoked by a subsequent instrument, however, any intent to revive an earlier will must be manifested by the revoking instrument. UPC § 2–509(c).

[100] *Cf.* Bailey v. Kennedy, 425 P.2d 304 (Colo.1967) (adopting an anti-revival rule to avoid this result).

requires "clear and convincing" evidence of the intent to revive.[101] In one case, the court found an intent to revive from the testator's statements to her attorney. But had the attorney advised the testator to execute a codicil to make her wishes clear, the case would not have had to go to the state supreme court on this question.

The UPC presumes against an intent to revive, so if there is *no* evidence as to intent, the testator dies intestate.[102] However, the presumption is reversed when the second instrument only partially revoked the first. Thus, if a codicil alters a will and then the codicil is destroyed, the provisions of the original will which the codicil had revised are reinstated, unless there is evidence that the testator did not so intend.[103]

Courts have inferred an intent to revive a will from a codicil which refers to the will which the testator had previously revoked.[104] But, on the other hand, if the testator revokes the will after executing the codicil one might infer that the testator just forgot about the codicil when he revoked the will, and neither should be probated.[105]

§ 4.4 Divorce

Roman law at one time provided that all wills were automatically revoked after ten years.[106] Anglo-American law has no such rule, but a change of circumstances after a will is executed may create doubt whether the will still reflects the testator's wishes. The UPC provides that a divorce or annulment of a marriage revokes any disposition of property "made by a divorced individual to his [or her] former spouse."[107] Although this was not the rule at common law,[108] many states have similar statutes. In a few states a divorce

---

[101] *Restatement (Third) of Property (Wills and Other Donative Transfers)* § 4.2, cmt. i (1998). *See also* White v. Wilbanks, 393 S.E.2d 182 (S.C.1990).

[102] *See also* May v. Estate of McCormick, 769 P.2d 395 (Wyo.1989) (intestacy where there is no evidence of an intent to revive). *Contra,* BGB (German Civil Code) § 2257 (intent to revive presumed); Italian Codice Civile art. 681 (same).

[103] UPC § 2–509(b). *See also* Fla.Stat. § 732.508(2); Wis.Stat. § 853.11(6)(a); Matter of Hering's Estate, 166 Cal.Rptr. 298 (App.1980). *Contra,* Will of Lake, 560 N.Y.S.2d 966 (Surr.1990). Hirsch points out that this distinction in the UPC can produce "odd" results. Hirsch, *supra* note 19, at 1096–97. *But see* In re Estate of Creech, 989 A.2d 185 (D.C. 2010) (revocation of a codicil did not revive will).

[104] In re Barrett's Estate, 260 N.E.2d 107 (Ill.App.1970). *See also* In re Estate of Stormont, 517 N.E.2d 259 (Ohio App.1986). But as Parry & Clark, *supra* note 82, at 117, observe, the reference to a revoked will in the codicil may simply have been a blunder.

[105] *Cf.* In re Estate of Smith, 378 N.W.2d 555 (Mich.App.1985) (dissenting opinion); In re Estate of King, 817 A.2d 297, 301 (N.H.2003); *Restatement (Third) of Property (Wills and Other Donative Transfers)* § 4.1, cmt. n (1998). As to whether destruction of a will can be used to show intent to revoke a codicil *see* Section 4.2, notes 42–43.

[106] R. Villers, *Rome et le Droit Privé* 472 (1977).

[107] UPC § 2–804(b)(1)(A). It also revokes any nomination of the former spouse as a fiduciary, such as executor or trustee. BGB (German Civil Code) section 2077 is similar to UPC § 2–804, but also covers cases where an action for divorce is pending when the testator dies, and devises to a fiancé when the engagement is later broken. *Compare* note 121 *infra,* and Section 4.5, note 132 et seq. For the rather complicated history of comparable English legislation *see* D. Parry & J. Clark, *The Law of Succession* 243–47 (10th ed. 1996).

[108] Hinders v. Hinders, 828 So.2d 1235 (Miss.2002) (provisions in a will for wife not revoked by later divorce); *cf.* Estate of Reap v. Malloy, 727 A.2d 326 (D.C.1999) (divorce revokes will only when accompanied by property settlement).

revokes the whole will,[109] but more commonly only the provisions relating to the former spouse are affected.[110]

Courts have applied such statutes even when the devisee was not married to the testator when the will was executed.[111] And, the fact that the testator cohabitated with the ex-spouse after the divorce does not matter.[112] Under the UPC, extrinsic evidence of a contrary intent is generally irrelevant,[113] but the provisions for the spouse are revived if the testator remarries the former spouse.[114]

Divorce only revokes a devise to the *testator's* spouse, or in some states, a relative of the spouse. Devises to an in-law who later divorced a relative of the testator are not affected. Thus, when property was devised to a nephew and "his wife Shirley," Shirley took even though she had divorced the nephew after the will was executed. "The designation of Shirley as [the nephew's] wife is merely descriptive and Shirley was an intended beneficiary . . . regardless of her marital status."[115] However, if Shirley had not been named in the will, many courts would have construed the devise to refer to a "wife" of the nephew whom he married after divorcing Shirley.[116]

The UPC revokes devises to relatives of the former spouse. Statutes without such provision have been construed to leave devises to the testator's step-children or former in-laws in effect despite a divorce between the testator and the spouse.[117] Thus, where testator devised his residuary estate to his wife "but if she predeceases me to her daughter" and after executing the will the

---

[109] Winebrenner v. Dorten, 825 S.W.2d 836 (Ky.1991); In re Crohn's Estate, 494 P.2d 258 (Or.App.1972); Estate of Liles, 435 A.2d 379 (D.C.App.1981).

[110] Carroll v. Israelson, 169 So.3d 239 (Fla. Dist. Ct. Appl 2015); Matter of Seymour's Estate, 600 P.2d 274 (N.M.1979); Roeske v. First Nat. Bank, 413 N.E.2d 476 (Ill.App.1980).

[111] In re Estate of Forrest, 706 N.E.2d 1043 (Ill.App.1999); In re Marriage of Duke, 549 N.E.2d 1096 (Ind.App.1990); Estate of Reeves, 284 Cal.Rptr. 650 (App.1991). *Contra,* Matter of Estate of Carroll, 749 P.2d 571 (Okl.App.1987).

[112] Estate of Reeves, 284 Cal.Rptr. 650 (App.1991); Pekol v. Estate of Pekol, 499 N.E.2d 88 (Ill.App.1986).

[113] UPC § 2–804(b) allows only for a contrary express provision in the will or "a court order, or a contract relating to the division of the marital estate made between the divorced individuals." German law is more open on this point, H. Brox, *Erbrecht* 135 (18th ed. 1999), as is the UPC itself on similar construction issues. *See* Section 7.1, note 28.

[114] UPC § 2–804(e). *See also* N.Y.EPTL § 5–1.4(2); Cal.Prob.Code § 6122(b).

[115] Estate of Kelly v. Stambaugh, 724 N.E.2d 1285, 1287 (Ill.App.2000). *See also* First Interstate Bank of Washington v. Lindberg, 746 P.2d 333 (Wash.App.1987); In re Estate of McGlone, 436 So.2d 441 (Fla.App.1983). *See also* Friedman v. Hannan, 987 A.2d 60 (Ct. App. Md. 2010) (gift to family member of testator's former wife revoked. In determining whether gift to family member is revoked, "a court should decide whether the testator in creating the provision was primarily motivated by the marriage or whether the testator had independent reason for the bequest.") *But see* Grady v. Grady, 395 So.2d 643 (Fla.App.1981). *Compare* devises to a named "spouse" who is not legally married. Section 2.12, note 602.

[116] Matter of Trust of Killian, 459 N.W.2d 497 (Iowa 1990); Wells Fargo Bank v. Marshall, 24 Cal.Rptr.2d 507 (App.1993). *But cf.* In re Erny's Trust, 202 A.2d 30 (Pa.1964) (trust for settlor's "wife" refers to his present wife, not the woman he later married). *See also* Section 2.12, note 605.

[117] Bloom v. Selfon, 555 A.2d 75 (Pa.1989) (substitute devise to testator's ex-husband's uncle); Porter v. Porter, 286 N.W.2d 649 (Iowa 1979) (ex-wife's son); In re Estate of Kerr, 520 N.W.2d 512 (Minn.App.1994). Some courts, however, have avoided this result on various theories. Estate of Hermon, 46 Cal.Rptr.2d 577 (App.1995); In re Estate of Jones, 18 Cal.Rptr.3d 637 (Cal. App. 3 Dist. 2004) (testator presumably intends to exclude children of former spouse as well); Estate of Liles, 435 A.2d 379 (D.C.App.1981).

testator divorced his wife, she was deemed to have predeceased the testator, and the residue passed to her daughter.[118]

The Restatement of Property calls for construing all statutes so as to reach the same result as the revised UPC.[119] Under the Code, the disqualified spouse and/or relatives are deemed to have disclaimed the devise, which generally produces the result which would occur if the former spouse (relative) had predeceased the testator.[120]

A separation that does not terminate the status of husband and wife does not revoke a devise to the spouse,[121] but a separation agreement may by its terms bar a spouse from claiming under the other spouse's will. This depends on how the agreement is drafted and construed. An agreement releasing "all claims or rights . . . by reason of the marriage between the parties with respect to any property" belonging to each other was held not to preclude the wife from taking under a will which the husband had previously executed; in order to revoke a prior devise a separation agreement must "employ language which clearly and unequivocally manifests" such an intent.[122] The UPC, however, presumes that "a waiver of 'all rights' " in the other spouse's property in a settlement entered into "after or in anticipation of separation or divorce" renounces provisions of a prior will of the other spouse.[123]

The UPC and many other statutes provide that apart from divorce "no change in circumstances . . . revokes a will,"[124] but as we have seen, an after-born child or later spouse of the testator may have rights in the estate.[125] We shall later discuss the effect of the death of a devisee or the transfer of property after a will is executed.[126]

§ 4.5 Gifts and Will Substitutes

Power to Revoke Gifts

A testator can revoke a will even though it contains no express power to revoke. Inter-vivos gifts, on the other hand, are irrevocable unless they were made in expectation of imminent death.[127] This exception comes from Roman law which allowed such gifts "causa mortis" to be revoked because they were

---

118 In re Estate of Nash, 220 S.W.3d 914 (Tex. 2007).

119 *Restatement (Third) of Property (Wills and Other Donative Transfers)* § 4.1, illus. 12 (1998).

120 UPC § 2–804(d). As to the effect of a disclaimer *see* Section 2.8.

121 UPC § 2–804(a)(2); Cal.Prob.Code § 6122(d). *But cf.* Estate of Lahey, 91 Cal.Rptr.2d 30 (App.1999) (legal separation terminates spouse's right to inherit on intestacy).

122 Matter of Estate of Maruccia, 429 N.E.2d 751 (N.Y.1981).

123 UPC § 2–213(d). *See also* Cal.Prob.Code § 145; Matter of Estate of Highgate, 348 N.W.2d 31 (Mich.App.1984). However, such a waiver is ineffective when the spouses remarry each other after they were divorced. Barnedt v. Wilder, 49 P.3d 1265 (Idaho App.2002); *cf.* note 114 *supra.*

124 UPC § 2–804(f). *See also* Mo.Stat. § 474.420; Cal.Prob.Code § 6122(e); Ind.Code § 29–1–5–8.

125 Sections 8.5 and 8.6.

126 *See* Sections 6.2 and 6.5.

127 Welton v. Gallagher, 630 P.2d 1077 (Haw.App.1981) (bonds given to defendant cannot be recovered where gift was not in contemplation of death); GME, Inc. v. Carter, 817 P.2d 183 (Idaho 1991); *Restatement (Second) of Contracts* § 332(1) (1981) (gratuitous assignment is irrevocable).

so much like wills.[128] Similarly under the Restatement of Property, gifts made "in apprehension of immediate death" are presumed to be revocable.[129]

A donor who repents having made a gift which was not causa mortis may be able to have it set aside on grounds that the donor lacked capacity or was subject to undue influence or fraud; these possibilities will be discussed later.[130] Also, gifts require donative intent, and statements indicating lack of such intent, even those emanating from a time after the alleged gift, may show no gift ever occurred. Thus, a friend's claim that the decedent had given her a watch was rejected because the decedent had "considered taking the watch with him to the nursing home, long after he purportedly gave it to" the claimant, and this was inconsistent with any donative intent.[131]

Courts also allow gifts to be revoked on the basis of an unsatisfied condition. Such a condition is implied for gifts connected with a contemplated marriage. The Restatement of Property allows a donor to recover an engagement ring if the donee breaks the engagement or the donor does so for a justified reason.[132] Many courts allow the donor to recover such gifts regardless of which party refused to go through with the marriage and the reason.[133] As one court said:

> It is difficult to see how the public policies involving divorce and the division of marital property are best served by no-fault principles, but broken engagements should require a fault-based determination as to the ownership of the engagement ring.[134]

Most of the cases involve engagement rings, but other forms of property may be recovered if they were given in contemplation of a marriage which never took place.[135] Wedding presents may be recoverable by the donors.[136]

[128] Justinian, *Institutes* 2.7.1–2. *See also* D. Parry & J. Clark, *The Law of Succession* 28 (10th ed. 1996) (England); Cal.Prob.Code § 5704. Even gifts made "without any thought of death" could be revoked if the donee proved to be "ungrateful" in specified ways. Some modern European codes also allow gifts to be revoked on this ground. French Code Civil art. 955; BGB (German Civil Code) art. 530; Italian Codice Civile art. 801. In Louisiana, gifts can be revoked for "ingratitude," but this is narrowly defined, *e.g.*, "cruel treatment, crimes or grievous injuries." La.Civ.Code art. 1557. Query if the results reached in Louisiana differ substantially from those under the common law. In Mack v. Evans, 804 So.2d 730, 734 (La.App.2001), the court held that because a gift was voidable for fraud, it was not necessary to consider a claim to set aside the same gift for ingratitude.

[129] However, if the donor survives and fails to revoke within a reasonable time thereafter, the right to revoke lapses. Also the circumstances, *e.g.*, a pattern of making irrevocable gifts to save taxes, may show an intent that the gift be irrevocable. *Restatement (Second) of Property (Donative Transfers)* § 31.3 (1990); *Restatement (Third) of Property (Wills and Other Donative Transfers)* § 6.2, cmt. zz (1998).

[130] As to incapacity *see* Section 5.1. As to undue influence *see* Section 5.3. As to fraud *see* Section 7.1, at note 77 et seq.

[131] In re Estate of Wittmond, 732 N.E.2d 659, 666 (Ill.App.2000).

[132] *Restatement (Second) of Property (Donative Transfers)* § 31.2, illus. 5–8 (1990).

[133] *See* Estate of Church v. Tubbs, 2006 WL 568335 (E.D. Mich. 2006). *See also Restatement (Third) of Property (Wills and Other Donative Transfers)* § 6.2, cmt. m (1998).

[134] Heiman v. Parrish, 942 P.2d 631, 638 (Kan.1997). *See also* Patterson v. Blanton, 672 N.E.2d 208 (Ohio App.1996); Meyer v. Mitnick, 625 N.W.2d 136 (Mich.App.2001). *Contra* Albinger v. Harris, 48 P.3d 711 (2002) (gift not revoked).

[135] Boydstun v. Loveless, 890 P.2d 267 (Colo.App.1995) (land put in joint tenancy with "wife").

[136] *Restatement (Third) of Property (Wills and Other Donative Transfers)* § 6.2, cmt. *l* (2001).

Conditions other than marriage are also enforced.[137] Parents often give property to a child on the understanding that the donee will support and care for them. If the child fails to do this, the donor can get the property back even if the deed of gift was not expressly conditional.[138] However, usually a condition in a gift must be manifested when the gift is made; a donor was not allowed to recover stock she had given to a hospital on the basis of a condition which she failed to state at the time of the gift.[139]

Despite the various situations in which gifts can be recovered, the basic rule is that gifts are irrevocable. Lawyers should make sure that clients understand this and discourage them from making gifts that could jeopardize their economic independence.[140]

Trusts

The Second Restatement of Trusts stated that living trusts could not be revoked unless the trust instrument reserved a power to revoke, but the Third Restatement presumes that a trust is revocable if the settlor "has retained a beneficial interest in the trust" on the ground that this may "protect the settlor from unanticipated, adverse tax consequences."[141] Some state statutes and the Uniform Trust Code (hereinafter referred to in the text and footnotes as the "UTC") as the "say that all trusts are revocable unless they otherwise provide."[142] Because many trusts are created with tax considerations in mind, and the tax consequences are radically different for revocable and irrevocable trusts,[143] most trust instruments make clear whether or not the trust was intended to be revocable.[144]

---

[137] Wilkin v. Wilkin, 688 N.E.2d 27 (Ohio App.1996) (money given for a course which the donee never took); Ewing v. Hladky Const., Inc., 48 P.3d 1086 (Wyo.2002) (gift of stock conditioned on donee's remaining employed by company).

[138] Trout v. Parker, 595 N.E.2d 1015 (Ohio App.1991); Almeida v. Almeida, 669 P.2d 174 (Haw.App.1983); Vincent v. Torrey, 417 N.E.2d 41 (Mass.App.1981); *Restatement (Second) of Contracts* § 372, illus. 3 (1981).

[139] Courts v. Annie Penn Memorial Hospital, 431 S.E.2d 864 (N.C.App.1993).

[140] J. Price, *Contemporary Estate Planning* § 7.2.1 (2d ed. 2000) (citing Shakespeare's King Lear).

[141] *See Restatement (Third) of Trusts* § 63, cmt. c (2001). (As to the taxation of irrevocable trusts where the settlor reserves a life interest see Section 15.4, notes 167 et seq.). *Compare Restatement (Second) Trusts* § 330 (1959). *See also* Goytizolo v. Moore, 604 A.2d 362 (Conn.App.1992); Nicosia v. Turzyn, 624 P.2d 499 (Nev.1981). Revocation with the consent of all the beneficiaries is discussed in Section 10.9, at note 482 et seq. Reformation (discussed at Section 7.4, at note 183 et seq.) may allow a power of revocation which was omitted by mistake to be enforced.

[142] Cal.Prob.Code § 15400; UTC § 602 (applicable only to instruments executed after the effective date of the Code). *See also* From the Heart v. African Methodist, 803 A.2d 548, 571 (Md.2002).

[143] *See* Section 15.3, note 73 et seq.

[144] Because "a well drafted trust spells out that the trust is revocable or irrevocable," the default rule "will be of importance primarily for . . . instruments drafted by non-lawyers (or dreadful lawyers)." Langbein, *The Uniform Trust Code*, 15 Trust Law International 66, 70 (2001). *Restatement (Third) of Trusts* § 63, cmt. c (2001), suggests that the filing or failure to file a gift tax return may indicate the settlor's intent on this point.

In Ike v. Doolittle, 70 Cal.Rptr.2d 887, 910 (App.1998), the court found that a trust which was stated to be revocable was actually intended to be irrevocable in order to reduce taxes, and reformed the trust accordingly.

Many trusts are created by two or more settlors, *e.g.*, a husband and wife. Such trusts raise the question whether *one of* the settlors can revoke. In California "if a trust is created by more than one settlor, each settlor may revoke the trust as to the portion of the trust contributed by that settlor."[145] However, one court has held that a trust which provided that during the life of the settlors it could be revoked "by the Settlors" implied that the surviving settlor could not revoke it.[146] The UTC suggests that if revocation of a trust by less than all the settlors "breaches an implied agreement not to revoke the trust," persons harmed thereby can sue for breach of contract.[147] Trusts created by married couples often expressly limit the power of the surviving settlor to revoke, usually for tax reasons,[148] but sometimes for the purpose of keeping the property out of the spouse's estate.

Some trusts by their terms allow revocation only with the consent of another, such as the trustee. According to the Third Restatement of Trusts, "a court may intervene if a person whose concurrence is required improperly withholds (or grants) the consent," *e.g.*, "in bad faith or from an improper motive."[149]

A power to revoke may only be exercised if the settlor has capacity, though in some situations it may be exercised on the settlor's behalf by a conservator or agent under a durable power.[150]

Bank account or Totten trusts[151] are presumed to be revocable: the terms of such trusts are typically so sketchy that it is reasonable to infer that a power to revoke was intended even if none was expressed.[152]

In order to revoke a trust the settlor must comply with any method of revocation specified in the trust instrument. A settlor reserved the right to alter a trust "by an instrument in writing signed by her and delivered during [her] life to the Trustees." After she died, an unsigned slip of paper was found clipped to the trust instrument, but this paper was not effective to change the beneficiary. "The term 'instrument in writing' suggests . . . substantially more

---

[145] Cal.Prob.Code § 15401(b); cf. UTC § 602(b); *Restatement (Third) of Trusts* § 63, cmt. k (2001). As to community property, either spouse can revoke, but the property withdrawn from the trust remains community property. Cal.Fam.Code § 761.

[146] L'Argent v. Barnett Bank, N.A., 730 So.2d 395 (Fla.App.1999). *See also* In re Herbst, 76 P.3d 888 (Ariz.App.2003) (when trust requires signature of "Grantors" to amend, amendment by one settlor is ineffective). *But see* Perrenoud v. Harman, 8 P.3d 293 (Utah App.2000) (power to revoke passes to surviving settlor).

[147] UTC § 602, comment. *Compare* claims that joint wills were made pursuant to an agreement not to revoke them. Section 3.9, at note 453.

[148] *E.g.*, Crook v. Contreras, 116 Cal.Rptr.2d 319 (App.2002).

[149] *Restatement (Third) of Trusts* § 63, cmt. j (2001). *See also* In re Estate of Mueller, 933 S.W.2d 903, 907 (Mo.App.1996) (requirement that amendments be "executed by the trustee" did not give the trustee a "veto power" over them). As to the tax consequences of a power to revoke with another's consent *see* Section 15.4, note 207.

[150] *Restatement (Third) of Trusts* § 63, cmt. *l* (2001). As to conservators and durable powers *see* Section 9.2. For suggested language making it clear that a trust can (or cannot) be revoked by a conservator or agent of the settlor *see* Price, *supra* note 14, at § 10.8.

[151] *See* Section 3.6, at note 351 et seq.

[152] *Restatement (Third) of Trusts* § 26 (2001); Terner v. Rand, 417 So.2d 303 (Fla.App.1982); Cal.Prob.Code § 5301(c). *But see* Underwood v. Bank of Huntsville, 494 So.2d 619 (Ala.1986) (deposit "as custodian" creates an irrevocable trust). Payable on death accounts are also revocable. UPC § 6–213.

than an unsigned scrap of paper." Moreover, the settlor had not delivered the writing to her co-trustee.[153] A court construed another trust which allowed changes by a signed writing "delivered to the Trustee" to require delivery during the settlor's lifetime, and, thus, an amendment delivered after the settlor died was invalid.[154] In another case, a person executed a will and a trust at the same time. The latter provided that it could be revoked by an instrument in writing. When the person died, neither the will nor the trust instrument could be found. The court held that the will was revoked pursuant to the presumption which arises when an executed will is missing;[155] the trust, however, was not revoked because there was no signed writing showing an intent to revoke the trust.[156]

Under the UTC, "substantial compliance" with the prescribed method of revocation is sufficient,[157] and some case law agrees.[158] If the trust does not provide for its method of revocation or the method prescribed is not expressly exclusive, then the UTC allows the revocable trust to be revoked by a later executed will or codicil that either expressly refers to the trust or devises property otherwise disposed of by the trust.[159] It also allows revocation "by any other method manifesting clear and convincing evidence of the settlor's intent."[160] A letter directing the trustee to deliver the trust assets to another was held to effectively revoke a trust even though it did not use the word "revoke."[161] Oral revocations have occasionally been recognized,[162] but

---

[153] Northwestern University v. McLoraine, 438 N.E.2d 1369 (Ill.App.1982). *See also Restatement (Second) of Trusts* § 330, cmt. j (1959); In re Estate of Tosh, 920 P.2d 1230 (Wash.App.1996); Cole ex rel. Cole Revocable Trust v. Cole, 75 P.3d 1280 (Mont.2003) (deed by one of several trustees ineffective to revoke trust). But when the settlor was the sole trustee, the delivery "requirement was automatically satisfied the moment" she signed the letter amending the trust. The letter was simply signed "Mom," but this was enough. Whittaker v. Stables, 791 N.E.2d 588, 592 (Ill.App.2003).

[154] Lourdes College v. Bishop, 703 N.E.2d 362 (Ohio Com.Pl.1997). *See also* In re Reid, 46 P.3d 188 (Okl.App.2002).

[155] *See* Section 4.2, note 54 et seq.

[156] Matter of Estate of Pilafas, 836 P.2d 420 (Ariz.App.1992). However, a signed writing which has been destroyed can be effective. In determining the contents of the missing writing, "all presumptions shall be taken against the spoliator." Whittaker v. Stables, 791 N.E.2d 588, 591 (Ill.App.2003).

[157] UTC § 602(c)(1). Because "substantial compliance" may not inform trustees that the trust has been revoked, they are protected from actions taken without knowledge of the revocation. *Id.* at § 602(g).

[158] Hauseman v. Koski, 857 P.2d 715 (Mont.1993) (signed and recorded instrument revoked a trust even though not mailed to the co-trustees until after the settlor died); Matter of Trust Estate of Daoang, 953 P.2d 959 (Haw.App.1998) (informal letter signed by settlor satisfied requirement of "another instrument" to amend trust). *See also Restatement (Third) of Trusts* § 63, cmt. i (2001) (specified method of revocation is not exclusive unless so stated; in any event substantial compliance suffices).

[159] UTC § 602(c)(2)(A).

[160] UTC § 602(c)(2)(B). Accord, *Restatement (Third) of Trusts* § 63, cmt. h (2001).

[161] Estate of Noell v. Norwest Bank Wyo., N.A., 960 P.2d 499 (Wyo.1998). The Third Restatement allows trustees to turn over trust property to the settlor even if the request "is not manifested in a manner by which the settlor could properly amend or revoke the trust." *Restatement (Third) of Trusts* § 74(a)(ii) (Prl.Drft.2003). But deeds of trust property executed by a settlor-trustee who neglected first to revoke the trust were held ineffective in Bongaards v. Millen, 793 N.E.2d 335, 339 (Mass.2003); Austin v. City of Alexandria, 574 S.E.2d 289 (Va.2003).

[162] Poltz v. Tyree, 705 P.2d 1229 (Wash.App.1985); Gabel v. Manetto, 427 A.2d 71 (N.J.Super.App.Div.1981); Barnette v. McNulty, 516 P.2d 583 (Ariz.App.1973).

California requires a writing signed by the settlor and delivered to the trustee.[163]

Insurance

Most modern life insurance policies expressly give the insured (the person on whose life the policy is based) the right to change the beneficiary.[164] The absence of such a provision in a policy may show an intention that there is no such right.[165] The right to designate the beneficiary is an incident of ownership of the policy, so an insured who assigns the ownership of the policy can no longer change the beneficiary, but the new owner can.[166] However, if the policy was simply assigned as security for a loan, the beneficiaries designated by the insured are entitled to any surplus after the loan is paid.[167]

Policies typically require that written notice be received by the insurer if the beneficiary is changed.[168] This protects the company from liability for paying the wrong person. "Substantial compliance" with this requirement is enough. When an insured signed a form to change the beneficiary but died suddenly before delivering the form to the insurer, the change was held effective. "When an insured has done everything within his power to effectuate a change of beneficiary, equity will not require exact compliance with all stated conditions" of the policy. Failure to deliver the form was not significant under the circumstances.[169] On the other hand, an insured who requested forms to change the beneficiary, but died without ever filling them out, had not substantially complied with the policy, and so the original beneficiary received the proceeds.[170]

Generally the insured cannot change the beneficiary of the policy by a provision in the insured's will.[171] However, given that the purpose of notification to the insurance company is to protect it against paying the wrong person, there appears to be no sound reason for prohibiting beneficiary changes by will. After all, the insurance company, assuming it learns of the will before distributing the insurance proceeds, can file an interpleader action allowing the beneficiary listed with the company and the beneficiary named in the will to litigate their entitlement to the proceeds. When insurers interplead competing claimants to the proceeds of a policy, this is usually held to

---

[163] Cal.Prob.Code § 15401(a)(2); *cf.* UTC § 602(c)(2)(B) (any method manifesting clear and convincing evidence of intent).

[164] *E.g.*, Graham v. Farmers New World Life Ins. Co., 841 P.2d 1165 (Okl.App.1992).

[165] *Restatement (Second) of Contracts* § 311, cmt. c (1981).

[166] American Western Life Ins. Co. v. Hooker, 622 P.2d 775 (Utah 1980). For the tax advantages of such a transfer of ownership of life insurance *see* Section 15.4, note 255 et seq.

[167] Prudential Ins. Co. of America v. Glass, 959 P.2d 586 (Okl.1998).

[168] *See also* Section 3.5, note 246 et seq. Mass.G.L. c. 175, § 123 requires in addition that a change of beneficiary form be "witnessed by a disinterested person."

[169] Connecticut Gen. Life Ins. Co. v. Gulley, 668 F.2d 325 (7th Cir.1982). *See also* In re Estate of Knickerbocker, 912 P.2d 969 (Utah 1996); Strauss v. Teachers Ins. & Annuity Ass'n, 639 N.E.2d 1106 (Mass.App.1994).

[170] Eschler v. Eschler, 849 P.2d 196 (Mont.1993). *See also* Hoopingarner v. Stenzel, 768 N.E.2d 772, 776 (Ill.App.2002); Penn Mutual Life Ins. Co. v. Abramson, 530 A.2d 1202 (D.C.App.1987) (oral expressions of intent to change the beneficiary insufficient).

[171] Lincoln Life and Annuity Co. of New York v. Caswell, 813 N.Y.S.2d 385 (1st Dept. 2006).

constitute a "waiver" by the insurer of strict compliance with policy terms,[172] but not always.[173]

Similar rules apply to the designation of beneficiaries under pension plans. Here the issue is complicated by the fact that ERISA, the federal statute which governs most pensions, supersedes state law. But one court has held that "the doctrine of substantial compliance . . . affects only the ultimate ownership of the benefits" and its "connection with ERISA is too tenuous . . . to trigger preemption."[174]

Joint Tenancy: Land

A person who puts land into joint tenancy is not usually allowed to get it back. When a husband bought a residence and took title in joint tenancy with his wife, she was awarded a half interest in the house when they later divorced. "When property is taken in joint tenancy by husband and wife . . . even when the purchase money is supplied by one spouse, . . . the presumption that a gift was intended [must be] overcome . . . by clear, convincing, and unmistakable evidence."[175] In California, whenever a spouse takes title to property in joint form with the other spouse, the property belongs to the community unless there is a written agreement or statement in the deed showing a contrary intent.[176]

A joint tenant, even though unable to revoke the other's interest, can destroy the *right of survivorship* and convert the property into a tenancy in common under which each tenant's share passes to his or her estate at death.[177] Thus, when a father put land into joint tenancy with his son, the latter was held to have an "irrevocably accrued right" only as to half the land so long as the father was alive because of the father's right to sever the joint tenancy.[178]

---

[172] Burkett v. Mott, 733 P.2d 673 (Ariz.App.1986); State Employees' Retirement System v. Taylor, 476 N.E.2d 749 (Ill.App.1985).

[173] McCarthy v. Aetna Life Ins. Co., 704 N.E.2d 557, 561 (N.Y.1998).

[174] BankAmerica Pension Plan v. McMath, 206 F.3d 821, 830 (9th Cir.2000). However, the Supreme Court has held that the administrator of an ERISA pension plan properly paid benefits to the employee's ex-wife even though she had waived her claim to them in a divorce settlement, because the employee had not complied with the plan's terms for changing the designated beneficiary. "The plan provided an easy way for [the employee] to change the beneficiary, but for whatever reason he did not . . . The plan administrator therefore did exactly what [ERISA] required." Kennedy v. Plan Adm'r for DuPont Sav. and Inv. Plan, 555 U.S. 285, 129 S.Ct. 865 (2009).

[175] In re Marriage of Wingader, 419 N.E.2d 611, 612 (Ill.App.1981). *See also* Helton v. Helton, 683 N.E.2d 1157 (Ohio App.1996); Bowen v. Bowen, 575 S.E.2d 553 (S.C.2003); Cunningham v. Hastings, 556 N.E.2d 12 (Ind.App.1990) (when land in joint tenancy sold on partition, person who paid for it is not entitled to be reimbursed for the price paid). However, the person who paid for the land may be able to impose a resulting trust on a joint tenant who did not pay for the land if donative intent can be disproved. *See* Section 6.4, at note 227 et seq.

[176] Cal.Fam.Code § 2581. This is stronger than the general presumption that all property acquired during the marriage is community. Section 8.8, note 390. However, the transaction may be upset by proof of undue influence. In re Marriage of Delaney, 4 Cal.Rptr.3d 378 (App.2003); Section 5.3.

[177] *Restatement (Second) Property (Donative Transfers)* § 31.1, illus. 16 (1990); Crowther v. Mower, 876 P.2d 876 (Utah App.1994).

[178] In re Estate of Antonopoulos, 993 P.2d 637, 644 (Kan.1999).

Historically joint tenants had to convey their interest to a third party in order to effectuate such a "severance," but modern courts have eliminated this requirement. A joint tenant's deed purporting to convey land from herself as grantor to herself as grantee "to dissolve any and all rights of survivorship" was held effective after her death against a claim by the other surviving co-tenant. The traditional requirement of conveyance to a third person in order to sever a joint tenancy was based on livery of seisin, and "just as livery of seisin has become obsolete, so should the ancient vestiges of that ceremony give way to modern conveyancing realities."[179] In California, however, a severance deed must be recorded to be effective. This requirement is designed to avoid the risk that a tenant might execute such a deed, keep it secret, and then destroy it if he turned out to be the surviving joint tenant.[180]

When both joint tenants join in selling land, does the right of survivorship attach to the proceeds or are they held as tenants in common? The cases on this issue are divided, except in saying that the result turns on what the parties intended, which is often hard to ascertain.[181]

In some states spouses can hold land as tenants by the entirety. Tenants by the entirety may not be allowed to sever; they hold as "tenants by the entirety" and "being considered as one person in law . . . neither the husband nor the wife can dispose of any part without the assent of the other but the whole must remain to the other."[182] This form of tenancy can exist only between spouses; a deed purporting to create a "tenancy by the entirety" creates only an ordinary joint tenancy if the parties are not legally married to each other.[183] Some states no longer recognize tenancy by the entirety at all.[184] A court upheld a wife's severance of a joint tenancy with her husband on the ground that tenancy by the entirety was "a peculiar and anomalous estate" which had been abolished by a statute "setting out and defining creation of other interests in detail" without mentioning tenancy by the entireties.[185]

A joint tenant's right to sever may be barred by contract[186] or by the terms of the document which created the joint tenancy. When land was devised to

---

179 Minonk State Bank v. Grassman, 447 N.E.2d 822 (Ill.1983). *See also* Riddle v. Harmon, 162 Cal.Rptr. 530 (App.1980); *Helmholz, Realism and Formalism in the Severance of Joint Tenancies*, 77 Neb.L.Rev. 1, 10–13 (1998). Conveyance to a straw man in order to sever a joint tenancy is not a prohibited "transfer" pending divorce proceedings. In re Estate of Hoffman, 653 N.W.2d 94 (S.D.2002).

180 Cal.Civ.Code § 683.2; In re Estate of England, 284 Cal.Rptr. 361 (App.1991) (unrecorded severance deed ineffective); Fetters, *An Invitation to Commit Fraud: Secret Destruction of Joint Tenant Survivorship Rights*, 55 Ford.L.Rev. 173 (1986).

181 Helmholz, *supra* note 179, at 15–20.

182 2 W. Blackstone, *Commentaries* 182 (1765). In Shwachman v. Meagher, 699 N.E.2d 16 (Mass.App.1998), the court cited and followed Blackstone in holding that a deed by the wife alone was void. It noted that the peculiar features of tenancy by the entirety had been abolished by statute, but the statute did not apply to existing tenancies. *But see* Evans v. Evans, 772 S.E.2d 576 (Va. 2015) (tenancy by entirety can be severed by the deed signed by only one spouse at least where one spouse conveys to the other).

183 Riccelli v. Forcinito, 595 A.2d 1322 (Pa.Super.1991).

184 Fay v. Smiley, 207 N.W. 369 (Iowa 1926).

185 Schimke v. Karlstad, 208 N.W.2d 710 (S.D.1973).

186 Alexander v. Snell, 424 N.E.2d 262 (Mass.App.1981). *But see* Register v. Coleman, 633 P.2d 418 (Ariz.1981) (enforcement of oral agreement barred by Statute of Frauds); Smolen for

children "as joint tenants and to the survivor of them," a conveyance by one child did not sever the joint tenancy so her surviving siblings succeeded to the land when she died.[187]

Joint Tenancy: Personal Property

Courts are more likely to regard joint tenancy in personal property as a will substitute rather than as an irrevocable gift to a joint tenant(s) who did not contribute to the acquisition of the property. For example, a woman bought certificates of deposit in the names of herself and her husband jointly. When her husband later changed the CDs into his own name, she sued him for conversion and prevailed. Although the agreement under which the CDs were issued allowed either party to withdraw the funds, this only discharged the bank from liability. "A deposit by one spouse into an account in the names of both, standing alone, does not constitute a gift to the other. The depositor is still deemed to be the owner of the funds" unless there is "evidence of donative intent."[188] In California, a joint account held by spouses is presumed to be community property, but either spouse can overcome this by showing that the funds came from his or her separate property.[189] The UPC says that while the parties are alive joint accounts belong to the party who contributed the funds "unless there is clear and convincing evidence of a different intent."[190] This means that the contributing party, while still alive, can withdraw the funds or change the form of the account,[191] and withdrawals by a noncontributing party can be recovered by the contributing party or his estate.[192]

Changes in the form of an account by a party authorized to make them require a signed written notice "received by the financial institution during the party's lifetime."[193] Many banks impose similar rules, which are like the standard clauses in insurance policies for change of beneficiary, so perhaps case law will develop a doctrine of "substantial compliance" in this area too.[194]

Smolen v. Smolen, 956 P.2d 128 (Nev.1998) (provision in divorce decree that land "remain in joint tenancy" did not bar severance by one party).

[187] Williams v. Studstill, 306 S.E.2d 633 (Ga.1983). *See also* Albro v. Allen, 454 N.W.2d 85 (Mich.1990) (no severance possible when deed expressly refers to right of survivorship); Hilterbrand v. Carter, 27 P.3d 1086 (Or.App.2001) (mother's putting land in joint tenancy with two children and their spouses created "cross-contingent remainders" which could not be destroyed).

[188] Myers v. Myers, 314 S.E.2d 809 (N.C.App.1984). *See also* In re Estate of Mayer, 664 N.E.2d 583 (Ohio App.1995); Estate of Lennon v. Lennon, 29 P.3d 1258, 1267 (Wash.App.2001) (estate can recover withdrawals by noncontributing party to joint account). *But see* Estate of Vogel, 684 N.E.2d 1035 (Ill.App.1997) (contributions are irrelevant where terms of agreement allows either party to withdraw funds).

[189] Cal.Prob.Code § 5305(b) (expressly trumping Family Code § 2581). Under UPC § 6–211(b) the contributions of spouses to a joint account are presumed to be equal.

[190] UPC § 6–211(b). *See also* Kinney v. Ewing, 492 P.2d 636 (N.M.1972).

[191] Campbell v. Black, 844 P.2d 759 (Kan.App.1993).

[192] Vaughn v. Bernhardt, 547 S.E.2d 869 (S.C.2001).

[193] UPC § 6–213. For a criticism of this requirement, *see* McGovern, *Nonprobate Transfers under the Revised Uniform Probate Code*, 55 Alb.L.Rev. 1329, 1335 (1992).

[194] *See* note 169 *supra*.

As to joint tenancy in personal property other than bank accounts some courts treat brokerage accounts like bank accounts,[195] although the common claim that a joint bank account was created simply for convenience in making deposits and withdrawals seems less apposite in this situation.[196] The UPC has different rules for securities than for accounts, but they are unclear on this issue.[197]

Divorce

In most states, provisions in a will in favor of the testator's spouse are revoked if they later divorce.[198] The assumption as to intent which underlies this rule applies also to will substitutes like insurance policies, but courts do not treat them the same way. For example, an ex-wife who had been named as beneficiary of her husband's POD account during the marriage was awarded the account after he died despite the fact that they had been divorced.[199]

Claims by ex-spouses are sometimes defeated on the basis of a waiver executed at the time of the divorce.[200] Despite the standard policy requirements of notice to the insurer, courts have barred spouses from claiming insurance when a separation agreement specifically mentioned it, even though the company was not notified.[201] But waiver arguments are often rejected on the ground that the language in the divorce settlement was too general.[202] A wife's agreement to waive all claims "in, to, or against the property" of her husband was held to preclude her from claiming as beneficiary of a trust listed in the agreement, but not as beneficiary of an insurance policy which was not so listed.[203] Even a provision in a divorce decree awarding a particular account to the husband was held not to bar his ex-wife's claim as the designated POD beneficiary after his death.[204] The UPC calls for a broad construction of a waiver of "all rights" in a separation agreement, but this does

---

[195] Parker v. Kokot, 793 P.2d 195, 200 (Idaho 1990); Lebitz-Freeman v. Lebitz, 803 A.2d 156 (N.J.Super.App.Div.2002).

[196] In In re Marriage of Orlando, 577 N.E.2d 1334 (Ill.App.1991), a wife's putting stock into joint tenancy was held to create a presumption of a gift which could be rebutted only by clear proof. *See also* Schmanski v. Schmanski, 984 P.2d 752 (Nev.1999) (separate property put into joint brokerage account becomes community, giving wife a share upon divorce).

[197] McGovern, *supra* note 193, at 1349.

[198] *See* Section 4.4.

[199] Matter of Estate of Leone, 860 P.2d 973 (Utah App.1993). *See also* Leahy v. Leahy-Schuett, 570 N.E.2d 407 (Ill.App.1991); Eredics v. Chase Manhattan Bank, 790 N.E.2d 1166 (N.Y.2003) (Totten trust); Schultz v. Schultz, 591 N.W.2d 212 (Iowa 1999). *But see* Kennedy v. Plan Adm'r for DuPont Sav. and Inv. Plan, 555 U.S. 285, 129 S.Ct. 865 (2009) (ERISA plan), *supra* note 174.

[200] Estate of Anello v. McQueen, 953 P.2d 1143 (Utah 1998) (IRA); Lelux v. Chernick, 694 N.E.2d 471 (Ohio App.1997), *abrogated on other grounds* (insurance and pension); Robson v. Electrical Contractors Ass'n, 727 N.E.2d 692 (Ill.App.1999) (pension).

[201] Curley v. Giltrop, 496 N.E.2d 224 (N.Y.1986); Conn v. Trow, 715 S.W.2d 152 (Tex.App.1986); Johnson v. Johnson, 746 P.2d 1061 (Idaho App.1987) (IRA account).

[202] Eschler v. Eschler, 849 P.2d 196 (Mont.1993); Eredics v. Chase Manhattan Bank, 790 N.E.2d 1166 (N.Y.2003) (Totten trust); Deida v. Murphy, 647 N.E.2d 1109 (Ill.App.1995).

[203] In re Marriage of Velasquez, 692 N.E.2d 841 (Ill.App.1998).

[204] Schultz v. Schultz, 591 N.W.2d 212 (Iowa 1999). *See also* Rishel v. Estate of Rishel ex rel. Gilbert, 781 N.E.2d 735, 742 (Ind.App.2003) (retirement benefits awarded to husband in property settlement go to wife as designated beneficiary when husband dies without changing beneficiary).

not apply to benefits to the former spouse in a living trust as distinguished from a will.[205]

While divorce proceedings are pending, it is common to restrain the spouses from disposing of their property. Such an order may preclude a spouse from changing the beneficiary designation on an insurance policy away from the other spouse.[206]

In many states divorce ends the right of survivorship between spouses who own property jointly.[207] Here too, the result may turn on the terms of the decree; a surviving husband succeeded to a house which, by the terms of the divorce decree was to remain in joint tenancy.[208] However, some courts have found an agreement to sever "from language that is ambiguous at best, and sometimes even from the conduct of the parties."[209]

Some statutes extend to all will substitutes the rule that divorce revokes devises. Under the UPC, a divorce "severs the interests of the former spouses in property held by them" as joint tenants, and revokes any revocable disposition made by one spouse to the other in a "governing instrument" which is defined to include trusts, insurance policies, POD accounts, and pension benefits as well as wills.[210] This presumption, unlike others in the Code, is not rebuttable by oral evidence of contrary intent. Thus, an ex-wife was cut out as beneficiary of an insurance policy by a divorce, despite the insured's statement that "he wanted to leave the designation the way it was."[211] As to pension benefits, ERISA preempts a state statute like this,[212] but some courts have reached the same result as a matter of federal common law, ERISA itself being silent on the question.[213]

Some courts have applied statutes providing for revocation of a will or bequest by divorce to will substitutes by analogy. Provisions in a revocable trust for the settlor's husband were held to be revoked when the settlor divorced him on the ground that it would be "incongruous" not to apply the

---

[205] Matter of Estate of Groesbeck, 935 P.2d 1255 (Utah 1997).

[206] Cal.Fam.Code § 2040(a); Nicholas v. Nicholas, 83 P.3d 214 (Kan.2004). *But see* Minnesota Mutual Life Ins. Co. v. Ensley, 174 F.3d 977 (9th Cir.1999).

[207] Matter of Estate of Ikuta, 639 P.2d 400 (Haw.1981); Goldman v. Goldman, 733 N.E.2d 200 (N.Y.2000) (divorce turns tenancy by the entirety into tenancy in common); 28 Pa.Stat. § 3507; Va.Code § 6.1–125.4 (joint account). *But see* Matter of Estate of Sander, 806 P.2d 545 (Mont.1991) (joint tenancy unaffected by divorce).

[208] In re Marriage of Dudek, 559 N.E.2d 1078 (Ill.App.1990). *See also* Estate of Dompke v. Dompke, 542 N.E.2d 1222 (Ill.App.1989) (joint account becomes husband's by terms of the decree); *cf.* In re Wax, 63 S.W.3d 668 (Mo.App.2001) (accounts said to be wife's "sole property" in separation agreement did not pass to ex-husband on wife's death, but other accounts in joint form did).

[209] Helmholz, *supra* note 179, at 23. *See also* Fitts v. Stokes, 841 So.2d 229, 232 (Ala.2002).

[210] UPC §§ 1–201(18), 2–804(b). In Henley v. Henley, 974 P.2d 362 (Wash.App.1999), the statute was held inapplicable to a divorce obtained in another jurisdiction. The effect of the UPC provision on joint bank accounts is unclear. McGovern, *supra* note 193, at 1340.

[211] Mearns v. Scharbach, 12 P.3d 1048 (Wash.App.2000). *See* also Section 4.4, note 115. Contrast the rules of construction in part 7 which apply "in the absence of a finding of a contrary intention." UPC § 2–701.

[212] Egelhoff v. Egelhoff, 532 U.S. 141 (2001).

[213] Weaver v. Keen, 43 S.W.3d 537, 545 (Tex.App.2001). *But see* Kennedy v. Plan Adm'r for DuPont Sav. and Inv. Plan, 555 U.S. 285, 129 S.Ct. 865 (2009) (ERISA plan), *supra* note 174.

statutory rule governing wills to this type of trust.[214] Another court held that a provision for a named spouse was ineffective after she divorced the settlor because the instrument referred to her as his "wife."[215]

Effect of Wills on Will Substitutes

Will provisions that purport to deal with property covered by a will substitute are often denied effect. For example, a purported devise of property held in joint tenancy is void, "for no testament takes effect till after the death of the testator and by such death the right of the survivor is already vested."[216] This rule, though ancient, seems questionable. Because a joint tenant can devise her interest "by using two pieces of paper ... [first an instrument severing the joint tenancy and then the will] . . . logic dictates that one piece of paper (the will) suffices where the election to sever is clearly expressed."[217] The contrary result appears to put form over substance.

A will may control joint tenancy property under the theory of an election if the will devises other property to the surviving joint tenant. "If a testator by his will assumes to dispose of the property of another person who is also made a beneficiary under the will," the devisee's acceptance of benefits under the will estops him from objecting to the disposition of his own property, including property acquired as surviving joint tenant.[218]

The Restatement of Trusts allows settlors of bank account trusts to revoke them by will,[219] but general language in a will may not suffice, *e.g.*, a devise of all the estate "of whatsoever nature" did not revoke the testator's bank account trusts.[220] Even when the intent to revoke a living trust is clear, it may be rejected for failure to satisfy a requirement in the trust that amendments be delivered to the trustee during the settlor's lifetime.[221] The UTC allows living

---

[214] Clymer v. Mayo, 473 N.E.2d 1084 (Mass.1985). *See also Restatement (Third) of Trusts* § 25, illus. 11 (2001); In re Estate of Davis, 589 N.E.2d 154 (Ill.App.1992).

[215] Offerman v. Rosile, 77 P.3d 504 (Kan.App.2003).

[216] 2 W. Blackstone, *Commentaries* 186 (1765). *See also* T. Littleton, *Tenures* § 287; In re Estate of England, 284 Cal.Rptr. 361 (App.1991) (will cannot sever joint tenancy); Matter of Estate of Ingram, 874 P.2d 1282 (Okl.1994) (CDs held in joint tenancy); Matter of Estate of Kokjohn, 531 N.W.2d 99 (Iowa 1995) (joint account).

[217] Mattis, *Joint Tenancy: Notice of Severance Mortgages and Survivorship,* 7 N.Ill.L.Rev. 41, 46 (1986). *See also* McGovern, *The Payable on Death Account and Other Will Substitutes,* 67 Nw.U.L.Rev. 7, 22 (1972).

[218] Citizens Nat. Bank v. Stasell, 408 N.E.2d 587 (Ind.App.1980). This theory has also been applied where the provisions of a will were inconsistent with the designation of an insurance beneficiary. Estate of Stalnaker, 479 A.2d 612 (Pa.Super.1984); Wis.Stat. § 853.17(2); *But see* Williamson v. Williamson, 657 N.E.2d 651 (Ill.App.1995) (refusing to require an election where the will did not require it expressly).

[219] *Restatement (Third) of Trusts* § 26, cmt. c (2001).

[220] Eredics v. Chase Manhattan Bank, 790 N.E.2d 1166 (N.Y.2003). *See also* Matter of Estate of Sanders, 929 P.2d 153 (Kan.1996) (trust not revoked by general language in will which did not refer to the trust); In re Estate of Furst, 55 P.3d 664 (Wash.App.2002) (same); In re Estate of Gloege, 649 N.W.2d 468 (Minn.App.2002) (statute allows will to revoke non-probate transfer only by "specific reference"); *Restatement (Third) of Trusts* § 26, illus. 7 (2001); Abernathy v. Latham, 545 S.E.2d 848, 851 (S.C.App.2001) (residuary clause in a will did not show clear evidence to defeat the right of survivorship in a joint account).

[221] One Valley Bank, Nat. Ass'n v. Hunt, 516 S.E.2d 516 (W.Va.1999). However, in In re Estate of Davis, 671 N.E.2d 1302 (Ohio App.1996), where the trust allowed the settlor to amend it during his lifetime, his will was held to be effective to do so because it "operated as an *in praesenti* instrument."

trusts to be revoked by will, but only if the trust does not provide an "exclusive" method of revocation.[222] Some states do not allow living trusts to be revoked by will at all.[223]

The UPC does not allow beneficiary designations in a P.O.D. account or a right of survivorship in a joint account to be altered by will.[224] A will directing who is to receive the proceeds of insurance has been held ineffective to change the beneficiary designation in the policy.[225] This allows banks and insurers to pay funds promptly after a depositor/insured's death without worrying about a possible will.

> It is in the public interest that an insurance company may pay a loss to the beneficiary designated in the policy as promptly after the death of the insured as may reasonably be done.... If paid to the beneficiary, a will might later be probated designating a different disposition of the fund, and it would be a risk that few companies would be willing to take.[226]

This concern is legitimate but could be better addressed by simply protecting any bank or insurer that makes payment without notice of the will. The UPC has several provisions protecting banks and other third parties who pay claims in good faith.[227] The Third Restatement of Property provides that payors who pay the beneficiary of record should be protected, but if they receive notice of the change of beneficiary designation in a will, they should comply with it.[228]

Lawyers who draft wills should ascertain what will substitutes the testator has made. Will substitutes are often made without legal advice by persons who use lawyers to draft their wills. While a testator is powerless to revoke irrevocable gifts, she can certainly take prior irrevocable gifts into account when determining what dispositions to make under her will. Also, with proper attention to formalities joint tenancies can be severed, revocable trusts revoked, and insurance beneficiaries changed so as to reflect the testator's current wishes. But this requires more than a duly executed will. A will failed to pass accounts which were the testator's principal asset to the intended beneficiaries because the drafter of the will "did not inquire about and was never informed that the accounts were jointly titled."[229] Lawyers who make

---

[222] UTC § 602(c).

[223] In re Last Will and Testament of Tamplin, 48 P.3d 471 (Alaska 2002); Cal.Prob.Code § 15401(a)(2).

[224] UPC § 6–213(b). *See also* Cal.Prob.Code § 5302(e); Matter of Estate of Ingram, 874 P.2d 1282 (Okl.1994) (CD in joint form); Matter of Estate of Kokjohn, 531 N.W.2d 99 (Iowa 1995) (joint account). *But see* Wash.Stat. § 11.11.020 ("any nonprobate asset specifically referred to in the owner's will" can be controlled by the will).

[225] Estate of Norwood, 443 N.W.2d 798 (Mich.App.1989); McCarthy v. Aetna Life Ins. Co., 704 N.E.2d 557 (N.Y.1998).

[226] McCarthy v. Aetna Life Ins. Co., *supra* note 225, at 560–561.

[227] UPC §§ 2–803(h), 2–804(g), 6–221–6–227. *See also* UTC § 602(g), protecting trustees who distribute without knowing that a trust has been revoked or amended.

[228] *Restatement (Third) of Property (Wills and Other Donative Transfers)* § 7.2, cmt. e (2001).

[229] Abernathy v. Latham, 545 S.E.2d 848, 849 (S.C.App.2001). *See also* D. Parry & J. Clark, *The Law of Succession* 11 (10th ed. 1996).

this mistake risk being sued for malpractice.[230] On the other hand, if the testator does *not* wish to disturb non-probate arrangements previously made, express confirmation of them in the will may be advisable to remove all doubt.[231]

§§ 4.6–5.0 are reserved for supplemental material.

[230] In Matter of McCoy, 419 N.W.2d 301 (Wis.App.1987) a settlor told the trustee she wanted to amend the trust. The trustee did not advise her that this required a writing. The trustee was held subject to suit by the intended beneficiary after the settlor died.

[231] J. Price, *supra* note 140, at § 4.13.

Chapter 5

INCAPACITY AND UNDUE INFLUENCE

Analysis

Sec.

5.1 Incapacity.
5.2 Conservatorship and Durable Powers of Attorney.
5.3 Undue Influence.
5.4 Role of Lawyers.

§ 5.1 Incapacity

Testamentary Capacity

Modern American statutes typically require that a testator be at least 18 years old to execute a valid will.[1] The same limitation applies to inter-vivos gifts. But if a minor who makes a gift fails to disaffirm it within a reasonable time after reaching majority, it becomes valid through ratification.[2] Some states also allow emancipated minors to execute a will.[3] In addition to an age requirement, most American statutes require that the testator be of "sound mind."[4] Few statutes, however, define that phrase. There are two possible challenges to a will on the basis that testator was not of "sound mind." A will could be challenged on the grounds that the testator either lacked mental capacity or suffered from an insane delusion. If the testator lacked mental capacity, the entire will is invalid; if, on the other hand, the will was a product

---

[1] UPC § 2–501; Cal.Prob.Code § 6100; *Restatement (Second) of Property (Donative Transfers)* § 34.4, cmt. a (1990); *Restatement (Third) of Property (Wills and Other Donative Transfers)* § 3.1, cmt. 10 (1998). Some countries provide a lower minimum age. E.g., BGB (German Civil Code) § 2229 (16). This can raise choice of law problems. *See* H. Flick & D. Piltz, *Der Internationale Erbfall* 46–50 (1999); 1 J. Schoenblum, *Multistate and Multinational Estate Planning* § 14.04 (2d ed.1999).

[2] *Restatement (Second) of Property (Donative Transfers)* § 34.4, cmt. b (1990); *Restatement (Third) of Property (Wills and Other Donative Transfers)* § 8.2, cmt. d (1998). Apparently, this also applies to wills executed by a minor who survives past reaching the age of majority without disaffirming the will. But *id.* § 18.1, illus. 5 suggests that this depends on "local law." UPC § 2–501 is not clear as to this.

[3] *See, e.g.*, Iowa Code § 633.3(17); 633.274.

[4] UPC § 2–501. Although the provision refers to "making" a will, the same standard applies to revoking one. Wood v. Bettis, 880 P.2d 961 (Or.App.1994) (destruction of will by testator who lacked capacity did not revoke it); *Restatement (Third) of Property (Wills and Other Donative Transfers)* § 8.1, cmt. c (2001). Merely because a conservator has been appointed for a ward does not mean the ward lacks testamentary capacity. If the ward has testamentary capacity, he may be barred from creating an inter-vivos trust but not a will. In re Estate of Gallavan, 89 P.3d 521 (Colo.App. 2004). There is a strong presumption in favor of finding testamentary capacity. See In re Estate of Phillips, 795 S.E.2d 273 (N.C. Ct. App. 2016).

In Louisiana, a testator must be literate in order to execute a "statutory" will. In re Succession of McClinton, 736 So.2d 906 (La.App.1999) (will rejected because testator was illiterate).

of an insane delusion, then only the portions, if any, affected by the insane delusion are invalid.[5]

The level of mental capacity to execute a will is not the same as is necessary for entering a contract or having a guardian appointed to administer one's property. Mental capacity to execute a will requires that the testator (1) know the nature and extent of the testator's property, (2) know the persons who are the "natural objects" of his bounty, *i.e.*, the persons with the highest moral claims to his property, and (3) understand the disposition being made of his property by his will.[6] In addition, the testator must be able to understand the relationship of those three elements to each other and to form an orderly disposition of his estate.[7] Persons with mental disease such as paranoia, paresis, senile dementia, Alzheimer's, and certain psychosis may not be able to execute a will. But, persons without mental disease may also lack capacity if, for other reasons, they cannot meet the four standards of capacity. In other words, it is not necessary that the testator has been diagnosed with a mental disease for a contest to be successful.

The California Probate Code defines capacity in words which closely approximate the common law:

> An individual is not mentally competent to make a will if at the time of making the will *either* of the following is true:
>
> (1) The individual does not have sufficient mental capacity to be able to (A) understand the nature of the testamentary act, (B) understand and recollect the nature of the individual's property,[8] or (C) remember and understand the individual's relations to living descendants, spouse, and parents, and those whose interests are affected by the will.[9]
>
> (2) The individual suffers from a mental disorder with symptoms including delusions or hallucinations, which delusions and hallucinations result in the individual's devising property in a way which, except for the existence of the delusions or hallucinations, the individual would not have done.[10]

Insane Delusion

A testator with an otherwise high degree of intelligence may suffer from an insane delusion.[11] Contests based upon an insane delusion do not often

---

[5] D.Parry & J. Clark, *The Law of Succession*, 61–62 (10th ed. 1996).

[6] In re Estate of Paigo, 863 N.Y.S.2d 508 (App. Div. 3rd Dept. 2008); Matter of Estate of Kumstar, 487 N.E.2d 271 (N.Y. 1985); Estate of Basich, 398 N.E.2d 1182 (Ill. App. Ct. 1979).

[7] T. Atkinison, *Handbook on the Law of Wills* (2d ed. 1953).

[8] *Cf.* Wood v. Smith, [1993] Ch. 90, 114 (finding incapacity when testator thought his estate was much smaller than it actually was). The size of an estate is often a relevant factor in making an intelligent disposition of it.

[9] *Compare* Bland v. Graves, 620 N.E.2d 920 (Ohio Ct. App.1993) (error to find incapacity from the testator's failure to know the names of her only relatives, second cousins with whom she had little contact).

[10] Cal.Prob.Code § 6100.5(a) (emphasis added).

[11] Contestants can assert both grounds, general incapacity and an insane delusion. Breeden v. Stone, 992 P.2d 1167 (Colo.2000).

succeed in upsetting a will, because a testator's mistaken belief is not an "insane delusion" if there was some rational basis for it. Thus, a testator's false belief that a child was not his was not an insane delusion because that belief did not defy "rational explanation" and was not "the product of a mental disorder."[12] On the other hand, a testator's belief that her nephews and niece were trying to kill her justified rejection of her will, because her belief was "without foundation or basis in fact . . . [and] too bizarre to be real."[13]

In order for the challenge to succeed, the will must be the product of the insane delusion.[14] In other words, the terms of the will must be explainable by reference to the insane delusion.[15] Thus, a will, allegedly motivated by an insane delusion that the contestant intended to harm the testator was probated when the court found that the testator had other reasons for the will: she wished a family business to continue and left most of her estate to a child who was also interested in its continuation.[16]

General Mental Incapacity, Additional Comments

When wills are challenged on capacity grounds, it is far more often for lack of general mental capacity rather than insane delusion. In fact, with a challenge based upon general mental incapacity contestants need not show that the will was the product of a delusion.[17] Mental incapacity may be congenital, or it may be brought on by disease or old age. The percentage of elderly in the population has dramatically increased and many challenges to capacity today arise from wills made by testators of advanced years.[18] However, a diagnosis of "senile dementia" and evidence of peculiar behavior are not incompatible with a finding of testamentary capacity because "the appropriate inquiry is whether the decedent was lucid and rational at the time the will was made."[19] Thus, if testator lacked capacity at different periods of

---

[12] Akers v. Hodel, 871 F.2d 924, 935 (10th Cir.1989). *See also* Dillon v. Phillips, 756 P.2d 1278 (Or.App.1988) ("at least a slight basis" for testator's belief that his children had stolen from him); Goodman v. Zimmerman, 32 Cal.Rptr.2d 419 (App.1994); Matter of Estate of Raney, 799 P.2d 986 (Kan.1990); In re Estate of Kottke, 6 P.3d 243, 247 (Alaska 2000). As to a simple mistaken belief by the testator, *see* Section 7.1, note 71 et seq.

[13] Matter of Estate of Killen, 937 P.2d 1368, 1373 (Ariz. Ct. App.1996). *See also* Matter of Estate of Watlack, 945 P.2d 1154 (Wash.App.1997) (no rational basis for testator's belief that his daughter had stolen from him).

[14] In re Estate of Berg, 783 N.W.2d 831 (S.D. 2010).

[15] Benjamin v. Woodring, 303 A.2d 779 (Md.1973); In re Agostini's Estate, 457 A.2d 861 (Pa.Super.1983); Spruance v. Northway, 601 S.W.2d 153, 157 (Tex.Civ.App.1980) (approved jury instructions). *Compare* Section 7.1, note 76.

[16] Matter of Yett's Estate, 606 P.2d 1174 (Or.App.1980). *See also* Goodman v. Zimmerman, 32 Cal.Rptr.2d 419 (App.1994); In re Estate of Nicholson, 644 N.E.2d 47 (Ill.App.1994); Breeden v. Stone, 992 P.2d 1167, 1173 (Colo.2000) (will probated despite testator's insane delusion).

[17] In re Estate of Washburn, 690 A.2d 1024 (N.H.1997).

[18] *See* Smith and Hager, *The Senile Testator: Medicolegal Aspects of Competency*, 13 Clev.-Mar.L.Rev. 397 (1964).

[19] In re Estate of Schlueter, 994 P.2d 937, 940 (Wyo.2000). Conversely, in Crittell v. Bingo, 36 P.3d 634, 641 (Alaska 2001), the court rejected a will, saying that "although there were many times during her last years in which [the testator] was competent, . . . at the time of the Will signing, she was not." It has been held sufficient that the testator had capacity when he gave instructions to his solicitor for drafting the will. Parry & Clark, *supra* note 5 at 60–61.

her life but when the will was actually signed had capacity, the will is valid.[20] Conversely, if the testator who was ordinarily of sound mind executes his will during a brief period when he is not, the will is invalid.

Medical evidence often is used to determine capacity. Experts who never saw the testator can render opinions based on the testator's medical records.[21] More common is testimony by doctors who treated the testator,[22] although this may encounter objections based on the doctor-patient evidentiary privilege unless that privilege is waived. One court denied a contestant permission to discover the testator's medical records because only the patient's executor could waive the privilege,[23] but another court removed an executor who refused to waive the privilege because she stood to benefit if the challenge to the will failed.[24] Some contestants, without success, have sought the testator's body exhumed for examination to find evidence of mental deterioration to support a claim of lack of mental capacity.[25]

Medical testimony is often either rejected or discounted because the doctor's contact with the patient was too far removed from the time when the will was executed. For example, testimony that the testator lacked capacity two years after the will was executed was rejected as "too remote," and a psychiatrist's testimony that the testator had "degenerative dementia" several weeks after the execution was admitted but deemed outweighed by witnesses to the will who testified affirmatively as to the testator's capacity.[26] Some estate planners advise that physicians be used as witnesses to a will if the testator's capacity is likely to be challenged.[27]

Subscribing witnesses, even if they are not experts, can offer an opinion about the testator's capacity.[28] The force of their testimony is enhanced if they

---

[20] Daly v. Hussey, 174 N.E. 916 (Mass. 1931); In re Estate of Rosen, 23 N.E.3d 116 (Mass. App. Ct. 2014).

[21] Roberts v. Baker, 463 S.E.2d 694 (Ga.1995); Matter of Estate of Kesler, 702 P.2d 86 (Utah 1985). In other cases contests based on such evidence have failed, however. Lucero v. Lucero, 884 P.2d 527 (N.M. Ct. App.1994); Morse v. Volz, 808 S.W.2d 424 (Mo. Ct. App.1991).

[22] *E.g.,* Estate of Verdi by Verdi v. Toland, 733 N.E.2d 25 (Ind. Ct. App.2000) (summary judgment for contestants reversed on basis of medical diagnosis of testator's suffering from "dementia of Alzheimer type").

[23] Cline v. Finney, 594 N.E.2d 1100 (Ohio Ct. App.1991).

[24] Pio v. Ramsier, 623 N.E.2d 174 (Ohio Ct. App.1993).

[25] Camilli v. Cemetery, 583 A.2d 417 (N.J.Super. Ct. Ch.Div.1990); Holm v. Superior Court (Misco), 232 Cal.Rptr. 432 (Cal. Ct. App.1986).

[26] Bishop v. Kenny, 466 S.E.2d 581 (Ga.1996). *See also* In re Estate of Farr, 49 P.3d 415, 427–8 (Kan.2002); Sanders v. Brooks, 611 So.2d 336 (Ala.1992); Quarterman v. Quarterman, 493 S.E.2d 146 (Ga.1997) (summary judgment for proponents when only evidence of incapacity related to a time years before will executed). However, in Jones v. LaFargue, 758 S.W.2d 320 (Tex.App.1988) a will was rejected based on testimony by doctors who had examined the testator 4 months after the will was executed.

[27] H. Tweed & W. Parsons, *Lifetime and Testamentary Estate Planning* 115 (10th ed. 1988); Wohl, *Guidelines for Avoiding Estate Litigation,* 19 Est.Plann. 67 (1992); Estate of Crossmore, TC Memo 1988–494 (discounting value of contestant's claim where doctors familiar with the testator had witnessed the will).

[28] Strong v. Holden, 697 S.E.2d 189 (Ga. 2010) (more weight given to testimony of attesting witnesses who questioned testator about content of will than to doctor who never examined patient and based entire testimony on testator's medications); In re Estate of Schlueter, 994 P.2d 937, 940 (Wyo.2000) (summary judgment for proponents based on affidavits of witnesses that testator had

knew the testator well or at least had a substantial conversation with the testator when the will was signed.[29] Courts tend to discount the testimony of witnesses whose contact with the testator was minimal.[30] Proponents of a will have used attestation clauses to undercut subscribing witnesses who testify that the testator *lacked* capacity.[31] Some lawyers make a tape recording of the execution to show that the testator was "making sense" at the relevant time.[32]

Capacity is a question of fact, and determinations of a trial court are accepted on appeal if supported by substantial evidence.[33]

Naturalness of Will

Roman law allowed a testator's children to assert claims that they had been unjustly disinherited "on the pretext that the testator was of unsound mind when he executed the will," although the real basis for the complaint was that the will showed "lack of family feeling."[34] Observers of American law have suggested that our rules on capacity represent a similar veiled limitation on testamentary freedom.[35] Juries are thought to be particularly prone to reject wills that they find unfair,[36] but references to "unnaturalness" as evidence of incapacity are also often found in judicial opinions. For example, a court upheld a finding of incapacity based upon the testator's failure to understand the natural objects of his bounty. "On the day the will was executed [testator] twice denied that he had a son . . . [The] devise to Dow [a non-relative] was unexpected and unnatural . . . The fact that the decedent made such an

---

testamentary capacity); In re Estate of Elam, 738 S.W.2d 169 (Tenn.1987); Lawrence v. First Nat. Bank, 516 So.2d 630 (Ala.1987).

[29] Beyer, *The Will Execution Ceremony*, 29 S.Tex.L.Rev. 413, 432 (1988).

[30] Bigej v. Boyer, 817 P.2d 760, 763 (Or.App.1991); Macaulay v. Wachovia Bank of SC, N.A., 569 S.E.2d 371, 376 (S.C.App.2002).

[31] In re Estate of Chlebos, 550 N.E.2d 1069 (Ill. Ct. App.1990). *See* Section 3.3.

[32] Patterson-Fowlkes v. Chancey, 732 S.E.2d 252 (Ga. 2012) (jury could rely on videotape of the will's execution to establish capacity where testator was questioned about disposition of property in the will); Central Bank-Granite City v. Ziaee, 544 N.E.2d 1121 (Ill.App.Ct. 1989); Hauck v. Seright, 964 P.2d 749, 755 (Mont.1998) (audiotape used to rebut claim of undue influence); In re Estate of Peterson, 439 N.W.2d 516 (Neb.1989); In re Estate of Smith, 827 So.2d 673, 676 (Miss.2002) (court relies on videotape of execution in finding capacity). For suggestions how to conduct such a videotaping *see* Kirtland, *Dealing With Mental Capacity Issues in Estate Planning*, 30 Est.Plann. 192, 196 (2003).

[33] In re Neville, 67 S.W.3d 522, 527 (Tex.App.2002); Riddell v. Edwards, 32 P.3d 4, 8 (Alaska 2001). *But see* Macaulay v. Wachovia Bank of SC, N.A., 569 S.E.2d 371, 376 (S.C. Ct. App.2002) (reversing a finding of incapacity).

[34] Justinian, *Institutes* 2.18.

[35] Fellows, *The Case Against Living Probate*, 78 Mich.L.Rev. 1066, 1070–73 (1980); Epstein, *Testamentary Capacity, Reasonableness and Family Maintenance: A Proposal for Meaningful Reform*, 35 Temp.L.Q. 231 (1962); Green, *Proof of Mental Incompetency and the Unexpressed Major Premise*, 53 Yale L.J. 271 (1944).

[36] Schoenblum, *Will Contests: An Empirical Study*, 22 Real Prop. Prob. & Trust J. 607, 626 (1987) (jury finds for contestants more often than judges do). Jury verdicts may be avoided or controlled by summary judgment or judgment n.o.v. Matter of Last Will of Dickey, 542 So.2d 903 (Miss.1989); Morse v. Volz, 808 S.W.2d 424 (Mo. Ct. App.1991); Quarterman v. Quarterman, 493 S.E.2d 146 (Ga.1997) (summary judgment); In re Estate of Wagner, 522 N.W.2d 159 (Neb.1994) (same).

unlikely disposition of his one-third share of the family farm may be given significant weight by the factfinder."[37]

A will which on its face seems unnatural may be upheld when a reason for the disposition appears. Thus, a will which disinherited the testator's grandchildren was probated after her attorney testified that the testator wanted to leave everything to her sister-in-law "because [she] had been good to her."[38] Some lawyers favor stating the reasons for an unusual disposition in the will itself.[39] Naturalness, one court has said, should be judged from the perspective of the testator, not the court or jury. "A will is unnatural when it is contrary to what *the testator,* from his known views, feelings, and intentions would have been expected to make"; a will "may differ from ordinary actions of men" and nevertheless not be "unnatural."[40]

Sudden changes in a testator's wishes are viewed with suspicion. A deed and will which altered an "estate plan of long standing" were voided for incapacity as "unnatural."[41] A testator who executed wills "just over three weeks apart [which] contained vastly different provisions" and differed from her contemporaneous statements of how she wished to dispose of her property was found to be incapacitated.[42] Conversely, if a disputed will is similar to prior wills, this helps to refute claims of incapacity, because this shows "that the testator (and grantor) had a constant and abiding scheme for the distribution of his property."[43]

§ 5.2 Conservatorship and Durable Powers of Attorney

All states have procedures for appointing a conservator or guardian for a person (sometimes referred to as a "ward," sometimes referred to as a "conservatee") who is unable to manage his or her property. A petition to have a conservator appointed in California is typical; it must allege "the inability of the proposed conservatee to substantially manage his or her own financial resources, or to resist fraud or undue influence."[44] Can someone for whom a

---

[37] Estate of Record, 534 A.2d 1319, 1322–23 (Me.1987). Likewise, a court invalidated a will for undue influence in part because the will excluded the testator's son with whom the testator had an extremely close relationship for most of the son's life. Kelly v. McNeel, 250 P.3d 1105 (Wyo. 2011).

[38] Doyle v. Schott, 582 N.E.2d 1057, 1060 (Ohio App.1989). *See also* In re Estate of Elam, 738 S.W.2d 169, 172 (Tenn.1987); Taylor v. Koslosky, 814 P.2d 985 (Mont.1991) (excluding child who had already received benefits); Hodges v. Genzone, 724 So.2d 521, 524 (Ala. Civ. App.1998) (will disinherited testator's daughters "because they had evicted [him] from his house").

[39] Gilfix, *Because It's About More Than Death and Taxes*, 142 Trusts & Estates, February 2003 p. 64.

[40] Matter of Estate of Bouchat, 679 P.2d 426 (Wash.App.1984).

[41] Matter of Guardianship & Conserv. of Estate of Tennant, 714 P.2d 122, 129 (Mont.1986). *See also* Crittell v. Bingo 36 P.3d 634, 642 (Alaska 2001).

[42] In re Estate of Washburn, 690 A.2d 1024, 1027 (N.H.1997); *cf.* Hauck v. Seright, 964 P.2d 749, 756 (Mont.1998) (inconsistent wills executed three days apart).

[43] In re Estate of Camin, 323 N.W.2d 827, 836 (Neb.1982). *See also* Matter of Estate of Luger, 797 P.2d 229 (Mont.1990); Costello v. Hall, 506 So.2d 293 (Miss.1987); Matter of Estate of Alexander, 749 P.2d 1052 (Kan.App.1988). Such a series of consistent wills may even deprive the heirs of standing to contest the last one. *See* Section 13.3, note 139.

[44] Cal.Prob.Code § 1821(a)(5). *Compare* the more elaborate formulation in UPC § 5–401(2) (2010 rev.).

conservator has been appointed make a will? In virtually all states the answer to this question is "yes."

> Ability to transact * * * business is not the legal standard of testamentary incapacity. * * * While * * * the existence of a conservatorship at the time a will was executed may have some bearing on the question of testamentary capacity, [it] * * * is not an adjudication of testamentary incapacity.[45]

Some courts consider a conservatorship as *evidence* of testamentary incapacity,[46] but others treat findings in the conservatorship proceedings as inadmissible hearsay in a will contest.[47] Conversely, the fact that proceedings to appoint a conservator for a testator were dismissed because he was found competent is not conclusive as to his testamentary capacity.[48] In many states a conservator can set aside gifts made by the ward during the conservatorship[49] even when the conservatorship was voluntary and, thus, involved no judicial finding of incapacity.[50] Under the Uniform Probate Code (hereinafter in the text and footnotes referred to as the "UPC"), appointment of a conservator "vests title in the conservator as trustee to all property of the protected person," and the conservatee's interest therein "is not assignable or transferable by the protected person."[51]

The distinction between wills and gifts raises the question of will substitutes. A statute depriving wards of power "to dispose of property in any manner other than by will" was held to apply to putting money in a joint

---

[45] Conservatorship of Bookasta, 265 Cal.Rptr. 1, 3 (App.1989). *See also* Estate of Ioupe, 878 P.2d 1168 (Utah App.1994); Matter of Estate of Oliver, 934 P.2d 144 (Kan.App.1997). In Oklahoma, however, a will of a person under guardianship must be signed in the presence of a judge. Myers v. Maxey, 915 P.2d 940 (Okl.App.1995).

[46] Wood v. Bettis, 880 P.2d 961 (Or.App.1994) (guardianship creates a rebuttable presumption of incapacity to revoke a will); Estate of Verdi by Verdi v. Toland, 733 N.E.2d 25 (Ind. Ct. App.2000) (court refers to appointment of guardian for testator in reversing summary judgment for proponents); In re Estate of Vanoni, 798 A.2d 203 (Pa.Super.2002) (proponents of will executed after testator has been adjudged incompetent must prove capacity by clear evidence); *Restatement (Third) of Property (Wills and Other Donative Transfers)* § 8.1, cmt. h (2001).

[47] In re Estate of Mask, 703 So.2d 852 (Miss.1997). *See also* Matter of Estate of Kesler, 702 P.2d 86, 96 (Utah 1985) (appointment based on physical infirmities has no probative value on testamentary capacity); In re Estate of Prescott, 8 P.3d 88, 94 (Mont.2000) (conservatorship "has no bearing on the issue" of testamentary capacity).

[48] Estate of Brown v. Fulp, 718 S.W.2d 588, 597 (Mo.App.1986); In re Estate of Wagner, 522 N.W.2d 159 (Neb.1994) (refusal to appoint conservator is not res judicata in will contest); Matter of Bo, 365 N.W.2d 847 (N.D.1985) (finding of incapacity despite termination of guardianship).

[49] Matter of Conservatorship of Marcotte, 756 P.2d 1091 (Kan.1988); O'Brien v. Dudenhoeffer, 19 Cal.Rptr.2d 826 (Cal. Ct. App.1993); Huntington Nat. Bank v. Toland, 594 N.E.2d 1103 (Ohio Ct. App.1991) (note signed by ward is unenforceable). The relevant statute may provide otherwise. Matter of Conservatorship of Spindle, 733 P.2d 388 (Okla.1986) (statute bars contracts but not gifts by conservatee). *Restatement (Third) of Property (Wills and Other Donative Transfers)* § 8.1, cmt. h (2001) speaks only of a "rebuttable presumption" of incapacity.

[50] Zobel by Hancox v. Fenendael, 379 N.W.2d 887 (Wis.App.1985).

[51] UPC §§ 5–421–22. In In re Estate of Gleeson, 655 N.W.2d 69 (N.D.2002), however, the court construed an earlier version of the UPC to allow a conservatee to consent to a transfer of an interest in property. An order for a *limited* conservatorship may specify that only part of the conservatee's property passes to the conservator. *Compare* Cal.Prob.Code § 1872: appointment "is an adjudication that the conservatee lacks the legal capacity to enter into or make any transaction" with certain exceptions, such as making a will, but the terms of the court order may broaden or restrict the conservatee's powers. *Id.* §§ 1871, 1873.

certificate of deposit; the court rejected a claim that the statute did not cover transfers that took effect at death.[52] But other courts have equated will substitutes with wills for this purpose. Changing the beneficiaries of P.O.D. accounts was held to be "in effect, a testamentary disposition similar to a will" and so the guardianship was "only prima facie evidence" of incapacity.[53]

The question of incapacity may also arise when the settlor of a revocable trust seeks to revoke or amend it. Some trust instruments provide a mechanism for determining capacity in order to avoid expensive and embarrassing court proceedings. For example, a settlor's attempt to amend a trust after she had moved into a nursing home was held ineffective because the trust by its terms was amendable only while the settlor was "competent." The trust instrument expressly provided that the settlor would be rendered incompetent if she was either admitted to a nursing home or was certified by a physician as a person who was unable to manage her own legal affairs.[54]

Even when no conservatorship has been created, gifts may be set aside if the donor was incapacitated at the time of the gift. A conservator later appointed for the donor can sue to rescind gifts made previously.[55] So may the donor's personal representative after the donor has died.[56] Such a suit may be barred, however, if the donor later recovered capacity and ratified the gift, and ratification may be inferred from failure to disaffirm.[57]

In determining the donor's capacity, courts usually apply the same standards to will substitutes and to wills.[58] The Restatement of Trusts agrees,[59] but suggests that "a standard slightly higher than that for a will" is appropriate for irrevocable gifts and trusts; as to these, the donor or settlor must be able to "understand the effects the disposition may have on the future financial security of the settlor/donor" and his or her dependents.[60] A gift which renders the donor a pauper is likely to appear "unnatural,"[61] whereas this is

---

[52] Matter of Conservatorship of Rininger, 500 N.W.2d 47 (Iowa 1993).

[53] Witt v. Ward, 573 N.E.2d 201 (Ohio Ct. App.1989). *See also* Campbell v. Black, 844 P.2d 759 (Kan.App.1993).

[54] Manning v. Glens Falls Nat. Bank, 697 N.Y.S.2d 203 (App.Div.1999). *See also* Uniform Custodial Trust Act § 10.

[55] Central Bank-Granite City v. Ziaee, 544 N.E.2d 1121 (Ill. Ct. App.1989) (guardian recovers damages from a person who persuaded ward to sell him property for a fraction of its value).

[56] Howe v. Johnston, 660 N.E.2d 380 (Mass. Ct. App.1996). In Olson v. Toy, 54 Cal.Rptr.2d 29 (Cal. Ct. App.1996), the devisees of the settlor of a living trust were allowed to bring suit to set aside the trust.

[57] *Restatement (Third) of Property (Wills and Other Donative Transfers)* § 8.1, cmt. g (2001).

[58] Bergen v. Travelers Ins. Co., 776 P.2d 659, 664 (Utah App.1989) (change of insurance beneficiary); Akerman v. Trosper, 420 N.E.2d 1148, 1151 (Ill. Ct, App.1981) (deed with life estate reserved); Lah v. Rogers, 707 N.E.2d 1208, 1214 (Ohio Ct. App.1998) (revocable trust amendment). As to the standard for testamentary capacity, *see* Section 5.1, notes 6–10.

[59] *Accord* Uniform Trust Code § 601.

[60] *Restatement (Third) of Trusts* § 11, cmts. b & c (2001). *See also* Bigej v. Boyer, 817 P.2d 760 (Or.App.1991); Hilbert v. Benson, 917 P.2d 1152 (Wyo.1996); *Restatement (Third) of Property (Wills and Other Donative Transfers)* § 8.1(c) (2001); *cf.* H. Brox, *Erbrecht* 59 (18th ed. 1999) (lower age for testamentary capacity than for inter-vivos transactions because testators need less protection).

[61] Christensen v. Britton, 784 P.2d 908, 912 (Mont.1989) *overruled on other grounds* (gift of house without reserving a place to live is unnatural).

not an issue in transfers which take effect at death, because "you can't take it with you."

The validity of wills is determined before the estate is distributed. In contrast, a long time may elapse between the making of an inter-vivos gift and a determination of the donor's capacity.[62] During this interval the donee may transfer the property to others or change position in reliance on the gift. If the donee sells the property to a bona fide purchaser for value, the latter is protected as against the claims of those who would set the gift aside.[63] But, persons to whom the donee had given property are not protected.[64] And, when a transfer occurs after the transferor-ward has been adjudicated incompetent, the judgment may constitute constructive notice of the ward's incapacity to make the transfer.[65] Even if a defendant is not a bona fide purchaser, however, equitable adjustments may be made to protect the purchaser's reasonable reliance on the validity of the transfer when it is rescinded.[66]

Transfers by Conservators

Some persons cannot meet even the relatively low standard that the law sets for testamentary capacity. Distribution of their property under the intestacy laws or under a will executed when they had capacity may produce an unsatisfactory solution.[67] Can a conservator make a will for such a person? The answer in nearly all jurisdictions has traditionally been no,[68] but there is now a slight trend the other way.[69] Conservators have previously been authorized to create revocable trusts, which are the functional equivalent of a will, for conservatees. According to the Restatement of Trusts, "prohibitions against will making are generally to be strictly construed" so as not to prohibit "other methods of . . . properly justified post-death disposition of estates of persons under disability."[70]

Many states allow conservators to make gifts of a conservatee's property. Irrevocable gifts can save income taxes (when the donee is in a lower tax

---

62 Howe v. Johnston, 660 N.E.2d 380 (Mass. Ct. App.1996) (suit brought to rescind transfer 6 years later; statute of limitations was tolled during donor's incompetence); Robertson v. Robertson, 654 P.2d 600 (Okl.1982) (similar).

63 First Interstate Bank v. First Wyo. Bank, 762 P.2d 379 (Wyo.1988) (mortgagee from buyer of land protected even though sale was voidable for incapacity); Cal.Fam.Code § 6713 (bona fide purchaser of goods transferred by a minor protected). *But see* Keville v. McKeever, 675 N.E.2d 417 (Mass.App.1997) (mortgagee of transferee not a bona fide purchaser).

64 Robertson v. Robertson, 654 P.2d 600 (Okl.1982).

65 Huntington Nat. Bank v. Toland, 594 N.E.2d 1103 (Ohio Ct. App.1991); *cf.* Cal.Prob.Code § 1875 (adjudication does not constitute notice until recorded in county where land located).

66 Keville v. McKeever, 675 N.E.2d 417 (Mass. Ct. App.1997); Citizens State Bank & Trust Co. v. Nolte, 601 P.2d 1110 (Kan.1979); *Restatement (Second) of Contracts* § 15(2) (1979); Cal.Civ.Code § 1692.

67 For the deficiencies of the intestacy statutes in many situations, *see* Section 2.3, at note 114 et seq.

68 *Restatement (Second) of Property (Donative Transfers)* § 34.5, cmt. b (1990); *cf.* In re Estate of Garrett, 100 S.W.3d 72, 76 (Ark.App.2003) (making a will is too "personal" to be performed by an agent).

69 Cal.Prob.Code § 2580(b)(13); UPC § 5–411(a)(7) (1998 rev); [England] Mental Health Act, 1983, § 96(1).

70 *Restatement (Third) of Trusts* § 11, cmt. f (2001). *See also Restatement (Second) of Property (Donative Transfers)* § 34.5, cmt. b (1990); Matter of Jones, 401 N.E.2d 351 (Mass.1980).

bracket than the donor) and transfer taxes as well.[71] Many statutes expressly mention tax savings as a justification for such gifts,[72] but these are not the only reason for them.[73] A court upheld the gift of a ward's property by his guardian-spouse to herself which would make the ward eligible for Medicaid. "There can be no quarreling with the [trial] court's determination that any person in Mr. Shah's condition would prefer that the costs of his care be paid by the state as opposed to his family."[74] A conservator may create a trust for the conservatee and her incompetent spouse who would otherwise take outright when the conservatee died.[75] The basic test expressed in an early case was "what it is likely the Lunatic himself would do, if he were in a capacity to act,"[76] or, as formulated more recently, "the likelihood from all the circumstances that the conservatee as a reasonably prudent person would take the proposed action if the conservatee had the capacity to do so."[77] This requires consideration of the relationship of the proposed donees to the conservatee; dependent family members have a strong claim, but others may also be included if the conservatee while competent had made gifts to them or they are named in the conservatee's will.[78] Such gifts should be authorized only if they leave enough property for the conservatee's prospective needs. Before approving them, the court must "determine by clear and convincing evidence that such actions are in the best interests of the protected person."[79]

The power to revoke a trust has been held to be "personal to the settlor" and thus not to be exercised by a conservator. Therefore, revocable trusts become irrevocable if the settlor becomes incompetent.[80] However, the latest version of the UPC expressly authorizes conservators (with court authorization) to exercise a power to revoke.[81]

---

[71] For example, by taking advantage of the annual exclusion. *See* Section 15.3, note 41.

[72] Conn.Gen.Stat. § 45a–655(e)(C) (minimization of income and estate taxes); 30 Okl.Stat. § 3–121(A)(3) (tax or estate planning); Cal.Prob.Code § 2580(a)(2) (minimizing current or prospective taxes). However, gifts made to qualify for welfare benefits are expressly disallowed by the Connecticut statute. Probate of Marcus, 509 A.2d 1 (Conn.1986). In Matter of Estate of Berry, 972 S.W.2d 324 (Mo. Ct. App.1998) the court disapproved proposed gifts which would have reduced both income and estate taxes where there was "no established pattern of giving" by the ward.

[73] Boone County State Bank v. Andrews, 446 N.E.2d 618, 620 (Ind.App.1983). *But cf.* Matter of Murray, 563 N.E.2d 217 (Mass.1990); Conservatorship of Hart, 279 Cal.Rptr. 249 (Cal. Ct. App.1991) (reversing approval of gifts which was based on a misunderstanding of conservatee's tax situation).

[74] In re Shah, 733 N.E.2d 1093, 1099 (N.Y.2000). *But see* note 72.

[75] *Restatement (Third) of Trusts* § 11, illus. 3 (2001).

[76] Ex parte Whitbread, 35 Eng.Rep. 878, 879 (1816).

[77] Cal.Prob.Code § 2583(k).

[78] Cal.Prob.Code § 2583; *Restatement (Second) of Property (Donative Transfers)* § 34.5, illus. 5 (1990) (gift to nephew of ward whom ward had supported in the past); In re Guardianship of Bohac, 380 So.2d 550 (Fla.App.1980) (disapproving proposed gifts to non-relative devisees to whom ward had made no prior gifts); Conn. Gen. Stat. § 45a–655(e) (gifts to non-relatives or charities if "the ward has made a previous gift").

[79] Guardianship of Garcia v. Garcia, 631 N.W.2d 464, 470 (Neb.2001).

[80] In re Guardianship of Lee, 982 P.2d 539, 541 (Okl.Civ.App.1999).

[81] UPC § 5–411(a)(4). *See also* Guardianship of Garcia v. Garcia, 631 N.W.2d 464, 470 (Neb.2001) (statute allows conservator to exercise settlor's power to amend trust). Cal.Prob.Code § 2580(b)(11) also allows conservators to exercise a power to revoke unless the trust shows an intent to reserve the right exclusively to the settlor.

Durable Powers of Attorney

Most statutes require prior court approval for gifts by conservators of a conservatee's property.[82] Because court proceedings are expensive and time consuming, as well as embarrassing to family members when they involve proof of a relative's incapacity, many people use durable powers of attorney to have their affairs managed if they become incompetent.[83] It has been estimated that about 70% of Americans over the age of 70 have executed such powers.[84] Agents under a power of attorney, like conservators, are fiduciaries, but unlike conservators they are created and usually function without court proceedings. An "attorney" is not necessarily or even usually a lawyer. In order to avoid confusion, a distinction is often made between "attorneys-in-fact" and "attorneys at law."[85]

Traditionally the powers of an agent/attorney ceased whenever the principal became incompetent.[86] This rule made powers of attorney useless as a device for managing an incompetent's property, and so it was changed by a Uniform Durable Power of Attorney Act of 1979 which was included in the UPC[87] and adopted (with variations) in most states. That act was superceded by the Uniform Power of Attorney Act of 2006.[88] Under the 1979 Act, a power of attorney is durable when it states that it "shall not be affected by the subsequent disability or incapacity of the principal" or words to that effect.[89] Conversely, under the Uniform Power of Attorney Act of 2006, a power of attorney is durable, meaning it is not terminated by the principal's incapacity, unless the power "expressly provides that it is terminated by the incapacity of the principal."[90]

Some persons prefer a "springing" power, which only comes into effect when the signer becomes incompetent. In order to avoid the need for a court determination of incompetence, a springing power may "be framed to confer authority commencing when two or more named persons . . . concur [in a signed writing] that the principal has become incapable of managing his affairs in a sensible and efficient manner."[91] The Uniform Power of Attorney Act specifically authorizes "springing powers"[92] and provides that, in the case of a

---

[82] Matter of Conservatorship of Rininger, 500 N.W.2d 47 (Iowa 1993) (conservator surcharged for transfers made without court approval); Matter of Estate of Leone, 860 P.2d 973 (Utah App.1993) (change of beneficiary by conservator without court approval ineffective).

[83] McGovern, *Trusts, Custodianships and Durable Powers of Attorney*, 27 Real Prop. Prob. & Trust J. 1 (1992). The rules governing durable powers for health care are somewhat different. They will be discussed in Section 9.3.

[84] Hook & Begley, *The Elder Law Durable Power of Attorney*, 29 Est.Plan. 538 (2002).

[85] Cal.Prob.Code § 4014(a): " 'Attorney-in-fact' means a person granted authority to act for the principal in a power of attorney, regardless of whether the person is known as an attorney-in-fact or agent."

[86] *Restatement (Second) of Agency* §§ 120, 122 (1958).

[87] UPC §§ 5–501 *et seq. See also,* Uniform Power of Attorney Act.

[88] Uniform Power of Attorney Act (2006), § 104.

[89] UPC § 5–501. Powers of attorney over bank accounts are durable unless they provide otherwise under UPC § 6–205.

[90] Uniform Power of Attorney Act (2006) § 104.

[91] UPC § 5–501, Comment. *See also* Cal.Prob.Code § 4129. For a sample provision to this effect, *see* J. Price, *Contemporary Estate Planning* § 4.35.7 (2d ed.2000).

[92] Uniform Power of Attorney Act (2006), § 109(a).

springing power, "the power may authorize one or more persons to determine in a writing or other record that the event or contingency" which causes the power to become effective has occurred.[93]

A durable power is effective only if it is executed while the principal is legally competent; someone who is already incompetent cannot confer a power.[94]

Conservators have such powers as are conferred by statute, sometimes modified by the terms of the court order appointing them. The powers conferred by a power of attorney, on the other hand, depend on the power's terms. Traditionally powers have been strictly construed,[95] and cannot be expanded by parol evidence of an intent to confer broader powers.[96] They are often interpreted not to allow the attorney to make gifts,[97] especially when the power is held by a family member who wishes to make gifts to himself or his family, because of the general prohibition against fiduciaries engaging in transactions in which they have a conflict of interest.[98] When a daughter used a power of attorney to convey her father's property to a trust in which she and her siblings had interests, the court held the trust invalid.

> Such self dealing by an agent, in the absence . . . of distinct authority from the principal expressly granted in the empowering instrument, has been continuously and uniformly denounced as one of the most profound breaches of fiduciary duty, irrespective of the agent's good faith.[99]

Other opinions have been more accommodating toward such transactions. When children under a power of attorney conferred by their mother made gifts to themselves and their families, the court approved this, saying that "the actions taken by the attorneys-in-fact . . . continue the grantor's practice of giving monetary gifts to the natural objects of her bounty and affection; . . . [and do] not deplete the grantor of the assets necessary for her to live her accustomed life-style [she died with an estate in excess of $1 million]; and . . . minimize the estate transfer tax, a goal the grantor desired."[100]

---

[93] *Id.* at § 109(b).

[94] Hagan v. Shore, 915 P.2d 435 (Or.App.1996); Testa v. Roberts, 542 N.E.2d 654 (Ohio Ct. App.1988). For suggested steps to guard against claims that the principal was incompetent when the power was executed, *see* Hook & Begley, *supra* note 84, at 539–40.

[95] McGovern, *supra* note 83, at 33; In re Guardianship of Mabry, 666 N.E.2d 16 (Ill.App.1996) (power to manage real estate did not include power to sell).

[96] In re Estate of Romanowski, 771 N.E.2d 966, 972 (Ill. Ct. App.2002).

[97] Estate of Casey, 948 F.2d 895 (4th Cir.1991); Townsend v. United States, 889 F. Supp. 369 (D.Neb.1995); Estate of Lennon v. Lennon, 29 P.3d 1258, 1267 (Wash.App.2001). Under the Uniform Power of Attorney Act (2006), § 201, the agent can make gifts if the power expressly authorized the agent to make gifts.

[98] Kunewa v. Joshua, 924 P.2d 559 (Haw.App.1996) (constructive trust imposed on child who used power to convey property to himself). As to the general prohibition against self-dealing by fiduciaries, *see* Section 12.1.

[99] Gagnon v. Coombs, 654 N.E.2d 54, 62 (Mass. Ct. App.1995). *See also* In re Conservatorship of Anderson v. Lasen, 628 N.W.2d 233, 239 (Neb.2001); Schubert v. Reynolds, 115 Cal.Rptr.2d 285 (App.2002).

[100] LeCraw v. LeCraw, 401 S.E.2d 697, 699 (Ga.1991). *See also* Estate of Ridenour v. C.I.R., 36 F.3d 332 (4th Cir.1994); Estate of Neff, TC Memo 1997–186. In In re Estate of Naumoff, 754 N.Y.S.2d 70 (App.Div.2003), the court held invalid most of the gifts to herself made by a child

An Alabama statute dictates that general powers be construed to allow the attorney to make gifts of the principal's property "to any individuals [or charitable organizations] including the attorney in fact" if the gifts will reduce the principal's estate tax and are "in accordance with the principal's personal history of making . . . lifetime gifts."[101] In California, on the other hand, any gifts of the principal's property by an agent must be "expressly authorized in the power of attorney."[102]

In summary, attorneys may want to advise clients to use durable powers in order to avoid conservatorship in case they become incompetent, but should exercise care in drafting them. As a protection against abuse, the power might require prior consultation with a lawyer and that transfers be "made in accordance with the principal's estate plan."[103] The planner should also consider authorizing the attorney to use the power to transfer the principal's property to a trust.[104]

§ 5.3 Undue Influence

Wills are often challenged as being the product of undue influence. In order to sustain a challenge of undue influence, the contestant must prove[105] that (1) the testator was susceptible to undue influence, (2) the alleged influencer had an opportunity to exercise undue influence over the testator, (3) the influencer had a disposition to influence unduly in order to procure an improper favor, and (4) the will reflects a disposition clearly appearing to be the product of the undue influence.[106] Courts recognize that the invalidity of the will depends upon a finding of "undue" influence, not merely influence.

> Undue influence sufficient to invalidate a will is '[t]he degree of influence necessary to be exerted over the mind of the testator to render it improper, [and] must from some cause or by some means be such as to induce him to act contrary to his wishes, and to make a different will and disposition of his estate from what he would have done if left entirely to his own discretion and judgment. That his free agency and independence must have been overcome, and that he must, by some dominion or control exercised over his mind, have been

---

under a power of attorney, but not those which were accompanied by similar gifts to her sibling. For a survey of more authorities, *see* Davis & Wade, *To Gift or Not to Gift*, 142 Trusts & Estates (July 2003) p. 20.

[101] Ala.Code 1975 § 26–1–2.1. *See also* Va. Code § 11–9.5. Such a power may be deemed to give the attorney a general power of appointment, thereby creating tax problems for him or her. *See* McGovern, *supra* note 53, at 38.

[102] Cal.Prob.Code § 4264; Estate of Huston, 60 Cal.Rptr.2d 217 (App.1997) (oral ratification of gift ineffective).

[103] Hook & Begley, *supra* note 84, at 542. For a form authorizing only gifts to the principal's descendants that will not incur a gift tax (Section 15.3, note 58 et seq.), *see* J. Price, *Contemporary Estate Planning* § 4.35.4 (2d ed. 2000).

[104] McGovern, *supra* note 83, compares the respective advantages of trusts and powers of attorney. *See also* Section 9.3.

[105] UPC § 3–407. *See also, Restatement (Third) of Property (Wills and Other Donative Transfers)* (2003), § 8.3, cmt. b.

[106] In re Will of Leisch, 267 N.W. 268 (Wis. 1936). *See also, Restatement (Third) of Property (Wills and Other Donative Transfers)* (2003), § 8.3, cmt. e. Closely associated with "undue influence" is fraud and duress both of which are also grounds to contest a will. *Id.* at comments i and j.

constrained to do what was against his will, and what he was unable to refuse and too weak to resist. But that moderate and reasonable solicitation, entreaty or persuasion, though yielded to, if done intelligently and from a conviction of duty, would not vitiate a will in other respects valid.'[107]

Because of the susceptibility requirement, it is often common for wills challenged on undue influence grounds also to be challenged on mental capacity grounds.

The standard for undue influence also applies to challenges to inter-vivos transfers.[108] Sometimes inter-vivos and testamentary transfers are challenged in the same proceedings, usually with the same result.[109] For instance, one heir successfully challenged a will, a deed, and an adoption by the decedent in the same suit.[110]

Sometimes only a particular provision of a will, rather than the entire will is challenged. A devise of $100,000 was found invalid because of the devisee's undue influence over the testator, but the rest of the will was probated because the tainted devise was "severable."[111] But courts sometimes conclude that the testator's intent would be better effectuated by invalidating the whole will when undue influence is found.[112]

Undue influence may also invalidate the revocation of a will.[113] If undue influence prevents the making of a will or gift, the intended beneficiaries have a tort action against the person whose influence frustrated the gift or will, even though this requires ascertaining the decedent's intent based on evidence which does not comply with the statutory requirements for a will.[114]

---

[107] Larocque v. O'Connor, 876 A.2d 1229, 1236 (Conn. Ct. App. 2005).

[108] Stockwell v. Stockwell, 790 N.W.2d 52 (S.D. 2010) (challenge to deed based upon undue influence grounds); In re Guardianship of Mowrer, 979 P.2d 156, 161 (Mont.1999); McPeak v. McPeak, 593 N.W.2d 180, 186 (Mich. Ct. App.1999) (rejecting claim that instruction given in an action regarding change of insurance beneficiaries was appropriate only for will contests). *Compare* the test(s) for incapacity. Section 5.1.

[109] In re Estate of Glennie, 265 P.3d 654 (Mont. 2011) (challenge to both probate of will and existing sales and lease agreements); McKee v. Stoddard, 780 P.2d 736 (Or. Ct. App.1989) (will and joint tenancy); Sun Bank/Miami, NA v. Hogarth, 536 So.2d 263 (Fla.App.1988) (will and trust). In Estate of Wenzel-Mosset by Gaukler v. Nickels, 575 N.W.2d 425 (N.D.1998), on the other hand, a change in bank accounts was found valid, but a will executed three days later was rejected for incapacity. *See also* Greenwood v. Camp, 738 N.Y.S.2d 452 (N.Y. Sup. Ct. App.Div.2002) (jury finding of undue influence on will not res judicata as to joint accounts established a week later).

[110] In re Estate of Reid, 825 So.2d 1 (Miss.2002).

[111] Estate of Lane, 492 So.2d 395 (Fla. Ct. App.1986). *See also* Estate of Hamilton v. Morris, 67 S.W.3d 786, 796 (Tenn. Ct. App.2001); In re Estate of Haneberg, 14 P.3d 1088, 1099 (Kan.2000).

[112] In re Estate of Marsh, 342 N.W.2d 373 (Neb.1984); Matter of Estate of Keeney, 908 P.2d 751, 755 (N.M. Ct. App.1995); *Restatement (Third) of Property (Wills and Other Donative Transfers)* § 8.3, cmt. d (2001). Some jurisdictions do not recognize partial invalidity. In re O'Loughlin's Estate, 183 N.W.2d 133 (Wis.1971).

[113] Cook v. Loftus, 414 N.E.2d 581 (Ind.Ct. App. 1981); Griffin v. Baucom, 328 S.E.2d 38 (N.C.Ct. App. 1985).

[114] *Restatement (Second) of Torts* § 774B (1977); Allen v. Hall, 974 P.2d 199 (Or.1999) (decedent's intent to devise property to plaintiff blocked by defendant's misrepresentations); Doughty v. Morris, 871 P.2d 380 (N.M.Ct. App. 1994). *Compare* the cases imposing a constructive trust in this situation. Section 7.1, note 77.

Claims of undue influence and mental incapacity are commonly combined. The same evidence may be relevant to both issues, because findings of undue influence are often predicated on the mental weakness of the testator/donor. "One who is infirm and mentally weak is more susceptible to influence than one who is not. . . ."[115] Conversely, if a testator was strong minded and intelligent, a finding of no undue influence is typical.[116] Expert testimony is occasionally heard, although this is less common in undue influence than in incapacity challenges.[117]

As in claims of incapacity, courts often stress the naturalness or unnaturalness of the disposition. In finding undue influence a court noted "the substantial bequest to [the devisee] is . . . suspicious," because "he was no more than a casual acquaintance" of the testator.[118] Another found undue influence because the will was a "radical deviation from [the testator's] previous testamentary scheme."[119] Conversely, in rejecting a claim of undue influence, courts often note that "the will's terms were reasonable and natural."[120] One observer has even suggested that contests based on undue influence act "as a form of forced heirship" requiring that property be left to a spouse or blood relatives.[121] Preferring one child to another is not necessarily evidence of unnaturalness suggesting undue influence,[122] but it may be.[123]

Relatively few wills are successfully challenged on undue influence grounds. According to one survey, only about one in a hundred wills are contested at all, and of those which are, the proponent has a "statistically overwhelming likelihood of success . . . Judges and juries are quite skeptical

---

[115] Boehm v. Allen, 506 N.W.2d 781, 784 (Iowa Ct. App. 1993). *See also* Pense v. Lindsey, 73 P.3d 168, 172 (Mont.2003); Crittell v. Bingo 36 P.3d 634, 642 (Alaska 2001). *But see* In re Estate of Harmon, 253 P.3d 821 (Mont. 2011) (testimony regarding testator's physical infirmities never asserted testator had reduced capacity and thus was insufficient to establish undue influence).

[116] Pascale v. Pascale, 549 A.2d 782 (N.J.1988) (donor was a shrewd businessman); Matter of Estate of Webb, 863 P.2d 1116 (Okl.1993) (testator/donor was "strong-minded"); Anderson v. Meadowcroft, 661 A.2d 726 (Md.1995) (claim dismissed for failure to allege that testator was "susceptible" to influence). *But see* In re Estate of Miller, 778 N.E.2d 262, 267 (Ill.Ct. App. 2002) (undue influence found even though decedent was legally competent).

[117] In re Estate of Hoover, 615 N.E.2d 736 (Ill.1993); Matter of Estate of Keeney, 908 P.2d 751 (N.M.Ct. App. 1995). *But see* Mache v. Mache, 578 N.E.2d 1253 (Ill.Ct. App. 1991) (no abuse of discretion not to hear expert testimony).

[118] Matter of Estate of Dankbar, 430 N.W.2d 124, 131 (Iowa 1988). *See also* Matter of Panek, 667 N.Y.S.2d 177 (App.Div.1997) (will gave proponents far more than their intestate share even though they were not close to testator); Montoya v. Torres, 823 P.2d 905 (N.M.1991) (gift to step-grandchild unnatural when donor had children of her own); In re Guardianship of Mowrer, 979 P.2d 156, 163 (Mont.1999) ("unnatural disposition of essentially all of" donor's property to donees).

[119] Hayes v. Apperson, 826 So.2d 798, 804 (Ala.2002); *cf.* Section 5.1, note 40 et seq.

[120] In re Estate of Shumway, 3 P.3d 977, 983 (Ariz.Ct. App. 1999); In re Estate of Wittman, 27 P.3d 35, 38 (Mont.2001) (will "makes sense under the circumstances"); Walker v. Roberds, 47 P.3d 911, 916 (Or.Ct. App. 2002) (will dividing estate equally between two sons was "natural and equitable"); In re Estate of Holcomb, 63 P.3d 9, 22 (Okl.2002) (will leaving all the estate to one child "in gratitude for [her] caretaking" upheld).

[121] Madoff, *Unmasking Undue Influence*, 81 Minn.L.Rev. 571, 611 (1997). For concerns that homophobia inspires some contests (with limited case support), *see* Massey, *Designation of Heirs: A Modest Proposal to Diminish Will Contests*, 37 Real Prop, Prob. & Trust J. 577, 584 (2003). *Restatement (Third) of Property (Wills and Other Donative Transfers)* § 8.3, cmt. f (2001) is careful to state that gifts to "unmarried partners" are not to be considered "unnatural."

[122] Cotten v. Cotten, 169 S.W.3d 824 (Tex. Ct. App. Dallas 2005).

[123] In re Estate of Schoppe, 710 N.W.2d 258 (Iowa Ct.App. 2005).

of" allegations of undue influence.[124] A substantial devise to a non-relative is not necessarily so "unnatural" as to warrant an inference of undue influence,[125] nor is unequal treatment of relatives, especially if there appears to have been a reason for it.[126]

In undue influence cases, courts often focus on the impropriety of the influencer's conduct. They admit evidence of the influencer's bad character,[127] or emphasize that "improper devices" were used to sway the testator, such as taking advantage of her belief in the supernatural by transmitting purported advice from dead relatives.[128] Claims of undue influence often involve misrepresentations made to the testator.[129] Courts distinguish between undue influence and "reasonable persuasion," *e.g.*, upholding a will even though the testator's sons had discussed the will with their mother and helped her change it; "theirs were the acts of dutiful sons [whose] mother . . . was aging and needed helpful information and even advice." If this were deemed to be undue influence, we would "have finally abolished the family ties of love and natural affection."[130] In upholding a devise to a wife, another court said:

> If a wife by her industry and virtue, and by the assistance which she has rendered her husband, has gained an ascendancy over the mind of her husband; . . . such influence, though it result in procuring a will in her favor . . . would not amount to undue influence.[131]

Duress, which is an extreme form of undue influence, requires an "unlawful" threat. When a husband induced his wife to deed him property by

---

124 Schoenblum, *Will Contests: An Empirical Study*, 22 Real Prop.Prob. & Trust J. 607, 625, 655 (1987). However, most of the wills studied left the estate to relatives of the testator; when the devise was to nonrelatives, the chances of a contestant's success were greater. *Id.* at 634, 659.

125 Matter of Estate of Gersbach, 960 P.2d 811 (N.M.1998); In re Estate of Squire, 6 P.3d 1060 (Okl.Civ.App.1999) (devise to charities, disinheriting cousins upheld).

126 Matter of Estate of Eggebrecht, 967 P.2d 388, 392 (Mont.1998) ("natural" to favor a grandson on whom decedent "primarily relied to assist her"); In re Camac, 751 N.Y.S.2d 435 (App.Div.2002) (rationale for favoring daughters "was clearly stated in the will"). *But see* Kelley v. Johns, 96 S.W.3d 189 (Tenn. Ct. App.2002) (jury finds devise of farm to one of nine children product of undue influence).

127 In re Estate of Herbert, 979 P.2d 39, 56 (Haw.1999); Warner v. Warner, 687 S.W.2d 856 (Ark.Ct. App. 1985). *But see* Estate of Garrett, 906 P.2d 254 (Nev.1995) (error to admit evidence of drug use by devisee).

128 Estate of Baker, 182 Cal.Rptr. 550 (Cal. Ct. App.1982).

129 Matter of Brown's Estate, 640 P.2d 1250 (Kan.1982) (beneficiary criticized other heirs and tried to prevent contact between them and the testator); Bryan v. Norton, 265 S.E.2d 282, 283 (Ga.1980) (pastor of testatrix's church told her "that her children did not care anything about her"); Rood v. Newberg, 718 N.E.2d 886 (Mass.Ct. App. 1999) (failure to correct testator's mistaken belief that son had stolen from testator); *cf.* Section 7.1, note 78 et seq.

130 Carter v. Carter, 526 So.2d 141, 143 (Fla.Ct. App. 1988). *See also* Nease v. Clark, 488 P.2d 1396 (Or.Ct. App. 1971) (influence arising from "gratitude and affection" is proper). *But see* Anderson v. Brinkerhoff, 756 P.2d 95 (Utah Ct. App. 1988) (deed voidable for undue influence by children despite their good motives and belief they were acting in mother's interest).

131 In re Estate of Mowdy, 973 P.2d 345, 347 (Okl.Civ.App.1998). *See also* In re Estate of Karmey, 658 N.W.2d 796, 799 (Mich.2003) (spouse's influence can "be great . . . without being 'undue' "). According to *Restatement (Second) of Torts* § 774B, cmt. c (1977), persuasion "by legitimate means" is not actionable. Similarly, in *Restatement (Second) of Contracts* § 177 (1979) undue influence involves "unfair" persuasion.

threatening to leave her, she could not avoid the deed for duress because he had not threatened to do an unlawful act.[132]

The person exerting undue influence need not be a beneficiary. When a husband induced his wife to deed land to his sisters, the wife could avoid the deed without proving that the sisters had been involved.

> A deed procured by undue influence is voidable regardless of whether the undue influence was exerted by the grantee or by someone else. . . . If, before the grantor takes steps to avoid the deed, the grantee therein conveys the premises to an innocent purchaser, a court of equity will extend protection to such a purchaser[133] . . . However, while an innocent purchaser is protected by equity, the initial grantee is not.[134]

The testimony of the subscribing witnesses to a will is less important in claims of undue influence than in claims of incapacity, because the witnesses would probably be unaware of influence exerted on the testator at times other than the moment of the will's execution.[135] When the execution of challenged documents had been videotaped, the court held that "while the tapes constitute strong evidence of capacity," they did not warrant a summary judgment for the contestants on the question of undue influence.[136] "Undue influence need not by exerted at the time a will is made; it is enough that it be operative at that time."[137] Because influence is typically exerted in secret, it may be established by circumstantial evidence.[138]

Presumption of Undue Influence

The burden of proving undue influence is on the contestants, but they can rely on a presumption of undue influence if a person in a "confidential relationship" with the testator participated in preparing the will.[139] Both

---

[132] Rubenstein v. Sela, 672 P.2d 492 (Ariz.Ct. App. 1983). *See also* Bailey v. Arlington Bank & Trust Co., 693 S.W.2d 787 (Tex.Ct. App. 1985); *Restatement (Second) of Property (Donative Transfers)* § 34.7, illus. 4 (1990); H. Brox, *Erbrecht* 142 (18th ed. 1999). However, *Restatement (Third) of Property (Wills and Other Donative Transfers)* § 8.3, cmt. i (2001) suggests that this might constitute undue influence.

[133] *Restatement, Second, of Contracts* § 177(3) (1979) protects a third party who "without reason to know of the undue influence either gives value or relies materially on the transaction." *Compare* Section 5.2, note 64.

[134] Bedree v. Bedree, 528 N.E.2d 1128, 1130 (Ind.Ct. App. 1988). *See also* Matter of Estate of Keeney, 908 P.2d 751, 755 (N.M.Ct. App. 1995); Matter of Estate of Maheras, 897 P.2d 268 (Okl.1995); *Restatement (Second) of Property (Donative Transfers)* § 34.7, cmt. a (1990). *But see*, In re Estate of Thornton, 922 So.2d 850 (Miss. Ct. App. 2006) (daughter did not influence her mother to leave property to a daughter's son).

[135] Succession of Hamiter, 519 So.2d 341, 347 (La.Ct. App. 1988) (testimony of subscribing witnesses discounted because they were unaware "of Mrs. Cox's relationship with" testator). *See also* In re Estate of Pedrick, 482 A.2d 215, 227 (Pa.1984) (dissenting opinion); In re Rosen, 747 N.Y.S.2d 99, 101 (App.Div.2002) (proper to consider events occurring after will execution in finding undue influence).

[136] Geduldig v. Posner, 743 A.2d 247, 259 (Md.Ct. Spec. App. 1999).

[137] Erb v. Lee, 430 N.E.2d 869, 872 (Mass.Ct. App. 1982).

[138] McDaniel v. McDaniel, 707 S.E.2d 60 (Ga. 2011); Montoya v. Torres, 823 P.2d 905, 910 (N.M.1991); Moore v. Smith, 582 A.2d 1237 (Md.1990); Crump v. Moss, 517 So.2d 609, 612 (Ala.1987).

[139] Kimbrough v. Estate of Kimbrough, 134 So.3d 281 (Miss. 2014). This presumption has also been applied to transfers other than wills. Doughty v. Morris, 871 P.2d 380 (N.M.Ct. App.

elements must be present; summary judgment was given to the proponents of a will despite the fact that they had a confidential relationship with the testator, when there was no evidence that they "were in any manner active or participated in the preparation or execution of the will."[140] However, some courts talk more generally about "suspicious circumstances" as the second ingredient in creating the presumption. The Third Restatement of Property uses this phrase, and participation in preparing the will is only one of many possible "suspicious circumstances."[141]

A will was upheld even though a child of the testator had participated in its preparation because "the normal relationship between a mentally competent parent and an adult child is not *per se* a confidential relationship."[142] Confidential relationship usually means an unequal one in which one party dominates the other.[143] Some relationships are confidential *per se,* such as that between guardian and ward,[144] doctor and patient,[145] and pastor and parishioner.[146] Surprisingly, in view of the casual way in which powers of attorney are often given to relatives, they have been held to establish a confidential relationship between the parties.[147] In other cases courts treat the existence of a confidential relationship as a question of fact.[148] Courts

---

1994) (joint bank accounts). In applying the presumption, revocable living trusts are treated like wills rather than like gifts. Upman v. Clarke, 753 A.2d 4, 12 (Md.2000). In England the presumption applies *only* to intervivos transfers. D. Parry & J. Clark, *The Law of Succession* 75 (10th ed. 1996). *See also,* In re Estate of Long, 846 N.W.2d 782 (S.D. 2014) (burden of proof on contestant to establish testator was susceptible to undue analysis).

[140] Matter of Estate of Brodbeck, 915 P.2d 145, 154 (Kan.Ct. App. 1996). *See also* Higgs v. Estate of Higgs, 892 S.W.2d 284 (Ark.Ct. App. 1995); In re Estate of Kottke, 6 P.3d 243, 247 (Alaska 2000) (no undue influence found despite confidential relationship because only slight participation in will making).

[141] *Restatement (Third) of Property (Wills and Other Donative Transfers)* § 8.3, cmt. h (2001).

[142] In re Estate of Elam, 738 S.W.2d 169, 173 (Tenn.1987). *See also* Heck v. Archer, 927 P.2d 495, 500 (Kan.Ct. App. 1996); Estate of Jones v. Jones, 759 P.2d 345 (Utah Ct. App. 1988) (even though beneficiary drafted the will); Matter of Estate of Neu, 588 N.E.2d 567 (Ind.Ct. App. 1992) (niece).

[143] *Restatement (Second) of Contracts* § 177 (1979) (a person "under the domination of another *or* [one who] is justified, by virtue of his relation with another in assuming that the other will not act inconsistently with his welfare"). *Compare* the use of the term in cases involving constructive trusts. Section 7.4, at note 206 et seq.

[144] Matter of Basich's Estate, 398 N.E.2d 1182 (Ill.Ct. App. 1979); Estate of Verdi by Verdi v. Toland, 733 N.E.2d 25 (Ind.Ct. App. 2000). Under Italian Codice Civile art. 596 a "tutore" is incapable of receiving a testamentary gift from the ward, unless they are related.

[145] Estate of McRae, 522 So.2d 731 (Miss.1988) (deed from patient to doctor set aside).

[146] Bryan v. Norton, 265 S.E.2d 282 (Ga.1980); Matter of Estate of Maheras, 897 P.2d 268 (Okl.1995) (devise to pastor's church); Roberts-Douglas v. Meares, 615 A.2d 1114 (D.C.Ct. App. 1992) (solicitation of contributions). *But see* Estate of Osborn, 470 N.E.2d 1114 (Ill.Ct. App. 1984). Gifts and devises to lawyers are discussed in Section 5.4, note 174 et seq.

[147] Smith v. Shafer, 623 N.E.2d 1261(Ohio Ct. App. 1993); In re Estate of Miller, 778 N.E.2d 262 (Ill.Ct. App. 2002) (non-probate transfers to attorney voided); Estate of Hamilton v. Morris, 67 S.W.3d 786, 793 (Tenn.Ct. App. 2001) (devise to attorney rejected). *But see* Napier v. Compton, 558 S.E.2d 593, 598 (W.Va.2001) (error to set aside gifts to son who had a power of attorney which he had never exercised); In re Estate of Farr, 49 P.3d 415, 431 (Kan.2002) (power of attorney is only "a persuasive fact in evaluating whether a confidential relationship existed"); Childress v. Currie, 74 S.W.3d 324 (Tenn.2002).

[148] Duncan v. Moore, 571 S.E.2d 771, 773 (Ga.2002).

sometimes distinguish between "confidential" and "fiduciary" relationships; they are particularly prone to avoid gifts made to a fiduciary.[149]

Statements concerning the relationship between spouses are hard to reconcile. In California "a husband and wife are subject to the general rules governing fiduciary relationships,"[150] and courts sometimes use similar language,[151] but one suggested that such a presumption "must be applied with caution as to marital relationships, because of the unique relationship between spouses."[152] Very few of the many wills that leave a large share of the estate to the testator's spouse are challenged, let alone set aside for undue influence.[153] Where a confidential relationship between spouses is recognized, it is "generally limited to second marriages where the children of the first marriage are disinherited."[154]

A presumption of undue influence allows contestants to escape summary judgment or a directed verdict.[155] The presumption can be rebutted, but some say that the fact finder must find undue influence unless the proponent produces contrary evidence,[156] while others assert that the presumption merely "makes a case which must be submitted to the jury," but does not "compel a finding for the contestant."[157] A will was probated on a jury's finding that the devisee was in a confidential relationship with the testator and "was active in procuring the will" but was not "unduly benefited."[158] A trust was

---

[149] Cleary v. Cleary, 692 N.E.2d 955 (Mass.1998) (insurance agent); *Restatement (Second) of Trusts* § 2, cmt. b (1959); Cal.Prob.Code § 16004(c) (transaction between trustee and beneficiary "by which the trustee obtains an advantage . . . is presumed to be a violation of the trustee's fiduciary duties.").

[150] Cal.Fam.Code § 721(b); In re Marriage of Haines, 39 Cal.Rptr.2d 673 (Cal. Ct. App. 1995) (deed from W to H subject to presumption of undue influence); In re Marriage of Delaney, 4 Cal.Rptr.3d 378 (Cal. Ct. App. 2003) (undue influence when H put property into joint tenancy with W).

[151] Matter of Estate of Banko, 622 N.E.2d 476, 479 (Ind.1993) (but presumption held inapplicable to a joint bank account); Krebs v. Krebs, 759 P.2d 77 (Idaho Ct. App. 1988) (same); Hughes v. Hughes, 634 P.2d 1271, 1275 (N.M.1981) (presumption was rebutted).

[152] In re Estate of Glogovsek, 618 N.E.2d 1231, 1237 (Ill.Ct. App. 1993). *See also* Morse v. Volz, 808 S.W.2d 424, 432 (Mo.Ct. App. 1991); In re Estate of Karmey, 658 N.W.2d 796, 799 (Mich.2003) (no presumption of undue influence from marital relationship).

[153] In Bratton v. Owens, 794 P.2d 423 (Okl.Ct. App. 1990) a deed from H to W was unsuccessfully challenged. In Matter of Estate of Montgomery, 881 S.W.2d 750, 756 (Tex.Ct. App. 1994), a will favoring a wife was upheld, the court noting that this was "not unusual." Occasionally, however, gifts or devises to a spouse, especially a second spouse, are found invalid for undue influence. McPeak v. McPeak, 593 N.W.2d 180 (Mich.Ct. App. 1999); Fields v. Mersack, 577 A.2d 376 (Md.Ct. App. 1990); *cf.* Riddell v. Edwards, 32 P.3d 4 (Alaska 2001) (incapacity).

[154] Madoff, *supra* note 121, at 602.

[155] In re Estate of Jessman, 554 N.E.2d 718 (Ill.Ct. App. 1990); Allen v. Dutton's Estate, 394 So.2d 132 (Fla.Ct. App. 1980).

[156] Estate of Hamilton v. Morris, 67 S.W.3d 786, 795 (Tenn.Ct. App. 2001) (summary judgment based on unrebutted presumption of undue influence); In re Last Will of Melson, 711 A.2d 783 (Del.1998) (burden shifts to proponent of will).

[157] Watson v. Warren, 751 S.W.2d 406, 410 (Mo.Ct. App. 1988). *See also* Bryan v. Norton, 265 S.E.2d 282, 284 (Ga.1980). In Upman v. Clarke, 753 A.2d 4, 9–10 (Md.2000), the court distinguished between inter-vivos gifts, where "the existence of a confidential relationship shifts the burden to the donee to show the fairness and reasonableness of the transaction," and wills.

[158] Estate of Sarabia, 270 Cal.Rptr. 560, 562 (Cal. Ct. App. 1990). Since Sarabia was decided California enacted Section 21350 of the Probate Code voiding testamentary provisions to a person who drafted the will and a person having a fiduciary relationship to the decedent "who transcribes

upheld against a claim of undue influence by a trust officer who enjoyed a "confidential relationship" with the settlor and who assisted in the preparation of the trust, because "the decedent provided all instructions regarding" the terms of the trust.[159] As with other questions of fact, in close cases appellate courts defer to the findings of the lower court or jury.[160]

§ 5.4 Role of Lawyers

Lawyer as Witness

Decisions in will contests upholding wills often rely on the testimony of the lawyer who drafted the will and supervised its execution.[161] This creates a problem when the same attorney represents the estate in a will contest. A lawyer in this situation was disqualified under DR 5–102 of the Code of Professional Responsibility:[162]

> (A) If after undertaking employment in contemplated or pending litigation, a lawyer learns . . . that he . . . ought to be called as a witness on behalf of his client, he shall withdraw from the conduct of the trial. . . .[163]

The rationale for the rule is that combining the disparate functions of witness and advocate may confuse the fact finder. It does not preclude the drafting attorney from representing the estate in administration after the contest is over.[164]

It is an impermissible conflict of interest for a lawyer who drafted a will to later represent persons who seek to contest the will.[165]

---

the instrument or causes it to be transcribed, or to the relative cohabitant, law partner; or employee of such drafter and transcriber."

[159] In re Estate of Squire, 6 P.3d 1060, 1063 (Okl.Civ.Ct. App. 1999). *See also* Estate of Stephens, 49 P.3d 1093 (Cal.2002) (the "act in question had its genesis in the mind of the" donor); In re Estate of Garrett, 100 S.W.3d 72, 75 (Ark.Ct. App. 2003).

[160] In re Estate of Holcomb, 63 P.3d 9 (Okl.2002). Verdicts can be directed, however, if the evidence of undue influence is deemed insufficient. In re Estate of Karmey, 658 N.W.2d 796 (Mich.2003).

[161] *E.g.*, Matter of Last Will of Dickey, 542 So.2d 903 (Miss.1989); Gala v. Magarinos, 665 N.Y.S.2d 95 (App.Div.1997); Morse v. Volz, 808 S.W.2d 424 (Mo.Ct. App. 1991). In Crittell v. Bingo 36 P.3d 634, 642 (Alaska 2001), the court in finding undue influence noted that "although [testator] had employed attorneys to draft her prior wills, the [challenged] will was produced without the aid of counsel." *See also* Estate of Shinkle, 119 Cal.Rptr.2d 42 (Cal. Ct. App.2002) (holding trust invalid, noting inter alia that it had not been reviewed by a lawyer). For suggestions as to how lawyers should act when planning estates for clients of marginal capacity, *see* Kirtland, *Dealing With Mental Capacity Issues in Estate Planning*, 30 Est.Plan. 192 (2003).

[162] Matter of Estate of Seegers, 733 P.2d 418 (Okl.Ct. App. 1986). *See also* Matter of Estate of McCoy, 844 P.2d 1131 (Alaska 1993); Matter of Will of O'Malley, 534 N.Y.S.2d 854 (Surr.1988).

[163] Model Rules of Professional Conduct 3.7 is similar: "A lawyer shall not act as advocate at a trial in which the lawyer is likely to be a necessary witness [with exceptions inter alia] where disqualification of the lawyer would work substantial hardship on the client." *See* Matter of Estate of Waters, 647 A.2d 1091 (Del.1994).

[164] Matter of Will of O'Malley, 534 N.Y.S.2d 854 (Surr.1988); Link, *Developments Regarding the Professional Responsibility of the Estate Administration Lawyer: The Effect of the Model Rules of Professional Conduct*, 26 Real Prop.Prob. & Trust L.J. 1, 98 (1991).

[165] Kirtland, *supra* note 161, at 197.

Undue Influence

A factor often mentioned when wills are contested for undue influence is whether or not the testator had "independent advice." The independent advisor most often mentioned in this connection is the lawyer who drafted the will.[166]

Lawyers unfortunately also often appear in a *negative* light in undue influence cases. In many rejected wills, the drafting lawyer was selected by the devisee rather than the testator, *e.g.,* the devisees "met with an attorney of their choice, not [the testator's], and discussed the planning of his estate." The drafter did not speak with the testator until the will was signed.[167]

Sometimes both the testator and a devisee are clients of the lawyer who drafts a will, for example when a lawyer represents several members of a family. In one such case the contestants argued that "a lawyer who drafts for one client a will that benefits another . . . creat[es] a strong presumption of undue influence."[168] The court rejected this argument; because the drafting lawyer "had known [the testator] for a number of years," she was "clearly the client." The devisees never discussed the will with the lawyer or the testator. To find an impermissible conflict of interest in this situation "would make it impossible for any lawyer . . . to draft a will for any family with which he was half-way familiar."[169] Another court, in rejecting a claim of undue influence, found that the lawyer had provided the father with "independent legal advice" even though he had also done work for the daughter-beneficiary.[170] Another court criticized a lawyer who had failed to disclose to his client, the donor, that he was representing the donee in another matter, but the gift was still valid because the donor "knew what he was doing."[171] Nevertheless there are risks for lawyers who represent several family members when the family quarrels. A lawyer who drafted a will for a father and misled the father's daughter about the will was sued by the latter. Although the lawyer had represented her in other matters, he had no duty to disclose the will's contents to the daughter. But, he owed her "the duty to deal with her in good faith and not actively misrepresent the will."[172]

---

[166] Matter of Estate of Wessels, 561 N.E.2d 1212, 1217 (Ill.Ct. App. 1990); Higgs v. Estate of Higgs, 892 S.W.2d 284, 287 (Ark.Ct. App. 1995); Matter of Estate of Gonzales, 775 P.2d 1300, 1303 (N.M.Ct. App. 1988).

[167] Matter of Estate of Bolinder, 864 P.2d 228, 232 (Kan.Ct. App. 1993). *See also* Matter of Estate of Carano, 868 P.2d 699 (Okl.1994) (assignment prepared by donee's lawyer who never talked with donor); Christensen v. Britton, 784 P.2d 908 (Mont.1989) (beneficiary took donor to her lawyer and was present in their discussions).

[168] Matter of Estate of Koch, 849 P.2d 977, 995 (Kan.Ct. App. 1993) (quoting Professor Charles Wolfram who was an expert witness for the contestants).

[169] *Id.* at 996. *See also* Blissard v. White, 515 So.2d 1196 (Miss.1987); In re Estate of Holcomb, 63 P.3d 9 (Okl.2002) (upholding will drawn by lawyer who also represented principal devisee).

[170] Matter of Estate of Wessels, 561 N.E.2d 1212, 1217 (Ill.Ct. App. 1990).

[171] Pascale v. Pascale, 549 A.2d 782, 791–92 (N.J.1988).

[172] Hotz v. Minyard, 403 S.E.2d 634, 637 (S.C.1991).

A devisee who pays a lawyer to draft a will for the testator creates a potential violation of the rules of the profession which in general prohibit lawyers from accepting compensation from someone other than the client.[173]

Particularly troubling are wills that benefit the drafting lawyer. Here the basis for a presumption of undue influence exists—a confidential relationship between attorney and client plus the lawyer's activity in preparing the will. Nevertheless, several such wills have been upheld, because the presumption of undue influence is rebuttable.[174]

Rules of the Profession

The rules of conduct governing the legal profession have become an important factor in this situation. The Model Code of Professional Responsibility[175] Disciplinary Rule (hereinafter DR) 5–101(A) provides: "Except with the consent of his client after full disclosure, a lawyer shall not accept employment if the exercise of his professional judgment on behalf of his client will be or reasonably may be affected by his own financial, business, property, or personal interests." The Ethical Consideration (hereinafter EC) 5–5 appended to this Rule states that a lawyer should urge any client to "secure disinterested advice from an independent, competent person" before accepting a gift from a client, and "[o]ther than in exceptional circumstances, a lawyer should insist that an instrument in which his client desires to name him beneficially be prepared by another lawyer selected by the client." This provision raises the question whether Ethical Considerations, as distinguished from the Rules, have obligatory force.[176]

The Model Rules of Professional Conduct,[177] promulgated by the American Bar Association in 1983, include a clearer prohibition in Rule 1.8(c): "a lawyer shall not prepare an instrument giving the lawyer or a person related to the lawyer as parent, child, sibling, or spouse any substantial gift from a client, including a testamentary gift, except where the client is related to the donee."[178] This rule was the basis for suspending a lawyer who drafted a codicil granting a company in which the lawyer's mother was a large shareholder an option to purchase the company's shares from the testator's estate. Although

---

[173] Model Rules of Professional Conduct 1.8(f). *See also* Estate of Gillespie, 903 P.2d 590 (Ariz.1995) (rejecting a will where the lawyer was selected and paid by the principal devisee).

[174] McGovern, *Undue Influence and Professional Responsibility*, 28 Real Property, Probate & Trust J. 643, 645 (1994). As to the presumption of undue influence, *see* Section 5.3, note 139 et seq. and accompanying text. Under Italian Codice Civile art. 597 devises to the notary who supervises the will execution are void. *See also* Underhill & Hayton, *Law of Trusts and Trustees* 216 (14th ed.1987) ("in the absence of independent advice, the presumption that the settlor was unduly influenced [in a gift to his or her solicitor] is . . . irrebuttable").

[175] The Model Code of Professional Responsibility was promulgated by the American Bar Association in 1972, and adopted in one form or another in 49 states. Today, however, it has been superceded by the Model Rules in most states. J. Price, *Contemporary Estate Planning* § 1.2.3 (2d ed. 2000).

[176] McGovern, *supra* note 174, at 651.

[177] As to the Model Rules, *see* Price, *supra* note 175, at § 1.2.1.

[178] In 2002, this provision was amended to include soliciting a gift, whether or not the preparation of an instrument was involved. The exception where "the client is related to the donee" was expanded to define "related" to "include a spouse, child, grandchild, parent, grandparent or other relative or individual with whom the lawyer or the client maintains a close, familial relationship."

it was not clear whether the option price was lower than the value of the stock when the codicil was drafted, "it was reasonably foreseeable" that the lawyer's mother would substantially benefit, which in fact she did.[179]

These rules have been cited in undue influence cases to show that a lawyer's conduct was "undue."[180] Model Rule 1.8(c) was the model for a provision in the California Probate Code that "no provision ... of any instrument shall be valid to make any donative transfer to ... the person who drafted the instrument" with exceptions.[181] Although the Model Rule only governs the legal profession, the California provision is not so limited.[182] It applies only to drafting instruments, but other gifts from clients to lawyers are subject to challenge for undue influence.[183] The Restatement of Law Governing Lawyers expressly bans (with exceptions) lawyers from preparing any instrument effecting a gift or devise from a client to the lawyer and accepting such a gift.[184]

The exception in the Model Rule "except where the client is related to the lawyer" has been defined somewhat more precisely in the California counterpart,[185] but it still raises troubling questions. May a relative draft an instrument giving the drafter more than his or her intestate share, *e.g.*, one of several children who drafts a will for a parent giving her the whole estate? Case law makes some allowances for kinship between the testator and the drafter. A trust drafted by the settlor's grandson which gave the grandson a remainder was upheld, the court finding there was no presumption of undue influence because they were related.[186] But kinship of the lawyer to the client is not an absolute defense to claims of undue influence.[187] The Restatement also makes an exception where the lawyer is related to the client, but only if "the gift is not significantly disproportionate to those given to donees similarly related to the donor."[188]

---

179 In re Watson, 733 N.E.2d 934, 937 (Ind.2000).

180 Matter of Estate of Dankbar, 430 N.W.2d 124 (Iowa 1988); Krischbaum v. Dillon, 567 N.E.2d 1291 (Ohio 1991); Pascale v. Pascale, 549 A.2d 782 (N.J.1988); *cf.* In re Succession of Parham, 755 So.2d 265 (La.Ct. App. 1999) (will ipso facto invalid because of lawyer's violation of Rule).

181 Cal.Prob.Code § 21350 *amended by* 2011 Cal.Legis.Ch. 296 (A.B. No. 1023) § 245.

182 Estate of Shinkle, 119 Cal.Rptr.2d 42 (Cal. Ct. App.2002) (trust for ombudsman at health care facility). *See also* In re Estate of Marks, 957 P.2d 235 (Wash.Ct. App. 1998) (applying Rule 1.8(c) to non-lawyers who helped testator draft will).

183 McGovern, *supra* note 174, at 658; In re Estate of Mapes, 738 S.W.2d 853 (Mo.1987) (joint bank account).

184 *Restatement (Third) of Law Governing Lawyers* § 127 (2000).

185 Cal.Prob.Code § 21350(b) *amended by* 2011 Cal.Legis.Ch. 296 (A.B. No. 1023) § 245.

186 Lah v. Rogers, 707 N.E.2d 1208, 1213 (Ohio Ct. App. 1998). *See also* Matter of Will of Wasson, 562 So.2d 74 (Miss.1990) (will drawn by testator's sister-in-law benefiting her children is upheld); In re Estate of Alexander, 749 P.2d 1052 (Kan.Ct. App. 1988) (will drawn by testator's daughter-in-law benefiting her husband upheld); Matter of Estate of Unke, 583 N.W.2d 145 (S.D.1998) (testator's son participated in drafting will).

187 Parker v. Marshall, 549 So.2d 463 (Ala.1989) (will rejected for undue influence by testator's lawyer-grandchild); Cleary v. Cleary, 692 N.E.2d 955 (Mass.1998) (fiduciary must justify benefit from transaction with beneficiary even though they were related); In re Last Will of Melson, 711 A.2d 783 (Del.1998) (presumption of undue influence when testator's son drafts will benefiting son's children).

188 *Restatement (Third) of Law Governing Lawyers* § 127(1) (2000). This qualification does not appear in subsection (2) involving lawyers who accept gifts without preparing an instrument.

Friends are *not* covered by the exception for relatives, but some courts have upheld wills when a drafter-devisee and the testator were close friends.[189] The Restatement puts "other natural object[s] of the client's generosity" in the same category as relatives.[190] When a lawyer drafted a will for a family friend which included a devise to himself, the court found no undue influence, but the lawyer was nevertheless reprimanded for violating a disciplinary rule.[191] In another case in which a lawyer was suspended for only 60 days for violating Model Rule 1.8(c), his "very close relationship" with the testator was cited as a "mitigating factor."[192]

Both the Model Rule and the California statute (but not the Restatement) bar devises to certain persons connected with the drafter, such as a spouse or child, but the terms differ.[193] Benefits to family members of the drafting attorney have also been held to raise a presumption of undue influence at common law.[194]

Neither the Model Rule nor the California statute cover instruments which designate the drafter as executor or trustee. This is not a "gift" or "donative transfer," because such fiduciaries are compensated for services rendered. "Such earned fees," one court remarked, "do not constitute the type of substantial economic benefit which gives rise to a presumption of undue influence."[195] But EC 5–6 of the Code of Professional Responsibility provides that "a lawyer should not consciously influence a client to name him as executor, trustee or lawyer in an instrument." When a will named the drafter and his son as co-executors, a court refused to appoint them, citing EC 5–6. In

---

Even when the lawyer prepares an instrument under which s/he receives a disproportionate share, the lawyer simply "bears the burden of persuading the tribunal that the gift was not the product of overreaching." *Id.*, cmt. e.

189 McGovern, *supra* note 174, at 659–60.

190 *Restatement (Third) of Law Governing Lawyers* § 127(1) (2000). In Attorney Grievance Comm'n v. Brooke, 821 A.2d 414 (Md.2003) an attorney was suspended for violating Rule 1.8(c) in drafting a will for an old friend in which he was the sole legatee. *But see* the revised version of the Model Rule, cited in note 178.

191 Clermont Cty. Bar Ass'n v. Bradford, 685 N.E.2d 515 (Ohio 1997). *See also* Disciplinary Proceeding Against Gillingham, 896 P.2d 656 (Wash.1995).

192 In re Watson, 733 N.E.2d 934, 937 (Ind.2000).

193 *Compare* revised Model Rule 1.8(c), note 175 *supra*, *with* Cal.Prob.Code § 21350(a)(2) *amended by* 2011 Cal.Legis.Ch. 296 (A.B. No. 1023) § 245. *Restatement (Third) of Law Governing Lawyers* § 127, cmt. d (2000) says only that the lawyer "may not improperly induce the gift to the lawyer or to a spouse, child, or similar beneficiary of the lawyer." It also allows a lawyer to recommend a charity favored by the lawyer. In Matter of Peeples, 374 S.E.2d 674 (S.C.1988), a lawyer was reprimanded under DR 5–101(A) of the Code for drafting a will which benefited his daughters despite a finding that he had exerted no undue influence.

194 Zachary v. Mills, 660 N.E.2d 1301, 1308 (Ill.Ct. App. 1996). In Estate of Auen, 35 Cal.Rptr.2d 557 (Cal. Ct. App.1994), a will and deed benefiting an attorney, her family and friends was voided for undue influence without reference to the statute.

195 Burke v. Kehr, 876 S.W.2d 718, 722 (Mo.Ct. App. 1994) (directed verdict for proponents of will which named drafter as executor). *See also* Kuster v. Schaumburg, 658 N.E.2d 462, 466 (Ill.Ct. App. 1995); *cf.* In re Estate of Howser, 639 N.W.2d 485, 488 (N.D.2002) (upholding will designating drafter as executor because "the presumption of undue influence had been rebutted"); *Restatement (Third) of Law Governing Lawyers* § 127, cmt. d (2000) (suggestion that client employ the lawyer is not solicitation of a gift). For a collection of ethical opinions on this issue, *see* J. Price, *supra* note 175, at § 1.6.7, at 57–59.

this case the appointment of co-executors would have increased the fees,[196] which the testator wished to keep low. Furthermore, because the testator had not previously known the drafter, his designation as executor was suspicious.[197] In California the drafter of a trust instrument who is designated as sole trustee is subject to removal unless the court finds no undue influence.[198] Of course, no lawyer should agree to serve as a fiduciary unless he or she is qualified for the job.[199]

Some lawyers have refused to draft a will under which they would benefit, but have been involved in the preparation of such a will by another lawyer. EC 5–5 provides that any will benefiting a lawyer should be "prepared by another lawyer selected by the client." Even this may not be enough. In one case a lawyer refused to draft a will naming himself as a devisee, but prepared a memorandum outlining the client's estate plan. The client found another lawyer who "prepared the will based principally upon [the first lawyer's] memo and a brief meeting" with the client. The court held that it was error to dismiss the contestants' challenge to the will, because "it could be inferred that [the testator] did not receive the benefit of counseling by an independent attorney."[200] In California, use of a second lawyer immunizes the transaction only if this lawyer certifies that:

> I am so disassociated from the interest of the transferee as to be in a position to advise my client impartially and confidentially as to the consequences of the transfer. On the basis of this counsel, I conclude that the transfer . . . [is] not the product of fraud, menace duress, or undue influence.[201]

Under the Restatement, however, it is enough if the client "has received independent advice, or has been encouraged and given a reasonable opportunity" to do so.[202]

Because of the perceived injury to the image of the bar when a lawyer benefits from a client's generosity, some courts conduct hearings over such wills even if no heir challenges them.[203] Lawyers may be disciplined for violating the rules of the profession, regardless of the result of any probate

---

[196] This is not always true when several fiduciaries are designated. *See* Section 14.5. In Matter of Bales, 608 N.E.2d 987 (Ind.1993), a drafter was named executor in a will which designated high fees. The lawyer was reprimanded and her fees reduced. *See also* Disciplinary Counsel v. Galinas, 666 N.E.2d 1083 (Ohio 1996); Matter of Eisenhauer, 689 N.E.2d 783 (Mass.1998). In Estate of Gerard v. Gerard, 911 P.2d 266 (Okl.1995), a designated trustee who would earn "substantial fees" was held to have exercised undue influence over a testator.

[197] Matter of Weinstock's Estate, 351 N.E.2d 647 (N.Y.1976). *See also* McGovern, *supra* note 174, at 668–73.

[198] Cal.Prob.Code § 15642(b)(6) *amended by* 2020 Cal.Legis.Serv.Ch. 36 (A.B. 3364).

[199] *See* Section 14.6, note 465.

[200] Matter of Henderson, 605 N.E.2d 323, 326 (N.Y.1992). *See also* In re Estate of Smith, 827 So.2d 673, 683 (Miss.2002). In Matter of Estate of Kern, 716 P.2d 528 (Kan.1986), a similar case, the will was upheld over a strong dissent, even though the first lawyer had also recommended the drafting attorney to the client. *See also* Vaupel v. Barr, 460 S.E.2d 431 (W.Va.1995).

[201] Cal.Prob.Code § 21351(b) *amended by* 2011 Cal.Legis.Ch. 296 (A.B. No. 1023) § 245.

[202] *Restatement (Third) of Law Governing Lawyers* § 127(2)(c) (2000). Independent advice, however, does not allow the lawyer-donee to draft the instrument effecting the transfer.

[203] Matter of Delorey, 529 N.Y.S.2d 153 (App.Div.1988) (will not probated even though uncontested); Estate of Lind, 257 Cal.Rptr. 853 (Cal. Ct. App.1989).

proceedings.[204] In England, solicitors have been stricken from the rolls for drafting wills under which they benefited without advising the testator to get independent advice.[205]

Lawyers also encounter ethical issues when drafting estate planning documents for two spouses. A firm drafted wills for a husband and wife who left their respective estates to each other. Later the firm learned that the husband had fathered a child out of wedlock. It wished to disclose this information to the wife, who had not known when executing her will "that the husband's illegitimate child may ultimately inherit her property." The firm cited Rules of Professional Conduct 1.4(b) requiring lawyers to "explain a matter to the extent reasonably necessary to permit the client to make informed decisions," which imposed on the attorney a "continuing duty to inform the client of any information important to him."[206] The husband objected on the basis of Rule 1.6(a), which says that "a lawyer shall not reveal information relating to the representation of a client unless the client consents." The court allowed the firm to make the disclosure, citing a local exception to the rule of nondisclosure when the lawyer reasonably believes disclosure is necessary "to rectify the consequences of the client's ... fraudulent act in furtherance of which the lawyer's services had been used."[207] The husband's failure to disclose the existence of the child "constitutes a fraud on his wife." The court also relied on a waiver signed by the couple when they engaged the firm, which provided that "information provided by one client could become available to the other."[208]

> An attorney, on commencing joint representation of co-clients, should agree explicitly with the clients on the sharing of confidential information. . . . [or] that unilateral confidences or other confidential information will be kept confidential by the attorney. . . . In the absence of an agreement to share confidential information with co-clients, the Restatement reposes the resolution of the lawyer's competing duties within the lawyer's discretion.[209]

However, the court noted decisions by Professional Ethics Committees of the New York and Florida bars which prohibited disclosure in somewhat similar situations.

Malpractice

At common law, a lawyer owed no duty to the client's potential heirs or beneficiaries and, thus, if, because of the lawyer's negligence, an heir or beneficiary was harmed, the heir or beneficiary had no cause of action in tort

---

204 Akron Bar Ass'n v. Parker, 557 N.E.2d 116 (Ohio 1990) (will contest settled, lawyer suspended); Matter of Eisenhauer, 689 N.E.2d 783 (Mass.1998); Attorney Grievance Comm'n v. Brooke, 821 A.2d 414 (Md.2003); *Restatement (Third) of Law Governing Lawyers* § 127, cmt. a (2000).

205 D. Parry & J. Clark, *The Law of Succession* 69 (10th ed. 1996).

206 A. v. B., 726 A.2d 924, 926 (N.J.1999).

207 This provision differed from the relevant Model Rule in other states which provided for "narrower disclosure."

208 *Id.* at 927–28.

209 *Id.* at 929, quoting *Restatement (Third) of Law Governing Lawyers* § 112, cmt. *l* (Proposed Final Draft No. 1, 1996).

against the lawyer. Furthermore, because the lawyer was not viewed as being in privity with the client's potential heirs or beneficiaries, they had no breach of contract action against the lawyer for the lawyer's negligence which adversely affected them. Today, however, most courts would allow the heir or beneficiary harmed by the lawyer's negligence to bring either a tort or breach of contract action against the lawyer.[210]

It has been suggested that lawyers should not prepare a will for a client whom they think is incapacitated, but such a rule is not found in the Model Rules.[211] Courts have rejected malpractice claims by heirs against lawyers who drafted a will for allegedly incapacitated testators on the ground that this would subject attorneys to "potentially conflicting duties to the client and to potential beneficiaries."[212] But lawyers who do sloppy work in *guarding against claims* of incapacity and undue influence can be liable for malpractice. A devisee-proponent who won a will contest then sued the drafter for negligence "in failing to firmly establish [the testator's] testamentary capacity and free will" thereby causing the proponent's expenses in defending the will to be "at least double what they should have been." The court held the complaint stated a cause of action, even though the devisee-proponent was not the defendant's client.[213]

§§ 5.5–6.0 are reserved for supplemental material.

---

[210] Lucas v. Hamm, 364 P.2d 685 (1961); Walker v. Lawson, 526 N.E.2d 968 (Ind. 1988); Schreiner v. Scoville, 410 N.W.2d 679 (Iowa 1987); Blair v. Ing, 21 P.3d 452 (Hawaii 2001). Some states, however, limit the right to sue to certain persons. *See* Hale v. Groce, 744 P.2d 1289 (Or. 1987) (plaintiff must show plaintiff was an intended beneficiary of the agreement between the testator and the lawyer); Mieras v. DeBona, 550 N.W.2d 202 (Mich. 1996) (limiting actions to those beneficiaries named in the will). Texas refused to abandon the common-law rule. *See* Barcelo v. Elliott, 923 S.W.2d 575 (Tex. 1996).

[211] J. Price, *supra* note 175, § 1.6.11. Model Rule 1.14 (Client Under Disability) does not seem to suggest this.

[212] Moore v. Anderson Zeigler, 135 Cal.Rptr.2d 888, 896 (Cal. Ct. App.2003). *See also* Logotheti v. Gordon, 607 N.E.2d 1015 (Mass.1993); Francis v. Piper, 597 N.W.2d 922 (Minn. Ct. App.1999); *Restatement (Third) of Law Governing Lawyers* § 51, illus. 4 (2000).

[213] Rathblott v. Levin, 697 F.Supp. 817 (D.N.J.1988). For suggested steps to take when a will is executed to guard against contests, *see* Price, *supra* note 175, at § 4.32.

Chapter 6

ADEMPTION, ABATEMENT, AND LAPSE

Analysis

Sec.

6.1 Classification of Devises.
6.2 Ademption.
6.3 Increases.
6.4 Abatement.
6.5 Lapse.

§ 6.1 Classification of Devises

Devises (or "bequests", see Section 1.1) under wills are classified as either general, specific, demonstrative, or residuary. The classification can affect a number of doctrines applicable to the law of wills, such as ademption, abatement, and increases.

A devise is general if it can be paid from the general assets of the estate.[1] The paradigm of the general devise is the gift of a sum of money, *e.g.*, I give Joe $10,000. Because this devise can be paid from general estate assets, it might (and most likely will be) paid by a check in the amount of $10,000. But it could also be paid by a distribution of property other than cash. In such a case, Joe would be fully paid if the asset distributed to him had a fair market value on the date it was distributed of $10,000.

A devise is specific if it is a devise of a specifically described item of property. The paradigm of the specific devise is the gift of a home or "my 100 shares of XYZ common stock." To be specific, the property that is the subject of the devise must be described in a way that its identity is readily identifiable, so that there is no mistaking what should be distributed to the beneficiary.

A devise that appears specific may actually be general.[2] This often occurs with gifts of stock not owned by the testator at the time the will was signed. If testator executes a will devising 100 shares of ABC stock to Jenna but owns no such stock when the will is signed, the devise is construed as general and constitutes a direction to the executor to use general estate assets to purchase 100 shares of ABC stock for Jenna.

A demonstrative devise is somewhat unusual. It is typically a gift of a specific sum of money to be paid from a particular fund, but it can be paid from general estate assets if the particular fund is insufficient to pay the devise.[3] A devise of $10,000 to Steve "to be paid to the extent possible from my account at

1 *See Restatement (Third) of Property (Wills and Other Donative Transfers)* § 5.1 (1999).

2 *Id.*, cmt. c.

3 *Id.*, cmt. d.

First Bank" is demonstrative. If the First Bank account has $10,000 or more in it at the testator's death, Steve will be paid from that account. But if the account only has $6,000 in it at the testator's death, Steve will be paid $6,000 from the account and $4,000 from general estate assets. Thus, this demonstrative devise is specific to the extent of $6,000 and general to the extent of $4,000.

Last, but surely not least, is the residuary devise. The residuary devise consists of all estate assets other than those used to satisfy the general, specific, and demonstrative devises. Because the general, specific, and demonstrative devises are often used to make remembrance gifts, the residue, in relationship to them, often is quite substantial. Typically, the residuary gift is easily identified by such language as "all the rest, residue, and remainder" of my estate, but in wills with no general, specific or demonstrative legacies, it may also be identified be a phrase such as, "I give my entire estate."

§ 6.2 Ademption

Ademption by Extinction

Sometimes after a will is executed but before the testator dies, a change occurs that makes distribution of a specific devise problematic. For example, suppose a will leaves "my IBM stock to my sister, Elizabeth," and the testator later sells the IBM stock. The devise of the stock is usually held to be "adeemed" (from the Latin *adimere:* to take away), so Elizabeth gets nothing.[4] Why? The testator's executor could buy equivalent IBM stock for Elizabeth with the money in the estate. Under Roman law, devises were adeemed only when the testator so intended,[5] but Chancellor Thurlow in the 18th century set the common law on a different path. Holding that the devise of a bond was adeemed when it was paid off before the testator died, the Chancellor said "there is nothing upon which the devise may operate. And I do not think that the question . . . turns on the intention of the testator."[6] Similar statements can be found in modern opinions, *e.g.*, "the testator's intent is not relevant where the property devised or bequeathed in his will is not part of his estate at death."[7] Such statements are misleading because, when one examines the

---

[4] Such "ademption by extinction" is sometimes contrasted with "ademption by satisfaction" when a testator gives something to a devisee, intending thereby to satisfy the devise. In re Estate of Hume, 984 S.W.2d 602, 604 (Tenn.1999); Uniform Probate Code [hereinafter UPC] § 2–609; *Restatement (Third) of Property (Wills and Other Donative Transfers)* § 5.4 (1999). The latter problem is discussed in Section 2.6, at note 222 et seq. Sales of property by an executor after the testator's death are discussed in Section 14.5.

[5] Justinian, *Institutes* 2.20.12. Earlier Roman lawyers had assumed that there was an intent to adeem in this situation. Gaius, *Institutes* 2.198. This is the rule of BGB (German Civil Code) § 2169, but there are many exceptions noted below. *See also* Italian Codice Civile art. 686 (rebuttable presumption of ademption); French Code Civil art. 1038 (alienation revokes a devise).

[6] Stanley v. Potter, 30 Eng.Rep. 83 (1789) *See also* In re Estate of Warman, 682 N.E.2d 557 (Ind.App.1997). Under BGB (German Civil Code) § 2173 the devisee of a pecuniary claim gets an equivalent sum if the claim is paid off before testator's death. A brief survey of the common law before Thurlow's decision appears in Lundwall, *The Case Against the Ademption by Extinction Rule: A Proposal for Reform*, 29 Gonz.L.Rev. 105, 106 (1993).

[7] In re Estate of Balter, 703 A.2d 1038, 1041 (Pa.Super.1997) (devise of ring adeemed when it could not be found after testator died). *See also* Wasserman v. Cohen, 606 N.E.2d 901, 902 (Mass.1993); In re Estate of Hume, 984 S.W.2d 602, 606 (Tenn.1999).

cases more closely, courts purportedly following the common-law identity theory "frequently manipulate doctrine to effectuate intent."[8]

The result may turn on how the devise is worded. When a will devised "my home located at 19 Holly Ridge" but the testator moved to another home before he died, the court held the devise was adeemed, distinguishing a devise of "the homestead upon which we are living," which would include the testator's home at the time of his death.[9] When a will describes property in general language, the devisee gets any property owned by the testator at death which meets the description whether or not the testator owned it when the will was executed.[10] This result can follow from either the facts of independent significance doctrine or from the rule of construction that a will speaks at the time of death.[11]

The common-law doctrine of ademption reflected the identity theory of ademption—that ademption occurred whenever the subject matter of the devise was not in the testator's probate estate.[12] A modern approach turns more on intent under which[13] property other than the expressed subject matter of a specific devise which is not in the probate estate can be distributed to the devisee if that would comport with the testator's intent. The Uniform Probate Code (hereinafter UPC) attempts to avoid the "harsh results" of the common-law identity theory of ademption where (in the view of the drafters) it would frustrate the testator's intent. For example, the UPC gives a specific devisee any property that the testator "acquired as a replacement for" the specifically devised asset, a rule that would presumably change the result in the "19 Holly Ridge" case.[14]

Classification of Devises

Only "specific" devises are subject to ademption by extinction. If a devise of stock is deemed "general," the executor must buy the shares for the devisee if the testator does not own them at death.[15] There is sometimes said to be a presumption that gifts of securities are general rather than specific,[16] but some

---

8 *Restatement (Third) of Property (Wills and Other Donative Transfers)* § 5.2, cmt. b (1999). Some opinions explicitly say that ademption turns on intention. *E.g.,* In re Estate of Poach, 600 N.W.2d 172, 177 (Neb.1999).

9 Matter of Estate of Brown, 922 S.W.2d 605, 608 (Tex.App.1996). For cases avoiding ademption by the "date-of-death" construction, *see* Lundwall, *supra* note 6, at 113.

10 *Restatement (Third) of Property (Wills and Other Donative Transfers)* § 5.2, cmt. e (1999); D. Parry & R. Kerridge, *The Law of Succession* 323–24 (13th ed. 2016) (discussing Wills Act § 24 requiring wills to be construed as if executed at the testator's death). *But cf.* Succession of Mydland, 653 So.2d 8 (La.App.1995) (devise of "all my interest" in a corporation does not include a corporate asset distributed to the testator when the corporation was dissolved).

11 Butler v. Dobbins, 53 A.2d 270, 271 (Me. 1947).

12 *See* In re Estate of Geary, 275 S.W.3d 835 (Tenn. Ct. App. 2008).

13 Brown v. Labow, 69 Cal. Rptr. 3d 417 (Cal. App. 2d Dist. 2007).

14 UPC § 2–606(a)(5).

15 In re Blomdahl's Will, 257 N.W. 152 (Wis.1934); Matter of Fitch's Will, 118 N.Y.S.2d 234 (App.Div.1952); *cf.* BGB (German Civil Code) § 2170 (Verschaffungsvermächtnis). However, even a general devise may fail if it refers to shares in a company which no longer exists. *Id.,* § 2171; Parry & Kerridge, *supra* note 10, at 252.

16 Lundwall, *supra* note 6, at 110; *Restatement (Third) of Property (Wills and Other Donative Transfers)* § 5.2, cmt. c (1999). Holtz v. Diesz, 68 P.3d 828, 833 (Mont.2003) is a rather extreme example; devises of a house and business were deemed "general" to avoid ademption (alternative holding).

devises of stock can only be classified as specific, *e.g.*, "all my IBM stock." A devise of a designated number of shares, on the other hand, is ambiguous if there is no indication that the shares were owned when the will was signed. But a devise of "my 147 shares of the stock of Wales Brothers" was held to be specific (and, thus, partially adeemed when the testator only owned 103 shares at death).[17] Even without the word "my," some courts would classify the devise as specific because the testator owned exactly 147 shares when she executed her will.[18]

A demonstrative devise is not subject to ademption. For example, a will left devises totaling $500,000 to eight individuals, designating a stock fund as the source of payment. The fund had only $46,000 in it when the testator died, but the designated individuals were paid the balance from the residuary estate because the devise was demonstrative.

> A demonstrative legacy is designated by a particular source and may be satisfied by other sources if the identified source is insufficient . . . 'Courts disfavor specific devises, for if the designated property is not part of the estate at death, the gift will generally be lost through ademption by extinction.' . . . An intention to create a specific legacy was not shown with clarity.[19]

Change in Form

Courts sometimes avoid an ademption on the theory that what occurred was a mere "change in form." Thus, a devise of "my interest in the investment plan with the United States National Bank" was not adeemed when the interest was distributed to the testator in the form of cash and stock, because this was a change "of form and not of substance."[20] An important basis for the decision was the fact that the distribution "was an event over which [the testator] had no control."[21] The UPC gives specific devisees of stock any securities which the testator later acquired "by reason of action initiated by the organization" and any securities acquired in another company by reason of a merger.[22] On the other hand, a testator's shifting a savings account to a certificate of deposit was held to cause an ademption.[23]

---

[17] Estate of Wales, 727 P.2d 536, 537 (Mont.1986). *See also* Estate of Bestwick, 426 A.2d 580 (Pa.1981); Boerstler v. Andrews, 506 N.E.2d 279 (Ohio App.1986).

[18] Matthews v. Matthews, 477 So.2d 391 (Ala.1985); In re Estate of Soles, 304 A.2d 97 (Pa.1973). *But see* Parry & Kerridge, *supra* note 10, at 251–252.

[19] In re Estate of Lung, 692 A.2d 1349, 1350 (D.C.App.1997). *See also* Smith v. Estate of Peters, 741 P.2d 1172 (Alaska 1987); Lavender v. Cooper, 285 S.E.2d 528 (Ga.1982). *But see* Estate of Norwood, 443 N.W.2d 798 (Mich.App.1989) (bequest of $6,000 from life insurance fails when no insurance in the estate).

[20] Stenkamp v. Stenkamp, 723 P.2d 336, 338 (Or.App.1986). *See also* Johnston v. Estate of Wheeler, 745 A.2d 345 (D.C.2000) (no ademption in roll-over of pension benefits to an IRA).

[21] "The fact that a testator did not initiate a change makes the application of the change-in-form principle more likely." *Restatement (Third) of Property (Wills and Other Donative Transfers)* § 5.2, cmt. d (1999). *Compare* the discussion of involuntary transfers *infra*.

[22] UPC § 2–605.

[23] Estate of Mayberry v. Mayberry, 886 S.W.2d 627 (Ark.1994). *See also* Church v. Morgan, 685 N.E.2d 809 (Ohio App.1996).

Usually to constitute a mere "change in form" the substitute for the devised property must be identifiable in the testator's estate.[24] Even under the UPC, a specific devisee does not get a distribution of *cash*, as distinguished from securities, resulting from a merger.[25] On the other hand, the mere fact that the proceeds of a sale can be identified in the testator's estate does not necessarily prevent an ademption. The devise of a house was adeemed even though the sales proceeds were paid only after the testator's death because the sale constituted "a 'material alteration' to the subject matter of the specific devise."[26] However, the UPC would alter this result; it gives specific devisees "any balance of the purchase price . . . owing from a purchaser at the time of the testator's death by reason of a 'sale of the devised property.' "[27]

Involuntary Transfers

Specifically devised assets are sometimes disposed of by a conservator after the testator has become incompetent. The UPC gives the specific devisee in this situation "a general pecuniary devise equal to the net sale price" of the asset sold, on the theory that an incapacitated testator could not have intended the devise to adeem.[28] Some courts reach this result without a statute,[29] but others only give the specific devisee whatever remains of the sales proceeds in the estate when the testator dies.[30]

The UPC's provision on ademption by extinction applies only to devises, but a similar rule has been applied to will substitutes.[31] When a conservator closed joint accounts that the conservatee had established for her niece and nephew, the court held that the conservator had exceeded his authority.

> The conservator's duty is to manage the estate during the conservatee's lifetime. It is not his function . . . to control disposition after death. . . . A conservator may withdraw funds from a joint

---

[24] Johnston v. Estate of Wheeler, 745 A.2d 345, 351 (D.C.App.2000) (emphasizing that the funds in question "remained segregated" from testator's other property).

[25] UPC § 2–605(b); Opperman v. Anderson, 782 S.W.2d 8 (Tex.App.1989).

[26] In re Estate of Hume, 984 S.W.2d 602, 605 (Tenn.1999). *See also* Kelley v. Neilson, 745 N.E.2d 952 (Mass.2001); Opperman v. Anderson, 782 S.W.2d 8 (Tex.App.1989); *Restatement (Third) of Property (Wills and Other Donative Transfers)* § 5.2, cmt. d (1999) (sale for cash is "too substantial" to be treated as a change of form even if tracing is possible).

[27] UPC § 2–606(a)(1). *See also* In re Estate of Poach, 600 N.W.2d 172 (Neb.1999) (property sold pursuant to exercise of an option after the testator died).

[28] UPC § 2–606(b). *See also* Matter of Estate of Gardner, 845 P.2d 1247 (N.M.App.1992); Cal.Prob.Code § 21134. The rule does not apply if the testator is judicially restored to capacity and survives thereafter by a year. UPC § 2–606(d); Oliver v. Estate of Oliver, 554 N.E.2d 8 (Ind.App.1990) (ademption found when testator's confusion "cleared up" after sale by conservator).

[29] Matter of Estate of Warren, 344 S.E.2d 795 (N.C.App.1986); Lundwall, *supra* note 6, at 115.

[30] In re Estate of Anton, 731 N.W.2d 19 (Iowa 2007); Matter of Estate of Swoyer, 439 N.W.2d 823 (S.D.1989); In re Graham's Estate, 533 P.2d 1318 (Kan.1975).

[31] UPC § 2–606 appears in Part 6, "Rules of Construction Applicable only to Wills," whereas Part 7 covers "Rules of Construction Applicable to Wills and Other Governing Instruments." However, *Restatement (Third) of Property (Wills and Other Donative Transfers)* § 5.2, cmt. i (1999) indicates that almost identical rules should "also apply to a will substitute, such as a revocable trust."

account only to provide what is necessary for the conservatee's maintenance.[32]

The UPC requires conservators to "take into account any estate plan" of the conservatee in utilizing funds for the conservatee's support.[33]

Today, many persons use durable powers of attorney to avoid conservatorship.[34] The UPC applies the same rule to conservators and to agents under a durable power of attorney who act for an incapacitated principal.[35] Without such a statutory mandate, courts have split over this issue.[36] Application of the UPC's rule requires a determination of whether the testator was competent at the time of the sale, but acts of an agent under a durable power are "presumed to be for an incapacitated principal."[37]

Involuntary loss may also arise from accident. When a specifically devised house was damaged by fire after the will was executed, the devisee was awarded the proceeds of an insurance policy on the house. Because the fire "did not occur through any voluntary act" of the testator, it "showed no change" in the testator's intention.[38] The UPC gives a specific devisee any insurance proceeds on lost property that are paid to the estate after the testator's death; even if the loss was uninsured, or the insurance has been paid and dissipated, the devisee may recover the value of the missing property "only to the extent it is established that ademption would be inconsistent with the testator's manifested plan of distribution."[39] The examples given in the accompanying comment distinguish between property stolen by a burglar (no ademption) and property given away by the testator (ademption). Thus, the UPC reflects a general presumption against ademption,[40] but the narrower exceptions to ademption in an earlier version of the UPC are still law in some states.[41]

---

[32] Matter of Estate of Briley, 825 P.2d 1181, 1183–84 (Kan.App.1992). *See also* Witt v. Ward, 573 N.E.2d 201 (Ohio App.1989); *Restatement (Second) of Property (Donative Transfers)* § 18.1, illus. 1 (1984). *But see* In re Conservatorship of Gobernatz, 603 N.W.2d 357, 360 (Minn.App.1999) (conservator properly terminated joint account of conservatee).

[33] UPC § 5–426. *See* Matter of Estate of Reinwald, 834 P.2d 1317 (Idaho 1992) (improper for conservator to eliminate POD beneficiary in renewing CD). For the circumstances in which a conservator can properly affect the conservator's estate plan *see* Section 5.2, at note 70 et seq.

[34] *See* Section 5.2, at note 83 et seq.

[35] UPC § 2–606(b). *See also* Cal.Prob.Code § 21134(a).

[36] *Compare* Funk v. Funk, 563 N.E.2d 127 (Ind.App.1990) (no equitable conversion from sale by agent while principal was comatose) *with* In re Estate of Hegel, 668 N.E.2d 474 (Ohio 1996) (devise adeemed by agent's sale under durable power).

[37] UPC § 2–606(e); *cf.* Chapman v. Chapman, 577 A.2d 775 (Me.1990) (finding ademption when there was no proof that the testator was incompetent when property was sold by an agent).

[38] White v. White, 251 A.2d 470, 473 (N.J.Super.Ch.Div.1969). *See also* In re Estate of Kolbinger, 529 N.E.2d 823 (Ill.App.1988); Lundwall, *supra* note 6, at 118 (citing cases both ways); *cf.* BGB (German Civil Code) §§ 2164(2), 2169(3) (any claims for damages to or replacement of devised property pass to devisee).

[39] UPC § 2–606.

[40] *See* UPC § 2–606(a)(6). In Holtz v. Diesz, 68 P.3d 828 (Mont.2003), the court relied inter alia on the UPC presumption in finding no ademption.

[41] *E.g.*, Cal.Prob.Code §§ 21133–34. For other statutes dealing with ademption in a limited way *see* Lundwall, *supra* note 6, at 119–22.

Other Factors

Even a testator who voluntarily disposes of a specifically devised asset may not intend to adeem the devise. A testator's decision to shift money from a savings account to a certificate of deposit in order to get a higher interest rate probably shows no intent to adeem.[42] But in some cases ademption reflects the testator's probable intent. The reason for a specific devise may disappear when the property is disposed of. When a business is devised to employees in the hope that they will carry it on, and the testator later sells the business, it seems reasonable to infer an intent to adeem.[43] The same applies to devises of items of sentimental value, like paintings or jewelry.[44] Many wills specifically devise the testator's house and tangible personal property in order to avoid putting them into a trust which holds the residue of the estate.[45] If the testator later sells the house, there is no reason why the sale proceeds should not go into the residuary trust, so ademption seems the proper result. Ademption also avoids administrative problems, *e.g.*, requiring the executor to determine the value of property that is no longer in the estate or the price of property that the testator sold many years before she died.

Drafters can avoid such problems by a using a different type of devise. "Competent estate planners generally try to avoid using specific devises when the testator's real desire is simply to allocate quantities of wealth among a group of individuals. General devises and fractional shares of the residuary estate are much more apt" for this purpose.[46] There is usually no good reason why a testator would want her sister to get her IBM stock, for example, rather than an equivalent amount of money or a fraction of the estate.

Income and Appreciation During Administration

The classification of devises affects the allocation of income received and changes in value that occur during the administration of an estate. For example, a will devised a motel to the testator's children, and the residue of his estate to his wife. The motel produced a profit of $10,000 during the estate's administration. This was held to pass to the testator's children as part of their

---

[42] *See* Re Dorman, [1994] 1 W.L.R. 282 (Ch.)(Eng.); *cf.* Holtz v. Diesz, 68 P.3d 828 (Mont.2003) (property sold to provide funds for testator's care, but not actually needed).

[43] Matter of Morrissey, 684 S.W.2d 876 (Mo.App.1984). *See also* Douglas v. Newell, 719 P.2d 971, 982 (Wyo.1986) (dissent); Alexander, *Ademption and the Domain of Formality in Wills Law*, 55 Alb.L.Rev. 1067, 1081 (1992).

[44] Ascher, *The 1990 Uniform Probate Code: Older and Better, or More like the Internal Revenue Code?*, 77 Minn.L.Rev. 639, 644 (1993); Johnston v. Estate of Wheeler, 745 A.2d 345, 352 (D.C.App.2000) (finding no ademption because devise was not "an heirloom of primarily sentimental value"). *But see Restatement (Third) of Property (Wills and Other Donative Transfers)* § 5.2, illus. 4–6 (1999) (no ademption when specifically devised jewelry is stolen).

[45] Unif. Statutory Will Act § 5. The fees paid to a professional trustee for managing investments of securities are usually an unnecessary expense as to a house.

[46] Ascher, *supra* note 44, at 644. *See also* Leach, *Cases and Text on the Law of Wills* 148 (2d ed. 1960). However, in some situations specific devises of tangible property may be advisable for income tax purposes. *See* Sherman, *All You Really Need to Know About Subchapter J You Learned from This Article*, 63 Mo.L.Rev. 1, 34 (1998). As to the potential liability by lawyers when an intended devise is frustrated by ademption, *see* Parry & Kerridge, *supra* note 10, at 365.

specific devise.[47] The Uniform Principal and Income Act similarly provides that specific devisees receive the net income and net principal receipts from the property devised which accrues during the period of administration.[48] General or pecuniary devises, on the other hand, do not share in the income earned by an estate during administration, but rather get interest, normally specified in a statute. The UPC provides "interest at the legal rate," which begins to run one year after the personal representative is appointed and does not depend on whether the estate actually realized income.[49]

Income of an estate that is not attributable to specifically devised property is divided among the residuary devisees and the trustee of any pecuniary devise in trust in proportion to their respective shares of the estate.[50] The question as to how a devise should be classified sometimes arises in this context, as when estate assets change in value during the administration of the estate. For example, a will devised "25% of my estate remaining after debts, funeral expenses, and expenses of administration, but before taxes." Was this a pecuniary devise not in trust to which no estate income was allocable or a fractional share of the residue which was entitled to some allocable portion of the estate's income?

> When the disposition is a specific amount, such as $10,000, it is clearly pecuniary. A disposition "determinable by means of a formula which is stated in the instrument" is also pecuniary. For example, a bequest of one-half of $20,000 can clearly be determined by means of a formula and is therefore a pecuniary disposition.[51]

Also this devise above appeared in Article Third of the will; in Article Fourth the testator disposed of her residuary estate in fractions, *i.e.*, 70 per cent to her son and 30 per cent to her son's descendants. Obviously if she had intended that the beneficiary of the devise in Article Third should share income during estate administration, she could have placed this disposition within her residuary clause.

---

47 Estate of Lindsey v. Taylor, 300 N.E.2d 572, 573 (Ill.App.1973). *See also* Matter of Estate of Meyer, 668 N.E.2d 263, 266 (Ind.App.1996) (growing crops pass to specific devisee of farm); Matter of Estate of Niehenke, 818 P.2d 1324, 1332 (Wash.1991).

48 Unif. Prin. and Inc. Act § 201(1) (1997). *See also* Parry & Kerridge, *supra* note 10, at 567; BGB (German Civil Code) § 2184. *But see* Matter of Estate of Hafferman, 442 N.W.2d 238, 240 (S.D.1989) (statute allows executor to use first 10 months' income from specifically devised farm to pay debts of the estate).

As to the treatment of dividends, rent and interest in computing income for this purpose *see* Section 10.6, note 246 et seq.

49 UPC § 3–904. The comment to this section states that at common law interest runs from the date of the testator's death. *Compare* the more complex rules set forth in Parry & Kerridge, *supra* note 10, at 570–74. In In re Estate of Miller, 437 N.W.2d 793, 797 (Neb.1989), the court interpreted such a statute not to apply when payment of the devise was postponed during a will contest. *Contra*, Matter of Estate of Vaden, 677 P.2d 659 (Okl.App.1983) (citing authority both ways).

50 Unif. Prin. and Inc. Act § 210(4) (1997).

51 Estate of McKee, 504 N.Y.S.2d 394, 395–96 (Surr.1986). Even pecuniary devises share in the estate income if they are "in trust." But the court held that this "pour over bequest" did not create a trust, but merely added to an existing trust and so did not qualify. *See also* Hanna v. Hanna, 619 S.W.2d 655 (Ark.1981) (devise of "assets which will equal one-half of my adjusted gross estate" is "clearly a true pecuniary bequest").

On the other hand, a devise of "such portion of my estate which shall result in an amount equal to one-half of my adjusted gross estate" to the testator's wife, followed by a devise of "the remaining undivided one-half of my estate" to the testator's children, was held to give the wife a "fractional residuary bequest" so she shared in the appreciation of the estate.[52]

Other Constructional Problems

Specific devises sometimes give rise to litigation concerning their scope. Wills often devise a house and "its contents" to a named beneficiary. Claims have been made, generally unsuccessfully, that this includes cash and securities found in the house.[53] But a similar phrase was construed to include valuable paintings in the house of artist Mark Rothko.[54] How much land is included in a devise "of my residence" when the house is located on a 40 acre tract?[55]

Does a devise of "cash on hand" include money in a checking account?[56] Do "the funds in my bank account" include a certificate of deposit?[57] Do "corporate stocks and bonds" include a municipal bond fund?[58] Do "automobiles" include a motor home?[59] Is an automobile included in "personal effects?"[60] What about cash found on the testator's person when he died?[61] Does a devise of "paintings" include icons painted on wood?[62]

The interpretation of words may be affected by their context. The words "personal property" normally encompass intangibles such as securities,[63] but when they appeared in a phrase following "household furniture and furnishings, books, pictures, silverware, my automobiles," etc., they were given a restricted construction under "the rule of ejusdem generis," *i.e.,* "general words following the enumeration of specific meaning are not to be construed in

---

[52] In re Estate of Parker, 180 N.W.2d 82 (Mich.App.1970). *See also,* S. Kurtz, *Allocation of Increases and Decreases to Fractional Share Marital Deduction Bequest,* 8 Real. Prop. Prob. & Tr. J. 450 (1973).

[53] Matter of Clark, 417 S.E.2d 856, 857 (S.C.1992) (cash); Last Will and Testament of Lawson v. Lambert, 792 So.2d 977, 978 (Miss.2001); *cf.* May v. Walter, 956 S.W.2d 138 (Tex.App.1997) ("tangible personal property contents" of a safe does not include a CD).

[54] In re Estate of Rothko, 352 N.Y.S.2d 574 (Surr.1974).

[55] East v. Estate of East, 785 N.E.2d 597 (Ind.App.2003).

[56] Yes, according to Matter of Estate of Farone, 482 N.E.2d 556 (N.Y.1985). *See also* Matter of Estate of Mitchell, 519 So.2d 430 (Miss.1988) ("cash" includes CDs); Matter of Estate of Flasted, 741 P.2d 750 (Mont.1987) ("cash and savings" includes a $150,000 note).

[57] Yes, according to Estate of Cushman, 501 A.2d 811 (Me.1985); Matter of Estate of Srubar, 728 S.W.2d 437 (Tex.App.1987).

[58] Yes, according to Longaker v. Evans, 32 S.W.3d 725, 736 (Tex.App.2000).

[59] Yes, according to Riggs v. Riggs, 507 So.2d 462 (Ala.1987). *See also* Matter of Estate of Crist, 434 N.W.2d 904 (Iowa App.1988) ("household goods and other chattels" includes excavating equipment).

[60] No, according to Matter of Estate of Roddy, 784 P.2d 841 (Colo.App.1989).

[61] Yes, according to Huskins v. Huskins, 517 S.E.2d 146, 151 (N.C.App.1999).

[62] Yes, according to McMillen v. McMillen, 784 N.E.2d 1130 (Mass.App.2003).

[63] Emmert v. Hearn, 522 A.2d 377 (Md.1987).

their widest extent but only as applying to things of the same kind," and, thus, did not include intangibles.[64]

Courts sometimes consider the identity of the devisees in resolving such questions. A devise of "all shares of common or preferred stock which I may own" to the testator's financial advisor was held not to include a cooperative apartment.

> Indisputably, for many commercial purposes the law treats a shareholder's interest in a cooperative apartment primarily as an interest in a corporation. Here, however, . . . the document manifests decedent's intent that her relatives take the interest in her residence.[65]

It is not usual in modern wills to describe each item of a testator's property, as in Shakespeare's famous devise of his "second-best bed" to his wife. However, objects of great value should be specifically mentioned, because they may be construed not to pass under general references to "household furnishings" or "personal effects."[66]

Specific devises of part of a larger tract of land have also generated litigation. When a husband devised to his wife thirty acres out of a tract of 164 acres, the court allowed the wife to select thirty acres because she was "the principal object" of the testator's bounty, but such devises have also been construed to make the devisee a tenant in common of the entire tract.[67]

Ordinarily, a testator would not have the power to dispose of property owned by the corporation, but some courts have given effect to devises of property owned by a corporation which the testator controls if they did not impair the rights of the corporation's creditors and minority shareholders.[68]

Because in all of these cases the particular language of a particular testator's will is being construed to ascertain the testator's intent, no case is necessarily predictive of the outcome of any other case. Furthermore, outwardly unusual or legally unexpected results may be justified by the particular facts of the case before the court. In other areas of will construction, such as lapse, the results tend to be more predictable because the courts construe the language of the will against the backdrop of a controlling statute.

Ademption by Satisfaction

Under the doctrine of ademption by satisfaction, if, after executing a will, the testator makes a gift to a devisee of either a specific or general devise in the will, the lifetime gift causes the testamentary gift to fail, in whole or in part, if that is what the testator intended. If the lifetime gift is of specifically

---

[64] Breckner v. Prestwood, 600 S.W.2d 52, 57 (Mo.App.1980). *See also* In re Estate of Mildrexter, 971 P.2d 758 (Kan.App.1999); Turner v. Reed, 518 S.E.2d 832 (Va.1999).

[65] Matter of Estate of Carmer, 525 N.E.2d 734, 736 (N.Y.1988).

[66] *Cf.* Matter of Brecklein's Estate, 637 P.2d 444 (Kan.App.1981) (gold coins not included in "belongings"); Griffin v. Gould, 432 N.E.2d 1031 (Ill.App.1982) (extrinsic evidence admissible to determine whether valuable statues were included as "articles of household ornament").

[67] Stephenson v. Rowe, 338 S.E.2d 301 (N.C.1986).

[68] Matter of Estate of Hatfield, 730 P.2d 696 (Wash.App.1986).

devised property, the devise also fails because it adeemed by extinction.[69] If the devise could have been paid from the general assets of the estate (as in the case of a general devise), it fails to the extent of the lifetime gift. If the donee-legatee is a child of the testator, a rebuttable presumption arises that the lifetime gift was in satisfaction of the devise.[70]

The UPC restricts the scope of ademption by satisfaction; it can occur only if (1) the will provided that the devise be reduced by the lifetime gift, (2) the testator by a writing executed contemporaneously with the lifetime gift stated that the gift was in lieu of the devise or that the gift's value should reduce the devise, or (3) the devisee acknowledged in writing that the gift was in satisfaction of the devise or its value should reduce the devise.[71] If the devisee predeceases the testator, a lifetime gift intended to be in satisfaction of the devise reduces or eliminates the amount of the gift that otherwise might have passed to the deceased legatee's descendants under the antilapse statute.[72]

§ 6.3 Increases

Events occurring after a will is executed sometimes increase the value of a specific devise. A devise of "my shares in the Putnam High Yield Trust" was held to include shares the testator bought after the will was executed.[73] Even when a will specifies a number of shares, the devisee may receive more as the result of a stock split. A devisee of "200 shares of Exxon" was awarded an additional 200 shares which the testator subsequently received in a stock split.[74] Some courts give a devisee of stock the additional shares only if the devise is characterized as specific,[75] but under the UPC it does not matter how the devise is characterized as long as the testator, at the time the will was executed, owned securities "that meet the description in the will."[76] Suppose a testator, who owns 200 shares of XYZ common stock, bequeaths "my 200 shares of XYZ common stock" to Bill. If between the date the will was signed and the testator's death, the stock of XYZ company split 2 for 1, Bill would get 400 shares as this was a specific devise. Bill would also get 400 shares if the devise

---

[69] In re Estate of Frank, 189 P.3d 834 (Wash. App. Div. 2008).

[70] In re Strand's Estate, 3 Pa. D. & C.3d 457 (Pa. Com.Pl. 1976); Carmichael v. Lathrop, 66 N.W. 350 (Mich. 1896).

[71] UPC § 2–609.

[72] *Id. See also Restatement (Third) of Property (Wills and Other Donative Transfers)* § 5.4, cmt. h (1999).

[73] Estate of Russell, 521 A.2d 677 (Me.1987). *See also* In re Succession of Lee, 831 So.2d 477, 480 (La.App.2002) (money added to devised account after will executed); *Restatement (Third) of Property (Wills and Other Donative Transfers)* § 5.2, cmt. e (1999).

[74] Shriners Hosp. for Crippled Children v. Coltrane, 465 So.2d 1073 (Miss.1985). *See also* Watson v. Santalucia, 427 S.E.2d 466 (W.Va.1993). In Matter of Estate of Holmes, 821 P.2d 300 (Colo.App.1991), the court even gave a devisee the benefit of a stock split which took place *before* the will was executed on the basis that the testator actually intended to include all of her stock in the company.

[75] Boerstler v. Andrews, 506 N.E.2d 279 (Ohio App.1986). In Polson v. Craig, 570 S.E.2d 190 (S.C.App.2002), the court gave lip service to this distinction, but it found a devise of "400 shares" was "specific" for this purpose. *Cf.* Section 6.2, notes 17–18.

[76] UPC § 2–605, cmt. *See also* In re Estate of Howard, 393 So.2d 81 (Fla.App.1981); Watson v. Santalucia, 427 S.E.2d 466 (W.Va.1993). Accord, *Restatement (Third) of Property: (Wills and Other Donative Transfers)* § 5.3 (1999), cmt. f.

had been merely, "I give Bill 200 shares of XYZ common stock,"[77] even though this were treated as a general devise. Under the UPC, however, if the testator owned no XYZ stock at the time the will was executed, Bill would receive only the 200 shares as a general devise.

Dividends paid in the stock of the distributing corporation, like stock splits, also go to a devisee of securities under the UPC although this was not the common-law rule.[78] On the other hand, dividends paid in cash to the testator during life do not pass to the devisee of the stock.

Many companies participate in so-called "dividend reinvestment programs" whereby cash dividends paid to shareholders are automatically re-invested in the company's shares. Under the UPC, if a testator devises a company's shares that he owns when he signed his will to a named devisee, the devisee also acquires the shares the testator later acquired as a result of the dividend reinvestment program.[79]

§ 6.4 Abatement

Sometimes there are insufficient assets in an estate to carry out all the testator's directions. Suppose a will leaves (1) "my XYZ stock to my sister Elizabeth," (2) "$10,000 to the First Presbyterian Church," and (3) "the residue of my estate to my descendants who survive me, by representation." When the testator dies, her estate contains the XYZ stock (hence there is no ademption problem), but the rest of her assets are worth only $8,000. Or suppose that her assets, apart from the XYZ stock, are worth $48,000 but claims against the estate amount to $40,000. Which of the devises should be abated to pay the claims?

Hierarchy of Devises

The UPC provides that "shares of distributees abate . . . in the following order: (1) property not disposed of by will; (2) residuary devises; (3) general devises; (4) specific devises."[80] This hierarchy of devises (specific, general, and residuary) comes from the common law[81] and is found in most abatement statutes.[82] In the case of a demonstrative devise, for abatement purposes, the gift is part specific, part general. It is specific to the extent of the particular source designated for payment of the devise, and general to the extent that it might have been paid from general estate assets.[83]

---

[77] *See also Restatement (Third) of Property (Wills and Other Donative Transfers)* § 5.3 (1999).

[78] First Nat. Bank v. Union Hospital, 183 N.E. 247 (Mass. 1932); Griffith v. Adams, 137 A. 20 (Conn. 1927). *Contra* Butler v. Dobbins, 53 A.2d 270 (1947).

[79] UPC § 2–605(a)(3).

[80] UPC § 3–902. *See also Restatement (Third) of Property (Wills and Other Donative Transfers)* § 1.1, cmt. f (1999). Courts sometimes confusingly refer to devises of a specific amount as "specific bequests", In re Estate of Passoff, 819 A.2d 26, 31 (N.J.Super.Ch.2002), but for purposes of the hierarchy in abatement the term refers to devises of specific property, like the IBM stock in the hypothetical.

[81] 2 W. Blackstone, *Commentaries* 512–13 (1766).

[82] Some statutes list devises in accordance with the "priority of *distribution*" as (1) specific, (2) general, (3) residuary, (4) intestate, 20 Pa.Stat. § 3541, but the result is the same.

[83] UPC § 3–902(a). *See also* Iowa Code § 633.436(2).

If the will disposes of the entire estate (as it usually does by virtue of a residuary devise), there is no property in the first category, *i.e.*, undisposed of property,[84] so the property that passes under the residuary clause abates first. In the hypothetical, therefore, the testator's descendants get nothing, the $10,000 general devise to the Presbyterian Church is partially abated in the amount of $2,000 leaving the church $8,000, and Elizabeth's specific devise of the XYZ stock is unaffected.[85]

Abatement among devises within each category is pro rata.[86] Thus, if the will had made two general devises[87] of $10,000 to Christina and $6,000 to Cal, and only $8,000 was available to pay them, Christina would receive $5,000 (being 10/16th of the available $8,000) and Cal would receive $3,000 (being 6/16th of the available $8,000).

What if a person owns property that does not pass through probate, such as a house or bank account in joint tenancy? In some jurisdictions such property is not subject to claims of creditors at all. Under the UPC, the decedent's creditors could reach the joint account, but only if other assets of the estate are insufficient, so if there is enough in the probate estate to pay claims, a surviving joint tenant would not have to contribute towards the payment of claims.[88] The Third Restatement of Property states merely that the decedent's creditor "may . . . be entitled "to have their claims satisfied out of the decedent's will substitutes, to the extent provided by applicable law."[89]

In most wills the residuary devisees are the persons closest to the testator's heart, *e.g.*, the testator's spouse and descendants, while pecuniary or specific devises are often made to friends, collateral relatives, or charities. The assumption made in the rules of abatement seems inconsistent with the assumptions underlying the rules of intestate succession where the spouse and descendants are preferred. However, to abate residuary devises last, or abate all devises pro rata, would present administrative problems. Often property that is specifically devised cannot readily be sold, or the testator does not want it to be sold. If specific devisees had to contribute to the payment of claims

---

[84] Contrary to what you might think on reading an abatement statute, property passing by nonprobate transfers is not in this category. Such property is dealt with elsewhere. *See* note 86 et seq.

[85] However, any expenses attributable to specifically devised property, such as property taxes on land, are deducted from the income which the devisee receives. *See* Section 6.2, note 48; Parry & Kerridge, *supra* note 10, at 568–69; Unif. Prin. and Inc. Act § 501(3) (1997).

[86] UPC § 3–902(a); Matter of Estate of Wales, 727 P.2d 536 (Mont.1986); In re Estate of Oberstar, 709 N.E.2d 872 (Ohio App.1998).

[87] To further confuse matters, such gifts are often referred to as "pecuniary" devises (or bequests), but they are not necessarily satisfied in money. Section 6.1, note 1. A provision forgiving a debt to the testator falls into the same category. In re Estate of Passoff, 819 A.2d 26 (N.J.Super.Ch.2002) (when estate insufficient, debt forgiveness ignored as well as pecuniary devises).

[88] *See* Section 13.6, at note 257 et seq.

[89] *Restatement (Third) of Property (Wills and Other Donative Transfers)* § 1.1, cmt. f (1999). *See also* Cal.Prob.Code § 19001 (revocable trusts); *Restatement (Third) of Trusts* § 26, cmt. d (1999).

against the estate, they might have to be sold. The residuary estate, on the other hand, usually contains cash or liquid assets more suitable for sale.[90]

Pecuniary devises could contribute to the payment of creditors' claims simply by a reduction in the amount. But when a will leaves "$10,000 to the Presbyterian Church" the testator probably expected the Church to get that amount and no less. This happens only if the residuary estate is the primary source for paying claims. Rarely do claims exhaust the residuary estate, so the testator's wishes are usually fulfilled by making the residue the primary source for paying claims.

Apportionment

In most estates the claims and the general and specific devises are small enough that even when they are all charged to the residue there is plenty left over for the residuary devisees. The spouse's elective share,[91] on the other hand (particularly when nonprobate assets are included in computing it), may seriously deplete the residue if liability is not apportioned. Therefore, the UPC departs from the normal order of abatement when the spouse claims an elective share; the spouse's claim is "equitably apportioned" among all the recipients of the decedent's estate, including nonprobate transferees.[92] Some states nevertheless follow the normal abatement rules in this situation,[93] but others like the UPC apportion liability.[94] The Third Restatement of Property suggests an open-ended rule: courts should allocate "liability as the decedent would probably have done had the decedent specifically addressed the question."[95]

The UPC generally follows the normal order of abatement when a pretermitted child or omitted spouse claims a share,[96] but in California, the share is taken from all devisees pro rata unless "the obvious intention of the testator . . . would be defeated" thereby.[97]

Liability for the federal estate tax is often apportioned among beneficiaries of an estate.[98] Failure to do this in cases where a considerable portion of the estate passes outside the residue might cause the residue to be

---

[90] In many estates life insurance is an important source of funds to pay taxes and other claims against the estate.

[91] As to the spousal elective share *see* Section 8.7.

[92] UPC § 2–207. *See also* Kilcoyne v. Reilly, 249 F.2d 472 (D.C.Cir.1957); Wilkinson v. Brune, 682 S.W.2d 107 (Mo.App.1984). An exception is made for property irrevocably transferred by the decedent within two years of death. This is included in the calculation of the spouse's share under § 2–205(3), but the transferred property is postponed in the apportionment under § 2–207(b).

[93] In re Estate of Brinkman, 326 N.E.2d 167 (Ill.App.1975); Winters National Bank & Trust Co. v. Riffe, 206 N.E.2d 212 (Ohio 1965); Iowa Code § 633.436.

[94] Kilcoyne v. Reilly, 249 F.2d 472 (D.C.Cir.1957); Wilkinson v. Brune, 682 S.W.2d 107 (Mo.App.1984).

[95] *Restatement (Third) of Property (Wills and Other Donative Transfers)* § 9.1, cmt. *l* (2003).

[96] UPC §§ 2–301(b), 2–302(d). *See also* Iowa Code § 633.436; *Restatement (Third) of Property (Wills and Other Donative Transfers)* § 9.5, cmt. f, § 9.6, cmt. b (2003). As to claims of pretermitted spouses and children *see* Sections 8.5 and 8.6.

[97] Cal.Prob.Code §§ 21612, 21623. *See also* N.Y.EPTL § 5–1.3(b).

[98] *See* UPC § 3–916(b). For a general discussion of the source of funds to pay the federal estate tax *see* J. Price & S. Donaldson, *Contemporary Estate Planning* §§ 4.28.9, 12.42–12.48 (2016).

completely abated.[99] On this issue also, the testator's intent controls[100] but is sometimes unclear. Sometimes there is a conflict between the will and the provisions of a revocable trust on the subject, because the drafter failed to coordinate the various parts of an estate plan.[101]

Classification

The classification of devises for purposes of abatement is sometimes problematic. When a will left $15,000 to the testator's son, and "all the rest of my property, including the rights to receive royalty distributions from the American Society of Composers, Authors and Publishers," to the testator's wife, the only asset in the estate was the testator's right to royalties. The wife claimed that her devise was specific, but the court classified it as residuary so the son's devise was preserved.[102] In another will, a devise of "a sum equal to 10% of the value of my estate" was held to be general devise of 10% of the estate to be computed before deducting claims.[103]

Contrary Intent

The specific/general/residuary order of abatement does not always reflect the testator's intent. Under the UPC, the statutory hierarchy can be overcome by an express contrary provision or by showing that it would defeat "the testamentary plan or the express or implied purpose of the devise."[104] A specific devise of personal property was held to abate prior to the residuary devises when the will specified "all debts . . . shall be paid from the personal property of my estate."[105]

Determining the testator's intent may be difficult. A will left a farm to the testator's son and "a portion of my estate equal in value to the value of the property passing to my son" to the testator's daughter. The son's devise was held to be specific and the daughter's general, with the result that the son ended up with more than his sister.[106] Perhaps the testator's "implied purpose"

---

[99] *E.g.*, In re Valma M. Hanson Revocable Trust, 779 N.E.2d 1218 (Ind.App.2002); In re Estate of Passoff, 819 A.2d 26, 27 (N.J.Super.Ch.2002).

[100] In re Estate of Kuralt, 68 P.3d 662 (Mont.2003) (taxes imposed on residue per provision in will despite apportionment statute).

[101] Matter of Estate of Pickrell, 806 P.2d 1007 (Kan.1991) (will imposes taxes on residue, but living trust calls for apportionment); In re Estate of Brownlee, 654 N.W.2d 206, 212 (S.D.2002).

[102] Matter of Deutsch's Estate, 644 P.2d 768 (Wyo.1982); *cf.* Parry & Kerridge, *supra* note 10, at 367.

[103] Williams v. Faucett, 579 So.2d 572 (Ala.1989). *Compare* Section 6.2, notes 51–52. In the civil law the heirs, including those designated by will, but not legatees, are liable for paying claims against the decedent BGB (German Civil Code) § 1967. Here too ambiguously drafted wills give rise to problems of interpretation. H. Brox & W. Walker, *Erbrecht* 195 (27th ed. 2016); BGB (German Civil Code) § 2087 (legacy of all or a fraction of testator's property is presumed to make the legatee an heir).

[104] UPC § 3–902(b). *See also* Cal.Prob.Code § 21400; N.Y.EPTL § 13–1.3(e); *cf.* Matter of Estate of Routh, 524 N.E.2d 46 (Ind.App.1988) (extrinsic evidence to show contrary intent is inadmissible).

[105] In re Estate of Ohrt, 585 N.W.2d 259 (Iowa 1998).

[106] Matter of Estate of Hale, 704 S.W.2d 725 (Tenn.App.1985). *See also* Koch v. James, 670 N.E.2d 113 (Ind.App.1996); Matter of Wernet's Estate, 596 P.2d 137 (Kan.1979).

to treat his children equally should have persuaded the court to ignore the preference for specific devises, but this is not obvious.[107]

In another case, a will left 30% of the residue, including the testator's funeral home stock, to the testator's wife. The stock was worth more than 30% of the estate. The court said the wife got only 30% of the estate because the testator "obviously intended" his children to get 70%.[108]

Some planners recommend that wills making substantial general devises include a clause that reduces the devises pro rata in case the testator's estate shrinks considerably in value after the will is executed, in order to avoid wiping out the residue.[109]

Other Factors

Factors other than the type of devise may affect the order of abatement. Historically, personal property was exhausted before real estate in paying claims. A few states retain vestiges of this idea,[110] but the UPC treats both types of property identically.[111]

Some states favor certain devisees in abatement. In Iowa, gifts to the testator's spouse abate last; even a specific devise to a child abates before a residuary devise to a spouse.[112] No such preference appears in the text of the UPC, but the comment to § 3–902 states that "it is commonly held, even in the absence of a statute, that general legacies to a [spouse], or to persons with respect to which the testator is in loco parentis, are to be preferred to other legacies *in the same class* because this accords with the probable purpose of the legacies."[113]

Exoneration

At common law, specific devisees could, if the property was subject to a mortgage on which the testator was personally liable, insist that the mortgage be "exonerated," *i.e.*, the mortgage be paid from the assets in the residuary estate.[114] The UPC, however, provides that "a specific devise passes subject to

---

[107] "A typical problem is . . . an older married couple had a home worth nearly $1 million but little else. The family home may have to be sold even though one or more of the children want to keep it in the family. Without other assets or life insurance [or a sale], there's no easy way to create three equal shares." Jurinsky, *Planning for the Medium-Sized Estate Presents Special Challenges*, 30 Est.Plan. 398, 403 (2003).

[108] West v. Francioni, 488 So.2d 571 (Fla.App.1986).

[109] J. Price & S. Donaldson, *Contemporary Estate Planning* § 4.17 (2016).

[110] 2 F. Pollock & F. Maitland, *A History of English Law* 345 (2d ed. 1898); Hurt v. Smith, 744 S.W.2d 1 (Tex.1987); Kan.Stat. § 59–1405.

[111] UPC § 3–902. *See also* Iowa Code § 633.436; N.Y. E.P.T.L. § 13–1.3; 20 Pa.Stat. § 3541(a); In re Estate of Oberstar, 709 N.E.2d 872, 874 (Ohio App.1998).

[112] Folkerds v. United States, 494 F.2d 749 (8th Cir.1974); Iowa Code § 633.436. *But see* In re Estate of Kraft, 186 N.W.2d 628 (Iowa 1971) (contrary intent shown).

[113] Emphasis added. *Compare* Cal.Prob.Code § 21402 (preference for relatives within specific and general devises). *Compare* In re Estate of Oberstar, 709 N.E.2d 872, 875 (Ohio App.1998) (refusing to give preference to general devise to relative over general devise to non-relative).

[114] Martin v. Johnson, 512 A.2d 1017 (D.C.App.1986); Paulus, *Exoneration of Specific Devises: Legislation vs. the Common Law,* 6 Willamette L.J. 53, 55 (1970). However, this could be altered by a contrary direction in the will. Gaymon v. Gaymon, 519 S.E.2d 142, 146 (Va.1999) (devise "subject to encumbrances").

any mortgage," absent evidence of the testator's contrary intent.[115] A direction in the will to "pay all my debts" is not enough to show an intent to exonerate specific devises.[116]

Often land subject to a mortgage was held in joint tenancy by the decedent and another. The UPC provision applies only to specific devises, but some courts have denied claims for exoneration or contribution against the decedent's estate by the surviving joint tenant.[117] Others hold that if both tenants were obligated on the mortgage, the survivor who pays the debt is entitled to contribution.[118]

If an insurance policy is pledged as collateral for a loan, some courts reimburse the beneficiary from the insured's estate if the pledgee collects the debt from the policy unless there is "evidence of an unequivocal intention on the part of the [decedent insured] that the proceeds of [the] policy be utilized as the primary fund for satisfaction of his indebtedness."[119]

§ 6.5 Lapse

A will leaves Blackacre "to Alice." If Alice was alive when testator's will was executed but dies before the testator, who gets Blackacre?[120] Several solutions are possible.

If Alice is dead, she cannot literally enjoy the devise—"you can't take it with you." Under the common law, if Alice predeceases the testator, the gift to her fails, just as in intestacy persons who predecease the decedent cannot inherit.[121] But, if the devise to Alice included an alternate devise to Alice's estate, *e.g.*, "if Alice predeceases me, then I give Blackacre to her estate" the gift does not fail but vests in her estate.

---

[115] UPC § 2–608. *See also* Cal.Prob.Code § 21131; Or.Rev.Stat. § 115.255; BGB (German Civil Code) § 2165; Vukmir v. Vukmir, 74 P.3d 918 (Alaska 2003) (same principle applied to option to purchase).

[116] UPC § 2–609; Or.Rev.Stat. § 115.001.

[117] Matter of Estate of Zahn, 702 A.2d 482 (N.J.Super.App.Div.1997); Mellor v. O'Connor, 712 A.2d 375 (R.I.1998); Wis.Stat. § 854.05 (if estate pays mortgage, can get subrogation from surviving joint tenant).

[118] Estate of Perry, 978 S.W.2d 28 (Mo.App.1998); Sarbacher v. McNamara, 564 A.2d 701 (D.C.App.1989); In re Estate of Shoaf, 750 N.E.2d 426 (Ind.App.2001). In Goldstein v. Ancell, 258 A.2d 93 (Conn.1969), where the survivor was not liable on the mortgage, she was allowed total exoneration. *See also* Ogan v. Ogan, 702 N.E.2d 472 (Ohio App.1997). In Matter of Estate of Brown, 764 P.2d 373 (Colo.App.1988), a direction in the will that "bequests be conveyed free of encumbrances" was extended to property passing in joint tenancy.

[119] Matter of Estate of Winstead, 493 N.E.2d 1183, 1189 (Ill.App.1986). *See also* Falk v. Vreeland Trading Corp., 325 S.E.2d 333 (S.C.App.1985).

[120] If Alice was dead when the will was signed, the devise to Alice was said to be void, but today, the treatment of void devises and lapsed devises is essentially the same.

[121] 2 W. Blackstone, *Commentaries* 513 (1766); *Restatement (Third) of Property (Wills and Other Donative Transfers)* § 1.2 (1999). The English Wills Act 1837 distributed the devised property as if the devisee had survived the testator, but in 1982 the Act was amended to give the devised property to the devisee's descendants, as is typical under American statutes. Administration of Justice Act 1982, § 19. *See also* BGB (German Civil Code) § 2069 which presumes that the testator intended that if the devisee is a descendant who dies before the testator the devise should pass to the devisee's descendants, who take in the proportions prescribed by the intestacy laws. Under Italian Codice Civile art. 467 the idea of representation (*see* Section 2.2, note 7) extends to wills so the result is similar to an American antilapse statute.

More commonly, however, potential gifts to estates arise in the case of inter-vivos instruments, often where the estate is not even named as an alternate beneficiary. For example, if a donor transfers land to his wife for her life, remainder to his son, the son has a vested remainder. If the son predeceases the wife, then upon her death, the land passes to the son's estate. Or, when a man had a bond registered in his name "as trustee for Audrey" and Audrey later predeceased the trustee, the bond passes to Audrey's estate because the gift was vested.[122] A similar result has been reached in construing wills made pursuant to a contract. A husband and wife executed a contractual will. The devisees named in the will who died after the wife but before the husband were held to have vested interests as soon as the wife died which passed to their estates.[123] On the other hand, a deed purporting to transfer land to a person who is dead when the deed is executed is generally held to be void, conveying no interest at all.

When property passes to the estate of a deceased person, the question arises whether the property is distributed to the deceased person's heirs or devisees. In the case of a vested inter-vivos gift, the answer is simple because when the holder of the vested interest dies, he or she has a property interest that is included in his probate estate and, thus, passes to whoever succeeds to the probate estate. But, in the case of a testamentary devise to the estate of a deceased person, such as the gift of Blackacre "to Alice's estate," some cases hold that Alice's will cannot dispose of the property by her will. The theory is that because she did not own Blackacre when she died, Blackacre did not become part of her estate so her will is irrelevant in determining the takers to Blackacre.[124] In states adopting that view, Blackacre passes to Alice's heirs rather than to the beneficiaries of her will. The UPC, however, rejects this view, allowing Alice's will to control who takes Blackacre, at least if the will purports to dispose of property acquired by her estate after her death.[125]

Antilapse Statutes

Today, all states have "antilapse" statutes that in many cases reject the common-law rule that gifts to persons who predecease the testator lapse. Most of these statutes provide that, unless the will otherwise provides, if a devisee predeceases the testator the devised property passes to any descendants of the devisee who survive the testator.[126] Descendants of the devisee more remote than children take by representation.[127]

---

[122] In re Estate of Zukerman, 578 N.E.2d 248 (Ill.App.1991). *See also* Detroit Bank & Trust Co. v. Grout, 289 N.W.2d 898 (Mich.App.1980); First Nat. Bank v. Anthony, 557 A.2d 957 (Me.1989).

[123] Matter of Estate of Anderson, 865 P.2d 1037, 1042 (Kan.App.1993). *See also* Young v. Young, 569 N.E.2d 1 (Ill.App.1991). *But* in Rape v. Lyerly, 215 S.E.2d 737 (N.C.1975), the rights of a promisee in who predeceased the testator were held to pass to her descendants under an antilapse statute.

[124] In re Estate of Braman, 258 A.2d 492 (Pa.1969). *Compare* the inability to give an expectancy. Section 3.5, at note 296 et seq.

[125] UPC § 2–602.

[126] *E.g.*, UPC § 2–603; N.Y. EPTL § 3–3.3; Calif.Prob.Code § 21110. A list of the antilapse statutes appears in a Statutory Note to *Restatement (Third) of Property (Wills and Other Donative Transfers)* § 5.5 (1999).

[127] *See* Section 2.2, at note 41.

Antilapse statutes differ both as to the identity of persons whose bequests are protected from lapse (the protected person) and as to the substituted takers of the bequest if it is saved from lapse. To illustrate, suppose that Alice, the devisee, has three children, Barbara, Ben, and Bill. Suppose further that Alice and her son Bill predecease the testator, but Barbara, Ben, and all six of Bill's children (Alice's grandchildren) survive the testator. Under the typical antilapse statute, property devised to Alice (the protected person) would pass to Alice's issue, here, one third to Barbara, one third to Ben, and one third to be distributed equally among Bill's six children, each taking a 1/18th interest.[128] All would take directly from the testator, so the devise would not be taxed in Alice's estate or be subject to the claims of her spouse or creditors.[129] The descendants take by representation of their deceased ancestor. For example, suppose the testator devises her residuary estate to her children, Jon and Julia, both of whom predecease the testator. Jon has two children who survive the testator and Julia has three. Although all five surviving grandchildren are equally related to the testator, they do not take equal one-fifth shares under a *per stirpes* system of representation. Rather, Jon's two children each share his half, each taking one fourth of the estate, and Julia's three children each share her half, each taking one-sixth.[130] In contrast, under the UPC's system of representation, the grandchildren would take equally.

Under most antilapse statutes, if the deceased devisee has no descendants who survive the testator, the statute is inapplicable,[131] and the devise lapses. Under almost all antilapse statutes, the deceased devisee has no ability to dispose of the gift by will. The Maryland statute, however, gives a lapsed devise to the persons who take by testate or intestate succession from the devisee. Thus, if Alice had left her estate to her husband by her will, in Maryland, he would take her devise.[132]

Antilapse statutes do not necessarily apply to every devisee in a will, *i.e.*, not every devisee is protected. Some statutes apply only to devisees who are descendants of the testator.[133] Others include devises to collateral relatives. The UPC applies to devises to "a grandparent or a lineal descendant of a

---

[128] The rules governing intestate distribution for children who were adopted or born out of wedlock also apply to antilapse statutes. UPC § 1–201(5); Meckstroth v. Robinson, 679 N.E.2d 744 (Ohio Com.Pl.1996) (child of devisee born out of wedlock takes under antilapse statute).

[129] *Restatement (Second) of Property (Donative Transfers)* § 27.1, cmt. e (1987). *Compare Restatement (Third) of Property (Wills and Other Donative Transfers)* § 5.5, cmt. b (1999). However, if Alice owed money to the testator, some authorities would allow the executor to set off this debt against the share which passes to her descendants under the statute. Chaffin, *The Time Gap in Wills: Problems Under Georgia's Lapse Statutes,* 6 Ga.L.Rev. 268, 276 (1971).

[130] *See* In re Estate of Mooney, 87 Cal.Rptr.3d 115 (Cal. App. 1st Dist. 2008). Contrast the result when these children take as heirs of a decedent who died intestate. See Section 1.3.

[131] Estate of Micheel, 577 N.W.2d 407 (Iowa 1998). Under the UPC, and in most states, a devise to a spouse would not be covered by the antilapse statute.

[132] Md. Code, Est. & Trusts, § 4–403; Rowe v. Rowe, 720 A.2d 1225 (Md.App.1998). The statute presents a circularity problem when the devisee's will leaves his estate to the testator. *See* Segal v. Himelfarb, 766 A.2d 233 (Md.App.2001) Even in Maryland the devise is not subject to claims of the devisee's creditors. Also, the administrative costs of passing property through the estate of a decedent are minimized because the property passes "directly . . . to those persons who would have taken the property" from the devisee. Md. Estates & Trusts Code § 4–403.

[133] Matter of Estate of Ross, 604 N.E.2d 982 (Ill.App.1992) (devise to siblings not covered); Matter of Will of Shannon, 587 N.Y.S.2d 76 (Surr.1992) (devise to cousins); Miss.Code § 91–5–7.

grandparent, or a stepchild" of the testator.[134] The Ohio statute covers any "relative of the testator."[135] The Iowa statute covers devises to any person, other than the testator's spouse.[136] Iowa's exclusion of a spouse is fairly typical,[137] but some statutes include the testator's spouse,[138] and some cover all devises.[139]

In a devise to a trust, the trust beneficiary rather than the trustee is treated as the devisee for purposes of the antilapse statute.[140] If a trustee designated in a will predeceases the testator, another trustee is appointed to administer the trust.[141]

Antilapse statutes have been applied to revocable trusts on the theory that they are much like wills. A revocable trust provided that, when the settlor died, the assets were to go to his mother. When she predeceased him, the court gave the property to his mother's granddaughter on the theory that "a gift to be enjoyed only upon or after the death of the donor is in practical effect a legacy," so the policy of the antilapse statute should control.[142] The Third Restatement of Property agrees that antilapse statutes "apply by analogy to revocable trusts and other will substitutes."[143]

Antilapse statutes focus on the question of whether a devisee survived the testator. If the devisee survives the testator, these statutes are silent regarding whether the devisee must survive some later date. But the UPC implies a condition of survival to the time of distribution for any "future interest under the terms of a trust," whether or not the trust is revocable.[144] In the case of a testamentary trust, this would include some time after the testator died. For example, suppose the testator devises property in trust to pay the income to David for life, remainder to Cy. Both David and Cy survive the testator so the wills antilapse statute is inapplicable. Nonetheless, the UPC implies a substitutional gift to Cy's descendants who survive David if Cy survives the testator but predeceases David. This substitutional gift applies not only to trusts but also to life insurance policies, pension plans, and POD or TOD registrations. Joint tenancies and joint bank accounts, on the other hand, are

---

[134] UPC § 2–603. *See also* Matter of Estate of Worsham, 859 P.2d 1134 (Okl.App.1993) (devise to sister covered); Tex.Prob.Code § 68.

[135] Ohio Rev.Code § 2107.52.

[136] Iowa Code §§ 633.273; 633.274.

[137] Matter of Estate of Hillman, 363 N.W.2d 588 (Wis.App.1985) (devise to brother-in-law not covered); Dye v. Battles, 112 Cal.Rptr.2d 362 (App.2001) (spouse not covered). However, UPC § 2–603 now covers devises to step-children of the testator. Cal.Prob.Code § 21110(c) covers all kindred of a spouse or former spouse of the testator.

[138] In re Thompson's Estate, 518 P.2d 393 (Kan.1974).

[139] Tenn.Code § 32–3–105; Ky.Rev.Stat. § 394.400.

[140] *Restatement (Third) of Trusts* § 8, cmt. a (2003). The contrary result reached in Portales Nat. Bank v. Bellin, 645 P.2d 986 (N.M.App.1982), was based on a provision of the UPC which has been changed.

[141] *See* Section 14.6, at note 362 et seq. as to the appointment of trustees.

[142] In re Estate of Button, 490 P.2d 731, 734 (Wash.1971). *See also* Tenn. Code § 32–3–105(b).

[143] *Restatement (Third) of Property (Wills and Other Donative Transfers)* § 5.5, cmt. p (1999). *See also Restatement (Third) of Trusts* § 25, cmt. e (2001).

[144] UPC § 2–707(b). This provision is limited to trusts, according to the official comment, so as not to impede the alienability of land. *See also* Section 11.1, note 34.

excluded.[145] In states that have no statute on this subject, courts have reached various results in construing inter-vivos instruments. Some courts hold that a beneficiary of a revocable trust who fails to survive the settlor has a vested interest, while others imply a condition of survivorship with no substitutional gift to the descendants of the deceased beneficiary.[146]

Contrary Intent

Antilapse statutes, like other rules of construction, do not apply if the will (or other governing instrument) shows that the testator (transferor) intended a different result.[147] If a will says "to Alice if she survives me, otherwise to Arthur," Arthur takes rather than Alice's descendants if Alice predeceases the testator.[148] The same result has been reached if the devise is more cryptic, "to Alice and/or Arthur."[149] If the will simply says "to Alice if she survives me," most courts would interpret this to mean the testator did not want the antilapse statute to apply,[150] but the UPC disagrees. Section 2–603(b)(3) of the UPC provides that ordinary words of survivorship "such as in a devise to an individual 'if he survives me,' or in a devise to 'my surviving children' " are insufficient to override the application of the statute.[151] Although the UPC's position has been criticized by some commentators,[152] several courts have reached this result, at least where refusal to apply the antilapse statute would cause a devise to fail, *e.g.* where a will left property "to my two brothers, or the survivor," and both brothers predeceased the testator, survived by descendants. The court awarded the property to the descendants of both brothers, saying:

> Had either [brother] outlived Testator, the antilapse statute would clearly not be applicable and the surviving brother would have received the entire estate.[153] . . . The language does not indicate, in

---

[145] UPC § 2–706. The statutory language is far from clear on this question. *See* McGovern, *Nonprobate Transfers Under the Revised Uniform Probate Code,* 55 Alb.L.Rev. 1329, 1340 (1992). Cal.Prob.Code § 21110 is similar in many ways to the UPC, and it expressly excludes joint tenancy. *Id.,* § 21104.

[146] In re Estate of Mendelson, 697 N.E.2d 1210 (Ill.App.1998) (land trust); *Cf.* In re Estate of Stratton, 674 A.2d 1281 (Vt.1996) (trust for beneficiary deceased at the time trust was created is void).

[147] As to the admissibility of extrinsic evidence to show contrary intent, *see* Section 7.1, note 26 et seq.

[148] *Restatement (Third) of Property (Wills and Other Donative Transfers)* § 5.5, illus. 4 (1999). However, if Arthur also predeceases the testator, the statute may apply. *See id.,* cmt. g.

[149] In re Estate of Massey, 721 A.2d 1033 (N.J.Super.Ch.Div.1998).

[150] Erlenbach v. Estate of Thompson, 954 P.2d 350 (Wash.App.1998) (trust for two sons "or the survivor of them"); Matter of Estate of Farris, 865 P.2d 1275 (Okl.App.1993); Estate of Berdrow, 7 Cal.Rptr.2d 37 (App.1992); Polen v. Baker, 752 N.E.2d 258 (Ohio 2001).

[151] UPC § 2–603(b)(3). *See also Restatement (Third) of Property (Wills and Other Donative Transfers)* § 5.5, cmt. h (1999); UPC §§ 2–706(b)(3), 2–707(b)(3).

[152] Ascher, *The 1990 Uniform Probate Code: Older and Better, or More like the Internal Revenue Code?,* 77 Minn. L. Rev. 639, 650 (1993); Begleiter, *Article II of the Uniform Probate Code and the Malpractice Revolution,* 59 Tenn.L.Rev. 101, 128 (1991).

[153] *Accord* Matter of Estate of Burruss, 394 N.W.2d 466 (Mich.App.1986); Erlenbach v. Estate of Thompson, 954 P.2d 350 (Wash.App.1998). However, this would not be true under UPC § 2–706 (surviving brother would take half; descendants of deceased brother would also take one-half). *See also* In re Will of Bybee, 896 S.W.2d 792 (Tenn.App.1994); In re Estate of Bulger, 586 N.E.2d 673 (Ill.App.1991).

the event of the death of both brothers before the death of the testator, an intent . . . to give a preference to the children of either.[154]

One court has concluded that the UPC's antilapse provision should not apply where the testator had expressed a survivorship contingency multiple times.[155] The court found that the frequent reference to survivorship was sufficient to show an intent that the antilapse statute not apply.

Some courts have held that the phrase "per capita" in a devise to a class shows an intent not to apply the statute,[156] but others disagree.[157] A devise of the residue of an estate "including lapsed gifts" was held to make the statute inapplicable to pre-residuary devises who died before the testator.[158] But the fact that a will contained another devise to a devisee's children did not preclude them from also taking under the antilapse statute.[159] Neither does a statement in a will that "I intentionally make no provision for persons not named herein."[160] The insertion of a "living" or "surviving" requirement can also be ambiguous when the will is silent on the time of survivorship. For example, a gift to "my living brothers and sisters" may mean the brothers and sisters living when the will is signed. In this case, a gift to a sister who predeceased the testator could be saved by an antilapse statute. Or the word "living" could refer to testator's death such that only brothers and sisters who survive the testator take, and any gift to those who predeceased the testator is not saved by an antilapse statute.[161] Courts often say that in order to overcome the antilapse statute, a will must use "clear and plain language" to this effect,[162] but query if this actually reflects the results of all the cases.

Class Gifts

A devise "to my daughters" without naming them is a class gift. A class gift implies a right of survivorship: if any daughter dies before the testator without descendants who survive the testator, her share will go to the other daughters. But if the deceased daughter had descendants who survive the testator, they take her share under most antilapse statutes, including the

---

[154] Early v. Bowen, 447 S.E.2d 167, 172 (N.C.App.1994). *See also* In re Estate of Ulrikson, 290 N.W.2d 757, 759 (Minn.1980). *But cf.* Matter of Estate of Simpson, 423 N.W.2d 28 (Iowa App.1988) (statute inapplicable in devise to siblings or the survivor of them when all predecease the testator).

[155] In re Estate of Raymond, 739 N.W.2d 889 (Mich. App. 2007).

[156] Matter of Estate of Wetsel, 546 N.Y.S.2d 243 (App.Div.1989).

[157] In re Estate of Delmege, 759 N.W.2d 812 (Iowa App. 2008); Rowe v. Rowe, 720 A.2d 1225 (Md.App.1998); Estate of Renner, 895 S.W.2d 180 (Mo.App.1995); Matter of Estate of Kinnamon, 837 P.2d 927 (Okl.App.1992).

[158] Estate of Salisbury, 143 Cal.Rptr. 81 (App.1978); *Restatement (Third) of Property (Wills and Other Donative Transfers)* § 5.5, illus. 7 (1999); Colombo v. Stevenson, 563 S.E.2d 591 (N.C.App.2002).

[159] In re Roberts' Estate, 88 Cal.Rptr. 396 (App.1970).

[160] South Shore Nat. Bank v. Berman, 294 N.E.2d 432 (Mass.App.1972). *See also* Kubiczky v. Wesbanco Bank Wheeling, 541 S.E.2d 334 (W.Va.2000); Lindsey v. Burkemper, 107 S.W.3d 354 (Mo.App.2003).

[161] Allen v. Talley, 949 S.W.2d 59 (Tex.App.1997).

[162] In re Estate of Kuruzovich, 78 S.W.3d 226, 227–228 (Mo.App.2002).

UPC, which expressly includes class gifts.[163] When the statutes are not clear, many courts apply them to class gifts, but some do not.[164]

If a class member was already dead when the testator signed the will, some statutes and cases do not give her share to her descendants, on the theory that if the testator had intended to include them, the will would have said so. A devisee's death *after* the will is executed is distinguishable because the testator may not have contemplated this possibility when signing the will.[165] But under the UPC, even the shares of class members who were already dead when the will was signed go to their descendants,[166] on the theory that strong evidence should be required before assuming a testator intended to disinherit a branch of the family (the descendants of the deceased class member) simply because one member died prematurely.

Similar questions arise in construing substitutional gifts in a will or trust. A trust provided for distribution to the settlor's children "with a share by right of representation for the surviving children of a deceased child." The court held that "deceased child" referred only to children living when the trust was executed who died thereafter,[167] but the Third Restatement of Property applies its rules of construction "whether the class member died before or after the donative document was executed."[168]

Substitute Gifts

If the antilapse statute does not apply, either because a devisee is not within the group of persons encompassed by it (*e.g.*, not related to the testator) or because the devisee had no surviving descendants, the property may pass under an alternative gift in the will. A devise "to Alice or her descendants" is usually interpreted as a gift to Alice's descendants who survive the testator if she fails to survive the testator, even if Alice is not covered by an antilapse statute.[169] A devise "to Alice *and* her *heirs*," on the other hand, is usually held to mean that Alice takes the property if she survives the testator, and her heirs take nothing if she does not.[170] But such language has occasionally been construed to create an alternative gift to the devisee's heirs, for example when

---

[163] UPC § 2–603(a)(4). *See also Restatement (Third) of Property (Wills and Other Donative Transfers)* § 5.5, cmt. j (1999).

[164] Matter of Kalouse's Estate, 282 N.W.2d 98 (Iowa 1979). England at one time did not apply the statute to class gifts, but the rule has been changed. Administration of Justice Act 1982, § 19.

[165] Haynes v. Williams, 686 S.W.2d 870 (Mo.App.1985); N.Y. EPTL § 3–3.3(a)(3); Calif.Prob.Code § 21110(a) (if testator knew of the death).

[166] UPC § 2–603(a)(2). *See also* Tenn.Code § 32–3–105; N.J.Stat. § 3B:3–35; *Reporter's Note to Restatement (Third) of Property (Wills and Other Donative Transfers)* § 15.2 (2011).

[167] Chipman v. Spitznagel, 728 P.2d 971 (Or.App.1986).

[168] *Restatement (Third) of Property (Wills and Other Donative Transfers)* § 15.2, cmt. a (2011). *See also* Estate of Elmer, 959 P.2d 701 (Wash.App.1998).

[169] In re Sibley's Trusts, L.R. 5 Ch.Div. 494 (1877); 3 *Amer. Law of Prop.* § 14.14, at 616.

[170] Estate of Straube v. Barber, 990 S.W.2d 40 (Mo.App.1999); In re Dumas' Estate, 379 A.2d 836 (N.H.1977). *Contra* Jackson v. Schultz, 151 A.2d 284 (Del. Ch. 1959). As to a devise "to A and his descendants" *see* Section 11.4, at note 169 et seq.

the drafter of the will admitted "that he did not know the difference between the words 'and heirs and assigns' and 'or heirs and assigns.' "[171]

Wills sometimes provide an alternative gift if the testator and devisee die simultaneously. Some courts construe such a gift to take effect even if the devisee predeceases the testator by a substantial period.[172] More commonly the provision is construed literally even if this results in property passing by intestacy.[173]

Class gift language implies a substitutional gift to the surviving members of the class (assuming the dead class member's share does not go to his descendants under an antilapse statute).[174] This is clear, but it is often unclear whether or not a devise *is* a "class gift." A gift to a group like "children" or "descendants" is, but a gift to named persons, *e.g.*, "to Alice and Arthur," is probably not, even if Alice and Arthur *could be* described as a class, *e.g.,* as the children of John. The argument against a class gift construction is even stronger if Alice and Arthur could not be so described or if their parents had other children as well.[175]

A devise "to Alice and Arthur" may be held to create a joint tenancy; if so, there is a right of survivorship more extensive than in an ordinary class gift in that if both survive the testator and one later dies without having severed the joint tenancy, the survivor owns the whole. On the other hand, if the devise is merely a class gift and does not create a joint tenancy, then, if both Alice and Arthur survive the testator, there is no right of survivorship. Upon the death of either after the testator, his or her respective share passes through his or her estate.[176] Only if one of them predeceased *the testator* would the survivor of them own the whole as the surviving member of the class. Modern law generally presumes against joint tenancy,[177] but not against class gifts.[178]

A devise "to my children, Alice and Arthur" points in different directions: "children" suggests a class gift, but the use of names suggests otherwise. Some cases hold that "where legatees are named as individuals and are also described as a class, the gift by name" controls, so that in a devise "to my sisters Ruth and Mary" Mary's share does not pass to Ruth if Mary dies without

---

171 In re Estate of Mangel, 186 N.W.2d 276, 282 (Wis.1971). *See also* Estate of Calden, 712 A.2d 522 (Me.1998) (devise to stepson "and his heirs" passed to stepson's widow when he predeceased testator); Noll v. Garber, 784 N.E.2d 388 (Ill.App.2003) (devise "to A and his heirs" ambiguous, may mean a substitutional gift to heirs).

172 Chambers v. Warren, 657 S.W.2d 3 (Tex.App.1983); New Mexico Boys Ranch, Inc. v. Hanvey, 643 P.2d 857 (N.M.1982); *cf.* Helmer v. Voss, 646 S.W.2d 738 (Mo.1983).

173 Naylor v. Koeppe, 686 S.W.2d 47 (Mo.App.1985); In re Estate of Corrigan, 358 N.W.2d 501 (Neb.1984); Larison v. Record, 512 N.E.2d 1251 (Ill.1987).

174 *Restatement (Third) of Property (Wills and Other Donative Transfers)* § 15.2, cmt. b (2011).

175 5 *Amer. Law Prop.* §§ 22.5–22.7; In re Estate of Haneberg, 14 P.3d 1088, 1095 (Kan.2000).

176 Cooley, *What Constitutes a Gift to a Class*, 49 Harv.L.Rev. 903, 922 (1936).

177 *See* Section 3.8, at note 424 et seq.

178 *See* UPC § 6–212(b)(2) (for treatment of POD accounts). *See also* Cal.Prob.Code § 5302(b); Morton v. McComb, 662 S.W.2d 471 (Ark.1983); King v. William M. King Family Ent., Inc., 515 So.2d 1241 (Ala.1987) (devise to children creates a tenancy in common among those who survived the testator).

descendants.[179] But there is also authority to the contrary.[180] The Third Restatement of Property presumes that the gift by name controls, but this presumption is rebuttable by language or circumstances establishing "that the transferor intended the beneficiaries to take as a class, i.e., as members of a group."[181] A devise "to Arthur and the children of Alice" is usually held to be a class gift, Arthur being treated as a member of the class, even though he is not a child of Alice.[182]

Even without names, a devise which states the number of recipients, *e.g.*, "to my *two* children," or designates the shares, *e.g.*, "one-half to each," has been held to show no intent to make a class gift,[183] but not always: a devise "to Bessie Sothman and Louise Fournier, to be equally divided between them" was held to be a class gift[184] as was a devise to a group of named relatives "share and share alike."

> The fact that the testator named the members does not compel the conclusion that it was not a class gift. . . . Nor does the addition of the phrase to "share and share alike." . . . That the testator intended a devise to a class is supported by the presumption that he did not intend to die partially intestate, [the result if this were not a class gift].[185]

Courts often cite a preference for a construction which avoids intestacy, but they often ignore it too.[186]

Courts sometimes compare different parts of the will in order to deduce the testator's intention. A devise to two named persons "or to the survivor of them should either predecease me" was used to show that the testator did not intend a class gift in another devise, because she "knew how to manifest an intent to create a class or survivorship gift" when she wanted it.[187]

---

179 McGill v. Johnson, 775 S.W.2d 826, 826 (Tex.App.1989).

180 Matter of Estate of Webster, 574 N.E.2d 245, 248 (Ill.App.1991); Sullivan v. Sullivan, 529 N.E.2d 890 (Mass.App.1988).

181 *Restatement (Third) of Property (Wills and Other Donative Transfers)* § 13.2(b)(2) (2011).

182 Matter of Kalouse's Estate, 282 N.W.2d 98 (Iowa 1979) ("to my first cousins and to Frank"); Allemand v. Weaver, 305 N.W.2d 7 (Neb.1981) (to named siblings "and the children of my deceased sister, Pearl").

183 Henderson v. Parker, 728 S.W.2d 768 (Tex.1987) ("our three sons"); Dawson v. Yucus, 239 N.E.2d 305 (Ill.App.1968) ("one-half to Stewart, a nephew, and one half to Gene, a nephew.").

184 Iozapavichus v. Fournier, 308 A.2d 573 (Me.1973). *See also* Estate of Frailey, 625 S.W.2d 241 (Mo.App.1981); In re Dumas' Estate, 379 A.2d 836 (N.H.1977).

185 Estate of Frailey, 625 S.W.2d 241, 243 (Mo.App.1981).

186 For cases in which courts rejected a class gift construction even though this created an intestacy *see* Brown v. Leadley, 401 N.E.2d 599 (Ill.App.1980); Moffett v. Howard, 392 So.2d 509 (Miss.1981). McGovern has argued elsewhere that the weight given to this factor should depend upon the circumstances, because intestacy is not necessarily a bad result. McGovern, *Facts and Rules and the Construction of Wills*, 26 UCLA L.Rev. 285, 307–10 (1978).

187 Dawson v. Yucus, 239 N.E.2d 305, 310 (Ill.App.1968); *cf.* Estate of Kehler, 411 A.2d 748 (Pa.1980) (devise to "surviving" siblings did not show intent to bar the antilapse statute where another devise was expressly stated to be void if the devisee predeceased); Estate of Straube v. Barber, 990 S.W.2d 40, 46 (Mo.App.1999) (devise "to H and her heirs" not a substitutional gift to heirs; other devises showed that testator "knew how to address the possibility that a legatee would predecease her.").

The Third Restatement of Property restates most of the traditional rules for determining what is or is not a class gift, but makes the question of less importance, because "a court need not classify a disposition . . . as a class gift in order to conclude that there is an implied gift over to the other beneficiary or beneficiaries."[188]

Residuary Clause

Suppose a will specifically devises Blackacre "to Alice, Arthur, and Andrew." Alice predeceases the testator and has no descendants who survive the testator, or is not in the group covered by the antilapse statute, and this language is not construed to create a class gift or a joint tenancy. Alice's share passes under the residuary clause of the will, if there is one. The UPC so provides,[189] and courts usually reach this result even without statutory authority.[190]

Under the common law, if a devise to Andrew and Arthur was a residuary devise and one of them died before the testator, the share that the deceased residuary devisee would have taken passes to the testator's heirs.[191] This was known as the "no residue of a residue rule." Under the UPC, however, "if the residue is devised to two or more persons, the share of a residuary devisee that fails for any reason passes to the other residuary devisee, or to the other residuary devisees in proportion to the interest of each in the remaining part of the residue."[192] This is known as the "residue of a residue rule." Many courts have reached the same result without a statute, either as a general rule,[193] or because they think that the particular testator so intended.[194] Disputes over whether particular language creates a "class gift" is thus often irrelevant when the devise appears in a residuary clause, but a dispute may arise as to what is a "residuary devise." A comment to the UPC says that a devise "of all my estate" constitutes a residuary devise for this purpose,[195] but what about a devise of "all of the contents of my apartment, furniture, rugs, silverware, china, jewelry, and other personal property?" A court was unsure whether this

---

[188] *Restatement (Third) of Property (Wills and Other Donative Transfers)* § 13.2, cmt. d (2011). Civil law also implies an intent to give to the surviving devisees, without regard to whether the devise was expressed as a "class gift." BGB (German Civil Code) §§ 2094, 2158; Italian Codice Civile art. 674–75. This is also true under the UPC for residuary gifts.

[189] UPC § 2–604(a). *See also* Cal.Prob.Code § 21111(a).

[190] 2 W. Blackstone, *Commentaries* 513 (1766); Wilkins v. Garza, 693 S.W.2d 553 (Tex.App.1985). Historically, a lapsed devise of land passed intestate instead of falling into the residue, but this rule is virtually obsolete. 5 *Amer.Law of Prop.* § 21.30.

[191] *See generally,* Atkinson, Wills (1953) at 784.

[192] UPC § 2–604(b). *See also* Estate of Straube v. Barber, 990 S.W.2d 40 (Mo.App.1999); Cal.Prob.Code § 21111(b); *Restatement (Third) of Property (Wills and Other Donative Transfers)* § 5.5, cmt. *o* (1999). Section 2–604 is subject to the antilapse provision, so if a residuary devisee has descendants they would take her share, assuming the devisee is in the group covered by the provision. *Id.*, illus. 15.

[193] Matter of Estate of Winslow, 934 P.2d 1001 (Kan.App.1997); In re Leavy's Estate, 442 A.2d 588 (N.H.1982).

[194] In re Dammann's Estate, 191 N.E.2d 452 (N.Y.1963); In re Estate of Kugler, 190 N.W.2d 883 (Wis.1971). There are similar decisions in England, but "prima facie" a failed share of the residue is held to pass intestate. Parry & Kerridge, *supra* note 10, at 379.

[195] UPC § 2–604, comment. *Accord* North Carolina Nat. Bank v. Apple, 383 S.E.2d 438 (N.C.App.1989). *But see* Matter of Estate of Allen, 388 N.W.2d 705 (Mich.App.1986).

was a residuary devise and remanded to hear extrinsic evidence of the testator's intent.[196]

Intestacy

As noted under the no residue of a residue rule, courts award a lapsed residuary devise to the testator's heirs rather than the surviving residuary devisees. The theory supporting this approach is that, because the heirs are the natural objects of the testator's bounty, any intent to exclude them should be more explicit.[197] (This argument is less persuasive in wills that expressly say that the heirs should get nothing or a specified limited amount.) Even under the UPC, the heirs (defined in § 2–711) take if *all* the residuary devisees predecease the testator without descendants who survive the testator.

In the case of a nonprobate transfer, such as a living trust, a joint bank account, or an insurance beneficiary designation, if the designated beneficiary fails to meet a condition of survivorship and no antilapse provision or substitutional gift applies, the property falls into the probate estate and ultimately passes to the heirs or devisees of the transferor (settlor, creator of the account, or insured).[198]

Other Causes of Devise Failures

A devise may fail for reasons other than the death of the devisee before the testator. A devise to an animal may be held invalid for public policy reasons.[199] A devise to a witness to the will may be void under a disinterested witness statute.[200] A devisee who disclaims or who divorces or murders the testator may forfeit his interest.[201] In these cases the devisee typically is treated as having died before the testator even though the devisee actually survived. When this occurs, the property subject to the failed devise may pass to the devisee's descendants under an antilapse statute or to another beneficiary named in the will whose gift was conditioned on the devisee predeceasing the testator. For example, a will left the estate to the testator's husband or, if he predeceased her, to her uncle. The testator and her husband were later divorced. Because of the divorce the husband was treated as having predeceased his former wife and the property passed to the uncle.

> The only reason for the predecease clause was to provide a fallback beneficiary in case the husband was no longer able to take under the will. Once the husband is barred by divorce from taking the gift, the time of his death no longer has any apparent significance.[202]

---

[196] District of Columbia v. Estate of Parsons, 590 A.2d 133 (D.C.App.1991).

[197] Betts By and Through Parker v. Parrish, 320 S.E.2d 662 (N.C.1984). Some courts rationalize the result simply by saying there can be "no residue of a residue." Block v. Edge, 608 S.W.2d 340 (Tex.Civ.App.1980); Moffett v. Howard, 392 So.2d 509 (Miss.1981); Matter of Estate of Hillman, 363 N.W.2d 588 (Wis.App.1985).

[198] *Restatement (Third) of Trusts* § 8, cmt. a (2001); UPC §§ 6–212(b)(2), 6–307.

[199] In re Estate of Russell, 444 P.2d 353 (Cal.1968).

[200] Dorfman v. Allen, 434 N.E.2d 1012 (Mass.1982); Section 3.3, at note 87 et seq.

[201] *See* Sections 2.7 (homicide), 2.8 (disclaimer), 4.4 (divorce).

[202] Bloom v. Selfon, 555 A.2d 75, 78 (Pa.1989). *See also* Porter v. Porter, 286 N.W.2d 649 (1979); Bowling v. Deaton, 507 N.E.2d 1152 (Ohio App.1986).

The UPC provides that the rules governing a predecease clause should also apply in cases of divorce, homicide, or disclaimer.[203] But some courts have held that a substitutional gift in the will "if A predeceases me" does not apply if the gift fails for another reason.[204]

Planning

A devise "to my descendants who survive me, by representation" duplicates the result of most antilapse statutes when a devise is made to children of the testator; the descendants of any child who predeceases the testator will take the child's share.[205] Such language is useful because the drafter cannot be sure what antilapse statute will apply, because the law may change or the testator may change domicile or acquire land in another state. A devise in this form may cause property to pass to minor children. *e.g.*, the children of a child who predeceases the testator. For such situations it is generally desirable to put the property into a trust for the minor(s), for reasons which will be explored in Section 9.2.

Many wills provide for lapse but fail to cover all the possibilities. For example, a devise "to Alice if she survives me, otherwise to Arthur," does not say what happens if neither survives the testator. Even a devise "to my descendants" may lapse if they all predecease the testator. A substitute gift to charity should be added if the testator does not want property to pass to the relatives who would inherit in intestacy.

Even the best drafted will may not reflect what the client actually wishes to happen when circumstances change after the will is drafted. For this reason, lawyers should urge clients to review their estate plans periodically.[206]

Simultaneous Death

Simultaneous, or nearly simultaneous, death is not uncommon; for example, spouses die in the same plane crash or automobile collision. When this occurs it may be necessary to determine which one(s) lived longer. A wife was the designated beneficiary of an insurance policy on her husband's life if she survived him. Both were poisoned and were unconscious on arrival at the hospital, where they never recovered. The insurance proceeds were awarded to the wife's estate based on a finding that she had survived her husband by a few hours, because her EEG on arrival at the hospital "was not flat but rather

---

[203] UPC § 2–804(d), § 2–803(e) (homicide). However, in the case of divorce, *relatives* of the divorced spouse are also deemed to disclaim. *See also* BGB (German Civil Code) § 2097 (provision of a substitute devise should be construed to cover all cases where primary devise fails); Italian Codice Civile art. 688 (same).

[204] Ray v. Tate, 252 S.E.2d 568 (S.C.1979); *cf.* Jones v. Bransford, 606 S.W.2d 118 (Ark.App.1980) (revoked devise does not "fail" and so does not pass into residue).

[205] *Cf.* Unif. Statutory Will Act § 7(a)(1). Representation should be defined to make clear what proportion each person takes. *Id.* § 1(5). More remote descendants do not share under this language if the testator's children survive. Section 2.2, note 48. This language can be adapted for the will of a testator who has no descendants and wishes to provide for collateral relatives, *e.g.*, "to the descendants of my parents."

[206] Feldman, *Reviewing Wills and Trusts: What Planners Should Look For*, 29 Est.Plann. 299 (2002). For a model transmittal letter with such an admonition *see* Price & Donaldson, *supra* note 98, at § 4.34.

it showed some delta waves of extremely low amplitude."[207] The result in the case would have been different under the UPC which says that a person who is required to survive under the terms of an instrument must survive by 120 hours.[208] This provision has been separately promulgated as the Revised Uniform Simultaneous Death Act. The original version of this Act simply said that if "there is no sufficient evidence that the two [persons] have died otherwise than simultaneously, the beneficiary shall be deemed not to have survived."[209]

The UPC, like the Revised Uniform Simultaneous Death Act, provides that for joint tenancies the property is split equally between the estates of the joint tenants. If the above-described case of the poisoned spouses had involved a joint bank account, half the account would have gone to the husband's probate estate and half to the wife's.[210]

Provisions in Instrument

Many wills and other instruments have provisions on simultaneous death that can supersede the statute. A husband's will left his estate to his wife, with alternative devisees designated if she "dies at the same time I do." The wife survived the testator by 38 hours. His property passed to her estate, because the will was held to override a statutory requirement of 120 hour survival.[211] After this case was decided the UPC was amended to provide that the 120 hour survival requirement applies unless the language about simultaneous death in the instrument "is operable under the facts of the case." Here the alternative devise is inoperable because the wife did survive the testator, but by less than 120 hours, so the alternative devisees would take.[212]

The 120 hour provision in the UPC was designed to cover most cases of near simultaneous death without unduly delaying distribution of an estate.[213]

---

[207] Janus v. Tarasewicz, 482 N.E.2d 418, 423 (Ill.App.1985). *See also* Estate of Fletcher, 94 T.C. 49 (1990) (H's bond POD W included in W's estate when she survived him by 3 hours). In In re Estates of Perry, 40 P.3d 492 (Okl.Civ.App.2001), the court held that survival could be proved by lay witnesses and only a preponderance of the evidence sufficed. Nevertheless, it reversed a trial court's finding that the wife had survived her husband for insufficient evidence. *See also* In re Estate of Parisi, 765 N.E.2d 123 (Ill.App.2002) (reviewing many cases, finding no sufficient evidence that daughter survived her father when both found dead).

[208] UPC § 2–702(b). A similar provision in the pre-1990 Code was limited to intestate succession and wills. § 2–104, 2–601. *Cf.* Cal.Prob.Code § 6403 (intestate succession); Parry & Kerridge, *supra* note 10, at 9 (spouse must survive by 28 days to inherit).

[209] Unif. Simultaneous Death Act § 2 (1940). At one time this version was in force in 45 states. In England, on the other hand, except in the case of spouses, persons are presumed to have died in the order of seniority, *i.e.*, the oldest first. Parry & Kerridge, *supra* note 10, at 348–49.

[210] UPC § 2–702(c); Unif. Simultaneous Death Act § 4 (1993). *Contra* Heirs of Ellis v. Estate of Ellis, 71 S.W.3d 705 (Tenn.2002) (because state had not adopted § 4 of USDA, spouse who survived by 3 days took all property held in tenancy by the entirety). In Estate of Jenkins, 504 N.E.2d 1178 (Ohio App.1985), the court interpreted an earlier version of the UPC to require that the parties' respective contributions to a joint account be the basis of allocation between their estates.

[211] Estate of Acord v. C.I.R., 946 F.2d 1473 (9th Cir.1991). *But cf.* Bratley v. Suburban Bank, 515 A.2d 236 (Md.App.1986) (similar will provision did not trump a statutory 30 day survival requirement).

[212] The example given in the comment to UPC § 2–702 has similar facts but no case is actually cited.

[213] Halbach & Waggoner, *The UPC's New Survivorship and Antilapse Provisions*, 55 Alb.L.Rev. 1091, 1098 (1992).

Some wills require survival by more than 120 hours. The Uniform Statutory Will Act says that any devisee who does not survive by 30 days or more is deemed to have predeceased the testator.[214] A longer period might delay distribution by creating uncertainty as to who should take, but estates are hardly ever distributed within 30 days of the decedent's death.

Some wills require devisees to survive until the property is distributed to them. A trust called for distribution to the settlor's son when she died "if he shall then be living." This was held to mean that the son had to survive until the trust was distributed; he survived the settlor only by a few weeks, so nothing passed to his estate, thereby fulfilling the settlor's wish to benefit her immediate family.[215] Such provisions raise problems of interpretation. In a case in which the executor had made partial distributions to the devisee before he died[216] the court held that the devise nevertheless failed because the will meant a "final, court-approved distribution or settlement of the estate."[217] Another litigated issue is whether an estate should have been distributed earlier; beneficiaries of the devisees' estates may argue that they should take despite failure to survive because distribution had been unreasonably delayed.[218]

The UPC's 120 hour survival requirement "avoids multiple administrations and in some instances prevents property from passing to persons not desired by the decedent."[219] This latter can occur when a will leaves property to the testator's spouse who survives briefly and the property of both spouses thereby passes to the surviving spouse's children by a prior marriage or to the spouse's collateral relatives.[220] On the other hand, a requirement of survival in a devise to a spouse may render it ineligible for the estate tax marital deduction; in larger estates this may be an overriding consideration.[221] Therefore some wills provide that in case of simultaneous death the spouse shall be deemed to have survived the testator. Such a provision would override the Uniform Simultaneous Death Act and UPC[222] and save the marital deduction if the spouses die simultaneously.[223]

---

[214] Unif. Statutory Will Act § 11.

[215] Chavin v. PNC Bank, 816 A.2d 781 (Del.2003).

[216] As to partial distributions while an estate is being administered *see* Section 14.3, note 218.

[217] Hintze v. Black, 873 P.2d 909, 911 (Idaho App.1994). *See also* In re Estate of Long, 918 P.2d 975 (Wash.App.1996).

[218] Matter of Estate of Johnson, 811 P.2d 360 (Ariz.App.1991); Estate of Justesen, 91 Cal.Rptr.2d 574 (App.1999); Estate of Carlson, 700 P.2d 771 (Wash.App.1985).

[219] UPC § 2–104, cmt.

[220] Matter of Estate of Villwock, 418 N.W.2d 1 (Wis.App.1987) (wife survived husband by a few minutes, so all property passed under her will to members of her family).

[221] *See* Section 15.4, note 291. In In re Estate of Keller, 46 P.3d 1135 (Kan.2002), a requirement of survival by 365 days in a devise to a spouse was reduced in order to save the marital deduction.

[222] Unif. Simultaneous Death Act § 6 (1993). According to *Restatement (Third) of Property (Wills and Other Donative Transfers)* § 1.2, cmt. e (1999), any "tax advantage in treating the other decedent as the survivor" should be a factor in judicial determinations even without such a clause.

[223] Treas.Reg. § 20.2056(e)–2(e); Estate of Gordon, 70 T.C. 404 (1978).

Definition of Death

Some cases raise the question of when death occurs for legal purposes. A will left property to a friend of the testator. The friend died on May 4. The testator's death occurred on May 6 according to the death certificate, but the friend's widow argued that the testator had died earlier; even though "a mechanical life support system was able to create a heart beat in [the testator] he in fact suffered a total and irreversible cessation of all functions of his brain, and was legally dead."[224] The death certificate is only prima facie evidence of the time of death,[225] but the widow's claim was rejected, because no expert testimony supported it. "How can a lay person whether judge or juror, be expected to reach a cogent and reliable conclusion from technically complex symptoms . . . without the assistance of expert knowledge of the brain's function and pathology?"

Disappearance

The time of death can also present a problem when a person disappears. The UPC provides that a person who has not been heard from for five years and whose absence "is not explained after diligent search or inquiry" is presumed to have died at the end of the 5 year period.[226] A similar common-law presumption operates after 7 years.[227] This period may be shortened in special situations. In 2002 a New York court probated the will of a man who had last been seen in the vicinity of the World Trade Center on September 11, 2001.[228]

§§ 6.6–7.0 are reserved for supplemental material.

---

[224] Estate of Sewart, 602 N.E.2d 1277, 1279 (Ill.App.1991). According to UPC § 1–107(1) death occurs when a person has sustained "either (i) irreversible cessation of circulatory and respiratory functions or (ii) irreversible cessation of all functions of the entire brain, including the brain stem." The same phrase appears in the widely-adopted Uniform Determination of Death Act § 1.

[225] *Id.*, at 1285. *Accord* UPC § 1–107(2); Unif. Simultaneous Death Act § 5(2) (1993); In re Estate of Price, 587 N.E.2d 995 (Ohio Com.Pl.1990) (deaths treated as simultaneous despite death certificates showing they were 27 minutes apart).

[226] UPC § 1–107(5). *See also* Cal.Prob.Code § 12401.

[227] In re Estate of King, 710 N.E.2d 1249 (Ill.App.1999).

[228] In re Death of LaFuente, 743 N.Y.S.2d 678 (Surr.2002), based on NY EPTL § 2–1.7 which allows a finding of death after a shorter period of absence when a person "was exposed to a specific peril of death."

Chapter 7

EXTRINSIC EVIDENCE

Analysis

Sec.

7.1 Wills: Mistake and Ambiguity.

7.2 Integration, Incorporation by Reference, Facts of Independent Significance, and Pour-Over Wills.

7.3 Will Substitutes.

7.4 Deeds of Land: Reformation, Constructive and Resulting Trusts.

---

§ 7.1 Wills: Mistake and Ambiguity

Policy and General Rules

Suppose that a will leaves property "to Kevin." Jenna attempts to show by evidence extrinsic to the will that the testator intended that she rather than Kevin should get the property. There are two possible bases for denying Jenna's claim. The first is the parol evidence rule which applies to wills as well as to other written documents.[1] A major reason for excluding parol evidence in construing contracts is that someone may have relied on the terms of the writing. Even when courts override the parol evidence rule to reform a writing, they protect persons who have relied on the writing.[2] The reliance argument generally does not arise with wills, because even though extrinsic evidence is offered to construe a will, other persons could not have reasonably relied on the language of the will to their detriment.[3]

The Statute of Wills provides another theoretical basis for excluding any evidence of the testator's intent that is not in a signed and attested writing. Courts admit oral evidence to correct mistakes in written contracts, even those that the Statute of Frauds requires to be in writing and signed.[4] But in the case of wills, the best source of evidence of the testator's intent—the testator—is dead when the will is probated.[5] Therefore, the law imposes more stringent

---

1 *E.g.,* Or.Rev.Stat. § 41.740: "When the terms of an agreement have been reduced to writing by the parties . . . there can be . . . no evidence of the terms of the agreement, other than the contents of the writing. . . . The term 'agreement' includes deeds and wills as well as acts. . . ."

2 *Restatement (Second) of Contracts* § 155 (1981).

3 Matter of Kalouse's Estate, 282 N.W.2d 98, 108 (Iowa 1979) (dissent); Langbein & Waggoner, *Reformation of Wills on the Ground of Mistake,* 130 U.Pa.L.Rev. 521, 569 (1982). *Compare* Section 2.7, discussing the protection of bona fide purchasers when succession is altered because of homicide.

4 *Restatement (Second) of Contracts* § 156 (1981); World of Sleep, Inc. v. Seidenfeld, 674 P.2d 1005 (Colo.App.1983).

5 Cornelison argues that even testimony by settlors of living trusts as to their intent may be unreliable, but it can be "cured in the crucible of cross examination." Cornelison, *Dead Man Talking: Are the Courts Ready to Listen?,* 35 Real Prop., Prob. and Trust J. 811, 815 (2001). But dead testators are not subject to cross examination.

formal requirements for wills than for contracts, *viz.* attestation as well as a signed writing. For the same reason, courts have traditionally been reluctant to allow extrinsic evidence in interpreting wills. A "will cannot be reformed to conform to any intent of the testator not expressed in it, no matter how clearly a different intent may be proved by extrinsic evidence . . . [I]f the rule were otherwise, . . . property would pass without a will in writing, which the law demands."[6]

Mistake

Nevertheless, courts admit extrinsic evidence of a testator's intent in some situations. The typical wills act says that wills must be in writing and signed, but it does not say that every signed writing must be probated. Thus, the statute does not bar courts from refusing to probate a will that was signed by mistake or a part of a will which was included by mistake.[7] Courts sometimes say that words inserted in a will by mistake may be struck out but words omitted by mistake may not be added to the will. Thus, if a will leaves property "to my brothers and sisters," and the word "brothers" was included by mistake, a court can delete it,[8] but if a devise to the testator's son was left out in error, the court cannot add it.[9]

The distinction between adding and deleting words offered for probate is explained by the wills act, but the policy considerations in both cases are the same.[10] Whether words are added or deleted, the same threat exists of untrustworthy evidence, unrebuttable by the testator. Moreover, striking words may have the same practical effect as adding them. For example, suppose a will left property to the testator's nephew and "Mabel Schneikert, his wife." The nephew's wife was named Evelyn. The court awarded the property to Evelyn, finding that she was the intended devisee, because it was possible to achieve the desired result by striking the words "Mabel Schneikert," leaving "a bequest to 'Raymond Schneikert and his wife.' . . . A mistake in description may be corrected by rejecting that which is shown to be false, but no words may be inserted."[11]

Some courts refuse to probate a will when extrinsic evidence shows that it was not meant to operate as a will. According to the Third Restatement of Property, a clear expression of testamentary intent in a document "raises a strong (but not irrebuttable) presumption" of testamentary intent that can be

---

[6] Matter of Estate of Frietze, 966 P.2d 183, 186 (N.M.App.1998). *See also* In re Reynette-James, [1976] 1 W.L.R. 161, 166 (Ch.1975).

[7] In re Estate of Herbert, 979 P.2d 39, 51–52 (Haw.1999); Matter of Estate of Smelser, 818 P.2d 822, 826 (Kan.App.1991); Estate of Gillespie, 903 P.2d 590, 592 (Ariz.1995) (will denied probate because testator did not know what it said). *But see* Estate of Smith, 71 Cal.Rptr.2d 424, 431 (App.1998) (will probated although testator allegedly intended a different distribution).

[8] In re Fenwick, [1972] V.R. 646. Contrast mistakes of fact, discussed *infra* at note 71.

[9] Knupp v. District of Columbia, 578 A.2d 702, 703 (D.C.App.1990) (name of residuary devisee omitted by mistake); First Interstate Bank v. Young, 853 P.2d 1324, 1328 (Or.App.1993); In re Estate of Smith, 599 N.E.2d 184 (Ill.App.1992).

[10] Warren, *Fraud, Undue Influence, and Mistake in Wills*, 41 Harv.L.Rev. 309, 333–34 (1928); Hirsch, *Inheritance and Inconsistency*, 57 Ohio St.L.J. 1057, 1098–1102 (1996).

[11] Breckheimer v. Kraft, 273 N.E.2d 468 (Ill.App.1971). For other cases raising the question which of two "wives" was intended *see* Section 2.12.

rebutted by clear contrary evidence.[12] Other courts disagree; one refused to admit evidence from a contestant that the testator "didn't really mean it; he was merely bluffing," because this "would leave every will open to attack as to the alleged testator's 'real' intent, and would deprive testators of any certainty as to the eventual disposition of their estates."[13]

Ambiguity

The rule barring courts from adding words omitted from a will is sometimes displaced by another rule that allows courts to use extrinsic evidence in order to resolve "latent ambiguities" in wills.[14] For example, a will left the testator's estate to his "nieces and nephews." The testator had only one niece and one nephew, but his wife had nineteen. He had told his lawyer that he wanted his estate to go to his 21 nephews and nieces including those of his wife. The court construed the will to include them even though words like "nieces and nephews" are normally construed to exclude relatives by marriage. "A latent ambiguity surfaced when the language of the devise did not square with the actual number of blood nieces and nephews," and extrinsic evidence could be used to resolve it.[15] Likewise, when a will expressed the testator's "desire" that an individual be allowed to buy property, the court used extrinsic evidence to decide whether this language was precatory.[16]

Wills that purport to devise property that the testator does not own may also be deemed "ambiguous." A testator who devised "all of the lots that I own on Suber Street" did not own any such land but owned other land known as "the Suber property." This "latent ambiguity" allowed extrinsic evidence of her intent to devise this property.[17] A similar mistake often arises in the designation of a devisee. A will left property to "Mary Beverly Peters of Spottsylvania." The testator had a niece named Mary *Beaumont* Peters in Spottsylvania, and a great niece named Mary Beaumont Peters who lived elsewhere. The court used extrinsic evidence to identify the person intended.[18] Mistakes in the designation of an intended devisee frequently occur in

---

[12] *Restatement (Third) of Property (Wills and Other Donative Transfers)* § 3.1, cmt. g (1999). *See also* Cal.Prob.Code § 6111.5 ("extrinsic evidence is admissible to determine whether a document constitutes a will"); *cf.* Fine v. Cohen, 623 N.E.2d 1134, 1138 (Mass.App.1993) (parol evidence admissible to show a trust was not intended to be binding).

[13] Matter of Estate of Duemeland, 528 N.W.2d 369 (N.D.1995). *See also* Taliaferro v. Taliaferro, 921 P.2d 803 (Kan.1996) (living trust).

[14] The statute cited in note 1 *supra* allows parol evidence "to explain an ambiguity."

[15] Matter of Estate of Anderson, 359 N.W.2d 479, 480 (Iowa 1984). *See also* Clymer v. Mayo, 473 N.E.2d 1084 (Mass.1985) (devise to the testator's "nephews and nieces" construed to include step-nephews and step-nieces since testator had none); In re Estate of Fabian, 483 S.E.2d 474, 476 (S.C.App.1997) (evidence that testator intended a nephew to be included in a devise "to my brothers and sisters"). *See also* Section 2.10.

[16] Gillespie v. Davis, 410 S.E.2d 613 (Va.1991). As to the distinction between precatory and mandatory terms *see* Section 3.6.

[17] Fenzel v. Floyd, 347 S.E.2d 105 (S.C.App.1986). *See also* Matter of Estate of Frietze, 966 P.2d 183 (N.M.App.1998) (same lot devised to two people; extrinsic evidence shows which was the intended devisee). *But see* Matter of Estate of Greenfield, 757 P.2d 1297 (Mont.1988) (devise of property which did not exist held unambiguous).

[18] Trustees of Wheaton College v. Peters, 677 N.E.2d 25 (Ill.App.1997). *See also* In re Black's Estate, 27 Cal.Rptr. 418 (App.1962) (devise to "University of Southern California known as The U.C.L.A."); Legare v. Legare, 490 S.E.2d 369 (Ga.1997).

charitable gifts,[19] and lawyers drafting such devises should exercise caution in ascertaining the intended charity's correct name and not simply rely on the testator's memory.

The foregoing examples represent "latent" ambiguities; they were not apparent until one looked outside the will and discovered that no devisee (or property owned by the testator) fit the description in the will. Some courts refuse to consider extrinsic evidence when the ambiguity is patent, *i.e.*, apparent on the face of the will.[20] But the distinction between latent and patent ambiguities seems irrelevant to the policy issues involved, and many courts reject it and allow for the admission of extrinsic evidence to resolve any ambiguity. For example, when a will left the residue of the estate to nine persons, each of whom was to receive a one-eighteenth share, a court used extrinsic evidence to resolve this dilemma, saying that "whenever an ambiguity in a will exists, be it latent or patent, extrinsic evidence is admissible."[21]

The exception allowing extrinsic evidence to resolve ambiguities can be stretched to swallow the rule generally prohibiting such evidence, because "ambiguity . . . is in the eyes of the beholder and can be perceived by those who are on the lookout practically anywhere."[22] But the mere fact that parties disagree on the proper interpretation of a will does not necessarily make a will "ambiguous."[23] Courts sometimes reject extrinsic evidence, asserting that the will in question is unambiguous. A will left property to the "blood heirs" of the testator. The court excluded evidence that the testator thought that his heirs were his sisters and his child, saying "there was no ambiguity in the will" because " 'blood heirs' meant those persons who were related by blood and who would take his real estate if he died intestate," in this case, only the testator's child.[24] The law has created rules of construction to deal with questions that arise frequently, like what "heirs" means, whether "children" includes adopted children or nonmarital children, etc.[25] Do such rules render "children" unambiguous or can extrinsic evidence be used to show that the testator intended something contrary to the rule of construction? The many cases raising this issue are hard to reconcile. When a rule of construction appears in a statute, the statutory language may specify where a contrary intent should

---

19 *E.g.*, National Society for the Prevention of Cruelty to Children v. Scottish National Society for the Prevention of Cruelty to Children, [1915] A.C. 207 (H.L.) (designation found unambiguous though extrinsic evidence showed testator intended a different institution); Ventura County Humane Society v. Holloway, 115 Cal.Rptr. 464 (App.1974) (drafter sued for malpractice in incorrect designation of charity).

20 Gafford v. Kirby, 512 So.2d 1356 (Ala.1987); In re Estate of Corrigan, 358 N.W.2d 501, 503 (Neb.1984); Breckner v. Prestwood, 600 S.W.2d 52 (Mo.App.1980).

21 In re Gibson's Estate, 312 N.E.2d 1, 3 (Ill.App.1974). *See also* Matter of Estate of Brown, 922 S.W.2d 605 (Tex.App.1996); Board of Regents v. Bates, 418 S.E.2d 8 (Ga.1992); Succession of Neff, 716 So.2d 410 (La.App.1998).

22 Hirsch, *supra* note 10, at 1120.

23 In re Estate of Brownlee, 654 N.W.2d 206, 210 (S.D.2002); East v. Estate of East, 785 N.E.2d 597, 601 (Ind.App.2003).

24 Brunson v. Citizens Bank and Trust Co., 752 S.W.2d 316 (Ky.App.1988). *See also* Estate of Straube v. Barber, 990 S.W.2d 40, 47 (Mo.App.1999). As to the meaning of "heirs" *see* Section 2.4. *Compare* the notion that when a statute is unambiguous, there can be no resort to legislative history in construing it. In re Estate of Snodgrass, 784 N.E.2d 431, 435 (Ill.App.2003).

25 *See* Sections 2.9 (nonmarital children), 2.10 (adopted children).

be found. For example, in California the construction rules govern if a contrary "intention of the transferor is not indicated by the instrument."[26] Conversely, the Uniform Probate Code simply says that its rules of construction apply "in the absence of a finding of a contrary intention." This wording was intended to allow extrinsic evidence to rebut the rules.[27] The perceived strength of the policy underlying a rule of construction may persuade a court to reject extrinsic evidence of a contrary intent.[28]

Ambiguous terms in a will are not always resolved on the basis of extrinsic evidence of the testator's intent, because such evidence often is unavailable. A devise of "living room furniture" raised the question whether this included lamps, vases, statues, and candlesticks. The court found a "wide divergence in the meaning given to 'furniture' " in various dictionaries and precedents, and so resolved the question by comparing terms used in other parts of the will which indicated that the testator intended this phrase to have a narrower scope.[29]

Even if a will is ambiguous, extrinsic evidence showing an intent totally at odds with the language of the will may be rejected. Thus, a will left paintings "to the New York Museum of Fine Arts" but there was no such museum. Evidence indicating that the testator meant the Boston Museum of Fine Arts was admitted, but other evidence indicating that she wanted her cousin to have the paintings was not, because the will showed a devise to a museum, not a person.[30]

The Second Restatement of Property adopted a more liberal position with respect to extrinsic evidence, allowing a "drafting error in carrying out . . . a testator's intention" to be reformed.[31] Indeed, there is a trend in this direction. For example, the Uniform Trust Code provides that:

> the court may reform the terms of a trust, even if unambiguous, to conform the terms to the settlor's intention if it is proved by clear and convincing evidence what the settlor's intention was and that the terms of the trust were affected by a mistake of fact or law, whether in expression or inducement.[32]

---

[26] Cal.Prob.Code § 21102(b). However, in 2002 a paragraph (c) was added to say that the section does not "limit the use of extrinsic evidence, to the extent otherwise authorized by law, to determine the intention" of the testator. *See also* Last Will and Testament of Lawson v. Lambert, 792 So.2d 977, 981 (Miss.2001) (extrinsic evidence inadmissible when statute provides for apportionment of taxes unless "the decedent's will directs" otherwise).

[27] Uniform Probate Code [hereinafter UPC] § 2–601.

[28] In re Estate of Brownlee, 654 N.W.2d 206, 212 (S.D.2002) ("the language of the will must be clear to override equitable apportionment").

[29] Kelly v. Estate of Johnson, 788 N.E.2d 933 (Ind.App.2003).

[30] Phipps v. Barbera, 498 N.E.2d 411, 412 (Mass.App.1986). *See also* Estate of Kaila, 114 Cal.Rptr.2d 865, 874 (App.2001) (extrinsic evidence must "show a meaning to which the language is reasonably susceptible").

[31] *Restatement (Second) of Property (Donative Transfers)* § 34.7, Comment d (1992). *See also* England, Administration of Justice Act, 1982, § 20. *But cf.* Dye v. Battles, 112 Cal.Rptr.2d 362 (App.2001) (rejecting reformation where the testator was allegedly mistaken about the intestacy law).

[32] Uniform Trust Code [hereinafter UTC] § 415. *See also Restatement (Third) of Trusts* § 62 (2003); In re Estate of Herceg, 747 N.Y.S.2d 901 (Surr.2002) (inserting name of devisee omitted by mistake).

Reformation of living trusts and deeds has long been accepted, and with the increasing use of such documents as will substitutes, there has been a trend to assimilate the rules governing all donative instruments.[33] For example, the Third Restatement of Property provides:

> A donative document, though unambiguous, may be reformed to conform the text to the donor's intention if it is established by clear and convincing evidence (1) that a mistake of fact or law, whether in expression or inducement, affected specific terms of the document; and (2) what the donor's intention was. In determining whether these elements have been established by clear and convincing evidence, direct evidence of intention contradicting the plain meaning of the text as well as other evidence of intention may be considered.[34]

Professors Langbein and Waggoner, who have long advocated this position, say that the risk of false testimony can be reduced by requiring clear and convincing evidence, a standard that is "pitched above the ordinary preponderance-of-the-evidence standard characteristic of most civil litigation."[35] Also, they find comfort in the fact that reformation of mistakes is an equitable matter, and, thus, the questions are tried by the court rather than a jury.[36]

Nature of the Evidence

In many cases the nature of the evidence offered to show the testator's intent affects the result. Although the question posed is whether extrinsic evidence is "admissible,"[37] the trial court usually has heard the evidence, and the strength of the evidence may determine the outcome.[38] In some cases, the evidence of a mistake is overwhelming, as when a husband and wife, executing wills at the same time, mistakenly each signed the other's will. The court reformed the two wills by substituting the proper names, saying that what had occurred was "so obvious, and what was intended so clear" that there was "absolutely no danger of fraud."[39] Reading the wills literally in this case would have produced an absurdity—a testator leaving property to himself![40]

Many courts distinguish between evidence of the circumstances and alleged declarations of the testator. In a will which created a trust to support

---

33 As to reformation in deeds and living trusts *see* Sections 7.3 and 7.4.

34 *Restatement (Third) of Property (Wills and Other Donative Transfers)* § 12.1 (2003).

35 Langbein & Waggoner, *supra* note 3, at 579. *See also* UTC § 415; *cf.* Phipps v. Barbera, 498 N.E.2d 411 (Mass.App.1986) (preponderance of evidence suffices when resolving a latent ambiguity).

36 *See infra* ("Constructive Trusts").

37 Even if evidence has been admitted without objection, it may be disregarded on the theory that the bar on parol evidence is a rule of substantive law. Matter of Kalouse's Estate, 282 N.W.2d 98, 105 (Iowa 1979); Tuttle v. Simpson, 735 S.W.2d 539 (Tex.App.1987).

38 *See*, McMillen v. McMillen, 784 N.E.2d 1130, 1132 (Mass.App.2003) ("after considering a fair amount of evidence extrinsic to the will, the judge ultimately concluded that the language in question was clear and unambiguous").

39 Matter of Snide, 418 N.E.2d 656, 657–58 (N.Y.1981). *But see* In re Pavlinko's Estate, 148 A.2d 528 (Pa.1959) (denying probate to both spouses' wills in this situation).

40 *See also* Ga.Code § 53–4–55 (in construing will courts may add or delete words where "a clause as it stands is unintelligible"); *cf.* Miller v. SRS, 64 P.3d 395, 404 (Kan.2003) (courts should avoid "absurd results arising from the literal reading of statutory terms").

the testator's wife, the question arose whether the trustee should consider the wife's own resources in deciding her needs.[41] The will was ambiguous on this point, but there was testimony that, according to the testator's instructions, the will should have contained the phrase "having in mind [the wife's] separate income." This testimony was excluded, because admitting such testimony would "subvert the very purpose of the Statute of Wills." However, it was proper to consider the amount that the testator had contributed to his wife's support while he was alive.[42] A similar distinction is suggested by some statutes, *e.g.*, the rules of construction control unless the intent of the testator "as indicated by the will and relevant circumstances is contrary."[43] Some courts say that the circumstances should be considered in deciding whether or not a will is ambiguous: "a court cannot determine whether the terms of a will are clear and definite in the first place until it considers the circumstances under which the will was made."[44] Some other courts, on the other hand, reject *any* extrinsic evidence when construing a will that they consider to be unambiguous.[45]

Evidence of some circumstances, *e.g.*, the age of the testator's children when he executed his will, is hard to manufacture. One may infer that the testator must have meant "youngest" when a will referred to the time when his "oldest" child should reach 30, because his oldest child already was already 30 when the will was signed.[46] When a will left "all to Danny" and three persons with that name claimed it, the court heard evidence as to which one had the "closest relationship to" the testator.[47] A devise to "my nieces and nephews" was construed to include nieces and nephews of the testator's spouse when "there had been a warm family relationship between" them and the testator.[48]

The identity of the drafter may affect the construction of technical words.[49] If a will was drafted by a non-lawyer, a devise of "all my money" may be

---

41 This is a recurring issue. *See* Section 10.7.

42 Estate of Utterback, 521 A.2d 1184, 1188 (Me.1987). *See also* Matter of Estate of Palizzi, 854 P.2d 1256 (Colo.1993).

43 N.J.Stat.Ann. § 3B:3–33–1. Ga.Code Ann. § 53–4–56 allows courts to hear evidence of "the circumstances surrounding the testator at the time of execution" to explain ambiguities, but courts have not felt restricted by this language. Legare v. Legare, 490 S.E.2d 369 (Ga.1997).

44 Estate of Anderson, 65 Cal.Rptr.2d 307, 316 (App.1997).

45 In re Ray Ellison Grandchildren Trust, 261 S.W.3d 111 (Tex. App. 2008); San Antonio Area Foundation v. Lang, 35 S.W.3d 636, 640 (Tex.2000); Flannery v. McNamara, 738 N.E.2d 739 (Mass. 2000).

46 Matter of Ikuta's Estate, 639 P.2d 400 (Haw.1981).

47 Succession of Bacot, 502 So.2d 1118 (La.App.1987). *See also* Transamerica Occidental Life Ins. Co. v. Burke, 368 S.E.2d 301 (W.Va.1988) ("children" includes stepchildren whom transferor treated as his own); Connecticut National Bank & Trust Co. v. Chadwick, 585 A.2d 1189 (Conn.1991) (adoptees for whom testator manifested affection are included); Estate of Christensen, 461 N.W.2d 469 (Iowa App.1990) ("children" does not include a child from whom testator was estranged).

48 Martin v. Palmer, 1 S.W.3d 875, 880 (Tex.App.1999). *See also* Matter of Will of Adair, 695 A.2d 250, 257 (N.J.1997) (noting evidence of "bitter feelings" between testator and her step-children in construing her will).

49 Cal.Prob.Code § 21122 (technical words to be interpreted in their technical sense unless "the instrument was drawn solely by the transferor [who] was unacquainted with their technical sense"); Estate of Starkey v. United States, 223 F.3d 694, 703 (7th Cir.2000) (noting lack of experience of the will drafter). *See also* Section 3.6.

construed to include all the testator's assets,[50] whereas a testator who worked in a county recording office was held not to intend to include real estate in a bequest of "personal effects."[51] A "peculiar vocabulary" of the testator may be considered, *e.g.*, the testator "customarily designated a particular person by a name other than" his real one, or customarily spoke of an unrelated person as his "niece."[52] More commonly, courts resort to a dictionary or to precedents to determine what a particular testator meant with respect to words used in a will.[53]

Even when the circumstantial evidence is uncontroverted, its bearing on intent is not always clear. Circumstantial evidence may show that one construction of a will treats all the testator's children equally, but some testators do not want this.[54] Courts in recent years have been willing to construe or reform wills to achieve tax benefits that (it is assumed) the testator would want.[55] For example, courts have reformed trusts in order to make them qualify for the federal estate tax marital deduction.[56] But some courts have refused to make such changes, doubting whether the testator was so focused on tax savings.[57] One court approved the division of a trust into separate trusts in order to minimize the generation skipping transfer tax, assuming there was an intent "on the part of most testators to save taxes,"[58] but refused to change

---

[50] *Restatement of Property* § 242, cmt. f (1940). *See also* Transamerica Occidental Life Ins. Co. v. Burke, 368 S.E.2d 301 (W.Va.1988) ("children" includes stepchildren when will is not drawn by a lawyer).

[51] Kaufhold v. McIver, 682 S.W.2d 660 (Tex.App.1984). *See also* Boston Safe Deposit & Trust Co. v. Wilbur, 728 N.E.2d 264, 269 (Mass.2000) (presume that technical terms used correctly in will drafted by a lawyer); Weller v. Tagge, 854 N.E.2d 443 (Mass. Ct. App. 2006); In re Estate of Goodwin, 739 N.Y.S.2d 239, 247 (Surr.2002) (emphasizing that drafter was a "meticulous and careful scrivener").

[52] *Restatement of Property* § 242, cmt. d (1940); *Restatement (Third) of Property (Wills and Other Donative Transfers)* § 11.2, cmt. r (2003).

[53] McMillen v. McMillen, 784 N.E.2d 1130, 1132 (Mass.App.2003) (resort to precedents and American Heritage Dictionary).

[54] *Compare* In re Estate of Seaton, 481 P.2d 567 (Wash.App.1971) *with* Steinke v. Novak, 441 N.E.2d 883 (Ill.App.1982).

[55] *See* UPC § 2–806 ("To achieve the transferor's tax objectives, the court may modify the terms of a governing instrument in a manner that is not contrary to the transferor's probable intention. The court may provide that the modification has retroactive effect"). *See also Restatement (Third) of Property (Wills and Other Donative Transfers)* § 12.2 (2003).

[56] Griffin v. Griffin, 832 P.2d 810 (Okl.1992); In re Substitute Indenture of Trust, 789 N.E.2d 1051 (Mass.2003). *See also* Loeser v. Talbot, 589 N.E.2d 301 (Mass.1992) (changing a general power into a special to avoid taxation in donee's estate); Simches v. Simches, 671 N.E.2d 1226 (Mass.1996) (gift to grandchildren changed to children in order to avoid generation skipping tax); UTC § 415 (court may modify trust in order to achieve settlor's tax objectives); In re Estate of Keller, 46 P.3d 1135 (Kan.2002) ("365" "construed" to mean "60" in order to save the marital deduction—*see* Section 15.4.).

State court decisions reforming wills for tax purposes are sometimes ignored in federal tax cases. Estate of Rapp, 140 F.3d 1211 (9th Cir.1998) (marital deduction denied despite state court reformation of will). In In re Harris Testamentary Trust, 69 P.3d 1109, 1111 (Kan.2003), a tax-reformation case was taken to the state supreme court in order to avoid the limitations of *Bosch* which, absent a supreme court determination, would have not allowed the trial court determination of property rights to be determinative in a federal tax matter. Reformation to qualify a trust for the estate tax charitable deduction is expressly countenanced by Int.Rev.Code § 2055(e)(3).

[57] Estate of Heim v. Commissioner, 914 F.2d 1322 (9th Cir.1990); Estate of Nicholson, 94 T.C. 666 (1990); Wisely v. United States, 893 F.2d 660 (4th Cir.1990).

[58] *See also* BankBoston v. Marlow, 701 N.E.2d 304 (Mass.1998).

the will in order to confer a general power of appointment on the testator's sons even though this would save "very substantial federal taxes" because it might allow the testator's grandchildren to lose their inheritance. The testator did not intend "to evade taxes at the cost of the dispository scheme."[59] Lawyers who draft estate plans that do not maximize tax savings because the client has other objectives should make this clear in writing to avoid later claims that "tax planning was overlooked."[60]

Some evidence of intent is more reliable than other evidence of intent. A court remanded a case for consideration of extrinsic evidence to resolve an ambiguity but said that "self-serving statements by [devisees] as to their understanding of the testator's intent would not be admissible."[61] Courts often rely on testimony by the attorney who drafted a will in determining what the testator intended,[62] even though the drafting attorney may have an interest in avoiding liability for malpractice if the testator's intent is frustrated.[63] Written extrinsic evidence seems more reliable than oral evidence. But these distinctions have not crystallized into firm rules.[64] Even a genuine written expression of a testator's wishes may have been intended as precatory rather than legally binding when it was not included in the will.[65]

Scope of Appellate Review

Questions of construction of a will are often resolved simply on the basis of the language of the will (plus any applicable rules of construction), either because no extrinsic evidence of the testator's intent is offered or because such evidence is inadmissible. These decisions are viewed differently on appeal from those in which a fact finder relied on extrinsic evidence. "Interpretation of a will generally is a question of law as long as the court determines the meaning of the document solely from its language and not from any surrounding circumstances."[66] But when a trial court properly considers extrinsic evidence in interpreting an ambiguous will, the appellate court does not "reweigh

---

[59] Matter of Estate of Branigan, 609 A.2d 431, 438 (N.J.1992).

[60] Berall, *Engagement Letters Clarify a Lawyer's Representation*, 30 Est.Plan. 315, 316 (2003).

[61] District of Columbia v. Estate of Parsons, 590 A.2d 133, 138 (D.C.App.1991).

[62] Danelczyk v. Tynek, 616 A.2d 1311 (N.J.Super.App.Div.1992); Ratchin v. Ratchin, 792 N.E.2d 116, 118 (Mass.2003); Skinner v. Moore, 940 S.W.2d 755 (Tex.App.1997); *cf.* Ike v. Doolittle, 70 Cal.Rptr.2d 887, 903 (App.1998) (drafter of living trust).

[63] *See* note 68 et seq.

[64] *Compare* In re Reynette-James, [1976] 1 W.L.R. 161, 168 (Ch. 1975) (reformation of wills should be allowed if there is "written contemporaneous evidence supporting the claim") *with* Matter of Estate of Bergau, 684 P.2d 734, 738 (Wash.App.1984) (ban on declarations includes testator's "written declarations not executed under the statute of wills"). In Matter of Estate of Frietze, 966 P.2d 183 (N.M.App.1998), the court allowed testimony by the drafting attorney to resolve an ambiguity in the will, but as to an issue where the will was clear, evidence from the same attorney was not allowed.

[65] Meister, *Kids and Money*, 141 Trusts & Estates (Nov. 2002) p. 45, recommends using "letters of wishes . . . providing useful guidelines that do not . . . carry the weight of law."

[66] Schreiber v. Kellogg, 50 F.3d 264, 266–67 (3d Cir.1995). *See also* In re Estate of Armijo, 31 P.3d 372, 375 (N.M.2001); In re Estate of Kuruzovich, 78 S.W.3d 226, 227 (Mo.App.2002).

conflicting evidence" and examines "the record only to determine whether substantial evidence exists to support the trial court's action."[67]

Malpractice

Malpractice suits have added a new dimension to the extrinsic evidence problem. Disappointed devisees have successfully sued attorneys for drafting wills that allegedly omitted a devise which the testator intended for them. "A lawyer who admits that he omitted from a will a residuary clause requested by the testator . . . has facially demonstrated an obvious lack of care and skill."[68] The net result is that "the intended beneficiaries receive what they would have gotten if the court could have implemented the defective will, but a pointless wealth transfer from the attorney to a third party also occurs."[69] This is one reason why reformation is a better vehicle than malpractice for remedying a mistake.[70]

Mistake of Fact

In contrast to the civil law,[71] American courts traditionally did not give relief when a will was alleged to have been made under a mistake of fact.[72] (If the mistake amounted to an "insane delusion," the traditional approach was different; this is discussed in treating incapacity.[73])

Materiality is the great difficulty. If a clause was omitted from a will by mistake, presumably the testator would have wanted it to be inserted if the omission had been noticed, but when a testator is mistaken as to a fact, it is often unclear what she would have desired had she known the truth. Mistakes of fact in a contract are distinguishable because they usually result in a markedly unequal exchange—*e.g.*, a $100,000 claim settled for $1,000 because the plaintiff mistook the extent of his injuries.[74] In wills, it is harder to determine what the testator would have done but for the mistake.

The Uniform Probate Code has long provided that, if a testator fails to provide in a will "for a living child solely because he believes the child to be dead," the child gets an intestate share.[75] This is a strong case for believing

---

[67] In re Estate of Pouser, 975 P.2d 704, 709 (Ariz.1999). *See also* Matter of Estate of Klein, 434 N.W.2d 560 (N.D.1989); In re Estate of Lord, 795 A.2d 700, 703 (Me.2002). A trial court's determination that a will is "ambiguous," thus, allowing extrinsic evidence, is a question of law. Estate of Kaila, 114 Cal.Rptr.2d 865, 874 (App.2001).

[68] Hamilton v. Needham, 519 A.2d 172, 175 (D.C.App.1986).

[69] Hirsch, *Inheritance Law, Legal Contraptions, and the Problem of Doctrinal Change*, 79 Or.L.Rev. 527, 558 (2000). This "pointless wealth transfer" may be avoided if the lawyer sued for malpractice can intervene in the will proceedings. *See* Matter of Estate of Lohr, 497 N.W.2d 730 (Wis.App.1993). In Estate of Hurst v. Hurst, 769 N.E.2d 55 (Ill.App.2002), a malpractice action against the drafter of a note was held not to give the affected persons an "adequate remedy" which would bar their claim for reformation of the note.

[70] See UPC § 2–805.

[71] The German Civil Code allows wills based on a material mistake of fact by the testator to be challenged. BGB § 2078; *cf.* Italian Codice Civile art. 624 (devise can be challenged if induced by a mistake of fact).

[72] In re Estate of Angier, 552 A.2d 1121 (Pa.Super.1989); In re Estate of Young, 738 N.Y.S.2d 100 (App.Div.2001); Witt v. Rosen, 765 S.W.2d 956 (Ark.1989) (gifts made to relatives).

[73] *See* Section 5.1.

[74] *Restatement (Second) of Contracts* § 152, illus. 12 (1981).

[75] UPC § 2–302(c). *See also* Calif.Prob.Code § 21622.

that a mistake was material, but even here the testator might have disinherited a child with whom she had no contact even had she known that her child was alive.[76]

Modern authorities, such as the Third Restatement of Property and the Uniform Probate Code (revised on this point in 2008), authorize reformation as a general remedy for a mistake of fact proved by clear and convincing evidence.[77]

Fraud

Courts are more receptive to claims of fraud than mistake. Here, too, it is necessary to show that the fraud induced the testator to make the devise,[78] but someone who misrepresents a fact to a testator probably thought the fact was material to the testator, and it is not implausible to assume he was right. Thus, a will which left the testator's property to her daughters was set aside because the daughters had told the testator that their father had left all his property to his sons.

> While a mistake as to an extrinsic fact made by the testator on his own affords no ground for setting aside a will, the situation is different when the mistake is caused by a misrepresentation made to him by a beneficiary. . . . It has also generally been held that in order to invalidate a will resulting from a misrepresentation of an extrinsic fact, it must be shown that the beneficiary knew the representation to be false. . . . We hold that there was no requirement under the facts of this case for the proof to show that [the daughters] knew that the statement . . . was false. . . . [I]t was made in reckless disregard of its truth or falsity, and no more should be required.[79]

Even nondisclosure may amount to fraud if there is a confidential relationship between the testator and another.[80] Claims of fraud are usually linked with undue influence; misrepresentations are regarded as a type of undue influence on the testator.[81] Other aspects of undue influence will be discussed in Section 5.3.

Constructive Trusts

The bar against adding words to a will does not apply to cases of wrongful conduct. A testator expressed a desire to make a new will leaving property to

---

[76] Matter of Araneo, 511 A.2d 1269 (N.J.Super.Law Div.1985).

[77] *See Restatement (Third) of Property (Wills and Other Donative Transfers)* § 12.1 (2003); UPC § 2–805.

[78] Edwards v. Shumate, 468 S.E.2d 23 (Ga.1996) (claim of fraud rejected because not shown to have affected will).

[79] Matter of Estate of Vick, 557 So.2d 760, 768–69 (Miss.1989). *See also* Geduldig v. Posner, 743 A.2d 247, 260–61 (Md.App.1999); *Restatement (Second) of Property (Donative Transfers)* § 34.7, cmt. c (1992).

[80] Rood v. Newberg, 718 N.E.2d 886, 893 (Mass.App.1999) (because of confidential relationship grandson had a duty to disclose to testator that she was mistaken in believing son had stolen from her); *Restatement (Third) of Property (Wills and Other Donative Transfers)* § 8.3, cmt. j (2003).

[81] In re Estate of Berry, 661 N.E.2d 1150, 1152 (Ill.App.1996); Matter of Estate of Lint, 957 P.2d 755, 765 (Wash.1998) (findings of fraud support conclusion of undue influence).

A, but *B*, the beneficiary of her existing will, prevented her from doing so by false representations and physical force. *A's* suit against *B* after the testator died alleging those facts was upheld. A devisee who "prevents the testator by fraud, duress, or undue influence from revoking the will and executing a new will in favor of another . . . holds the property thus acquired under constructive trust for the intended legatee." The statute of wills was no bar because "the will has full effect" but "equity, in order to defeat fraud, raises a trust in favor of those intended to be benefitted by the testator."[82]

Constructive trusts (like other trusts) were historically enforced in equity and, thus, there is no right to trial by jury. This may explain why courts allow oral evidence of a decedent's intent in such suits. The hostility to such evidence is partly based on the fear that inexperienced juries cannot assess it adequately. But the jurisdictional boundaries between law and equity are increasingly ignored, as probate courts become courts of general jurisdiction.[83] The Second Restatement of Torts allows a tort suit against anyone who "by fraud, duress or other tortious means intentionally prevents another from receiving from a third person an inheritance or gift that he would otherwise receive" if there is reasonably certain proof that such a devise or bequest would have been made.[84]

The Third Restatement of Property extends the constructive-trust remedy to mistake, for example where the testator performed a revocatory act on the wrong document.[85]

Promises

Constructive trusts also are imposed on devisees who promised the testator that they would give the devised property to another person. A mother with an incompetent child, Josh, left half her estate to Josh's sister, Sally, who agreed to look after Josh. When Sally refused to do so, the court imposed a constructive trust on her.[86]

The trustee's promise need not be connected with making a will. If a decedent leaves a will unchanged in reliance on a devisee's promise—or makes no will at all, relying on an heir's promise to give property to another—courts will impose a constructive trust.[87] But the decedent's wishes must show an intent to impose an obligation on the devisee and not be merely precatory.[88] Furthermore, the wishes must be communicated to the devisee or heir during

---

[82] Latham v. Father Divine, 85 N.E.2d 168 (N.Y.1949). *See also Restatement (Third) of Property (Wills and Other Donative Transfers)* § 8.3, cmt. *l* (2003). *Compare* Section 2.7.

[83] In re Will of Artope, 545 N.Y.S.2d 670 (Surr.1989) (probate court has jurisdiction over claim that devisee had agreed to transfer property to another). *See also* Matter of Lembach's Estate, 622 P.2d 606 (Colo.App.1980).

[84] *Restatement (Second) of Torts* § 774B (1979). Followed in Davison v. Feuerherd, 391 So.2d 799 (Fla.App.1980).

[85] *Restatement (Third) of Property (Wills and Other Donative Transfers)* § 4.1, cmt. f (1999).

[86] Kauzlarich v. Landrum, 274 N.E.2d 915 (Ill.App.1971); *cf. Restatement (Second) of Contracts* § 69 (1981).

[87] Kramer v. Freedman, 272 So.2d 195 (Fla.App.1973); *Restatement (Third) of Trusts* § 18(2) (2001).

[88] *Id.*, cmt. d. As to precatory language, *see* Section 3.6.

the decedent's lifetime.[89] This restriction seems odd, because a devisee would seem to be unjustly enriched by taking property that was intended for another even if she learned of this intent only after the decedent's death (assuming she has not changed her position in reliance on the devise).[90]

It is difficult to reconcile the enforcement of constructive trusts based on oral statements of a testator with the statutory requirements for wills or the requirement of a writing for contracts to make a will.[91] Courts impose a high standard of proof for a constructive trust. "The agreement to hold property in trust must be shown by clear and convincing evidence . . . because the proof must . . . substitute for the normal statutory requirements of the Wills Act."[92] Interested testimony may be excluded in some states by a Dead Man's Act.[93]

The term "trust" is somewhat misleading in the context of a constructive trust, because the devisee upon whom the trust is imposed does not act like a normal trustee who manages property for the beneficiaries. Rather, the devisee is ordered to turn the property over to the beneficiary. If continuing management duties are contemplated, the devisee who has refused to act as agreed, thus making a suit to impose the trust necessary, is usually replaced by another trustee.[94]

This type of constructive trust has a long history, under various names. It closely resembles the *fideicommissum* of Roman law.

> Instead of making a legacy directly to an intended beneficiary, a testator could entrust (*committere*) to the faith (*fides*) of an intermediary . . . that property should be conveyed to a beneficiary. . . . Initially . . . the only entitlement the beneficiary had was a moral one which was not enforceable in the courts. That changed when the emperor Augustus introduced a jurisdiction charged with the enforcement of such trusts.[95]

Blackstone in the 18th century saw a link between the Roman *fideicommissum* and the English trust, asserting that medieval chancellors, who were familiar with Roman law, had "assumed the jurisdiction, which Augustus had vested in his praetor, of compelling the execution of such trusts in the court of chancery."[96]

---

[89] *Id.*, cmt. f. However, the trust is enforceable if the devisee knows that she is to hold property in trust even if she learns the identity of the beneficiary only after the testator dies. *Id.*, cmt. e.

[90] Because "evidence of testamentary intent (the true desideratum) is essentially equivalent" in all these cases, Professor Hirsch also finds the constructive trust to be "an imperfect antidote" to this problem. Hirsch, *Inheritance Law, Legal Contraptions, and the Problem of Doctrinal Change*, 79 Or.L.Rev. 527, 558 (2000).

[91] *See* Section 3.9.

[92] *Restatement (Third) of Trusts* § 18, cmt. h (2003).

[93] Kamberos v. Magnuson, 510 N.E.2d 112 (Ill.App.1987).

[94] *Restatement (Third) of Trusts* § 18, cmt. b (2003).

[95] Johnston, *Trusts and Trust-like Devices in Roman Law*, in Itinera Fiduciae (ed. Helmholz/Zimmermann 1998), pp. 45–46.

[96] 2 W. Blackstone, *Commentaries* 328 (1766). One objection to the connection seen by Blackstone between the English trust and the Roman *fideicommissum* was that the latter was

Semi-Secret Trusts

Some wills show on their face that a devisee was intended to give the devise to others who are not identified in the will. These are sometimes called "semi-secret" trusts as contrasted with "secret" trusts in which the will gives no clue that a trust was intended. Strangely, secret trusts can be enforced under constructive trust principles whereas semi-secret trusts typically are not. Arguably, semi-secret trusts provide a stronger case for enforcement because extrinsic evidence showing the intended beneficiaries is not inconsistent with the will but rather supplements it, rather like resolving a patent ambiguity. The Third Restatement of Trusts makes semi-secret trusts enforceable and dispenses with the higher burden of proof required for constructive trusts in this situation.[97] But some courts, contrary to the Restatement, refuse to enforce semi-secret trusts. When a will directed the executor to distribute the estate "in accordance with the verbal guidelines last given by me," the court held this was invalid, because the "guidelines" were not "in writing and attested in conformity with the statute on wills."[98] Refusal to enforce a semi-secret trust does not leave the devisee unjustly enriched because he does not get to keep the property.[99] But the result leaves the *testator's heirs* unjustly enriched, because they will get property that was not intended for them.[100]

When there is no evidence of the testator's wishes in a semi-secret trust, the devised property ordinarily passes by intestacy,[101] but if the will indicates that some kind of charitable trust was intended, the property will be applied to charitable purposes generally if the specific purpose which the testator intended cannot be identified.[102]

§ 7.2 Integration, Incorporation by Reference, Facts of Independent Significance, and Pour-Over Wills

Multi-page wills can be probated even though only the last page is signed. The earlier pages are "integrated" into the will if they were present when the will was executed.[103] Ordinarily, the pages of a multi-page are stapled together.

---

always created by will, whereas the medieval use arose when (and largely because) wills of land were not allowed. *See* Section 8.2.

Generally speaking, the civil law is more receptive to parol evidence than the common law, probably because it has no civil jury. For an interesting treatment of this subject by the 14th century jurist Bartolus, *see* Graziadei, *The Development of Fiducia in Italian and French Law from the 14th Century to the End of the Ancient Regime*, in Itinera Fiduciae (ed. Helmholz/Zimmermann 1998), pp. 335–37.

97 *Restatement (Third) of Trusts* § 18, cmt. c, h (2003).

98 Matter of Reiman's Estate, 450 N.E.2d 928 (Ill.App.1983).

99 *Id. See also* In re Estate of Liginger, 111 N.W.2d 407 (Wis.1961).

100 *Restatement (Third) of Trusts* § 18, cmt. a (2003).

101 Estate of Bruner, 691 A.2d 530 (Pa.Super.1997); *Restatement (Third) of Trusts* § 18, cmt. e (2003).

102 Estate of Carper, 415 N.Y.S.2d 550 (App.Div.1979); *Restatement (Second) of Trusts* § 358, cmt. e (1959). For the application of *cy pres* to save a charitable gift, *see* Section 10.10.

103 Estate of Beale, 113 N.W.2d 380 (Wis.1962); *Restatement (Third) of Property (Wills and Other Donative Transfers)* § 3.5 (1999). For techniques to assure that all the unsigned pages will be integrated, *see* Section 3.2.

But, even if they are not, if the pages are internally coherent, a presumption arises that the pages were present when the will was signed.[104]

Other writings, even if not present at the time of execution, can also be probated if they were incorporated into a will by reference.[105] Ordinarily, an unattested document containing testamentary dispositions can be incorporated by reference into a will if the document was in existence when the will was signed *and* the will refers to the document to be incorporated. For example, a will, later republished by a codicil, recited that the testator wished to leave shares of stock to certain relatives and that he would place them "in envelopes bearing the name of each such relative and leave [the envelopes] in my Safe Deposit Box." Although the writing on the envelopes was not signed and attested, the envelopes were in existence when the codicil was signed. The court held that they were incorporated by reference into the will.[106] This case highlights the consequence of the doctrine of republication by codicil in that it was clear that all of the envelopes were in existence when the codicil was signed, while the evidence was less clear that the envelopes were in existence when the will was signed.

Attempts to incorporate by reference fail if the identification in the will is not sufficiently precise. An attempt by the proponents of an unexecuted will to have it incorporated by reference in a duly executed codicil failed. Although the codicil was stapled to the will and both were inserted in an envelope that had typed on the outside "WILL OF LAWRENCE NORTON AND CODICIL TO WILL OF LAWRENCE NORTON," there was no reference within the codicil itself that clearly designated the will as the document to be incorporated.[107]

Other courts have been less strict in permitting incorporation especially if extrinsic evidence shows that the document in question was the one mentioned in the will.[108] Even a misdescription in the will is not necessarily fatal. A will referring to a letter "dated March 25, 1932" was held to incorporate a letter dated July 3, 1933, because the letter was found with the will, its terms fit the will, and no other letter was found. This provided "reasonable certainty" that the letter was the one referred to in the will.[109]

---

[104] *Restatement (Third) of Property (Wills and Other Donative Transfers)* § 3.5, cmt. c (1999).

[105] This is the normal effect of incorporation by reference, but according to *Restatement (Third) of Property (Wills and Other Donative Transfers)* § 3.6, cmt. h (1999) the incorporated document is "treated as part of the will for purposes of" distributing the estate, but "need not be offered for probate nor be made part of the public record."

[106] Smith v. Weitzel, 338 S.W.2d 628 (Tenn.App.1960). *See also* Clark v. Greenhalge, 582 N.E.2d 949 (Mass.1991); Matter of Estate of Sneed, 953 P.2d 1111 (Okl.1998). New York is one of the few states which does not recognize incorporation by reference. In re Philip, 596 N.Y.S.2d 146 (App.Div.1993). *But cf.* In re Estate of Schmidt, 619 N.Y.S.2d 245 (Surr.1994) (statutory exception for published fee schedules).

[107] Matter of Estate of Norton, 410 S.E.2d 484, 485 (N.C.1991). *See also* Estate of Sweet, 519 A.2d 1260 (Me.1987).

[108] In re Estate of McGahee, 550 So.2d 83 (Fla.App.1989) (paper clipped to the will).

[109] Simon v. Grayson, 102 P.2d 1081, 1083 (Cal.1940). In Clark v. Greenhalge, 582 N.E.2d 949 (Mass.1991), a will referring to a "memorandum" was held to incorporate a notebook of the testator.

Republication by Codicil

A codicil which refers to an earlier will is said to "republish" it. This can cure defects to a previous validly executed will. For example, suppose Kevin signs a will bequeathing $50,000 to his friend, Andrew, who is also one of two witnesses to the will. In most states, Andrew's bequest fails because of an interested witness statute. However, if Kevin later executes a codicil witnessed by Steve and Jenna and the codicil republishes the will, then the bequest to Andrew is valid. If a duly executed codicil refers to an unattested will, the terms of the will could be given effect under the doctrine of incorporation by reference.[110] Incorporation of a typewritten document into a holographic codicil does not destroy the codicil's holographic character. Even when a holographic "codicil" appeared on the same page as the typewritten will, both were probated under the theory that the codicil incorporated the will by reference.[111]

Future Documents

To be incorporated by reference the document must have been in existence when the testator signed the will. This limitation prevents testators from using the doctrine to change their wills informally through unattested documents prepared after the will was signed. Thus, when a will left property to a friend to distribute "to the persons named in a letter or memorandum of instructions which I shall leave addressed to her," the letter could not be admitted to probate.[112] It is not enough that the document *might have been* in existence before the will was executed; its prior existence must be proved.[113] The Third Restatement of Property aids the proponent with a number of presumptions. It provides that:

> a writing that is dated on or before the day that the will was executed is presumed to have been in existence when the will was executed. If the will refers to a writing as existing when the will was executed, . . . a writing that fits the will's description but is undated is presumed to have been in existence when the will was executed. On the other hand, if the will clearly refers to a writing as one that does not currently exist but will be prepared in the future, the writing cannot be incorporated by reference.[114]

---

[110] *Restatement (Third) of Property (Wills and Other Donative Transfers)* § 3.6, cmt. d (1999); Allen v. Maddock, 14 Eng.Rep. 757 (1858). In *Maddock*, only one will was found. If there had been several, identifying which one was meant would have been a problem. *See* In re Erbach's Estate, 164 N.W.2d 238 (Wis.1969). *Compare* use of codicils to revive a will which has been revoked or to postdate a will for purposes of a pretermitted heir or omitted spouse claim. *See* Sections 4.3, 8.5, and 8.6.

[111] Johnson v. Johnson, 279 P.2d 928 (Okl.1954). *See also* In re Foxworth's Estate, 50 Cal.Rptr. 237 (App.1966); *Restatement (Third) of Property (Wills and Other Donative Transfers)* § 3.6, cmt. f (1999).

[112] Hastings v. Bridge, 164 A. 906 (N.H.1933); In re Estate of Richardson, 50 P.3d 584, 589 (Okl.App.2002).

[113] Tierce v. Macedonia United Meth. Church, 519 So.2d 451, 456 (Ala.1987).

[114] *Restatement (Third) of Property (Wills and Other Donative Transfers)* § 3.6, cmt. b (1999).

Courts sometimes say that the incorporated document must also *be referred to in the will as an existing document.*[115] The Uniform Probate Code rejects this position. It allows for incorporation by reference if the will "manifests this intent" and describes the writing sufficiently to permit its identification.[116]

When a codicil "republishes" an earlier will, a document produced between the time of execution of the will and the codicil can be incorporated. For example, when a will executed in May referred to a letter which was written the following July, the letter was admitted because a codicil executed in November had republished the will.[117]

Lists of Tangible Personalty

The Uniform Probate Code, pursuant to its "broader policy of . . . relaxing formalities of execution," allows wills to refer to a "written statement or list to dispose of items of tangible personal property" if the list is signed by the testator, even if it was prepared or altered after the execution of the will.[118] The restriction to tangible personal property seems to reflect the idea that less formality should be required for property of relatively small value, as in most estates is tangible personalty.[119] The requirement that the list be signed by the testator distinguishes this from incorporation by reference, because wills can incorporate unsigned writings or writings by someone other than the testator. The Uniform Statutory Will Act, for example, is designed to be incorporated by reference in wills.[120]

Facts of Independent Significance

If a will leaves property "to my wife" without naming her, a court may resort to evidence outside the will in order to identify the wife, even if she married the testator after the will was executed. The Uniform Probate Code, like the common law, allows wills to "dispose of property by reference to acts and events that have significance apart from their effect upon the dispositions made by the will, whether they occur before or after the execution of the

---

[115] Bryan's Appeal, 58 A. 748, 750 (Conn.1904). *See also* Estate of Sweet, 519 A.2d 1260 (Me.1987) ("reference in the will must clearly and precisely describe the extrinsic writing"); Ohio Rev.Code § 2107.05; *Restatement (Third) of Trusts* § 14, cmt. b (2003).

[116] UPC § 2–510, comment; Cal.Prob.Code § 6130; *Restatement (Third) of Property (Wills and Other Donative Transfers)* § 3.6, cmt. a (1999).

[117] Simon v. Grayson, 102 P.2d 1081 (Cal.1940). *See also* Clark v. Greenhalge, 582 N.E.2d 949 (Mass.1991); *Restatement (Third) of Property (Wills and Other Donative Transfers)* § 3.5 (1999).

[118] UPC § 2–513. For the slight differences between the original and revised version of this provision, *see Restatement (Third) of Property (Wills and Other Donative Transfers)* § 3.9, cmt. b and c (1999). In Wilkins v. Wilkins, 48 P.3d 644 (Idaho 2002), such a memorandum was held to be valid despite a later will expressly revoking prior wills. In In re Estate of Blodgett, 95 S.W.3d 79 (Mo.2003), a gift of "all tangible property" in a trust amendment was held to be effective under this provision.

[119] *Compare* the exemption of sales of goods for less than $500 from the Statute of Frauds. Uniform Commercial Code § 2–201. In Burkett v. Mott, 733 P.2d 673 (Ariz.App.1986), a $10,000 insurance policy was held to be covered by UPC § 2–513, a questionable result under the statutory language. *Cf.* Matter of Estate of Harrington, 850 P.2d 158 (Colo.App.1993) (note attempting to devise $25,000 not covered).

[120] Uniform Statutory Will Act § 3.

will."[121] The rationale is that such facts are not likely to be seriously disputed.[122] Courts have allowed devises even of the contents of a house or of a safe-deposit box under this theory, but not an unattested writing of the testator.[123]

In some cases, a testamentary gift can be upheld just as well under the canon of construction that a will speaks at the time of the testator's death. Thus, in the case of a devise to "my wife" where the testator was not married when the will was signed, the devise could be sustained under either the facts of independent significance doctrine or the canon that a will speaks at the time of death. But what of unattested acts that the will specifically refers to as having testamentary significance, such as a bequest to any "person I may hire in the future to manage my company." Here the hiring of such person after the will is signed clearly has testamentary significance as that hiring (a nontestamentary act) affects how the estate will be distributed. But it also has significance apart from its testamentary effect in that it also provides a business manager for testator's company. This unattested act can be validated under the facts of independent significance doctrine.

Pour-Over Wills

The doctrines of incorporation by reference and facts of independent significance have been used to validate a modern estate planning device, the "pour-over" will. To illustrate, suppose a couple who had created a revocable trust later executed wills leaving property to the trustees of the trust to be held pursuant to the terms of the trust. Thus, the ultimate beneficiaries of the wills could only be ascertained by looking at the trust instrument, which was not executed with the formalities prescribed for wills. The couple amended the trust after executing their wills. Could property passing under their wills be governed by the terms of this subsequent amendment of the trust? Earlier cases had refused to allow this, based on the restrictions against incorporating future documents.[124] But this court upheld the pour-over devise by treating the trust as a fact of independent significance; because the trust contained assets other than those which the will poured into it, its terms had independent significance.[125] But if the assets in the trust have only nominal value prior to

---

[121] UPC § 2–512. *See also Restatement (Third) of Trusts* § 14, cmt. b (2003); Calif.Prob.Code § 6131.

[122] Professor Hirsch finds the doctrine of facts of independent significance "perverse." Hirsch, *Inheritance and Inconsistency*, 57 Ohio St.L.J. 1057, 1084 (1996). It is not often expressly invoked in the cases, but no one seriously doubts that a devise "to my children," for example, can encompass a child born after the will was executed. *See* Section 11.2.

[123] *Restatement (Second) of Trusts* § 54, illus. 5 (1959); Matter of Estate of Nelson, 419 N.W.2d 915, 916 (N.D.1988) ("personal items used in connection with my farm"); *Restatement (Third) of Property (Wills and Other Donative Transfers)* § 3.7, cmt. c, e (1999).

[124] Koeninger v. Toledo Trust Co., 197 N.E. 419 (Ohio App.1934); Old Colony Trust Co. v. Cleveland, 196 N.E. 920 (Mass.1935).

[125] Second Bank-State Street Trust Co. v. Pinion, 170 N.E.2d 350 (Mass.1960). *See also* Canal Nat. Bank v. Chapman, 171 A.2d 919 (Me.1961); *Restatement (Third) of Property (Wills and Other Donative Transfers)* § 3.8, cmt. d (1999). *But see* South Carolina Nat. Bank of Charleston v. Copeland, 149 S.E.2d 615 (S.C.1966).

the pour-over, this makes the "independent significance" of the trust questionable.[126]

The difficulties posed by the incorporation by reference and the facts of independent significance doctrines have led most states to adopt statutes which expressly authorize pour-over wills. The Uniform Probate Code allows them "regardless of the existence, size, or character of the corpus of the trust."[127] Theoretically even a pour-over to an oral trust could be justified on the basis of independent significance, but the Code requires that the trust terms be "set forth in a written instrument." But the trust can be amended after the pour-over will is executed.[128] In an earlier version of the Uniform Probate Code, unchanged in some states, the trust instrument must be "executed before or concurrently with the execution of the testator's will,"[129] but even a later-executed trust, if funded, might be accepted as a fact of independent significance.[130]

Pour-over devises have been accepted by courts and legislatures because they perform a useful function, allowing various parts of an estate plan to be consolidated. Many persons wish to put some of their assets into an inter-vivos trust and have other assets pass to a trust for the same beneficiaries when they die.[131] Or a testator may wish to add assets to a trust created by another person. Spouses may wish to put their respective assets into a trust for their common children. Administrative costs can be reduced by consolidating the trusts of the two spouses.[132] The wife can leave her estate to the trust created by her husband's will and vice versa, depending on who dies first. Or a parent may wish to add property to a trust created by a child for the parent's grandchildren. The Uniform Probate Code allows a pour-over to a trust created by "another individual's will" if the testator of the latter will predeceased the testator of the pour-over devise.[133]

---

[126] *Restatement (Third) of Trusts* § 19, cmt. h (2003).

[127] UPC § 2–511. This provision is copied from the Uniform Testamentary Additions to Trusts Act which has been widely adopted. *See* Estate of Harper, 93 T.C. 368, 376 (1989) (pour over to a nominally funded trust is valid under statute). In Tyson v. Henry, 514 S.E.2d 564 (N.C.App.1999) the terms of a trust were given effect as having been incorporated by reference in a pour-over will even though no property had been transferred to the trust.

[128] UPC § 2–511(a).

[129] Cal.Prob.Code § 6300; Tierce v. Macedonia United Meth. Church, 519 So.2d 451 (Ala.1987) (devise to a trust "to be made" fails).

[130] *Restatement (Third) of Property (Wills and Other Donative Transfers)* § 3.8, illus. 1 (1999).

[131] The advantages of avoiding probate by using a living trust rather than a will to dispose of assets are discussed in Section 10.1. Despite these advantages, it is often inconvenient to put *all* of the settlor's assets into a living trust, particularly assets acquired after the trust is executed. An attempt by the terms of the trust to include assets later acquired by the settlor would probably fail. On the other hand, some of the advantages of avoiding probate are lost when assets are left to pass under the pour-over will. Feldman, *Reviewing Wills and Trusts: What Planners Should Look For*, 29 Est.Plan. 299, 300 (2002).

[132] *Cf.* Cal.Prob.Code § 15411 (court can authorize combining two trusts which are "substantially similar"). In Matter of Will of Marcus, 552 N.Y.S.2d 546 (Surr.1990), the court authorized such a consolidation, emphasizing its advantages, without statutory authority. *See also* Matter of Will of Daniels, 799 P.2d 479 (Kan.1990); Section 10.9.

[133] UPC § 2–511. *See also* Cal.Prob.Code § 6300.

Many states subject testamentary trusts to close court supervision. Under the theory of incorporation by reference, the trust receiving poured-over assets from the decedent's estate would be a testamentary trust subject to supervision.[134] To avoid that result, the Uniform Probate Code provides that property passing under a pour-over devise "is not held under a testamentary trust of the testator, but it becomes a part of the trust to which it is devised."[135] However, for some purposes, the pour-over will and receptacle trusts are treated as a unit. The probate court has been held to have jurisdiction to determine the validity of both when they are challenged for undue influence.[136] A provision in a trust for a spouse has been held to bar her claim to have been pretermitted in the pour-over will.[137] And where the settlor of a pour-over trust and her husband divorced, the court found that the trust and will were part of a comprehensive estate plan and revoked the husband's interest under the trust under a statute that on its face only applied to wills.[138]

If a settlor revokes the receptacle trust before dying, the Uniform Probate Code provides that the pour-over devise lapses unless the will otherwise provides.[139] But in Illinois, the devise takes effect "according to the terms . . . of the trust as they existed at the time of termination."[140]

Pour-Up Trusts

The parts of an estate plan can also be merged by going in the other direction, *i.e.*, by making an insurance policy or death benefit under a pension plan payable to the trustee under a will.[141] This technique has the advantage of not having to draft two documents, a will and a trust, so the drafter and testator can focus their attention on the terms of the will which controls all the testator's assets.

---

134 Note, *The Pour-Over Trust in Missouri*, 48 Mo.L.Rev. 523, 528 (1983). As to court supervision of testamentary trusts, *see* Section 14.3.

135 UPC § 2–511(b). *See also Restatement (Second) of Trusts* § 54, cmt. k (1959); *Restatement (Third) of Property (Wills and Other Donative Transfers)* § 3.8, cmt. e (1999).

136 Sun Bank/Miami, N.A. v. Hogarth, 536 So.2d 263 (Fla.App.1988). *See also* Davisson v. Indiana Nat. Bank, 493 N.E.2d 1311 (Ind.App.1986) (trust instrument discoverable for a will contest).

137 In re Estate of Norem, 561 So.2d 434 (Fla.App.1990). *But see* Estate of Harper, 93 T.C. 368 (1989) (wife can take under trust and elect against the will); In re Estate of Richardson, 50 P.3d 584 (Okla.App.2002) (stated intent to disinherit son in a receptacle trust did not defeat son's claim as pretermitted heir).

138 Clymer v. Mayo, 473 N.E.2d 1084 (Mass. 1985).

139 UPC § 2–511(c). *See also* Cal.Prob.Code § 6300; *cf. Restatement (Third) Trusts* § 19, cmt. f (2001). In Estate of Rose v. Loucks, 772 S.W.2d 886 (Mo.App.1989), this was held to apply even though the testator had created a similar trust after revoking the original one.

140 In re Estate of Stern, 636 N.E.2d 939, 942 (Ill.App.1994).

141 *Restatement (Third) of Trusts* § 19, cmt. a(2) (2001); *Restatement (Third) of Property (Wills and Other Donative Transfers)* § 3.8, cmt. f (1999). Use of this device will not cause the loss of the probate-avoidance advantages available to insurance and pensions under statutes like Cal.Prob.Code §§ 6323–24. For further discussion of the alternatives *see* J. Price & S. Donaldson, *Contemporary Estate Planning* § 6.20 (2019).

§ 7.3 Will Substitutes

Comparison with Wills

In cases involving wills, extrinsic evidence is generally excluded because the testator is unable to contradict possibly perjured testimony about his or her intent. Will substitutes present a similar problem, but a more liberal admission of extrinsic evidence may be appropriate for them. Most wills are made-to-order for the testator, while the terms of multiple party accounts (joint, trust, or P.O.D.) usually appear on printed forms drafted primarily to protect the bank rather than to express the depositor's intention.[142] As one court said of a bank account signature card, "it can hardly be expected to accurately express the intentions and relationships between the joint tenants about which the depository [bank] typically has little, if any, knowledge."[143]

Many persons open joint accounts simply for the convenience of having another party make deposits and withdrawals for them, without any intent that this other party succeed to the account when the depositor dies.[144] Nevertheless, some statutes exclude extrinsic evidence of intent. A woman added a friend's name to a joint account, but her will, executed at about the same time, recited that the joint accounts were "for convenience purposes only and without the intent of conveying any interest therein to the joint signator." Nevertheless, the friend was awarded the money in the account after the testator died on the basis of a statute providing that deposits in a joint account "shall in the absence of fraud or undue influence, be conclusive evidence" of the depositor's intent to vest title to the deposit in the survivor.[145] Some courts reach this result without a statute on the basis of the parol evidence rule.[146] One court, after reviewing the case law, concluded:

"Our efforts to determine survivorship rights by a *post-mortem* evaluation of extrinsic evidence of depositor intent are flawed to the point of offering no predictability. . . . [I]t is imperative that the depositor know that the opening of such an account is conclusive of his intent to transfer a survivorship interest."[147]

---

[142] Anderson v. Baker, 641 P.2d 1035, 1039 (Mont.1982). When handwritten words conflict with the printed portion of a form, the handwritten words control. Isbell v. Williams, 738 S.W.2d 20 (Tex.App.1987). This distinction between wills and will substitutes is undercut to some extent by the growing use of printed will forms.

[143] In re Estate of Silver, 1 P.3d 358, 361 (Mont.2000). *See also* Blaircom v. Hires, 423 N.E.2d 609, 612 (Ind.1981) (dissent).

[144] McGovern, *The Payable on Death Account and Other Will Substitutes,* 67 Nw.U.L.Rev. 7, 17 (1972); Hines, *Personal Property Joint Tenancies,* 54 Minn.L.Rev. 509, 530–51 (1969); James v. Elder, 368 S.E.2d 570 (Ga.App.1988) (finding that joint account just set up for convenience); Matter of Estate of Savage, 631 N.E.2d 797 (Ill.App.1994) (same).

[145] Baker v. Leonard, 843 P.2d 1050 (Wash.1993). The statute had later been altered but the court said the statute in effect when the account was opened controlled. *See also* In re Estate of Hill, 931 P.2d 1320 (Mont.1997); *cf.* Childs v. First National Bank, 410 S.E.2d 17 (S.C.App.1991) (account goes to survivor unless written evidence of contrary intent). In Seidl v. Estate of Michelsen, 487 So.2d 336 (Fla.App.1986), the court avoided a similar result by a strained reading of the statute.

[146] Cooper v. Crabb, 587 So.2d 236 (Miss.1991); Jeschke v. United States, 814 F.2d 568, 574 (10th Cir.1987); In re Estate of Fields, 46 P.3d 176, 179 (Okl.Civ.App.2001); *cf.* Section 7.1.

[147] Wright v. Bloom, 635 N.E.2d 31, 37 (Ohio 1994). Followed in Robinson v. Delfino, 710 A.2d 154, 161 (R.I.1998), at least if "survivorship rights are specifically provided for" in the terms

The Uniform Probate Code says that sums in a joint account on death of a party "belong to the surviving party or parties."[148] This seems to make the form of the account conclusive.[149] However, a comment to the Code says that it "permit[s] a court to implement the intentions of the parties to a joint account . . . if it finds that the account was opened solely for the convenience of a party who supplied all [of the] funds . . . and intended no present gift or death benefit for the other party."[150]

The dichotomy between "gift" and "convenience" is found in many opinions, *e.g.*, "if the intent to transfer a present interest to the named survivors . . . is lacking, it will reduce the account to one of convenience only, and no survivorship right will be found."[151] But persons who create joint accounts often want the other party to make deposits and withdrawals for them *and also* receive the balance in the account when they die.[152] Moreover, the absence of any possible convenience motive when stock is put into joint tenancy may reinforce the belief that the survivor was intended to enjoy the property. "Unlike a bank account, stocks may be liquidated only with the signature of both joint tenants. . . . Thus, stocks registered in joint tenancy are substantially less 'convenient' than joint bank accounts."[153]

Courts sometimes use a constructive trust to effectuate a decedent's intent. When a father with six children put property into joint tenancy with one daughter, a court imposed a constructive trust on the daughter after the father died. Although parol evidence was not admissible "to explain or vary the terms of the instrument" that created the joint tenancy, the daughter held the property as a constructive trustee because the father intended to benefit all his children and she had "accepted title on that basis."[154] This theory usually requires proof of wrongdoing by the "trustee" and, thus, does not apply if the survivor was unaware of the decedent's wishes.[155] However, when an insured named his brother the beneficiary of life insurance and left an unwitnessed

---

of the account and there is no "evidence of fraud, undue influence, duress, or lack of mental capacity." Where there is evidence of undue influence or incapacity, however, the terms of the account are not conclusive. Gotthardt v. Candle, 723 N.E.2d 1144 (Ohio App.1999). *See* Sections 5.1 & 5.3.

[148] UPC § 6–212(a).

[149] There is no language in the text comparable to that appearing in an early version of the Code (still in effect in some states) that says that the survivor gets the funds "unless there is clear and convincing evidence of a different intention." UPC (pre-1989) § 6–104(a). *See also* Cal.Prob.Code § 5302(a). The old UPC had certain anomalies, *e.g.* it distinguished between joint and P.O.D. accounts. *See* Graves v. Summit Bank, 541 N.E.2d 974 (Ind.App.1989) (can show contrary intent in a joint account, but not a P.O.D. account); McGovern, *Nonprobate Transfers under the Revised Uniform Probate Code*, 55 Alb.L.Rev. 1329, 1338 (1992).

[150] UPC § 6–212, comment. For a commentary on this comment, *see* McGovern, *supra* note 149, at 1339.

[151] Offret v. DiDomenico, 623 N.E.2d 128, 130 (Ohio App.1993). *See also* Gershaw v. Gershfield, 751 N.E.2d 424, 434 (Mass.App.2001).

[152] Matter of Estate of Savage, 631 N.E.2d 797, 802 (Ill.App.1994) (dissenting opinion).

[153] In re Estate of Flecken, 640 N.E.2d 1329, 1332 (Ill.App.1994). *See also* Matter of Estate of Savage, 631 N.E.2d 797, 802 (Ill.App.1994) (convenience explanation inapplicable to CDs); Rood v. Newberg, 718 N.E.2d 886, 894 (Mass.App.1999) (convenience explanation rejected for P.O.D. account).

[154] Winsor v. Powell, 497 P.2d 292 (Kan.1972). *See also* Estate of Zins by Kelsch v. Zins, 420 N.W.2d 729 (N.D.1988); In re Estate of Vittorio, 546 N.W.2d 751 (Minn.App.1996); Section 7.1.

[155] Baker v. Leonard, 843 P.2d 1050, 1054 (Wash.1993); *cf.* Section 7.1.

will stating that the brother should hold the proceeds for the insured's wife and children, the court held that an effective express trust was created even if the brother had not known the insured's wishes.

> It was not necessary . . . to have notified the trustee and obtained his consent to act before designating him as such in the policies. Having accepted the trust, which he might have disclaimed, it was the duty of the [brother] . . . to carry out its provisions.[156]

Courts are more likely to reject extrinsic evidence when they construe a "custom-made" trust rather than a printed form. Even though the statute of wills does not apply to inter-vivos transfers, the parol evidence rule does. Therefore, "the settlor's intention . . . must be ascertained by analyzing the trust instrument. . . . Only when the trust instrument is ambiguous can a court consider extrinsic evidence."[157] It is hard to reconcile this idea with the equally well-accepted principle that trusts, like contracts, can be reformed to correct mistakes in the writing.[158] For example, a court reformed a trust "to effectuate the actual intent of the settlor" when "due to a scrivener's error" it would have been "subject to nearly $400,000 in otherwise avoidable taxes."[159] Another court reformed a trust for a mistake, saying that even though "wills cannot be reformed," inter-vivos trusts "may be reformed after the death of the settlor for a unilateral[160] drafting mistake."[161]

Type of Evidence

Trusts can be reformed only if there is " 'full, clear, and decisive proof' of mistake."[162] Similarly, evidence of intent inconsistent with the form of a bank account must be "clear and convincing."[163] Similar principles apply to gifts under the Uniform Transfers to Minors Act.[164] A father who had established accounts for his children under the Act later claimed that he never intended to make a gift and did not understand the effect of signing the signature cards.

---

[156] Duncan by Duncan v. Duncan, 884 S.W.2d 383, 388 (Mo.App.1994).

[157] First Nat. Bank v. Anthony, 557 A.2d 957, 960 (Me.1989). *See also* Malachowski v. Bank One, Indianapolis, 590 N.E.2d 559 (Ind.1992); Mercury Bay Boating v. San Diego Yacht, 557 N.E.2d 87 (N.Y.1990).

In the case of "Totten" trusts, however, written evidence of intent is so sketchy that extrinsic evidence is admissible to rebut the inferences of intent made by the law. *See Restatement (Third) of Trusts* § 26, cmt. a (2003); Section 5.5.

[158] *Restatement (Third) of Trusts* § 62 (2003); *Restatement (Second) of Contracts* § 155 (1981); UTC § 415.

[159] Loeser v. Talbot, 589 N.E.2d 301 (Mass.1992). *See also* Griffin v. Griffin, 832 P.2d 810 (Okl.1992).

[160] In contracts, the mistake must usually be "mutual," *i.e.*, shared by both parties, *Restatement (Second) of Contracts* § 155 (1981). Donative transfers are different. *See* Section 7.4.

[161] In re Estate of Robinson, 720 So.2d 540, 541, 543 (Fla.App.1998). As to extending reformation to wills *see* Section 7.1.

[162] Loeser v. Talbot, 589 N.E.2d 301, 304 (Mass.1992). *See also Restatement (Second) of Contracts* § 155, cmt. c (1981). *See also* UTC § 415 (reformation permitted to conform trust terms to settlor's intent "if it is proved by clear and convincing evidence what the settlor's intention was and that the terms of the trust were affected by a mistake of fact or law, whether in expression or inducement").

[163] Calif.Prob.Code § 5302; Matter of Estate of Martin, 559 N.E.2d 1112, 1114 (Ill.App.1990); In re Estate of Combee, 583 So.2d 708 (Fla.App.1991).

[164] As to this Act, *see* Section 10.5.

The court held that his signature "did not create an irrebuttable presumption of intent," but "clear, convincing, unequivocal and unmistakable evidence" was required to overcome it and the father's testimony failed to meet this standard.[165]

Courts tend to view extrinsic evidence offered by an interested party with suspicion. For example, a man opened a joint account with his sister; after he died, an affidavit by his brother that the decedent had told him that he wanted his estate divided equally among his brothers and sisters and had created the account only for convenience was held to be "not admissible without corroboration."[166]

Declarations of intention by the decedent are admissible,[167] but courts usually give greater weight to the circumstances.[168] The fact that a written disposition appears unnatural may indicate that the decedent intended something else. Thus, when a person with minor children named his father beneficiary of an insurance policy, the court found that he intended the father to hold the proceeds in trust for the insured's children, because it would have been "unnatural for the insured to have designated his father as beneficiary without having a corresponding intent that these proceeds be used for the benefit of his minor sons."[169] When a father put one child's name on a bank account which amounted to over two-thirds of the father's assets, the account was awarded to the father's estate, because "no reason is shown why he would make such a sizeable gift" to one child.[170] But a child was allowed to take as surviving joint tenant when he "had a very close relationship" with his mother whereas his sisters "seldom helped his mother" and " 'fought like cats and dogs.' " Also, in that case the disputed property constituted a relatively small fraction of the mother's estate. She "could well have intended to favor the child closest to her by giving him the two CDs [held jointly] while still giving substantial benefits to the others."[171]

Some courts focus exclusively on evidence of a depositor's intent when the account was created. The fact that a "controversy [between the parties] began *after*" the accounts were established is irrelevant.[172] A later change in circumstances cannot be considered "even though the court may believe that the settlor would change the terms of the distribution if he was aware of the

---

165 Heath by Heath v. Heath, 493 N.E.2d 97, 101 (Ill.App.1986). *See also* Golden v. Golden, 434 So.2d 978 (Fla.App.1983); Gordon v. Gordon, 419 N.Y.S.2d 684 (App.Div.1979). But in State v. Keith, 610 N.E.2d 1017 (Ohio App.1991) extrinsic evidence was successfully used to show lack of donative intent in a purported transfer under the Act.

166 Sawyer v. Lancaster, 719 S.W.2d 346, 350 (Tex.App.1986). *See also* In re Estate of Lambert, 785 N.E.2d 1129 (Ind.App.2003) (interested testimony barred by Dead Man statute); James v. Elder, 368 S.E.2d 570, 572 (Ga.App.1988) ("the trial judge was authorized, if not required, to reject [testimony] as self-serving").

167 Pontius v. Nadolske, 584 N.E.2d 1228 (Ohio App.1989).

168 *Compare* Section 7.1.

169 Rosen v. Rosen, 167 So.2d 70, 73 (Fla.App.1964).

170 Estate of Stanley v. Sandiford, 337 S.E.2d 248, 251 (S.C.App.1985). *See also* Matter of Estate of Abbot, 510 N.E.2d 619 (Ill.App.1987) (joint account would create "a gross disparity" among children).

171 Matter of Estate of Lewis, 549 N.E.2d 960, 961, 964 (Ill.App.1990).

172 Rasmussen v. LaMagdelaine, 566 N.E.2d 864, 870 (Ill.App.1991).

changed circumstances."[173] Subsequent evidence of a settlor's intent has been held inadmissible even to resolve an ambiguity because this "would allow a settlor to revoke or modify a trust at his pleasure."[174] But most courts are not so strict. "The critical question is the intent of the alleged donor at the time the account was created . . . but subsequent events may be considered as [having a] bearing on" this.[175] When a father put his daughters' names on a brokerage account in 1980 and his will executed in 1984 left the accounts in trust for his wife, the will showed he had put his daughters' names on the account "simply for his business or personal convenience" rather than as a gift to them.[176]

Protection of Third Parties

When extrinsic evidence of intent contradicts a writing, third parties who have reasonably relied on the writing are protected.[177] Under the Uniform Probate Code, a bank is not liable if it pays sums in a multiple-party account according to the terms of the account, even if the terms do not reflect the decedent's intention, unless the bank has previously received written notice not to do so.[178]

§ 7.4 Deeds of Land: Reformation, Constructive and Resulting Trusts

If Andrew executes a deed which conveys land to Bob, can Andrew or a third person show by evidence outside the deed that *Bob* was not intended to keep the land? The parol evidence rule may bar such evidence,[179] but there are theories that can be used to get around the rule.

Just as a will may be denied probate on the basis of extrinsic evidence that the maker had no testamentary intent,[180] parol evidence can be used to show that a deed was not intended to operate according to its terms. For example, a mother who had deeded land to her daughter was allowed to cancel the deed on the ground that she had signed the deed only to avoid probate with no intent to give the daughter a present interest.[181] Parol evidence can also show that a deed was conditional on a promise of support of the grantor.[182] A fortiori,

---

[173] In re Estate of Deupree, 54 P.3d 542, 547 (N.M.App.2002).

[174] Bonney v. Granger, 356 S.E.2d 138, 143 (S.C.App.1987).

[175] In re Estate of Blom, 600 N.E.2d 427, 429 (Ill.App.1992).

[176] Parker v. Kokot, 793 P.2d 195, 201 (Idaho 1990). *See also* Matter of Estate of Savage, 631 N.E.2d 797 (Ill.App.1994); Derman v. Dreznick, 546 A.2d 1091 (N.J.Super.App.Div.1988). This reasoning undercuts the rule that a will cannot alter the terms of a joint account. *See* Section 4.5. An earlier will of the depositor was used to show that he did not intend to give the survivor the proceeds of a joint account in Hopper v. Rech, 375 N.W.2d 538, 542 (Minn.App.1985).

[177] *Restatement (Second) of Contracts* § 155, cmt. f (1981).

[178] UPC § 6–226. *See also* Calif.Prob.Code § 5405.

[179] Rubenstein v. Sela, 672 P.2d 492 (Ariz.App.1983); Mahrenholz v. County Board of School Trustees, 466 N.E.2d 322 (Ill.App.1984). Parol evidence may be admissible, however, to resolve an ambiguity in the deed. Bledsoe v. Hill, 747 P.2d 10 (Colo.App.1987); *cf.* Section 7.1.

[180] *See* Section 7.1.

[181] Myers v. Weems, 876 P.2d 861 (Or.App.1994). *See also* Anderson v. Brinkerhoff, 756 P.2d 95 (Utah App.1988); *cf.* Fine v. Cohen, 623 N.E.2d 1134 (Mass.App.1993) (parol evidence showed "trust" was not intended to be binding).

[182] *See* Section 4.5.

someone who is induced by fraud to sign a paper which he does not realize is a deed can have it set aside.[183]

Reformation

Another well-settled exception to the parol evidence rule allows mistakes in a deed to be reformed. For example, when a deed was intended for a husband alone but was made out by mistake to the husband and his wife, the husband's executor was able to have it reformed.[184]

Some cases say the mistake must be as to the words in the deed rather than their legal effect; for example, the fact that the maker of a deed did not understand the legal significance of joint tenancy does not warrant reformation.[185] But the Second Restatement of Contracts says that "if the parties are mistaken with respect to the legal effect of the language that they have used, the writing may be reformed to reflect the intended effect."[186]

Relief may be denied if the mistake was the product of "supine negligence." A person cannot claim "he did not understand what he was signing when there was nothing to prevent him from merely reading the deed to discover its contents."[187] But grantors who had difficulty in communicating in the English language and did not understand the legal implications of the term "life estate" were able to have a deed reformed.[188]

Opinions differ as to whether or not the mistake must be mutual. The Second Restatement of Contracts generally gives relief only when "*both* parties as to" a writing are mistaken.[189] An uncle who deeded land to his niece, thinking that he was signing a will, got no relief because she did not share his mistake.[190] When a husband put a house in joint tenancy with his wife, his executor was not allowed to recover the house on proof that he had not intended

---

183 Pedersen v. Bibioff, 828 P.2d 1113 (Wash.App.1992). *See also Restatement (Second) of Contracts* § 163 (1981) (no effective assent to a contract where its character is misrepresented); *Restatement (Third) of Property (Wills and Other Donative Transfers)* § 8.3(a) (2003) (donative transfer induced by fraud may be set aside). Even mistake as to the contents of the document not induced by fraud may suffice to make it voidable.

184 Geissel v. Galbraith, 695 P.2d 1316 (Nev.1985). *See also* Matter of Estate of Vadney, 634 N.E.2d 976 (N.Y.1994) (deed reformed to add "as joint tenants"); *Restatement (Third) of Property (Wills and Other Donative Transfers)* § 8.3, cmt. k (2003). *But see* Groh v. Ballard, 965 S.W.2d 872 (Mo.App.1998) (interpreting a statute which made deeds voidable for "fraud, duress, or undue influence" as precluding reformation for mistake). As to the extension of the idea of reformation to wills, *see* Section 7.1.

185 Boone v. Grier, 688 P.2d 1070 (Ariz.App.1984).

186 *Restatement (Second) of Contracts* § 155, cmt. a (1981). *See also* West One Trust Co. v. Morrison, 861 P.2d 1058 (Utah App.1993) (reformation allowed where parties did not understand meaning of "joint tenants"); Estate of Hurst v. Hurst, 769 N.E.2d 55, 62 (Ill.App.2002) (rejecting a distinction between mistakes of fact and law in reforming a note intended to create a joint tenancy).

187 Yohe v. Yohe, 353 A.2d 417, 420 (Pa.1976). *See also* Briggs v. Liddell, 699 P.2d 770, 773 (Utah 1985) (no reformation unless "the error occurred despite . . . exercise of due care"); Wright v. Blevins, 705 P.2d 113 (Mont.1985) (no relief to party who signs a deed without reading it); Henkle v. Henkle, 600 N.E.2d 791 (Ohio App.1991). *But see* Eisenhart v. Lobb, 647 N.W.2d 96, 106 (Neb.App.2002) (negligence in executing deed does not bar reformation).

188 Yano v. Yano, 697 P.2d 1132, 1134–35 (Ariz.App.1985).

189 *Restatement (Second) of Contracts* § 155 (1981).

190 Felonenko v. Siomka, 637 P.2d 1338, 1341 (Or.App.1981). *See also* Briggs v. Liddell, 699 P.2d 770 (Utah 1985) (unilateral mistake does not allow reformation of an insurance policy); Henkle v. Henkle, 600 N.E.2d 791 (Ohio App.1991).

to create a joint tenancy; his "hidden intention," undisclosed to his wife, was irrelevant.[191] However, some courts allow reformation of unilateral mistakes in a gratuitous transfer on the ground that "the expectations of a donee are less worthy of protection than are those of a transferee who gives value for the property" (unless the donee has changed position in reliance upon the transfer).[192]

Reformation is equitable relief and "equity will not ordinarily aid a volunteer," *i.e.*, the intended recipient of a gift may be barred from seeking reformation.[193] But when a father deeded land to his children "for $10 and love and affection," the children were able to have the deed reformed to include property which had been omitted by mistake; "any nominal consideration accompanied by 'love and affection' is sufficient."[194] Also, a donee has been permitted to sue the donor's heirs for reformation where the donor himself would not have opposed it.[195]

Courts distinguish between mistakes as to the contents of a deed and mistakes of fact; they generally refuse to upset deeds simply because the grantor acted under an erroneous factual supposition. For example, a father gave his son land under which gas was later discovered; the donee's sister claimed that "had the father known of the valuable oil and gas deposits he would have divided them equally between son and daughter," but her claim was rejected as resting on "speculation or conjecture."[196] However, the Third Restatement of Property provides that a mistake of fact proven by clear and convincing evidence will justify reforming a donative transfer, whether by deed or will.[197]

Constructive Trusts

Constructive trusts are imposed on devisees who promised the testator to give the property to another person and refused to do so.[198] A similar rule

---

[191] Estate of Levine, 178 Cal.Rptr. 275 (App.1981). *See also* Schulz v. Miller, 837 P.2d 71 (Wyo.1992); Estate of Gallio, 39 Cal.Rptr.2d 470 (App.1995).

[192] Yohe v. Yohe, 353 A.2d 417, 424 (Pa.1976) (concurring opinion). *See also* Yano v. Yano, 697 P.2d 1132 (Ariz.App.1985); Shoemaker v. Estate of Freeman, 967 P.2d 871, 876 (Okl.1998); *Restatement (Third) of Trusts* § 62, cmt. a (2003); *Restatement (Second) of Contracts* § 155, cmt. b (1981); *cf.* Estate of Hurst v. Hurst, 769 N.E.2d 55, 62 (Ill.App.2002) (irrelevant whether maker of note was a party to a mistake by payees, because maker "had no interest in whether [payees] held the note as joint tenants").

[193] *Restatement (Second) of Contracts* § 155, cmt. d (1981).

[194] Snyder v. Peterson, 814 P.2d 1204, 1208 (Wash.App.1991). *See also* Roots v. Uppole, 400 N.E.2d 1003 (Ill.App.1980).

[195] Zabolotny v. Fedorenko, 315 N.W.2d 668 (N.D.1982).

[196] Thomas v. Reid, 608 P.2d 1123, 1124 (N.M.1980). *See also* Harmston v. Harmston, 680 P.2d 751 (Utah 1984); Getty v. Getty, 232 Cal.Rptr. 603, 614 (App.1986). But in Berger v. United States, 487 F.Supp. 49 (W.D.Pa.1980), a settlor was allowed to rescind a trust which he had created under the mistaken belief he was going to obtain a government position.

[197] *Restatement (Third) of Property (Wills and Other Donative Transfers)* § 12.1 (2003). The same conclusions are even more strongly stated in the case of fraudulent representations. *See also* Section 7.1.

[198] *See* Section 7.1.

applies to inter-vivos transfers where the transferee at the time of the transfer[199] promised to hold the land for the transferor or for a third person.

In any event, the categories of cases in which constructive trusts are imposed on transfers by deed are the following.

First, a constructive trust will be imposed on a grantee who was guilty of fraud.[200] In England, *any* breach of promise constitutes "fraud,"[201] but American courts define fraud to include only promises that were made without any intent to perform when the promise was made. This can be inferred from refusal to perform a promise,[202] but a grantee who intended to perform and later changed his mind is not guilty of fraud,[203] although this distinction is blurred in cases that impose a trust on the basis of "constructive fraud."[204]

A constructive trust is also imposed if the grantor and grantee were in a "confidential relation to [each other]."[205] Arguably, such a relationship exists whenever a transferor intended to create a trust, for trust and confidence are synonyms. But courts usually "require additional evidence of confidence in the relation between [the settlor and trustee] before they will impose a constructive trust."[206] However, confidential relationship is an elastic term. Many cases involve transfers between members of the same family. In New York, a confidential relationship is always held to exist among family members, but this is not true in Massachusetts.[207] A confidential relationship has been found to exist between unrelated friends,[208] whereas close relatives are sometimes found not to have such a relationship.[209]

---

[199] A promise made *after* the transfer does not give rise to a constructive trust. Walsh v. Walsh, 841 P.2d 831 (Wyo.1992). However, a declaration of trust, if in writing, may be enforceable. *See* Section 3.6.

[200] *Restatement (Second) of Trusts* § 44(1)(a) (trust for settlor), § 45(1)(a) (trust for third person); *Restatement (Third) of Trusts* § 24(2)(a) (2003); Guy v. Guy, 411 S.E.2d 403 (N.C.App.1991).

[201] Davies, *Constructive Trusts, Contracts and Estoppels,* 7 Adelaide L.Rev. 200, 207 (1980); *cf.* Masino v. Sechrest, 66 N.W.2d 740 (Wis.1954) (to hold property contrary to the terms of an agreement is "constructive fraud").

[202] *Restatement (Third) of Trusts* § 24, cmt. d (2003); March v. Gerstenschlager, 436 S.W.2d 6 (Mo.1969).

[203] Nessralla v. Peck, 532 N.E.2d 685 (Mass.1989); *Restatement (Third) of Trusts* § 24, cmt. e (2003) (refusal to perform promise is "some but not conclusive evidence of" fraud).

[204] Baizley v. Baizley, 734 A.2d 1117, 1118 (Me.1999).

[205] *Restatement (Second) of Trusts* §§ 44(1)(b), 45(1)(b) (1959); *Restatement (Third) of Trusts* § 24(2)(b) (2003); Estates of Kalwitz v. Kalwitz, 717 N.E.2d 904, 913 (Ind.App.1999) (confidential relationship creates "constructive fraud").

[206] *Restatement (Second) of Trusts* § 44, cmt. c (1959). *See also Restatement (Third) of Trusts* § 24, cmt. f (2003).

[207] Rudow v. Fogel, 426 N.E.2d 155, 157 (Mass.App.1981). In Gulack v. Gulack, 620 A.2d 181 (Conn.App.1993) the court found a confidential relationship between two brothers in "a close knit family"). *See also* Baizley v. Baizley, 734 A.2d 1117, 1119 (Me.1999) ("familial relationship" creates "a relationship of trust"). A confidential relationship is commonly found between spouses. Rajanna v. KRR Investments, Inc., 810 S.W.2d 548 (Mo.App.1991); Matter of Estate of McKim, 807 P.2d 215 (N.M.1991).

[208] David v. Russo, 415 N.E.2d 531 (Ill.App.1980); Thomasi v. Koch, 660 P.2d 806 (Wyo.1983); Klein v. Shaw, 706 P.2d 1348 (Idaho App.1985).

[209] Beelman v. Beelman, 460 N.E.2d 55 (Ill.App.1984); Meskell v. Meskell, 243 N.E.2d 804 (Mass.1969).

Some opinions suggest that a "confidential relationship" denotes an unequal one. A court refused to impose a constructive trust when a woman conveyed land to her fiancé/cohabitant, because "the doctrine of confidential relationship . . . implies a position of superiority occupied by one of the parties over the other" whereas the parties in the case had an "equal relationship."[210] This seems to confuse undue influence (where the idea of a "confidential relationship" also plays an important role)[211] with the question whether oral promises should be enforced. Another court held that while there was no confidential relationship between a father and daughter to support a claim of undue influence, "for the purposes of imposing a constructive trust, a confidential relationship can be based on an agreement between the owner of property and another who will distribute the owner's property in a specified manner."[212] A rationale for enforcing such promises is that the confidential relationship renders plausible a claim that the parties made an agreement without reducing it to writing. "The existence of the confidential and fiduciary relationship . . . was precisely the reason for their failure to have an express agreement to convey. Strength of this relationship is shown by lack of . . . such an agreement."[213] The argument becomes circular: the absence of a writing indicates the existence of a confidential relationship which makes a writing unnecessary.

Constructive trusts are also imposed when oral evidence shows that a deed was intended only as a mortgage.[214] This may be explained by the fact that mortgagors are usually needy, and so may sign anything in order to get the loan, including a deed which incorrectly states the intent of the parties.[215]

Oral trusts are also enforced on an "estoppel" theory when a beneficiary has relied on the trust to his detriment. For example, after a father deeded a farm to his two oldest children with the intent that they hold it for all his children, the younger children worked to improve the farm. The trust was enforceable because the trustees had "induced others to change their position."[216]

When a deed conveys land from Alice to Bill, any attempt to show that Connie was actually supposed to enjoy the land would seem to violate the parol evidence rule, but courts hold otherwise. "Where realty is conveyed by a deed which . . . does not stipulate . . . that the grantee named therein shall take the equitable as well as the legal title, the parol evidence rule does not preclude the establishment of a parol trust."[217] Section 7 of the Statute of Frauds which

---

[210] Mattes v. Olearain, 759 P.2d 1177, 1179 (Utah App.1988). *See also* Estates of Kalwitz v. Kalwitz, 717 N.E.2d 904, 913 (Ind.App.1999) (confidential relationship arises "where one party dominates a weaker party"); Badger Bldg. Corp. v. Gregoric, 430 N.E.2d 561 (Ill.App.1981).

[211] *See* Section 5.3.

[212] Heck v. Archer, 927 P.2d 495, 502 (Kan.App.1996).

[213] Thompson v. Nesheim, 159 N.W.2d 910, 918 (Minn.1968).

[214] Beelman v. Beelman, 460 N.E.2d 55 (Ill.App.1984); McGill v. Biggs, 434 N.E.2d 772 (Ill.App.1982).

[215] 1 A. Scott & M. Ascher, *Scott and Ascher on Trusts*, § 6.11.3 (5th ed. 2006).

[216] Potucek v. Potucek, 719 P.2d 14, 18 (Kan.App.1986). *See also Restatement (Third) of Trusts* § 24, cmt. c (2003).

[217] Kelley v. Kelley, 575 S.W.2d 612, 616 (Tex.Civ.App.1978). *See also Restatement (Third) of Trusts* § 21 (2003); Schaneman v. Wright, 470 N.W.2d 566 (Neb.1991).

requires that trusts of land "shall be manifested and proved" by a signed writing poses a more serious problem to the enforcement of oral trusts of land. Most American jurisdictions have adopted Section 7 (with minor variations in language), along with Section 8 which excepts trusts which "arise or result by the implication or construction of law."[218] Courts have made such extensive use of the exception in Section 8 for "resulting" and "constructive" trusts that the rule of Section 7 has become almost, but not quite, meaningless.

Decisions in the few American states which have not adopted Sections 7 and 8 of the Statute of Frauds are inconsistent. Some courts hold that these provisions are part of the common law,[219] but in other states the failure to enact these provisions has led courts to enforce oral trusts of land.[220]

The Uniform Trusts Act provides that if land is conveyed "by deed to a person on a trust which is unenforceable on account of the Statute of Frauds," a trustee who fails to perform the trust "shall be under a duty to convey the real property to the settlor or his successor in interest."[221] This prevents the trustee from being unjustly enriched but does not effectuate the settlor's intent if the intent was to benefit a third party. The Third Restatement of Trusts adopts a modified form of this rule, which, it says, provides "an appropriate balance between competing policies. It prevents unjust enrichment and yet gives force to the Statute of Frauds" by not enforcing the trust absent fraud, confidential relationship, or estoppel. Under the Restatement, if the original settlor has died without repudiating the trust, "the transferee can be compelled to hold the property ... upon constructive trust for ... the intended beneficiaries."[222]

Resulting Trusts

The Statute of Frauds allows enforcement of resulting as well as constructive trusts which may contradict the written evidence of title. Resulting trusts arise in several situations. For example, when an express trust fails to provide what to do with property in a certain situation, there may be a resulting trust for the settlor.[223] There is also a "purchase money" resulting trust. "Where the property is purchased and the title is taken in the name of one person, but the purchase price is paid by another, . . . [the person] who furnished the consideration money is presumed to intend to acquire a corresponding beneficial interest in the lands purchased."[224] Some courts apply

---

[218] *Restatement (Third) of Trusts* § 22, cmt. a (2003); Cal.Prob. Code §§ 15003, 15206.

[219] Bassett v. Bassett, 798 P.2d 160, 163 (N.M.1990).

[220] Ellis v. Vespoint, 403 S.E.2d 542 (N.C.App.1991); Linger v. Rohr, 383 S.E.2d 825 (W.Va.1989).

[221] Uniform Trusts Act § 16. This Act, promulgated in 1937, is not to be confused with the Uniform Trust Code, promulgated in 2000.

[222] *Restatement (Third) of Trusts* § 24, cmt. h (2003).

[223] *Id.*, § 8.

[224] Browder v. Hite, 602 S.W.2d 489, 492 (Tenn.App.1980). *See also* Hofferkamp v. Brehm, 652 N.E.2d 1381, 1388 (Ill.App.1995); Hilliard v. Hilliard, 844 P.2d 54 (Mont.1992); *Restatement (Third) of Trusts* § 9 (2001). When the parties intend to give a beneficial interest to a person other than the payer, this is treated as a constructive trust. *Id.*, cmt. c.

the same rules to resulting and constructive trusts or confuse the two,[225] but the Restatement distinguishes between them; it requires fraud or a breach of a confidential relation to enforce a constructive trust but not for a resulting trust.[226] Why? Professor Scott suggested that in resulting trusts the intention of the parties "is evidenced by the circumstances of the transaction rather than by the language of the parties" and so there was not "the same danger of perjured testimony."[227] However, the inference that should be derived from circumstances is not obvious. At one time, whenever deeds were given without consideration, courts presumed that the donee was intended to hold the land in trust, but today they presume that the transferor intended to make a gift to the transferee.[228] Why then do they presume a trust was intended when a person pays for land which is deeded to another?

Perhaps the distinction is based on the fact that a deed normally means what it says and the signer should understand this. But when a buyer of land instructs the seller to put title in the name of a third person, this instruction is often not reflected in a signed writing; the grantor signs the deed but not the person who pays the price.[229]

The differing legal treatment of resulting and constructive trusts is not of great practical significance. If a gratuitous conveyance was intended to create a trust, the beneficiary can usually prove "fraud" or a "confidential relation" and thereby enforce the trust. Conversely, the presumption of a purchase-money resulting trust can be rebutted by evidence that the payer intended to give the land to the person in whose name title was placed.[230]

When the person who pays for land and the transferee named in the deed are related by blood or marriage, courts presume that the payer intended a gift rather than to create a trust. According to the Restatement, the presumption of a gift arises when the transferee was a "spouse,[231] descendant, or other natural object of the bounty" of the person who paid the price.[232] The gift-presumption has also been applied to a mother-in-law who paid for a house

---

[225] Leonard v. Counts, 272 S.E.2d 190, 195 (Va.1980); Yates v. Taylor, 791 P.2d 924, 926 (Wash.App.1990) ("constructive trust" arises when one person pays and title is taken in the name of another).

[226] *Compare Restatement (Third) of Trusts* § 9 *with id.* § 24 (2003). *See also Restatement (Third) of Property (Wills and Other Donative Transfers)* § 12.1 (2003) (constructive trust as a remedy for mistake in addition to being a remedy for fraud).

[227] 5 A. Scott, *The Law of Trusts*, § 440, at 144 (4th ed. Fratcher 1989).

[228] *Restatement (Third) of Trusts* § 9, cmt. a (2003).

[229] The payer "was not the grantor, and we do not have the evidentiary protection of his signing a deed before independent witnesses." Hofferkamp v. Brehm, 652 N.E.2d 1381, 1389 (Ill.App.1995).

[230] *Restatement (Third) of Trusts* § 9(1)(a) (2003); Thor v. McDearmid, 817 P.2d 1380 (Wash.App.1991); Erb v. Kohnke, 824 P.2d 903 (Idaho App.1992).

[231] In the *Restatement (Second) of Trusts* § 442, the comparable words were "*wife*, child, or other natural object." *See* Tarkington v. Tarkington, 272 S.E.2d 99 (N.C.1980) (no gift presumed when wife buys land in names of both spouses). However, more recent cases generally reject any such gender-based distinction. In re Estate of Koch, 697 N.E.2d 931, 933 (Ill.App.1998).

[232] *Restatement (Third) of Trusts* § 9(2) (2003). *See also* Minn.Stat. § 501B.07(2); Wachter v. Wachter, 357 S.E.2d 38 (W.Va.1987) (gift presumed when wife pays for land put in husband's name); Matter of Estate of Lettengarver, 813 P.2d 468 (Mont.1991) (joint funds used to buy house put into W's name); Durward v. Nelson, 481 N.W.2d 586 (N.D.1992) (parents pay for land deeded to their son and his wife).

which was conveyed to her son-in-law,[233] but not an aunt who bought a home for her nephew.[234] Such distinctions seem arbitrary, but they are not important because evidence of the parties' actual intent is always admissible.[235] However, the presumption of a gift is not overcome by one party's "after-the-fact testimony that" no gift was intended; proof of a "common understanding" of the parties is required.[236]

Some state statutes appear to abolish the purchase-money resulting trust. In Kentucky, "when a deed is made to one person, and the consideration is paid by another no use or trust results in favor of the latter."[237] But this law has been held to bar only trusts that arise "from the naked fact that a person has furnished consideration to buy land," and not proof of an "agreement establishing a trust."[238]

A purchase money resulting trust can arise from a sale on credit. For example, a court imposed a trust when a mother and son agreed that a house would be deeded to the son in order to qualify for a veteran's loan, but the mother would make all the payments and own the house. Where the price is not paid at the time of purchase, "the party seeking imposition of the trust must have incurred an absolute obligation to pay [it] as a part of the original transaction," but she "need not be obligated directly to the grantee's lender; it is sufficient if [she] is obligated to the grantee, pursuant to a promise made before title passes, to make payments to the grantee."[239] But if there is no such agreement before title passes, a resulting trust does not arise in favor of someone who furnishes funds to the owner subsequent to the purchase.[240]

If someone pays part of the price of land, the resulting trust presumption arises only as to part,[241] but the land is not beneficially owned in proportion to contributions if the parties intended otherwise. For example, when two brothers contributed to the acquisition of land and title was taken in the name of one, he held half in trust for his brother even though they had not paid equal

---

[233] Matter of Estate of Hock, 655 P.2d 1111 (Utah 1982).

[234] Peterson v. Kabrich, 691 P.2d 1360 (Mont.1984). *See also* Blalak v. Mid Valley Transp., Inc., 858 P.2d 683 (Ariz.App.1993) (no gift presumed when daughter pays for land put in mother's name); Hofferkamp v. Brehm, 652 N.E.2d 1381 (Ill.App.1995) (no presumption when parties are engaged but not married); *cf.* Rakhman v. Zusstone, 957 S.W.2d 241 (Ky.1997) (gift presumed between unmarried cohabitants).

[235] *Restatement (Third) of Trusts* § 9, cmt. c (2003); Treschak v. Yorkville Nat. Bank, 604 N.E.2d 1081 (Ill.App.1992); Hilliard v. Hilliard, 844 P.2d 54 (Mont.1992).

[236] Valladee v. Valladee, 718 P.2d 206, 209 (Ariz.App.1986). Under Cal.Fam.Code § 2581 property held jointly by spouses is presumed to be community unless there is evidence in writing to the contrary.

[237] Ky.Rev.Stat. § 381.170.

[238] Horn v. Horn, 562 S.W.2d 319, 320 (Ky.App.1978). *See also Restatement (Third) of Trusts* § 9, cmt. d (2003).

[239] Watkins v. Watkins, 351 S.E.2d 331, 334 (N.C.App.1986). *See also Restatement (Third) of Trusts* § 9, cmt. e (2003); Stone v. McCarthy, 511 N.E.2d 780 (Ill.App.1987); Simmons v. Smith, 482 N.E.2d 887 (Mass.App.1985).

[240] Leicht v. Quirin, 558 N.E.2d 715 (Ill.App.1990); Workman v. Douglas, 419 N.E.2d 1340, 1345 (Ind.App.1981); Gitto v. Gitto, 778 P.2d 906 (Mont.1989); *Restatement (Third) of Trusts* § 9, cmt. e (2003).

[241] *Restatement (Third) of Trusts* § 9, cmt. c (2003); Bassett v. Bassett, 798 P.2d 160 (N.M.1990); Yates v. Taylor, 791 P.2d 924 (Wash.App.1990).

portions, because the evidence showed that "from the inception . . . the brothers looked upon themselves as equal partners."[242]

Nature of Proof

Before granting reformation, courts require that the evidence of mistake in a deed be clear and convincing. Reformation is denied, for example, if the donor's testimony is equivocal and unsupported by disinterested witnesses.[243] Claims to a resulting or constructive trust also require evidence that is "clear, convincing, unequivocal, and unmistakable."[244] Appellate courts generally defer to findings by a trial court, however. An appellate court, while saying that "proof of an oral trust must be [of] the clearest and most convincing character," affirmed a decision imposing a trust because "this case turns primarily on the credibility of witnesses" and "a court of review which cannot view the witness . . . ought not to reverse that finding absent 'clear, concrete, and convincing evidence to the contrary.' "[245] It is the *trial* court which must be satisfied that the proof was clear and convincing.[246] Testimony by interested witnesses can be "clear and convincing,"[247] but it may be excluded under a Dead Man statute.[248] Proof sometimes falls short of the clear and convincing standard, not because the testimony is conflicting but because it shows that the parties' intentions were indefinite or vague.[249]

Proof is often circumstantial. The fact that a deed was given for an inadequate consideration is evidence that it was intended as a mortgage.[250] A grantor's staying in possession is evidence that he intended to retain a beneficial interest in property. Thus, a father who had put land in his son's name was able to impose a resulting trust despite the presumption of a gift which arises in this situation, because he had collected the rents, paid the insurance and taxes, maintained the property, and otherwise treated it as his own.[251]

---

[242] Bassett v. Bassett, 798 P.2d 160, 168 (N.M.1990).

[243] In re LaRocca's Trust Estate, 192 A.2d 409 (Pa.1963). *See also Restatement (Second) of Contracts* § 155, cmt. c (1981).

[244] In re Estate of McCormick, 634 N.E.2d 341, 345 (Ill.App.1994). According to *Restatement (Third) of Trusts* § 24, cmt. h(1) (2003), clear and convincing evidence is needed to show that a trust was intended (when the deed does not indicate such an intent), but "a preponderance of the evidence is then sufficient to establish the intended interests of the beneficiaries." *See also id.* § 9, cmt. f (as to resulting trusts).

[245] Browder v. Hite, 602 S.W.2d 489, 495 (Tenn.App.1980). *See also* Bassett v. Bassett, 798 P.2d 160, 164 (N.M.1990); Greenwald v. Spring Hill Ford, Inc., 527 N.E.2d 1095 (Ill.App.1988).

[246] Thomasi v. Koch, 660 P.2d 806, 811 (Wyo.1983). *But cf.* Matter of Estate of Hock, 655 P.2d 1111, 1114 (Utah 1982) ("smaller quantum of contrary evidence" suffices to upset trial court's finding when it must be "based upon a clear and convincing standard").

[247] Fenton v. Walter, 612 S.W.2d 17 (Mo.App.1981).

[248] Thompson v. Nesheim, 159 N.W.2d 910 (Minn.1968); Parks v. Zions First Nat. Bank, 673 P.2d 590, 606 (Utah 1983).

[249] Workman v. Douglas, 419 N.E.2d 1340, 1346 (Ind.App.1981) ("the agreement was not sufficiently definite to enforce"); Engel v. Breske, 681 P.2d 263 (Wash.App.1984) (intent was "very loose, very indefinite").

[250] McGill v. Biggs, 434 N.E.2d 772, 774 (Ill.App.1982).

[251] Hilliard v. Hilliard, 844 P.2d 54, 58 (Mont.1992). *See also* In re Estate of Koch, 697 N.E.2d 931 (Ill.App.1998) (husband's continued management of property put in wife's name shows no gift intended); Levin v. Smith, 513 A.2d 1292, 1298 (Del.1986) (grantee's treating his sister as half owner for years confirms claim of a constructive trust for her); Eisenhart v. Lobb, 647 N.W.2d

Statements of intent are also admissible if they relate to the time when the property was transferred. A person who conveys land with the intent that the grantee own it beneficially cannot later declare that the grantee holds in trust; this would be tantamount to revoking an irrevocable gift. After a mother conveyed land to her daughter, the daughter's brothers were unable to have a trust imposed when their evidence of the mother's intent came from conversations which occurred after the deed to the daughter was delivered.[252] However, many courts admit statements of intent after a deed was executed on the theory that "while intention at the time of the conveyance of the property controls, . . . subsequent acts and conduct are admissible to show intention at the time of the transaction."[253]

Litigation concerning oral trusts can arise long after the trust was created, because the statute of limitations does not start to run at that time. For example, when land was conveyed in 1986, and suit was brought to impose a constructive trust in 1995, the action was not barred by a six-year statute of limitations because the statute started to run only when the transferee "disclosed his intention not to return the land."[254]

Clean Hands

Courts of equity sometimes deny relief to plaintiffs who have "unclean hands." This defense is frequently asserted in suits to enforce constructive and resulting trusts because the suits often involve attempts to disguise ownership. For example, a man who titled land in his brother's name in order to avoid attachments under outstanding judgments was not allowed to enforce a resulting trust. "A party who conveys his property in order to keep it from judgment creditors cannot . . . seek assistance from the courts" after his "fraudulent purpose . . . has been accomplished."[255] Many courts reject the clean-hands defense, however, sometimes on the ground that even if the settlor intended to defraud creditors, none were actually harmed by the transaction.[256] Others say that harm to third persons such as creditors is irrelevant to a suit against the trustee.[257] Others reject the defense on the ground that the defendants' fault was greater than the plaintiff's,[258] *e.g.*, because the defendant

---

96, 106 (Neb.App.2002) (wife's lack of participation in a farm supports claim that her name was included on deed by mistake).

[252] Fowler v. Montgomery, 326 S.E.2d 765, 766–67 (Ga.1985). *See also* Groden v. Kelley, 415 N.E.2d 850, 853 (Mass.1981) (statements of settlor after trust execution inadmissible to show his intent); Section 3.6, note 362.

[253] Ashbaugh v. Ashbaugh, 152 S.E.2d 888, 892 (Ga.1966). *See also* Key v. Key, 443 N.E.2d 812 (Ill.App.1982); Beelman v. Beelman, 460 N.E.2d 55 (Ill.App.1984); *Restatement (Third) of Trusts* § 9, cmt. c (2003).

[254] Estates of Kalwitz v. Kalwitz, 717 N.E.2d 904, 914 (Ind.App.1999). *See also* Dombek v. Reiman, 748 N.Y.S.2d 630 (App.Div.2002); Rajanna v. KRR Investments, Inc., 810 S.W.2d 548 (Mo.App.1991); *cf. Restatement (Third) of Trusts* § 98, cmt. b (2012) (laches).

[255] American Nat. Bank and Trust v. Vinson, 653 N.E.2d 13, 15 (Ill.App.1995). *See also Restatement (Third) of Trusts* § 9, cmt. g (2003); Senter v. Furman, 265 S.E.2d 784 (Ga.1980); Kauffman-Harmon v. Kauffman, 36 P.3d 408, 413 (Mont.2001).

[256] Garcia v. Marquez, 684 P.2d 513, 516 (N.M.1984); Thomasi v. Koch, 660 P.2d 806 (Wyo.1983); Hilliard v. Hilliard, 844 P.2d 54 (Mont.1992).

[257] Beelman v. Beelman, 460 N.E.2d 55, 58 (Ill.App.1984); Fenton v. Walter, 612 S.W.2d 17 (Mo.App.1981); Kostelnik v. Roberts, 680 S.W.2d 532 (Tex.App.1984).

[258] Locken v. Locken, 650 P.2d 803, 805 (Nev.1982).

suggested the transfer,[259] or there was "great inequality of condition" between the parties.[260] Sometimes courts simply say that refusing to enforce the trust would "compound the defendant's wrong."[261] The result may depend on how "seriously against public policy" the transaction appears to be.[262] The Third Restatement says the question is whether "the policy against unjust enrichment of the transferee is outweighed by the policy against giving relief to a person who has entered into an illegal transaction."[263] Because acceptance or rejection of the clean-hands defense is a discretionary matter,[264] the result in a given case is hard to predict.

Third Parties

The law often protects third persons who have relied on a deed which does not reflect the intention of the parties. Thus, reformation of deeds is not granted if "rights of third parties, such as good faith purchasers for value, will be unfairly affected."[265] However, when because of fraud the grantor did not understand that the document was a deed, it is void, and even a bona fide purchaser from the grantee does not acquire title to the land.[266]

If Joe conveys property to Ryan or pays for land which is put in Ryan's name, even if they intended that Ryan hold the property in trust, a bona fide purchaser for value from Ryan takes free of the beneficiary's claims.[267] However, the beneficiary can impress a trust on the sale proceeds or hold the trustee personally liable.[268] The trust can also be enforced against transferees who had notice of the trust. When a person put title in his brother's name and the brother later sold it to another, the latter's claim to be a bona fide purchaser was rejected, because the settlor's "continuous, open and obvious possession of the property" gave him "constructive notice" of the trust.[269] Even persons who acquire property from the trustee without notice are not protected unless they paid value for the purchase.[270]

---

[259] Samuelson v. Ingraham, 77 Cal.Rptr. 750, 753 (App.1969).

[260] Hinson v. Hinson, 343 S.E.2d 266, 274 (N.C.App.1986). *See also* Estates of Kalwitz v. Kalwitz, 717 N.E.2d 904, 913–14 (Ind.App.1999).

[261] Chapman v. Citizens and Southern Nat. Bank, 395 S.E.2d 446, 454 (S.C.App.1990).

[262] *Restatement (Third) of Trusts* § 9, cmt. g (2003); Granado v. Granado, 760 P.2d 148, 152 (N.M.1988) (policy against felons holding liquor licenses had been "relaxed" by the legislature); Leeks v. Leeks, 570 A.2d 271, 276 (D.C.App.1989).

[263] *Restatement (Third) of Trusts* § 9(1)(b) (2003). In accepting the clean hands defense in Kauffman-Harmon v. Kauffman, 36 P.3d 408, 413 (Mont.2001), the court noted that the defendants "will not be unjustly enriched" because they "have expended substantial amounts of personal time and finances" in reliance on their ownership of the gifted property.

[264] Carter v. Carter, 210 So.2d 800 (Ala.1968); Key v. Key, 443 N.E.2d 812, 817 (Ill.App.1982); Kostelnik v. Roberts, 680 S.W.2d 532, 536 (Tex.App.1984).

[265] *Restatement (Second) of Contracts* § 155 (1981). *See also* Unif. Trust Code § 1006 (trustee protected in relying on written terms of trust).

[266] Pedersen v. Bibioff, 828 P.2d 1113 (Wash.App.1992); *Restatement (Second) of Contracts* § 163, cmt. c (1981).

[267] *Restatement (Third) of Trusts* § 108, cmt. c (2012); N.Y. EPTL, § 7–3.2. As to the defense of bona fide purchase from trustees in general, *see* Section 14.9.

[268] McMahon v. McMahon, 422 N.E.2d 1150, 1153 (Ill.App.1981).

[269] American Nat. Bank and Trust v. Vinson, 653 N.E.2d 13, 16 (Ill.App.1995).

[270] Granado v. Granado, 760 P.2d 148 (N.M.1988); French v. French, 606 P.2d 830 (Ariz.App.1980); Ashton v. Ashton, 733 P.2d 147 (Utah 1987).

Creditors of a trustee who relied on the trustee's apparent ownership may be allowed to satisfy their claims out of the trust property. "The actual owner of trust property will be estopped from claiming a resulting trust in the property where the record owner obtained credit upon the strength of ownership,"[271] but some courts say this applies only if the beneficiary knew of the creditors' reliance.[272] If the trustee fulfills the oral trust by conveying the property to the beneficiary, the trustee's creditors cannot attack this as a fraudulent conveyance. The Statute of Frauds "only precludes judicial enforcement of the oral trust; it does not render it void as between parties to the trust who desire to abide by the terms of their oral agreement."[273] However, courts view with suspicion claims that a debtor's property was held in trust for another member of the debtor's family.[274]

If a trustee becomes bankrupt, the equitable interests of the beneficiaries are preserved,[275] but the trustee in bankruptcy has powers of avoidance equivalent to those of a bona fide purchaser for value that may defeat the rights of the beneficiaries.[276] But a beneficiary's possession of property may give constructive notice that defeats a claim of bona fide purchase and, thus, the avoidance power of the bankruptcy trustee.[277]

§§ 7.5–8.0 are reserved for supplemental material.

---

[271] Gary-Wheaton Bank v. Meyer, 473 N.E.2d 548, 555 (Ill.App.1984). *See also Restatement (Third) of Trusts* § 9, cmt. f (2003); N.Y. EPTL § 7–3.2.

[272] John Deere Indus. Equipment Co. v. Gentile, 459 N.E.2d 611 (Ohio App.1983). Beneficiaries of a resulting trust prevailed over the trustee's creditors in Armendaris Water Dev. Co. v. Rainwater, 781 P.2d 799 (N.M.App.1989); Treschak v. Yorkville Nat. Bank, 604 N.E.2d 1081 (Ill.App.1992).

[273] Ward v. Grant, 401 N.E.2d 160, 163 (Mass.App.1980). *See also* In re Gustie, 36 B.R. 473 (D.Mass.1984).

[274] Anderson v. Ferris, 470 N.E.2d 518 (Ill.App.1984); Gary-Wheaton Bank v. Meyer, 473 N.E.2d 548 (Ill.App.1984).

[275] 11 U.S.C. § 541(d).

[276] *Id.* § 544; *cf.* In re Crabtree, 871 F.2d 36 (6th Cir.1989) (equitable interest voided under a state statute because not recorded).

[277] In re Sale Guaranty Corp., 220 B.R. 660 (9th Cir.BAP Cal.1998).

Chapter 8

LIMITS ON TESTAMENTARY POWER

Analysis

Sec.

8.1 Policy Considerations.
8.2 History and Comparative Law.
8.3 Survival of Claims for Support.
8.4 Family Allowance and Homestead.
8.5 Pretermitted Heirs.
8.6 Omitted Spouse.
8.7 Elective Share.
8.8 Community Property.
8.9 Waivers.
8.10 Negative Limitations.

§ 8.1 Policy Considerations

This chapter discusses the question: how much freedom should an owner have to dispose of property? It has been argued that society should restrict this freedom in order to prevent excessive inequality of wealth.[1] This argument is usually rejected today on the ground that there are better ways to deal with the unequal distribution of wealth, such as progressive taxation.[2]

A more cogent reason for limiting an owner's power of disposition arises from the duty of parents to support their children and of spouses to support each other.[3] These obligations have long been recognized. Blackstone said the duty of parents to support their children was "a principle of natural law,"[4] so parents should be obligated to leave their children "at least a necessary subsistence."[5] As we shall see, this suggestion has been adopted in many jurisdictions of the British Commonwealth, but it is not the law in most American states.[6]

---

[1] 2 W. Blackstone, *Commentaries* 373–74 (1766). *See also* Succession of Steckler, 665 So.2d 561, 564 (La.App.1995) (forced heirship is designed to prevent "the cummulation [sic] of excessively large fortunes through primogeniture and entailment").

[2] Le Van, *Alternatives to Forced Heirship,* 52 Tul.L.Rev. 29, 44 (1977); Nathan, *An Assault on the Citadel: A Rejection of Forced Heirship,* 52 Tul.L.Rev. 5, 6–7 (1977).

[3] *E.g.*, Cal.Family Code §§ 3900 (duty of parents to support child); 4300 (duty to support spouse).

[4] 1 W. Blackstone, *Commentaries* 435 (1765). However, the common law did not provide adequate remedies to enforce this duty. Foster, Freed & Midonnick, *Child Support: The Quick and the Dead,* 26 Syr.L.Rev. 1157 (1975).

[5] 1 W. Blackstone, *Commentaries* 438 (1765).

[6] *See* Section 8.2.

Spouses v. Children

In most states, spouses receive more protection against disinheritance than children.[7] In a way this is not surprising[8] because spouses can provide for their support by contract when they marry or support themselves after the marriage ends,[9] whereas children have no such opportunity when they enter a family. Furthermore, providing greater protection for spouses reflects a societal recognition of the important contribution that both spouses make to the accumulation of family wealth. On the other hand, few argue that parents should not be able to disinherit adult, competent children, whereas a strong case can be made that minor children should be protected from disinheritance.[10] On the other hand, barring disinheritance of minor children can often lead to inefficient results because minors are incapable of managing property. Thus, any property that they inherit must be managed by a guardian or conservator. Guardianship is inconvenient and expensive, and many parents seek to avoid it by leaving all their property to the other spouse in the expectation that he or she will use it to support or raise their children. A will that leaves all of the estate to the testator's spouse technically disinherits the testator's children, but why should the law upset this sensible estate plan?[11]

The surviving spouse is normally competent to manage any property received from the decedent's estate. Also, spouses have another basis for claiming a share of the decedent's estate, in addition to the obligation of support. Usually both spouses contribute to the accumulation of property during a marriage, even if all of the property is held in the name of one spouse. The elective share given to spouses is

> based upon two rationales: (1) contribution—which recognizes that no matter what role a spouse plays in marriage, he or she has made some contribution towards the acquisition of property of the deceased spouse and (2) support—which recognizes that the surviving spouse will need support after the death of his or her spouse.[12]

The decedent's children, on the other hand, normally have made no such contribution.[13]

If the surviving spouse is the other parent of the decedent's children, the claims of the spouse and the children usually coincide. The share given to the

---

[7] Only Georgia permits a spouse to be disinherited. Kwestel & Seplowitz, *Testamentary Substitutes—A Time for Statutory Clarification*, 23 Real Prop. Prob. Tr. J. 467, 468 (1988). As to the elective share, *see* Section 8.7. The spouse's claim to half the community property is the elective share's counterpart in the eight community property states. *See* Section 8.8.

[8] Batts, *I Didn't Ask to be Born*, 41 Hast.L.J. 1197, 1198 (1990) (finding the American protection of spouses hard to reconcile with the lack of protection to children).

[9] Rein, *A More Rational System for the Protection of Family Members from Disinheritance*, 15 Gonz. L. Rev. 11, 47 (1979).

[10] *See* Cal. Family Code § 3910 (duty of parents to support an incapacitated child of whatever age).

[11] Chaffin, *A Reappraisal of the Wealth Transmission Process*, 10 Ga.L.Rev. 447, 475 (1976); Foster, Freed & Midonnick, *supra* note 4, at 1186.

[12] Mongold v. Mayle, 452 S.E.2d 444, 447 (W.Va.1994). *See* In re Estate of Hjersted, 175 P.3d 810, 824 (Kan. 2008) (partnership theory of marriage).

[13] A child who has helped a parent in a business or provided care may have an enforceable claim against the estate if the parent agreed in return to leave property to the child at death.

spouse will indirectly provide for the children; the spouse will, indeed *must*, use the property awarded for the children's support if they are minors. But with the increase in multiple marriages, the surviving spouse sometimes is not the parent of the decedent's children and there may be hostility between them; stepparents cannot be counted on to provide for their stepchildren.[14] Most litigation today about the spouse's forced share arises in this context.

Arguments for Free Disposition

Arguments against the claims of spouses and children to share in an estate against the decedent's wishes have been made for centuries. The author(s) of the treatise known as Bracton in the 13th century asserted that men would have no incentive to work and save if they were compelled to leave their property at death to their widows and children.[15] Similar arguments have been made in modern times.[16] However, the law compels persons while they are alive to support dependents even though this may deter work or saving. Moreover, a person's duty to pay debts survives death, so why shouldn't the duty to support survive as well?[17]

The author(s) of Bracton also argued that freedom of testation gave wives and children an incentive to treat the testator well.[18] Blackstone made a similar point. When children could not be disinherited they became "disobedient and headstrong."[19] King Lear was mistreated by two of his daughters as soon as their share of his estate was secure.[20] On the other hand, some parents use their testamentary freedom to control the lives of their children in an unappealing way, for example by disinheriting a child who adopts a religion or marries a person the parent dislikes.[21] Arguably the law should allow a person to disinherit a child or spouse only for certain misconduct.[22]

A better argument for testamentary freedom is that it permits more intelligent estate planning than the rigid rules of intestate succession: "the parent more often than not will know better how to dispose of his property than will the state [which imposes] an inflexible blanket rule."[23] Such planning is

---

[14] Oldham, *What Does the U.S. System Regarding Inheritance Rights of Children Reveal about American Families?* 33 Family L.Q. 265, 269–70 (1999).

[15] 2 Bracton, *De Legibus et Consuetudinibus Angliae* 181 (Thorne ed. 1968).

[16] Macey, *Private Trusts for the Provision of Private Goods*, 37 Emory L.J. 295, 297 (1988); Cahn, *Restraints on Disinheritance,* 85 U.Pa.L.Rev. 139, 145 (1936).

[17] Rein, *supra* note 9, at 18–19.

[18] *See* note 15 *supra.*

[19] 2 W. Blackstone, *Commentaries* 12 (1766). *See also* Nathan, *supra* note 2, at 15. Thomas Jefferson made a similar point in justifying the abolition of the fee tail in Virginia. Sherman, *Posthumous Meddling: An Instrumentalist Theory of Testamentary Restraints on Contractual and Religious Choices*, 99 U.Ill.L.Rev. 1273, 1286 (1999). As to the fee tail, *see* Section 11.4.

[20] For a modern case, reminiscent of Lear, *see* Matter of Succession of Chaney, 413 So.2d 936 (La.App.1982).

[21] *E.g.,* Shapira v. Union Nat. Bank, 315 N.E.2d 825 (Ohio Com.Pl.1974); In re Estate of Feinberg, 919 N.E.2d 888 (Ill. 2009); 1 W. Blackstone, *Commentaries* 437 (1765). For the validity of such provisions, *see* Section 8.10.

[22] Thus, BGB (German Civil Code) §§ 2333 specifies grounds for which a spouse, parent or descendant may be deprived of the forced share.

[23] Nathan, *supra* note 2, at 19.

not limited to punishing family members for conduct of which the testator disapproves. A will may depart from the equal treatment of children mandated by the intestacy laws in order to take account of their differing needs (and behaviors). Or a testator who has provided for one child by lifetime gifts may leave this child less than the others to equalize the property passing to all of the testator's children during life and at death, because the law of advancements,[24] applicable when a decedent dies intestate, is a crude alternative for reflecting this desire. Or a testator may wish to provide for children equally but in different ways, for example, by leaving a family business to one child and equivalent assets to the others.[25] Or, a testator may wish to leave property in trust for a child or spouse who is unable to handle property.[26] Why should the law allow a child or spouse to upset reasonable wills like these?

Fixed-Share v. Discretionary Restraints

Restraints on testamentary freedom are of two types: (1) fixed share and (2) discretionary. Today, the most important limitation on testamentary freedom in the United States relates to a spouse's right to an elective share or community property share. Elective and community shares generally are a fraction of the estate. The elective share has been justified as designed "to secure a minimal means of sustenance for the surviving spouse, and to relieve the State of providing support in a situation where advanced age or infirmities make the surviving spouse unable to provide his or her own support,"[27] but the elective share imperfectly fits this rationale.

> [As] a means of assuring a degree of support for the surviving spouse . . . the forced share is a very crude instrument, because the costs of living and financial resources of the widow or widower are irrelevant, as are lifetime gifts the decedent may have made to the spouse. . . . Also, the fraction of the estate to which the surviving spouse is entitled does not vary with the size of the estate. . . . One-third of an estate of $1,000,000 may enable a spouse to live in the accustomed style, but one-third of an estate of $200,000 may not.[28]

A similar objection can be made against the forced share given to children in the civil law. Napoleon's proposal that the share should vary with the size of their parents' estate was rejected by the drafters of the "Napoleonic" Code because it "would require an expensive and often uncertain appraisal" of the estate.[29]

---

[24] *See* Section 2.6.

[25] Nathan, *supra* note 2, at 16.

[26] The advantage of trusts over alternative forms of property management are further explored in Section 10.5.

[27] Montgomery v. Estate of Montgomery, 677 N.E.2d 571, 581 (Ind.App.1997).

[28] E. Halbach ed., *Death, Taxes and Family Property* 111–12 (1977). *See also* Oldham, *supra* note 14, at 269–70. Some of these objections do not apply to the Uniform Probate Code. *See* Section 8.7.

[29] Lemann, *In Defense of Forced Heirship,* 52 Tul.L.Rev. 20, 23–24 (1977). Professor Haskell proposed a similar scheme. Haskell, *The Power of Disinheritance: Proposal for Reform,* 52 Geo.L.J. 499, 519 (1964).

The fixed-share schemes that protect the surviving spouse in America are easy to administer, but they often give a spouse more or less than is necessary for support. Some states reduce the surviving spouse's share by gifts received from the decedent or by the spouse's other resources, however acquired.[30] Even these statutes correlate only imperfectly with the need for support because they ignore the spouse's earning capacity. Also, support needs can change over time, for example if the spouse remarries or dies. And yet virtually all American statutes give the spouse a lump sum and take no account of later changes in circumstances.[31]

These objections to a fixed share do not all apply to the alternative rationale for the spouse's share, viz., recognition of the spouse's contributions to the estate. A spouse who helped to build up an estate should not be denied a share in it on the ground that the spouse is self-supporting. Nor should the decedent be allowed to put the spouse's share into a trust without the spouse's consent (assuming that the spouse is not incapacitated). However, if the spouse's contribution to the accumulation of property justifies the forced share, the share ought to depend upon the length of the marriage. If a marriage has lasted only a few weeks, the surviving spouse would have contributed very little, but would receive a large portion of the estate under most American statutes.

The family maintenance system common in the British commonwealth gives courts discretion to make awards from an estate to a spouse or child for whom the decedent's will fails to make adequate provision. The claimant's need is the primary determinant. The claimants' other resources, including earning capacity, are considered.[32] Awards can take the form of periodic payments that can be altered as needs change.[33] Need, however, is not the only factor; indeed, a spouse does not have to show need at all.[34] The contribution made by a spouse (including "looking after the home and caring for the family") and the length of the marriage are taken into account.[35] The conduct of an applicant may also be considered.

Some fixed-share statutes bar claimants who have engaged in specified misconduct. The Statute of Westminster of 1285 provided that a wife who left her husband and lived in adultery lost her right to dower.[36] Some states today bar a spouse who abandoned the other spouse from claiming an elective share in the estate.[37] Courts tend to construe such statutes strictly, so as to avoid a

---

[30] *See* Section 8.7.

[31] The family allowance provides a relatively unimportant exception to this statement. *See* Section 8.4.

[32] Inheritance (Provision for Family and Dependants) Act, 1975, § 3(1)(a), (6). For the history of this provision, *see* D. Parry & R. Kerridge, *The Law of Succession* 183–85 (13th ed. 2016).

[33] Laufer, *Flexible Restraints on Testamentary Freedom*, 69 Harv.L.Rev. 277, 293 (1955); New Zealand, Family Protection Act, 1955, § 12; England, Inheritance (Provision for Family and Dependants) Act, 1975, § 6.

[34] Inheritance (Provision for Family and Dependants) Act, 1975, § 1(2).

[35] *Id.* § 3(2).

[36] Statute of Westminster II, 13 Edw. I, ch. 34.

[37] N.Y. EPTL § 5–1.2(a)(5); Ind.Code § 29–1–2–15; N.C.Gen.Stat. § 31A–1(a)(2)(3); Purce v. Patterson, 654 S.E.2d 885 (Va. 2008).

forfeiture.[38] And in the absence of a statutory provision, courts have refused to hold that desertion bars a spouse's claims to an elective share.[39]

Discretionary statutes avoid many of the traditional objections to limitations on testamentary freedom. They do *not* disrupt intelligent estate plans by imposing an "inflexible blanket rule" modeled on the laws of intestate succession. In fact, discretionary statutes recognize that intestacy statutes may be unsuitable and allow courts to vary the statutory disposition.[40] Many American writers have urged that statutes of this type be adopted in the United States.[41] Others object that these statutes would promote litigation because courts would be "without guideposts or rules."[42] But, American courts regularly make similar discretionary determinations when they fix alimony and child support or divide property in divorce proceedings. For example, under the Model Marriage and Divorce Act, courts are to "equitably apportion" the spouses' property, considering among other things "the duration of the marriage . . . [and the] employability, estate, liabilities, and needs of each of the parties" and "the contribution or dissipation of each party" in their property.[43] The English Inheritance Act requires courts to treat the division of property at death and divorce in similar fashion.[44]

Discretionary statutes may lead to excessive litigation but, because wills which disinherit children or spouses are much rarer than divorce,[45] there would be few occasions to litigate under a discretionary statute designed to deal with this problem.[46] A statute protecting disinherited children might not actually increase the incidence of litigation in American law because such children often contest wills today on the ground that the testator was incapacitated or subject to undue influence.[47]

Nevertheless, in the comments to the Uniform Probate Code, the drafters rejected the idea of modeling the spouse's elective share on divorce law. "Although all or almost all states now follow the so-called equitable-distribution system upon divorce, there is considerable variation among the

---

38 In re Harris' Estate, 391 N.W.2d 487 (Mich.App.1986) (husband who occasionally visited his wife was not "absent" for a year, and so could claim an elective share). *See also* In re Estate of Kostick, 526 A.2d 746 (Pa.1987); In re Estate of Montgomery, 528 S.E.2d 618 (N.C.App.2000) (wife who left her husband not barred without "repeated" acts of adultery). The statutes give courts no discretion to reduce a share in proportion to the severity of the wrongdoing. Spitko, *An Accrual/Multi-Factor Approach to Intestate Inheritance Rights for Unmarried Committed Partners*, 81 Or.L.Rev. 255, 278 (2002).

39 Petition of Shiflett, 490 S.E.2d 902, 908 (W.Va.1997); Estate of Miller v. Miller, 768 P.2d 373 (Okl.App.1988)).

40 New Zealand, Family Protection Act, 1955, § 4; England, Inheritance (Provision for Family and Dependants) Act, 1975, § 1.

41 Laufer, *supra* note 33, Rein, *supra* note 9, at 47; Cahn, *supra* note 16, at 147; Niles, *Probate Reform in California,* 31 Hastings L.J. 185, 198–99 (1979).

42 Chaffin, *supra* note 11, at 462.

43 Model Marriage and Divorce Act § 307. Also, many American wrongful death statutes give courts broad discretion to distribute damages among the decedent's family. *See* Section 2.5.

44 Inheritance (Provision for Family and Dependants) Act, 1975, § 3(2).

45 Browder, *Recent Patterns of Testate Succession in the United States and England,* 67 Mich.L.Rev. 1303, 1305–08 (1969).

46 Plager, *The Spouse's Nonbarrable Share: A Solution in Search of a Problem,* 33 U.Chi.L.Rev. 681, 715 (1966).

47 Rein, *supra* note 9, at 54. As to incapacity and undue influence, *see* Sections 5.1, 5.3.

states in the details," and so the system was not compatible "with a uniform laws project striving to achieve uniformity within the probate system." Uniformity was important "in order to prevent a spouse bent on disinheritance from domicile shopping by relocating property to a state with fewer safeguards against this sort of behavior." Also, equitable distribution involves giving weight to fault in some states, and this is unfair "when death terminates the marriage [and] only the surviving spouse can testify as to . . . fault."[48] Claims that the different legal treatment of property upon divorce and death violates equal protection guarantees under the Constitution have been rejected.[49]

The drafters of the Uniform Probate Code were probably correct to conclude that "the consensus of national legal thinking would not accept a solution for the problem of spousal disinheritance that conferred so much discretion on the judicial system."[50] American legislatures have failed to adopt several proposed discretionary statutes like those of the British commonwealth. A similar anti-discretionary statute bias also is evident at the federal level as exemplified by the fact that when Congress empowered the Secretary of the Interior to approve wills disposing of Indian lands, the Supreme Court construed the statute to prohibit the Secretary from disapproving a will "simply because of a subjective feeling that the disposition of the estate was not 'just and equitable.' "[51]

Inter Vivos Transfers

If spouses or children should be able to upset a will which disinherits them, should they also be allowed to attack transfers which the decedent made while alive? One might distinguish between transfers made for consideration and transfers made as gifts. To upset sales would impede commerce and be unfair to purchasers who paid value. Moreover, the assets available for support of the seller's dependents are not depleted by a sale, because the sale proceeds take the place of the property sold. A right based on a spouse's contribution to the acquisition of property raises different considerations. Community property states, where the spouse's claim rests on a contribution theory, often allow one spouse to attack even sales of community real property made by the other.[52] On the other hand, a spouse whose claim is predicated on the duty of support should not be allowed to dictate which assets are used to fulfill that duty as long as adequate support is provided. Thus, the Uniform Probate Code allows a surviving spouse to attack only those lifetime transfers for which the decedent did not receive adequate consideration.[53]

---

[48] Waggoner, *The Multiple Marriage Society*, 76 Iowa L.Rev. 223, 242–44 (1991). *See also* Bongaards v. Millen, 793 N.E.2d 335, 346 (Mass.2003) ("case-specific" rules governing division of property at divorce inapplicable to "mathematical calculation" of spousal elective share).

[49] Hamilton v. Hamilton, 879 S.W.2d 416, 418 (Ark.1994).

[50] Wellman, *Arkansas and the Uniform Probate Code*, 2 U. of Ark. at Little Rock L.J. 1, 13 (1979).

[51] Tooahnippah v. Hickel, 397 U.S. 598, 610 (1970).

[52] Neumann v. McMillan, 629 P.2d 1214 (Nev.1981); Padilla v. Roller, 608 P.2d 1116 (N.M.1980); Rev.Code Wash. § 26.16.030; Cal.Fam.Code § 1102 (real property).

[53] Uniform Probate Code [hereinafter UPC] § 2–208(a). *See also* Inheritance (Provision for Family and Dependants) Act, 1975, § 10(2) (allowing court to reach property transferred within 6 years of death where the transferee did not give "full valuable consideration").

Perhaps even donees should be protected from some claims of the donor's family. Small gifts, like ordinary Christmas presents, should not be subject to attack.[54] Even as to more substantial gifts, donees may be unfairly prejudiced if they are forced to return property which was given to them years earlier. Many states, therefore, only allow surviving spouses a share of the property which the decedent owned at death. But the line between transfers during life and those which take effect at death is often blurred. How should one classify a gift made by a husband two days before he died? Or a trust created by a wife under which she reserved the income for her life and a power to revoke the trust until she died? In recent years such "will substitutes," which purport to be present gifts but which have virtually no effect until death, have become increasingly popular. They were originally not encompassed by the family maintenance statutes of the British Commonwealth,[55] but later amendments have empowered courts to reach them.[56] Many states now allow spouses to reach transfers made during life which are will-like in substance.[57]

§ 8.2 History and Comparative Law

Land

Wills of land and personal property followed different paths historically. Originally the common law limited a parent's right to give away land. Distinctions were made between land which the parent had acquired as distinguished from land which had been inherited. Likewise, there was a distinction between gifts within the family and gifts to strangers.[58] These rules disappeared early in the 13th century,[59] probably because the rise of primogeniture, under which all of a parent's land descended to the eldest son, created pressure to allow parents to make gifts to younger children.[60]

The freedom acquired in the 13th century to transfer land did not extend to wills. Land could not be devised by will until the Statute of Wills of 1540.[61] Blackstone attributed this rule to feudalism:

> Before the [Norman] conquest [of 1066 which introduced feudalism into England], lands were devisable by will. But, upon the introduction of the military tenures, the restraint of devising lands naturally took place, as a branch of the feudal doctrine of non-alienation without the consent of the lord.... The reason of conferring the feud being the personal abilities of the feudatory to

---

54 Even in community property states, small gifts of community property by one spouse are often allowed. Redfearn v. Ford, 579 S.W.2d 295 (Tex.Civ.App.1979).

55 Laufer, *supra* note 33, at 299.

56 Inheritance (Provision for Family and Dependants) Act, 1975, § 8–10.

57 *See* Section 8.7.

58 Glanvill, *Tractatus de Legibus* 69–71 (G. Hall ed. 1965).

59 A claim that a father could not give away all his inheritance seems to have been accepted in 6 Curia Regis Rolls 201 (1212), but was rejected in 13 Curia Regis Rolls pl. 1588 (1229).

60 T. Plucknett, *A Concise History of the Common Law* 528 (5th ed. 1956); Simes, *Public Policy and the Dead Hand* 10–11 (1955). Primogeniture survived in England until the 20th century, but almost from the beginning American states provided for equal treatment of an intestate's children. *Compare* the argument in Section 3.1 that wills allow better estate planning than the rules of intestate succession.

61 Glanvill, *supra* note 58, at 69–70.

> serve in war, it was not fit that he should be at liberty to transfer this gift . . . to others who might prove less able.[62]

Although this explanation resembles the modern justification for the rule which allows landlords to restrain alienation by tenants under a lease,[63] there are difficulties with it. A feudal lord's concern with the personal abilities of tenants would apply to all transfers of land, but in 1290 the statute Quia Emptores allowed tenants to alienate their land inter vivos without the lord's permission,[64] whereas the prohibition on devises continued for another two and a half centuries.

Feudal opposition to wills in the later Middle Ages focused not on concern with the "personal abilities" of the tenant, but on the feudal incidents, such as wardship, which gave lords the profits of land when it descended to a minor heir. If tenants could make wills, they could avoid wardship by devising land away from a minor heir.

For the author(s) of the treatise known as Glanvill in the 12th century, the prohibition against wills was a logical consequence of the rule that land could only be transferred by delivery, commonly known as livery of seisin.[65] The law required delivery perhaps because juries originally relied on their own knowledge in rendering verdicts rather than the testimony of witnesses produced in court. If possession of land was not delivered to the donee, the neighbors would not learn of the gift. A will, however, takes effect only when the testator dies, so delivery is impossible. Juries knew who had been in possession of land but were not competent to decide whether a decedent had made a will.[66] Only the church courts, which did not employ juries, could probate wills.[67] But the common law would not allow church courts to deal with *land*.[68] Thus, it may be that the medieval prohibition on wills of land rested, at least in part, on the inadequacy of the jury.

Uses

The prohibition on devises was evaded in the 15th century by uses. If John wanted to devise land to Arthur, he would deliver seisin to Tom and Dick "to the use" of John's last will and declare in his will that the land should pass to Arthur when John died.[69] If the feoffees Tom and Dick failed to carry out John's will, the Chancellor would compel them to do so. Why? Blackstone said the Chancellors enforced wills because they were usually ecclesiastics who wanted

---

[62] 2 W. Blackstone, *Commentaries* 57, 373 (1766).

[63] *See* Section 12.8.

[64] 18 Edw. 1, c. 1 (1290). For the background of this statute, *see* D. Sutherland, *The Assize of Novel Disseisin* 86–95 (1973).

[65] Glanvill, *supra* note 58, at 69.

[66] Plucknett, *supra* note 60, at 736.

[67] Glanvill, *supra* note 58, at 81. For further discussion of the history of probate, *see* Section 13.2.

[68] 2 Bracton, *De Legibus* 70, 149; Plucknett, *supra* note 60, at 737.

[69] The Roman will originally developed along similar lines, but the Roman counterpart to the English feoffee to uses (Tom and Dick in the hypothetical in the text), ultimately became a mere witness to the will whereas the feoffee to uses developed into the modern trustee. Zimmermann, *Heres Fiduciarius?*, in Itinera Fiduciae 268–70 (ed. Helmholz & Zimmermann 1998).

to foster devises for religious purposes: "as the popish clergy then generally sat in the court of chancery, they considered that men . . . at their death would choose to dispose of [their land] to those who, according to the superstition of the times, could intercede for their happiness in another world."[70] However, most 15th century wills were designed to provide for the testator's wife or younger children rather than the church.[71] The inadequacy of juries to deal with wills was irrelevant because the Chancellor did not use them; he examined witnesses under oath to ascertain the testator's intent.[72] The fact that uses, the ancestor of modern trusts, were originally enforced by the Chancellor in Equity still affects the enforcement of trusts today, where trial is not usually by jury.[73] It may also explain the absence of trusts in the civil law, which has no tradition of separate courts of law and equity.[74]

In the early 16th century, Henry VIII sought to end uses in order to maximize his revenue as a feudal lord. He induced the judges (who at this time held office at the King's pleasure) to hold that the devise of a use was "void."[75] This decision unsettled titles to much of the English land which for more than a century had been passing by devise and induced Parliament to enact the famous Statute of Uses. This statute validated all wills previously made, but effectually barred wills thereafter by providing that when land was held in use the legal title should pass to the beneficiary.[76] This made it impossible to evade the common-law prohibition on wills.

The preamble of the Statute reiterated many of Glanvill's arguments against wills made 350 years before. They were "for the most part made by such persons as be visited with sickness, in their extreme agonies and pains . . . at which times they . . . dispose indiscreetly and unadvisedly their lands." They injured both lords and heirs: "many heirs have been unjustly . . . disinherited, the lords have lost their wards" and other feudal incidents.

However, the abolition of wills produced a popular outcry. In an uprising in 1536 the rebels demanded that the Statute of Uses be repealed.[77] Henry VIII had to consent to the Statute of Wills of 1540 which allowed wills but protected the interests of feudal lords to some extent. A person who held land by knight service could only dispose of two-thirds of it; as to the other third, the lord's

---

70 2 W. Blackstone, *Commentaries* 375 (1766).

71 For examples of such wills, *see* K. Digby, *Introduction to the History of the Law of Real Property* 333–36 (4th ed. 1892); A. Kiralfy, *A Source Book of English Law* 266–67 (1957).

72 *Ibid.* Juries today are often used to try will contests, *see* Section 13.3, but for centuries juries' knowledge of the facts has depended on evidence produced in court rather than their own knowledge.

73 *See* Section 14.8.

74 *But see* Section 7.1 (possible Roman law origin for trusts); M. Lupoi, *Trusts: A Comparative Study* 4 (2000) (absence of separate courts of Equity no bar to civil law recognition of trusts).

75 Re Lord Dacre, 93 Sel.Soc. 228 (1536).

76 Statute of Uses, 27 Hen. 8, c. 10, § 9 (1536).

77 Plucknett, *supra* note 60, at 587. The Statute was not repealed, and is still invoked occasionally today, but loopholes were found which made the modern trust possible. *See* F. Maitland, *Equity* 38–42 (1909).

right to wardship and other feudal incidents was expressly preserved.[78] This limitation became obsolete in 1660 when the feudal incidents were abolished.[79]

Personal Property

Feudal considerations did not apply to personal property, which originally was much less important than land. The common law conceded jurisdiction over testaments of personal property to the church courts, which did not employ jury trial, and allowed wills. There were, however, limitations on a testator's right to disinherit his wife[80] and children. In the 12th century, a decedent's movables were divided into three equal parts: one for his children, one for his wife, and a third "over which he has free power of disposition." If the testator died without a wife he could dispose of half of his personalty.[81] The treatise known as Bracton restated these rules in the next century, but said that they did not apply if there was a local custom to the contrary.[82]

In the later Middle Ages the situation described by the Bracton treatise was reversed. Freedom of testation became the general rule; a widow or children who sought a forced share had to allege a local custom. By the end of the fourteenth century such local customs had largely ceased to be in force.[83] They were eliminated by statutes in the late 17th and early 18th centuries.[84] Before then, the differing rules in different localities had allowed evasion of local restrictions.[85] A similar problem exists in the United States today. Our 51 jurisdictions offer opportunities for a determined parent or spouse to evade restrictions on testamentary freedom. State restrictions on disinheritance may simply encourage a flight of property to jurisdictions where testamentary freedom is less impaired.[86]

Modern British Law

In the British Commonwealth, instead of the medieval fixed share, modern legislatures, beginning with New Zealand in 1900,[87] have established discretionary controls to protect spouses and children.[88] The New Zealand Family Protection Act of 1955 also allows claims by parents. The English statute includes step-children who were "treated by the deceased as a child,"

---

[78] Statute of Wills, 32 Henry 8, c. 1, § 4 (1540). The power of devising lands held by "socage" tenure was not limited because wardship did not apply to them, because "no military or other personal service being required, there is no occasion for the lord to take the profits, in order to provide a proper substitute for his infant tenant." 2 W. Blackstone, *Commentaries* 88 (1766).

[79] 12 Car. 2, c. 24, § 1 (1660).

[80] At common law a husband acquired title to his wife's personal property upon marriage, 2 W. Blackstone, *Commentaries* 433 (1766). Therefore there was no occasion to consider the wife's right to disinherit her husband.

[81] Glanvill, *supra* note 58, at 80.

[82] Bracton, *supra* note 68, at 180–81.

[83] Helmholz, *Legitim in English Legal History,* [1984] U. of Ill.L.Rev. 659, 660, 667. However, church courts provided some protection to children who were needy. *Id.* at 669–70.

[84] 2 W. Blackstone, *Commentaries* 492–93 (1766).

[85] 11 Geo. 1, c. 18, § 1 (1724).

[86] As to the rules governing choice of law, *see* Section 1.2.

[87] Laufer, *Flexible Restraints on Testamentary Freedom,* 69 Harv.L.Rev. 277, 282 (1955).

[88] *See* Section 8.1.

former spouses, and any other person who was "being maintained" by the decedent.[89]

Civil Law

The fixed share for children described by the Glanvill and Bracton treatises in medieval England still exists throughout much of the world. A "testator is required under Islamic inheritance law to leave various heirs, including distant relatives, specified percentages of his wealth."[90] The German Civil Code gives heirs a forced share equivalent to one half of their intestate share.[91] The French Civil Code of 1804 prescribed fixed shares in order to prevent parents from reinstituting primogeniture by leaving all their property to the eldest son; the leaders of the French Revolution associated primogeniture with aristocracy and considered it contrary to their egalitarian ideals.[92] The share reserved for children, known as the *legitime,* varies with the number of children; a parent with one child can dispose of half his estate, but if there are three children the disposable share is only one fourth.[93] Even if a testator has no children, a share is reserved for any surviving ascendants (parents, grandparents, etc.).[94] The *legitime* is protected against inter vivosinter vivos gifts as well as wills,[95] but insurance is exempt; if a parent designates a stranger as beneficiary of an insurance policy, the children cannot claim a share of the proceeds.[96] In Germany, unlike France, a child can be disinherited for four specified "just causes" which must be set forth in the will,[97] and a parent can put the child's forced share into something like a trust.[98] If a will leaves property to a forced heir, he or she is put to an election

---

89 Inheritance (Provision for Family and Dependants) Act, 1975, § 1(1).

90 Schoenblum, *The Role of Legal Doctrine in the Decline of the Islamic Waqf: A Comparison with the Trust,* 32 Vand.J. Transnational Law 1191, 1196–97 (1999).

91 BGB (German Civil Code) § 2303. Arguably this share is protected by the German constitution. H. Brox & W. Walker, *Erbrecht* 15–16 (27th ed. 2016). The hindrance of the forced share to intelligent estate planning can be avoided by persuading an heir to renounce the right during the decedent's lifetime. BGB (German Civil Code) § 2346.

92 H. Maine, *Ancient Law* 187 (World Classics ed. 1931). Contrast the modern attempt of the United States to deal with the opposite problem—the "fractionation" of Indian lands—by "regulating the[ir] descent and devise." Hodel v. Irving, 481 U.S. 704, 718 (1987). Under the original Revolutionary legislation, a person with children could devise only a tenth of his property. J. Brissaud, *A History of French Private Law* § 518, at 747 (R. Howell tr. 1912). The Napoleonic Code, the basis of modern French law, is less restrictive.

93 French Code Civil art. 913. A larger share can be left to the testator's spouse for life. *Id.* art. 1094–1.

94 French Code Civil art. 914.

95 French Code Civil art. 922–23.

96 A. Braun & A. Röthel, *Passing Wealth on Death: Will-Substitutes in Comparative Perspective* 172 (2016).

97 BGB (German Civil Code) § 2333. A similar provision once in force in Louisiana gave rise to much litigation. Succession of Del Buno, 665 So.2d 172 (La.App.1995) (disinheritance for failure to communicate with testator upheld); Ambrose Succession v. Ambrose, 548 So.2d 37 (La.App.1989) (disinheritance for "cruelty" allowed); Succession of Steckler, 665 So.2d 561 (La.App.1995) (disinheritance disallowed, because child had sent parent at least two Christmas cards and a birthday card).

98 BGB (German Civil Code) § 2338; *cf.* Lorio, *Louisiana Trusts: The Experience of a Civil Law Jurisdiction with the Trust,* 42 La.L.Rev. 1721, 1735–36 (1982).

between the will and the *legitime*, as under the American elective share scheme for spouses.[99]

Louisiana once had similar rules, but they have been watered down considerably in recent years. Since 1981, only descendants of the decedent, and since 1995, only children who are under age 24 or "who, because of mental incapacity or physical infirmity, are incapable of taking care of" themselves, are protected.[100] China also provides a mandatory share only for "heirs who are unable to work and have no source of income."[101]

Because forced heirship is common in most of the world, American courts have had to deal with choice-of-law problems. When the will of a French domiciliary executed in Paris disinheriting her son provided that it should be "regulated by the laws of the State of New York," a New York court denied the son's claim to a *legitime*, saying that there was "a significant distinction between enforcing a . . . spouse's elective share, which differs only in degree from our own law . . . and enforcing a descendant's forced share which runs counter to our local policy."[102] Not surprisingly courts in Europe look less favorably on attempts to evade the forced share, *e.g.*, by transferring title to land in France to a corporation in order to have it governed by the law of the testator's domicile, New York.[103]

§ 8.3 Survival of Claims for Support

Litigation occasionally arises about whether a parent's duty to support a child survives the parent's death. Typically, the issue arises upon a father's death but even then the issue rarely arises if the father at death is married to the child's mother. In such a case, usually the decedent leaves all or most of the estate to the surviving spouse. If the decedent does not, the surviving spouse in most states can claim a share of it.[104] The surviving spouse will use the property to support the child. Indeed, the surviving spouse can be compelled to do so because parents are obligated to support their children.[105]

---

99 Italian Codice Civile art. 550; *cf.* BGB (German Civil Code) § 2307. *See also* Section 8.7, *infra.*

100 An earlier attempt by the legislature to limit forced heirship to such children was held unconstitutional in Succession of Lauga, 624 So.2d 1156 (La.1993). The constitutional protection of forced heirship was thereafter limited in 1995. La. Const. Art. 12, § 5. The forced share is one-half if there are two or more children, one-fourth if there is only one child. La.Civ.Code art. 1495.

101 Foster, *The Dark Side of Trusts: Challenges to Chinese Inheritance Law*, 2 Wash.U. Global Studies L.Rev. 151, 174 (2003).

102 Estate of Renard, 437 N.E.2d 860 (N.Y.Sur. 1981). *See also* Sanchez v. Sanchez De Davila, 547 So.2d 943 (Fla.App.1989) (claim to forced heirship under Venezuela law of bank account in Florida); Matter of Estate of Wright, 637 A.2d 106 (Me.1994) (claim under Swiss law rejected where will said Maine law should govern). However, American courts have on occasion recognized claims by children to a forced share under civil law. Nahar v. Nahar, 656 So.2d 225 (Fla.App.1995) (applying Dutch law to a Florida bank account because the owner was domiciled in the Netherlands Antilles).

103 J-P. Béraudo, *Les Trusts Anglo-Saxons et le Droit Francais* 210–11 (1992); H. Flick & D. Piltz, *Der Internationale Erbfall* 37–38 (1999).

104 For the elective share and community property rights of spouses, *see* Sections 8.7, 8.8.

105 H. Clark, *The Law of Domestic Relations* § 6.2 (2d ed. 1988); Cal.Family Code § 3900 (father and mother have equal responsibility to support their child).

However, if the parents are divorced when one dies, or if they were never married, the surviving parent is not a surviving "spouse" entitled to a share of the estate. Fathers' wills often do not provide for children by a former marriage or for nonmarital children. Normally at the time of divorce, the parent is ordered or agrees to make payments for the child's support. Whether the obligation of child support survives a parent's death may depend on the terms of the agreement or divorce decree; if it is silent, the obligation to make future payments expires at death in many, but not in all, states. For example, a father who was obligated by an Indiana divorce decree to pay child support died in Ohio while the children were still minors.[106] Under Ohio law, his obligation terminated at death,[107] because the divorce decree made no provision for this,[108] but under Indiana law, the obligation continued.[109] This gave rise to the further question whether the Indiana decree would be given effect in Ohio. Ordinarily judgments subject to modification (as support orders typically are) are not entitled to full faith and credit, but this limitation did not apply to accrued claims for support that were due at death.[110]

Many of the traditional justifications for freedom of testation do not apply in this situation. The disinheritance of children here is not merely the "technical" one which occurs when a spouse leaves everything to the other parent of the decedent's children.[111] The disadvantage of guardianship for minors is irrelevant because support payments typically go to the other parent for the benefit of the children, so a guardianship is not needed.[112] Reluctance to confer discretion on courts is not a valid objection to enforcing a duty of support which was fixed at the time of the divorce or in a paternity action in the case of nonmarital children. However, an adjustment in a prior support order may be called for by the changed circumstances produced by the parent's death. Life insurance proceeds or Social Security benefits may render continuation of the support payments no longer necessary. For example, when a father who was obligated to pay monthly child support died, the child began receiving Social Security payments of $768. Although this did not extinguish the father's obligation, the executor of his estate could seek to have it modified

---

106 Barnett v. Barnett, 619 N.E.2d 38 (Ohio App.1993).

107 However, accrued claims for support due at death can be enforced from the obligor's estate. Connin v. Bailey, 472 N.E.2d 328 (Ohio 1984); Benson v. Patterson, 830 A.2d 966 (Pa. 2003) (obligation terminated at death).

108 *Compare* Gilford v. Wurster, 493 N.E.2d 258 (Ohio App. 1983) (construing support obligation in a separation agreement to survive death).

109 *See also* In re Marriage of Perry, 68 Cal.Rptr.2d 445 (Cal. App.Dist. 4. 1997) ("a child support obligation survives the death of the supporting parent and is a charge against his or her estate" and can also be paid from the assets of a revocable trust—the functional equivalent of an estate); Kiken v. Kiken, 694 A.2d 557 (N.J.1997) (same); L.W.K. v. E.R.C., 735 N.E.2d 359 (Mass.2000) (support order in a paternity action against the father of a child born out of wedlock enforceable against the father's estate). For further statutes and cases on both sides of this question, *see* Oldham, *What Does the U.S. System Regarding Inheritance Rights of Children Reveal about American Families?* 33 Family L.Q. 265, 271 (1999).

110 *Accord*, Adair v. Martin, 595 S.W.2d 513 (Tex.1980).

111 *See* Section 8.1.

112 H. Clark, *The Law of Domestic Relations* § 17.1 (2d ed. 1988); L.W.K. v. E.R.C., 735 N.E.2d 359, 362 (Mass.2000).

because of the changed circumstances.[113] If a parent has remarried and incurred obligations to a new family, enforcing the duty to support children by the prior marriage might deplete the estate at the expense of the new dependents.[114]

The Model Marriage and Divorce Act attempts to reconcile these competing considerations: provisions in a divorce decree or agreement for child support are not terminated by the death of the obligated parent (unless the decree so provides), but the "amount of support may be modified . . . to the extent just and appropriate in the circumstances."[115] This statute only protects children of a testator who has been divorced. A claim that this was an unconstitutional denial of equal protection was rejected on the ground that disinheritance by parents who have not been divorced is alleviated by the other parent's right to a share of the decedent's estate.[116] A similar argument was used to justify special protection for a nonmarital child.[117]

Alimony

The duty to pay alimony to a former spouse usually ceases when the payer dies,[118] but an agreement may provide otherwise, either expressly or by implication.[119] For example, an agreement to pay annual support until a wife remarried or died was held to create a claim against the husband's estate, because the explicit "criteria for termination were remarriage or death of the ex-wife," not the husband's death.[120] But another court rejected this reasoning, saying that when an agreement contains "no unequivocal direction to pay after death, . . . [the] preference that maintenance obligations terminate upon death of the payor should ordinarily prevail." However, the court refused to grant summary judgment for the husband's estate; because the wife had not been represented by counsel when the separation agreement was drafted, "the omission of the recommended and customary explicit clause providing for the circumstance of the death of the payor . . . ought not to be deemed . . . a complete or reliable manifestation of intent for both contracting parties."[121]

---

[113] In re Marriage of Bertrand, 39 Cal.Rptr.2d 151 (App.1995). Courts have responded to this situation in various ways. In re Marriage of Meek, 669 P.2d 628 (Colo.App.1983) (proper to terminate support obligation because of Social Security benefits); Gilford v. Wurster, 493 N.E.2d 258 (Ohio App.1983) (Social Security payments credited to obligation); Pessein v. Pessein, 846 P.2d 1385 (Wash.App.1993) (obligation is not reduced by Social Security payments).

[114] H. Clark, *The Law of Domestic Relations* § 17.2 (2d ed. 1988).

[115] Model Marriage and Divorce Act § 316(c). In In re Matter of Marriage of Perry, 68 Cal.Rptr.2d 445, 449 (Cal. App. Dist. 4. 1997) the court deferred deciding whether a court could order a post-death upward modification of a child support order but mused that a post-death upward adjustment "would severely destabilize estate planning."

[116] Kujawinski v. Kujawinski, 376 N.E.2d 1382 (Ill.1978).

[117] L.W.K. v. E.R.C., 735 N.E.2d 359, 365–66 (Mass.2000).

[118] Holley v. Holley, 969 So.2d 842 (Miss. 2007); Hendricks v. Hendricks, 817 P.2d 1339 (Or.App.1991); Barron v. Puzo, 610 N.E.2d 973 (Mass.1993). *Contra,* BGB (German Civil Code) § 1586b (limited liability of payer's estate).

[119] Braun v. Braun, 865 N.E.2d 814 (Mass. App. 2007); Palmer v. Palmer, 170 P.3d 676 (Ariz. App. Div. 2007); In re Last Will and Testament of Sheppard, 757 So.2d 173 (Miss.2000).

[120] Lipe v. Lipe, 728 P.2d 1124, 1127 (Wyo.1986). *See also* In re Estate of Bartlett, 485 N.E.2d 566 (Ill.App.1985).

[121] Matter of Riconda, 688 N.E.2d 248, 252–53 (N.Y.1997).

As the foregoing opinion indicates, lawyers who negotiate divorce settlements that provide for support payments should anticipate that the payer may die while the children or ex-spouse still need support. A provision for continuation of payments from the obligor's estate is not an adequate solution, because the estate may be inadequate—even if the obligor currently earns a high income, that income will cease at death. Also, it is generally undesirable to keep an estate open to continue periodic payments. The Model Marriage and Divorce Act deals with the latter problem by allowing an obligation to be "commuted into a lump sum payment."[122] Many divorce settlements require a parent to maintain life insurance for the benefit of children whom the divorcing parent is obligated to support.[123] The California Family Code provides that unless otherwise agreed, obligations to support a spouse terminate "upon the death of either party,"[124] but a court may order payment of an amount "sufficient to purchase an annuity . . . or to maintain insurance for the benefit of the supported spouse on the life of the spouse required to make the payment of support" or to establish a trust for support.[125] Such a provision can provide security that the claim will be paid[126] and avoid having to keep an estate open.

§ 8.4 Family Allowance and Homestead

Family Allowance

A decedent's assets are frozen while the estate is administered. During this time, claims against the estate are ascertained and paid.[127] But the decedent's family cannot be left to starve while the claims of creditors are ascertained, so the law provides an allowance for their support during administration. This idea is as old as the Magna Carta, which allowed a widow to remain in her husband's home for forty days after his death while dower was being assigned to her.[128]

---

[122] Model Marriage and Divorce Act § 316(c).

[123] In re Estate of Downey, 687 N.E.2d 339 (Ill.App.1997) (noting a conflict in the cases as to whether a court could order such a provision, but clearly "the parties may voluntarily agree to do so").

[124] Cal. Family Code § 4337. However, under § 3952, if a parent with a support obligation dies leaving a *child* "chargeable to the county or . . . confined in a state institution," the county or state can get reimbursement from the parent's estate.

Model Marriage and Divorce Act § 316 also distinguishes between "maintenance" of a spouse, which terminates on the death of either party, and "support" for a child, which is "terminated by emancipation of the child but not by the death of a parent."

[125] Cal.Family Code § 4360. *See also* In re Marriage of Perry, 68 Cal.Rptr.2d 445 (App.1997) (support payments ordered from trust created by father before his death); Benson v. Benson, 977 P.2d 88, 94–5 (Alaska 1999) (proper to order father who had been dilatory in making support payments to create a trust to satisfy them).

[126] But if the father who is obligated to keep insurance in force nevertheless allows the policy to lapse, it may be necessary to enforce the claim against his probate estate. Tintocalis v. Tintocalis, 25 Cal.Rptr.2d 655 (App.1993); Kiltz v. Kiltz, 708 N.E.2d 600 (Ind.App.1999).

[127] For the payment of claims against an estate, *see* Section 13.5.

[128] Magna Carta cap. 7 (1215). For modern reflections of the widow's "quarantine," *see* Matter of Estate of Stroh, 392 N.W.2d 192 (Mich.App.1986) (widow entitled to remain in home rent-free until dower assigned); Cal.Prob.Code § 6500 (spouse and minor children can remain in dwelling until 60 days after inventory of the estates filed).

Today, the family allowance provides for a decedent's spouse and children while the estate is being settled. While some statutes give allowances only to minor children,[129] the Uniform Probate Code covers "minor children whom the decedent was obligated to support and children who were in fact being supported by the decedent."[130] The allowance is paid to the surviving spouse "for the use of" the children, but if a child is not living with the spouse, "the allowance may be made partially to the child or the child's guardian or other person having the child's care and custody."[131]

The size of the allowance varies. The Uniform Probate Code gives "a reasonable allowance."[132] According to the comment, "account should be taken of the previous standard of living" in deciding what is "reasonable." An Illinois statute says that the allowance shall be "suited to the condition in life of the surviving spouse and to the condition of the estate."[133] The allowance can be very substantial if the claimants were accustomed to "the finer things of life." William Randolph Hearst's widow received an allowance of $10,000 per month.[134]

If the spouse and children have sufficient other resources, the Texas Probate Code bars them from receiving a family allowance.[135] The Uniform Probate Code comments say that "account should be taken of . . . the nature of other resources available to the family."[136] Some courts distinguish between a spouse's independent means, which do not bar an award, and benefits derived from the decedent, which do.[137] Some courts also consider a spouse's earning capacity.[138] A spouse's remarriage precludes the spouse from receiving an award in some states.[139]

---

[129] Tex.Est.Code § 353.101; Ohio Rev.Code § 2106.13; Ga.Code § 53–3–1; Md.Estates and Trusts Code § 3–201(b).

[130] UPC § 2–404. *See also* 755 ILCS 5/15–1 (minor and adult dependent children); Calif.Prob.Code § 6540 (includes adult dependent children and parents); Or.Rev.Stat. § 114.015; *cf.* In re Estate of Degner, 518 N.E.2d 400 (Ill.App.1987) ("dependent" includes an adult child unable to support herself even though decedent had not been supporting her).

[131] UPC § 2–404. *Cf.* 755 ILCS 5/15–2(a) (award to child not residing with spouse goes to "such person as the court directs").

[132] UPC § 2–404. Cal.Prob.Code § 6540 is similar.

[133] 755 ILCS 5/15–1(a).

[134] T. Atkinson, *Handbook of the Law of Wills* 134 (2d ed. 1953). *Compare* Howard v. Howard, 257 S.E.2d 336 (Ga.App.1979) ($45,000 awarded to widow for "year's support"); Matter of Estate of Hamilton, 869 P.2d 971 (Utah App.1994) ($1,000 a month for 24 months); Matter of Estate of Lettengarver, 813 P.2d 468 (Mont.1991) ($6,000 award).

[135] Tex.Est.Code § 353.101(d). *Cf.* Calif.Prob.Code § 6540(c) (claimants without "reasonable maintenance from other sources" are given preference). *Compare* the consideration of other resources in determining needs in trusts for support, discussed in Section 10.7, at note 304 et seq.

[136] UPC § 2–404, comment. *Cf.* In re Estate of Wentworth, 452 N.W.2d 714 (Minn.App.1990) (proper to deny allowance to spouse with other means of support); Matter of Estate of Wheat, 955 P.2d 1339 (Kan.App.1998) (proper to deny allowance to spouse and children who received substantial life insurance proceeds).

[137] Matter of Estate of Caffrey, 458 N.E.2d 1147 (Ill.App.1983). In Matter of Estate of Parkhill, 548 N.E.2d 821 (Ill.App.1989), a widower was given the minimum allowance because he had received over $249,000 from assets held in joint tenancy with the decedent.

[138] In re Estate of O'Neill, 432 N.E.2d 1111 (Ill.App.1982); Ga.Code § 53–3–7(c)(1).

[139] *Id.* § 53–3–2(a).

Some statutes fix the amount of the family allowance, leaving nothing to the court's discretion,[140] and others provide for a minimum award.[141] The Uniform Probate Code allows the decedent's personal representative to determine the allowance at up to $27,000 (indexed for inflation, see UPC § 1–109) but a court may order a smaller or larger allowance on petition by an interested person.[142] Where statutes designate a specific amount, periodic adjustment should be made to compensate for the effects of inflation.[143]

Appeals from a trial court order fixing the family allowance rarely succeed.[144] Because the allowance is designed to meet immediate needs of the family, time-consuming appellate review is inappropriate.[145]

The American family allowance resembles family maintenance legislation in the British Commonwealth,[146] but the American allowance provides support only "during the period of administration" of the estate[147] or for some fixed period following the decedent's death.[148]

Many statutes, including the Uniform Probate Code, provide that the allowance may be paid in installments. Under the Code, payments cease if a recipient dies before all the installments are paid,[149] but in some states any unpaid family allowance passes to the spouse's estate.[150]

The family allowance takes precedence over nearly all claims against the estate. In this respect it provides more protection to spouses than the elective share, which is based on the net estate.[151] However, the family allowance may be limited if an estate is insolvent. Under the Uniform Probate Code, the allowance "may not continue for longer than one year if the estate is inadequate to discharge allowed claims."[152]

---

140 Md.Estates and Trusts Code § 3–201 ($10,000 for spouse and $5,000 for each minor child); Ohio Code § 2106.13(A) ($40,000); Ind.Code § 29–1–4–1 ($25,000).

141 755 ILCS 5/15–1(a) ($20,000 to spouse plus $10,000 for each eligible minor child).

142 UPC §§ 2–404; 2–405.

143 The UPC guideline was raised from $6,000 to $18,000 in 1990, and then raised again in 2008. UPC § 2–405, comment.

144 In re Marriage of Meek, 669 P.2d 628 (Colo.App.1983) (applying abuse of discretion standard to affirm lower court decision); Matter of Estate of Buhler, 607 P.2d 956 (Ariz.1980); Matter of Estate of Lettengarver, 813 P.2d 468 (Mont.1991).

145 *See* Calif.Prob.Code § 6545 (no stay of payment of family allowance pending appeal).

146 *See* Section 8.1.

147 UPC § 2–404. *See also* Cal.Prob.Code § 6543(a) (allowance terminates when estate is distributed); Matter of Estate of Bell, 833 P.2d 294 (Okl.App.1992) (court lacks discretion to continue support allowance once statutory purpose is met).

148 Iowa Code § 633.374 (12 month period following the decedent's death).

149 UPC § 2–404(b).

150 755 ILCS 5/15–1(a); Matter of Estate of Gray, 505 N.E.2d 806 (Ind.App.1987). This seems inconsistent with the support rationale of the family allowance, but it allows the allowance to qualify for the federal estate tax marital deduction. Estate of Radel, 88 T.C. 1143 (1987).

151 UPC § 2–404; *cf.* Cal.Prob.Code § 11420(a)(5); Estate of Rosenberger, 495 N.W.2d 234 (Minn.App.1993) (family maintenance allowed even though estate is under attachment to creditor); Timothy C. Wirt, M.D., P.C. v. Prout, 754 P.2d 429 (Colo.App.1988); Matter of Estate of Wilhelm, 760 P.2d 718 (Mont.1988) (family allowance supersedes creditor's lien on deceased debtor's property).

152 UPC § 2–404(a). *See also* Calif.Prob.Code § 6543(a); Or.Rev.Stat. § 114.065. In Matter of Estate of Caffrey, 458 N.E.2d 1147 (Ill.App.1983), an award was reduced when it appeared it would render the estate insolvent.

In some states, the family allowance is payable only out of assets which the decedent owned, and if the decedent's property was mortgaged or held in trust, the rights of the mortgagee or trust beneficiary are superior.[153] Although the family allowance is usually payable only out of the probate estate, the Uniform Probate Code allows many nonprobate assets (*e.g.*, joint bank accounts) to be reached to pay the allowance if the probate estate is insufficient.[154] Other nonprobate assets, such as life insurance, are not reachable to satisfy the family allowance, however.[155] The right of a spouse to satisfy the elective share from such assets is more extensive.[156]

The family of a decedent is entitled to an allowance even if they are disinherited by the decedent's will. If the will provides for them, they can take under the will and claim an allowance too, unless the will expressly provides that they must elect between the two.[157] In this respect, the family allowance differs from the elective share.[158]

Homestead; Exempt Property

The Uniform Probate Code has two other provisions for spouses and children: a "homestead allowance" and one for "exempt property." Exemptions from execution existed at common law, but homestead is a uniquely American contribution which goes back to a 1839 statute of the Republic of Texas.[159] Homestead and exempt property, like the family allowance, take precedence over claims of creditors and any will of the decedent.[160] The amounts involved are relatively small. The UPC homestead allowance gives the spouse $22,500 (indexed for inflation, see UPC § 1–109), and, if there is no surviving spouse, the same amount is divided among the "minor and dependent" children.[161] Exempt property is $15,000 (indexed for inflation, see UPC § 1–109).[162]

---

[153] Parson v. Parson, 56 Cal.Rptr.2d 686 (App.1996); Hughes v. Hughes, 314 S.E.2d 920 (Ga.App.1984).

[154] UPC § 6–102; Matter of Estate of Wagley, 760 P.2d 316 (Utah 1988). *See also* Kroslack v. Estate of Kroslack, 504 N.E.2d 1024 (Ind.1987); In re Estate of Sieh, 745 N.W.2d 477 (Iowa 2008) (spouse's allowance can be paid from assets of a revocable trust). For the right of creditors to reach non-probate assets, *see* Section 13.6.

[155] In re Estate of Agans, 998 P.2d 449 (Ariz.App.1999).

[156] *See* Section 8.7.

[157] UPC § 2–404(b); 755 ILCS 5/15–1(b); Sanders v. Pierce, 979 S.W.2d 457 (Ky.App.1998) (widow's exemption); Russell v. Hall, 266 S.E.2d 491 (Ga.1980); *cf.* In re Estate of Reddick, 657 N.E.2d 531 (Ohio App.1995) (will put spouse to an election). If the decedent had no will, the family allowance is not charged against the recipient's intestate share. Matter of Estate of Bowman, 609 P.2d 663 (Idaho 1980); Hiers v. Estate of Hiers, 628 S.E.2d 653, 656 (Ga. App. 2006) (bequest to spouse in lieu of year's support puts spouse to an election).

[158] *See* Section 8.7.

[159] Matter of Estate of Dodge, 685 P.2d 260, 263 (Colo.App.1984).

[160] UPC §§ 2–402, 2–403; In re Estate of Martelle, 32 P.3d 758 (Mont.2001); In re Estate of Lane, 188 P.3d 23 (Kan. App. 2008). Florida allows a devisee who is not an heir to take advantage of the homestead exemption. Snyder v. Davis, 699 So.2d 999 (Fla.1997). A constructive trust can be imposed on homestead property which was wrongfully acquired. Kostelnik v. Roberts, 680 S.W.2d 532 (Tex.App.1984).

[161] UPC § 2–402, comment.

[162] UPC § 2–403. This amount goes, in the absence of a spouse, to the "children"—it is not restricted to minors and dependent children.

However, these amounts are not dependent upon need,[163] and are not affected by other provisions made for the claimant by the decedent.[164]

In some states, homestead is more substantial.[165] The Arkansas Constitution provides a homestead of up to one acre of land in cities and 160 acres elsewhere without regard to value, but widows only get a life estate and children only a right to the income until they are 21.[166] In Iowa, the homestead includes the debtor's principal dwelling house and up to forty acres depending on whether the house is located on a city or rural plat.[167] The surviving spouse's rights in the estate may equal a fee or a life estate in the homestead depending upon certain circumstances. Homestead is available only if the decedent owned a residence; a family living in rental property derives no benefit from it.[168] The homestead and exempt property allowance under the Uniform Probate Code, on the other hand, do not depend on the "type of property in the decedent's estate."[169] Under Section 2–403 of the Uniform Probate Code, exempt property is taken primarily "in household furniture, automobiles, furnishings, appliances, and personal effects," but if necessary, other assets are used to satisfy the exempt property allowance.

Some homestead laws protect children,[170] but under the Uniform Probate Code homestead and exempt property go only to the surviving spouse; children benefit only if no spouse survives.[171]

Even though homestead and the exempt property take precedence over claims of creditors, they may provide less protection than the elective share provides with respect to property that is not in the probate estate.[172] But some

---

[163] In re Estate of Wentworth, 452 N.W.2d 714 (Minn.App.1990) (proper to deny family allowance but not homestead and exempt property claim on basis that spouse had sufficient resources of her own).

[164] In re Estate of Martelle, 32 P.3d 758 (Mont.2001) (widow entitled to homestead allowance even though the residence passed to her in joint tenancy).

[165] Fla. Const. art. 10, § 4(a)(1) (homestead for residence of up to one half-acre in municipality, and 160 acres elsewhere). UPC § 2–402A preserves the constitutional right of homestead in those states where it exists. In Matter of Estate of Heimbach, 847 P.2d 824 (Okl.App.1993), a widow was awarded an 80 acre farm for life as homestead, even though the decedent had devised it to his children by a prior marriage.

[166] Ark.Const. art. 9, §§ 4–6. *Cf.* Carolina Production Credit Ass'n v. Rogers, 318 S.E.2d 357 (S.C.1984) (widow loses homestead when she remarries). In contrast, under the UPC if a wife dies before receiving her homestead allowance her executor can claim it. Matter of Estate of Merkel, 618 P.2d 872 (Mont.1980).

[167] Iowa Code §§ 561.1, 561.2.

[168] Brantley & Effland, *Inheritance, the Share of the Surviving Spouse, and Wills: Arkansas Law and the Uniform Probate Code Compared,* 3 U.Ark. at Little Rock L.J. 361, 388 (1980).

[169] *Restatement (Third) of Property (Wills and Other Donative Transfers)* § 1.1, cmt. j (1999); UPC § 2–402; In re Estate of Martelle, 32 P.3d 758, 762 (Mont.2001) (widow entitled to homestead allowance even though the residence passed to her in joint tenancy). Washington provides a discretionary award "in lieu of" homestead when the decedent does not own a home. In re Estate of Martin, 655 P.2d 1211 (Wash.App.1983).

[170] In re Estate of Finch, 401 So.2d 1308 (Fla.1981).

[171] *Cf.* In re Estate of Garwood, 38 P.3d 362 (Wash.App.2002) (when surviving spouse, to whom the decedent's estate was devised, did not petition for homestead, adult child by a prior marriage could not).

[172] Estate of Overmire v. American Nat. Red Cross, 794 P.2d 518 (Wash.App.1990) (no award in lieu of homestead out of revocable trust). This result may be changed if a state has adopted UPC § 6–102, as proposed in 1998.

states protect homestead against inter vivosinter vivos conveyances by one spouse without the other's consent.[173] In Iowa, the lifetime conveyance of a homestead is void if the non-owning spouse does not join in the conveyance.[174] The non-owning spouse's consent is necessary even if the homestead was acquired by the owning spouse prior to the marriage.[175]

§ 8.5 Pretermitted Heirs

Most American states today have "pretermitted" or "omitted heir"[176] statutes, based on the assumption that the failure to mention a child in a will was an oversight, so the omitted child should get a share of the estate in order to fulfill the testator's true intent. The idea goes back to Roman law, in which an intestate heir had to be expressly disinherited if the testator intended that the heir receive no share.[177] The common law rejected this rule, but held that if a testator married *and* had a child after executing a will, the will was revoked.[178] American pretermitted heir statutes, which began in the 18th century,[179] do not depend on the testator's marrying subsequent to the will.

Variations in the Statutes

Pretermitted heir statutes differ on several points.[180]

1. *Are all children covered, or only those born or adopted after the will was executed?* Many statutes, including the Uniform Probate Code, cover only children who were born after the will was executed.[181] Others are not so limited.[182] It is questionable whether statutes that include all children are consistent with the testator's probable intent.

> A childless testator may occasionally fail to focus on the possibility that he may have children after execution of his will. But ... forgetting about the existence of a child one already has is on a par with misplacing a house—not very likely.[183]

---

[173] Fla.Const. art. 10, § 4(c); Sims v. Cox, 611 So.2d 339 (Ala.1992) (deed of homestead to daughter not signed by wife is voidable); Ray v. American Nat. Bank & Trust Co., 894 P.2d 1056 (Okl.1994) (deed of homestead not signed by wife is voidable); Besnilian v. Wilkinson, 25 P.3d 187 (Nev.2001); Taylor v. Maness, 941 So.2d 559 (Fla. App. 2006).

[174] Iowa Code § 561.13; Martin v. Martin, 720 N.W.2d 732 (Iowa 2006).

[175] Yeager v. Lucy, 998 So.2d 460 (Ala. 2008) (the court applied this rule even though husband had abandoned wife after she conveyed to her children without his signature).

[176] UPC § 2–302 uses the term "omitted." *See also* Cal.Prob.Code § 21620.

[177] Justinian, *Institutes* 2.13. Originally the rule applied only to sons of the testator, but Justinian abolished this discrimination between the sexes. Modern civil law systems commonly have provisions similar to the American pretermitted heir statutes, founded on the idea that the omission of the heir was an oversight.

[178] 2 W. Blackstone, *Commentaries* 502–03 (1766); Pascucci v. Alsop, 147 F.2d 880 (D.C.Cir.1945).

[179] Matthews, *Pretermitted Heirs: An Analysis of the Statutes,* 29 Colum.L.Rev. 748, 753 (1929).

[180] For a comprehensive list of the statutes, *see* Reporter's Note to *Restatement (Third) of Property (Wills and Other Donative Transfers)* § 9.6 (2003).

[181] UPC § 2–302.

[182] 84 Okl. St. § 132. *See* In re Estate of Richardson, 50 P.3d 584 (Okl.Civ.App.2002).

[183] Rein, *A More Rational System for the Protection of Family Members Against Disinheritance,* 15 Gonz.L.Rev. 11, 24–25 (1979). *See also* Matthews, *supra* note 179, at 752; Evans,

On the other hand, providing a share for an omitted child who was alive when the will was executed may be consistent with intent if the testator mistakenly believed that the child was dead at that time. The Uniform Probate Code covers such children.[184] Is this mistaken belief distinguishable from a testator's mistaken belief that a child was not his? Case law generally provides no relief for such mistakes of fact.[185]

The date of the child's birth, not conception, is controlling; even when a testator was five months pregnant when she executed her will, her child qualified as afterborn under a pretermitted heir statute.[186] For an adopted child, the date of adoption rather than the date of birth controls.[187] No inference of intent to disinherit can be drawn from failure to provide for a person who was not the testator's child when the will was executed.[188]

When, after the execution of a will and the subsequent birth of a child, a testator executes a codicil to the earlier will, the child is no longer regarded as afterborn. The execution of a codicil is said to "republish" the will as of the date of the codicil.[189] Thus, if the child is also omitted by the codicil, the child cannot claim a statutory share created in favor of afterborn children.

2. *Is the statute limited to children or are more remote descendants included?* The Uniform Probate Code and many other statutes only protect omitted children,[190] but some statutes also cover issue of a deceased child.[191]

3. *What evidence is admissible to show that the disinheritance was intentional?* Some courts admit any evidence of the testator's actual intent. Thus, in one case there was a statute giving a share to an omitted child unless it appeared from all the facts and circumstances that the omission was intentional. The court rejected the three daughters' claim to a pretermitted child share on the basis of testimony that the testator had had no contact with them for 15 years before he died and had represented himself to the world as a single man.[192] But under many statutes, evidence of an intent to disinherit

---

Should Pretermitted Children Be Entitled to Inherit?, 31 Calif.L.Rev. 263, 269 (1943); Niles, *Probate Reform in California,* 31 Hast.L.J. 185, 197 (1979).

[184] UPC § 2–302(c). *See also* Cal.Prob.Code § 21622; Ohio Rev.Code § 2107.34; *cf.* Wis.Stat. § 853.25(2) (child omitted "by mistake or accident"). A child who claims under this provision has the burden of proving the testator's mistake, at least when there is no reason to suppose the testator thought the child was dead. Estate of Della Sala, 86 Cal.Rptr.2d 569 (App.1999).

[185] *See* Section 7.1.

[186] DeCoste v. Superior Court, 470 P.2d 457 (Ariz.1970).

[187] However, where a beneficiary of a specific bequest under the will was adopted by the testator after the will was executed, the adoptee could not claim as a pretermitted heir. Ozuna v. Wells Fargo Bank, 123 S.W.3d 429 (Tex. App. 2003).

[188] UPC § 2–302; Tex.Est.Code § 255.053; N.Y. EPTL § 5–3.2; Estate of Turkington, 195 Cal.Rptr. 178 (App.1983).

[189] Azcunce v. Estate of Azcunce, 586 So.2d 1216 (Fla.App.1991). *But see Restatement (Third) of Property (Wills and Other Donative Transfers)* § 3.4, illus. 3 (1999) (disapproving the result in Azcunce).

[190] UPC § 2–302; Cal.Prob.Code § 21620.

[191] Ohio Rev.Code § 2107.34; Wis.Stat. § 853.25(1)(d); Matter of Estate of Woodward, 807 P.2d 262 (Okl.1991) (grandchildren take as pretermitted heirs).

[192] In re Estate of Blank, 219 N.W.2d 815 (N.D.1974). *See also* Matter of Estate of Flowers, 848 P.2d 1146 (Okl.1993) (remand for consideration of extrinsic evidence of intent). *But see* In re

the child must appear in the will.[193] Under such a statute, the daughters' claim would have been allowed because the will made no reference to testator's children.

The Uniform Probate Code says that it must appear "*from the will* that the omission was intentional," unless "the testator provided for the . . . child by transfer outside the will" which was intended to "be in lieu of a testamentary provision." This intent can be "shown by the testator's statements or . . . inferred from the amount of the transfer or other evidence."[194] Thus, oral statements by a testator showing an intent to disinherit a child are admissible if, but only if, they are connected with a non-probate transfer to the child.[195]

The Code also bars claims by omitted children when the will devises "all or substantially all the estate to another parent of the omitted child."[196] Presumably in this situation the other parent will use the property for the benefit of the children, so they are not really disinherited.[197]

Language in the will can also bar claims by a pretermitted heir. Blackstone mentioned a "groundless vulgar error" that a testator had to leave "the heir a shilling or some other express legacy, in order to disinherit him effectually."[198] This belief still persists; many wills make nominal devises to persons whom the testator wishes to disinherit.[199] But a will which simply says "I do not wish to provide for my son Arthur" or "I have made no provision for my son Arthur in this will for good and sufficient reasons known best to me" is sufficient, because all statutes bar claims by an expressly disinherited heir.[200]

Estate of Richardson, 50 P.3d 584, 587 (Okl.Civ.App.2002) (evidence of intent to disinherit child "must appear from the four corners of the will" even though statute did not so provide).

[193] In re Estate of Treloar, 859 A.2d 1162 (N.H. 2004); Estate of Jones v. Jones, 759 P.2d 345 (Utah App.1988), reversed on other grounds, Matter of Estate of Jones, 858 P.2d 983 (Utah 1993). For a general discussion of the use of extrinsic evidence to determine a testator's intent, *see* Section 7.1.

[194] UPC § 2–302(b). *See also* Cal.Prob.Code § 21621. *But see* In re Estate of Came, 529 A.2d 962 (N.H.1987) (beneficiary of $500,000 trust also takes as pretermitted heir).

[195] Contrast the rule governing gifts to an heir which the UPC allows to be charged against the heir only if the donor's intent to do so is expressed in writing. *See* Section 2.6, note 195. Contrast also UPC § 2–601, comment: "evidence extrinsic to the will . . . is admissible for the purpose of rebutting the rules of construction in Part 6" (where most of the assumptions about intent are placed).

[196] UPC § 2–302(a)(1); *cf.* Cal.Prob.Code § 21621(b) (applicable only when testator had some children when the will was executed).

[197] If the will devises all or substantially all of the estate to another parent but that parent does not survive the testator, or that parent survives the testator but is not entitled to take under the will, then the omitted child can claim under the will.

[198] 2 W. Blackstone, *Commentaries* 503 (1766).

[199] Matter of Estate of Hilton, 649 P.2d 488 (N.M.App.1982); In re Estate of Cooke, 524 P.2d 176 (Idaho 1973).

[200] Such a clause may not be effective if the will fails to give the property to someone else, however. *See* Section 8.10. It may also be desirable to recite the reason for disinheriting a child in order that the will not appear "unnatural" and, thus, become subject to claims of incapacity or undue influence. *See* Section 5.1. However, if the reasons stated in the will for the disinheritance are libelous, the child may have an action for damages.

It has also been held to bar a claim by Arthur's children even if the statute allows more remote issue to claim as pretermitted.[201]

There has been much litigation about what language is sufficient to bar heirs who are not mentioned by name in the will. The cases are hard to reconcile, and the language of each will differs. Generally speaking, courts are reluctant to treat "boilerplate" provisions as showing an intent to disinherit children. For example, a statement that "all other persons are excluded from receiving anything from my estate," was held insufficient to bar grandchildren from claiming under a pretermitted heir statute.[202] But, when a will provides a class gift for the testator's "descendants," a child who is not mentioned by name is not pretermitted because that child, even though born after the will was executed, would be included in the class gift. This is true even if the provision for the children is conditional on an event that does not occur, for example "to my wife, Mary, if she survives me, otherwise to my descendants." If Mary survives, the descendants take nothing, but they were not overlooked.[203] If the will had merely left the entire estate to Mary with no gift over, the practical result would be the same as it would be with an alternative gift to the "descendants," because if she did not survive, the testator's descendants would take by intestacy, but the afterborn child is protected by the intestacy statute in this case.

Even a substantial devise in a will to a person whom the testator later adopts (but a devise valued at less than would be the adopted child's afterborn child share) does not bar a pretermitted-heir claim; courts assume that the testator's failure to change the will to give the devisee more after the adoption was an oversight.[204]

4. *What does a pretermitted heir take?* In a few states the birth of a child to the testator revokes a previous will.[205] This result seems "too drastic," because an afterborn child can be given a share of the estate while leaving the rest of the will intact.[206] In most states, pretermitted heirs receive their intestate share.[207] This may amount to the whole estate,[208] but this depends on the surrounding facts. For example, in community property states where all

---

[201] In re Estate of Laura, 690 A.2d 1011 (N.H.1997). Cf. In re Estate of Treloar, 859 A.2d 1162 (N.H. 2004) (naming one child in a will but not the other is not an implicit disinheriting of the other child and other child can claim as pretermitted heir).

[202] Matter of Estate of Woodward, 807 P.2d 262 (Okl.1991); In re Estate of Cooke, 524 P.2d 176 (Idaho 1973) ($1 to any other person who claims against estate).

[203] Leatherwood v. Meisch, 759 S.W.2d 559 (Ark.1988); Estate of Norwood, 443 N.W.2d 798 (Mich.App.1989); Matter of Estate of Broughton, 828 P.2d 443 (Okl.App.1991). *But see* Robinson v. Mays, 610 S.W.2d 885 (Ark.1981).

[204] Brown v. Crawford, 699 P.2d 162 (Okl.App.1984); Estate of Marshall, 621 P.2d 187 (Wash.App.1980); Estate of Turkington, 195 Cal.Rptr. 178 (App.1983). *Contra*, Ozuna v. Wells Fargo Bank, NA, 123 S.W.3d 429 (Tex. App. 2003).

[205] Ga.Code § 53–4–48; Talley v. Succession of Stuckey, 614 So.2d 55 (La.1993). This was also the effect at common law of marriage and birth of issue subsequent to the will.

[206] Chaffin, *A Reappraisal of the Wealth Transmission Process*, 10 Ga.L.Rev. 447, 473 (1976).

[207] Cal.Prob.Code § 21620; 755 ILCS 5/4–10.

[208] Even if the intestate share of the pretermitted heirs is 100%, the will may contain administrative provisions which make its admission to probate significant. *See* Estate of Shimun, 136 Cal.Rptr. 668 (App.1977).

the community property usually passes to the spouse on intestacy, the share of a pretermitted child may be zero.[209]

Giving pretermitted heirs an intestate share may produce a questionable result. Suppose a will leaves $3,000 each to the testator's two children, A and B, and the rest of the large estate to charity. A daughter C is born later, and all three children survive the testator. C's intestate share would give her more than her older siblings, but it is doubtful that testator would have intended this.[210] The Uniform Probate Code only gives C a share equal to that of her siblings, whose shares would abate ratably to make up C's share, so each child would get $2,000.[211] A Wisconsin statute gives courts discretion to "make such provision for the omitted child or issue out of the estate as it deems would best accord with the intent of the testator."[212]

5. *Nonprobate property.* Pretermitted heir statutes typically do not apply to a decedent's nonprobate property. For example, a man had life insurance on his life which designated his "children, Robert and Tamara" as the beneficiaries. He later had a third child who claimed a share of the insurance proceeds. This situation fits within the rationale of the pretermitted heir statutes but is not covered by them because they refer only to *wills,* so the afterborn child takes none of the insurance proceeds.[213] Although the Uniform Probate Code extends many rules of construction for wills to will substitutes,[214] it does not do so for pretermitted heirs.[215] The lawyerly solution to the problem, namely to use class gift language which is sufficiently expansive to include afterborn children, may not be available because "some insurance companies and plan administrators have been reluctant to accept class-gift designations, preferring instead that the beneficiaries be individually designated by name and Social Security number."[216]

Drafting Suggestions

Although pretermitted heir statutes are designed to carry out the testator's probable intent, they often fail to do so. The harm that they can cause is reduced by the limitations in the Uniform Probate Code, which restricts claims to afterborn children and excepts wills that leave everything to the other parent of the children. But these limitations may not apply if the testator dies domiciled in a state where a different statute controls.[217]

---

[209] Rein, *supra* note 183, at 35.

[210] Matthews, *supra* note 179, at 751–52; Rein, *supra* note 184, at 34.

[211] UPC § 2–302(a)(2). *See also* Md.Estates and Trusts Code § 3–302(a); N.Y. EPTL § 5–3.2(a)(1)(B).

[212] Wis.Stat. § 853.25(5). *See also* Rev.Code Wash. § 11.12.091(3).

[213] Penn Mutual Life Ins. Co. v. Abramson, 530 A.2d 1202 (D.C.App.1987). *See also* Matter of Guardianship of Koors, 656 N.E.2d 530 (Ind.App.1995); Matter of Estate of Cayo, 342 N.W.2d 785 (Wis.App.1983) (refusing to apply statute to a living trust).

[214] *See* UPC § 2–701 et seq. *See also* Uniform Trust Code [hereinafter UTC] § 112, comment.

[215] McGovern, *Nonprobate Transfers Under the Revised Uniform Probate Code,* 55 Alb.L.Rev. 1329, 1339–46 (1992).

[216] *Restatement (Third) of Property (Wills and Other Donative Transfers)* Scope Note to Division 5 (2011).

[217] In Royce v. Estate of Denby, 379 A.2d 1256 (N.H.1977), a will was saved from claims by a child only because the court applied the law of New York, where the testator was domiciled when

Malpractice Potential

Lawyers whose negligence causes a will to be upset by a pretermitted heir's claim may be liable to the devisees for malpractice.[218] Lawyers can usually guard against the problem at which pretermitted heir statutes are aimed—unintended omission of an afterborn child—by using class gifts. If a will leaves the estate "to my descendants"[219] instead of "to Arthur and Andrew," an afterborn child would not have to (and could not) invoke a pretermitted heir statute. Some testators object to an impersonal reference to "descendants" but a will can alleviate this by naming the testator's existing children while making it clear that afterborn children are also included in a devise. If the client wishes to disinherit children born after the execution of the will the following clause may be useful: "I intentionally make no provision in the will for any child born or adopted by me after the execution of this will."

§ 8.6 Omitted Spouse

At common law a *woman's* will was revoked by her marriage but a *man's* will was not revoked unless he also had afterborn children. The distinction was based on a rule which has disappeared today—the incapacity of a married woman to make a will.[220] The distinction was eliminated in England by the Wills Act of 1837 which provided that marriage revoked any existing will of *either spouse*.[221] This rule prevails in some states today,[222] but in others a will is revoked only if the testator (of either sex) later marries *and* has a child.[223]

Many statutes give an intestate share to an omitted spouse like an omitted child. This is not the same as revoking the will, even when the spouse's intestate share amounts to the entire estate, because administrative provisions in the will are still effective.[224] While the spouse may be entitled to a share of the intestate share as an omitted spouse, the spouse has no claim to nonprobate assets, such as assets held in a revocable trust.[225] Also, any omitted

---

she executed the will, rather than the law of New Hampshire, where she died. For a general discussion of choice of law, *see* Section 1.2.

[218] Leak-Gilbert v. Fahle, 55 P.3d 1054 (Okl.2002). This case also holds, however, that lawyers can rely on information supplied by the testator if they ask the proper questions; they need not independently investigate the testator's family situation.

[219] As to the extent to which afterborn children are included in a class gift, *see* Section 11.3. A common mistake is to use the word "children" in place of "descendants." "Descendants" provides for the children of a child who dies prematurely, which is presumably what most testators desire. *See* Section 6.5.

[220] Parker v. Hall, 362 So.2d 875 (Ala.1978) (holding unconstitutional a statute which made the same distinction).

[221] Wills Act, 1 Vict. c. 26, § 18 (1837). This rule still prevails in England, unless when the will was made the testator was expecting to marry. Administration of Justice Act, 1982, § 18.

[222] R.I.Gen.Laws § 33–5–9 (unless will made in contemplation of marriage). This statute applies even though the spouse predeceases the testator. Under Ore.Rev.Stat. § 112.305, a subsequent marriage revokes the will only if the spouse survives the testator. In Knott v. Garriott, 784 S.W.2d 603 (Ky.App.1989) a marriage which was later annulled was held not to revoke a prior will.

[223] Kan.Stat. § 59–610; Md.Estates and Trusts Code § 4–105(3); Tenn.Code § 32–1–201(4).

[224] Matter of Estate of Coleman, 718 P.2d 702 (N.M.App.1986); Matter of Estate of Groves, 788 P.2d 127 (Ariz.App.1990).

[225] Bell v. Estate of Bell, 181 P.3d 708 (N.M. App. 2008).

spouse's claim disappears if the new spouse predeceases the testator or they are divorced before the testator dies.

There are similarities between Section 2–301 of the Uniform Probate Code, giving an intestate share to a spouse who marries the testator after a will is executed, and Section 2–302, protecting afterborn children, which was discussed in the preceding section.[226] In both situations, a codicil which "republishes" the will after the marriage or birth can bar the claim of the spouse or child.[227] There are also differences between the two provisions. A spouse who is omitted from a will because the testator mistakenly believes the spouse is dead is not covered by the Code, but under Section 2–302(c) a child in the same situation is. The Code bars the spouse where there is evidence from or outside of the will that "the will was made in contemplation of the testator's marriage,"[228] but there is no comparable bar on a child whose birth was contemplated when the will was executed.[229]

An omitted-spouse statute has been held to apply to a remarriage to a former spouse,[230] but according to a comment to the Uniform Probate Code the statute applies only if the will was executed "when [the spouses] were not married to each other but not a will executed during a prior marriage."[231] Thus, if Jenna and Paul are married but then divorce and thereafter Jenna executes a will that omits Paul, he is entitled to an omitted spouse's share if they were to remarry each other after the execution of Jenna's will.

Because the underlying theory in the provisions for omitted spouses and children is the correction of an oversight, both rules are subject to evidence that the omission was intentional. Both sections use virtually identical language covering a "transfer outside the will" intended to "be in lieu of a testamentary provision."[232] Under this proviso a widow who had received a $230,000 gift from the testator was held not to be an omitted spouse,[233] but a widow who received survivorship rights in her husband's pension automatically without any action by him was also allowed to claim as an omitted spouse.[234]

---

[226] *See also* Cal.Prob.Code § 21610 (omitted spouse) and § 21620 (omitted child). Both were modeled on earlier versions of the UPC.

[227] In re Estate of Wells, 983 P.2d 279 (Kan.App.1999); Matter of Estate of Ivancovich, 728 P.2d 661 (Ariz.App.1986). *But see* Matter of Will of Marinus, 493 A.2d 44 (N.J.Super.App.Div.1985) (later codicil which does not refer to earlier will does not bar spouse's claim).

[228] UPC § 2–301(a)(1). Similar language appears in R.I.Gen.Laws § 33–5–9, but not in Cal.Prob.Code § 21610, which was based on an earlier version of the UPC. In Estate of Dennis, 714 S.W.2d 661 (Mo.App.1986), the court rejected a claim by an omitted spouse when the will was executed on the same day as the marriage. *See also* Erickson v. Erickson, 716 A.2d 92 (Conn.1998) (will executed 2 days before marriage). *But see* Matter of Estate of Wagley, 760 P.2d 316 (Utah 1988) (claim allowed where marriage took place 5 days after will executed).

[229] *See* Section 8.5.

[230] Stevenson v. United States National Bank, 695 P.2d 77 (Or.App.1985).

[231] Presumably this means "a prior marriage to the surviving spouse." In any event, one may wonder if the text supports the comment.

[232] UPC §§ 2–301(a)(3), 2–302(b)(2).

[233] Matter of Estate of Bartell, 776 P.2d 885 (Utah 1989). *See also* Matter of Estate of Taggart, 619 P.2d 562 (N.M.App.1980).

[234] Noble v. McNerney, 419 N.W.2d 424, 432–33 (Mich.App.1988). *See also* Estate of Shannon, 274 Cal.Rptr. 338 (App.1990).

An intent not to provide for the spouse may be manifested in the will itself. (As discussed in the next section, an express disinheritance would not preclude a claim to an *elective share*.) The relevant language in the Uniform Probate Code is similar, though not identical, for spouses and children.[235] General language disinheriting heirs is not sufficient.[236] A frequent source of litigation arises where the will executed prior to the marriage includes a devise (usually relatively small) to a friend whom the testator later marries. Most courts have held that such devises do not bar an omitted spouse claim unless the will was made in contemplation of the marriage,[237] but there are also contrary decisions.[238] The comment to Section 2–301 of the Uniform Probate Code says the section should apply even "if the person the decedent later married was a devisee in his or her premarital will." But, "the value of any such devise . . . must be counted toward and not be in addition to the ultimate share" which the spouse receives.

The Uniform Probate Code also bars an omitted spouse from taking property that the testator's premarital will leaves to children of a prior marriage on the theory that the failure to provide for the spouse in this situation is not likely to be an oversight.[239] Here the spouse can still claim an elective share[240] but, because the size of the elective share under the Code varies depending upon the length of the marriage, it can be rather small if the marriage is of short duration. Furthermore, if the omitted spouse also claims an elective share, any amounts payable to the spouse on an omitted spouse claim reduce the amount of the elective share claim.[241]

In several states, a testator's marriage has no effect on a will.[242] Arguably spouses need no other protection than the elective share. However, the elective share is usually smaller than the intestate share of an omitted spouse. Under the Uniform Probate Code, the omitted spouse's share and the elective share are measured against different bases. The omitted spouse's share is a share of the probate estate only; the elective share, on the other hand, can include both probate and nonprobate assets. If the decedent's only assets are in the decedent's probate estate of $500,000 and the spouse could claim the entire probate estate as an omitted spouse, this would clearly be preferable to claiming an elective share against the probate estate as the maximum amount

---

235 UPC § 2–301(a)(2) ("the will expresses the intention that it is to be effective notwithstanding any subsequent marriage"). *Compare* § 2–302(b)(1) ("it appears from the will that the omission was intentional").

236 Estate of Katleman, 16 Cal.Rptr.2d 468 (App.1993). A spouse has even been allowed a share despite a provision that "this will shall not be affected by any subsequent marriage." Estate of Green, 174 Cal.Rptr. 654 (App.1981).

237 Miles v. Miles, 440 S.E.2d 882 (S.C.1994); In re Estate of Deoneseus, 906 P.2d 922 (Wash.1995); In re Estate of Gaspelin, 542 So.2d 1023 (Fla.App.1989).

238 Estate of Christensen v. Christensen, 655 P.2d 646 (Utah 1982); Matter of Estate of Keeven, 716 P.2d 1224 (Idaho 1986); Porter v. Porter, 726 P.2d 459 (Wash.1986); In re Estate of Moi, 151 P.3d 995 (Wash.App. 2006).

239 Waggoner, *The Multiple Marriage Society*, 76 Iowa L.Rev. 223, 254 (1991).

240 In re Estate of Sprenkle-Hill, 703 N.W.2d 191 (Mich.App.2005); Mongold v. Mayle, 452 S.E.2d 444 (W.Va.1994).

241 UPC § 2–301, comment.

242 McKnight v. McKnight, 267 So.2d 315 (Miss.1972); 755 ILCS 5/4–7(b); N.Y.E.P.T.L. § 5–1.3(a) (omitted spouse share applies only if will executed before 1930).

of the elective share would only be $250,000. But if the decedent leaves a probate estate of $1,000,000 but an augmented estate of $2,500,000 (consisting of the $1,000,000 intestate estate, plus a $1,500,000 revocable trust), the omitted spouse could claim both an omitted spouse's share and an elective share. However, the omitted spouse's $1,250,000 elective share (assuming the spouse was entitled to 1/2 of the augmented estate) would be reduced by the $1,000,000 omitted spouse share, thus, entitling the spouse to collect only $250,000 from the revocable trust.[243]

Omitted spouse statutes have been the cause of malpractice actions against lawyers who drafted wills that failed to include a provision as to the testator's impending marriage.[244] Even if no marriage is impending, the testator should be advised to review the will if he or she should later marry. Such a warning appears in the California Statutory Will.[245]

§ 8.7 Elective Share

Historical Introduction; Gender Discrimination

At common law the rights of surviving spouses depended on their sex. A widow received *dower*, a life estate in one-third of lands which her husband owned.[246] A widower received *curtesy*, a life estate in *all* the lands which his wife owned, but only if issue were born of the marriage.[247] Maitland attributed the unequal treatment of husbands and wives to the interest of feudal lords in seeing that services were performed; the widow's share was smaller because she could not perform military service (under the then prevailing customs of war).[248]

In most states today, distinctions between the sexes have been eliminated. Statutes that differentiate between the rights of widows and widowers have been held to be an unconstitutional denial of equal protection.[249] Some states still retain the name "dower," but the husband and wife usually receive equivalent shares by that name different from those provided by the common law.[250]

---

243 UPC § 2–209(a)(1).

244 Heyer v. Flaig, 449 P.2d 161 (Cal.1969). *See also* McAbee v. Edwards, 340 So.2d 1167 (Fla.App.1976).

245 Calif.Prob.Code § 6240(12).

246 2 W. Blackstone, *Commentaries* 129 (1766).

247 *Id.* at 126. For a brief history of dower and curtesy, *see* A. Simpson, *A History of the Land Law* 68–70 (2d ed. 1986).

248 2 F. Pollock & F. Maitland, *History of English Law* 419 (2d ed. 1898).

249 Montgomery v. Estate of Montgomery, 677 N.E.2d 571 (Ind.App.1997); Stokes v. Stokes, 613 S.W.2d 372 (Ark.1981); Hall v. McBride, 416 So.2d 986 (Ala.1982); In re Estate of Reed's, 354 So.2d 864 (Fla.1978) (family allowance to widow only). *But see* Matter of Baer's Estate, 562 P.2d 614 (Utah 1977) (greater rights for widows justified by "the disparity between economic capabilities of" men and women). In In re Miltenberger Estate, 737 N.W.2d 513, 518 (2007), the court upheld the Michigan dower statute stating "it remains an unfortunate fact that there are still circumstances in which the surviving wife may be significantly disadvantaged, in a way that surviving husbands generally are not."

250 N.J.Stat. § 3B:28–1 (1/2 of land held by decedent in 1980 for life).

Deficiencies of Dower

Dower did not adequately protect the surviving spouse. It attached only to land, but today the chief or only form of wealth in many families is personal property.[251] Because dower attached to all land the husband owned (technically "was seised of") at any time during marriage, it gave the wife a "veto . . . over all her husband's transactions involving his real property."[252] Because dower was only a life estate, widows could not sell the land without the consent of the persons who would succeed to it after her death.[253]

Modern statutes usually give a surviving spouse (husband or wife) a fee interest instead of a life estate,[254] but only in property that the decedent owned at death. Many statutes like the Uniform Probate Code explicitly abolish dower and curtesy and replace it with an "elective share."[255]

Purpose of Elective Share

By preventing a spouse's complete disinheritance, elective share statutes serve at least two purposes. They recognize that the surviving spouse may have contributed significantly to the accumulation of the deceased spouse's wealth. They also help assure the spouse will have some assets to provide for the spouse's future support. As such, they minimize or eliminate the likelihood of the spouse seeking support from the state. At the same time, however, when properly structured, elective share statutes can "prevent the surviving spouse from needlessly overriding the decedent's legitimate intent to benefit others."[256]

Size of Elective Share

The elective share is computed in various ways in different states. Sometimes it equals the spouse's intestate share, or is a fraction thereof, but in the Uniform Probate Code the intestate and elective shares are computed differently. The size of a spouse's intestate share under Section 2–102 of the Code depends, for example, on whether the decedent was survived by no issue of their marriage or issue of a prior marriage. This is irrelevant under the Code to the size of the elective share.[257]

---

[251] Chaffin, *A Reappraisal of the Wealth Transmission Process,* 10 Ga.L.Rev. 447, 457 (1976); Haskell, *The Premarital Estate Contract and Public Policy,* 57 N.C.L.Rev. 415, 421 (1979); Matter of Estate of Cole, 491 A.2d 770 (N.J.Super.Ch.Div.1984).

[252] Clark, *The Recapture of Testamentary Substitutes to Preserve the Spouse's Elective Share,* 2 Conn.L.Rev. 513, 516–17 (1970). In Sterling v. Wilson, 621 N.E.2d 767 (Ohio App.1993), a contract to sell land was held unenforceable because the seller's wife refused to release her dower rights. This problem can also occur in community property states. *See* Section 8.8.

[253] As to the disadvantages of legal life estates, *see* Section 10.5.

[254] *But see* R.I.Gen.Laws § 33–25–2 (surviving spouse gets life estate in land); In re Seifert's Estate, 242 A.2d 64 (N.H.1968) (direction to sell land in will did not convert it into personal property, so husband who took elective share got only a life interest).

[255] UPC § 2–112. *See also* Md. Estates and Trusts Code § 3–202; 755 ILCS § 5/2–9.

[256] In re Estate of Hjersted, 175 P.3d 810, 823–24 (Kan. 2008).

[257] But not in all states. *See* In re Estate of White, 651 N.E.2d 324 (Ind.App.1995) (widow limited to life estate where decedent had children by a prior marriage). Many states give a larger elective share if the decedent has no issue. Ohio Rev.Code § 2106.01(c); 755 ILCS § 5/2–8(a).

On the other hand, the size of the Code's elective share depends on the length of the spouses' marriage.[258] This factor recognizes, in part, the partnership theory as a justification for any elective share, namely that a surviving spouse is entitled to an elective share because of the spouse's important contributions to the accumulation of the spouses' wealth. Thus, the Code provides that a surviving spouse is entitled to 50% of the "marital-property portion" of the decedent's augmented estate. The marital-property portion depends upon the length of the marriage. For example, for marriages of 15 years or longer, the marital-property portion is 100%; for marriages of ten years, the marital-property portion is 60%; and for a marriage of less than one year, the marital-property portion is 3%.

The greater complexity of the elective share as compared with the intestate share is justified by the fact that "intestacy affects so many estates of small size" whereas "elections are the exception in estate practice" and so "a more individuated system" to accommodate different size estates can be tolerated.[259]

Both the intestate share (when the spouse is not entitled to the entire estate) and the elective share give the surviving spouse a percentage of the estate, with a guaranteed minimum amount. In the case of the elective share, the minimum amount is fixed at $75,000. But unlike intestacy, in the elective share the surviving spouse's own assets are taken into account, such that even in a long marriage, if the surviving spouse is wealthier than the decedent, the elective share may amount to nothing.[260]

The Code's elective share is atypical of American law in several respects, and it remains to be seen how many states will adopt it given the reach and complexities of its provisions. Even though the Code's elective share may not be widely adopted, the partnership theory it uses to justify, in part, the computation of the elective share has been adopted in many states in when dividing property between divorcing spouses.[261] It is also similar in many ways to the community property system which is discussed in the next Section.

The Code's elective share is the same for real and personal property. This is consistent with the trend to eliminate distinctions between the two, although they survive in a few states.[262]

---

[258] UPC §§ 2–202(a); 2–203. Apparently years when the spouses were living separately still count as years of marriage. *See id.* § 2–802 (divorce but not decree of separation terminates spousal status); *cf.* Section 3.8 (community property). In In re Estate of Antonopoulos, 993 P.2d 637, 647 (Kan.1999) a spouse increased her elective share from 15 to 30% by proving a common-law marriage preceded the formal marriage by 5 years.

In Arkansas, a spouse who was married to the decedent for less than a year can claim no elective share, but otherwise the length of the marriage is irrelevant. Shaw v. Shaw, 989 S.W.2d 919 (Ark.1999).

[259] L. Waggoner, *Marital Property Rights in Transition*, 59 Mo.L.Rev. 21, 55 (1994).

[260] In re Estate of Karnen, 607 N.W.2d 32 (S.D.2000) (husband not entitled to elective share in 50 year marriage because he had substantial assets of his own).

[261] UPC Article II, Part 2, general comment.

[262] Ky.Rev.Stat. § 392.020.

Unlike the family allowance, the spouse's elective share is subject to claims against the decedent's estate.[263] In this respect, common-law dower was more advantageous; even though it gave the widow only a life estate, dower came ahead of her husband's creditors.

Nonprobate Assets

Common-law dower gave a widow a life estate in lands of which her husband was seised at any time during the marriage, including land which the husband had conveyed away before he died.[264] Many modern elective share statutes only include assets owned by the decedent at death, the so-called "probate" estate. This allowed spouses to evade the elective share by using will substitutes or inter vivos gifts to deplete the estate prior to death.[265] Lawyers drafting instruments for a married client should be aware of the possibility of the estate plan being upset by a spousal election and consider possible steps to avoid this. One firm was sued for malpractice after a client's widow exercised her elective share rights to upset an estate plan. Had the lawyer

> properly advised Mr. Adreme concerning Mrs. Adreme's possible exercise of her spousal share, he could have protected the [childrens'] residuary interest in the . . . trust intended by Mr. Adreme . . . [U]nder Kansas law, Mr. Adreme could have created an irrevocable QTIP trust or a joint tenancy with right of survivorship to the appellants in order to defeat Mrs. Adreme's right of election, [as explained in an article titled] *The Capricious Operation of the Kansas Elective Share: Feast or Famine for the Surviving Spouse?*[266]

Efforts to avoid the elective share may fail. Some courts have subjected property that the decedent transferred before death to the elective share on the theory that the transfer was "illusory." Generally, an "illusory" transfer is one in which there has been a change in the form of ownership but the transferor's economic interest in the property both before and after the transfer is essentially the same.[267] Thus, revocable living trusts are frequently characterized as illusory. Even though the transferred assets are owned by a trust and not the settlor, the only thing standing between the settlor and absolute ownership of the trust assets is a piece of paper stating: "I revoke the trust."[268] The Third Restatement of Property and the Third Restatement of

---

[263] UPC § 2–204; Winkelfoos v. Mann, 475 N.E.2d 509 (Ohio App.1984); 755 ILCS § 5/2–8(a) (after payment of all just claims). As to the family allowance, *see* Section 8.4.

[264] 2 W. Blackstone, *Commentaries* 132 (1766). For a modern application, *see* Matter of Estate of Stroh, 392 N.W.2d 192 (Mich.App.1986).

[265] Friedberg v. Sunbank/Miami, N.A., 648 So.2d 204 (Fla.App.1994) (assets in charitable trust or medical trust not subject to elective share); Soltis v. First of America Bank of Muskegon, 513 N.W.2d 148 (Mich.App.1994) (revocable trust not subject to elective share; court recognizes its holding circumvents purpose of elective share but noted legislature refused to adopt UPC augmented estate concept). *Contra*, Sieh v. Sieh, 713 N.W.2d 194 (Iowa 2006). Contrast with Friedberg as well, the protection of the forced share in the civil law against inter vivos transfers. *See* Section 8.2.

[266] Johnson v. Sandler, Balkin, Hellman & Weinstein, P.C., 958 S.W.2d 42, 53 (Mo.App.1997).

[267] Dreher v. Dreher, 634 S.E.2d 646 (S.C. 2006).

[268] *Id.*; Johnson v. Farmers & Merchants Bank, 379 S.E.2d 752 (W.Va.1989); Seifert v. Southern Nat. Bank, 409 S.E.2d 337 (S.C.1991) (later superseded by statute). In Pezza v. Pezza, 690 A.2d 345 (R.I.1997), the court adopted the "illusory transfer" test, but held that a trust was

Trusts both allow a surviving spouse to reach the assets of any revocable trust created by the decedent.[269] If a trust is illusory, either the entire trust is invalidated[270] and the assets become part of the probate estate or only enough assets to fund the elective share are diverted to the spouse from the persons who would otherwise be beneficiaries of the trust.[271] The latter is the better view, particularly where the beneficiaries of the probate estate and those named in the trust differ. The issue here is protecting the spouse, not benefiting the estate beneficiaries over the trust beneficiaries.

A second approach to nonprobate transfers focuses on "fraud." A Tennessee statute makes voidable "any conveyances made fraudulently . . . with an intent to defeat the surviving spouse of his . . . elective share."[272] Because anyone who makes a gift knows that it will reduce his estate and thereby partially "defeat" the elective share of the donor's spouse, this seems to be a questionable criterion.[273]

"Fraud" suggests the idea of a fraudulent conveyance, which creditors can set aside if the conveyance renders the transferor insolvent.[274] But because the elective share is a percentage of the estate, if a husband reduces his estate by transfers, his estate can still literally satisfy the elective share. Thus, the analogy to a fraudulent conveyance is hard to apply. The term "fraud" also suggests that the result should turn on whether the transfer was concealed from the other spouse, but this is only occasionally mentioned in the cases.[275]

Some courts interpret the "fraud" test to allow "reasonable" transfers that do not "substantially" deplete the probate estate.[276] Even if nearly all of a settlor's property is put into an inter vivos trust, the trust may still be upheld if it makes a substantial provision for the settlor's spouse.[277] On the other

---

not subject to the elective share when the settlor had surrendered his right to revoke the trust before he died. Pezza was later overturned by statute. R.I. Gen. Laws § 33–5–2.

[269] *Restatement (Third) of Property (Wills and Other Donative Transfers* § 9.1, cmt. i (2003); *Restatement (Third) of Trusts* § 25, cmt. d (2003).

[270] Newman v. Dore, 9 N.E.2d 966 (N.Y. 1937).

[271] Dreher v. Dreher, 634 S.E.2d 646 (S.C. 2006); Montgomery v. Michaels, 301 N.E.2d 465 (Ill. 1973).

[272] Tenn.Code § 31–105. *See also* Wis.Stat. § 861.17; 755 ILCS § 25/1; Mo.Stat. § 474.150; *cf.* In re Estate of Weitzman, 724 N.E.2d 1120 (Ind.App.2000) (result turns on whether husband in creating a revocable trust intended to defeat wife's elective share).

[273] In re Estate of Mocny, 630 N.E.2d 87 (Ill.App.1993) (intent to defeat elective share is irrelevant under "fraud" statute); *But see* Harris v. Rock, 799 S.W.2d 10 (Ky.1990). *See also* In re Estate of Defilippis, 683 N.E.2d 453, 458 (Ill.App.1997), where the court said "intent to defraud the surviving spouse . . . does not involve the traditional meaning of fraud," but rather "refers to a transfer that is illusory." This is a curious interpretation of the Illinois statute which expressly rejects an "illusory" transfer test.

[274] *See* Section 10.8.

[275] Clay v. Woods, 487 N.E.2d 1106 (Ill.App.1985) (no fraud because decedent informed his spouse); Matter of Estate of Froman, 803 S.W.2d 176 (Mo.App.1991) (fraud found where transfer concealed from spouse). In many cases, however, it is unclear (and apparently considered irrelevant) whether the other spouse knew about the transfer before the decedent died.

[276] Windsor v. Leonard, 475 F.2d 932 (D.C.Cir.1973) ($190,000 transferred to trust considered reasonable because $110,000 left in probate estate). *See also* Warren v. Compton, 626 S.W.2d 12, 18 (Tenn.App.1981) ("the amount of the transfers in relation to the total estate is not so great as to infer fraudulent intent").

[277] Richards v. Worthen Bank & Trust Co., 552 S.W.2d 228 (Ark.1977).

hand, fraud may be "implied in law from transfers of a disproportionate and unreasonable amount of assets" by the decedent.[278]

Some statutes explicitly include certain nonprobate property in computing the elective share. The Uniform Probate Code gives spouses a share of the "augmented estate." The augmented estate includes the probate estate and property transferred by the decedent during lifetime if the transfer was made within two years of the decedent's death.[279] It also includes property transferred by the decedent at any time during the decedent's life, if the decedent reserved either the right to revoke the transfer or reserved the income from the transferred property for life.[280] It also includes joint tenancies, to the extent of the "decedent's fractional interest" therein.[281] The fractional interest is presumptively based on the number of joint tenants, *e.g.*, if there are two, the decedent's interest is assumed to be one half,[282] but this may be altered due to the source of the funds in a joint account. Thus, if the surviving party contributed all the funds, the decedent would have no fractional interest for purposes of computing the augmented estate.[283]

The Uniform Probate Code is modeled on the Internal Revenue Code, which includes such lifetime transfers in a decedent's "gross" estate for tax purposes.[284] Before 1990, the Uniform Probate Code exempted life insurance and pensions from the augmented estate,[285] but now insurance is expressly included if the decedent owned the policy at death.[286] Most pensions are subject to federal law (ERISA) which requires that they be taken in the form of an annuity which benefits the employee's surviving spouse.[287] Individual

---

[278] Russell v. Walz, 458 N.E.2d 1172, 1185 (Ind.App.1984).

[279] UPC § 2–205(3). *See also* Dunnewind v. Cook, 697 N.E.2d 485 (Ind.App.1998) (irrevocable trust created after settlor learned she was terminally ill subject to elective share).

[280] UPC § 2–205(2). *See also* N.Y. EPTL § 5–1.1(b)(1)(E); 20 Pa.Stat. § 2203(a). In Bongaards v. Millen, 793 N.E.2d 335, 348 (Mass.2003), the court accepted a similar judicially created rule, but refused to extend it to a trust created by decedent's mother even though decedent had a power to terminate it, rejecting *Restatement (Third) of Property (Wills and Other Donative Transfers)* § 9.1(c) (2003).

[281] UPC § 2–205(1)(B). *Restatement (Third) of Property (Wills and Other Donative Transfers)* § 9.1(c) (2003) purports to restate similar rules as part of the common law, but this is somewhat wide of the mark. *Cf.* note 34. Absent a statute, a surviving spouse cannot reach property held in joint tenancy by the decedent and another. In re Estate of Mocny, 630 N.E.2d 87 (Ill.App.1993); Smith v. McCall, 477 S.E.2d 475 (S.C.App.1996); *cf.* Estate of Bruce, 538 A.2d 923 (Pa.Super.1988) (widow can reach husband's half of tenancy in common); In re Estate of Tyler, 536 N.E.2d 1188 (Ohio App.1987) (joint account created only for convenience included in probate estate—*see* Section 4.5).

[282] In re Estate of Hart, 801 A.2d 599 (Pa.Super.2002) (wife can reach husband's half interest in land given by his parents to husband and his son as joint tenants).

[283] UPC § 2–205, comment, examples 4, 6–7; In re Estate of Antonopoulos, 993 P.2d 637 (Kan.1999) (remand to consider contributions of surviving joint tenant, a child of the decedent by a prior marriage).

[284] *Compare* 12 Del.Code § 902 which bases the spouse's share on the "gross estate for federal estate tax purposes." As to what this includes, *see* Section 15.4.

[285] UPC § 2–202(1) (pre-1990). Insurance is excluded from the New York and Pennsylvania statutes N.Y. EPTL § 5–1.1(b)(2); 20 Pa.Stat. § 2203(b)(2). *See also* Taliaferro v. Taliaferro, 843 P.2d 240 (Kan.1992); Graham v. Farmers New World Life Ins. Co., 841 P.2d 1165 (Okl.App.1992).

[286] UPC § 2–205(1)(D); *cf.* Section 8.2.

[287] 29 U.S.C. § 1055(a); Matter of Estate of Harrison, 967 P.2d 1091 (Kan.App.1998); In re Lefkowitz, 767 F.Supp. 501 (S.D.N.Y.1991) (death benefits under pension plan must go to widow even though daughter named as beneficiary).

retirement accounts (IRAs) are not subject to this requirement, but they have been held subject to the elective share.[288]

The Uniform Probate Code formerly included in the augmented estate only property which was transferred "during marriage,"[289] but the present version also includes assets subject to the decedent's control at the time of death, regardless of when they were transferred.[290] Some courts have upset conveyances made by a spouse to a third party on the eve of marriage as fraudulent.[291]

The Uniform Probate Code excludes from the augmented estate property transferred "to the extent that the decedent received adequate and full consideration in money or money's worth."[292] Thus, unlike common-law dower and community property (in some states), the elective share is not an obstacle to sales. Also if a donee of property included in the augmented estate sells it to a third party, the latter is not subject to claims by the surviving spouse.[293]

Other Benefits Conferred on Spouse

If a husband's will leaves Blackacre to his wife, what effect will this have on her elective share? The law might allow her to take *both* her elective share *and* Blackacre unless the will made the devise conditional on waiving the elective share. This was the common-law rule as to dower,[294] and the same rule still applies to the family allowance,[295] homestead, and Social Security benefits.[296]

A second position would require the wife to elect between the will and her statutory share. This is the rule in most states today; hence the term *elective* share.[297] In such states, the surviving spouse chooses the benefits passing to the spouse under the will or the elective share.

---

[288] Matter of Estate of Luken, 551 N.W.2d 794 (N.D.1996); McCarty v. State Bank, 795 P.2d 940 (Kan.App.1990).

[289] UPC § 2–202(1) (pre-1990). *See also* Estate of Kotz, 406 A.2d 524 (Pa.1979) (spouse can't attack a joint tenancy created 8 years prior to marriage); De Werthein v. Gotlib, 594 N.Y.S.2d 230 (App.Div.1993) (Totten trust).

[290] UPC § 2–205(1); In re Estate of Antonopoulos, 993 P.2d 637 (Kan.1999) (property put in joint tenancy prior to marriage included in augmented estate).

[291] Estate of Tomaso v. Tomaso, 402 N.E.2d 702 (Ill.App.1980); Efird v. Efird, 791 S.W.2d 713 (Ark.App.1990); Wis.Stat. § 861.17. *Contra,* Perlberg v. Perlberg, 247 N.E.2d 306 (Ohio 1969); Matter of Estate of Scheiner, 535 N.Y.S.2d 920 (Surr.1988). *See generally* Seplowitz, *Transfers Prior to Marriage and the UPC's Redesigned Elective Share—Why the Partnership Is Not Yet Complete,* 25 Ind.L.Rev. 1 (1991).

[292] UPC § 2–208(a)(1).

[293] UPC § 2–210(a); Limb v. Aldridge, 978 P.2d 365 (Okl.Civ.App.1998) (bona fide purchaser from beneficiary of revocable trust not subject to claim by settlor's spouse).

[294] Brown v. Parry, 21 Eng.Rep. 438 (1787) (Ch.). However, an intent to make the spouse elect may be inferred from the will. Carolina Production Credit Ass'n v. Rogers, 318 S.E.2d 357 (S.C.1984); In re Estate of Switzer, 599 A.2d 358 (Vt.1991).

[295] UPC § 2–404(b). This Section also allows a spouse to claim both the family allowance and an elective share. *Accord,* Estate of Calcutt v. Calcutt, 576 N.E.2d 1288 (Ind.App.1991). This is not true in all states. Brown v. Sammons, 743 S.W.2d 23 (Ky.1988).

[296] UPC §§ 2–206, 2–402; In re Estate of Antonopoulos, 993 P.2d 637, 646 (Kan.1999).

[297] Matter of Estate of Spurgeon, 572 N.W.2d 595 (Iowa 1998) (wife's election bars her from taking devise under will even though she was not entitled to a statutory share because of waiver);

A third approach, adopted by the Uniform Probate Code, simply reduces the spouse's statutory share by the value of any devise to the spouse.[298] If the value of devises to a spouse equal or exceed the statutory share the spouse receives nothing more, but if the devise is worth $100,000, for example, and the elective share amounts to $150,000, the spouse gets the devise and an additional $50,000 from other assets in the augmented estate.

Many wills create a trust in which the testator's spouse gets the income for life with a remainder at the spouse's death passing to others. Valuation of the spouse's interest in this case is problematic, because no one knows how long the spouse will live. Furthermore, if the trustee has discretion over payments to the spouse, no one knows how the trustee will exercise this discretion. In one case a widow's interest, based on her age, was valued (by referring to tax tables)[299] at 86% of the value of the trust assets despite her objection that much of the trust consisted of assets which were producing no income.[300] Since 1993, the Uniform Probate Code has allowed spouses to avoid this problem by disclaiming any devises; they are not charged with devises which they disclaim.[301]

What if a husband instead of *devising* Blackacre to his wife, puts it into joint tenancy with her? Many states ignore nonprobate transfers to the spouse and would allow the widow to take her full elective share in addition to Blackacre.[302] The Uniform Probate Code, on the other hand, includes property owned by the surviving spouse at the decedent's death in the calculating the elective share.[303] The theory of the Code is that marriage is an "unspoken bargain" in which the spouses "agree that each is to enjoy a half interest in the fruits of the marriage, *i.e.*, in the property nominally acquired by and titled in the sole name of either partner during the marriage (other than in property acquired by gift or inheritance)." However, the parenthetical exception for property acquired by gift or inheritance (also found in community property systems)[304] is actually ignored in the Code in the interest of ease of administration. The Code uses a "mechanically determined approximation system [in which] . . . there is no need to identify which of the couple's property

---

Hannah v. Hannah, 824 S.W.2d 866 (Ky.1992). This is made clear in most statutes. *E.g.,* 755 ILCS § 5/2–8(a) ("if a will is renounced" spouse gets a share).

[298] UPC § 2–209(a).

[299] *See* Section 15.3.

[300] In re Estate of Myers, 594 N.W.2d 563, 570 (Neb.1999). *See also* In re Estate of Karnen, 607 N.W.2d 32 (S.D.2000). The Code does not expressly deal with the valuation of interests for life or of future interest, but comments suggest the commuted value is the value to be taken into account in valuing limited interests passing to the spouse or others. *See* UPC § 2–207, comment.

[301] UPC § 2–209, comment. *See* Bloom, *The Treatment of Trust and other Partial Interests of the Surviving Spouse under the Redesigned Elective-Share System,* 55 Alb.L.Rev. 941 (1992); Matter of Estate of Grasseschi, 776 P.2d 1136 (Colo.App.1989) (disclaimer is effective if made within the time allotted for the spouse's election). Not all UPC states have adopted this change. In re Estate of Karnen, 607 N.W.2d 32, 37 (S.D.2000).

[302] Gallagher v. Evert, 577 S.E.2d 217, 221 (S.C.App.2002); Estate of Harper, 93 T.C. 368 (1989). King v. King, 613 N.E.2d 251 (Ohio App.1992).

[303] UPC §§ 2–207, 2–209(a)(2).

[304] *See* Section 8.8.

was earned during the marriage and which was acquired prior to the marriage or acquired . . . by gift or inheritance."[305]

Making the Election

Spouses have a limited period in which to choose whether to take the elective share. Under the Uniform Probate Code, the spouse must claim an elective share within nine months after the decedent's death or within six months after the probate of the decedent's will, whichever comes later.[306] The court may extend the time in which to make an election. Even after the time has expired, courts have allowed an election where the spouse's failure to elect was deemed excusable.[307] A spouse who fails to act in time only gets the benefits provided in the decedent's will,[308] but courts have given relief to spouses who made an unwise election in ignorance of relevant facts, such as the size of the decedent's estate.[309]

A lawyer can help a surviving spouse choose intelligently whether to claim the elective share, but if the lawyer drafted the decedent's will, an ethical problem is raised by Rule 1.9 of the Model Rules of Professional Conduct: "a lawyer who has formerly represented a client in a matter shall not thereafter (a) represent another person in the same or a substantially related matter in which the other person's interests are materially adverse to the interests of the former client. . . ." One court held that an attorney who drafted a will could properly advise the testator's widow of her right to an elective share,[310] but another reprimanded a lawyer who had drafted wills for a husband and wife and then represented the husband's estate against which the wife claimed an elective share.[311] It may be advisable for the surviving spouse to have independent counsel, because the attorney for the estate may feel an obligation to preserve the testator's estate plan.[312] If the spouse does not have independent counsel, the attorney for the estate should observe Model Rule 4.3: "in dealing on behalf of a client with a person who is not represented by counsel, a lawyer shall not state or imply that the lawyer is disinterested."

What factors should the spouse (and the lawyer) consider? A simple comparison between the size of the elective share and the benefits given to the spouse by the will is clearly relevant but not always determinative. Suppose that the decedent's will creates a bypass trust which gives a widow the income

---

305 UPC, Part 2, general comment.

306 UPC § 2–211. *Compare* the material in Section 2.8 on the time allowed for disclaimers.

307 Matter of Estate of Hessenflow, 909 P.2d 662 (Kan.App.1995) (period extended because of executor's inappropriate actions); *cf.* In re Estate of Kruegel, 551 N.W.2d 718 (Minn.1996) (no abuse of discretion to deny late petition).

308 In re Estate of Goodlett, 588 N.E.2d 367 (Ill.App.1992); Hutton v. Rygalski, 574 N.E.2d 1128 (Ohio App.1989); In re Estate of Delaney, 819 A.2d 968, 984 (D.C.2003).

309 In re Estate of Tensfeldt, 839 So.2d 720, 726 (Fla.App.2003) (time extended while controversy over size of the estate is being litigated).

310 Walton v. Davy, 586 A.2d 760, 767 (Md.App.1991).

311 Matter of Robak, 654 N.E.2d 731 (Ind.1995).

312 Benjamin, *Post-Mortem Strategies Extend Planning Prospects,* 19 Est.Plan. 24 (1992); Link, *Developments Regarding the Professional Responsibility of the Estate Administration Lawyer: The Effect of the Model Rules of Professional Conduct,* 26 Real Prop. Prob. and Tr. J. 1, 73 (1991). For a more extensive discussion of the ethical problems when lawyers represent both spouses, *see* Section 8.9.

for her life, with the corpus to be distributed at her death to their children.[313] If the widow has enough property to generate an estate tax when she dies, she may decide not to take an elective share even if it would give her more money, because the additional money would be taxed in her estate at death. The widow's failure to take an elective share, like a disclaimer, does not constitute a taxable transfer.[314] On the other hand, if the decedent husband's estate is large enough to incur an estate tax and his will does not qualify for the marital deduction,[315] the widow may wish to elect against the will in order to reduce the taxes on her husband's estate.

If the beneficiaries of the husband's will are also objects of the widow's bounty, such as their common children, the widow's decision will probably turn on such tax considerations, but she may also be affected by the form of the devise in her husband's will. If it creates a trust for her, is she happy with the designated trustee or would she prefer to manage the assets herself? (This is not an issue if the widow herself is designated the trustee, as is often the case.) Is she happy with the allocation of assets in the will? Some wills provide a substantial share for the spouse but allocate particular assets, like a family business, to others.[316] A surviving spouse may wish to elect against the will in order to reduce the assets passing to the decedent's devisees. This is not uncommon when the marriage was childless and/or the spouses have children by prior marriages.

Election by Conservator

If the surviving spouse is legally incompetent, a conservator (guardian) must decide on the spouse's behalf whether to elect against the will,[317] although agents under a durable power of attorney previously executed by the spouse have been allowed to make the election.[318] If the spouse has no conservator, the time for making an election may be tolled until one is appointed.[319] A conservator's decision to claim an elective share requires court approval, which may be withheld if the conservatee does not need the additional money for support.[320] But some states allow conservators to elect

---

[313] *See* Section 15.4.

[314] As to disclaimers, *see* Section 2.8. As we shall see in the next section, the rule is otherwise with respect to the surviving spouse's share of community property.

[315] As to the marital deduction, *see* Section 15.4.

[316] *See* Section 8.1. In this situation, the spouse may not be able to use the elective share to obtain a portion of each asset in the estate. In re Estate of Murphy, 464 N.E.2d 1057 (Ill.1984). UPC § 2–210(a) allows persons who have received nonprobate transfers and who must contribute to making up the elective share an option "to pay the value of the amount for which he [or she] is liable" and retain the property.

[317] In In re Estate of Disney, 550 N.W.2d 919 (Neb.1996), a devisee claimed that the spouse who elected against the will lacked capacity, but the court rejected the claim. *See also* Jones v. Peacock, 591 S.E.2d 83 (Va. 2004) (burden on executor to establish husband lacked capacity).

[318] In re Estate of Schriver, 441 So.2d 1105 (Fla.App.1983); UPC § 2–212(a). As to durable powers, *see* Section 9.3.

[319] In re Estate of Owens, 450 S.E.2d 2 (N.C.App.1994).

[320] In re Estate of Wentworth, 452 N.W.2d 714 (Minn.App.1990); Matter of Guardianship of Scott, 658 P.2d 1150 (Okl.1983); UPC § 2–203 (pre-1990) (for the present UPC solution, *see infra*); In re Estate of Pendleton, 753 N.E.2d 237 (Ohio App.2001) (no election against will which completely disinherited disabled spouse). *Compare* the material in Section 2.8 on the problem of disclaimers by fiduciaries.

against a will whenever this is in the conservatee's "best interests."[321] The Uniform Probate Code allows conservators to claim the share, but the funds then go into a trust for the spouse's support and, when the spouse dies, the funds are returned to the decedent's estate to pass under the will.[322] This removes any incentive to claim an elective share in order to benefit the spouse's children by a prior marriage or other relatives.

In most states, if a spouse dies before making the election, the right to elect disappears and cannot be exercised by the spouse's personal representative.[323] But if the spouse files the election and dies while the claim is being litigated, it can be pursued by the spouse's personal representative.[324] The latter result is arguably inconsistent with the support rationale of the elective share, but not if the elective share is designed to recognize the spouse's contributions to the decedent's wealth.[325]

The right of election cannot be asserted by a creditor of the spouse even if the spouse is insolvent.[326] Failure to exercise a right to an elective share, like a disclaimer, is not a transfer for purposes of the gift or estate tax,[327] but it may render the spouse ineligible for state welfare benefits.[328]

Choice of Law

Differences between state laws on the spouse's elective share may raise the question of which law to apply. Different laws may apply to an estate that includes both real and personal property, with the law of the situs state governing issues respecting the land and the law of the decedent's domiciliary state governing issues respecting the personalty.[329] When a state in which land is situated provides an elective share of 50%, should its computation of the elective share take into account the decedent's personal property or land in other states passing to the spouse? The authorities disagree on this question.[330]

---

[321] McElroy v. Taylor, 977 S.W.2d 929, 932 (Ky.1998); Spencer v. Williams, 569 A.2d 1194 (D.C.App.1990).

[322] UPC § 2–212. This provision applies also if the election is made by an agent under a durable power for an incompetent spouse.

[323] Kirkeby v. Covenant House, 970 P.2d 241, 248 (Or.App.1998) (purpose of election is to financially benefit spouse, not the spouse's estate); Sarbacher v. McNamara, 564 A.2d 701 (D.C.App.1989); Matter of Estate of Thompson, 475 N.E.2d 1135 (Ill.App.1985).

[324] Will of Sayre, 415 S.E.2d 263 (W.Va.1992); Smail v. Hutchins, 491 So.2d 301 (Fla.App.1986); Gallagher v. Evert, 577 S.E.2d 217, 221 (S.C.App.2002). *But see* In re Estate of Bilse, 746 A.2d 1090 (N.J.Super.Ch.Div.1999) (heirs of widower only entitled to amount needed for his support for the balance of his life).

[325] *See* Section 8.1.

[326] Matter of Savage's Estate, 650 S.W.2d 346 (Mo.App.1983). *Compare* the material in Section 2.8 on the frustration of creditors' claims by a disclaimer.

[327] Rev.Rul.74–492, 1974–2 C.B. 298.

[328] Tannler v. DHSS, 564 N.W.2d 735 (Wis.1997) (Medicaid benefits denied because of failure to make spousal election). *See also* Miller v. SRS, 64 P.3d 395, 404 (Kan.2003) (spouse deemed settlor of husband's testamentary trust which became a MQT); Estate of Wyinegar, 711 A.2d 492 (Pa.Super.1998) (guardian of incompetent spouse must elect because otherwise the spouse would be ineligible for benefits). *But see* Bradley v. Hill, 457 S.W.2d 212 (Mo.App.1970).

[329] In re Estate of Pericles, 641 N.E.2d 10, 13 (Ill.App.1994) (out of state land excluded in computing elective share under law of domicile). *See also* Section 1.2.

[330] J. Schoenblum, *Multistate and Multinational Estate Planning* § 10.14 (2016). In Matter of Estate of Rhoades, 607 N.Y.S.2d 893 (Sup.Ct.1994) the widow of a Florida domiciliary was

A spouse is not usually allowed to take under a will in one state and elect against it in another.[331] The Uniform Probate Code provides that the law of the decedent's domicile governs the elective share as to all of a decedent's property.[332] However, when a decedent made nonprobate transfers in another state, the state of the decedent's domicile may not have jurisdiction over the transferees.[333] If ancillary proceedings in another state are necessary, that state may not agree that the law of the decedent's domicile at death controls.[334]

Changes in the law may also raise problems. Most courts apply the law in effect when the testator dies in determining the elective share.[335] But when a Massachusetts court decided to subject revocable trusts to the surviving spouse's elective share, it did so only as to trusts created after the date of the opinion in order to protect persons who had relied on older cases to the contrary.[336] Similarly, statutes abolishing dower typically make an exception for rights already vested.[337]

§ 8.8 Community Property

Significance of Community Property

In Alaska, Arizona, California, Idaho, Louisiana, Nevada, New Mexico, Texas, Washington, and Wisconsin, the community property system provides a counterpart to the elective share. In California, for example, when a married person dies, "one-half of the community property belongs to the surviving spouse and the other one-half belongs to the decedent."[338] This may produce the same result as the spouse's elective share of 50% of the augmented estate under the Uniform Probate Code for long-term marriages, but this depends on how a couple's property is classified, because a spouse in a community property

---

caught between Florida law which took no account of out-of-state realty and New York law which gave no rights to spouses of decedents domiciled elsewhere.

[331] Schoenblum, *supra* note 330, at § 10.09; In re Estate of Conrad, 422 N.E.2d 884 (Ill.App.1981) (failure to renounce will in state of domicile bars claim to elective share of land in Illinois).

[332] UPC § 2–202(d). In Estate of Brown, 955 S.W.2d 940 (Mo.App.1997), on the other hand, the widower of a woman who died domiciled in Missouri was barred from an elective share on the basis of a waiver which he had executed in Kansas which was effective under Kansas law. As to waivers generally, *see* Section 8.9.

[333] Matter of Estate of Ducey, 787 P.2d 749 (Mont.1990); Toledo Trust Co. v. National Bank of Detroit, 362 N.E.2d 273 (Ohio App.1976).

[334] National Shawmut Bank v. Cumming, 91 N.E.2d 337 (Mass.1950) (applying Massachusetts law to deny widow a share of living trust of Vermont domiciliary); De Werthein v. Gotlib, 594 N.Y.S.2d 230 (App.Div.1993) (applying New York law to defeat claims of widow of Argentinian).

[335] In re Estate of Peterson, 381 N.W.2d 109, 115 (Neb.1986). *But see* In re Estate of Pendleton, 753 N.E.2d 237, 240 (Ohio App.2001) (applying statute passed after testator died on theory that change was "procedural").

[336] Sullivan v. Burkin, 460 N.E.2d 572, 577 (Mass.1984). *See also* Matter of Novitt's Estate, 549 P.2d 805 (Colo.App.1976). For a more extended discussion of change in the law, *see* Section 1.3.

[337] Tenn.Code § 31–2–102; N.J.Stat. § 3B:28–1 (preserving dower in land if husband was seised in 1980).

[338] Cal.Prob.Code § 100.

state usually has no rights in the other spouse's separate property if the other spouse devises or gives it to a third person.[339]

The classification of a spouse's property as either community or separate is relevant for several purposes. The rules of intestate succession distinguish between community and separate property. In most community property states, if the deceased spouse dies intestate, the surviving spouse takes decedent's half of the community, thus getting all of the community property. However, the surviving spouse's share of the separate property is ordinarily smaller, particularly where decedent had surviving descendants. The spouse may also receive all of the separate property if the intestate had no descendants or other close relatives, but the division of community property does not depend on the absence of descendants.[340]

Community property states also restrict inter vivos transfers of community property, so courts may have to decide whether property was community or separate in the context of a challenge to a conveyance by one spouse.

Even if a testator leaves all of his or her property to the other spouse, it may make a difference whether this property was separate or community. Because one-half of the community property already belongs to each spouse, there is no taxable transfer of this half.[341] If either spouse earns income during the marriage, one-half of it is attributed to the other spouse for income tax purposes. Some litigation involving community property concerns taxes.[342] However, this is less common, because the marital deduction often produces the same tax result for separate property. In fact, the marital deduction was designed to reduce the disparity between the tax treatment of residents of community and separate property states.[343]

The classification of a couple's property as community or separate may affect its allocation in a divorce.[344] Because divorce is more common today than disinheritance of a spouse by will, most classification cases arise in the context of a divorce. However, the division of community property at divorce varies in different states. California divides community property equally between the spouses, but in Arizona it is "equitably" divided at divorce.[345]

The classification of property may also affect the rights of creditors. For example, expenses of a husband's last illness were held to be a "community

---

339 Cal.Fam.Code § 752. However, a surviving spouse receives a substantial share of the decedent's separate property if the decedent died intestate.

340 Calif.Prob.Code § 6401; Uniform Prob.Code § 2–102A. Even if the decedent had a will, the surviving spouse may claim an intestate share of the estate as an "omitted" spouse if the will fails to mention the spouse. *See* Section 8.6.

341 *See* Section 15.4.

342 Keller v. Department of Revenue, 642 P.2d 284 (Or.1982) (half of husband's income attributed to wife for tax purposes, because it was community property); Estate of Cavenaugh v. Commissioner, 51 F.3d 597 (5th Cir.1995) (error to include all insurance proceeds in H's taxable estate, because wife had a community property interest).

343 H. Weinstock, *Planning an Estate* § 4.2 (4th ed. 1995).

344 Hatcher v. Hatcher, 933 P.2d 1222 (Ariz.App.1996) (division of property in divorce reversed due to erroneous classification of property as separate).

345 *Compare* Calif.Fam.Code § 2550 *with* Ariz.Rev.Stat. § 25–318.

debt" which could be satisfied out of his widow's share of the community property but not out of her separate property.[346]

History and Rationale

The ultimate origin of community property lies in the customs of some of the Germanic tribes which overran the Roman Empire. Community property today exists in many countries of Europe,[347] but it never took hold in England for reasons which are unclear.[348]

The American states which were once under Spanish rule chose to adopt community property even though they rejected everything else in the civil law tradition (except for Louisiana), because they considered the common-law rules governing marital property unfair. The common law held that a wife's property belonged to her husband. The choice of community property improved the rights of married women.[349]

Nevertheless, American courts originally treated the wife's interest in community property as only an expectancy until the husband died. This was a perversion of the Spanish community property system[350] and ended when the tax advantages of the Spanish system were recognized.

> If the community was equally owned by the spouses, then only one-half the community would be includible in the decedent spouse's estate. If, however, the husband was regarded as owner of all the community his wife taking no interest until his death, 100 percent of the community would be part of the husband's taxable estate. A similar problem was presented in the income tax context . . . To the extent that state law regarded the spouses as equal owners, the spouses could divide the community [income] for tax purposes, each separately reporting one half. This allowed the use of a considerably lower tax rate. . . .[351]

To achieve these tax advantages, community property states began to treat spouses as having "present, existing" interests in community property.[352]

From this history one might infer that community property is a "tax gimmick" which is no longer useful because the marital deduction confers

---

[346] Samaritan Health System v. Caldwell, 957 P.2d 1373 (Ariz.App.1998); Abbett Elec. Corp. v. Storek, 27 Cal.Rptr.2d 845 (App.1994) (distinguishing between community property and joint tenancy with regard to rights of husband's creditors); Nichols Hills Bank v. McCool, 701 P.2d 1114 (Wash.1985) (contract creditor of husband cannot reach his share of community property).

[347] Rheinstein, *Division of Marital Property,* 12 Wil.L.J. 413, 419–20 (1975).

[348] Donahue, *What Causes Fundamental Legal Ideas,* 78 Mich.L.Rev. 59 (1979).

[349] Prager, *The Persistence of Separate Property Concepts in California's Community Property System, 1849–1975,* 24 UCLA L.Rev. 1, 6, 10 (1976).

[350] *But cf.* 2 R. David, *Le Droit Francais* 81 (1960) (characterizing the wife's interest in community property in France as an expectancy: "uxor non est proprie socia sed speratur fore").

[351] Prager, *supra* note 349, at 60.

[352] *Id.* at 63. This has made it difficult to alter the rules of community property retroactively. *See also* Model Marital Property Act, prefatory note: "A provision effecting automatic reclassification of [property owned when the Act takes effect] would amount to retroactive legislation and would risk constitutional attack."

similar advantages in separate property states.[353] However, community property continues to flourish. In fact, there is a trend in all states toward the community property approach in dividing marital assets at divorce.[354] Many states now give special treatment to "marital property," which is much like community property.[355] In 1983 a Uniform Marital Property Act was promulgated, which Wisconsin has adopted, and which was the model for an elective community property system adopted by Alaska.[356] Community property thinking inspired the provisions of the Uniform Probate Code governing the elective share.[357] Proposals have also been advanced to improve Social Security by "drawing on community property concepts" to "treat each spouse as earning one half of the couple's total wages earned during the marriage, for purposes of determining social security benefits."[358]

The community property system recognizes the contributions to marital wealth of a spouse who does not earn wages, such as a housewife. "Why should a wife working as keeper of the home and nurse of the children be in a less favorable position than the married woman who works outside the home . . . and accumulates her own savings? Does not the housewife through her work enable the husband to earn money and accumulate his savings?"[359] Community property rules do not always benefit a spouse; when a couple has little community property, the spouse has few rights, but arguably this is as it should be. Property which "was not acquired because of the performance of marital duties . . . should not be available for the survivor to share."[360] However, some have criticized the community property system for failing to give a needy surviving spouse any rights in the decedent's separate property.[361] The Uniform Probate Code attempts to meet this objection by including in the elective share a supplemental amount to reflect the "spouses' mutual duties of support."[362]

---

[353] There continue to be certain income and estate tax advantages in community property. Reinecke, *Community Property Issues for Non-Community Property Practitioners,* 28 ACTEC Journal 224, 232–33 (2002); Estate of Young, 110 T.C. 297 (1998) (discount in value for tax purposes available for community property but not joint tenancy); Burke & McCouch, *Estate Tax Repeal: Through the Looking Glass,* 22 Va. Tax Rev. 187, 202 (2002) (arguing for full step-up in basis for all community property even though only half included in decedent's taxable estate).

[354] Note, 28 UCLA L.Rev. 1365, 1369 (1981); Reppy, *Community Property in the U.S. Supreme Court,* 10 Comm.Prop.L.J. 93, 119 (1983).

[355] Model Marital Property Act, prefatory note. *See also* In re Marriage of Smith, 405 N.E.2d 884 (Ill.App.1980) (citing cases from community property states in defining "marital property.")

[356] Wis.Stat. § 766.001 et seq.; Reinecke, *supra* note 353, at 225.

[357] *See* Section 8.7.

[358] Burke & McCouch, *Women, Fairness, and Social Security,* 82 Iowa L.Rev. 1209, 1232 (1997).

[359] Rheinstein, *supra* note 347, at 420. *See also* Model Marital Property Act, prefatory note ("marriage is a partnership to which each spouse makes a different but equally important contribution").

[360] Greene, *Comparison of the Property Aspects of the Community and Common Law Marital Property Systems,* 13 Creighton L.Rev. 71, 110 (1979). *See also* 84 Okl.Stat. § 44 (elective share limited to property "acquired by the joint industry of the husband and wife during coverture").

[361] Niles, *Probate Reform in California,* 31 Hastings L.J. 185, 193 (1979). As to the support rationale of the elective share, *see* Section 8.1.

[362] UPC § 2–202(b). The quoted rationale for this provision appears in the general comment to Article II, Part 2, of the Code.

The community property system also has been criticized because it raises difficult factual questions and gives rise to much litigation.[363] The Uniform Probate Code, while adopting the basic rationale of community property, uses "a mechanically determined approximation system" which only considers the length of the marriage without having "to identify which of the couple's property was earned during the marriage and which was acquired prior to the marriage or acquired during the marriage by gift or inheritance."[364]

As more wives enter the workforce,[365] issues have arisen in separate property states like those issues in identifying community property. When both spouses are employed and commingle their earnings, a wife, for example, may claim that assets held in her husband's name were actually hers because she paid for them.[366] The increasing number of married women employed outside the home has reduced the disparities between the two systems.

Classification of Property

In some European countries, all of the assets of both spouses are community property; but under the Spanish system, which is the basis of the rules in American community property states, community property is limited to acquisitions due to the gainful activity of either spouse during marriage. What a spouse owned prior to marriage or acquired during marriage by inheritance or gift remains separate property.[367] This principle is common to all American community property systems, but the answers to more specific questions vary in different states.

Assume a wife owns land as separate property and leases it to a tenant while she is married. Spanish law would treat the rent she receives as community property and so would some American states,[368] but in other states income from separate property is separate.[369] If the land rises in value during the marriage, the appreciation will be separate property in all states,[370] unless

---

[363] An estate planner can help to avoid this by advising couples to keep their separate and community property segregated. J. Price & S. Donaldson, *Contemporary Estate Planning* § 3.25 (2019).

[364] The quoted rationale appears in the general comment to Article II, Part 2, of the UPC. For other differences between the UPC and community property, *see* notes 403–13 *infra*.

[365] "Between 1950 and 1992 the percentage of women in the workforce rose from 33.9 to 57.8." Burke & McCouch, *supra* note 358, at 1224 n. 88.

[366] Parks v. Zions First National Bank, 673 P.2d 590 (Utah 1983); Adams v. Jankouskas, 452 A.2d 148 (Del.1982). As to the "purchase money resulting trust" which may arise in this situation, *see* Section 7.4.

[367] Rheinstein, *supra* note 347, at 419; Calif.Fam.Code §§ 760, 770; Idaho Code § 32–903, 32–906; Lay, *A Survey of Community Property,* 51 Iowa L.Rev. 625, 626, 629–30 (1966). *See also* Model Marital Property Act § 4(f), (g).

[368] Swope v. Swope, 739 P.2d 273, 283 (Idaho 1987); Alsenz v. Alsenz, 101 S.W.3d 648, 654 (Tex.App.2003) (royalties from husband's patent granted prior to marriage are community property).

[369] Lay, *supra* note 367, at 630; Bayer v. Bayer, 800 P.2d 216, 222 (N.M.App.1990) (contrasting Arizona and New Mexico rules); Cross, *Community Property: A Comparison of the Systems in Washington and Louisiana,* 39 La.L.Rev. 479, 484 (1979); *cf.* Model Marital Property Act § 4(d) (all income earned during marriage is marital property).

[370] *Cf.* Note, 28 UCLA L.Rev. 1365, 1386 (1981) (arguing that "all appreciation in the value of [a] home since the date of the marriage" should be community property, but noting that "this rule is not followed anywhere today"); In re Balanson, 25 P.3d 28, 42 (Colo.2001) (appreciation in separate property is marital property upon divorce). *See also* Model Marital Property Act § 4(g)(3).

the increase was due to the expenditure of community funds or labor on improvements. When a wife owned land prior to marriage, and $20,000 in community funds were used to build a home on the land which enhanced its value by $54,000, the community was awarded an interest measured by this enhancement in value.[371] Another court in a similar case adopted a flexible approach:

> in most cases simple reimbursement without interest is the appropriate measure for ... improvements, [but] where the improvements actually decrease the value of the property, reimbursement may be too generous a measure. Alternatively, reimbursement may be too stingy a measure where the vast bulk of appreciation is due to the improvements.[372]

In the converse case, when separate funds are used to improve community property, California gives the spouse whose funds were used reimbursement "without interest or adjustment for change in monetary values."[373]

If a spouse's separate property is subject to a mortgage at the time of the marriage and community funds are used to reduce the mortgage, some states simply reimburse the community for the amount paid,[374] but others give the community an interest in the property proportional to its contribution to the total price paid.[375]

Sometimes a spouse owns a business at the beginning of a marriage and works for it during the marriage. If the spouse services were not adequately compensated by the business but those services increased the value of the business, the community acquires a share of the business according to some

---

[371] Anderson v. Gilliland, 684 S.W.2d 673 (Tex.1985). *See also* Portillo v. Shappie, 636 P.2d 878 (N.M.1981); Honnas v. Honnas, 648 P.2d 1045 (Ariz.1982); Elam v. Elam, 650 P.2d 213 (Wash.1982).

[372] Malmquist v. Malmquist, 792 P.2d 372, 382–83 (Nev.1990). In In re Marriage of Wolfe, 110 Cal.Rptr.2d 921 (App.2001), where there was no "claim to the enhanced value of a separate asset attributable to a community-funded improvement nor . . . a claim that the improvement is without value," the wife was awarded one half of the amount of community funds expended in improving the husband's separate property. *See also* In re Marriage of Allen, 116 Cal.Rptr.2d 887 (App.2002) (accepting a claim for reimbursement to the community, but remanding for a determination of the amount).

[373] Cal.Fam.Code § 2640. The reimbursement "may not exceed the net value of the property at the time of the division." This provision applies only in dividing property at divorce. In Bono v. Clark, 128 Cal.Rptr.2d 31, 45 (App.2002), the court said that the different treatment of separate and community property contributions was "anomalous" but nevertheless followed the principle applied in the cases in note 376 where community property had been used to improve a husband's separate property.

[374] Pringle v. Pringle, 712 P.2d 727, 728 (Idaho App.1985); In re Marriage of Wakefield, 763 P.2d 459 (Wash.App.1988).

[375] Drahos v. Rens, 717 P.2d 927 (Ariz.App.1985); Malmquist v. Malmquist, 792 P.2d 372 (Nev.1990). The court in In re Marriage of Chumbley, 74 P.3d 129 (Wash.2003), applied the same principle to apportion stock bought with separate funds in exercising an option owned by the community.

courts.[376] Other courts only reimburse the community for the value of the services.[377]

Classification issues also arise when a spouse owns life insurance prior to marriage and premiums are paid during the marriage. Many courts hold that "the proceeds will be separate property or community property in proportion to the percentage of total premiums which have been paid with separate or community funds."[378] In Texas, however, if a policy began as separate property it remains so, and the community is only reimbursed for the premiums paid with community funds.[379] For term insurance, the source of the funds used to pay the most recent premium on the policy is determinative.[380]

If a couple separates but does not divorce, states differ as to how their earnings during separation are classified. For example, a husband deserted his wife in the 1950s in Texas. He "married" another woman in 1984 and thereafter won $2.5 million in a lottery. The husband then died in the State of Washington. Under Washington law, a wife has no community property interest in the husband's earnings after the couple's separation,[381] but arguably Texas law governed because, under Texas law, the community continues until a divorce.[382] Although this rule seems inconsistent with the rationale of community property, it "avoids the factual issue of when the couple began living apart, and provides appropriate treatment for the on-again-off-again manner in which some couples try to resolve their differences and patch up their marriages."[383]

If a spouse recovers damages for personal injury, compensation for pain and suffering is regarded as separate property, but amounts given to replace lost earnings during the marriage are community property because the earnings themselves would have been community property.[384] Many states

---

[376] Lindemann v. Lindemann, 960 P.2d 966 (Wash.App.1998) (increase in value of husband's separate business attributable to his labor during marriage divided upon separation); Smith v. Smith, 837 P.2d 869 (N.M.App.1992).

[377] Jensen v. Jensen, 665 S.W.2d 107 (Tex.1984).

[378] Porter v. Porter, 726 P.2d 459, 463 (Wash.1986). *See also* Lay, *supra* note 371, at 637.

[379] Rev. Rul. 80–242, 1980–2 Cum.Bull 799; McCurdy v. McCurdy, 372 S.W.2d 381 (Tex.Civ.App.1963).

[380] Matter of Estate of Bellingham, 933 P.2d 425 (Wash.App.1997); Phillips v. Wellborn, 552 P.2d 471 (N.M.1976). As to the difference between term and ordinary life insurance, *see* J. Price & S. Donaldson, *supra* note 363, at § 6.8. For a more detailed discussion of the alternate ways of apportioning insurance, *see id.*, §§ 6.14–.15.

[381] *See also* Cal.Fam.Code § 771 (earnings of a spouse "while living separate and apart from the other spouse" are separate property); *cf.* Aetna Life Ins. Co. v. Boober, 784 P.2d 186 (Wash.App.1990) (community continues even though spouses are living apart if their conduct does not show an intent to renounce the community).

[382] Seizer v. Sessions, 940 P.2d 261 (Wash.1997). The court noted that Texas would also give a share to the putative spouse. (On putative spouses, see Section 2.12.) The court held that Washington law governed, but remanded for a trial as to whether *both* spouses' conduct showed that the marriage was over; mere desertion by one did not indicate a defunct marriage.

[383] Lynch v. Lynch, 791 P.2d 653, 655 (Ariz.App.1990). *See also* In re Marriage of von der Nuell, 28 Cal.Rptr.2d 447 (App.1994) (couple not "separated" under Family Code when they continued to go out even though living apart).

[384] In re Marriage of Hilt, 704 P.2d 672, 676 (Wash.App.1985); Hatcher v. Hatcher, 933 P.2d 1222 (Ariz.App.1996) (distinguishing between earnings during marriage and those after divorce). It may be difficult to allocate an award between these elements. In Brown v. Brown, 675 P.2d 1207,

treat worker's compensation benefits and disability pensions the same way, but some classify them as community property only if they are attributable to premiums paid during the marriage.[385]

Questions of fact in classifying property are often resolved by a presumption that everything acquired during a marriage is community property.[386] This presumption applies even though title to an asset (*e.g.*, a stock certificate) is in only one spouse's name.[387] But a spouse can establish that property is separate by tracing its source.[388] When a man owned Texaco stock prior to marriage, sold it during the marriage, and used the proceeds to buy other stock, the new stock was held to be his separate property even though acquired during the marriage.[389] But when a wife had a savings account prior to marriage into which community property was deposited, the whole account was held to be community at divorce because she "did not sustain her burden of demonstrating which portion of the monies in the account retained their separate character."[390]

Classification may be altered by agreement between the spouses. In California, a couple may, with or without consideration, "transmute separate property of either spouse to community property" or vice versa. This requires an "express declaration" accepted by the spouse adversely affected.[391] But such an agreement is sometimes inferred from conduct. If a husband uses his separate property to buy a house and takes title in the names of both spouses, many courts would infer that he intended the house to be community property.[392]

Nonprobate Transfers

Because each spouse has a present interest, transfers of community property by one spouse may be voidable by the other. Thus, a deed by a husband of a home to his children from a former marriage was held voidable

---

1209 (Wash.1984), an action for personal injury was pending when a couple divorced. The court said that "allocation of the damages should proceed upon special interrogatories" to the jury.

[385] Douglas v. Douglas, 686 P.2d 260 (N.M.App.1984).

[386] In Estate of Hull v. Williams, 885 P.2d 1153, 1157–58 (Idaho App.1994), the court applied this presumption even though the marriage had lasted only 8 years and the date of acquisition of the property was unclear.

[387] Matter of Estate of Mundell, 857 P.2d 631 (Idaho 1993) (husband owns half interest in IRA accounts listed in wife's name); C & L Lumber and Supply, Inc. v. Texas American Bank, 795 P.2d 502 (N.M.1990) (land conveyed by deed to husband as his separate property is community property, because deed not signed by wife).

[388] Cooper v. Cooper, 635 P.2d 850, 853 (Ariz.1981); Cal.Prob.Code § 5305 (bank accounts); *cf.* Model Marital Property Act §§ 4(b), 14(a).

[389] Estate of Hanau v. Hanau, 730 S.W.2d 663 (Tex.1987). *See also* Estate of Kenly, TC Memo 1996–516.

[390] Cooper v. Cooper, 635 P.2d 850 (Ariz.1981).

[391] Cal.Fam.Code §§ 850, 852. *See also* Bosone v. Bosone, 768 P.2d 1022 (Wash.App.1989) (separate property converted to community by agreement). As to the tax consequences of such a transmutation, *see* J. Price & Donaldson, *supra* note 363, at § 3.34.1–.2.

[392] Schmanski v. Schmanski, 984 P.2d 752, 755 (Nev.1999) (separate property put into a joint brokerage account was transmitted to community property). In California the presumption that property held in both spouses' names is community property can only be rebutted by a writing in divorce cases. Calif.Fam.Code § 2581.

by his widow because the home was community property.[393] This gives more protection to spouses than the elective share, which encompasses only a decedent spouse's probate estate in some states.[394] Even the Uniform Probate Code's "augmented estate" would not have included the home in this case if the transfer occurred more than two years before the husband died.

Insurance payable to a named beneficiary is a classic example of a nonprobate asset. Many separate property states exclude insurance proceeds payable to someone other than the spouse from the elective share, but, in community property states, spouses who show that an insurance policy was purchased with community funds can get half the proceeds even if the insured designated someone else as the beneficiary.[395]

However, there are limits on a spouse's rights to upset transfers of community property. Third parties who deal in good faith with one spouse may be free from claims by the other spouse. An insurance company which pays a beneficiary designated by an insured spouse is not liable if it had no notice of the other spouse's community property rights.[396] Purchasers of community real property held in the name of one spouse are protected if they bought "in good faith without knowledge of the marital relation."[397]

A transfer may also be upheld as a legitimate exercise of the transferor-spouse's managerial powers. A widow's attack on her husband's transfer of beehives to his son was rejected, because the transfers were compensation for the son's work in the business, and either spouse could bind the community property by contract.[398] Similarly, a court rejected a husband's challenge of his wife's selection of a payment option under her pension plan which increased payments during her lifetime but gave nothing to the husband when she died.[399]

This rationale may produce the same result as the Uniform Probate Code's exclusion from the augmented estate of transfers made by a spouse for consideration,[400] but the parallel is not complete. Many community property states require the consent of both spouses for all transfers of real estate, even

---

[393] Bosone v. Bosone, 768 P.2d 1022 (Wash.App.1989). *See also* Estate of Hull v. Williams, 885 P.2d 1153 (Idaho App.1994); Ackel v. Ackel, 595 So.2d 739 (La.App.1992) (gift of stock voidable by non-consenting spouse).

[394] *See* Section 8.7.

[395] Aetna Life Ins. Co. v. Boober, 784 P.2d 186 (Wash.App.1990). *But see* Egelhoff v. Egelhoff, 532 U.S. 141 (2001) (state law revoking by divorce the designation of former spouse as beneficiary of a life insurance policy invalid as applied to an ERISA plan).

[396] Leonard v. Occidental Life Ins. Co., 106 Cal.Rptr. 899 (App.1973). *See also* Cal.Fam.Code § 755 (payment under an employee retirement plan discharges payer who has received no written notice of community property rights).

[397] Calif.Fam.Code § 1102; *cf.* Model Marital Property Act § 9.

[398] Mundell v. Stellmon, 825 P.2d 510 (Idaho App.1992).

[399] O'Hara v. State ex rel. Public Employees Retirement Board, 764 P.2d 489 (Nev.1988); Brown v. Boeing Co., 622 P.2d 1313 (Wash.App.1980).

[400] UPC § 2–208(a).

sales.[401] On the other hand, some states permit gifts of community property by one spouse if they are not "excessive."[402]

Differences Between Community Property and Elective Share

All community property states give each spouse one-half of the community property, regardless of whether or not the decedent spouse had surviving children, whereas the existence of children is a relevant factor in determining the elective share in some states.[403] Children may provide a reason to reduce a spouse's claim for support, because children are also entitled to support, but community property claims are based on the spouse's contribution to the acquisition of property.

There are other peculiar rules of community property law which grow out of this contribution rationale. Separate property states only give an elective share to a *surviving* spouse, and the right to elect is lost if the survivor dies before exercising it.[404] Community property rights, on the other hand, do not usually turn on survival. Thus, the estate of a wife who predeceased her husband was awarded one half of the retirement benefits provided by the husband's employer because they were community property.[405]

In separate property states, the conservator of an incompetent spouse may be denied the right to an elective share if it is not necessary for the spouse's support.[406] Under a community property system, a failure to claim the surviving spouse's share of the community would be regarded as a gift to whoever succeeded to that share, and the spouse's lack of need would not by itself justify such a gift.[407]

If a will devises property to a spouse, in most separate property jurisdictions the spouse must renounce the devise in order to get the elective share, or the value of the devise is charged against it.[408] In community property states, however, normally the spouse can keep half of the community property and get the devise too. Each spouse already *owns* half of the community property, and devisees do not have to surrender property which they own in

---

[401] Cal.Fam.Code § 1102; Arch, Ltd. v. Yu, 766 P.2d 911 (N.M.1988) (contract to exchange land signed by only one spouse is unenforceable).

[402] Street v. Skipper, 887 S.W.2d 78 (Tex.App.1994) (designation of estate as beneficiary of insurance upheld because not "unfair" to the spouse); Fernandez v. Fernandez, 806 P.2d 582 (N.M.App.1991). *Compare* Model Marital Property Act § 6 allowing gifts of marital property by one spouse up to $500 a year, or more if "the gift is reasonable in amount considering the economic position of the spouses." *See also* La.Civ.Code art 2349 (allowing a "customary gift of a value commensurate with the economic position of the spouses"); Succession of Caraway, 639 So.2d 415 (La.App.1994).

[403] *See* Section 8.7.

[404] *See* Section 8.7.

[405] In re Estate of MacDonald, 794 P.2d 911 (Cal.1990). However, this result is precluded by federal law as to plans governed by ERISA. Boggs v. Boggs, 520 U.S. 833 (1997); Ablamis v. Roper, 937 F.2d 1450 (9th Cir.1991).

[406] *See* Section 8.7.

[407] As to gifts by conservators of an incompetent, *see* Section 5.2.

[408] *See* Section 8.7.

order to take under a will.[409] If a will simply leaves "one half my estate to my wife," courts assume that the testator "intended only to dispose of his own interest (his separate property and one-half of the community property), and no election is necessary, no matter how liberal the provision is for the wife." However, the spouse *is* put to an election if the testator purported to dispose of both his and his spouse's share of the community property.[410] The same rule applies outside the context of community property when *A*'s will purports to devise *B*'s property to *C* and leaves other property to *B*: *B* must allow her property to pass to *C* if she wishes to take under the will.[411]

If a testator owns community property, the will should make clear whether or not the spouse must elect. Some testators want to put both halves of the community into a trust, either because they do not think the spouse can manage the property, or because they want to have a unified management of all the community property, or in order to save probate costs when the spouse dies. Although a testator cannot dispose of more than one half of the community property against the other spouse's wishes, the other spouse often does not object, particularly if he or she was used to letting the decedent manage their property and does not wish to undertake the burdens of management.[412] Such acquiescence by the surviving spouse is less likely if the will leaves community property to the decedent's children by another marriage or to other relatives, but even in such cases, the benefits to the surviving spouse from taking under the will may exceed the spouse's community property rights. Unless a widow, for example, is quite old, the income from all the community property for life (as a typical trust provides) may be worth more than the remainder interest in the spouse's half of the community property.[413]

Choice of Law

Although people often move to or from community property states, there is not much case law on how conflicts between the laws of separate and community property states should be resolved.[414] The traditional rule that the law of the situs governs land may apply here,[415] but there is a trend to have domicile control even land. California defines community property as "all

---

[409] In Chesnin v. Fischler, 717 P.2d 298 (Wash.App.1986), a wife used community property to create two joint accounts, one with her husband, the other with her sister. The husband was allowed to keep his account while claiming a share in the one for his sister-in-law. Contrast UPC § 2–209(a).

[410] Smith v. Smith, 657 S.W.2d 457 (Tex.App.1983); In re Estate of Patton, 494 P.2d 238 (Wash.App.1972).

[411] *Restatement (Third) of Property (Wills and Other Donative Transfers)* § 6.1, cmt. f (2003).

[412] Kahn & Gallo, *The Widow's Election*, 24 Stan.L.Rev. 531, 536–38 (1972). J. Price & S. Donaldson, *supra* note 363, at § 9.29, suggests that "a widow's election plan should be used only if it is understood by the husband and wife and is completely acceptable to them."

[413] *Compare* the discussion in Section 8.7, notes 299 et seq. The income, estate and gift tax consequences of a "widow's election" in community property states are complicated and still not entirely clear. For an extended discussion, *see* H. Weinstock, *Planning an Estate* §§ 5.18–5.31 (4th ed. 1995).

[414] The dearth of conflict cases may arise from the fact that in many situations the two systems produce the same result. *E.g.,* In re Succession of Hubbard, 803 So.2d 1074, 1081 (La.App.2001).

[415] In In re Crichton's Estate, 228 N.E.2d 799 (N.Y.1967), a husband died domiciled in New York, owning land in Louisiana. His widow's claim to half the Louisiana land as community property was conceded. *See also* Millikin Trust Co. v. Jarvis, 180 N.E.2d 759 (Ill.App.1962).

property, real or personal, *wherever situated*, acquired by a married person during the marriage *while domiciled in this state*."[416] If a non-domiciliary buys land in California, the law of the owner's domicile governs the rights of the owner's surviving spouse.[417]

Everyone agrees that domicile should at least control personal property, but couples often change domicile. In England, domicile at the time of marriage controls. If a couple marries in France, all of their property is community property even though they later move to England.[418] In the United States, however, domicile at the time property is acquired determines whether it is community or separate.[419] Thus, if a couple buys stock while living in a separate property state, it remains the separate property of the acquiring spouse if they later move to a community property state.[420] This rule may leave a spouse "caught between two radically different systems and protected by neither,"[421] because the elective share of the separate property state is unavailable if the decedent spouse was domiciled elsewhere at death, and the community property system of the new domicile is of no use if all the decedent's assets are separate property. California and Idaho have solved this dilemma by the concept of "quasi-community" property: property acquired in another state is treated "as if" the decedent acquirer had been domiciled in the community property state.[422] As with community property, the surviving spouse is entitled to half of the quasi-community property despite the decedent's will, and inherits all of it if the decedent had no will.[423] But unlike true community property, if the acquiring spouse gives away quasi-community property during life, the other spouse has no claim unless the transfer had testamentary characteristics. The test is similar to the test used for including property in the augmented estate under the Uniform Probate Code.[424]

---

[416] Cal.Fam.Code § 760 (emphasis added). For a more general discussion of domicile v. situs as determining choice of law, *see* Section 1.2.

[417] Calif.Prob.Code § 120.

[418] De Nicols v. Curlier, [1900] A.C. 21 (1899); Juenger, *Marital Property and the Conflict of Laws*, 81 Colum.L.Rev. 1061, 1072 (1981); Schoenblum, *Multistate and Multinational Estate Planning* § 10.24[A] (2016).

[419] Matter of Unanue, 710 A.2d 1036, 1039 (N.J.Super.App.Div.1998) (even though couple married in Puerto Rico, property acquired while domiciled in N.J. was not community). If the couple have separate domiciles, that of the acquiring spouse controls. Seizer v. Sessions, 940 P.2d 261, 265 (Wash.1997) (following *Restatement (Second) Conflicts of Law* § 258, cmt. c (1971)).

[420] Brenholdt v. Brenholdt, 612 P.2d 1300 (N.M.1980); *Restatement (Second) of Conflict of Laws* §§ 258, 259 (1971); Estate of Hanau v. Hanau, 730 S.W.2d 663 (Tex.1987); In re Marriage of Moore and Ferrie, 18 Cal.Rptr.2d 543, 547 (App.1993).

[421] Rein, *A More Rational System for the Protection of Family Members Against Disinheritance,* 15 Gonz.L.Rev. 11, 42 (1979). For such a case, *see* Pouliot v. Cloutier, [1944] 3 D.L.R. 737, involving a couple married in New Hampshire who later settled in Quebec.

[422] Calif.Prob.Code § 66; Idaho Code § 15–2–201; *cf.* In re Succession of Hubbard, 803 So.2d 1074 (La.App.2001) (stock acquired while domiciled in Florida is community property for purposes of intestate succession when owner died in Louisiana). This does not apply to real property located outside the state.

[423] Cal.Prob.Code §§ 101, 6401(b).

[424] Calif.Prob.Code § 102. This section is modeled on the pre-1990 UPC, and thus it excludes life insurance and pensions. *Cf.* Idaho Code § 15–2–202. Dean Price and Professor Donaldson suggest that spouses "with a stable marriage who move from a common law state to a community property state" should by agreement transform their property into true community property to

When the move is in the other direction—from a community property state to a separate property state—the spouse may receive *too much* protection rather than too little. If a couple acquires stock while domiciled in a community property state, it continues to be community property if they move to a separate property state.[425] Can a surviving spouse also claim an elective share in the decedent's half of the community property? A Uniform Disposition of Community Property Rights at Death Act would preserve the surviving spouse's share of the community property but bars an elective share in the decedent's half of the community.[426]

Community property interests may be preempted by federal law. Several decisions of the United States Supreme Court have dealt with the relationship between federal and state law in this area, but the underlying principles remain unclear. When a husband used community funds to purchase United States Savings Bonds payable on death to his brother, this did not deprive the widow of her rights under state law.[427] But the Court rejected a claim by an Army officer's widow to half the proceeds of a National Service Life Insurance Policy purchased with community funds; a federal statute which said the proceeds went to the named beneficiary was held to supersede state community property law.[428] The Court also rejected community property claims asserted against military retirement pay[429] and benefits under the Railroad Retirement Act,[430] but here the Court misread congressional intent, for the relevant statutes were later amended to change the result.[431] ERISA has also been held to supersede community property claims in undistributed pension benefits.[432]

---

take advantage of the step up in basis allowed by Int.Rev.Code § 1014(b). J. Price & S. Donaldson, *supra* note 363, at § 3.26.

425 Devine v. Devine, 711 P.2d 1034 (Wash.App.1985); Scoles et al., *Conflict of Laws* § 14.9 (2000); G. Miller, *International Aspects of Succession* 97 (2000).

426 Uniform Disposition of Community Property Rights at Death Act § 3 (14 adoptions). In Estate of Bach, 548 N.Y.S.2d 871 (Surr.1989) a widow was awarded half of her husband's estate based on Bolivian community property law under the Uniform Act. For a detailed discussion of the Act, *see* Schoenblum, *supra* note 418, at § 10.21[G].

In Beaudoin v. Trudel, [1937] 1 D.L.R. 216 (Ont.C.A.1936), a wife died intestate after the couple moved from Quebec to Ontario; her husband was awarded half of the community property and also a share of her half under Ontario law. The Uniform Act would allow this; it only bars the surviving spouse's taking an *elective share* in the decedent's half.

427 Yiatchos v. Yiatchos, 376 U.S. 306 (1964).

428 Wissner v. Wissner, 338 U.S. 655 (1950). The California Supreme Court was able to perceive a distinction between this and a very similar insurance program for civilian employees of the federal government in Carlson v. Carlson, 521 P.2d 1114, 1115–1116 (Cal.1974).

429 McCarty v. McCarty, 453 U.S. 210 (1981) (later superseded by statute).

430 Hisquierdo v. Hisquierdo, 439 U.S. 572 (1979) (later superseded by statute). *See also* Wisner v. Wisner, 631 P.2d 115 (Ariz.App.1981) (Social Security).

431 Uniformed Services Former Spouses' Protection Act, 10 U.S.C. § 1408. This Act has been held to exclude retirement pay which a spouse receives as a result of waiving disability benefits, despite the Court's inability to perceive a policy reason for the distinction. Mansell v. Mansell, 490 U.S. 581 (1989). *See also* In re Marriage of Kraft, 832 P.2d 871 (Wash.1992).

432 Boggs v. Boggs, 520 U.S. 833 (1997); Barnett v. Barnett, 67 S.W.3d 107, 121 (Tex.2001). As to the possible conflict between community property and copyright laws, *see* Nimmer, *Copyright Ownership by the Marital Community*, 36 UCLA L.Rev. 383 (1988).

§ 8.9 Waivers

Agreements between spouses to limit the survivor's claim to an elective share are increasingly common as more persons enter into second marriages and wish to protect the inheritance of children of a prior marriage from the new spouse. (Nearly all of the cases involving waivers arise from a second marriage where one or both spouses have children by a prior union.) Even in community property states, where property owned prior to the marriage is not subject to a forced share, parties may wish to provide that property that would otherwise be community property shall be separate or to allow one spouse to dispose of all of the community assets.

Time of the Waiver

Waiver agreements may be made before or during a marriage.[433] The rules governing the two situations may be the same or may differ, depending on the relevant law. The Uniform Premarital and Marital Agreements Act, promulgated in 2012, treats "premarital agreements and marital agreements under the same set of principles and requirements."[434] (With respect to the waiver of a surviving spouse's elective share, the relevant provisions of the Uniform Premarital and Marital Agreements Act have been incorporated into the Uniform Probate Code.) In contrast, the prior uniform act on point—the Uniform Premarital Agreements Act of 1983—covered only premarital agreements, not marital agreements. That older Act is still the law in several states. California, for example, has enacted the Uniform Premarital Agreement Act[435] and somewhat different provisions governing marital agreements.[436]

The California Family Code expresses an idea which can also be found in judicial opinions in other states: spouses occupy "confidential relations with each other . . . and neither shall take unfair advantage of the other."[437] At least according to one judicial opinion in California, the situation of parties who are not yet married is arguably different.

> Although persons, once they are married, are in a fiduciary relationship to one another . . . so that . . . the advantaged party bears the burden of demonstrating that the agreement was not obtained through undue influence . . . a different burden applies under the Uniform Act in the premarital setting. Even where the premarital

---

[433] For a discussion of several situations in which postnuptial agreements may be useful, *see* Siegel-Baum & Averill, *Postnuptial Agreements Can Resolve Personal and Estate Planning Issues*, 29 Est. Plan. 405 (2002). As to the choice of law applicable to such agreements, *see*, Schoenblum, supra note 418, at § 10.08. *See also*, In re Estate of Smid, 756 N.W.2d 1 (S.D. 2008) (postmarital waiver valid where voluntary, not unconscionable, spouse reasonably informed, and no undue influence).

[434] Unif. Premarital and Marital Agreements Act, prefatory note.

[435] Cal.Fam.Code §§ 1600 et seq.

[436] Cal.Prob.Code §§ 140–47. Section 140 indicates that these provisions apply to all agreements "whether signed before or during marriage" but Section 147(c) indicates that premarital agreements are *not* covered. In re Estate of Gagnier, 26 Cal.Rptr.2d 128, 131 (App.1993), holds that different rules apply to pre-and postnuptial agreements. *See also* Fla.Stat. § 732.702(2) (disclosure required for postnuptial agreements only).

[437] Cal.Fam.Code § 721(b).

agreement clearly advantages one of the parties, the party challenging the agreement bears the burden of demonstrating that the agreement was not entered into voluntarily.[438]

Agreements made after a couple has separated and are anticipating divorce are less likely to be affected by undue confidence in the other spouse.[439] As one court noted in upholding such an agreement, the wife "was in a position of knowledge that is far superior to that of a young bride signing an agreement *before* the marriage."[440]

A surviving spouse may also waive rights in the estate after the other spouse has died. Although this situation is not directly covered by statute, it can involve abuses of confidence. A widow's release of any claims against her husband's estate was held not binding because the executor, a child by a prior marriage, "failed to disclose the facts which would enable [the widow] to make a free and understanding consent."[441] In contrast, a husband's waiver of rights in his deceased wife's estate without consideration was held binding, because before signing he "was advised of his legal rights" and had "thoroughly reviewed" the inventory of her estate.[442]

Formal Requirements

Oral or unsigned waivers contained in an agreement in consideration of marriage are unenforceable in most states under the Statute of Frauds.[443] Furthermore, under Section 2–213 of the Uniform Probate Code, the spouse's right of election can be waived "only by a written agreement signed by the surviving spouse."[444] However, some oral agreements have been enforced on an "estoppel" theory despite such statutes.[445]

ERISA requires that a spouse's waiver of rights in a pension must be "witnessed by a plan representative or a notary public."[446] Comparable agreements must be executed before a notary in Europe,[447] where the notaries, being members of the legal profession, play a more important role than in the

---

438 In re Marriage of Bonds, 5 P.3d 815, 831 (Cal.2000).

439 Estate of Gibson, 269 Cal.Rptr. 48 (App.1990).

440 Davis v. Miller, 7 P.3d 1223, 1233 (Kan.2000).

441 Matter of Estate of Hessenflow, 909 P.2d 662, 672 (Kan.App.1995). *See also* Matter of Estate of Geer, 629 P.2d 458 (Wash.App.1981).

442 In re Estate of Ferguson, 730 N.E.2d 1205, 1211 (Ill.App.2000). On the ethical problems of attorneys who advise the surviving spouse, *see* Section 8.7.

443 Clark, *Antenuptial Contracts*, 50 U.Colo.L.Rev. 141, 142 (1979); *Restatement (Second) of Contracts* § 124, illus. 3 (1981).

444 *See also Restatement (Third) of Property (Wills and Other Donative Transfers)* § 9.4(a) (2003); Ind.Code § 29–1–3–6; Calif.Prob.Code § 142; Estate of Calcutt v. Calcutt, 576 N.E.2d 1288, 1292 (Ind.App.1991) (oral waiver unenforceable).

445 Estate of Sheldon, 142 Cal.Rptr. 119, 125 (App.1977); Brown v. Boeing Co., 622 P.2d 1313, 1317 (Wash.App.1980).

446 29 U.S.C. § 1055(c)(2)(A).

447 BGB (German Civil Code) § 1410 (marriage contract affecting property rights must be executed before a notary), § 2348 (same for disclaimer of the right to a forced share). In France premarital agreements must be notarized. Code Civil art. 1394. In Matter of Estate of Halmaghi, 457 N.W.2d 356 (Mich.App.1990), the court set aside a prenuptial agreement executed before a German notary, taking a dim view of the protective value of the notary.

United States.[448] Historically, married women in England could waive dower only before a judge who would examine them to make sure that they were acting voluntarily.[449] This is not necessary today,[450] but New York requires that a waiver of the spouse's elective rights must be acknowledged like a deed.[451]

Section 2–208 of the Uniform Probate Code excludes from the augmented estate (and thus the elective share) property which the decedent transferred "with the written joinder of" the surviving spouse. This section says nothing about the disclosure requirements for waivers, to be discussed presently. California also provides for a "spouse's written consent to . . . a nonprobate transfer of community property on death,"[452] but such consent can be avoided by showing fraud or undue influence.[453] This is also true of a consent to transfers under the Uniform Probate Code, because "the principles of law and equity supplement" its provisions.[454]

Disclosure

A common theme in the statutes and case law concerning waivers of a surviving spouse's elective share is the need for disclosure. The Uniform Premarital and Marital Agreements Act and the Uniform Probate Code provide that a waiver of an elective share is not enforceable if the surviving spouse proves that (1) the waiver was involuntary or the result of duress, (2) the surviving spouse did not have access to independent legal representation, (3) unless the surviving spouse had access to independent legal representation, the waiver did not include an explanation in plain language of the rights being waived, or (4) the surviving spouse did not receive adequate financial disclosure.[455]

Some judicial opinions suggest that disclosure is necessary only if the agreement is unfair. The Pennsylvania Supreme court at one time denied that agreements must "make reasonable provision *and* [be] entered into after full and fair disclosure. . . . An agreement can survive if *either* (but not necessarily

---

[448] On the role of continental notaries in executing wills, *see* Section 3.3.

[449] Y.B. 18 Edw. 4, f. 4, pl. 11 (1478); 2 W. Blackstone, *Commentaries* 351 (1766).

[450] However, in Louisiana an agreement made during marriage to alter the community property regime needs court approval. La.Civ.Code art. 2329. *See also* French Code Civil art. 1397. Apparently, this arises from the historical incapacity of married women, which prevailed in France as well as England.

[451] N.Y.EPTL § 5–1.1(f)(2). *See also* Wash.Rev.Code § 26.16.120 (agreement on disposition of community property must be acknowledged like a deed).

[452] Such consent is revocable during the marriage, in contrast to a "declaration" transmuting community into separate property. In 1990, the California Supreme Court held that a wife's consent to her husband's designation of a beneficiary of community property did not bind her estate because she did not expressly declare an intent to transmute the property. In re Estate of MacDonald, 794 P.2d 911 (Cal.1990). The relevant statutes were thereafter amended to provide that even without such an express declaration, a consent to a transfer could not be revoked after the death of either spouse. Cal.Prob.Code §§ 5022, 5030; Cal.Fam.Code §§ 850, 852.

[453] Cal.Prob.Code § 5015.

[454] UPC § 1–103.

[455] Unif. Premarital and Marital Agreements Act § 9; UPC § 2–213. But in Estate of Brown, 955 S.W.2d 940, 943–44 (Mo.App.1997), the court rejected a widower's challenge of a waiver for lack of disclosure on the ground that this was not required by Kansas law which controlled.

both) of these requirements is satisfied."[456] But more recently that court backed away from its earlier position that courts should inquire into the reasonableness of the provisions. While the court appeared to continue to support the necessity of full disclosure, it stated that "absent fraud, misrepresentation, or duress, spouses should be bound by the terms of their agreements."[457] Under the Third Restatement of Property, however, an "unconscionable" agreement is unenforceable even if voluntary.[458]

Sometimes a party attacks an agreement which recites such disclosure, denying that the disclosure actually occurred. Many courts view such claims with suspicion,[459] but others hold that the recital of disclosure is not conclusive.[460]

In community property states, a spouse's knowledge about the other spouse's separate property seems irrelevant, because spouses have no rights in the other spouse's separate property.[461]

In all states, one may question whether a spouse's knowledge of the other spouse's wealth should matter unless the spouse understands his or her *rights* in that wealth, *i.e.*, what is actually being surrendered by the waiver. Some courts stress the business experience (or lack thereof) of the party who challenges the waiver. For example, a wife was bound who had "been involved in various businesses . . . and was not unaware of the importance or effect of binding legal documents,"[462] whereas a wife who was "extremely unsophisticated" in business was not bound.[463] Some opinions suggest that waivers are valid only if the signer was aware of the rights being waived.[464] Arguably (unless one indulges in the fiction that everyone knows the law) the waiving party must have received legal advice.[465] The California Probate Code makes waivers binding when the spouse was "represented by independent legal counsel at the time of signing the waiver," but they can also be upheld

---

456 In re Estate of Geyer, 533 A.2d 423, 427 (Pa.1987). *See also* Sasarak v. Sasarak, 586 N.E.2d 172 (Ohio App.1990) (even though amount received was "disproportionate" to widow's rights, valid because of full disclosure). But cf. Matter of Estate of Halmaghi, 457 N.W.2d 356, 357 (Mich.App.1990) (small provision for wife raises a presumption of nondisclosure).

457 Simeone v. Simeone, 581 A.2d 162, 165 (Pa 1990).

458 *Restatement (Third) of Property (Wills and Other Donative Transfers)* § 9.4, cmt. k (2003). *See also* Ind.Code § 29–1–3–6(a) (both "full disclosure" and "fair consideration" needed).

459 In Matter of Estate of Thies, 903 P.2d 186, 190 (Mont.1995), a widow attacking the agreement lost because the trial court found her story not credible. *See also* Matter of Baggerley's Estate, 635 P.2d 1333, 1335 (Okl.App.1981).

460 Bohnke v. Estate of Bohnke, 454 N.E.2d 446, 449 (Ind.App.1983) (waiver failed to disclose the nature and extent of the rights being waived); Matter of Estate of Halmaghi, 457 N.W.2d 356, 357 (Mich.App.1990) (contract in German, wife was Romanian).

461 *See* Section 8.8.

462 Matter of Estate of Ascherl, 445 N.W.2d 391, 393 (Iowa App.1989). *See also* Elgar v. Elgar, 679 A.2d 937, 943 (Conn.1996) ("both parties were experienced business people").

463 Sogg v. Nevada State Bank, 832 P.2d 781, 785 (Nev.1992). *See also* In re Estate of Grassman, 158 N.W.2d 673, 675 (Neb.1968) (husband "inexperienced in business and legal affairs").

464 Jarvis v. Jarvis, 824 P.2d 213 (Kan.App.1991); Matter of Estate of Halmaghi, 457 N.W.2d 356, 357 (Mich.App.1990).

465 Matter of Estate of Crawford, 730 P.2d 675, 678 (Wash.1986) (unfair prenuptial agreement invalid unless entered "upon the advice of independent counsel"); Matter of Estate of Halmaghi, 457 N.W.2d 356, 358 (Mich.App.1990).

without this.[466] Some courts question the propriety of waivers prepared by a lawyer for one spouse when the other has no lawyer.

> The agreement was prepared entirely by decedent's counsel . . . To have upheld this agreement, the court would have had to have found that Blair, her fiancé's attorney, adequately advised her. [The court cites EC 5–15 of the Code of Professional Responsibility limiting a lawyer's representation of clients with conflicting interests.] Blair did not fully explain the potential conflict or recommend that appellant obtain other counsel before signing the agreement.[467]

A lawyer who advised his stepmother to waive her right to take against her husband's will was held to have violated the Rules of Professional Conduct and was suspended from practice, because his interest as a beneficiary of his father's will "jeopardized his ability to provide objective legal advice to his stepmother."[468] The California Supreme Court, however, rejected a claim that "a premarital agreement in which one party is not represented by independent counsel should be subjected to strict scrutiny for voluntariness." In this case the lawyer for the prospective husband had suggested to his fiancée that she get her own counsel but she declined to do so. He then explained to her that she was giving up her community property rights under the agreement. The court held that the "rule of professional conduct prohibiting counsel for one party from giving legal advice to an opposing party who is unrepresented" did not preclude enforcement of the contract. It was proper "for the attorney to take steps to ensure that the premarital agreement will be enforceable" and he had done this.[469]

Most spouses in deciding whether or not to waive their rights would want to know who will benefit thereby.[470] A widow may be willing to allow her husband to leave property to his children, but not to his mistress. In California, a spouse's consent to a nonprobate transfer of community property is revoked if the other spouse later changes the beneficiary of the transfer.[471]

Fairness

According to the Uniform Premarital and Marital Agreements Act, an agreement requires no "consideration" but is unenforceable if the party against whom the enforcement is sought proves (1) the agreement was involuntary or the result of duress, (2) the party did not have access to independent legal

---

[466] Cal.Prob.Code §§ 143–44; In re Estate of Gagnier, 26 Cal.Rptr.2d 128 (App.1993). In other states the fact that a spouse had independent counsel is often mentioned as a factor in upholding the agreement. Matter of Marriage of Yager, 963 P.2d 137, 139 (Or.App.1998); Davis v. Miller, 7 P.3d 1223, 1231 (Kan.2000). Under *Restatement (Third) of Property (Wills and Other Donative Transfers)* § 9.4(c) (2003) a rebuttable presumption of validity arises if the spouse "was represented by independent legal counsel."

[467] Rowland v. Rowland, 599 N.E.2d 315, 319 (Ohio App.1991). *See also* Matter of Marriage of Leathers, 789 P.2d 263, 266 (Or.1990) (dissenting opinion); Briggs v. Wyoming Nat. Bank, 836 P.2d 263, 267–72 (Wyo.1992) (dissenting opinion). For more discussion of the ethical issues, *see* McGovern, *Undue Influence and Professional Responsibility*, 28 Real Prop. Prob. and Trust J. 643, 665–68 (1994); J. Price & S. Donaldson, *Contemporary Estate Planning* § 1.6.7 (2019).

[468] Matter of Taylor, 693 N.E.2d 526, 528 (Ind.1998).

[469] In re Marriage of Bonds, 5 P.3d 815, 821, 833 (Cal.2000) (later superseded by statute).

[470] *See* Section 8.7.

[471] Cal.Prob.Code § 5023. *See also* 26 U.S.C. § 417(a)(2) (pension plan).

representation, (3) unless the party had access to independent legal representation, the agreement did not include an explanation in plain language of the rights being waived, or (4) the party did not receive adequate financial disclosure; moreover, a court may still decline to enforce an agreement if the agreement is "unconscionable."[472] Even without a statute, courts often say that the marriage itself provides consideration for the waiver in premarital agreements.[473] Even in postnuptial agreements, courts usually have no difficulty in finding consideration.[474]

Courts often refuse to enforce agreements they consider unfair. The question arises, however, whether "unfairness" is determined at the time the agreement is signed or at the time one of the spouse's dies? Most courts hold it is the former, enforcing agreements that were fair when signed, even those that ultimately give the spouse substantially less than the spouse's intestate or elective share.[475] "Antenuptial agreements are favored by the law . . . It was no more than equitable that the prospective husband should, at the time he made the contract, provide that his estate should go to his children by a former wife."[476] This argument is especially persuasive when the legal rights of a spouse seem unduly great, *e.g.*, a large share of an estate after a short marriage. This is less likely to be the case when a state has a phased-in percentage for the elective share. Furthermore, as noted above, issues of fairness are balanced by disclosure, so that an agreement providing nothing for a surviving spouse (which may not seem fair) is enforceable if there had been full disclosure.

Under the Uniform Premarital and Marital Agreements Act, unconscionability is determined "at the time of signing" the agreement, but there is also a bracketed provision in the Act that would empower a court to take a second look and deny enforcement if enforcement of the agreement "would result in substantial hardship for a party because of a material change in circumstances arising after the agreement was signed."[477]

Are the standards different in community property states? One court found unfair and, thus, unenforceable an agreement by which the wife waived all rights "by virtue of the expenditure of community funds or community labor" on the husband's separate property, because this allowed the husband "effectively to foreclose the accumulation of any significant community

[472] Unif. Premarital and Marital Agreements Act § 9.

[473] Beatty v. Beatty, 555 N.E.2d 184 (Ind.App.1990).

[474] Matter of Estate of Brosseau, 531 N.E.2d 158, 160 (Ill.App.1988) (consideration in mutual release of rights in the other spouse's estate); Matter of Estate of Beesley, 883 P.2d 1343, 1348 (Utah 1994) (benefits to spouse in agreement supplied consideration).

[475] Davis v. Miller, 7 P.3d 1223, 1232 (Kan.2000), rejecting a claim that a settlement which gave the wife over $1 million was unconscionable, without discussing what she might have received without the agreement). *But see* In re Estate of Geyer, 533 A.2d 423 (Pa.1987); Estate of Mader, 89 Cal.Rptr. 787, 792 (App.1970) (presumption of undue influence when agreement gives wife "less than she would receive by way of her community property rights").

[476] Beatty v. Beatty, 555 N.E.2d 184, 188–89 (Ind.App.1990). *See also* Matter of Baggerley's Estate, 635 P.2d 1333, 1335–36 (Okl.App.1981) ("the antenuptial pact was aimed at achieving a natural and entirely appropriate end—the protection of the inheritance rights of his daughter").

[477] Unif. Premarital and Marital Agreements Act § 9(f).

[property]" in a 10-year marriage.[478] On the other hand, an agreement which allowed a husband to put his wife's half of the community property into a trust which made "ample provision" for her and over which she had a power of appointment, was found to be "fair" and enforceable even though she had no independent counsel.[479]

California law allows courts to modify an agreement; courts are not limited to either enforcing or invalidating it entirely.[480] This more flexible approach is followed in England's family maintenance scheme[481] and by state courts in divorce cases.[482]

A decedent's failure to perform the consideration promised for a spouse's waiver does not necessarily make the waiver ineffective. Thus, when a husband failed to name his wife as beneficiary of an insurance policy as promised, the court nevertheless enforced her waiver, because the husband's breach could be "remedied by a money judgment."[483]

Construction

An enforceable agreement may raise problems of construction. For example, an agreement that "all property owned by each party at the time of the marriage would remain the separate property of each" was held not to bar the husband from claiming a statutory surviving spouse's allowance from his wife's estate.[484] The Uniform Probate Code, however, presumes that "a waiver of 'all rights,' or equivalent language, in the property or estate of a present or prospective spouse" covers claims to a family allowance, an elective or intestate share,[485] or any devise under a will executed before the waiver.[486] But it does not preclude a spouse from receiving gifts made by the other spouse after the waiver.[487]

---

478 Matter of Marriage of Foran, 834 P.2d 1081, 1086 (Wash.App.1992).

479 Whitney v. Seattle-First Nat. Bank, 579 P.2d 937 (Wash.1978).

480 Calif.Prob.Code § 144(b); *cf.* Uniform Commercial Code § 2–302.

481 Inheritance (Provision for Family and Dependants) Act § 2(1)(f) (1975).

482 Osborne v. Osborne, 428 N.E.2d 810 (Mass.1981); Gross v. Gross, 464 N.E.2d 500 (Ohio 1984).

483 Brees v. Cramer, 586 A.2d 1284, 1289 (Md.1991). *See also* In re Estate of Cummings, 425 A.2d 340 (Pa.1981); Gillilan's Estate v. Gillilan's Estate, 406 N.E.2d 981 (Ind.App.1980).

484 Estate of Calcutt v. Calcutt, 576 N.E.2d 1288 (Ind.App.1991). *See also* Matter of Estate of Zimmerman, 579 N.W.2d 591 (N.D.1998) (elective share); Steele v. Steele, 623 So.2d 1140 (Ala.1993) (wrongful death proceeds); Hunter v. Clark, 687 S.W.2d 811 (Tex.App.1985) (homestead). *But see* Estate of Dennis, 714 S.W.2d 661 (Mo.App.1986) (elective share rights precluded by waiver).

485 This is true even though the agreement was not executed with the formalities prescribed for a will. Matter of Estate of Beesley, 883 P.2d 1343 (Utah 1994). In Matter of Estate of Lindsay, 957 P.2d 818 (Wash.App.1998), a broadly worded separation agreement was held to bar a spouse's claim to homestead even though homestead was not specifically mentioned.

486 UPC § 2–213(h). *See also* Cal.Prob.Code § 145. In Matter of Estate of Hansen, 910 P.2d 1281 (Wash.1996), such an agreement was held to bar a claim as an omitted spouse because it showed that the decedent did not intend to provide for the spouse.

487 Bowen v. Bowen, 575 S.E.2d 553 (S.C.2003).

§ 8.10 Negative Limitations

Mortmain

In the 13th century when the feudal system was in full sway, lords complained against tenants who alienated land into "mortmain" by giving it to religious institutions such as monasteries. These complaints culminated in the Statute of Mortmain of 1279.[488] Though the term mortmain literally means "dead hand" (Latin: *mortuus manus*), the lords' complaint was that religious corporations did *not* die, so the lord had no chance to profit from wardship which arose when a tenant left a minor heir or escheat when a tenant died without heirs. The feudal basis for the original Statute of Mortmain was made clear by the remedy: forfeiture to the lord of whom the land was held. The donor's heirs had no standing to complain of the gift.[489]

A mortmain statute of a different sort was enacted in 1736, which reflected the law's historic concern with death-bed wills. The statute provided that all gifts of land to charity had to be made by a deed sealed and delivered at least twelve months before the donor died.[490]

Both of these statutes have been repealed in England, and neither became part of the common law in America,[491] but several American states until recently had "mortmain" statutes based on the 1736 law. The underlying purpose was to prevent wills made by dying persons under undue influence, but the statutes operated arbitrarily. Most have since been repealed or held unconstitutional.[492] For example, when a daughter invoked a mortmain statute to attack her mother's will leaving property to a hospital, the court held that the statute violated the state constitution.

> The statute does not protect against overreaching by unscrupulous lawyers, doctors, nurses, housekeepers, companions, or others with a greater opportunity to influence a testator . . . Nor is it rational to apply the statute in cases where the testator dies suddenly due to an accident during the six-month period after making the charitable bequest . . . Artful will drafting easily defeats the effect of the statute: If the testator names anybody other than a spouse or lineal descendant to take the charitable devise in the event that the charitable devise fails, nobody would have standing to petition to avoid the charitable devise.[493]

---

[488] 7 Edw. 1, stat. 2, c. 13 (1279). For the background of the statute, *see* D. Sutherland, *The Assize of Novel Disseisin* 88 (1973).

[489] Y.B. 20 & 21 Edw. 1 R.S. 262 (1292). Similar feudal concerns played a role in the history of wills. *See* Section 8.2.

[490] Charitable Uses Act, 9 Geo. 2, c. 36 (1736). *Compare* the recitals about death-bed wills in the Statute of Uses quoted in Section 8.2.

[491] *Restatement (Second) of Trusts* § 362 (1959).

[492] The Ohio statute was repealed in 1985 and held unconstitutional in 1986, but prospectively only. It was used in Wendell v. AmeriTrust Co., N.A., 630 N.E.2d 368 (Ohio 1994), to invalidate a charitable remainder created in 1942.

[493] Shriners Hospitals v. Zrillic, 563 So.2d 64, 69–70 (Fla.1990). Other decisions holding mortmain statutes invalid are In re Cavill's Estate, 329 A.2d 503 (Pa.1974); Estate of French, 365 A.2d 621 (D.C.App.1976); Shriners' Hospital for Crippled Children v. Hester, 492 N.E.2d 153 (Ohio 1986).

Mortmain statutes were easily avoided by the use of will substitutes. The original mortmain statutes covered any form of conveyance, but the American counterparts covered only wills. Revocable trusts and even death-bed gifts were immune.[494]

Despite the virtual disappearance of mortmain statutes, modern law continues to invalidate wills or other transfers made under undue influence. This will be discussed in Section 5.3.

Negative Wills

A negative will is a will in which the testator does not dispose of property but attempts to merely exclude a person from inheriting what otherwise would be the person's intestate share. A testator's will left his estate to his wife and declared his intention to exclude his children. The wife predeceased the testator and so could not take.[495] The testator's children were allowed to take under intestacy laws despite the disinheritance clause in the will on the ground that "a testator cannot disinherit his heirs by words alone, but in order to do so, the property must be given to somebody else."[496] The Uniform Probate Code, on the other hand, specifically authorizes "so-called negative wills, [reversing] the usually accepted common-law rule, which defeats a testator's intent for no sufficient reason."[497] Under the Code, the disinherited heirs' shares pass as if they had disclaimed, *i.e.,* they are deemed to have predeceased the testator.[498] Thus, under the Code in the preceding case, the testator's property would have passed to the descendants of the testator's disinherited children, if any, or to his collateral relatives, or if he had none, to the state by escheat. Maybe this is what the testator would have wanted, but it seems more likely that he disinherited his children only to make sure his wife took his entire estate.[499] If this was the reason the testator disinherited his children, then he would probably have wanted them to take when his wife could not. One court accepted this view in a similar case despite a statute based on the Uniform Probate Code.

> The plain language of the will indicates that [the testator] wanted to disinherit his other heirs if [his brother, the sole devisee] was alive, but there is no indication that [the testator] wanted to disinherit them if [his brother] predeceased [the testator]. . . . Can it honestly

---

[494] In re Estate of Katz, 528 So.2d 422 (Fla.App.1988); Matter of Estate of Kirk, 907 P.2d 794 (Idaho 1995); Bible Ministry Ass'n v. Merritt, 391 So.2d 641 (Miss.1980). *Contra, Restatement (Third) of Trusts* § 25, cmt. d (2003).

[495] The effect of a devisee predeceasing the testator is discussed in Section 6.5.

[496] Estate of Baxter, 827 P.2d 184, 187 (Okl.App.1992). *See also*, Harrison v. Harrison, 120 S.W.3d 144 (Ark. App. 2003); Cook v. Estate of Seeman, 858 S.W.2d 114 (Ark.1993); Matter of Estate of Krokowsky, 896 P.2d 247 (Ariz.1995); In re Estate of Jackson, 793 S.W.2d 259 (Tenn.App.1990); McClain v. Hardy, 56 P.3d 501 (Or.App.2002) (noting that state had not adopted UPC provision cited in note 502).

[497] UPC § 2–101(b), comment. *See also Restatement (Third) of Property (Wills and Other Donative Transfers)* § 2.7 (1999).

[498] UPC § 2–1106(b)(3)(B). *See also Restatement (Third) of Property (Wills and Other Donative Transfers)* § 2.7, cmt. c (1999).

[499] In many states they might have taken as omitted heirs if they had not been mentioned in the will. *See* Section 3.5. In some cases giving the disinherited heir's share to his or her issue, as prescribed by the UPC, may not reflect the testator's real intent.

be said . . . that [the testator] intended the State to have his property if his brother did not survive him? If he had had such a bizarre intent, would he have left any doubt?[500]

Even without a statute like the Uniform Probate Code, some courts give effect to disinheritance clauses by construing them as implied gifts to another person. For example, a will which said "I leave nothing to my husband" was held to be an implied devise to the testator's children.[501]

Conditions Relating to Marriage and Divorce

Some testators try to use wills to control the lives of the devisees. Roman jurists disputed whether a devise contingent on marrying Titus' daughter was valid.[502] American courts have had to deal with similar provisions. For example, a will left a house to the testator's fiancée "so long as she remains unmarried."[503] This arguably violates public policy. The Second Restatement of Property invalidates restrictions in instruments that are "designed to prevent the acquisition or retention of" property "in the event of any first marriage of the transferee."[504] The idea has roots in Roman and canon law, but "what may have been the Roman policy—encouraging the growth of the population—can hardly be a strong policy today; nor in the light of our separation of church and state would we feel comfortable following a rule . . . striking down marriage restraints because they encourage immoral cohabitation." Still, "we are reluctant to brook any interference with the marriage choice of the parties to the marriage."[505] Nevertheless, such conditions are valid if "the dominant motive of the transferor is to provide support until marriage" rather than to induce the transferee to remain unmarried.[506] Evidence as to motive is admissible, and a recital in the instrument itself is not conclusive.[507] The Third Restatement of Trusts, noting that such provisions "may reflect a mixture of motives," says they may be "judicially reformed to accomplish the permissible objectives . . . while removing or minimizing socially undesirable effects," for example, by replacing a condition with a provision allowing a trustee to exercise discretion to provide for needs.[508]

Regardless of motive, some restraints on marriage are acceptable. Devises conditioned on the testator's surviving spouse remaining unmarried are

---

[500] Matter of Estate of Jetter, 570 N.W.2d 26, 31 (S.D.1997).

[501] In re Thomas, (1984) 1 W.L.R. 237 (1983).

[502] Gaius, *Institutes* 2.235; Justinian, *Institutes* 2.20.36.

[503] Matter of Estate of Romero, 847 P.2d 319 (N.M.App.1993).

[504] *Restatement (Second) of Property (Donative Transfers)* § 6.1 (1983). *See also* Cal.Civ.Code § 711; Ga.Code § 19–3–6.

[505] *Restatement (Second) of Property (Donative Transfers)* Introductory Note to ch. 6 (1983).

[506] Thus the court in *Romero, supra* note 503, remanded for a determination of the testator's motive. Professor Sherman would reject consideration of motive, not only because of the difficulty of proof; for him "it is an offensive spectacle for the state, at the behest of a dead person, to shift wealth from B to A as a reward" for complying with the decedent's wishes both as to marriage and divorce. Sherman, *Posthumous Meddling: An Instrumentalist Theory of Testamentary Restraints on Contractual and Religious Choices*, 99 U.Ill.L.Rev. 1273, 1311 (1999).

[507] *Restatement (Second) of Property (Donative Transfers)* § 6.1, cmt. e (1983).

[508] *Restatement (Third) of Trusts* § 29, cmt. j (2003).

allowed.[509] Although this rule is supported by case law,[510] the drafters of the Second Restatement of Property appear to be uncomfortable with it; they note that its "possible harshness" is alleviated by the right of a spouse to take against the will. Also, the fact that such devises do not qualify for the federal estate tax marital deduction operates to deter them.[511] The only legitimate justification for such a condition is to preserve property for the testator's children, and so the rule "may come to be applied" only if the testator is survived by descendants.[512]

The Restatement also allows partial restraints, *i.e.*, those which restrict "some, but not all, first marriages" of the devisee so long as they do not "unreasonably limit" the freedom to marry. Under this theory a court allowed a devise to the testator's son "only if he is married . . . to a Jewish girl."[513] Restrictions which impose difficult problems of interpretation on the courts may be rejected. A court, in upholding a devise to descendants who were "members in good standing of the Presbyterian Church," distinguished a will which required the devisees to "remain faithful" to a specified religion.[514] Problems of interpretation can be reduced by using a trustee to decide if the condition has been met, but this technique was held invalid when it created a conflict of interest, as was the case where trustees took an alternative bequest if the primary beneficiary married without their consent.[515] On the other hand, a condition that a beneficiary's wife "continues to worship according to the Jewish faith" was upheld where the instrument stipulated that any questions on this were to be submitted to the chief rabbi in London.[516]

The Restatement invalidates conditions where the testator's "dominant motive" was to break up a family relationship.[517] When a will devised a house

---

[509] *Id.*, illus. 1; *Restatement (Second) of Property (Donative Transfers)* § 6.3 (1983).

[510] Matter of 1942 Gerald H. Lewis Trust, 652 P.2d 1106 (Colo.App.1982); Wilbur v. Campbell, 192 So.2d 721 (Ala.1966). For state statutes dealing with this question and the cases construing them, *see* Statutory Note to Section 6.3, *Restatement (Second) of Property (Donative Transfers)* (1983).

[511] *See* Section 15.4.

[512] *Restatement (Second) of Property (Donative Transfers)* § 6.3, cmts. c, e (1983). In Estate of Guidotti, 109 Cal.Rptr.2d 674 (App.2001) a provision whereby the testator's wife lost her benefits under a trust if she remarried was held to be invalid. Otherwise it would have disqualified the trust for the marital deduction.

[513] Shapira v. Union Nat. Bank, 315 N.E.2d 825 (Ohio Com.Pl.1974). *See also* Taylor v. Rapp, 124 S.E.2d 271 (Ga.1962) (daughter disinherited if she marries a named individual); In re Keffalas' Estate, 233 A.2d 248 (Pa.1967) (to daughter if she marries a Greek). *But see Restatement (Second) of Property (Donative Transfers)* § 6.2, illus. 1 (restraint invalid when child was already engaged to designated individual), 3 (restraint invalid when child unlikely to marry someone of the designated religion) (1983); *Restatement (Third) of Trusts* § 29, illus. 3 (2001). Sherman says "it is hard to find" cases holding "a partial restraint to be unreasonable;" for him the whole approach "astonishingly . . . unsatisfactory." Sherman, *supra* note 506, at 1320–21.

[514] In re Estate of Laning, 339 A.2d 520 (Pa.1975). *See also Restatement (Second) of Property (Donative Transfers)* § 6.2, illus. 4 (1983) (requirement that daughter marry "her social equal" is too vague).

[515] In re Liberman, 18 N.E.2d 658 (N.Y.1939); *Restatement (Second) of Property (Donative Transfers)* § 6.2, cmt. e (1983).

[516] In re Tuck's Settlement Trusts, [1978] Ch. 49 (Ct.App.).

[517] *Restatement (Second) of Property (Donative Transfers)* § 7.2, cmt. e (1983). *See also Restatement (Third) of Trusts* § 29, cmt. j (2001); Jiles v. Flegel, 291 N.E.2d 300 (Ill.App.1972) (devise to adopted children on condition they use name of their biological father).

to the testator's children on condition that their mother not live in it, the court remanded the case for a finding as to the testator's motive, suggesting that the prohibition may have been only "a recognition of . . . 'almost an impossible situation' ", *i.e.,* the testator's fiancée and his ex-wife living in the same house.[518]

Conditions designed to induce divorce or separation are also invalid, but not if the "dominant motive . . . is to provide support in the event of separation or divorce."[519] The Restatement says that today's more liberal rules for divorce do not "indicate an abandonment of the policy of preventing outsiders from inducing the break-up of a marriage by offers of wealth."[520] But recent cases suggest that courts are willing to countenance just that if it seems appropriate under the circumstances. A court sustained a trust under which the settlor's daughter got nothing until she reached 65 or her husband died or they were divorced. The court held the condition valid, noting that the daughter's husband "had tricked [the settlor] into investing $10,000 in a worthless venture" and his "financial affairs were under Federal investigation."[521] Another court in a similar case said "not every encouragement of divorce is objectionable"; parents can do this when they seek to advance what they "reasonably believe to be their child's welfare."[522] The Third Restatement of Trusts says that a "reasonable concern over the spouse's financial irresponsibility or apparent gambling or substance addiction" may provide a legitimate motive for such a provision, and that courts may modify objectionable provisions so as to satisfy the settlor's reasonable objectives without invalidating a provision completely.[523]

Conditions designed to control the custody of children may also be invalid. Thus, a trust for the testator's grandchildren provided that the funds should pass to another if certain persons became their guardian. This was held to be against a public policy to choose guardians on the basis of the best interests of the child.[524]

In *Marion v. Davis,*[525] testator created a trust for his wife and then provided that if any successor beneficiary should "attempt to place my wife in a nursing" home, that beneficiary's share under the trust would be forfeited. The court upheld the forfeiture provision against the argument that it violated public policy.

Conditions which do not affect the beneficiary's conduct after the testator's death are allowed. For example, a devise to a daughter to take effect only if "at the time of my death, she is married to and living with her husband" was upheld, because "public policy regarding restraints on marriage should

---

[518] Matter of Estate of Romero, 847 P.2d 319, 322–23 (N.M.App.1993).

[519] *Restatement (Second) of Property (Donative Transfers)* § 7.1 (1983); In re Gerbing's Estate, 337 N.E.2d 29 (Ill.1975) (to son if he divorces his wife—invalid condition); In re Keffalas' Estate, 233 A.2d 248 (Pa.1967) (to married daughter if she remarries a Greek—invalid condition).

[520] *Restatement (Second) Property (Donative Transfers)* § 7.1, cmt. b (1983).

[521] Matter of Estate of Donner, 623 A.2d 307 (N.J.Super.App.Div.1993).

[522] Hall v. Eaton, 631 N.E.2d 805 (Ill.App.1994).

[523] *Restatement (Third) of Trusts* § 29, cmt. j (2003).

[524] Stewart v. RepublicBank, Dallas, N.A., 698 S.W.2d 786 (Tex.App.1985).

[525] 106 S.W.3d 860 (Tex. App. Dallas 2003).

only be concerned with continuing inducements" whereas in this case the "rights become absolutely fixed at [the testator's] death."[526]

The Second Restatement of Property allows conditions designed to affect other types of conduct, such as religious practices[527] and the choice of education or career,[528] unless they are too indefinite.[529] Professor Sherman notes that "religious conditions almost invariably present interpretive problems. How, for instance, does a court, unable to read minds, determine whether a legatee has complied with a condition requiring 'adherence' to a particular faith?"[530] The Third Restatement of Trusts suggests that the "risk of excessive influence on a serious and fundamentally personal decision" may justify a policy restraint. A further limitation on such terms may be found in the Uniform Trust Code requirement that all trust terms must be "for the benefit of" the beneficiaries.[531] Recent cases on this issue are too infrequent to derive firm conclusions. It is also hard to derive from the cases a clear rule as to what happens in the event that a condition is held to be invalid; does the devisee get the property whether or not he complies with the condition or does the gift fail?[532]

Destruction of Property

Virgil's will directed his executors to destroy his poem, the Aeneid. They refused to do so, and it has become a classic of world literature.[533] The law will not assist a decedent in carrying out eccentric wishes. "A settlor may destroy his own Rembrandt. But he cannot establish a trust and order his trustees to destroy it. Society will not assist him to waste economic assets."[534] Such restraints on ownership rights are not needed for the living who have a natural desire to preserve what they own, but the law must impose checks on a *decedent's* "extravagance or eccentricity."[535]

---

[526] In re Estate of Heller, 159 N.W.2d 82, 85 (Wis.1968). *See also Restatement (Second) of Property (Donative Transfers)* § 6.1, cmt. c (1983); *Restatement (Third) of Trusts* § 29, cmt. i(2) (2003). Professor Sherman, however, rejects this distinction; he "would invalidate even testamentary restraints aimed only at personal conduct occurring before the testator's death." Sherman, *supra* note 510, at 1304.

[527] 1 W. Blackstone, *Commentaries* 437 (1765) describes two English statutes directed at any Catholic or Jewish father who "shall refuse to allow his protestant child a fitting maintenance, with a view to compel him to change his religion," but these provisions were repealed by Religious Opinions Relief Act, 8 & 9 Vict. ch. 59 (1846).

[528] *Restatement (Second) of Property (Donative Transfers)* §§ 8.1–8.3 (1983).

[529] *Id.*, § 8.1, cmt. e, § 8.2, illus. 4.

[530] Sherman, *supra* note 506, at 1314. He also raises, but ultimately rejects the idea that court enforcement of such conditions is unconstitutional.

[531] UTC § 404. *See* Langbein, *The Uniform Trust Code*, 15 Trust Law Int. 66, 78 (2001).

[532] The various possibilities are discussed in Sherman, *supra* note 506, at 1322–26.

[533] Zabel, *The Wills of Literary Figures*, 128 Trusts and Estates 59 (Sept. 1989). Franz Kafka's novel, *Der Prozess* (The Trial) is another classic which was published posthumously against the express wishes of the author.

[534] E. Halbach ed., *Death, Taxes, and Family Property* 126 (1977).

[535] Eyerman v. Mercantile Trust Co., N.A., 524 S.W.2d 210, 215, 217 (Mo.App.1975).

Directions in a will as to how the testator's body is to be disposed of, *e.g.*, by cremation, are normally respected,[536] but testators who seek to devote an immense fortune to the erection of a tomb like the pyramids or the Mausoleum[537] may run afoul of the restrictions on trusts for noncharitable purposes.[538] A will provision that "can only gratify the vanity of the testators, who have no claim to be immortalised, but who possess the means. . . . to provide for more substantial monuments to themselves than many that are erected to famous persons by public subscription" was held invalid.[539]

Provisions in a will restricting a devisee's use of land may be enforced only if "the restrictions are confined within reasonable bounds." If not, a court "may refashion the restrictions so that they are reasonable."[540]

Courts have refused to respect provisions for trust administration which they find "capricious," such as a requirement that the trustees and their spouses be Protestants. "Public policy does not permit a settlor to burden the judicial system with the responsibility to keep watch over every one of his personal vagaries that is unrelated to any proper trust purpose."[541] From this perspective, the trust purpose is all important. Presumably such a requirement imposed on the trustees of a trust to run a school for training Protestant ministers would not be unrelated to the trust purpose.

§§ 8.11–9.0 are reserved for supplemental material.

---

[536] Cottingham v. McKee, 821 So.2d 169 (Ala.2001). It is advisable to express such wishes in a writing outside the will, because often a will is not read until after the body is disposed of. J. Price & S. Donaldson, *Contemporary Estate Planning* § 4.11 (2019).

[537] Erected for King Mausolus by his widow about 350 B.C. and one of the seven wonders of the ancient world.

[538] *See* Section 10.10.

[539] McCaig's Trustees v. Kirk-Session of the United Free Church, 1915 Sess.Cas. 426, 434 (Scot.2d Div.).

[540] Crowell v. Shelton, 948 P.2d 313, 316 (Okl.1997) (restriction that land "never be used for residential or commercial development"). As to restraints on alienation, *see* Section 12.8.

[541] In re Estate of Coleman, 317 A.2d 631, 633 (Pa.1974). *See also Restatement (Third) of Trusts* § 29, cmt. m (2003). As to provisions restricting the *beneficiaries* of a charitable trust to a particular religion, race or gender, *see* Section 10.10. As to the courts' power to modify administration provisions of a trust when circumstances change, *see* Section 10.9.

Chapter 9

PLANNING FOR INCAPACITY

Analysis

Sec.

9.1 Introduction.
9.2 Guardianship.
9.3 The Durable Power of Attorney.
9.4 End-of-Life Decision Making.
9.5 Advance Health-Care Directives.
9.6 Family Consent Laws.
9.7 Anatomical Gifts.

---

§ 9.1 Introduction

Over the past couple of decades, estate planning practice has changed dramatically. Federal estate and gift tax planning has receded in importance as the estate tax exemption has increased from $60,000 in 1976 to $11,700,000 in 2021, with the amount to be increased even further for subsequent inflation.[1] Litigation involving estates and trust matters has increased dramatically, giving birth to a new law practice specialty, that of fiduciary litigation. But perhaps most importantly, fueled by concerns that individuals are living longer than formerly but not necessarily in a state of good health, planning for incapacity has become part of the standard estate planning counseling session. In addition to a will and possibly revocable trust, it is customary for a client to sign a durable power of attorney for property management[2] and some type of advance health-care directive.[3] Less commonly, the client will sign a document indicating an intent to be an organ or tissue donor.[4] For those who fail to plan, the law's traditional answer was for the court to appoint a guardian or conservator.[5] But because proof of incapacity is required before making an appointment for an adult, appointing a guardian or conservator can be an expensive and time-consuming procedure. Even so, because guardians and conservators are supervised by the court, guardianship or conservatorship may provide more protection against abuse than a durable power of attorney, whose principal advantage and vice is lack of supervision of the agent's actions. For individuals who fail to plan, a majority of states have enacted statutes authorizing specified family members or close friends to make health-care decisions on the incapacitated individual's behalf.[6] These family

---

[1] *See* Section 15.1.

[2] For a discussion, *see* Section 9.3.

[3] For a discussion, *see* Section 9.5.

[4] For a discussion, *see* Section 9.7.

[5] For a discussion, *see* Section 9.2.

[6] For a discussion, *see* Section 9.6.

consent statutes can work well in most cases but sometimes not so well if the person the statute designates to make decisions is not qualified or is not the person the incapacitated individual would have selected.

§ 9.2 Guardianship

Overview

Guardianship is a judicial process that transfers decisionmaking authority over an individual deemed incapable of managing his or her personal or financial affairs (a "ward,") to another person (the "guardian"). Guardians may be appointed for both minors and adults.

Modern guardianship has its roots in English common law, which was brought to America in Colonial times. Under English common law, the doctrine of *parens patriae* (parent of the country) allowed the courts to assume control of and appoint guardians for "infants" (minors) and "incompetents" (incapacitated adults).[7] Today, state law controls the appointment of guardians, and guardians are appointed by state courts. Because each state is free to enact its own laws, state guardianship laws vary, even on basic terminology. Under the Uniform Guardianship and Protective Proceedings Act (UGPPA), enacted in about a third of the states, a "guardian" makes personal care decisions, while a "conservator" manages property.[8] But in many other states, the court-appointed manager is referred to as either a "guardian of the person" or "guardian of the property." In California and Connecticut, "conservators" make decisions for adults, whether on property or personal matters, and "guardians" make decisions for minors.

States also vary on procedures for appointment of guardians. Procedures for appointment of a guardian of a minor are different from and generally less detailed than procedures for an adult appointment. Procedures for minors are less detailed because the incapacity of a minor is presumed, while the incapacity of an adult must be proved.[9]

Types of Guardianship

There are several types of guardianship. Under a plenary or full guardianship, the guardian is granted comprehensive decision-making authority over an individual's personal care, property, or both. Under a limited guardianship, as its name implies, the guardian is granted only limited and specified powers regarding an individual's personal care or property. A guardian of the person makes decisions with respect to the ward's personal care. The guardian ordinarily will determine where the ward will live and will arrange for the ward's medical care. The guardian of the property manages the

---

[7] For historical background, *see* Krasik, *The Lights of Science and Experience: Historical Perspectives on Legal Attitudes Toward the Role of Medical Expertise in Guardianship of the Elderly*, 33 Am. J. Leg. Hist. 201 (1989).

[8] For a discussion of the 1997 revision of this Act, *see* English & Morgan, *The Uniform Guardianship and Protective Proceedings Act (1997)*, 11 NAELA Quarterly 3 (1998).

[9] For a discussion of guardianship for minors, *see* English, *Minors' Guardianship in an Age of Multiple Marriage*, 29 Heckerling Inst. on Est. Plan. ¶ 5–1 (1995).

ward's finances. The guardian will disburse funds for the ward's care, will handle the ward's investments, and will determine which assets must be sold.

Guardians are typically appointed for an extended period—until a minor attains the age of majority, or until an adult individual's death or recovery of capacity. Under a temporary or emergency guardianship, however, the guardianship lasts for only a short period of days or months. Because temporary or emergency guardians are appointed for only a short term and often on an emergency basis, the procedures for appointment are more expedited than for a regular, longer-term appointment.[10] Limited and temporary or emergency guardianships are the exception, not the rule, however. The term "guardianship," without qualification, usually refers to a plenary or full guardianship.

Guardianship, which requires a proceeding before a court before an appointment may be made, must be distinguished from other uses of the term. It is sometimes said that parents, by virtue of their custodial rights, are the natural guardians of their minor children, although this term is falling into disuse. Also, the role of a guardian is very different from that of a guardian ad litem. A guardian ad litem is an individual, often an attorney, who is usually appointed for the sole purpose of representing another person in a particular court proceeding, such as in a dispute over the validity of a will.

Guardianship of Adults

Appointment of a guardian for an adult is very different from appointment of a guardian for a minor. A minor, by legal definition, lacks the capacity to manage his or her own personal or financial affairs. An adult, however, is presumed to have such capacity. Before a guardian may be appointed for an adult, it must be established to a court's satisfaction that the adult individual lacks capacity to make his or her own decisions. The procedures for the appointment of a guardian of an adult are therefore more detailed.

Guardianship of adults is an issue of growing importance. The reason for this is changing demographics. Approximately 80 percent of adult guardianship appointments are made for individuals age sixty or older.[11] This segment of the population is rapidly increasing. Between 2010 and 2050, the percentage of Americans age 65 or older is expected to increase from 13% to 20.9%.[12] Guardians are also frequently appointed for adults with developmental disabilities and adults with serious mental illnesses.

Guardians may be appointed only for adults who are determined to lack capacity. Capacity is a legal standard, not a clinical one. Professionals such as physicians, psychologists, and social workers may be asked to provide evidence concerning the individual's medical condition and ability to perform certain tasks, but the determination of whether an individual lacks legal capacity to make the individual's own decisions must be made by a court.

---

[10] For one approach, *see* UGPPA (1997) § 318.

[11] Commission on the Mentally Disabled/Commission on Legal Problems of the Elderly, *Guardianship: An Agenda for Reform* (1989).

[12] U.S. Census Bureau, *Current Population Reports, P23–212, 65+ in the United States: 2010*.

The definition of incapacity was traditionally based on a categorical approach: Did the individual have a specified impairment such as mental deficiency, mental retardation, or infirmity of advanced age? In most states, however, the definitions have moved away from such labels and conclusory statements. The growing trend is to focus on the individual's ability to make decisions with respect to self-care and management of property. If the individual is unable to make such decisions, then a guardian may be appointed if the individual's needs cannot be met by any less restrictive means.[13]

Guardianship of an adult is initiated by filing a written petition with a court, requesting that a guardian be appointed. The petition may request the appointment of a guardian of the person, a guardian of the property, or both. The same person may be appointed as guardian of the person and guardian of the property, or different persons may be appointed. The individual for whom guardianship is sought (the "respondent") must be given notice of the petition and has the right to contest the requested appointment. In many states an attorney must be appointed to represent the respondent. The court may also appoint a "visitor" to make an independent investigation on whether guardianship is appropriate or order that the respondent be examined by a physician, psychologist, or other qualified professional.

The procedure for appointment of a guardian concludes with a determination by the court. The judge considers the evidence and either makes the appointment, rejects the appointment, or orders that the respondent's needs be met by other means. In some states, the respondent may request that certain issues be determined by a jury. As with minors, the guardian will usually be a close family member. Before making the selection, however, the court will usually consider the ward's preferences.[14]

The role of the appointed guardian has traditionally been to act in the ward's best interests. Under this model, the guardian must make an objective determination of what is best for the ward and act accordingly. Whether this determination conflicts with the ward's current or prior expressed wishes is not a factor in this situation.

However, other approaches have become increasingly important. Under the least restrictive alternative model, the guardian may exercise authority only to the extent necessitated by the ward's limitations. The guardian must select the alternative least restrictive of the ward's independence and freedom. The guardian must also encourage the ward to participate in making decisions. A third approach is the substituted judgment model. The guardian must make the decision the ward would have made had the ward still had capacity. Under

---

13 For a discussion of the various legal tests for determining capacity, *see* Villavicencio & Cuello, *Standards and Basic Principles of Examining and Evaluating Capacity in Guardianship Proceedings*, 26 St. Thomas L.Rev. 64 (2013); Anderer, *Determining Competency in Guardianship Proceedings*, Washington, DC: American Bar Association (1990). For a discussion of clinical assessment methods, *see* Grisso, *Evaluating Competencies: Forensic Assessments and Instruments* (2d ed. 2002).

14 *See, e.g.*, UGPPA (1997) § 310(a)(2) ("person nominated as guardian by the respondent, including the respondent's most recent nomination made in a durable power of attorney, if at the time of the nomination the respondent had sufficient capacity to express a preference.")

this approach, the ward's prior expressed wishes and personal values are important factors to be considered.[15]

Many adult guardianships continue for the ward's lifetime and are terminated only by death. Upon the ward's death, the court will discharge the guardian, and the ward's assets will be distributed under the ward's will or to the ward's heirs. Guardianships are not necessarily lifelong, however. The ward may recover capacity, in whole or in part, or other changed circumstances may suggest that guardianship is no longer needed. In all states, a ward may request termination of the guardianship. To protect this right, many states provide that the ward's request need not be made by a formal petition but may be made by informal letter.

The decision to seek guardianship of an adult should never be made lightly. The position of guardian is a heavy responsibility. The ward, because he or she has been found to lack legal capacity, may lose many basic rights, including the right to vote, to travel, to decide where to live, to divorce or marry, to keep and care for children, and even to drive a car.[16]

Similar to children, incapacitated adults are sometimes moved to different states or countries and appointment of a guardian will be sought in the new locale. Sometimes the move is arranged by a child who disagrees with his or her siblings on what care is best for the parent. Such moves raise serious issues as to which state's court has jurisdiction to make an appointment. Traditionally, a guardian could be appointed by the court in which the respondent was domiciled or physically present, leading to the possibility that courts in two different states might appoint a guardian for the same person. The Uniform Adult Guardianship and Protective Proceedings Jurisdiction Act, completed in 2007 and enacted in 48 jurisdictions as of late 2020, seeks to minimize such jurisdictional conflicts by generally limiting jurisdiction for the appointment of a guardian or conservator to the courts of only one state.

Further reforms of guardianship law have occurred. In 2017, the UGPPA was replaced by the renamed Uniform Guardianship, Conservatorship, and Other Protective Arrangements Act (UGCOPAA). The charge to the committee that drafted UGCOPAA was to consider revising UGPPA in light of the recommendations of the Third Guardianship Summit held in 2011.[17] An important theme of this Summit was to encourage use of supported decision-making as an alternative to guardianship. Under supported decision-making, the ability of the individual to make decisions is not stripped away and granted to a guardian. Instead, the individual with a disability will continue to make decisions but with the "support" or "assistance" from a network of family and

---

[15] *See generally* Frolik, *Plenary Guardianship: An Analysis, a Critique, and a Proposal for Reform*, 23 Ariz. L. Rev. 599 (1981).

[16] *See* Parry, *Incompetency, Guardianship, and Restoration*, in The Mentally Disabled and the Law (1985).

[17] For the text of the standards and recommendations, *see Third National Guardianship Summit Standards and Recommendations*, 2012 Utah L. Rev. 1191. For the specific issues being addressed in the revision of the UGPPA, *see* English, *Amending the Uniform Guardianship and Protective Proceedings Act to Implement the Standards and Recommendations of the Third National Guardianship Summit*, 12 NAELA J. 33 (2016).

professionals (the "supporters").[18] Although a relatively new concept in the United States, supported decision-making is recognized in Canada and a number of European countries.[19] The concept gained general currency following approval of the 2006 U.N. Convention on the Rights of Persons With Disabilities. Article 12(3) of that Convention requires that countries that are parties to the Convention "shall take appropriate measures to provide access by persons with disabilities to the support they may require in exercising their legal capacity."[20] As of late 2020, the Convention had been ratified or acceded to by 182 countries although not by the United States.[21]

§ 9.3 The Durable Power of Attorney

The durable power of attorney for financial affairs, along with the revocable living trust, are the principal alternatives to guardianship of an individual's property. The growth of the durable power has been truly remarkable. From a little used device only a few decades ago, the power of attorney has become a standard part of the estate planning package.

Under a power of attorney, a person called a "principal" grants to an "agent" or "attorney-in-fact" the powers as specified in the document. The powers granted may relate to health care and/or finances, although the growing practice is to address finances and health care in separate documents.[22] Under the Uniform Durable Power of Attorney Act, which has been widely enacted in the states, a power is durable if it provides either that the agent's authority continues in effect despite the principal's incapacity (termed an "immediately effective" power), or if it provides that the agent's authority springs into effect upon the principal's incapacity (termed a "springing" power).[23] Immediately effective powers are recognized by statute in all states, and a majority of state statutes expressly recognize springing powers.

Principals appointing agents is not a new phenomenon but is part of the common law of agency. However, at common law a power of attorney was revoked upon the principal's incapacity.[24] The purpose of the durable power statutes, enacted in all states, is to allow a principal to overcome this common law limitation. But the durable power of attorney statutes do not override the common law rule that a power of attorney is automatically revoked upon the

---

[18] *See* Kohn, Blumenthal & Campbell, *Supported Decision-Making: A Viable Alternative to Guardianship*, 117 Penn. St. L. Rev. (2013).

[19] *See* Then, *Evolution and Innovation in Guardianship Laws: Assisted Decision-Making*, 35 Sydney L. Rev. 133, 148–54 (2013).

[20] For discussions of this provision, *see* Perlin, *"Strikers for the Guardians and Protectors of the Mind": The Convention of the Rights of Persons With Mental Disabilities and the Future of Guardianship Law*, 117 Penn. St. L. Rev. 1159 (2013); Dinerstein, *Implementing Legal Capacity Under Article 12 of the UN Convention on the Rights of Persons With Disabilities: The Difficult Road From Guardianship to Supported Decision-Making*, 19(2) Human Rights Brief 8 (2012).

[21] A copy of the Convention and related documents can be accessed at www.un.org.

[22] Durable powers of attorney for health care are discussed in Section 9.5.

[23] For a discussion of the Uniform Durable Power of Attorney Act (UDPAA), *see* English, *The UPC and the New Durable Powers*, 27 Real. Prop. Prob. & Tr. J. 333, 337–45 (1992).

[24] *Restatement (Third) Agency* § 3.08 (2006).

principal's death.[25] Consequently, a durable power of attorney is not an alternative to probate.

The following are some drafting and counseling issues to be considered in advising clients on durable powers of attorney:

Does the Document Contain the Required Language?

A majority of the durable power of attorney statutes were formerly patterned after the Uniform Durable Power of Attorney Act (UDPAA). Under the UDPAA, a power of attorney is not durable unless it contains certain prescribed language or its equivalent. To create an immediately effective power, the document must state "this power of attorney shall not be affected by the subsequent disability of the principal." To create a springing power of attorney, the document must state "this power of attorney shall become effective upon the disability of the principal."[26]

The Uniform Power of Attorney Act (UPOAA), completed in 2006 and enacted in 27 states as of late 2020, dispenses with the durability requirement. Under this Act, all powers of attorney are durable unless the document states otherwise.[27]

What Are the Execution Requirements?

The UDPAA and the later UPOAA do not impose execution requirements except for the principal's signature, a pattern followed by a majority of the states. But a minority of states impose specific execution requirements. California, for example, requires that the power of attorney must be either notarized or signed by two witnesses.[28] Despite the absence of execution requirements, it is advisable to have the power notarized. Notarization may increase the chance of acceptance. In most states, notarization is also required to record the power of attorney in connection with a real estate transaction.[29]

Which Is Better, an Immediately Effective or a Springing Power?

Opinion varies, with the principal determinant being concerns about third-party acceptance of powers of attorney. With a springing power, an extra element for third parties to ponder is introduced—a possible issue as to whether the principal is indeed incapacitated. If the principal is not yet incapacitated, an agent under a springing power is without authority and a financial institution or other third party might be liable for accepting the power. To counteract concerns about third party refusal, a springing power

---

25 *Restatement (Third) Agency* § 3.07.

26 UDPAA § 1.

27 Unif.Power Atty. Act (UPOAA) § 104. For an analysis of the Act by the Act's Reporter, *see* Whitton, *The Uniform Power of Attorney Act: Striking a Balance Between Autonomy and Protection*, 1 Phoenix L. Rev. 343 (2008). *See also* Hook & Johnson, *The Uniform Power of Attorney Act*, 45 Real Prop. Tr. & Est. L.J. 283 (2010); Vallario, *The Uniform Power of Attorney Act: Not a One-Size-Fits-All Solution*, 43 U. Balt. L. Rev. 85 (2014); Odom, McDonald & Underwood, *Financial Powers of Attorney: Increased Oversight by States and Banks to Prevent Abuse*, Prob. & Prop., Nov./Dec. 2016, at 8.

28 Cal.Prob.Code § 4121.

29 For the importance of recording transactions with respect to real property, *see* Section 3.5, note 233 et seq.

should always specify a method for determining the principal's incapacity, for example, a determination by the family physician in conjunction with the agent. If a physician or other professional is chosen to make the evaluation, the document should protect the physician for making a good faith evaluation and should protect the third party for relying on such a determination. The California statute specifies a procedure for implementing a springing power and protects a third party in relying on a declaration that the event or contingency springing the agent's authority has occurred.[30]

Should You Use Your State's Statutory Form?

A growing number of states have enacted so-called statutory short forms, and such a form is included in the UPOAA.[31] The name is apt. The form is short, consisting primarily of a series of boxes to check. The powers of the agent granted by the particular check marks, such as a power to engage in "real estate transactions," are then laid out in detail in the underlying statute.[32] Use of a common form promotes acceptance by third parties. Perhaps the answer depends on the quality of the form. The Illinois statutory short-form[33] enjoys wide acceptance among practitioners. Some other statutory short-forms have been less successful.

Grant Agent Authority to Fund Living Trust

Because trust assets are titled in the name of the trustee, trustees of living trusts encounter less third-party reluctance than do agents acting under durable powers, where title to assets normally remains in the name of the principal. The revocable living trust may therefore be more effective than a durable power of attorney as an incapacity planning device. A living trust is only effective to the extent that it is funded, however. Despite the best of intentions, assets are often found outside the trust. For a client with a living trust, a power of attorney with a trust funding provision should be a standard part of the plan.[34] The Missouri statute authorizes an agent to fund an existing trust even if not expressly authorized in the power of attorney.[35]

Update the Power Periodically

Due to possible concerns by third parties as to whether a power of attorney is still in effect or is otherwise stale, the principal should periodically re-execute the power or at least sign in the margin that the power is still in effect.

Have Agent Sign Acceptance

An agent, like any other appointed fiduciary, is not obligated to accept the office. Having the agent sign an acceptance reduces the likelihood that the agent will decline when the need arises. Also, involving the agent in the process

---

30 Cal.Prob.Code § 4129.

31 Unif. Power Atty. Act §§ 301–302.

32 For a discussion of the statutory short forms, *see* English, *The UPC and the New Durable Powers*, 27 Real Prop. Prob. & Tr. J. at 345–54.

33 755 Ill. Comp. Stat. 45/3–1.

34 For the methods for transferring property to a trustee, *see* Section 3.6.

35 Mo. Rev. Stat. § 404.710(6).

will encourage the principal to discuss his or her wishes with the agent, making the power better fit the client's particular needs.

Appoint Successor Agents

The reason for this step is obvious. However, the now superseded Uniform Statutory Power of Attorney Act,[36] still in effect in several states including California, omits this vital provision.[37]

Nominate the Agent as Guardian

Should a guardianship become necessary, the agent is likely the person whom the principal would want to serve as guardian or conservator. More importantly, the nomination of the agent as guardian will reduce the chance that a disgruntled family member will use a guardianship or conservatorship to thwart the agent's authority. In nearly all states, either by specific statute or judicial practice, the court will grant the ward's nominee a first preference to act as guardian or conservator.[38]

Exercise Great Care in Granting an Agent Authority to Make Gifts

There are numerous reasons why an agent might be granted authority to make gifts. By making gifts, the agent can facilitate qualification for Medicaid and other government benefits. In addition, the estate tax savings from annual exclusion gifts can be dramatic.[39] Due to the substantial repeal of the rule pulling back gifts made within three years of death into the gross estate, substantial sums often can be funneled out of the gross estate shortly before death. Because the individual is frequently incapacitated during this final stage of life, a durable power of attorney with gifting authority may be essential to meet estate planning goals. It is generally held that a grant of general authority ("agent can do whatever I could have done if competent") does not authorize the making of gifts. An express gifting provision is required.[40]

But a liberal grant of gift giving authority may invite abuse. Numerous questions should be considered. May the agent make gifts for the agent's own benefit, whether directly or in discharge of a legal obligation of support? Should the authority to make gifts be subject to an annual exclusion cap? Should the standard for gifts be the principal's prior pattern of giving? Should all family lines be treated equally, or may the agent favor one group over another? Is the agent allowed to support family members, such as adult children, who are no longer legal dependents but who were being supported by the principal? Should

---

[36] The Uniform Statutory Power of Attorney Act, approved in 1988, was replaced by the Uniform Power of Attorney Act, which contains a statutory form that provides a space to designate successor agents. *Compare* Unif. Power of Atty. Act § 301 *with* Unif. Statutory Power of Atty. Act § 1.

[37] Cal.Prob.Code § 4401.

[38] *See, e.g.*, Unif. Guardianship & Protective Proceedings Act §§ 310, 413.

[39] For a discussion of the annual exclusion, *see* Section 15.3, note 59 et seq.

[40] The leading case is Estate of Casey v. Commissioner, 948 F.2d 895 (4th Cir. 1991). This rule is also codified in many state statutes. *See*, e.g., Unif. Power of Atty. Act § 201; Cal.Prob.Code § 4264; Mo. Rev. Stat. § 404.710(6). Alabama authorizes an agent to make annual exclusion and charitable gifts without express authority in the power of attorney. Ala. Code § 26–1–2.1.

the agent have authority to transfer assets in order to qualify the principal for government benefits?

Be Mindful of the Risk of Abuse

If the principal is competent, the principal is in a position to monitor the actions of the agent. But the principal is incapacitated, the agent lacks oversight. A 2000 survey by AARP found that 45% of individuals over age 50 have signed powers of attorney, a percentage that increases to three-fourths for individuals over age 80,[41] a prime age for when elder abuse may and does occur. Counselors should be mindful of this risk when advising on powers of attorney. Abuse by agents under powers of attorney is a growing problem. To reduce the risk of abuse, consideration should be given to appointing someone in the power of attorney to be kept notified of the agent's actions. Other reform ideas, such as requiring that powers of attorney be filed in a public registry, have not taken hold in the US.[42] One useful provision, found in the UPOAA and in numerous state statutes, is the addition of a special court procedure allowing a wide range of individuals to demand an accounting by an agent or to request other relief.[43]

§ 9.4 End-of-Life Decision Making

"Every human being of adult years and sound mind has a right to determine what shall be done with his own body."[44] These oft-quoted words of Judge (later Justice) Benjamin Cardozo, taken from a case where a physician performed an operation allegedly without the patient's consent, have become the foundation for the law of "informed consent." Under the doctrine of informed consent, an adult competent patient has the right to have the risks and benefits of proposed medical treatment explained to her before that treatment is provided, and the right to either refuse or accept the proposed treatment. The right to refuse or accept medical treatment can be grounded in either the common law, statutes or in state constitutions. In *Cruzan v. Director, Missouri Department of Health*[45] the Justices of the United States Supreme Court, excepting Justice Scalia, either stated or strongly implied that the right of a competent adult patient to refuse medical treatment was a constitutionally protected "liberty" interest.

The ethical and moral dilemmas surrounding the right to refuse medical treatment, whatever its source, were not seriously tested until medical

---

[41] AARP Research Group, *Where There is a Will . . . Legal Documents Among the 50+ Population: Findings From an AARP Survey* (2000).

[42] *See generally* Rhein, *No One in Charge: DPAs and the Failure to Protect Incapacitated Principals*, 17 Elder L.J. 165 (2009); Craft, *Preventing Exploitation and Preserving Autonomy: Making Springing Powers of Attorney the Standard*, 44 U.Balt. L.Rev. 407 (2015); Stiegel & Klem, *Power of Attorney Abuse, What States Can Do About It*, AARP Public Policy Institute (2008).

[43] UPOAA § 116 (petition may be filed, among others, by a person who demonstrates sufficient interest in the principal's welfare); Mo. Rev. Stat. § 404.727.1 (similar).

[44] Schloendorff v. Society of New York Hospital, 105 N.E. 92, 93 (1914).

[45] 497 U.S. 261, 278 (1990). *See Cruzan* at 287 (O'Connor concurring); at 304–05 (Brennan, Marshall and Blackmun dissenting); at 331 (Stevens dissenting).

technologies made it possible to physically sustain the life of a person in a persistent vegetative state.[46]

These dilemmas were first brought to wide public attention in the well-known case of *In the Matter of Karen Quinlan*.[47] Karen Ann Quinlan, age 22, stopped breathing for at least two 15-minute periods. As a result, the flow of blood to her brain ceased, destroying her cortex but not her brain stem. She was diagnosed as being in a persistent vegetative state "with the capacity to maintain the vegetative parts of neurological function but"[48] no longer having any cognitive function. Karen was connected to a respirator to assist her in breathing and to feeding tubes to provide her with food and hydration. Karen's doctors believed that she had no reasonable hope of recovery and would likely die if she were removed from the respirator. Her father sought to be appointed her legal guardian for the purpose, among other things, of directing her health care providers to remove her from the respirator. Karen's father did not seek removal of the feeding tubes. The New Jersey court found that Karen had a constitutionally protected right of privacy which would have permitted her, had she been competent, to demand that the life-sustaining procedures be withdrawn even if withdrawal would result in her death. This right of privacy was not extinguished when Karen became incompetent. Consequently, to effectuate this right it was necessary that someone else be allowed to exercise it on Karen's behalf, in this case her father as her court-appointed guardian. The court did not engage in an extended discussion of the standards to be used by her guardian in determining whether the respirator should be removed. Rather, the court concluded that the guardian had the right to require the removal of the respirator if Karen's attending physicians, with the consent of an appropriate ethics committee, were of the view that there was "no reasonable possibility of Karen's ever emerging from her present comatose condition to a cognitive, sapient state."[49]

Later cases from New Jersey and many other states have developed standards to guide decisionmakers. In addition, *Quinlan* sparked a national interest in both living wills and durable health care powers of attorney (sometimes called "advance directives") which has ultimately led to the adoption of statutes throughout the country designed to empower patients to have health care decisions consistent with their wishes made on their behalf.

When patients are unable to express their own health care decisions, those decisions may be expressed by a so-called "surrogate," "proxy," or "agent."[50] For

---

[46] "The distinguishing feature of a patient in a persistent vegetative state is wakefulness without awareness. These patients commonly make sporadic movements, spontaneously blink their eyes and have heightened reflex responses, but they cannot voluntarily respond to stimuli." Mack v. Mack, 618 A.2d 744, 746 (Md.1993).

[47] 355 A.2d at 647 (1976).

[48] 355 A.2d at 654.

[49] 355 A.2d. at 671.

[50] As used in this chapter, a "surrogate" could be either a family member to whom health care providers customarily look for guidance in making medical decisions for a patient lacking decision making capacity or a person authorized by statute, the courts or under a durable health care power to make decisions on behalf of a patient.

While there have been many well publicized court cases involving surrogate decision making in the health care arena, the overwhelming majority of decisions to withdraw life support are made

example, in *Quinlan* the surrogate was Karen's guardian. Generally, surrogates make decisions by complying with either the substituted judgement or the best interest standard.

Under the "substituted judgement" standard, the surrogate is expected to make the decision that the patient would have made if the patient had decision making capacity. To this end, the surrogate should consider the patient's previously expressed preferences, if any, as well as the patient's known values and interests.[51] The substituted judgement standard presumes that the patient had once been competent to express his or her preferences and values.

A surrogate's decision might be challenged on the grounds that the patient's preferences cannot be ascertained. This was the core of the dispute in *Cruzan v. Director, Missouri Department of Health*.[52] Nancy Cruzan was in a persistent vegetative state unable to breathe or be nourished without the use of a respirator and feeding tube. Her parents, after a considerable period of time, asked that the feeding tube be withdrawn, knowing that if it were withdrawn, Nancy would die. The employees at the state hospital where Nancy resided refused to honor that request. Her parents, acting as Nancy's court-appointed guardians, then sued in state court.

The *Cruzan* trial court found that Nancy had a "fundamental right" under state and federal law to "refuse or direct the withdrawal of 'death prolonging procedures.' " It also found that in at least one conversation Nancy had with a friend, Nancy evidenced her intent not to be maintained on life-sustaining technologies. This, in the trial court's view, was sufficient to permit her parents to withdraw based on the substituted judgement standard.

On appeal from an order in the parents' favor, the Missouri Supreme Court reversed. It rejected the substituted judgement approach, holding that any decision to withdraw life support from Nancy must be based upon clear and convincing evidence of Nancy's actual expressed wishes, and that Nancy's conversation with her friend was insufficiently persuasive.[53] The parents appealed that decision to the United States Supreme Court which held that the United States Constitution did not prevent the Missouri Supreme Court from imposing this heightened "clear and convincing" standard. While the Court did not decide whether a person had a constitutional right to die or a right to direct the withholding or withdrawal of life-sustaining treatment, it stated in dicta that "for purposes of this case, we assume that the United States Constitution would grant a competent person a constitutionally protected right to refuse lifesaving hydration and nutrition."[54] Similarly, despite this limitation to competent persons, many state courts have held that protection

at the bedside by physicians working in concert with patients, if able, and their families. The reported cases should not create the impression that these matters are frequently litigated.

[51] *See generally* In re Fiori, 673 A.2d 905 (Pa.1996).

[52] 497 U.S. 261 (1990).

[53] *But see* Conservatorship of Drabick, 245 Cal.Rptr. 840 (App.1988) (conservator has authority to remove life support without court permission and can make a decision on behalf of patient without need for evidence of intent to be "clear and convincing.")

[54] 497 U.S. at 278.

for withdrawing or withholding treatment from incompetent persons can be found or grounded either in state constitutions or state statutes.

In *Cruzan*, the Supreme Court concluded that Missouri's interest in the preservation of life was sufficiently strong to allow it to err on the side of life by disallowing withdrawal of treatment unless the patient had clearly and convincingly expressed her wishes on the matter.[55] In addition to preservation of life, other countervailing factors that states have taken into account include the protection of the interests of innocent third parties, the maintenance of the ethical integrity of the medical profession, and the prevention of suicide.[56] Whether a state may constitutionally prohibit physician assistance in suicide has also been tested in the Supreme Court. The Court held that a ban was constitutional.[57] An attempt by the Justice Department to strike down Oregon's physician-assisted suicide law on the basis that it violated the federal controlled substances act was rejected, however.[58] As of late 2020, physician assistance in suicide was recognized by statute in eight states and the District of Columbia.[59]

Cruzan is important because it emphasizes the importance of planning for end-of-life decision making. *Cruzan* implicitly supports the need for persons to clearly express their end-of-life decisions through the execution of durable powers of attorney for health care and other forms of advance directive.[60]

Use of either the expressed wishes or substituted judgement standard is illogical in cases where the patient *never* had decisionmaking capacity. This, for example, could be the true in the case of infants, young minors, or individuals with severe developmental disabilities. Use of the substituted judgement standard may also be inappropriate where there is little or no evidence that a patient who once had decisionmaking capacity had any preferences, values or interest that would inform the decision to be made. For such patients the best interest standard is more appropriate.

The best interest standard seeks what is best for the patient without regard to what the patient would have preferred. However, some courts find the use of a best interest test inappropriate because "it lets another make a determination of the patient's quality of life, thereby undermining the

---

[55] 497 U.S. at 280.

[56] Superintendent of Belchertown State School v. Saikewicz, 370 N.E.2d 417, 426 (Mass.1977).

[57] Washington v. Glucksberg, 521 U.S. 702 (1997); Vacco v. Quill, 521 U.S. 793 (1997).

[58] Gonzales v. Oregon, 546 U.S. 243 (2006).

[59] California, Colorado, District of Columbia, Hawaii, Maine, New Jersey, Oregon, Vermont, and Washington.

[60] Justice O'Connor opined that states might be required to respect the decisions of dulydesignated surrogate decisionmakers. She stated: "In my view, such a duty may well be constitutionally required to protect the patient's liberty interest in refusing medical treatment. Few individuals provide explicit oral or written instructions regarding their intent to refuse medical treatment should they become incompetent. States which decline to consider any evidence other than such instructions may frequently fail to honor a patient's intent. Such failures might be avoided if the State considered an equally probative source of evidence: the patient's appointment of a proxy to make health care decisions on her behalf. Delegating the authority to make medical decisions to a family member or friend is becoming a common method of planning for the future." 546 U.S. at 289.

foundation of self-determination and inviolability of the person upon which the right to refuse medical treatment stands."[61]

The most comprehensive approach on standards for withdrawing life-sustaining treatment has been developed by the New Jersey courts, particularly in the case of *In re Matter of Conroy*.[62] First, and in recognition of the patient's autonomy rights, life-sustaining treatment may be withdrawn or withheld "when it is clear that the particular patient would have refused the treatment under the circumstances involved."[63] The patient's intent may be evidenced by a living will, oral declarations, a power of attorney for health care, the patient's reactions to the medical treatment others received or deduced from the patient's religious beliefs or from other decisions the patient might have made with respect to his or her medical treatment. The probative value of the evidence varies depending upon several factors, including the "remoteness, consistency, and thoughtfulness of the prior statements or actions and the maturity of the person at the time of the statements or acts."[64] For persons who had never clearly expressed their wishes, the court adopted two additional tests—the limited objective best interest test and the pure objective best interest test.

Under the limited objective best interest test, life support may be withheld or withdrawn where "there is some trustworthy evidence that the patient would have refused the treatment, and the decision-maker is satisfied that it is clear that the burdens of the patient's continued life with the treatment outweigh the benefits of that life for him."[65] This test allows for the termination of treatment when the patient's intent expressed before he or she became incompetent is ambiguous but it is clear that the life sustaining treatment would merely prolong the patient's suffering.

Absent any trustworthy evidence of the patient's intent or any evidence of the patient's intent, the decision maker employs the pure objective best interest test. Here again there is a balance between the net burdens of treatment and the benefits. If the burdens outweigh the benefits, treatment may be withdrawn if "the recurring, unavoidable and severe pain of the patient's life with the treatment . . . [is such] that the effect of administering the life-sustaining treatment would be inhumane."[66]

The New Jersey court, in *In re Jobes*,[67] later backed away from the pure objective test for patients in a persistent vegetative state who are incapable of feeling pain. For these patients, the court held that the decision of close and caring family members or a close friend should control and their right to decide is not limited by a balancing of benefits and burdens.

---

[61] Mack v. Mack, 618 A.2d 744, 758 (Md.1993) (quoting from In re Estate of Longeway, 549 N.E.2d 292, 299 (Ill.1989)). *But see* In re K.I. 735 A.2d 448 (D.C.1999) (best interest standard governs to determine whether guardian ad litem could seek a DNR order for a neglected minor).

[62] 486 A.2d 1209 (N.J.1985).

[63] 486 A.2d at 1229.

[64] 486 A.2d at 1230.

[65] 486 A.2d at 1231.

[66] 486 A.2d at 1232.

[67] In re Jobes, 529 A.2d 434 (1987).

Less important to the development of legal standards is the well-known case of Terri Schiavo. Despite attempts by both the Florida Legislature and Congress to overturn court orders allowing withdrawal of artificial nutrition and hydration, the Florida courts were applying well-settled principles. Under Florida law, the husband had the right to make the decision to withdraw artificial nutrition and hydration from his wife, who was in a persistent vegetative state. This case was factually similar to a prior case of the Florida Supreme Court.[68]

§ 9.5 Advance Health-Care Directives

Because of the respect and deference given to a once-competent patient's expressed wishes respecting medical procedures and treatment, lawyers should be keenly aware of the importance of having their clients communicate their wishes and desires respecting the health care they receive when the clients are no longer are able to communicate themselves. Lawyers who practice estate planning almost always discuss such advance directives with their clients.

Since *Quinlan* and *Cruzan*, all states have enacted statutes authorizing individuals to designate agents, surrogates, or proxies to make health care decisions on their behalf when they are no longer capable of making their own decisions[69] and nearly all states have enacted statutes authorizing the use of living wills,[70] in which the declarant gives written instructions specifying the circumstances under which life-sustaining treatment may be withheld or withdrawn. The Uniform Law Commissioners have promulgated two uniform acts in this area. The Uniform Rights of the Terminally Ill Act, last revised in 1989, authorizes the use of living wills. This Act was superseded by the Uniform Health-Care Decisions Act, completed in 1993, which takes a more comprehensive approach. It authorizes the use of both types of advance directives: an "instruction directive," under which a patient may give health-care instructions on any matter; and a "proxy directive," under which the patient designates an agent to make health-care decisions.[71]

A living will is legally effective when it is executed but becomes operative only after it is communicated to the attending physician and the declarant is determined to have a terminal condition and is no longer capable of making decisions regarding the use of life-sustaining procedures.[72]

Living wills usually are easy to revoke. They can be revoked orally or by a writing and often without regard to the declarant's mental or physical

---

[68] In re Guardianship of Browning, 568 So. 2d (Fla. 1990). There are so many *Schiavo* opinions at both the state and federal levels, that it is easier to understand the case by reading a chronology. For a straightforward chronology with a minimum of editorializing, *see Federal and Florida Judicial and Legislative Involvement in the Theresa Schiavo Case*, 33 Fla. St. U. L. Rev. 356 (2005).

[69] For an analysis of the statutes, *see* English, *The UPC and the New Durable Powers*, 27 Real Prop. Prob. & Tr. J. 333, 361–404 (1992).

[70] For an analysis of the living will statutes, *see* Gelfand, *Living Will Statutes: The First Decade*, 1987 Wis. L. Rev. 737.

[71] For an analysis of the Uniform Health-Care Decisions Act, *see* English & Meisel, *Uniform Health Care Decisions Act Gives New Guidance*, Est. Plan., Nov./Dec. 1994, at 355.

[72] Unif. Rights of the Terminally Ill Act (URTIA) § 3.

condition. However, to protect health care providers, it is generally provided that a revocation is effective only "upon its communication to the attending physician or other health-care provider by the declarant or a witness to revocation."[73]

While state laws differ, a typical living will provides that if the maker has an "incurable and irreversible" condition that will result in death within "a relatively short time"[74] or, as some states add, if the maker becomes "unconscious and, to a reasonable degree of medical certainty . . . will not regain consciousness,"[75] then life-sustaining or life-prolonging procedures be withheld or withdrawn.[76] Even though the quoted phrases are fraught with ambiguity, there is little case law to suggest that they have become the subject of much litigation. The language of living will statutes necessarily clothes the physician with a great deal of authority to determine whether the declarant has a medical condition described in the living will.

The effectiveness of living wills is open to question, however. Studies have found that a majority of patients fail to give their living wills to their physicians and a majority of living wills that physicians do see fail to cover the clinical realities the patients face.[77] These studies buttress the general conclusion that the durable power of attorney for health care is a more effective device.

The durable power of attorney for health care is conceptually broader in scope than the living will in that it permits an agent designated by the principal to make any health-care decision for the principal whenever the principal is unable to make a health care decision for himself.[78] Durable powers of attorney for health care generally become operative whenever the principal is incapable of making a health-care decision. They are not limited to cases where the principal has a terminal condition. Generally, the agent can be any competent adult, although many statutes prohibit the principal's physician or an employee of the physician from being designated as an agent. Whether principals are capable of making health-care decisions is usually determined by the principal's primary physician.[79]

Under the Uniform Health-Care Decisions Act, the decision of the agent should comport with the principal's expressed instructions or other wishes to the extent known, or, if there are none, then in accordance with the agent's judgement of the principal's best interest.[80] Given that the agent's first duty is to make a decision consistent with the principal's wishes, it is important that the durable power adequately reflect the desires of the principal, or that those desires be communicated to the agent by some other means. The agent's

---

73 URTIA § 4.

74 Unif. Health-Care Decisions Act (UHCDA) § 4; URTIA § 2.

75 UHCDA § 4.

76 UHCDA § 4.

77 A list of studies is included in *Defective Directives, Struggling With End-of-Life Care*, amednews.com, posted Jan. 5, 2009.

78 UHCDA §§ 2(b) & 4.

79 UHCDA §§ 2(c) & 4.

80 UHCDA § 2(e).

powers can be limited in most any way by the terms of the power of attorney for health care, although often a principal will want the agent to make decisions to the fullest extent possible in all situations where the principal is unable to act.

Lawyers who prepare these health care documents for their clients often combine the health care power with specific instructions to guide the agent's decision. A combination document provides a written expression of the principal's intent, particularly when end-of-life decision making is required, that not only guides the agent but can also address concerns the agent might have in making a decision that could end the principal's life.

Federal legislation has been enacted to facilitate the use of advance directives. Under the Patient Self-Determination Act,[81] hospitals receiving funds from either Medicare or Medicaid (thus almost all hospitals) must advise patients of their rights to refuse medical care when they are admitted as a patient. The hospital must also ask the patient if he or she has an advance directive and must document any such document in the patient's medical records.

Despite their great promise, it has been difficult to implement advance directives in practice. The directive may not make its way into the medical record or may not be consulted when needed. Also, the legal language in which directives are often written may be difficult for medical personnel to implement. As a supplement to the advance directive, the Physician's Order for Life-Sustaining Treatment (POLST) was developed. The POLST is prepared collaboratively by the physician in consultation with a patient in the last stages of life, or if the patient is mentally incapacitated, in consultation with the patient's guardian, agent, or family member. Because the medical order is prepared with the involvement of the physician and uses language that physicians understand, the chance that the order will be implemented when needed is far higher than if the patient had signed an advance directive alone.[82]

§ 9.6 Family Consent Laws

Because most patients have not executed any type of advance directive, physicians and other health care providers must often look to family members as alternative decision makers. In the absence of express statutory authority empowering family members to make health care decisions for an incapacitated relative, there is a concern that physicians may risk liability for relying on a family member's decision. These concerns are reduced in jurisdictions that have adopted some form of family consent statute.[83] Some of these statutes apply only to end-of-life decision making, while others apply to

---

[81] §§ 4206, 4751, Omnibus Reconciliation Act of 1990, Pub L No. 101–508 (Nov. 5, 1990).

[82] *See generally* Hoffman, *Portable Medical Order Sets (POLST): Ethical and Legal Landscape*, 15 NAELA J. 91; Blix & Tolle; *POLST: Co-Piloting, Not Hijacking, the Advance Directive*, 15 NAELA J. 103 (2019); Jennison, *Reflections on the Graying of America: Implications of Physician Orders for Life-Sustaining Treatment*, 12 Rutgers J.L. & Pol'y 295 (2015); Wolf, Maag & Gallant, *The Physician Orders for Life-Sustaining Treatment (POLST) Coming Soon to a Health Care Community Near You*, 49 Real Prop. Tr. & Est. L.J. 71 (2014).

[83] *See* Judith Areen, *The Legal Status of Consent Obtained from Families of Adult Patients to Withhold or Withdraw Treatment*, 258 J.Am.Med. Ass'n 229 (1987).

all health care decisions.[84] The Uniform Health-Care Decisions Act contains a typical provision.[85] Absent a court-appointed guardian or agent under a durable power of attorney for health care, health care decisions for an incapacitated patient may be made by a designated family member or family members. The typical priority among family members is the spouse, then an adult child or majority of adult children, followed by parents and then adult siblings. Many statutes permit close friends to make decisions if family members are unavailable. More challenging is making health-care decisions for patients who lack family or close friends.[86] For these patients, hospital ethics committees can play an important role.

§ 9.7 Anatomical Gifts

The ability to transplant organs, eyes, and tissue to save or enhance human life requires that individuals be able to donate their body parts for transplant purposes. The common-law rule that individuals had no property rights in their body parts created a potential bar to donation. The bar was effectively removed in 1968 with the adoption of the first of three Uniform Anatomical Gift Acts, the most recent version of which was promulgated by the Uniform Law Commission in 2006 and which has been adopted in all but a few states.

Under the Uniform Anatomical Gift Act, an adult individual or certain minors may donate one or more or all of the individual's organs, eyes, or tissue during the individual's life by signing a document of gift.[87] A document of gift could be a driver's license or other writing or an electronic entry on an electronically maintained donor registry.[88] Unless the individual revokes the gift, the gift is effective at the individual's death and cannot be altered by the individual's surviving family members,[89] even if they are personally opposed to donation. This policy reflects the Act's commitment to respecting an individual's autonomous decision to be a donor.

While there has been an exponentially increasing number of individuals who have executed documents of gift, particularly with the advent of electronic databases, many individuals die without having signed a document of gift. In such case, their health care agent or surviving family members (in a statutory listed priority) may donate the deceased's body parts for transplant or research purposes[90] unless the individual, during her life, signed a refusal providing that in no event did the individual wish to be an organ donor.[91] Here again, the Act reflects respect for the individual's autonomous decision not to be a donor.

---

84 For the statutes, *see* Meisel, The Right to Die § 2.06[D] (2d ed. 1995 & 2003 Supp.).

85 UHCDA § 5.

86 *See* Karp & Wood, *Incapacitated and Alone: Healthcare Decision Making for Unbefriended Older People*, 31 Human Rights 20 (2004).

87 Unif. Anatomical Gift Act (UAGA) § 4.

88 UAGA § 2(6).

89 UAGA § 8(a).

90 UAGA § 9.

91 UAGA § 7.

Where the document of gift reflects in only a general way the donor's intent to be an organ donor, such as by a marking on the driver's license stating nothing more than "organ donor," the Uniform Anatomical Gift Act sets forth default interpretative rules. Generally, these rules are that if the document of gift does not specify the purpose of the anatomical gift, as might be the case if the only evidence of the gift is a notation on a driver's license, "organ donor," the gift is of the donor's organs, eyes, and tissue and these can only be used for transplant or therapy purposes.[92] In other words, if an individual wants to make her organs, eyes, and tissue available for research greater specificity is required in the document of gift.

An anatomical gift can be made directly to a named individual so long as that individual will personally use the gift for transplantation or therapy,[93] but this rarely occurs because a donor is unlikely to know an identifiable individual in need of the donor's parts. In most cases, anatomical gifts, upon the donor's death, pass into the "system," meaning that donated tissue goes to a tissue bank, eyes to an eye bank, and organs to an organ procurement organization.[94] Organs that pass to an organ procurement organization are sent by that organization to patients in need of those organs. In the United States the identity of patients in need of organs is largely controlled by an organization known as UNOS (United Network for Organ Sharing) which has well-defined rules based upon widely accepted medical criteria that identity potential organ recipients. These rules are necessary because not every organ can be safely transplanted into every patient in need of an organ. For example, the patient in need of an organ and the donor of that organ must have compatible blood types. The rules allocating organs also differ depending on which organ is being allocated for a variety of medical and practical reasons.

By federal law[95] as well as the Uniform Anatomical Gift Act[96] it is illegal in the United States to buy and sell organs for transplant purposes. Thus, the entire transplant system in the United States depends upon altruism, not markets. Because of the continuing shortage of organs required to save the lives of people in need of organs, there continues to be a lively debate in this country whether sales of organs should be allowed and no doubt that debate will continue. In other Western countries, mainly in Europe, there is a presumed consent system. Under that system, all individuals are presumed to be organ donors at death unless, in some countries, they opted out of the system prior to their deaths or, in other countries, they or their families opted out of the system. Thus, in Europe an individual is a donor unless the individual opts out whereas in the United States an individual is not a donor unless the individual or her family opts in. Whether the United States should convert to the opt out systems has also been widely debated, but to date no state has adopted an opt in system along the European model.

---

[92] UAGA § 11(e).

[93] UAGA § 11(a)(2).

[94] UAGA § 11(g).

[95] National Organ Transplant Act, 42 U.S.C. § 274(e).

[96] UAGA § 16.

An individual might sign a living will directing that her life not be prolonged by life support systems. She might also sign a document of gift making an anatomical gift. There sometimes can be a tension in carrying out the dictates of both documents because it may be necessary to administer life support systems that prolong the individual's life in order to preserve the organs for transplant purposes. If the donor's health care documents do not contain directives to resolve this conflict, such as language stating: "I do not want life support systems withdrawn if their administration is necessary to preserve my organs for transplant purposes," someone must determine whether the donor should be maintained on life support systems to further the donor's intent to be an organ donor or whether the life support should be withdrawn consistent with the directive in the living will even if withdrawal could lead to the loss of organs for transplant purposes. The Uniform Anatomical Gift seeks to resolve this potential problem by empowering the health care agent or, if none, another health care surrogate decisionmaker for the donor to make the decision.[97] However, pending this final decision, measures necessary to ensure the medical suitability of the organ may not be withheld or withdrawn unless administering such measures would be inconsistent with appropriate end of life care, in other words would be harmful to the patient-donor.[98]

[97] UAGA § 21.

[98] UAGA § 21.

Chapter 10

TRUSTS

Analysis

Sec.

10.1 Introduction.
10.2 The Uniform Trust Code.
10.3 Creation of Trusts.
10.4 The Revocable Trust.
10.5 Revocable Trust Alternatives.
10.6 Principal and Income.
10.7 Discretionary Trusts.
10.8 Spendthrift Provisions and Creditor Claims.
10.9 Modification and Termination of Trusts.
10.10 Charitable Trusts.

---

§ 10.1 Introduction

The word "trust" is used for many property arrangements that have little in common with each other apart from the fact that they were historically enforced by the Chancellor in the Court of Equity. Courts, for example, have imposed "constructive trusts" to avoid unjust enrichment when a person would otherwise profit from having murdered a decedent.[1] The trusts to be discussed in this chapter, on the other hand, are deliberately created by a person called the settlor and are sometimes referred to as "express" trusts as opposed to a constructive trust, which is imposed by law and is part of the law of remedies. The word settlor is related to the words "settle" and "settlement," which at one time were commonly used terms to describe any disposition of property.[2]

Trusts are a form of transfer, usually gratuitous,[3] either *inter-vivos* (from the Latin: "between the living"), or testamentary if created by will. People can make gifts without using a trust, but trusts can provide important advantages. The Restatement of Trusts mentions five common reasons for using trusts: "[1] the avoidance of probate, [2] providing property management for those who cannot, ought not or wish not to manage for themselves, [3] providing for the limited and successive enjoyment of property over several generations, . . . [4]

---

1 *See* Section 2.7, note 221 et seq. *See also infra* notes 12–13.

2 Simpson, *An Introduction to the History of the Land Law* 218–24 (1961) (discussion of "the family settlement").

3 Trusts are also used as devices for conducting business or investment activities, but this book does not deal with such trusts. They are also excluded from the Restatement of Trusts, *Restatement (Third) of Trusts* § 1, cmt. b (2003), but not from the Uniform Trust Code ("UTC"). *See* UTC § 102 cmt.

the saving of taxes and [5] the insulation of the trust property from the claims of the beneficiaries' creditors."[4]

An express trust is an extremely flexible method of disposing of property and providing for the changing needs of persons who are to benefit from that property. In essence, the legal and equitable interests in the property are split, with the legal ownership being held by one or more trustees and the equitable ownership (the beneficial use) of the property being held by one or more beneficiaries. The trustee of the property has a fiduciary duty to hold the property and act for the benefit of the beneficiaries.[5]

To create a trust, there must be a creator, or *settlor*, who expresses an intent to create a trust. There must be trust property or *res*. And there must be one or more beneficiaries. No trust will fail for want of a trustee—the court will appoint one—but it will fail if it lacks an identifiable beneficiary. Although trusts are almost always created with documentation, a written trust document is not required in most states. An oral declaration of a trust will suffice except where the Statute of Frauds requires a writing or the trust is to be created under a will. A trust may be created by a settlor without notice to or acceptance by a beneficiary.[6]

Trusts are useful devices for estate planning because the settlor can provide for ongoing oversight of the gift. Discretion—or flexibility in administration—can be given to the trustees to provide for changing needs of the beneficiaries or for unforeseen circumstances that affect the trust property.[7] Trusts may be created with minimal funding, adding additional funding later; almost any property may be placed in trust and may be divided into present and future beneficial interests. Trusts may be either revocable or irrevocable. Revocable (living) trusts, which the settlor has the right to modify or terminate, have become a popular strategy for passing property at death without going through probate, or court administration.[8]

The trust originated in medieval England, apparently from a desire to make gifts to medieval church orders in England which were prohibited by their vows from owning property. A legal gift was therefore made to certain responsible persons, who were mandated to hold the property to the *use* of the friars. This was in most cases an unenforceable system, although the Chancellor eventually did try to take jurisdiction. Uses became more popular in England when the Statute of Uses was passed in 1535. King Henry VIII was trying to abolish uses by enacting the statute, which turned equitable uses into legal interests and extinguished the interests of the parties to whom the property was legally conveyed. However, there were many loopholes in the operation of the statute, the most notable of these being that the Statute of Uses did not execute active trusts. That meant that if the "trustee" had an

---

[4] *Restatement (Third) of Trusts* § 27, cmt. b(1) (2003). Creditors' rights with respect to trusts are discussed in Section 10.8.

[5] For the fiduciary duties of the trustee, *see* Sections 14.1–14.4.

[6] For the requirements for creating a trust, *see* Section 10.3.

[7] For discussion of discretionary provisions, *see* Section 10.7.

[8] For discussion of revocable trusts, *see* Section 10.4. For alternatives to the revocable trust, *see* Section 10.5.

active duty—to determine and distribute income, to collect rents, to do anything other than just hold the property and perform ministerial duties—the use could not be extinguished and would be enforced by the courts.[9]

The terms of an express trust are enforceable by the trust's beneficiaries. An honorary trust is a trust for a specific noncharitable purpose without any ascertainable human beneficiaries, such as to provide care for a designated animal or for the care and upkeep of cemetery or other burial property. An honorary trust traditionally has been unenforceable because there is no human beneficiary;[10] but under the Uniform Trust Code (UTC) and many state statutes, such trusts can be enforced by the court or by a person appointed in the trust document or by the court.[11]

Constructive and resulting trusts are remedial devices imposed by the courts or by operation of law. A constructive trust is imposed by a court to prevent the unjust enrichment of one who wrongfully acquires property, for example, if an inheritance was obtained through fraud. The wrongful holder of the property is deemed to hold the equitable interest in trust for the true owner (or successors in interest). Upon the court's imposition of the constructive trust, the wrongful holder is automatically divested of legal title. Title will then vest in the true owner or successor.[12]

A resulting trust arises in situations where the settlor fails to dispose of all the equitable interests in property. The inference is that the settlor intends the equitable interest to revert back to her rather than to other transferees. If all other interests in the trust have expired, the trustee of a resulting trust has a duty to transfer the trust property or reversionary interest in the trust property back to the settlor. A resulting trust also arises when an express trust is invalid in whole or part; the trustee to whom the property was transferred holds it in a resulting trust for the settlor.[13]

§ 10.2 The Uniform Trust Code[14]

The Uniform Trust Code (UTC), which was approved by the Uniform Law Commission in 2000, is the first effort to provide the states with a comprehensive model for codifying their law on trusts.[15] The drafting of the UTC was prompted by the much greater use of trusts in recent years. This greater use of the trust, and consequent rise in the number of day-to-day questions involving trusts, led to a recognition by the Commissioners that the trust law in most states was thin, with many gaps between the few statutes

---

[9] *See* Maitland, *Equity* Lecture III (1913).

[10] *See Restatement (Third) of Trusts* § 47 (2003).

[11] Unif. Trust Code (UTC) §§ 408, 409, discussed in Section 10.10, note 607 et seq.

[12] *See* Scott & Fratcher, *The Law of Trusts* § 462 (4th ed. 1989).

[13] For a discussion of the various types of resulting trusts, *see Restatement (Third) of Trusts* § 7–9 (2003).

[14] This section is based generally on English, *The Uniform Trust Code: Significant Provisions and Policy Issues*, 67 Mo. L. Rev. 143, 144–49, 155 (2002).

[15] For an overview of the UTC, *see* English, *The Uniform Trust Code: Significant Provisions and Policy Issues*, 67 Mo. L. Rev. 143 (2002). For a look at the UTC twenty years after its original approval, *see* Cooper, *Foreword: Twenty Years of the Uniform Trust Code*, 45 ACTEC L.J. 1 (2019), which is the foreword to an issue of the ACTEC Journal devoted entirely to the UTC.

and reported cases. It also led to a recognition that previous uniform acts relating to trusts, while numerous, are fragmentary. The primary source of trust law prior to the UTC was the Restatement of Trusts and the multivolume treatises by Scott[16] and Bogert,[17] sources that fail to address numerous practical issues and that on others sometimes provide insufficient guidance. The purpose of the UTC is to update, fill out, and systematize the American law of trusts.[18] The UTC will enable states that enact it to specify their rules on trust law with precision and in an accessible source. Through 2020, the UTC has been enacted in the District of Columbia and in 34 states.[19]

Related Uniform Acts

The UTC is only one of several uniform acts that have over time converted trust law from common law to primarily statute law.[20] The most important of these other uniform acts is the 1994 Uniform Prudent Investor Act, enacted in forty-four states and in the District of Columbia through 2020.[21] That Act codifies the Restatement, Third, of Trusts: Prudent Investor Rule (1992). The Uniform Prudent Investor Act prescribes a trustee's duties with regard to the management and investment of trust property. The UTC expands on this by also specifying the trustee's duties regarding distributions to beneficiaries. Given its importance and already widespread acceptance, the UTC does not modify the smaller Uniform Prudent Investor Act but incorporates it without change.[22]

The UTC also does not supersede the Uniform Custodial Trust Act, approved in 1987 and discussed in this chapter,[23] and the Uniform Fiduciary Income and Principal Act,[24] which was approved in 2018 in replacement of the predecessor 1997 Uniform Principal and Income Act. The Uniform Statutory Rule Against Perpetuities,[25] and the Uniform Testamentary Additions to Trusts Act,[26] although they impact trusts, also relate to wills and other types of property disposition and are similarly unaffected by the UTC.

Relationship to the Restatement

Restatements, which are written and approved by a national body of lawyers comprising the members of the American Law Institute ("ALI"), serve a proactive role close to that of uniform acts. A Restatement is more than a document that collects and summarizes, in one place, the common law on a particular subject. Rather, where the decisions of the courts conflict, a Restatement strives to delineate the better rule. It also tries to fill in gaps in

---

16 Scott & Fratcher, *The Law of Trusts* (4th ed. 1987).

17 Bogert, *The Law of Trusts and Trustees.*

18 UTC Prefatory Note.

19 A list of enacting jurisdictions can be found at www.uniformlaws.org.

20 *See* Langbein, *Why Did Trust Law Become Statute Law in the United States*, 58 Ala. L. Rev. 1069 (2007).

21 For a discussion of this Act, *see* Section 14.2.

22 UTC art. 9 general, cmt.

23 Section 10.5.

24 Section 10.6.

25 *See* Section 12.4.

26 *See* Section 7.2.

the law, to promote the rule the court should apply when it encounters an issue for the first time. The hope is that the courts of the different states, by relying on the Restatement as a primary guide for decision, will adopt uniform rules of decision over time.[27]

The Restatement, Second, of Trusts was published by the American Law Institute in 1959.[28] Beginning in the late 1980s, work on the Restatement Third began. The portion of the Restatement Third relating to the prudent investor rule and other investment topics was published in 1992.[29] Others portions of the Restatement were thereafter periodically approved. The project was finally completed and published in 2012.[30]

Restatements are not statutes. Until accepted by the courts of a particular state, the courts are free to, and often do, adopt a different rule. By contrast, uniform acts, when enacted, become mandatory rules of law that can be relied on and are easily accessible to a state's citizens. The UTC thus serves an important educational function. For the first time, legal practitioners in many states will be able to determine their state's law on trusts. Furthermore, there are numerous practical issues that are best addressed by specific legislation, such as the UTC, instead of by a more discretionary guideline, such as a Restatement.

Relationship to the Common Law

The UTC is supplemented by the common law of trusts, including principles of equity.[31] The Restatement of Trusts is the most complete and accessible reference in which to locate this common law. The common law of trusts is not static but includes the contemporary and evolving rules of decision developed by the courts in the exercise of their power to adapt the law to new situations and changing conditions. It also includes the traditional and broad equitable jurisdiction of the court, which the UTC in no way restricts.[32] The statutory text of the UTC is also supplemented by its comments, which, like the comments to any uniform act, may be relied on as a guide for interpretation.[33]

Default Act

Most of American trust law consists of rules subject to override by the terms of the trust. The UTC is no exception. Nearly all the Code's provisions are subject to override in the terms of the trust. But prior to the UTC, neither the Restatement, treatise writers, nor state legislatures had attempted to

---

[27] *See, e.g.*, In re Estate of Somers, 89 P.3d 898, 904 (Kan.2004) ("When there is no law directly on point, Kansas courts turn to the Restatement of Trusts.").

[28] *See Restatement (Second) of Trusts* (1959).

[29] *See Restatement (Third) of Trusts (Prudent Investor Rule)* (1992). For a discussion of trustee investments, *see* Section 14.2.

[30] §§ 1–69 was published in 2003, §§ 70–92 in 2007, and §§ 93–111 in 2012.

[31] UTC § 106.

[32] UTC§ 106, cmt. For an example, *see* In re Hrnicek, 792 N.W. 2d 143 (Neb. 2010), where the court, after acknowledging that the UTC did not address, the issue, applied the common law doctrine of retention to offset a debt a beneficiary owed the trust against the beneficiary's share.

[33] See J. Davies, *Legislative Law and Process in a Nutshell* § 55–4 (2d ed. 1986); 2 Norman Singer, *Statutory Construction* § 52.05 (6th ed. 2000).

describe the principles of law that are *not* subject to the settlor's control. The UTC collects these principles in Section 105. Included are the requirements for creating a trust;[34] the rights of third parties in their dealings with the trustee;[35] the power of the court to take certain actions with respect to a trust's administration such as to remove a trustee;[36] the power of the court to modify or terminate a trust on specified grounds;[37] a trustee's obligation to act in good faith, and in accordance with the terms and purposes of the trust and the interests of the beneficiaries;[38] and the trustee's duty to keep the beneficiaries informed of certain matters relating to the trust's administration.[39]

§ 10.3 Creation of Trusts

Because the provisions of the UTC on creation of trusts largely codify the common law and are similar to the comparable provisions of the Restatement of Trusts, this section will mostly use the UTC as the basis for discussion.

Categories

Most of the Code's provisions on the requirements for creating an express trust are straightforward and fairly conventional. The UTC divides trusts into three categories—private, charitable, and honorary. Private trusts require an ascertainable beneficiary, charitable trusts by their very nature are created for the public at large.[40] Honorary trusts include trusts for animals and other trusts for a noncharitable purpose, such as maintenance of a cemetery lot. "Honorary" trusts were not enforceable at common law because there was no beneficiary capable of enforcing them and hence were honorary only. Honorary trusts are enforceable under the UTC, however.[41]

Methods of Creation[42]

Trusts are created by a transfer of property to another person as trustee, either during the settlor's lifetime ("inter-vivos" trust) or at death pursuant to provisions of the settlor's will ("testamentary" trust). A testamentary trust is typically funded upon the closing of the settlor's probate estate. For an inter-vivos trust, the property necessary to create the trust need not be transferred contemporaneously with the signing of the trust document.[43] Local property law may need to be consulted. For example, it has been held that a trust was

---

34 UTC § 105(b)(1). For the requirements, *see* Section 10.3.

35 UTC § 105(b)(11). For rights of third parties, *see* Section 14.9.

36 UTC § 105(b)(13). For issues relating to trustee removal, *see* Section 14.6.

37 UTC § 105(b)(4). For the provisions on trust modification and termination, *see* Section 10.9.

38 UTC § 105(b)(2)–(3). For an application, *see* Rafert v. Meyer, 859 N.W.2d 332 (Neb. 2015) (exculpatory clause unenforceable to extent it waived trustee's obligation to act in good faith).

39 UTC § 105(b)(8)–(9). For the duty to keep the beneficiaries informed, *see* Section 14.3. For additional background on Section 105, *see* Langbein, *Mandatory Rules in Law of Trusts*, 98 Nw. U. L. Rev. 1105 (2004).

40 Charitable trusts are discussed in Section 10.10.

41 UTC §§ 408–409, discussed in Section 10.10, notes 607 et seq.

42 *See* UTC § 401. *See also Restatement (Third) of Trusts* § 10 (2003).

43 UTC § 401, cmt.

created upon recordation of a deed that was never personally delivered to the trustee.[44]

Settlors may also designate themselves as trustee. If so, no transfer of title to property is involved. The settlor will hold title to the property both before and after the trust's creation, although after the trust's creation the settlor's title will be subject to a fiduciary obligation on behalf of the trust's beneficiaries.

Trusts are frequently created pursuant to authority granted by statute or court order.[45] Examples include the holding of a spouse's elective share in trust,[46] a conservator's creation of a trust to qualify the protected person for Medicaid benefits,[47] and trusts created to hold wrongful death benefits.[48] Under some power of attorney statutes, the settlor may delegate authority to create a trust to an agent under a durable power of attorney.[49]

Less commonly, trusts are created pursuant to the exercise of a power of appointment.[50]

Property

Any legally cognizable interest in any real or personal property, tangible or intangible, may be transferred into trust.[51] This includes not only money—as little as one cent—or a piece of land in fee simple, but also contingent remainders and other future interests, stocks, choses in action, mineral rights, leaseholds, life insurance policies and insurance beneficiary designations.[52] However, property must be specifically identified in order to create a trust.[53] It is not sufficient to gratuitously agree to make a gift without indicating the source and setting it aside. The requirement of an identifiable res creates a fiduciary duty as to that property, meaning it cannot be commingled or used as the trustee's own.[54] Usually, assets will be reregistered from the name of the settlor into the name of the trustee using the formalities normally required for title transfer, such as a deed in the case of real estate. However, problems can be encountered in the case of self-declarations of trust where the settlor

---

[44] Manning v. Snyder, 2009 WL 792821 (Tenn. Ct. App., Mar. 26, 2009). *Compare* Nevitt v. Rotham, 762 S.E. 2d 267 (N.C. Ct. App. 2014), in which the trust failed because the unrecorded deed was not delivered.

[45] UTC § 102, which specifies the scope of the Code, states that the trusts to which the Code applies include "trusts created pursuant to a statute, judgment, or decree that requires the trust to be administered in the manner of an express trust."

[46] Unif. Probate Code (UPC) § 2–212; In re Honigman, 168 N.E.2d 676 (N.Y. 1960). For the elective share, *see* Section 8.7.

[47] Unif. Guardianship & Protective Proceedings Act § 411(a)(4). For a discussion of guardianship, *see* Section 9.2.

[48] *Restatement (Second) of Trusts* § 17, cmt. i (1959).

[49] *See, e.g.*, Unif. Power Atty. Act § 201(a)(1). For a discussion of durable powers of attorney, *see* Section 9.3.

[50] For a discussion of powers of appointment, *see* Section 11.5.

[51] *Restatement (Third) of Trusts* § 40 (2003).

[52] *See* Gordon v. Portland Trust Bank, 271 P.2d 653 (Or. 1954) (designation of trustee as revocable beneficiary of life insurance policy a sufficient property interest to support creation of trust).

[53] *Restatement (Third) of Trusts* § 40, cmt. e (2003).

[54] For a discussion of the prohibition against commingling, *see* Section 14.4.

still holds title but in a different capacity. A description such as "the bulk of my securities" is too indefinite to make the securities part of the trust.[55] But assets listed by title on a schedule attached to a self-declaration of trust instrument will be considered part of the trust even though the stock certificates and other evidence of title is still in the settlor's individual name.[56] However, to assure ease of later transfer it is best to formally reregister each of the assets.[57]

Capacity

Whatever method may have been employed to create a trust, a settlor must have the requisite capacity.[58] The level of capacity required to create a trust differs depending on the type of trust being created. Because a testamentary trust is created pursuant to provisions of the testator's will, the settlor (or testator in this case) must have had testamentary capacity at the time of the will's execution.[59] To create an irrevocable inter-vivos trust (either by transfer or declaration), the settlor must ordinarily have had the capacity to make an outright gift. This is generally considered a slightly higher standard than testamentary capacity and requires an understanding of the effect of the transfer on the donor and donor's dependents. But context can make a difference. For example, contractual capacity would ordinarily be required to create a trust directed by a divorce settlement.[60]

To create a revocable inter-vivos trust, there is a split of authority on the level of capacity needed. The decided trend, codified in the UTC, is to follow the law of wills, on the theory that these trusts are used primarily as will substitutes.[61] The alternate view is that the capacity level should be that of an irrevocable trust because these trusts, unlike wills, are used to manage property during the settlor's lifetime.[62]

To create a trust by exercise of a power of appointment, the settlor must have the level of capacity needed for an outright transfer of a like type.[63] So, for example, a person may exercise a testamentary power only if that person (donee of the current power) has testamentary capacity. A donee of a power may appoint to another to hold as a trustee of a revocable trust only if the donee has testamentary or gift making capacity, whichever is the standard in that jurisdiction. And a donee of a power may create an irrevocable trust only

---

55 *Restatement (Third) of Trusts* § 40, cmt. e (2003).

56 Estate of Heggstad, 20 Cal.Rptr.2d 433 (App.1993); Taliaferro v. Taliaferro, 921 P.2d 803 (Kan.1996).

57 UTC § 401, cmt.

58 UTC § 402(a)(1).

59 For the test for determining testamentary capacity, *see* Section 5.1.

60 See *Restatement (Third) of Trusts* § 11, cmt. c (2003).

61 UTC § 601; Kelley v. First State Bank of Princeton, 401 N.E.2d 247, 261 (Ill. App. Ct.1980); Maimonides School v. Coles, 881 N.E.2d 778 (Mass. App. Ct.2008); Upman v. Clarke, 753 A.2d 4 (Md. 2000); *Restatement (Third) of Trusts* § 11(2) (2003); *Restatement (Third) of Property (Wills and Other Donative Transfers)* § 8.1 (2003).

62 *See, e.g.*, In re Estate of Head, 615 P.2d 271, 274 (N.M. Ct. App.1980). *See* Frolik & Radford, *"Sufficient" Capacity: The Contrasting Capacity Requirements for Different Documents*, 2 NAELA J. 303 (2006).

63 *Restatement (Third) of Trusts* § 11, cmt. d (2003).

if the donee has the capacity to transfer like property outright as a gift or, if more appropriate, through commercial or contractual disposition.

Persons who do not have legal capacity to transfer property—minors and incompetent adults—may make a transfer in trust, but the transfer is voidable. The settlor may ratify the transfer upon (re)attaining capacity or, after the settlor's death, the transfer may be ratified by those to whom the property would pass if the transfer were voided.[64]

Intention

To make a will, the testator must have testamentary intent.[65] Similarly, to create a trust, the settlor must have the intention to create a trust relationship,[66] but it is not necessary for the settlor to use the term "trust" or "trustee" or to understand the legal requirements for creating a trust.[67] On the other hand, using the correct terms will usually but not necessarily indicate the required intent.[68] The settlor's intent must be communicated—it cannot be a secret, undisclosed intent—but that communication may be generic and need not be directed specifically at the trustee or beneficiaries.[69] There must be an intent to create a present trust, that is, it cannot be an intent to create a trust sometime in the future. Precatory language, expressing the donor's suggested use or disposition of property, is not sufficient to create a trust. Whether the donor intended to impose legal obligations on the transferee or merely wanted to express a moral duty or nonbinding wish is often a matter for judicial interpretation.[70]

Active Duties

Under the Statute of Uses, passive uses were executed thereby converting the equitable use into a legal title. The failure of the Statute to execute active uses is what gave rise to the modern trust.[71] Absent active trustee duties (the modern equivalent of "active use"), no trust is created, or if the trustee formerly had active duties but is now passive, the trust will terminate. To constitute an active duty, the trustee must have more than mere ministerial duties to perform. If not, the trust will be invalidated in favor of an outright gift to the beneficiaries. Ministerial duties include the mandatory distribution of income with no discretion as to the amount distributed to each of the beneficiaries.

---

64 *Restatement (Third) of Trusts* § 11, cmt. e (2003).

65 *See* Section 3.1, note 12.

66 UTC § 402(a)(2). For the intention requirement, *see Restatement (Third) of Trusts* § 13 (2003).

67 No particular manner of expression is necessary to manifest the intention to create a trust. Bogert & Hess, *The Law of Trusts and Trustees* § 45 (3rd ed. 2007).

68 *See, e.g.*, In re Mannara, 785 N.Y.S.2d 274 (Sur.Ct.2004).

69 But only such manifestations of intent as are admissible as proof in a judicial proceeding may be considered. *See* UTC § 103(17) & cmt. (definition of "terms of a trust"); Franke & Moody, *The Terms of the Trust: Extrinsic Evidence of Settlor Intent*, 40 ACTEC L.J. 1 (2014), . *See also* In re Cable Family Trust dated June 10, 1987, 231 P.3d 108 (N.M. 2010) (citing this UTC provision, court holds that testimony of drafting attorney admissible in determining whether joint trust was revocable by the surviving spouse).

70 It is "immaterial whether or not the settlor knows that the intended relationship is called a trust, and whether or not the settlor knows the precise characteristics of the trust relationship." *Restatement (Third) of Trusts* § 13, cmt. a (2003). *See also* Section 3.6.

71 *See* Section 10.1, note 9.

However, any obligation to manage the money by collecting rents, investing the principal, insuring the property, etc., and any grant of discretion to the trustee as to the amount or timing of distributions would be considered active duties and validate the trust.[72]

Definite Beneficiary

A definite beneficiary is a legal person (human or entity) or ascertainable class that is capable of enforcing the trust. A trust must have a definite beneficiary unless it is a charitable trust, a trust for the care of an animal, or a trust for another valid noncharitable purpose.[73] The purpose of this requirement is to assure that there is someone capable of enforcing the trust. There is no need to apply the requirement to charitable trusts. The attorney general is capable of enforcing a charitable trust.[74] With respect to a trust for an animal or other valid noncharitable purpose, the UTC provides a method of enforcement.[75]

The beneficiaries do not have to be currently identified so long as they are identifiable within the period of the Rule Against Perpetuities.[76] In fact, they may be as yet unborn so long as they are ascertainable through a class or other designation. For example, a trust for the members of State University's graduating class of 2030 would be acceptable because the beneficiaries will be ascertainable even though the members of the class have not yet been admitted to the university. Until they are identified, the court can appoint someone to represent their interests.

Under traditional doctrine, a trust was not created if the trustee was required to select from among an indefinite class. Such a provision was an imperative power which failed because there was no beneficiary capable of enforcement.[77] Such a power is valid under the UTC, which allows a settlor to empower the trustee to select the beneficiaries even if the class from whom the selection may be made cannot be ascertained so long as if there is at least one person who can meet the description.[78]

Doctrine of Merger

No trust is created, or a trust terminates, if the same person is, or later becomes, the sole beneficiary and sole trustee.[79] If the trustee is the sole beneficiary of the trust, there would then be no independent party to enforce the settlor's terms. The legal and equitable interests therefore would merge in the beneficiary to constitute an outright gift. To understand the doctrine of merger, it is essential to understand the situations in which the doctrine would *not* apply. The doctrine does not apply if settlor A creates a trust naming A as

---

[72] *See generally Restatement (Third) of Trusts* § 6 (2003).

[73] UTC § 402(a)(3).

[74] For a discussion of charitable trusts, *see* Section 10.10.

[75] UTC §§ 408, 409. *See* Section 10.10, note 607 et seq.

[76] UTC § 402(b).

[77] The most famous case is Clark v. Campbell, 133 A. 166 (N.H. 1926), in which the testator wished to leave various items of tangible personal property to his "friends," which the court deemed too indefinite, causing the disposition to fail.

[78] UTC § 402(c).

[79] UTC § 402(a)(5).

trustee and life beneficiary but provides that upon A's death the trust be distributed to B. The doctrine does not apply because A does not hold all beneficial interests. They are divided between A and B. Nor does the doctrine apply if settlor A creates a trust naming A and B as trustees even though A is the sole beneficiary. The doctrine does not apply because legal title would be in A and B jointly as trustees, and not solely in A. A rare example where the doctrine would be applicable is if settlor A were sole trustee, sole beneficiary for life, and with the remainder payable to A's probate estate. In this case, A would be both sole trustee and sole beneficiary of all interests and no trust would be created.[80]

Trust Purpose

A trust must have a purpose that is lawful, not contrary to public policy, and possible to achieve[81] A trust with a purpose that is unlawful or against public policy is invalid. Depending on when the violation occurred, the trust may be invalid at its inception or it may become invalid at a later date. The invalidity may also affect only particular provisions. Purposes violative of public policy include those that tend to encourage criminal or tortious conduct, that interfere with freedom to marry or encourage divorce, that limit religious freedom, or which are frivolous or capricious.[82]

Pursuant to the *Restatement (Third) of Trusts*, provisions that are invalid include provisions that tend to encourage disruption of a family relationship or discourage formation or resumption of such a relationship. Included are provisions terminating a beneficiary's interest if the beneficiary should marry a person not of a certain religion, provisions encouraging or discouraging divorce, and provisions rewarding a beneficiary for embracing or rejecting particular religions.[83] The *Restatement Third* position has been rejected by at least one prominent court, concluding that intent should trump public policy concerns.[84]

Less controversial are so-called "incentive" or "B average trusts," which encourage behavior, usually relating to employment and educational achievement, that do not implicate sensitive issues of religion, marriage, and divorce.[85] In addition, it is widely accepted that provisions directing

[80] On the doctrine of merger generally, *see Restatement (Third) of Trusts* § 69 (2007). For a modern application, *see* Chicago Police Sergeant's Association v. Pallohusky, 128 N.E.3d 436 (Ill. Ct. App. 2019).

[81] UTC § 404.

[82] For an explication of the requirement that a trust must not have a purpose that is unlawful or against public policy, *see Restatement (Third) of Trusts* §§ 27–30 (2003). For a discussion of comparable restrictions under the law of wills, *see* Section 8.10.

[83] *See Restatement (Third) of Trusts* § 29, cmts. d–f (2003).

[84] In re Estate of Feinberg, 919 N.E.2d 888 (Ill.2009) (provision upheld that terminated interest of beneficiaries who married outside Jewish faith and whose spouse did not convert within one year). Macklin, *The Puzzling Case of Max Feinberg: An Analysis of Conditions in Partial Restraint of Marriage*, 43 J. Marshall L. Rev. 265 (2010); Cundiff & Copans, *In re Estate of Feinberg: When Legal Fees Consume an Estate-Restrictive Clauses Are Moot*, 35 ACTEC J. 255 (2009).

[85] Responding to client interest, the incentive trust has attracted wide interest among estate planners but has received a more skeptical reception among academics. *See* Joshua Tate, *Conditional Love and the Inflexibility Problem*, 41 Real Prop. Prob. & Tr. J. 445 (2006).

destruction of property are invalid, such as a direction that testator's house be razed.[86]

Contest

Testamentary trusts, because they are contained in a will, are subject to the same grounds as contest of a will. If the will is contested and invalidated, then so is the testamentary trust.

Like a will, the creation of an inter-vivos trust may be contested on grounds that the settlor lacked capacity or was acting under undue influence or duress.[87] Whether or not a settlor revoked a trust can also be contested on similar grounds.[88] Unlike a will, an inter-vivos trust also can be set aside on the ground of mistake[89] but not contested on grounds of lack of proper execution. There are no required formalities to execute an inter-vivos trust document unless the state has enacted special execution requirements.[90]

Identity of Trustee

Individuals and corporate trust entities may serve as trustee, either singly or jointly. The trustee should be capable of performing the duties of a trustee. In some cases, it may be that appointment of more than one trustee is optimal. For example, if there is a large estate to be administered, it may be advantageous to have a professional trust department as trustee; but if, in addition, the trustee is given discretion as to how to distribute assets, then a relative or someone else who is familiar with the beneficiaries should perhaps also serve as co-trustee. To plan for the resignation or death of a trustee, including instances where the settlor serves as trustee, it is to the settlor's advantage to name a successor trustee. However, no trust will fail for lack of a trustee; the court has the authority to appoint trustees if there is an otherwise valid trust.[91]

Oral Trusts; Statute of Frauds

There are no formal execution requirements for a written inter-vivos trust document. Furthermore, while not encouraged, a trust may be created by an oral statement unless a written document is required by some other statute,

---

86 Eyerman v. Mercantile Trust Co., 524 S.W.2d 210 (Mo.Ct.App.1975). *See also* Section 8.10, note 533 et seq.

87 UTC § 406. This section is similar to *Restatement (Third) of Property (Wills and Other Donative Transfers)* § 8.3 (2003). For the grounds for contesting a will, *see* Sections 5.1 & 5.3. For cases claiming that the settlor was fraudulently induced to create an inter-vivos trust, *see* In re Passarelli Family Trust, 206 A.3d 1188 (Pa. Super. 2017); Ward v. Fogel, 768 S.E. 2d 292 (N.C. Ct. App. 2014). In In re Estate of Hedke, 775 N.W.2d 13 (Neb. 2005), son's confidential relationship with his mother, coupled with "badges of fraud" gave rise to a presumption of undue influence in the execution of the trust and various property transfers to the son.

88 Davis v. Young, 190 P.3d 23 (Utah Ct. App. 2008) (settlor lacked mental capacity to revoke trust and purported revocation was procured by constructive fraud of grandson).

89 *Restatement (Third) of Trusts* § 12 (2003).

90 The best known exception is Florida, which provides that the post-death dispositive provisions of a revocable trust are invalid unless the trust instrument was executed with the formalities of a will. Fla. Stat. Ann. § 736.0403(b).

91 *Restatement (Third) of Trusts* § 31 (2003). For further discussion of the selection of fiduciaries, *see* Section 14.6.

such as a Statute of Frauds.[92] The Statutes of Frauds requires that a trust of real property or transfer of real property to a trust must be evidenced by a writing.[93] To provide some protection against fraud, the UTC requires that the creation of an oral trust and its terms must be evidenced by clear and convincing evidence.[94]

Secret/Semisecret Trusts

Unless the Statute of Frauds requires that the trust be in writing, an inter-vivos trust may be created by an oral declaration. But if the testator attempts to create a trust by will, oral statements of the testator and other extrinsic evidence may not be used to complete the terms of an otherwise incomplete trust ("semisecret trust") or to establish that what otherwise appears to be an outright devise was intended to be held in trust ("secret trust"). To allow the testator's oral supplementation or other extrinsic evidence to be considered would violate the command of the Statute of Wills that only those words in front of the testator at the time of the will's execution may be considered.

Given that the terms of the intended trust cannot be carried out, the issue then becomes what to do with the property to prevent unjust enrichment. If the testator clearly intends to and does create a trust relationship but fails to set forth in the will the purpose and beneficiaries to whom the equitable interest belongs ("semisecret trust"), the traditional view is that the attempted trust fails and property is returned to the testator (or testator's successors).[95] The Restatement has long taken the position, however, that the trustee holds it on a constructive trust for the benefit of the intended beneficiaries.[96]

On the other hand, where the will makes what appears to be an outright devise, but the grantee, in a separate interaction, promises to hold the property for the benefit of others ("secret trust"), extrinsic evidence is allowed to prove that the grantee is not personally entitled to the proceeds. Once evidence of unjust enrichment is before the court, a constructive trust will be imposed for the benefit of the intended beneficiaries.[97]

§ 10.4 The Revocable Trust

Avoiding Probate

A "living trust" is a revocable trust in which the settlor usually but not always declares themselves trustee. If properly funded and the trust document contains post-death dispositive provisions, the living trust can be a very effective technique for avoiding probate. For many persons of modest means

---

92 For the law of oral trusts generally, *see Restatement (Third) of Trusts* § 20 (2003).

93 *See also* Section 3.6, note 360 et seq. For a list of the state Statutes of Frauds, *see* Bogert, *The Law of Trusts and Trustees* §§ 62–64 (2d ed. Rev. 1984).

94 UTC § 407. For cases upholding a clear and convincing evidence standard for creating an oral trust, *see Restatement (Third) of Trusts* § 20 Reporter's Notes (2003).

95 The leading case is Olliffe v. Wells, 130 Mass. 221 (1881).

96 *Restatement (Third) of Trusts* § 18 (2003); *Restatement (Second) of Trusts* § 55 (1959). *See also* Section 7.1, note 96 et seq.

97 *Restatement (Third) of Trusts* § 18 (2003). *See also* Section 7.1, note 86 et seq.

who do not use lawyers, most of their wealth passes through non-probate channels.[98]

Why this concern for "avoiding probate"? The reasons for avoiding probate are stronger in some states than in others. They depend on the client's objectives and situation. One should *not* assume that avoiding probate for all assets of all clients is desirable.

Living trusts do not have to be executed with all of the formalities prescribed for wills,[99] but this is not a significant advantage since compliance with these formalities is not burdensome. Living trusts may be challenged for incapacity or undue influence just like wills, and the standards are similar.[100] However, many states require that heirs be notified before a will is admitted to probate, whereas no such notice is given to persons adversely affected by a living trust. In many states will contests are tried by jury, and juries may be more prone than judges to reject wills that they find "unnatural." Trusts may be "more resistant to capacity challenges" than wills because they "belong to the jury-free realm of equity law."[101] However, successful contests of either wills or living trusts are rare.[102] But wills have one advantage over trusts; the time limits on contesting wills are usually much shorter than those governing non-probate transfers.[103]

When wills are probated after the testator dies, they become public documents open to inspection by all.[104] To a publicity-shy family this can cause concern. However, such publicity is not a concern in most families, and the public is rarely interested in ascertaining the average citizen's estate plan.[105]

Probate may be costlier than nonprobate transfers. In some states the fees of executors and their attorneys are based on the size of the "probate" estate, and thus can be reduced by nonprobate transfers. But there is a growing trend against basing fees simply on the size of the probate estate.[106] A living trust often requires additional work by lawyers, such as transferring title of assets to the trust, and the fees for this work may offset some of the savings in probate

---

[98] Langbein, *The Uniform Trust Code: Codification of the Law of Trusts in the United States*, 15 Trust Law International 66, 70 (2001).

[99] *See* Section 3.6, note 360 et seq. A *testamentary* trust, on the other hand, is not valid if the will which purports to create it cannot be probated. Florida, however, requires that a living trust be executed with the formalities of a will. *See* Section 10.3, note 90.

[100] *See* Section 5.2, note 58; Section 10.3, note 87 et seq.

[101] Langbein, *Living Probate: the Conservatorship Model*, 77 Mich.L.Rev. 63, 67 (1978). As to trial by jury in will contests, *see* Section § 13.3, note 91 et seq.

[102] *See* Section 5.3, note 124.

[103] Anderson v. Marquette Nat'l Bank, 518 N.E.2d 196 (Ill.App.1987) (attack on amendment to revocable trust allowed even though time limit for contesting settlor's will had expired). As to the time limits on contesting wills, *see* Section 13.3, note 97 et seq. *But see* UTC § 604, discussed *infra* notes 133–135.

[104] During the testator's lifetime, the will in America is a secret document, unless the testator chooses to reveal its contents. Cf. Cal.Prob.Code § 2586 (court may order production of the will of a living conservatee when relevant to exercising its powers of substituted judgment).

[105] Engel, *The Pros and Cons of Living Trusts as Compared to Wills*, 29 Est.Plan. 155, 164 (2002).

[106] *See* Section 14.7, note 503 et seq.; Engel, 29 Est. Plan. at 158 (lawyers' fees often based on value of gross rather than probate estate).

costs.[107] The delay involved while property of a decedent is being administered is a source of popular dissatisfaction with probate,[108] but this dissatisfaction should not be exaggerated. The needs of the beneficiaries of the estate during the period of administration can be met by the family allowance[109] and by partial distributions.

Living trusts are occasionally used to escape limitations on testamentary freedom imposed by the spouse's elective share. However, many states allow surviving spouses to claim a share of assets in a revocable trust as well as the probate estate.[110]

Creditors of a testator can reach the probate estate to satisfy their claims. In some states, creditors of the settlor of a revocable trust have no comparable right, but this is no longer true in many jurisdictions.[111] In any event, creditors are not a major consideration in a majority of estates.

Another possible reason for using living trusts is that some states subject testamentary trusts to close court supervision and this can create costs and delays. But the number of states in which close court supervision is required is declining and under the UTC no trust, whether revocable or irrevocable, is "subject to continuing court supervision unless ordered by the court."[112]

Many persons wish to have some assets pass by nonprobate transfer and others pass under their will. In this situation it is important to coordinate the various parts of the estate plan. Pour-over wills can be used for this purpose.[113]

Revocable trusts are also used sometimes by persons who wish to unburden themselves of the responsibilities of managing their property by turning it over to a trustee. However, in most situations the settlor serves as the initial trustee. When the settlor is named as initial trustee, it is important that a successor trustee be designated to carry out the transfer to the desired beneficiaries after the settlor-trustee's death.

Saving Taxes

Revocable living trusts have no tax advantages. If the settlor retains the power to revoke the trust the trust income continues to be taxed to the settlor,[114] and the trust property is taxed in the settlor's gross estate at

---

[107] Weinstock, *Planning an Estate* § 6.7 (4th ed. 1995); Price & Donaldson, *Contemporary Estate Planning* § 10.13 (2014 ed.). Some lawyers leave the job of transferring assets to the trust to the client, but the lawyer should make sure that the job gets done. Feldman, *Reviewing Wills and Trusts: What Planners Should Look For*, 29 Est.Plan. 299 (2002). As to the malpractice risk when they fail to do so, *see* Section 3.6, note 328.

[108] Norman Dacey, the author of a popular book on living trusts, estimates that it takes from two to five years to clear the average estate through probate. N. Dacey, *How to Avoid Probate* 14 (updated edition 1983). As to steps some states have taken to avoid such delays, *see* Section 14.3, note 253 et seq.

[109] *See* Section 8.4.

[110] *See* Section 8.7, note 267 et seq.

[111] *See* Section 13.6, note 256 et seq.

[112] UTC § 201(b).

[113] *See* Section 7.2, note 124 et seq.

[114] For a more precise description of the income tax treatment of so-called "grantor" trusts, *see* Section 15.7; Sherman, *All You Really Need to Know About Subchapter J You Learned from This Article*, 63 Mo.L.Rev. 1, 30–31 (1998).

death.[115] Irrevocable transfers, on the other hand, can save both income and transfer taxes. These savings do not usually require the use of a trust; an outright gift normally has the same effect, but an irrevocable trust may be more advantageous than other forms of gift for non-tax reasons.

UTC Provisions[116]

Because the extensive use of revocable trust is a recent phenomenon, beginning decades if not centuries after most traditional trust law was formulated, there are numerous issues involving such trusts that have yet to be adequately addressed in the case law or state statutes. The provisions of the UTC on revocable trusts fill in many of these gaps and are among the Code's most important and innovative provisions. The biggest change is a reversal of the common law presumption that trusts are irrevocable. Reflecting the increasing if not predominant use of the revocable trust in the United States, the UTC follows the lead of California and several other states in providing that a trust is revocable absent contrary language in the terms of the trust.[117] Professional drafters routinely state whether a trust is revocable or irrevocable. Providing a presumption in the statute is therefore most relevant to self-drafted trusts or trusts prepared by less competent counsel. These trusts, when silent, are usually intended to be revocable. Because the Code's presumption of revocability will reverse the rule in most jurisdictions, the presumption applies only to trust instruments executed on or after the date of UTC enactment.[118]

The UTC treats the revocable trust in most respects as the functional equivalent of a will, at least while the settlor is alive. Following the trend in the case law, the capacity requirement for creating a trust is the same as that for a will. The capacity standard for wills also applies to revocation, amendment, adding property to the trust, or otherwise directing the actions of the trustee.[119] In addition, while the settlor has capacity, the settlor has the same control over the trust that a testator has over a will and the testator's own property. Notices that would otherwise be given to the beneficiaries must instead be given to the settlor, and all other rights that the beneficiaries might have are within the settlor's exclusive control. The settlor is authorized to give binding consents on a beneficiary's behalf, and access to the trust document is also within the settlor's control.[120] Just as the devisees under the will of a living testator do not have a right to be informed of their prospective devise, neither do the beneficiaries of a revocable trust. Under the UTC, however, the settlor's authority over the beneficiaries terminates upon the earlier of the settlor's

115 *See* Section 15.4, note 203 et seq.

116 This portion of the section is based generally on English, *The Uniform Trust Code: Significant Provisions and Policy Issues*, 67 Mo. L. Rev. 143, 186–93 (2002).

117 UTC § 602(a). The most recent revision of the Restatement of Trusts provides that a trust is presumed revocable if the settlor has retained a beneficial interest. *See Restatement (Third) of Trusts* § 63, cmt. c (2003).

118 UTC § 602(a). The UTC otherwise generally applies to trust instruments executed prior to enactment. *See* UTC § 801. For a discussion of the retroactivity of statutory reforms, *see* Section 1.3.

119 UTC § 601, which is patterned after *Restatement (Third) of Trusts* § 11(1) (2003). For the capacity requirements for trusts generally, *see* Section 10.3, note 58 et seq.

120 UTC § 603(a).

death or settlor's loss of capacity. Thereafter, unless provided otherwise in the terms of the trust, the beneficiaries may assert their rights as beneficiaries[121] but the remainder beneficiaries lack standing to contest the trustee's actions for any period while the settlor was alive and competent.[122] This provision of the UTC and the more general problem of protecting a settlor of declining capacity from abuse has attracted significant commentary.[123]

This provision on beneficiary notice highlights the dual nature of the revocable trust and the policy tension that can result. One view is that a revocable trust should in all instances be treated the same as a will. Because the devisees under a will have no right to know of the devise no matter how incapacitated the testator, then neither should the beneficiaries of a revocable trust. The other approach emphasizes the use of a trust as a lifetime management device. Those holding this view argue that for the beneficiaries to protect their rights, disclosure of the trust upon the settlor's incapacity should be required. The provision as finally drafted was a compromise. Settlors for whom confidentiality is important can so provide in the terms of the trust. Otherwise, upon the settlor's incapacity, the beneficiaries are entitled to learn of the trust.[124]

Revocation of a trust differs fundamentally from revocation of a will. Because a will is not effective until death, revocation of a will cannot affect an existing fiduciary relationship. With a trust, however, because a revocation will terminate an already existing fiduciary relationship, there is a need to protect a trustee who might act without knowledge that the trust has been revoked. There is also a need to protect trustees against the risk that they will misperceive the settlor's intent and mistakenly assume that an informal document or communication constitutes a revocation when that was not in fact the settlor's intent. To protect trustees against these risks, drafters habitually insert provisions providing that a revocable trust may be revoked only by delivery to the trustee of a formal revoking document. Some courts require strict compliance with the stated formalities. Other courts, recognizing that the formalities were inserted primarily for the trustee's and not the settlor's benefit, will accept other methods of revocation as long as the settlor's intent is clear[125]

---

[121] UTC § 603(b).

[122] The leading case is Ex parte Synovus Trust Co., N.A., 41 So.3d 70 (Ala. 2009) (no standing to challenge trustee's decisions for period when settlor was alive and competent). *See also* Hilgendorf v. Estate of Coleman, 201 So.3d 1262 (Fla. Dist. Ct. App. 2016); Tseng v. Tseng, 352 P.3d 74 (Ore. Ct. App. 2015); Gunther v. Gunther, 350 S.W.3d 44 (Mo. Ct. App. 2014) (same); Manon v. Orr, 856 N.W.2d 106 (Neb. 2014) (because Nebraska deleted reference to capacity in its version of UTC § 603, beneficiaries lacked standing to sue trustee even though settlor was allegedly incompetent).

[123] *See* Wick, *The Expressive, Protective Estate Planning Strategy: A New Paradigm for Estate Planning Design and Administration*, 27 Elder L.J. 115 (2019); McGouch, *Revocable Trusts and Fiduciary Accountability*, 26 Elder L.J. 1 (2018); Ausness, *A "Mere Expectancy?", What Rights Do Beneficiaries of a Revocable Trust Have Prior to the Death of the Settlor?*, 32 Quinnipiac Prob. L.J. 376 (2019).

[124] *See* Berry, English & Fitzsimons, *Longmeyer Exposes (or Creates) Uncertainty About the Duty to Inform Remainder Beneficiaries of a Revocable Trust*, 35 ACTEC J. 125 (2009).

[125] *See Restatement (Third) of Trusts* § 63 Reporter's Notes to cmts. h–j (2003). *See also* Section 4.5.

The UTC tries to effectuate the settlor's intent to the maximum extent possible while at the same time protecting a trustee against inadvertent liability. Unless the terms of the trust make a specified method of revocation exclusive, the UTC provides that a trust may be revoked by substantially complying with the method specified in the trust's terms or by any other method manifesting clear and convincing evidence of the settlor's intent,[126] including by a later will or codicil[127] or informal letter.[128] However, to protect the trustee, a trustee is immunized for actions taken without knowledge of the revocation or amendment.[129] Typically, the trust instrument will provide that the trust may be revoked by a written instrument delivered to the trustee. The courts have struggled on how to apply such a trust provision when the settlor is also trustee and must therefore deliver an instrument to himself or herself.[130]

The UTC also addresses the extent to which a guardian, conservator, or agent under a durable power of attorney may exercise the power to revoke or amend on behalf of an incapacitated settlor. Because most revocable trusts are created with the intent that management of the settlor's assets will be handled by the trustee and not by a subsequently appointed guardian or conservator, a guardian or conservator should not succeed automatically to the settlor's power to revoke the trust. Requiring that the guardian or conservator first obtain court permission is appropriate and the UTC so requires.[131] Similarly, when a settlor creates both a revocable trust and a durable power of attorney, the power of attorney is usually intended to supplement and not supersede the trust. Implementing this presumption, the UTC allows the settlor's agent to revoke or amend the trust only to the extent expressly authorized either in the trust or power of attorney.[132] An express provision is required because most settlors usually intend that the revocable trust, and not the power of attorney, function as the settlor's principal property management device. The power of

---

[126] UTC § 602(c).

[127] UTC § 602(c)(2)(A). The later will or codicil must expressly refer to the trust or specifically devise property that would otherwise pass under the trust. *See* Barlow v. Olguin, 329 P.3d 733 (N.M. Ct. App. 2014) (because the trust instrument did not make delivery of an instrument to the trustee the exclusive method of revocation, the trust was revoked by a later will that specifically referred to the trust and devised property subject to the trust; alternatively, even if the trust terms were deemed exclusive, settlor complied when he signed and delivered his will to himself).

[128] *See* Barrenger v. Barrenger, 2017 WL 1967490 (Mich. Ct. App., May 11, 2017) (signed letter sufficient); Rouner v. Wise, 446 S.W.3d 242 (Mo. 2014) (letter containing precatory language not sufficient); In re Hoisington Living Trust, 2017 WL 4750644 (Tenn. Ct. App., Oct. 19, 2017) (handwritten notations directly on trust instrument not sufficient). In Pena v. Dey, 39 Cal. App. 5th 546 (2019), the court concluded that an unsigned Post-it note was not sufficient.

[129] UTC § 602(g).

[130] In re Estate of Field, 953 A.2d 1281 (Pa. Super. 2008) (trust amendment validly delivered when she placed replacement pages in a binder containing her other estate planning documents even though amendment was unsigned); In re Estate of Weinen, 2013 N.J. Super Unpublished LEXIS 509 (N.J. Super. Ct., Feb. 12, 2013) (settlor would have effectively amended trust when she delivered her will, which contained amendment of trust, to herself, but because the will was determined to be the product of undue influence, the trust amendment ultimately failed).

[131] UTC § 602(f). Under the UTC, a "conservator" is appointed by the court to manage the ward's party, a "guardian" to make decisions with respect to the ward's personal affairs. *See* UTC § 103. For a discussion of guardianship, *see* Section 9.2.

[132] UTC § 602(e), which is similar to *Restatement (Third) of Trusts* § 63, cmt. *l* (2003). For a discussion of powers of attorney, *see* Section 9.3.

attorney is usually intended as a backup for assets not transferred to the revocable trust or to address specific topics, such as the power to sign tax returns or apply for government benefits, which may be beyond the authority of a trustee or are not customarily granted to a trustee.

Contest of a will is typically barred under one of two alternative statutes. Normally, a contest is barred following some period of time following notice of probate, ranging from two to six months. In addition, many states bar a contest after a specified period of time following the settlor's death, whether or not the will was probated or notice of probate given. The most commonly enacted time limit is three years following the testator's death.[133] Prior to the UTC, few states had limitation periods on contest of a revocable trust. Section 604 corrects this omission. The section is designed to allow an adequate time in which to bring a contest while at the same time permitting the expeditious distribution of the trust property following the settlor's death. A potential contestant must file a contest within the earlier of 120 days following receipt of an optional notice or three years following the settlor's death.[134] For those not receiving notice, three years should be ample time in which to determine whether they have an interest that will be affected by the trust. These time limits have been placed in brackets, however, with the suggestion made in the comments that states should substitute the periods under their comparable will contest statutes.[135] The thought here is that the state's contest period should be the same for wills and revocable trusts.

Rules of Construction

Rules of construction attribute intention to individual donors based on assumptions of common intention. Rules of construction are found both in enacted statutes and in judicial decisions. Rules of construction can involve the meaning to be given to particular language in a document such as the words "heirs" or "issue." Rules of construction can address situations the donor failed to anticipate, such as failure to anticipate the predecease of a beneficiary or to specify the source from which expenses are to be paid. Rules of construction also can make assumptions about how a donor would have revised donative documents in light of specified events occurring after execution. These include rules dealing with the effect of a divorce and the effect on a specific devisee if the devised property is disposed of during the donor's lifetime.[136]

Most states have enacted numerous statutes on the construction of wills. Most states have not enacted rules of construction applicable to revocable trusts and other nonprobate devices. While the Code's drafters concluded that the rules of construction for revocable trusts and, to a lesser extent, irrevocable trusts, ought to be the same as the rules for wills, the drafters realized that any effort on their part to draft detailed rules for trusts would not succeed. The rules on construction for wills vary radically among the states. Any detailed

---

[133] *See, e.g.*, UPC § 3–108. *See also* Section 13.3, note 98 et seq.

[134] UTC § 604(a). The drafters rejected the approach taken in California, which mandates notice. *Compare* Cal.Prob.Code § 16061.7.

[135] UTC § 604, cmt.

[136] *See* UTC § 112, cmt.

rules on trusts that the drafters might have developed could have matched the rules for wills in only a limited number of states.

Instead of including detailed rules of construction for revocable trusts, Section 112 of the UTC is a general provision providing that the enacting jurisdiction's rules of construction for wills apply, as appropriate, to the construction of trusts. Interpreting this section, two courts have held that the state's statute on pretermitted heirs under the law of wills does not extend to revocable trusts.[137]

Section 112 of the UTC was placed in brackets with the suggestion made in the comment that an enacting jurisdiction might be better served by enacting specific rules of construction for trusts. The key is the language in Section 112 stating that the rules on wills apply to trusts "as appropriate." This phrase masks some very difficult questions. Not all will construction rules should necessarily be applied to trusts. Also, even those that should apply may require modification due to the legal distinctions between wills and trusts.[138]

The 1990 revision of the UPC extends many but not all rules of will construction to revocable trusts. Topics covered include requirement of survival by 120 hours;[139] the meaning of a specific reference requirement in a power of appointment;[140] construction of class gifts;[141] survivorship with respect to future interests;[142] abolition of the doctrine of worthier title;[143] and the meaning of specific words including "descendants,"[144] "by representation,"[145] and "heirs."[146]

Joint Revocable Trusts

Formerly common only in community property states primarily to dispose of community property, joint revocable trusts are increasingly created in non-community property states. They are particularly useful for transferring joint tenancy or entireties property into trust. When drafting such a trust, it is important to clarify the extent to which a surviving spouse may revoke the trust. May the spouse revoke the entire trust or only the settlor's proportionate share.[147] Under the UTC, the default rule is that either spouse may revoke the

---

[137] In re Craig Living Trust, 194 A.3d 967 (N.H. 2018); In re Trust under Deed of Kulig, 175 A.3d 222 (Pa. 2017).

[138] An example of a rule requiring modification is the disposition of the share of a predeceased devisee, or so-called antilapse statute. Applying the antilapse statute for wills to revocable trusts runs into property classification issues. Devises under a will, because not effective until death, are classified as present interests. On the other hand, because a revocable trust is created at the instant it receives property, dispositions at the death of the settlor are classified as future interests. Most existing antilapse statutes apply only to present interests.

[139] UPC § 2–702.

[140] UPC § 2–704.

[141] UPC § 2–705.

[142] UPC § 2–707.

[143] UPC § 2–710.

[144] UPC § 2–708.

[145] UPC § 2–709.

[146] UPC § 2–711.

[147] For background on joint revocable trusts, *see* Turner, *Joint Revocable Trusts: New Flexibility in an Old Form*, Prob. & Prop., July/Aug. 2005, at 49; Martin, *The Joint Trust: Estate Planning in a New Environment*, 39 Real Prop. Prob. & Tr. J. 275 (2004); Merk, *Joint Revocable*

trust to the extent of that spouse's contribution.[148] Entireties property transferred into such a trust may retain its protection from creditor claims,[149] particularly if the state passes a statute to assure that result.[150]

§ 10.5 Revocable Trust Alternatives

Living trusts are not the only device available to avoid probate. Joint tenancy is often used for the same reason. Nevertheless, most estate planners warn against its use.[151] Joint bank accounts are often created or alleged to have been created only for convenience, with no intent that the survivor own the account when the depositor dies. This has caused courts much difficulty.[152] Revocable trusts are less open to such disputes.

The idea often expressed that joint tenancy gives a "present interest" to both (all) parties creates additional problems. If the other joint owner(s) become(s) incompetent, a conservatorship may be needed to deal with the property. Creditors of any joint tenant may have claims against the property.[153] If the parties have a falling out, the ability of the creator of a joint account to revoke the joint account is unclear, whereas the power of a settlor to revoke a trust is usually expressly reserved (or negated) in the trust instrument.[154]

TOD registration of securities, POD bank accounts, and the designation of beneficiaries of insurance policies and pension plans allow nonprobate transfer without a trust or the disadvantages of joint tenancy.[155] Nevertheless, securities, bank accounts, and insurance benefits are often put into a trust to accomplish objectives other than avoiding probate.

Insurance proceeds can be put into a trust in several ways. They can be made payable to the insured's estate and pass with other assets into a testamentary trust although this will subject the proceeds to probate and possible creditor claims and could subject the proceeds to an inheritance tax. Another alternative is to have the proceeds paid directly to trustees named in the insured's will. In some states this has some of the advantages of avoiding

---

Trusts for Married Couples Domiciles in Common-Law Property States, 32 Real Prop. Prob. & Tr. J. 345 (1997); Thede, *The ABCs of Joint Trusts*, Prob. & Prop., Jan./Feb. 1997, at 57.

[148] UTC § 602(b). *See* Kane v. Locklin, 2017 WL 4700389 (Kan. Ct. App., Oct. 20, 2017) (trust terms unambiguously required joint action).

[149] *See, e.g.*, In re Bellingroehr, 403 B.R. 818 (Bankr. W.D. Mo. 2009).

[150] Mo. Rev. Stat. § 456.950; Blase, *The Missouri Qualified Spousal Trust: A Potential Estate Planning Panacea*, 68 Mo. B. 144 (2012).

[151] Weinstock, *Planning an Estate* § 6.22 (4th ed. 1995); Price & Donaldson, *Contemporary Estate Planning* §§ 3.11.1–.2, 3.21 (2014 ed.) (listing advantages and disadvantages of joint tenancy).

[152] Robinson v. Delfino, 710 A.2d 154, 160 (R.I.1998). As to the admissibility of extrinsic evidence to show the depositor's intent, *see* Section 7.3, note 145 et seq.

[153] *See* Section 13.6, note 262 et seq.

[154] *See* Section 4.5, note 153 et seq.

[155] *See* Section 3.7.

probate.[156] Most planners prefer to create a revocable living trust and designate the trustee of that trust as beneficiary of the insurance policy.[157]

Need for Management

Trusts are frequently used to manage property for persons who are legally incompetent, either minors or adults who have been adjudicated incompetent by the court, or for persons who are legally competent but unable (in the settlor's opinion) to handle property well. Many parents want property held in trust for children until they reach an age well beyond eighteen, the age of majority. Even for fully competent family members, a trust can provide unified management of a family business.[158] A living trust can also help persons who are concerned about their own possible future incompetence. In this case someone other than the settlor must be designated as trustee, either initially or upon defined circumstances, such as whenever a physician certifies that the settlor is no longer capable. This can avoid the expense and embarrassment of judicial proceedings to have the settlor declared incompetent.[159]

Knowledgeable estate planners prefer trusts to guardianship or conservatorship for minors or incompetent adults.[160] Guardians/conservators typically must file a bond, periodically account to a court and, in many states, obtain court approval for sales, investments and distributions.[161] Trustees are also fiduciaries who handle property belonging to others, and so the law regulates their activities as well, but trustees are generally freer from court control than guardians. A settlor can choose to take risks with property which he puts into a trust, *e.g.*, by waiving bond,[162] whereas restrictions on guardians cannot generally be waived.

Guardianship for minors has the additional disadvantage that it terminates when the child reaches the age of majority[163] even though most parents probably do not think an 18-year-old is mature enough to manage a substantial amount of property. Trusts may continue until any age the settlor wishes, even for the beneficiary's lifetime.

Because of the advantages of trusts over guardianships some states allow courts to create trusts for money awarded to minors or other incapacitated

---

[156] *E.g.*, Cal.Prob.Code § 6323 (insurance payable to testamentary trustee is not subject to administration).

[157] As to the validity of such insurance trusts, *see* Section 3.6, note 341.

[158] Van Pelt, *Saving a Family Business for Future Generations,* 141 Tr. & Est.41 (2002).

[159] McGovern, *Trusts, Custodianships, and Durable Powers of Attorney*, 27 Real Prop. Prob. & Trust J. 1, 4 (1992).

[160] Even if all a testator's property is left in trust, a guardian *of the person* of any minor children may be necessary if both parents die while the children are minors. For the duties of a guardian of the person (basically a surrogate parent), *see* UPC § 5–209. A parent can appoint such a guardian by a will or other writing signed and attested by 2 witnesses. UPC § 5–202.

[161] McGovern, 27 Real Prop. Prob. & Tr.J. at 4; Cal.Prob.Code §§ 2320 (bond), 2540 (sales), 2620 (accounting in court), 2570 (investments). The UPC reduces the differences between trusts and conservators. *See, e.g.*, UPC § 5–425(a) (conservator has "all of the powers . . . conferred by law on trustees").

[162] As to bond, *see* Section 14.6, note 433 et seq.

[163] UPC § 5–431(a).

persons in a lawsuit.[164] The UPC puts the elective share taken for an incompetent spouse into a trust.[165]

Custodianships

The Uniform Transfers to Minors Act (UTMA) provides another way to have property managed for minors. Under this Act, the donor designates a "custodian" for a minor to whom the property is given. A custodian "has all the rights, powers, and authority over the custodial property that unmarried adult owners have over their own property," to be held, however, in a fiduciary capacity.[166] Custodians are not required to give a bond or make periodic court accountings.[167] The UTMA is principally directed at gifts but also covers other ways that property is transferred to minors. For example, a person can create a custodianship by a will.[168] The Act allows payment to a custodian, *e.g.*, if an insurance beneficiary is a minor when the policy matures or if a minor has a tort claim.[169] The Act also allows personal representatives and trustees to distribute to a custodian when this is "in the best interests of the minor" to whom property is to be distributed.[170] For example, an administrator of an intestate decedent could distribute the share of a minor heir to a custodian and thereby avoid the need for a court-appointed guardian.

Custodians operate very much like trustees.[171] The Restatement of Trusts says that custodians "are subject to the rules of trust law" except where the statute otherwise provides.[172] Custodianship is a useful alternative to a trust for smaller amounts of money or property, because a custodianship can be established without having to draft a trust instrument. If a father, for example, wants to give his daughter a few shares of stock, he can simply have the stock registered in the name of custodian (who can be himself or another adult) "as custodian for [the daughter] under the [state] Uniform Transfers to Minors Act."[173] This designation by incorporating by reference the provisions of the Act confers all necessary powers on the custodian,[174] including discretion to "expend for the minor's benefit so much of the custodial property as the custodian considers advisable" without court order.[175]

A custodianship can be created only for one person,[176] whereas a settlor can create a trust for a group of persons and give the trustee discretion to make

---

[164] *E.g.*, Tex.Prop.Code § 142.005; Cal.Prob.Code § 3604 (special needs trust).

[165] *See* Section 8.7, note 322.

[166] Unif. Transfers to Minors Act (UTMA) § 13(a). As to the tax consequences of gifts to minors under the Act, *see* Price & Donaldson, *Contemporary Estate Planning* § 7.35 (2014 ed.).

[167] UTMA §§ 15(c), 19. As to accountings by other fiduciaries, *see* Section 14.3.

[168] UTMA § 5.

[169] UTMA § 7.

[170] UTMA § 6. This requires court approval if the transfer involves more than $10,000.

[171] McGovern, *Trusts, Custodianships, and Durable Powers of Attorney*, 27 Real Prop. Prob. & Tr. J. at 6–10, discusses the similarities and differences between custodians and trustees.

[172] *Restatement (Third) of Trusts* § 5, cmt. a(1) (2003).

[173] UTMA § 9.

[174] UTMA § 11(c).

[175] UTMA § 14.

[176] UTMA § 10.

unequal distributions among them based on differing need, conduct or other factors.[177]

Custodianships normally end when the beneficiary reaches age 21.[178] For parents who wish to postpone distribution until their children are older, a trust is necessary. If the minor dies during a custodianship, the property passes to the minor's estate.[179] A trust can provide for distribution to others when a beneficiary dies—indeed one purpose of many trusts is to keep the trust assets out of the beneficiary's estate at death.[180]

Custodial Trusts

The Uniform Custodial Trust Act, which is targeted at adults, has been widely enacted but is not widely used. The Act allows standard trust provisions to be automatically incorporated into the terms of a trust simply by referring to the Act in the instrument. The Act designates the fiduciary as a "custodial trustee" and gives the beneficiary more powers than a minor has under the UTMA. For example, a beneficiary of a custodial trust who is not incapacitated may terminate the trust on demand[181] and can give the custodial trustee binding instructions for investments or management.[182] Thus this device is not appropriate if the intended beneficiary is a spendthrift.[183] If the beneficiary does not terminate the trust before he/she dies, the trustee must distribute the property as directed in writing by the beneficiary when the latter dies.[184] Thus custodial trusts, unlike custodianships under the Transfers to Minors Act, can avoid transmission of assets through the beneficiary's probate estate.

Durable Powers of Attorney[185]

The durable power of attorney allows a "principal" to designate an "agent" to manage the principal's property either currently or in the event of incapacity. Agents, like trustees, are fiduciaries who act for others. Traditionally an agent's powers ceased when the principal became incompetent.[186] This made agency useless for managing property for an incompetent. As a response, the durable power of attorney concept developed. Durable powers of attorney were authorized in the UPC, which was approved in 1969, and were later separately approved in the Uniform Durable Power of Attorney Act, which was promulgated in 1979, and which was in turn superseded by the Uniform Power of Attorney Act, approved in 2006. The term "attorney" in this context is equivalent to agent and has nothing to do with

---

177 McGovern, *Trusts, Custodianships, and Durable Powers of Attorney*, 27 Real Prop. Prob. & Tr. J. at 14–16. Discretionary trusts are further discussed in Section 10.7.

178 Termination at 18 may be required in some circumstances. UTMA § 20. The California version allows extension to age 25 in some circumstances. Cal.Prob.Code § 3920.5.

179 UTMA § 20.

180 *See* Section 10.4.

181 Unif. Custodial Trust Act (UCTA) § 2(e).

182 UCTA § 7(b).

183 Spendthrift trusts are discussed in Section 10.8.

184 UCTA § 17.

185 Durable powers of attorney are discussed in more detail in Section 9.3.

186 *Restatement (Second) of Agency* § 122 (1958).

being a "attorney at law."[187] Although durable powers are usually better than guardianship, a court may appoint a guardian to manage the property of a person with a durable power when an appointment is in the principal's best interest because of questionable conduct by the designated attorney.[188]

Agents are like trustees in many respects; they manage property on behalf of the principal just as trustees manage property for the beneficiary(ies). However, while trustees (like custodians) have many powers implied either by common law or a statute like the UTC,[189] most state durable power statutes do not confer any power on the agent unless there is authorizing language in the power of attorney document. Therefore, to determine the scope of the agent's authority, one must look to the terms of the power and to the law of agency . . . Agency law only sparingly implies powers and strictly construes express powers.[190]

A "durable" power of attorney terminates when the principal dies.[191] Since trusts continue to operate after the settlor dies, they can also function as will substitutes, but a power of attorney cannot. On the other hand, an agent can act under a power of attorney without the principal transferring property to the agent; whereas a living trust may fail if the trustee does not obtain title to the property.[192] The respective advantages of trusts and agency can be combined by executing a power of attorney authorizing the attorney to transfer the principal's assets into a trust.

Legal Life Estates

A testator or donor can create a legal life estate instead of a trust, but knowledgeable estate planners do not recommend legal life estates.

The law imposes duties on life tenants to protect the remainder interests. If legal life tenants allow property to deteriorate, they can be sued for waste.[193] In some circumstances they may be required to post a bond.[194] But "unlike a trustee, a life tenant as such does not stand in a fiduciary relationship to the other beneficiaries of successive legal interests."[195] Trustees who are financially responsible provide better protection for remainder beneficiaries than legal life tenants. Trustees have extensive powers over property held in trust, but life tenants and remaindermen "may deal only with their own respective interests" in the property.[196] If a third party injures the property,

---

[187] " 'Attorney-in-fact' means a person granted authority to act for the principal in a power of attorney, regardless of whether the person is known as an attorney-in-fact or agent, or by some other term." Cal.Prob.Code § 4014(a).

[188] In re Conservatorship of Anderson v. Lasen, 628 N.W.2d 233 (Neb.2001).

[189] UTC §§ 815–816. Trustees' powers of sale, investment, etc., are discussed in Section 14.5.

[190] McGovern, *Trusts, Custodianships, and Durable Powers of Attorney*, 27 Real Prop. Prob. & Trust J. at 32–33.

[191] UPC § 5B–110(a)(1).

[192] *See* Section 3.6, notes 320 et seq.

[193] Moore v. Phillips, 627 P.2d 831 (Kan.App.1981).

[194] Cf. Matter of Estate of Jud, 710 P.2d 1241, 1248 (Kan.1985) (rejecting a demand for a bond "in the absence of a showing of danger of loss or waste"). *Compare* the obligation of trustees to provide a bond. Section 14.6, note 433 et seq.

[195] *Restatement (Third) of Trusts* § 5, cmt. b (2003).

[196] *Restatement (Third) of Trusts* § 5, cmt. b.

the life tenant might only seek recovery for the damage to her interest, leaving the remaindermen with a separate claim.[197] A trustee, on the other hand, would sue on behalf of all the beneficiaries.[198] Life tenants may not commit "waste" but they have no duty to take out insurance to cover the remainder interests,[199] whereas trustees are bound to insure the property for the benefit of all.[200] Trustees must furnish information to the beneficiaries as to their administration of the trust,[201] but legal life tenants have no comparable obligation unless the remaindermen can show "there is real danger of destruction of the estate."[202]

Remedies against life tenants who commit waste are problematic when the succeeding interests are contingent as they often are. For example, parents left land to their daughter for life, with a remainder to her surviving issue. When the daughter sold timber standing on the property, her grandson sought relief. The court refused to award him damages because his interest was uncertain; he would have none if he failed to survive the life tenant.[203]

While the remedies available to remainder interests are often restricted, a life tenant's ability to exploit land is also limited. The best use of land may require a long-term lease. Trustees can usually execute leases extending beyond the term of the trust,[204] but life tenants can convey only what they have; if they die during the term of a lease, the remaindermen can expel the lessee.[205] Many statutes allow courts to authorize life tenants to sell property, for example, a sale binding upon all parties can be authorized if it "appears to the court to be necessary or expedient."[206] Some courts have ordered such sales even without statutory authorization.[207] Court proceedings are expensive, however. They can be avoided if the instrument that creates the life estate gives the life tenant a power of sale,[208] but a narrowly drafted power may be insufficient. On the other hand, broadly drafted powers may allow the tenant to destroy the remainder. A tenant with "full and unrestricted power to sell, convey, dispose of, or expend all or any part of said property" was allowed to give the property away.[209]

---

[197] *Restatement (First) of Property* § 118 (1936).

[198] *Restatement (Third) of Trusts* § 107 (2012).

[199] Keith Estate v. Keith, 647 S.E.2d 731 (W. Va.2007) (life tenant who insures property can keep all the proceeds when property is destroyed by fire).

[200] *Restatement (Third) of Trusts* § 76, cmt. d (2007); *Restatement (Second) of Trusts* § 176, cmt. b (1959).

[201] *Restatement (Third) of Trusts,* § 82 (2007); Section 14.3.

[202] Holley v. Marks, 535 S.W.2d 861, 862 (Tenn.1976).

[203] Pedro v. January, 494 P.2d 868, 875 (Or.1972).

[204] *See* Section 14.5, note 370 et seq.

[205] *Restatement (First) of Property* § 124 (1936).

[206] Mass.Gen.Laws c. 183, § 49. *See also* N.C.Stat. § 41–11; *Restatement (First) of Property* § 124, comment i (1936); In re Estate of Sauer, 753 N.Y.S.2d 318 (Sur.2002) (ordering sale on petition of life tenant pursuant to a statute).

[207] Alsup v. Montoya, 488 S.W.2d 725 (Tenn.1972); Ball v. Curtis, 637 S.W.2d 571 (Ark.1982); Jackson v. Breton, 484 A.2d 256 (Me.1984).

[208] Ware v. Green, 691 S.W.2d 167 (Ark.1985).

[209] Kelly v. Lansford, 572 S.W.2d 369 (Tex.Civ.App.1978).

Trustees usually have power to sell trust property when appropriate, but they cannot give it away without adequate consideration.[210] When property in a trust is sold, the proceeds are retained in the trust. Legal life tenants with a power of sale, unlike trustees, are not obligated to keep the sale proceeds separate from their own property, and if the proceeds cannot be identified when the life tenant dies, the remainder fails.[211] Some drafters therefore stipulate that if assets are sold, the life tenant shall become a trustee of the proceeds.[212]

Because trusts and legal life estates perform the same function, an instrument which creates a life estate may be construed to create a trust. A will which left property to the testator's wife for life accompanied by a direction that the executors "handle my estate during the life of my wife," was held to create a trust by implication.[213] English legislation converts all life estates to trusts even for land.[214] Such forcing of legal life estates into the trust mold coincides with the common advice of estate planners to use a trust whenever one wishes to create successive interests in property.

§ 10.6 Principal and Income

Suppose that a woman creates a trust which provides that the trustee shall pay the income to her husband for life, and upon his death, convey the principal to her issue. The trustee will receive dividends, interest, rent, proceeds of property sold, etc. Are these receipts income to be distributed to the husband, or principal to be retained in trust for the settlor's issue? When the trust incurs expenses, such as trustee's fees or taxes, which account is charged with them? These problems arise repeatedly in the administration of trusts. Trustees need a clear answer. In case of doubt, they can apply to a court for instructions, but this is expensive. In most states a statute answers most questions. There are no less than three Uniform Principal and Income Acts. The first was promulgated in 1931, the second in 1962, and a third dating from 1997, which supersedes the prior Acts and had 47 adoptions through 2016.[215] A fourth, the Uniform Fiduciary Income and Principal Act, was approved in 2018. There are also numerous provisions on income and principal allocation in the second Restatement of Trusts. Given that the Uniform Principal and Income Act largely supplanted the Restatement in this area, the drafters of the Third Restatement have included only limited discussion of principal and income issues.[216]

---

210 On trustee's powers of sale, *see* Section 14.5, note 343 et seq.

211 South Side T. & S. Bank v. South Side T. & S. Bank, 284 N.E.2d 61 (Ill.App.1972).

212 *Restatement (Third) of Trusts* § 5, cmt. b (2003).

213 Perfect U. Lodge v. Interfirst Bank, 748 S.W.2d 218 (Tex.1988).

214 Maudsley, *Escaping the Tyranny of Common Law Estates*, 42 Mo.L.Rev. 355 (1977).

215 *See* www.uniformlaws.org.

216 *Restatement (Third) of Trusts* § 109 (Duty to Account for Principal and Income), § 110 (Determining Principal and Income), § 111 (Duty to Distribute to Income Beneficiaries Amounts Appropriate to Duty of Impartiality) (2012).

Purpose of Act

The purpose of the 2018 Uniform Fiduciary Income and Principal and prior Uniform Principal and Income Acts is to determine:

- How income earned during administration of a decedent's estate is to be distributed to trusts and to persons entitled to outright devises of specific property, pecuniary gifts, and the residue;
- When an income interest in a trust begins and how receipts received after that date are to be allocated;
- Upon termination of an income interest, who is entitled to the income that has been collected but not yet distributed, or that is due but not yet collected, or that has accrued but is not yet due; and
- After an income interest begins and before it ends, how receipts and disbursements are to be allocated between principal and income.[217]

General Principles

The law of principal and income consists of many detailed rules, not all of which can be treated here. A few general principles underlie these rules. First, the settlor's intent controls. The provisions of the Act are subject to contrary directions in the trust.[218] However, it is sometimes not clear whether a testator or settlor intended to depart from the established rules. For example, a provision in a will for payment of the income to the testator's wife "after deduction for the costs and expenses of the trustee" was held not to override the general rule of the governing Act that trustees' fees should be charged half to income and half to principal, and that capital gains taxes and brokerage commissions be charged entirely to principal.[219]

Some wills give the trustee discretion in making allocations between principal and income. A fiduciary may exercise such a discretionary power even if the exercise of the power produces a result different from the one required or permitted by the Act.[220] It often is not clear how far such discretion extends. A trustee was not allowed to allocate capital gain to an income beneficiary under a provision empowering the trustee to determine "whether any money coming into its hands shall be treated as" principal or income because "proceeds from the sale of trust securities are principal. Where proper allocation is not a matter of honest doubt the trustees are not authorized to make allocations contrary to law."[221] On the other hand, another court upheld a trustees' decision to allocate litigation expenses to income rather than principal.[222]

---

[217] Unif. Principal & Income Act (UPAIA) (1997) Prefatory Note.

[218] UFIPA (2018) § 103(a)(1); UPAIA (1997) § 103(a)(1). For an application of this provision, *see* Goodwine v. Goodwine, 819 N.E. 2d 824 (Ind. Ct. App. 2004).

[219] Venables v. Seattle-First Nat'l Bank, 808 P.2d 769 (Wash.App.1991).

[220] UFIPA (2018) § 201(b); UPAIA (1997) § 103(a)(2).

[221] Englund v. First Nat'l Bank, 381 So.2d 8, 11 (Ala.1980).

[222] du Pont v. Southern Nat'l Bank, 771 F.2d 874, 887 (5th Cir.1985).

The definition of income for tax purposes influences the allocation of trust receipts. For example, a decision to deduct estate administration expenses on a trust's income tax return[223] instead of on the decedent's estate tax return can impact the income and principal beneficiaries differently. If deducted on the estate tax return, the estate tax, which is payable from principal, is reduced and the principal beneficiaries benefit.[224] The method whereby one group of beneficiaries reimburses another group of beneficiaries for the effect of tax elections is referred to as an equitable adjustment. The 2018 and 1997 Acts allow trustees to make "adjustments between principal and income to offset the shifting of tax benefits between income beneficiaries and successor beneficiaries" in some instances and requires them in others.[225]

A common theme is that receipts should be allocated so that the value of the principal is preserved and everything else is income. For example, under the 1997 Act proceeds from the sale of timber are allocated to income "to the extent that the amount of timber removed does not exceed the rate of growth of the timber."[226]

Courts sometimes suggest that doubtful allocation questions should be resolved in favor of the income beneficiaries because they are "the primary objects of [the settlor's] bounty."[227] However, the uniform act provides that in cases for which no rule is provided, receipts shall be added to principal.[228] A comment to the 1997 Act-notes that the allocation to principal serves the long-term interest of all beneficiaries since additions to principal will produce more income in the future.[229]

Administrative convenience is an important factor in allocation. Because trustees must make decisions frequently, an easily applicable rule is better than one that requires difficult calculations or knowledge that is not readily available. For example, a trustee may rely on statements by a corporation as to the character of the distribution made by the corporation.[230]

Another underlying concept is the desirability of a relatively steady stream of "income," rather than wide fluctuations from year to year. Corporate distributions amounting to more than 20% of the fair market value of the fiduciary's interest in the entity are allocated to principal.[231] The Act charges "ordinary repairs" and "regularly recurring" property taxes to income.[232] but "disbursements relating to environmental matters" are charged against principal "on the assumption that they will usually be extraordinary in nature."[233]

---

[223] For an explanation of this tax election, *see* Section 15.4, text following note 270.

[224] UFIPA (2018) § 502; UPAIA (1997) § 502.

[225] UFIPA (2018) § 507; UPAIA (1997) § 506.

[226] UFIPA (2018) § 412(a)(1); UPAIA (1997) § 412(a)(1).

[227] Matter of Kuehn, 308 N.W.2d 398, 400 (S.D.1981).

[228] UFIPA (2018) § 201(c)(1); UPAIA (1997) § 103(a)(4).

[229] UPAIA (1997) § 103(a)(4), cmt.

[230] UFIPA (2018) § 401(e)(1); UPAIA (1997) § 401(f).

[231] UFIPA (2018) § 401(e)(2); UPAIA (1997) § 401(d)(2) (20% of gross assets).

[232] UFIPA (2018) §§ 501(3), 502(a)(8); UPAIA (1997) §§ 501(3), 502(a)(7).

[233] UPAIA (1997) § 502(a)(7), cmt.

Specific Rules: Proceeds of Sale

When property is sold the proceeds are allocated to principal, including capital gains which are taxed as income under federal law.[234] However, part of the proceeds of a sale may be treated as income if the property had not been producing adequate income before it was sold. The 1962 Uniform Act provided for an adjustment in the income account for property "which has not produced an average net income of at least 1% per year of its inventory value."[235] The 1997 Act rejects such special treatment for underproductive assets because it "conflicts with the basic precept" of the Prudent Investor Act which requires that the trust portfolio be considered as a whole in assessing productivity.[236] Instead, the 2018 and 1997 Acts empower trustees to make adjustments between principal and income in order to be "fair and reasonable to all beneficiaries."[237] A trustee may invest the trust assets entirely in growth stocks that produce little dividend income. The trustee may do this and at the same time transfer (an unspecified amount of) cash from principal to income in order to provide the income beneficiary "the degree of beneficial enjoyment normally accorded a person who is the income beneficiary of a trust."[238] This provision leaves much to the trustee's discretion (subject to judicial review for "abuse of discretion"),[239] but has the advantage that the income beneficiaries do not have to wait until unproductive property is sold in order to get their "fair share." This provision is restricted where it would create a conflict of interest because the trustee is also a beneficiary or would cause tax problems.

Corporate Distributions

Under both the 2018 and 1997 Acts, cash dividends are generally income and other distributions including stock dividends are principal. Distributions in "property other than money" are principal, as is a distribution of money which exceeds 20% of the distributor's assets (1997 Act),[240] updated in the 2018 Act to 20% of the fair market value of the fiduciary's interest in the entity.[241] Cash dividends are generally income, but a distribution made in total liquidation of a corporation is usually principal even if paid in cash.[242]

The 2018 and 1997 Acts gives trustees holding an unincorporated business leeway to decide the extent to which receipts should be allocated to income,[243] "just as the board of directors of a corporation owned entirely by the trust decides the amount of annual dividends to be paid to the trust."[244] This discretion is not unnecessarily unlimited. When a trust holds a controlling

---

[234] As to the treatment of capital gains in the taxation of trust income, *see* Section 15.6, note 386 et seq.

[235] UPAIA (1962) § 12(a).

[236] UPAIA (1997) § 413, cmt. As to the Prudent Investor Act, *see* Section 14.2.

[237] UFIPA (2018) § 203; UFIPA § 104 &, cmt.

[238] UPAIA (1997) § 104, cmt., ex. 3.

[239] UFIPA (2018) § 202; UPIA (1997) § 105.

[240] UPAIA (1997) § 401.

[241] UFIPA § 401(e)(2) (2018). The update is in part due to cases such as Hasso v. Hasso, 55 Cal.Rptr.3d 667 (App. 2007), and In re Estate of Thomas, 21 Cal.Rptr.3d 741 (App. 2004).

[242] UFIPA (2018) § 401(a)(1)(B), (d)(3); UPAIA (1997) § 401(c)(3).

[243] UFIPA (2018) § 403: UFIPA (1997) § 403.

[244] UPAIA (1997) § 403, cmt.

interest in a corporation, courts can "pierce the corporate veil" and treat corporate earnings as trust income even though they have not been declared as dividends.[245]

Interest paid on bonds is income. Proceeds received on redemption or sale are principal without adjustment even if the bonds were purchased at a premium or discount.[246]

Wasting Assets

The counterpart to under-or unproductive property is a "wasting asset," one which is destined to lose its value over time. Oil wells, for example, eventually run dry. If all the receipts from such a "wasting asset" are classified as income, principal would not be preserved. The 1962 Uniform Act, apportioned oil royalties 27 ½% to principal as an allowance for depletion, and the remainder is income.[247] The 1997 Act replaces this with a 90% allocation of receipts to principal[248] The drafters of the 2018 Act, recognizing that a precise percentage formula is unlikely to reflect economic realities, provided that the trustee is to allocate "equitably."[249]

Can trustees establish a reserve for depreciation for buildings? Must they? The 1962 Uniform Act required trustees to set up "a reasonable allowance for depreciation . . . under generally accepted accounting principles" for property acquired by trustees after the Act took effect.[250] The 2018 and 1997 Acts, on the other hand, simply permits trustees to create a reserve for depreciation.[251] The comment notes that such a reserve "has been resisted by many trustees" because it is "not needed to protect the remainder beneficiaries if the value of the land is increasing."[252]

Planning, Power to Adjust, and Unitrusts

Most principal and income questions have been settled by statute. Settlors or testators who do not like the statutory rules can provide otherwise, but to ascertain a client's views on all allocation issues would require a good deal of time that could better be spent on other questions.

Trusts can be drafted so that distributions do not depend on classification of items as income or principal. Most trusts allow invasion of principal to meet the needs of the "income" beneficiaries. A settlor may wish to have *all* distributions based on need, but as discussed in the next section, controversies about "need" may be harder to resolve than questions about what is "income." On the other hand, making distributions depend on "income" may distort investment decisions. The allocation between principal and income required in many trusts is "profoundly inconsistent with the portfolio paradigm" of modern

---

[245] Matter of Estate of Butterfield, 341 N.W.2d 453, 462 (Mich.1983).

[246] UFIPA (2018) § 406; UPAIA (1997) § 406.

[247] UPAIA (1962) § 9(a)(3). The 1931 Act, § 9, allocated all oil royalties to principal. The figure in the 1962 Act was derived from the rule then used for computing income for tax purposes.

[248] UPAIA (1997) § 411.

[249] UFIPA (2018) § 411(a)(3).

[250] UPAIA (1962) § 13(a)(2).

[251] UFIPA (2018) § 503; UPAIA (1997) § 503.

[252] UPAIA (1997) § 503, cmt.

investment theory.[253] The desire to produce adequate income for the income beneficiaries may result in over investment in bonds that pay high interest but no appreciation potential, but under investment in stocks, which may pay little or no dividends but have high appreciation potential. The 2018 and 1997 Acts attempt to avoid this problem by empowering trustees to make the necessary adjustments between principal and income "if the trustee manages trust assets as a prudent investor."[254] A long list of factors is provided for trustees to consider in deciding whether to exercise this power to adjust.[255]

It is also possible to draft a trust so that benefits are allocated without regard to either accounting income or need. Under a "unitrust," the beneficiary receives a distribution each year equal to a specified percentage of the trust's value. Under an "annuity" trust, the beneficiary receives a distribution each year equal to a specified percentage of the trust's initial value. Both these techniques were developed in the context of charitable remainder trusts. Trusts *must* use one of these distribution methods if a charitable remainder is to qualify for a federal income, estate or gift tax deduction.[256] The unitrust has become increasingly popular among estate planners, and numerous states have adopted legislation authorizing trustees to convert "income" trusts to unitrusts.[257] Unitrusts can achieve the same goal as the discretion accorded trustees under the 2018 and 1997 Acts to make adjustments between principal and income, but they give trustees less open-ended discretion.[258] Other estate planners are more skeptical about unitrusts, pointing out the problems that can arise in trying to apply the percentage to trusts that contain assets that are hard to value. Also, when a trust holds assets that produce little or no income, the trustee may have to sell assets to make the mandated distributions.[259] The unitrust concept and related power to adjust has generated a large amount of commentary.[260]

---

[253] Gordon, *The Puzzling Persistence of the Constrained Prudent Man Rule*, 62 N.Y.U.L.Rev. 52, 101 (1987). Trust investments are further discussed in Section 14.2.

[254] UFIPA (2018) § 203; UPAIA (1997) § 104(a) & Prefatory Note.

[255] UFIFA (2018) § 203(e); UPAIA (1997) § 104(b). Despite the broad authority given to the trustee to make adjustments, the case law on the power to adjust is relatively sparse. *See* McKenzie v. Vanderpoel, 61 Cal. Rptr. 3d 129 (App. 2007); Orpheus Trust, 179 P. 3d 562 (Nev. 2008). *See generally* Sager, *Litigation and the Total Return Trust*, 35 ACTEC J. 206 (2009).

[256] *See* Section 15.4, note 274 et seq.

[257] *See, e.g.* In re Estate of Ives, 745 N.Y.S.2d 904 (Sur.2002) (income trust converted to a 4% unitrust under N.Y.EPTL § 11–2.4).

[258] Welch, *Brave New World of Total Return Laws*, 141 Tr. & Est. 24 (2002). *Compare supra* notes 238–239.

[259] Golden, *Total Return Unitrusts: Is This a Solution in Search of a Problem?*, 28 ACTEC Journal 121 (2002).

[260] Medlin, *Limitations on the Trustee's Power to Adjust*, 42 Real Prop. Prob. & Tr. J. 717 (2008); Nenno, *The Power to Adjust and Total-Return Unitrust Statutes: State Developments and Tax Considerations*, 42 Real Prop. Prob. & Tr. J. 657 (2008); Cline, *Uniform Prudent Investor and Principal and Income Acts, Changing the Trust Landscape*, 42 Real Prop. Prob. & Tr. J. 611 (2008); Volkmer, *Nebraska's "Total Return Trust" Statute; Unitrust Conversion and the Challenges of Managing a Trust and Drafting a Trust*, 40 Creighton L. Rev. 135 (2006); DiRusso & Sablone, *Statutory Techniques for Balancing the Interests of Trust Beneficiaries*, 39 U.S.F.L.Rev. 21 (2005); Arakaki, *Promoting Trustee Adherence to the Fiduciary Duty if Impartiality: A Case for Enacting Unitrust Conversion Statutes in Conjunction With Equitable Adjustment Statutes*, 28 U. Haw. L. Rev. 105 (2005); Wolf, *Total Return Trusts-Can Your Clients Afford Anything Less*, 33 Real Prop

The most significant change between the 2018 and 1997 Acts is the addition of a unitrust provision.[261] The 2018 Act grants the trustee the power to convert an income interest into a unitrust.[262] The 2018 Act also applies to a trust originally drafted as a unitrust except to the extent the terms of the trust are inconsistent with the 2018 Act.[263] Advance notice of a proposed conversion must be given to the beneficiaries. In the event of an objection, either the trustee or beneficiary may petition the court to approve or disapprove the conversion.[264] While a common unitrust rate is 4% of the trust's value per year, the 2018 Act does not set a specific rate.

§ 10.7 Discretionary Trusts

Reasons for Discretion

A major advantage of trusts over guardianship is that trustees, unlike guardians, can be given discretion to make distributions from time to time to different beneficiaries. Many trusts are designed to last for an extended period of time, but they may be unable to meet the beneficiaries' changing needs unless the trustee is allowed flexibility.[265] A power to distribute principal (sometimes called corpus) to an income beneficiary is very common. Powers to accumulate income and add it to principal, or to "sprinkle" income and principal among a group of beneficiaries, are also used with increasing frequency. The financial needs of children vary as they grow up. One who is entering college usually needs more than siblings who are living at home attending public schools. Parents typically consider such differences in need in allocating their resources. If the parents die before their children are grown, a trustee can do the same. In this situation the question arises whether the trustee should take earlier discretionary distributions into account when all the trust assets are finally distributed upon termination. If the settlor intends this, the trust instrument should make this clear, because courts will normally assume the settlor intended otherwise.[266]

Discretionary trusts offer income tax advantages. Because income of a trust is normally taxed to the person who receives it,[267] trustees can reduce the total taxes paid by a family by distributing income to family members who are in lower tax brackets—children instead of their parents, for example, if the children are still in school and the parents have well-paying jobs. "It is normally appropriate, and often necessary, for a trustee to take tax

Prob. & Tr. J. 131 (1998); Wolf, *Defeating the Duty to Disappoint Equally-The Total Return Trust*, 32 Real Prop. Prob. & Tr. J. 45 (1997).

[261] UFIFA (2018) Art. 3.

[262] UFIFA (2018) § 302(a)(1).

[263] UFIPA (2018) § 302(a)(2).

[264] UFIPA (2018) §§ 303, 304.

[265] Price & Donaldson, *Contemporary Estate Planning* § 10.2 (2014 ed.).

[266] If the trust is silent, the earlier distributions are not treated as advancements. New England Merchants Nat'l Bank v. Morin, 449 N.E.2d 682 (Mass.App.1983); *Restatement (Third) of Trusts* § 50, cmt. f (2003). However, trustees can make loans to beneficiaries in lieu of outright distributions. *Restatement (Third) of Trusts* § 50, cmt. d.

[267] Section 15.6.

considerations into account in determining what discretionary decisions to make."[268]

Giving trustees discretion over distributions of income is not usually advisable when a beneficiary is likely to need all the trust income, because disputes may arise between the beneficiaries and trustee as to how this discretion is exercised. As always, careful drafting can reduce the risk of such litigation.

Judicial Review of Trustee's Discretion[269]

Judicial review of trustees' decisions takes several forms. Sometimes a remainderman seeks to enjoin a trustee from distributing principal to an income beneficiary[270] or to surcharge the trustee for distributions previously made.[271] Conversely, a beneficiary may complain of a trustee's refusal to make distributions. Courts may order trustees to make distributions[272] or make up for payments that should have been made in the past,[273] including payments to the estate of a beneficiary who has since died.[274] Courts may also "deny or diminish the trustee's compensation, . . . or even remove the trustee for repeated or serious abuse of the discretionary power."[275] Courts sometimes "issue instructions to clarify the standards or guidelines applicable to" discretionary powers,[276] but "if a matter rests within the sound discretion of the trustee, . . . the court will ordinarily not instruct the trustee how to exercise that discretion," because this is the trustee's primary responsibility.[277] In proceedings for instructions, the trustee's duty of impartiality towards the different beneficiaries requires that the trustee "not become an advocate but remain neutral."[278]

Reported cases involving claims by beneficiaries that trustees were too stingy or overly generous in exercising discretion are relatively uncommon, because courts rarely overrule trustees' decisions. "[A] trustee's exercise of

---

268 *Restatement (Third) of Trusts* § 50, cmt. e (2003).

269 The leading article on judicial review of a trustee's decisions on discretionary distributions is Halbach, *Problems of Discretion in Discretionary Trusts*, 61 Colum. L. Rev. 1425 (1961). Professor Halbach later served as the reporter for the Restatement (Third) of Trusts. For an update on the Halbach article, *see* Ausness, *Discretionary Trusts: An Update*, 43 ACTEC L.J. 231 (2018). For comments on the Ausness article and a response, *see* Beyer, *Reactions to Discretionary Trusts: An Update*, 43 ACTEC L.J. 435 (2018); Bove, *Commentary on Discretionary Trusts: An Update*, 43 ACTEC L.J. 441 (2018); and Ausness, *My Response to Beyer and Bove*, 43 ACTEC L.J. 447 (2018).

270 Ballenger v. Ballenger, 694 S.W.2d 72 (Tex.App.1985).

271 Austin v. United States Bank of Washington, 869 P.2d 404 (Wash.App.1994).

272 Kolodney v. Kolodney, 503 A.2d 625 (Conn.App.1986).

273 Matter of Estate of Lindgren, 885 P.2d 1280, 1283 (Mont.1994); Matter of Estate of McCart, 847 P.2d 184 (Colo.App.1992).

274 Marsman v. Nasca, 573 N.E.2d 1025 (Mass.App.1991); Third Nat'l Bank v. Brown, 691 S.W.2d 557 (Tenn.App.1985).

275 *Restatement (Third) of Trusts* § 50, cmt. b (2003). As to the compensation and removal of trustees and other fiduciaries, *see* Sections 14.6–14.7.

276 Barnett Banks Trust Co. v. Herr, 546 So.2d 755 (Fla.App.1989); Godfrey v. Chandley, 811 P.2d 1248 (Kan.1991) (declaratory judgment); Hertel ex rel. Hertel v. Nationsbank N.A., 37 S.W.3d 408 (Mo.App.2001) (same).

277 *Restatement (Third) of Trusts* § 71, cmt. d (2007).

278 *Restatement (Third) of Trusts d.* § 79, cmt. d.

discretion should not be overruled by a court unless the trustee has clearly abused the discretion granted him under the trust instrument or acted arbitrarily."[279] If a trial court upholds the trustee, the chances of success on appeal are limited, because the question of whether the trustee has abused discretion is one of fact.[280] However, courts do occasionally overturn trustees' decisions, even if the trust instrument gives the trustee "sole discretion." For example, a trustee was ordered to increase payments to a beneficiary from $1,000 to $2,500 a month because the trust instrument referred to the beneficiary's "comfortable maintenance and support" showed that the "trustee's discretion was not intended to be absolute" despite the words "sole discretion."[281] The trustee has a duty of impartiality toward the beneficiaries; this does not mean that all beneficiaries must receive equal amounts, but the trustee must investigate the needs of them all.[282]

A clause which purports to relieve a trustee from accountability for its decisions is ineffective.[283] A settlor who really intended a trustee to be absolutely free of supervision would make an outright gift. A *trust* connotes *some* judicial control over the trustee.[284]

Courts do *not* defer to a trustee's interpretation of ambiguous language in a trust instrument. When a company construed the terms of its pension plan as not to provide benefits to employees who lost their jobs when plants were sold, the court refused to apply "a deferential standard of review appropriate when a trustee exercises discretionary powers . . . Courts construe terms in trust agreements without deferring to either party's interpretation."[285]

Language of Instrument

In reviewing a trustee's action, the language of the trust instrument is important in determining whether the trust contains language under which the "existence or non-existence, the definiteness or indefiniteness, of an external standard by which the reasonableness of the trustee's conduct can be judged."[286] No grant of discretion is ever absolute but is always subject to court review. The UTC requires that a trustee must exercise a discretionary power in good faith and with regard to the purposes of the trust and the beneficial interests of the beneficiaries as specified in the terms of the trust.[287] This

---

[279] NationsBank of Virginia v. Estate of Grandy, 450 S.E.2d 140, 143 (Va.1994).

[280] In the Matter of Campbell's Trusts, 258 N.W.2d 856 (Minn.1977). Conversely, a trial court's decision that a trustee abused its discretion "will be disturbed on appeal only if . . . manifestly wrong." Gulf Nat'l Bank v. Sturtevant, 511 So.2d 936 (Miss.1987); Matter of Estate of McCart, 847 P.2d 184 (Colo.App.1992).

[281] Kolodney v. Kolodney, 503 A.2d 625, 627 (Conn.App.1986). *See also* UTC § 814(a) (despite "absolute" discretion, trustee must act "in good faith and with regard to the purposes of the trust").

[282] *Restatement (Third) of Trusts* § 79, cmt. c.

[283] *Restatement (Third) of Trusts* § 50, cmt. c (2003); *cf.* UTC § 105(b) (limiting the Code provisions which the trust terms can override).

[284] When the terms of a "trust" are extremely vague, a court may find that in fact no trust was intended, and the "trustee" can keep the property. *See* Section 3.6, note 378 et seq.

[285] Firestone Tire and Rubber Co. v. Bruch, 489 U.S. 101, 111–12 (1989).

[286] *Restatement (Second) of Trusts* § 187, cmt. d (1959). *See also Restatement (Third) of Trusts* § 50, cmt. b (2003).

[287] UTC § 814(a).

standard applies notwithstanding the breadth of discretion granted to a trustee in the terms of the trust, including the use of such terms as "absolute," "sole," or "uncontrolled."[288] The extent to which such language of extended discretion relieves a trustee from normal judicial supervision and control is a matter for interpretation. Even under the broadest grant of discretion, the trustee must always act honestly and in the state of mind contemplated by the settlor.[289]

The authors of a 50 state survey on the enforcement of discretionary provisions concluded that the states could be divided into two groups, "restrained jurisdictions" whose courts will review the trustee's exercise of discretion only for bad faith or fraud, and "more aggressive jurisdictions" whose courts will apply a standard of prudence even to language of extended discretion.[290] But many cases are difficult to so categorize because litigation in this area often turns on the interpretation of particular words and is hard to predict. If an instrument directs a trustee to pay whatever amount it "deems necessary for the support" of a beneficiary, a court will order the trustee to increase payments if the court finds that they were inadequate for support.[291] On the other hand, if the instrument says that trustees are to make distributions as they "deem best," judicial review is very limited.[292] Thus a trustee's decision to distribute to a beneficiary so he could provide for his step-children was upheld where the instrument allowed the trustee to invade principal "for the benefit of" the designated beneficiaries. "The word 'benefit' . . . is more comprehensive than the word 'support.' "[293] According to the Restatement, "benefit" may "authorize discretionary expenditures that fall beyond the usual scope of a support-related standard," but it does not necessarily authorize courts to *compel* such distributions when a trustee does not choose to make them.[294]

The word "support" is defined by reference to the beneficiary's station in life; the trustee is bound to maintain the beneficiary "in accordance with the standard of living which was normal for him before he became a beneficiary of the trust."[295] The size of the trust may also be relevant in determining the appropriate level of support. Where a beneficiary over time comes to enjoy a higher standard of living, this "may become the appropriate standard of support if consistent with the trust's level of productivity." Conversely, "a lower level of distributions may be justifiable if the trust estate is modest relative to the probable future needs of the beneficiary."[296]

---

[288] UTC § 814(a).

[289] *Restatement (Third) of Trusts* § 50, cmt. c (2003).

[290] Taback & Pratt, *When the Rubber Meets the Road: A Discussion Regarding a Trustee's Exercise of Discretion*, 49 Real Prop. Tr. & Est. L. J. 491 (2015).

[291] Kolodney v. Kolodney, 503 A.2d 625 (Conn.App.1986); Matter of Estate of Lindgren, 885 P.2d 1280 (Mont.1994); Marsman v. Nasca, 573 N.E.2d 1025 (Mass.App.1991).

[292] American Cancer Soc. v. Hammerstein, 631 S.W.2d 858 (Mo.App.1981); First Nat'l Bank v. Department of Health, 399 A.2d 891 (Md.1979).

[293] Ewing v. Ruml, 892 F.2d 168, 172–73 (2d Cir.1989).

[294] *Restatement (Third) of Trusts* § 50, cmt. d (2003).

[295] Marsman v. Nasca, 573 N.E.2d 1025, 1030 (Mass.App.1991).

[296] *Restatement (Third) of Trusts* § 50, cmt. e (2003).

It is not clear how much weight references to the beneficiary's "comfort" or "happiness" carry. Any words may be limited by their context. The word "comfort," when "part of a clause referencing the support, maintenance and education of the beneficiary" meant only what was "reasonably necessary to maintain the beneficiary in his accustomed manner of living."[297]

Review of trustees' discretionary decisions sometimes reflects assumptions that the settlor preferred certain beneficiaries. A trustee's denial of a payment requested by the settlor's widow was upheld when the settlor's "children were his primary concern and any provision for his wife . . . was clearly secondary,"[298] whereas invasion of principal for a widow was approved where "the testator was concerned primarily with his wife's comfort and any residue to others was secondary."[299] The trust instrument may indicate the settlor's preferences. Even without such a clause, a spouse or child of the settlor is more likely to prevail than other beneficiaries.[300]

Courts may distinguish between income and principal even when the trust instrument gives the trustee the same powers over both. A trustee who was directed to "distribute to my spouse . . . as much of the income and principal . . . as the trustee believes desirable" for his support, was surcharged for excessive distributions of principal whereas the income payments were not considered unreasonable.[301] Another trustee under a similar clause was rebuked for stinginess when it accumulated much of the trust income.[302] A refusal to invade principal can actually serve the long term interests of a beneficiary who requests it, because "a reduction of principal could leave the beneficiary in want later in life."[303]

Many trusts name a beneficiary as trustee. The resultant conflict of interest may affect judicial review of trustees' decisions. A trustee who refused to make payments to the settlor's spouse was held to have "acted with improper motives and with a clear conflict of interest . . . by seeking to preserve the trust funds for himself and his heirs as remaindermen."[304] Some jurisdictions even prohibit trustees from participating in decisions where they have such a conflict of interest; a disinterested co-trustee must act in their place.[305] But most courts defer to the judgment of the settlor who created the conflict of interest apparently believing that the beneficiary-trustee would act fairly and approve exercise of discretionary powers from which the trustee benefits if they are deemed reasonable.[306] Naming a beneficiary as trustee can result in adverse tax consequences, in particular a risk that the beneficiary-trustee will

---

[297] Estate of Vissering v. Commissioner, 990 F.2d 578, 581 (10th Cir.1993).

[298] In re Flyer's Will, 245 N.E.2d 718, 720 (N.Y.1969).

[299] Hart v. Connors, 228 N.E.2d 273, 275 (Ill.App.1967).

[300] *Restatement (Third) of Trusts* § 50, cmt. f (2003).

[301] Dunkley v. Peoples Bank & Trust Co., 728 F.Supp. 547, 564 (W.D.Ark.1989).

[302] Old Colony Trust Company v. Rodd, 254 N.E.2d 886, 890 (Mass.1970).

[303] Emmert v. Old Nat'l Bank, 246 S.E.2d 236 (W.Va.1978).

[304] Matter of Estate of McCart, 847 P.2d 184, 186 (Colo.App.1992).

[305] Matter of Estate of Seidman, 395 N.Y.S.2d 674 (App.Div.1977); First Union Nat'l Bank v. Cisa, 361 S.E.2d 615 (S.C.1987).

[306] E.g., Bracken v. Block, 561 N.E.2d 1273 (Ill.App.1990); *Restatement (Third) of Trusts* § 50 illus. 1 (2003).

be deemed to possess a taxable general power of appointment.[307] However, because of this risk, the UTC and many state statutes convert an otherwise taxable power of appointment into a non-taxable power by limiting a beneficiary-trustee's discretion to make distributions to "an ascertainable standard relating to the trustee's health, education, support or maintenance within the meaning of . . . the Internal Revenue Code."[308]

Other Resources of Beneficiary

Claims for support raise the question whether other resources of the beneficiary should be considered. If a trust provides for the support of a person who needs $50,000 a year and has a job which pays $35,000 a year, should the trustee take the beneficiary's earnings into account? potential earnings if the beneficiary refuses to maximize his or her earning potential? income from assets which the beneficiary owns outside the trust? Should the trustee require the beneficiary to sell such assets before resorting to the trust?

The judicial opinions that discuss this issue are hard to reconcile, because the language of the governing instrument and the circumstances vary in every case.[309] The Restatement of Trusts presumes that the trustee "is to consider other resources but has some discretion in the matter."[310] A trustee who distributed principal to a beneficiary without determining what other funds she might have was held to have shown "reckless disregard" for the rights of the remaindermen.[311] On the other hand, a trustee was not required to inquire into the beneficiary's other resources even though the trustee's discretion was to be exercised for the beneficiary's "proper support, care, and maintenance."[312]

Some courts distinguish between income and principal; a trustee should consider the beneficiary's income from all sources, but the beneficiary's own principal need not be depleted before resorting to the trust.[313] It is undesirable to force beneficiaries to sell assets which are not readily marketable to raise needed funds. Yet sometimes it is the trust which holds illiquid assets which would have to be sold to satisfy a request for a distribution of principal.

Should trustees consider a beneficiary's right to support from a parent or spouse? The Restatement presumes that "the trustee is to take account of a parental duty to support a youthful beneficiary" on the ground that "only the parents would be likely to be benefitted if the trustee provides what the child is entitled to in any event."[314]

---

[307] *See* Section 15.4 note 241 et seq.

[308] UTC § 814(b).

[309] Hertel ex rel. Hertel v. Nationsbank N.A., 37 S.W.3d 408, 412 (Mo. Ct. App.2001) (variations in circumstances and language make it impossible to state a general rule).

[310] *Restatement (Third) of Trusts* § 50, cmt. e (2003). For a discussion to the Restatement Third approach to the consideration of other resources and a comparison to the Restatement Second, *see* Geierman, *Discretionary Dilemma: Trustee Consideration of Beneficiary's Financial Resources*, Prob. & Prop., Jan./Feb. 2020, at 40,

[311] Feibelman v. Worthen Nat'l Bank, N.A., 20 F.3d 835 (8th Cir.1994).

[312] In re Raggio Family Trust, 460 P.3d 969 (Nev. 2020).

[313] Barnett Banks Trust Co. v. Herr, 546 So.2d 755 (Fla.App.1989); Hart v. Connors, 228 N.E.2d 273 (Ill.App.1967).

[314] *Restatement (Third) of Trusts* § 50, cmt. e (2003).

Uniform Trust Code

The UTC and its comments provide significance guidance on the administration of discretionary trusts:[315]

"[A] grant of discretion establishes a range within which the trustee may act. The greater the grant of discretion, the broader the range." The comment further notes that . . . "whether the trustee has a duty in a given situation to make a distribution depends on the exact language used, whether the standard grants discretion and its breadth, whether the discretion is coupled with a standard, whether the beneficiary has other available resources, and, more broadly, the overriding purposes of the trust."[316]

In addition, despite trust provisions giving the trustee broad discretion, the UTC requires that the trustee always administer a trust in good faith and in accordance with the trust terms, the trust purposes, and the interests of the trust beneficiaries.[317]

Finally, in administering trusts with two or more beneficiaries, the UTC requires that the trustee "act impartially in investing, managing, and distributing the trust property, giving due regard to the beneficiaries' respective interests.[318] . . . "[T]he duty to act impartially does not mean that the trustee must treat the beneficiaries equally. Rather, the trustee must treat the beneficiaries equitably in light of the purposes and terms of the trust."[319]

Drafting

The drafter of a discretionary trust should deal with the question of outside resources.[320] One possibility is to give the trustee leeway to consider any income or other resources of the beneficiary that are known to the trustee and are reasonably available. Assuming the settlor wishes to provide maximum flexibility, a clause which authorizes a trustee to use funds for a group of persons, such as the settlor's children, should make clear that (1) not every member of the group must receive a distribution,[321] and (2) the income need not all be distributed.

Some commentators suggest that professional trustees tend to be conservative in making discretionary distributions for various reasons, such as fear of surcharge.[322] If the settlor is concerned that the trustee may be too conservative in making distributions, language indicative of generosity may help, for example, a recital that certain beneficiaries are settlor's "primary concern." Or a beneficiary can be made a co-trustee or be given power to remove

---

[315] The following quote is from Geierman, *Discretionary Dilemma: Trustee Consideration of Beneficiary Resources*, Prob. & Prop., Jan./Feb. 2020, at 40, 41.

[316] UTC § 814, cmt.

[317] *See* UTC §§ 105(b)(2), 801 & 814(a).

[318] UTC § 803.

[319] UTC § 803, cmt.

[320] For suggested language, *see* Geierman, *Discretionary Dilemma: Trustee Consideration of Beneficiary Resources*, Prob. & Prop., Jan./Feb. 2020, at 40.

[321] As to the distinction between "exclusive" and "non-exclusive" powers, *see* Section 11.5, notes 244–246.

[322] Danforth, *Rethinking the Law of Creditors' Rights in Trusts*, 53 Hastings L.J. 287, 357–58 (2002).

the trustee and appoint another. If there are co-trustees, there may be a deadlock if they cannot agree[323] unless an odd number of trustees is named.

Factors Other than Need

Discretion usually involves an assessment of beneficiaries' needs, but the settlor may want other factors considered as well, in which event clauses framed in terms of "support" may not be adequate. Even if all the beneficiaries have more income than they need for support, it may be desirable to distribute trust income to one who is in a lower income-tax bracket than the others. A discretionary power which is not limited by any standard can avoid the "troublesome question whether distributions can properly be made purely for tax reasons to selected beneficiaries."[324] Settlors may also wish a trustee to consider the beneficiary's ability to handle funds. Many trusts provide for distribution when a beneficiary attains a certain age. Since settlors can rarely predict when beneficiaries will achieve maturity, it may be better to let the trustee decide when a beneficiary is mature enough to receive the principal.

More recently some planners have suggested "incentive trusts" which depart from the idea that distributions should be designed to maintain the beneficiaries' standard of living. In its place such trusts seek to "encourage certain types of behavior," e.g., "providing a monthly payment to the stay-at-home mom, . . . [or] denying distributions if a child fails a drug test."[325]

Single v. Separate Trusts

Related to the question of discretionary versus fixed-benefit trusts is the question *how many* trusts should be created. Is it better to create a single trust for all the beneficiaries (the testator/settlor's children, for example), or separate trusts for each? This depends on whether the settlor wants the children to receive equal benefits or prefers to allow the trustee to give more to one child than to another based on need or some other criterion. This choice often depends upon the ages of the children and on the size of the trust estate. If a modest fund is being used to provide for young children, because one child may have greater need than the others in a particular year, a single trust with discretion in the trustee is usually desirable. At the other extreme is a large estate held in trust for children of full age. Most parents want their children to receive equal shares in this situation, so separate trusts for each child are more suitable (assuming that the children's shares are held in trust and not distributed to them outright). With separate trusts, the trustee can satisfy reasonable requests by one child for early distribution of his or her share (for example, to buy a house or start a business), without affecting the shares of the child's siblings.[326]

---

[323] As to resolving deadlocks when there is more than one trustee, *see* Section 14.6, note 472 et seq.

[324] *Restatement (Third) of Trusts* § 50, cmt. e (2001).

[325] Tate, *Conditional Love: Incentive Trusts and the Inflexibility Problem*, 41 Real Prop. Prob. & Tr. J. 445 (2006); Stephens, *Incentive Trusts: Considerations, Uses and Alternatives*, 29 ACTEC J. 59 (2003). *See also* Section 10.3, notes 85–86.

[326] As to the possibility of combining or separating existing trusts, *see* Section 10.9, notes 482–484. A will may provide that separate trusts be administered as a unit for investment purposes. Price & Donaldson, Contemporary Estate Planning § 4.25.4 (2014 ed.).

Some settlors provide for single and separate trusts at different stages; a single trust for the children so long as they are all young in which the trustee distributes income and principal as necessary for their support and education, accumulating any excess income. When all of the children have reached a specified age, the trustee divides the property into separate trusts for each child (or distributes the trust assets outright at that point).

Indefinite Beneficiaries

A trust sometimes fails because the trustee has *too much* discretion in choosing beneficiaries on the theory that a trust must have ascertainable beneficiaries to enforce it.[327] For example, a woman left her estate to her sister "to distribute among my heirs, named legatees, and such other persons she may deem deserving in such proportion as she shall deem just." This language was held to be insufficiently definite.[328] Also insufficient was a residuary clause directing that the estate "be divided among my close friends"[329]

The vice in these cases was the lack of ascertainable beneficiaries, not the trustee's discretion. A will can authorize trustees to distribute property "among my surviving children . . . in such manner as [they] . . . consider to be most appropriate."[330] In this case the children are the beneficiaries even though no one of them is certain to receive anything. The trust beneficiaries need not be named in the trust instrument; a trust for a class like "my children" is valid even if the class includes persons not born when the trust is created.[331]

Courts have resorted to various techniques to save trusts from invalidity on the grounds of uncertainty. Vague terms may be ignored when they are appended to more definite ones. When a will directed trustees to distribute to "worthy charities, institutions and individuals," the court avoided invalidity by using a limiting construction. "The word 'worthy,' as used by the testatrix, was meant by her to refer only to an institution which would fall within the legal definition of charity."[332] The term "relatives" may be construed to mean heirs in order to avoid uncertainty; the limits of the class are fixed by the laws of intestate succession.[333] The word "family" may also be construed in this way.[334] Invalidity can also be avoided if the troublesome language is construed as an outright devise with precatory suggestions rather than a trust. When a will left the estate to a woman "to divide and disperse as she sees fit," the court held that she took the property outright.[335]

---

[327] *See* Section 10.3, notes 73–78.

[328] In re Kradwell's Estate, 170 N.W.2d 773 (Wis.1969).

[329] Re Connor, 10 Dom.L.R.3d 5, 11 (Alberta 1970).

[330] Deal v. Huddleston, 702 S.W.2d 404 (Ark.1986).

[331] *Restatement (Third) of Trusts* § 45 (2003). This is subject to the Rule Against Perpetuities, discussed in Chapter 12.

[332] Newick v. Mason, 581 A.2d 1269 (Me.1990).

[333] *Restatement (Third) of Trusts* § 45, cmt. d (2003).

[334] McLendon v. Priest, 376 S.E.2d 679 (Ga.1989) (contract to leave property to spouse's "family" construed to mean heirs); UPC § 2–711.

[335] Tucker v. Bradford, 599 So.2d 611 (Ala.1992).

Trusts must have definite beneficiaries but no such requirement exists for powers of appointment.[336] The UTC avoids the dilemma of trusts with indefinite beneficiaries by deeming that a direction to a trustee to distribute property among an indefinite group of persons gives the trustee the power but no duty to distribute the property to the persons the trustee may select.[337] The fear that the trustee may appropriate the property if there are no beneficiaries to enforce the trust is illusory, because those who would take upon failure of the power can compel the trustee to convey the property to them if the trustee does not make distribution within a reasonable period.[338]

Medicaid Eligibility

A frequently litigated issue in recent years has been the effect of a discretionary trust on a beneficiary's eligibility for Medicaid benefits. The analysis depends on whether the trust was created by someone else, such as a parent, for the benefit of the Medicaid recipient ("third party" trust), or whether the trust was created by the Medicaid applicant or by someone else using the Medicaid applicant's funds ("self-settled" or "first party") trust. The issue is not one of trust law but rather of Medicaid law, although the Medicaid statute adopts certain trust law principles. The question for either type of trust is the extent to which the beneficiary's interest in the trust constitutes an "available resource." In most states, an individual is ineligible for Medicaid if the individual has more than $2,000 in available resources.

Revocable Trusts

While a trust is revocable, the income and trust principal is treated as an available resource of the settlor even if the settlor is not named as a beneficiary.[339]

Third-Party Trusts

In the case of trusts established by a third party such as a parent, the beneficiary's interest is treated as an available resource if the beneficiary under state trust law "has the legal ability to make such sum available for support and maintenance."[340] The case law in the states is not consistent but certain general conclusions can be drawn. Mandatory income interests and directions to pay for the beneficiary's support constitute available resources because of the beneficiary's right to demand distributions. Interests that are totally discretionary do not disqualify the beneficiary for Medicaid. The most difficult cases are what might be referred to as "discretionary support" trusts,[341] under which the language of discretion is tied to a support standard. The results of these cases are hard to predict.[342]

---

[336] For a general discussion of powers of appointment, *see* Section 11.5.

[337] UTC § 402(c); *Restatement (Third) of Trusts* § 46 (2001).

[338] UTC § 402(c). *See also Restatement (Third) of Trusts* § 46, cmt. g (2003).

[339] *See, e.g.*, Bonta v. Burke, 120 Cal.Rptr.2d 72 (App.2002).

[340] 45 C.F.R. § 233.20(a)(3)(ii)(D).

[341] *See* Abravanel, *Discretionary Support Trusts*, 68 Iowa L. Rev. 273 (1983).

[342] For the case law, *see* Kruse, *Third Party and Self-Settled Trusts: Planning for the Elderly and Disabled Client* (ABA 3d ed. 2003).

First-Party Trusts

If an individual creates a trust for the individual's own benefit, or if someone else creates a trust with the individual's funds, the rules are less favorable. Any income or principal that *could* in the exercise of the trustee's discretion be distributed to the beneficiary will be treated as an available resource for Medicaid purposes.[343] Consequently, if the trustee has discretion to distribute income or principal to the beneficiary, the entire trust will be considered an available resource even if the trustee never makes a distribution.[344]

But federal law recognizes some important exceptions, one of which is referred to as a (d)(4)(A) trust.[345] A (d)(4)(A) trust is not treated as an available resource and the trustee is able to disburse for a beneficiary's special needs not otherwise covered by Medicaid. To qualify as a (d)(4)(A) trust, the irrevocable trust must have been created by a disabled individual under age 65 or by a parent, grandparent, guardian, or court using the assets of a disabled individual under age 65. Furthermore, the trust must have a "pay back" provision under which the State will receive all amounts remaining in the trust upon the death of such individual up to an amount of Medicaid benefits paid on behalf of the individual.

Trusts for Spouses

Trusts for spouses are subject to special rules. An irrevocable inter-vivos trust created by a spouse of a Medicaid beneficiary, including a trust that was revocable while the settlor was living, is treated the same as if it had been created by the beneficiary—it is deemed an available resource to the extent the trustee can exercise discretion on the recipient's behalf. But a testamentary trust created by a spouse is treated under the regular third-party trust rules. If the trust is discretionary and not subject to a standard, the trust will usually not be treated as an available resource.[346]

§ 10.8 Spendthrift Provisions and Creditor Claims

Like they can against other debtors, creditors of a trustee can obtain a judgment against the trustee for which the trustee may be able to seek reimbursement from the trust.[347] Far more complicated and addressed in this section is the extent to which the interests in a trust may be reached to satisfy claims of creditors of the settlor, and also creditor claims against beneficiaries other than the settlor.

Creditors of Settlor

Creditors can in general only reach property that belongs to their debtor. Legal title to trust property is in the trustee, not the beneficiary. If *S* creates a trust which requires the trustee to pay the income and principal to others, *S's*

---

[343] 42 U.S.C. § 1396p(d).

[344] *See, e.g.*, Masterson v. Department Social Services, 969 S.W.2d 746 (Mo.1998).

[345] 42 U.S.C. § 1396p(d)(4)(A).

[346] 42 U.S.C. § 1395p(d)(2)(A).

[347] *See* Section 14.9.

creditors have no right to reach the trust unless the creation of a trust involved a fraudulent conveyance. Creditors were allowed to reach an irrevocable trust which the debtor had created for his children on the basis of a statute providing that "every conveyance made . . . by a person who is, or will thereby be rendered, insolvent is fraudulent as to creditors" if the conveyance was made without "fair consideration."[348] Most states have similar statutes, many of which are based on the Uniform Fraudulent Transfer Act.[349] These statutes cover all gratuitous transfers, including the creation of trusts.

Even when the creation of a trust was not a fraudulent conveyance, if the settlor reserves the right to revoke the trust, most states allow the settlor's creditors to reach the trust, either by virtue of a statute[350] or by case law.[351] Even after the settlor has died and the power to revoke has expired, many authorities allow the settlor's creditors to reach the trust assets, at least if the settlor's probate estate is insufficient to satisfy claims.[352]

Even if a trust is irrevocable, if the settlor creates a "self-settled" trust under which the settlor has reserved a beneficial interest, then in most states the creditors of the settlor can reach that interest. Thus, if a trust provides that the trustee shall pay the income to the settlor for her life, remainder to her children, her creditors can reach her income interest. They can also reach the principal if the trustee has discretion to distribute it to the settlor. According to the Restatement, where the trustee:

> has discretionary authority to pay to the settlor . . . as much of the income and principal as the trustee may determine appropriate, creditors of the settlor can reach the maximum amount the trustee, in the proper exercise of fiduciary discretion, could pay to . . . the settlor.[353]

Courts generally interpret this rule to give the settlor's creditors access to all the trust principal, presumably on the theory that the trustee could properly pay all of a settlor's debts under such a power,[354] and at least one court has held that the creditors can still reach the trust after the settlor's death.[355] Also, the settlor's creditors can reach the settlor's beneficial interest irrespective of whether the trust document contains a spendthrift provision purportedly barring creditor claims.[356] The reasons generally advanced for allowing the settlor's creditors to reach the settlor's interest—for example, a

---

[348] Territorial Sav. & Loan Ass'n v. Baird, 781 P.2d 452 (Utah App.1989).

[349] *Restatement, Second, of Property (Donative Transfers)* § 34.3 Statutory Note (1992).

[350] UTC § 505(a)(1). For an overview of the creditor provisions of the UTC, addressing this and other topics, *see* Danforth, *Article 5 of the UTC and the Future of Creditor Rights in Trusts*, 27 Cardozo L. Rev. 2551 (2006).

[351] *Restatement (Third) of Trusts* § 25, cmt. e (2003); Spetz v. New York State Dep't of Health, 737 N.Y.S.2d 524 (Sup.2002).

[352] For a discussion, *see* Section 13.6, note 256 et seq.

[353] *Restatement (Third) of Trusts* § 60, cmt. f (2003). Similar language appeared in *Restatement (Second) of Trusts* § 156 (1959) and is found in UTC § 505(a)(2).

[354] In re Robbins, 826 F.2d 293 (4th Cir.1987) (bankruptcy); State v. Hawes, 564 N.Y.S.2d 637 (App.Div.1991); Giles v. Ingrum, 583 So.2d 1287 (Ala.1991) (claim allowed after settlor's death).

[355] De Prins v. Michaeles, 154 N.E.3d 921 (Mass. 2020).

[356] UTC § 505(a)(2); *Restatement (Third) of Trusts* § 58(2) (2003).

debtor should not be allowed to "have his cake and eat it too"[357]—apply to *all* spendthrift trusts, and ERISA's immunity of pension trusts from creditors includes plans built up by contributions of the employee-beneficiary.[358]

The special rule for self-settled trusts occasionally raises the question "who *was* the settlor of the trust?" Under the UTC, a "settlor" is defined as a person "who creates, or contributes property to, a trust."[359] Consequently, the name listed on the document as settlor may not be determinative. For example, a son who contributed personal funds to restore a plantation house in a trust created by his parents was held to be a "settlor" to the extent of his contribution.[360]

The general refusal to allow self-settled spendthrift trusts is not worldwide. Professor LoPucki notes that "more than a half-dozen nations compete for foreign investment by . . . providing havens for judgment debtors from their foreign creditors . . . by validating self-settled spendthrift trusts." According to one estimate "this offshore trust industry already administers a trillion dollars in assets." He discusses various strategies creditors might invoke to reach such assets but concludes that they are not likely to succeed.[361] One possibility is that the debtor-settlor may be held in contempt for failing to repatriate funds which placed into an offshore trust.[362] Also, assets placed in an offshore situs that have a US situs, such as real property, are subject to seizure to satisfy a domestic judgment.[363]

Beginning with Alaska in 1997, numerous American states have followed the lead of these foreign jurisdictions by allowing self-settled spendthrift trusts, presumably to attract trust business which might otherwise go abroad or flee to another asset protection state.[364] The effect of such statutes on creditors in other states is not fully resolved. Because of the full faith and credit clause of the American constitution, trusts set up in an American jurisdiction may not offer debtors as much protection against judgments in other states as an "offshore" trust.[365] An Alaska statute purporting to deprive courts of other states of jurisdiction was denied enforcement in the case of an Alaska trust

---

[357] Matter of Shurley, 115 F.3d 333, 337 (5th Cir.1997).

[358] Patterson v. Shumate, 504 U.S. 753 (1992) (exemption under ERISA does not depend on plan qualifying as spendthrift trust under state law).

[359] UTC § 103(15).

[360] In re Tait, 2008 WL 4183341 (Bankr. S.D. Ala., Sept. 10, 2008). *See also Restatement (Third) of Trusts* § 58, cmt. f (2003).

[361] LoPucki, *The Death of Liability*, 106 Yale L.J. 1, 33 (1996). For a more recent survey, *see* Ausness, *The Offshore Asset Protection Trust: A Prudent Financial Planning Device or the Last Refuge of a Scoundrel*, 45 Duq. L. Rev. 47 (2007).

[362] Federal Trade Commission v. Affordable Media, LLC, 179 F.3d 1228 (9th Cir.1999).

[363] Rush University Medical Center v. Sessions, 980 N.E.2d 45 (Ill. 2012).

[364] The early statutes are discussed and criticized in Boxx, *Gray's Ghost—A Conversation About the Onshore Trust*, 85 Iowa L. Rev. 1195 (2000). *See also* Danforth, *Rethinking the Law of Creditors' Rights in Trusts*, 53 Hastings L.J. 287, 306–26 (2002) (discussing both domestic and foreign "asset-protection trusts"). Danforth is not so critical of such trusts as Boxx, pointing out their resemblance to other asset protection devices such as family partnerships, tenancy by the entirety, etc. Danforth, 53 Hastings L.J. at 360–66. For a later survey, covering the first 12 enactments, *see* Shaftel, *Comparison of the Twelve Domestic Asset Protection Statutes*, 34 ACTEC L.J. 293 (2009). For an even later survey, *see* Hood, *Domestic Asset Protection Trusts: A Debtor's Friend and Creditor's Foe*, 13 Brooklyn J. Corp. Fin. & Com. L. 443 (2019).

[365] Boxx, 85 Iowa L. Rev. at 1209; Danforth, 53 Hastings L.J. at 322–23.

that held Montana real estate.[366] On the other hand, the South Dakota Supreme Court refused to give full faith and credit to a California judgment for child support that was asserted against a trust that had been moved from California to South Dakota after the entry of the judgment.[367]

If several persons contribute property to a trust, each is treated as the settlor of a portion reflecting the contributions of each.[368] An individual can be classified as a settlor even though not listed as a settlor in the trust document. Nor need the contribution be made at the creation of the trust. A son who contributed personal funds to restore a plantation house owned by a trust created by his parents was held to be a settlor of the trust to the extent of his contribution. Consequently, this proportionate share of the trust was reachable by the bankruptcy trustee to pay the son's personal debts.[369]

Beneficiaries Other than the Settlor

Creditors of beneficiaries other than the settlor traditionally were required to resort to "equitable" remedies and show that their legal remedies were inadequate to reach the beneficiary's interest.[370] In accordance with the traditions of equity, courts have discretion in deciding how to use the beneficiary's interest to satisfy claims. The UTC says that the court may award a creditor "such relief as is appropriate under the circumstances."[371] Where the debtor-beneficiary is entitled to the trust income "the court will normally direct the trustee to make the payments to the creditor until the claim . . . is satisfied," but it may award less than all the income to the creditor, leaving some for the basic needs of the beneficiary.[372] The court may alternatively order a sale of the beneficiary's interest, particularly when it is a future interest which produces no current income.[373] If "the uncertainty or remoteness of the interest [is] such that its forced sale would produce little relative to its value to the beneficiary," the court may simply give creditors "a lien on the beneficiary's interest, to be realized if and when it falls into possession."[374]

If the trustee has discretion to pay principal or income to a debtor other than the settlor, the creditor's rights are limited.[375] Where "the beneficiary has no right to a disbursement from the trust other than what the trustee in his sole discretion chooses to distribute, the beneficiary's creditors cannot compel the trustee to pay," but (as we have seen) "where the settlor is a beneficiary of

---

[366] Toni 1 Trust, by Tangwall v. Wacker, 413 P.3d 1199 (Alaska 2018).

[367] In re Cleopatra Cameron Gift Trust, 831 N.W.2d 244 (S.D. 2019).

[368] UTC § 103(15).

[369] In re Tait, 2008 WL 4183341 (Bankr. S.D. Ala., Sept. 10, 2008).

[370] This has been changed by statute in some states. *Restatement (Third) of Trusts* § 56, cmt. e (2003).

[371] UTC § 501.

[372] *Restatement (Third) of Trusts* § 56, cmt. e (2003). *See, e.g.*, King v. King, 434 P.3d 502 (Ore. Ct. App. 2018) (notwithstanding spendthrift provision, successor trustee could pay judgment against predecessor trustee from predecessor's income interest in trust).

[373] *Restatement (Third) of Trusts* § 56, cmt. e (2003).

[374] *Restatement (Third) of Trusts* § 56, cmt. e.

[375] For an overview of this topic, *see* Newman, *Trust Law in the Twenty-First Century: Challenges to Fiduciary Accountability*, 29 Quinnipiac Prob. L. J. 261, 280–86 (2016).

the trust, the creditors can reach the maximum amount that the trustee could pay to the beneficiary."[376]

Even a tax lien does not attach to a discretionary trust created by someone other than the beneficiary, because the beneficiary "does not have 'property' or any 'right to property' in nondistributed trust property before the trustees have exercised their discretionary powers of distribution."[377] Absent a valid spendthrift provision, creditors can get an order directing the trustee to pay them rather than the beneficiary if the trustee decides to exercise the discretion in the beneficiary's favor. A trustee who makes distributions to a beneficiary in disregard of the order will be liable to the beneficiary's creditors.[378]

The Second Restatement of Trusts distinguished between "trusts for support" and "discretionary trusts;" certain creditors could reach the beneficiary's interest in a support trust, for example, those who had supplied "necessaries" to the beneficiary.[379] Courts have had great difficulty in applying this distinction,[380] because many trusts direct the trustee to support a beneficiary but also give the trustee discretion in determining the appropriate level of support. The Third Restatement rejects the distinction and gives creditors of a beneficiary of a discretionary trust "judicial protection from abuse of discretion by the trustee."[381] This view has some judicial support. One court stated, in reversing the dismissal of an attempt by a beneficiary's creditor to reach her interest in a discretionary trust:

> When a trustee has the absolute discretion to withhold from the beneficiary all payments, . . . the trust . . . is beyond the reach of his creditors who stand in his shoes. . . . [But here] the wording of the trust requires the trustee to pay to [the beneficiary] as much of the trust income as is necessary to maintain her 'in accordance with her station in life.' . . . Because [the beneficiary] can demand payment from the trustee, so may her creditors who 'stand in her shoes.'[382]

The UTC, on the other hand, does not allow creditors to compel a trustee to make a discretionary distribution even if the trustee "has abused the discretion." The beneficiary can get judicial relief in such cases, but not creditors of the beneficiary, unless the claim is for support by a child, spouse,

---

376 In re Johannes Trust, 479 N.W.2d 25, 28 (Mich.App.1991). Compare the question whether a trust disqualifies a beneficiary from receiving Medicaid benefits. *See* Section 10.7.

377 United States v. O'Shaugnessy, 517 N.W.2d 574, 578 (Minn.1994). *See also* Landmark First Nat'l Bank of Fort Lauderdale v. Haves, 467 So.2d 839 (Fla.App.1985).

378 Wilcox v. Gentry, 867 P.2d 281 (Kan.1994); Cal.Prob.Code § 15303(b); *Restatement (Third) of Trusts* § 60, cmt. c (2003).

379 *Restatement (Second) of Trusts* §§ 154, 155, 157 (1959).

380 Smith v. Smith, 517 N.W.2d 394 (Neb.1994); State ex rel. Secretary of SRS v. Jackson, 822 P.2d 1033 (Kan.1991). *See generally* Abravanel, *Discretionary Support Trusts*, 68 Iowa L. Rev. 273 (1983).

381 *Restatement (Third) of Trusts* § 60, cmt. e (2001).

382 Goforth v. Gee, 975 S.W.2d 448, 450 (Ky.1998). As to judicial review of discretionary decisions by trustees, *see* Section 10.7, note 269 et seq.

or former spouse of the beneficiary, in which case the court may direct the trustee to distribute "such amount as is equitable under the circumstances."[383]

In any event, courts are unlikely to find that a trustee has abused discretion when the issue is raised by a beneficiary's creditors, particularly if the discretion is not controlled by a standard like support. Courts tend to defer to the trustee's decisions in any event, and even under the Third Restatement "a trustee's refusal to make distributions might not constitute an abuse against . . . a creditor even when . . . a decision to refuse distributions to the beneficiary might have constituted an abuse."[384]

The Restatement gives creditors more rights when the beneficiary by the terms of the trust has authority, as trustee or otherwise, "to determine his or her own benefits" even if this authority is restricted by a standard. In this situation the beneficiary's creditors, like the creditors of the settlor, can reach "the maximum amount" that the beneficiary can properly take.[385] Case support for this rule is thin;[386] some courts hold that a beneficiary's power is not reachable by creditors if the beneficiary does not choose to exercise it.[387] The UTC insulates a trustee-beneficiary from creditor claims in such circumstances if the trustee-beneficiary's discretion is limited by an ascertainable standard relating to health, education, support, or maintenance.[388] This provision was included to protect standard marital deduction planning in situations where the spouse is named trustee.[389]

Spendthrift Provisions

Spendthrift provisions, when effective, prohibit a beneficiary from assigning the beneficiary's interest and preclude an attachment of the interest by the beneficiary's creditor. The UTC clarifies that to be valid, a spendthrift provision must restrain both voluntary (action by beneficiary) and involuntary (action by creditor) transfer.[390] A spendthrift provision provides only limited protection to the beneficiary. The creditor may pounce upon the trust funds as soon as distribution is made. But even funds retained in trust are not always protected. Numerous exceptions to spendthrift protection are recognized,

---

[383] UTC § 504(c)(2). For a discussion of the provisions of the UTC relating to creditor claims against discretionary interests, *see* Newman, *Spendthrift and Discretionary Trusts: Alive and Well Under the Uniform Trust Code*, 40 Real Prop. Prob. & Tr. J. 567 (2005).

[384] *Restatement (Third) of Trusts* § 60, cmt. e (2001).

[385] *Restatement (Third) of Trusts* § 60, cmt. g (2001). The rule does not apply if the power is held jointly by the beneficiary and another.

[386] *Compare* Morrison v. Doyle, 582 N.W.2d 237 (Minn.1998) (beneficiary's powers do not allow his creditors to reach his interest) with In re Baldwin, 142 B.R. 210 (Bkrtcy.S.D.Ohio 1992) (spendthrift provision ineffective when beneficiary had power to replace the trustee and control investments).

[387] University National Bank v. Rhoadarmer, 827 P.2d 561 (Colo.App.1991).

[388] UTC §§ 103(2), 504(e); In re Skubitz, 2014 WL 222103 (Bankr. D. Kan, Jan. 21, 2014) (trust had ascertainable standard and trustee-beneficiary's interest was protected from claims); Diamond v. Trawick, 497 B.R. 572 (Bankr. C.D. Ca. 2013) (trust did not have ascertainable standard and trustee-beneficiary's interest was therefore subject to claims).

[389] UTC § 504, cmt.

[390] UTC § 502(a); Atkins v. Marks, 288 S.W.3d 356 (Tenn. Ct. App. 2008) (spendthrift provision invalid because it restrains only involuntary and not voluntary transfer).

depending on the type of creditor, the category of beneficiary, or the time when the claim was made.[391]

A spendthrift provision, despite the name, rarely contains the word "spendthrift." A typical provision says:

> Every beneficiary hereof is hereby restrained from anticipating, assigning, selling or otherwise disposing of his or her interest in the Trust, and none of the interests of the beneficiaries hereunder shall be subject to the claims of creditors or other persons.[392]

Under the UTC, a settlor can avoid such a lengthy statement by saying simply, "this is a spendthrift trust."[393] Furthermore, an intent to impose a spendthrift restriction can be inferred; it need not be stated expressly.[394]

Some state statutes make all trusts spendthrift. Washington exempts from execution "property held in trust for a judgment debtor" unless the debtor created the trust.[395] In most states, however, if the trust instrument does not contain a spendthrift provision, beneficiaries' interests that are not dependent on the trustee's discretion are subject to claims of the beneficiaries' creditors.[396]

England does not give effect to spendthrift provisions,[397] but almost all American states do give them effect.[398] In states that recognize them, spendthrift provisions keep the beneficiary's interest out of the reach of creditors in bankruptcy.[399]

Debate has raged over spendthrift trusts ever since they first appeared over a century ago. One commonly used argument for their validity focuses on the settlor's intent:

> A property owner should have the right to dispose of her property as she chooses. . . . A beneficiary owns no greater interest in the trust property than the settlor has given him. In the case of a spendthrift trust, the settlor has not given the beneficiary an alienable interest.[400]

The premise of this reasoning is questionable, because the right of property owners to dispose of property is limited by "public policy," which has traditionally curtailed the ability of transferors to restrict alienation.[401] Another rationale for spendthrift trusts compares them to laws exempting a

---

[391] English, *The Uniform Trust Code: Significant Provisions and Policy Issues*, 67 Mo. L. Rev. 143, 180 (2002)

[392] Council v. Owens, 770 S.W.2d 193, 194–95 (Ark.App.1989).

[393] UTC § 502(b); Diamond v. Trawick, 497 B.R. 572 (Bankr. C.D. Ca. 2013) (rule of construction applied).

[394] *Restatement (Third) of Trusts* § 58, cmt. b (2003).

[395] Rev.Code Wash. § 6.32.250.

[396] Henderson v. Collins, 267 S.E.2d 202 (Ga.1980); Chandler v. Hale, 377 A.2d 318 (Conn.1977); *Restatement (Third) of Trusts* § 56 (2003).

[397] Brandon v. Robinson, 34 Eng.Rep. 379 (1811).

[398] *Restatement (Third) of Trusts* § 58 (2003).

[399] Matter of Shurley, 115 F.3d 333 (5th Cir.1997); 11 U.S.C. § 541(c)(2).

[400] Scott v. Bank One Trust Co., 577 N.E.2d 1077, 1082, 1084 (Ohio 1991).

[401] Emanuel, *Spendthrift Trusts: It's Time to Codify the Compromise*, 72 Neb.L.Rev. 179, 192–94 (1993). As to the validity of restraints on alienation generally, *see* Section 12.8.

portion of a debtor's property from execution.[402] This analogy has been challenged on the ground that exemption laws "apply equally to all members of society" whereas spendthrift trusts are a privilege of the few who have relatives with enough property to create trusts. Also, exemption laws only keep debtors "from absolute poverty" and allow creditors to reach the balance of their property, whereas spendthrift trusts "permit the children of rich men to live in debt and luxury at the same time."[403]

A New York statute which has been copied in several states attempts to meet this objection by allowing creditors to reach trust income in excess of the amount necessary for the beneficiary's support.[404] This statute has been construed to exempt large amounts of income from execution on the ground that they were necessary to support the beneficiary's "station-in-life."[405] In revising the Bankruptcy Code in 1978 Congress considered, but ultimately rejected, a provision that would have made spendthrift trusts valid in bankruptcy only to the extent necessary for the debtor's support.[406]

Spendthrift trusts have also been justified by analogy to the protection that the law confers on minors and incapacitated adults. A spendthrift provision allows a settlor to secure "the object of his affection . . . from . . . his own improvidence, or incapacity for self-protection."[407] But spendthrift provisions are inserted in many trusts without regard to the beneficiaries' actual capacity for self-protection, and often apply to persons whom the settlor never knew.[408] It is often said that creditors have no reason to complain about spendthrift provisions because they can have notice of them. This argument has been challenged on the ground that inter-vivos trusts of personal property are not matters of public record.[409] The paucity of legislation restricting spendthrift trusts suggests that creditors, who are not slow to seek favorable legislation on other issues, do not regard spendthrift protection as a serious problem.

After income or principal from a spendthrift trust has actually been distributed to a beneficiary it becomes subject to creditors' claims.[410] Even if no distribution has yet taken place, but the beneficiary has the right to demand it—for example, she has reached the age specified in the trust instrument for distribution, the beneficiary's creditors can reach it despite the spendthrift provision.[411] But to protect a trust from an immediate attachment as soon as a payment becomes due, whether the payment is periodic or upon termination of

[402] Nichols v. Eaton, 91 U.S. 716, 726 (1875). *See* Section 8.4, note 159 et seq.

[403] Bushman, *The (In)Validity of Spendthrift Trusts*, 47 Ore.L.Rev. 304, 312 (1968).

[404] N.Y.EPTL § 7–3.4. *See also* Cal.Prob.Code § 15307.

[405] Griswold, *Spendthrift Trusts* §§ 378, 379 (1936); Powell, *The Rule Against Perpetuities and Spendthrift Trusts in New York*, 71 Colum.L.Rev. 688, 699 (1971).

[406] Matter of Goff, 706 F.2d 574, 582 (5th Cir.1983).

[407] Nichols v. Eaton, 91 U.S. 716, at 727 (1875).

[408] Hirsch, *Spendthrift Trusts and Public Policy: Economic and Cognitive Perspectives*, 73 Wash. U.L. Q. 1, 44 (1995).

[409] Bushman, *(In)Validity of Spendthrift Trusts*, 47 Ore.L.Rev. at 315; Wicker, *Spendthrift Trusts*, 10 Gonz.L.Rev. 1, 3 (1974); Emanuel, *Spendthrift Trusts: It's Time to Codify the Compromise*, 72 Neb.L.Rev. at 192–94.

[410] *Restatement (Third) of Trusts* § 58, cmt. d (2003).

[411] Brent v. State Cent. Collection Unit, 537 A.2d 227 (Md.1988).

the trust, the UTC provides that spendthrift protection is lost only after the trustee has had a reasonable time in which to make the distribution.[412] In California, however, creditors may request that the trustee make payments directly to the creditor once the amount to be distributed to the beneficiary has been determined.[413]

Although the money in a spendthrift trust will eventually become subject to claims against the beneficiary, it may be hard for creditors to collect money after it reaches the beneficiary's hands, particularly if the beneficiary is really a spendthrift. Creditors can reach the money after it is distributed "assuming they can find it, for in practice what may follow is a game of hide and seek."[414]

Protective Trusts

Perhaps creditor groups have not vigorously opposed spendthrift trusts because the alternative is no better for them. Jurisdictions that do not allow spendthrift trusts permit "protective" trusts that provide that if a creditor seeks to reach a beneficiary's interest it is forfeited, or it becomes discretionary with the trustee whether to pay the beneficiary.[415] Opponents of spendthrift trusts object that they allow debtors not to pay creditors and still retain their property. This is not true of protective trusts, but the distinction makes little practical difference to creditors.

Exception Creditors

Some claims override spendthrift provisions. Creditors who supply necessaries to a beneficiary can reach the beneficiary's interest despite a spendthrift clause.[416] Both the settlor and society have an interest in having beneficiaries provided with necessaries, and this might not happen if those who furnished them could not collect from the trust. The UTC rejects the "necessaries" exception on the basis that nearly all cases involve claims by governmental entities for providing care, the reimbursement for which the UTC drafters concluded was a topic best addressed by separate legislation.[417]

Many states create an exception for persons who have rendered services to protect the beneficiary's interest in the trust.[418] An attorney who represented a beneficiary in a suit to surcharge the trustee could reach the beneficiary's interest to collect his fee despite a spendthrift provision.[419]

---

[412] UTC § 506; In re Hilgers, 371 B.R. 465 (B.A.P. 10th Cir. 2007), aff'd, 279 Fed. Appr. 662 (10th Cir. 2008) (applying provision to terminated trust).

[413] Blech v. Blech, 38 Cal App. 5th 941 (2019) (interpreting Cal.Prob.Code § 15301(b)).

[414] Hirsch, *Spendthrift Trusts and Public Policy: Economic and Cognitive Perspectives*, 73 Wash. U.L. Q. at 2.

[415] *Restatement (Third) of Trusts* § 57 (2003). As to the distinction between "forfeiture" and "disabling" restraints, *see* Section 12.8, note 305 et seq.

[416] *Restatement (Third) of Trusts* § 59(b) (2003).

[417] UTC § 503, cmt. For a discussion of the provisions of the UTC relating to spendthrift protection, *see* Newman, *Spendthrift and Discretionary Trusts: Alive and Well Under the Uniform Trust Code*, 40 Real Prop. Prob. & Tr. J. 567, 569–82 (2005).

[418] UTC § 503(b)(2); *Restatement (Third) of Trusts* § 59(b) (2003).

[419] Schreiber v. Kellogg, 50 F.3d 264 (3d Cir.1995); Evans & Luptak v. Obolensky, 487 N.W.2d 521 (Mich.App.1992)

The UTC[420] and Restatement,[421] as well as many cases and state statutes, allow claims for alimony and child support to be asserted against spendthrift trusts.[422] The exception is sometimes predicated on the settlor's probable intent,[423] but this is questionable at least as to alimony, the recipient of which is not related to the settlor. The Restatement bases the exception "on policy considerations;" the settlor's intent "is neither the rationale nor the limit of this exception."[424] Some say that a spouse and children "are in quite a different position from ordinary creditors who have voluntary extended credit." Furthermore, "unless the interest of the beneficiary can be reached, the state may be called upon for their support."[425] The *beneficiary* may also become dependent on state support if the spendthrift trust is dissipated. Perhaps for this reason, support claims can be satisfied from a spendthrift trust only after taking account of "the beneficiary's actual need for some part of the distributions."[426] The Florida District Court of Appeals, however, held that the state's policy in encouraging the use of trusts for individuals with special needs did not prevent a child support claimant from reaching the trust.[427]

A somewhat related issue is to extent to which a beneficiary's interest in a trust can be considered in dividing the beneficiary's property in the event of a divorce. A decision of the Massachusetts Court of Appeals that a beneficiary's interest in a discretionary trust was divisible as marital property was later reversed by the Massachusetts Supreme Court, which concluded that the beneficiary's interest was not "fixed and enforceable."[428] The question whether tort claims should be subject to a spendthrift provision has been discussed in the literature, but there is little case law. In a case in which the beneficiary of a spendthrift trust had seriously injured a man by drunken driving, the court held that the spendthrift provision did not immunize his interest. It cited a tort victim's lack of opportunity to investigate the tortfeasor's credit, and the policy reflected in the federal Bankruptcy Act, which denies discharges for claims "based on 'willful and malicious' injuries."[429] The Restatement approves the result in this case, but the Reporter's Note comments that the case was overturned by later legislation.[430] A recurring problem in interpreting statutes is whether references to *some* situations where spendthrift provisions are not recognized precludes courts from creating other exceptions. The exceptions listed in the Restatement for spendthrift trusts, on the other hand, are

---

[420] UTC § 503(b)(1).

[421] *Restatement (Third) of Trusts* § 59(a) (2003).

[422] Ex parte Boykin, 656 So.2d 821 (Ala.Civ.App.1994) (child support but not alimony in gross); Council v. Owens, 770 S.W.2d 193 (Ark.App.1989) (alimony); Cal.Prob.Code § 15305.

[423] Howard v. Spragins, 350 So.2d 318, 322 (Ala.1977); Hurley v. Hurley, 309 N.W.2d 225, 228 (Mich.App.1981).

[424] *Restatement (Third) of Trusts*, 59, cmt. b (2003).

[425] Council v. Owens, 770 S.W.2d 193, 197 (Ark.App.1989).

[426] *Restatement (Third) of Trusts* § 59, cmt. b (2003).

[427] Alexander v. Harris, 278 So. 3d 721 (Fla. Dist. Ct. App. 2019).

[428] Pfannenstiehl v. Pfannenstiehl, 37 N.E. 3d 15 (Mass. Ct. App. 2015), *rev'd*, 55 N.E. 3d 933 (Mass. 2019).

[429] Sligh v. First Nat'l Bank of Holmes County, 704 So.2d 1020, 1028 (Miss.1997). Ga.Code Ann. § 53–12–28(c) exempts "tort judgments" generally from the bar of a spendthrift provision.

[430] *Restatement (Third) of Trusts* § 59 Reporter's Note (2003), citing Miss.Code § 91–5–903. The UTC also declines to create an exception for tort claimants. *See* UTC § 503, cmt.

expressly stated to be "not exclusive," because "special circumstances or evolving policy may justify recognition of others."[431]

Liens for unpaid federal taxes are held generally to override a spendthrift or protective provision.[432] Both the UTC and the Restatement refers generally to "governmental claimants . . . to the extent provided by federal law or an applicable state statute."[433]

Voluntary Transfers

Absent a spendthrift provision, interests in trusts are normally transferable by the beneficiaries. Spendthrift provisions typically bar transfers by the beneficiary as well as claims by the beneficiary's creditors. According to the Restatement, "for reasons of policy, a spendthrift restraint that seeks only to prevent creditors from reaching the beneficiary's interests, while allowing the beneficiary to transfer the interest, is invalid,"[434] but there is case law to the contrary.[435] Even the Restatement allows beneficiaries of spendthrift trusts to *disclaim* or *release* their interest[436] on the theory that because the disposition of the released interest is "supplied by the settlor, . . . not by the renouncing beneficiary," releases do not "involve the type of risks that concern a settlor."[437]

If a beneficiary purports to assign an unassignable interest, the assignment can be revoked, but a trustee who has been paying to the assignee is protected from liability for having made such prior payments.[438]

Planning

Many lawyers routinely insert spendthrift provisions in all trusts.[439] This is a questionable practice because many beneficiaries may prove to be responsible, and the ability to transfer their trust interest gives them additional financial flexibility. On the other hand, a spendthrift clause can serve to prevent improvident transfers and the unwise use of credit. It is difficult to resolve these competing considerations, because settlors of long-

---

431 *Restatement (Third) of Trusts* § 59, cmt. a(2) (2003).

432 United States v. Grimm, 865 F.Supp. 1303 (N.D.Ind.1994); Bank One Ohio Trust Co., N.A. v. United States, 80 F.3d 173 (6th Cir.1996). In Kraft v. Commissioner, 142 T.C. 259 (2014), the Service did not need to rely on federal preemption in order to reach the trust. Because the trustee of the settlor's trust had discretion to distribute all of the trust property to the settlor, the Service was able to reach the trust under UTC § 505(a)(2), the same as an ordinary creditor.

433 UTC § 503(a)(3); *Restatement (Third) of Trusts* § 59, cmt. a(1) (2003). *See also* Cal.Prob.Code § 15306(a) (reimbursement of the state or local public entity for support furnished the beneficiary); Ga.Code Ann. § 53–12–80(d)(2) ("governmental claims").

434 *Restatement (Third) of Trusts* § 58, cmt. b (2003). The UTC has a similar provision. UTC § 502(a).

435 Bank of New England v. Strandlund, 529 N.E.2d 394 (Mass.1988).

436 *Restatement (Third) of Trusts* § 58, cmt. c (2003). As to disclaimers, *see* UPC § 2–1105; Cal.Prob.Code § 286.

437 An attempt by a beneficiary to transfer his interest to another can not qualify as a renunciation. Lundgren v. Hoglund, 711 P.2d 809, 814 (Mont.1985).

438 *Restatement (Third) of Trusts* § 58, cmt. d(1) (2003); Matter of Will of Link, 462 N.Y.S.2d 582 (Sur.1983).

439 Farr & Wright, *An Estate Planner's Handbook* 451 (4th ed. 1979); Hirsch, *Spendthrift Trusts and Public Policy: Economic and Cognitive Perspectives*, 73 Wash. U.L. Q. at 3.

term trusts cannot know whether the beneficiaries, who are often young children or even unborn, will turn out to be spendthrifts.

A discretionary trust may better achieve the settlor's goals than a fixed income spendthrift trust. Discretionary trusts may be more effective against claims like alimony which prevail over a spendthrift provision. They also avoid the problem of an unassignable mandatory income interest held by a beneficiary in a high tax bracket, because the trustee of a discretionary trust can take account of tax consequences in deciding how to distribute income.

Pensions

Of particular importance, in view of the vast number of persons entitled to pension benefits, is the federal Employee Retirement Income Security Act of 1974 (ERISA), which covers nearly all pension plans and requires that benefits under the plan must be unassignable.[440] The limitations on spendthrift trusts as to claims for alimony and child support have counterparts with respect to pensions; for example, ERISA allows spouses to garnish pension benefits in order to collect a maintenance obligation.[441] Similar to private trusts, the protection against creditors does not extend to pension money after it is distributed to the beneficiary.[442] Unlike private trusts, however, the ineffectiveness of spendthrift provisions in self-settled trusts is not matched by a like restriction on pension plans to which an employee has contributed or to which an employer has contributed on an employee's behalf.

§ 10.9 Modification and Termination of Trusts

Numerous reasons exist why it might be appropriate to modify a trust or to terminate a trust earlier than as provided in the trusts' terms. Perhaps the trust was inappropriate because the drafter had incomplete or inaccurate information, or a mistake was made in the drafting. Circumstances can also change. Children may grow up more financially independent than expected or the opposite may occur. The beneficiaries might develop drug or alcohol problems or mental health issues or suffer an incapacitating injury. The law might change, such as changes in the tax law or changes in the rules on Medicaid eligibility. Families also change. Divorce, remarriage, and blended families may suggest than a change in the estate plan might be appropriate.[443]

The need to modify a trust can be reduced if flexibility is built into the trusts' terms.[444] The trustee can be given discretion concerning distributions to beneficiaries,[445] beneficiaries can be given powers of appointment to change the trust terms,[446] the trust can be designed to give a trust protector the ability

---

[440] 29 U.S.C. § 1056(d).

[441] 29 U.S.C. § 1056(d)(3).

[442] Brosamer v. Mark, 561 N.E.2d 767 (Ind.1990).

[443] Barnes, *Repairing Broken Trusts and Other Fallen Estate Plans*, Est Plan., Nov. 2014, at 3.

[444] Fox, *How "Revocable" is "Irrevocable"? Obtaining Flexibility in Irrevocable Trusts*, 33 Ohio Northern.U.L. Rev. 943 (2007).

[445] Discussed in Section 10.7.

[446] Discussed in Section 11.5.

to modify the trust,[447] and, in many states and perhaps at common law, a trustee may be able to decant the trust to a new trust with different terms.[448]

This Section begins with a discussion of the various grounds for judicial modification and termination followed by a discussion of the ability of the beneficiaries to modify or terminate a trust and a few miscellaneous topics. When representing a client seeking a modification or termination, all grounds should be considered. Frequently, a trust may arguably be terminated or modified under more than one ground. Most trusts, of course, terminate as provided in the terms of the trust or, in the case of a revocable trust, upon the settlor's decision to revoke.

Achievement or Failure of Purpose

To create a trust the trust must have a purpose that is lawful, not contrary to public policy, and possible to achieve.[449] The flip side of this is also relevant. An otherwise valid trust terminates or is subject to modification if its purpose becomes unlawful or contrary to public policy or its purpose has been achieved.[450]

Unanticipated Circumstances

Most trusts are set up to last for a considerable period after the settlor has died; they extend "the dead hand [of the settlor] into the future where needs and circumstances cannot be predicted."[451] To some extent the rigidity of the "dead hand" can be alleviated by giving trustees wide discretion or by giving powers of appointment.[452] Nevertheless, circumstances may change after a trust is created, and the trust terms may not reflect what the settlor would have wanted under the new circumstances. Courts have power to allow deviations from the terms of a charitable trust under the *cy pres* doctrine,[453] but they have been more hesitant to allow deviations from the terms of a private trust, particularly dispositive provisions. For example, a trust created in 1935 provided annuities for designated individuals. Over the years inflation sharply reduced the value of the annuities, and a beneficiary sought a court order to have hers increased from $5,000 to $14,034 to reflect changes in the Consumer Price Index. The charitable remaindermen refused to consent, and the court said that it was "without power to modify the trust . . . in the absence of the agreement of all the parties in interest" even though it was "difficult to conceive . . . any rational argument that such an adjustment would be contrary to the wishes of the testatrix."[454] Another court refused to allow a trustee to

---

[447] Trust Protectors are discussed in 14.4.

[448] Discussed *infra* notes 550 et seq.

[449] Discussed in 10.3.

[450] UTC § 410(a). *See, e.g.,* Guardianship & Conservatorship of Novotny, 904 N.W.2d 346 (S.D. 2017) (trust created to hold share of missing beneficiary of terminated trust could itself be terminated when beneficiary was found).

[451] Haskell, *Justifying the Principle of Distributive Deviation in the Law of Trusts,* 18 Hast.L.J. 267, 291 (1967). An important limitation on the dead hand is the Rule Against Perpetuities, which is discussed in Chapter 12.

[452] Discussed in Section 11.5.

[453] *See* Section 10.10, note 637 et seq.

[454] New England Merchants Nat'l Bank v. Kann, 294 N.E.2d 390, 392–93 (Mass.1973). *See also* Shire v. Unknown/Undiscovered Heirs, 907 N.W. 2d 263 (Neb. 2018), where a request to

accumulate trust income which exceeded the needs of an income beneficiary who had become incompetent, so that a guardian had to be appointed to receive the excess income.[455] "When the intention of a settlor is plainly expressed . . . the Court will not go outside the instrument in an attempt to give effect to what it conceives to have been the actual intent or motive of the settlor."[456]

The results in the above cases are not surprising. Traditionally, a court could modify the administrative but not dispositive terms of a trust. Both the UTC[457] and Restatement Third[458] eliminate this restriction and allow a court to modify both the administrative *and* dispositive terms of a trust. Before ordering a modification or termination, however, the court must not only find that there are circumstances not anticipated by the settlor but also that modification or termination will further the purposes of the trust. To the extent practicable, the modification must be made in accordance with the settlor's probable intention.[459] Examples where modification of dispositive provisions might be appropriate include failure to anticipate economic change like inflation or the incapacity of a beneficiary,[460] the very situations above where modification was denied under the more restrictive approach.[461] Or modification of the dispositive provisions to increase support of a beneficiary might be appropriate if the beneficiary has become unable to provide for support due to poor health or serious injury.[462] Under the UTC provision, the a court has approved a partial termination in favor of a charitable remainder beneficiary when the size of the trust had grown from $120,000 to $3,000,000, well more than needed to fund a fixed annuity to the life beneficiary.[463] Also, a court approved modification of a trust that severely restricted a child's beneficial interest because of the settlor's mistaken belief that a more generous provision would have jeopardized the child's eligibility for Social Security benefits.[464] Under the UTC, if the unanticipated circumstances lead to the termination of the trust, the trustee must distribute the property in a manner consistent with the purposes of the trust.[465] Typically, such terminating distributions will be made to the beneficiaries in proportion to the actuarial value of their interests, although the UTC does not so prescribe.[466]

---

increase a life annuitant's payment of $500 per month was denied when the consent of the unknown and undiscovered heirs could not be obtained.

[455] As to the problem of distributions by a fiduciary to an incompetent, *see* Section 14.3, note 251 et seq.

[456] Taylor v. Hutchinson, 497 P.2d 527, 530 (Ariz. App.1972). *See also* Appeal of Harrell, 801 P.2d 852 (Or.App.1990) (refusal to extend duration of trust for developmentally disabled adult).

[457] UTC § 412(a). For discussion of the UTC provisions, *see* Chester, *Modification and Termination of Trusts in the 21st Century: The Trust Code Leads a Quiet Revolution*, 35 Real Prop. Prob. & Tr. J. 697 (2001).

[458] *Restatement (Third) of Trusts* § 66(1) (2003).

[459] UTC § 412(a).

[460] *Restatement (Third) of Trusts* § 66, cmt. b (2003).

[461] See *supra* notes 434–436.

[462] *Restatement (Third) of Trusts* § 66, cmt. b (2003).

[463] In re Estate of Somers, 89 P.3d 898 (Kan. 2004).

[464] In re Revocable Trust of Moeder, 2012 WL 5328124 (Ind. Ct. App., Oct. 30, 2012).

[465] UTC § 412(c).

[466] UTC § 412, cmt.

A particularly useful application of the unanticipated circumstances doctrine is the modification into a special needs trust of a trust that would otherwise be distributed to the beneficiary and thereby terminate the beneficiary's eligibility for governmental assistance. By modifying and extending the trust, the beneficiary may qualify for governmental benefits because the special needs trust will not be treated as a countable asset.[467] The courts are divided on whether the unanticipated circumstances doctrine can be used for this purpose.[468]

Certain state statutes predating the UTC also permitted selected modification of dispositive terms. The best known is in New York, which allows courts to "make an allowance from principal to any income beneficiary whose support or education is not sufficiently provided for" if this would "effectuate the intention" of the settlor.[469]

Because many trusts are created to save or avoid estate taxes, and the future of the estate tax is uncertain, it has been suggested that the trustee (or perhaps another) should be authorized to terminate trusts if the purpose for which they were created has become irrelevant.[470]

The reluctance of the courts to modify dispositive terms does not apply to administrative terms. Courts have long modified administrative terms, when, owing to circumstances not anticipated by the settlor, compliance with the trust's terms "would defeat or substantially impair the accomplishment of the purposes of the trust."[471] The UTC goes even further, allowing the court to modify any administrative term whenever continuation of the trust on its existing terms would be impracticable, wasteful, or impair the trust's administration.[472] Unlike the case with dispositive provisions, modification of an administrative term may be ordered whether or not there are circumstances not anticipated by the settlor.

There are numerous case examples authorizing such *administrative deviation*. Some trusts prohibit sale of the trust assets or of a particular asset by the trustee. Although such a restriction is valid, courts may overrule it when the circumstances change. For example, a will left a farm in trust and authorized the trustees to lease the land but not to sell it. Years later new highways turned the land into highly desirable commercial property. A buyer offered $473,960 for the land which was producing an income from farming of only $3,000 a year. The court authorized a sale, because under the changed circumstances "no landowner . . . in his right mind would continue to use this

---

[467] For a discussion of special needs trust, *see* Section 10.7.

[468] *Compare* In re Riddell, 157 P. 3d 888 (Wash. Ct. App. 2007) (trust extended beyond age 35 on account of beneficiary's unanticipated mental illness), *with* In re Ruby G. Owen Trust, 418 S.W. 3d 421 (Ark. Ct. App. 2012) (trust for beneficiary with unanticipated mental illness not extended).

[469] N.Y.EPTL § 7–1.6(b).

[470] Grassi, *Drafting Flexibility Into Trusts Helps Cope With Uncertainty*, 29 Est. Plan. 347 (2002).

[471] *Restatement (Second) of Trusts* § 167 (1959); *Restatement (Third) of Trusts* § 66 (2003).

[472] UTC § 412(b). The standard under Section 412(b) is similar to the standard for applying *cy pres* to a charitable trust. *See* UTC § 413(a), discussed in Section 10.10. Subsection (b), unlike subsection (a), does not have a direct precedent in the common law.

land for agricultural purposes."[473] Similarly, a restriction against sale of certain real estate in an 1815 charitable trust was lifted when it was determined that because the city had undergone drastic changes since the trust was founded the land was no longer appropriate for educational purposes.[474]

Courts may also remove restrictions on trust investments if circumstances change after the trust was created. Professor Langbein predicts that new trends in trust investment law[475] "will result in less deference to the wishes of the trust settlor [who] . . . attempts to impose a manifestly stupid investment restriction on the trust," even in cases in which there has been no unanticipated change of circumstances, based on the idea that the terms of "a private trust must be for the benefit of the beneficiaries."[476] However, the Uniform Prudent Investor Act restates the traditional view that the permissible investments may be restricted by the provisions of a trust.[477]

Uneconomic Trusts

When a professional trustee is used, the costs of a trust can outweigh the advantages when only a small amount is left in the trust. The UTC and numerous state statutes allow premature termination of trusts whose continued operation has become uneconomical. Under the UTC, a court "may modify or terminate a trust or remove and appoint a different trustee if it determines that the value of the trust property is insufficient to justify the cost of administration."[478] The UTC and many state statutes also authorize a trustee, following notice to the beneficiaries, to terminate a trust without prior court approval if its value is below $50,000.[479] If termination is necessary, the assets are to be distributed in a manner consistent with the purposes of the trust.[480] The same objectives can be achieved by an appropriate provision in the trust authorizing termination if the trustee concludes that administration is uneconomic or the value of the trust falls below a specified figure.[481]

Division/Consolidation

Another type of modification which does not alter the shares of the beneficiaries is the consolidation of separate trusts or the division of a trust into separate trusts. The UTC and numerous state statutes authorize such consolidation or division. Under the UTC, the trustee, following notice to the beneficiaries, may combine two or more trusts into a single trust or divide a

---

473 Ex parte Guaranty Bank & Trust Co., 177 S.E.2d 358, 360 (S.C.1970).

474 City of Augusta v. Attorney General, 943 A.2d 582 (Me. 2008) (applying UTC provision).

475 Discussed in Section 14.2.

476 Langbein, *The Uniform Prudent Investor Act and the Future of Trust Investing*, 81 Iowa L.Rev. 641, 663 (1996). *See also Restatement (Third) of Trusts* § 27(2) (2003); UTC § 404.

477 Unif. Prudent Investor Act § 1(b).

478 UTC § 414(b). In In re Estate of Brown, 87 Va. Cir. 353 (2013), the court, applying this provision, denied a requested elimination of a requirement that the trust always have an institutional trustee because the trust document made clear that the settlor intended that the trust always have an institutional trustee.

479 UTC § 414(a). Many states enacting the UTC have increased this limit. *See, e.g.*, Mo. Rev. Stat. § 456.4–414 ($100,000).

480 UTC § 414(c).

481 Price & Donaldson, *Contemporary Estate Planning* § 4.24.6 (2014 ed.).

trust into two or more separate trusts, if the result does not impair rights of any beneficiary or adversely affect achievement of the purposes of the trust.[482]

Division of trusts may achieve significant tax advantages, facilitate making appropriate investments, and allow the trustee to make distributions to one beneficiary without affecting the shares of the others.[483] Consolidation on the other hand may reduce trustee fees where the trustee charges a minimum fee for each trust. These advantages have persuaded courts to allow division and consolidation even without statutory authorization.[484]

Reformation[485]

Judicial reformation of inter-vivos instruments to correct for a mistake of law or fact is a long-established remedy. Reformation is available under the UTC[486] and Restatement (Third) of Property[487] whether the mistake is one of expression or one of inducement. A mistake of expression occurs when the terms of the trust misstate the settlor's intention, fail to include a term that was intended to be included, or include a term that was intended to be excluded. A mistake in the inducement occurs when the terms of the trust accurately reflect what the settlor intended to be included or excluded but this intention was based on a mistake of fact or law.[488] Mistakes of expression are frequently caused by scriveners' errors while mistakes of inducement often trace to errors of the settlor.

Reformation is different from resolving an ambiguity. Resolving an ambiguity involves the interpretation of language already in the instrument. Reformation, on the other hand, may involve the addition of language not originally in the instrument, or the deletion of language originally included by mistake if the addition or deletion is necessary to conform the instrument to the settlor's intent. Because reformation may involve the addition of language to the instrument, or the deletion of language that may appear clear on its face, reliance on extrinsic evidence is essential. To guard against the possibility of unreliable or contrived evidence in such circumstance, the UTC and Restatement require the higher standard of clear and convincing proof before allowing a reformation.[489]

Under the UTC and Restatement, the court, in determining the settlor's original intent, may consider evidence relevant to the settlor's intention even though it contradicts an apparent plain meaning of the text. The objective of

---

[482] UTC § 417. For an application, *see* Keybank, N.A. v. Thalman, 2016 WL 2587143 (Ohio Ct. App., May 5, 2018).

[483] Fleet National Bank v. Marquis, 771 N.E.2d 133 (Mass.2002) (trust split in order to minimize GST—*see* Section 15.5).

[484] Matter of Estate of Branigan, 609 A.2d 431 (N.J.1992); Matter of Will of Kaskel, 549 N.Y.S.2d 587 (Sur.1989); *Restatement (Third) of Trusts* § 68 Reporter's Note (2003). For further discussion of trust merger and division, *see* Price, *Contemporary Estate Planning* § 4.25.7.

[485] The discussion of reformation is based on English, *The Uniform Trust Code: Significant Provisions and Policy Issues*, 67 Mo. L. Rev. 143, 174–75 (2002).

[486] UTC § 415.

[487] See *Restatement (Third) of Property (Wills and Other Donative Transfers)* § 12.1 (2003).

[488] See *Restatement (Third) of Property (Wills and Other Donative Transfers)* § 12.1, cmt. i.

[489] UTC § 415; *Restatement (Third) of Property (Wills and Other Donative Transfers)* § 12.1, cmt. e (2003).

the plain meaning rule, to protect against fraudulent testimony, is satisfied by the requirement of clear and convincing proof.[490] Consistent with the Restatement[491] but unlike the common law, the UTC extends the doctrine of reformation to testamentary as well as inter-vivos trusts.[492] This extension to the testamentary trust represents a major change in the law. Traditionally, wills cannot be reformed on account of mistake.[493]

The types of reformation cases which have arisen under the UTC include a misunderstanding that a distribution to a beneficiary's "brothers and sisters" could result in distribution of the trust property outside of the settlors' bloodlines,[494] a scrivener error in drafting a joint revocable trust resulting in an extra distribution to a beneficiary,[495] and uncertainty on the face of the trust document whether a grandchild was entitled to take which was resolved in the negative once extrinsic evidence was considered,[496] and reformation of a trust the settlor had drafted herself which failed to dispose of the remainder after the deaths of two life beneficiaries.[497]

Tax Modifications[498]

In another provision derived from the Restatement (Third) of Property,[499] the UTC expands the court's ability to modify a trust to achieve the settlor's tax objectives. The court may modify the trust in any manner not contrary to the settlor's probable intention. The court may also give the modification retroactive effect.[500] This broad authority is appropriate because the settlor's objective—to achieve tax savings of a particular type—is usually abundantly clear. The other grounds for modification or termination, where applicable, can also be used to secure modifications for tax reasons.

Whether a modification made by the court will be recognized under federal tax law is a matter of federal law. Absent specific statutory or regulatory authority recognizing a state court modification, binding recognition for federal tax purposes is normally given only to modifications made prior to the taxing event, for example, the death of the testator or settlor in the case of the federal estate tax.[501] Otherwise, under the *Bosch* case, the state court determination is binding on the IRS only if it is a decision of the state's highest court.[502] Recognizing this, Kansas formerly had a procedure allowing quick access to

---

490 *Restatement (Third) of Property (Wills and Other Donative Transfers)* § 12.1, cmt. d & Reporter's Note. *See also* John H. Langbein & Lawrence W. Waggoner, *Reformation of Wills on the Ground of Mistake: Change of Direction in American Law?*, 130 U. Pa. L. Rev. 521 (1982).

491 *Restatement (Third) of Property (Wills and Other Donative Transfers)* § 12.1 (2003).

492 UTC § 415.

493 *See* Section 7.1.

494 Clairmont v. Larson, 831 N.W.2d 388 (N.D. 2013).

495 Frakes v. Nay, 273 P.3d 137 (Or. Ct. App. 2011).

496 Becker v. Brozek-Robinson, 2012 WL 5519211 (Kan. Ct. App., Nov. 9, 2012).

497 In re Trust of O'Donnell, 815 N.W.2d 640 (Neb. Ct. App. 2012).

498 The discussion of tax modifications is based on English, *The Uniform Trust Code: Significant Provisions and Policy Issues*, 67 Mo. L. Rev.at 175–76.

499 *Restatement (Third) of Property (Wills and Other Donative Transfers)* § 12.2 (2003).

500 UTC § 416.

501 *See* Rev. Rul. 73–142, 1973–1 C.B. 405.

502 Commissioner v. Estate of Bosch, 387 U.S. 456 (1967).

the state's supreme court to secure modification of a trust even though there was no dispute between the trustee and beneficiaries as to the requested relief.[503]

Termination by Beneficiaries

Under traditional doctrine, a trust could also be terminated by unanimous agreement of the beneficiaries acting alone but only if the trust no longer serves a material purpose.[504] Under the UTC and Third Restatement, a trust can be modified or terminated by the beneficiaries acting alone only if the modification or termination is not inconsistent with a material purpose.[505] The UTC provisions are limited to noncharitable irrevocable trusts.[506] The Restatement and common law are not so limited. Under both the UTC and Restatement, partial termination may be allowed even if not all beneficiaries agree.[507] Thus when all the beneficiaries except one annuitant sought to terminate a trust, the court directed the trustee to retain enough funds to pay the annuity and distribute the rest of the trust assets, because it was not "necessary to maintain intact a trust corpus of more than $900,000 to fund" a $12,000 annuity.[508]

Under traditional doctrine, a trust may be modified or terminated by unanimous agreement of the settlor and all beneficiaries.[509] Unlike termination or modification by the beneficiaries acting alone, termination or modification with the concurrence of the settlor does not require a finding that the trust or the provision to be modified no longer serve a material purpose. No finding of failure of material purpose is required because all parties with a possible interest in the trust's continuation, both the settlor and beneficiaries, agree there is no further need for the trust.[510]

The ability of the beneficiaries to modify or terminate a trust does not require consent of the trustee.[511] However, a trustee who concludes that the beneficiaries lack adequate grounds has standing to object to a proposed termination or modification.[512] A settlor who wishes to make sure that a trust will not be terminated prematurely should select a trustee who has enough "backbone" to refuse an improper request by a beneficiary. Under the UTC but

---

[503] Kansas cases decided under UTC § 416 include In re Harris Testamentary Trust, 69 P.3d 1109 (Kan. 2003); and In re Paul F. Suhr Trust, 2010 WL 198467 (Kan., Jan. 15, 2010).

[504] *Restatement (Second) of Trusts* § 337 (1959).

[505] UTC § 411(b); *Restatement (Third) of Trusts* § 65(2) (2003).

[506] UTC § 411(a)–(b).

[507] UTC § 411(e); *Restatement (Third) of Trusts* § 65, cmt. c (2003); *Restatement (Second) of Trusts* §§ 338(2) & 340(2) (1959).

[508] Matter of Boright, 377 N.W.2d 9, 13 (Minn.1985).

[509] *Accord,* UTC § 411(a); *Restatement (Third) of Trusts* § 65(2) (2003); *Restatement (Second) of Trusts* § 338(2) (1959).

[510] Matter of Edwards Irrevocable Trust, 966 P.2d 810 (Okl.Civ.App.1998); Phillips v. Lowe, 639 S.W.2d 782 (Ky.1982); Johnson v. First Nat'l Bank, 386 So.2d 1112 (Miss.1980).

[511] Hein v. Hein, 543 N.W.2d 19, 20 (Mich.App.1995).

[512] UTC § 410(b); American National Bank v. Miller, 899 P.2d 1337 (Wyo.1995).

not common law, the settlor has standing to challenge a proposed beneficiary action.[513] A petition may also be filed by a beneficiary.[514]

Upon termination of a trust by the beneficiaries, whether with or without the settlor's consent, the trust property is to be distributed as the beneficiaries agree.[515]

Material Purpose Doctrine

Even if all the beneficiaries consent, termination is not allowed if continuance of the trust is necessary to carry out a material purpose of the trust[516] or termination would be inconsistent with a material purpose of the trust.[517] This limitation does not exist in England[518] or in a few of the United States,[519] but most American jurisdictions follow the leading case, *Claflin v. Claflin*,[520] which involved a testamentary trust for the settlor's son who was to get the corpus at age 30. The son sought to compel the trustees to give him the trust assets when he was only 24. The court dismissed his suit, even though he was the sole beneficiary, because "the purposes of the trust have not been accomplished."

The dominant idea of *Claflin* is that the settlor's wishes should be followed. If circumstances not contemplated by the settlor arise after the trust was created, courts recognize that the settlor's intent might best be carried out by departing from the terms of the trust. However, in *Claflin,* "nothing [had] happened which the testator did not anticipate," but in another case, where "the testator did not foresee the bountiful accumulations" which the trust was accruing, the court held that early termination would "serve the testator's ultimate objective."[521] Some judges, however, apply the *Claflin* rule rather

---

[513] UTC § 410(b). This is contrary to *Restatement (Second) of Trusts* § 391 (1959), which does not mention and presumably precludes a settlor from bringing an action. Section 410(b) also grants a settlor standing to petition the court under Section 413 to apply *cy pres* to modify the settlor's charitable trust. *See* Section 10.10.

[514] UTC § 410. *See also* Kryder v. Kryder, 2012 WL 1866376 (Ohio Ct. App., May 23, 2012) (although UTC § 410 does not use the word "only," anyone who is not the trustee or a beneficiary lacks standing to bring an action).

[515] UTC § 411(d).

[516] *Restatement (Second) of Trusts* § 337(2) (1959).

[517] UTC § 411(b)(1); *Restatement (Third) of Trusts,* § 65(2) (2003).

[518] Maitland, *Equity* 53 (1913); Goulding v. James, [1997] 2 All E.R. 239 (C.A.).

[519] Mo. Rev. Stat. § 456.4B–411 (termination allowed upon agreement of all adult and competent beneficiaries if the court concludes that the interests of other beneficiaries will be adequately protected; Cal.Prob.Code § 15403(b) (termination allowed where reason for it "outweighs the interest in accomplishing a material purpose of the trust"). For a comparison of the UTC with the virtually identical predecessor to the current Missouri provision, *see* Walker, *Get Your Dead Hands Off Me: Beneficiaries' Rights to Terminate or Modify a Trust Under the Uniform Trust Code,* 67 Mo.L.Rev. 443 (2002).

[520] 20 N.E. 454 (Mass.1889). Prior to Claflin, American courts had followed the English view. Alexander, *The Dead Hand and the Law of Trusts in the Nineteenth Century,* 37 Stan.L.Rev. 1189, 1201 (1985). Even where the Claflin doctrine is accepted, it does not apply after the trust has endured for the period allowed by the Rule Against Perpetuities. *Restatement (Third) of Trusts* § 29, cmt. h(1) (2003); *Restatement (Second) of Trusts* § 62, cmt. *o* (1959).

[521] In re Bayley Trust, 250 A.2d 516 (Vt.1969).

strictly and refuse to "speculate on what the settlor might have done" under changed circumstances.[522]

The result turns on the "purposes of the trust." A trust may have multiple purposes, and, at least in a few states and under the Restatement Third, their relative importance must be weighed; the beneficiaries can compel a modification unless it "would frustrate a material purpose of the trust *and* the reasons for modification are outweighed by such material purpose."[523] Occasionally trust purposes are recited in the trust instrument, for example, a trust "for the education of the children,"[524] but usually they must be inferred from the beneficial interests created by the trust.[525] Extrinsic evidence may also be used.[526] For example, the beneficiaries of a trust were allowed to terminate it when they produced testimony that the settlor had created the trust in order "to keep the money away from [her daughter's] alcoholic husband." Because the husband was now dead "that purpose no longer exists and termination of the trust was proper."[527]

If a trust calls for distribution when a beneficiary reaches a specified age, the settlor's purpose was probably to postpone distribution until the beneficiary was mature enough to handle the money.[528] In a trust, for example, "to A for life, remainder to her children," on the other hand, it is presumed "in the absence of circumstances indicating a further purpose" other than providing for successive enjoyment, the beneficiaries (if they can be ascertained and are *sui juris*) can compel termination.[529] But a trust purpose to provide a lifetime income coupled with a grant of discretion was deemed a material purpose even though the primary purpose of the trust, to provide for the educational needs of a beneficiary's children, had been accomplished.[530] In addition, a spendthrift provision in the trust is often deemed to show a purpose which bars early termination, because this would frustrate "the testator's obvious purpose to protect the [beneficiary] against his own improvidence."[531] But under the UTC, a spendthrift provision, while a factor, is not automatically presumed to constitute a material purpose.[532]

---

[522] Trabits v. First Nat'l Bank, 345 So.2d 1347 (Ala.1977); Frost Nat'l Bank of San Antonio v. Newton, 554 S.W.2d 149 (Tex.1977).

[523] In re Mark K. Eggebrecht Irrevocable Trust, 4 P.3d 1207, 1210 (Mont.2000) (position of trust advisor eliminated). *See also Restatement (Third) of Trusts* § 65 (2003). Cal.Prob.Code § 15403(b).

[524] Appeal of Gannon, 631 A.2d 176, 186 (Pa.Super.1993).

[525] *Restatement (Third) of Trusts* Ch. 6, Int. Note (2003).

[526] *Restatement (Second) of Trusts* § 337, cmt. e (1959).

[527] Matter of Harbaugh's Estate, 646 P.2d 498 (Kan.1982).

[528] *Restatement (Third) of Trusts* § 65, illus. 5 (2003).

[529] *Restatement (Third) of Trusts* § 65, cmt. d. *See* Saunders v. AMG National Trust Bank, 88 Va. Cir. 389 (2014), where the court applies this Restatement provision.

[530] In re Estate of Brown, 528 A.2d 572 (Vt. 1987).

[531] In re Estate of Davis, 297 A.2d 451, 455 (Pa.1972). For a discussion of spendthrift provisions, *see* Section 10.8, note 390 et seq.

[532] UTC § 411(c), although this provision was placed in brackets, recognizing that there are different views on whether this provision is appropriate. Some UTC states have omitted this provision, e.g., Mo. Rev. Stat § 456.4A–411. Other states have flipped the presumption and provide that a spendthrift provision is presumed to be a material purpose, *e.g.*, Ark. Code § 28–73–411(c). In In re Pike Family Trusts, 38 A.3d 329 (Me. 2012), the court, applying UTC § 411(c) as originally

If a purpose of the trust is to protect against a beneficiary's improvidence, can the beneficiary show that the settlor was mistaken about this? According to the Restatement Second, if a trust was created "solely on account of a physical or mental disability of the beneficiary," removal of the disability warrants termination of the trust.[533] Many drafters routinely insert spendthrift provisions without real consideration of the abilities of the beneficiaries, who are often infants or unborn when the trust is drafted. Therefore, to make them a litmus test of trust purposes is unfortunate. The California Probate Code makes a spendthrift provision "a factor" but not conclusive in deciding whether to modify or terminate a trust.[534] Under the UTC, a spendthrift provision is not presumed to constitute a material purpose.[535]

Sometimes trusts are terminated pursuant to settlement agreements of contests brought on such grounds as lack of capacity or undue influence. If the interested parties agree on a settlement by which a former trust beneficiary will receive property free of trust, the settlement may be approved even if the trust, including the spendthrift provision, is destroyed in the process.[536] The UPC allows courts to approve settlements "even though [they] may affect a trust or an inalienable interest."[537] However, some courts deny requests for early termination of trusts even in this situation.[538]

Professor Fogel is of the view that termination or modification by consent of the beneficiaries should not be allowed. He believes that situations where beneficiaries should be allowed to terminate or modify the trust are also situations where the trust could be modified or terminated due to circumstances not anticipated by the settlor.[539]

Obtaining Unanimous Consent

Very often trust beneficiaries are members of the same family and get along with one another. They may all agree that a trust should be modified or terminated. However, many trusts have minor, unborn or unascertained beneficiaries whose existence makes unanimous consent impossible. For example, a court refused to terminate a trust for the settlor's son with a reminder to his children because the son's after-born children could not join in the settlement agreement.[540]

A disposition in a trust to the "heirs" of someone other than the settlor can cause particular difficulties in obtaining consent. If the trust makes provision

---

written, concluded that the spendthrift provision did not constitute a material purpose. A similar result was reached in Saunders v. AMG National Trust Bank, 88 Va. Cir. 389 (2014).

533 *Restatement (Second) Trusts* § 337, cmt. h (1959).

534 Cal.Prob.Code § 15409(b).

535 UTC § 411(c). *See also Restatement (Third) of Trusts* § 65, cmt. e (2003).

536 Budin v. Levy, 180 N.E.2d 74 (Mass.1962).

537 UPC § 3–1101; *Restatement (Third) of Trusts* § 65, cmt. h (2003).

538 Adams v. Link, 145 A.2d 753 (Conn.1958); Fleisch v. First American Bank, 710 N.E.2d 1281 (Ill.App.1999) (denying termination based on a settlement in the absence of "a bona fide family dispute").

539 Fogel, *Terminating or Modifying Irrevocable Trusts by Consent of the Beneficiaries—A Proposal to Respect the Primacy of the Settlor's Intent*, 50 Real Prop. Tr. & Est. L.J. 337 (2016).

540 In re Testamentary Trust of Hasch, 721 N.E.2d 1111, 1113 (Ohio App.1999).

for A for life, remainder to A's heirs, the beneficiaries of the trust will not be finally known until A's death.

Various legal doctrines have been devised to reduce but not necessarily overcome these problems. Some courts accept proof negating the possibility of future children. For example, a trust provided for its termination when all of the settlor's grandchildren attained age 30. The beneficiaries sought to terminate the trust when the settlor's existing grandchildren were over 30 and her only children were daughters aged 65 and 70. The trustee resisted termination, citing the possibility that the aged daughters might give birth to children (settlor's grandchildren) who would be denied a share were the petition to terminate be granted. The court, however, granted the petition, concluding that the fertile octogenarian rule "had its origin at a time when medical knowledge was meager" and should be rebuttable today.[541] This modern view, however, is not universally followed.[542]

Normally more effective, however, are doctrines allowing a substitute to give a consent on behalf of beneficiaries who are incapable of giving consents on their own behalf. Such representation was not traditionally permitted in a trust termination or modification matter, however.[543] Such rejection of representation was not universal, however, and the trend in the law is to allow all types of representation for beneficiaries who are incapable of giving a consent or who are unascertained or unborn. It has been held that a guardian ad litem appointed to represent minor, unborn or unascertained trust beneficiaries may approve a modification of a trust's terms.[544] The UTC and some state statutes authorize guardians ad litem to consent on the basis of "general family benefit accruing to living members of the beneficiary's family" without focusing solely on the immediate interests of the persons they represent.[545] Missouri has adopted a version of the English Variation of Trusts Act, under which a court may approve trust modifications on behalf of persons unborn or otherwise incapable of consenting unless the modification would not "be for the benefit of the person" affected.[546]

The UTC recognizes other bases for representation.[547] The UTC provides not only for representation by fiduciaries such as guardians, conservators, or agents under durable powers of attorney,[548] but also for what is known as

[541] Korten v. Chicago City Bank and Trust Co., 533 N.E.2d 102, 103 (Ill.App.1988).

[542] *Compare Restatement (Second) of Trusts* § 340, cmt. e (1959); In re Ransom's Estate, 214 A.2d 521 (N.J.Super.App.Div.1965); Estate of Weeks, 402 A.2d 657 (Pa.1979).

[543] *Restatement (Second) of Trusts* § 337(1) (1959) (beneficiary must not be under incapacity). The discussion of representation concepts in this Section is partially derived from English, *The Uniform Trust Code: Significant Provisions and Policy Issues*, 67 Mo. L. Rev. 143, 158–62 (2002).

[544] Connecticut Bank and Trust Co. v. Coffin, 563 A.2d 1323 (Conn.1989); *Restatement (Third) of Trusts* § 65, cmt. b (2003).

[545] UTC § 305(c); Cal.Prob.Code § 15405.

[546] Variation of Trusts Act, 1958, c. 53, § 1. *See also* Mo. Rev. Stat. § 456.4–411A.

[547] On representation generally, with a focus on the provisions of the UTC and UPC, *see* 14.8, note 707 et seq.

[548] UTC § 303. Representation by a guardian is allowed only if a conservator for the ward has not been appointed. *See* UTC § 303(2). Representation by an agent is permitted only if the agent has authority to act with respect to the particular matter or dispute. *See* UTC § 303(3).

virtual representation, under which an otherwise unrepresented person (such as a child who may not yet be born) may be represented and bound by another beneficiary with a substantially identical interest with respect to the particular matter or dispute.[549]

Decanting[550]

In *Phipps v. Palm Beach Trust Company*,[551] the individual trustee had "sole and absolute" discretion to direct distributions to the settlor's descendants. The trustee did not make distributions directly to the beneficiaries but instead directed that the trust assets be distributed to a second trust for the same beneficiaries but upon slightly different terms. The *Phipps* court concluded that a trustee's power to make distributions to a beneficiary in fee simple included the power to distribute a lesser estate unless the trust instrument expressly provides otherwise.[552] Out of *Phipps* and other similar cases,[553] the technique known as decanting arose. Like the process of decanting (pouring) wine from the bottle to a glass, decanting of a trust involves the transfer of assets from one trust to a newly created second trust for the same beneficiaries although upon different terms. While originating in case law, decanting is today largely regulated by statute, with the first enacted in New York in 1992.[554] Subsequently, decanting statutes have been enacted in over twenty other states and the Uniform Law Commission in 2015 approved a Uniform Trust Decanting Act.[555]

There are many reasons why a decanting might be beneficial, most of which would otherwise require court approval. Reasons might include the need to update, modernize, or amend trust provisions in older trusts, to modify a trust on account of changed circumstances, to fix errors and ambiguities, and

---

[549] UTC § 304. In addition to unborns, under the Code, virtual representation may be used to bind beneficiaries who are minors, incapacitated, or whose identity or location is unknown and is not reasonably ascertainable.

[550] For discussions of decanting, *see* Wolf, DeLuca & O'Brien, *A More Suitable Vessel: Trust Decanting and the Future of Trust Modification in Nebraska*, 53 Creighton L. Rev. 751 (2020); Sterk, *Trust Decanting: A Critical Perspective*, 38 Cardozo L. Rev. 1993 (2017); Culp & Mellen, *Trust Decanting: An Overview and Introduction to Creative Planning Opportunities*, 45 Real Prop. Tr. & Est. L.J. 1 (2010); Willms, *Decanting Trusts: Irrevocable, Not Unchangeable*, 6 Est. Plan. & Community Prop. L.J. 35 (2013); Simmons, *Decanting and Its Alternatives: Remodeling and Revamping Irrevocable Trusts*, 55 S.D.L. Rev. 253 (2010).

[551] 196 So. 299 (Fla.1940).

[552] The court analogized the trustee's discretionary power to a type of special power of appointment, a topic discussed in Section 11.5. Under the Second Restatements of Property, the holder of a power with authority to transfer an unlimited interest also has the power to transfer anything less. *Restatement (Second) of Property: Donative Transfers* § 19.3 (1986). The *Third Restatement of Property* clarifies that this includes the power to appoint in further trust. *Third (Restatement) of Property: Wills & Other Donative Transfers* § 19.14 (2011).

[553] In re Estate of Spencer, 232 N.W.2d 491, 493–95 (Iowa 1975); Wiedenmeyer v. Johnson, 254 A.2d 534 (N.J.Super.Ct. App. Div. 1969); Bagley, *Trusts-Trustee's Decanting Power Derived From Irrevocable Trust Language*—Morse v. Kraft, 992 N.E.2d 1021 (Mass. 2013).

[554] N.Y. Est. Powers & Trusts Law § 10–6.6(b). *See* Restrepo, *New York's Decanting Statute: Helping as Old Vintage Come to Life or Spoiling the Settlor's Fine Wine?*, 34 Pace L. Rev. 479 (2014).

[555] For an analysis of the decanting statutes, *see* Lockett & Blumeyer, *Sour Grapes: When Decanting Gives Rise to Litigation*, Prob. & Prop., Sept./Oct. 2019, at 26.

to qualify a trust for tax benefits or a special needs beneficiary for Medicaid.[556] The state statutes, nearly all of which predate the approval of the Uniform Trust Decanting Act, vary on numerous details, a key difference being whether the beneficiaries are entitled to advance notice of a proposed decanting. In order to decant, the trustee must have discretion with regard to distributions although the state statutes vary on whether this discretion must be absolute or whether the discretion may be narrower. Because the decanting power is held by a trustee, the trustee remains subject to fiduciary duties, which would allow a beneficiary to successfully object if the decanting violated such obligations as the duty of loyalty[557] or the duty to act with prudence.[558]

A body of caselaw on trust decanting has begun to develop. Following the lead of *Phipps*, broad discretionary authority in the trust instrument has been construed to authorize a decanting even absent a decanting statute.[559] A decanting that eliminated the interests of future beneficiaries was found to violate the duty of impartiality and was held to be void.[560] A decanting dividing a charitable trust into two similar charitable trusts was permitted but the decanting could not be ordered over the objection of a co-trustee.[561]

Planning

The *Claflin* rule makes it possible in most American states for a trust to continue for as long as the settlor desires up to the limits imposed by the Rule Against Perpetuities.[562] Cases in which beneficiaries seek to terminate trusts are often a result of poor planning when the trust was created. When a court terminates a trust because its purposes have ceased, better drafting might have created a more flexible trust which could have been terminated without costly litigation. The UTC makes it easier to modify trusts than formerly and the use of decanting, which allows a trustee to proceed without court approval, makes it even easier. The repeal of the Rule Against Perpetuities in many states has made it possible for trusts to last longer than formerly, increasing the likelihood that circumstances will arise for which the trust was not designed[563] and also increasing the need to modify the trust.

§ 10.10 Charitable Trusts

Charitable gifts may be made in numerous ways. The donor may create and transfer property to a non-profit corporation. The donor may make an outright gift to charity in the donor's will. The donor may transfer property

---

[556] In In re Kroll, 971 N.Y.S.2d 863 (N.Y.Surr. 2013), the court approved the use of decanting to create a special needs trust in order to qualify the beneficiary for Medicaid.

[557] Discussed in 14.1.

[558] Discussed in 14.4.

[559] Morse v. Kraft, 992 N.E.2d 1021 (2013); Ferri v. Powell-Ferri, 72 N.E.3d 541 (Mass. 2017).

[560] Hodges v. Johnson, 177 A.3d 86 (N.H. 2017).

[561] In re Fund for Encouragement of Self Reliance, 440 P.3d 30 (Nev. 2019).

[562] For limits posed by the Rule Against Perpetuities, *see* Chapter 12. A trust can be terminated after the period allowed by the Rule has expired. *Restatement (Second) of Trusts* § 62, cmt. e (1959).

[563] Dukeminier & Krier, *The Rise of the Perpetual Trust*, 50 UCLA L.Rev. 1303, 1331 (2003); Section 12.4.

directly to a charity but subject its use to various restrictions. Finally, the donor may create a charitable trust.

Charitable trusts are an exception to the general rule that trusts must have definite beneficiaries.[564] Identifiable beneficiaries are not needed to enforce charitable trusts because a public official, the attorney general, has the authority to enforce the trust.[565] Charitable trusts are allowed to go on forever, despite the Rule Against Perpetuities.[566] Because terms laid down by the settlor often become out of date over the centuries, courts authorize deviations from the terms of charitable trusts under a power known as *cy pres,* the old French spelling of *si près,* "as near."[567] Such modifications are supposed to stay "as near" to the trust terms as possible under the changed circumstances, although modern courts in fact do not always "adopt that scheme which is as nearly as possible like that designated by the terms of the gift."[568]

Charitable trusts are important in estate planning because of their tax advantages.[569] Also, many persons without a spouse or close relatives may prefer that their property pass to charity instead of to distant relatives who would take by intestacy.

Definition of Charitable

Because of the peculiar rules governing charitable trusts, courts sometimes must decide whether a particular trust is charitable. According to the Restatement a trust is charitable "if its accomplishment is of such social interest to the community as to justify permitting the property to be devoted to the [designated] purpose in perpetuity."[570] Alternatively, charity is sometimes defined by a list of purposes recognized as charitable. Such a list appeared in the Statute of Charitable Uses of 1601. Although "never intended to provide an exhaustive definition," this list "still exerts a strong pull on the modern concept of charity."[571] Some items on this list appear rather quaint today, such as the "marriages of true maids."[572] Some purposes not on the 1601 list are considered charitable today, such as the prevention of cruelty to animals.[573] A more current list appears in the UTC: "(a) the relief of poverty; (b) the advancement of education; (c) the advancement of religion; (d) the

---

[564] Section 10.3, note 73 et seq.; *Restatement (Third) of Trusts* § 28, cmt. c (2003) (charitable trust valid though it has no definite beneficiaries).

[565] *See infra* note 614 et seq.

[566] *Restatement (Third) of Trusts* § 28, cmt. d (2003); Section 12.6, note 211.

[567] Because of its French origin, cy rhymes with "sea" rather than "sigh" (although usage on this point is varied), and the final "s" in pres is not pronounced.

[568] *Restatement (Second) Trusts* § 399, cmt. b (1959). The point is made more forcefully in *Restatement (Third) of Trusts* § 67, cmt. d (2003).

[569] As to the estate tax charitable deduction, *see* Section 15.4, note 271 et seq. For a more comprehensive discussion of the tax aspects of charitable giving, *see* Price & Donaldson, *Contemporary Estate Planning* ch. 8 (2014 ed.).

[570] *Restatement (Third) of Trusts* § 28, cmt. a (2003).

[571] Bright, *Charity and Trusts for the Public Benefit—Time for a Re-think?*, The Conveyancer 28, 31 (1989).

[572] Statute, 43 Eliz. I, c. 4 (1601).

[573] Green's Will Trusts, [1985] 3 All E.R. 455 (Ch.1984).

promotion of health; (e) governmental or municipal purposes; (f) other purposes the achievement of which is beneficial to the community."[574]

Even purposes on this list are not charitable if they do not benefit the public. "A college for pickpockets is no charity" said an English court in refusing to hold charitable a trust under George Bernard Shaw's will to reform the alphabet to make spelling phonetic. "I do not think that the fact that the testator and a number of other people are of the opinion that the step would be a benefit proves the case, for undoubtedly there are a great many more people . . . who think the exact contrary."[575]

American courts define charity more broadly. Trusts to promote change in the law, such as one to promote the Equal Rights Amendment or to advance the cause of socialism, have been held charitable.[576] The definition of "charity" for private law purposes is broader than the tax definition[577] although a practitioner should keep the tax definition in mind because much charitable giving is motivated by a desire for a tax deduction. A trust to promote socialism was deemed charitable even though the trustees were authorized "to use the trust assets for non-charitable purposes," because this phrase merely meant that the trust "not be limited to those entities or causes which would . . . qualify as tax-exempt."[578]

There are limits to how far even American courts will go in finding trusts charitable, however. A trust to distribute the income to children in the first three grades of a school to further their education was held not to be charitable, since the "admonition to the children" to use the money for education "would be wholly impotent" in the light of "childhood impulses."[579] Nor could the trust be regarded as one for the relief of poverty because distributions were not limited to needy children.[580] The social benefit in the scheme was not sufficient "to justify its existence in perpetuity as a charitable trust."

A trust cannot qualify as charitable if the class of potential recipients is too narrow, for example, a trust "for the education of my descendants."[581] But

---

574 UTC § 405(a). This list is identical to that in *Restatement (Third) of Trusts* § 28 (2003).

575 Re Shaw, [1957] 1 All E.R. 745, 752 (Ch.). The holding in this case is contrary to *Restatement (Third) of Trusts* § 28, cmt. h, illus. 5 (2003). Amnesty International was held not to be a charity in McGovern v. Attorney-General, [1982] Ch. 321 (1981). However, the promotion of faith healing has been deemed charitable. Re Le Cren Clarke, [1996] 1 All E.R. 715 (Ch.D.).

576 Estate of Breeden, 256 Cal.Rptr. 813 (App.1989); Register of Wills v. Cook, 216 A.2d 542 (Md.1966); *Restatement (Third) of Trusts* § 28, cmt. *l* (2003).

577 *Cf. Restatement (Third) of Trusts* § 28, cmt. a.

578 In re Estate of Breeden, 256 Cal.Rptr. 813, 818 (App.1989). In Fund for the Study and Economic Growth v. Internal Rev. Serv., 161 F.3d 755 (D.C.Cir.1998), an organization seeking to replace the income tax with a flat tax was held not to qualify for a tax deduction. *Restatement (Third) of Trusts* § 28 Reporter's Note to cmt. *l* (2003), suggests the result in this case might be different under "the more lenient rules of trust law."

579 Shenandoah Valley Nat'l Bank v. Taylor, 63 S.E.2d 786, 791 (Va.1951).

580 However, a trust can be "for the relief of poverty" even though it does not state specifically that the beneficiaries must be poor. A trust for the benefit of "widows and orphans" is ordinarily interpreted as meaning "poor widows and orphans." *Restatement (Third) of Trusts* § 28, cmt. g (2003).

581 In re Compton, [1945] Ch. 123; *Restatement (Third) of Trusts* § 28, cmt. a(1) (2003). But cf. Runser v. Lippi, 664 N.E.2d 1355 (Ohio App.1995) (trust for scholarships for needy persons, with preference given to settlor's nieces and nephews).

a settlor can select a favored group, such as a small community.[582] Even payment to one individual may involve enough social benefit to make the trust charitable, as in a trust to provide medical education for a person who agreed to practice in a small town, or a prize for an individual who has done something useful.[583] A trust to maintain the tomb of the testator or his family is not charitable, but the perpetual upkeep of a *public* cemetery or a monument to a "notable person" is charitable.[584] A trust to provide for the settlor's pets is not charitable, but one for the prevention of cruelty to animals in general is considered to be charitable.[585]

Racial, Gender and Religious Limitations

The will of Stephen Girard in 1831 created a college for "poor white male orphans," naming the city of Philadelphia as trustee. Over a century later the Supreme Court held that the governmental trustee's refusal to admit African Americans was state action forbidden by the 14th Amendment's equal protection clause.[586] Arguably, the state's involvement in enforcing restrictions in charitable trusts should subject them all to the 14th Amendment. No court has yet so held,[587] but they have been quick to find unconstitutional state action when racially restrictive trusts are challenged.[588] When a private trustee sought instructions from a court on whether to abide by racial restrictions, the court said that any advice it gave to comply with them would constitute state action.[589] Absent state action, racially discriminatory charities have been held to be charitable for purposes of trust law.[590] Such trusts are rare, however, because they do not qualify for federal tax benefits[591] and most charitable giving today is substantially tax-motivated.

A trust which provides benefits only for blacks can be upheld by analogy to state affirmative action programs. When a will created a scholarship fund for a "white female student," the racial restriction was stricken but the limitation to females was upheld on the ground that this "benign

---

[582] *Restatement (Third) of Trusts* § 28, cmt. f (2001).

[583] *Restatement (Third) of Trusts* § 28, cmt. f; Estate of Bunch v. Heirs of Bunch, 485 So.2d 284 (Miss.1986).

[584] *Restatement (Second) of Trusts* § 374, cmt. h (1959). *See also Restatement (Third) of Trusts* § 28, cmt. *l* (2003). Trusts for masses for the settlor's soul are considered charitable. In re Hetherington, [1990] Ch. 1 (1989); *Restatement (Third) of Trusts* § 28, cmt. i (2003).

[585] In re McNeill's Estate, 41 Cal.Rptr. 139 (App.1964); *Restatement (Third) of Trusts* § 28, cmt. *l* (2003). Trusts for the care of an animal or a grave may be sustained as "honorary." *See infra* note 602 et seq.

[586] Commonwealth of Pennsylvania v. Board of Directors, 353 U.S. 230 (1957).

[587] Adams, *Racial and Religious Discrimination in Charitable Trusts*, 25 Clev.State L.Rev. 1, 13 (1976); cf. Lockwood v. Killian, 375 A.2d 998, 1005 (Conn.1977).

[588] Trammell v. Elliott, 199 S.E.2d 194 (Ga.1973); Dunbar v. Board of Trustees, 461 P.2d 28 (Colo.1969); Connecticut Bank & Trust Co. v. Cyril and Julia C. Johnson Mem. Hosp., 294 A.2d 586 (Conn.Super.1972).

[589] Bank of Delaware v. Buckson, 255 A.2d 710 (Del.Ch.1969).

[590] Swanson, *Discriminatory Charitable Trusts: Time for a Legislative Solution*, 48 U.Pitt.L.Rev. 153, 158 (1986).

[591] Bob Jones University v. United States, 461 U.S. 574 (1983); Estate of Clopton, 93 T.C. 275 (1989).

discrimination . . . does not subvert equal opportunity but rather promotes it by compensating for past acts of discrimination."[592]

The Restatement of Trusts allows beneficiaries of a charitable trust to be "limited to the inhabitants of a particular place" or "to persons of a particular sex or religion."[593] Gender limitations have also been removed under *cy pres* when they caused a dearth of eligible claimants, for example, a scholarship designated for a "male member" of a church was expanded to include females when no qualified male applied.[594]

Salvaging Non-Charitable Trusts

If the words "benevolent" or "philanthropic" are used to describe the trust purposes, English courts have held the trust invalid on the grounds that these terms are broader than charitable,[595] but modern American courts construe such terms as synonymous with charitable.[596]

A trust which has both charitable and non-charitable objectives may be sustained in part if a clear part can be allocated to each. A will left property to a foundation which was to pay specified amounts to certain individuals and use the rest "to aid the blind." The devises to individuals were "no impediment to the remaining portion of the trust." Such a "mixed trust" fails only where "there is no method of apportionment" between the charitable and other purposes.[597] Other courts have sustained "mixed" trusts by disregarding the references to noncharitable objects.[598] But a will directing the executors to distribute the residue to "whatever person or charitable organization they determine" was held to fail for indefiniteness.[599]

Devises that are restricted to charitable purposes, on the other hand, can be quite open-ended, such as "to charity" or "to such charitable organizations as my trustee shall select."[600] Even if the will fails to name a trustee, or if the designated trustee fails to act, the court normally appoints a trustee.[601]

---

592 Trustees of University of Delaware v. Gebelein, 420 A.2d 1191 (Del.Ch.1980). *See also* Swanson, 48 U.Pitt. L.Rev. at 188; *Restatement (Third) of Trusts* § 28, cmt. f (2003) (only "invidious" discrimination is against public policy, no objection to "affirmative action").

593 *Restatement (Third) of Trusts* § 28, cmt. f.

594 Wesley United Methodist Church v. Harvard College, 316 N.E.2d 620 (Mass.1974).

595 Chichester Diocesan Fund v. Simpson, [1944] A.C. 341 (H.L.). For many similar examples, *see* Underhill & Hayton, *Law Relating to Trusts and Trustees* 65–66 (14th ed. 1987).

596 Wilson v. Flowers, 277 A.2d 199 (N.J.1971).

597 In re Teubert's Estate, 298 S.E.2d 456, 463–64 (W.Va.1982). *See also Restatement (Third) of Trusts* § 28, cmt. e (2003).

598 Newick v. Mason, 581 A.2d 1269 (Me.1990); *Restatement, Second, of Trusts* § 389(2) (1959); English Charitable Trusts (Validation) Act, 1954, § 1; Estate of Starkey v. United States, 223 F.3d 694 (7th Cir.2000) (devise to a designated church and "missionaries" was a charitable devise to the church); cf. *Restatement (Third) of Trusts* § 28 illus. 3 (2003).

599 Klassen v. Klassen, [1986] 5 W.W.R. 746 (Sask.Q.B.). *But cf.* Section 10.7, notes 320–321.

600 Lancaster v. Merchants Nat'l Bank, 961 F.2d 713 (8th Cir.1992); *Restatement (Third) of Trusts* § 28, cmt. a (2003).

601 *Cf.* Morton v. Potts, 781 N.E.2d 43 (Mass.App.2003) (trust for "charitable organizations designated by the Donor" is effective even though she failed to designate any).

Honorary Trusts

Honorary trusts are noncharitable trusts created for a proper trust purpose but without an enforceable interest. The most common examples are trusts created to benefit an individual animal[602] or a trust created to maintain a relative's burial plot.[603] A trust created to benefit animals generally or a cemetery as a whole might qualify as a charitable trust but a trust for an individual animal or deceased individual is not eligible.[604] Because neither an animal or deceased individual may petition the court, the beneficiary's interest was unenforceable and the trust was not a valid trust at common law. However, the trustee had power to carry out the terms of the trust if the trustee was so inclined but was otherwise free to ignore the settlor's wishes. Hence the trust was no more than an unenforceable power of appointment,[605] and was therefore "honorary" only, binding only the trustee's conscience.[606]

Both the UPC and UTC convert honorary trusts into real trusts by allowing the settlor to appoint someone to enforce the beneficiary's interest.[607] A trust for the care of an animal is valid for the life of the animal,[608] and a trust for another noncharitable purpose without an ascertainable beneficiary may be created but is valid for only 21 years.[609] A great majority of states have enacted either the UPC version, the UTC version, or some combination. Because honorary trusts are often funded with far more property than needed to carry out the intended purpose, disposition of excess funds is a frequent issue. Both the UPC and UTC address this concern. Absent a provision disposing of excess funds in the terms of the trust, property not required for the intended use must be distributed to the settlor, if then living, otherwise to the settlor's successors in interest.[610] Successors in interest for this purpose would include the beneficiaries under the settlor's will, if the settlor has a will, or in the absence of an effective will provision, the settlor's heirs.

The drafters of the UTC specifically elected not to follow the offshore islands in their liberal authorization of the noncharitable purpose (NCP) trust.[611] The noncharitable purpose trust contemplated in the UTC is one created for a benevolent but noncharitable purpose, and even then it is

---

[602] *See, e.g.*, In re Searight's Estate, 95 N.E.2d 779 (Ohio App. 1950) (where the testator provided $1,000 to be used for care of her dog Trixie, to be disbursed at a rate of 75 cents/day).

[603] Trusts for perpetual care are often validated by provisions in a state's cemetery statutes. *See, e.g.*, Perry v. Twentieth Street Bank, 206 S.E.2d 421, 423 (W.Va.1974).

[604] *See Restatement (Third) of Trusts*, § 28, cmt. *l* (2003).

[605] For discussion of powers of appointment, *see* Section 11.5.

[606] For a discussion of the common law doctrine, *see Restatement (Third) of Trusts* § 47 (2003); Hirsch, *Bequests for Purposes: A Unified Theory*, 56 Wash. & Lee L. Rev. 33 (1999).

[607] UPC § 2–907(c)(4); UTC §§ 408(b), 409(2). *See* Carnabuci, *Avoiding the Fate of Argos: The Duty of Pet Trust Protectors in Connecticut*, 31 Quinnipiac Prob. L. Rev. 281 (2018).

[608] UPC § 2–907; UTC § 408. *See* Cave, *Trusts: Monkeying Around With Out Pets' Futures: Why Oklahoma Should Adopt a Pet Trust Statute*, 55 Okla. L. Rev. 627 (2002).

[609] UPC § 2–907; UTC § 409, For a discussion, *see* Ausness, *Non-Charitable Purpose Trusts: Past, Present, and Future*, 51 Real Prop. Tr. & Est. L.J. 321 (2016).

[610] UPC § 2–907(c)(6); UTC §§ 408(c), 409(3).

[611] For a discussion, *see* Bove, *The Purpose of Purpose Trusts*, Prob. & Prop., May/June 2004, at 34.

enforceable for only a limited duration.[612] The stewardship trust, enacted by statute in Oregon in 2019, allows a business with a non-charitable purpose to be held in trust without any limit on the trust's duration. The concept is particularly appropriate for mission-driven businesses. The original stimulus for the Oregon statute was to assist a business engaged in organic farming.[613]

Standing to Enforce Charitable Trusts

The Attorney General's standing to enforce charitable trusts originated under English common law and was then brought to the Colonies.[614] The Attorney General has standing even when charitable organizations are named beneficiaries. A suit by the Attorney General is not precluded by a prior judgment approving the conduct of a charitable trustee if the Attorney General was not a party.[615]

Although it has been stated that the Attorney General has the same right to information from the trustees of a charitable trust as the beneficiary of a private trust,[616] practice varies in the states on the extent to which the Attorney General must be notified of trust administration.[617] In addition, the Uniform Supervision of Trustees for Charitable Purposes Act requires charitable trustees to register with the Attorney General and file periodic reports. Four states have adopted this Act, and nineteen others have enacted similar legislation.[618] But these statutes exempt many charities, such as educational and religious institutions. Their effectiveness is also limited by inadequate staffing. In California, for example, three auditors had 29,000 registrants to monitor.[619]

The standing of persons other than the Attorney General to enforce charitable trusts is restricted. A suit by residents and taxpayers of San Francisco alleging breaches of trust by the trustees of the city's fine arts museums was dismissed.

"Because the beneficiaries of charitable trusts . . . are ordinarily indefinite, the attorney General has primary responsibility for the supervision of charitable trusts, and generally he is the proper party to enforce them. . . .

---

[612] For further explication on the limited recognition of purpose trusts in the United States, *see Restatement (Third) of Trusts* § 48 (2003).

[613] Gary, The Oregon Stewardship Trust: A New Type of Purpose Trust that Enables Steward-Ownership of a Business, 88 U. Cin. L. Rev. 707 (2019).

[614] *Restatement (Third) of Trusts* § 94 (2012).

[615] In re Los Angeles County Pioneer Soc'y, 257 P.2d 1 (Cal.1953). *But see* Loring v. Marshall, 484 N.E.2d 1315 (Mass.1985) (adverse will construction binding on charities even though Attorney General not a party); Israel v. National Board of YMCA, 369 A.2d 646 (R.I.1977) (N.Y. judgment binding even though R.I. Attorney General not a party).

[616] State v. Taylor, 362 P.2d 247 (Wash.1961). As to a trust beneficiary's right to information, *see* Section 14.3.

[617] Section 110(d) of the UTC provides that the attorney general has the rights of a qualified beneficiary of a trust, one of which would include being kept informed of the trust's administration, but this provision was placed in brackets on the assumption that states are likely to vary this provision. *See* UTC § 110, cmt.

[618] Bell & Bell, *Supervision of Charitable Trusts in California*, 32 Hast.L.J. 433, 438 (1980).

[619] Bell & Bell, 32 Hast.L.J. at 438.

This limitation on standing arises from the need to protect the trustee from vexatious litigation."[620]

Another court dismissed a suit by an unsuccessful applicant for a scholarship; because there were over 930 contenders, "this action would only open the door to similar actions by other unsuccessful nominees."[621]

Particularly helpful in analyzing such cases is the *Blasko* test, a five-factor formula developed by the authors of a 1993 law review article.[622] The five factors are (1) the extraordinary nature of the acts complained of and the remedy sought; (2) presence of bad faith; (3) attorney general's availability and effectiveness; (4) nature of the benefitted class and its relationship to the charity; and (5) subjective factors and social desirability. In a case involving a trust created by the founder of the Christian Science Church, the *Blasko* test was applied to deny standing to a potential trust beneficiary.[623]

Even settlors have traditionally been denied standing to enforce charitable trusts,[624] but there is now contrary authority both in the cases and in the UTC, motivated in large part by the demonstrated inability of state Attorneys General to monitor compliance with restrictions in charitable gifts.[625] But attempts to extend the UTC's donor standing to charitable corporations have failed. While charitable corporations are subject to certain trust law doctrines, such as the doctrine of *cy pres*, different rules apply to governance issues.[626]

The Restatement allows beneficiaries with a "special interest" in a charitable trust to sue.[627] A common case involves a trust created to provide financial support to a university. Should the trustee default, the university would be deemed to have a special interest and could sue to enforce the trust. The special interest doctrine is necessary because charitable trusts, being created for the benefit of society at large, do not have beneficiaries in the usual sense. A trust created to support a specific public charity is the easy case. Other

---

[620] Hardman v. Feinstein, 240 Cal.Rptr. 483, 485 (App.1987).

[621] Kania v. Chatham, 254 S.E.2d 528, 530 (N.C.1979).

[622] Blasko, Crossley & Lloyd, *Standing to Sue in the Charitable Sector*, 28 U.S.F.L. Rev. 37 (1993).

[623] In re Trust of Mary Baker Eddy, 212 A.3d 414 (N.H. 2019).

[624] Carl J. Herzog Foundation v. University of Bridgeport, 699 A.2d 995 (Conn.1997); *Restatement (Second) of Trusts* § 391, cmt. e (1959).

[625] UTC § 405(c); Smithers v. St. Luke's-Roosevelt Hosp. Center, 723 N.Y.S.2d 426 (App.Div.2001). In Smithers, the settlor's widow and personal representative was allowed to sue, the court noting the lack of diligence in the Attorney-General's oversight in this case.

[626] Courtenay C. & Lucy Patten Davis Foundation v. Colorado State University Research Foundation, 320 P.3d 1115 (Wyo. 2014); Hardt v. Vitae Foundation, Inc., 302 S.W.3d 133 (Mo.Ct.App. 2009); Dodge v. Trustees of Randolph Macon Woman's College, 661 S.E.2d 805 (Va, 2008). For an article discussing the UTC provision, *see* Chester, *Grantor Standing to Enforce Charitable Transfers Under Section 405(c) of the Uniform Trust Code and Related Law: How Important Is It and How Extensive Should It Be*, 37 Real Prob. Prob. & Tr. J. 611 (2003). For articles discussing donor standing, primarily with respect to charitable corporations, *see* Brody, *From the Dead Hand to the Living Dead: The Conundrum of Charitable Donor Standing*, 41 Ga. L. Rev. 1183 (2007); Weisbrod, *Reservations About Charitable Standing: Should The Law Allow Charitable Donors to Reserve the Right to Enforce a Gift Restriction?*, 42 Real Prop. Prob. & Tr. J. 245 (2007); Goodwin, *Donor Standing to Enforce Charitable Gifts: Civil Society vs. Donor Empowerment*, 58 Vanderbilt L. Rev. 1093 (2005).

[627] *Restatement (Third) of Trusts* § 94 (2012).

cases test the boundaries. Where a trust instrument "suggested" that trust funds be allocated to certain charities, one of the rejected applicants was held to have such a special interest. The plaintiff was "entitled to some kind of minimal review" as to whether the trustee had abused its discretion.[628]

When there are several trustees, charitable trustees can act by a majority vote,[629] but the minority can sue for a breach of trust, even when the Attorney General has refused to act because he believes that the challenged conduct is not "detrimental to the public interest." Standing is restricted in order to avoid harassing litigation, but a suit by co-trustees poses no such threat since they are few in number.[630]

Some courts are more liberal in conferring standing on the ground that otherwise breaches of trust may go unremedied. One way to deal with the problem of over-worked Attorneys General without opening the door to a flood of litigation is to allow individuals to sue "on the relation of" the Attorney General with the latter's permission, or to bring a petition for mandamus to require the AG's office to perform its duty.[631] Some courts act *sua sponte*. "A judge is not precluded from exercising his authority because the Attorney General has had the opportunity to object to an account but has not done so."[632] Some estate planners suggest inserting a "gift over" to another charity if specified conditions are violated in order to give the substituted charity an incentive to monitor compliance with the conditions.[633]

Restricted Gifts to Charitable Entities

Many charitable gifts to established organizations impose restrictions on the use of the money or property given. Even though the gift was not expressly made in trust, a donee who "is directed by the terms of the gift to devote the property to a particular one of its purposes is under a duty, enforceable at the suit of the Attorney General" to do so.[634] Even if the gift was by its specific terms unrestricted, the property must not be diverted from the purposes of the organization as set forth in its articles of incorporation.[635]

Courts are reluctant to find that a donor intended to restrict the use of property, particularly when considerable time has elapsed since the date of the gift. Land was given in 1827 to a church "on condition that the same . . . shall

---

[628] St. John's-St. Luke Evangelical Church v. National Bank of Detroit, 283 N.W.2d 852 (Mich.App.1979).

[629] Richards v. Midkiff, 396 P.2d 49 (Haw.1964); *Restatement (Second) of Trusts* § 391 (1959). As to private trusts, *see* Section 14.6, note 84 et seq. The Restatement Third and the UTC provide that a trustee may act by majority vote with regard to any type of trust, charitable or private. *Restatement (Third) of Trusts* § 39 (2003); UTC § 703(a).

[630] Holt v. College of Osteopathic Physicians & Surgeons, 394 P.2d 932 (Cal.1964); Takabuki v. Ching, 695 P.2d 319 (Haw.1985); Belcher v. Conway, 425 A.2d 1254 (Conn.1979).

[631] The court suggested these alternatives in rejecting a petition brought by an individual to have a successor trustee appointed for a charitable trust in Arman v. Bank of America, N.T. & S.A., 88 Cal.Rptr.2d 410, 416 (App.1999). *See also Restatement (Third) of Trusts* § 94, cmt. e (2012).

[632] In re Will of Crabtree, 795 N.E.2d 1157, 1169 (Mass.2003).

[633] Tucker, *When Charities Disappoint*, 141 Tr. & Est. 44 (2002). As to the effect of such a gift over on the application of *cy pres*, *see* infra note 659 et seq.

[634] *Restatement (Second) of Trusts* § 348, cmt. f (1959).

[635] In re Connolly's Estate, 121 Cal.Rptr. 325 (App.1975); Greil Memorial Hospital v. First Ala. Bank, 387 So.2d 778 (Ala.1980); Blocker v. State, 718 S.W.2d 409 (Tex.App.1986).

be used for . . . the erection and maintenance thereon of a house of public worship." A century and a half later a court held that the donee was no longer subject to the condition. "Because a reasonable time has passed, the condition on the use of the tract has been fulfilled."[636]

Removing Restrictions Under Cy Pres Power

The traditional doctrine of *cy pres* is most succinctly stated in the Restatement (Second) of Trusts:

> If property is given in trust to be applied to a particular charitable purpose, and it is or becomes impossible or impracticable or illegal to carry out the particular purpose, and if the settlor manifested a more general intention to devote the property to charitable purposes, the trust will not fail but the court will direct the application of the property to some charitable purpose that falls within the general charitable intention of the settlor.[637]

Under the traditional doctrine, if the settlor did not manifest a general charitable intention, the trust failed and the trust property would be returned to the settlor or, because the settlor is usually dead, to the settlor's successors. Within the universe of *cy pres* cases, failure to apply *cy pres* is very rare but occasionally does occur. Money which was raised for a bone marrow transplant for a victim of leukemia who died before the operation could be performed was returned to the donors, because the solicitation for donations "was solely directed to . . . one operative procedure for one specified beneficiary."[638] This result was reached despite the "administrative difficulties in locating the present whereabouts of some contributors," many of whom were anonymous.[639]

The question whether a settlor had a "general charitable intent" beyond the specific purpose mentioned amounts to asking what the settlor would want to have done under the circumstances. This question is hard to answer because the settlor did not contemplate the circumstances which have come to pass.[640] Because the courts nearly always apply *cy pres* no matter how particular the settlor's original charitable scheme,[641] both the UTC and Restatement (Third) of Trusts direct the use of *cy pres* unless the trust explicitly provides to the contrary.[642]

---

[636] Independent Congregational Society v. Davenport, 381 A.2d 1137 (Me.1978). *See also* Section 3.6, note 388 et seq.

[637] *Restatement (Second) of Trusts* § 399 (1959).

[638] Matter of Gonzalez, 621 A.2d 94, 96–97 (N.J.Super.Ch.1992).

[639] *Compare* N.Y.EPTL § 8–1.1(j) (if more than 1,000 contributors, unexpended funds after five years shall be applied *cy pres*). If *cy pres* does not apply and the contributors cannot be located, *Restatement (Third) of Trusts* § 67, cmt. f (2003) says the money may go to the state.

[640] In re Estate of Thompson, 414 A.2d 881, 886 (Me.1980).

[641] *See, e.g.*, Obermeyer v. Bank of America, N.A., 140 S.W.3d 18 (Mo.2004), in which the court applied *cy pres* to a disposition to the Dental Alumni Development Fund, even though both the Fund and the dental school it supported had ceased to exist. The lower appellate court had held that the settlor's intent was so specific that the settlor did not have a general charitable intent and the trust had failed. *See* Obermeyer v. Bank of America, N.A., 2003 WL 22004833 (Mo.Ct. App., Aug. 26, 2003).

[642] UTC § 413(a); *Restatement (Third) of Trusts* § 67, cmt. b (2003).

Cy pres cases arise in a myriad of different situations. One common situation is where because of passage of time the charitable gift is not working as effectively as had been originally anticipated. A common solution is to expand the class of possible recipients. For example, a will probated in 1899 left property for a home for "orphans between the ages of 6 and 10, an orphan being defined as one whose father is dead." Seventy years later a court expanded this to include children between the ages of 6 and 18 who had been deprived of parental care for any reason. The number of applicants who qualified under the terms of the will had been declining.[643] Similarly, a trust for "defraying the cost of hospitalization" was modified to allow use "for broader health care purposes" because "today, third-party payment of hospitalization costs is nearly universal."[644]

Although courts are more willing to deviate from the terms of an old gift,[645] more recent ones are also modified on occasion. When a will devised property to a hospital which ceased to operate while the testator's estate was still in administration, the executor was directed to distribute the property to another hospital, "so that the charitable purpose of the testator will not fail."[646]

Courts have used *cy pres* to eliminate racial restrictions in gifts even where no state action was involved. The founder of Rice University said that it was to be for the "white inhabitants" of Texas. The limitation was removed because "under present conditions no university that discriminates . . . on the basis of race could attain or retain the status of a university of the first class."[647] When a will left money to Amherst for scholarships for "Protestant, Gentile" boys, the restriction was eliminated because Amherst refused to accept the gift otherwise.[648]

When trust funds exceed what is necessary for the stated purpose of the trust, the excess can be applied *cy pres,* as when a will left money for two annual scholarships and the fund produced enough income for more.[649] Conversely, if funds are insufficient for the project designated by the settlor, the funds may be applied *cy pres* for a more modest purpose. For instance, a will left $150,000 for the erection of a hospital. Since "the average capital expenditure to construct and equip one hospital *bed* . . . is between $150,000–$180,000," the money was used "to renovate and equip existing facilities."[650]

---

[643] Dunbar v. Board of Trust. of George W. Clayton Col., 461 P.2d 28, 31 (Colo.1969).

[644] Matter of Estate of Vallery, 883 P.2d 24, 29 (Colo.App.1993).

[645] *Restatement (Third) of Trusts* § 67, cmt. d (2003); In re Estes Estate, 523 N.W.2d 863, 869 (Mich.App.1994) (rejecting *cy pres,* noting that only 21 years had elapsed since testator died); UTC § 413(b) (distinguishing trusts in existence for over 21 years from others).

[646] Stockert v. Council on World Service, 427 S.E.2d 236 (W.Va.1993).

[647] Coffee v. William Marsh Rice University, 408 S.W.2d 269, 286 (Tex.Civ.App.1966). *See also* Home for Incurables v. University of Maryland Medical System Corp., 797 A.2d 746 (Md.2002) (racial restriction in a gift to a hospital removed as violative of a state statute).

[648] Howard Savings Inst. v. Peep, 170 A.2d 39 (N.J.1961). *Accord, Restatement (Third) of Trusts* § 67, cmt. c (2003).

[649] Estate of Puckett, 168 Cal.Rptr. 311 (App.1980); *Restatement (Third) of Trusts* § 67, cmt. c (2003).

[650] Matter of Estate of Craig, 848 P.2d 313, 317, 322 (Ariz.App.1992). *See also Restatement (Third) of Trusts* § 67, cmt. c (2003).

Cy pres is also used when the settlor's original purpose has been accomplished. A testator who died in 1861 left money "to create a public sentiment that will put an end to negro slavery." After the Thirteenth Amendment did this, the money was applied to support the education of freedmen.[651]

Cy pres has been invoked when money is left to an entity, such as the "Cancer Research Fund," which does not exist. Since the testator intended to benefit cancer research, the money was given to the American Cancer Society.[652] *Cy pres* has also been applied when a charitable corporation goes out of existence.[653] On the other hand, when a charity is dissolved in a merger, the funds may simply pass to the successor organization.[654]

Just as judges may classify a purpose as charitable even if they feel the purpose is unwise, they are also reluctant to modify a charitable trust simply because they disagree with its terms. A petition by the trustee of a trust "for the inhabitants of the City of Oshkosh" to extend benefits to persons living in adjacent areas was rejected. "Cy-pres does not warrant a court substituting a different plan for that set forth in the trust instrument solely because the trustee, or court, or both, believe the substituted plan to be a better plan."[655]

Professor Simes thought that courts were too hesitant to apply *cy pres*. Simes proposed that after thirty years courts should have an enlarged *cy pres* power to modify charitable trusts "not only if the original purpose was found impracticable but also if . . . the amount to be expended is out of all proportion to its value to society."[656] The Third Restatement of Trusts and the UTC allow the use of *cy pres* simply because a trust purpose is "wasteful."[657]

The presumption against intestacy is sometimes used to support *cy pres*.[658] This argument is inapplicable when the failure of a charitable gift causes the property to go to another devisee under the will. If the substituted legatee is a charity the argument against *cy pres* is even stronger, since the public will benefit in any event. Nonetheless, it is usually held that "the presence or absence of a gift over is merely one factor among many in determining whether the testator had a general charitable intent."[659] The Third Restatement if more definitive, "A trust provision expressing the settlor's own intention of an alternative charitable purpose will be carried out, without the need to apply the *cy pres* doctrine."[660]

---

651 Jackson v. Phillips, 96 Mass. 539 (1867).

652 In re Tomlinson's Estate, 359 N.E.2d 109 (Ill.1976).

653 In re Connolly's Estate, 121 Cal.Rptr. 325 (App.1975); Alexander v. Georgia Baptist Foundation, Inc., 266 S.E.2d 165 (Ga.1980); *Restatement (Third) of Trusts* § 67, cmt. e (2003).

654 Washington Hospital v. Riggs Nat'l Bank, 575 A.2d 719 (D.C.1990); Colgan v. Sisters of St. Joseph, 604 N.E.2d 989 (Ill.App.1992); Cowden v. Sovran Bank/Central South, 816 S.W.2d 741 (Tenn.1991).

655 In re Oshkosh Foundation, 213 N.W.2d 54, 57 (Wis.1973).

656 Simes, *Public Policy and the Dead Hand* 139 (1955).

657 UTC § 413(a); *Restatement (Third) of Trusts* § 67 (2001).

658 In re Estate of Rood, 200 N.W.2d 728 (Mich.App.1972).

659 Home For Incurables v. University of Maryland Medical System Corp., 797 A.2d 746 (Md.2002); *Restatement (Second) of Trusts* § 399, cmt. c (1959).

660 *Restatement (Third) of Trusts* § 67, cmt. b (2003).

Most courts admit extrinsic evidence on this issue. When a will left money to Amherst for a scholarship with religious restrictions unacceptable to Amherst, the court removed the restrictions rather than have the money pass intestate because of evidence that the testator's heirs were distant relatives with whom he had little contact, he regularly contributed to Amherst and attended reunions of his graduating class, and was not actively interested in any church.[661] Conversely, a donor's long-term association with Syracuse Medical College was held to show he intended the property to revert rather than go to another school when the designated college went out of existence.[662]

The other grounds for modifying trusts, in particular unanticipated circumstances, are also applicable to charitable trusts.[663] The Restatement Second distinguishes between *cy pres* and "deviation" from the terms of a trust with respect to administration[664] although there is an overlap between the two. Many trusts to which *cy pres* is applied on the basis that the settlor's charitable scheme has become impracticable could also have been modified on account of unanticipated circumstances. However, there are situations where *cy pres* may be unavailable but administrative deviation will nonetheless be applicable. One is where the court refuses to apply *cy pres* because the will directed a gift over in case the charitable purpose failed. For example, in one case a will devised a house and land in trust for use as a convalescent home, "and if used for any other purpose [it] shall revert to my heirs." Upon the later destruction of the house, the court, concluding that applying *cy pres* would violate the will, instead applied administrative deviation to modify the trust.[665] A second situation is in the minority of states where *cy pres* can be applied only if the settlor's charitable purpose has failed instead of merely becoming impracticable.[666]

Trustees are not supposed to deviate from trust terms without first obtaining court approval,[667] but courts sometimes ratify deviations which have already occurred.[668] In exercising their *cy pres* powers, courts give weight to the trustee's views, but they are not bound to follow the views of either the trustee or of the Attorney General.[669]

Planning

A trust is often not the best vehicle for administering a charitable gift. An alternative is to create a not-for-profit corporation. A court has rejected the

---

661 Howard Savings Inst. v. Peep, 170 A.2d 39, 46 (N.J.1961).

662 Application of Syracuse University, 148 N.E.2d 671 (N.Y.1958). *But see* Obermeyer v. Bank of America, N.A., 140 S.W.3d 18 (Mo.2004), in which court applied *cy pres* to a disposition to the Dental Alumni Development Fund, even though both the Fund and the dental school it supported had ceased to exist.

663 For these grounds, *see* Section 10.9.

664 *Restatement (Second) of Trusts* §§ 381, 399 (1959).

665 Wigglesworth v. Cowles, 648 N.E.2d 1289, 1294 (Mass.App.1995).

666 *See* English, *The Uniform Trust Code (2000) and Its Application to Ohio*, 30 Cap. U. L. Rev. 1, 18–19 (2002).

667 Cinnaminson Tp. v. First Camden Nat'l Bank & Trust Co., 238 A.2d 701 (N.J.Super.Ch.1968); *Restatement (Second) of Trusts* § 399, cmt. e (1959).

668 Wigglesworth v. Cowles, 648 N.E.2d 1289 (Mass.App.1995); *Restatement (Third) of Trusts* § 67, cmt. d (2003).

669 *Restatement (Third) of Trusts* § 67, cmt. f.

argument that all trust rules should apply by analogy to charitable corporations because they "are created for the same purpose" By using the form of a charitable corporation, the donor intends to "invoke the far more flexible and adaptable principles of corporate law."[670] On the other hand, certain charitable trust doctrines, particularly the *cy pres* doctrine, do apply to charitable corporations.[671]

Donors with specific wishes may often carry out their plans most efficiently by making a restricted gift directly to a charitable organization. That way, the administrative costs of a trust or non-for-profit organization can be avoided. However, donors should be aware that such restrictions may ultimately hamper fulfillment of their charitable objectives, perhaps necessitating court proceedings to remove the restrictions.

---

[670] Oberly v. Kirby, 592 A.2d 445, 466–67 (Del.1991).

[671] *Restatement (Third) of Trusts* § 67, cmt. e (2003).

Chapter 11

FUTURE INTERESTS

Analysis

Sec.

11.1 Conditions of Survival.

11.2 Rule of Convenience.

11.3 Gifts to Heirs.

11.4 Continuing Effect of Old Rules.

11.5 Powers of Appointment.

§ 11.1 Conditions of Survival

Many wills and trusts create future interests, for example "to my spouse for life, remainder to our children." If a child fails to survive the testator, a question of lapse arises (*see* Section 6.5). This section discusses what happens if a remainderman survives the testator or settlor[1] but dies during the life of the life beneficiary or prior to some other time fixed for distribution, such as "when she reaches age 25."[2] If the interest is "vested," it passes to the remainderman's estate to be disposed of by his or her will[3] or to the heirs of a remainderman who died intestate. But a court may find a condition that remaindermen must survive the life beneficiary. If so, the court must decide what happens to the share of a remainderman who fails to survive. Most antilapse statutes[4] apply only to devisees who predecease the testator and so are irrelevant in this situation. A remainder "to our children" is a class gift, so any children who survive will take the shares of children who did not. If no class member survives, or if the remainder was to an individual who failed to survive, the particular remainder will fail and be disposed of under the rules for failed dispositions. In the case of a will, the failed remainder will usually pass to the residuary devisees or other residuary devisees, if any, or by intestacy to the testator's heirs.[5] If a remainder created by a revocable inter

---

1 Generally speaking, the rules are the same whether the instrument is a will or an inter vivos trust, Trackman v. Ringer, 529 N.E.2d 647, 649 (Ill.App.1988), and whether the future interest is legal or equitable, with some exceptions.

2 Normally the question is whether the remainderman survived the life beneficiary, but in National City Bank v. Beyer, 729 N.E.2d 711, 715–716 (Ohio 2000), the interest of a remainderman who died a few months after the life beneficiary was held to be divested by a gift over "[i]f such beneficiary dies before the assets . . . [have] been fully distributed."

3 It is also possible, but rare, for remainders to be transferred inter vivos, assuming that there is no spendthrift restraint in the trust. *Restatement (Third) of Trusts* § 51 (2003).

4 As to antilapse statutes, *see* Section 6.5.

5 As to what constitutes a "class gift," and whether a failed residuary gift passes intestate or to other residuary devisees, *see* Section 6.5.

vivos trust fails, typically a "resulting trust" in favor of the settlor or settlor's successors will arise.[6]

Vested or Contingent

The question whether a remainderman must survive the life interest in order to take is often posed as "was the remainder vested or contingent?" This terminology is convenient but misleading, because (1) even vested remainders may be conditioned on survival, and (2) not all contingent remainders are conditioned on survival. As to the first point, if a will provides "remainder to my children, but if any child dies before my spouse, his or her share shall go to his or her children," the children's remainder is not *contingent* on survival, but *vested subject to divestment* for failure to survive.[7] In contrast, a remainder "to our then-living children" is *contingent.* In the first case, the condition of survival is *subsequent;* in the second, the condition is *precedent.*[8] The distinction between conditions precedent and subsequent has practical significance only in jurisdictions which prohibit the transfer of contingent remainders.

> Whether a remainder is contingent or vested depends upon the language employed. If the conditional element is incorporated into the description of . . . the remaindermen, then the remainder is contingent; but if, after words giving a vested interest, a clause is added divesting it, the remainder is vested. Thus, on a devise to A for life, remainder to his children, but if any child dies in the lifetime of A his share is to go to those who survive, the share of each child is vested, subject to be divested by its death.[9] But on a devise to A for life, remainder to such of his children as survive him, the remainder is contingent.[10]

Most states avoid such verbal niceties and allow both vested and contingent remainders to be transferred. "The holder of a contingent future interest in a clear and growing majority of states . . . has property of which present disposition can be made."[11]

Contingent remainders are not always conditioned on survival. A will left land to the testator's granddaughter for life, with a remainder to her descendants if she had any, "and if not, then to Asbury Fletcher." The granddaughter died without descendants. Asbury predeceased her. The court held that Asbury did not get the property because his remainder was

---

[6] *Restatement (Third) of Trusts* § 7 illus. 1 (2003).

[7] *Restatement of Property* § 253, illus. 1 (1940); National City Bank v. Beyer, 729 N.E.2d 711, 716 (Ohio 2000). *But see* Webb v. Underhill, 882 P.2d 127, 130 (Or.App.1994).

[8] Language about survival can come after the designation of the takers and still be deemed "precedent." A remainder "to B's children who survive B" is contingent. *Restatement of Property* § 278 illus. 1 (1940).

[9] *See also* Scott v. Brunson, 569 S.E.2d 385, 388 (S.C.App.2002) (devise to son, but if he does not appear within 10 years, to others is "vested" and reachable by creditor).

[10] Goodwine State Bank v. Mullins, 625 N.E.2d 1056, 1074 (Ill.App.1993) (quoting Danz v. Danz, 26 N.E.2d 872, 874 (Ill.1940) (quoting John Chipman Gray, The Rule Against Perpetuities 86 (3d ed. 1915))).

[11] *Restatement (Third) of Trusts* § 41, cmt. a (2003). In these jurisdictions contingent remainders are no longer regarded as "expectancies."

"contingent."[12] As a dissenting opinion observed, however, a remainder may be subject to a condition (the death of the granddaughter without descendants) that renders it contingent without being subject to a further condition that the remainderman survive the termination of the life estate. Most courts agree with this dissent: a remainder not expressly conditioned on survival is not implicitly conditioned on survival.[13]

Preference for Early Vesting

Some courts give little weight to precedents in construing wills on the ground that the language of every will differs. "Cases construing remainders created by wills are almost as countless as grains of sand on the seashore," but they have little "controlling force . . . because no two wills are alike."[14] Other courts, however, rely on general rules of construction, either statutory or common law. According to one commonly cited rule, the law favors the early vesting of estates.[15] Coke expressed this idea in the 17th century: "the law always delights in the vesting of estates, and contingencies are odious in the law, and are the causes of troubles."[16] Some states have codified the preference for a vested construction,[17] but several writers have attacked it,[18] and courts have begun to question it. For example, "the maxim favoring early vesting of remainders . . . frequently . . . frustrates what the ordinary settlor would have intended" and "should no longer be followed . . . without question."[19] The Uniform Probate Code (hereinafter UPC) presumes that a "future interest under the terms of a trust is contingent on the beneficiary's surviving the distribution date."[20] The UPC justifies a survivorship requirement as avoiding "cumbersome and costly distributions to and through the estates of deceased beneficiaries of future interests."[21] The Third Restatement of Property does not automatically presume a contingency but does provide that "an express condition of survival that is ambiguous regarding the time to which survival is

---

[12] Fletcher v. Hurdle, 536 S.W.2d 109, 113 (Ark.1976). *See also* Rushing v. Mann, 910 S.W.2d 672, 674 (Ark.1995).

[13] *See Restatement of Property* § 261 (1940); Temple Beth Israel v. Feiss, 2 P.3d 388, 390–91 (Or.App.2000); Evans v. Giles, 415 N.E.2d 354, 358 (Ill.1980); In re Ferry's Estate, 361 P.2d 900, 905 (Cal.1961).

[14] Clark v. Strother, 385 S.E.2d 578, 582 (Va.1989). *See also* In re Estate of Long, 918 P.2d 975, 978 (Wash.App.1996).

[15] Summers v. Summers, 699 N.E.2d 958, 962 (Ohio App.1997); Warren v. Albrecht, 571 N.E.2d 1179, 1181 (Ill.App.1991); Matter of Estate of Sprinchorn, 546 N.Y.S.2d 256, 258 (App.Div.1989); William M. McGovern, *Facts and Rules in the Construction of Wills*, 26 UCLA L. Rev. 285, 285 (1978).

[16] Roberts v. Roberts, 80 Eng.Rep. 1002, 1009 (K.B.1613).

[17] Okl.Stat. tit. 84, § 175.

[18] Verner F. Chaffin, *Descendible Future Interests in Georgia: The Effect of the Preference for Early Vesting*, 7 Ga. L. Rev. 443 (1973); Edward H. Rabin, *The Law Favors the Vesting of Estates. Why?* 65 Colum. L. Rev. 467 (1965); Daniel M. Schuyler, *Drafting, Tax, and Other Consequences of the Rule of Early Vesting*, 46 Ill. L. Rev. 407 (1951).

[19] Harris Trust & Savings Bank v. Beach, 513 N.E.2d 833, 839–840 (Ill.1987).

[20] Uniform Probate Code [hereinafter UPC] § 2–707(b). This and all other rules of construction in the Code are subject to "a finding of contrary intention." *Id.* § 2–701.

[21] *Id.* § 2–707, cmt.

required is construed to require the beneficiary or beneficiaries to survive the distribution date."[22]

Many rules of law are based on an assumption that persons want their property to go to their relatives. Intestacy statutes provide only for the decedent's relatives, plus the decedent's spouse.[23] Most antilapse statutes apply only to relatives and make a substitutional gift to the devisee's surviving descendants, so that a lapsed devise will pass to relatives of the testator.[24] Courts sometimes refer to "the common desire" to favor relatives as a relevant factor in construing instruments.[25]

A remainder which is held to be vested may pass to a spouse or other devisees of the remainderman who are unrelated to the testator. This provides an argument for construing such a remainder as contingent. A remainder to the testator's grandnieces and grandnephews was held to be contingent on survival because otherwise "persons not of [the] testatrix' blood line, or even corporate institutions, might be the ultimate distributees."[26]

This reasoning has been challenged. Even if a remainder is contingent on survival, a remainderman who *does* survive and whose interest then vests can give or devise the property to a person unrelated to the testator. Testators who are disturbed by this possibility can limit the remainderman's interest to a life estate.[27]

Arguments Supporting Vested Construction

(1) Promoting Alienability

An argument *in favor of* a vested construction is that it "enables property to be freely transferred at the earliest possible date."[28] However, the question whether a remainder was contingent on survival usually arises after the life tenant has died, at which time the property is alienable whichever construction is chosen. Moreover, even before the life estate expires, the ability to transfer property burdened with a remainder does not often turn on whether the remainder is vested or contingent. Nearly all jurisdictions allow contingent as well as vested remainders to be assigned.[29] Furthermore, most future interests today are beneficial interests in a trust, under which the trustee has the power to sell the trust assets,[30] and the beneficiaries' interests are inalienable

---

[22] *Restatement (Third) of Property (Wills and Other Donative Transfers)* § 26.4 (2011).

[23] *See* Sections 2.1 & 2.2.

[24] *See* Section 6.5.

[25] 5 *American Law of Property* § 21.3 (A. James Casner ed., 1952).

[26] In re Trust of Walker, 116 N.W.2d 106, 109 (Wis.1962). *See also* Lamb v. NationsBank, N.A., 507 S.E.2d 457, 460 (Ga.1998); National City Bank v. Beyer, 729 N.E.2d 711, 716 (Ohio 2000) (testator wanted property to "remain in the family."). In Browning v. Sacrison, 518 P.2d 656, 659 (Or.1974), this general feeling was reinforced by expressions of hostility in the will to an in-law of the testator.

[27] *See* Laura E. Cunningham, *The Hazards of Tinkering with the Common Law of Future Interests: The California Experience*, 48 Hastings L.J. 667, 700 (1997).

[28] In re Krooss, 99 N.E.2d 222, 224 (N.Y.1951). Conversely, the presence of a spendthrift restraint is sometimes advanced as an argument that the settlor/testator wanted an interest to be contingent. National City Bank v. Beyer, 729 N.E.2d 711, 716 (Ohio 2000).

[29] *Restatement (Third) of Trusts* § 41, cmt. a (2003).

[30] As to sales by trustees, *see* Section 14.5.

because of the inclusion of spendthrift provisions. Although courts have traditionally applied the preference for early vesting to trusts as well as to legal remainders,[31] the UPC distinguishes between the two. It implies a condition of survivorship only for future interests in a trust, because "the ability of the parties to sell the land would be impaired if not destroyed" if legal remainders were contingent.[32]

(2) Avoiding Intestacy

Courts sometimes hold remainders vested in order to avoid an intestacy. "The abhorrence of courts to intestacy under a will may be likened unto the abhorrence of nature to a vacuum."[33] If a remainder devised to "children" in the residuary clause of a will is contingent on surviving the life beneficiary, the property will pass to the testator's heirs by intestacy if all the children predecease the life tenant, unless a substitutional devise is added.[34] The property may even escheat to the state if the testator has no surviving relatives.[35]

However, contingent remainders which are given to a class do not create an intestacy if at least one member of the class survives the life beneficiary. Some courts treat *all* class gifts as contingent on survival: if "a gift to a class is postponed until after the termination of a preceding estate, as a rule, those members of the class, and those only, take who are in existence when . . . the time for distribution comes."[36] Most courts, however, treat class gifts the same as gifts to individuals in deciding whether to imply a requirement of survivorship. The Third Restatement of Property provides that in a gift to a single-generation class such as children or the like, a class member who "fails to survive the distribution date . . . is not excluded from the class" absent language or circumstances indicating a contrary intent.[37]

Intestacy may give property to an heir whom the testator wished to disinherit. One court construed a remainder as vested when intestacy would

---

[31] Summers v. Summers, 699 N.E.2d 958, 962 (Ohio App.1997); In re Trust Under Will of Holt, 491 N.W.2d 25, 29 (Minn.App.1992); Trackman v. Ringer, 529 N.E.2d 647, 649 (Ill.App.1988).

[32] UPC § 2–707, cmt.; *See also* Edward C. Halbach & Lawrence W. Waggoner, *The UPC's New Survivorship and Antilapse Provisions*, 55 Alb. L. Rev. 1091, 1132 (1992).

[33] Coddington v. Stone, 9 S.E.2d 420, 424 (N.C.1940). *See also* Matter of Estate of Sprinchorn, 546 N.Y.S.2d 256, 258 (App.Div.1989); In re Trust of Lane, 592 A.2d 492, 496–498 (Md.1991); *Restatement of Property* § 255 (1940). More generally, courts prefer a construction that results in a complete disposition. *Restatement (Third) of Property (Wills and Other Donative Transfers)* § 11.3, cmt. i (2003).

[34] In re Estate of Cruikshank, 746 N.Y.S.2d 769, 775 (Surr.2002) (citing presumption against intestacy in holding a remainder vested). However, if the remainder is in a pre-residuary devise, its failure may simply cause the property to pass under the residuary clause of the will. Temple Beth Israel v. Feiss, 2 P.3d 388, 395 (Or.App.2000).

[35] Jesse Dukeminier, *The Uniform Probate Code Upends the Law of Remainders*, 94 Mich. L. Rev. 148, 158 (1995). As to escheat, *see* Section 2.2.

[36] Wilkes v. Wilkes, 488 S.W.2d 398, 405 (Tex.1972). *See also* In re Trust of Walker, 116 N.W.2d 106, 109–10 (Wis.1962); *cf.* In re Estate of Cruikshank, 746 N.Y.S.2d 769, 773 (Surr.2002) (in a gift *to named individuals* the presumption of vesting is "almost irrebuttable").

[37] *Restatement (Third) of Property (Wills and Other Donative Transfers)* § 15.4 (2011). *See also* Hofing v. Willis, 201 N.E.2d 852, 856 (Ill.1964) (overruling earlier cases); Hartford National Bank & Trust Co. v. Birge, 266 A.2d 373, 378 (Conn.1970); Halbach, *Issues About Issue: Some Recurrent Class Gift Problems,* 48 Mo. L. Rev. 333, 363 (1983).

have frustrated "the testator's expressed intention that his three daughters should each receive $1 'and no more.' "[38]

(3) Protecting Remoter Issue

Intestacy laws and antilapse statutes assume that decedents want the descendants of a deceased relative to take in their place.[39] A vested construction may produce the same result. However, a deceased remainderman may leave his estate to someone else or the estate may be diminished by claims of creditors and/or a spouse, and by death taxes. A remainderman's descendants can be protected better by a direct substitutional gift to them in the manner of the antilapse statutes. The UPC provides such a substitutional gift[40] but the Restatement does not.[41]

Courts sometimes achieve the same result by construing the word "children" in a will or trust to include the children of a deceased child.[42] This result is particularly attractive if the gift would otherwise fail because there are no eligible children,[43] or where the gift is to "children per stirpes," where "per stirpes" makes no sense if "children" is interpreted literally.[44] But courts usually follow "normal usage" under which "the term 'children' does not include grandchildren or more remote descendants."[45] Nor does "grandchildren" include great-grandchildren, and "cousins" does not include first cousins once-removed.[46]

A gift to "descendants," on the other hand, encompasses descendants of all generations, children, grandchildren, etc.[47] Courts have traditionally construed remainders to "descendants" or "issue," in contrast to one-generation classes like "children," as conditioned on survival of the preceding interests,

---

[38] In re Ferry's Estate, 361 P.2d 900, 905–06 (Cal.1961). However, in *In re Gautier's Will*, 146 N.E.2d 771, 774 (N.Y.1957) the court rejected a similar argument.

[39] *See* Sections 2.2 and 6.5.

[40] UPC § 2–707(b)(2). Thus the Restatement calls the vested construction a "crude and costly means of protecting the deceased class member's descendants," *Restatement (Third) of Property (Wills and Other Donative Transfers)* § 15.4, cmt. e (2011), and prefers the antilapse approach of the UPC if a court is "willing to adopt" it. *Id.*, cmt. i.

[41] *Restatement (Third) of Property (Wills and Other Donative Transfers)* § 15.4 (2011). A motion to adopt the UPC's approach was defeated by the ALI membership. ALI Reporter, Fall 2004, at 13.

[42] Cox v. Forristall, 640 P.2d 878, 884–85 (Kan.App.1982).

[43] Matter of Estate of Jenkins, 904 P.2d 1316, 1321 (Colo.1995).

[44] Matter of Estate of Broughton, 828 P.2d 443, 444–45 (Okl.App.1991); *Restatement (Third) of Property (Wills and Other Donative Transfers)* § 14.1, cmt. g(1) (2011); *Restatement (Second) of Property (Donative Transfers)* § 28.1, cmt. i (1988); In re Estate of Garrett, 756 N.E.2d 920, 925 (Ill.App.2001).

[45] *Restatement (Third) of Property (Wills and Other Donative Transfers)* § 14.1(1) (2011); *Restatement (Second) of Property (Donative Transfers)* § 25.1, cmt. a (1988). *See also* Matter of Gustafson, 547 N.E.2d 1152, 1154 (N.Y.1989); Lamb v. NationsBank, N.A., 507 S.E.2d 457, 459 (Ga.1998).

[46] *Restatement (Third) of Property (Wills and Other Donative Transfers)* § 14.1, cmt. *l* (2011); *Restatement (Second) of Property (Donative Transfers)* § 25.8 (1988); Matter of Shields, 552 N.W.2d 581, 585 (Minn.App.1996); Harris Trust and Sav. Bank v. Beach, 495 N.E.2d 1173, 1180 (Ill.App.1986).

[47] *Restatement (Third) of Property (Wills and Other Donative Transfers)* § 14.3 (2011). As to how property is divided among "issue" or "descendants," see Section 2.2.

because in this situation this construction does *not* disinherit descendants of deceased class members.[48]

The UPC's extension of the antilapse statute to future interests in effect converts gifts "to children" into gifts "to descendants."

The extension of antilapse statutes to future interests has not escaped criticism. Professor Dukeminier says that it leads to a "loss of flexibility." If a remainderman, B's interest is vested:

> B can devise the remainder to B's children in such shares and upon such terms as appear wise. If B's children are minors, B can devise the remainder in trust for the children until they reach majority, avoiding conservatorship.[49] If one of B's children is disabled and supported by the state in a state institution, B can devise the child's share in a trust, . . . thus avoiding the state's seizure of the child's full share as the child's creditor,[50] as section 2–707 [of the UPC] would allow.[51]

Professor Waggoner counters that there is no evidence that "beneficiaries of transmissible future interests do any of the things that Dukeminier's article suggests," and even if they did, "circumstances . . . might change in unpredictable ways between [B's] death and the distribution date" (at the death of the life beneficiary).[52]

Drafting Errors

Doubts about the testator's/settlor's intent do not arise if the governing instrument is well drafted. Most future interest disputes arise because the will or trust did not deal adequately with the problem of survival. It apparently never occurred to some drafters that a remainderman might die before the life tenant, but silence on this subject may be deemed to show an intent that the remainder be indefeasibly vested; otherwise the will would have said "if then living" or the like.[53] The argument is strengthened when another gift in the same will expressly requires survival.[54] On the other hand, implying a condition of survival in class gifts can be justified on literalistic grounds: if a

---

48 *Restatement (Third) of Property (Wills and Other Donative Transfers)* § 15.3, *cmt.* b (2011); *Restatement (Second) of Property (Donative Transfers)* § 28.2 (1988); Webb v. Underhill, 882 P.2d 127, 131 (Or.App.1994); In re Estate of Cruikshank, 746 N.Y.S.2d 769, 772 (Surr.2002).

49 For the advantages of a trust over conservatorship *see* Section 10.5. The result favored by Dukeminier in this situation can also be reached under the power given by the Third Restatement of Trusts to modify trusts. *See Restatement (Third) of Trusts* § 66, illus. 6 (2003).

50 As to the effect of a trust for a child who is receiving state aid, *see* Section 10.7.

51 Dukeminier, *supra* note 35, at 151. Professor Waggoner himself once expressed similar views. Lawrence W. Waggoner, *Future Interests Legislation: Implied Conditions of Survivorship and Substitutionary Gifts Under the New Illinois "Anti-Lapse" Provision*, 1969 U. Ill. L.F. 423, 437–38 (1969). But see the following note.

52 Lawrence W. Waggoner, *The Uniform Probate Code Extends Antilapse-Type Protection to Poorly Drafted Trusts*, 94 Mich. L. Rev. 2309, 2331–32 (1996).

53 *See* Matter of Estate of Ruhland, 452 N.W.2d 417, 421 (Iowa 1990).

54 In re Estate of Benson, 285 A.2d 101, 106 (Pa.1971).

gift to "children" is deemed vested, persons who are not "children" will take a share through the estate of a deceased child.[55]

Gifts of future interests typically are expressed in words which look to the future, like "then." Such words are not usually construed to postpone vesting. A will gave the testator's son a life estate and "at his death the remainder shall vest in his children." A daughter of the son who predeceased him was held to have a vested interest; the phrase about vesting at the son's death was said to refer only to the date when the remainder would be distributed.[56]

A spendthrift clause occasionally has been held to show that beneficiaries did not have vested interests, on the theory that allowing a remainder to pass through the beneficiary's estate would violate the prohibition on alienation.[57] This argument is almost always rejected, however.[58] A spendthrift clause prevents an inter vivos transfer of the beneficiary's interest[59] but does not bar the devise of a vested remainder.[60]

"To Alice at 30"

Many trusts provide for distribution of the trust assets to a beneficiary when he or she reaches a specified age such as 30. What if the beneficiary dies before she reaches 30? A famous 17th century case said that if money was "to be paid" to the beneficiary at age 30 her interest was vested, but a bequest to her "at age 30" was not.[61] This subtle distinction has little to recommend it,[62] but it found its way into the Second Restatement of Property.[63] The Third Restatement partially abandons this distinction: "Language providing that the share is 'to be paid at' a specified age is treated as a factor but not necessarily a controlling factor suggesting that there is no condition of survival to the specified age."[64]

Some courts say that, if the trust also gives the beneficiary income from the trust before she reaches 30, this indicates that her interest in the corpus is vested,[65] but one may question whether this really affects decisions, because remainders are often held to be vested when the remaindermen had no prior right to income.

---

[55] In re Trust of Walker, 116 N.W.2d 106, 109 (Wis.1962). *See also* Temple Beth Israel v. Feiss, 2 P.3d 388, 391–92 (Or.App.2000) (vested construction rejected because, in the court's view, it could not literally be carried out).

[56] Rudy v. Wagner, 198 N.W.2d 75, 79 (Neb.1972). *See also* Dauer v. Butera, 642 N.E.2d 848, 851 (Ill.App.1994); Hinds v. McNair, 413 N.E.2d 586, 601 (Ind.App.1980).

[57] In re Robinson's Estate, 68 Cal.Rptr. 420, 425 (App.1968). As to spendthrift provisions, *see* Section 10.8.

[58] In re Benson's Estate, 285 A.2d 101, 106 (Pa.1971); Trugman v. Klein, 226 N.E.2d 521, 527 (Ill.App.1967).

[59] *Restatement (Third) of Trusts* § 58 (2003); *Restatement (Second) of Property (Donative Transfers)* § 25.1, illus. 4 (1988).

[60] *Restatement (Third) of Trusts* § 58, cmt. g (2003).

[61] Clobberie's Case, 86 Eng. Rep. 476 (Ch.1677).

[62] McGovern, *supra* note 15, at 316.

[63] *Restatement (Second) of Property (Donative Transfers)* § 27.3, cmt. f (1988).

[64] *Restatement (Third) of Property (Wills and Other Donative Transfers)* § 26.6, cmt. e (2011).

[65] Brown v. Am. Fletcher Nat. Bank, 519 N.E.2d 166, 168 (Ind.App.1988).

"Surviving"

Many wills and trusts attach words like "surviving" to a remainder. The word is ambiguous, since every person who is born alive survives *someone. Whom* must the remaindermen survive? A will left a remainder to three named sisters-in-law, with the proviso that if any "is not in life, . . . their share be added to the share of any surviving sister-in-law." All three sisters-in-law survived the testator but only one was still living when the life beneficiary died. The court held that she took the whole remainder, deeming that the word "surviving" referred to the death of the life beneficiary, despite a statute saying that "words of survivorship shall refer to the death of the testator in order to vest remainders unless a manifest intention to the contrary shall appear."[66] Some cases interpret "surviving" to refer to the time of the testator's death,[67] but the UPC "codifies the predominant . . . position that survival relates to the distribution date;"[68] even words of survivorship that expressly "relate to . . . an earlier time" (such as the testator's death) do not prevent the implied condition that remaindermen must survive to the date of distribution.[69] Ambiguities can be avoided if the instrument provides for distribution to those who are "then living" on the specified distribution date.

Gifts on Death Without Children or Issue

References to "death" or "decease" in a will, like "surviving," often fail to make clear the point in time to which they refer. The problem arises in three kinds of cases.

(1) *Remainderman Dies Before Life Tenant.* A will left a remainder "to my sister, and in case of her predecease, to her son." The sister survived the testator but not the life tenant. The court held that sister's remainder failed.[70] Despite the general preference for early vesting, most courts would agree.[71]

(2) *Remainderman Dies After Life Tenant.* A will left a remainder to the testator's stepsons and "in the event that any of them should die without issue," his share should go "to the survivors." One of the stepsons survived the life tenant and died without issue years later. The court held that his share was not divested and passed under his will. A "devise over if the remainderman should die without issue . . . is to be taken as referring to the remainderman's death prior to the termination of the intervening estate," because otherwise the remaindermen would have only a life estate, whereas the will gave them a

---

[66] Lemmons v. Lawson, 468 S.E.2d 749, 750–51 (Ga.1996), *abrogated by* Swanson v. Swanson, 514 S.E.2d 822 (Ga.1999). *See also* Matter of Gustafson, 547 N.E.2d 1152, 1154–55 (N.Y.1989); Harris Trust and Sav. Bank v. Beach, 495 N.E.2d 1173, 1179–80 (Ill.App.1986); Theodore Short Trust v. Fuller, 7 S.W.3d 482, 490 (Mo.App.1999).

[67] Swanson v. Swanson, 514 S.E.2d 822, 825 (Ga.1999) (decision in *Lemmons, see* previous note, was "flawed"); Pechin v. Medd, 476 N.E.2d 526, 529–30 (Ind.App.1985); Matter of Mulholland's Estate, 432 N.Y.S.2d 76, 78 (Surr.1980).

[68] UPC § 2–707, cmt.

[69] UPC § 2–707(b)(3). *Contra* DiFilippo v. DiFilippo, 640 N.E.2d 1120, 1123 (Mass.App.1994) (remainder vests at testator's death when a substitutional gift provided "should my . . . brother pre-decease me").

[70] Mueller v. Forsyth, 235 N.E.2d 645, 646, 649 (Ill.App.1968).

[71] Canoy v. Canoy, 520 S.E.2d 128, 132 (N.C.App.1999); Ruth v. First Nat. Bank, 197 S.E.2d 699, 700 (Ga.1973); Browning v. Sacrison, 518 P.2d 656, 660 (Or.1974); *Restatement of Property* § 264 (1940).

fee simple.[72] Some courts have reached the opposite result on the ground that if the testator wanted the substitutional gift to apply only if the remainderman predeceased the life tenant, the will would have said so.[73]

(3) *Immediate Devise*. A woman devised a farm to her son Alvin, but if "Alvin should die without leaving children, I devise the farm to my two daughters." Alvin died without issue 27 years after the testator. The court held that the gift over applied only if Alvin predeceased the testator.[74] The California Probate Code agrees: "a transfer of a present or future interest that refers to a person's death 'with' or 'without issue' . . . refers to that person's being dead at the time the transfer takes effect in enjoyment."[75]

Historically, gifts over upon a devisee's death without issue were deemed to apply if the devisee *or any descendant of his* ever died without issue. With respect to realty this "indefinite failure of issue" construction gave the devisee a fee tail followed by a remainder. As to personal property, a fee tail was not recognized, and the succeeding interest was invalid under the Rule Against Perpetuities, since a descendant of the devisee might die without issue centuries later.[76] Modern law rejects indefinite failure of issue in favor of the "definite" failure of issue construction under which "death" refers only to the named devisee and not to any of his descendants.[77]

Sometimes the devise of a life estate is followed only by a gift over "if the life tenant dies without issue." What happens if the life tenant is survived by issue? Most courts imply a gift to the issue in order to avoid an intestacy.[78] However, in a devise "to A *in fee,* and if he dies without issue, to B," no gift to A's issue is implied because there is no gap to be filled; the property becomes part of A's estate if he is survived by issue.[79]

"To A or His Children (Heirs)"

A remainder given to "my children, or their issue (or heirs)," is usually construed to give the share of any child who fails to survive the life beneficiary

---

[72] Stanley v. Brietz, 612 S.W.2d 699, 701 (Tex.Civ.App.1981). *See also Restatement (Third) of Property (Wills and Other Donative Transfers)* § 26.8 (2011); *Restatement of Property* § 269 (1940); Thomas v. Thomas, 294 S.E.2d 795, 799 (Va.1982).

[73] Adams v. Vidal, 60 So.2d 545, 548 (Fla.1952); Ford v. Thomas, 633 S.W.2d 58, 60 (Ky.1982).

[74] Lones v. Winzer, 486 S.W.2d 758, 760 (Tenn.App.1971).

[75] Cal.Prob.Code § 21112.

[76] Hayes v. Hammond, 143 N.E.2d 693, 697 (Mass.1957); *Restatement of Property* § 243 illus. 3 (1940). For a full discussion of the Rule Against Perpetuities, *see* Chapter 12. The fee tail is discussed in Section 11.4.

[77] *Restatement (Third) of Property (Wills and Other Donative Transfers)* § 26.8, illus. 1 (2011); *Restatement of Property* § 266 (1940); Minn. Stat. Ann. § 500.14(1); Kan. Stat. Ann. § 58–504.

[78] *Restatement (Third) of Property (Wills and Other Donative Transfers)* § 26.9, cmt. b (2011); *Restatement of Property* § 272 (1940); 5 *American Law of Property* § 21.34 (A. James Casner ed., 1952).

[79] Erickson v. Reinbold, 493 P.2d 794, 801 (Wash.App.1972).

to his or her issue (or heirs).[80] Such language should not be confused with devises "to A *and* his heirs" or "to A *and* his children."[81]

Some wills provide a substitutional gift to the children of a remainderman who fails to survive the life tenant but do not say what should happen if a remainderman dies *without* children. For example, the disposition is "to A for life, then to A's children, but if a child of A dies before A leaving descendants who survive A, such deceased child's share shall be paid per stirpes to such deceased child's descendants." Many courts hold that in this situation the interest of the remainderman is vested and, if the remainderman dies without descendants, the interest passes through the deceased remainderman's estate because the divesting condition never occurred.[82] However, the Second Restatement of Property says that "because of the undesirability of having the gift pass through the deceased [class] member's estate" it should go to the other members of the class.[83]

The Third Restatement takes a more complex approach. If, as in the above example, the remainder is in the form of a class gift, the result is the same: the interest of a child who predeceases without issue passes to the remaining class members.[84] However, if the remainder is not in the form of a class gift, the result depends on whether the condition of survival is restricted or unrestricted. An unrestricted condition of survival is expressed through disjunctive language: "To A for life, then to A's children or their descendants." A restricted condition of survival is expressed through supplanting language: "To A for life, then to A's children, but if a child of A dies before A leaving descendants who survive A, to such deceased child's descendants." Unrestricted conditions of survival are unequivocal. By contrast, a restricted condition of survival divests the interest of the remainderman only upon two conditions: the remainderman's (1) predecease (2) with descendants surviving the life tenant.[85]

Some wills impose a requirement of survival on the primary remainderman but not on the persons designated as substitute takers. A will devised a remainder to the descendants of the testator's nephew, or, "if no such descendants are then living . . . [to] the other beneficiaries of this will." The express condition of survival imposed on the nephew's descendants was deemed to show an intent to impose the same requirement on the other

---

[80] Rowett v. McFarland, 394 N.W.2d 298, 302–04 (S.D.1986); *Restatement (Third) of Property (Wills and Other Donative Transfers)* § 26.5 (2011); *Restatement of Property* § 252 (1940).

[81] As to "A and his heirs" or "A and his children," see Section 11.4.

[82] Swanson v. Swanson, 514 S.E.2d 822, 825 (Ga.1999); Matter of Estate of Sprinchorn, 546 N.Y.S.2d 256, 258 (App.Div.1989) (remainder to niece and her daughter or the survivor vests in their estates when both predecease life beneficiary); Matter of Blough's Estate, 378 A.2d 276, 280–81 (Pa.1977); *Restatement of Property* § 254 (1940).

[83] *Restatement (Second) of Property (Donative Transfers)* § 27.3, cmt. e (1988). *See also* Warren Boynton State Bank v. Wallbaum, 493 N.E.2d 21, 26 (Ill.App.1986), *rev'd*, 528 N.E.2d 640 (Ill. 1988).

[84] *Restatement (Third) of Property (Wills and other Donative Transfers)* § 26.5, illus. 3 & Reporter's Note (2011).

[85] *Restatement (Third) of Property (Wills and other Donative Transfers)* § 26.5, cmt. c (2011).

beneficiaries,[86] but other courts have drawn the opposite inference, holding that the substitute takers do *not* have to survive.[87]

Planning

One court has suggested that "a pervasive cloud of uncertainty" surrounds the law of future interests, leading courts to "determine an equitable distribution and thereafter fill in the blanks with appropriate bits and pieces of the law . . . in order to reach the desired result."[88] It seems proper for courts to adopt a construction that leads to a "desired result" when the language of a will is open to more than one interpretation,[89] but what might be deemed a desired result is often not certain.

Drafters can avoid such dilemmas by (1) stating clearly whether survivorship is required; (2) specifying with certainty the person, class, or event that must be survived; and (3) saying what happens if the survivorship condition is not met.

Lawyers should use formulas from the better formbooks in preparing wills and trusts with future interests. It is inefficient and risky to draft wills "from scratch"; the future interest cases strewn though the reports demonstrate the many chances for error.

Income Interests

Similar constructional problems arise when income is payable to several beneficiaries and one of them dies before the trust terminates. A trust called for the payment of income to the "child or children" of the settlor's daughter "during their lives." One of the daughter's children died without issue after receiving income for several years. What should the trustee do with the income the deceased child had been receiving?

> Courts in other jurisdictions have reached a variety of solutions. . . . Some courts have ordered the income to be paid to the surviving income beneficiaries under the doctrine of implication of cross remainders, as a gift to a class, or as an implied joint tenancy. Other courts have ordered the income to be paid to the deceased beneficiary's estate until the death of the last income beneficiary[90] . . . . Other courts have ordered the income to be paid to the remaindermen. . . . Finally, some courts have ordered the income to be accumulated until the death of the last income beneficiary.[91]

---

[86] Irish v. Profitt, 330 N.E.2d 861, 871–72 (Ill.App.1975). *See also* Lamb v. NationsBank, N.A., 507 S.E.2d 457, 459 (Ga.1998).

[87] Mueller v. Forsyth, 235 N.E.2d 645, 649 (Ill.App.1968); *Restatement (Third) of Property (Wills and Other Donative Transfers)* § 26.3, cmt. f (2011); *Restatement of Property* § 250, illus. 4, § 252, cmt. f (1940).

[88] Warren-Boynton State Bank v. Wallbaum, 528 N.E.2d 640, 643 (Ill.1988).

[89] McGovern, *supra* note 15, at 321.

[90] *See, e.g.*, Oak Park Trust & Savings Bank v. Baumann, 438 N.E.2d 1354, 1358 (Ill.App.1982); Prince v. Prince, 239 N.E.2d 18, 20–21 (Mass.1968); Matter of Lopez, 636 P.2d 731, 738 (Haw.1981); Wing v. Wachovia Bank & Trust Co., 272 S.E.2d 90, 95 (N.C.1980).

[91] Trust Agreement of Westervelt v. First Interstate Bank, 551 N.E.2d 1180, 1185 (Ind.App.1990) (citation omitted).

The court in this case adopted the first mentioned possibility for Mr. Westervelt's trust.[92] Would it have done so if the deceased child was survived by issue? Not necessarily, under the Third Restatement of Property. The Third Restatement of Property recognizes the traditional rule of an implied cross remainder to living income beneficiaries, but provides an exception where the remainder in trust principal is in favor of the income beneficiaries' issue. In such cases, the Restatement Third of Property presumes an income interest in favor of the deceased beneficiary's living issue, finding this solution "more consistent with the transferor's overall plan of disposition,"[93] a solution like that of the UPC for future interests.

Because of the conflicting authorities, it is hard to predict the result a court will choose. The best *drafting* solution is probably to allow the trustee to sprinkle income among the beneficiaries. This language would permit the trustee to refrain from distributing income to a decedent's estate and to give it directly to the decedent's children or the decedent's siblings or accumulate it in the trustee's discretion.

§ 11.2 Rule of Convenience

The primary concern of this chapter so far has been remaindermen who die too soon, that is, before the preceding interest terminates. This section deals with the opposite problem: persons who are born too late to be included in a class gift even though they literally fall within its terms. For example, suppose a will created a trust for "the children of Ralph," the testator's son. The trustee was to use income and principal for the children's support and education and to distribute a share of the principal to each child at age 25. When the testator died Ralph had five children, but he later adopted another. The 6th child was allowed to share in the trust.

> If a testamentary gift to a class is in general terms . . . , the death of the testator will, as a general rule, fix the time for distribution, and close the class.[94] . . . However, if the gift is . . . to be distributed at a later determinable date, the class members who are in being at the testator's death take a vested interest in the fund then, subject to the addition of members of the class who are born after the testator's death but before the time provided for distribution.[95]

Ralph's 6th child was adopted before Ralph's oldest child reached 25. Any child born or adopted after Ralph's oldest child reached 25 would be excluded under

---

[92] *Id. See also* Svenson v. First Nat. Bank of Boston, 363 N.E.2d 1129, 1134 (Mass.App.1977); Littwin v. Littwin, 498 N.E.2d 544, 547 (Ill.App.1986).

[93] *Restatement (Third) of Property (Wills and Other Donative Transfers)* § 26.9, cmt. e(1) (2011). *Accord Restatement (Third) of Trusts* § 49, cmt. c(3) (2003).

[94] Thus if there had been a simple devise to "the children of Ralph," the after-born 6th child would have been excluded. *Accord Restatement (Third) of Property (Wills and Other Donative Transfers)* § 15.1 (2011).

[95] Cent. Trust Co. of N. Ohio, N.A. v. Smith, 553 N.E.2d 265, 271 (Ohio 1990). *Accord* In re Testamentary Trust of Hasch, 721 N.E.2d 1111, 1113 (Ohio App.1999); S. C. Nat. Bank v. Johnson, 197 S.E.2d 668, 670 (S.C.1973); *Restatement (Third) of Property (Wills and Other Donative Transfers)* § 15.1, cmt. f (2011).

the "rule of convenience,"[96] even though it would be possible to redivide the trust assets each time a child reached age 25 based on the number of children age 25 or younger at the time without upsetting any distributions previously made. This solution, of course, might give the eldest child more than the younger siblings.

Under the "rule of convenience," a class that is still physiologically open will close earlier when any class member is entitled to possession or enjoyment. So in the example above, when Ralph's oldest child attained age 25 and could demand her share, the class closed. This rule excluding after-born class members is called the "rule of convenience" because it avoids "the otherwise necessary complex safeguards in favor of possible but as yet not conceived or adopted takers."[97] The rule is not often invoked because most class gifts are to groups which close naturally at the time of distribution. When a will devises property "to my children," no class members will be born after the will takes effect.[98] In an outright devise "to my grandchildren," on the other hand, if the testator is survived by children, grandchildren may be born after the testator dies, but they would be excluded by the rule of convenience.

The rule turns on the time when distribution is made. In a future interest, the class closes when the gift takes effect in enjoyment, for example, at the end of a preceding life estate.[99] In some instruments the time of distribution is ambiguous, such as "when my youngest grandchild reaches [or when all of my grandchildren have reached] age 21." Has this time arrived when all of the transferor's *living* grandchildren have reached 21, if children of the transferor are still alive? A later grandchild may turn out to be the "youngest," so one might want to postpone distribution until all the children are dead at which point the youngest grandchild can be identified with certainty.[100] However, the quoted language is generally read to call for distribution when there is no living grandchild under 21.[101] Although this interpretation cuts off any grandchild born thereafter, few parents have children after their youngest living child reaches 21. In the unusual situation in which after-born or adopted class members are a likely possibility, the Third Restatement of Property suggests the class should remain open.[102]

A direction to distribute "when the youngest grandchild reaches 21" also presents a problem if the youngest grandchild dies before reaching 21. In that

---

[96] In re Estate of Evans, 80 N.W.2d 408, 416 (Wis.1957); *Restatement (Third) of Property (Wills and Other Donative Transfers)* § 15.1, cmt. f (2011); *Restatement (Second) of Property (Donative Transfers)* § 26.2, cmt. m (1988); *cf.* In re Silberman's Will, 242 N.E.2d 736, 742 (N.Y.1968) (will provided class would close when eldest grandchild reached 21).

[97] *Restatement (Second) of Property (Donative Transfers)* § 26.1, cmt. a (1988). *See also Restatement (Third) of Property (Wills and Other Donative Transfers)* § 15.1, cmt. d (2011).

[98] As to posthumous children, *see infra* note 109 *et seq.*

[99] *Restatement (Third) of Property (Wills and Other Donative Transfers)* § 15.1, cmt. f (2011). *Cf.* Section 6.5.

[100] 5 *American Law of Property* § 22.44 (A. James Casner ed., 1952); *See generally* Sheridan v. Blume, 125 N.E. 353 (Ill.1919).

[101] S.C. Nat. Bank v. Johnson, 197 S.E.2d 668, 672 (S.C.1973); Lux v. Lux, 288 A.2d 701, 707 (R.I.1972); *Restatement (Third) of Property (Wills and Other Donative Transfers)* § 15.1, cmt. *o* (2011); *Restatement (Second) of Property (Donative Transfers)* § 26.2, cmt. *o* (1988).

[102] *Restatement (Third) of Property (Wills and Other Donative Transfers)* § 15.1, cmt. *o* (2011).

case, the trust will normally terminate when the *next* youngest grandchild reaches 21,[103] because the testator's probable purpose was to avoid distribution to persons under 21. This is achieved if distribution is put off only until no living distributee is under 21.

If an interest preceding the class gift is disclaimed, many courts hold that the disclaimer "accelerates" the remainder and closes the class.[104]

Income

Many trusts provide for the distribution of income to or among a class. A distribution of an income installment does not close the class (other than for that installment of income) because "there is no . . . real inconvenience in allowing the class to remain open to those children born after the distribution of income begins. . . . Each distribution of income can be made to the children . . . living at that time,"[105] treating the income interest as "a series of" gifts.[106]

Posthumous and Adopted Children

When a class "closes" under the rule of convenience, any child who has then been *conceived* is included in the class if the child is later born alive. This may delay the fixing of shares for a few months, but this is not a significant inconvenience.[107] Similarly intestacy statutes include as heirs persons who were conceived before but born after the decedent's death.[108] Recently, the courts have been grappling with the question of whether a posthumously-conceived child may inherit from the deceased father.[109] Developments in assisted reproductive technology also have implications for class gifts and the class closing rules. The Third Restatement of Property provides:

> In cases in which the distribution date is the deceased parent's death, a child produced posthumously by assisted reproduction is treated as in being at the decedent's death, for purposes of the class-closing rules, if the child was born in utero within a reasonable time after the decedent's death. . . . Determining whether birth or pregnancy occurred within a reasonable time after the decedent's death requires a balancing of the interest in final settlement of trusts and estates and allowing the surviving spouse or domestic partner time to grieve before making a decision whether to go forward with an assisted-reproduction procedure, and how soon after death an attempt was

---

103 *Restatement (Second) of Property (Donative Transfers)* § 26.2, cmt. *o* (1988).

104 Pate v. Ford, 376 S.E.2d 775, 777 (S.C.1989); *Restatement (Third) of Property (Wills and Other Donative Transfers)* § 15.1, illus. 4 (2011); *Restatement (Second) of Property (Donative Transfers)* § 26.1, cmt. j (1988).

105 Hamilton Nat. Bank v. Hutcheson, 357 F.Supp. 114, 119–20 (E.D.Tenn.1973) (quoting Lewis Simes, Law of Future Interests 211 (2d ed. 1966)). *See also* Cent. Trust Co. of N. Ohio, N.A. v. Smith, 553 N.E.2d 265, 273 (Ohio 1990).

106 *Restatement (Third) of Property (Wills and Other Donative Transfers)* § 15.1, cmt. p (2011); *Restatement (Second) of Property (Donative Transfers)* § 26.1, cmt. f (1988).

107 *Restatement (Third) of Property (Wills and Other Donative Transfers)* § 15.1, cmt. h (2011); *Restatement (Second) of Property (Donative Transfers)* § 26.1, cmt. c (1988).

108 UPC § 2–104(b)(2); Cal.Prob.Code § 6407.

109 *See, e.g.*, Woodward v. Comm'r of Soc. Sec., 760 N.E.2d 257, 270 (Mass.2002); In re Estate of Kolacy, 753 A.2d 1257, 1259–64 (N.J.Super.Ch.Div.2000).

made to produce a pregnancy through assisted reproduction, whether successful or not.[110]

If a person enters a class by adoption, the crucial date is the date of adoption, not birth; any child adopted after the class closed is excluded regardless of the date of birth.[111]

Exceptions to the Rule of Convenience

The rule of convenience is a rule of construction and does not apply if "the language or circumstances establish that the transferor had a different intention."[112] Courts rarely find such a "contrary intent"; the rule of convenience creates a "stronger" presumption of intent than the preference for early vesting. A court applied the rule of convenience even to a trust for "all" of the settlor's children who attained the age of 21 "whether now living, or hereafter to be born." The quoted words were held to refer only to children born after the trust was executed but before the date of distribution.[113] Devises under a will to children "who may hereafter be born or adopted" may also be construed to refer only to children born after the will is executed and before the testator dies.[114]

No Class Members in Being

To avoid rendering a gift totally ineffective, courts do not apply the rule of convenience when no class member is alive at the time of distribution. In such cases all class members get a share whenever born.[115] Thus if a will devises property "to the children of Charles" and Charles has two children when the testator dies, a third child born a year later is excluded, but if Charles has no children when the testator dies and three are born thereafter, they all get a share in spite of any inconvenience this creates. However, the Third Restatement of Property rejects this "traditional rule" if the birth of after-born class members is "improbable . . . because of the age or physical condition of the prospective parent."[116]

Class Gifts v. Individual Gifts

The terms of an instrument may limit a class more narrowly than does the rule of convenience. When a will divided the estate "equally between my three grandchildren Francis, Manley, and Willie," a fourth grandchild was not allowed a share even though he was born prior to distribution, because the use of names and the number "three" showed that the testator did not intend a

---

[110] *Restatement (Third) of Property (Wills and Other Donative Transfers)* § 15.1, cmt. j (2011).

[111] In re Silberman's Will, 242 N.E.2d 736, 742 (N.Y.1968). As to the right of adoptees generally to inherit or take under a class gift, see Section 2.10.

[112] *Restatement (Third) of Property (Wills and Other Donative Transfers)* § 15.1 (2011); *Restatement (Second) of Property (Donative Transfers)* § 26.1 (1988).

[113] In re Wernher's Settlement Trusts, [1961] 1 All E.R. 184, 189–90 (Ch.1960).

[114] *Restatement (Second) of Property (Donative Transfers)* § 26.1, illus. 22–23 (1988).

[115] *Restatement (Third) of Property (Wills and Other Donative Transfers)* § 15.1, cmt. k (2011); *Restatement (Second) of Property (Donative Transfers)* §§ 26.1(2), 26.2(2) (1988).

[116] *Restatement (Third) of Property (Wills and Other Donative Transfers)* § 15.1, cmt. k (2011).

class gift.[117] Courts have reached this result even when a will alternates between general language ("the children of R") and specific ("[names], the children of R").[118]

Planning

Most commentators agree with the rule of convenience.[119] The rule reasonably reconciles the inclusive intent indicated by class-gift language with the inconvenience of preserving an interest for unborn beneficiaries, but it may not provide the best solution to the problem in a particular situation. Suppose land is devised to "the children of Charles," and Charles has one child but plans to have more. Why should his later children be excluded? Conversely, suppose that Charles is fifty and a bachelor who has no intention of marrying. Why should the title to the land be kept in abeyance for his lifetime to protect children who are not likely to materialize? Some courts would allow proof that Charles cannot have further children,[120] but even if he can, the possibility might be too improbable to justify the inconvenience of protecting their interest.

§ 11.3 Gifts to Heirs

A well-drafted instrument that creates future interests contingent on survival should leave no gaps in the event that the designated remaindermen fail to survive. Many drafters use the intestacy statutes for this purpose but clarify that the heirs who are to take are those persons who would be entitled to take as heirs had the testator or other designated person died at the time of distribution instead of on the date of their actual death. It is the simple gift to the "heirs" of the testator or of another person that raises problems of construction that will be discussed in this section.

Intestacy statutes usually allow very remote relatives to inherit (if no closer relatives survive)[121] whereas the testator may prefer that the estate go to a charity. On the other hand, intestacy statutes list descendants and collateral relatives of a decedent in the order that most testators prefer, incorporate a requirement of survival of the ancestor, and provide for representation of deceased relatives by their descendants. Thus, if a will leaves property "to Alice for life, remainder to her heirs," a child of Alice who predeceased her would get no share,[122] but any children of the deceased child would take the share by representation.[123] In this respect a devise to "heirs" is

---

[117] Platt v. Romesburg, 348 S.E.2d 536, 536–37 (S.C.App.1986). *See also* Penn Mut. Life Ins. Co. v. Abramson, 530 A.2d 1202, 1210–13 (D.C.1987).

[118] Retseck v. Fowler State Bank, 782 N.E.2d 1022, 1026–27 (Ind.App.2003); Estate of Hurst v. Hurst, 769 N.E.2d 55, 66 (Ill.App.2002) (devise to "my children. My children are A and B" excludes two unnamed children of testator).

[119] Halbach, *supra* note 37, at 358–61.

[120] *See* Section 10.9.

[121] *See* Section 2.2.

[122] Tootle v. Tootle, 490 N.E.2d 878, 882 (Ohio 1986).

[123] Dempsey v. Dempsey, 795 N.E.2d 996, 1000 (Ill.App.2003). *See also* Section 2.2.

like one to "descendants," but "heirs" normally includes a spouse[124] and collateral relatives if the designated ancestor is not survived by descendants.

Time of Determination

Suppose that a will or trust creates a remainder in the heirs of someone who dies before the life tenant. For example, suppose a trust gives a life interest to the settlor and then a remainder to the heirs of the settlor's children. What happens if a child of the settlor dies before the settlor? At least one court has held that the remainder interest became vested in the child's heirs when the child died because "vested estates are to be favored. . . . Unless a contrary intention appears, a gift in a will to the heirs of a person . . . will be construed as a gift to such heirs determined as of the time of death of that person."[125] Some courts have reached similar conclusions in construing remainders to the heirs of the testator; the heirs were to be determined as of the testator's death.[126]

An immediate devise, such as "to the heirs of Alice," can also raise the question when the heirs should be determined. If Alice predeceased the testator and was survived by children who also predeceased the testator, they would not take under the devise because courts usually determine "heirs" in this situation at the time of the testator's death.[127] If instead Alice survives the testator, courts usually give the property to those persons who *would have been* Alice's heirs if she had died when the testator did; otherwise distribution would have to be postponed until Alice's actual death.[128]

The Third Restatement of Property and the UPC take a consistent position focusing on the time of distribution. As a default rule of construction, "heirs" are to be determined as if the ancestor "died when the disposition is to take effect in possession or enjoyment."[129]

Change in Law

Since the statutes governing intestate succession vary, an undefined reference to "heirs" raises the question which state's statute should control.[130] Also, the intestacy law of a given state may change. When a testator died with a will leaving a remainder to the "heirs of my children," the relevant state law did not give husbands an intestate share of their wife's land, but when the testator's daughter later died, it did. The court found the testator intended to

---

[124] *See* Section 2.4.

[125] Matter of Dodge Testamentary Trust, 330 N.W.2d 72, 81 (Mich.App.1982) (quoting In re Estate of Jamieson, 132 N.W.2d 1, 4, 12 (Mich. 1965)). *See also* Estate of Woodworth v. Regents of the Univ. of Cal., 22 Cal. Rptr.2d 676, 678–81 (App.1993); Hess v. Proffer, 87 S.W.3d 432, 434–35 (Mo.App.2002).

[126] Tate v. Kennedy, 578 So.2d 1079, 1083 (Ala.1991).

[127] *Restatement (Third) of Property (Wills and Other Donative Transfers)* § 16.1, illus. 3 (2011); *Restatement (Second) of Property (Donative Transfers)* § 29.4, cmt. g (1988); UPC § 2–711 (which also applies to present gifts to heirs).

[128] *Restatement (Third) of Property (Wills and Other Donative Transfers)* § 16.1, illus. 2 (2011); *Restatement (Second) of Property (Donative Transfers)* § 29.4, cmt. c (1988).

[129] UPC § 2–711; *Restatement (Third) of Property (Wills and Other Donative Transfers)* § 16.1 (2011). *See also* Cal.Prob.Code § 21114.

[130] *See* Section 2.4.

apply the intestacy laws in effect when each child died.[131] But another court, construing a trust created in 1929 which gave a remainder to the heirs of the settlor's grandson, determined heirs as of the grandson's death but used the law in effect in 1929 in doing so.[132]

A designation in the will of the relevant law may affect the time when the heirs are determined as well. A devise "to my heirs according to the Statute . . . of the State of Illinois in effect at the time of the death" of the life tenant was held to show an intent that the heirs be determined as of the life tenant's death.[133]

§ 11.4 Continuing Effect of Old Rules

Heirs as a Word of Limitation

Historically, one had to use the word "heirs" in order to convey land in fee simple; a conveyance "to John in fee simple" gave him only a life estate.[134] This is no longer true, but many drafters still use "heirs" to indicate that a donee or devisee should get a fee simple. In this case "heirs" is a word of "limitation" because it limits (*i.e.*, defines) John's estate. Heirs acquire an interest under an instrument only if "heirs" is used as a "word of purchase."[135]

In a gift "to John and his heirs," John's heirs get no interest,[136] but slightly different wording can change the result. A devise to the testator's grandson "and *at his death* to his heirs" was held to give the grandson a life estate with a remainder in his children.[137] A devise "to A and his heirs" is sometimes construed as a substitutional gift to the heirs if A predeceases the testator; *a fortiori* if the will says "to A *or* his heirs."[138]

Construing "heirs" as a word of limitation facilitates alienation of property, because one need not necessarily wait until the ancestor dies to determine the interested parties. However, future interests are allowed to impede alienation if they stay within the limits of the Rule Against Perpetuities. Therefore, courts today usually construe heirs as a word of

---

[131] Matter of Dodge Testamentary Trust, 330 N.W.2d 72, 83 (Mich.App.1982). *See also Restatement (Third) of Property (Wills and Other Donative Transfers)* § 16.1, cmt. g (2011); *Restatement (Second) of Property (Donative Transfers)* § 29.3 (1988).

[132] National City Bank of Cleveland v. Ford, 299 N.E.2d 310, 314 (Ohio Com.Pl.1973). *See also* In re Johnson's Will, 301 N.Y.S.2d 174, 176 (App.Div.1969); *cf.* In re Matter of Estate of Hughlett, 446 N.E.2d 887, 891 (Ill.App.1983) (law at date of execution of will).

[133] Spaugh v. Ferguson, 264 N.E.2d 542, 549 (Ill.App.1970). *See also Restatement (Third) of Property (Wills and Other Donative Transfers)* § 16.1, cmt. *l* (2011).

[134] Littleton, Tenures § 1 (Eugene Wambaugh ed., 1903); 2 W. Blackstone, *Commentaries* 107 (1766); *cf. Restatement of Property* § 27 (1936).

[135] *Restatement (Third) of Property (Wills and Other Donative Transfers)* § 16.1, cmt. a (2011). Purchase in this context does not mean "acquire for money." Even if land is given to "heirs," they are "purchasers" if they were intended to get an interest. 2 W. Blackstone, *Commentaries* 241 (1766).

[136] *Restatement (Third) of Property (Wills and Other Donative Transfers)* § 16.1, cmt. a (2011); *Restatement (Second) of Property (Donative Transfers)* § 29.7, cmt. a (1988). *See also* Estate of Straube v. Barber, 990 S.W.2d 40, 45 (Mo.App.1999); In re White's Estate, 238 A.2d 791, 794 (Vt.1968).

[137] Cheuvront v. Haley, 444 S.W.2d 734, 736–37 (Ky.1969).

[138] Rowett v. McFarland, 394 N.W.2d 298, 305 (S.D.1986). *See also* Section 6.5.

purchase if they think it was intended as such, even though this may impede a transfer of property.

Fee Tail

The tension between the law's desire to promote alienability and the desire of some donors to keep property in the family surfaced in the 13th century with limitations of the type "to A and the heirs of his (her) body." Courts construed such words as giving A a fee simple conditional on having issue; if A had no issue, the land would revert to the donor (or pass to a remainderman if one was designated), but if A had issue s/he could transfer the property.[139] The statute *De Donis Conditionalibus* 1285 rejected this construction as being contrary to the donor's intention, and allowed A's issue to recover the land if A alienated it.[140] The interest created by limitations "to A and the heirs of his (her) body" became known as a "fee tail." The statute *De Donis* did not make clear how far the restraint on alienation in a fee tail extended. A could not convey the land, but could her children? her grandchildren? Eventually the courts held that a fee tail was perpetual; if, for example, A's *great grandson* sold the land, *his* children could upset the sale.[141] Courts soon regretted this perpetual restraint on alienation and allowed a fee tail to be conveyed by a complex legal proceeding involving many fictitious allegations. In the 18th century, Blackstone praised the courts for "unriveting the fetters of estates-tail, which were attended with a legion of mischiefs to the commonwealth," but he lamented the "awkward shifts [necessary] . . . to get the better of that stubborn statute *de donis*".[142]

Most American states have adopted a statutory solution to the problem of gifts "to A and the heirs of his/her body."[143] These statutes vary, but in general they allow alienation to be restrained, if at all, for only one generation. A devise to the testator's daughter "and the heirs of her body" was held to give her by virtue of a statute a fee simple, defeasible if she died without issue, because the will contained a gift over "in the event of the death of my said daughter without bodily heirs."[144] In some states these words would give the daughter a life estate with a remainder to her issue.[145]

Since the phrase "heirs of her body" is subject to several possible constructions, drafters should avoid it. If a donor wishes to keep property in the family, a gift "to my daughter for life, remainder to her descendants who survive her" makes this clear. (The instrument should also provide an

[139] 2 Bracton, *De Legibus* 68 (George E. Woodbine ed., 1915). In Prichard v. Dep't of Revenue, 164 N.W.2d 113, 122 (Iowa 1969), the court applied the same rule to hold that if A had issue, the property was taxable in her estate at death.

[140] Statute of Westminster II, 13 Edw. 1, c. 1 (1285).

[141] T.F.T. Plucknett, *A Concise History of the Common Law* 552–54 (5th ed. 1956).

[142] 2 W. Blackstone, *Commentaries* 360 (1766).

[143] *Restatement (Third) of Property (Wills and Other Donative Transfers)* § 16.2, Reporter's Note (2011); *Restatement (Second) of Property (Donative Transfers)* § 30.1, Statutory Note par. 7 (1988). In Dempsey v. Dempsey, 795 N.E.2d 996, 999 (Ill.App.2003), such a statute was held inapplicable to a gift "to heirs of the body of my son . . . *in fee simple*." (emphasis added).

[144] Russell v. Russell, 399 S.E.2d 415, 418 (N.C.App.1991). *See also* Cal.Civ.Code §§ 763–64.

[145] Williams v. Kimes, 949 S.W.2d 899, 899 (Mo.1997); Sligh v. Plair, 569 S.W.2d 58, 60 (Ark.1978).

alternative remainder in case the daughter dies without surviving descendants.)

The Rule in Shelley's Case

A settlor created a trust for his grandson for life "and upon his death to the heirs of his body." The court held these words gave the grandson a fee tail under the notorious Rule in Shelley's Case.

> Where a freehold is limited to one for life, and, by the same instrument, the inheritance is limited . . . to his heirs, or to the heirs of his body, the first taker takes the whole estate, either in fee simple or in fee tail; and the words "heirs," or "heirs of his body" are words of limitation, and not words of purchase.[146]

Technically, under the Rule in Shelley's Case, the disposition to the grandson's heirs was converted into a remainder in the grandson. The grandson's life estate and remainder were then merged, resulting in a fee tail.

Applying the Rule in this case probably produced a good result; it allowed an adopted child of the grandson to take because a statute converted the grandson's fee tail into a life estate with a remainder to his "issue," and "issue" included adoptees even though "heirs of his body" did not.[147] The original Rule in Shelley's Case was created for a very different purpose: to prevent evasions of the medieval equivalent of the estate tax.[148] It has also been invoked by the Internal Revenue Service for the same reason,[149] but skilled drafters can easily avoid the Rule, and creating traps for clients of unskilled drafters in order to generate tax revenue seems unfair.

Another rationale for the Rule is that it promotes alienability.[150] When land was left to the testator's son for life and "at his death his heirs take the fee simple title," the Rule gave the son a fee simple which he could convey over the protest of his children.[151] The promotion of alienability is a worthy purpose, but the Rule is nevertheless in disrepute because it is so arbitrary. A devise "to my son for life, remainder to his heirs," imposes no greater restriction on alienability than a devise "to my son for life, remainder to his descendants."

---

[146] Soc'y Nat. Bank v. Jacobson, 560 N.E.2d 217, 221 (Ohio 1990) (quoting King v. Beck, 12 Ohio 390, 471 (Ohio 1843)).

[147] *Cf.* Section 2.10.

[148] 2 W. Blackstone, *Commentaries* 242 (1766); *Restatement (Second) of Property (Donative Transfers)* § 30.1, cmt. a (1988). Some have questioned this theory of the Rule's origin. Bruce Ziff & M.M. Litman, *Shelley's Rule in a Modern Context: Clearing the 'Heir'*, 34 U. Toronto L.J. 170, 175–76 (1984). One thing is clear: the Rule is much older than the 17th century case from which its name is derived.

[149] Estate of Forrest, TC Memo 1990–464. The rule was held inapplicable, however, because the word "heirs" was construed to mean "children." *Id.*

[150] *Restatement (Third) of Property (Wills and Other Donative Transfers)* § 16.2, cmt. b (2011).

[151] Toler v. Harbour, 589 S.W.2d 529, 532 (Tex.Civ.App.1979). If the remainder in this case had been to "the heirs of the body" of the son, the effect of the Rule would depend on how the jurisdiction treated estates in fee tail.

But the Rule in Shelley's Case does not apply to the latter because it only covers remainders to "heirs."[152]

The Rule in Shelley's Case has been abolished in most states by statute and is repudiated by the Third Restatement of Property.[153] Because abolition of the Rule has generally been prospective, it occasionally appears in recent cases involving older instruments.[154]

Most rules of construction apply both to land and to personal property, but the Rule in Shelley's Case typically applies only to land.[155] The Rule applies both to wills and deeds, and to legal interests as well as equitable interests in trust.

Doctrine of Worthier Title

The Doctrine of Worthier Title, like the Rule in Shelley's Case, holds that the word "heirs" is not a word of purchase but rather a word of limitation. Under the Doctrine of Worthier Title, an inter vivos transfer that purports to create a remainder in the grantor's heirs is converted into a reversion in the grantor. Like the Rule in Shelley's Case, the Doctrine of Worthier Title helped preserve the feudal incidents that accrued when land passed by descent rather than purchase.[156] (Acquisition by descent was considered a "worthier title," hence the name.) Both rules promote alienability and may permit early termination of trusts by eliminating any interest in the heirs of a living person.[157]

Whereas the Rule in Shelley's Case applies to remainders to the "heirs" of a life tenant, the Doctrine of Worthier Title applies to the "heirs" of the grantor in a deed or the settlor of an inter vivos trust.[158] Many commentators condemn

---

[152] Harper v. Springfield, 578 S.W.2d 824, 826 (Tex.Civ.App.1979); *Restatement (Second) of Property (Donative Transfers)* § 30.1, cmt. g (1988); Estate of Forrest, TC Memo 1990–464.

[153] *Restatement (Third) of Property (Wills and Other Donative Transfers)* § 16.2 (2011). The Third Restatement of Trusts takes a similar approach. *Restatement (Third) of Trusts* § 49, cmt. a (2003).

[154] *See, e.g.*, City Bank & Trust Co. in Dixon v. Morrissey, 454 N.E.2d 1195, 1198 (Ill.App.1983) (1952 will); Soc'y Nat. Bank v. Jacobson, 560 N.E.2d 217, 218 (Ohio 1990) (1931 trust).

[155] *Restatement (Third) of Property (Wills and Other Donative Transfers)* § 16.2, cmt. a (2011); *Restatement (Second) of Property (Donative Transfers)* § 30.1(3) (1988). *But see* Soc'y Nat. Bank v. Jacobson, 560 N.E.2d 217, 218 (Ohio 1990) (local version of rule covers personal property as well).

[156] 1 *American Law of Property* § 4.19 (A. James Casner ed., 1952). Similarly, both rules may cause property to be subject to death taxes today. McGovern, *supra* note 15, at 304.

[157] *Restatement (Second) of Property (Donative Transfers)* § 30.2, cmt. a (1988); Bixby v. California Trust Co., 202 P.2d 1018, 1019 (Cal.1949).

[158] The Doctrine of Worthier Title, like the Rule in Shelley's Case, originally applied to wills as well as inter vivos conveyances, so that if a will left property to the testator's heir, the heir took by descent as if the testator died intestate. At one time, the difference between taking by will and by descent was often significant. Today it rarely is. Where it is significant, courts have rejected the Doctrine of Worthier Title as to wills on the ground that it would frustrate the testator's intent. *Restatement (Second) of Property (Donative Transfers)* § 30.2, cmt. j (1988); City Nat. Bank of Birmingham v. Andrews, 355 So.2d 341, 343–44 (Ala.1978); Matter of Campbell, 319 N.W.2d 275, 278 (Iowa 1982).

both rules,[159] but the Doctrine of Worthier Title had defenders,[160] and it has been extended to personal property whereas the Rule in Shelley's Case generally applied only to *land*.[161]

The Rule in Shelley's Case overrides the donor's intention, but the Doctrine of Worthier Title, where it is still recognized, is today typically regarded as a rule of construction which gives way to an indication of contrary intent.[162] Its influence is declining, however. The Rule is totally repudiated in the Third Restatement.[163] The UPC abolishes the doctrine both "as a rule of law and as a rule of construction."[164] Its principal role in modern cases has been to allow settlors to modify or terminate trusts which purport to give an interest to their "heirs."

The Doctrine of Worthier Title, even where it is still recognized, does not apply if the settlor's "heirs" are ascertained at a time other than the settlor's death. A trust for the settlor's wife provided that upon her death the property was to be distributed "among my heirs." A claim by devisees under the settlor's will under the Doctrine of Worthier Title was rejected, since the court construed the trust to refer to the heirs determined at the wife's death rather than the settlor's death.[165]

Nor does the Doctrine apply to gifts to the settlor's "descendants" as distinguished from "heirs." Modern substitutes for the Doctrine make the same distinction. A New York statute which provides that "persons described only as the heirs, next of kin or distributees" of the settlor have no interest in a trust was held inapplicable to a remainder to the settlor's "issue;" even though the settlor's issue would have been his heirs, the two terms were not the same.[166]

Wild's Case: "To Charles and His Children"

A devise "to Charles and his children" invokes Wild's Case,[167] a 16th-century decision almost as celebrated as Shelley's Case. The court in *dicta* pronounced two resolutions. First, "if A devises his land[168] to [Charles] and to his children or issue, and [Charles] hath not any issue at the time of the

---

[159] "There is no more reason" for the Doctrine of Worthier Title than for "its close cousin, the Rule in Shelley's Case." C. Dent Bostwick, *Loosening the Grip of the Dead Hand,* 32 Vand. L. Rev. 1061, 1075 (1979). *See also* Thomas P. Gallanis, *The Future of Future Interests,* 60 Wash. & Lee L. Rev. 513 (2003).

[160] Joseph W. Morris, *The Inter vivos Branch of the Worthier Title Doctrine,* 2 Okla. L. Rev. 133, 174 (1949); Edward H. Warren, *A Remainder to the Grantor's Heirs,* 22 Tex. L. Rev. 22, 23 (1943); 3 Richard R. Powell, *The Law of Real Property* § 31.08 (Michael Allan Wolf ed., 2000).

[161] *Restatement (Third) of Property (Wills and Other Donative Transfers)* § 16.3, cmt. a (2011).

[162] *Id.*

[163] *Id.*

[164] UPC § 2–710. *See also* Cal.Prob.Code § 21108; *Restatement (Third) of Property (Wills and Other Donative Transfers)* § 16.3 (2011).

[165] Harris Trust & Sav. Bank v. Beach, 513 N.E.2d 833, 842 (Ill.1987). *See also Restatement (Second) of Property (Donative Transfers)* § 30.2, illus. 1 (1988).

[166] In re Dodge's Trust, 250 N.E.2d 849, 854–855 (N.Y. 1969).

[167] 77 Eng. Rep. 277 (K.B.1599).

[168] Although these resolutions apply by their terms only to *devises* of *land,* they have also been applied to deeds and to gifts of personal property. Ronald C. Link, *The Rule in Wild's Case in North Carolina,* 55 N.C. L. Rev. 751, 773, 783 (1977).

devise,"[169] Charles gets a fee tail. Second, if Charles *does* have issue at the time of the devise, they take joint interests with Charles, cutting out any after-born children.

These resolutions reflect a tension between the "manifest intent" that Charles' children take, and the inconvenience of giving an interest to unborn children. The first resolution, if applied today in states where a fee tail is turned into a fee simple,[170] would give the children no interest, just like a devise "to Charles and his *heirs*" or "Charles *or* his children," *i.e.,* as if "children" was intended as a word of limitation, or as a substitutional gift to take effect only if Charles died before the testator.[171] If the transferor intended to give Charles' children an interest, this could be accomplished by interpreting the words as giving Charles a life estate with a remainder to his children. The Second Restatement of Property adopts this solution.[172] An immediate gift to the children would exclude after-borns, whereas the life-estate-remainder construction includes them all by postponing distribution to them until Charles dies.

The second resolution in Wild's Case, which gives Charles and his children (if he has any) immediate interests, is still widely followed,[173] but the Restatements adopt the life-estate-remainder construction here too.[174] This postpones alienability during Charles' lifetime,[175] but it allows later-born children to share.

§ 11.5 Powers of Appointment

Definitions

We have previously discussed certain powers, such as the power to revoke a trust.[176] Powers can also be conferred by one person on another. If John's will gives Mary a power of appointment, John is the "donor" of the power and Mary is the "powerholder" (or, in older parlance, the "donee" of the power) even if she

---

[169] Modern American cases apply this test at the time of the testator's death rather than when the will was executed. *Id.* at 771.

[170] *See supra* note 144.

[171] Link, *supra* note 168, at 762.

[172] *Restatement (Second) of Property (Donative Transfers)* § 28.3 (1988). The *Restatement (Third) of Property (Wills and Other Donative Transfers)* § 14.2, cmt. f (2011) agrees unless the words "tenants in common" are added, which are presumptively deemed to create concurrent and not successive interests. *Id.*, cmt. f(1).

[173] In re Parant's Will, 240 N.Y.S.2d 558, 564 (Surr.1963); Link, *supra* note 168, at 820.

[174] *Restatement (Third) of Property (Wills and Other Donative Transfers)* § 14.2, cmt. f (2011); *Restatement (Second) of Property (Donative Transfers)* § 28.3 (1988). *See also* Neb. Rev. Stat. § 76–113; Kan. Stat. § 58–505.

[175] In Ellingrod v. Trombla, 95 N.W.2d 635, 637 (Neb.1959), land was devised "to my daughter . . . and her descendants." The daughter was unable to sell the land because under the governing statute she only got a life estate. *Id.* at 640. But as to the possibility of sale by a legal life tenant compare Section 10.5.

[176] *See* Section 4.5. *Restatement (Third) of Property (Wills and Other Donative Transfers)* § 17.1, cmt. e (2011), and *Restatement (Second) of Property (Donative Transfers)* § 11.1, cmt. c (1988), classify powers of revocation as a type of power of appointment.

cannot benefit from exercise of the power.[177] If a power is reserved, the donor and the powerholder are the same person.

A trustee who has discretion in distributing income or principal is sometimes said to have a power of appointment, but a trustee's distributive power is not the type of power of appointment discussed in this section. Rather, this section addresses powers held in a nonfiduciary capacity. Trustees' decisions are subject to court control whereas the appointments made under a power of appointment are generally not reviewable.[178] The Third Restatement of Property addresses this confusion by describing fiduciary powers as nondiscretionary powers of appointment,[179] while the Uniform Powers of Appointment Act excludes fiduciary powers from the definition of a power of appointment altogether.[180]

Powers of appointment are of two types: "general" and "nongeneral."[181] A powerholder who can appoint to herself or to her estate has a general power. If she can appoint to anyone in the world *except* herself, her estate, or the creditors of either, her power is nongeneral.[182] Nongeneral powers often are more focused, such as to appoint among her descendants. If no limits are expressed in the instrument which creates a power, it is construed to be general. Thus a beneficiary who was given power to appoint "to such person or persons as she may designate," was held to have a general power and could appoint to creditors.[183]

A power is "testamentary" if the powerholder can appoint only by a will. If powers are "presently exercisable," the powerholder can make an appointment by will or by an inter vivos instrument that would be sufficient to transfer the assets had the appointed assets been owned by the powerholder.[184] Such an inter vivos appointment is sometimes referred to as a transfer by "deed."[185]

---

[177] *Restatement (Third) of Property (Wills and Other Donative Transfers)* § 17.1, cmt. a (2011). *See also* Unif. Powers of Appointment Act § 102(4), (14); Cal.Prob.Code § 610.

[178] As to judicial review of trustee decisions, *see* Section 10.7.

[179] *Restatement (Third) of Property (Wills and Other Donative Transfers)* § 17.1, cmt. g (2011).

[180] Unif. Powers of Appointment Act § 102(13) and, cmt.

[181] *Restatement (Third) of Property (Wills and Other Donative Transfers)* § 17.3 (2011) . *See also* Unif. Powers of Appointment Act § 102(6), (10). Older authorities refer to nongeneral powers as "special" powers. *E.g.*, Cal.Prob.Code § 611; N.Y. Est. Powers & Trusts Law § 10–3.2.

[182] The line closely tracks the one made for tax purposes. *See* Section 15.4.

[183] Dickinson v. Wilmington Trust Co., 734 A.2d 605, 610–11 (Del.Ch.1999). *See also* First Union Nat. Bank v. Ingold, 523 S.E.2d 725, 728 (N.C.App.1999); Mittleman's Estate v. Comm'r of Internal Revenue, 522 F.2d 132, 135–140 (D.C.Cir.1975); Wis. Stat. § 702.02(5); Mich. Comp. Laws § 556.112(h). *But see* Hillman v. Hillman, 744 N.E.2d 1078, 1081 (Mass.2001) (ambiguous power construed as nongeneral in order to avoid adverse tax consequences).

[184] *Restatement (Third) of Property (Wills and Other Donative Transfers)* § 17.4, cmt. e (2011). The instrument must be sufficient to transfer the assets had the appointed assets been owned by the powerholder. *Id. See also* Unif. Powers of Appointment Act § 102(15) and, cmt.

[185] *Restatement (Third) of Property (Wills and Other Donative Transfers)* § 17.4, cmt. e (2011). *See also* Unif. Powers of Appointment Act § 102, cmt.

Relation Back

The exercise of a power of appointment is typically deemed to "relate back" to the donor, so that the appointee takes directly from the donor. The powerholder thus is viewed as akin to an agent who "fills in the blanks" in the donor's will or trust, and not as the owner of the appointed assets. When the executors of the powerholder sought to include the appointed assets in the powerholder's probate estate, the court refused, saying that to treat a power as "an interest in property" would hinder "one of the most useful tools in estate planning."[186]

For centuries, courts have used the relation-back concept to avoid rules they dislike. It was "an ingenious trick by which conveyancers circumvented the declared policy of the law or . . . a device by which the courts assisted progress during a period in which statutory reform was slow."[187] Many of these historical uses of powers are no longer relevant. Courts still invoke relation back, but they do not apply the concept in all situations.[188] The Third Restatement of Property rejects relation back as a general theory, preferring instead to focus directly on the question of whether the donor or the powerholder should be treated as the owner of the appointive property. Applying this rationale, the Restatement concludes that relation back is never applicable to presently exercisable general powers. To the extent the doctrine still has predictive value, it is largely limited to nongeneral powers.[189]

Taxes

Before 1942, powers were distinguished from property under the federal estate tax. Appointive assets were not taxed in the powerholder's estate unless the power was exercised. Today, however, appointive assets are taxed in the powerholder's estate whether or not the power is exercised, if the power is general and was created after 1942.[190] Nongeneral powers, on the other hand, are not taxed even if they are exercised.[191]

Powers are treated as equivalent to ownership for some income tax purposes. A person with "a power exercisable solely by himself to vest the corpus or the income" of a trust in himself is taxed on the trust income even if it is accumulated or paid to someone else.[192] Even nongeneral powers, if reserved by the settlor, may cause the settlor to be taxed on the trust income.[193]

---

[186] In re Wylie's Estate, 342 So.2d 996, 999 (Fla.App.1977). *Accord* Aurora Nat. Bank v. Old Second Nat. Bank, 375 N.E.2d 544, 549 (Ill.App.1978).

[187] 5 *American Law of Property* § 23.13 (A. James Casner ed., 1952).

[188] *Restatement (Second) of Property (Donative Transfers)*, Part V, Introductory Note (1988); Margaret M. Mahoney, *Elective Share Statutes: The Right to Elect Against Property Subject to a General Power of Appointment in the Decedent*, 55 Notre Dame Law. 99, 107–10 (1979).

[189] *Restatement (Third) of Property (Wills and Other Donative Transfers)* § 17.4, cmt. f(2) (2011).

[190] However, a tax on assets subject to a general power can be avoided by a qualified disclaimer. *See* I.R.C. § 2518 (2012); Section 2.8.

[191] *See* Section 15.4. However, appointive assets are not always subject to *state inheritance tax* when the powerholder dies even if the power is general. In re Estate of Nelson, 571 N.W.2d 269, 273 (Neb.1997).

[192] I.R.C. § 678 (2012).

[193] *Id.* § 674; *see* Section 15.7.

Rights of Creditors

State laws vary as to the rights of creditors of the powerholder. Factors determining whether a creditor may reach appointive property include the type of power in question and whether it has been exercised. Creditor rights are greatest with respect to presently exercisable general powers of appointment ("powers of withdrawal") under which the powerholder can take title to the appointive assets at any time. Traditionally, such a power was subject to creditor claims only if the power was exercised,[194] but the modern trend is to subject such powers to claims of the powerholder's creditors whether or not the power has been exercised. The Third Restatement subjects such powers of withdrawal to creditor claims to the extent the powerholder's own property is insufficient.[195] In New York, there are no limitations; the powerholder's creditors may reach "property covered by a general power of appointment . . . which is presently exercisable" to the same extent as if owned directly.[196] The Uniform Trust Code (hereinafter UTC) also generally subjects property subject to a power of withdrawal to creditor claims during any period that the power can be exercised.[197]

Creditors have greater rights over appointive assets if the donor created the general power for himself:

> A settlor, who has reserved to himself the income for life and a general power of appointment over the remainder . . . has retained 'all the substantial incidents of ownership' and . . . therefore 'it would be contrary to public policy to allow him . . . to prevent creditors from reaching the property.'[198]

Creditor claims against other types of powers of appointment are more limited. Property subject to a nongeneral power is exempt from creditor claims,[199] even in bankruptcy.[200] Property subject to a general testamentary power of appointment was traditionally reachable by the powerholder's creditors only if the power was exercised[201] but the Third Restatement subjects

---

194 *See Restatement (Second) of Property (Donative Transfers)* § 13.2 (1986).

195 *Restatement (Third) of Property (Wills and Other Donative Transfers)* § 22.3(a) (2011). *See also* Unif. Powers of Appointment Act § 501(d).

196 N.Y. Est. Powers & Trusts § 10–7.2. *See also* Cal.Prob.Code § 682. For a list of similar statutes, *see Restatement (Second) of Property (Donative Transfers)* § 13.2, Statutory Note (1988).

197 Uniform Trust Code [hereinafter UTC] § 505(b)(1). The UTC treats a power of withdrawal as the functional equivalent of a power of revocation. Because during the settlor's lifetime property subject to a power of revocation is subject to claims of the settlor's creditors, UTC § 505(a)(1), so is property subject to a power of withdrawal. This is also the approach taken in *Restatement (Third) of Trusts* § 56, cmt. b (2003). The UTC does not address creditor issues with respect to property subject to a nongeneral power of appointment or a testamentary general power of appointment. Not discussed here is the exception created under the UTC provision for the holders of Crummey and "5 and 5" powers. *See* UTC § 505 cmt.

198 United States v. Ritter, 558 F.2d 1165, 1167 (4th Cir.1977) (quoting *Restatement of Property* § 328, cmt. a (1940)). *Accord Restatement (Third) of Property (Wills and Other Donative Transfers)* § 22.2 (2011); Unif. Powers of Appointment Act § 501(d); Cal.Prob.Code § 683.

199 *Restatement (Third) of Property (Wills and Other Donative Transfers)* § 22.1 (2011); Unif. Powers of Appointment Act § 504; Cal.Prob.Code § 681; N.Y. Est. Powers & Trusts § 10–7.1.

200 11 U.S.C. § 541(b)(1) (2014).

201 *Restatement (Second) of Property (Donative Transfers)* § 13.4 (1988).

even unexercised testamentary general powers to creditor claims to the extent the powerholder's estate is otherwise insufficient.[202]

Spouse's Rights

The relation back concept traditionally was held to prevent a powerholder's spouse from including appointive assets in the elective share.[203] The Third Restatement, however, subjects to the elective share all presently exercisable general powers of appointment.[204] The UPC elective share statute, upon which many state elective share statutes are modeled, includes in the assets subject to the elective share (1) property over which the decedent spouse "held a presently exercisable general power of appointment," and (2) property transferred during the marriage in which the decedent reserved a general power, including a testamentary power.[205]

The powers held by a decedent spouse are less important in community property states. Spouses have no claim to the decedent's separate property in any event, whereas they can upset gifts of community property even if the donor reserved no power at all.[206]

Capacity

Today the rules governing capacity are generally the same for the exercise of powers and the transfer of property. A powerholder can make an effective appointment "if the [powerholder] has capacity to make a similar transfer of owned property."[207] The tendency to set a lower standard for capacity for wills than for inter vivos gifts[208] applies to powers as well. A woman who had power to appoint the principal of a trust made an appointment while she was under a conservatorship. Even though conservatees were not competent to make present gifts, this appointment was considered to be "testamentary in nature," because it took effect only when the powerholder died.[209]

When the holder of a presently exercisable power is under conservatorship, a conservator can exercise the power on the powerholder's behalf, although this generally requires court approval.[210] Testamentary

---

[202] *Restatement (Third) of Property (Wills and Other Donative Transfers)* § 22.3(b) (2011). *See also* Unif. Powers of Appointment Act § 501(d).

[203] Reno v. Reno, 626 P.2d 552, 556 (Wyo.1981).

[204] *Restatement (Third) of Property (Wills and Other Donative Transfers)* § 23.1(1) (2011). *See also* Unif. Powers of Appointment Act §§ 501, 502 and accompanying comments.

[205] UPC § 2–205. In Matter of Reynolds, 664 N.E.2d 1209, 1211 (N.Y.1996), a similar statute was construed to allow a widower to reach a trust created by his wife in which she had reserved a broad nongeneral power.

[206] *See* Section 8.8.

[207] *Restatement (Third) of Property (Wills and Other Donative Transfers)* § 19.8(a) (2011). *See also* Unif. Powers of Appointment Act § 301, cmt.; Cal.Prob.Code § 625. As to the general requirements for capacity, *see* Section 5.1.

[208] *See* Section 5.1.

[209] In re Wood's Estate, 108 Cal. Rptr. 522, 534 (App.1973).

[210] UPC § 5–411(a)(3); Cal.Prob.Code § 2580(b)(3); *Restatement (Third) of Property (Wills and Other Donative Transfers)* § 19.8, cmt. f (2011); Wilhelm v. Zepp, 447 A.2d 123, 126 (Md.App.1982). As to gifts by conservators, *see* Section 5.2.

powers are more problematic because most states deny conservators the power to make a will for the protected person.[211]

Formalities

The instrument granting a power usually specifies that it shall be exercised "by will," "by deed," or by "written instrument." This means a will, deed, or other written instrument that complies with the legal requirements prescribed for such instruments,[212] but substantial compliance may suffice. Thus, when the holder of a testamentary power exercised it by a will which had only two witnesses instead of the three then required by law, the court upheld her appointment, citing the Restatement of Property, which allows substantial compliance with the manner of appointment imposed by the donor.[213]

When a donor adds formal requirements to those imposed by the law,[214] *e.g.*, that any instrument exercising the power be delivered to the trustee, substantial compliance may suffice. When a powerholder signed an instrument exercising a power and gave it to her attorney, who failed to deliver it to the trustee until after the powerholder died, the court upheld the exercise, saying that all the purposes of the delivery requirement had been satisfied since the trustee had not distributed the funds before receiving the instrument.[215]

Contracts to Exercise Powers

A promise by the holder of a testamentary power to exercise the power in a particular way is unenforceable. The Third Restatement justifies this rule on the ground that the donor manifested "an intent that the selection of the appointees . . . be made in the light of the circumstances" existing when the powerholder dies.[216] The Restatement does allow powerholders to *release* a testamentary power by an inter vivos document. A release is not supposed to

---

[211] *But see* UPC § 5–411(a)(7) (court may authorize conservator to make, amend, or revoke protected person's will).

[212] *Restatement (Third) of Property (Wills and Other Donative Transfers)* § 19.9 (2011). *See also* Unif. Powers of Appointment Act § 301(1). Thus a codicil which was not executed in conformity with the statutory requirements for wills was held ineffective to exercise a testamentary power. In re Estate of Scott, 77 P.3d 906, 910 (Colo.App.2003).

[213] Estate of McNeill, 463 A.2d 782, 784–85 (Me.1983) (citing *Restatement (Second) of Property (Donative Transfers)* § 18.3 (1986)). The Third Restatement also adopts a substantial compliance approach. *See Restatement (Third) of Property (Wills and Other Donative Transfers)* § 19.10 and cmt. b (2011). *See also* Unif. Powers of Appointment Act § 304.

[214] *Restatement (Third) of Property (Wills and Other Donative Transfers)* § 19.10, cmt. c (2011). *See also* Unif. Powers of Appointment Act § 304, cmt.; Cal.Prob.Code § 630.

[215] In re Wood's Estate, 108 Cal. Rptr. 522, 536 (App.1973). *See also* In re Meyer, 987 P.2d 822, 826–828 (Ariz.App.1999) (power effectively exercised even though powerholder's will was not probated within three months of death as required by power); *Restatement (Third) of Property (Wills and Other Donative Transfers)* § 19.10, illus. 4 (2011) (appointment by will of power exercisable by inter vivos instrument).

[216] *Restatement (Third) of Property (Wills and Other Donative Transfers)* § 21.2, cmt. a (2011). *See also* Unif. Powers of Appointment Act § 406; In re Brown's Estate, 306 N.E.2d 781, 786 (N.Y.1973) (promise in divorce settlement to exercise power in favor of a son unenforceable); Cal.Prob.Code § 660.

defeat the donor's intent because it "operates negatively" whereas an appointment "operates affirmatively."[217]

Intent to Exercise

The question whether a powerholder intended to exercise a power is often litigated. For example, the will of a holder of a general testamentary power of appointment left "all the residue of my estate of every kind and nature to a trust." The court followed the presumption of non-exercise in the UPC, which is based on the idea that "the donor would prefer to have the property pass under his trust instrument" to the designated takers in default of appointment.[218] Reflecting this rationale, both the UPC and Third Restatement provide that the presumption of non-exercise of a general testamentary power does not apply if the document omits takers in default of appointment.[219] In New York, a power is exercised if the powerholder "leaves a will disposing of all of his property" unless a contrary intention "appears expressly or by necessary implication."[220]

Many instruments conferring powers state that the power can only be exercised if the holder specifically refers to the power. Such provisions have been strictly construed by some courts, more liberally by others. A will which devised all the powerholder's property "including any property over which I may have a power of appointment" was held a sufficient exercise, even though it did not identify the power.[221] Other courts on similar facts have held the power was not exercised on the ground that "where the controlling requirements are clearly stated in the donor's will, the [powerholder's] intent is irrelevant if she fails to comply with those requirements."[222] The UPC analyzes such cases under a doctrine of substantial compliance; a specific reference requirement will be satisfied "if the powerholder knows of and intends to exercise the power . . . [and] the powerholder's manner of attempted exercise does not impair a material purpose of the donor in imposing the requirement."[223]

---

[217] *Restatement (Second) of Property (Donative Transfers)* § 14.1, cmt. a, § 16.2, cmt. a (1986). *Restatement (Third) of Property (Wills and Other Donative Transfers)* § 20.1 (2011) is similar. *See also* Unif. Powers of Appointment Act § 402; Wood v. Am. Sec. & Trust Co., 253 F. Supp. 592, 594–95 (D.D.C.1966); Cal.Prob.Code § 661; *cf. Restatement (Third) of Trusts* § 58, cmt. c (2003) (beneficiary can release an interest even though a spendthrift provision bars its transfer).

[218] Matter of Estate of Allen, 772 P.2d 297, 299 (Mont.1989).

[219] UPC § 2–610; *Restatement (Third) of Property (Wills and Other Donative Transfers)* § 19.4 (2011). *See also* Unif. Powers of Appointment Act § 302.

[220] N.Y. Est. Powers & Trusts § 10–6.1(a)(4). *See also* First Union Nat. Bank v. Ingold, 523 S.E.2d 725, 728 (N.C.App.1999) (based on a N.C. statute); (English) Wills Act 1837, § 27, 7 Wm. 4 & 1 Vict., ch. 26. For a list of both types of statutes, see *Restatement (Second) of Property (Donative Transfers)* § 17.3, Statutory Note (1986).

[221] McKelvy v. Terry, 346 N.E.2d 912, 916 (Mass.1976). *See also* Wright v. Greenberg, 2 S.W.3d 666, 672 (Tex.App.1999).

[222] Matter of Smith's Estate, 585 P.2d 319, 321 (Colo.App.1978). *See also* Matter of Estate of Burgess, 836 P.2d 1386, 1391 (Utah App.1992); In re Shenkman, 737 N.Y.S.2d 39, 39 (App.Div.2002).

[223] UPC § 2–704. *See also* Unif. Powers of Appointment Act § 304; In re Estate of Carter, 760 N.E.2d 1171, 1174 (Ind.App.2002) ("it is not essential to refer in express terms to the power, if an intention to execute it otherwise plainly appears").

Some courts consider extrinsic evidence in ascertaining the powerholder's intent, such as evidence of discussions with the drafting attorney.[224] Extrinsic evidence is admissible in determining the powerholder's intent in accordance with the rules generally on interpretation of wills, trusts, and other donative documents.[225]

The Third Restatement specifically mentions "any relevant evidence of intent," with the primary focus to be "on the [powerholder's] intention when the [powerholder] executed the dispositive provision."[226] These include the adverse tax consequences of exercising the power,[227] "an extremely close and affectionate relationship" between the donor, powerholder, and the beneficiary of the powerholder's will,[228] and the extent of the powerholder's own property. One court concluded that a powerholder must have intended to exercise a power when her will made pecuniary devises totaling $90,000 and left the residue to five individuals, because the pecuniary devises alone would have exhausted the powerholder's owned assets.[229] A specific devise of property over which the powerholder has a power of appointment, *e.g.*, "I leave Blackacre to Alice," will be deemed an exercise.[230] Conversely, an intent *not* to exercise a nongeneral power may be inferred if a devise includes persons who are not permissible appointees.[231]

The fact that the powerholder's will was executed before the power was created is not determinative. A woman executed a will, and two years later her mother died with a will giving her a power of appointment. The court held that the daughter's will had exercised the power, just as a devise of "all my property" includes property which a testator acquired after executing her will.[232]

---

224 Motes/Henes Trust v. Motes, 761 S.W.2d 938, 940 (Ark.1988); McKelvy v. Terry, 346 N.E.2d 912, 916 (Mass.1976).

225 *Restatement (Third) of Property (Wills and Other Donative Transfers)* § 19.5, cmt. a (2011). For a general discussion of the use of extrinsic evidence in construing ambiguous wills *see* Section 7.1.

226 *Restatement (Third) of Property (Wills and Other Donative Transfers)* § 19.5, cmt. a (2011).

227 *But see* In re Jaekel's Estate, 227 A.2d 851, 858 (Pa.1967) (finding an exercise despite adverse tax consequences).

228 Bank of N.Y. v. Black, 139 A.2d 393, 400 (N.J.1958).

229 Little Red Schoolhouse for Special Children, Inc. v. Citizens & Southern Nat. Bank, 197 S.E.2d 342, 343 (Ga.1973). *See also Restatement (Third) of Property (Wills and Other Donative Transfers)* § 19.5, cmt. b (2011); First Nat. Bank v. Ettlinger, 465 F.2d 343, 350 (7th Cir.1972). *But see* DiSesa v. Hickey, 278 A.2d 785, 791 (Conn.1971).

230 *Restatement (Third) of Property (Wills and Other Donative Transfers)* § 19.3 (2011); In re Estate of Carter, 760 N.E.2d 1171, 1175 (Ind.App.2002); Brouse v. Old Phoenix Nat. Bank, 495 N.E.2d 42, 45 (Ohio App.1985). *See also* Unif. Powers of Appointment Act § 301, cmt.

231 MacLean v. Citizens Fidelity Bank & Trust Co., 437 S.W.2d 766, 768 (Ky.1969). *But see* United Cal. Bank v. Bottler, 94 Cal. Rptr. 227 (App.1971).

232 In re Buck Trust, 277 A.2d 717, 720 (Del.Ch.1971) *See also* Motes/Henes Trust v. Motes, 761 S.W.2d 938, 940 (Ark.1988); Wetherill v. Basham, 3 P.3d 1118, 1122–23 (Ariz.App.2000) (attempt to amend trust held to exercise a later acquired power of appointment); *Restatement (Third) of Property (Wills and Other Donative Transfers)* § 19.6 (2011); Unif. Powers of Appointment Act § 303. However, the terms of the power may preclude exercise by an earlier instrument. *See*, e.g., Cal.Prob.Code § 642.

Lapse

If the powerholder appoints to a person who predeceases her, the appointment lapses, but an antilapse statute may apply.[233] A testator gave his wife a nongeneral power of appointment, which she exercised to appoint to the donor's brother. The appointment failed because the brother predeceased the powerholder; he had survived the testator, but (despite the relation back theory) an appointee must survive the powerholder as well as the donor in order to take. The brother's children claimed the property under an antilapse statute, but the statute applied only if a devisee who was "a relative of the testator" and the brother was not related to the powerholder.[234] Also, the brother's children were not permissible appointees, since the powerholder was only authorized to appoint to the brother.[235] The UPC removes these difficulties. The antilapse statute applies if the appointee is related to "either the testator or the donor" of the power, and, unless the power expressly provides otherwise, "a surviving descendant of a deceased appointee . . . can be substituted for the appointee . . . whether or not the descendant is an object of the power."[236] Many antilapse statutes do not specifically address powers of appointments. The Third and Second Restatements of Property encourage courts, in construing such statutes, to interpret them in a way that antilapse achieves the same results as the UPC provision.[237]

Limitations on Nongeneral Powers

Nongeneral powers often restrict appointments to a defined group such as "descendants." Courts interpret such words the same way they would construe a gift to the same class. A power given to the testator's son to appoint to "one or more of my descendants" was held not to include an adult whom the son had adopted.[238] Most courts would not permit appointment to a grandchild if the power says "children."[239] A power to appoint among "issue" was held not to allow an appointment to grandchildren whose parents were alive.[240] This seems wrong. Ordinarily, children of living parents do not share in a gift to "issue,"[241] but a powerholder who elects to appoint to them presumably thought the advantages outweighed the possible disadvantages.

Appointments in trust, or the creation of further powers of appointment, are sometimes held invalid. When a will directed the trustee to pay the funds "free from trust, to and among [the] children or issue [of the testator's

---

[233] On antilapse statutes, *see* Section 6.5.

[234] Dow v. Atwood, 260 A.2d 437, 441 (Me.1969).

[235] *See also* Daniel v. Brown, 159 S.E. 209, 210 (Va.1931); Mich.Comp.Laws § 556.130.

[236] UPC § 2–603(b)(5).

[237] *Restatement (Third) of Property (Wills and Other Donative Transfers)* § 19.12 (2011); *Restatement (Second) of Property (Donative Transfers)* § 18.6 (1986). *See also* Unif. Powers of Appointment Act § 306, cmt.

[238] Cross v. Cross, 532 N.E.2d 486, 489 (Ill.App.1988). On the inclusion of adoptees in class gifts, *see* Section 2.10.

[239] Equitable Trust Co. v. Foulke, 40 A.2d 713, 717 (Del.Ch.1945); *Restatement (Second) of Property (Donative Transfers)* § 20.1, illus. 4 (1986).

[240] Kramer v. Freedman, 346 So.2d 1216, 1217 (Fla.App.1977). *Contra Restatement (Second) of Property (Donative Transfers)* § 24.2, cmt. d (1986).

[241] *See* Section 2.2.

daughter] as she may appoint," the daughter was not permitted to use the power to create a trust for her children.[242] The Third Restatement, however, presumes that a powerholder is intended to have "the same breadth of discretion in appointment to permissible appointees that the powerholder has in the disposition of . . . owned property."[243]

If a nongeneral power is construed to be "nonexclusive" the powerholder must include every object of the power in an appointment. This requirement seems inconsistent with the very idea of a power, yet some cases have construed powers to be "nonexclusive."[244] Can the powerholder satisfy the requirement by a nominal appointment or must each permissible appointee of the power receive a substantial share? The Third Restatement and some statutes avoid this problem by providing that powers are "exclusive" unless the donor provides that an appointment must benefit each permissible appointee or one or more designated permissible appointees.[245] Most recent cases have construed questionable powers as exclusive.[246]

An appointment to a permissible appointee may be upset if the powerholder's motive was to benefit an impermissible appointee. Thus if a powerholder has a power to appoint among her issue, her appointment to a child who has agreed to give part of the property to the powerholder's sister may be disallowed as a "fraud on the power."[247]

The drafter of the powerholder's will should note any limits on the power. If a powerholder wishes to benefit an impermissible appointee, she can use her own property (if she has some) to accomplish this. Courts sometimes validate the exercise of a power by "marshalling" after the powerholder has died. A holder of a power to appoint to her heirs appointed to a trust which could be used to pay claims against her estate. The appointment was upheld by utilizing the appointive assets exclusively for the permissible appointees by "selective allocation or marshalling," while using the powerholder's own property to fulfill objectives not authorized by the power.[248]

Marshalling does not work if the powerholder does not have sufficient property to satisfy the gifts to impermissible appointees. If, under these circumstances, she appoints half the appointive assets to a permissible appointee and the other half to an impermissible appointee, courts usually give

---

[242] Loring v. Karri-Davies, 357 N.E.2d 11, 15 (Mass.1976).

[243] *Restatement (Third) of Property (Wills and Other Donative Transfers)* § 19.14, cmt. a (2011). *See also* Unif. Powers of Appointment Act § 305; Cal.Prob.Code § 650; Matter of Moore, 493 N.Y.S.2d 924, 927 (Sup.1985).

[244] 5 *American Law of Property* § 23.57 (A. James Casner ed., 1952).

[245] *Restatement (Third) of Property (Wills and Other Donative Transfers)* § 17.5 (2011). *See also* Unif. Powers of Appointment Act § 205(c); Wis.Stat. § 702.07; Cal.Prob.Code § 652.

[246] Ferrell-French v. Ferrell, 691 So.2d 500, 502 (Fla.App.1997); First Nat. Bank of Arizona v. First Nat. Bank of Birmingham, 348 So.2d 1041, 1048 (Ala.1977).

[247] *Restatement (Third) of Property (Wills and Other Donative Transfers)* § 19.16 (2011); Horne v. Title Ins. & Trust Co., 79 F.Supp. 91, 95 (S.D.Cal.1948). *See also* Unif. Powers of Appointment Act § 307(b) and accompanying comment.

[248] Dollar Savings & Trust Co. v. First Nat. Bank, 285 N.E.2d 768, 772 (Ohio Com.Pl.1972). *See also Restatement (Third) of Property (Wills and Other Donative Transfers)* § 19.19 (2011); Unif. Powers of Appointment Act § 308.

effect to the valid part of the appointment,[249] but not if this would distort the powerholder's intent.[250]

Failure to Appoint Effectively

A well-drafted power should include a gift in default of appointment. Even if it does not, if the power is nongeneral, a gift in default of appointment to the permissible appointees is often implied if the class is defined and the class members are not so numerous as to be unmanageable.[251] A trust called for distribution as the settlor might appoint by will among seven named persons. When the settlor failed to exercise the power, the assets were equally divided among the seven permissible appointees.[252]

If the holder of a general power fails to exercise it and no gift in default of appointment is expressed, the appointive assets traditionally reverted to the donor's estate,[253] but the Third Restatement changes the rule to provide that the appointive property passes instead to the powerholder or the powerholder's estate.[254] But an *ineffective appointment* (as contrasted with failure to exercise) may "capture" the assets in the powerholder's estate and even override a gift in default of appointment. A man gave his wife a general testamentary power with a gift in default of appointment to his son. The wife's will left her property, including the appointive assets, to devisees who all predeceased her without issue, so the appointment lapsed. The court held that the appointive property passed to the wife's estate and not to the taker in default.[255]

Choice of Law

Because the rules governing powers vary in different states, choice of law may be crucial. The logic of the relation-back theory suggests that the law of the donor's domicile should control, and many cases so hold,[256] but recent cases

---

[249] First Nat. Bank of Ariz. v. First Nat. Bank of Birmingham, 348 So.2d 1041, 1046 (Ala.1977); *Restatement (Third) of Property (Wills and Other Donative Transfers)* § 19.20 (2011); N.Y. Est. Powers & Trusts § 10–6.6(a); Cal.Prob.Code § 670.

[250] Equitable Trust Co. v. Foulke, 40 A.2d 713, 718–19 (Del.Ch.1945). *See also Restatement (Third) of Property (Wills and Other Donative Transfers)* § 19.20, cmt. b (2011).

[251] *Restatement (Third) of Property (Wills and Other Donative Transfers)* § 19.23 & cmt. c (2011). *See also* Unif. Powers of Appointment Act § 311 &, cmt.

[252] Schroeder v. Herbert C. Coe Trust, 437 N.W.2d 178, 182 (S.D.1989). *See also* Loring v. Marshall, 484 N.E.2d 1315, 1318–19 (Mass.1985); In re Spencer's Estate, 232 N.W.2d 491, 498–99 (Iowa 1975).

[253] *Restatement (Second) of Property (Donative Transfers)* § 24.1 (1986); Cal.Prob.Code § 672.

[254] *Restatement (Third) of Property (Wills and Other Donative Transfers)* § 19.22 (2011). *See also* Unif. Powers of Appointment Act § 310(2)(A).

[255] Estate of Eddy v. Wong, 176 Cal. Rptr. 598, 610–11 (App.1981), *vacated*, 184 Cal. Rptr. 521 (1982). *See also Restatement (Third) of Property (Wills and Other Donative Transfers)* § 19.21 (2011); Unif. Powers of Appointment Act § 309; Cal.Prob.Code § 672(b). Capture does not apply to nongeneral powers. As to capture when an appointment violates the Rule Against Perpetuities, *see* Section 12.5.

On rehearing in *Estate of Eddy*, the court held that the powerholder had not satisfied a specific reference requirement in the donor's will and so had not exercised the power, and thus the gift passed under the gift in default of appointment after all. Estate of Eddy, 184 Cal. Rptr. 521, 527–28 (App.1982).

[256] Beals v. State St. Bank & Trust Co., 326 N.E.2d 896, 899–900 (Mass.1975); Will of Brown, 466 N.Y.S.2d 988, 991 (Surr.1983); First Nat. Bank of Ariz. v. First Nat. Bank of Birmingham, 348 So.2d 1041, 1045 (Ala.1977).

have applied to the exercise of powers the law of the powerholder's domicile. The powerholder's will "should be construed according to the laws under which his will was drafted and with which he was presumably most familiar, those of his own domicile."[257] To questions of exercise, the Third Restatement also applies the law of the powerholder's domicile.[258]

Choice of law can also be an issue when the law has changed. A husband gave his wife a general testamentary power of appointment at a time when a statute presumed that a devise of all the testator's property exercised a power. Prior to the wife's death the statute was altered to reverse the presumption. The wife's will did not mention the power. The court held that she had not exercised it, saying "the law in effect at the time of the exercise of a power of appointment controls its exercise, rather than the law in effect at its creation."[259]

Powers and Planning: Creation of Powers

Powers of appointment provide flexibility to deal with changing conditions.[260] If a husband, for example, gives his wife a power, she can adjust their estate plan to account for circumstances which arise after his death. As one lawyer has noted:

> Drafters should recognize that circumstances can change dramatically in the time between the husband's death and the wife's later death, and should provide for a means of adjustment. For example, it may appear best that the children not share equally. Perhaps there is a richly deserving person, such as a daughter-in-law or son-in-law, who would not share in the boilerplate remainder given to 'my then living descendants.' Perhaps the surviving spouse would choose to make a charitable bequest. Perhaps the interest of one descendant should be sheltered by a continuing trust.[261]

The same argument for flexibility applies if the husband, not the wife, survives. The arguments for including powers for appointment in a trust are stronger the longer the trust is expected to last.[262]

It is true that ownership also provides flexibility. If the wife leaves property to her husband outright he can dispose of it in the light of the circumstances existing when he dies. Powers have some advantages over

---

[257] White v. United States, 680 F.2d 1156, 1159 (7th Cir.1982). *See also* Toledo Trust Co. v. Santa Barbara Foundation, 512 N.E.2d 664, 667 (Ohio 1987); *cf.* First Nat. Bank v. Ettlinger, 465 F.2d 343, 346–349 (7th Cir.1972).

[258] *Restatement (Third) of Property (Wills and Other Donative Transfers)* § 19.1, cmt. e (2011), citing *Restatement (Second) Conflict of Laws* § 275, cmt. c (1971). *See also* Unif. Powers of Appointment Act § 103(2).

[259] Hund v. Holmes, 235 N.W.2d 331, 334 (Mich.1975). *See also* Cal.Prob.Code § 601; Matter of Moore, 493 N.Y.S.2d 924, 927 (Sup.1985).

[260] W. Bryan Bolich, *The Power of Appointment: Tool of Estate Planning and Drafting,* 1964 Duke L.J. 32, 39–40 (1964); Edward C. Halbach, *The Use of Powers of Appointment in Estate Planning,* 45 Iowa L.Rev. 691, 692 (1960).

[261] Harrison Gardner, *Designing Wills and Trust Instruments to Provide Maximum Flexibility,* 18 Est. Plan. 138, 138 (1991).

[262] Jesse Dukeminier & James E. Krier, *The Rise of the Perpetual Trust,* 50 UCLA L. Rev. 1303, 1341 (2003).

ownership, however. Various types of power are appropriate for different purposes. If the husband wishes to keep property out of his wife's taxable estate and still allow her to alter the disposition at her death, he can give her a *nongeneral* power. A donor may also wish to use a nongeneral power in order to limit the powerholder's choices for non-tax reasons, such as to allow her to provide for their descendants but not to give the property to her other relatives or a second husband.

The donor may have absolute confidence that the powerholder will dispose intelligently of the property at death but fear that he will dissipate it during his lifetime if he owns it outright. If so, a spendthrift trust with a general *testamentary* power is the solution; a *presently exercisable* power would not achieve the donor's objective.

Even if a donor has full confidence in the powerholder's ability to handle property and is unconcerned with avoiding taxation in the powerholder's estate, the donor may prefer to put property in trust (1) to free the powerholder from the burden of managing it and (2) to avoid the non-tax costs of passing assets through the powerholder's probate estate.[263] In this situation, a presently exercisable general power may be appropriate because it would allow the powerholder to take the property out of the trust if the trustee is not doing a good job.[264] A presently exercisable power also allows the powerholder to make gifts which may reduce the powerholder's taxable estate.[265]

A parent may also wish to give children powers of appointment, particularly if property will be held in trust for their lifetimes because of the likelihood of a change of circumstances after the donor's death. Even if the children's trusts terminate when they reach an age such as 30, it may be desirable to allow them to appoint the property to a spouse or to a trust if they die prior to termination, because any descendants of the child in this situation would almost certainly be minors.

If the children are given *general* powers, the assets will be taxable in their estates. This is not necessarily a disadvantage; without any power the property may be subject to a generation-skipping tax which is higher than the estate tax.[266] On the other hand, the donor may wish to give the children only nongeneral powers in order to keep the property in the family.

Powers of appointment have one disadvantage as compared with ownership. The Rule Against Perpetuities in most states starts to run at the donor's death as to interests created by the powerholder's exercise of a non-

---

[263] For the advantages of avoiding probate, *see* Section 10.4.

[264] Another alternative is to give the beneficiary power to remove the trustee and appoint another one.

[265] As to the possible tax advantages of inter vivos gifts as compared with transmission at death see J. Price & S. Donaldson, *Contemporary Estate Planning* §§ 2.44–.45 (2019).

[266] *See* Eileen Caulfield Schwab, *General Powers of Appointment May Cause Unexpected Tax*, 19 Est. Plan. 75, 80 (1992). In Matter of Will of Lewis, 544 N.Y.S.2d 719, 723 (Surr.1989), the court reformed a trust by adding a general power in order to qualify for a GSTT exemption. As to the generation-skipping transfer tax, *see* Section 15.5.

presently exercisable general power, whereas if the powerholder owns the property outright, she can use lives in being at *her* death as measuring lives.[267]

Many persons who confer testamentary powers require that the powerholders refer to the power specifically in their wills in order to exercise it. Otherwise, a powerholder may exercise the power inadvertently by a general devise of "all my property" or may violate the Rule Against Perpetuities or exceed the limits of the power. These risks are diminished if the donor requires a specific reference to the instrument creating the power for the powerholder effectively to exercise the power. The donor may also wish to require that the power be exercised by a will executed subsequent to the donor's death. Powers are designed to enable the powerholder to alter arrangements if circumstances change after the donor dies, but unless restricted a will executed before the donor dies can exercise them.

The donor may want to require the powerholder to deliver any instrument exercising the power to the trustee so that the trustee will know whether the power has been exercised and can distribute the assets immediately after the powerholder dies without risking liability for a distribution to the wrong person.[268]

Beware of drafting nongeneral powers too narrowly. Allowing appointment only to "children" precludes appointment to the descendants of a deceased child. Many testators may want their children to be able to appoint to their spouse as well as their descendants. The powerholder should be authorized to make appointments in trust and to create further powers.[269]

Dealing with Powers

If you are drafting a will for the holder of a power of appointment, the client must decide whether to exercise the power. A key factor in this decision is the gift in default of appointment. The powerholder may be happy to let the assets pass under the gift in default, but she may prefer to leave the property to someone else or to put assets into a trust. If there is no gift in default of appointment in the instrument creating the power, or if it is ambiguous, exercising the power is desirable to avoid litigation.

Exercising a power may subject the appointive property to an otherwise avoidable state inheritance or estate tax or to claims of the powerholder's creditors. Avoiding creditors' claims is relevant only if (1) the powerholder is insolvent and (2) the governing law makes the rights of the powerholder's creditors depend on exercise.

If a powerholder intends to exercise a testamentary power, the powerholder's will should refer specifically to the power and to its exercise. The

---

[267] *See* Section 12.5.

[268] For the risk incurred by trustee's of liability for distributing to the wrong person, *see* Section 14.3.

[269] For a model nongeneral testamentary power, see Price & Donaldson, *supra* note 265, at § 10.23.

drafter should ascertain the limits of the power and be careful not to violate the Rule Against Perpetuities.[270]

Often lawyers draft wills for clients who have no powers of appointment (that they know of) but who may acquire one later. Should a will expressly exercise or *refrain from* exercising unknown powers? Professor Rabin argued in favor of exercise: "The testator-[powerholder] ordinarily wishes to benefit his legatees to the maximum extent of his ability. . . . A failure to dispose of unknown or after-acquired appointive property is as unnatural as a failure to dispose of unknown or after-acquired owned property."[271] The contrary view warns that such a blind exercise is "likely to violate some limitation on the power . . . or to produce a violation of the rules regulating perpetuities."[272]

§§ 11.6–12.0 are reserved for supplemental material.

[270] As to the application of the Rule to powers of appointment, *see* Section 12.5.

[271] Edward H. Rabin, *Blind Exercise of Powers of Appointment*, 51 Cornell L.Q. 1, 2 (1965). *See* also John H. Martin, *The Draftsman Views Wills for a Young Family*, 54 N.C. L. Rev. 277, 294 (1976).

[272] *Use and Drafting of Powers of Appointment*, 1 Real Prop., Prob. & Tr. L. J. 307, 318 (1966).

Chapter 12

THE RULE AGAINST PERPETUITIES

Analysis

Sec.

12.1 History and Policy of the Rule.
12.2 Operation of the Rule.
12.3 Planning to Avoid the Rule.
12.4 Modern Reforms.
12.5 Powers and the Rule.
12.6 Gifts to Charity; Reversionary Interests.
12.7 Commercial Transactions.
12.8 Restraints on Alienation.
12.9 Accumulations.

§ 12.1 History and Policy of the Rule

The Fee Tail

The first "perpetuity" so-called in the law was created by the Statute *De donis* 1285 which provided that, if land was conveyed "to A and the heirs of his body," A could not alienate it, and, as courts later held, neither could A's issue ad infinitum. When courts began to allow the fee tail to be barred,[1] landowners looked for new ways to keep land in the hands of their families. One method was to attach to a fee tail a proviso that an attempt to bar it would cause a forfeiture. Courts refused to give effect to such provisos, calling them "perpetuities" and "utterly void and against the law."[2]

Destructibility of Contingent Remainders

Landowners also used contingent remainders to keep land in the family. This was frustrated by the doctrine of destructibility of contingent remainders. For example, a testator devised land to his son Robert "for his life, and afterwards to the next heir male of Robert."[3] When Robert conveyed the land to a stranger, this destroyed the remainder in his heir, because contingent remainders had to vest when (or before) the preceding estate ended. Robert's conveyance of a fee put an immediate end to his life estate,[4] and Robert's "next

[1] *See* Section 11.4.

[2] Corbet's Case, 76 Eng.Rep. 187 (1599).

[3] Use of the word "heir" in place of "heirs" in the will avoided the rule in Shelley's Case (*see* Section 11.4) which would have given Robert a fee tail, because in England the rule applied only when the whole line of heirs in successive generations was designated, not just the person(s) who inherited when the life tenant died. Re Rynard, 31 O.R.2d 257 (1980).

[4] This rule was originally designed to protect future interests, but it later had the opposite effect. W. McGovern, *The Historical Conception of a Lease for Years,* 23 UCLA L.Rev. 501, 517 (1976).

heir male" could not be ascertained until Robert died.[5] Similarly, a remainder to Robert's "children who survive to the age of 21" would be destroyed if his children were under 21 when Robert died.[6]

A leading case on the destructibility of contingent remainders alludes to the "inconveniences" arising from "these perpetuities."[7] But the destructibility of contingent remainders operated "arbitrarily"[8] because there were so many exceptions. The destructibility rule did not apply to trusts,[9] and a form of trust to preserve contingent remainders arose in the 17th century "in order to secure in family settlements a provision for the future children of an intended marriage, who before were usually left to the mercy of the particular tenant for life."[10] Destructibility fostered alienability to some extent but also placed "a premium on the drafting skills" of lawyers who knew how to avoid it.[11]

The destructibility of contingent remainders still operates occasionally,[12] but it has been abolished by statute in many states,[13] and some courts have rejected it even without a statute as "a relic of the feudal past, which has no justification or support in modern society."[14]

Executory Interests

Lawyers in the 17th century came up with various ways to avoid the destructibility of contingent remainders. A father with two sons, William and Thomas, devised land "to Thomas and his heirs" with a proviso that, if Thomas died without issue, William should have the land. Thomas suffered a common recovery (the traditional device for breaking a fee tail), but this was held to be ineffective because Thomas had a fee *simple*; the land was "devised to him *and his heirs*." Since Thomas had a fee simple, William's interest was not a *remainder*, because "one fee cannot be in remainder after another." Thomas' interest was rather an "executory devise," and executory devises, unlike remainders, were not destructible. One judge thought that executory interests *should* be destructible "for otherwise it would be a mischievous kind of perpetuity," but he was outvoted by his colleagues.[15] As Blackstone later explained it: "if a man devises land to A and his heirs; but, if he dies before the age of twenty one, then to B and his heirs: this remainder [in B], though void in a deed [because no "remainder" can follow a fee simple], is good by way of

---

5 Archer's Case, 76 Eng.Rep. 146 (1597). *Compare* the modern treatment of a gift to the heirs of a living person. *See* Section 11.3.

6 Festing v. Allen, 12 Mees & W. 279 (1843).

7 Chudleigh's Case, 76 Eng.Rep. 270, 322 (1595).

8 Abo Petroleum Corp. v. Amstutz, 600 P.2d 278, 281 (N.M.1979).

9 Abbiss v. Burney, 17 Ch.Div. 211 (Ct.App.1881).

10 2 W. Blackstone, *Commentaries* 172 (1766).

11 Abo Petroleum Corp. v. Amstutz, 600 P.2d 278, 280 (N.M.1979).

12 Belleville National Bank v. Trauernicht, 445 N.E.2d 958 (Ill.App.1983) (abolition of destructibility in 1921 was prospective, so remainder in life tenant's heirs created in a 1913 deed was destroyed when life tenant conveyed her interest).

13 1 *Amer.Law of Prop.* § 4.63.

14 Abo Petroleum Corp. v. Amstutz, 600 P.2d 278, 281 (N.M.1979).

15 Pells v. Brown, 79 Eng.Rep. 504, 506 (1620).

executory devise"; such an executory devise "cannot be barred by a recovery, suffered before it commences."[16]

Later in the 17th century a trust for the Duke of Norfolk came before Chancellor Nottingham. The basic plan again involved a gift to a younger son if his elder brother died without issue. The common-law judges, whom Nottingham consulted, advised him that the limitation was void[17] but Nottingham did not wish to frustrate the father's intent to provide for his younger son. He and the judges agreed that the same rule should apply in law and in equity. This distinguishes the Rule Against Perpetuities from the destructibility of contingent remainders, which did not apply to trusts. Nottingham also agreed with the judges that "perpetuities" were undesirable because they "fight against God, for they pretend to such a Stability in human Affairs as the Nature of them admits not of." But as to where the line should be drawn, the Chancellor had no clear answer: "I will stop wherever any visible Inconvenience doth appear, for the just Bounds of a Fee-simple upon a Fee-simple are not yet determined." He rejected the technical distinctions which had prevailed in the common law. "These are Words, and but Words, there is not any real Difference at all, but the Reason of Mankind will laugh at it. . . . Pray let us so resolve Cases here, that they may stand with the Reason of Mankind when they are debated abroad."

Lives in Being, plus 21 Years

The Duke of Norfolk's Case held only that "where it is within the Compass of one Life, that the Contingency is to happen, there is no Danger of a Perpetuity." Further details of the modern Rule Against Perpetuities were worked out during the succeeding century and a half. The "one Life" was expanded to many lives, on the ground that this did not greatly expand the restraint: "let the lives be never so many, there must be a survivor, and so it is but the length of that life; [for Twisden [J.] used to say, the candles were all lighted at once]. . . ."[18] The persons used as measuring lives did not have to be beneficiaries of the interest, because the Rule was designed to avoid keeping "property for too great a length of time out of commerce. The length of time will not be greater or less, whether the lives taken have any interest or have not." Children in gestation when a testator died could be used as measuring lives because "the space of time between the death of the father and the birth of the posthumous son was so short that no inconvenience could ensue."[19]

Twenty one years was added to the period of the Rule in a case involving a devise to the "eldest son of my daughter Mary who attains the age of twenty one years." The son's interest was not certain to vest during any life in being at the testator's death since he might be under 21 when Mary died. Nevertheless this did not restrain "the power of alienation . . . longer than the law would restrain it viz. during the infancy of" Mary's son, who could not make

---

[16] 2 W. Blackstone, *Commentaries* 173 (1766).

[17] 22 Eng.Rep. 931, 940 (1682). For a fuller discussion of this case, *see* G. Haskins, *Extending the Grasp of the Dead Hand*, 126 U.Pa.L.Rev. 19, 35 (1977).

[18] Scatterwood v. Edge, 91 Eng.Rep. 203, 203 (1699).

[19] Thellusson v. Woodford, 32 Eng.Rep. 1030, 1040–41 (H.L. 1805).

a conveyance so long as he was a minor.[20] This reasoning suggests that a postponement of vesting beyond lives in being must be connected with the minority of a beneficiary, but the law soon came to permit an absolute term of 21 years.[21] The period of gestation, on the other hand, is limited to actual children in gestation; a limitation which postpones vesting for 21 years and nine months without reference to any actual child is invalid.[22]

The modern Rule Against Perpetuities has thus moved from Nottingham's general idea of "stopping when any visible inconvenience doth appear" to a more precise rule which can be concisely expressed as follows:

> No interest in property shall be valid unless it must vest, if at all, not later than 21 years after one or more lives in being at the creation of the estate and any period of gestation involved.[23]

The Rule Against Perpetuities is more comprehensive than its predecessor, the rule of destructibility of contingent remainders: the Rule Against Perpetuities applies to trusts and legal interests, to real and personal property, and to executory interests as well as remainders. But it has the same unfortunate quality of constituting a trap which only careful drafters can avoid.[24]

Policy Behind the Rule: Alienability

Early cases attributed the Rule Against Perpetuities to the public interest in keeping property alienable or "in commerce." Perpetuities were defined as limitations which make "an estate unalienable, though all mankind join in the conveyance."[25] More recently a court said that the "purpose of the Rule Against Perpetuities [is] to facilitate the free alienation of property which in turn helps assure its proper maintenance and changing use as dictated by the changing circumstances of its various owners and of society as a whole."[26] Even persons who question whether the operations of a free market foster society's best interests should support the Rule, because it favors "free marketability versus restrictions imposed by an erratic testator; not free enterprise versus governmental regulation."[27]

A New York statute invalidates any suspension of the power of alienation which lasts longer than lives in being plus 21 years. The power of alienation is "suspended" within the meaning of this statute "when there are no persons in

---

[20] Stephens v. Stephens, 25 Eng.Rep. 751, 752 (1736).

[21] *Restatement (Second) of Property (Donative Transfers)* § 1.1, cmt. a (1983).

[22] Cadell v. Palmer, 6 Eng.Rep. 956 (1833); *Restatement of Property* § 374, cmt. *o* (1944); 6 *Amer.Law of Prop.* § 24.15.

[23] N.Y. EPTL § 9–1.1(b).

[24] This has been largely altered by modern reforms that are discussed in Section 12.4.

[25] Scatterwood v. Edge, 91 Eng.Rep. 203, 203 (1699).

[26] Klugh v. United States, 588 F.2d 45, 53 (4th Cir.1978). *See also* Norton v. Georgia R.R. Bank & Trust Co., 322 S.E.2d 870, 873 (Ga.1984) ("to prevent property from being tied up for an unreasonable length of time and to prohibit unreasonable restraints upon the alienation of property"). However, there is a separate rule dealing with unreasonable restraints on alienation. *See* Section 12.8.

[27] L. Simes, *Public Policy and the Dead Hand* 38 (1955).

being by whom an absolute fee . . . can be conveyed."[28] Similar statutes in some other states replace the Rule Against Perpetuities,[29] but in New York interests may be invalid under the Rule Against Perpetuities even though they do not suspend the power of alienation. A perpetual option was held invalid under the Rule even though it did not suspend the power of alienation, because the optionor and optionee could join to convey the land.[30] Even though sale is theoretically possible when all interests in property are held by living, identifiable persons, the owners are not likely to join in a sale if their individual interests are contingent because they will not be able to agree on how to allocate the sales proceeds.[31]

In considering whether the Rule should be applied to a property interest subject to a right of first refusal, one court refused to extend the Rule to such interests on the basis that the right did not impact the marketability of the property "[b]ecause the holder of a right of first refusal may only choose to purchase property on the same terms as a bona fide offer".[32]

Trusts

Concerns about alienability are reduced when property is held in trust where the trustee has a power of sale.[33] Some states do not apply the Rule to trusts if the trustee can sell the trust assets.[34] In many states, however, a trustee's power to sell property does not take the case out of the Rule Against Perpetuities.[35] Professor Simes suggests the reason is that trustees "cannot invest the funds as freely as a person who owns it beneficially." Trustees are not supposed to speculate with trust assets, but society needs "risk investments to further social and economic advancement."[36] However, as Professor Haskell has observed,

> Family trusts, however, constitute a very small portion of available investment capital. Pension trusts . . . constitute a much larger portion . . . and are exempted from the Rule Against Perpetuities by statute as they must be if they are to function. . . . There is no

---

[28] N.Y. EPTL § 9–1.1(a).

[29] Idaho Code § 55–111; Wis.Stat.§ 700.16.

[30] Buffalo Seminary v. McCarthy, 451 N.Y.S.2d 457 (App.Div.1982).

[31] Simes, *supra* note 27, at 37–38. *See also* J. Morris & W. Leach, *The Rule Against Perpetuities* 14 (1962); *Restatement of Property* § 370, cmt. i (1940).

[32] Bortolotti v. Hayden, 866 N.E.2d 882, 889 (Mass. 2007). Accord *Restatement (Third) of Property (Servitudes)* § 3.3, cmt. a (2000).

[33] As to sales by trustees, *see* Section 14.5.

[34] Wis.Stat. § 700.16(3); In re Walker's Will, 45 N.W.2d 94 (Wis.1950); *cf.* Del.Stat. tit. 25, § 503 (Rule not applicable to trusts but they must terminate after 110 years). Other states have moved in this direction in order to attract trust business.

[35] *Restatement of Property* § 370, cmt. p (1940); Simes, *supra* note 27, at 55.

[36] *Id.* at 60. (Simes, writing in 1955, used nuclear energy as an example.) *See also* In re Chun Quan Yee Hop's Estate, 469 P.2d 183, 186 (Haw.1970) (Rule channels wealth "into open commerce without subjecting it to the limited discretion of a trustee"). As to investments by trustees, *see* Section 14.2.

shortage of risk capital now. If a shortage of risk capital should develop, family trusts would be a very small part of the problem.[37]

Even if getting property out of trust is a goal worth pursuing, the Rule Against Perpetuities does not accomplish it. The Rule allows trusts to last forever if all the beneficial interests are vested.[38] A trust that allowed the trustee to retain shares of the testator's great-grandchildren until they reached age 25 was upheld. The challenge to the trust was based on

> an apparent misunderstanding as to exactly when an interest vests. In general, the word "vest" is used to mean either a vesting in possession or a vesting in interest. . . . Vesting in possession connotes an immediate, existing right of present enjoyment, while vesting in interest implies a presently fixed right to future enjoyment. . . . For an interest to vest within the meaning of the rule the interest [need only] be vested in interest.[39]

Thus the "possibility that the great grandchildren will not obtain actual possession of the trust principal" within the period allowed by the Rule did not matter, since they would have "an absolute right to ultimately receive a share."[40]

Wealth Concentration

Morris and Leach asserted that the Rule Against Perpetuities prevented "enormous concentrations of land in the hands of a very few and thereby brought it about that England never suffered unbearably from those conditions which elsewhere have produced violent social revolution."[41] The Rule, by freeing up property, may allow the rich to lose their wealth. A similar argument praises the Rule for assuring "the normal operation of the competitive struggle," preventing "persons less fit" from retaining property disproportionate to their skills.[42] But the role of the Rule in promoting social Darwinism or in preventing undue concentration of wealth is small. Morris and Leach themselves concede that the existence of progressive taxation today would render "the Rule (if this is its sole object) quite unnecessary."[43]

The estate tax itself depends to some extent on the Rule. If persons had unlimited freedom to do so they might create trusts for their children, grand-

---

[37] P. Haskell, *A Proposal for a Simple and Socially Effective Rule Against Perpetuities*, 66 N.C.L.Rev. 545, 558–59 (1988). *See also* J. Dukeminier & J. Krier, *The Rise of the Perpetual Trust*, 50 UCLA L.Rev. 1303, 1324 (2003).

[38] However, after the period of the Rule, the beneficiaries can compel termination of the trust. *Restatement (Third) of Trusts* § 29, cmt. h(1) (2003). Thus the *Claflin* rule, *see* Section 10.9, no longer applies as of that point.

[39] Brown v. American Fletcher Nat. Bank, 519 N.E.2d 166, 168 (Ind.App.1988).

[40] *Id. See also* May v. Hunt, 404 So.2d 1373 (Miss.1981) (trust created in 1973 to last until 2022 was valid because remainder was vested in settlor's children). *See also* Schuyler, *The Statute Concerning Perpetuities*, 65 Nw.U.L.Rev. 3, 6–7 (1970); *Restatement of Property* § 378 (1944).

[41] Morris & Leach, *supra* note 31, at 11–12. *Compare* the discussion of the European experience at *infra* note 46 et seq.

[42] *Restatement of Property*, Int. Note p. 2132 (1944). This "exaltation of self-reliance . . . is today an axiom that most thinkers reject." A. Hirsch & W. Wang, *A Qualitative Theory of the Dead Hand*, 68 Ind.L.J. 1, 44 (1992).

[43] Morris & Leach, *supra* note 31, at 15.

children, great-grandchildren, etc., and so avoid the estate tax for centuries. The Rule Against Perpetuities prevents this. But tax law does not really need the Rule. Today the generation-skipping transfer tax reaches successive interests even before the period allowed by the Rule runs out.[44] Professors Dukeminier and Krier argue that the enactment of the GSTT made "perpetual trusts . . . more attractive."[45] This seems odd, because the GSTT (despite its generous exemptions) limits rather than expands the tax advantages of long term trusts. Nevertheless, the current movement away from the Rule (discussed in Section 12.4) has coincided (by and large) with the appearance of the GSTT.

Social equality has played a larger role in the history of the European counterpart to the common-law perpetuity, the *fideicommissum*. Roman law allowed a testator to designate "the beneficiary (for example) of land under his will as a *fiduciarius* under a *fideicommissum* in favor of a further beneficiary. . . . [T]he initial beneficiary would enjoy the land during his lifetime but would have to die intestate with respect to it; . . . its fate was already regulated by the settlor's will. The same arrangement might extend over several generations."[46]

On the Continent, the *fideicommissum* reappeared in modern times, where it was associated with the aristocracy, as indicated by the title of a leading treatise on the subject: *Tractatus de Fideicommissis Familiarum Nobilium*.[47] In France a similar institution known as the "substitution" was defended by Montesquieu in the 18th century as necessary to maintain an hereditary aristocracy, even though it interfered with commerce.[48] This "justification" did not carry weight with the leaders of the French revolution, and so substitutions were abolished.[49] The end of the German Fideikomiss was associated with another revolution and appeared in the Constitution of the Weimar Republic of 1919.[50]

Even Professor Leach, an effective advocate of reforming the Rule, did not propose its abolition. He concluded that "on the whole the Rule does more good

---

[44] For the generation-skipping transfer tax *see* Section 15.5. As to the uneasy relationship between the GSTT and the Rule *see* I. Bloom & J. Dukeminier, *Perpetuities Reformers Beware: the USRAP Tax Trap,* 25 Real Prop. Trust J. 203 (1990).

[45] Dukeminier & Krier, *supra* note 37, at 1315.

[46] D.Johnston, *Trusts and Trust-like Devices in Roman Law*, in Itinera Fiduciae (ed.Helmholz/Zimmermann 1998), p. 49. Justinian limited fideicommissa to four generations, a very generous limit by common-law standards!

[47] K. Luig, *Philipp Knipschildt und das Familienfideikommiss im Zeitalter des Usus modernus*, in Itinera Fiduciae (ed.Helmholz/Zimmermann 1998), p. 362–87. The book was first published in 1626 and was cited as the "standard work" as late as 1868.

[48] Montesquieu, *De l'Esprit des Lois*, bk. 5, ch. 9.

[49] J. Brissaud, *A History of French Private Law* 732 (1912). This provision was retained in a modified form in the Napoleonic Code, which allows property to be tied up for one generation. Code Civil art. 896, 1048–49. The prohibition on substitutions (without the exceptions) was carried over into the Louisiana Civil Code, where it was interpreted to forbid trusts, which were only allowed by a constitutional amendment of 1921. *See* J. Wisdom, *A Trust Code in the Civil Law,* 13 Tul.L.Rev. 70, 72–3 (1938).

[50] Constitution of 1919, art. 155. Fideikomisse had previously been abolished in Article 170 of the Frankfurt Constitution of 1849, but that constitution did not come into force because of the collapse of the 1848–49 revolution.

than harm, though the policy considerations underlying it are much weaker than they were 300 or 100 years ago."[51]

Fair Balance Between Generations

The most persuasive argument for the Rule today is that it "strikes a fair balance between the desires of members of the present generation, and similar desires of succeeding generations" to control the property.[52] If parents could tie up their property in perpetuity, their descendants would have no power over it, and the descendants' claim to control property is as strong as the parents. Furthermore, long-term arrangements for controlling property often become inappropriate as conditions change. Benjamin Franklin's 200-year charitable trust[53] turned out to be unsuited to the 20th-century. If noncharitable trusts were allowed to go on for so long a period, they would present similar problems. As Chancellor Nottingham noted, perpetuities "pretend to such a Stability in human Affairs as the Nature of them admits not of."

Arguably the Rule is too lax. Is it really a "fair balance" between generations when parents can tie up property so that their descendants who are lives in being have no power over it?[54] The Rule's limits have been explained on the ground that a "father could realistically and perhaps wisely, assess the capabilities of *living* members of his family" but "could know nothing of unborn persons. Hence, the father was permitted control only so long as his judgment was informed with an understanding of the capabilities and needs of persons alive when the judgment was made."[55] But increasing life spans have stretched lives in being plus 21 years to about a century. Can testators really be familiar with the capacities of descendants in being at their death for such a long time? European scholars object to the trust because it allows too much dead-hand control.[56] Professor Waggoner agrees that the Rule is "overpermissive" in allowing "donors in some cases to extend control through or into generations completely unknown and unseen by them," but he adds that there is almost "no enthusiasm" among knowledgeable persons "for tightening up" the Rule to make it coincide more precisely with its rationale.[57]

John Chipman Gray, who wrote an often-cited treatise on the Rule, delighted in the Rule's precision. Whereas on most legal issues "there is no exact standard to which appeal can be made," the Rule was different:

---

[51] Morris & Leach, *supra* note 31, at 18. *See also Powell on Real Property* § 71.02.

[52] Simes, *supra* note 27, at 58. *See also* Matter of Estate of Anderson, 541 So.2d 423, 428 (Miss.1989).

[53] *See* Section 10.10.

[54] P. Wiedenbeck, *Missouri's Repeal of the Claflin Doctrine—New View of the Policy Against Perpetuities* 50 Mo.L.Rev. 805, 828 (1985).

[55] J. Dukeminier, *A Modern Guide to Perpetuities,* 74 Cal.L.Rev. 1867, 1870 (1986). *See also* Wiedenbeck, *supra* note 54, at 832–33; S. Kurtz, The Iowa Rule Against Perpetuities: A State of Little or No Law, 65 Iowa L. Rev. 177 (1979).

[56] E.g., H. Flick & D. Piltz, *Der Internationale Erbfall* 244 (1999). However, the drafters of China's new trust law chose not to include any restrictions on trust duration. F. Foster, *The Dark Side of Trusts: Challenges to Chinese Inheritance Law,* 2 Wash.U. Global Studies L.Rev. 151, 157 (2003).

[57] L. Waggoner, *The Uniform Statutory Rule Against Perpetuities,* 21 Real Prop.Prob. & Tr. L.J. 569, 586–89 (1986).

> [I]f a decision agrees with [the Rule] it is right; if it does not agree with it, it is wrong. . . . If the answer to a problem does not square with the multiplication table one may call it wrong, although it be the work of Sir Isaac Newton; and so if a decision conflicts with the Rule Against Perpetuities, one may call it wrong, however learned and able the court that has pronounced it.[58]

By Gray's time, the Rule had come a long way from the initial tentative formulation of Chancellor Nottingham.[59] The mathematical precision of the developed Rule had an unfortunate effect on the Rule as an instrument of policy. It caused many trusts to fail even though they did not violate the policy behind the Rule, while those "who know[ ] the Rule well" are able to "violate its spirit" while complying with the letter.[60]

§ 12.2 Operation of the Rule

Starting Point

The Rule is easy to memorize but difficult to apply in practice. In testing an instrument for a Rule violation one should first determine when the period begins to run. For wills, this is the time of the testator's death, regardless of when the will was executed. For revocable trusts, this is the time when there no longer is a power of revocation, typically the settlor's death. For irrevocable trusts or deeds, it is the time of execution of the instrument (or delivery if required).[61] Some perpetuities violations occur because the drafter overlooked the difference between wills and inter vivos transfers. Suppose an irrevocable trust was to last until the death of the last surviving grandchild of the Grantor who shall be living *at the time of his death*. This would have been all right had this been a will or a revocable trust, but this trust was irrevocable, and so a grandchild born after its execution could not serve as a validating life, and the Rule was violated.[62]

After determining the starting date, determine whether there is any possibility that the trust in question[63] will continue beyond lives in being at the starting date plus 21 years. If not, there is no problem.

While termed a "Rule:"

> The Rule Against Perpetuities is not a rule of construction. Instead, it is a positive mandate of law to be applied irrespective of the intent of the grantor.[64]

---

58 J. Gray, *The Rule Against Perpetuities* xi (4th ed. 1942).

59 *See supra* note 17 et seq.

60 Morris & Leach, *supra* note 31, at 13.

61 *See Restatement (Second) of Property (Donative Transfers)* § 1.2 (1983).

62 Ryan v. Ward, 64 A.2d 258, 260 (Md.1949).

63 The Rule applies also to legal interests, but most modern cases involve trusts so it is convenient to use them as examples.

64 Washington State Grange v. Brandt, 148 P.3d 1069, 1074 (Wash. Ct. App. 2006).

Is It Possible for the Trust to Continue Beyond Lives in Being plus 21 Years?

Any possibility, however remote, that the trust may continue beyond lives in being plus 21 years raises the specter of an infraction of the Rule in its traditional form.[65] Five types of cases occur with some frequency:

(1) Period in Gross

A testamentary trust was to continue for 25 years after the testator's death, following which the assets were to be distributed to the then living descendants of her husband's brothers and sisters. This violated the Rule because there was the possibility of vesting after a life in being plus 21 years.[66] This shows how the letter and the spirit of the Rule often diverge. A valid trust can be drafted in which the drafter designates a group of lives in being and provides that 21 years after the death of the survivor of them the trust will terminate. Such a trust will probably endure for about a century, and will not violate the Rule, but one which is certain to last for 25 years does.

(2) Age Contingencies

A testamentary trust provided that "when the youngest living child of my son has reached the age of 25 years," the assets should be distributed to the son's then living descendants. Because it was possible that the son's youngest child (born after the testator's death) would not reach 25 until more than 21 years after every life in being at the testator's death had died, the Rule was violated.[67] Infractions like this are not unusual, because many testators do not want their grandchildren to receive property as soon as they reach 21, believing that they will not be ready to handle property at that age. Some have suggested that the 21-year period allowed by the Rule should be increased so as not to "prematurely force capital into the hands of persons not mature enough to handle it."[68]

A trust to last until all the testator's grandchildren (or other class which includes potential afterborn persons) complete their education seems like a sensible arrangement, but may likewise violate the Rule.[69]

Even an interest which vests when the youngest *child of the testator* reaches 25 may violate the Rule in an irrevocable trust.[70] An interest which vests at age 21 may also violate the Rule if it involves grandchildren of a living

---

[65] *Restatement of Property* § 370, cmt. k (1944). This has been changed today in many states by the adoption of "wait and see." *See* Section 12.4.

[66] However, the court saved the trust by reducing the term to 21 years. Berry v. Union Nat. Bank, 262 S.E.2d 766 (W.Va.1980). *See* Section 12.4.

[67] Hagemann v. National Bank and Trust Co., 237 S.E.2d 388 (Va.1977). *See also* Merrill v. Wimmer, 481 N.E.2d 1294 (Ind.1985).

[68] D. Schuyler, *The Statute Concerning Perpetuities,* 65 Nw.U.L.Rev. 3, 19 (1970). *See also* Morris & Leach, *supra* note 31 at 69; 6 *Amer.Law of Prop.* § 24.16.

[69] Sheats v. Johnson, 189 S.E.2d 856 (Ga.1972) (trust terminates when youngest grandchild completes education).

[70] *Cf.* Second Bank-State Street Trust Co. v. Second Bank-State Street Trust Co., 140 N.E.2d 201 (Mass.1957) (trust to terminate when settlor's youngest child reached 21).

person.[71] On the other hand, age designations over 21 are permissible when they relate to a class which contains only lives in being. A testamentary trust which was to terminate when "the youngest of my grandnephews and grandnieces is fifty years old" did not violate the Rule because it was construed to mean only those grandnieces and grandnephews who were alive when the testator died.[72]

(3) Two-Generation Trust

Many Rule violations arise from trusts which are designed to last for two generations, *e.g.*, the lives of the testator's children and grandchildren. Such trusts may violate the Rule even if the testator has no afterborn grandchildren, because some might have been born.

> At the time of his death the testator was survived by three children and five grandchildren. . . . There remained the possibility that another grandchild would be born. . . . The law looks forward from the time the limitation is made to see what may be, not backward to see what has been. It regards the possible, not the actual.[73]

However, if the testator's children all predecease him, such a testamentary trust does not violate the Rule because the possibility of an after born grandchild is eliminated even when one "looks forward from the time the limitation is made."[74]

Sometimes a trust is saved by construing it to exclude afterborn class members. A testamentary trust to terminate "upon the death of my last surviving grandchild" was valid because the court held the testator meant only those grandchildren whom he had named previously in the will. Because they were lives in being, the Rule was not violated.[75]

Courts sometimes rely on circumstances to reach this result, *e.g.*, the testator's children were so old when the will was drafted that they were unlikely to have further children.[76] This construction is questionable, however, because of the class gift language; if the testator had meant only grandchildren then living wouldn't the will have named them instead of referring generically to grandchildren?[77] Thus, most courts construe such trusts to include any

---

[71] Ward v. Van der Loeff, [1924] A.C. 653 (remainder to nieces and nephews of testator who reached 21 invalid when testator's parents were living when he died).

[72] Estate of Grove, 138 Cal.Rptr. 684 (App.1977). *See also* Underwood v. MacKendree, 251 S.E.2d 264 (Ga.1978).

[73] Connecticut Bank & Trust Co. v. Brody, 392 A.2d 445, 450 (Conn.1978). The result in this case would also be changed by a "wait-and-see" approach.

[74] *Restatement of Property* § 374, cmt. j, § 384, illus. 3 (1944); 6 *Amer.Law of Prop.* § 24.24.

[75] Southern Bank & Trust Co. v. Brown, 246 S.E.2d 598 (S.C.1978). *See also* Cotham v. First Nat. Bank, 697 S.W.2d 101 (Ark.1985); Newick v. Mason, 581 A.2d 1269 (Me.1990); Abrams v. Templeton, 465 S.E.2d 117 (S.C.App.1995).

[76] *Restatement of Property* § 377 illus. 3, 4 (1944); Morris & Leach, *supra* note 31, at 79; 6 *Amer. Law of Prop.* § 24.22.

[77] *Cf.* Sheats v. Johnson, 189 S.E.2d 856, 859 (Ga.1972); In re Ghiglia's Estate, 116 Cal.Rptr. 827, 831 (App.1974).

grandchildren born after the testator's death, even when this creates a perpetuities violation.[78]

(4) Unborn Spouse

A will provided a secondary income interest "to the wife of my son," followed by a contingent remainder at her death. The court held that because the son might marry a woman who was not yet born or conceived when the testator died, the trust violated the Rule.[79]

Some courts avoid this result by construing the will to refer only to the son's wife living at the time the will took effect,[80] but this construction is subject to the objection that if the testator meant that, the will would have said so or named the wife instead of using a generic term such as "wife," "husband," or "spouse."[81]

(5) Administrative Contingencies

When a will created a trust which was to terminate five years after the testator's estate was distributed, the heirs claimed that the Rule was violated because the distribution might be delayed too long.[82] Some courts find that the Rule is not violated by such a provision because the law requires administration to proceed expeditiously, so it cannot possibly last for more than 21 years after the testator dies. Others reject this reasoning on the ground that the Rule requires "absolute certainty," and distribution of a decedent's estate is subject to many possible delays.[83]

Are the Interests Vested?

Even if a trust may continue beyond lives in being, the Rule is still not violated if all the interests must vest in interest (rather than vest in possession) in sufficient time. This is because the Rule applies to future interests in property, but only if they are contingent (nonvested). A trust for the testator's daughters and their children was to last "until each of said grandchildren shall reach the age of 25 years, when [such] grandchild shall receive his or her share of the principal." This did not violate the Rule.

> Another grandchild could conceivably been born and been less than four years old at [the death of the lives in being. However] the testator's will can be construed to intend vesting in each grandchild immediately at birth, with only distribution delayed until age 25.[84]

---

[78] *E.g.*, Fleet National Bank v. Colt, 529 A.2d 122, 126 (R.I.1987).

[79] Pound v. Shorter, 377 S.E.2d 854, 856 (Ga.1989). *See also* Dickerson v. Union Nat. Bank, 595 S.W.2d 677 (Ark.1980).

[80] In re Chemical Bank, 395 N.Y.S.2d 917 (Sup.1977) (irrevocable trust for settlor's "widow" meant his present wife so Rule not violated).

[81] *Compare* Section 2.12.

[82] The trust beneficiaries made a substantial payment to the heirs to settle this claim and sought reimbursement from the attorney who had drafted the questionable will. Lucas v. Hamm, 364 P.2d 685 (Cal.1961).

[83] Prime v. Hyne, 67 Cal.Rptr. 170, 173 (App.1968); L. Waggoner, *Perpetuity Reform*, 81 Mich.L.Rev. 1718, 1741 (1983).

[84] Foley v. Evans, 570 N.E.2d 179, 181 (Mass.App.1991). *See also* White v. National Bank & Trust Co., 186 S.E.2d 21 (Va.1972) (25 year trust valid because remainder to John's "heirs"

A similar trust included a further provision that if any grandchild died before reaching 25, the share should go to his or her descendants. This gift over violated the Rule, but the preceding clause, providing for distribution to the grandchildren at age 25, was upheld. In other words, the invalidity of the divestiture clause left the grandchildren with an indefeasibly vested remainder.[85]

Class Closing

A class gift is not "vested" for purposes of the Rule so long as more persons can become members of the class.[86] A testamentary trust was to last until all the testator's grandnieces and grandnephews reached 35, whereupon the assets would be distributed to them. Their interest was not conditioned on survival, but it nevertheless violated the Rule, because the testator's brother survived him, and so could have had afterborn children who produced more grandnieces and grandnephews. The class would not close until distribution was made, and that was not certain to occur in time.[87]

Any gift to the grandchildren (or more remote issue) of living persons risks violation of the Rule, but may be saved by the rule of convenience. A devise to the testator's daughter for life, remainder to his great grandchildren was upheld; even though more great-grandchildren might be born after lives in being, because the testator was survived by one great-grandchild, the rule of convenience would close the class when the daughter died.[88] Usually a class remains open until the time for distribution under the rule of convenience, but some courts construe gifts more narrowly in order to avoid perpetuities violations. For example, the devise of an annuity to the "issue of *N*" was construed to mean only *N*'s issue living at the testator's death; this construction made the devise valid.[89]

Effect of the Rule on Construction

The mathematical certainty of the Rule Against Perpetuities often evaporates when it is applied to actual instruments because the question whether the Rule was violated turns on cloudy constructional questions, such as when "heirs" are determined, or when a class closes, or whether there was a condition of survival. If the Rule is violated under one construction but not under another, should this affect the way a court resolves the construction? According to John Chipman Gray, "every provision in a will or settlement is to be construed as if the Rule did not exist and then to the provision so construed

---

vested when John died); Deiss v. Deiss, 536 N.E.2d 120, 124 (Ill.App.1989); Brown v. American Fletcher National Bank, 519 N.E.2d 166 (Ind.App.1988).

[85] Thornhill v. Riegg, 383 S.E.2d 447, 452 (N.C.App.1989). *See also* Lanier v. Lanier, 126 S.E.2d 776 (Ga.1962). This result turns on the way the will is worded. As to the distinction between contingent and vested subject to divestment, *see* Section 11.1.

[86] Morris & Leach, *supra* note 31, at 1; *Restatement of Property* § 371(1)(b), § 383 (1944).

[87] Abram v. Wilson, 220 N.E.2d 739 (Ohio Prob.1966). As to when a class closes, *see* Section 11.2.

[88] In re Greenwood's Will, 268 A.2d 867 (Del.1970). *See also* Austin v. Dobbins, 252 S.E.2d 588, 593 (Va.1979).

[89] In re Trust of Criss, 329 N.W.2d 842 (Neb.1983).

the Rule is to be remorselessly applied."[90] Many modern courts do not follow Gray's approach. A court construed a will to refer only to grandnieces and grandnephews alive when the testator died because "a document should be interpreted if feasible to avoid the conclusion that it violates the rule against perpetuities."[91]

Much depends on how ambiguous is the instrument. No one can claim that "25" is ambiguous and really means "21."[92] (*Reforming* 25 to 21 is another matter which we shall discuss later.[93]) But "grandnephews" *can* mean "grandnephews alive at my death" if other language in the will or the circumstances indicate(s) the testator had this in mind.

Effect of Rule Violation

Infractions of the Rule usually appear in the residuary clause of a will and result in property passing intestate. Claims that the Rule was violated are typically raised by heirs who hope to get property outright when it was left in trust. This effort may fail even if a Rule violation is found because normally the violation does not invalidate the income interests of the trust but only the remainder interests which were to vest in the distant future. "The rule against perpetuities voids only those interests vesting beyond the perpetuities period. The remaining valid interests take effect."[94]

If the violation appears in a pre-residuary clause, the property simply falls into the residue.[95] In an inter vivos trust, invalidity of an interest may create a resulting trust for the settlor which means that the property passes under the settlor's will, if the settlor had one.[96] Some statutes provide that a Rule violation results in "vesting the fee in the last taker under the legal limitations;" under this approach, a person designated as a life beneficiary can get the remainder as well.[97] This avoids a distribution to the testator's heirs long after the testator's death.

When application of the Rule produces an intestacy, this may not seriously disrupt the testator's estate plan. Many wills create a trust for the testator's heirs, and a successful invocation of the Rule simply gives them their inheritance outright rather than in trust. But when the beneficiaries of the challenged will are not the testator's heirs, the distortion of the testator's wishes when a Rule violation is found can be extreme.[98]

---

[90] Quoted in Hagemann v. National Bank and Trust Co., 237 S.E.2d 388, 393 (Va.1977). *See also* First Alabama Bank v. Adams, 382 So.2d 1104, 1107 (Ala.1980).

[91] Estate of Grove, 138 Cal.Rptr. 684, 688 (1977). *See also* Southern Bank & Trust Co. v. Brown, 246 S.E.2d 598, 601 (S.C.1978); *Restatement of Property* § 375 (1944).

[92] *Id.*, cmt. b (will must be "ambiguous" and the construction "possible").

[93] *See* Section 12.4.

[94] White v. Fleet Bank of Maine, 739 A.2d 373, 378 (Me.1999).

[95] Brownell v. Edmunds, 209 F.2d 349 (4th Cir.1953); *Restatement of Property* § 403, cmt. c (1944).

[96] Ryan v. Ward, 64 A.2d 258 (Md.1949).

[97] Pound v. Shorter, 377 S.E.2d 854 (Ga.1989). The Georgia statute was repealed in 1990. *Cf.* 20 Pa.Stat. § 6105(c).

[98] Berry v. Union Nat. Bank, 262 S.E.2d 766 (W.Va.1980).

Courts sometimes use a doctrine called "infectious invalidity" to strike down even interests which are valid in order better to effectuate the testator's intent. For example, a will created trusts for the testator's three children. The termination provision for two of them violated the Rule. The one for the third child's trust did not but the court struck it down also:

> [E]ven if the provisions for Walter be valid, . . . they cannot be permitted to stand alone, because such would result in significant distortion or defeat of the Testator's underlying objectives. . . . [The] underlying plan of [the] Testator was for his three children to have equal shares . . . If the provisions for Walter are permitted to stand, . . . Walter will share equally with Judith and Denis under the laws of intestate succession . . . while also receiving the income for life in the remaining one-third—a grossly distorted result.[99]

When a remainder is held to violate the Rule, the preceding income interests may also be stricken as "inextricably intertwined" with them.[100] If the trust was created in order to bypass the estates of the testator's children, and if the Rule violation causes the remainder to fall to the children as intestate property, why should the trusts be established at all? On the other hand, the testator may have had another purpose which would be defeated by early termination. When a remainder after a life estate in the testator's grandson was held invalid, the court declined to void the life estate itself, because a spendthrift provision in the trust showed that "the testator's obvious purpose was to protect the [grandson] against his own improvidence," and this would be frustrated by an outright distribution to him.[101]

When an executory interest is held to violate the Rule, the preceding interest will normally become indefeasibly vested.[102] However, where a fee simple determinable is followed by an invalid executory interest, only the executory interest is stricken, not the determinability.[103] Thus, the fee remains determinable and a possibility of reverter vests in the grantor by operation of law.[104]

Separability of Class Gifts

Most infractions of the Rule involve class gifts. Courts generally refuse to sever them to hold the interests of some class members valid while others are invalid. A will left property to the testator's grandchildren who attained the age of 25. He had five grandchildren when he died, and three more were born thereafter. The interests of the grandchildren who were alive when the testator died were certain to vest, if at all, in time because they were lives in being. The interest of the afterborn grandchildren might vest too late. The court refused

---

[99] Merrill v. Wimmer, 481 N.E.2d 1294, 1299–1300 (Ind.1985). *See also Restatement of Property* § 402, illus. 3 (1944).

[100] Connecticut Bank & Trust Co. v. Brody, 392 A.2d 445, 451 (Conn.1978).

[101] In re Estate of Davis, 297 A.2d 451, 455 (Pa.1972). *See also Restatement of Property* § 386, illus. 5 (1944). *Compare* Section 10.9.

[102] Washington State Grange v. Brandt, 148 P.3d 1069, 1075 (Wash. Ct. App. 2006); In re Estate of Dees, 308 P.2d 90 (1957).

[103] First Universalist Society v. Boland, 29 N.E. 524 (Mass. 1892).

[104] City of Klamath Falls v. Bell, 490 P.2d 515, 518 (Or. App. 1971).

to distinguish between the two groups. The testator thought that he could "include afterborn grandchildren and also postpone the vesting till twenty-five. But if he had been informed that he could not do both, can I say that the alteration he would have made would have been to leave out the afterborn grandchildren ... I should think quite the contrary."[105] This decision established the "all-or-nothing" rule under which if a gift is invalid as to one class member it is invalid as to all.[106]

Gifts to "sub-classes" are treated differently. A trust provided for the testator's daughter and grandchildren, with a remainder to more remote descendants upon the death of each grandchild. When one grandchild died, the remainder was challenged under the Rule.[107] The court invoked "the doctrine of vertical separability" under which the remainder to the descendants of any grandchild who was alive at the testator's death was separable from the remainder to the descendants of an afterborn grandchild. "Because [this grandchild] was a life in being at the time of the will's [taking effect], the remainder to his issue was valid and any possible void remainder interest to [issue of] afterborn children of his mother . . . was separable."[108] But in a case in which life estates in the testator's grandchildren were followed by a remainder to their descendants, the court refused to separate the remainders because the will did:

> not indicate any intention that each of his grandchildren should have a separate life estate in a separate share and that each such separate share should vest separately at the death of such grandchild in the issue of that grandchild. Rather the entire corpus of the trust . . . was to be held for the benefit of his grandchildren as a class until the last of them should die at which time the same undivided corpus should, as a remainder, vest in his great-grandchildren per capita.[109]

Separability is an appealing way to avoid the Rule if no afterborn beneficiaries are born, because no one loses thereby.[110] But when afterborn grandchildren actually appear, courts are reluctant to treat subclasses differently, and so they adopt an "all or nothing" approach. A trust for the children of testator's daughter provided that at the death of each child, the principal from which the child had been receiving income should go to his or her descendants. The daughter had five children, one of whom was born after

---

[105] Leake v. Robinson, 35 Eng.Rep. 979, 989 (1817).

[106] *Restatement of Property* § 371, cmt. a (1944); In re Ghiglia's Estate, 116 Cal.Rptr. 827 (App.1974); Abram v. Wilson, 220 N.E.2d 739 (Ohio Prob.1966); *cf.* Carter v. Berry, 140 So.2d 843 (Miss.1962).

[107] The challenge was made by the widow of the deceased grandchild. She was not included in the remainder, but as the grandchild's devisee she would take under the Pennsylvania statute cited at *supra* note 97 if the remainder was invalid.

[108] In re Estate of Weaver, 572 A.2d 1249, 1256 (Pa.Super.1990). *See also* First Alabama Bank v. Adams, 382 So.2d 1104 (Ala.1980).

[109] Connecticut Bank and Trust Co. v. Brody, 392 A.2d 445, 452 (Conn.1978). *See also* North Carolina Nat. Bank v. Norris, 203 S.E.2d 657, 659 (N.C.App.1974); *Restatement of Property* § 376 illus. 2 (1944). Even if distribution is postponed until the last grandchild dies if a per stirpes rather than per capita distribution is called for, the gift may be considered separable. *Id.* § 389, cmt. g; Second Bank-State Street Trust Co. v. Second Bank-State Street Trust Co., 140 N.E.2d 201, 206 (Mass.1957). As to the distinction between per stirpes and per capita, *see* Section 2.2.

[110] *Cf. Restatement of Property* § 389, cmt. a (1944).

the testator died. The remainder to his descendants was held invalid. When two of his elder brothers later died, even though they were in being when the testator died, the remainders to their descendants were also stricken, because to separate their remainders from the one previously held invalid would distort the testator's plan for "absolute equality on a stirpital basis" among his descendants. This differed from cases in which separability led to a "perfect result . . . because all grandchildren were born in the testator's lifetime and [so] the whole of the testator's disposition could be sustained."[111]

Alternative Contingencies

A Rule violation can be avoided if the instrument expresses alternate contingencies. For example, a trust was to last until the death of the settlor's two sons, or until their youngest child reached 25, "whichever event shall occur last." The youngest grandchild might not reach 25 until after lives in being plus 21 years, but the court refused to hold the trust invalid. "Where a limitation is made to take effect on two alternative events, one of which is too remote and the other valid, . . . the gift . . . will be allowed to take effect on the happening of the [valid] one."[112] If the youngest grandchild was 25 when the sons died, the trust would terminate under the first alternative which was valid because the sons were lives in being. But if the youngest grandchild was not then 25, the second alternative would apply and the remainder would be invalid.

This avenue of escape from the Rule is available only if the instrument expresses alternative contingencies. A trust which was to end upon the death of the beneficiaries, including the "widow" of the testator's son, was held invalid because the will did not *say* that the trust was to terminate "upon the death of my son *or* upon the death of his widow," even though what the will said was equivalent to this.[113] Thus, Chancellor Nottingham's dictum that "real Differences" rather than "Words" should be determinative does not always characterize the modern Rule.[114]

§ 12.3 Planning to Avoid the Rule

Bad Ways to Avoid the Rule

The Rule has an impact on drafting even though it produces relatively few reported cases. Many lawyers unnecessarily distort sensible estate plans in order to avoid Rule violations. Some suggested "prescriptions for avoiding violation of the Rule"[115] are questionable. For example:

---

[111] In re Morton's Estate, 312 A.2d 26, 27 (Pa.1973). *See also Restatement (Second) of Property (Donative Transfers)* § 1.5, cmt. g (1983).

[112] Application of Wolfsohn, 339 N.Y.S.2d 755, 759 (App.Div.1973). *See also* Earle v. International Paper Co., 429 So.2d 989, 997 (Ala.1983) (concurring opinion); *Restatement (Second) of Property (Donative Transfers)* § 1.4, cmt. *o* (1983).

[113] Easton v. Hall, 154 N.E. 216, 220 (Ill.1926). *See also Restatement of Property* § 377 illus. 3 (1944).

[114] *See* Section 12.1.

[115] R. Link, *The Rule Against Perpetuities in North Carolina,* 57 N.C.L.Rev. 727, 817 (1979). *See also* 6 *Amer.Law of Prop.* § 24.7.

1. "Beware of gifts to grandchildren." Such gifts may be desirable if settlors do not want property to pass outright to their children for tax or other reasons.

2. "Describe beneficiaries by name rather than by class designation." This may exclude afterborn grandchildren, a result most testators would want to avoid.[116]

3. "Beware of gifts contingent upon the taker attaining an age over twenty-one." A distribution at age 21 may be premature. How many fortunes have been dissipated after they were distributed to beneficiaries at age 21 in order to avoid the Rule?[117]

4. "Avoid gifts conditioned on the survival of the 'widow' of a named person." Surely it would be unfortunate if all widows (and widowers) were excluded from wills because of the Rule. Naming a relative's current spouse avoids the Rule, but excluding a later spouse of a relative may also produce a questionable result.

Saving Clauses

A saving clause avoids Rule violations without producing such undesirable side effects.[118] For example, a saving clause saved a trust for the testator's daughter and her children which provided that each child's share vested at age 30. The trial court reduced the age to 21 in order to avoid violating the Rule, but the appellate court reversed, because this change

> creates possibilities that the trust property could pass out of the decedent's family or that a beneficiary could gain either absolute ownership or control over the disposition of the trust property earlier than was intended by the decedent. . . . [A saving clause made this unnecessary. It] provides that all trusts created by the will are to terminate on the date limited by the applicable Rule Against Perpetuities . . . and any remaining corpus is to be distributed to those persons then entitled to receive income from the trust.[119]

Saving clauses have two parts: a termination provision and a direction for distribution. The termination clause in the foregoing case failed to make clear what "the date limited" by the Rule was. Lives in being plus 21 years, of course, but *what* lives? The court found the relevant measuring life was the testator's daughter, so the trust would have to end 21 years after she died. But the Rule allows more than one measuring life, and so a well-drafted saving clause should specify a *reasonable number* of measuring lives *e.g.* "twenty one years after the death of all of my descendants living at the time of my death." Vesting cannot be postponed until "the death of the last survivor of all persons who

---

[116] In some states afterborn grandchildren might claim an intestate share under a pretermitted heir statute which might also be undesirable. *See* Section 8.5.

[117] *See* Section 10.5.

[118] W. McGovern, *Perpetuities Pitfalls and How Best to Avoid Them,* 6 Real Prop., Prob. & Tr. L. J. 155, 175 (1971).

[119] In re Estate of Burrough, 521 F.2d 277, 280 (D.C.Cir.1975). *See also* Norton v. Georgia R.R. Bank & Trust, 322 S.E.2d 870, 875 (Ga.1984) (trust for testator's children, grandchildren and great grandchildren valid under saving clause).

shall be living at my death." The administrative difficulty of determining the survivor of very large groups has led courts to hold clauses like this void.[120] An English court allowed a clause which used the "descendants of Queen Victoria alive at my death," even though these numbered 120 when the testator died (in 1926), and they were "scattered over the entire continent of Europe," and some had fallen into "penury and obscurity," which made tracing them extremely difficult.[121]

No testator should use such a large group as measuring lives, and very few do.[122] A trust which goes on for "as long as the law allows" imposes dead-hand control on an unforeseeable future. Saving clauses can usefully prevent frustration of a more limited objective, such as holding property in trust until grandchildren reach age 30. A saving clause makes this valid because, if the unlikely event happens (expiration of lives in being designated in the saving clause plus 21 years before the grandchildren reach 30), the trust terminates. A well-drafted termination provision in a saving clause might say "unless sooner terminated in accordance with its provisions,[123] this trust shall terminate 21 years after the death of the last survivor of my spouse and my issue who are living at the time of my death." An unmarried testator could designate "the descendants of my parents who are living at the time of my death" (or some other comparable group) instead. An irrevocable trust should refer to "descendants now living," or name the measuring lives.[124]

If the trust terminates under the saving clause, to whom should distribution be made? If this is not made clear, the clause may be ineffective.[125] Many saving clauses provide that, upon termination, the assets should be "distributed to the persons then entitled to the income."[126] In most situations this makes sense. If a trust for children and grandchildren with a remainder to their descendants is still operating for an afterborn grandchild 21 years after the designated measuring lives expired, distribution to the afterborn grandchild would come close to the testator's plan since the grandchild would probably leave it to his or her children at death. But if the income beneficiary at the time of termination under the saving clause is an "unborn widow," giving

---

[120] In re Moore, [1901] 1 Ch. 936. According to *Restatement (Second) of Property (Donative Transfers)* § 1.3, cmt. a (1983), if "the number of lives specified in the saving clause is unreasonable" a court may select "a reasonable number" out of the specified group, rather than avoiding the clause.

[121] In re Villar, [1929] 1 Ch. 243. One of these descendants was Anastasia, Czar Nicholas' daughter, the date of whose death remains unclear. Morris & Leach, *supra* note 31, at 61 (1962).

[122] J. Dukeminier, *The Uniform Statutory Rule Against Perpetuities: Ninety Years in Limbo*, 34 UCLA L.Rev. 1023, 1030 (1987). However, some lawyers tout trusts as a "unique opportunity to create a family asset pool which may be enjoyed by the creator's family into perpetuity without shrinkage caused by transfer taxes or loss due to divorce or other creditor claims." S. Oshins & J. Blattmacher, *The Megatrust: An Ideal Family Wealth Preservation Tool*, 130 Trusts & Estates 20, 30 (1991).

[123] This phrase is important, because it is undesirable to keep a trust going for the full length allowed by the Rule. *See* note 129.

[124] *See* Section 12.2. If the will is exercising a power of appointment, *see* Section 12.5.

[125] Hagemann v. National Bank & Trust Co., 237 S.E.2d 388, 392 (Va.1977).

[126] E.g., In re Burrough's Estate, 521 F.2d 277, 279 (D.C.Cir.1975).

the trust assets to her outright may frustrate a settlor's wish to keep property in the family.[127]

Duration of Trusts

Although the Rule allows trusts to continue beyond lives in being plus 21 years if all the interests are vested,[128] knowledgeable estate planners advise against keeping trusts going so long.[129] Courts occasionally misunderstand the Rule and erroneously hold trusts invalid simply because they last too long.[130] Also, if the trust gives the trustee discretion to accumulate income, invade principal, or sprinkle income, the beneficiaries' interests are contingent upon the trustee's discretion, and so their interests are invalid if the trust continues beyond the period of the Rule.[131]

A saving clause, therefore, ought to terminate any trust which is still operating when the period of the Rule ends. This will be unfortunate if a distributee is then a minor, but in most cases the trust will actually terminate not under the saving clause but at a time when all the distributees are mature.[132]

§ 12.4 Modern Reforms

Wait and See

Late in his career, Professor Leach became a zealous crusader for reforming the Rule.[133] He attacked its focus on possibilities rather than actual facts. "[T]he public interest is not damaged by a tying up of property that *might have* exceeded the period of perpetuities." Therefore, courts should "wait and see" whether the contingency happens within the period of the Rule.[134] This idea had been adopted in a Pennsylvania statute which provided that the Rule should be "measured by actual rather than possible events."[135] Since then, it had been accepted in some judicial decisions. A court upheld a 25 year trust because when it decided the case (about 5 years after the testator died), the

---

[127] *See* McGovern, *supra* note 118, at 159.

[128] *See* Section 12.2.

[129] McGovern, *supra* note 118, at 176; Link, *supra* note 115, at 818.

[130] Burton v. Hicks, 136 S.E.2d 759 (Ga.1964) (25 year trust "void" under Rule even though interests vested).

[131] Arrowsmith v. Mercantile-Safe Deposit, 545 A.2d 674, 677 (Md.1988); Abram v. Wilson, 220 N.E.2d 739, 742 (Ohio Prob.1966); *Restatement (Third) of Trusts* § 29, cmt. h (2003); *Restatement (Second) of Trusts* § 62, cmt. q (1959); W. Bolich, *The Power of Appointment: Tool of Estate Planning and Drafting,* [1964] Duke L.J. 32, 61–62; Morris & Leach, *supra* note 31, at 143–44. This is ironic, since such flexible trusts are less subject to the objection of dead hand control. See generally Hirsch & Wang, *supra* note 42.

[132] A clause retaining in trust the share of any distributee under disability may be desirable for this remote possibility. The clause should provide for distribution to the distributee's estate in case the share is not fully distributed prior to the distributee's death. Such a clause *ought not* to violate the Rule, since the interest retained in trust is vested.

[133] Leach's previous articles about the Rule were principally descriptive. W. Leach, *Perpetuities in a Nutshell,* 51 Harv.L.Rev. 638 (1938); *cf.* W. Leach, *The Rule Against Perpetuities and Gifts to Classes,* 51 Harv.L.Rev. 1329 (1938) (attacking Leake v. Robinson).

[134] W. Leach, *Perpetuities in Perspective: Ending the Rule's Reign of Terror*, 65 Harv.L.Rev. 721, 729–30 (1952) (emphasis added).

[135] 20 Pa.Stat. § 6104(b).

trust had less than 20 years to run and there were then "a host of" persons alive who were born before the testator died.[136]

Time of Decision

The courts in these cases did not actually *wait* to see what would happen; by the time the litigation arose it had become clear that the trust would not last beyond twenty one years plus lives in being. Would the court have waited to see what happened if the will had been challenged just after the testator died? This raises an issue which is related to but distinct from wait and see: should courts decide whether a remainder is valid before the time comes to distribute it? Leach argued that they should not. Because remainders are usually given to persons who are unborn, under age, or unascertained, an early decision requires that these persons be represented by a guardian ad litem, whereas if the court postpones the decision, the remaindermen can choose their own advocate.[137] (Any judgment in which affected parties were not adequately represented would not bind them.)[138] Other knowledgeable authorities disagreed.[139] Postponing a decision keeps title uncertain, and it seems unfair to persons who would take if an instrument is invalid to say "the property may belong to you, but we will not decide this until you are dead and *then* you will get your property."

Even if the time of decision is not deliberately postponed, often no one raises the perpetuities question until after the relevant facts have become clear. In this situation distributions may already have taken place. The 1964 English Perpetuities Act provided that any ultimate determination of invalidity would not affect previous distributions.[140]

Who Are the Measuring Lives?

Some courts have rejected "wait and see."[141] The great difficulty with the concept is determining the appropriate measuring lives. Professor Simes illustrated the problem by a hypothetical devise "to my descendants living 120 years after my death." At the end of 120 years should a court uphold the devise if it discovers *any person* in the world who was alive at the testator's death who died at age 100?[142] Courts have had to answer an analogous problem in construing trusts that by their terms were to last "for as long as is legally possible." One court held that the measuring lives for such a trust were the

136 In re Estate of Anderson, 541 So.2d 423, 433 (Miss.1989). *See also* Hansen v. Stroecker, 699 P.2d 871, 875 (Alaska 1985); Merchants Nat. Bank v. Curtis, 97 A.2d 207, 212 (N.H.1953).

137 W. Leach, *supra* note 134, at 729. *See also* Trust Agreement of Westervelt v. First Interstate Bank, 551 N.E.2d 1180, 1183 (Ind.App.1990); Dewire v. Haveles, 534 N.E.2d 782, 785 (Mass.1989) (declining to decide possible invalidity of remainder under the Rule).

138 *See* Section 14.8.

139 P. Mechem, *Further Thoughts on the Pennsylvania Perpetuities Legislation*, 107 U.Pa.L.Rev. 965, 979–80 (1959); L. Simes, *Is the Rule Against Perpetuities Doomed?*, 52 Mich.L.Rev. 179, 183 (1953).

140 Perpetuities and Accumulations Act 1964, § 3(1). *See also* Unif. Statutory Rule Against Perpetuities § 1, cmt. Perhaps courts would reach this result even without such a statute. D. Powell, *Florida's Statutory Rule Against Perpetuities*, 11 U.Fla.St.U.L.Rev. 767, 813n (1984). As to the recovery of property erroneously distributed to a beneficiary, *see* Section 14.3.

141 Pound v. Shorter, 377 S.E.2d 854, 856 (Ga.1989).

142 Simes, *supra* note 139, at 187. *See also* Mechem, *supra* note 139, at 981–82.

testator's children, not including the testator's grandchildren alive at his death even though they were beneficiaries of the trust. As a result the trust would end after 78 years.[143]

The "possibilities" approach of the common-law Rule avoids the dilemma of picking measuring lives. Even a *25-year* postponement of vesting (without a saving clause) violates the common-law Rule because *whoever* is picked as a measuring life in advance *may* die within 4 years. Taking advantage of hindsight under "wait and see" can substantially lengthen the time during which property is tied up even though the period of the Rule remains nominally the same unless the measuring lives are limited.

A Kentucky statute attempted to solve this problem by providing that "the period shall not be measured by any lives whose continuance does not have a causal relationship to the vesting or failure of the interest."[144] Professor Dukeminier believed this was clear; he "had no trouble in identifying the causally-related measuring lives" in the standard perpetuities hypotheticals,[145] but Professor Waggoner wrote that this test "leaves so many questions in doubt" that it would breed much litigation.[146]

The Uniform Statutory Rule Against Perpetuities ("USRAP"), promulgated in 1986 and at one time adopted in about half the states, accepts wait and see but rejects the use of measuring lives because of the difficulty of defining and keeping track of them. Instead the USRAP validates any interest which "either vests or terminates within 90 years after its creation."[147] The 90-year period was selected as

> a reasonable approximation of . . . the period of time that would, on average, be produced through the use of a set of actual measuring lives identified by statute and then adding the traditional 21 year tack-on period after the death of the survivor.[148]

Professor Dukeminier criticized the USRAP for inviting "lawyers unconversant with the law of future interests to create long-term ninety-year trusts [which] may lack the flexible powers an experienced estate planner gives to the trustee and beneficiaries to deal with changing circumstances over a long period of

---

[143] Matter of Estate of Holt, 857 P.2d 1355 (Hawaii 1993). *See also* In re Burrough's Estate, 521 F.2d 277, 280 (D.C.Cir.1975) (testator's daughter used as measuring life under similar clause); *cf.* White v. Fleet Bank of Maine, 739 A.2d 373, 379 (Me.1999) (grandchildren and great-grandchild living at testator's death used).

[144] Ky.Rev.Stat. § 381.216, repealed by Ky. Laws 2010 (H.B. 199), ch. 21, § 14. Iowa adopts the Restatement (Second)'s measuring lives list. *See* S. Kurtz, *The Iowa Rule Against Perpetuities—Reform at Last, Restatement Style, Wait-and-See and* Cy Pres, 69 Iowa. L. Rev. 705 (1984).

[145] J. Dukeminier, *Perpetuities: The Measuring Lives*, 85 Colum.L.Rev. 1648, 1674 (1985). *See also* Fleet Nat. Bank v. Colt, 529 A.2d 122, 130 (R.I.1987) (two-generation trust sustained because grandchildren alive when testator died were still living when interest vested).

[146] L. Waggoner, *Perpetuities: A Perspective on Wait-and-See*, 85 Colum.L.Rev. 1714, 1724 (1985). *See also* R. Maudsley, *Perpetuities: Reforming the Common-Law Rule—How to Wait and See*, 60 Cornell L.Rev. 355, 375 (1975).

[147] Unif. Statutory Rule Against Perpetuities § 1(a)(2). Interests which would be valid under the common-law Rule continue to be valid under the USRAP.

[148] *Id.* at Prefatory Note.

years."[149] Professor Fellows, on the other hand, after studying how the USRAP would have affected perpetuities cases decided during the period 1984–89, concluded that the statute

> avoids unwarranted interference with a transferor's estate plan while guaranteeing that a trust does not last too long. . . . Only in unusual family situations in which adult children [of the testator] had not yet had their own children [when the testator died] did the ninety year rule result in a substantially longer perpetuity period. . . . This is a small cost to pay for the administrative simplicity obtained by the ninety-year rule.[150]

Professor Fellows argued that legislatures need not worry that drafters will use the statute to establish "dynastic trusts." Professor Fellows cited the example of Wisconsin which abolished the rule in 1969, but has not become a "perpetuity haven."[151] In a posthumously published article, Professor Dukeminier countered that the recent rash of actual and proposed legislation to allow trusts to last for "125 years, or 150, or 360, or 1000, or forever" suggests that many settlors in fact plan to create such trusts.[152]

Cy Pres

Leach also espoused a second reform of the Rule, often called *cy pres* by analogy to the doctrine which allows courts to modify charitable trusts to meet changing circumstances.[153] "If a gift in the will or trust threatens to tie up property for too long a period, why should we invalidate it in toto? Why not cut it down to size?"[154] *Cy pres* extends the idea that ambiguous instruments should be *construed* so as to avoid violating the Rule; it allows unambiguous terms to be reformed, *e.g.*, changing "age 40" to "age 21." (Reformation in this sense should not be confused with altering the terms of an instrument so as to correct a mistake in transcribing the maker's intention.)[155] This idea had already been adopted by a court in 1891 which cured a perpetuities violation by reducing the age from 40 to 21 in a trust for the testator's grandchildren.[156] A New York statute providing for this result[157] saved a trust for the testator's grandchildren by reducing the age of distribution from 35 to 21.[158]

---

[149] J. Dukeminier, *A Modern Guide to Perpetuities*, 74 Cal.L.Rev. 1867, 1886 (1986). *See also* J. Dukeminier, *The Uniform Statutory Rule Against Perpetuities: Ninety Years in Limbo,* 34 UCLA L.Rev. 1023 (1987).

[150] M. Fellows, *Testing Perpetuity Reforms: A Study of Perpetuity Cases 1984–89,* 25 Real Prop. Prob. & Tr. J. 597, 598 (1991).

[151] *Id.* at 602, 653.

[152] J. Dukeminier & J. Krier, *The Rise of the Perpetual Trust,* 50 UCLA L.Rev. 1303, 1309–10 (2003).

[153] *See* Section 10.10.

[154] Leach, *supra* note 134, at 734–35.

[155] *See* Section 7.1.

[156] Edgerly v. Barker, 31 A. 900 (N.H.1891).

[157] N.Y. EPTL § 9–1.2. See also 765 ILCS § 305/4(c)(2). A similar provision appeared in the English Law of Property Act 1925, 15 Geo. 5 c. 20, § 163.

[158] Matter of Estate of Kreuzer, 674 N.Y.S.2d 505, 508 (App.Div.1998). The court in this case rejected "wait and see;" while it was possible that the gifts would be distributed within the perpetuities period, "the 'what might have been' doctrine . . . requires us to consider all possibilities as of the testator's death."

Some statutes give courts a more general authorization to reform instruments, not limited to reducing a designated age to 21.[159] Others combine *cy pres* with wait and see. The Uniform Statutory Rule adopts this approach.[160] Wait and see is applied first. In most cases, this renders alteration in the instrument unnecessary,[161] but not always. A will purported to create a "perpetual" trust for scholarships "to any blood heirs of my husband or myself."[162] The court apparently assumed that the term "blood heirs" was not limited to descendants living at the testator's death,[163] and thus the trust might go on forever. Reformation was necessary because wait and see could not avoid the perpetuities problem.[164] The reformation consisted in directing that any remaining principal be distributed "twenty-one years after the death of the last heir of the testator or her husband who was living at the time of the testator's death."[165]

Some courts have reformed wills to avoid a Rule violation even without statutory authority,[166] but others have refused to do so.[167] Some criticize the idea as too vague.[168] For instance, in a case involving an age contingency over 21, a court might reduce the specified age to 21, or it might confine the relevant class to persons born before the testator's death,[169] or it might leave the specified distribution date and class intact but make the interests vest prior to the trust termination.[170] Perhaps the testator would have preferred to do *nothing* and let the interests fail rather than modify the will.[171]

Professor Browder suggested that the best way to reform wills was to insert a perpetuities saving clause.[172] This would allow any reasonable estate plan to be carried out unchanged. *Cy pres*, when implemented by inserting a

---

[159] Mo.Stat. § 442.555(2); Tex.Prop.Code § 5.043.

[160] Unif. Statutory Rule Against Perpetuities § 3. *See also* Iowa Code § 558.68(3); Ohio Rev.Stat. § 2131.08(C).

[161] Unif. Statutory Rule Against Perpetuities § 3, cmt. *See also* Fellows, *supra* note 150, at 610.

[162] Matter of Estate of Keenan, 519 N.W.2d 373, 375 (Iowa 1994). Because of the limitation to relatives, the trust could not qualify as charitable. *See* Section 10.10.

[163] *Compare* Section 12.2.

[164] Query: if none of the heirs living at the testator's death had descendants, wouldn't the trust terminate within lives in being?

[165] Matter of Estate of Keenan, *supra* note 162 at 375 (Iowa 1994). Distribution was to be "to the testator's heirs at law." Presumably this means those who would have been the testator's heirs had she then died. *Cf.* Section 11.3.

[166] Berry v. Union Nat. Bank, 262 S.E.2d 766, 771 (W.Va.1980) (25 year trust reduced to 21 years); In re Chun Quan Yee Hop's Estate, 469 P.2d 183 (Haw.1970) (30 years reduced to 21); Carter v. Berry, 140 So.2d 843 (Miss.1962).

[167] Hagemann v. National Bank and Trust Co., 237 S.E.2d 388, 392n (Va.1977).

[168] D. Schuyler, *The Statute Concerning Perpetuities,* 65 Nw.U.L.Rev. 3, 24 (1970); R. Powell, *The Rule Against Perpetuities and Spendthrift Trust in New York,* 71 Colum.L.Rev. 688, 694 (1971); L. Simes, *Public Policy and the Dead Hand* 78 (1955).

[169] Estate of Grove, 138 Cal.Rptr. 684, 689 (App.1977).

[170] Foley v. Evans, 570 N.E.2d 179, 181 (Mass.App.1991).

[171] W. McGovern, *Facts and Rules in the Construction of Wills,* 26 UCLA L.Rev. 285, 312–14 (1978); University of Louisville v. Isert, 742 S.W.2d 571 (Ky.App.1987) (refusing to apply reformation statute).

[172] O. Browder, *Construction, Reformation, and the Rule Against Perpetuities,* 62 Mich.L.Rev. 1, 6 (1963). *See also* Unif. Statutory Rule Against Perpetuities § 5, cmt.

saving clause, is virtually the same as wait and see.[173] An Illinois statute following this approach terminated trusts[174] violating the Rule 21 years after the death of the last to die of all the beneficiaries alive when the trust began.[175]

The Uniform Statutory Rule is only prospective with respect to wait and see, whereas it provides for reformation even of existing instruments.[176] A case arose under the statute involving a will which devised land to the testator's son and his children for their lives with a remainder to the testator's great-grandchildren. The son had no further children after the testator died, but the wait and see provisions of the USRAP did not apply to this 1915 will. The court reformed the will, however, to restrict the grandchildren to those "who are alive at the time of my death."[177] This produced the same result.

Repeal

The foregoing suggestions for avoiding the pitfalls of the traditional Rule do not satisfy those who (for whatever reason) want to create perpetual (or very long-term) trusts. Over the past couple of decades many American states have repealed or substantially modified the Rule in an effort to retain or attract trust business to their respective states. By careful planning, a married couple may shelter $23.4 million in trust (based on the 2021 exemption of $11.7 million per person) and theoretically hold it in trust in perpetuity without assessment of GST tax.[178] These repeal or substantial repeal statutes take one of the following three forms:[179]

Perpetual Trust States: These states allow trusts to be created in perpetuity; although legal interests in real estate generally remain subject to the rule;

Multi-Century Trust States: These states allow trusts to exist for very long periods, such as 360 to 1,000 years;

Opt-Out States: These states allow the trust drafter to opt out of the Rule or to create a trust for a very long time but trusts that fail to opt out remain subject to the common-law Rule or some reform version.

The Third Restatement

The drafters of the Third Restatement were critical of the common-law Rule. Yet they believed that it is socially desirable to place limits on the

---

[173] L. Waggoner, *Perpetuity Reform*, 81 Mich.L.Rev. 1718, 1781 (1983) (the Restatement version of wait and see "automatically interjects a well-conceived saving clause into every instrument").

[174] The drafters believed that wait and see would make property inalienable for too long unless a trustee had power to sell during the waiting period. Schuyler, *supra* note 168, at 22.

[175] 765 ILCS 305/5. The heirs are determined as of the date of distribution rather than at the testator's death. *Cf.* note 165.

[176] Unif. Statutory Rule Against Perpetuities § 5. For a general discussion of retroactivity of Perpetuities reform statutes, *see* Section 1.3.

[177] Abrams v. Templeton, 465 S.E.2d 117 (S.C.App.1995).

[178] For the history, *see Restatement (Third) of Property (Wills and Other Donative Transfers)* Ch. 27 Intro. Note (2011); J. Dukeminier & J. Krier, *The Rise of the Perpetual Trust*, 50 UCLA L.Rev. 1303 (2003). For discussion of the GST tax, *see* Section 15.5.

[179] For a list of the states, *see* T. Gallanis, *Estates, Future Interests, and Powers of Appointment in a Nutshell* § 5.15 (6th ed. 2018).

duration of trusts.[180] The Third Restatement dispenses with the lives in being concept and the wait and see reform which it spawned. Rather, the Restatement bases the perpetuities period on the lifetimes of the beneficiaries who are up to two generations below the settlor whether or not the beneficiary was alive on the date the trust was created.[181] For beneficiaries unrelated to the settlor, generation assignment would be based on the 25-year age spans (12 1/2 years above and below the settlor) used in the GST tax.[182] The perpetuities period expires at the death of the last such beneficiary. For beneficiaries who are under age 30 at the expiration of the perpetuities period, shares may be maintained in trust until they reach that age.[183]

Upon the expiration of the perpetuities period, any interest violating the revised Rule is subject to judicial modification under *cy pres* principles as discussed above.[184]

The revised Rule does not generally apply to nondonative transfers, to trusts for charitable purposes, to honorary trusts and to trusts for the care of an animal if the trust duration is limited by other law, and to trusts for pensions and other benefit plans.[185] The Third Restatement approach does not currently reflect the law of any state.

§ 12.5 Powers and the Rule

Exercise of Power—Starting Point

The starting point for determining the validity under the Rule of interests created by the exercise of a power of appointment depends on the type of power; general powers which are presently exercisable are differentiated from other powers. An irrevocable trust gave the settlor's son a testamentary power of appointment which he exercised by creating a trust for his children for their lives with remainder to their descendants. The court, following the conception of "relation back,"[186] said the terms of the powerholder's will must be considered as if they had been contained in the trust creating the power, and so the "period of the Rule is calculated from the date of the deed of trust creating the power and not from the exercise of the power by the will."[187] This premise made the appointment invalid, since the powerholder's children were born after the trust which conferred the power was executed. If a power is not presently exercisable, even if it is a general power, the appointive assets are

---

[180] *Restatement (Third) of Property (Wills and Other Donative Transfers)* Ch. 27 Intro. Note (2011).

[181] *Id.* at § 27.1(b)(1).

[182] *Id.* at § 27.1, cmt. f.

[183] *Id.* at § 27.1(a).

[184] *Id.* at § 27.2.

[185] *Id.* at § 27.3. Nondonative transfers to which the Rule still applies include trusts or other property dispositions arising out of marital, divorce, and separation agreements, contracts to make or not to revoke a will or trust, a contract to exercise or not exercise a power of appointment, and a transfer in satisfaction of a duty of support. *Id.*

[186] *See* Section 11.5.

[187] Arrowsmith v. Mercantile-Safe Deposit, 545 A.2d 674, 678 (Md.1988).

not treated as belonging to the powerholder for purposes of the Rule.[188] There is some contrary authority with respect to general testamentary powers,[189] but the Uniform Statutory Rule agrees with most authorities that an interest created by the exercise of a power is deemed to have been created at the time the power was created, unless the power allows the powerholder "to become the unqualified beneficial owner."[190] The exception for presently exercisable general powers applies also at common law. When the powerholder exercised the power to create trusts that were to terminate 21 years after "the death of the survivor of her descendants in being at the time of her [the powerholder's] death," the trusts were valid because the powerholder also had power to withdraw the assets from the trust during her lifetime,

> Where a trust beneficiary is granted . . . an unqualified lifetime power to withdraw for his own use . . . the trust principal, the period of the rule with respect to nonvested interests which may be created by his exercise of [a] testamentary power does not begin to run until the termination of his unqualified power of withdrawal . . . even though (as appears to have been the case here) such beneficiary may make little use of his lifetime power of withdrawal.[191]

As to interests created by exercise of nongeneral powers, almost all states agree that the period of the Rule starts when the power was created.[192] This is consistent with the tax avoidance rationale of the Rule,[193] because *nongeneral* powers do not normally cause the appointive assets to be taxable in the powerholder's estate.[194] In Delaware, however, interests created by exercise of any power, whether general or special, were "deemed to have been created at the time of the exercise and not at the time of the creation of such power of appointment."[195] The Delaware rule inspired a special provision of the Internal Revenue Code to deal with the tax-evasion possibilities it presented, a provision that may create a tax trap for persons taking advantage of the new legislation designed to abolish the Rule.[196]

---

[188] Second Nat. Bank v. Harris Trust and Savings Bank, 283 A.2d 226 (Conn.Sup.1971); In re Bird's Estate, 37 Cal.Rptr. 288 (App.1964); N.Y. EPTL § 10–8.1(a); *Restatement (Second) of Property (Donative Transfers)* § 1.2, cmt. d (1983).

[189] Industrial Nat. Bank v. Barrett, 220 A.2d 517 (R.I.1966); Wis.Stat. § 700.16(c); S.D.Laws § 43–5–5.

[190] Unif. Statutory Rule Against Perpetuities § 2.

[191] In re Moore, 493 N.Y.S.2d 924, 928 (Sup.1985). The starting date for the Rule is postponed only if the general power is unlimited. A "5 and 5 power" allowing a trust beneficiary to invade corpus to the extent of $5,000 or 5% has no effect on the Rule. Unif. Statutory Rule Against Perpetuities, § 2, cmt. ex. 4.

[192] United Cal. Bank v. Bottler, 94 Cal.Rptr. 227 (App.1971); N.Y. EPTL § 10–8.1(a)(2); Wis.Stat. § 700.16(c); S.D.Laws § 43–5–5; *Restatement (Second) of Property (Donative Transfers)* § 1.2 illus. 11 (1983).

[193] *See* Section 12.1.

[194] *See* Section 11.5.

[195] Del.Code tit. 25, § 501. Now modified by id. at § 504. An ambiguous Ohio statute also might be read to change the rule but it was interpreted otherwise in Dollar Savings & Trust Co. v. First Nat. Bank, 285 N.E.2d 768, 778 (Ohio Com.Pl.1972); C. Johnson & F. Williams, *Application of the Rule Against Perpetuities to Powers of Appointment: Ohio Style,* 5 U.Day L.Rev. 39 (1980).

[196] I.R.C. § 2041(a)(3) (exercise of a power is taxable if it creates another power which can postpone vesting beyond the period of the Rule); J. Dukeminier & J. Krier, *The Rise of the Perpetual Trust,* 50 UCLA L.Rev. 1303, 1333 (2003).

Second Look

All jurisdictions allow a "second-look" at the facts when a power of any kind is exercised, even though the starting period for the Rule is the date on which the power was created.

> When the permissible period of the rule against perpetuities must be computed from the time of the creation of the power of appointment, facts and circumstances existing on the effective date of the instrument exercising the power shall be taken into account in determining the validity of the interests created by the instrument exercising the power.[197]

If, for example, a powerholder exercises a testamentary power given by a parent by creating trusts for the lives of the powerholder's children, the second look will validate the trusts if the powerholder's children were born before the power was created because they would have been lives in being at the starting date. The second look is a limited form of "wait and see,"[198] but even opponents of wait and see favor the second look. A decision on the validity of interests created by exercise of a power must inevitably be postponed until the powerholder exercises the power. Therefore, "it would be silly for a court to refuse to look at the course of events during this unavoidable interval" in determining whether the Rule was violated.[199]

Second look does not go as far as wait and see. If the powerholder exercises a power to create trusts that use persons who were born after the power was created as measuring lives, the second look does no good.[200] Under wait and see, however, such a trust would be valid if the afterborn persons happened to die within 21 years after the death of the last to die of the lives in being when the power was created (or within 90 years of creation of the power under the Uniform Statutory Rule).[201]

Capture

When an appointment violates the Rule, the property may pass under a gift in default of appointment in the instrument which created the power,[202] but some courts have avoided this result by invoking "capture." When a powerholder exercised a power to create trusts for children born after the power was created, the invalid remainders in the trusts were replaced by a gift to the powerholder's heirs, on the theory that the powerholder "has manifested

---

[197] N.Y. EPTL § 10–8.3. See also Wis.Stat. § 700.16(1)(c). Courts have also taken a second look in passing on gifts in default of appointment as well as interests created by exercise. Sears v. Coolidge, 108 N.E.2d 563, 566 (Mass.1952). *See also* In re Frank, 389 A.2d 536, 541 (Pa.1978).

[198] In fact, some courts use the terms interchangeably. Harrison v. Marcus, 486 N.E.2d 710, 715n (Mass.1985).

[199] *Powell on Real Property* § 73.11[3]. Professor Powell opposed wait and see.

[200] Second Nat. Bank v. Harris Trust and Savings Bank, 283 A.2d 226 (Conn.Sup.1971); United California Bank v. Bottler, 94 Cal.Rptr. 227 (App.1971).

[201] *Restatement (Second) of Property (Donative Transfers)* § 1.4, cmt. *l* (1983).

[202] Matter of Will of Grunebaum, 471 N.Y.S.2d 513, 515 (Surr.1984); Arrowsmith v. Mercantile-Safe Deposit and Trust Company, 545 A.2d 674, 677 (Md.1988).

an intent wholly to withdraw the appointive property from the operation of the instrument creating the power."[203]

Capture applies only to general powers. If a nongeneral power is invalidly exercised, the property passes to the takers in default of appointment. For example, a father gave his son a nongeneral power which he exercised to create a trust for his daughter for life with remainder to her descendants. The daughter was born after the power was created, so despite a "second look" the remainder was invalid, but not the daughter's life interest. After the daughter's death, the property passed under the father's gift in default of appointment to the son's descendants. Because the power was nongeneral, the court did not apply capture, but the result was the same, because the daughter was both the taker in default of appointment and the powerholder's heir.[204]

Choice of Law

The law in effect at the date a power is exercised determines the validity of the exercise. This has allowed courts to use modern reform statutes to avoid or soften the consequences of a Rule violation.[205]

Planning

What can the creator of a power do to prevent the powerholder from violating the Rule in exercising it?[206] A requirement that the powerholder specifically refer to the power may help to avoid violations of the Rule arising from an inadvertent exercise. Donees who deliberately exercise a power may forget that the period began to run at the time the power was created. A reminder in the power itself might avoid this mental lapse if the drafter of the powerholder's will examines the terms of the power when providing for its exercise.[207] The donor should also consider giving the powerholder a presently exercisable general power, so that the Rule will not begin to run until the powerholder's death. This solution is unsuitable, however, if the donor is using a nongeneral power in order to keep the assets out of the powerholder's taxable estate or fears that the powerholder might use a presently exercisable power to squander the trust assets.[208]

In drafting a will for the holder of a power (other than a presently exercisable general power), the perpetuities saving clause must refer to lives in being when the power was created,[209] rather than persons living at the testator's) death. A powerholder with substantial property of her own who wishes to create trusts for persons who were born after the power was created

---

[203] Amerige v. Attorney General, 88 N.E.2d 126, 131 (Mass.1949). *See also Restatement (Second) of Property (Donative Transfers)* § 23.2 (1983); Cal.Prob.Code § 672(b). For other examples of "capture," *see* Section 11.5.

[204] United California Bank v. Bottler, 94 Cal.Rptr. 227, 232 (App.1971).

[205] Dollar Savings & Trust Co. v. First Nat. Bank, 285 N.E.2d 768 (Ohio Com.Pl.1972); In re Morgan Guaranty Trust Co., 269 N.E.2d 571, 573 (N.Y.1971). *See also* Section 11.5.

[206] *See* generally, W. McGovern, *Perpetuities Pitfalls and How Best to Avoid Them,* 6 Real Prop. Prob. & Tr. J. 155, 168–70 (1971).

[207] 6 *Amer.Law of Prop.* § 24.7.

[208] For further discussion of the use of various kinds of powers in planning, *see* Section 11.5.

[209] H. Tweed & W. Parsons, *Lifetime and Testamentary Estate Planning* 121–22 (10th ed. 1988).

should use the power to pay claims or make outright bequests (if the power allows this) and use her own property for the trusts. If the powerholder fails to do this, a court may sometimes do it by marshalling.[210]

§ 12.6 Gifts to Charity; Reversionary Interests

Duration of Trusts

Charitable trusts are allowed to be perpetual,[211] and courts can utilize their *cy pres* power to modify terms which become obsolete.[212] The public interest in supporting charities is also said to justify exempting charitable trusts from the Rule.[213] Nevertheless, the Rule sometimes has been applied to frustrate charitable gifts or provisions connected with them.

Vesting

Future interests given to a charity must vest within the period prescribed by the Rule if they are preceded by a noncharitable interest.[214] A trust was created in 1976 to accumulate the income for the settlor's son, who had never returned from action in World War II; if the son did not appear by the year 2020, the trustees were to establish a foundation for cruelly treated animals. The court upheld this charitable gift only because of a statute that allowed testators to substitute 80 years in place of the Rule's lives in being plus 21 years.[215]

If the charity's interest vests in time, it need not actually receive the gift within the period of the Rule. The same rule applies to private trusts,[216] but courts are especially prone to treat charitable gifts as "vested." A trust for the lives of the testator's grandchildren and their children provided a gift at their death to Mt. Zion Methodist Church and "to an orphan or childrens home or homes selected" by the trustee. The charitable remainders were held valid because they vested at the testator's death.[217] This is clear as to Mt. Zion Methodist Church, but it is questionable to say that the homes to be selected by the trustee had vested interests.[218] Similarly, a devise to a hospital "to be organized" after the testator's death did not infringe the Rule; the

---

[210] *Restatement (Second) of Property (Donative Transfers)* § 22.1 (1983).

[211] Brown v. Ryan, 788 N.E.2d 1183, 1191 (Ill.App.2003).

[212] *See* Section 10.10 as to *cy pres* and as to the time limits on trusts for non-charitable purposes ("honorary" trusts).

[213] Matter of Estate of Kirk, 907 P.2d 794, 805–06 (Idaho 1995).

[214] *Restatement (Second) of Property (Donative Transfers)* § 1.6 (1983); J. Morris & W. Leach, *The Rule Against Perpetuities* 186–88 (2d ed. 1962). Several American statutes appear to exempt charitable gifts from the Rule altogether, but it is not clear whether they go beyond the common-law described in the text. E.g., Mich.Comp.Laws § 554.351(1) (no gift for charitable uses "shall be invalid . . . by reason of the same contravening any statute or rule against perpetuities").

[215] In re Green's Will Trusts, [1985] 3 All E.R. 455 (1984). *Compare* Section 12.2, note 66.

[216] *See* Section 12.2.

[217] Burt v. Commercial Bank & Trust Co., 260 S.E.2d 306, 310 (Ga.1979).

[218] *Compare* Arrowsmith v. Mercantile-Safe Deposit and Trust Co., 545 A.2d 674, 677 (Md.1988) (income interests in individuals not vested because distributions were discretionary).

"organizational details" were not considered conditions precedent and so the gift was vested.[219]

Executory Interests Following a Charitable Gift

Gifts over to a noncharitable beneficiary if a charity ceases to use the property can violate the Rule. A testator who died in 1931 left money for a hospital; if the hospital ceased to operate, the funds were to "become the absolute property of my friend George Green." When the hospital ceased to operate in 1975, the provision for George Green was held invalid. "Where property is given in trust for charitable purposes, and it is provided that on the happening of a designated event the property shall go to a noncharity, the gift over is subject to the rule against perpetuities and will be void unless it necessarily vests within the period of the rule."[220]

A wait and see approach might have changed this result; under the Uniform Statutory Rule, since the gift to George Green actually vested within 90 years, it would have been valid.[221] However, under the Uniform Trust Code a provision in a charitable trust for distribution to a noncharitable beneficiary can only be given effect "if fewer than 21 years have elapsed" since the trust was created.[222]

If the gift over in this case had been to another charity instead of an individual, it would be valid under a special exception to the Rule.[223] Some commentators have questioned this exception because it applies even if an event unrelated to charity causes the shift from one charity to another, *e.g.*, a gift for UCLA, but if it "should neglect to keep the testator's grave in repair the property" should go to USC.[224]

Effect of Invalid Executory Interest

If the gift to a noncharitable beneficiary following a charitable gift is invalid, what happens to the property? Several answers are possible. Some cases have allowed the charitable donee to keep the property free of the restriction, on the theory that when a divesting condition is invalid under the Rule, the prior interest becomes absolute.[225] Land was given to a city for a park with a gift over to the donor's heirs if the land was not used as a park. The heirs' interest was invalid under the Rule, and the city was held to have "an

---

[219] Rice v. Stanley, 327 N.E.2d 774, 779–80 (Ohio 1975). *See also Restatement (Second) of Trusts* § 401, cmt. j (1959).

[220] Nelson v. Kring, 592 P.2d 438, 442 (Kan.1979). Accord, *Restatement (Second) of Property (Donative Transfers)* § 1.6, cmt. c (1983).

[221] As to the Uniform Statutory Rule Against Perpetuities, *see* Section 12.4. In Harrison v. Marcus, 486 N.E.2d 710, 715 (Mass.1985), the court used wait and see to avoid a similar perpetuities problem.

[222] Uniform Trust Code [hereinafter UTC] § 409(1). Most charitable trusts are designed to get a tax deduction and so the application of the limitation will be rare, since any gift over to an individual may cause the deduction to be lost. *See* Section 15.4.

[223] *Restatement (Second) of Property (Donative Transfers)* § 1.6 (1983); Unif. Statutory Rule Against Perpetuities § 4(5).

[224] *Restatement (Second) of Trusts* § 401 illus. 3 (1959). As to trusts for the perpetual care of graves, *see* Section 10.10.

[225] *Compare* Section 12.2 on cases holding that the invalidity of a divestiture clause makes the preceding interest indefeasibly vested.

absolute fee simple title to the property . . . devoid of all conditions or restrictions."[226]

Another possibility is to order the trustee to comply with the terms of the charitable trust. A trust "for the relief of aged needy and deserving women and couples" provided that if the funds were not used for this purpose, they should go to named individuals. When the trust ceased to operate, the gift to the individuals was held invalid, and the court appointed new trustees to carry out the testator's charitable intent.[227] Even in cases where the Rule is not involved, courts often refuse to treat language of "condition" literally, believing that the donor used it simply to compel the performance of a duty.[228]

Where compliance with the terms of a gift is impossible, *e.g.*, the land given for a park is taken by eminent domain to build a highway, the court may apply the proceeds to a related purpose under *cy pres*.[229] This traditionally required a finding that the testator had a "broader charitable intent" beyond the specified purpose.[230]

Possibility of Reverter

The invalidity of a gift to a third person sometimes causes property to revert to the donor/testator or his or her successors.[231] This does not violate the Rule because future interests reserved by the grantor or testator, as distinguished from those given to third persons, are not subject to the Rule.[232] Some modern commentators have criticized this exception, saying that interests reserved by the grantor tie up property "in precisely the manner which the Rule Against Perpetuities was designed to prevent."[233] Such interests, unlike interests in unborn children, do not suspend the power of alienation because the grantor, or the grantor's successor, can at any time join in a conveyance of the property affected, but that is also true of many executory interests that are invalid under the Rule.[234] Nevertheless the Second Restatement of Property reaffirms the exemption for reversionary interests and the Uniform Statutory Rule leaves it undisturbed.[235]

---

[226] Standard Knitting Mills, Inc. v. Allen, 424 S.W.2d 796, 800 (Tenn.1967); *Restatement (Second) of Property (Donative Transfers)* § 1.5, cmt. b (1983).

[227] Davenport v. Attorney General, 280 N.E.2d 193, 198 (Mass.1972).

[228] *See* Section 3.6.

[229] State v. Rand, 366 A.2d 183 (Me.1976).

[230] Nelson v. Kring, 592 P.2d 438, 444 (Kan.1979) (rejecting *cy pres* because no such intent). The UTC presumes that the settlor has a general charitable intention, *see* Section 10.10.

[231] *Restatement (Second) of Trusts* § 401, cmt. d (1959); Nelson v. Kring, 592 P.2d 438, 444 (Kan.1979). For 16th century statement of this idea, *see* C. St. German, *Doctor and Student* (91 Sel.Soc.) 219 (1974).

[232] Howson v. Crombie St. Congregational Church, 590 N.E.2d 687, 689 (Mass.1992); Nelson v. Kring, 592 P.2d 438, 442 (Kan.1979); Commerce Union Bank v. Warren County, 707 S.W.2d 854 (Tenn.1986); City of Klamath Falls v. Bell, 490 P.2d 515 (Or.App.1971).

[233] Morris & Leach, The Rule Against Perpetuities at 213 (1962). *See also* V. Chaffin, *The Rule Against Perpetuities as Applied to Georgia Wills*, 16 Ga.L.Rev. 235, 318 (1982); L. Simes, *Public Policy and the Dead Hand* 70 (1955); M. Fellows, *Testing Perpetuities Reforms: A Study of Perpetuities Cases 1984–89*, 25 Real Prop.Prob. & Tr. J. 597, 667 (1991).

[234] *See* Section 12.1.

[235] *Restatement (Second) of Property (Donative Transfers)* § 1.4, cmt. c (1983); Unif. Statutory Rule Against Perpetuities § 4, cmt., subsection 7.

The desire to support charity may explain this, because reversionary interests are often linked to charitable gifts. "The public benefits from our determination not to apply the rule here," because otherwise "grantors would not freely give their properties for public use."[236] Also, the Rule's period of lives in being plus 21 years is not appropriate for such interests, as distinguished from trusts for children and grandchildren or other individuals. Leach attacked the exemption of reversionary interests, but suggested that a special rule for them was a better solution than subjecting them to the common-law Rule.[237]

Reverter Statutes

An Illinois statute provides that possibilities of reverter and rights of entry for breach of a condition shall be valid only for 40 years.[238] Unlike the Rule Against Perpetuities, the statute does not invalidate an interest completely if it is too remote, but rather cuts it down to 40 years. A similar Massachusetts statute allowed 30 years for both reversionary and executory interests, thus eliminating the common law's disparate treatment of the two.[239]

The Illinois statute applies to interests previously created. Some courts have held such retroactive statutes amount to an unconstitutional taking from persons who owned the reversionary interests when the statute was enacted,[240] but the Illinois Supreme Court upheld the statute on the ground that possibilities of reverter were not property but only "an expectation."[241] If the statute were not applied retroactively, possibilities would remain as "clogs on title," making property unmarketable. This inconvenience outweighed the slight value of these interests to their owners.[242]

Some legislatures have enacted similar statutes which extend to existing interests unless the owner records a reservation of rights within a brief period after the statute is passed. Many owners, being unaware of such statutes, have failed to record their claims and thus lost them. Courts have upheld such

---

[236] Central Del. Cty. Auth. v. Greyhound Corp., 563 A.2d 139, 145 (Pa.Super.1989). (This decision was later reversed, 588 A.2d 485 (Pa.1991).) Some statutes which restrict possibilities of reverter make an exception for conveyances to charity. Fla.Stat. § 689.18(5); Mich.Comp.Laws § 554.64(c). However, at common law "the exemption from the Rule is equally applicable where the determinable fee is given to a non-charity." 6 *Amer.Law of Prop.* § 24.17, at 56.

[237] W. Leach, *Perpetuities in Perspective: Ending the Rule's Reign of Terror*, 65 Harv.L.Rev. 721, 745 (1952). *See also Restatement (Second) of Property (Donative Transfers)* § 1.4, cmt. c (1983); Unif. Statutory Rule Against Perpetuities § 4, cmt.

[238] 765 ILCS 330/4.

[239] Oak's Oil Serv. v. Massachusetts Bay Transp. Auth., 447 N.E.2d 27, 30 (Mass.App.1983). It has been held not to apply to a trust where the trustee holds title in fee simple absolute, subject to an equitable obligation to return the property to the settlors. Harrison v. Marcus, 486 N.E.2d 710 (Mass.1985).

[240] Biltmore Village v. Royal Biltmore Village, 71 So.2d 727 (Fla.1954). Followed in Board of Education v. Miles, 207 N.E.2d 181 (N.Y.1965). Florida courts, however, have applied the statute to a possibility of reverter created *after* its enactment. J.C. Vereen & Sons, Inc. v. City of Miami, 397 So.2d 979 (Fla.App.1981).

[241] *Compare* Section 3.5 on the idea that "expectancies" are not "property" and so cannot be gratuitously transferred.

[242] Trustees of Schools of Township No. 1 v. Batdorf, 130 N.E.2d 111, 114–15 (Ill.1955). *See also* Hiddleston v. Nebraska Jewish Education Soc'y., 186 N.W.2d 904 (Neb.1971). For a general discussion of retroactive legislation, *see* Section 1.3.

statutes.[243] "The requirement that a holder of a reversionary interest file a notice of intent to preserve that interest creates a minimal burden. . . . The benefit to the state is great in that marketability of title is improved."[244]

Transfers of Possibilities and Rights of Entry

The common-law distinction between executory interests (subject to the Rule) and reversionary interests (exempt from the Rule) becomes absurd when a grantor transfers a reversionary interest. A woman conveyed land to a church for use as a parsonage; if the church ceased to use the land for religious purposes, it was to "revert to me, or if I should be deceased, then to the persons who at such time would be entitled to the residue of my estate."[245] The successors to the grantor's residuary devisees recovered the land after it ceased to be used for religious purposes. Their interest did not violate the Rule because they took as devisees of the grantor's right of entry,[246] which was valid as an interest reserved by the grantor. Because the grantor was dead, her right passed under the residuary clause of her will.[247] In other words, although the Rule invalidated the executory interest in the deed, the same persons took as devisees of the grantor. Here the Rule turns on "mere words," rather than "real differences."[248]

The result hinges on the transferability of reversionary interests. In the 15th century, rights of entry could not be assigned. If the grantor attempted to do so, they were destroyed on the theory that the assignee could not enforce them (because they were non-assignable) and neither could the grantor because he had given the interest away.[249] The First Restatement of Property distinguished between rights of entry, which were not assignable, and possibilities of reverter which were.[250] This distinction raises difficult questions of classification because many deeds use language that does not neatly fit into either category.[251]

---

[243] Brookline v. Carey, 245 N.E.2d 446 (Mass.1969); Presbytery of Southeast Iowa v. Harris, 226 N.W.2d 232 (Iowa 1975); Kilpatrick v. Snow Mountain Pine Co., 805 P.2d 137 (Or.App.1991).

[244] Walton v. City of Red Bluff, 3 Cal.Rptr.2d 275, 285 (App.1991). However, the court in this case did not actually apply the statute because it had not been properly pleaded.

[245] Howson v. Crombie St. Congregational Church, 590 N.E.2d 687, 688 (Mass.1992).

[246] *Id.* at 689 n. A statute limiting reverters was inapplicable because the deed preceded the statute and the grantor had protected her interest by recording.

[247] *See also* Nelson v. Kring, 592 P.2d 438, 444 (Kan.1979); *Restatement of Property* § 403, illus. 2 (1944). *But cf.* J. Dukeminier, *Cleansing the Stables of Property,* 65 Iowa L.Rev. 151, 174 (1979) (testator should not be allowed "by one clause [to] retain a possibility of reverter and subsequently transfer it by another clause").

[248] The result to which Chancellor Nottingham sought to avoid in the Duke of Norfolk's Case. *See* Section 12.1.

[249] T. Littleton, *Tenures* § 347.

[250] *Restatement of Property* §§ 159–60 (1936). The rule that a purported assignment destroyed a right of entry appeared originally in Section 160, cmt. c, but this was changed in 1947. *See* 1 *Amer.Law of Prop.* § 4.69. The idea reappears as an alternative holding in Kilpatrick v. Snow Mountain Pine Co., 805 P.2d 137, 139 (Or.App.1991).

[251] Fennell v. Foskey, 225 S.E.2d 231, 233 (Ga.1976) (deed interpreted to create an alienable possibility of reverter rather than an inalienable right of entry).

Many modern statutes make rights of entry alienable in keeping with the trend to allow transfer of all interests,[252] but an Illinois statute makes *both* possibilities of reverter and rights of entry inalienable.[253] This statute has been said to reduce the "nuisance value" of such interests,[254] but why making them inalienable accomplishes this is unclear, unless an attempt to alienate destroys the interest.

§ 12.7 Commercial Transactions

The Rule Against Perpetuities was not applied to commercial transactions until late in its history. In more recent years, however, the reported cases involving the Rule in commercial transactions has outnumbered those in donative transfers,[255] perhaps because the lawyers who handle commercial transactions are less familiar with the Rule and the ways to avoid it.

Options

The Rule applies only to property, not to contracts to pay money. Thus a provision in a land sale requiring the buyer to pay the seller 10% of the gross sale price if he ever resold the land did not infringe the Rule, which

> does not affect the making of contracts which do not create rights of property. Thus a promise to A to pay him or his executors or administrators a sum of money on a future event is good, although such event may not happen within twenty-one years after lives in being.[256]

Options to buy land or unique goods, on the other hand, because they give the optionee a right to specific performance even against third persons, are deemed to create property interests and are subject to the Rule. An option is invalid if it might have been exercised beyond the period of the Rule.[257] This includes options to repurchase given to a seller, despite the general exemption from the Rule for interests reserved by a grantor.[258]

Options are frequently denied enforcement even though the optionee seeks to exercise the option only a few years after the option was created. Some courts have applied "wait and see" to make the option enforceable,[259] but others

---

[252] *Restatement of Property* § 160, cmt. d (1936); 1 *Amer.Law of Prop.* § 4.68; Cal.Civ.Code § 1046; Oak's Oil Serv., Inc. v. Massachusetts Bay Transp. Auth., 447 N.E.2d 27 (Mass.App.1983).

[253] 765 ILCS 330/1. *See also* Neb.Rev.Stat. § 76–299.

[254] 1 *Amer.Law of Prop.* § 4.68. *See also Restatement of Property* § 160, cmt. a (1936).

[255] I. Bloom, *Perpetuities Refinement: There Is an Alternative*, 62 Wash.L.Rev. 23, 76 (1987).

[256] Kerley v. Nu-West, Inc., 762 P.2d 631, 637 (Ariz.App.1988).

[257] Stuart Kingston, Inc. v. Robinson, 596 A.2d 1378 (Del.1991); Symphony Space v. Pergola Properties, 669 N.E.2d 799 (N.Y.1996); Low v. Spellman, 629 A.2d 57 (Me.1993) (right of repurchase); Mizell v. Greensboro Jaycees, 412 S.E.2d 904 (N.C.App.1992) (25 year right of first refusal).

[258] First Huntington National Bank v. Gideon-Broh Realty Co. 79 S.E.2d 675, 684 (W.Va. 1953). All the cases in the previous note involved rights reserved by a seller. *Cf.* J. Dukeminier, *A Modern Guide to Perpetuities*, 74 Cal.L.Rev. 1867, 1909 (1986) ("not easy to explain" why a grantor who must pay to reenter is subject to the Rule). As to the exemption of reserved interests, *see* Section 12.6, note 231 et seq.

[259] Colby v. Colby, 596 A.2d 901 (Vt.1990); Gartley v. Ricketts, 760 P.2d 143 (N.M.1988). As to "wait and see," *see* Section 12.4.

have refused to do so.[260] Other theories have been used to validate options. One is to imply a time limit for exercise of the option.

> Where the parties have explicitly fixed a period of time [for exercise] longer than that permitted by the rule, a reasonable time cannot be implied. . . . Use of a general term, however, such as "any time," does not necessarily preclude the implication of a reasonable time. . . . A contrary interpretation is disfavored because it would create a perpetuities problem unnecessarily, . . . enabling the [promissors] to escape the enforcement of a contract they entered into freely.[261]

This construction is particularly appealing if the jurisdiction permits courts to construe or reform instruments so as to avoid violations of the Rule.[262] However, some courts have refused to imply a reasonable time limit on the ground that if the parties had intended this they would have said so in the contract.[263]

Some options are so expressed that a court can separate valid from invalid parts. When a lease gave the lessee the right to demand additional space "after the fifth, tenth, fifteenth, twentieth or twenty-fifth anniversary of the commencement of the term of this lease," the court treated this as five options of which the first four were valid.[264] However, a single option will not be divided into annual components so as to make it valid for 21 years.[265]

Options are often saved by finding that they were "personal" to the optionor or optionee, so they will expire within a life in being.

> The fact that the agreement is made binding on the heirs and assigns of [the optionor] but not on the heirs and assigns of [the optionee] supports the conclusion that the parties . . . intended [it] . . . to expire on [the optionee's] death.[266]

But this construction was rejected as to an option which by its terms extended to the heirs and assigns of both parties.[267]

---

[260] Symphony Space v. Pergola Properties, 669 N.E.2d 799, 808 (N.Y.1996) (no wait and see statute); Low v. Spellman, 629 A.2d 57 (Me.1993) (conveyance was prior to wait and see statute); Buck v. Banks, 668 N.E.2d 1259, 1261 (Ind.App.1996).

[261] Peterson v. Tremain, 621 N.E.2d 385, 387 (Mass.App.1993). *See also* Byke Const. Co., Inc. v. Miller, 680 P.2d 193 (Ariz.App.1984); Ryland Group, Inc. v. Wills, 331 S.E.2d 399 (Va.1985). This argument can backfire; if the optionee has waited more than a reasonable time to enforce it, enforcement will be denied for that reason. Lawson v. Redmoor Corp., 679 P.2d 972 (Wash.App.1984).

[262] Matter of Estate of Crowl, 737 P.2d 911, 914 (Okl.1987). As to construing or reforming instruments so as to avoid perpetuities violations, *see* Section 12.4.

[263] Shaffer v. Reed, 437 So.2d 98 (Ala.1983); Buffalo Seminary v. McCarthy, 451 N.Y.S.2d 457 (App.Div.1982).

[264] Crossroads Shopping Center v. Montgomery Ward & Co., Inc., 646 P.2d 330 (Colo.1981).

[265] Certified Corp. v. GTE Products Corp., 467 N.E.2d 1336 (Mass.1984).

[266] Stratman v. Sheetz, 573 N.E.2d 776, 779 (Ohio App.1989). *See also* Gore v. Beren, 867 P.2d 330 (Kan.1994); Morrison v. Piper, 566 N.E.2d 643 (N.Y.1990); Marcy v. Markiewicz, 599 N.E.2d 1051, 1058 (Ill.App.1992).

[267] Buck v. Banks, 668 N.E.2d 1259 (Ind.App.1996); Shaffer v. Reed, 437 So.2d 98 (Ala.1983).

Rights of First Refusal

Under a right of first refusal, the seller may sell property to whomever the seller wishes but must first offer the property on the same terms to the holder of the refusal right. The Rule arguably applies to such rights. The right is contingent upon the seller deciding to sell, and unless the refusal right is limited to a period measurable by specified lives, might be exercised beyond the period of the Rule. Some courts have applied the Rule to rights of first refusal.[268] But the decided trend in the case law, and the position taken by the Third Restatement of Property is that rights of refusal do not violate the Rule because they are "compatible with the policies of commerce and utilization of land."[269]

Leases and Covenants

Long-term leases that give the lessee an option to purchase have been held not to infringe the Rule. Whereas options unconnected with a lease deter "the free marketability of the real estate and the possibility of its development," an option in a lease gives the lessee an incentive to develop the property fully. To hold it invalid under the Rule "could very well have a reverse effect."[270] By similar reasoning, perpetual options to renew a lease do not violate the Rule,[271] but an option to buy additional land *is* subject to the Rule.[272]

Restrictive covenants limiting the use of land are also exempt from the Rule.[273] The policy against dead-hand control is effectuated here by refusing to enforce covenants that have become out of date.[274] Indeed, many courts hold that covenants running with the land do not violate the Rule because they vest immediately in those against whom the covenants run.[275]

Policy Analysis—USRAP

Some have questioned whether the Rule is appropriate in commercial cases. It is troubling to let a party get out of a bargain for which he received

---

[268] *See*, e.g., Stuart Kingston, Inc. v. Robinson, 596 A.2d 1378, 1384–85 (Del. 1991).

[269] CS-Lakeview at Gwinnett, Inc. v. Simon Property Group, Inc., 642 S.E.2d 393, 397 (Ga. App. 2007). See also Bortolotti v. Hayden, 866 N.E.2d 882, 889 (Mass. 2007); Randolph v. Reisig, 727 N.W.2d 388 (Mich. App. 2006); *Restatement (Third) of Property (Servitudes)* § 3.3, cmt. a (2000).

[270] St. Regis Paper Co. v. Brown, 276 S.E.2d 24, 25 (Ga.1981). *See also* Coomler v. Shell Oil Co., 814 P.2d 184 (Or.App.1991); Stenke v. Masland Development Co., Inc., 394 N.W.2d 418 (Mich.App.1986); W. Leach, *Perpetuities in Perspective*, 65 Harv.L.Rev. 721, 738 (1952).

[271] Camerlo v. Howard Johnson Co., 710 F.2d 987 (3d Cir.1983); Dixon v. Rivers, 245 S.E.2d 572 (N.C.App.1978); *Restatement of Property* § 395 (1944).

[272] Crossroads Shopping Center v. Montgomery Ward & Co., Inc., 646 P.2d 330 (Colo.1981).

[273] State v. Reece, 374 S.W.2d 686 (Tex.Civ.App.1964); Lowry v. Norris Lake Shores Development Corp., 203 S.E.2d 171 (Ga.1974); *Restatement of Property* § 399 (1944).

[274] *Id.*, cmt. d; Nutis v. Schottenstein Trustees, 534 N.E.2d 380, 385 (Ohio App.1987) (residence restriction no longer enforceable because of change in character of neighborhood); Lacer v. Navajo County, 687 P.2d 404, 411 (Ariz.App.1983).

[275] Malone v. Guynes, 250 S.W.3d 260 (Ark. App. 2007); AAM/US Bank LLC v. Lake Carroll Ass'n, 869 N.E.2d 1065, 1083–88 (Ill. Ct. App. 2007); Schafer v. Deszcz, 698 N.E.2d 60, 62 (Ohio Ct. App. 1997).

valuable consideration because of the Rule.[276] One seller who had sold property below its market value in return for an option to repurchase attempted to rescind the whole transaction when the option was held invalid. Rescission was denied on the ground that "it would lead to the same result as enforcing the option"[277] and so the buyer got a windfall. Perhaps if the consideration paid for an option was clearly identifiable, it could be recovered to avoid unjust enrichment, but it is usually an inseparable part of a larger transaction.

The Rule may be necessary to limit foolish dispositions by a capricious testator, but when two parties with conflicting interests make a contract, their self-interest should protect against unreasonable restrictions.[278] The Uniform Statutory Rule Against Perpetuities exempts interests "arising out of a nondonative transfer" from the Rule on the ground that the period of the Rule is "not suitable" for them. The drafters acknowledged that options may restrain alienability or "provide a disincentive to improve the property," but suggested that their duration could be controlled by a special statute like the Illinois 40-year limit on options.[279]

One court invoked the USRAP in upholding a contract provision challenged under the Rule, finding that "neither the Legislature nor this court can perceive any danger . . . requiring continued application of the rule to nondonative commercial transactions."[280] On the other hand, another court struck down an option on the theory that the USRAP exemption left the transaction subject to the common-law Rule.[281]

§ 12.8 Restraints on Alienation

History and Rationale

Closely related to the Rule Against Perpetuities is a much older rule against restraints on alienation which appeared in the 15th century, about two hundred years before the Duke of Norfolk's Case.[282]

> If a feoffment is made on condition that the feoffee not alienate the property to anyone, the condition is void, for when a man is enfeoffed of lands or tenements, he has power to alienate them to anyone by law [so] if this condition were good, the condition would take away the power which the law gives him, which would be against reason.[283]

The rule is often stated in the same conclusory terms today: "the power of alienation is necessarily incident to every estate in fee, and a condition in a devise of lands in fee simple altogether preventing alienation, is repugnant to

[276] J. Morris & W. Leach, *The Rule Against Perpetuities* 224 (2d ed. 1962); M. Fellows, *Testing Perpetuities Reforms: A Study of Perpetuities Cases 1984–89*, 25 Real Prop.Prob. and T.J. 597, 665 (1991); *cf.* Martin v. Prairie Rod and Gun Club, 348 N.E.2d 306, 310 (Ill.App.1976).

[277] Symphony Space v. Pergola Properties, 669 N.E.2d 799, 809 (N.Y.1996).

[278] Morris & Leach, *supra* note 276, at 224; 6 *Amer. Law of Prop.* § 24.56, at 144.

[279] Unif. Statutory Rule Against Perpetuities § 4(1), cmt.; *see also* Section 12.6.

[280] Juliano & Sons v. Chevron, U.S.A., 593 A.2d 814, 819 (N.J.Super.App.Div.1991).

[281] Buck v. Banks, 668 N.E.2d 1259 (Ind.App.1996).

[282] *See* Section 12.1.

[283] T. Littleton, *Tenures* § 360.

the estate and void."[284] This "rationale" for the rule begs the question why the power of alienation is "necessarily incident to" a fee simple. The rationale can be turned on its head. When a provision in a deed giving the seller the right to repurchase property if the buyer ever offered it for sale was claimed to be "repugnant" to the buyer's fee, the court disagreed, saying that the buyer's estate was not "a fee simple absolute" but only a "a fee simple defeasible."[285]

Reconciling the cases requires an understanding of the policy behind this rule against restraints on alienation. It is commonly said that the rule is designed to keep property alienable in order to allow "the utilization of land in the most effective manner."[286] Because this policy also underlies the Rule Against Perpetuities,[287] courts sometimes examine a provision under both rules,[288] but the conclusion is not always the same. A provision in a deed requiring the grantor's consent to sell the land was held not to violate the Rule Against Perpetuities under a "wait and see" statute, but the provision was nevertheless invalid as an unreasonable restraint on alienation.[289] Conversely, a provision may violate the Rule Against Perpetuities but not constitute an invalid restraint.

Reasonableness

Although courts sometimes say that even "reasonable" restraints on alienation are invalid,[290] many decisions upholding restraints rest, expressly or implicitly, on the idea of reasonableness. The Second Restatement of Property says that in general a restraint is valid if "under all the circumstances of the case, [it] is found to be reasonable."[291] Two factors determine whether a restraint is reasonable. First, does it serve a purpose which the court finds worthy? One court found a restraint invalid because it served "no worthwhile purpose . . . other than to allow [the grantor] to 'keep property in the family,' "[292] while another court upheld a provision which was "reasonably designed to attain or encourage accepted social or economic ends."[293] A second factor is how substantial a bar to alienability the restraint presents. Courts balance these factors. "The greater the quantum of restraint that results from enforcement of a given clause, the greater must be the justification for that enforcement."[294]

---

[284] Hankins v. Mathews, 425 S.W.2d 608, 610 (Tenn.1968). *See also* Kenney v. Morgan, 325 A.2d 419, 422 (Md.App.1974); Cast v. National Bank, 183 N.W.2d 485, 489 (Neb.1971); Cal.Civ.Code § 711 (conditions restraining alienation are void "when repugnant to the interest created").

[285] Floyd v. Hoover, 234 S.E.2d 89 (Ga.App.1977).

[286] 6 *Amer. Law of Prop.* § 26.3.

[287] *See* Section 12.1.

[288] Colby v. Colby, 596 A.2d 901 (Vt.1990) (repurchase option valid under both analyses); Low v. Spellman, 629 A.2d 57 (Me.1993) (repurchase option invalid under both analyses).

[289] Gartley v. Ricketts, 760 P.2d 143 (N.M.1988).

[290] White v. White, 251 A.2d 470, 473 (N.J.Super.Ch.Div.1969); Andrews v. Hall, 58 N.W.2d 201, 203 (Neb.1953); *Restatement of Property* § 406, cmt. p (1944).

[291] *Restatement (Second) of Property (Donative Transfers)* § 4.2(3) (1983).

[292] Gartley v. Ricketts, 760 P.2d 143, 146 (N.M.1988).

[293] Kerley v. Nu-West, Inc., 762 P.2d 631, 635 (Ariz.App.1988).

[294] Carma Developers (California), Inc. v. Marathon Development California, Inc., 826 P.2d 710, 716 (Cal.1992).

1. *Partial Restraints.* A restraint which simply forbids alienation to one person, or a small group, is valid.[295] But a restraint is not valid simply because it allows the land to be transferred to a small group, such as the testator's descendants.[296] The size of the group is not necessarily determinative. If the prohibited group contains the probable purchasers of the land, even though a small number, the restraint is invalid, and the converse is also true.[297] At one time restraints on alienation based on race were held to be reasonable, but in 1948 the Supreme Court invalidated them under the 14th Amendment.[298]

2. *Restraints on Use.* Courts distinguish between restraints on alienation and restrictions on use.[299] When the deed of land stipulated that if the grantee failed to use the land or sold it, the land should revert to the grantor, the court held that the restraint on sale was invalid, but the condition on use was not.[300] Restraints on use are exempt because they cease to be enforceable when they become obsolete. Some restrictions on use are held invalid, however, because their practical effect is to restrain alienation. Provisions that require a devisee to occupy property as his residence have been held invalid on this reasoning.[301]

3. *Life Estates.* A restraint is not valid just because it is limited in time,[302] but restraints on alienation of a *limited interest* such as a life estate are permitted. A devise to the testator's children, with the proviso that none could convey his or her interest "during the lifetime of any of my children . . . and after the death of the last of my children, the said property shall be owned by my grandchildren," was upheld as a restraint on a life estate; although the will did not expressly devise a life estate to the children, that was its effect.[303] Life estates differ from a fee simple because they are hard to sell anyway—few purchasers want to buy an interest which will end when the life tenant dies.[304]

The Second Restatement distinguishes between forfeiture and disabling restraints in this connection. A provision that simply says "the grantee shall not alienate the land" is a disabling restraint; a forfeiture restraint is one which says the grantee shall lose the land if he tries to alienate it. As to a fee simple, both types of restraint are invalid. As to life estates, forfeiture

---

[295] T. Littleton, *Tenures* § 361; Pritchett v. Turner, 437 So.2d 104 (Ala.1983) (forfeiture if devisees convey land to testator's ex-wife); *Restatement (Second) of Property (Donative Transfers)* § 4.2 illus. 3 (1983).

[296] Wise v. Poston, 316 S.E.2d 412, 415 (S.C.App.1984); Williams v. Williams, 73 S.W.3d 376 (Tex.App.2002). *Cf.* Section 8.10 on restraints on marriage.

[297] *Restatement (Second) of Property (Donative Transfers)* § 4.2, cmt. r (1983).

[298] Shelley v. Kraemer, 334 U.S. 1 (1948); *see also* Niemann v. Vaughn Community Church, 77 P.3d 1208 (Wash.App.2003) (statute bars restraint on alienation to persons of a particular creed).

[299] *Restatement (Second) of Property (Donative Transfers)* § 3.4 (1983).

[300] Mountain Brow Lodge No. 82 v. Toscano, 64 Cal.Rptr. 816 (App.1967).

[301] Cast v. National Bank of Commerce, 183 N.W.2d 485 (Neb.1971); *Restatement (Second) of Property (Donative Transfers)* § 3.4 illus. 4 (1983).

[302] Beauchamp v. Beauchamp, 574 So.2d 18 (Miss.1990) (restraint on sale for lives plus 30 years invalid); *Restatement (Second) of Property (Donative Transfers)* § 4.1, illus. 3, § 4.2, illus. 14 (1983); Williams v. Williams, 73 S.W.3d 376 (Tex.App.2002) (restraint for lifetimes of testator's children); Imerys Marble Co. v. J.M. Huber Corp., 577 S.E.2d 555 (Ga.2003) (same).

[303] Wise v. Poston, 316 S.E.2d 412 (S.C.App.1984).

[304] *Restatement (Second) of Property (Donative Transfers)* § 4.2, cmt. c (1983).

restraints are permitted, but disabling restraints are not,[305] "because if effective they enable the person restrained to deny the validity of such person's own transfer."[306] Some courts, however, allow even disabling restraints on a life estate.[307] Some courts obliterate the distinction by *implying* a forfeiture provision whenever a will restrains alienation by a life tenant.[308] Spendthrift trusts are disabling restraints on equitable interests and are permitted in all states.[309]

4. *Future Interests.* Restraints on the alienation of future interests are often upheld[310] because "a future interest from its very nature is not as marketable as a present interest."[311] Also, the restraint serves a useful purpose, namely protecting against improvident dispositions, because future interests are often sold at a large discount.[312]

5. *Contract for Deed; Lease.* Contracts to sell land that allow the buyer to take possession and pay the price in installments usually prohibit the buyer from transferring his interest without the seller's consent. These provisions are upheld because of the seller's legitimate concern with possible waste committed by an unreliable assignee while the price remains unpaid.[313] The law allows restraints on assignment by a lessee for years for similar reasons. However, many courts hold that a lessor may not "unreasonably" withhold consent to an attempted assignment.[314] Others disagree.[315]

6. *Transfer with Consent.* According to the First Restatement of Property, a restraint is objectionable even if it allows transfer with another's consent; otherwise, all forfeiture restraints would be valid because the person to whom property would pass upon forfeiture can always consent to forego his claim.[316] The Second Restatement, however, allows restraints which permit

---

[305] *Id.*, § 4.1 (disabling restraints), § 4.2 (forfeiture restraint); Carma Developers v. Marathon Dev., 826 P.2d 710, 718 (Cal.1992) (forfeiture restraints are viewed more favorably than comparable disabling restraints).

[306] *Restatement (Second) of Property (Donative Transfers)* § 4.1, cmt. a (1983).

[307] Estate of Kelly, 193 So.2d 575, 578 (Miss.1967).

[308] Atkinson v. Kish, 420 S.W.2d 104, 109 (Ky.1967); *cf. Restatement of Property* § 419 (1944) (ambiguous restraint construed not to be disabling).

[309] *See* Section 10.8. "Protective trusts" operate as forfeiture restraints and are allowed even where spendthrift provisions are not. *Id.*

[310] E.g., Lowrance v. Whitfield, 752 S.W.2d 129 (Tex.App.1988).

[311] *Restatement (Second) of Property (Donative Transfers)* § 4.2, cmt. u (1983).

[312] 6 *Amer. Law of Prop.* § 26.54.

[313] Carey v. Lincoln Loan Co., 998 P.2d 724, 732 (Or.App.2000).

[314] *Restatement (Second) of Property (Landlord and Tenant)* § 15.2(2) (1977); Bert Bidwell Inv. v. LaSalle and Schiffer, 797 P.2d 811 (Colo.App.1990); *cf.* Cheney v. Jemmett, 693 P.2d 1031 (Idaho 1984) (seller under land sale contract cannot unreasonably withhold consent to assignment); Carey v. Lincoln Loan Co., 998 P.2d 724, 732 (Or.App.2000) (seller's right to refuse to consent to assignment is "tempered by the duty of good faith").

[315] First Federal Sav. Bank v. Key Markets, 559 N.E.2d 600 (Ind.1990); 21 Merchants Row Corp. v. Merchants Row, 587 N.E.2d 788 (Mass.1992). In Carma Developers (California), Inc. v. Marathon Development California, Inc., 826 P.2d 710 (Cal.1992) the court held it was not unreasonable for a lessor to invoke such a clause "in order to appropriate to itself the increased rental value of the property."

[316] *Restatement of Property* § 406 illus. 1 (1944). *See also* Gartley v. Ricketts, 760 P.2d 143 (N.M.1988) (clause requiring grantor's consent to transfer invalid); Williams v. Williams, 73 S.W.3d 376 (Tex.App.2002) (restraint which allows sale with consent of testator's children is invalid).

alienation with another's consent if they are reasonable. If a father gives property to his son and requires consent by a family friend to any transfer until the son reaches 40, this restraint is considered to serve a reasonable purpose and is allowed.[317]

7. *Preemptive Rights.* Options are sometimes held invalid as unreasonable restraints on alienation,[318] but preemptive provisions giving "a right of first refusal" if property is offered for sale are not regarded as restraints if their terms are reasonable as to price and other conditions.[319] When a deed provided that, if the grantee wished to sell the land, the grantor could repurchase it for the price the grantee had paid, this was held an invalid restraint. Although "a repurchase option at market or appraised value" is permissible, a "fixed price" option is not because it "discourages any improvements of the land by the existing property owner."[320] However, some courts have upheld even fixed-price options,[321] while others have invalidated preemptive rights which were based on current value.[322]

8. *Trusts.* Reasonable restraints against the alienation of trust property by the trustee are valid,[323] but they may be overridden if, owing to a change of circumstances, the purpose of the trust would be defeated or substantially impaired unless the property is sold.[324]

Courts do not as a general rule cut down unreasonable restraints to make them reasonable. However, when a will devised land to a daughter for life, remainder to her children provided that the land was not to be sold until the children reached age 45, the court, by analogy to *cy pres* in perpetuities cases,[325] held that the restriction was invalid only to the extent that it continued beyond the daughter's lifetime.[326]

---

[317] *Restatement (Second) of Property (Donative Transfers)* § 4.1 illus. 11 (1983). *See also id.* at § 4.2, cmt. p.

[318] Low v. Spellman, 629 A.2d 57 (Me.1993) (option to repurchase); Urquhart v. Teller, 958 P.2d 714 (Mont.1998). They may also be held to violate the Rule Against Perpetuities. *See* Section 12.7.

[319] *Restatement (Second) of Property (Donative Transfers)* § 4.4 (1981). *See also* Wildenstein & Co., Inc. v. Wallis, 595 N.E.2d 828 (N.Y.1992); Lorentzen v. Smith, 5 P.3d 1082, 1086 (N.M.App.2000).

[320] Iglehart v. Phillips, 383 So.2d 610, 615 (Fla.1980). *See also Restatement (Second) of Property (Donative Transfers)* § 4.4 illus. 4 (1983).

[321] McDonald v. Moore, 790 P.2d 213 (Wash.App.1990); Colby v. Colby, 596 A.2d 901 (Vt.1990).

[322] Holien v. Trydahl, 134 N.W.2d 851 (N.D.1965); Atchison v. City of Englewood, 463 P.2d 297 (Colo.1969).

[323] Ohio Society for Crippled Children & Adults, Inc. v. McElroy, 191 N.E.2d 543 (Ohio 1963).

[324] *See Restatement (Third) of Trusts* § 66 (2003), § 86, cmt. c (2007). *See also* Section 10.9.

[325] *See* Section 12.4.

[326] In re Kelly's Estate, 193 So.2d 575 (Miss.1967). But see Beauchamp v. Beauchamp, 574 So.2d 18 (Miss.1990) (applying Wisconsin law making restraint totally void).

Planning

Some cases suggest that for commercial transactions the rule against restraints should completely replace the Rule Against Perpetuities.[327] Insofar as restraints on alienation are upheld where "reasonable," mechanical applications of the rule which undercut its policy are infrequent. Perhaps for this reason, the trend to soften the Rule Against Perpetuities has not gone nearly so far with regard to restraints on alienation. Nevertheless, the rule against restraints on alienation may nevertheless frustrate a reasonable plan if the drafter is not sophisticated. When a restraint on alienation is held invalid, often the objective could have been accomplished by use of a trust, as to which the limits are more generous. For example, a will provision that land should not be "sold, given away or in any way disposed of" for 20 years was held to be an invalid restraint. The court acknowledged that spendthrift trusts are valid, but said that this rule did not apply when the will "fails to create a 'trust' in unmistakable terms."[328]

§ 12.9 Accumulations

Common Law

Thellusson v. Woodford,[329] the leading case on the legality of accumulations of income, involved a trust which directed that the income be accumulated for nine lives. The House of Lords saw no policy objection to this and upheld the trust. "The rents and profits are not to be locked up, and made no use of. . . . The effect is only to invest them from time to time in land: so that the fund is not only in a constant course of accumulation, but also in a constant course of circulation."[330] Some have objected that, because of limitations of trust investments, "there is not the same freedom of the use of such income in the economy in the hands of the trustee as there would be in the hands of the trust beneficiary."[331] Also, accumulations of income in a trust may allow huge fortunes to be amassed contrary to the law's policy against extreme inequality of wealth.[332] However, as with the Rule Against Perpetuities itself, this problem can be dealt with by tax law.[333] Present law, for example, discourages accumulating income in a trust by taxing it at higher rates than those imposed on income distributed to beneficiaries.[334]

---

[327] Metropolitan Transp. Auth. v. Bruken Realty Corp., 492 N.E.2d 379, 384 (N.Y.1986); Hartnett v. Jones, 629 P.2d 1357, 1363 (Wyo.1981). *See also* Unif. Statutory Rule Against Perpetuities § 4, cmt.

[328] Baskin v. Commerce Union Bank, 715 S.W.2d 350, 352 (Tenn.App.1986).

[329] 32 Eng.Rep. 1030 (1805).

[330] *Id.* at 1044. *See also* J. Macey, *Private Trusts for the Provision of Private Goods*, 37 Emory L.J. 295, 311 (1988).

[331] *Restatement (Second) of Property (Donative Transfers)* § 2.2, cmt. e (1983).

[332] *Restatement (Second) of Property (Donative Transfers)* § 2.2, cmt. e (1983). In fact, Thelluson's trust grew far less than had been predicted, partly because of the costs of litigation. "The legal profession, mindful as always of the public weal, did its best to ensure that the accumulation did not exceed reasonable limits." J. Morris & W. Leach, *The Rule Against Perpetuities* 267 (2d ed. 1962).

[333] *See* Section 12.1.

[334] *See* Section 15.6.

Even before the House of Lords rendered its decision upholding the Thelluson trust, Parliament passed a statute which prospectively imposed stringent time limits on accumulations.[335] Some American states followed suit,[336] but nearly all these American statutes have since been repealed. Commentators have generally condemned them. The Thelluson Act "has proved to be one of the most difficult Acts on the Statute Book to apply. It has produced a vast mass of intricate case law" and "frustrates the quite reasonable dispositive schemes of settlors."[337] In criticizing a former New York statute, Professor Powell noted that "directions for the accumulation of income often serve desired and justifiable purposes . . . It is often most unsuitable to have income of a trust fund accumulated until a child becomes twenty one,[338] and then to have the funds so accumulated dumped into the inexperienced hands of this child on his twenty-first birthday."[339]

Today virtually all states allow trusts to accumulate income for the period of the Rule Against Perpetuities but no longer.[340] An accumulation "is valid until the period of the rule . . . expires;" "any accumulation thereafter is invalid." Any income released by the invalidity of the direction to accumulate is to be applied to effectuate the settlor's intent to the extent possible.[341] But a recent case, relying on a 19th century precedent, held that the direction to accumulate was void ab initio, and the income should pass intestate.[342]

Trusts that call for excessive accumulations usually also create contingent interests that violate the Rule Against Perpetuities. For example, a trust gave 70% of the income to the settlor's daughter and 30% was to be accumulated; when the daughter died, or when her youngest child reached 23, whichever occurred last, the trust assets were to be distributed to the daughter's then living descendants. Because of the possibility that the daughter might have an afterborn child, the trust violated the Rule, but by modifying the trust so it would terminate when the daughter died, both the accumulation provision and the remainder were saved.[343] Probably no such modification of the trust would have been necessary under wait and see,[344] but a court recently refused to apply a "wait and see" statute to save a provision for accumulation in a trust.[345]

Presumption Against Accumulation

Hostility to accumulation of income may affect construction of a trust. A court construed an ambiguous trust as authorizing the trustee to distribute income rather than accumulating it because of "the general policy against

---

[335] 39 & 40 Geo. 3, c. 98 (1800).

[336] 6 *Amer. Law of Prop.* § 25.100; *Powell on Real Property* ¶ 834.

[337] Morris & Leach, *supra* note 31, at 304. *See also* L. Simes, *Public Policy and the Dead Hand* 100 (1955).

[338] Even under the restrictive statutes, accumulation of income for a minor was permitted.

[339] Quoted in Will of Cheney, 379 N.Y.S.2d 346, 348–349 (Surr.1976).

[340] *Restatement (Second) of Property (Donative Transfers)* § 2.2(1) (1983). *See also* Estate of Freeman, 404 P.2d 222 (Kan.1965); 6 *Amer. Law of Prop.* § 24.65.

[341] *Restatement (Second) of Property (Donative Transfers)* § 2.2(3) (1983).

[342] White v. Fleet Bank of Maine, 739 A.2d 373 (Me.1999).

[343] Estate of Foster, 376 P.2d 784 (Kan.1962).

[344] *Restatement (Second) of Property (Donative Transfers)* § 2.2(1) (1983).

[345] White v. Fleet Bank of Maine, 739 A.2d 373, 380 (Me.1999).

accumulations."[346] Nevertheless, courts often find an implied direction to accumulate trust income. A direction to pay the testator's grandchildren as much income as was needed for their support was held to imply that income in excess of their needs should be accumulated.[347]

Charitable Trusts

An accumulation in a charitable trust can continue beyond the period of the Rule Against Perpetuities.[348] This is justified by the social utility of charities and the thought that gifts to charity will be encouraged if prospective givers can determine the details of the gift.[349] Also, the common-law Rule based on measuring lives makes little sense in a charitable trust.[350]

Even in charitable trusts, courts will not allow "unreasonable" accumulations. A settlor who believed that endowments for government could replace taxation created a trust to accumulate income for 500 years; in the year 2444 the principal and accumulated income was to go to the state of Pennsylvania. This was held to be "unreasonable, contrary to public policy, and void."[351] Other courts have simply whittled down directions for excessive accumulation. A trust to accumulate income until the funds were large enough to build a 40-bed rest home was modified by reducing the size of the rest home so as to allow earlier distribution.[352]

It is not easy to predict when courts will find a provision for accumulation to be "unreasonable." One court upheld a trust which required 25% of the income to be accumulated *forever*.[353] A reasonable purpose for an accumulation, such as a desire to have funds adequate for a project, is relevant.[354] Views of what is reasonable may alter as conditions change. When "continued accumulation no longer furthers the purpose of the trust" courts may order it to cease.[355]

§§ 12.10–13.0 are reserved for supplemental material.

---

[346] In re Trust Estate of Daoang, 953 P.2d 959, 968 (Haw.App.1998). *See also* Rogerson v. Wheeling Dollar Sav. & Trust Co., 222 S.E.2d 816 (W.Va.1976); In re Estate of Krebs, 483 A.2d 919 (Pa.Super.1984).

[347] Will of Cheney, 379 N.Y.S.2d 346, 348 (Surr.1976). *See also* Godfrey v. Chandley, 811 P.2d 1248 (Kan.1991); Jones v. Heritage Pullman Bank & Trust Co., 518 N.E.2d 178 (Ill.App.1987) (income in excess of annuity).

[348] *Restatement (Second) of Property (Donative Transfers)* § 2.2(2) (1983); Estate of Puckett, 168 Cal.Rptr. 311, 315 (App.1980); Matter of Booker, 682 P.2d 320, 324 (Wash.App.1984).

[349] *Restatement of Property* § 442, cmt. a (1944).

[350] *Compare* Sections 12.6 and 12.7 regarding the argument for exempting possibilities of reverter and commercial transactions from the Rule.

[351] Trusts of Holdeen, 403 A.2d 978, 980 (Pa.1979). *See also Restatement (Second) of Property (Donative Transfers)* § 2.2(2) (1983).

[352] In re Booker, 682 P.2d 320 (Wash.App.1984).

[353] Mercantile Trust Co. Nat. Ass'n v. Shriners' Hosp., 551 S.W.2d 864 (Mo.App.1977).

[354] In re Estes Estate, 523 N.W.2d 863, 869 (Mich.App.1994) (upholding indefinite accumulation to build a new church); Estate of James, 199 A.2d 275, 279 (Pa.1964).

[355] Mercantile Trust Co. Nat. Ass'n v. Shriners' Hosp., 551 S.W.2d 864, 868 (Mo.App.1977). *See also Restatement of Property* § 442, cmt. a (1944).

Chapter 13

PROBATE ISSUES

Analysis

Sec.

13.1 Probate Process.
13.2 Necessity for Administration.
13.3 Will Contests.
13.4 Ancillary Administration.
13.5 Claims Against Estate.
13.6 Claims Against Nonprobate Assets.

§ 13.1 Probate Process

This chapter focuses on issues relating only to decedent's estates. Administrative issues relevant to both estates and trusts are discussed in Chapter 14—Fiduciary Duties and Administration.

Necessity for Probate

When an individual dies, most nonprobate assets can be transferred relatively easily. To collect on life insurance and retirement benefits, ordinarily all that is required is the furnishing of a death certificate and the filing of a claim form with the insurance company or retirement plan administrator. To change title to jointly owned or tenancy by the entireties real estate, practice varies by state but in many states all that is necessary is to file with the land records an affidavit reciting the death to which a copy of the death certificate will be attached. Often these documents are not filed until the surviving joint tenant or spouse sells the property. Administering property in a revocable living trust is more complicated. If the settlor was trustee until her death, the successor trustee will first normally sign an acceptance of office.[1] Once in office, the successor will need to verify the assets held in the trust, pay the decedent's debts and expenses as directed in the trust document, and then distribute the trust assets to the beneficiaries. Absent a dispute, it is usually not necessary for the trustee to go to court.

The process is not so simple for assets that the decedent held in the decedent's individual name. Unlike nonprobate assets, where the document of title recites to whom title will pass, establishing to whom title to individually owned assets will pass must be proved in court unless an expedited small estate's procedure is available.[2] Title to these "probate" assets will pass as provided in a valid will. If the decedent did not leave a valid will, title will pass

[1] For a typical statute on trustee acceptance, *see* Unif. Trust Code (UTC) § 701. *See also* Section 14.6, note 390.

[2] For a discussion of small estates procedures, *see* Section 13.2.

to the heirs. "Probate" has both a technical and a colloquial meaning. Technically, "probate" is the process by which the court will validate a will. "Administration" is the process occurring thereafter where the personal representative appointed to administer the estate will collect assets, pay debts and expenses, and distribute what is left to the devisees in the case of a will or the heirs if the decedent died intestate. However, the term "probate" is often used more broadly to refer to the entire process of probate and administration. When someone complains about delays in probate, it is usually not complaints about delays in obtaining a court hearing to prove the will but delays in completing the subsequent process of administration.

The court will not only enter an order admitting the will to probate but also enter an order appointing a personal representative. In the case of a will, if the court appoints the person whom the testator has nominated in the will, that person was traditionally referred to as an "executor." If the person nominated in the will does not or cannot accept the office, the court will appoint someone else based on a statutory list.[3] This substitute was traditionally referred to as an administrator with the will annexed or administrator cum testatamento annexo. If the original executor leaves office before completing the job and the will does not provide for the appointment of a successor, the successor appointed by the court was traditionally referred to as an administrator de bonis non. The modern tendency is to bypass this terminology confusion and to refer to anyone appointed by the court to administer the estate as a "personal representative."[4] The term "personal representative" is used whether the decedent died testate or intestate, although for intestate decedents the traditional term "administrator" is often still employed.

The court responsible for proving wills, appointing personal representatives, and supervising administration is called the probate court, from the Latin *probare,* to prove. These courts are normally organized in one of two ways. Under the more restrictive model, the court of probate has both limited and specialized jurisdiction. The court can hear probate matters but lacks jurisdiction to resolve other matters that might arise in the litigation. For that, the plaintiff or petitioner would need to seek relief in another court. For example, a specialized court of probate could determine heirs but not impose a constructive trust denying the heir an inheritance because she had intentionally killed her husband. For that, relief had to be requested from a court of chancery.[5]

A second model is to grant the court general jurisdiction but to then divide the court into separate divisions such as probate, chancery, and criminal for purposes of administrative convenience. This is the model followed in California, for example.[6] An advantage of this model is that the probate court,

---

[3] *See, e.g.*, Unif. Probate Code (UPC) § 3–203.

[4] UPC § 1–201.

[5] In re Estate of Mahoney, 220 A.2d 475 (Vt. 1966). *See also* In re Estate of Cooney, 454 P.3d 1190 (Mont. 2019) (district court sitting in probate did not have jurisdiction to adjudicate contract to make a will).

[6] Cal.Prob.Code § 7050 and Law Revision Commission Comment. As to the traditional limitation on probate courts, *see* Sections 3.9, note 505 et seq.; 2.7, note 225 et seq.

because it has general jurisdiction, can provide equitable relief, such as issue injunctions.[7]

The notion that only a "probate" court can determine the validity of a will goes back to the time when jurisdiction over wills of personal property belonged to the ecclesiastical courts, the ancestor of today's probate court. The ecclesiastical court had no jurisdiction over land, and so wills of land were not probated; their validity was determined in ordinary actions to try title, such as ejectment.[8] Although wills were probated in an ecclesiastical court, probate had no effect on devises of land in the will; an heir could assert that the will was invalid even though it had been probated.[9]

Having two courts pass on the validity of the same will made no sense.[10] In keeping with the modern trend to assimilate the rules for land and personal property,[11] the English Court Probate Act of 1857 made the probate of a will, or a decree that a will was invalid, binding as to all the testator's property.[12] The assimilation of land and personal property might have been accomplished by abolishing probate altogether, and having the validity of wills tried in any court whenever it became relevant in a proceeding. Other forms of transfer are handled in this way: if a person conveys a home by deed, no probate of the deed is necessary. Absent a dispute, everyone assumes the deed is valid. Why then should a will always have to be proved in court before it may determine title to property? Why not wait and see if anyone complains and decide the matter then? But requiring probate may promote efficiency. Because a will often affects many persons, it could give rise to many lawsuits between heirs and devisees, whereas a single probate proceeding binds them all. "A will contest is a proceeding in rem, the res being the estate of the deceased . . . The principle . . . is to determine in one proceeding . . . who is entitled to inherit the property. . . ."[13]

Multi-State Probate

Because probate is an *in rem* proceeding,[14] a decree admitting a will to probate binds persons living in other states, assuming the court has jurisdiction over them. A will can be probated either in the state where (a) the testator was domiciled at death, or (b) assets of the testator are located.[15] Thus,

---

[7] *See, e.g.*, In re Estate of Owens, 413 P.3d 255 (Colo. Ct. App. 2017) (probate court could set aside payable-on-death transfers and impose a constructive trust).

[8] 3 Amer. Law of Prop. § 14.35 (1952).

[9] Ash v. Calvert, 170 Eng.Rep. 1193 (1810).

[10] However, as we shall see, this can happen today when a testator has property in different states. *See infra* note 14 et seq.

[11] For example, as to intestate succession, *see* Section 2.1, notes 3 et seq.

[12] Court of Probate Act, 1857, 20 & 21 Vict. c. 77, § 62.

[13] Green v. Higdon, 891 S.W.2d 220, 222 (Tenn.App.1994).

[14] 3 Amer. Law of Prop. § 14.37, at 720 (1952).

[15] *Restatement (Second) of Conflict of Laws* § 314 (1971); E. Scoles & P. Hay, *Conflict of Laws* §§ 22.1–.2 (2d ed. 1992); UPC § 3–201(a).

a Wisconsin court had jurisdiction to probate the will of a testator who was domiciled in Arizona because the testator owned property in Wisconsin.[16]

Determinations of domicile can be problematic.[17] The location of property can also be unclear. An Oregon court refused to probate the will of a testator domiciled in Massachusetts based on a note which the testator held secured by a mortgage on Oregon land; because the note was personal property, its situs was the decedent's domicile.[18] But the Uniform Probate Code says that debts evidenced by paper are located "where the instrument is."[19]

Even though probate operates in rem, proceedings in two states may be necessary[20] and may reach different outcomes. The heirs of a woman whose will had been probated in Florida had standing to contest her will in Kentucky where she owned land. "A contest of a foreign will in another state, where the real estate affected by the will is located, does not violate full faith and credit required under the Federal Constitution."[21] The result might have been different if the dispute had involved personal property or if the contestants had been served in the Florida proceedings.[22] Some states recognize foreign probate decrees even as to local land. The Uniform Probate Code (UPC) makes a final order determining testacy by a court of the decedent's domicile determinative elsewhere.[23] According to the comment, this "adds nothing to existing law as applied to cases where the parties . . . were also personally before the local court," but it "extends present law" in cases involving "local land."[24] California similarly recognizes wills established in another jurisdiction including a foreign country, except one which does not "provide impartial tribunals" or "due process of law."[25] Both the California and Uniform Probate Code provisions apply only if the other probate was in the state of the decedent's domicile,[26] and only if all interested persons were given notice and an opportunity to contest the will.[27]

---

16 Matter of Estate of Warner, 468 N.W.2d 736 (Wis.App.1991). *But see* In re Seyse, 803 A.2d 694 (N.J.Super.App.Div.2002) (probate jurisdiction transferred to state of decedent's domicile).

17 *See* Section 1.2, note 143 et seq.

18 West v. White, 758 P.2d 424, 426 (Or.App.1988).

19 UPC § 3–201(d). *See also* Section 1.2, note 127 et seq.

20 Cooper v. Tosco Corp., Lion Oil Div., 613 S.W.2d 831 (Ark.1981) (probate in Louisiana not effective as to Arkansas land).

21 Marr v. Hendrix, 952 S.W.2d 693, 695 (Ky.1997). *See also* Estate of Read, 768 P.2d 566 (Wyo. 1989); In re Roberg's Estate, 396 So.2d 235 (Fla. App. 1981).

22 Estate of Waitzman, 507 So.2d 24 (Miss.1987) (contest of will probated in Florida not permitted because personal property involved); *Restatement (Second) of Conflict of Laws* § 317 (1971).

23 UPC § 3–408.

24 UPC § 3–408, cmt.

25 Cal.Prob.Code §§ 12522–23. Judgments in foreign countries are not covered by the "full faith and credit" clause of the U.S. Constitution, but they may nevertheless be recognized.

26 In re Estate of Stein, 896 P.2d 740 (Wash. App. 1995) (Oregon probate binding only as to assets in Oregon, since decedent was domiciled in Washington); In re Reed's Estate, 664 P.2d 824 (Kan. 1983) (probate in Indiana no bar to contest in Kansas where testator was domiciled).

27 In re Estate of Farley, 397 N.W.2d 409 (Minn. App. 1986) (Texas probate decree not binding when only "posted courthouse notice given").

Notice of Probate

Historically, there were two forms of probate, "common" in which no notice to the testator's heirs was given, and "solemn" which did require notice. This dual system still prevails in many states.[28] The Georgia Code, for instance, provides that "the probate of a will may be in either common or solemn form." Common form probate occurs "without notice to anyone" and "is not conclusive upon anyone" until four years have elapsed. Solemn form probate "requires due notice to all the heirs of the testator" and "is conclusive upon all parties notified."[29] The UPC provides similar options, but uses the terms "informal" and "formal" to describe them.[30] Orders in formal proceedings are "final as to all persons,"[31] whereas wills which have been informally probated may be contested within the later of 12 months following the informal probate or 3 years after the decedent's death.[32] Even if a will is informally probated, the personal representative, after being appointed, must notify the heirs and devisees.[33]

Some state courts have held that a statute of limitations on contest of a will cannot be constitutionally applied to bar a contest by an unnotified heir. Actual notice is required to bar a claim by an heir who is known or reasonably ascertainable; notice by publication suffices as to heirs who are not reasonably ascertainable,[34] such as a distant relative whom the decedent had never mentioned,[35] but not as to heirs whose identity is known to the executor of the will. Other courts have rejected the due process argument on the basis that heirs have a "mere expectancy" which is "not entitled to constitutional protection."[36] The cases turn on whether *Tulsa Professional Collection Services, Inc. v. Pope*,[37] which addresses notice to a decedent's creditors, is also applicable to notice to heirs.

Although informal probate is not immediately conclusive, it has legal consequences beyond triggering a limitation period on contest. One who deals with the executor under an informally probated will in good faith, for example, by purchasing property of the estate, is protected even if the probate of the will is later set aside.[38] A critic has argued that informal probate allows "a clean out of estate assets at the expense of creditors and beneficiaries" by proponents

---

[28] Chaffin & Barwick, *The Probate and Establishment of Domestic and Foreign Wills,* 13 Ga.L.Rev. 133, 141 (1978).

[29] Ga.Code §§ 53–5–15 to 53–5–22.

[30] UPC §§ 3–301, 3–401.

[31] UPC § 3–412; In re Estate of Gaines, 830 P.2d 569 (N.M.App. 1992) (proponent bound by order in formal proceedings finding will invalid).

[32] UPC § 3–108(a)(3); Viera v. Estate of Cantu, 940 P.2d 190 (informally probated will may be challenged as being made under undue influence).

[33] UPC § 3–705.

[34] Estate of Beck v. Engene, 557 N.W.2d 270 (Iowa 1996); In re Estate of Carter, 4 Cal.Rptr.3d 490, 492 (App.2003) (notice to reasonable ascertainable heirs before estate distributed is required by constitution as well as statute).

[35] Matter of Estate of Daily, 555 N.W.2d 254 (Iowa App.1996).

[36] Matter of Estate of Wilson, 610 N.E.2d 851, 858 (Ind.App.1993). *Compare* Section 12.6, note 243 et seq. (upholding retroactive abolition of possibilities of reverter).

[37] 485 U.S. 478 (1988).

[38] Ky.Rev.Stat. § 395.330; Cal.Prob.Code § 8272(b).

of an invalid will,[39] but the drafters of the Uniform Probate Code believed that informal probate had been proved satisfactory by "accumulated experience," and feared that people would avoid probate altogether if it was made "more awkward than non-probate alternatives which are freely available" such as joint tenancy.[40] In order to deter "misuse [of] the no-notice feature of informal proceedings," applicants are required to file a verified statement that they believe that the will being offered was validly executed and was the decedent's last will.[41] The rules of professional conduct provide a sanction against abuse by lawyers. A lawyer who filed a will for probate without disclosing the existence of a later will was suspended from practice for violating the Code of Professional Responsibility. "All judges regularly rely on the candor, honesty and integrity of the lawyer in handling ex parte matters which are presented to them. . . . Judges must be able to rely on the integrity of the lawyer."[42]

§ 13.2 Necessity for Administration

Probate and Administration

When a will is admitted to probate, the court appoints a personal representative to administer the testator's estate. Probate and administration are thus closely connected. But probate of a will usually takes little time (absent a contest) whereas administration of an estate typically lasts for many months or even years. Thus, the widespread desire to "avoid probate"[43] is more appropriately directed at administration.

The connection between probate and administration is not inevitable: "The fact that the latter is customarily carried on in connection with the former, at the same time, and in the same court, is likely to lead to the conclusion that the two constitute a single proceeding. . . . A will may be probated without being followed by administration."[44] Conversely, administration is necessary even if there is no will to probate. The decedent's heirs must be determined, and a personal representative appointed to administer the estate.

History and Comparative Law

Administration of estates is designed to assure that claims against the decedent are paid before the assets are distributed to the heirs or devisees. Originally only personal property went to the executor; land passed directly to the devisees or heirs without administration. England extended

---

[39] Parker, *No-Notice Probate and Non-Intervention Administration Under the Code,* 2 Conn.L.Rev. 546, 556 (1970).

[40] Wellman, *The Uniform Probate Code: Blueprint for Reform in the 70's,* 2 Conn.L.Rev. 453, 497–99 (1970).

[41] UPC § 3–301, cmt.

[42] In re Conduct of Hedrick, 822 P.2d 1187, 1190 (Or.1991). *See also* Cincinnati Bar Ass'n v. Lowery, 567 N.E.2d 1038 (Ohio 1991); Model Rules of Professional Conduct 3.3(d) (in ex parte proceedings "a lawyer shall inform the tribunal of all material facts known to the lawyer").

[43] *See* Section 10.4.

[44] Basye, *Dispensing with Administration,* 44 Mich.L.Rev. 329, 424 (1945); *cf.* UPC § 3–401 (petition for probate "may, but need not, involve a request for appointment of a personal representative").

administration to land only in 1897.[45] Some American states preserve vestiges of the old distinction between land and personal property with respect to administration, but the practical effects are limited: "title" to land may technically pass directly to the decedent's heirs or devisees but under modern statutes the personal representative has extensive powers over the land.[46]

Administration is not the only possible way for the law to assure that a decedent's creditors are paid. Creditors could be allowed to sue the debtor's heirs or devisees, but such suits give rise to problems. If an intestate has several heirs, must creditors seek a proportionate amount from each, or can they collect the whole from any heir? If the decedent died insolvent, his heirs and devisees should not be personally liable for his debts. Conversely, if the estate is solvent but the heirs and devisees are not, creditors of the estate would be prejudiced if they were limited to claims against the latter. Creditors should share the decedent's assets in a rational order; certain claims have priority, and creditors in the same class should get the same share.[47] Devises abate in a prescribed order to pay claims against a testator.[48] Without administration this might require a series of lawsuits.

Administration consequently helps to handle the payment of claims in a fair way. In the great majority of cases, however, the decedent is not insolvent, and administration is a needless expense. This breeds general disrespect for law and lawyers, because the only direct contact which many persons have with our legal system involves administration of decedents' estates.[49]

The civil law system of continental Europe usually dispenses with administration. This informality is despite the fact that the countries of Europe are usually regarded as being fond of paternalistic governmental interference with private affairs, while in the United States the traditional hostility to governmental meddling has tended to keep state supervision of private matters at a minimum. Yet, with respect to the transfer of property upon death, the roles are curiously reversed. While in Europe judicial or judicially supervised administration of decedents' estates constitutes a comparatively rare exception, in the United States it is theoretically required in every case.[50]

Louisiana follows the civil law system and "probably has the least expensive system in the nation" for succession.[51] Heirs may seek administration in order to avoid personal liability when the decedent was

---

[45] Land Transfer Act, 1897, 60 & 61 Vict. c. 65, § 1; 3 *Amer. Law of Prop.* § 14.6 (1952).

[46] 3 *Amer. Law of Prop.* § 14.7, at 578 (1952).

[47] For claimant priority, *see* Section 13.5, note 198 et seq.

[48] For discussion of abatement, *see* Section 6.4.

[49] Link, *Probate and Administration of Small Estates in Georgia,* 6 Ga.L.Rev. 74, 75 (1971); Merrill, *The Proposed Model Small Estates Act,* 5 Okl.L.Rev. 49 (1952). However, popular satisfaction with the work of lawyers in this field actually is high. Stein & Fierstein, *The Role of the Attorney in Estate Administration,* 68 Minn.L.Rev. 1107, 1224 (1984).

[50] Rheinstein, *The Model Probate Code: A Critique,* 48 Colum.L.Rev. 534, 538 (1948). Thus in Germany a decedent's property passes directly to his heirs, although he *can* by will designate a Testamentsvollstrecker to administer the property. BGB (German Civil Code) §§ 857, 2197.

[51] Sarpy, *Probate Economy and Celerity in Louisiana,* 34 La.L.Rev. 523, 524 (1974). The low cost is attributable to the absence of an executor's fee and a reduction in attorney's fees. Sarpy, 34 La. L. Rev. at 528.

insolvent, but this is infrequent.[52] If creditors fear that lack of administration will jeopardize their rights, they can apply for appointment as personal representative, but this also rarely happens.[53] Creditors in other states have shown a similar lack of concern about will substitutes which avoid administration.[54]

The Louisiana statute inspired the drafters of the UPC to in 1982 add provisions authorizing universal succession under which the beneficiaries take title to assets subject to creditor claims without the need to appoint a personal representative.[55] But this statute is more theoretical than real. The UPC system of universal succession has not been enacted in any state. Much more energy has been expended on developing alternatives to probate than on further simplifying the probate system. A probate system built on civil law concepts is unlikely to spread beyond Louisiana.[56]

Practical Problems in Avoiding Administration

Usually, the heirs or devisees can enjoy a decedent's tangible personal property without bothering to have the estate administered, but they cannot collect choses in action like a bank account or securities registered in the decedent's name. "The executor or administrator of a decedent's estate has standing to file suit on behalf of a decedent, but the legatees, heirs, and devisees have no such standing," because the court cannot be sure that they are the sole claimants to the estate.[57] Persons who owe money to a decedent sometimes voluntarily pay the decedent's successors without administration,[58] but in doing this they run the risk that an administrator will later sue them on the same obligation. Payment to the decedent's heirs is no defense to such a suit.[59] Thus, a decedent's debtors have standing to petition for administration of the estate so they will know whom to pay.[60]

Heirs or devisees may be able to take possession of the decedent's land without having the estate administered, but if they want to sell or mortgage the land, third persons should be reluctant to deal with them, for good reason.[61]

---

[52] Sarpy, 34 La. L. Rev. at 528.

[53] Sarpy, 34 La. L. Rev. at 535.

[54] "If modern creditors had needed to use probate very much, they would have applied their considerable political muscle to suppress the nonprobate system. Instead they have acquiesced without struggle. . . ." Langbein, *The Nonprobate Revolution and the Future of the Law of Succession*, 97 Harv. L. Rev. 1108, 1125 (1984).

[55] UPC § 3–312 to 3–322. For an overview of these provisions and arguments in favor of universal succession, *see* Sneddon, *Beyond the Personal Representative: The Potential for Succession Without Administration*, 50 S. Tex. L. Rev. 449 (2009).

[56] For the challenges in further simplifying probate when the creation of non-probate transfer is such an easy alternative, *see* Martin, *Non-Judicial Estate Settlement*, 45 U. Mich. J.L. Reform 965 (2012); Martin, *Reconfiguring Estate Settlement*, 94 Minn. L. Rev. 42 (2009).

[57] McGill v. Lazzaro, 416 N.E.2d 29, 31 (Ill.App.1980). In Louisiana, on the other hand, heirs can sue on a decedent creditor's obligation if they establish their right to inherit. Taboni ex rel. Taboni v. Estate of Longo, 810 So.2d 1142 (La.2002).

[58] Basye, *Dispensing With Administration*, 44 Mich. L. Rev. at 399, 405.

[59] Basye, 44 Mich. L. Rev. at 334. But courts will deny a second recovery where the estate has ample funds to pay debts. Basye, 44 Mich. L. Rev. at 398.

[60] Matter of Windholz, 809 S.W.2d 30 (Mo.App.1991).

[61] Costigan, *Problems Preliminary to Administration*, [1951] U.Ill.L.F. 357, 361; Siedel v. Snider, 44 N.W.2d 687 (Iowa 1950) (heir does not have marketable title without administration).

For example, a mortgage executed by an heir was later held to be subordinate to a claim by a creditor of the decedent.[62] But lapse of time may give heirs or devisees marketable title without administration, and heirs have been allowed to sue debtors of the decedent on the theory that "the non-existence of creditors [of the decedent] will be presumed from the mere lapse of time."[63]

Small Estates

The expense of administration is particularly burdensome for small estates because the cost represents a larger percentage of the estate,[64] and the beneficiaries are usually needier. If an estate is smaller than the statutory exemptions,[65] the rationale for administration—protection of creditors—does not apply. Therefore, many states exempt small estates from administration. The statutes are of two types, "collection by affidavit" and "summary distribution."[66]

Collection by affidavit requires no court action.[67] Suppose a wife's will leaves her entire estate to her husband. When she dies, she had a small bank account in her own name and a claim for unpaid wages. Under many state small estates affidavit provisions, the husband would have to wait thirty days after the wife died before attempting to collect these claims. This waiting period allows the decedent's creditors to initiate administration if they think it necessary. Then the widower can execute an affidavit stating that he is entitled to payment and that the estate is less than the statutory amount, which under the UPC is only $25,000.[68] If the bank and employer pay the widower when he produces the affidavits, they are discharged from liability, even if the facts asserted in the affidavit turn out to be untrue.[69] If they refuse to pay the widower when he produces the affidavit, he can sue them.[70] If a creditor of the decedent later initiates proceedings to have the estate administered, the widower must account for the money he received.

In many states the ceiling on "small estates" for which this procedure is available is much higher than $25,000; California allows a probate estate of up to $150,000 to be collected in this way.[71] On the other hand, some statutes cover only particular kinds of property, such as bank accounts, statutes that

---

62 Janes v. Commerce Federal Savings & Loan Ass'n, 639 S.W.2d 490 (Tex.App.1982). *See also* VCF v. McClellan, 69 P.3d 274, 280 (Okl. Civ. App. 2002) (heir's transfer of truck did not give possession to support a storage lien).

63 Basye, *Dispensing With Administration*, 44 Mich. L. Rev. at 397. In Parsons v. Tickner, 37 Cal.Rptr.2d 810 (App.1995), the court allowed an heir to sue years after an estate had been closed.

64 Merrill, *The Proposed Model Small Estates Act*, 50 Okl. L. Rev. at 49; Link, *Probate and Administration of Small Estates in Georgia*, 6 Ga. L. Rev. at 79.

65 *See* Section 8.4, note 159 et seq.

66 For a listing and analysis of the state statutes, *see* Blumberg, *51 Flavors: A Survey of Small Estate Procedures Across the Country*, Prob. & Prop., July/Aug. 2014, at 31.

67 *See* UPC §§ 3–1201, 3–1202, which have influenced legislation in states which have not adopted the whole Code. Johnson, *Wills, Trusts & Estates*, 68 Va.L.Rev. 521, 529 (1982).

68 UPC § 3–1201(a)(1).

69 UPC § 3–1202; Clark v. Unknown Heirs of Osborn, 782 P.2d 1384 (Okl.1989).

70 UPC § 3–1202. As a practical matter, if the debtor insists on the estate being administered it may be cheaper to comply than to sue. Johnson, 68 Va. L. Rev. at 530.

71 Cal.Prob.Code § 13100.

were promoted by banks so they could more easily "clear their books."[72] The UPC affidavit can be used by any successor, whereas in some states only the decedent's spouse and children can collect by affidavit.[73]

The affidavit procedure is open to abuse. An heir (or alleged heir) could execute a false affidavit, collect the money, and disappear.[74] A Missouri statute requires claimants to file a bond in an amount approved by court conditioned on paying claims against the decedent.[75] In Arkansas, the claimant must file the affidavit with the clerk of the probate court.[76]

The affidavit procedure allowed by the UPC does not cover land, even if its value is small. The drafters believed it was unnecessary "since the appointment of a personal representative may be obtained easily under the Code."[77] The UPC approach is not universal, however. California provides an affidavit procedure for clearing title to land which is worth less than $50,000.[78] Arkansas and Missouri take encumbrances into account in valuing the estate, potentially permitting real property of significant value to pass under their small estate procedure.[79]

The UPC allows summary distribution in certain cases after administration has begun. Suppose a widow has the decedent's will probated, is appointed personal representative, and files an inventory of the estate assets which shows that the estate is so small that nothing would be left for ordinary creditors after paying the family allowance and other exemptions and preferred claims like funeral expenses. On these facts she can distribute the estate immediately.[80] Many states have similar provisions, though they often require that a court determine the relevant facts before any distribution.[81]

Larger Estates

Some states allow even large estates to escape administration. If an estate consists entirely of community property which passes to the surviving spouse, in several states no administration is necessary.[82] In California, even separate property need not be administered if the spouse gets it outright.[83] A spouse who receives property without administration, like heirs under the civil law system, becomes personally liable for the decedent's obligations to the extent

---

72 Basye, 44 Mich. L. Rev. at 401; Link, 6 Ga. L. Rev. at 87.

73 UPC § 3–1201, cmt.; 20 Pa.Stat. § 3101 (spouse, child, parents, or siblings); Ohio Rev.Code § 2113.04 (wages up to $5,000 to spouse, adult children, or parents).

74 Basye, *Dispensing With Administration*, 44 Mich. L. Rev. at 370. *See also* Sullivan & Hack, *Streamlining Probate*, 51 Marq.L.Rev. 150, 153 (1967).

75 Mo.Rev.Stat. § 473.097.1(3).

76 Ark.Code § 28–41–101.

77 UPC § 3–1201, cmt.

78 Cal.Prob.Code § 13200.

79 Ark. Code § 28–41–101 (net value of $100,000); Mo. Rev. Stat. § 473.097 (net value of $40,000).

80 UPC § 3–1203.

81 Fla.Stat. § 735.301; Ark.Code § 28–41–103.

82 Basye, 44 Mich. L. Rev. at 382–84.

83 Cal.Prob.Code § 13500.

of the property received.[84] In order to avoid personal liability, the spouse can elect to have the property administered.[85]

§ 13.3 Will Contests

A will may be contested on a variety of grounds, including lack of capacity, undue influence, insane delusion, fraud, or lack of proper execution.[86] Despite the numerous grounds, relatively few wills are contested.[87]

Some states allow wills to be contested even after they have been probated with notice to the heirs. For example, in Ohio, a will which has been probated can be contested for up to three months.[88] Allowing wills that have already been probated still to be contested may reflect lack of confidence in probate judges, who in some states are lay persons, whereas will contests usually take place in a court of general jurisdiction.[89] Under the Uniform Probate Code informal probate is handled by a Registrar, who is not necessarily a judge,[90] whereas formal testacy proceedings are heard by a judge who has "the same qualifications as a judge of the court of general jurisdiction."[91]

The ecclesiastical courts which probated wills of personal property did not use jury trial, whereas devises of land were tried in actions at law in which juries were used.[92] Today, most courts hold that constitutional provisions preserving the right to jury trial do not apply to will contests.[93] Nevertheless, many states provide for it;[94] in others, jury trial is discretionary, or the verdict is only advisory.[95] Some commentators suggest that juries in will contests are "more disposed to work equity for the disinherited" than to follow the law.[96] Professor Schoenblum's empirical study suggested that "whether judgment was reached by a judge or jury, it was more likely than not to be in favor of the

---

[84] Cal.Prob.Code §§ 13550–51; *cf.* BGB (German Civil Code) § 1967(I) (heir liable for decedent's debts), § 1975 (liability limited when estate is insolvent). The spouse's liability is subject to the same defenses as would be available if the claim were asserted in probate proceedings, such as the one year limitation running from the date of the death of the decedent spouse. Collection Bureau of San Jose v. Rumsey, 6 P.3d 713 (Cal.2000).

[85] Cal.Prob.Code § 13502.

[86] For a discussion of the various grounds for contesting a will, *see* Ch. 5.

[87] "Will contests rarely occur, perhaps on the order of one in a hundred or so cases." Schoenblum, *Will Contests: An Empirical Study*, 22 Real Prop. Prob. & Tr. J. 607, 614 (1987).

[88] Ohio Rev.Code §§ 2107.71, 2107.76.

[89] Simes, *The Function of Will Contests*, 44 Mich. L. Rev. 503, 541 (1946). *See also* Chaffin & Barwick, *The Probate and Establishment of Domestic and Foreign Wills*, 13 Ga. L.Rev. 133 (1978).

[90] UPC §§ 1–307, 3–301.

[91] UPC §§ 1–309, 3–401.

[92] Brook v. Warde, 73 Eng.Rep. 702 (K.B.1571).

[93] In re Estate of Johnson, 820 A.2d 535 (D.C.2003); Petition of Atkins, 493 A.2d 1203 (N.H.1985); Riddell v. Edwards, 32 P.3d 4, 8 (Alaska 2001).

[94] Mo.Rev.Stat. § 473.083.7; Matter of Estate of Ruther, 631 P.2d 1330, 1332 (N.M.App.1981).

[95] UPC § 1–306(b); Cal.Prob.Code § 8252(b) (abolishing trial by jury in will contests).

[96] Langbein, *Living Probate: The Conservatorship Model,* 77 Mich.L.Rev. 63, 65 (1978).

proponent" of the will, but jury trials "appear to improve materially the [contestants'] chances for success."[97]

Time Limits on Contest

The time limits for contest of a probated will are typically quite short; for example, three months from the date of probate[98] or six months after first publication of notice that letters of office have been granted.[99] These short limitations provide a counter argument to the common advice to avoid probate to minimize the risk of a successful contest. "If circumstances suggest the possibilities of such a contest, the commencement of probate proceedings is advisable to bar the right of contest."[100] Some statutes provide comparable short limits to contests of revocable trusts. Under the Uniform Trust Code (UTC), contests of a revocable trust after the settlor dies are barred 120 days after the trustee sent the potential contestants a notice of the time allowed for contest, accompanied by a copy of the trust instrument.[101]

Some courts allow an untimely contest in cases of fraud. For example, the proponent of a will sent a notice of probate to the testator's heirs but told their mother that "everything was fine . . . the boys' interests were well represented." He neglected to tell her that the will gave him most of the estate. The court set aside the probate even though the period for will contests had expired, because of the proponent's "extrinsic fraud," defined as fraud which prevents a party "from presenting all of his case to the court."[102] Another court held that even "intrinsic fraud"—alleged probate of a forged will—allowed a contest after the limit expired, but only if the contestant had been diligent in pursuing the claim after she should have discovered the fraud.[103] The Uniform Probate Code allows relief "whenever fraud has been perpetrated in connection with any proceeding" under the Code, if proceedings are brought within 2 years of discovery of the fraud.[104]

Some courts grant relief on a tort or constructive trust theory after the time for a will contest is over. Other courts hold that tort claims are precluded by a probate decree,[105] or have rejected them on the ground that a will contest

[97] Schoenblum, *Will Contests: An Empirical Study*, 22 Real Prop. Prob. & Tr. J. at 626–27 (1987). *See generally*, Athanas, *The Pros and Cons of Jury Trials in Will Contests*, 1990 U. Chi. L. F. 529 (1990).

[98] Ohio Rev.Code § 2107.76.

[99] Mo. Rev. Stat. § 473.087.1.

[100] Parks, *Varied Duties Face the Successor Trustee of a Revocable Trust*, 19 Est.Plan. 203, 206 (1992).

[101] UTC § 604(a)(2). *See also* Cal.Prob.Code § 16061.8.

[102] Estate of Sanders, 710 P.2d 232 (Cal.1985). *See also* Anderson v. Marquette National Bank, 518 N.E.2d 196 (Ill. App. 1987); Carrell v. Ellingwood, 423 N.E.2d 630 (Ind. App. 1981). *But cf.* Young v. Thompson, 794 N.E.2d 446 (Ind.App.2003) (heirs had no right to rely on erroneous statement of attorney for the estate as to time within which they could contest will); Matter of Estate of Taylor, 675 P.2d 944 (Mont.1984) (no untimely probate on ground of estoppel; devisee's only remedy is to sue heir).

[103] In re Estate of Delaney, 819 A.2d 968, 980–82 (D.C.2003).

[104] UPC § 1–106; *cf.* Section 14.8, note 650 et seq.

[105] In re Estate of Hendrix, 134 Wash.App. 1007 (2006). *See also* Jurgensen v. Haslinger, 692 N.E.2d 347 (Ill.App.1998) (no tort action lies against witnesses who allegedly testified falsely in probate proceedings). *See also* Jurgensen v. Haslinger, 692 N.E.2d 347 (Ill. App. 1998) (no tort

provides an adequate remedy for the plaintiff's claim.[106] Where it is found that a will contest does not provide an adequate remedy, both actions have been allowed to proceed, *e.g.*, where a will contest would not result in recovery of nonprobate assets alleged to have been fraudulently transferred.[107]

Under the "probate exception" to federal jurisdiction, federal courts do not have jurisdiction to hear will contests. They do, however, have jurisdiction to entertain estate-related actions for tortious interference or other matters not representing a direct claim to assets in the custody of the probate court.[108] The federal court also has jurisdiction to determine the validity of beneficiary designations on payable-on-death accounts, even though the accounts would have become probate assets had it found the beneficiary designations to be invalid.[109]

Expiration of the time limit on will contests does not bar raising questions of will construction[110] or even claims that a will provision was invalid as a matter of public policy because it conditioned benefits on the devisee getting a divorce.[111] A claim that a devise to the testator's spouse was revoked by divorce was held not covered by the limit on contests,[112] but another court held that a claim that the testator's marriage revoked the will was barred.[113]

Courts are divided as to whether attempting to probate a later-discovered will after an earlier one has been probated amounts to a "contest" within the meaning of the time limit.[114] The Uniform Probate Code allows even a formal testacy order to be modified if proponents of a later will show that "they were unaware of its existence at the time of the earlier proceeding."[115] In California, the later will may be admitted to probate, but it cannot "affect property previously distributed."[116]

---

action lies against witnesses who allegedly testified falsely in probate proceedings); Baars v. Campbell University, 558 S.E.2d 871, 877 (N.C. App. 2002).

[106] Minton v. Sackett, 671 N.E.2d 160 (Ind.App.1996); Geduldig v. Posner, 743 A.2d 247, 257 (Md.App.1999); Wilson v. Fritchy, 55 P.3d 997 (N.M.App.2002).

[107] Peralta v. Peralta, 131 P.3d 81 (N.M.App.2005); Martin v. Martin, 687 So.2d 903 (Fla.Ct.App.1997); In re Estate of Jeziorski, 516 N.E.2d 422 (Ill.Ct.App.1987).

[108] Marshall v. Marshall, 547 U.S. 293 (2006). For an analysis of *Marshall*, *see* Penzer & Santaro, *Second Circuit Clarifies Scope of Probate Exception to Federal Jurisdiction*, 80 N.Y.S.B.J. 52 (2008) (discussing post-Marshall case law); Graves, Marshall v. Marshall: *The Past, Present, and Future of the Probate Exception to Federal Jurisdiction*, 59 Ala. L. Rev. 1643 (2008); Dougherty, Marshall v. Marshall: *Playmates, Prenupts, and the Probate Exception*, 61 Ark. L. Rev. 329 (2008).

[109] Kinder Morgan, Inc. v. Crout, 814 Fed. Appx. 811 (5th Cir. 2020).

[110] Matter of Estate of Worsham, 859 P.2d 1134 (Okl.App.1993).

[111] Hall v. Eaton, 631 N.E.2d 805, 807 (Ill.App.1994).

[112] In re Marriage of Duke, 549 N.E.2d 1096, 1101 (Ind.App.1990). *See also* Succession of Austin, 527 So.2d 483 (La.App.1988) (revocation by birth of children); *cf.* In re Estate of Delaney, 819 A.2d 968, 984 (D.C.2003) (claim to elective share).

[113] Martin v. Kenworthy, 759 P.2d 335 (Or.App.1988).

[114] *Compare* Coussee v. Estate of Efston, 633 N.E.2d 815 (Ill.App.1994) *with* In re Will of Fields, 570 So.2d 1202 (Miss.1990).

[115] UPC § 3–412(1).

[116] Cal.Prob.Code § 8226(b).

Ante-Mortem Probate

Courts generally refuse to determine the validity of a will while the testator is alive.[117] Many have argued that such determinations should be permitted so that the testator's capacity can be better evaluated by the fact finder.[118] The question may become moot if the testator later revokes the will or dies without an estate, but declaratory judgments of issues which may become moot are generally permitted if the potential benefits of a decision outweigh the costs.[119] Ante-mortem probate has not caught on, however. Only a few states have enacted statutes allowing ante-mortem probate.[120]

Any order obtained in an ante-mortem proceeding may be of limited effectiveness. If the will is found to be invalid, the testator could circumvent the order by executing a new will or by disposing of the estate by non-probate transfers. Conversely, heirs might be able to contest a will which had been declared valid on the ground that the testator was later prevented from revoking it by undue influence.[121] Perhaps more problematic is the fact that the testators do not want to disclose the contents of their will during their lifetime, but a proceeding to approve a will would usually require that the contents be revealed because they may constitute relevant evidence.[122] Finally, the existing statutes do not allow heirs to institute proceedings for a declaration that a will is invalid.[123] Perhaps for these reasons, ante-mortem probate is not commonly used in the few states that allow it.

Binding Effect on Persons Under Legal Disability

Heirs under disability often get additional time to file a contest. In Ohio, probate of a will becomes binding after three months except as to persons "under any legal disability" for whom the three-month period begins to run only when the disability is removed.[124] This may leave the disposition of an estate in doubt for a considerable time. The UPC circumvents this problem by allowing parties under a legal disability to be bound by representation. Orders against a trustee in probate proceedings bind the trust beneficiaries "to the extent that there is no conflict of interest between them."[125]

The UPC also facilitates compromise of controversies concerning wills by providing for court approval thereof which makes a written agreement binding

---

[117] Burcham v. Burcham, 1 P.3d 756 (Colo.App.2000); Conservatorship of Bookasta, 265 Cal.Rptr. 1 (App.1989) (determination of invalidity reversed); Lawver v. Lawvor, 740 P.2d 1220 (Or.App.1987). *See also* Claveloux v. Bacotti, 778 So.2d 399 (Fla.App.2001) (action for tortious interference with expectancy dismissed because testator was still living).

[118] Leopold & Beyer, *Ante-Mortem Probate: A Viable Alternative*, 43 Ark. L. Rev. 131 (1990); Fink, *Ante-Mortem Probate Revisited*, 37 Ohio St.L.J. 264, 266 (1978); Langbein, *Living Probate: The Conservatorship Model*, 77 Mich. L. Rev. at 67.

[119] Fink, 37 Ohio St. L.J. at 278–79.

[120] N.D. Code § 30.1–08.1–01; Ohio Rev.Code § 2107.081; Ark.Code § 28–40–201.

[121] Fellows, *The Case Against Living Probate*, 78 Mich. L. Rev. 1066, 1080, 1095 (1978).

[122] Fink, 37 Ohio St. L.J. at 290.

[123] Corron v. Corron, 531 N.E.2d 708 (Ohio 1988).

[124] Ohio Rev.Code § 2107.76. *See also* 58 Okl. Stat. § 67; N.C. Gen. Stat. § 31–32.

[125] UPC § 1–403(2). *See also* Fifth Third Bank v. Fifth Third Bank, 602 N.E.2d 325, 328 (Ohio App. 1991). *But cf.* Schlosser v. Schlosser, 578 N.E.2d 1203 (Ill.App.1991) (default judgment against trustee not binding on beneficiaries who were not made parties).

even on persons "unborn, unascertained or who could not be located."[126] Minor children can be bound by the agreement of their parents if their interests do not conflict; if they do, the agreement may be approved by a guardian ad litem for the children.[127] Before approving an agreement, the court must find that its effect on persons "represented by fiduciaries or other representatives is just and reasonable."[128] The Arizona Court of Appeals has held that if the agreement affects distribution of the estate, it must be signed by the all of the competent adult beneficiaries and claimants whose interests would be affected.[129] Commentators have suggested that perhaps the UPC should be amended to incorporate the more flexible and more comprehensive settlement provisions of the Uniform Trust Code.[130]

Time Limits on Probate

Many states limit the time within which a will must be probated after the testator dies. A will which was discovered 5 years after the testator died could not be probated under the UPC because the UPC requires that probate proceedings be commenced within three years of the testator's death regardless of when the will was discovered.[131] Some states allow wills to be probated at any time. An Oklahoma court probated a will 12 years after the testator died.[132] But an exception may be recognized if probate of the will was withheld by someone who would benefit from the will's suppression, and late probate has been allowed when a clerk of court misplaced a will the testator had deposited with the clerk for safekeeping.[133]

Delay in probating a will may mislead third parties. Therefore, many statutes protect bona fide purchasers or mortgagees from an heir if a will is not probated or recorded within a specified time after the testator's death.[134] Courts have protected bona fide purchasers even without a statute.[135] Court proceedings based on the assumption that a person died intestate may lead purchasers to think that his heirs have title. Therefore, the UPC bars probate

---

[126] UPC §§ 3–1101, 3–1102. An agreement between persons sui juris does not require court approval. Matter of Estate of Grimm, 784 P.2d 1238 (Utah App.1989).

[127] In re Estate of Truhn, 394 N.W.2d 864 (Minn.App.1986).

[128] UPC § 3–1102(3). *See also* Hunter v. Newsom, 468 S.E.2d 802, 807 (N.C.App.1996) (denying approval to settlement as "unfair to the remainder interests of the unborn and unknown heir").

[129] In re Estate of Riley, 266 P.3d 1078 (Ariz. Ct. App. 2011).

[130] Avraham & Avraham, *In re Estate of Riley: Protecting Beneficiaries' Rights in a Probate Estate*, 54 Ariz. L. Rev. 567, 575 (2012). For the comparable provisions of the UTC, *see* 14.8, notes 707 et seq.

[131] UPC § 3–108; Matter of Estate of Wood, 710 P.2d 476 (Ariz.App.1985). See also Martin v. Martin, 883 P.2d 673 (Haw. App. 1994); In re Estate of Thompson, 962 P.2d 564 (Kan. App. 1997). *But cf.* Matter of Estate of McGrew, 906 S.W.2d 53 (Tex.App.1995) (5-year limit on probate not applicable when proponent not "in default" for not offering it earlier).

[132] Mitchell v. Cloyes, 620 P.2d 398 (Okl.1980). *See also* In re Estate of Schafroth, 598 N.E.2d 479 (Ill. App. 1992) (will probated 8 years after testator died).

[133] In re Estate of Oroke, 445 P. 3d 742 (Kan. 2019).

[134] N.C.Stat. § 31–39; Ohio Rev.Code § 2107.47; Kan.Stat. § 59–618. In Cooper v. Tosco Corp., Lion Oil Div., 613 S.W.2d 831 (Ark. 1981), a similar statute was held to protect a purchaser from an heir even though he was not *bona fide*.

[135] Last Will and Testament of Welch v. Welch, 2020 WL 6111010 (N.M. Ct. App., Oct. 15, 2020); Thomas v. Harper, 218 S.E.2d 832 (Ga.1975); Eckland v. Jankowski, 95 N.E.2d 342 (Ill.1950).

of a will after a court enters a decree of distribution to the heirs,[136] but this is not true in all states.[137]

Standing

Courts allow wills to be contested only by persons with a financial interest in the contest. A contest by the testator's grandchild was dismissed on the ground that she was not a "person interested;" she was not an heir, because the testator's children had survived him.[138] A devisee under an earlier will has standing to contest a later one,[139] but not if both wills leave her the same amount.[140] The testator's heirs may have standing, even if the testator left more than one will disinheriting them.[141] But one court rejected a contest by an heir, saying, "when an at least facially valid previous will is before the court, the burden is on the potential heir at law who wishes to contest a will to show that the previous will which excluded the contestant was invalid."[142]

Courts are split on the question whether an heir's creditors can contest a will if the heir does not.[143] An heir's right to contest a will survives and passes to his heirs or devisees.[144] But an heir who accepts devised property or appointment as a fiduciary is estopped from contesting the will.[145]

Fiduciaries have been allowed to contest wills in some cases but not in others. A trustee designated in the will was not permitted to challenge a codicil, because it did not affect the property interests passing to the trustee. The wish to manage the trust and receive trustee's fees did not give the trustee

---

[136] UPC § 3–412(3)(A). *But see* Last Will and Testament of Welch v. Welch, 2020 WL 6111010 (N.M. Ct. App., Oct. 15, 2020) (decree not a bar when decree void because of failure of petitioner to adequately notify other interested parties).

[137] Gross v. Slye, 360 So.2d 333 (Ala.1978); Matter of Estate of Cornelius, 465 N.E.2d 1033 (Ill.App.1984); 3 *Amer. Law of Prop.* § 14.39, at 733.

[138] Martone v. Martone, 509 S.E.2d 302, 306 (Va.1999). *See also* Taylor v. Estate of Taylor, 770 P.2d 163 (Utah App. 1989) (testator's brother has no standing since he was not his heir); York v. Nunley, 610 N.E.2d 576 (Ohio App. 1992) (child raised but not adopted by testator); *cf.* In re Estate of Peters, 29 P.3d 90 (Wyo. 2001) (parent cannot challenge appointment of administrator when decedent was survived by children).

[139] Spicer v. Estate of Spicer, 935 S.W.2d 576 (Ark.App.1996); Estate of Malcolm, 602 N.E.2d 41 (Ill.App.1992); Estate of Auen, 35 Cal.Rptr.2d 557 (App.1994).

[140] Miller v. Todd, 447 S.E.2d 9 (W.Va.1994).

[141] Power v. Scott, 837 So.2d 202, 206 (Miss.App.2002); Rienhardt v. Kelly, 917 P.2d 963 (N.M.App.1996); In re Estate of Schlenker, 789 N.E.2d 456 (Ill.App.2003).

[142] Cates v. Fricker, 529 So.2d 1253 (Fla. Ct. App.1988). *See also* Wehrheim v. Golden Pond Assisted Living Facility, 905 So.2d 1002 (Fla. Dist. Ct. App. 2005).

[143] Hirsch, *The Problem of the Insolvent Heir*, 74 Cornell L.Rev. 587, 645–51 (1989). *Cf.* In re Bentley, 120 B.R. 712 (Bkrtcy.S.D.N.Y. 1990) (heir's trustee in bankruptcy has standing to contest will but refused to do so because no basis for a contest); In re Estate of Oelberg, 414 N.W.2d 672 (Iowa App. 1987) (judgment creditor of devisee can challenge appointment of executor).

[144] Sheldone v. Marino, 501 N.E.2d 504 (Mass.1986); Kinsella v. Landa, 600 S.W.2d 104 (Mo.App.1980). *But see* In re Estate of Davis, 467 N.E.2d 402 (Ill. App. 1984) (right to contest is not assignable inter-vivos); In re Will of Calhoun, 267 S.E.2d 385 (N.C. App. 1980) (legatee of legatee cannot contest later will); In re Estate of Pearson, 319 N.W.2d 248 (Iowa 1982) (heir's wife cannot contest will).

[145] Matter of Estate of Joffe, 493 N.E.2d 70 (Ill.App.1986); Marine v. Johnson, 437 A.2d 694 (Md.App.1981); Matter of Estate of McDaniel, 935 S.W.2d 827 (Tex.App.1996). In In re Beglinger Trust, 561 N.W.2d 130 (Mich.App.1997), the court applied a similar rule to one who had accepted benefits from a trust and then sought to challenge its validity.

standing.[146] Personal representatives have been allowed to contest a will on behalf of the heirs or beneficiaries of an earlier will.[147] But the UPC does not allow personal representative to seek probate of a will if all of the devisees object.[148]

Attorney's Fees

Successful contestants of a will may recover attorney's fees from the estate. Normally in the United States the prevailing party in a lawsuit does not recover attorney's fees, but if attorney's fees were not paid from the estate, distributees who benefited from the contest without participating in it would be unjustly enriched.[149]

The UPC allows personal representatives reimbursement for attorney's fees from the estate for any proceeding prosecuted or defended "in good faith" regardless of the outcome.[150] This may allow executors under two wills both to be reimbursed for their expenses in a contest as to which will should be probated.[151] Many states have similar statutes, under which even if a will is rejected, the proponent can be reimbursed for attorney's fees.[152] Some courts deny fees for attorneys hired by beneficiaries as distinguished from a personal representative.[153]

Forfeiture Clauses

Many commentators have deplored will contests. Few are successful and the cost of litigation may force a settlement even when a contest has no merit. Some testators seek to deter contests by including a clause in their wills providing that devisees who contest the will lose their devises.[154] Under the UPC these provisions are unenforceable "if probable cause exists for instituting

---

[146] Matter of Estate of Getty, 149 Cal.Rptr. 656 (App.1978). *But see* In re Estate of Milward, 73 P.3d 155, 158 (Kan.App.2003) (executor has standing to challenge a codicil naming another executor); Leone Hall Price Foundation v. Baker, 577 S.E.2d 779 (Ga.2003) (charitable trustee can object to settlement of will contest despite approval of Attorney General). *Compare* a trustee's standing to oppose termination of a trust. *See* Section 10.9, note 511 et seq.

[147] Toon v. Gerth, 735 N.E.2d 314, 320 (Ind. App.2000) (executor of earlier will); Matter of Estate of Beal, 769 P.2d 150, 152 (Okl.1989); Matter of Estate of Campbell, 673 P.2d 645, 649 (Wyo.1983). *But see* In re Read's Estate, 664 P.2d 824, 833 (Kan. 1983) (administrator has no standing).

[148] UPC § 3–720, cmt. *See also* In re Estate of Baldwin, 745 N.Y.S.2d 265 (App.Div.2002) (executor denied standing to contest later will when beneficiaries of earlier will settle); Matter of Estate of Wise, 890 P.2d 744 (Kan.App.1995) (executor cannot challenge settlement reached by testator's heir and devisee).

[149] In re Estate of Foster, 699 P.2d 638 (N.M.App.1985). If the contestants are the sole beneficiaries, this rationale is inapplicable. Rogers v. Rogers, 691 P.2d 114 (Or. App. 1984).

[150] UPC § 3–720.

[151] Enders v. Parker, 66 P.3d 11 (Alaska 2003).

[152] In re Estate of Austin, 553 N.W.2d 632 (Mich.App.1996); Dunnuck v. Mosser, 546 N.E.2d 1291 (Ind.App.1989) (devisee who unsuccessfully contested later will awarded fees); Matter of Estate of Killen, 937 P.2d 1375 (Ariz.App.1996). In Estate of Clark v. Foster & Good, 568 N.E.2d 1098 (Ind.App.1991) attorney's fees were awarded to both sides in a will contest.

[153] In re Estate of Zonas, 536 N.E.2d 642 (Ohio 1989).

[154] *See* Beyer, et al. *The Fine Art of Intimidating Disgruntled Beneficiaries with In Terrorem Clauses*, 51 S.M.U. L.Rev. 225 (1998).

proceedings."[155] "Probable cause" requires a reasonable, not merely a good faith, belief that the will is invalid.[156] Many cases apply a similar test,[157] but some courts enforce the clause even if the contestant had probable cause[158] and in some states forfeiture clauses are ineffective in all cases.[159] If the will is actually found invalid, the issue of enforcement becomes moot because the forfeiture clause fails along with the rest of the will.

What acts are covered by a forfeiture provision has occasioned much litigation. Forfeiture provisions have been applied not only to the person who brought the contest but to others who aided the contestant.[160] A clause that by its terms covered any beneficiary who "directly or indirectly initiates legal action to contest or attack the validity of this will" has been held to cover an attempt to probate a later will.[161] A suit to construe a will is not a "contest" within the meaning of a forfeiture clause.[162] Nor is a claim to assets in the testator's estate. For example, a claim that land was held in joint tenancy and did not pass under the will does not constitute a contest of the will.[163] Forfeiture provisions have been held inapplicable to attacks on a fiduciary named in a will, such as a petition seeking removal.[164] Forfeiture provisions are narrowly construed,[165] but a broadly drafted one will be given effect (subject to any probable cause limitation).[166]

The use of forfeiture clauses is not limited to wills. They are increasingly being included in trust documents. With regards to enforcement, the courts tend to look to their analogous law on forfeiture clauses in wills, which are not necessarily a good fit.[167]

---

155 UPC § 3–905; In re Estate of Mumby, 982 P.2d 1219 (Wash.App.1999) (clause effective where bad faith found). *See also Restatement (Third) of Property (Wills and Other Donative Transfers)* § 8.5 (2003); Beyer, 51 S.M.U.L. Rev. at 247–49.

156 In re Estate of Shumway, 3 P.3d 977, 986 (Ariz.App.1999). On appeal, however, the supreme court found that the contestant did have probable cause. Rodriguez v. Gavette, 9 P.3d 1062 (Ariz.2000).

157 Matter of Estate of Campbell, 876 P.2d 212 (Kan.App.1994); Hannam v. Brown, 956 P.2d 794 (Nev.1998) (no forfeiture when contestant had probable cause); Hammer v. Powers, 819 S.W.2d 669 (Tex.App.1991) (clause enforced when contestant fails to prove probable cause).

158 Larson v. Naslund, 700 P.2d 276 (Or.App.1985); Briggs v. Wyoming Nat'l Bank, 836 P.2d 263 (Wyo.1992) (revocable trust); Beyer, 51 S.M.U.L. Rev. at 245–47.

159 Ind.Code § 29–1–6–2; Fla.Stat. § 732.517.

160 In re Estate of Simpson, 595 A.2d 94, 100 (Pa.Super.1991); *Restatement (Third) of Property (Wills and Other Donative Transfers)* § 8.5, cmt. e (2003).

161 In re Estate of Peppler, 971 P.2d 694, 696 (Colo.App.1998); Estate of Gonzalez, 126 Cal.Rptr.2d 332 (App.2002).

162 Reed v. Reed, 569 S.W.2d 645 (Tex.Civ.App.1978).

163 Jacobs-Zorne v. Superior Court (Swonetz), 54 Cal.Rptr.2d 385 (App.1996); Matter of Ikuta's Estate, 639 P.2d 400 (Haw.1981).

164 McLendon v. McLendon, 862 S.W.2d 662, 678 (Tex.App.1993); Estate of Wojtalewicz, 418 N.E.2d 418 (Ill.App.1981) ("good faith" challenge to appointment of executor); Matter of Estate of Zarrow, 688 P.2d 47 (Okl.1984) (suit against executor for breach of fiduciary duty).

165 Cal.Prob.Code § 21304 ("a no-contest clause shall be strictly construed"); Haley v. Pickelsimer, 134 S.E.2d 697, 702 (N.C.1964); *Restatement (Third) of Property (Wills and Other Donative Transfers)* § 8.5, cmt. d (2003).

166 Estate of Pittman, 73 Cal.Rptr.2d 622, 631 (App.1998).

167 Gordon, *Forfeiting Trust*, 57 William & Mary L. Rev. 455 (2015).

§ 13.4 Ancillary Administration

Rationale and an Example

The problems of seeking probate of the will and appointment of a personal representative are multiplied if the decedent owned assets in several states. Suppose the decedent was a domiciliary of Maryland, but owned land in Georgia, a bank account in Virginia, stock in a Pennsylvania corporation, and had a tort claim against a resident of Illinois. If a Maryland court appoints the husband personal representative of the will, will the personal representative be able to collect assets and pursue litigation in other states without seeking appointment as a personal representative in the other states in a proceeding known as ancillary administration? The answer will vary depending on the type of asset in question and the rigor with which the state follows the principle that personal representatives are "clothed with authority to administer only such assets as are within the jurisdiction of the court" which appoints them.[168]

This limitation on the powers of personal representatives is usually explained by the need to protect local creditors of the decedent from the need to go to the decedent's domicile to collect their claims.[169] Many have questioned whether this is enough to justify the burden of ancillary administration. Professor Basye called ancillary administration "a wasteful expenditure of time, effort and expense."[170] Often there are no local creditors in the state of ancillary administration, or they are quickly paid and need no protection.[171]

The UPC lessens the need for ancillary administration by giving personal representatives appointed in the state of the decedent's domicile standing to sue in the courts of other jurisdictions.[172] Such a "foreign" personal representative thereby acquires "all powers of a local personal representative," including the right to sue, by filing a copy of their appointment.[173] By taking this action "a foreign personal representative submits personally to the jurisdiction of the Courts of this state,"[174] and so is subject to suit by local creditors. This makes appointment as personal representative in the ancillary jurisdiction unnecessary. Perhaps reflecting the attitudes of a different era, "foreign" in the context of an ancillary administration refers to a different state, not different country.

---

168 Eikel v. Burton, 530 S.W.2d 907, 908 (Tex.Civ.App.1975). *See also* In re Estate of Widmeyer, 741 S.W.2d 758 (Mo. App. 1987). In Eikel, the defendant's failure to object to the plaintiff's standing in the trial court was held to be irrelevant, since "the question is fundamental, going to the jurisdiction of the court," but in Shaw v. Stutchman, 771 P.2d 156 (Nev. 1989), the court held that the defense was waived by failure to raise it in time.

169 Eikel 530 S.W.2d at 909; Chaffin & Barwick, *The Probate and Establishment of Domestic and Foreign Wills,* 13 Ga.L.Rev. 133, 173 (1978); *Restatement (Second) of Conflict of Laws* § 354, cmt. a (1971).

170 Basye, *Dispensing With Administration,* 44 Mich.L.Rev. 329, 409 (1945). *See also* E. Scoles & P. Hay, *Conflict of Laws* § 22.14 (2d ed. 1992).

171 Atkinson, *The Uniform Ancillary Administration and Probate Acts,* 67 Harv.L.Rev. 619, 623 (1954).

172 UPC § 3–703(c). An ancillary administrator, who was appointed by a state in which the decedent was not domiciled but had property, cannot sue to collect property in other states. Matter of Stern, 696 N.E.2d 984 (N.Y.1998).

173 This applies only if no local administration is pending. UPC § 4–204.

174 UPC § 4–301. *See also Restatement (Second) of Conflict of Laws* § 358, cmt. g (1971).

Particular Assets

In practice, the need for ancillary administration depends upon the type of asset and the state where it is located.

1. *Pennsylvania Stock.* If the decedent's interest is represented by a stock certificate in the personal representative's possession that is registered in the decedent's name, the personal representative can have it transferred without ancillary administration. The Second Restatement of Conflicts allows corporations to transfer shares on their books "to any executor or administrator of the decedent who surrenders [the] share certificate" and allows an executor or administrator to sue a corporation which refuses to transfer the shares.[175]

2. *Virginia Bank Account.* Generally, a bank will automatically close a bank account when presented with a copy of the domiciliary letters of appointment, but the extent to which payment to a foreign executor legally discharges a debtor is unclear in many states. The Second Restatement says such payment discharges the debtor "in the absence of knowledge of the appointment of a local executor or administrator,"[176] but not all cases agree.[177] Under the UPC, the bank could safely pay the executor if it waited 60 days after the testator died and got an affidavit from the executor that no local administration was pending.[178] Virginia has a similar statute but it requires publication of notice prior to payment if the amount exceeds $25,000.[179]

3. *Georgia Land.* A personal representative may be able to take possession of the land without dealing with a third party like a bank or the transfer agent of a corporation. If she does so, she can sue trespassers without ancillary administration. Because of her possession the cause of action is regarded as belonging to her as an individual.[180] If she tries to sell the land, however, prospective purchasers will most likely question her title.[181] Consequently, ancillary administration would ordinarily be required except that Georgia is among the states that allow foreign executors to sell land in the state without having to seek a local appointment.[182]

4. *Illinois Tort Claim.* The personal representative may seek to be appointed ancillary administrator in Illinois on the theory that the tort claim

---

[175] *Restatement (Second) of Conflict of Laws* § 324, cmt. c (1971).

[176] *Restatement (Second) of Conflicts of Law* § 329.

[177] Atkinson, *The Uniform Ancillary Administration and Probate Acts*, 67 Harv. L.Rev. at 620.

[178] UPC § 4–201. Compare the affidavit procedure for collecting assets in small estates without any administration. *See* Section 13.2, note 64 et seq.

[179] Va.Code § 64.2–609.

[180] Currie, *The Multiple Personality of the Dead: Executors, Administrators, and the Conflict of Laws*, 33 U. Chicago L. Rev. 429 (1966). Currie adds that this is "arrant nonsense" given the rationale of protecting local creditors, but the distinction is well settled. *Restatement (Second) of Conflicts* § 330 (1971).

[181] Allen v. Amoco Production Co. 833 P.2d 1199 (N.M.App.1992) (deed by Colorado executor ineffective as to New Mexico land); Leggett v. Church of St. Pius, 619 S.W.2d 191 (Tex.Civ.App.1981) (deed to Texas mineral interest by Minnesota executor ineffective); Bell v. King, Phipps & Assoc., P.C., 337 S.E.2d 364 (Ga.App.1985) (Florida executor "had no authority to convey" Georgia land—*but see* note 182).

[182] Ga.Code Ann. § 53–5–42.

constitutes property in Illinois.[183] "The situs of intangible personal estate is . . . where the debtor resides, if there is no instrument evidencing the . . . chose in action[184] . . . A 'cause of action' against an Illinois resident . . . may constitute an asset of an estate."[185]

Identity of Ancillary Administrator

If ancillary administration is necessary, the burden is reduced if the domiciliary representative can also act as the ancillary administrator. However, some states require that administrators be residents of the appointing state.[186] The cost of ancillary administration is increased when different persons must be appointed in each state.[187] The UPC gives a personal representative appointed by the decedent's domicile priority in being appointed ancillary representative if one is needed.[188]

Claims Against a Decedent

Suppose that a resident of Michigan has a claim against a person who died domiciled in Maryland. She could file her claim in Maryland,[189] but she might prefer to sue in Michigan. As a creditor of the decedent, she could begin ancillary administration in Michigan if the decedent owned property there. But if the decedent does not have enough assets in Michigan to satisfy the claim, a Michigan judgment may be worthless in other states. "A judgment against one executor or administrator does not make the facts found by the court in the action res judicata in an action against another executor or administrator of the same decedent."[190] This rule has been much criticized and is changed by the Uniform Probate Code which treats multi-state estates as a unit: "an adjudication rendered in any jurisdiction in favor of or against any personal representative of the estate is as binding on the local personal representative as if he were a party."[191]

Suit Against Foreign Representative

Claimants cannot sue a personal representative of a decedent outside the state which appointed the representative unless a statute provides otherwise. Statutes in many jurisdictions change this rule. The UPC allows domiciliary

---

183 Either domicile or property in a state are the bases of probate jurisdiction. Section 1.2; *cf.* Matter of Guardianship of Bowers, 624 N.Y.S.2d 750 (Sur.1995) (N.Y. has jurisdiction to appoint a guardian to collect N.Y. property of Arizona resident).

184 *See also* UPC § 3–201(d); *cf.* Section 1.2, note 130 et seq.

185 In re Estate of Hoffman, 286 N.E.2d 103, 104 (Ill.App.1972).

186 As to non-resident personal representatives generally, *see* Section 14.6, note 417 et seq.

187 Currie, *The Multiple Personality of the Dead: Executors, Administration, and the Conflict of Laws*, 33 U. Chicago L. Rev. at 433.

188 UPC §§ 3–203(g), 3–611(b); In re Estate of Kuralt, 30 P.3d 345 (Mont.2001) (error not to appoint domiciliary executors to administer Montana property).

189 But the Maryland court might stay proceedings on the claim if it could be tried more conveniently in the state where the tort occurred. V-1 Oil Co. v. Ranck, 767 P.2d 612 (Wyo.1989).

190 *Restatement (Second) of Conflict of Laws* § 356, cmt. b (1971).

191 UPC § 4–401. *See also* Beacham v. Palmer, 523 N.E.2d 1007 (Ill.App.1988) (dismissal of suit against ancillary administrator bars suit against domiciliary).

personal representatives to be sued in any state in which the decedent could have been sued at death.[192]

Distribution of Ancillary Assets

If a decedent had assets in another state and an ancillary administrator collects them, should the administrator, after paying local creditors, remit the balance to the domiciliary executor for distribution there? Yes, under the UPC if the decedent's successors "are identified pursuant to the local law of" the state of ancillary administration.[193] But an Oklahoma court ordered the ancillary administrator of a Texas decedent to distribute the Oklahoma assets directly to the decedent's widow who claimed an elective share of the estate, on the ground that transmitting them to the Texas executor for distribution under to the decedent's will "would defeat the public policy of" Oklahoma.[194]

Planning

The inconvenience of ancillary administration is sometimes advanced as an argument for using will substitutes,[195] because trustees of inter-vivos trusts are not normally appointed by a court, and even a trustee who is so appointed can sue outside the state of appointment.[196] However, if this is the only reason for avoiding probate, the planner should consider whether it will really be a problem in the particular estate. Depending on the nature and location of the client's assets, ancillary administration may be no great inconvenience, or not necessary at all if the relevant states have statutes like the UPC.

§ 13.5 Claims Against Estate

A primary duty of a personal representative is to pay claims against the estate. For most estates, the estate assets are adequate to pay claims and the validity of creditor claims are not at issue. For these estates, the personal representative will typically pay creditors without insisting that they file claims. But if the estate is insufficient to pay all claims or a creditor's bill is in dispute, a prudent personal representative will wait for the creditor to file a claim to sort out priorities or establish the validity of the debt. Traditionally, claims must be filed with the court although the UPC allows claims to be filed directly with the personal representative.[197]

Priorities and Preferences

If its assets are insufficient to pay all claims, the law establishes priorities among creditors. Section 3–805 of the UPC requires payment in the following order: (1) expenses of administration, (2) funeral expenses, (3) debts and taxes

---

192 UPC § 3–703(c). *Compare* Martel v. Stafford, 992 F.2d 1244 (1st Cir.1993) (testator had insufficient contacts) *with* Moore v. Healy, 745 F.Supp. 791 (D.Mass.1990) (testator had sufficient contacts).

193 UPC § 3–816.

194 Estate of Miller v. Miller, 768 P.2d 373, 377 (Okl.App.1988). Under UPC § 2–202, however, the state of the decedent's domicile (Texas) would have governed the widow's elective share, even as to real property in another state.

195 Keydel, *Funding the Revocable Trust*, 14 Prob.Notes 98, 105 (1988).

196 4 Scott & Fratcher, *Trusts* § 280.6 (4th ed. 1989).

197 UPC § 3–806.

preferred under federal law,[198] (4) medical expenses of the decedent's last illness, (5) claims preferred under other state laws, (6) other claims. Claims in the same class must receive an equal pro-rata share.[199] The execution of judgments against a decedent are stayed by death, but not the enforcement of mortgages or other liens.[200] If the mortgage is insufficient to satisfy the claim, the mortgagee can claim the balance as a general creditor.[201]

When a decedent was in bankruptcy at the time of death, the bankruptcy court retains jurisdiction over the decedent's assets and applies bankruptcy rules which differ somewhat from state laws governing insolvent decedent estates.[202]

Normally neither the heirs and devisees nor the personal representative are personally liable for claims against the estate,[203] but a personal representative may incur liability if "due to negligence or wilful default" claims are paid in "such manner so as to deprive the injured claimant of priority."[204]

Non-Claim Statutes

Personal representatives must know the extent of the claims against an estate; otherwise, they may pay a claim in full or distribute to an heir or devisee and later discover that there are not enough assets to satisfy all claims. "Non-claim" statutes protect a personal representative from this possibility by requiring that creditors be notified of the estate proceeding and then barring their claims if not filed within specified time periods. The UPC allows personal representatives to publish in a newspaper of general circulation a notice to creditors to present their claims within four months "or be forever barred."[205] Such statutes were typical in the United States until 1988 when the Supreme Court in Tulsa Professional Collection Services, Inc. v. Pope,[206] held a similar statute unconstitutional because it barred claims without giving adequate notice to creditors. Statutes of limitations bar claims without any notice, but they are "self-executing," whereas non-claim statutes are triggered by "significant state action," the probate court's appointment of a personal representative. Creditors are often unaware of the debtor's death or of the probate proceedings and are unlikely to see "an advertisement in small type

---

[198] The preference for administrative and funeral expenses has been upheld despite a federal statute giving priority to federal claims. Martin v. Dennett, 626 P.2d 473 (Utah 1981).

[199] UPC § 3–805(b).

[200] UPC § 3–812; Lundgren v. Gaudiane, 782 P.2d 285, 288 (Alaska 1989).

[201] UPC § 3–809.

[202] Fed.R.Bank.Proc. 1015.

[203] Bailey v. Cherokee County Appraisal Dist., 862 S.W.2d 581 (Tex.1993) (heirs not personally liable for property taxes on decedent's property during the period of administration). However, under the civil law, the heirs are liable for the decedent's debts and if the decedent died insolvent, the heirs can limit their liability to the decedent's assets. BGB (German Civil Code) §§ 1967(1), 1975.

[204] UPC § 3–807(b). *See also* In re Robinson ex rel. Snell, 754 N.Y.S.2d 525 (Sur.2003) (executor liable to claimant with statutory priority for using estate funds to pay another creditor). *Compare* the liability of fiduciaries for improper distributions to beneficiaries. *See* Section 14.3, note 230 et seq.

[205] UPC § 3–801(a). This bar extends to "the estate, the personal representative, and the heirs and devisees of the decedent." UPC § 3–803(a).

[206] 485 U.S. 478 (1988).

inserted in the back pages of a newspaper." Such notice by publication is sufficient only for creditors who are not "reasonably ascertainable" by the personal representative. Personal representatives must make "a good-faith search of decedent's personal and business financial records . . . in attempting to discover claims."[207] Some unnotified claimants have been barred on the ground that they were not reasonably ascertainable.[208] The courts are split on whether the creditor's knowledge that an estate administration proceeding has been opened is sufficient to excuse notice to the creditor.[209] On the other hand, mere knowledge of the decedent's death has been held insufficient to bar a claimant who was not notified of the time within which claims had to be filed.[210] An important and perhaps obvious distinguishing factor among the cases is whether the creditor had documentation of the debt.[211] The drafters of the UPC responded to the *Tulsa* decision by making the traditional publication of notice to creditors optional, on the ground that it "is quite expensive in some populous areas" and under *Tulsa* "is useless except as to bar unknown creditors."[212] The UPC also allows the personal representative to give notice to creditors "by mail or other delivery." This notice bars creditors 60 days "after the mailing or other delivery." To avoid the claim bar, a creditor may either file a claim with the clerk of court or deliver or mail to the personal representative "a written statement of the claim, indicating its basis."[213]

The UPC also bars all claims, whether or not notice was given, which are not filed within one year after the decedent's death.[214] Similar statutes have been enacted in many other states.[215] Because these latter statutes run from the decedent's death, these statutes are "self-executing" and have withstood constitutional challenge.[216]

---

207 Matter of Estate of Anderson, 615 N.E.2d 1197, 1206 (Ill.App.1993).

208 U.S. Trust Co. v. Haig, 694 So. 2d 769 (Fla. Dist. Ct. App. 1997); Matter of Estate of Ragsdale, 879 P.2d 1145 (Kan.App.1994); Jones v. Sun Bank/Miami, N.A., 609 So.2d 98 (Fla. Dist. Ct. App. 1992); In re Estate of Thompson, 484 N.W.2d 258 (Minn.App.1992).

209 *Knowledge of estate excused notice to claimant:* Venturi v. Taylor, 41 Cal.Rptr.2d 272, 276 (App.1995); Matter of Estate of Sutherland, 593 N.E.2d 955 (Ill.App.1992); *Knowledge of estate did not excuse notice to claimant:* In re Estate of Kotowski, 704 N.W.2d 522 (Minn.App.2005); In re Estate of Emery, 606 N.W.2d 750 (Neb.2000); Armstrong v. Armstrong, 130 F.R.D. 449 (D.Colo.1990).

210 In re Estate of Malone, 556 N.E.2d 678 (Ill.App.1990); Matter of Estate of Anderson, 821 P.2d 1169 (Utah 1991). *But see* In re Estate of Reynolds, 970 P.2d 537, 545 (Kan.1998). For an analysis of the case law of a particular jurisdiction, namely Florida, on who is and who is not a known or reasonably ascertainable creditor, *see* Karibjanian & Galler, *Revisiting Pope and Creditors' Rights*, Prob. & Prop., Sept./Oct. 2016, at 40; Camp, *Pope's Projeny*, 28 Nova L. Rev. 157 (2003).

211 *Compare* Jones v. Sun Bank/Miami, N.A., 609 So. 2d 98 (Fla. Dist Ct. App.,1992); *with* Miller v. Estate of Baer, 837 So.2d 448 (Fla. Dist. Ct. App. 2002), and Strulowitz v. Cadle Company, II, Inc., 839 So.2d 876 (Fla. Dist. Ct. App. 2003).

212 UPC § 3–801, cmt.

213 UPC § 3–804. A writing with the name of the claimant and the amount of the claim without stating the basis for it was held insufficient under a similar statute. Villegas v. McBride, 50 P.3d 678 (Wash.App.2002).

214 UPC § 3–803(a).

215 *See, e.g.*, Mo. Rev. Stat. § 473.444.

216 *See, e.g.*, State ex rel. Houska v. Dickhaner, 323 S.W.3d 29 (Mo.2010).

There are several exceptions to the non-claim bar.

1. *Suit Pending.* A claimant who had a suit pending against the decedent at the time of the decedent's death need not present the claim in the estate proceedings under the UPC.[217] Some courts have held otherwise, however, on the ground that personal representatives should not be forced to search the court records to discover suits against the deceased.[218]

2. *Claims Arising After Death.* Claims which arise after the decedent's death are treated differently. Under the UPC they can be presented within 4 months after performance is due (contracts) or the claim arises (other claims).[219] But some states impose no special claim bar for claims arising after death.[220]

Claims which are only potential at the time of the decedent's death are troublesome. For example, a partner guaranteed the debt of a partnership. The partnership defaulted after the partner died. The court allowed a claim on the guaranty after the non-claim period had run, saying: "The filing of a contingent claim . . . is not required. . . . To reserve against such contingencies may greatly impede the full distribution of an estate . . . contrary to the policy of speedy and efficient administration of estates.[221] Many non-claim statutes, however, expressly apply to claims "whether due, or to become due, absolute or contingent."[222] This means contingent claims must be *presented,* but they are not necessarily *paid* during administration because it is difficult to ascertain the amount due. Under the UPC, the claimant may accept the present value of the claim "taking any uncertainty into account," or can insist on an arrangement for future payment, such as a bond from the distributees of the estate.[223]

3. *Governmental Claims.* The UPC non-claim provision expressly includes claims by the state or its agencies,[224] but some states treat them as

---

217 UPC § 3–804(2); Reese v. Reese, 637 P.2d 1183 (Mont.1981).

218 In re Worrell's Estate, 442 N.E.2d 211 (Ill.1982). *See also* Fox v. Woods, 382 So.2d 1118 (Ala.1980) (suit pending in a foreign jurisdiction). *But cf.* Berke v. First Nat. Bank & Trust Co., 397 N.E.2d 842 (Ill.1979) (substitution of executor for defendant in pending action satisfies statute).

219 UPC § 3–803(b); In Matter of Estate of Scott, 735 P.2d 924 (Colo.App.1986) (claim for reformation of deed given by executor "arises" only when mistake is discovered).

220 In Cardwell v. Estate of Kirkendall, 712 N.E.2d 1047, 1049 (Ind. App.1999), a letter sent to the executor's attorney was held to satisfy a similar statute. *See also* In re Estate of Tollison, 463 S.E.2d 611 (S.C. App. 1995). But not a letter sent to the decedent under the assumption he was still alive. In re Estate of Beider, 645 N.E.2d 553 (Ill. App. 1994).

221 Security S & L v. Estate of Kite, 857 P.2d 430, 433 (Colo.App.1992). *But see* Poleson v. Wills, 998 P.2d 469 (Colo.App.2000) (malpractice claim against lawyer for failure to shield client from liability which arose after lawyer died barred by non-claim statute); Eresian v. Mattei, 750 N.E.2d 30 (Mass.App.2001) (claim which matured 8 years after debtor died barred because estate had been distributed).

222 UPC § 3–803(a).

223 UPC § 3–810(b); *cf.* Ind.Code § 29–1–14–8 (creditor can sue distributees if contingent claim becomes absolute after estate distributed); Iowa Code § 633.427 (same); *cf.* Cohen v. Cronin, 346 N.E.2d 524 (N.Y.1976) (fund to pay contingent claim retained when balance of estate distributed).

224 UPC § 3–803(a).

exceptions.[225] The federal government is not subject to state non-claim statutes,[226] but the Internal Revenue Code contains comparable provisions discharging a personal representative from liability for unpaid taxes of which the Service fails to notify the personal representative within nine months of a request therefor.[227]

4. *Recoupment.* If an estate sues on a claim due to the estate, many courts allow the debtor to assert by recoupment a claim against the estate even if the period allowed by the non-claim statute has expired,[228] but there is also contrary authority.[229]

5. *Insurance.* Most non-claim statutes apply to tort as well as contract claims, but such a statute does not apply to the extent the tort is covered by liability insurance: "a failure to file within the statutory period bars only the right to enforce any liability of the estate beyond the limits of the insurance policy."[230]

6. *Debts and Expense Provision.* A direction in the will to pay the decedent's debts does not extend the time limit for filing claims. A claim against an estate for services rendered during the testator's last illness was rejected as untimely even though the will directed the executor "to pay the expenses of my last sickness . . . and all of my other just debts."[231]

7. *Property.* If a personal representative erroneously inventories property which did not belong to the testator, the owner need not file a claim within the non-claim period to protect her property.[232] The "property" exception has been held to cover claims for specific performance of contracts,[233] including contracts to devise property,[234] and even a claim for rescission by a purchaser who could trace the price paid.[235] Also, persons holding mortgages

---

[225] In re Estate of Cahill, 131 S.W.3d 859 (Mo.Ct.App.2004); Ohio Dept. of Human Services v. Eastman, 763 N.E.2d 193 (Ohio App.2001); *cf.* State ex rel. Department of Human Resources v. Payne, 970 P.2d 266 (Or.App.1998) (time limit on suit after rejection of claim by personal representative not applicable to claim by state agency); Cal.Prob.Code §§ 9200 et seq. (special time periods prescribed for claims by various "public entities").

[226] United States v. Summerlin, 310 U.S. 414 (1940).

[227] Int. Rev. Code §§ 2204, 6905; *cf.* Bank of Kansas City v. District Director, 721 S.W.2d 226 (Mo.App.W.D.1986).

[228] Estate of Ruehl v. Ruehl, 623 N.E.2d 741 (Ohio Mun.1993); In re Estate of Massie, 353 N.W.2d 735 (Neb.1984).

[229] In re Estate of Kremer, 546 N.E.2d 1047, 1052 (Ill.App.1989).

[230] Corlett v. Smith, 763 P.2d 1172, 1174–75 (N.M.App.1988). *But cf.* Turner v. Lo Shee Pang's Estate, 631 P.2d 1010 (Wash.App.1981) (even claim covered by insurance is barred after 18 months). *See also* In re Daigle's Estate, 634 P.2d 71 (Colo. 1981). But cf. Turner v. Lo Shee Pang's Estate, 631 P.2d 1010 (Wash. App. 1981) (even claim covered by insurance is barred after 18 months; Scott v. Scott, 918 P.2d 198 (Wyo. 1996).

[231] In re Bachand's Estate, 307 N.W.2d 140 (S.D.1981). *See also* Farm Credit Bank v. Brown, 577 N.E.2d 906, 912 (Ill. App. 1991).

[232] In re Estate of Kolbinger, 529 N.E.2d 823, 827 (Ill.App.1988); Lewis v. Steinreich, 652 N.E.2d 981, 984 (Ohio 1995); Gottwig v. Blaine, 795 P.2d 1196, 1199 (Wash.App.1990).

[233] Hackmann v. Dawley, 663 N.E.2d 1342 (Ohio App.1995).

[234] In re Shepley's Estate, 645 P.2d 605 (Utah 1982); O'Steen v. Wineberg's Estate, 640 P.2d 28 (Wash.App.1982); L.G. v. F.G.H., 729 S.W.2d 634 (Mo.App.1987). *But see* In re Estate of Berg, 713 N.W.2d 87 (N.D. 2006); Young v. Wheeler. 676 P.2d 748 (Kan. 1984); Grossman v. Selawacz, 417 So.2d 728 (Fla. Dist. Ct. App. 1982) (promise to sell unidentifiable property).

[235] Pay Less Drug Stores v. Bechdolt, 155 Cal.Rptr. 58 (App.1979).

and other security interests in estate assets are not required to present their claims unless their security is insufficient and they wish to collect the deficiency from the decedent's other assets.[236]

8. *Estoppel.* Sometimes a personal representative is "estopped" to raise the non-claim bar, for example, "where an estate . . . makes representations to the claimant which lead the claimant to believe that it is not necessary to protect his claim by filing a creditor's claim."[237] Other courts have rejected estoppel claims on the ground that "the personal representative is a trustee of the estate for the benefit of its creditors and heirs, and as such cannot by his conduct waive any provision of a statute affecting their substantial rights."[238] The UPC allows personal representatives to "waive any defense of limitations available to the estate" only "with the consent of all whose interests would be affected."[239]

Statute of Limitations

Non-claim statutes can operate more harshly than ordinary statutes of limitations, which often do not run until a claimant has reason to know of the claim or are tolled while a claimant is unable to sue. Non-claim statutes resemble statutes of limitation but they have different purposes and operate independently. A claim that is presented within the limits of a non-claim statute may be dismissed because the statute of limitations has run and vice-versa. If a claim is not yet due—for example, a note payable in 2020, the non-claim period may expire even before the statute of limitations starts to run, because the former is designed "not to prevent the litigation of stale claims, but to facilitate the speedy settlement of estates."[240]

Special provisions apply when a debtor dies while the statute of limitations is running, because the creditor has no one to sue until administration of the debtor's estate begins. The Uniform Probate Code suspends the running of any statute of limitations for four months following the decedent's death. Presentation of a claim is treated as "equivalent to commencement of a proceeding," so the statute of limitations stops running when a claim is presented.[241] But if the personal representative "disallows" a

---

[236] UPC § 3–803(c)(1); WYHY Federal Credit Union v. Burchell, 643 P.2d 471 (Wyo.1982); Estate of Ripley v. Mortgage One Corp., 16 S.W.3d 593 (Mo.App.1999) (mortgagee entitled to lien on proceeds of sale of mortgaged property despite failure to file claim in time).

[237] Boyer v. Sparboe, 867 P.2d 1116, 1119–20 (Mont.1994). *See also* De Avila v. Estate of DeHerrera, 75 P.3d 1144 (Colo. App. 2003).

[238] In re Estate of Ongaro, 998 P.2d 1097, 1104 (Colo.2000). *See also* Estate of Decker v. Farm Credit Services, 684 N.E.2d 1137 (Ind.1997) (court is without power to extend limits of non-claim statute). *See also* Estate of Decker v. Farm Credit Services, 684 N.E.2d 1137 (Ind. 1997) (court is without power to extend limits of non-claim statute); Secrest v. Citizens National Bank, 796 N.E.2d 999 (Ohio App. 1999).

[239] UPC § 3–802(a).

[240] State v. Goldfarb, 278 A.2d 818, 821 (Conn.1971).

[241] UPC § 3–802. *See also* Brown v. Eiguren, 628 P.2d 299 (Nev.1981) (can sue within one year of appointment of personal representative if claim not barred when decedent dies); Shearer v. Pla-Boy Inc., 538 N.E.2d 247 (Ind. App. 1989).

claim which has been timely presented, the claimant must bring suit within 60 days.[242]

Court Approval

In some states courts closely supervise the payment of claims by personal representatives, like other aspects of administration. In Mississippi, claims against an estate must be "registered, probated, and allowed" in court, and personal representatives may be surcharged for paying an otherwise valid claim which was not "probated, allowed and registered."[243] The UPC in keeping with its goal to simplify administration, allows personal representatives to "pay any just claim which has not been barred, with or without presentation."[244] A personal representative can compromise claims if it appears to be "for the best interest of the estate."[245] Many states make special provisions for any claims that personal representatives have against the estate because of the conflict of interest involved. In Ohio, such claims must be "proved to and allowed by the probate court" after notice to the decedent's heirs and devisees.[246]

Personal representatives may be surcharged for paying invalid claims,[247] but the UPC allows them to "satisfy written charitable pledges of the decedent" even if they are not binding obligations or properly presented "if in the judgment of the personal representative the decedent would have wanted the pledges completed."[248]

§ 13.6 Claims Against Nonprobate Assets

Traditionally, nonprobate assets were not reachable by general creditors of the decedent even if the probate estate was insufficient to pay claims. But as the growing use of nonprobate transfers decreases the pool of probate assets, state legislatures and courts have increasingly subjected nonprobate assets to creditor claims.

Uniform Probate Code

The most comprehensive approach it taken in UPC § 6–102, which was added to the Code in 1998.[249] This provision subjects beneficiaries of nonprobate transfers to liability to the extent of the property received if the

---

242 UPC § 3–806. *See also* First Interstate Bank v. Haynes, 699 P.2d 1168 (Or. App. 1985); In re Estate of Levine, 700 P.2d 883 (Ariz. App. 1985); In re Estate of Mayfield, 771 P.2d 179 (N.M. 1989).

243 Miss.Code §§ 91–7–151, 91–7–155; Harper v. Harper, 491 So.2d 189 (Miss.1986).

244 UPC § 3–807(b). However, a personal representative risks personal liability if claims are paid before the non-claim period expires and the estate is insolvent.

245 UPC § 3–813; Matter of Estate of Vertin, 352 N.W.2d 200 (N.D.1984). Trustees have a similar power. UTC §§ 811, cmt., 816(14); *Restatement (Third) of Trusts* § 78, cmt. d (2007).

246 Ohio Rev.Code § 2117.01. *See also* Ind.Code § 29–1–14–17 (special personal representative appointed unless all interested persons consent in writing to claim). *Compare* the need for court authorization for other types of self-dealing. *See* Section 14.1, note 22 et seq.

247 Estate of Sturm, 246 Cal.Rptr. 852 (App.1988) (claims paid which were time-barred); Estate of Stellwag v. Kennedy, 817 S.W.2d 466 (Mo.App.1990) (same).

248 UPC § 3–715(4).

249 For an analysis of this provision, *see* Gagliardi, *Remembering the Creditor at Death: Aligning Probate and Nonprobate Transfers*, 41 Real Prop. Prob. & Tr. J. 819 (2007).

debtor's probate estate is insufficient to satisfy claims. Survivorship interests in joint tenancy in real estate are expressly excluded from the reach of creditors of a deceased joint tenant.[250] Also excludable is life insurance eligible for statutory exemptions.[251]

Claimants entitled to recover under Section 6–102 include not only creditors but also a spouse or children entitled to statutory allowances.[252] Creditors who wish to reach nonprobate assets under the UPC cannot do so directly. Instead, they must notify the personal representative to proceed on their behalf. This prevents a free-for-all among creditors and assures that the statutory priorities in paying claims of an insolvent estate will control.[253]

Subjecting nonprobate transfers to creditors' claims can have unpleasant consequences for transferees. For example, a surviving party to a joint bank account withdraws and spends the funds without knowing that the decedent died insolvent. Should a creditor later successfully pursue a claim against the joint tenant, the joint tenant may be forced to make restitution. This does not happen when property passes through probate because the property is usually not distributed until all claims against the estate have been paid.[254] To guard against undue hardship, the UPC imposes a limit of one year from the decedent's death on enforcement of claims against non-probate transferees.[255]

Revocable Trusts

An increasing number of courts and state legislatures allow the decedent's creditors to reach the assets of a trust that was revocable by the decedent at death, at least if the settlor's probate estate is insufficient to satisfy claims.[256] Under the UPC, this is part of a comprehensive statute potentially allowing the creditor to reach other non-probate assets.[257] Under the Uniform Trust Code (UTC), the provision pertains only to revocable trusts.[258] Both the UPC and UTC also allow creditors to reach the revocable trust and, in the case of the UPC, other non-probate assets, in satisfaction of statutory allowances, which would include the family allowance, homestead and exempt property.[259] The California Probate Code imposes time limits on claims against a revocable

---

250 On the other hand, property held in joint tenancy is included in the "estate" of a decedent who has received Medicaid for purposes of reimbursement claims under 42 U.S.C. § 1396p(b)(4)(B).

251 UPC § 6–102(b) & cmt., par. 2.

252 UPC § 6–102(b).

253 As to these priorities, *see* Section 13.5, note 198 et seq.

254 However, UPC § 3–909 contemplates recovery from a distributee when property is improperly distributed. California Probate Code § 11622 allows courts to require a bond from persons who receive an early distribution "conditioned on payment of the distributee's proper share of the debts of the estate."

255 UPC § 6–102(h).

256 UPC § 6–102; Cal.Prob.Code § 19001; Matter of Estate of Nagel, 580 N.W.2d 810 (Iowa 1998); State Street Bank v. Reiser, 389 N.E.2d 768 (Mass. App.1979); UTC § 505(a)(3); *Restatement (Second) of Property (Donative Transfers)* § 34.3(3) (1992);. *Restatement (Third) of Trusts* § 25, cmt. e (2001).

257 UPC § 6–102.

258 UTC § 505(a)(3).

259 But not the elective share of the surviving spouse. In re Estate of Chrisp, 759 N.W.2d 87 (Neb. 2009).

trust after the settlor's death[260] analogous to those on claims against a deceased debtor's probate estate.[261]

Joint Tenancy

Traditionally, property in joint tenancy cannot be reached by creditors of a joint tenant after that joint tenant's death, even if the husband had mortgaged or pledged the property,[262] although this rule has been changed by statute in some states.[263] If a lien is foreclosed by sale before the joint tenant dies, this severs the joint tenancy so the creditor prevails.[264] But sophisticated creditors can protect themselves by getting all joint tenants to sign a note when they extend credit.[265]

Tenancy by the Entirety

In some states when land is held jointly by two spouses as tenants by the entirety, creditors of one spouse cannot reach it either during the spouse's lifetime or after death.[266] Even where tenancy by the entirety is recognized, federal tax liens against one spouse can be enforced.[267]

Multiple-Person Bank Accounts

The UPC multiple-person account provisions, which have been widely enacted in the states, subjects joint and payable-on-death bank accounts to claims if the decedent debtor's probate estate is insufficient to satisfy them.[268] However, this provision was not extended to securities registered in TOD form when the Code authorized this form of nonprobate transfer in 1989.[269] But the pendulum swung again in 2009. The Uniform Real Property Transfer on Death Act, approved in 2009, imposes liability on the beneficiary of a TOD deed for claims to the extent the probate estate is insufficient.[270]

---

[260] Cal.Prob.Code § 19100; *cf.* Dobler v. Arluk Medical Center Indus. Group, 107 Cal.Rptr.2d 478 (App.2001) (timely filing of claim in probate proceedings satisfies statute and allows creditor to proceed against trust assets).

[261] *See* Section 13.5, note 201 et seq.

[262] Webster v. Mauz, 702 P.2d 297 (Colo.App.1985); In re Certificates of Deposit, 569 N.E.2d 484 (Ohio 1991); Kalk v. Security Pacific Bank Washington, 894 P.2d 559 (Wash.1995). *Contra,* Heffernan v. Wollaston Credit Union, 567 N.E.2d 933, 939 (Mass.App.1991); Dieden v. Schmidt, 128 Cal.Rptr.2d 365 (App.2002) (lien created before property put into joint tenancy survives joint tenant's death).

[263] Wis.Stat. § 700.24; Conn.Gen.Stat. § 47–14e. If a state follows the theory that a mortgage conveys "title" to the mortgagee, the mortgage severs the joint tenancy even if it is later paid off. Mattis, *Joint Tenancy: Notice of Severance; Mortgages and Survivorship,* 7 N.Ill.U.L.Rev. 41, 47–48 (1986).

[264] Jolley v. Corry, 671 P.2d 139 (Utah 1983).

[265] Bahler v. Doenges, 499 N.E.2d 35 (Ohio App.1986) (land held by the entireties subject to liens against both spouses).

[266] *See also* Central Nat'l Bank v. Fitzwilliam, 465 N.E.2d 408 (Ohio 1984); Hinchee v. Security Nat. Bank, 624 P.2d 821 (Alaska 1981); Matter of Savage's Estate, 650 S.W.2d 346 (Mo.App.1983); Effland, *Creditors and Non-Probate Assets,* 48 Mo.L.Rev. 431, 437 (1983); Danforth, *Rethinking the Law of Creditors' Rights in Trusts,* 53 Hastings L.J. 287, 333–37 (2002).

[267] United States v. Craft, 535 U.S. 274 (2002).

[268] UPC § 6–215 (1989). This provision was superseded by Section 6–102, discussed *supra* note 246 et seq., but remains in effect in numerous states.

[269] McGovern, *Nonprobate Transfers Under the Revised Uniform Probate Code,* 55 Alb.L.Rev. 1329, 1347 (1992).

[270] Unif. Real Property Transfer on Death Act § 15.

Life Insurance

Many states exempt life insurance policies in whole or in part from claims of the insured's creditors except when paid to the decedent's estate.[271] Life insurance can provide greater protection against creditors than trusts. In the case of a revocable trust, in most states, the settlor's creditors can reach the trust assets both during the settlor's life and at death.[272] But in many states creditors of the insured may not reach the cash surrender value during the insured's life[273] or the proceeds at death.[274] Some states limit the amount exempt from creditor claims. In California, the loan value of unmatured life insurance policies is exempt from creditors only up to $9,700, and the proceeds of matured policies only "to the extent reasonably necessary for the support of the judgment debtor and the spouse and dependents of the judgment debtor."[275] But care should be designated on how the beneficiary is designated. If the life insurance is payable to the probate estate, the insurance is normally subject to claims of the decedent's creditors. The same result may occur if the insurance is payable to a revocable trust that is reachable by the decedent's creditors, particularly if the insurance is available to pay the decedent's debts.[276]

---

[271] Estate of Chiesi v. First Citizens Bank, 613 N.E.2d 14 (Ind.1993).

[272] *See supra* note 251 et seq.

[273] In re Marriage of Gedgaudas, 978 P.2d 677 (Colo.App.1999) (cash surrender value of insurance exempt up to $25,000). In contrast to term insurance "cash value insurance provides insurance protection and a fund that is sheltered from creditors and that accumulates earnings . . . free of tax to the policy owner . . . which is available to the policy owner prior to maturity of the policy." Price, *Contemporary Estate Planning* § 6.8 (2014 ed.).

[274] In re Estate of Grigg, 545 N.E.2d 160, 161 (Ill.App.1989).

[275] Cal.Code Civ.Proc. § 704.100.

[276] Difilippo v. Reed, 269 P.3d 1189 (Ariz. Ct. App. 2012) (insurance exemption statute controls over UTC unless protection of insurance exemption statute waived in trust document).

Chapter 14

FIDUCIARY DUTIES AND ADMINISTRATION

Analysis

Sec.

14.1 Duty of Loyalty.
14.2 Investments.
14.3 Duty to Inform and Account.
14.4 Other Duties.
14.5 Administrative Powers.
14.6 Selection of Fiduciary.
14.7 Compensation.
14.8 Remedies of Beneficiaries.
14.9 Relationships with Third Parties.

§ 14.1 Duty of Loyalty

Trustees must "administer the trust solely in the interests of the beneficiaries."[1] This so-called "duty of loyalty" also applies to other fiduciaries, including personal representatives[2] and agents under powers of attorney.[3] Similar language in ERISA governs fiduciaries of pension plans.[4]

The duty of loyalty proscribes transactions in which the trustee places the interests of anyone, either the trustee itself or of others, above the interests of the beneficiaries. Transactions in which the trustee uses trust assets for the trustee's own personal benefit are characterized as "self-dealing." Self-dealing includes the purchase of trust assets by the trustee, the sale of the trustee's own assets to the trust, the trustee's leasing of trust assets, and the trustee's "borrowing" of trust funds.[5] Because of the risks involved to the beneficiaries' interests, self-dealing is subject to a *no further inquiry* rule, which was formulated in its modern form in a famous opinion of Judge Cardozo.[6] A self-dealing transaction is voidable by the beneficiaries regardless of whether the trustee was acting in good faith and the transaction was reasonable. The beneficiaries may hold the trustee accountable for any profit made, compel the

---

1 Unif. Trust Code (UTC) § 802(a); *Restatement (Third) of Trusts* § 78(1) (2007).For an analysis of the duty of loyalty under the UTC, *see* Newman, *Trust Law in the Twenty-First Century: Challenges to Fiduciary Accountability*, 29 Quinnipiac Prob. L.J. 261, 273–80 (2016).

2 *See, e.g.*, In re Rothko, 372 N.E.2d 291 (N.Y.1977).

3 First National Bank v. Cooper, 312 S.E.2d 607 (Ga.1984) (agent cannot use principal's property to secure loan to agent).

4 29 U.S.C. § 1104(a)(1).

5 *Restatement (Third) of Trusts* § 78, cmt. d (2007).

6 Meinhard v. Salmon, 164 N.E. 545 (N.Y.1928).

return of the property to the trust or, if the property has been transferred to a bona fide purchaser, compel the trustee to restore the lost value. Because self-dealing transactions are only "voidable," the beneficiaries can affirm them. "If the transaction proves profitable to the trust, . . . the beneficiary will likely allow it to stand."[7] The opportunities to speculate at the fiduciary's expense by postponing their choice to affirm or disaffirm may be barred either by a statute of limitations or laches defense if the beneficiaries wait too long.[8]

It does not matter that a disinterested co-trustee approved a self-dealing transaction.[9] In this respect trustees differ from directors of corporations, who also are fiduciaries. A court approved a charitable corporation's exchange of stock with a company which had the same directors. For corporations such transactions are valid if approved by disinterested directors or if the directors establish the fairness of the transaction. "The founder of a charitable trust . . . imposes upon its trustees the strict and unyielding rules principles of trust law. By contrast, the founder of a charitable corporation . . . invokes the far more flexible and adaptable principles of corporate law."[10]

The duty of loyalty goes beyond self-dealing. The statement often quoted that one may not serve two masters is applicable here. Even though the trustee may not be engaged in a transaction with the trust *individually*, there may nonetheless be a violation of the duty of loyalty if the trustee is acting on behalf of *others* to whom the trustee also owes obligations. For example, duty of loyalty issues arise often when a personal representative or trustee has ties to a company which deals with the estate or trust. An executor's sale of stock to a company of which he was an officer and director was set aside under a statute barring executors from buying estate property "directly or indirectly."[11] A trustee was surcharged for making investments in companies of which he was the president.[12] However, some conflicts of interest are deemed insubstantial; a court vacated a sale of stock by a corporate trustee to its president but not a sale to a stockholder of the trustee.[13] The key here is establishing that a transaction was affected by the conflict of interest.[14] Additionally, trustees may not "personally acquire a business that competes with the business activities

---

[7] UTC § 802, cmt.

[8] *See* Section 14.8, note 738 et seq.; *cf.* UTC § 802(b)(3) (beneficiaries' claims barred by running of statute of limitations).

[9] Matter of Garwood's Estate, 400 N.E.2d 758 (Ind.1980) (sale by co-executors to one of them voided); Stegemeier v. Magness, 728 A.2d 557 (Del.1999) (sale by estate to company owned by an administrator is voidable although approved by a disinterested administrator).

[10] Oberly v. Kirby, 592 A.2d 445, 466–67 (Del.1991).

[11] In re Estate of Martin, 86 Cal.Rptr.2d 37 (App.1999). *See also* Furr v. Hall, 553 S.W. 2d 666 (Tex. Civ. App. 1977); Lincoln National Bank v. Shriners Hospitals, 588 N.E.2d 597 (Ind. App. 1992); UTC § 802(c)(4) (transaction with a business entity in which the trustee has an interest that might affect the trustee's best judgment).

[12] Wheeler v. Mann, 763 P.2d 758 (Utah 1988). *See also* In re Estate of Stowell, 595 A.2d 1022 (Me. 1991) (loans by executor to companies in which he was interested).

[13] Steiner v. Hawaiian Trust Co., 393 P.2d 96, 104 (Haw.1964). As to transactions between a bank trustee and its commercial customers, compare Brock v. Citizens Bank, 841 F.2d 344 (10th Cir. 1988) (loan by trustee to persons who had borrowed from bank allowed) with InterFirst State Bank Dallas, N.A. v. Risser, 739 S.W.2d 882 (Tex. App. 1987) (sale of stock at inadequate price to commercial customer at inadequate price to commercial customer of trustee warrants punitive damages).

[14] UTC § 802(b).

of the trust" or acquire stock in a company in which the trustee owns so a large block of stock that there would be "a temptation to consider the trustee's own advantage" in deciding whether to sell or retain the stock.[15]

Lawyers who represent a family with a business may also encounter conflicts of interest. A lawyer who represented an estate was held liable for a below-market-value sale made by the estate to a client of the lawyer; the lawyer had recommended the sale without disclosing the conflict of interest.[16] Lawyers involved in self-dealing while acting as fiduciaries have been subjected to discipline under the rules of professional conduct.[17]

There is some uncertainty on how to apply the duty of loyalty to transactions between the trustee and relatives of the trustee. Should the relative be treated as the trustee's alter ego, in which case the transaction is voidable under the no further inquiry rule? Or is the relationship irrelevant? Does the closeness of the relationship make a difference? Courts have classified a sale to an executor's spouse as self-dealing,[18] but are split on whether to apply the duty to transactions with a fiduciary's children.[19]

The Uniform Trust Code (UTC) creates an intermediate category for transactions with relatives. A transaction between the trustee and the trustee's spouse, descendants, siblings, parents, or their spouses is presumed to be affected by a conflict of interest. Also presumptively affected by a conflict of interest are transactions with the trustee's agent or attorney and any business entity in which the trustee, or person that owns a significant interest in, the trustee, has an interest that might affect the trustee's best judgment.[20] As stated in the comments, "[a]mong the factors tending to rebut the presumption are whether the consideration was fair and whether the other terms of the transaction are similar to those that would be transacted with an independent party."[21]

Exceptions: Court Approval

Probably the most often quoted passage in a judicial opinion about trustees dealt with the duty of loyalty. "A trustee is held to something stricter than the morals of the market place. Uncompromising rigidity has been the attitude of courts of equity when petitioned to undermine the rule of undivided

---

15 *Restatement (Third) of Trusts* § 78, cmt. e (2007).

16 Kelly v. Foster, 813 P.2d 598 (Wash.App.1991).

17 In re Conduct of Carey, 767 P.2d 438 (Or.1989) (lawyer reprimanded for lending money as guardian to his secretary); Office of Disciplinary Counsel v. Kurtz, 693 N.E.2d 1080 (Ohio 1998) (lawyer-trustee suspended for lending trust funds to self); In re Gordon, 524 N.E.2d 547 (Ill.1988) (attorney for estate suspended for lending estate funds to a person for whom he had guaranteed a loan); In re Cohen, 8 P.3d 429 (Colo.1999) (lawyer suspended for loan of trust funds to company which lawyer represented).

18 Hartman v. Hartle, 122 A. 615 (N.J. Ct. Ch. 1923).

19 In re Estate of Hughes, 641 N.E.2d 248, 251 (Ohio App.1994) (not self-dealing); Cudworth v. Cudworth, 312 N.W.2d 331 (N.D.1981) (self-dealing).

20 UTC § 802(c). *See also Restatement (Third) of Trusts* § 78, cmt. e (2007).

21 UTC § 802, cmt. For the debate concerning whether UTC § 802(c) is an appropriate provision, *compare* Langbein, *Questioning the Trust Law Duty of Loyalty: Sole Interest or Best Interest*, 114 Yale L.J. 929 (2005), *with* Leslie, *In Defense of the No Further Inquiry Rule: A Response to Professor Langbein*, 47 Wm. & Mary L. Rev. 541 (2005).

loyalty by particular exceptions."[22] In fact, the "rule of undivided loyalty" is subject to numerous exceptions. Otherwise, it would pose serious difficulties for estates or trusts which need to sell property for which there is an inadequate market, like a family corporation, where the fiduciary may be the most likely buyer.[23]

The UTC permits transactions that would otherwise violate the duty of loyalty if "the transaction is authorized by the terms of the trust; . . . the transaction was approved by the court; . . . [or] the beneficiary consented to the trustee's conduct, ratified the transaction, or released the trustee."[24] Courts usually approve such transactions only when the advantages are clear, *e.g.*, if "there are no other available purchasers willing to pay the same price the trustee is willing to pay."[25] Approval need not precede the transaction. A conservator's sale of a house to his daughter, though not approved by a court at the time, was not subject to challenge because "his acts as conservator . . . were approved by the court in its orders approving his annual accountings."[26]

Authorization in Instrument

Self-dealing is proper if it is authorized by the will or trust,[27] but a broadly drafted power may not be sufficient. A court set aside sales by an executor to himself even though the will allowed the executor to sell to "any purchaser."[28] Even explicit authorization for self-dealing does not permit a trustee to "act in bad faith or unfairly."[29] A trust allowed the trustees to lease trust property to their automobile dealership, but they were surcharged for making the lease without any "determination whether the rental rates were reasonable in the current market."[30] However, sales which are personally advantageous to the

---

22 Meinhard v. Salmon, 164 N.E. 545, 546 (N.Y.1928) (Cardozo J.). The parties in this case were coventurers rather than trustees but this made no difference to Cardozo J. For a critique of the "rhetorical excesses of fiduciary law, exemplified in Cardozo's incessantly cited opinion in *Meinhard v. Salmon,*" *see* Langbein, *The Contractarian Basis of Trust Law,* 105 Yale L.J. 625, 658 (1995).

23 Wellman, *Punitive Surcharges Against Disloyal Fiduciaries,* 77 Mich.L.Rev. 95, 114 (1978). *See also Restatement (Third) of Trusts* § 78, cmt. b (2007) (rejecting idea that there are no exceptions to duty of loyalty).

24 UTC § 802(b); *Restatement (Third) of Trusts* § 78, cmt. c (2007). *See., e.g.,* In re CVR 1997 Irrevocable Trust, 42 P.3d 605, 609 (Ariz. App. 2002) (trustee "properly resolved any conflict: of interest by obtaining "instructions from the probate court").

25 Wachovia Bank and Trust Co. v. Johnston, 153 S.E.2d 449, 460 (N.C.1967).

26 Matter of Conservatorship of Holman, 849 P.2d 140, 142 (Kan.App.1993). For circumstances where court approval of an account is not a defense to a breach of fiduciary duty, *see* Section 14.8, note 678 et seq.

27 UTC § 802(b)(1). For a suggested clause authorizing self-dealing with respect to works of art in an estate, *see* Hader, *Making the Intangible Tangible: Planning for Intellectual Property,* 29 Est. Plan. 574, 576 (2002). The author suggests that even with this clause, "it may nevertheless be prudent for the fiduciary to obtain court approval.

28 Powell v. Thorsen, 322 S.E.2d 261, 263 (Ga.1984). *See also* Furr v. Hall, 553 S.W.2d 666, 672 (Tex. Civ. App. 1977).

29 *Restatement (Third) of Trusts* § 78, cmt. c(2) (2007).

30 Mest v. Dugan, 790 P.2d 38, 41 (Or.App.1990). *See also* Estate of Blouin, 490 A.2d 1212 (Me. 1985) (sale by executor to himself at below market value set aside).

fiduciary may be found to have been authorized, *e.g.*, when the will or a contract gave an executor an option to buy property at a favorable price.[31]

Authorization for self-dealing can be inferred from the circumstances. A court upheld a sale by trustees of stock to a company of which a trustee was an officer and director. The settlor "was fully aware of his brother's interest in the closely-held family corporations. Yet he chose to nominate his brother . . . as Co-Trustee of trusts whose primary assets were stock in those same corporations. . . . [T]he settlor must have understood that his Co-Trustee would take into consideration the interests of the corporation as well as the interest of the beneficiary in making any decisions concerning the family corporations' stock held by the Trusts."[32] Of course, a good drafter should not leave such questions to inference. If conflict of interest issues arise when planning an estate, and if the client intends to authorize the transaction, a carefully tailored provision is appropriate.[33]

Statutory Exceptions

The UTC and many state statutes allow banks serving as trustee to deposit trust funds in their own banking department.[34] Nevertheless, a bank trustee was surcharged for keeping excessive sums on self-deposit. "A bank-trustee does not commit a per se breach of trust by depositing with itself . . . cash which it holds as trustee," but it should not leave cash unproductive except for overriding liquidity needs. The court refused to accept as a defense "the practices of even a majority of commercial banks which operated trust departments because of the inherent conflicts of interest" in this situation.[35]

A corporate trustee holding its own stock in the trust also raises conflict of interest problems; the trustee may hold on to the stock in order to avoid depressing its value, or to bar a take-over by a purchaser who plans to install a new management.[36] The Restatement prohibits corporate trustees from purchasing their own shares for the trust even "if received from the settlor, unless such purchase or retention is expressly or impliedly authorized by the terms of the trust or by statute."[37] Many state statutes allow corporate trustees

---

[31] McPherson v. Dauenhauer, 69 P.3d 733 (Or.App.2003); Matter of Estate of Hensley, 413 N.E.2d 315 (Ind.App.1980).

[32] Huntington Nat'l Bank v. Wolfe, 651 N.E.2d 458, 464 (Ohio App.1994). *See also* Goldman v. Rubin, 441 A.2d 713 (Md. 1982); Langbein, *The Contractarian Basis of Trust Law*, 105 Yale L.H. at 658. Although UTC § 802(b)(1) speaks of the duty of loyalty being overridden "by the terms of the trust," the comment says that such an override can sometimes be "implied."

[33] Price, *Contemporary Estate Planning* § 10.45.3 (2014 ed.).

[34] UTC § 802(h)(4); Cal.Prob.Code § 16225; Tex.Prop.Code § 113.007; 12 Code Fed.Reg. § 9.10(b) (governing national banks). *See also* UPC § 5–425(b)(6) (conservators); *Restatement (Third) of Trusts* § 78, cmt. c(6) (2007) (altering the prohibition in *Restatement (Second) of Trusts* § 170, cmt. m).

[35] Maryland Nat'l Bank v. Cummins, 588 A.2d 1205, 1213 (Md.1991). *See also* Cal.Prob.Code § 9705 (trust company which self-deposits must pay the prevailing rate of interest on such deposits).

[36] Hallgring, *The Uniform Trustees' Powers Act and the Basic Principles of Fiduciary Responsibility*, 41 Wash.L.Rev. 801, 813 (1966). Federal law prohibits national banks which hold their own stock as trustee from voting it in the election of directors. 12 U.S.C. § 61.

[37] *Restatement (Third) of Trusts* § 78, cmt. e(2) (2007) (similar); First Ala. Bank v. Spragins, 515 So.2d 962 (Ala.1987) (trustee surcharged for retaining its own stock). *Contra*, Elmhurst Nat. Bank v. Glos, 241 N.E.2d 121 (Ill.App.1968). A general authorization to retain investments may be held to include the trustee's own stock. In re Heidenreich's Will, 378 N.Y.S.2d 982 (Surr. 1976).

to retain but not to purchase their own shares.[38] Absent such a state statute or specific retention provision in the trust instrument, the corporate trustee should ordinarily sell its shares or should the beneficiaries insist that the shares be retained, obtain those beneficiaries' written consent.[39]

Self-Hiring

Some states do not allow a person to get compensation as both personal representative and attorney, but the advantages in this arrangement have induced many states to allow it.[40] The Uniform Probate Code (UPC) permits personal representatives to employ attorneys "even if they are associated with the personal representative"[41] The Third Restatement of Trusts is more guarded; trustees can be compensated for services to the trust as an attorney "when it is advantageous that the trustee rather than another perform those services."[42]

Many statutes authorize corporate fiduciaries to invest in their own use mutual funds for which they charge a separate management fee to the trust or estate.[43] Under the UTC, such investments are not presumptively a violation of the duty of loyalty if they otherwise comply with the Uniform Prudent Investor Act.[44] A comment to the UTC suggests that the fact a separate management fee is charged for such mutual fund investments "may be taken into account" in setting the trustee's regular compensation.[45]

Other fact patterns may arise. In one case, the trustee hired himself to plan an auction of trust property and at the subsequent auction attempted to buy the property at below market value.[46]

Fiduciaries Acting in Two Capacities

Often the same fiduciary acts in two capacities for the same beneficiaries, *e.g.*, as executor and trustee, or as trustee of several trusts for the same family. Can the ABC Bank as trustee of an insurance trust buy assets from itself as the executor of the insured's probate estate? Allowing such a transaction can provide a market for hard to sell assets, and the potential conflict of interest is

---

However, even a specific authorization to retain stock of the corporate fiduciary may be subject to a general requirement of prudence. Robertson v. Central Jersey Bank & Trust Co., 47 F.3d 1268 (3rd Cir. 1995).

[38] Tex.Prop.Code § 113.055; Ky.Rev.Stat. § 386.025; Mo.Stat. § 362.550.5. *But cf.* Ind. Code § 30–4–3–7(a)(4) (trustee cannot purchase or retain own stock).

[39] Under UTC § 1009, a trustee is protected from liability if the consenting beneficiary knew of the beneficiary's rights and of the material facts relating to the potential breach.

[40] *See* Section 14.7, note 578.

[41] Unif. Probate Code (UPC) § 3–715(21).

[42] *Restatement (Third) of Trusts* § 38, cmt. d (2003). As to the salaries of trustees who serve a company in which the trust holds stock, *see* Section 14.7, note 549 et seq.

[43] *E.g.*, Estate of Vail v. First of America Trust, 722 N.E.2d 248, 252 (Ill.App.1999) (upholding such an investment as authorized by statute); UTC § 802(f); *Restatement (Third) of Trusts* § 78, cmt. c(8) (2007). Most of these statutes refer to funds that are registered under the Investment Company Act. Specific authorization in the trust instrument may be needed for investments in unregistered alternative investments. Morgan & Morris, *Trust Worthy?*, Tr. & Est., July 2003, at 55.

[44] UTC § 802(f).

[45] UTC § 802, cmt.

[46] Nelsen v. Nelsen, 2013 WL 646481 (Kan. Ct. App., Feb. 15, 2013).

attenuated because the Bank has no personal interest in the matter. The California Probate Code allows sales and exchanges between two trusts where the same trustee administers both if the transaction is "fair and reasonable with respect to the beneficiaries of both trusts" and the beneficiaries are properly notified.[47] The UTC provides that the fact the trustee is acting in another fiduciary capacity "does not preclude a transaction between a trust and another trust, decedent's estate, or conservatorship of which the trustee is a fiduciary."[48]

Closelyheld Business

Decedents who own a closelyheld business frequently place their businesses in trust. In addition to acting as trustee, the trustee may also be named as a corporate director or control who is named as corporate director. These fiduciary roles vary and can come into conflict.[49] The trustee owes fiduciary obligations to the trust's beneficiaries and the directors of the corporation owe fiduciary obligations to the shareholders. In *Betty Weldon*,[50] co-trustees, in their capacity as directors of a losing horse breeding operation, voted to sell the trust's interest in the company. While such an action might appear to be prudent and an appropriate exercise of business judgment under corporate law, the sale violated the trustee's obligation to carry out the terms of the trust, which indicated an intent that the settlor's business be continued. The court removed the trustees and enjoined the sale. But the application of the trustee standard to the conduct of a trustee also acting as a corporate director is not universal. Some courts would have instead applied the business judgment rule.[51]

Contracts Between Fiduciary and Beneficiary

Duty of loyalty issues can also arise when a trustee engages in a transaction with a beneficiary concerning property that is not part of the trust, *e.g.*, a beneficiary agrees to purchase personal assets of the trustee. The concern here is that the beneficiary will be induced or pressured to give the trustee sweeter terms in return for better treatment by the trustee. While such transactions are not per se violations of the duty of loyalty, an executor can, for example, buy stock from a legatee;[52] the Second Restatement of Trusts requires trustees who contract with a beneficiary "on the trustee's own account" to "deal fairly" and communicate to the beneficiary all material facts in connection with the transaction.[53] The UTC provides that a transaction with a beneficiary not concerning trust property in which the trustee "obtains an

---

[47] Cal.Prob.Code § 16002(b). *See also* 760 ILCS § 5/4.15; 12 Code Fed.Regs. § 9.12(d).

[48] UTC § 802(h)(3). *See also Restatement (Third) of Trusts* § 78, cmt. c(7) (2007).

[49] *See generally* Smith, *The Critical Resource Theory of Fiduciary Duty*, 55 Vand. L. Rev. 1399 (2002).

[50] In re Betty G. Weldon Revocable Trust, 231 S.W.3d 158 (Mo. Ct. App. 2007).

[51] The cases are collected in Ferges, *A Dichoyomy of Fiduciary Duties: What Hat Does a Trustee Wae While Managing the Trust's Business?*, Prob. & Prop., July/August 2018, at 34.

[52] Matter of Winslow's Estate, 636 P.2d 505 (Wash.App.1981); In re Estate of Neisewander, 474 N.E.2d 1378 (Ill.App.1985).

[53] *Restatement (Second) of Trusts* § 170(2) (1959). *See* now *Restatement (Third) of Trusts* § 78(3) & cmt. g (2007).

advantage is voidable by the beneficiary unless the trustee establishes that the transaction was fair to the beneficiary."[54]

§ 14.2 Investments

Fiduciaries have a power and a duty to invest. Fiduciaries can be surcharged or removed for failure to invest and for making improper investments. This section will discuss the basic rules pertaining to investing. The remedies against fiduciaries who have acted improperly in investing or otherwise committed a breach of trust are discussed in Section 12.8.

Different Fiduciaries

The rules on investment governing trustees, personal representatives, conservators, custodians under the Uniform Transfers to Minors Act, and directors of charitable corporations[55] are sometimes similar but are often distinctly different. Some state statutes on investments apply to all "fiduciaries,"[56] but the "investment authority and responsibilities" of personal representatives are generally "more limited than those of trustees,"[57] typically requiring that the personal representative "close out the estate as quickly as possible."[58] The Uniform Prudent Investor Act covers only trustees, but the drafters suggest that states may adapt it to "other fiduciary regimes, taking account of such changed circumstances as the relatively short duration of most executorships."[59] However, many wills give the same investment powers to the personal representative as are given to trustees.

Terms of the Instrument

The will or trust instrument is a primary source of the rules controlling investments. The Uniform Prudent Investor Act provides "a default rule, [which] may be expanded, restricted eliminated or otherwise altered by the provisions of a trust."[60] The Third Restatement of Trusts requires trustees to "conform to the terms of the trust directing or restricting investments."[61] However, courts may authorize trustees to ignore such terms when circumstances have changed, and trustees may even have a duty to seek such authorization.[62] Sometimes fiduciaries invoke a term in the instrument to justify what would otherwise be an improper investment. A complaint that a

---

[54] UTC § 802(d).

[55] Today, charitable corporations are in most states governed by the Uniform Prudent Management of Institutional Funds Act (UPMIFA). Agents are also fiduciaries, but they differ from trustees in that they generally must follow the instructions of the principal and the assets remain titled in the principal's name. McGovern, *Trusts, Custodianships and Durable Powers of Attorney*, 27 Real Prop.Prob. & T.J. 1, 28–30 (1992).

[56] Matter of Estate of Janes, 681 N.E.2d 332, 336 (N.Y.1997) (imposing liability on an executor under such a statute).

[57] *Restatement (Third) of Trusts* § 5, cmt. c (2003).

[58] Matter of Estate of Pirie, 492 N.E.2d 884, 893 (Ill.App.1986). *See also* Hamilton v. Nielsen, 678 F.2d 709, 712 (7th Cir. 1982). *But see* Matter of Estate of Donner, 626 N.E.2d 922 (N.Y.1993) (executor surcharged for failure to sell stock in declining market).

[59] Unif. Prudent Investor Act (UPIA) Prefatory Note.

[60] UPIA § 2(b).

[61] *Restatement (Third) of Trusts* § 91(b) (2007).

[62] *Restatement (Third) of Trusts* § 91, cmt. e. For modification of a trust because of unanticipated circumstances, *see* Section 10.9, note 451 et seq.

trustee had failed to diversify investments and invested in speculative securities was dismissed when a provision in the will which authorized the trustee to invest "in any type of real or personal property . . . regardless of diversification or state laws" was held to "waive the application of the prudent man rule."[63] As this example illustrates, the drafter should exercise care that standard boiler plate investment language included in the trust document matches the settlor's actual intent. Liability under the Uniform Prudent Investor Act has been excused because the trustee was granted "broadest discretion" with respect to investment decisions,[64] was granted "broad discretion" to retain the assets originally transferred to the trust,[65] was authorized to invest "regardless of diversification and regardless of whether the property would be considered a proper trust investment,"[66] or was authorized to invest "without regard to conflict of interest, risk, lack of diversification, or unproductivity."[67]

Many trust documents created by the owners of closelyheld businesses contain provisions expressly authorizing the trustee to retain the business. Some provisions merely authorize the trustee to retain the interest, while others mandate that the interest be retained. A trustee faced with such a provision is well served to ask the beneficiaries to specifically authorize the retention of the interest. Better yet, prior to agreeing to serve as trustee, the trustee should request that the settlor immunize the trustee from potential liability. A considerable body of case law on the effectiveness of such retention provisions has developed which should be consulted by counsel for both the settlor and trustee.[68]

Court Approval

Prior court approval for investments by trustees is not usually required.[69] Such a requirement for conservators is common,[70] but the UPC allows conservators "without Court authorization or confirmation [to] invest and reinvest funds of the estate as would a trustee."[71] The need for court approval may turn on the type of investment. The UPC generally allows personal representatives to invest without court order, but court approval is needed to continue operating an unincorporated business for more than four months.[72] Even when it is not required, fiduciaries may seek court approval for a questionable investment decision. Courts are open to instruct trustees in

---

[63] Hoffman v. First Virginia Bank, 263 S.E.2d 402, 407 (Va.1980).

[64] Donato v. BankBoston, N.A., 110 F. Supp. 2d 42 (D.R.I. 2000).

[65] Atwood v. Atwood, 25 P.3d 936 (Okla. Civ. App. 2001).

[66] Carter v. Carter, 965 N.E.2d 1146 (Ill. Ct. App. 2012).

[67] French v. Wachovia Bank, 722 F.3d 1079 (7th Cir. 2013).

[68] The cases are collected in Klein, *Duty to Diversify*, NY Law Journal, Sept. 22. 2008. For a lengthier treatment, *see* Cooper, *Speak Clearly and Listen Well: Negating the Duty to Diversity*, 33 Ohio N.U.L.Rev. 903 (2007).

[69] UTC § 201(b) ("A trust is not subject to continuing judicial supervision"); Cal.Prob.Code § 17209 (administration of trust "free of judicial intervention").

[70] Cal.Prob.Code § 2570 (conservator may invest "after authorization by order of the court"); Conservatorship of Coffey, 231 Cal. Rptr. 421, 424 (App. 1986) (conservator surcharged for allowing insurance policy to lapse without court approval).

[71] UPC § 5–425(b)(5).

[72] UPC § 3–715(24). *See also* Cal.Prob.Code § 16222.

doubtful questions,[73] but excessive resort to courts is discouraged. A trustee can get instructions only "if there is reasonable doubt as to the extent of his powers or duties of the trusteeship," and courts will not ordinarily instruct a trustee on how to exercise discretion.[74]

Legal List v. "Prudent Man (Person)"

Historically the law has followed one of two approaches to controlling investments, the legal list and the "prudent man (person)" rule. Legal lists vary, but they tend to be conservative ever since the disastrous burst of the South Sea Bubble in the early 18th century, following which Chancellors "developed a restricted list of presumptively proper trust investments, initially government bonds, later well-secured first mortgages. Only in 1961 was the English statute amended to allow trustees to invest in equities . . . subject to a ceiling of half the trust fund."[75] In the United States, each state had its own rules but the predominant view was long the one which appeared in the Restatement Second of Trusts: absent a statute or trust terms providing otherwise, a trustee could "make such investments as a prudent man would make of his own property having in view the preservation of the estate and the amount and regularity of the income to be derived."[76] This formula, which goes back to a famous 19th century Massachusetts case,[77] has been adapted with variations in many statutes, such as the Uniform Transfers to Minors Act, where the "prudent man" dealing with "his own property" became "a prudent person dealing with the property of another."[78]

Studies showed that the return on trust investments in "prudent man/person" states, which generally allow investment in common stocks, was almost double those in states controlled by legal lists. A particularly prominent example is *Woodward School for Girls*,[79] involving a trust created in 1822 by President John Quincy Adams, in which the trust was invested almost entirely in fixed income instruments even following Massachusetts' enactment of the Uniform Prudent Investor Act. Given the poor performance of the legal list approach, most states have abandoned legal lists, at least for trustees.[80] "During the depression years of 1930–1940, bonds and mortgages [included on most legal lists] suffered as well as common stocks [often excluded or limited], but unlike stocks, bonds and mortgages failed to recover their value once

---

73 Cal.Prob.Code §§ 17200(b)(6), 17209.

74 *Restatement (Third) of Trusts* § 71 & cmt. d (2007). *See also* Section 10.7, note 272.

75 Langbein, *The Uniform Prudent Investor Act and the Future of Trust Investing*, 81 Iowa L.Rev. 641, 643 (1996). For a similar American statute, *see* Ohio Rev.Code § 2109.37. The leading legal list case is King v. Talbot, 40 N.Y. 76 (1869).

76 *Restatement (Second) of Trusts* § 227(a) (1959). Even when governed by a legal list, a trustee was supposed to use prudence in selecting among investments on the list. *Restatement (Second) of Trusts* § 227, cmt. p.

77 Harvard College v. Amory, 26 Mass. (9 Pick.) 446 (1830).

78 Unif. Transfers to Minors Act § 12(b). The Uniform Prudent Investor Act, on the other hand, rejects any distinction between a person "investing for another and investing on his or her own account." Unif.Prudent Investor Act § 2, cmt.

79 Woodward School for Girls v. City of Quincy, 13 N.E.3d 579 (Mass.2014)

80 Begleiter, *Does the Prudent Investor Really Need the Uniform Prudent Investor Act—An Empirical Study of Trust Investment Practices*, 51 Me.L.Rev. 27, 32 (1999). The dichotomy between "legal lists" and "prudent person" states is somewhat misleading, since some legal lists allow a broad range of investments, and conversely, "prudence" can be narrowly interpreted.

conditions improved."[81] Although the trustee in *Woodward* apparently paid no attention to the enactment of the Uniform Prudent Investor Act, its enactment has led to an increase in the portion of trust portfolios invested in stocks.[82]

Fiduciary's Expertise

The "prudent person" standard is used in many contexts. The UTC requires trustees to "administer the trust as a prudent person would."[83] The UPC uses a similar formula for personal representatives,[84] as does ERISA for managers of pension funds.[85] The standard is objective. A family member who served as trustee without compensation was surcharged for failing to invest funds despite her "good faith."[86] The Third Restatement justifies this harsh seeming rule by emphasizing "the importance of obtaining competent guidance and assistance sufficient to meet the standards."[87]

A higher standard is imposed on professional fiduciaries. The UTC, the UPC, and the Uniform Prudent Investor Act agree that "if the trustee has special skills or is named trustee on the basis of representations of special skills or expertise, he is under a duty to use those skills."[88]

Speculation

Prudence is sometimes regarded as a question of fact with deference given to a trial court's findings on the issue.[89] But courts operating under the standard have tended to formulate specific sub-rules for determining prudence, *e.g.*, trustees should not invest in second mortgages or buy land for resale.[90] Although prudent persons often make speculative investments if the possible rewards outweigh the risk, fiduciaries were not supposed to do this. The Second Restatement of Trusts barred "purchase of securities for

---

[81] Fleming, *Prudent Investments,* 12 Real Prop. Prob. & Trust L.J. 243, 244–45 (1977). *See also* Gordon, *The Puzzling Persistence of the Constrained Prudent Man Rule,* 62 N.Y.U.L.Rev. 52, 87 (1987).

[82] Sitkoff & Schanzenbach, *The Prudent Investor Rule and Trust Asset Allocation: An Empirical Analysis,* 35 ACTEC J. 314 (2010).

[83] UTC § 804.

[84] UPC § 3–703.

[85] 29 U.S.C. § 1104(a)(1)(B).

[86] Witmer v. Blair, 588 S.W.2d 222 (Mo. Ct. App.1979). *See also* Cal.Prob.Code § 16041 (standard of care not affected by lack of compensation); Buder v. Sartore, 774 P.2d 1383 (Colo. 1989) (father acting as uncompensated custodian surcharged for losing investment). *But see* Section 14.8, note 618 et seq. In Vento v. Colorado National Bank-Pueblo, 907 P.2d 642 (Colo. App. 1995), a trustee was surcharged for failing to consult coal mining experts during the negotiations for a mineral lease which resulted in terms unfavorable to the trust.

[87] *Restatement (Third) of Trusts* § 77, cmt. b (2007). As to reliance on expert advice as a defense to liability claims, *see* Section 14.8, note 632 et seq. In Vento v. Colorado National Bank-Pueblo, 907 P.2d 642 (Colo. App. 1995), a trustee was surcharged for failing to consult coal mining experts during the negotiations for a mineral lease which resulted in terms unfavorable to the trust.

[88] UTC § 806; UPIA § 2(f). *See also Restatement (Third) of Trusts* § 90, cmt. d (2007).

[89] Matter of Trusts Created by Hormel, 504 N.W.2d 505, 512 (Minn.App.1993); Matter of Estate of Donner, 626 N.E.2d 922, 927 (N.Y.1993); Malachowski v. Bank One, 667 N.E.2d 780, 788 (Ind.App.1996).

[90] *Restatement (Second) of Trusts* § 227, cmt. f, h (1959); In re Estate of Munger, 309 A.2d 205 (N.J. 1973) (investment in real estate improper); In re Estate of Collins, 139 Cal. Rptr. 644, 648 (App. 1977) (junior mortgage); Langbein & Posner, *Market Funds and Trust Investment Law,* Am. Bar. Fdn. Res. J. 1, 3 (1976).

speculation" and "in new and untried enterprises."[91] A court surcharged fiduciaries for buying real estate investment trusts (REITs) because they had existed "for only a short period" and so "there was no solid history of a productive return." The prospectuses had said that REITs "were subject to substantial risks," whereas "the primary objective of a trustee should be preservation of the trust."[92]

Fiduciaries who followed the crowd were considered prudent. The Second Restatement of Trusts said trustees could invest in stocks which "prudent men in the community are accustomed to invest in."[93] A court refused to surcharge a trustee for investing in Penn Central despite its disastrous performance because "the stock was widely held . . . by financial institutions and common trust funds." Another losing investment was upheld because "33 common trust funds" held the same stock.[94]

This aversion to "speculation" and penchant for sticking to well-trodden paths has disappeared in the Third Restatement which expressly approves speculative and "unconventional" investments.[95] The Uniform Prudent Investor Act, which was promulgated in 1994, has been widely adopted.[96] The Act allows trustees to invest "in any kind of property or type of investment," and "disavows the emphasis in older law on avoiding 'speculative' or 'risky' investments."[97] Newer investment products, such as derivatives[98] and alternative investments[99] can also potentially qualify as prudent.

Diversification

The Uniform Prudent Investor Act requires that in investing trustees "exercise caution"[100] but the Act's answer to risk is not to avoid "speculative" investments but to require that trustees diversify. Trustees "diversify the investments of the trust."[101] One of the central findings of Modern Portfolio Theory is "that there are huge and essentially costless gains to diversifying the portfolio thoroughly."[102]

---

91 *Restatement (Second) of Trusts* § 227, cmt. f.

92 Matter of Newhoff's Will, 435 N.Y.S.2d 632, 636 (Sur.1980). *See also* In re Goldstick, 581 N.Y.S. 2d 165, 171 (App. Div. 1992) (investment in company with no earnings history).

93 *Restatement (Second) of Trusts* § 227, cmt. m (1959).

94 Chase v. Pevear, 419 N.E.2d 1358, 1368–69 (Mass.1981).

95 *Restatement (Third) of Trusts* § 90, cmt. e (2007). For the history and the development of the doctrine of speculative investments, *see* Dobris, *Speculations on the Idea of "Speculative" Trust Investing: An Essay*, 39 Real Prop. Prob. & Tr. J. 439 (2004).

96 The Act has been enacted in 46 jurisdictions. Unif. Prudent Investor Act Refs & Annos, ULA PRUDENT INV Refs & Annos (2016).

97 UPIA § 2(e) &, cmt.

98 Aalberts & Poon, *Derivatives and the Modern Prudent Investor Rule: Too Risky or Too Necessary*, 67 Ohio St. L.J. 525 (2006).

99 Ruce, *The Trustee and the Prudent Investor: The Emerging Acceptance of Alternative Investments*, 53 S. Tex. L. Rev. 653 (2012).

100 UPIA § 2(a).

101 UPIA § 3.

102 Langbein, 81 Iowa L. Rev. at 647. This theory is briefly summarized in this article and in more detail in Langbein & Posner, *Market Funds and Trust Investment Law*, Am. Bar Fdn. Res. J. 1, 3 (1976).

A requirement of diversification was already present in earlier law, *e.g.*, the Second Restatement of Trusts[103] and ERISA.[104] It remains to be seen how much weight courts will give to the increased emphasis on diversification in the Third Restatement and the Uniform Prudent Investor Act. A court in 1997 refused to surcharge a trustee who had failed to dispose of real property which made up the bulk of a trust's assets because the "land was placed in the trust by the settlor and comprised a majority of the trust, thus indicating the settlor's intent that the land remain the primary asset of the trust."[105] But another court in the same year surcharged executors who delayed selling a block of Kodak stock which made up 71% of the portfolio because risk "is significantly exacerbated when a portfolio is heavily concentrated in one such growth stock."[106]

Most cases of underdiversification involve portfolios which the fiduciary received in this condition, and so the need to diversify must be balanced against possible reasons for retaining an asset.[107] The Uniform Prudent Investor Act does not require diversification if "the trustee reasonably determines that, because of special circumstances the purposes of the trust would be better served without diversifying." The comment suggests as a possible special circumstance the tax costs of selling low-basis stock in order to diversify.[108] A weak market for an asset may be another. A court refused to surcharge trustees for failure to sell realty in an undiversified portfolio because the absence of a strong market meant that a sale would have been at a sacrifice.[109] The retention of a closelyheld business may also qualify. The circumstances of the settlor and the settlor's family, who are often employed in the business, may suggest that the settlor wished the business to be retained even though the trust document failed to address the issue.[110] Attempts to justify the long-term retention of large blocks of publiclytraded securities have less prospect of success.[111]

---

[103] *Restatement (Second) of Trusts* § 228 (1959). The idea now appears in *Restatement (Third) of Trusts* § 90(b) (2007).

[104] 29 U.S.C. § 1104(a)(1)(C); Brock v. Citizens Bank of Clovis, 841 F.2d 344 (10th Cir. 1988) (pension trustee's investing over 65% of assets in real estate mortgages violated ERISA).

[105] Matter of Estate of Maxedon, 946 P.2d 104, 109 (Kan. App.1997). *See also* In re Trusts Created by Hormel, 504 N.W.2d 505 (Minn. App. 1993); Atwood v. Atwood, 25 P.3d 936, 944 (Okl. Civ. App. 2001) (authorization to retain investments justified trustee's failure to diversify).

[106] Matter of Estate of Janes, 681 N.E.2d 332, 338 (N.Y.1997). *See also* In re Estate of Cooper, 913 P.2d 393 (Wash. App. 1996) (trustee surcharged for investing 87% in bonds).

[107] Kiziah, *The Trustee's Duty to Diversity: An Examination of the Developing Case Law*, 36 ACTEC L.J. 357 (2010).

[108] UPIA § 3 &, cmt. *See also Restatement (Third) of Trusts* § 92, cmt. a (2007). Langbein, however, suggests that fiduciaries can use "derivatives" to reduce risk in an underdiversified portfolio without realizing capital gains. Langbein, *The Uniform Prudent Investor Act and the Future of Trust Investing*, 81 Iowa L. Rev. at 661.

[109] In re Estate of Cavin, 728 A.2d 92, 100 (D.C. App.1999).

[110] *See* In re HSBC Bank, USA, 952 N.Y.S.2d 740 (Surr. Ct. 2006), in which the closely-held position constituted 60% of the trust assets. *See also* Regions Bank v. Lowery, 101 So. 3d 210 (Ala. 2012), where the court concluded that the trustee acted prudently even though the primary trust asset, a stand of timber, was damaged by an unexpected hurricane.

[111] *See., e.g.*, In re Estate of Kenney, 64 Misc.3d 1232(A) (Sur. Ct., Albany Cnty. 2019) (executor surcharged $3.5 million for retaining portfolio consisting of 86% General Electric stock).

Many statutes and judicial opinions apply different standards to new investments and retention of received asset.[112] The Second Restatement of Trusts required trustees to dispose of assets which would be improper investments "within a reasonable time," but an authorization in the trust instrument to retain property contributed by the settlor to the trust (a common provision) could be construed as abrogating the requirement of diversification.[113] The Third Restatement and the Uniform Prudent Investor Act are less approving of fiduciaries' maintaining the status quo. Trustees must "within a reasonable time" review the portfolio and bring it into compliance with the Act.[114] Even if an initial investment is proper, trustees may be surcharged for loss arising from failure to monitor the investment.[115] A general authorization in a trust to retain investments "does not ordinarily abrogate the trustee's duty with respect to diversification." Even an authorization to retain a specific investment ("my XYZ stock") does not control "if retention would otherwise be imprudent."[116] But there are cases to the contrary.[117]

How far does the duty to diversify extend? The Third Restatement leaves this open. One of its illustrations approves a portfolio of 20 carefully selected stocks, noting that diversification "is not simply a matter of numbers."[118] But it also touts the advantages of index funds which match the performance of the market as a whole.[119] "Studies have found that professionally managed institutional portfolios as a group actually underperformed the broad stock

---

[112] Gardner v. Cox, 843 P.2d 469, 471–72 (Or. App.1992) (distinguishing between buying and retaining a "speculative" investment); Estate of Weingart, 182 Cal. Rptr. 369, 375 (App.1982). For purposes of this distinction a new security which is received in place of a security originally held by virtue of a reorganization or the like can be viewed as a retention if the new security is "substantially equivalent" to the old one. Donato v. BankBoston, N.A., 110 F.Supp. 2d 42, 51 (D.R.I. 2000).

[113] *Restatement (Second) of Trusts* § 230, cmt. j (1959). *See also* Atwood v. Atwood, 25 P.3d 936, 944 (Okl. Civ. App. 2001) (authorization to retain investments justified trustee's failure to diversify); Wood v. U.S. Bank, N.A., 828 N.E.2d 1072 (Ohio App. 2005) (trustee authorized to retain investments not liable unless abuse of discretion).

[114] UPIA § 4. *See also* In re Saxton, 712 N.Y.S.2d 225 (App. Div. 2000) (trustee surcharged for retaining 100% investment in IBM stock).

[115] Republic National Bank v. Araujo, 697 So.2d 164, 166 (Fla.App.1997).

[116] *Restatement (Third) of Trusts* § 92, cmt. d (2007). *See also* Rutanen v. Ballard, 678 N.E.2d 133, 139 (Mass. 1997) (general authorization to retain property does not warrant retention of underproductive asset).

[117] For a comprehensive discussion of inception assets, including both statues and cases, *see* Kiziah, Singleton, and Marshall, *The Persistent Preference for Inception Assets*, 40 ACTEC L.J. 151 (2014).

[118] *Restatement (Third) of Trusts* § 90 illus. 14 (2007). *See also* UPIA § 3, cmt.: "there is no automatic rule for identifying how much diversification is enough." In In re HSBC Bank, USA, 952 N.Y.S.2d 740 (Surr. Ct. 2006), the court found that a portfolio consisting of four publicly traded stocks and a 60% interest in a closely held business was adequately diversified. For mathematical models for measuring diversification, *see* Moses, Singleton & Marshall, *Measuring the Effectiveness of a Trust Portfolio's Diversification*, 35 ACTEC J. 303 (2009).

[119] *Restatement (Third) of Trusts* § 90, cmt. h (2007). It has been suggested that because the "United States capital markets now represent only one-half of the world's capital markets, . . . diversification into international markets may . . . be required under the UPIA's prudent investor rule" even though this presents special problems. Bendremer, *Modern Portfolio Theory and International Investments Under the Uniform Prudent Investor Act*, 35 Real Prob. Prob. & Tr. J. 791, 792 (2001).

market averages such as the Standard and Poor's 500 stock index."[120] This is so because stock markets are efficient; since everything knowable about a publicly traded security is already reflected in its price,[121] research in attempting to pick the "best" stocks is a waste of money.[122] However, there are also "inefficient" markets, like real estate, where investment without prior inquiry would be imprudent.[123] Assets of this type should not be rejected because "vigorous research and investigation to introduce assets from less efficient markets into the trust portfolio can . . . contribute to its overall diversification."[124] The debate between the advocates of passive versus active investing is a continuing one.[125] Perhaps the best answer is that the particular investment strategy should be tailored to the purposes of the individual trust.[126] However, because higher fees are charged for active investing, the trustee's duty to not incur unreasonable costs[127] gives the edge to the passive approach.

Because a small portfolio is hard to diversify, many banks have established "common trust" or "proprietary mutual" funds which pool the assets of many small trusts to facilitate diversification. Mutual funds provide another way to diversify. This type of investment delegates the trustee's responsibility to the manager of the mutual fund. The Uniform Prudent Investor Act and the Third Restatement reject the idea that such a delegation is improper, in part because of the advantages of mutual funds, and in part because prudent investments in new areas beyond the expertise of the typical trustee may require reliance on the expertise of others.[128]

Adapting Investments to the Circumstances

One reason for the modern rejection of the traditional aversion to "speculation" is the recognition that the situations of beneficiaries differ widely. Some persons are more risk averse than others, partly because they are in varying financial situations. Prudence requires fiduciaries to consider *inter alia* a beneficiary's "ability to absorb losses in the event an investment is

---

[120] Langbein, *The Uniform Prudent Investor Act and the Future of Trust Investing*, 81 Iowa L. Rev. at 655.

[121] Langbein, *The Uniform Prudent Investor Act and the Future of Trust Investing*, 81 Iowa L. Rev. at 657. *See also* Halbach, *Trust Investment Law in the Third Restatement*, 27 Real Prop. Prob. & Tr. J. 407, 425 (1992).

[122] Halbach, 27 Real Prop. Prob. & Tr.J. at 447.

[123] Langbein, 81 Iowa L. Rev. at 658.

[124] *Restatement (Third) of Trusts* § 90, cmt. h (2007).

[125] *See* Harmon & Fisher, *The Prudence of Passivity: An Argument for Default Passive Management in Trust Investing*, 44 ACTEC L.J. 147 (2019), and the responses, Ayres & Fox, *Strengthening the Passivity Default*, 44 ACTEC L.J. 289 (2019); Radigan & Hillman, *Brief Comment on Trustee Prudence and Passive Investing*, 44 ACTEC L.J. 297 (2019); and Rizzo & Lord, *Prudence of Passivity vs. Prudence of Process: Can a Default Approach be Prudent?*, 44 ACTEC L.J. 301 (2019).

[126] *See* UPIA § 2(a) ("A trustee shall invest and manage the trust assets as a prudent investor would, by considering the purposes, terms, and distribution requirements, and other circumstances of the trust.").

[127] UTC § 805.

[128] UPIA § 9; *Restatement (Third) of Trusts* § 90, cmt. j (2007). *See also* UTC § 807.

unsuccessful."[129] A trust "to support an elderly widow of modest means will have a lower risk tolerance than a trust to accumulate for a young scion of great wealth."[130]

The goal of investing in the Second Restatement was "preservation of the estate and the amount and regularity of the income."[131] This remains true in the Third Restatement only for those trusts in which distributions are based on trust income.[132] Many beneficiaries are more concerned about protecting against inflation than about a regular income and prefer non-dividend-paying growth stocks to high-yield bonds. Investments of this type were not allowed by the Second Restatement, which only permitted trustees to invest in stock that paid "regular dividends."[133] On similar principles a trustee was ordered to sell a farm which was worth $1.5 million but produced only $1,265 in income.[134]

The Third Restatement notes that in many trusts, distributions do not depend on the trust's income and so the trustee should be free "to disregard income productivity in managing investments."[135] Even in private trusts in which income is important to some beneficiaries, it is the trust estate as a whole, not any particular investment, that must be productive. The Uniform Prudent Investor Act requires that individual investments "be evaluated not in isolation but in the context of the trust portfolio as a whole."[136] This allows trustees to hold one or more non-income producing investments if the portfolio as a whole produces a reasonable income. Under the Uniform Principal and Income Act, § 104, the trustee can adjust between the income and principal accounts as necessary to make up any deficiency in the income.[137]

Investments that are expected to appreciate even if they produce no income are justifiable, but not a failure to invest at all, *e.g.*, leaving money in a checking account. Many fiduciaries have been surcharged for this, including a bank that did not invest cash receipts until they amounted to $1,000.[138] Even executors have been surcharged for leaving estate funds in a checking account.[139] On the other hand, liquidity can be a legitimate concern for

---

129 Erlich v. First Nat'l Bank, 505 A.2d 220, 235 (N.J.Super.L.1984) (imprudent to invest in a single stock for a person who had little income and few assets apart from investment).

130 UPIA § 2, cmt.

131 *Restatement (Second) of Trusts* § 227 (1959).

132 *Restatement (Third) of Trusts* § 79(2) (2007).

133 *Restatement (Second) of Trusts* § 227, cmt. m (1959).

134 Sturgis v. Stinson, 404 S.E.2d 56 (Va.1991). *See also* Perfect Union Lodge v. Interfirst Bank, 748 S.W.2d 218 (Tex. 1988) (order to sell land which produced less than 1% of its value in income); Rutanen v. Ballard, 678 N.E.2d 133 (Mass. 1997) (trustee surcharged for retaining underproductive property).

135 *Restatement (Third) of Trusts* § 90, cmt. i (2007); Shear v. Gabovitch, 685 N.E.2d 1168, 1185 (Mass. App. 1997) (proper for trustee to hold stock paying no dividends since settlor implicitly authorized this).

136 UPIA § 2(b).

137 Discussed in Section 10.6.

138 Maryland Nat'l Bank v. Cummins, 588 A.2d 1205, 1210–12 (Md.1991).

139 Cooper v. Jones, 435 N.Y.S.2d 830, 834 (App.Div.1981); Whitaker v. Estate of Whitaker, 663 N.E.2d 681, 686 (Ohio App.1995).

fiduciaries.[140] California allows trustees to keep in a checking account amounts "reasonably necessary for the orderly administration of the trust."[141]

The beneficiaries of a trust often have conflicting interests with respect to investments, *e.g.*, income beneficiaries who wish the trust to produce more income and remaindermen who are concerned only with the principal. Trustees are supposed to keep these interests in balance, to be "impartial" in such conflicts.[142] A trustee was surcharged for investing 87% of the assets in bonds because "the prudent investor standard requires that the trustee maintain a balance between the rights of the income beneficiaries with those of the remainderman."[143]

The Uniform Prudent Investor Act directs trustees to consider the "tax consequences of investment decisions;" for example, "it may be prudent for the trust to buy lower-yielding tax-exempt securities for high tax-bracket taxpayers." However, such choices may have different impact on beneficiaries in different tax situations and so the trustee must balance the varying interests.[144] In some cases tensions between beneficiaries can be reduced by dividing trusts. One court divided a trust to accommodate the different investment wishes of two beneficiaries.[145]

Under the Second Restatement "preservation of the estate" (along with production of income) was the goal of trust investment, but under the new rules, preservation of the estate in the traditional sense is not enough. The Uniform Prudent Investor Act speaks of "total return from income and the appreciation of capital."[146] The Third Restatement describes the goal as preservation of the "real value" of the trust property, *i.e.*, "seeking to avoid the loss of the trust estate's purchasing power due to inflation."[147]

Social Investing

Professor Scott argued that in choosing investments, trustees could avoid securities of corporations whose actions were "contrary to fundamental and generally accepted ethical principles. They may consider such matters as pollution, race discrimination, fair employment and consumer responsibility," just as directors of corporations could contribute corporate funds to charity.[148] Professor Langbein and Judge Posner on the other hand argue that any consideration of social objectives is inconsistent with the trustees' duty "to

---

140 UPIA § 2(c)(7).

141 Cal.Prob.Code § 16225(e).

142 *Restatement (Third) of Trusts* § 90, cmt. c (2007); UPIA § 6. The duty of impartiality is not limited to investments. UTC § 803; Section 10.7, note 282.

143 Matter of Estate of Cooper, 913 P.2d 393, 398 (Wash.App.1996).

144 UPIA § 2(c)(3) &, cmt.

145 In re Siegel, 665 N.Y.S.2d 813 (Sur.1997).

146 UPIA § 2(c)(5).

147 *Restatement (Third) of Trusts* § 90, cmt. e (2007).

148 3 Scott & Fratcher, *Trusts* § 227.17 (4th ed. 1987). *See also* Ravikoff & Curzan, *Social Responsibility in Investment and the Prudent Man Rule*, 68 Cal. L. Rev. 518 (1980); Dobris, *Arguments in Favor of Fiduciary Divestment of "South African" Securities*, 65 Neb. L.Rev. 209 (1986).

administer the trust *solely* in the interest of the beneficiary."[149] They particularly objected to pension funds divesting their holdings in companies which did business in South Africa during the apartheid era, because this would leave the portfolio less than optimally diversified.[150]

The Third Restatement of Trusts accepts the Langbein/Posner view: a trustee's investment decisions "must not be motivated by a purpose of advancing or expressing the trustee's personal views concerning social or political issues."[151] The same idea appears in a comment in the Uniform Prudent Investor Act, the text of which reiterates the trustee's duty to manage the trust "solely in the interest of the beneficiaries."[152]

Discussion on this issue has focused primarily on pension funds, perhaps because of their vast size.[153] Most pension funds are governed by ERISA which, like trust law, requires fiduciaries to act "solely in the interests of the participants and beneficiaries."[154] ERISA does not apply to pension funds for state employees, but many states, including California, have similar provisions.[155]

Charitable trusts differ from private trusts because social benefits *are* their objective and they have no private beneficiaries. However, money which is given for one charitable purpose cannot be diverted to another, and any investing decision must be justified "on grounds of advancing" one of the trust purposes.[156]

Nonetheless, the debate continues over whether social investing is a permitted strategy under the Uniform Prudent Investor Act.[157] There is also increased sophistication among financial firms concerning social investing, including in the terminology employed. A common overall term for this strategy is impact investing, but this term may include program related investments ("PRIs"), mission related investments ("MRIs"), socially responsible investments ("SRIs"), sustainable investments, investments that

---

[149] Langbein & Posner, *Social Investing and the Law of Trusts*, 79 Mich. L.Rev. 71, 96–98 (1979).

[150] Langbein & Posner, 79 Mich. L.Rev. at 85. For a more recent discussion of the issue, *see* Sanders, *Resolving the Conflict Between Fiduciary Duties and Socially Responsible Investing*, 35 Pace L. Rev. 535 (2014).

[151] *Restatement (Third) of Trusts* § 90, cmt. c (2007).

[152] Unif. Prudent Investor Act § 5, cmt. which asserts that proponents of social investing generally argue only that "particular schemes of social investing may not result in below-market returns."

[153] "There has been little pressure on trustees of individual trusts to adopt social investing." Langbein & Posner, *Social Investing and the Law of Trusts*, 79 Mich.L.Rev. at 96–98.

[154] 29 U.S.C. § 1104(a)(1).

[155] Cal. Const. art. 16, § 17.

[156] *Restatement (Third) of Trusts* § 90, cmt. c (2007); Langbein & Posner, *Social Investing and the Law of Trusts*, 79 Mich.L.Rev. at 96–98. *But see* Gadsden, *The Hershey Power Play*, Tr. & Est., Nov. 2002, at 8, in which a state attorney general blocked a sale of stock needed for diversification in the trust portfolio of a school because it threatened a loss of jobs in the community.

[157] *See* Schanzenbach & Sitkoff, *Reconciling Fiduciary Duty and Social Conscience: The Law and Economics of ESG Investing by a Trustee*, 72 Stan. L. Rev. 381 (2020); Gary, *Best Interests in the Long Term: Fiduciary Duties and ESG Integration*, 90 U. Colo. L. Rev. 731 (2019); Clark & Kirkpatrick, *Impact Investing Under the Uniform Prudent Investor Act*, Prob. & Prop., March/April 2018, at 32.

consider environmental, social and governance ("ESG") factors, and economically targeted investments ("ETIs").[158]

Family Business

Retention of a family business may subject a fiduciary to surcharge. The administrator of the estate of the sole shareholder of a company was surcharged for continuing to operate the business at a loss. "[A] personal representative commits a breach of trust by continuing to operate a trade or business on behalf of an estate in the absence of testamentary direction."[159] Because the success of such a business often depends on the ability of its manager, it may be imprudent to continue the business after he or she dies.[160]

Some courts apply this rule only to *unincorporated* businesses because their unlimited liability may deplete the whole estate. A court refused to surcharge an executor who continued to operate a company without court approval on the ground that a statute requiring approval for continuing a "business" did not apply to an incorporated business.[161] The UPC requires court approval to continue an unincorporated business for more than 4 months, but an incorporated business can be operated "throughout the period of administration" if no potential distributee objects.[162]

The Uniform Prudent Investor Act provides that "interests in closely held enterprises" may be permissible trust investments,[163] and "the wish to retain a family business" may even override the duty to diversify.[164] But according to the Third Restatement, a trustee cannot continue a business of the settlor "unless authority to do so is expressly or impliedly granted by terms of the trust, or unless . . . it is prudent to do so."[165] A lawyer whose client owns a business should make special provision for this in the will or trust. A sale of the business may be the best solution, but a mere authorization (or direction) to sell may be hard to carry out after the client dies, so the client may need to negotiate a "buy-out" agreement with others associated with the business.[166]

Evaluating Performance

Relatively few reported decisions have appeared since the promulgation of the Third Restatement and the Uniform Prudent Investor Act, so it remains to be seen how courts will interpret them. Older decisions surcharging fiduciaries for speculative investments are obsolete under the new rules. Older

---

[158] The terms are defined in McDowell, *Fiduciary Duties in an Age of Impact Investing*, 44 Pen. & Ben. Rptr.(BNA) 1151 (2017).

[159] In re Kurkowski's Estate, 409 A.2d 357, 361 (Pa.1979). *See also* Estate of Baldwin, 442 A.2d 529 (Me.1982).

[160] Fortune v. First Union Nat'l Bank, 359 S.E.2d 801, 805 (N.C.App.1987).

[161] Harper v. Harper, 491 So.2d 189, 195 (Miss.1986). *See also* In re Estes' Estate, 654 P.2d 4, 13 (Ariz. App. 1982).

[162] UPC § 3–715(24).

[163] UPIA § 2(c)(4).

[164] UPIA § 3, cmt.

[165] *Restatement (Third) of Trusts* § 92, cmt. e (2007). UTC § 816(6) empowers trustees to continue a business, but the exercise of this power is subject to the general requirement of prudence in § 804.

[166] For a detailed discussion of buy-sell agreements for closely held businesses, *see* Price & Donaldson, *Contemporary Estate Planning* §§ 11.6–11.12. (2014 ed.).

decisions stated that the fact that a portfolio showed substantial overall increase in value did "not insulate the trustee from responsibility for imprudence with respect to individual investments."[167] These statements cannot be squared with the Uniform Prudent Investor Act's instruction that trustees' decisions "must be evaluated not in isolation, but in the context of the trust portfolio as a whole."[168]

The Act also says that a trustee's actions must not be judged "by hindsight;" the fact that a portfolio has gone down in value does not necessarily or even imply that the trustee has been imprudent.[169] But how then is a fiduciary's prudence to be assessed? Professor Langbein noted that the cases "give great weight to the trustee's internal procedures for investing and monitoring investments; . . . the courts have sometimes been willing to treat this paper trail as presumptive evidence of prudence."[170]

Professor Langbein suggests that under the Uniform Prudent Investor Act a "paper trail" cannot excuse a seriously underdiversified portfolio, and trustees who "persistently underperform" comparable funds may be found imprudent.[171] Is this consistent with the command not to use "hindsight" in evaluating trustees? The Act requires trustees to have "an overall investment strategy."[172] But presumably the absence of a defensible strategy will not cause a trustee whose investment performance was above average to be surcharged. In any event, the risk of surcharge is not the only incentive for fiduciaries to perform well; "continued inadequacies in matters of investment" is grounds for removing trustees.[173] However courts interpret the Act, it will change the investment practices of trustees by opening up a broader range of investments.[174]

§ 14.3 Duty to Inform and Account

Duty to Inform[175]

The duty to keep the beneficiaries reasonably informed of the administration of the trust is a fundamental duty of a trustee, for only by being informed can the beneficiaries know of and enforce their interests.[176] An

---

[167] In re Bank of New York, 323 N.E.2d 700, 703 (N.Y.1974); Chase v. Pevear, 419 N.E.2d 1358, 1366 (Mass.1981).

[168] UPIA § 2(b). *See also Restatement (Third) of Trusts* § 90(a) (2007).

[169] UPIA § 8. *See also Restatement (Third) of Trusts* § 90, cmt. b (2007). Despite such statements (which are common in judicial opinions) "courts have a pronounced propensity to evaluate the prudence or imprudence of a trustee's investment decision on the basis of information that the trustee could not have known at the time she made the decision." Alexander, *A Cognitive Theory of Fiduciary Relationships*, 85 Cornell L.Rev. 767, 783 (2000) (describing illustrative cases).

[170] Langbein, *The Uniform Prudent Investor Act and the Future of Trust Investing*, 81 Iowa L. Rev. at 662.

[171] Langbein, 81 Iowa L. Rev. at 655.

[172] UPIA § 2(b).

[173] *Restatement (Third) of Trusts* § 37, cmt. e (2001).

[174] Begleiter, *Does the Prudent Investor Really Need the Uniform Prudent Investor Act—An Empirical Study of Trust Investment Practices*, 51 Me. L. Rev. 27 (1999).

[175] Portions of the following discussion are based on English, *The Uniform Trust Code: Significant Provisions and Policy Issues*, 67 Mo. L. Rev. 143, 199–203 (2002).

[176] For background, *see* Gallanis, *The Trustee's Duty to Inform*, 85 N.C. L. Rev. 1595 (2007); Fitzsimons, *Navigating the Trustee's Duty to Disclose*, Prob. & Prop., Jan./Feb. 2009, at 40; Ruce,

exception to this rule is the so-called "blind trust," in which a beneficiary—usually the settlor—is deliberately kept uninformed about the trust's investments in order to promote public confidence in the integrity of his or her decisions as a government official, for example.[177] Another exception is that trustees may withhold from beneficiaries an opinion of counsel which they have obtained for their own protection.[178] A final and very important exception is that the beneficiaries of a revocable trust are not entitled to information concerning the trust as long as the settlor is still alive.[179] The UTC, however, grants the beneficiaries rights to information in the event of the settlor's incapacity,[180] an approach that can work well if the settlor's incapacity is clear,[181] less well so if the settlor's incapacity is in doubt.[182]

The most complete statement of the duty is in the UTC,[183] which codifies this common law obligation but at the same time adds detail and makes the duty more precise. An initial question faced by the UTC drafters is which beneficiaries must be kept informed? Those to whom income must be currently distributed is the most obvious category but what about beneficiaries who may receive distributions only in the discretion of the trustee or upon termination of the trust. The UTC draws the line based on its concept of "qualified beneficiaries," a defined term that includes beneficiaries who are currently eligible to receive distributions, even if in the trustee's discretion, and those who would receive the trust were it to terminate currently.[184] The principal beneficiaries excluded are those holding remote future interests.[185]

The Trustee and the Remainderman: The Trustee's Duty to Inform, 46 Real Prop. Prob. & Tr. J. 173 (2011); Millard, *The Trustee's Duty to Inform and Report Under the Uniform Trust Code,* 40 Real Prop. Prob. & Tr. J. 373 (2005); Foster, *Privacy and the Elusive Quest for Uniformity in the Law of Trusts,* 38 Ariz. St. L.J. 713 (2006).

[177] Ballard, *The Shortsightedness of Blind Trusts,* 56 U. Kan. L. Rev. 43 (2007); Ianni, *Blind Trusts Offer Clients Customized Wealth Planning* 30 Est.Plan. 319 (2003).

[178] *Restatement (Third) of Trusts* § 82, cmt. f (2007); Symmons v. O'Keeffe, 644 N.E.2d 631, 639–40 (Mass.1995); Huie v. DeShazo, 922 S.W.2d 920 (Tex.1996). But the advice of counsel must ordinarily be disclosed if it relates to ordinary administration. *See* In re Kipnis Section 3.4 Trust, 329 P.3d 1055 (Ariz. Ct. App. 2014). *See generally* Bartolacci, Short & Talen, *The Attorney-Client Privilege and the Fiduciary Exception: Why Frank Discussions Between Fiduciaries and Their Attorneys Should Be Protected,* 48 Real Prop. Tr. & Est. L. J. 1 (2013).

[179] Montrone v. Valley Bank and Trust Co., 875 P.2d 557 (Utah App.1994); Cal.Prob.Code § 16064(b); In re Malasky, 736 N.Y.S.2d 151 (App.Div.2002).

[180] UTC § 603; *Restatement (Third) of Trusts* § 74, cmt. e (2007).

[181] The UTC/Restatement approach would have reversed the result in Johnson v. Kotyck, 90 Cal.Rptr.2d 99 (App.1999), where the court dismissed a beneficiary's claim for an accounting by the trustee of a revocable trust for a settlor for whom a conservator had been appointed.

[182] Berry, English & Fitzsimons, *Longmeyer Exposes (or Creates) Uncertainty About the Duty to Inform Remainder Beneficiaries of a Revocable Trust,* 35 ACTEC J. 125 (2009), discussing J. P. Morgan Chase Bank, N.A. v. Longmeyer, 275 S.W.3d 697 (Ky.2009).

[183] UTC § 813. For an overview of the duty to keep the beneficiaries informed under the UTC, *see* Newman, *Trust Law in the Twenty-First Century: Challenges to Fiduciary Accountability,* 29 Quinnipiac Prob. L.J. 261, 267–72 (2016).

[184] UTC § 103(13). The Restatement is less specific, providing that the trustee's obligation extends to "representative" beneficiaries, which is defined as "a limited number of beneficiaries whose interests and concerns are fairly representative of—*i.e.*, likely to coincide with—those of the trust beneficiaries generally." *Restatement (Third) of Trusts* § 82(a)(1) (2007).

[185] There has been relatively little caselaw on the definition of qualified beneficiary. *But see* Brown v. Brown, 2013 WL 1619687 (Tenn. Ct. App., April 16, 2013). For a discussion of and suggested revisions of the definition, *see* Edgar, *What is a Qualified Beneficiary?,* 45 ACTEC L. Rev. 23 (2019).

Nonqualified beneficiaries are entitled to information from the trustee only upon a specific request.

The UTC imposes a general obligation on the trustee to "keep the qualified beneficiaries reasonably informed about the administration of the trust and of the material facts necessary for them to protect their interests."[186] This general obligation is ordinarily satisfied by providing the beneficiary with a copy of the trustee's annual report.[187] However, special circumstances may dictate that the trustee provide additional information. For example, "the trustee may be required to provide advance notice of transactions involving real estate, closely-held business interests, and other assets that are difficult to value or to replace."[188]

In addition to the general obligation, the UTC imposes several specific notice requirements. A trustee is required to notify the qualified beneficiaries that they are beneficiaries and of the trustee's acceptance of office[189] and of any change in the method for computing, or the rate of, the trustee's compensation.[190] Regular reporting by the trustee to the current beneficiaries is required. Unless the beneficiary has waived its receipt,[191] the trustee must furnish the current beneficiaries at least annually with "a report of the trust property, liabilities, receipts, and disbursements, including the source and amount of the trustee's compensation, a listing of the trust assets and, if feasible, the market value of the trust assets."[192] The report need not be in the detailed format required for a judicial accounting but may be more informal.[193] However, merely sending the beneficiary a copy of the trust's income tax return is insufficient.[194] The key is whether the report and other information provided by the trustee is sufficient to keep the current beneficiaries reasonably informed of administration. Mandatory reporting is limited to the current beneficiaries because they are most likely to have the greatest interest in the day-to-day activities of the trust.[195]

---

[186] UTC § 813(a). This duty has been extended to ERISA fiduciaries. Langbein, *What ERISA Means by "Equitable": The Supreme Court's Trail of Error in Russell, Mertens, and Great West*, 103 Colum. L. Rev. 1317, 1326 (2003).

[187] UTC § 813, cmt.

[188] UTC § 813, cmt. *See also* In re Green Charitable Trust, 431 N.W.2d 492 (Mich.Ct.App.1988); Allard v. Pacific National Bank, 663 P.2d 104 (Wash.1983).

[189] UTC § 813(b). For the procedure for accepting office, *see* UTC § 701; Section 14.6. *See* McNeil v. McNeil, 798 A.2d 503, 510 (Del.2002) (trustees properly surcharged for failure to tell beneficiary that he was one).

[190] UTC § 813(b)(4). The UTC does not specify a trustee's compensation other than that it must be reasonable. *See* UTC § 708(a); Section 14.7, note 506 et seq.

[191] UTC § 813(d).

[192] UTC § 813(c), which defines the current beneficiaries as the "distributees or permissible distributees of trust income or principal." Mandatory reporting is limited to current beneficiaries because they are most likely to have the greatest interest in the day-to-day activities of the trust. UTC § 813, cmt.

[193] In re Goar, 2012 WL 6738678 (Ariz. Ct. App., Dec. 31, 2012).

[194] In re Rolf H. Brennemann Testamentary Trust, 849 N.W.2d 458 (Neb. 2014).

[195] UTC § 813, cmt.

The trustee must also promptly respond to any beneficiary's request for information, unless unreasonable under the circumstances.[196] Requiring that the trustee respond to a beneficiary's request for information is premised on the assumption that the beneficiary should be allowed to make an independent assessment of what information is relevant to protecting the beneficiary's interest.[197]

This includes a requirement that the trustee provide a beneficiary upon request with a copy of the trust instrument.[198] The drafting committee rejected the more limited approach of letting the trustee decide which provisions are material to the beneficiary's interest; the trustee's version of what is material may differ markedly from what a beneficiary might find relevant. Requiring disclosure of the entire instrument upon demand is consistent with case law.[199] However, like most provisions of the UTC, the requirement that the beneficiary be furnished with a copy of the entire trust instrument may be waived in the terms of the trust.[200]

The most discussed issue during the drafting of the UTC and subsequent to its approval is the extent to which a settlor may waive the above disclosure requirements. Under the UTC, most of the specific disclosure requirements are waivable. Not waivable is the trustee's obligation to notify the qualified beneficiaries age 25 or older of the existence of the trust, of the identity of the trustee, and of the right to request trustee's reports.[201] With respect to any beneficiary regardless of age, the trustee also may not waive the trustee's obligation to respond to a request for a trustee's report and other information reasonably related to the trust's administration.[202] In other words, if a beneficiary finds out about the trust and makes a request for information, the trustee must respond to the request even if the trustee was not obligated to inform the beneficiary about the trust in the first instance. This provision proved to be so controversial that in 2004 the Commissioners placed the waiver provision in brackets signaling that its enactment is optional.[203]

In states where the UTC is not in effect, clauses in a trust relieving the trustee from any duty to report have been held invalid, assuming that a true trust was intended rather than a gift to the "trustee."[204] A statement in a trust that "trustees need keep no accounts" did not preclude a court from ordering

---

[196] UTC § 813(a). For a case where the trustee failed to respond sufficiently to a beneficiary's request, *see* McHenry v. McHenry, 88 N.E.3d 1222 (Ohio Ct. App. 2017).

[197] UTC § 813, cmt.

[198] UTC § 813(b)(1).

[199] *See* Taylor v. Nationsbank Corp., 481 S.E.2d 358 (N.C.Ct.App.1997); Fletcher v. Fletcher, 480 S.E.2d 488 (Va.1997).

[200] UTC § 105(b)(8).

[201] UTC § 105(b)(8).

[202] UTC § 105(b)(9). For an application of this provision, *see* McHenry v. McHenry, 88 N.E.3d 1222 (Ohio Ct. App. 2017).

[203] UTC § 105, cmt. For a discussion of the various approaches taken with respect to the enactment of UTC § 105(b)(8)–(9), *see* Justak & Rhodes, *UTC's Duty to Inform and Report at 20-How Mandatory is Transparency*, 45 ACTEC L.J. 49 (2019).

[204] McNeil v. McNeil, 798 A.2d 503, 509 (Del.2002); Briggs v. Crowley, 224 N.E.2d 417 (Mass.1967). As to whether words in an instrument actually create a trust or are merely precatory, *see* Section 3.6, note 378 et seq.

the trustees to account, because a "settlor who attempts to create a trust without any accountability in the trustee is contradicting himself."[205] Under the Third Restatement, despite a waiver provision, a beneficiary is "always entitled . . . to request such information . . . as is reasonably necessary to enable the beneficiary to redress a breach of trust and to prevent or redress a breach of trust and otherwise to enforce his or her rights under the trust."[206] In *Wilson v. Wilson*,[207] the comparable and almost identical language in the Second Restatement was applied to require disclosure even though the trust document had totally waived any requirement to keep the beneficiaries informed of administration.[208]

The failure to keep the beneficiaries informed can be the basis for an award of attorney's fees against the trustee even though the beneficiary did not otherwise suffer harm. In the absence of information, "the beneficiary had little choice but to file litigation to resolve any doubts about the trust's administration.[209]

Accounting in Court

Reporting to the beneficiaries must be distinguished from accounting in court. Guardians/conservators must file accounts periodically in court.[210] Many states require court accountings for personal representatives administering the estate under supervised administration.[211] In California, even "independent" executors and administrators must get court approval of accounts.[212] Under the UPC, on the other hand, if administration is not "supervised," the personal representative can close an estate simply by filing a statement that an account has been given to the distributees, although the personal representative or any interested person can ask for court review of the account.[213] Cautious fiduciaries may seek the "greater protection" afforded by court approval of accounts even when it is not required.[214]

Some states require court accounting by testamentary trustees although court supervision of testamentary trusts has come under attack. Some trustees charge higher fees for testamentary trusts because of the cost of court accountings, which also focus "unwanted publicity" on the beneficiaries' financial affairs. These disadvantages are not justified by the protection they afford.[215] Many states have reduced or eliminated periodic judicial review of trustees' accounts. The UTC makes trust administration free of judicial supervision unless ordered by the court.[216] Beneficiaries are entitled to an

---

[205] Raak v. Raak, 428 N.W.2d 778, 780 (Mich.App.1988).

[206] *Restatement (Third) of Trusts* § 82, cmt. a(2) (2007).

[207] 690 S.E.2d 710 (N.C. Ct. App. 2010).

[208] *Restatement (Second) of Trusts* § 173, cmt. c (1959).

[209] In re Estate of Forgey, 906 N.W.2d 618, 639 (Neb. 2018).

[210] *See, e.g.*, Cal.Prob.Code § 2620.

[211] Tex. Est. Code § 359.

[212] Cal.Prob.Code § 10501(a)(3).

[213] UPC §§ 3–1001, 3–1003(a).

[214] UPC § 3–1005, cmt.

[215] Westfall, *Nonjudicial Settlement of Trustees Accounts*, 71 Harv.L.Rev. 40, 49–50 (1957).

[216] UTC § 201(b).

annual report, but copies do not have to be filed in court.[217] Courts have jurisdiction, however, when it is "invoked by an interested person" to "intervene in the administration of a trust."[218] The drafters of the UTC chose the term "report" instead of "accounting" to avoid an "inference that the report must be prepared in any particular format or with a high degree of formality."[219]

Even states that require court accountings allow interested parties to waive them,[220] but beneficiaries who are unborn, unascertained, or minors cannot approve or waive accounts. In addition, the fee of a guardian ad litem to represent such beneficiaries is often a significant cost. Under the UPC, guardians ad litem are appointed only if "representation of the interest otherwise would be inadequate."[221] The UTC authorizes binding settlements to be obtained in a nonjudicial settlement.[222] A provision in the trust instrument allowing one or more adult beneficiaries to approve accounts can avoid the cost of a guardian ad litem. Approval by such a designated beneficiary discharges the trustee if (i) the approval was not given "in bad faith nor in casual disregard of the interests or rights of the non-assenting beneficiary, and (ii) the accounting appropriately discloses material issues about the trustee's conduct."[223] But such a provision was held ineffective in a case where the settlor was the trustee and only adult beneficiary, since it would effectively negate the trustee's duty to account.[224]

Recordkeeping

To prepare an accounting and to otherwise keep the beneficiaries informed of administration requires that a trustee keep adequate records. Consequently, "[a] trustee has a duty to maintain clear, complete, and accurate books and records regarding the trust property and the administration of the trust."[225] To enable the beneficiaries to verify the accuracy of the information provided, a trustee must also "permit beneficiaries on a reasonable basis to inspect trust documents, records, and property holdings."[226]

---

[217] UTC § 813.

[218] UTC § 201(b). *See also* Cal.Prob.Code § 17200(a)(5).

[219] UTC § 813, cmt. For cases on what constitutes an adequate report under the UTC, *see* Meyers v. First Tennessee Bank, 503 S.W.3d 365 (Tenn. Ct. App. 2016); In re Rolf H. Brennemann Testamentary Trust, 849 N.W.2d 458 (Neb. 2014); In re Goar, 2012 WL 6738678 (Ariz. Ct. App. 2012).

[220] Cal.Prob.Code § 10954 (waiver of account by person entitled to distribution).

[221] UPC § 1–403(4).

[222] Nonjudicial settlements and virtual representation and other methods of representation are discussed in Section 14.8, note 707 et seq.

[223] *Restatement (Third) of Trusts* § 83, cmt. d (2007).

[224] In re Malasky, 736 N.Y.S.2d 151 (App.Div.2002).

[225] *Restatement (Third) of Trusts* § 83 (2007). *See also* UTC § 810(a). For cases where the trustee was remiss in this duty, *see* In re Rolf H. Brennemann Testamentary Trust, 849 N.W.2d 458 (Neb. 2014); In re Estate of Hedke, 775 N.W.2d 13 (Neb. 2009); Nelsen v. Nelsen, 2013 WL 646481 (Kan. Ct. App., Feb. 16, 2013); Green v. Lombard, 343 A.2d 905, 911 (Md. Ct. Spec. App. 1975).

[226] *Restatement (Third) of Trusts* § 82(a)(2) (2007).

Decree of Distribution

Normally when a court approves a final account it also enters a decree of distribution.[227] Partial distributions during administration may also be authorized, if the estate is clearly solvent, though a bond may be required of the distributees.[228] The UPC allows personal representatives to distribute assets of the estate without court authorization,[229] but many states do not. Even in independent administration, California requires court supervision for preliminary and final distributions.[230] No such order is generally required for distributions by trustees,[231] but a beneficiary can get a court order if a distribution is improperly made or withheld and trustees in doubt as to a distribution can seek instructions from the court.[232]

A decree of distribution made without proper notice to interested parties does not bind them. Furthermore, notice may be "effected by publication only if the address or identity of the person is unknown and cannot be obtained with reasonable diligence."[233] Also, a notice of a hearing does not satisfy the requirements of due process if it does not "provide sufficient information that will allow the [recipient] intelligently to ascertain the issue the hearing will address . . . and what one stands to lose . . . through non-attendance."[234] Even a minor who was represented by a guardian may sometimes get relief against a decree. A will left one third of the testator's estate to his wife, two thirds in trust for his minor sons. A guardian ad litem appointed for the sons raised no questions when the executors distributed more than a third of the estate to the wife. The guardian's "compensation was $100, indicative of a minimum effort involved in checking the documents for their facial regularity." The sons, after they came of age, had standing to sue the trustees for failing to obtain their proper share of the estate. "Equitable relief from a valid judgment will be granted . . . if there was no fair trial because [a party] was subject to an incapacity and was so poorly represented that there was no substantial presentation of his case."[235]

---

[227] *E.g.,* Cal.Prob.Code § 11641 (personal representative may distribute estate "when an order settling a final account and for distribution is entered"). A trustee can withhold final distribution until its accounts are approved. First Midwest Bank/Joliet v. Dempsey, 509 N.E.2d 791 (Ill. App. 1987).

[228] Cal.Prob.Code §§ 11620–11622. *See also* UPC § 3–505 (supervised administration). A trial court's order granting or denying a petition for partial distribution will be affirmed absent an abuse of discretion. In re Estate of Beard, 84 Cal. Rptr.2d 276, 293–94 (App.1999) (partial distribution with bond approved).

[229] Unless the administration is "supervised." UPC §§ 3–504, 3–704.

[230] Cal.Prob.Code § 10501(a)(4).

[231] Trust administration is to proceed "free of judicial intervention." Cal.Prob.Code § 17209.

[232] Cal.Prob.Code § 17200(a)(6). As to petitions for instructions, *see Restatement (Third) of Trusts* § 71 (2007).

[233] Matter of Estate of Hoffas, 422 N.W.2d 391, 395 (N.D.1988). *See also* Section 14.8, note 689.

[234] Booth v. McKnight, 70 P.3d 855, 865 (Okl.2003).

[235] In re Wickman's Will, 289 So.2d 788 (Fla.App.1974). Perhaps the proper defendant in this case was the guardian ad litem. "A number of decisions solemnly declare that he is liable to his ward for negligence in the performance of [his] duty [to assert claims] but it is difficult to find decisions in which liability was in fact imposed." Westfall, *Nonjudicial Settlement of Trustees Accounts*, 71 Harv.L.Rev. at 45.

A decree can also be attacked on the ground that it purported to determine title to property which did not belong to the decedent. "A probate court may only determine who takes property owned by the decedent."[236] But the UPC, in keeping with a trend to expand the limits of the probate court's jurisdiction, allows the court "to determine title to property alleged to belong to the estate."[237]

Some courts ignore a mistaken decree if the court which rendered it failed to focus on the relevant issue. Collateral attack on a judgment is barred if "the court had actually construed a will, albeit erroneously," but not if the court "made an obvious mistake."[238] Finally, a decree of distribution has been set aside for "extrinsic fraud" when the applicant for an estate failed to reveal the existence of a closer heir of the decedent.[239]

Liability for Improper Distribution

Fiduciaries can be held liable for making distributions to the wrong person. When a trust gave the settlor's wife the income so long as she remained unmarried, and she remarried and failed to notify the trustee which continued to pay her the income, the trustee was held liable to the remaindermen for these payments because it failed to make reasonable efforts to ascertain the true state of the facts.[240] The UTC and some statutes protect trustees who make erroneous distributions without knowledge of a relevant fact like marriage, divorce, or death.[241] The Third Restatement provides that a trustee is not liable "for a misdelivery resulting from a reasonable, good faith reliance" on the terms of the trust, but if the trust terms are ambiguous, the trustee must apply to a court for instructions.[242] The Third Restatement also protects trustees who make payments under a trust which is later held invalid or revoked unless they knew or had reason to suspect the true situation.[243] The UTC provides similar protection to the trustee of a revocable trust that is later invalidated.[244] The UPC exonerates personal representatives for distributions which were "authorized at the time," *e.g.*, a distribution of apparently intestate assets to the heirs when a will is later probated.[245]

Whether or not a personal representative who makes an erroneous distribution is protected, the person who receives it is liable under the UPC unless the distribution can "no longer can be questioned because of

---

[236] Apple v. Kile, 457 N.E.2d 254, 258 (Ind.App.1983).

[237] UPC § 3–105.

[238] Loberg v. Alford, 372 N.W.2d 912, 918 (N.D.1985).

[239] Estate of McGuigan, 99 Cal.Rptr.2d 887 (App.2000).

[240] National Academy of Sciences v. Cambridge Trust Co., 346 N.E.2d 879, 884 (Mass.1976). *See also* Deluca v. Jordan, 781 N.E.2d 849 (Mass. App. 2003) (administrator surcharged for erroneous distribution based on heir's forged signature).

[241] UTC § 1007; Texas Prop.Code § 114.004; Wash.Rev.Code § 11.98.100. Such claims may also be limited by a statute of limitations. Toombs v. Daniels, 361 N.W.2d 801, 810 (Minn. 1985) (claim of wrongfully excluded beneficiary limited to last 6 years' income).

[242] *Restatement (Third) of Trusts* § 76, cmt. f (2007).

[243] *Restatement (Third) of Trusts* § 76, cmt. f. *See also Restatement, Second, of Trusts* § 226A (1959); *cf.* Wilcox v. Waldman, 744 P.2d 444 (Ariz. App. 1987) (filing suit not enough to create reasonable doubt as to validity of trust).

[244] UTC § 604(b).

[245] UPC § 3–703.

adjudication, estoppel, or limitation."[246] The Restatement of Trusts has a similar provision for trustees.[247] A court decree surcharging a trustee for excessive payments to a beneficiary also directed the recipient to return to the money improperly distributed to him.[248] A fiduciary has been allowed to sue a third party who supplied him with false information which led to the wrongful distribution.[249]

Retainer

When a devisee or heir owes money to the decedent, personal representatives can normally set off this debt against any distribution to which the debtor is entitled. But under the UPC, personal representatives cannot thereby indirectly collect an unenforceable debt, because the debtor "has the benefit of any defense which would be available to him in a direct proceeding for recovery of the debt," such as a statute of limitations or a discharge in bankruptcy.[250]

Distributions to Incompetents

Fiduciaries who distribute to persons who are legally incapacitated risk having to pay again. A trustee was surcharged for permitting an incompetent settlor to withdraw funds from a revocable trust when "the trustee should have known of the settlor's incompetency." However, the trustee was not liable for earlier distributions, since "the facts do not indicate that the bank knew or should have known" that the distributee was incompetent at the time.[251]

To be safe, personal representatives usually must distribute shares of a minor heir or devisee to a guardian or conservator,[252] but many states have "facility of payment" statutes to avoid the need for guardianship when only small amounts are involved.[253] The UPC allows "a person required to transfer money or property to a minor" to do so "as to an amount or value not exceeding $10,000 a year, by transferring it to . . . a person who has the care and custody of the minor with whom the minor resides." The recipient must apply the money for the minor's support and turn over any balance to the minor at majority.[254] The UTC authorizes trustees to pay amounts distributable to a beneficiary "under a legal disability or who the trustee reasonably believes is

---

[246] UPC § 3–909.

[247] *Restatement (Third) of Trusts* § 104, cmt. g(3) (2012). *See also* UTC § 604(c); Tex. Prop. Code § 114.031(a)(4); In re Estate of Berger, 520 N.E.2d 690 (Ill. App. 1987) (conservator's surety).

[248] Dunkley v. Peoples Bank & Trust Co., 728 F.Supp. 547, 564 (W.D.Ark.1989); Brent v. Smathers, 547 So.2d 683, 686 (Fla.App.1989).

[249] Deluca v. Jordan, 781 N.E.2d 849, 856 (Mass.App.2003).

[250] UPC § 3–903; Matter of Will of Cargill, 420 N.W.2d 268 (Minn.App.1988) (trustee cannot withhold income to satisfy claim against beneficiary which was discharged in bankruptcy). *But see* Estate of Randeris v. Randeris, 523 N.W.2d 600 (Iowa App. 1994); In re De Laurentiis Entertainment Group, Inc., 963 F.2d 1269, 1274 (9th Cir. 1992) (a discharged debt can be used as setoff outside probate).

[251] Cloud v. United States Nat'l Bank, 570 P.2d 350, 355–56 (Or.1977). *Restatement (Second) of Contracts* §§ 14–15 (1981) distinguishes between persons dealing with minors and adult incompetents.

[252] Matter of Estate of Roberts, 426 N.E.2d 269, 272 (Ill.App.1981) (trustee directed to distribute to conservator of incompetent beneficiary).

[253] UPC § 5–104, cmt.

[254] UPC § 5–104.

incapacitated" to the beneficiary or, in order of priority: (1) a guardian or conservator; (2) a custodian under the Uniform Transfers to Minors or Custodial Trust Acts, or (3) an adult relative or other person responsible for the beneficiary's care, "to be expended on the beneficiary's behalf."[255] The trustee may also retain any distributions as a separate fund but subject to the beneficiary's continuing right to withdraw the distribution.[256] Many trusts and wills contain broad facility of payment powers similar to the UTC.

Distribution in Kind

Distributions are sometimes made in cash, sometimes in kind. The UPC provides that assets of an estate "shall be distributed in kind to the extent possible" but a pecuniary or a residuary devisee can object to such distribution.[257] Distributions in kind to satisfy pecuniary devises raise the problem of valuation. Suppose a will leaves $10,000 to the testator's sister and the executor proposes to satisfy this by distributing shares of XYZ stock. The stock must be valued to know how many shares the sister should receive. Assets are valued for this purpose at the date of distribution.[258] Thus if the assets of an estate appreciate or depreciate during administration, the benefit or burden of the change falls on the residuary and specific devisees, not pecuniary devisees.

When heirs or residuary devisees are entitled to fractional shares, can a fiduciary make non-pro-rata distributions, *e.g.*, all the XYZ stock to one, and other assets of comparable value to the others? The UTC authorizes trustees to make such non-pro-rata distributions,[259] but the UPC gives each residuary beneficiary a right "to his proportionate share of each asset constituting the residue."[260] Non-pro-rata distributions may be desirable to avoid divided ownership, but they too raise valuation problems.

The UPC and UTC seek to reduce controversies over the form of distributions by allowing trustees to send the beneficiaries a proposal for distribution, which terminates their right to object if they do not do so within 30 days.[261]

---

[255] UTC § 816(21).

[256] UTC § 816(21)(D). *See also Restatement (Third) of Trusts* § 49, cmt. c(2) (2003).

[257] UPC § 3–906. *See also* Estate of Lindberg, 388 N.E.2d 148, 156 (Ill. App.1979) (executor has duty to sell when residuary beneficiary objects to distribution in kind). *See also Restatement (Second) of Trusts* § 346 (1959) (beneficiary can control whether distribution is in cash or kind).

[258] UPC § 3–906(a)(2)(B); Van Schaack v. American South Bank, N.A., 530 So. 2d 740, 744 (Ala. 1988). When multiple distributions are made in installments, multiple valuations are necessary. Williams v. Harrington, 460 So.2d 533 (Fla. App. 1984). As to the income tax consequences of such distributions, *see* Sherman, *All You Really Need to Know About Subchapter J You Learned from This Article*, 63 Mo.L.Rev. 1, 44–6 (1998).

[259] UTC § 816(22). *See also* Cal.Prob.Code § 16246; In re Estate of Meyer, 802 P.2d 148, 153 (Wash.App.1990). For the desirability of authorizing such distributions in order to prevent the realization of capital gains when they occur, *see* Price, *Contemporary Estate Planning* § 4.28.6 (2014 ed.).

[260] UPC § 3–906, cmt.

[261] UPC § 3–906(b); UTC § 817(a).

Delay in Distribution

One of the most common complaints about lawyers and the legal system is delay in distribution of assets in administration. This is a commonly cited reason for the widespread popular desire to avoid probate.[262] Some states penalize personal representative who unduly delay distribution. Illinois charges them 10% interest per year on the value of any assets not distributed two years after their appointment unless good cause for the delay is shown.[263] California courts can reduce the personal representatives' compensation for such delays.[264] Delays have also been the basis for disciplining attorneys who were responsible for them.[265] However, courts have shown their customary deference to reasonable decisions by fiduciaries.[266] And the UTC goes further by clarifying that upon the event terminating a trust, the trustee's obligation to expeditiously terminate a trust is subject to the proviso that a trustee may "retain a reasonable reserve to pay debts, expenses, and taxes."[267] A trustee who delays distribution following termination for more than a reasonable time may be charged with the costs of the delay.[268]

§ 14.4 Other Duties

Trustees and other fiduciaries are subject to numerous other duties.

Prudence

While the duty to act with prudence is principally associated with investment decisions, discussed in Section 12.2, the duty applies to all aspects of administration. The most widely and modern accepted statement of the duty is found in the Restatement (Third) of Trusts.[269] Approved by the American Law Institute in 1990, the duty requires a "trustee to invest and manage the funds of the trust as a prudent person would, by considering the purposes, terms, distribution requirements, and other circumstances of the trust." In satisfying this standard, the trustee must "exercise reasonable care, skill, and caution."[270] This standard was then copied nearly verbatim in the Uniform Prudent Investor Act,[271] approved in 1994, and then generalized and made applicable to all aspects of trust administration in both the Uniform Trust

---

[262] *See* Section 10.4, note 108 et seq.

[263] 755 ILCS 5/24–10.

[264] Cal.Prob.Code § 12205; Estate of Heller, 9 Cal. Rptr.2d 274, 276 (App. 1992).

[265] Committee on Professional Ethics v. Winkel, 415 N.W.2d 601 (Iowa 1987) (attorney reprimanded for allowing an estate to remain open for seven years).

[266] Estate of Vail v. First of America Trust, 722 N.E.2d 248 (Ill.App.1999) (finding of good cause for delay in distributing estate upheld); Shriners Hospitals v. Robbins, 450 So.2d 798, 802 (Ala.1984) (refusal to impose liability on trustee for delay in distribution). As to the income tax consequences of delayed distribution of an estate, *see* Sherman, *All You Really Need to Know About Subchapter J You Learned from This Article*, 63 Mo.L.Rev. at 44–6.

[267] UTC § 817(b).

[268] In re Estate of Hedke, 775 N.W.2d 13 (Neb. 2009).

[269] *Restatement (Third) of Trusts* § 90 (2007). The late date of the volume is attributable to editorial updating. The prudent investor rule was approved by the American Law Institute in 1990.

[270] *Restatement (Third) of Trusts* § 90.

[271] Unif. Prudent Investor Act (UPIA) § 2(a).

Code,[272] approved in 2000, and in a different section of the Third Restatement.[273]

The Third Restatement has a different emphasis than the Second Restatement. The Second Restatement can be read as applying the same standard—that which a "man of ordinary prudence [would exercise] in dealing with his own property"[274]—regardless of the type or purposes of the trust. The Third Restatement more appropriately bases the standard on the purposes and other circumstances of the particular trust.

Although there is an extensive body of caselaw on prudence in making investments, there is less caselaw on prudence in other aspects of trust administration. Examples of alleged imprudence in states that have enacted the UTC include payment of excessive storage charges for a beneficiary's tangible personal property,[275] and failure to insure and otherwise take steps to protect standing timber.[276]

Both the Second and Third Restatements assume that the settlor has selected a trustee of ordinary skills. However, a trustee "who has special skills or expertise, or is named trustee in reliance on the trustee's representation that the trustee has special skills or expertise," is held to a standard based on those skills or expertise.[277]

The duty to act with prudence and the other duties of the trustee do not depend on whether the trustee receives compensation.[278] A settlor who wishes to modify a trustee's standard of care may do so but there is a limit. An exculpatory clause is unenforceable to the extent it exculpates a trustee from liability "for breach of trust committed in bad faith or with reckless indifference to the purposes of the trust or to the interests of the beneficiaries."[279]

Duty to Administer Trust

Following acceptance of the trusteeship, the trustee must administer the trust in good faith, and in accordance with its terms and purposes and the interests of the beneficiaries and other applicable law.[280] Under the UTC, this duty may not be waived in the terms of the trust.[281] Once the trustee has

---

[272] UTC § 804.

[273] *Restatement (Third) of Trusts* § 77(1) (2007).

[274] *Restatement (Second) of Trusts* § 174, cmt. a (1959).

[275] Passero v. Fitzsimmons, 81 N.E.3d 814 (Mass Ct. App. 2017) (trustee found liable)

[276] Regions Bank v. Lowrey, 101 So.3d 210 (Ala. 2012) (trustee not found liable, risk of severe hurricane damage was less than 1%).

[277] UTC § 806, which is similar to Unif. Prudent Investor Act § 2(f), *Restatement (Third) of Trusts* § 77(3) (2007), and *Restatement (Second) of Trusts* § 174 (1959).

[278] *Restatement (Third) of Trusts* § 70, cmt. d(1) (2007).

[279] UTC § 1008(a)(1). The Third Restatement substitutes "indifference" for "reckless indifference" and adds that an exculpatory provision cannot relieve a trustee of accountability for profits derived from the breach of trust. *Restatement (Third) of Trusts* § 96(1) (2012). For a more detailed discussion of exculpatory provisions, *see* Section 14.8, note 655 et seq.

[280] UTC § 801. *See also Restatement (Third) of Trusts* § 76(1) (2007).

[281] UTC § 105(b)(2).

accepted the trusteeship, the duty to administer the trust continues as long as the trustee is in office.[282]

Costs of Administration

In administering a trust, a trustee may only incur costs that reasonably relate "to the trust property, the purposes of the trust, and the skills of the trustee:"[283]

The duty not to incur unreasonable costs applies when a trustee decides whether and how to delegate to agents, in addition to other aspects of trust administration. In deciding whether and how to delegate, the trustee must be alert to balancing projected benefits against the likely costs. To protect the beneficiary against excessive costs, the trustee should also be alert to adjusting compensation for functions that the trustee has delegated to others.[284]

Delegation

It is often necessary if not essential that a trustee delegate authority to agents such as attorneys, accountants, real estate managers and investment advisors. Despite this necessity, the much-criticized former law, referred to as the "non-delegation" rule,[285] placed a premium on the frequently arbitrary distinction between discretionary functions that were thought to be nondelegable versus ministerial functions that the trustee was allowed to delegate. The Second Restatement admitted in a comment that "There is not a clear-cut line dividing the acts which a trustee can properly delegate from those which he cannot properly delegate."[286] Significantly, a trustee was forbidden to delegate the authority "to select investments."[287]

The Third Restatement,[288] and even more so, the Uniform Prudent Investor Act[289] and UTC,[290] have reversed the former approach by encouraging and protecting the trustee in making delegations appropriate to the facts and circumstances of the particular trust. A trustee may delegate duties and powers that a prudent trustee of comparable skills could properly delegate under the circumstances.[291] For example, delegating some administrative and reporting duties might be prudent for a family trustee but unnecessary for a corporate trustee. Although a trustee is not mandated to delegate any specific function, failure to delegate may result in the trustee committing a breach of trust if the trustee is incapable of performing the function.

---

282 *Restatement (Third) of Trusts* § 76, cmt. a (2007).

283 UTC § 805. *See also* UPIA § 7; *Restatement (Third) of Trusts* § 88 (2007).

284 UTC § 805, cmt.

285 *Restatement (Second) of Trusts* § 171 (1959).

286 *Restatement (Second) of Trusts* § 171, cmt. d.

287 *Restatement (Second) of Trusts* § 171, cmt. h. For discussion and criticism of the "non-delegation" rule, *see* Langbein, *Reversing the Nondelegation Rule of Trust-Investment Law*, 59 Mo.L.Rev. 105 (1994).

288 *Restatement (Third) of Trusts* § 80 (2007). An earlier version, approved by the American Law Institute in 1990, was first published by the ALI in *Restatement (Third) of Trusts (Prudent Investor Rule)* § 227, cmt. j (1992).

289 UPIA § 9.

290 UTC § 807.

291 UPIA § 9(a); UTC § 807(a).

The Third Restatement also established standards for making a delegation. In making a delegation, a trustee must exercise reasonable care, skill, and caution in selecting an agent, in establishing the scope and terms of the delegation consistent with the purposes and terms of the trust, and in periodically reviewing the agent's performance and compliance with the terms of the delegation.[292] Assuming that the trustee meets this obligation, the trustee is not liable to the beneficiaries no matter how improper the actions of the agent.[293] However, the agent can be held liable to the beneficiaries for failing to exercise reasonable care.[294]

Powers to Direct

Trusts frequently grant to other persons the power to direct the trustee's actions. The settlor of a revocable trust, through the settlor's power of revocation, retains, at least indirectly, the authority to direct the trustee's actions. Many revocable trusts provide that the trustee is to make distributions as the settlor may direct. Powers to direct a trustee's actions are also frequently granted to third parties. The "adviser," "trust protector," or "director" may be granted authority in the trust to make decisions with respect to distributions, to select trust investments, or to manage a closely held business. Sometimes the powers granted are more extensive, such as granting the third party the right to remove and replace the trustee or to even modify or terminate the trust.[295]Section 808 of the UTC, which addresses powers to direct the trustee is, like most other duties under the UTC, subject to modification or negation in the terms of the trust. Section 808(a) addresses the authority of the settlor of a revocable trust. While a trust is revocable, the trustee may follow a direction of the settlor that is contrary to the terms of the trust and is protected from liability for doing so.[296] The trustee may also insist that the settlor formally amend the trust so that the direction conforms to the trust's stated terms. The directions given by the settlor during life can also bind the trustee after the settlor's death. A direction given during lifetime to pay the university tuition of a relative required the trustee to pay the tuition bill for the three semesters falling after the settlor's death.[297]

Section 808(b) ratifies the use of the more common types of powers to direct, whether granted to a third person or retained by the settlor of an irrevocable trust. To encourage the trustee to honor the exercise of a power to

---

[292] UPIA § 9(a)(1)–(3); UTC § 807(a)(1)–(3).

[293] UPIA § 9(c); UTC § 807(c).

[294] UPIA § 9(b); UTC § 807(b).

[295] For background on trust protectors, *see* Miller, *Regularizing the Trust Protector,* 103 Iowa L. Rev. 2097 (2018); Newman, *Trust Law in the Twenty-First Century: Challenges to Fiduciary Accountability,* 29 Quinnipiac L. Rev. 261, 292–307 (2016); Frolik, *Trust Protectors: Why They Have Become "The Next Big Thing,"* 50 Real Prop. Tr. & Est. L. J. 267 (2015); Ausness, *The Role of Trust Protectors in American Trust Law,* 45 Real Prop. Tr. & Est. L.J. 319 (2010); Sterk, *Trust Protectors, Agency Costs, and Fiduciary Duty,* 27 Cardozo L. Rev. 2761 (2006). While the protector may be a single individual, some of these trusts have detailed governance structures with separate protectors or committees for investments and distributions among other details. These structures are discussed in Duncan & Sarafa, *Achieve the Promise and Limit the Risk-of-Multi-Participant Trusts,* 36 ACTEC L.J. 769 (2011). For a case involving such a multi-participant structure, *see* Shelton v. Tamposi, 62 A.3d 741 (N.H. 2013).

[296] McGinley v. Bank of America, N.A., 209 P.3d 1148 (2005).

[297] Kritchman v. Wolk, 152 So.3d 628 (Fla. Dist. Ct. App. 2014).

direct, Section 808(b) imposes only minimal oversight responsibility on the trustee. A trustee may refuse the direction only if the attempted exercise would be "manifestly contrary to the terms of the trust or the trustee knows that the attempted exercise would constitute a serious breach of a fiduciary duty owed by the holder of the power to the beneficiaries of the trust."

Section 808(c) ratifies the recent trend to grant "trust protectors" broad authority not only to direct the actions of the trustee but also to modify or terminate the trust. Section 808(c) clarifies that the terms of a trust may confer on any person, including the trustee, a power to direct the modification or termination of the trust. The holder of the power to direct is usually acting on behalf of others, whether the power is limited to direction of specific acts or more broadly authorizes the power holder to modify or terminate the trust.

The desire for more certainty than provided by Section 808 led many states to enact more detailed directed trust statutes with the Delaware statute being the best known.[298] In 2017, the Uniform Law Commission replaced Section 808(b)–(c) with the more detailed Uniform Directed Trust Act (UDTA) that is separate from but coordinates with the UTC.[299] The most noticeable feature of UDTA is a lowering of a trustee's standard of care. Under UDTA, a trustee may be held liable only for "willful misconduct," a standard that was borrowed from the Delaware statute.[300] Section 808(a) of the UTC, which addresses the authority of a settlor of a revocable trust to direct the actions of a trustee, was not impacted by the approval of the UDTA. Section 808(a) was instead moved to Section 603(a).

Collect, Control and Protection of Trust Property

A trustee has a duty to "take reasonable steps to take control of and protect the trust property."[301] This duty normally requires that the trustee take possession of the personal property belonging to the trust, obtain appropriate insurance, and secure payment of any choses in action. Like other trustee duties, the duty to control and protect is subject to modification in terms of the trust. For example, the settlor may provide that the spouse may occupy the settlor's former residence rent-free, in which event the spouse's occupancy would prevent the trustee from taking possession.[302]

A trustee must take reasonable steps to enforce claims of the trust and to defend against claims made against the trust. It may not be reasonable to enforce a claim depending on the likelihood of recovery and the cost of suit and

[298] 2 Del. C. § 3313.

[299] For analyses of UDTA, *see* Morley & Sitkoff, *Making Directed Trusts Work: The Uniform Directed Trust Act,* 44 ACTEC L.J. 3 (2019); Reames, *Beyond UTC Section 808 and the Uniform Directed Trust Act,* 45 ACTEC L. J. 61 (2019); Ditelberg, *Am I My Brother's Keeper: Willful Misconduct and the Directed Trustee Under the Uniform Directed Trust Act,* 44 ACTEC L.J. 207 (2019); Spica, *From Strength to Strength: A Comment on Morley and Sitkoff's Making Directed Trusts Work,* 44 ACTEC L.J. 215 (2019).

[300] UDTA §§ 9, 10.

[301] UTC § 809; *Restatement (Third) of Trusts* § 76(2)(b) (2007).

[302] *See* UTC § 809, cmt.

enforcement. It might also be more reasonable to settle an action or suffer a default rather than to defend an action.[303]

A trustee must also take reasonable steps to compel a former trustee or other person to deliver trust property to the trustee and to redress a breach of trust known to the trustee to have been committed by a former trustee.[304] However, pursuit of a claim is not required if the amount of the claim, costs of suit and enforcement, and likelihood of recovery, make such action uneconomic.[305] Under the UTC, a successor trustee need only redress breaches of trust "known" to have been committed by the predecessor.[306] Under the second Restatement, the successor trustee could be held liable if the trustee knew or should have known of a situation constituting a breach of trust.[307] Pursuing claims against a predecessor fiduciary may be expensive or unwise due to family dynamics. Consequently, consideration should sometimes be given to obtaining consent from the beneficiaries protecting the trustee from potential liability for failing to pursue a claim.[308] The obligation to pursue a predecessor trustee can also be waived or limited in the terms of the trust.[309]

Identification of Trust Property

The duty to adequately identify trust property is implicit in the requirements that a trustee act with prudence and with loyalty toward the beneficiaries' interests. Without such a requirement, trust property could easily be lost through commingling with the property of the trustee or others or even misappropriated by the trustee.

The duty to adequately identify trust property is in fact two duties—the prohibition against mingling and the duty to earmark. The prohibition against mingling requires that a trustee at all times keep the trust property separate from the trustee's own property. The duty to earmark, in its traditional formulation, required the trustee to make certain that the property is identified as property of the trust.[310] Concluding that this standard was not particularly informative, the UTC drafters decided to make it more precise by requiring that the interest of the trust must appear in the records of a third party, such as a bank, brokerage firm, transfer agent, or recorder of deed.[311] Because of the serious risk of mistake or misappropriation even if disclosure is made to the beneficiaries, showing the interest of the trust solely in the trustee's own internal records is insufficient.[312] Earmarking is not practical for all types of assets. For assets not subject to registration or recording, such as

---

[303] UTC § 811 & cmt. *See also Restatement (Third) of Trusts* § 76, cmt. d (2007).

[304] UTC § 812. *See also Restatement (Third) of Trusts* § 76, cmt. d (2007); *Restatement (Second) of Trusts* § 223 (1959).

[305] UTC § 812, cmt.

[306] UTC § 812.

[307] *Restatement (Second) of Trusts* § 223(2)(a) (1959).

[308] The effect of beneficiary consent, which is addressed in UTC § 1009, is discussed in Section 14.8, note 695 et seq.

[309] UTC § 105.

[310] *See Restatement (Third) of Trusts* § 84 (2007). *See also Restatement (Second) of Trusts* § 179 (1959).

[311] UTC § 810(c) & cmt.

[312] UTC § 810, cmt.

tangible personal property and bearer bonds, arranging for the trust's ownership interest to be reflected on the records of a third-party custodian would not be feasible. For this reason, the UTC waives separate recordkeeping for assets for which separate identification is infeasible.[313]

§ 14.5 Administrative Powers

A power differs from a duty. A duty imposes an obligation or a mandatory prohibition. A power, on the other hand, is a discretion, the exercise of which is not obligatory.[314] Historically, the powers granted to trustees were "typically few, since the trustees' job was simply to hold and then to convey to the remainder beneficiaries."[315] The role of trusts has expanded over the years and the demands on trustees have greatly increased with trustees now required to provide active management instead of being mere title holders. Yet, the leading treatise writers, Professors Scott and Bogert, when describing a trustee's powers, have used open-ended language such as a trustee has all powers "necessary" to carry out the purposes of the trust, leaving trustees, beneficiaries and third parties uncertain as to exactly what authority the trustee had.[316] In reaction, drafters added trustee power lists consisting of pages of mind-numbing detail. Also, the Uniform Law Commissioners in 1964 promulgated the Uniform Trustees' Powers Act, containing a detailed list of powers automatically bestowed upon a trustee except to the extent modified in the trust terms. This Act and similar trustees' powers legislation was eventually enacted in nearly all states.[317]

Powers legislation is not limited to trustees. The UPC contains comprehensive powers lists for both personal representatives[318] and conservators.[319] Numerous non-UPC states have also enacted detailed powers lists for fiduciaries other than trustees, particularly in their independent administration statutes.[320] The difficulty with most such legislation, however, is that a fiduciary's authority to engage in particular transactions is sometimes assumed not to exist unless it is specifically enumerated in the list, thereby resulting in even longer powers lists and inquiries by third parties to verify that the document contains express language authorizing particular transactions.[321]

---

313 UTC § 810(c).

314 UTC § 815, cmt.

315 Langbein, *The Contractarian Basis of the Law of Trusts*, 105 Yale L.J. 625, 640 (1995).

316 For a short but good summary of this history, *see Restatement (Third) of Trusts* § 85, cmt. a (2007). For the restrictive approach of the treatise writers and prior versions of the Restatement, *see Restatement (Third) of Trusts* § 85 Reporter's Note to, cmt. a.

317 For background on the Act, *see* Haskell, *Problems with the Uniform Trustees' Powers Act*, 32 Law & Contemp.Probs. 168 (1967); Hallgring, *Uniform Trustees' Powers Act and the Basic Principles of Fiduciary Responsibility*, 41 Wash.L.Rev. 801 (1966); Horowitz, *Uniform Trustees' Powers Act*, 41 Wash.L.Rev. 1 (1966); Fratcher, *Trustees' Powers Legislation*, 37 N.Y.U.L.Rev. 627 (1962).

318 UPC § 3–715.

319 UPC § 5–425.

320 *See, e.g.*, Mo. Rev. Stat. § 473.810.

321 UTC § 815, cmt.

The UTC is intended to change this attitude. Sections 815 and 816 specify a trustee's powers with respect to the administration of the trust. Section 815(a) is intended to grant trustees the broadest possible powers. "This broad authority is denoted in part by granting the trustee the powers of an unmarried competent owner of individually owned property, unlimited by restrictions that might be placed on it by marriage, disability, or cotenancy."[322] The trustee may also exercise the powers conferred by the terms of the trust, and, except as limited by the terms of the trust, any other powers conferred by the UTC and any other powers appropriate to properly manage, invest, and distribute the trust property. The trustee's authority is not unlimited, however. Under section 815(b), the exercise of a power is subject to the fiduciary duties prescribed by the UTC, including whether its exercise is prudent in a particular circumstance. All the trustee's powers under the UTC are exercisable without court approval.[323] This is in contrast to the necessity in many states for other fiduciaries, such as personal representatives and conservators, to get prior court approval for certain actions.[324]

The UTC drafters could have arguably stopped at this point. If a trustee has all powers that persons can exercise with respect to their own property, why would any additional authority be necessary? The drafters, however, recognized the reality that persons with whom trustees must deal would continue, at least for a time, to insist on a detailed powers list. It is "easier to obtain the co-operation of transactional parties when the trustee can point to specific statutory authority that does not require any thought or interpretation in the application."[325] Section 816 contains such a detailed list, all of which may be altered or supplemented in the terms of the trust.[326] There are also a number of other trustee powers scattered throughout the UTC that are subsumed under section 815.[327]

The Third Restatement copies its powers provision after the UTC. Except as limited by the terms of the trust or statute, a trustee has all powers that a competent unmarried individual has with respect to their own property, as well as any additional powers conferred in the terms of the trust, granted by statute or recognized elsewhere in the Restatement.[328] The exercise of all such powers is subject to fiduciary duties, however.[329] The Restatement adds helpfully that all such powers pass to a substitute or successor trustee unless otherwise provided in the terms of the trust.[330]

---

[322] UTC § 815, cmt.

[323] UTC § 815(a).

[324] *See* Section 14.2, notes 69–74 (investments); *infra* note 343 et seq. (sale of property by personal representative); Mo. Rev. Stat. § 475.235 (sale of real estate by conservator).

[325] Langbein, *The Uniform Trust Code,* 15 Trust Law International 66, 71 (2001).

[326] UTC § 105.

[327] *See* UTC §§ 108(c) (transfer of principal place of administration); 414(a) (termination of uneconomic trust with value less than $50,000); 417 (combination and division of trusts); 703(e) (delegation to cotrustee); 802(h) (exception to duty of loyalty); 807 (delegation to agent of powers and duties); 810(d) (joint investments); and Article 9 (Uniform Prudent Investor Act).

[328] *Restatement (Third) of Trusts* § 85 (2007).

[329] *Restatement (Third) of Trusts* § 86 (2007).

[330] *Restatement (Third) of Trusts* § 85(2) (2007). This Restatement position is consistent with case law and many state statutes. *See* Section 14.6, note 490 et seq.

Specific Powers

Reference should be made to Section 816 of the UTC or other powers legislation for the full breadth of powers that can be granted to a fiduciary and the types of assets that a fiduciary may be called upon to manage. Instead of comprehensive coverage, the following discussion focuses on a limited number of discrete issues.

Digital Assets[331]

With nearly all Americans having a digital presence, an increasingly important issue is how digital accounts and assets will be accessed and managed upon the death or incapacity of the owner. The Revised Uniform Access to Digital Assets Act addresses the authority of a personal representative, attorney-in-fact under a power of attorney, conservator, and trustee to access and manage these assets.

Under the Act, a "custodian" is "a person that carries, maintains, processes, receives, or stores a digital asset of a user."[332] "Digital asset" is in turn expansively defined as "an electronic record in which an individual has a right or interest."[333] Not under the Act but under the federal Stored Communications Act (SCA),[334] a distinction is made between "public" custodians, such as Google, which makes its service available to the general public, and "private" custodians, such as a bank, university, or employer, which limit electronic access to a defined and restricted audience. Under the SCA, it is a criminal offense for the custodian to disclose the contents of a communication to anyone other than the customer or subscriber without the express consent of the customer or subscriber.[335] Because public custodians took the view that a fiduciary for a customer or subscriber was not covered by the SCA, public custodians were habitually denying access by fiduciaries. The strictures on disclosure, however, are less severe for what is known as the "catalogue," which is a listing of persons with whom the customer or subscriber communicated, the time and date, and the recipient's email address, but not the content of the message.[336]

Upon the death or incapacity of an individual, the fiduciary's first concern is gaining access to the electronic accounts. Ideally, the individual will have kept a log of the passwords or arranged for cloud storage and made certain that a trusted person is aware of the cloud storage account. But assuming the fiduciary has adequate information to access the account, obtaining necessary information from employers and financial institutions has not generally been an issue. Refusal to access has mostly occurred with public custodians.

---

[331] The discussion of digital assets is adapted from English, Specific Assets-Digital Assets, 2 Missouri Probate Law & Practice § 783.50 (Supp. 2020). Reprinted here with permission of the publisher, Thomson Reuters.

[332] RUFADAA § 2(8).

[333] RUFADAA § 2(10).

[334] U.S.C.A. §§ 2701 to 2712.

[335] U.S.C.A. § 2702.

[336] RUFADAA § 2(4).

The Revised Uniform Fiduciary Access to Digital Assets Act (RUFADAA) was approved by the Uniform Law Commission in 2015. The term "Revised" is used because RUFADAA replaced the unsuccessful Uniform Fiduciary Access to Digital Assets Act, which was approved in 2014 and used a different approach.

Under RUFADAA, an opt-in approach is used. A custodian may deny access to the electronic content unless the user has somehow signified consent. One way a user may signify consent is through use of an "online tool" where the user may indicate who is to have access. A direction in an online tool overrides a contrary direction in a will, trust, or power of attorney.[337]

A second way a user may signify consent to the disclosure of electronic content is by granting the fiduciary access in the will, trust, or power of attorney. The provision inserted into the document should preferably track the language of the Act itself and make clear that the fiduciary may access the content of the electronic communication in addition to accessing the catalogue of the communication.[338]

Beyond that, access to the content depends on the type of fiduciary. A personal representative and conservator may gain access to the content by obtaining a court order.[339] Access by a trustee varies depending on whether the trustee is the original user of the account.[340] No provision is made in the Act for access by an attorney-in-fact who lack express authority in the power of attorney.[341] In any of these cases, the custodian may request proper proof of authority before granting the fiduciary access.

Less of a hurdle applies to access to the catalogue of communications as opposed to content. If the fiduciary presents proper proof of authority, access to the catalogue is permitted.[342]

Power to Sell

Can a personal representative or trustee sell assets of the estate or trust or must they be preserved for distribution in kind to the beneficiaries the estate is closed or the trust terminated? While the governing instrument may limit the fiduciary's authority, most wills and trusts confer broad powers of sale on the executor or trustee. Some instruments are silent on this question, however, but for these, the applicable powers legislation normally confers the necessary authority.[343] The Third Restatement of Trusts implies a power of sale for trustees unless the terms of the trust or the circumstances indicate "that assets of the trust are to be retained in specie."[344] Some statutes are more restrictive.

---

337 RUFADAA § 4(a).

338 RUFADAA § 4(b).

339 RUFADAA §§ 7, 14.

340 RUFADAA §§ 11, 12.

341 RUFADAA § 9.

342 RUFADAA §§ 8, 10, 13, 14(2).

343 UTC § 816(2) (trustees); UPC § 3–715(6) (personal representatives); UPC § 5–425(b)(7) (conservators).

344 *Restatement (Third) of Trusts (Prudent Investor Rule)* § 190 (1992).

In Illinois trustees have broad powers of sale,[345] but personal representatives may sell property only "by leave of court and upon such terms as the court directs" unless the will gives a power of sale.[346] Additionally, most powers legislation expressly authorizes executors and trustees to sell on credit,[347] but some impose special requirements.[348]

Courts are reluctant to allow personal representatives to sell property which the will specifically devised, even when a will confers a broad power of sale.[349] The statutory power of sale given to personal representatives in many states allow such sales only when needed to raise money to pay debts.[350] The UPC is not so restricted, but it provides that "the distributable assets of a decedent's estate shall be distributed in kind to the extent possible."[351]

A sale may be necessary to effectuate distribution when an estate or trust terminates. An executor was permitted to sell land even though the will said "it is my desire that the farm land which I own remain in the family." The court found that the "desire" was merely precatory,[352] and that a sale would be "in the best interests of the estate;" because the children to whom the land was devised did not get along, shared ownership would be inconvenient.[353] A sale can take place after the termination date of a trust, since trustees' powers continue for a reasonable period to allow "winding up" of the trust.[354]

Courts' willingness to infer a power to sell may depend on the type of property involved. A court refused to authorize a transfer of a ward's home by her guardian, saying that "transfers of a ward's real property should be disfavored."[355] Some wills and trusts prohibit sale. These restrictions are valid,[356] but courts may overrule them when circumstances have changed.[357]

---

345 760 ILCS 5/4.01.

346 755 ILCS 5/20–4(a), 5/20–15.

347 UTC § 816(2); UPC § 3–715(23).

348 Cal.Prob.Code §§ 10257–10258 (on credit sale of personal property buyer must pay 25% down, but court may waive this if to the advantage of the estate), § 10315 (on credit sale of land, buyer's note must be secured by mortgage on the property).

349 Lowell v. Bouchillon, 271 S.E.2d 498, 499 (Ga.1980). *See also* Maier v. Henning, 578 A.2d 1279, 1282 (Pa. 1990); Diana v. Bentsen, 677 So.2d 1374 (Fla. App. 1996) (error to order sale of specifically devised stock where not needed to pay debts); Koch v. James, 616 N.E.2d 759 (Ind. App. 1993) (same); 755 ILCS § 5/20–4(b).

350 3 *Amer. Law of Prop.* § 14.27 (1952); In re Bettis' Estate, 340 A.2d 57 (Vt.1975) (sale of land by administrator voided because not necessary to pay debts); Duffy v. Heffernan, 459 N.E.2d 898 (Ohio App.1983) (where sale not needed to pay debts, 50% of interested persons must consent).

351 UPC § 3–906.

352 *See* Section 3.6, note 378 et seq.

353 In re Estate of Zimbleman, 539 N.W.2d 67, 70 (N.D.1995). *See also* In re Estate of Kunzler, 699 P.2d 1388 (Idaho 1985). In Huntington National Bank v. Wolfe, 651 N.E.2d 458, 462 (Ohio App. 1994), the court upheld a decision by trustees to sell shares in lieu of distributing them to a beneficiary who might "manage it in a way that would be hostile" to the interests of the company.

354 *Restatement (Third) of Trusts* § 89 (2007); UTC § 816(26); Cal.Prob.Code § 15407(b). *But see* In re Nathan Trust, 638 N.E.2d 789 (Ind. 1994).

355 In re Guardianship of Mabry, 666 N.E.2d 16, 21–22 (Ill.App.1996).

356 *See* Section 12.8, note 323.

357 *See* Section 12.8, note 324.

Normally fiduciaries do not have to notify or get the consent of beneficiaries before selling property,[358] but such a requirement may be found in the terms of an instrument.[359] Certainly it is good policy for fiduciaries to consult the beneficiaries about the sale of a major asset. One commentator has observed that most investment problems involving fiduciaries can be traced to ineffective communication between the fiduciary and the beneficiaries.[360]

Sales can be challenged because the price is too low[361] or fiduciaries can be surcharged for leasing property at less than its rental value.[362] Executors have also been surcharged for delaying a sale by asking too high a price.[363] But it is not always necessary for a fiduciary to accept the highest offer.[364] It may even be prudent for a trustee to abandon property. The UTC allows trustees to abandon or disclaim property which is "of insufficient value to justify its . . . continued administration" or because it "may have environmental liability attached to it."[365]

Many states require sales by personal representatives to be confirmed by a court.[366] Sometimes fiduciaries contract to sell property, and before the sale is confirmed another buyer offers a higher price. Some courts refuse to confirm the sale when this occurs,[367] but others hold that if the sale was for a "reasonable value" it should be confirmed despite the later offer.[368] However, many state statutes allow sales by personal representatives without the

---

[358] In re Estate of Hughes, 641 N.E.2d 248, 251 (Ohio App.1994) (will conferred a power of sale); Shear v. Gabovitch, 685 N.E.2d 1168, 1189 (Mass.App.1997) (judgment as to propriety of a sale lies "with the trustees, not with the beneficiaries"); Rock Springs Land and Timber, Inc. v. Lore, 75 P.3d 614, 620 (Wyo. 2003) (beneficiaries' consent is not required).

[359] Papiernik v. Papiernik, 544 N.E.2d 664 (Ohio 1989) (refusal to remove requirement of advisor's consent to a sale).

[360] Willis, *Steps to Protect the Fiduciary from Liability for Investment Decisions*, 16 Est.Plan 228, 229 (1989); Gallagher, *The Trustee's Role in Selling a Closely Held Business*, Trust & Estates 35, 40 (Sept. 1990). In Allard v. Pacific Nat'l Bank, 663 P.2d 104, 110 (Wash.1983), the court in surcharging a trustee for an improper sale said that it should have consulted the beneficiaries, even though their consent was not required. *Compare* UTC § 813, cmt. ("trustee may be required to provide advance notice of transactions involving real estate, closely held business interest, and other assets that are difficult to value or replace").

[361] Allard v. Pacific Nat'l Bank, 663 P.2d 104, 111 (Wash.1983). *See also* Murphy v. Central Bank and Trust Co., 699 P.2d 13 (Colo. App. 1985); Estate of Blouin, 490 A.2d 1212 (Me. 1985) (executor surcharged for sale at inadequate price); In re Estate of Hughes, 515 A.2d 581 (Pa. Super. 1986) (injunction against executor's sale at too low a price).

[362] Mest v. Dugan, 790 P.2d 38 (Or.App.1990). See also Forest Guardians v. Wells, 34 P.3d 364 (Ariz. 2001) (trustee's decision not to consider higher bid reversed).

[363] Sims v. Heath, 577 S.E.2d 789, 791 (Ga.App.2002).

[364] Aloha Lumber Corp. v. University of Alaska, 994 P.2d 991, 1000 (Alaska 1999). *See also* Forest Guardians v. Wells, 34 P.3d 364, 371 (Ariz. 2001) (highest bid by potential lessee "is not necessarily the best bid").

[365] UTC § 816(12), (13); *cf. Restatement (Third) of Trusts* § 86, cmt. f (2007); Seven G Ranching Co. v. Stewart Title, 627 P.2d 1088, 1090 (Ariz.App.1981).

[366] Matter of Estate of Ostrander, 910 P.2d 865 (Kan.App.1996) (sale of trailer without court approval set aside); *cf.* In re Estate of Hughes, 641 N.E.2d 248, 251 (Ohio App.1994) (no court approval needed when will confers a power of sale).

[367] Kapur v. Scientific Gas Products, Inc., 454 N.E.2d 1294 (Mass.App.1983) (court refused to approve executor's sale after higher bid received). *See also* Cal.Prob.Code § 10311 (substantially higher bid precludes confirmation).

[368] Stanton v. Sayre, 461 N.E.2d 3, 7 (Ohio App.1983). *See also* In re Estate of Hughes, 538 A.2d 470 (Pa. 1988) (sale for $42,000 approved despite later offer of $60,000); Rock Springs Land and Timber, Inc. v. Lore, 75 P.3d 614 (Wyo. 2003).

necessity of seeking court confirmation. The UPC authorizes personal representatives to "proceed expeditiously" in administering an estate "without adjudication, order or direction of the Court."[369]

Leases and Options

The UPC allows personal representatives to "lease any real or personal property of the estate," and the UTC gives a similar power to trustees.[370] Some statutes are more restrictive, on the theory that the beneficiaries should not be saddled with a lease which extends beyond the closing of the estate or trust.[371] The Third but not Second Restatement of Trusts allows leases for a term extending beyond the probable duration of the trust.[372]

Fiduciaries may lack power to grant an option. "A fiduciary's authority to sell real estate does not normally include authority to grant an option to purchase it" unless "inclusion of an option agreement in a lease is clearly necessary to make the most advantageous arrangement."[373] Other courts, however, have assumed with little discussion that a power to sell or lease included a power to grant options.[374] The UPC and UTC authorize personal representatives and trustees to execute leases "with or without option to purchase or renew,"[375] but some statutes are more restrictive.[376]

Principal Place of Administration[377]

Determining a trust's principal place of administration is important for a variety of reasons. It may determine which state's income tax applies to the trust.[378] It will establish which court has primary jurisdiction concerning trust administrative matters[379] or venue for bringing a proceeding.[380] Locating a

---

[369] UPC § 3–704. As to the extent to which a fiduciary who gets court approval of a transaction is protected thereby, *see* Section 14.8, note 678 et seq.

[370] UPC § 3–715(23); UTC § 816(9).

[371] *See, e.g.*, N.Y.EPTL §§ 11–1.1(b)(5)(C), 11–1.1(c); Cal.Prob.Code §§ 9941, 9947.

[372] *Compare Restatement (Third) of Trusts* § 86, cmt. c(1) (2007) *with Restatement (Second) of Trusts* § 189, cmt. c, d (1959).

[373] Nelson v. Maiorana, 478 N.E.2d 945, 948 (Mass.1985).

[374] Jost v. Burr, 590 N.E.2d 828, 832 (Ohio App.1990). *See also* Aloha Lumber Corp. V. University of Alaska, 994 P.2d 991, 1000 (Alaska 1999) (upholding trustee's grant of right of first refusal).

[375] UPC § 3–715(9); UTC § 816(9).

[376] 20 Pa.Stat. § 3354 (testamentary power of sale does not include granting an option without court order); N.Y.EPTL § 11–1.1(b)(7) (fiduciaries can grant options for up to 6 months).

[377] Portions of the following discussion are based on English, *The Uniform Trust Code: Significant Provisions and Policy Issues*, 67 Mo. L. Rev. 143, 155–58 (2002).

[378] For the effect of place of administration on the state's authority to tax a trust, *see* Bradley E.S. Fogel, *What Have You Done for Me Lately? Constitutional Limitations on State Taxation of Trusts*, 32 U. Rich. L. Rev. 165 (1998).

[379] *See* UTC § 202(a): "[b]y accepting the trusteeship of a trust having its principal place of administration in this State or by moving the principal place of administration to this State, the trustee submits personally to the jurisdiction of the courts of this State regarding any matter involving the trust."

[380] Under UTC § 204, venue for bringing a proceeding is in the county of the trust's principal place of administration unless the trust has no trustee or the trust was created by will and the decedent's estate is not yet closed. It has been held that this statute, being more specific, prevails over a state's general venue statute. State ex rel. Board of Curators University of Missouri v. Green, 576 S.W. 3d 183 (Mo. 2019); Betts v. Ginlickson, 445 P.3d 1223 (Mont. 2019).

principal place of administration in a particular jurisdiction also makes it more likely that the particular jurisdiction's law will govern the trust.[381]

As trust administration has become more complex, determining a trust's principal place of administration has become more difficult. Co-trustees may be located in different states, or a corporate trustee's personal trust officers may be located in one state, its investment division in another, and its operations facilities yet somewhere else. Also, a variety of nontrustees, such as advisors and trust protectors, may play a role in the trust's administration. Concluding that the fact situations were simply too diverse to allow the development of a straightforward statutory test, the drafters of the UTC did not attempt to define principal place of administration.[382] However, the UTC otherwise facilitates the locating of a trust in a particular jurisdiction. First, a provision in the trust terms designating the principal place of administration is valid and controlling if "a trustee's principal place of business is located in or a trustee is a resident of the designated jurisdiction or, all or part of the trust's administration occurs in the designated place."[383] Second, for trust instruments failing to address the subject, the UTC grants the trustee a power and specifies a procedure for transferring the principal place of administration, whether to another state or country.[384] The transfer must facilitate the trust's administration, and the trustee must inform the qualified beneficiaries of the transfer at least sixty days in advance. The transfer may proceed as long as no qualified beneficiary objects by the date specified in the notice. If a qualified beneficiary objects, the trustee must obtain a court order. "Qualified beneficiary," a defined term used frequently in the UTC, excludes a beneficiary with a remote remainder interest.[385] Should the trustee decline or be ineligible to act in the new jurisdiction, the UTC authorizes the appointment of a new trustee in connection with the transfer.[386]

§ 14.6 Selection of Fiduciary

A fiduciary is a person who is entrusted with another's property; the word comes from the Latin *fiducia,* trust. This chapter is primarily concerned with personal representatives of a decedent (executors and administrators) and trustees, but agents under a power of attorney, custodians under the Uniform

---

[381] For a discussion of the legal background behind principal place of administration and the issues addressed in Section 108, *see* VA Scott & Fratcher, *The Law of Trusts* §§ 610–615 (4th ed. 1989). For a discussion of choice of law issues for trusts, wills, and other donative documents, *see* Section 1.2.

[382] For such an attempt, *see* Cal.Prob.Code § 17002, which provides that the principal place of administration is the usual place where the day-to-day activity of the trust is carried on by the trustee or its representative primarily responsible for its administration. If there is no such usual place, the principal place of administration in the case of a trust with a single trustee is the trustee's residence or usual place of business. In the case of a trust having more than one trustee, the principal place of administration is the residence or usual place of business of any of the trustees as agreed upon by them. In the absence of an agreement, the principal place of administration is the residence or usual place of business of any of the cotrustees.

[383] UTC § 108(a).

[384] UTC § 108(b)–(e).

[385] For a discussion, *see* Section 14.3, note 184.

[386] UTC § 108(f).

Transfers to Minors Act, and conservators of minors and incapacitated adults perform similar functions and are subject to many of the same rules.[387]

Court Appointment

Personal representatives and conservators acquire their powers by court appointment,[388] but trustees under an inter-vivos trust need no court appointment, nor do agents under a power of attorney or custodians under the Uniform Transfers to Minors Act. Some states require court appointment of testamentary trustees, but most do not.[389] Trustees of inter-vivos trusts accept appointment either by signing a written acceptance or simply by starting to do the job.[390]

Even where a court is not involved in the initial designation of a fiduciary, court proceedings may be necessary to remove a fiduciary or to designate a successor when the original fiduciary is unable or unwilling to continue to serve, such as if the trustee dies. The death of a trustee does not terminate a trust unless the trust's creation or continuation depends on that specific person serving as trustee.[391] Consequently, the court will often be required to appoint a successor if the will or trust does not specify a procedure for filling the vacancy. The Uniform Transfers to Minors Act allows custodians to designate a successor by a written instrument,[392] but personal representatives and trustees cannot designate their own successors unless the governing instrument so authorizes.[393]

Another possibility is to empower the beneficiaries to designate a new fiduciary. Absent authorization in the instrument beneficiaries were not entitled at common law to name a new fiduciary,[394] although courts, in selecting fiduciaries, do give weight to the beneficiaries' wishes.[395] Often some beneficiaries of a trust or estate are minors or unascertained persons who cannot act. The UTC gets around this difficulty by allowing a vacancy in the office of trustee to be filled by unanimous agreement of the qualified beneficiaries,[396] and includes a representation provision authorizing consent

---

[387] As to custodianships, *see* Section 10.5. As to powers of attorney, *see* Sections 9.3 and 10.5. As to the differing uses of the words "conservator" and "guardian", *see* Section 1.1.

[388] *E.g.*, UPC §§ 3–103, § 5–401. As to the differing uses of the words "conservator" and "guardian," *see* Section 1.1. As to the selection of a guardian of the person, *see* Section 9.2.

[389] *Restatement (Third) of Trusts* § 34(1) (2003) (except as required by statute, trustee needs no court appointment).

[390] UTC § 701. Applied in In re Hamilton Living Trust, 471 S.W.3d 203 (Ark. 2015) (although bank custodian sent letters declining appointment as successor trustee, because it took actions beyond preserving the trust property, it was deemed to have accepted the trusteeship).

[391] *Restatement (Third) of Trusts* § 31 (2003).

[392] Unif. Transfers to Minors Act § 18(b).

[393] Cal.Prob.Code § 8422 (executor cannot designate a successor unless the will so provides). Alternative ways to provide for the designation of successor trustees in a trust instrument are suggested in Scroggin, *Restraining an Inheritance Can Accomplish a Client's Objectives*, 30 Est. Plan. 124, 128 (2003).

[394] *Restatement (Third) of Trusts* § 34, cmt. c(1) (2003). But under Uniform Transfers to Minors Act § 18(d), a minor who has attained age 14 can designate a successor custodian.

[395] *Restatement (Third) of Trusts* § 34, cmt. f(1) (2003).

[396] UTC § 704(c). The definition of "qualified beneficiary" excludes those holding remote remainder interests. *See* UTC § 103(13); 14.3, note 185.

to be given by substitutes on behalf of beneficiaries unable to consent.[397] If the qualified beneficiaries cannot agree, the appointment will be made by the court.[398] It is always best to address the issue of succession in the trust document.

Administrators and Executors

State statutes provide priorities for the choice of an administrator when someone dies intestate. The UPC gives priority to the decedent's spouse, but permits courts to depart from the statute and appoint "any suitable person." Persons eligible for appointment may instead nominate another.[399] Under a similar statute, a court chose the decedent's brother instead of his widow because her claim to certain property in the estate "created a conflict of interest that rendered her unfit."[400] Under these circumstances, the trial court's choice was not an "abuse of discretion." (Appellate courts commonly defer to the determinations of lower courts in the appointment and removal of fiduciaries.)[401]

When a will fails to designate an executor, or the designated executor cannot or will not serve, the court appoints an administrator "with will annexed" (sometimes designated in Latin: *cum testamento annexo* or simply *cta*). Under the UPC, the devisees under the will have priority over heirs in seeking appointment or in nominating an administrator with will annexed.[402]

Executors are by definition nominated in a will to carry out its terms. They too must be appointed by a court, but courts normally appoint the person named in the will unless the nominee is disqualified. Because the executor was the testator's personal choice, some courts impose a higher standard to remove an executor than to remove an administrator.[403] In appointing conservators, most conservatorship statutes require that the appointing court defer to persons nominated by the protected person if the latter is over 14 and "has sufficient capacity to express a preference."[404]

Conflicts of Interest

Conflict of interest is sometimes a basis for disqualifying a fiduciary, but in making this decision the court will consider whether the conflict was apparent to the testator or settlor who nominated the fiduciary. When a will designated the testator's child by a prior marriage as a trustee as well as

---

[397] UTC Art. 3, discussed in Section 14.8, note 707 et seq.

[398] For a case where this occurred, *see* Brown v. Brown, 2013 WL 1619687 (Tenn. Ct. App., April 16, 2013).

[399] UPC § 3–203(b). A similar (but not identical) list of priorities for the appointment of conservators appears in UPC § 5–413.

[400] Ayala v. Martinez, 883 S.W.2d 270, 272 (Tex.App.1994). *Compare infra* note 405.

[401] In re Estate of Posey, 548 N.E.2d 1205, 1207 (Ind.App.1990) (appointment of bank rather than decedent's brother); In re Estate of Pfahler, 581 N.E.2d 602, 603 (Ohio App.1989) (refusal to appoint designated executor).

[402] UPC § 3–203(a); *cf.* Cal.Prob.Code § 8441(b).

[403] *See* Wolfe v. Young, 521 S.W.3d 598 (Ky. Ct. App. 2017).

[404] UPC § 5–413(a)(2). *See also* Cal.Prob.Code § 1810; Guardianship of Smith, 684 N.E.2d 613 (Mass. App. 1997) (error not to appoint guardian nominated in ward's durable power of attorney).

remainderman, the court held it was an error not to appoint the child.[405] A conflict which was "unknown to the settlor at the time of the designation, or that came into being at a later time" presents a stronger case for removing the fiduciary or refusing to appoint.[406]

A conflict of interest can be removed without completely disqualifying the fiduciary, *e.g.*, by restricting the fiduciary's powers. When a conflict of interest arose between a trustee and the beneficiaries with respect to particular litigation, a court "suspended the trustee's powers regarding only the litigation and appointed a 'trustee ad litem' with limited powers to conduct the litigation."[407]

Even if a testator or settlor believes that a family member is sufficiently fair-minded to overlook his or her selfish interests, use of a family member as trustee can have adverse estate tax consequences if the beneficiary-trustee can distribute principal to herself. For this reason, the UTC automatically limits the trustee's discretion in such cases to "an ascertainable standard relating to [the beneficiary's] health, education, support or maintenance,"[408] a limitation which solves the estate tax issue and also limits the trustee's ability to favor the trustee's own interests over the interests of the other beneficiaries.

Other Grounds for Removal or Refusal to Appoint

Another ground for removing or not appointing a designated executor or trustee is hostility between the fiduciary and the beneficiaries. A court refused to appoint the executor designated in a will who had acted so abrasively toward the testator's wife and children that "there was no way" they could get along with him.[409] If a trustee has broad discretion in making distributions, hostility between the trustee and a particular beneficiary may make the trustee unsuitable.[410] But hostility is not always grounds for removal. "There are many trusts in which no trustee could fully perform his duty without incurring the hostility of some of the beneficiaries."[411] Trial courts have wide discretion on

---

[405] Lovett v. Peavy, 316 S.E.2d 754, 757 (Ga.1984). *See also* Schildberg v. Schildberg, 461 N.W.2d 186, 192 (Iowa 1990); Symmons v. O'Keeffe, 664 N.E.2d 631, 638n (Mass. 1995); *Restatement (Third) of Trusts* § 37, cmt. f (2003).

[406] *Restatement (Third) of Trusts* § 37, cmt. f(1); Estate of Hammer, 24 Cal. Rptr.2d 190 (App. 1993) (husband of devisee later involved in acrimonious divorce with her); Shriners Hospitals v. Gardiner, 733 P.2d 1110, 1114 (Ariz. 1987).

[407] Getty v. Getty, 252 Cal.Rptr. 342, 346 (App.1988). *See also* In re Sauter's estate, 615 P.2d 875 (Mont.1980) (special administrator appointed to handle claim involving conflict of interest); Stilwell v. Estate of Crosby, 519 So.2d 68, 69 (Fla. App. 1988); *Restatement (Third) of Trusts* § 37, cmt. g (2003).

[408] UTC § 814(b). The particular language of limitation is copied from I.R.C. § 2041(b)(1)(A). For further discussion of the estate tax issue, *see* 15.4, notes 234 et seq.

[409] Matter of Petty's Estate, 608 P.2d 987, 995 (Kan.1980). *See also* Kerper v. Kerper, 780 P.2d 923, 938 (Wyo. 1989); In re Estate of Greenheck, 27 P.3d 42, 46 (Mont.2001) (hostility between co-executors justifies removal in order to facilitate administration of the estate).

[410] Shear v. Gabovitch, 685 N.E.2d 1168, 1193 (Mass.App.1997); Matter of Brecklein's Estate, 637 P.2d 444, 452 (Kan.App.1981).

[411] Edinburg v. Cavers, 492 N.E.2d 1171, 1181 (Mass.App.1986). *See also Restatement (Third) of Trusts* § 37, cmt. e(1) (2003); Pontrello v. Estate of Kepler, 528 So.2d 441,444 (Fla. App. 1988) (error to refuse to appoint designated executor on grounds of hostility of testator's family). In Holst v. Purdy, 844 P.2d 229 (Or. App.1992), the court refused to remove a designated executor-trustee but ordered him to post a bond).

this issue[412] so it is hard to reconcile all the cases, but the extent of the hostility and the reason for it are important factors. One court refused to remove a trustee, noting that the "hostility was primarily created by the beneficiaries."[413]

A change of circumstances after a will or trust is executed may throw in question the suitability of the designated fiduciary. In most states, when a testator marries or has a child after executing a will, the new spouse or child may be entitled to a share of the estate despite the will,[414] but unless the statute revokes a will in this situation the named executor is still appointed.[415] If the testator divorces a spouse who is designated as a fiduciary in an instrument, however, the divorce revokes the designation under the Uniform Probate Code.[416] The UTC has a more general provision for replacement of trustees when "there has been a substantial change of circumstances."[417]

If an executor or trustee becomes insolvent, his creditors cannot reach property which he holds as a fiduciary,[418] but there is a risk that assets of the estate or trust will become confused with those of the fiduciary, so courts will often remove insolvent fiduciaries.[419] Trustees and personal representatives can also be removed for misconduct in office.[420] The Third Restatement of Trusts lists as grounds for removing a trustee "repeated or flagrant failure or

---

412 Matter of Trust Created by Hill, 499 N.W.2d 475, 486 (Minn.App.1993); Helgason v. Merriman, 36 P.3d 703, 704 (Alaska 2001) (trial court's findings reversed only if "clearly erroneous"). *But cf.* Rennacker v. Rennacker, 509 N.E.2d 798 (Ill. App. 1987) (abuse of discretion not to remove trustee because of extreme hostility); In re Estate of Robbin, 747 P.2d 869 (Mont. 1987) (abuse of discretion to remove executor who had divorced legatee).

413 Akin v. Dahl, 661 S.W.2d 911, 914 (Tex.1983).

414 *See* Sections 8.5, 8.6.

415 Matter of Bowman's Estate, 609 P.2d 663, 666 (Idaho 1980) (error to appoint testator's husband whom she married after will executed when will named another executor). *See also* State ex rel. First National Bank v. Skow, 284 N.W.2d 74 (Wis. 1979) (even though testator's children were minors when will was executed because they are now of age they may be appointed).

416 UPC § 2–804(b). *See also* Cal.Prob.Code § 6122 (wills), § 4154 (power of attorney); McClinton v. Sullivan, 438 S.E.2d 71 (Ga. 1994) (refusal to appoint spouse as administrator when action for divorce pending at death). Homicide also negates the killer's nomination as fiduciary. UPC § 2–803(c)(1); Cal.Prob.Code § 250(b)(3).

417 UTC § 706(b)(4). "Changed circumstances justifying removal of a trustee might include a substantial change in the character of the service or location of the trustee. A corporate reorganization of an institutional trustee is not itself a change of circumstances if it does not affect the service provided the individual trust account." UTC § 706, cmt. Before removing the trustee, the court must also find that removal best serves the interests of the beneficiaries and is not inconsistent with a material purpose of the trust. UTC § 706(b)(4).

Among the situations found by the courts to be sufficient to remove the trustee for substantial change of circumstances: move by family to another state coupled with a corporate trustee that had gone through six mergers, In re McKinney, 67 A.3d 834 (Pa. Super. Ct. 2013); continued efforts by the settlor to regain control of the trust assets, In re Vincent J. Fumo Irrevocable Children's Trust, 104 A.3d 535 (Pa. Super Ct. 2014); and family disharmony regarding the settlor's care, In re Mlynarczyk Living Trust, 2011 WL 4104976 (Mich. Ct. App., Sept. 15, 2011).

418 UTC § 507.

419 *Restatement (Third) of Trusts* § 37, cmt. e (2003); Cal.Prob.Code § 15642(b); In re Quinlan's Estate, 273 A.2d 340 (Pa.1971).

420 Altshuler v. Minkus-Whalen, 579 N.E.2d 1369 (Mass.App.1991) (administrator removed for failure to tell court of the existence of other heirs); Smith v. Underwood, 437 S.E.2d 512, 517 (N.C.App.1993) (trustee removed for failure to file accounts, commingling); In re Estate of Townsend, 793 P.2d 818 (Mont. 1990).

delay in providing accountings or information to the beneficiaries, gross or continued under performance of investments," and "unwarranted preference" toward certain beneficiaries or "a pattern of indifference" toward others.[421] Courts do not remove fiduciaries who have been guilty of only minor wrongs,[422] but the UTC does allow removal for lackluster performance: "persistent failure to administer the trust effectively."[423]

Some trust documents give designated beneficiaries the right to remove a trustee with whom they are dissatisfied and appoint another. In this case no ground for the removal is necessary.[424] Such a provision can allow adjustments to changing circumstances, *e.g.*, such as a decline in the quality of a trustee's services but short of grounds for judicial removal. Such a removal provision may also give a trustee an incentive to be more attentive to trust administration. On the other hand, there are risks that the power will be improperly used, *e.g.*, as a "threat [in order] to receive larger distributions." Thus, it may be desirable to "limit the pool of candidates for trustees to . . . institutions . . . likely to have the desired experience, objectivity and capabilities".[425]

The UTC contains two other grounds for removal. One is deadlock among co-trustees even if neither trustee has committed a breach of trust.[426] Such a deadlock can paralyze trust administration. The deadlock can be eliminated by removing one or sometimes both trustees.[427]

The UTC also gives the court discretion to remove a trustee upon request of the qualified beneficiaries but only if the court finds that removal of the trustee best serves the interests of all of the beneficiaries, is not inconsistent with a material purpose of the trust, and a suitable cotrustee or successor trustee is available. In *Davis v. U.S. Bank, N.A.*,[428] the court removed a Missouri corporate trustee and appointed a Delaware corporate trustee as a replacement. The corporate trustee removed had become trustee because a series of bank mergers, the family had moved to the East Coast where the

---

[421] *Restatement (Third) of Trusts* § 37, cmt. e (2003); McNeil v. McNeil, 798 A.2d 503, 513 (Del.2002) (removal and surcharge of trustee who failed to keep beneficiary informed upheld).

[422] *Restatement (Third) of Trusts* § 37, cmt. e (2003); In re Estate of Ehlers, 911 P.2d 1017 (Wash.App.1996) (trustee not removed for delay in filing account).

[423] UTC § 706(b)(3). "A 'persistent failure to administer the trust effectively' might include a long-term pattern of mediocre performance, such as consistently poor investment results when compared to comparable trusts." UTC § 706, cmt. In In re Trust of Socha, 783 N.W.2d 800 (Neb. Ct. App. 2010), the court applied this ground to remove trustees who had kept a trust open following its termination date and had failed to provide the beneficiary with information. In addition, the trustees had continued to pay their own administration expenses, had hired family members to provide trust services, and had purchased trust assets for themselves.

[424] *Restatement (Third) of Trusts* § 37, cmt. c (2003). As to the tax problems in giving beneficiaries a removal power if not carefully circumscribed, *see* Price, *Contemporary Estate Planning* § 10.27 (2014 ed.).

[425] Moore, *Trustees Under a Microscope*, Tr. & Est., July 2003, at 44.

[426] UTC § 706(b)(2) ("lack of cooperation among cotrustees substantially impairs the administration of the trust")

[427] UTC § 706(b)(2) was applied to remove one of two trustees in In re Charles C. Wells Revocable Trust, 734 N.W.2d 323 (Neb.2007). In addition to disagreeing with his brother, who was the other trustee, the removed trustee had failed to pay rent on his personal use of trust property, paid personal debts out of the trust, and pledged trust real estate to secure personal loans.

[428] 243 S.W.3d 425 (Mo. Ct. App. 2007).

successor trustee was located, and the successor trustee charged less in commissions and was as qualified as the trustee being removed. On the other hand, in *In re Fenske*,[429] where the trustee was a bank with whom the settlor had a close personal relationship, the qualified beneficiaries' request to remove the trustee was denied. The selection of the particular trustee was a material purpose of the trust.

A fiduciary who has become incompetent, *e.g.*, by dementia, can be removed.[430] In order to avoid court proceedings, many trusts provide that the certificate of designated individuals shall be conclusive that the trustee is no longer qualified to serve.[431] However, including a removal procedure in the trust instrument does not usurp the ability of the court to remove the trustee.[432]

Bond

Another expense in many estates is the requirement that personal representatives file a bond. The amount of the bond is generally based on the value of the personal property of the estate, but if land is sold the bond is increased.[433] The bond usually must have sureties, because the executor or administrator may be unable to pay a surcharge imposed for mismanagement, in which case the sureties are liable to the extent of the bond, with a right of reimbursement against the fiduciary.[434] The sureties naturally charge a fee for this, the cost of which is born by the estate.[435] No bond is required when a corporation is the fiduciary, because corporations must have substantial assets in order to be licensed to act as fiduciaries.[436]

A will can waive bond, but even if it does, a court may "for good cause" require one.[437] The testator's confidence in the designated executor may prove to be mistaken, or the fiduciary designated in the instrument may not actually serve.[438]

The business of acting as surety for bonds is substantial, and in many states, sureties have lobbied for retaining the bond requirement.[439] Most estate

---

[429] 930 N.W.2d 43 (Neb. 2019).

[430] *Restatement (Third) of Trusts* § 37, cmt. e (2003).

[431] Buchanan & Buchanan, *Strategies for Clients Residing in Nursing Homes*, 20 Est. Plan. 27, 30 (1993). In Manning v. Glens Falls National Bank, 697 N.Y.S.2d 203 (App. Div. 1999), a similar clause was used to nullify a settlor's attempted exercise of a power to remove a trustee while the settlor was in a nursing home.

[432] Wallace v. Comprehensive Personal Care Services, Inc., 306 So. 3d 207 (Fla. Dist. Ct. App. 2020).

[433] Cal.Prob.Code § 8482.

[434] Cal.Prob.Code § 8488; UPC § 3–606.

[435] Cal.Prob.Code § 8486.

[436] Cal.Prob.Code § 301; UTC § 702(c).

[437] Cal.Prob.Code § 8481 (personal representatives), § 15602(a)(2) (waiver of bond for trustee is ineffective if a bond is "necessary to protect the interests of the beneficiaries"); *cf.* Section 10.5, note 190 (bond for life tenants).

[438] Cal.Prob.Code § 15602(a)(3) (waiver of bond ineffective as to "a trustee not named in the instrument").

[439] Wellman, *Recent Developments in the Struggle for Probate Reform*, 79 Mich.L.Rev. 501, 523 (1981).

planners believe a bond is usually not worth the expense.[440] The UPC rejects "the idea that a bond always should be required of a probate fiduciary" and allows courts to dispense with a bond if it is not necessary, even if the will does not waive it.[441]

Bond requirements tend to be more relaxed for trustees. In California, executors must give a bond unless the will waives it whereas trustees do not have to give a bond unless the trust instrument requires one.[442] This is also the rule for trustees under the UTC and the Third Restatement of Trusts,[443] but in New York testamentary trustees must file bond unless the will excuses it.[444] For conservators, on the other hand, bond requirements are usually more strict than those for personal representatives; here the beneficiary of the arrangement (the protected person) is incapable of waiving the requirement.[445]

Nonresidents

Some wills designate a person residing in another state as fiduciary. Nonresidence is usually not disqualifying,[446] but a few statutes do disqualify nonresidents. California disqualifies persons who are not residents of the United States from serving as administrator, but not as executor, presumably out of respect for the wishes of the testator.[447] Some states have reciprocity provisions; a foreign bank can be appointed only if its home state would do the same in the converse situation.[448] Others condition the appointment of a nonresident on naming a resident co-fiduciary.[449] Some allow only nonresident fiduciaries who are related to the decedent by blood or marriage. A Florida statute of this type was upheld, but several judges dissented on the ground that the statute was "arbitrary and irrational" because "a close personal advisor" was "a far more rational choice by the decedent than the choice of remote [relatives] which the statute would allow."[450]

A fiduciary ought to be subject to process in the state of appointment, but this can be accomplished simply by requiring out-of-state fiduciaries to consent to local jurisdiction.[451] A Louisiana court appointed an Arkansas resident as

---

[440] Price, *Contemporary Estate Planning* at § 4.25.2 (2014 ed.).

[441] UPC § 3–603, cmt.

[442] Cal.Prob.Code § 15602.

[443] UTC § 702(a); *Restatement (Third) of Trusts* § 34(3) (2003).

[444] N.Y.Surr.Ct.Proc.Act § 806. *See also* Tex. Prob. Code § 113.058(b).

[445] *Compare* Cal.Prob.Code §§ 2320–2321 (bond required except for good cause) *with* UPC § 5–415 (court may order bond).

[446] *Restatement (Third) of Trusts* § 32, cmt. d (2003); In re Farnsworth's Estate, 241 A.2d 204 (N.H.1968) (trust assets distributed to N.Y. bank); Munford v. Maclellan, 373 S.E.2d 368 (Ga.1988) (refusal to remove nonresident trustee).

[447] Cal.Prob.Code § 8402(a)(4); In re Estate of Damskog, 1 Cal.Rptr.2d 653 (App.1991) (heir residing in Norway cannot even nominate administrator).

[448] Matter of Estate of Westpfal, 531 N.Y.S.2d 81 (Sur.1988) (appointment of Florida bank for land in New York upheld); Ohio Rev. Code § 2109.21B.

[449] Estate of White, 509 N.Y.S.2d 252 (Sur.1986) (nondomiciliary alien can act as trustee only if a N.Y. resident also serves); Matter of Estate of Oelberg, 414 N.W.2d 672 (Iowa App.1987) (resident co-executor appointed).

[450] In re Greenberg's Estate, 390 So.2d 40, 51 (Fla.1980).

[451] UPC § 3–602; Cal.Prob.Code § 8572; Md. Est. & Tr. Code § 5–105(b)(6).

trustee, noting that "the Long Arm Statute would be available for the purpose of service of process."[452]

Distance between the fiduciary and beneficiary or the property which the fiduciary administers may make a fiduciary unsuitable. An Arkansas court removed a resident of New York City as trustee of a trust operating a farm in Arkansas, saying she was "not qualified to make farming decisions."[453] A New York court approved a transfer of the situs of a trust to California after the beneficiaries had moved to that state.[454] The UTC provision authorizing transfer of the principal place of administration was discussed in the immediately preceding section. The Third Restatement of Trusts lists "geographic inconvenience" as a possible ground for removing a trustee.[455]

Corporations

A corporation, usually a bank,[456] is often appointed as executor, trustee, or conservator. Many states impose special regulations on corporate fiduciaries. A corporation not so licensed is subject to removal.[457] National banks engaging in the trust business are regulated by the Comptroller of Currency, which can order a bank to discontinue its trust business because of bad practices.[458]

Whereas individual fiduciaries may die or become incompetent before the job is over, this is not a problem with corporations, so instruments often name a bank as successor fiduciary if a designated individual(s) can no longer act. If a bank merges with another, normally the successor bank assumes the fiduciary functions of the predecessor without a formal new appointment.[459] Although "from a legal sense" banks provide continuity, personnel changes at a particular bank may create a "lack of communications continuity in the eye of the customer."[460]

Banks charge for their services, whereas individual family members often do not despite their right to claim compensation. These perceived cost savings may lead to a push toward the choice of an individual. But executors' and

---

[452] Succession of Batton v. Prince, 384 So.2d 506 (La.App.1980). *See also* UTC § 202(a) (by accepting trusteeship, trustee submits to court's jurisdiction).

[453] Ashman v. Pickens, 674 S.W.2d 4, 5 (Ark.App.1984). *See also* In re Estate of Ikuta, 639 P.2d 400 (Haw.1981) (appointing a resident of Hawaii, where trust had property, as cotrustee where existing trustee lived in California).

[454] In re Weinberger's Trust, 250 N.Y.S.2d 887 (App.Div.1964). Absent such a transfer, the beneficiaries may be unable to sue the trustee in their new state of residence. Rose v. Firstar Bank, 819 A.2d 1247 (R.I.2003). A change of situs may also reduce state income taxes on capital gains. Moore, *Trustees Under a Microscope*, Tr. & Est., July 2003, at 44, 49.

[455] *Restatement (Third) of Trusts* § 37, cmt. e (2003).

[456] The connection between banking and trust business is somewhat accidental. The earliest corporate trustees were often insurance companies. 2 Scott & Fratcher, *Trusts* § 96.5 (4th ed. Fratcher 1987).

[457] Erwin & Erwin v. Bronson, 844 P.2d 269 (Or.App.1992); Ozee v. American Council on Gift Annuities, 888 F.Supp. 1318 (N.D.Tex.1995).

[458] Central Nat'l Bank v. United States Dept. of Treasury, 912 F.2d 897 (7th Cir.1990).

[459] 12 U.S.C. § 215(e) (consolidated national bank continues to hold fiduciary offices without court order).

[460] Buchanan, *Choosing Executors and Trustees*, Tr. & Est., Aug. 1980, at 26, 27; Dukeminier & Krier, *The Rise of the Perpetual Trust*, 50 U.C.L.A. L.Rev. 1303, 1338 (2003).

trustees' fees are deductible for tax purposes, so part of the cost is borne by the government. In small estates, however, a professional's fee may be prohibitive. Professionals generally charge a minimum fee to discourage small estates and trusts or refuse to handle them altogether.[461] The cost-saving in using a family member may be offset by the need for professional advice. If an individual fiduciary must hire an investment counselor, its fee may be equivalent to that of a professional trustee who provides investment expertise as part of the job.[462] But some believe that trust beneficiaries can "procure equally good management of assets, and at a much lower cost, by investing in index funds."[463]

If a corporate fiduciary mismanages a trust or estate, it usually can pay for any damages imposed on it. An individual is more likely to be judgment-proof. This risk can be avoided by having the individual give a bond with sureties, but the cost of such a bond reduces the cost-advantage of having an individual fiduciary.[464]

Professional fiduciaries are expected to be experts in making investments and are held to higher standards than individuals.[465] "Serving as executor or trustee is neither an honor, nor a game for beginners to play. [It] requires technical skills [and] experience."[466] If the trust is to operate a business, an individual familiar with the business may be a better choice for trustee than a bank.[467]

Multiple Fiduciaries

Appointing multiple fiduciaries allows the particular skills of various persons to be utilized. A corporate trustee may be best suited to handle records and perform routine administration while a business associate may have desirable investment skills and a family friend or relative may be the best person to exercise discretion over distributions.[468] Using a family member as co-trustee may also have psychological benefits. A spouse or child may resent a testator's putting "his or her" inheritance in a trust; such resentment may be reduced if the beneficiary is named co-trustee.[469] A cofiduciary can also watch after and act as a check on the other fiduciaries. Under the UTC, a cotrustee must "exercise reasonable care to: (1) prevent a cotrustee from committing a

---

[461] Olsen & Sharman, *Practical and Tax Considerations in Deciding Who Should Be a Trustee,* 8 Est.Plan. 214, 219 (1981).

[462] Bromberg & Fortson, *Selection of a Trustee: Tax and Other Considerations,* 19 Sw.L.J. 523, 530 (1965). As to the right of a fiduciary to hire agents and advisors with trust funds, *see* Section 14.4, note 273 et seq.

[463] Dukeminier & Krier, 50 U.C.L.A.L.Rev. at 1337.

[464] As to bonds, *see supra* note 433 et seq.

[465] *See* Section 14.2, note 88.

[466] McEachern, *Corporate Fiduciaries Can Be an Attorney's Best Friend,* Tr. & Est., Apr. 1989, at 30.

[467] Bromberg & Fortson, *Selection of a Trustee: Tax and Other Considerations,* 19 Sw. L. J. 523, 532 (1965).

[468] Bromberg & Fortson, 19 Sw.L.J. at 547.

[469] Bromberg & Fortson, 19 Sw.L.J. at 533.

serious breach of trust; and (2) compel a cotrustee to redress a serious breach of trust."[470]

Multiple fiduciaries also have disadvantages. Unless the additional executors or trustees serve without compensation, the total fees may be higher.[471] If the co-fiduciaries disagree, court proceedings may be needed to resolve the deadlock.[472] The chance of a deadlock can sometimes be reduced by designating an uneven number of fiduciaries. Absent such a provision the result can vary. According to the Second Restatement of Trusts, if there are two or more trustees, all of them must agree to exercise their powers,[473] but the UTC, Third Restatement, and many other statutes provide for majority rule.[474] At common law, each executor could exercise many powers without the others' concurrence,[475] but the UPC provides that all personal representatives must concur in an action unless the will provides otherwise.[476] This can create problems even if there is no actual disagreement among the fiduciaries, because the failure of all fiduciaries to join may invalidate a transaction.[477] When all fiduciaries must sign every document, efficient administration is impaired.[478] This can be avoided by providing in the document that a majority vote is sufficient or by authorizing fiduciaries to delegate routine matters to a co-fiduciary. Under the UTC, a cotrustee may delegate to another cotrustee the performance of any function the settlor did not reasonably expect the cotrustees to perform jointly.[479]

Unless the will or trust requires that a successor be appointed when a cofiduciary ceases to act the others can usually continue without any need to appoint a successor.[480] The Third Restatement of Trusts says that when one of several trustees ceases to act a "replacement trustee is required, only if the settlor manifested an intention, or it is conducive to the proper administration of the trust that the number of trustees be maintained."[481] When a replacement trustee is appointed, courts should give weight to the recommendations of the existing trustees.[482]

---

[470] UTC § 703(g). *See also Restatement (Third) of Trusts* § 81(2) (2007).

[471] *See* Section 14.7, note 584 et seq.

[472] *Restatement (Third) of Trusts* § 39, cmt. e (2003).

[473] *Restatement (Second) of Trusts* § 194, cmt. a (1959). *See also* Cal.Prob.Code § 15620. For charitable trusts, majority rules. *Restatement (Second) of Trusts* § 383 (1959).

[474] UTC § 703(a); *Restatement (Third) of Trusts* § 39 (2003); 760 ILCS § 5/10; N.Y.EPTL § 10–10.7; Edwards v. Edwards, 71 Cal. Rptr.2d 653 (App.1988) (majority controls as to voting stock under Corporation Code which trumps Probate Code).

[475] Maitland, *Equity* 93–94 (1913); 2 Blackstone, *Commentaries* *510 (1765). *But cf.* 3 *Amer. Law of Prop.* § 14.28, at 689–90.

[476] UPC § 3–717.

[477] Walter E. Wilhite Revocable Living Trust v. Northwest Yearly Meeting Pension Fund, 916 P.2d 1264, 1271 (Idaho 1996); Farmers State Bank v. Harmon, 778 F.2d 543 (10th Cir.1985) (guarantee signed by one of two trustees is ineffective).

[478] Fratcher, *Trustees' Powers Legislation,* 37 N.Y.U.L.Rev. 627, 640 (1962).

[479] UTC § 703(e). For further discussion of delegation, *see* Section 14.8, at note 672 et seq.

[480] UPC § 3–718. UTC § 703(b) is similar.

[481] *Restatement (Third) of Trusts* § 34, cmt. d (2003). *See also* UTC § 704(e); Rubinson v. Rubinson, 620 N.E.2d 1271, 1278 (Ill.App.1993) (act by remaining trustee is valid).

[482] In re Will of Crabtree, 795 N.E.2d 1157, 1164 (Mass.2003).

Resignation

A person will not be appointed executor or trustee over the person's objection.[483] A trustee who has not accepted the office may reject it,[484] but a fiduciary who has accepted the office ordinarily needs court approval to resign unless the trust instrument provides otherwise or all the beneficiaries consent.[485] Some trust instruments allow a trustee to resign simply by giving notice to the current income beneficiaries.[486] This obviates the need for court proceedings that are wasteful because requests to resign are usually approved.[487] Both the UPC and UTC allow a personal representative or fiduciary to resign upon the giving of a notice but the resignation is not fully effective until the successor takes office.[488] The resigning trustee remains subject to fiduciary duties until a successor takes office.[489]

Successor's Powers

The powers conferred by an instrument on a fiduciary are usually not construed as personal to the original trustee or executor, *i.e.*, a successor can also exercise them. Many statutes presume that successor fiduciaries were intended to have the same powers.[490] The UPC gives successor personal representatives the same powers as the original except for any power "expressly made personal to the executor named in the will."[491] The Third Restatement of Trusts similarly allows successor trustees to exercise powers conferred on the original trustee unless the trust provides otherwise, but such a restrictive intent can possibly be inferred "by an appearance from the terms of the trust that the settlor placed some particular confidence in the original trustee"[492]

---

[483] McCarthy v. Poulsen, 219 Cal.Rptr. 375 (App.1985) (error to force settlors to become trustees); In re Estate of Cavalier, 582 A.2d 1125 (Pa.Super.1990).

[484] UTC § 701(b); *Restatement (Third) of Trusts* § 35(2) (2003). Acceptance of the office of trustee may be inferred from conduct. *Id.* § 35(1). As to the possible liability of a person who has promised to serve but then declines to act, *see Restatement (Third) of Trusts* § 35, cmt. b (2003).

[485] *Restatement (Third) of Trusts* § 36 (2003). *But cf.* Unif. Transfers to Minors Act § 18(c) (custodian can resign by giving notice); Cal.Prob.Code § 15640 (consent of adult income beneficiaries sufficient for resignation); UTC § 705(a)(1) (trustee may resign by giving 30 day notice to "qualified beneficiaries"—these are defined in § 103(12)).

[486] Shaffer, *The Planning and Drafting of Wills and Trusts* 235 (2d ed. 1979); Tweed & Parsons, *Lifetime and Testamentary Estate Planning* 102 (10th ed. 1988).

[487] In re White, 484 A.2d 763, 766 (Pa.1984); Oregon Bank v. Hendricksen, 515 P.2d 1328 (Or.1973) (trustee allowed to resign because stipulated compensation was too low).

[488] UPC § 3–610(c); UTC § 705. In Wortman v. Hutaff, 2012 WL 379752 (N.C. Super. Ct, Jan. 30, 2012), the trustee filed a statement of resignation with the clerk. The court held that the resignation was ineffective because the trustee had not complied with the procedure specified in UTC § 705.

[489] UTC § 707; Republic National Bank & Trust Co. v. Bruce, 105 S.W.2d 882 (Tex. Civ. App. 1937).

[490] Fratcher, *Trustees' Powers Legislation,* 37 N.Y.U.L.Rev. 627, 638 (1962); N.Y.EPTL § 11–1.1(b)(12); Wis.Stat. § 701.17(3); cf. Cal.Prob.Code § 8442 (administrator with the will annexed has same powers as executor except as to "discretionary powers not conferred by law").

[491] UPC § 3–716.

[492] *Restatement (Third) of Trusts* § 85, cmt. d (2007).

Attorney's Role

Testators and settlors often ask attorneys for advice as to who should be named as executor or trustee. A designation of the attorney who drafted the will as a fiduciary sometimes is challenged for undue influence or as a violation of the rules of professional conduct.[493]

Knowledgeable estate attorneys disagree about the propriety of attorneys serving as executors. Professor Stein suggests that it is "usually more efficient than the ordinary division of labor" between the personal representative and the estate's attorney; "potential communication difficulties are obviated. The attorney-representative is in a position to act quickly because it is unnecessary to wait for a lay representative to be informed and to participate." On the other hand, many time-consuming tasks of a personal representative require no legal expertise,[494] while others require skills that many lawyers lack. An "attorney who becomes a fiduciary must become financially sophisticated with investments and capable of evaluating the competence and prudence of [any] in-house or advisory service."[495] The trend to allow trustees to delegate investment functions to experts may lead to a greater willingness on the part of lawyers to serve as trustees.[496]

Even lawyers who do not serve as fiduciaries profit from being chosen as attorneys for the executor or trustee. A provision in a will directing the executor to hire a particular attorney is usually held unenforceable on the ground that the executor should have "unfettered discretion to select an attorney."[497] Corporate executors typically hire the attorney who drafted the will to handle administration, but this practice has been criticized.[498] A California court looked more favorably on the practice and refused to remove as executor a bank which had hired the drafter of the will as attorney for the estate, stating that "the lawyer with familiarity of the testator's property is a reasonable choice."[499]

---

[493] McGovern, *Undue Influence and Professional Responsibility*, 28 Real Prop.Prob. & Tr.J. 643, 670 (1994); Section 5.4, note 195 et seq. In Matter of Bales, 608 N.E.2d 987 (Ind.1993), a lawyer who drafted a will which named her executor and provided a high fee was reprimanded. A drafter-executor to whom the will gave discretion to distribute the estate to charities of his choice was held to be a "substantial beneficiary" thus raising a presumption of undue influence. Allen v. Estate of Allen, 394 So.2d 132 (Fla.App.1980).

[494] Stein & Fierstein, *The Role of the Attorney in the Administration of the Estate*, 68 Minn.L. Rev. 1107, 1164 (1984).

[495] *Draft Statement of Principles Attorneys Acting as Other Fiduciaries*, Tr. & Est., Dec. 1988, at 27.

[496] Langbein, *The Uniform Prudent Investor Act and the Future of Trust Investing*, 81 Iowa L.Rev. 641, 666 (1996). As to delegation, *see* Section 14.4, note 285 et seq.

[497] In re Estate of Deardoff, 461 N.E.2d 1292, 1293 (Ohio 1984). *See also* Johnston, *An Ethical Analysis of Common Estate Planning Practices*, 45 Ohio St. L.J. 57, 105 (1984); Hawaiian Trust Co., Ltd. v. Hogan, 623 P.2d 450 (Haw.App.1981). But see In re Devroy's estate, 325 N.W.2d 345 (Wis. 1982) (condition on appointment of as executor that he retain Y as attorney upheld); La. Rev.Stat. § 9:2448 (designation of attorney in will is binding on executor).

[498] Johnston, *An Ethical Analysis of Common Estate Planning Practices*, 45 Ohio St. L. J. at 115. *See also* Wolfram, *Modern Legal Ethics* § 8.12.4 (1986).

[499] Matter of Estate of Effron, 173 Cal.Rptr. 93, 102 (App.1981). *But cf.* Wis.Stat.§ 856.31 (beneficiaries receiving majority of interests of estate can select attorney for a corporate executor).

§ 14.7 Compensation

An important factor in choosing a fiduciary is cost. This section deals with the fees of personal representatives, trustees, and their attorneys. It is convenient to talk about fiduciary fees in general, but the rules are not the same for all fiduciaries. For example, in California, the fees of personal representatives and their attorneys are based on a percentage of the estate,[500] but trustees, custodians and conservators are allowed "reasonable" compensation.[501] A donor who acts as custodian under the Uniform Transfers to Minors Act can receive no compensation,[502] but there is no such limitation on settlors who act as trustee.

Size of the Estate

In many states, fiduciary fees are based on the size of the estate or trust. New York allows personal representatives commissions on a sliding scale, starting at 5% of the first $100,000 down to 2% of property in excess of $5,000,000.[503] Trustees are entitled to annual fees of $10.50 per $1,000 of principal up to $400,000, $4.50 per $1,000 for the next $600,000, and $3 per $1,000 for the rest.[504] Thus, fees for larger trusts are higher in amount, but smaller in proportion to the trust assets. Many trustees charge a minimum fee for each trust handled. This may make the use of a professional trustee uneconomical for small trusts and provides a reason to consolidate smaller trusts with the same beneficiaries.[505]

The UPC does not base fiduciary fees on a percentage of the estate but rather provides for "reasonable compensation."[506] The UTC and Third Restatement of Trusts also apply a reasonable compensation standard,[507] as does the Uniform Transfers to Minors Act for custodians.[508]

Is there a substantial practical difference between a "reasonable fee" and a percentage of the estate (or income)? A Florida court reversed an award of administrator's fees based on a percentage of the estate under a "reasonable compensation" statute, because "the amount of the probate estate . . . was not intended to be the sole controlling factor."[509] Most percentage fee provisions allow "further compensation" for any "extraordinary services" provided by the

---

[500] Cal.Prob.Code §§ 10800, 10810.

[501] Cal.Prob.Code §§ 15681 (trustee), 3915(b) (custodian), 2640 (guardian and conservator).

[502] Unif. Transfers to Minors Act § 15(b).

[503] N.Y.Surr.Ct.Proc. Act § 2307.

[504] N.Y.Surr.Ct.Proc.Act. § 2309.

[505] *See* Section 10.9, note 460.

[506] UPC § 3–719 (personal representatives), § 5–413 (conservators). *See also* Ind.Code § 29–1–10–13.

[507] UTC § 708; *Restatement (Third) of Trusts* § 38 (2003).

[508] Unif. Transfers to Minors Act § 15(b).

[509] In re Estate of Platt, 586 So.2d 328, 336 (Fla.1991). *See also* Ford v. Peoples Trust & Savings Bank, 651 N.E.2d 1193 (Ind. App.1995) (fees in large estate excessive given the time required).

fiduciary.[510] Some statutory percentage fees, on the other hand, are expressed as a maximum.[511]

"Reasonable compensation" takes custom into account,[512] and courts rely on expert testimony in passing on fees.[513] Professional trustees customarily base their fees on a percentage of the income and principal of the trust. A termination fee of 2% of the trust assets was upheld under a "reasonable compensation" statute: "In determining what is reasonable a trial court should look to the practices of other trust institutions in the state," most of which charged such a fee.[514] But a termination fee in another case was denied because it was not considered part of the trustee's "ordinary and reasonable fees."[515]

State and local bar associations used to issue fee schedules which based lawyers' fees on the size of the estate[516] until the Supreme Court held that such fee schedules violated the antitrust laws.[517] This decision contributed to a trend to base fees on factors other than the size of the estate.[518] But a California court upheld that state's statutory percentage fee system for both executors and attorneys. The anti-trust laws did not apply because the statute constituted state action. The legislature "after expending enormous energy" studying the issue had concluded that its system was "both cost effective and fair," because it saved judicial time which would otherwise be spent establishing reasonable fees, favored small estates, and encouraged the efficient use of time.[519]

The Third Restatement of Trusts lists the "amount and character of the trust property" as a factor in determining a reasonable fee along with the "responsibility and risk assumed in administering the trust."[520] But holding a

---

[510] Cal.Prob.Code § 10801(a); Wis.Stat. § 857.05(2); In re Estate of Barber, 779 P.2d 477, 488 (Mont. 1989) (additional fees for extraordinary services as attorney).

[511] Ark.Code § 28–48–108(a); Iowa Code § 633.197; Md. Est. & Tr. Code § 7–601(b); Estate of Stone, 768 P.2d 334 (Mont.1989) (fee claim based on statutory maximum allowed).

[512] *Restatement (Third) of Trusts* § 38, cmt. c(1) (2003); UTC § 708, cmt.; Appeal of Wickersham, 594 N.E.2d 498, 502 (Ind. App.1992) (attorney's fees "higher than those customarily charged" reduced); In re Estate of Berthot, 59 P.3d 1080, 1087 (Mont.2002) (fees "consistent with the fees generally charged by corporate fiduciaries" upheld).

[513] Estate of McClenahan v. Biberstein, 671 N.E.2d 482, 484 (Ind.App.1996) (attorney's fee).

[514] Matter of Trusts Under Will of Dwan, 371 N.W.2d 641, 642–43 (Minn.App.1985). *See also* UTC § 708, cmt., suggesting termination fee may be excessive when trust transferred to successor trustee instead of terminated. In Lehmann v. Bank of America, N.A., 427 S.W. 3d 315 (Mo. Ct. App. 2014), the corporate trustee was denied a termination fee when the trust was transferred to a successor trustee because the trust had not in fact been terminated.

[515] In re William Dankworth Trust, 2014 WL 7475202 (Ohio Ct. App., Dec. 29, 2014).

[516] *Fiduciary and Probate Counsel Fees in the Wake of Goldfarb*, 13 Real Prop.Prob. & Tr.J. 238 (1978) (hereinafter cited as *Fiduciary Fees*).

[517] Goldfarb v. Virginia State Bar, 421 U.S. 773 (1975).

[518] In re Estate of Secoy, 484 N.E.2d 160, 164 (Ohio App.1984) (noting a "general retreat from fee schedules" following *Goldfarb*).

[519] Estate of Effron, 173 Cal.Rptr. 93, 99 (App.1981). *See also* Stein & Fierstein, *The Role of the Attorney in Estate Administration*, 68 Minn.L.Rev. 1107, 1178 (1984) (lawyers' time in justifying fee may increase cost of administration).

[520] *Restatement (Third) of Trusts* § 38, cmt. c(1) (2003). *See also* UTC § 708, cmt.

block of stock in a public company may involve little effort compared to managing a small business.[521]

Basing trustee's fees on the value of the trust principal rewards trustees who make shrewd investments, just as the compensation of mutual fund managers is often based on the value of the fund.[522] But percentage formulas also create perverse incentives. Lawyers whose fees are based on the size of the probate estate have an incentive not to advise clients to avoid probate.[523]

Professor Stein has observed, "folklore in some legal communities suggests . . . that attorneys price estate planning services cheaply in the expectation that they will later be retained to provide the more profitable estate administration services."[524] But Stein's study found that "whatever the historical pattern, . . . estate planning services are now priced similarly to estate administration and other legal services performed by the attorney." The study also found that fees in California based on a percentage of the estate were comparable to fees charged in states with a reasonable compensation system.[525]

Other Factors

What factors other than the size of the estate are relevant in determining a reasonable fee? The Third Restatement of Trusts mentions "the time devoted to trust duties."[526] The ABA Model Rules of Professional Conduct make "the time and labor required" as well as "the experience, reputation, and ability of the lawyer" as relevant factors in determining a reasonable lawyer's fee.[527] A fee claimed by a personal representative was rejected on the ground that "there was no evidence of the time spent in performing the claimed services."[528] On the other hand, fees exceeding the assets remaining in an estate were allowed in a case where "although an inordinate amount of time was spent by the attorneys for the estate, the time spent was reasonable and necessary" under

---

[521] Matter of Trusts Under Will of Dwan, 371 N.W.2d 641, 643–44 (Minn.App.1985) (dissent); Martin, *Professional Responsibility and Probate Practices*, 1975 Wis.L.Rev. 911, 944; Adams, *Professional Fees: The Consumer's Perspective*, Tr. & Est., May, 2002, at 64 (trustee fees should be adjusted for type of property in trust, and be reduced for "self-directed" trust where trustee has no investment responsibility).

[522] However, trustees' fees are not as "performance based" as those of some investment advisors. Gordon, *The Puzzling Persistence of the Constrained Prudent Man Rule*, 62 N.Y.U.L.Rev. 52, 82 (1987).

[523] In Matter of Tobin, 628 N.E.2d 1268 (Mass.1994) a lawyer was suspended, among other reasons, for advising probate of an estate where all the assets were held in joint tenancy.

[524] Stein & Fierstein, *The Role of the Attorney in Estate Administration*, 68 Minn.L.Rev. at 1193. *See also* Johnston, *An Ethical Analysis of Common Estate Planning Practices—Is Good Business Bad Ethics?*, 45 Ohio St.L.J. 57, 102 (1984); *Developments regarding the Professional Responsibility of the Estate Planning Lawyer: the Effect of the Model Rules of Professional Conduct*, 22 Real Prop.Prob & Tr.J. 1, 5 (1987).

[525] Stein & Fierstein, 68 Minn.L.Rev. at 1188, 1193.

[526] *Restatement (Third) of Trusts* § 38, cmt. c(1) (2003).

[527] Rule 1.5(a)(1). *See also* Minn.Stat. § 525.515(b)(1).

[528] Noble v. McNerney, 419 N.W.2d 424, 430 (Mich.App.1988); Estate of Stone, 768 P.2d 334, 336 (Mont.1989) (claim for fees by attorney-executor who kept no time logs rejected); In re Estate of Konopka, 498 N.W.2d 853 (Wis.App. 1993). *But see* In re Estate of Salus, 617 A.2d 737, 743 (Pa.Super.1992) (trustee awarded fee despite lack of time records); Estate of McClenahan v. Biberstein, 671 N.E.2d 482, 486 (Ind.App.1996) (same for attorney); Andrews v. Gorby, 675 A.2d 449, 455 (Conn.1996).

the circumstances.[529] However, no statute fixes fees on a per hour basis, and courts have also resisted this notion. A claim for attorney's fees based on 364.5 hours of work in administering an estate was rejected because "a number of routine matters had occupied an inordinate amount" of time.[530] This is a common theme in cases in which the attorney also serves as executor, or the executor is a family member who lets the lawyer do all the work.[531]

Family members and friends who act as trustees are entitled to reasonable compensation, but usually at a lower rate under a reasonable compensation standard which takes into account "the trustee's skill, experience and facilities."[532] Family members should make clear up front whether they expect to receive compensation or compensation may be deemed to have been waived by course of conduct.[533] Family members and others named as a fiduciary should also not delay billing too long, although in one case a bill for 12 years of work was approved.[534]

Poor performance may cause a reduction or even total loss of fees. An executor was denied all compensation because of unjustified delays in closing an estate.[535] The fees of a trustee which had improperly left cash in a checking account were reduced by 10% in addition to surcharging the trustee for the loss suffered by the trust.[536] The Third Restatement includes "the quality of the trustee's performance" as a relevant consideration in determining compensation.[537] But fiduciaries who acted in good faith and performed valuable services may receive a fee despite a breach of duty.[538]

---

[529] In re Estate of Schaffer, 656 N.E.2d 368, 372 (Ohio App.1995).

[530] Matter of Estate of Larson, 694 P.2d 1051, 1055–59 (Wash.1985). *See also* In re Estate of Miller, 556 N.E.2d 568, 571 (Ill. App. 1990); In re Estate of Quinn, 830 P.2d 282, 285 (Utah App.1992).

[531] Estate of Coughlin, 633 N.Y.S.2d 610 (App.Div.1995); Matter of Estate of Mathwig, 843 P.2d 1112, 1113 (Wash.App.1993); *cf.* Price & Donaldson, *Contemporary Estate Planning* § 4.26.1 (2014 ed.) (drafter should advise client that designating an individual fiduciary may require lawyer to do more work and entitle lawyer to more compensation).

[532] *Restatement (Third) of Trusts* § 38, cmt. c(1) (2003). *See also* Shear v. Gabovitch, 685 N.E.2d 1168, 1192 (Mass.App.1997) (proper claim by individual trustee to fees based on a corporate fiduciary fee schedule).

[533] Meeks v. Successor Trustees of Marital Trust, 2010 WL 3420546 (Tenn. Ct. App. 2010).

[534] Lyons ex rel. Lawing v. Holder, 163 P.3d 343 (Kan. Ct. App. 2007).

[535] Estate of Heller, 9 Cal.Rptr.2d 274 (App.1992). *See also* Lowery v. Evonuk, 767 P.2d 489 (Or.App.1989) (trustee). In In re Estate of McCool, 553 A.2d 761 (N.H.1988) an executor was denied compensation because he had a conflict of interest as lawyer for persons with claims against the estate.

[536] Maryland Nat'l Bank v. Cummins, 588 A.2d 1205, 1219–20 (Md.1991). In In re Consupak, Inc., 87 B.R. 529 (Bkrtcy.N.D.Ill. 1988), a bankruptcy trustee was surcharged for leaving money in a checking account and the fee of the attorney for the trustee was reduced for failure to advise the trustee of his duty.

[537] *Restatement (Third) of Trusts* § 38, cmt. c(1) (2003). *See also* UTC § 1001(b)(8), allowing courts to "reduce or deny compensation" as a remedy for breach.

[538] Burch v. Dodge, 608 P.2d 1032 (Kan.App.1980) (since surcharge will make estate whole, no abuse of discretion to award trustee a fee); Matter of Estate of Bartlett, 680 P.2d 369 (Okl.1984) (fee should be reduced only if administrator failed to perform duties, not for an improper sale); Matter of Trust of Grover, 710 P.2d 597 (Idaho 1985) (family member trustee gets compensation despite failure to keep records); In re Saxton, 712 N.Y.S.2d 225, 233 (App.Div.2000) (abuse of discretion to deny compensation to a trustee who was surcharged but without a "finding of self-dealing or fraud").

Claims by attorneys for fees for services performed for a trust have been denied on the ground that they had a conflict of interest in representing both a trustee and a beneficiary with adverse interests.[539]

Contract

Fees of fiduciaries or the attorney for an estate are often not discussed at the time a will or trust is drafted, even though this would be a desirable practice.[540] ABA Model Rule 1.5(b) says that "the basis or rate of the [lawyer's] fee shall be communicated to the client . . . before or within a reasonable time after commencing the representation."[541] This does not apply to the fee of the attorney for the estate who is not the testator's client, but when the executor engages a lawyer for the estate, the latter should provide the executor with a "written explanation of the basis upon which the lawyer's fee will be determined."[542]

A provision in an instrument stating what a fiduciary or lawyer is to receive may preclude a claim for more. The Third Restatement of Trusts provides, however, that although a trustee's compensation is "ordinarily governed" by such a provision, if the amount specified "is or becomes unreasonably high or unreasonably low, the court may allow a smaller or higher compensation."[543] The Uniform Trust Code provides for similar relief.[544] Such relief is denied if a trustee has agreed with the settlor to act for a certain compensation, and such an agreement may be inferred when a trustee accepts a trust which contains such a provision.[545] Even in this case a "substantial and unanticipated change" in the circumstances may warrant ignoring it.[546]

Under the UPC, "if a will provides for compensation of the personal representative and there is no contract regarding compensation, he may renounce the provision before qualifying and be entitled to reasonable compensation."[547] Because fiduciaries have a right to take their fee before the

---

[539] Crawford & Lewis v. Boatmen's Trust Co., 1 S.W.3d 417 (Ark.1999).

[540] McGovern, *Undue Influence and Professional Responsibility*, 28 Real Prop.Prob. & Tr. J. 643, 672 (1994). Massachusetts encourages this practice by requiring fiduciaries who know that someone intends to designate them to provide the customer with a statement of their current charges. Mass.Ann.Laws c. 203, § 4B(f).

[541] ABA Model Rules of Professional Conduct 1.5(b).

[542] Price & Donaldson, *Contemporary Estate Planning* § 12.2.1 (2014 ed.).

[543] *Restatement (Third) of Trusts* § 38, cmt. e (2003). UTC § 708(b) and Cal.Prob.Code § 15680(b)(2) also allow upward or downward adjustment.

[544] UTC § 709(b)(2).

[545] For cases enforcing such a contractual limitation on compensation *outside* the instrument, *see* Lowy v. Kessler, 522 So.2d 917 (Fla.App.1988) (executor); Rutanen v. Ballard, 678 N.E.2d 133, 142 (Mass.1997) (trustee).

[546] *Compare* other cases of deviations from the terms of a trust when circumstances change. Section 10.9, note 451 et seq.

[547] UPC § 3–719. However, a comment to the Code says that "if a will provision is framed as a condition on the nomination, it could not be renounced." In re Estate of Schuldt, 428 N.W.2d 251, 255 (S.D. 1988), the court held that a stipulation in a will about the compensation of the attorney for the estate was not binding on the ground that "it is the [personal] representative who contracts for the services, not the testator."

assets of a trust or estate are distributed,[548] a trustee who distributes assets without deducting a fee may be deemed to have waived any claim to one.[549]

A provision for an unreasonably *high* fee for a fiduciary may be valid as a devise or gift,[550] but is subject to attack for undue influence. An attorney who drafted a will that named him as executor with a designated fee was limited to reasonable compensation because of the "fiduciary relationship" between lawyer and client.[551]

Fiduciaries and attorneys sometimes contract with the beneficiaries of an estate for higher than normal fees. Professor Stein notes that attorneys may properly charge a fee to the recipients of the nonprobate assets rather than burdening the probate estate with the fee for the attorney's services.[552] The Third Restatement allows trustees to contract for an enlarged fee from the trust beneficiaries if they "disclose all the relevant circumstances" and the agreement is not "unfair."[553]

Compensation of Agents

Fiduciaries often seek reimbursement for the cost of hiring others to assist them. A trustee's right to reimbursement depends on "how the advisor's employment relates to the responsibilities reasonably expected of" the trustee.[554] Thus, a court approved an arrangement whereby a bank trustee delegated its investment function to an investment advisor and charged only a considerably reduced "custody account fee."[555] But the fees of an accountant were charged against an executor's commission rather than the estate on the theory that "if one hires a professional to assist in carrying out one of the

---

548 *Restatement (Third) of Trusts* § 38, cmt. b (2003).

549 *Restatement (Third) of Trusts* § 38, cmt. g; Rutanen v. Ballard, 678 N.E.2d 133, 142 (Mass.1997); McCormick v. McCormick, 536 N.E.2d 419, 435 (Ill.App.1988). However, mere failure to claim a fee prior to termination of a trust was held not to be a waiver in In re Estate of Salus, 617 A.2d 737, 741 (Pa.Super.1992).

550 If the will is ambiguous on the point, the Restatement presumes that a devise to a person who is also designated as a fiduciary is in addition to compensation and is not conditioned on the devisee's acceptance of the trusteeship. *Restatement (Third) of Trusts* § 38, cmt. e (2003).

551 Andrews v. Gorby, 675 A.2d 449, 454 (Conn.1996); *cf.* Matter of Bales, 608 N.E.2d 987 (Ind.1993) (lawyer reprimanded for drafting a will providing high compensation for her services as executor and attorney). As to will provisions for the drafter, *see* Section 5.4, note 174.

552 Stein & Fierstein, *The Role of the Attorney in Estate Administration*, 68 Minn.L.Rev. at 1179. *Compare* the common rule apportioning death taxes between probate and nonprobate distributees. Section 6.4, note 98 et seq.

553 *Restatement (Third) of Trusts* § 38, cmt. f (2003). Under UTC § 802(h)(1) and Cal.Prob.Code § 16004(c) the general suspicion of contracts between trustees and beneficiaries does not apply to contracts for the trustee's compensation. But Cal.Prob.Code § 10803 makes an agreement between a personal representative and devisees or heirs for higher compensation void. *See also* Haw.Rev.Stat. § 607–18(c) (agreement for higher compensation for trustee is void); In re Estate of Konopka, 498 N.W.2d 853 (Wis.App.1993) (fee contract between beneficiary of estate and attorney rejected as "unreasonable").

554 *Restatement (Third) of Trusts* § 38, illus. 1 (2003). *See also* Unif. Prudent Investor Act § 9, cmt.

555 Matter of Estate of Younker, 663 N.Y.S.2d 946 (Sur.1997). *See also* Chase v. Pevear, 419 N.E.2d 1358, 1364–65 (Mass.1981).

ordinary duties of being a personal representative," the latter's fees should be adjusted accordingly.[556]

Attorney's Fees

Trustees and personal representatives can be indemnified for reasonable attorney's fees but only if the services benefited the trust or estate rather than the fiduciary personally. The line between the two is sometimes fuzzy. An executor who was also a principal beneficiary of a contested will was denied reimbursement for her attorney's fees in an appeal from a decree rejecting the will because "the appeal promoted only the [executor's] personal interests."[557] On the other hand, a trustee who successfully resisted an attempt to remove and surcharge it was awarded attorney's fees.[558] Partial reimbursement of attorney's fees may be allowed when trustees prevail as to part but not all of the claims made against them.[559] The UPC allows personal representatives reasonable attorney's fees when they "defend or prosecute any proceeding in good faith, whether successful or not."[560]

Some courts deny attorney's fees incurred in litigation over the amount of the fiduciary's compensation,[561] but others disagree, reasoning that if fiduciaries are not reimbursed for such expenses, "their compensation for the underlying services may be effectively diluted."[562]

Courts also award attorney's fees from an estate to beneficiaries who are not fiduciaries. The attorneys for two heirs recovered fees from the estate under the "common fund" theory; there would otherwise be "an unfair advantage to the other [heirs] who are entitled to share in the fund and who should bear their share of the burden of the recovery."[563] When beneficiaries

---

[556] In re Estate of Billings, 278 Cal.Rptr. 439, 442 (App.1991). As to the deductibility of fees paid for investment advice for income tax purposes, *see* Sherman, *All You Really Need to Know About Subchapter J You Learned from This Article*, 63 Mo.L.Rev. 1, 10–11 (1998).

[557] Matter of Estate of Jones, 492 N.W.2d 723, 727 (Iowa App.1992). *See also* In re Estate of Meyer, 802 P.2d 148, 154 (Wash.App.1990). *But see* Shepherd v. Mazzetti, 545 A.2d 621, 623–24 (Del.1988) (executor-devisee entitled to attorney's fees in unsuccessfully resisting claim against the estate).

[558] Matter of Trust Created by Hill, 499 N.W.2d 475, 494 (Minn.App.1993). *See also* Lucas v. Mannering, 745 S.W.2d 654 (Ky.App.1987); Morrison v. Watkins, 889 P.2d 140 (Kan.App.1995). But in In re Estate of Morris, 949 P.2d 401, 403 (Wash.App.1998), the court denied a similar claim by an executor on the ground that since estate administration is relatively short-term, the executor's desire to keep the job did not provide "a substantial benefit" to the estate. In In re Trust Created Under Mitchell, 788 N.E.2d 433, 439 (Ind.App.2003), the court upheld denial of attorney's fees to a trustee who successfully resisted removal attempt, but was "not without blame in fostering a hostile relationship" with the beneficiaries.

[559] Leigh v. Engle, 858 F.2d 361, 369 (7th Cir.1988) (ERISA); Matter of Estate of Cassity, 165 Cal.Rptr. 88, 91 (App.1980).

[560] UPC § 3–720; *cf.* In re Estate of Stowell, 595 A.2d 1022 (Me.1991) (this does not allow a fiduciary to recover fees from "litigation that results from the fiduciary's misconduct"). Payment may be made even prior to the conclusion of the proceedings in question. National Wildlife Federation v. Foster, 575 A.2d 776, 781–83 (Md. App.1990).

[561] Matter of Trust of Grover, 710 P.2d 597, 602 (Idaho 1985); Matter of Estate of Larson, 694 P.2d 1051 (Wash.1985) (attorney can't charge estate for time spent in justifying his own fee); In re Estate of Inlow, 735 N.E.2d 240, 250 (Ind.App.2000) (same); In re Estate of Petesch, 62 P.3d 674, 680 (Kan.App.2003).

[562] In re Estate of Trynin, 782 P.2d 232, 238 (Cal.1989).

[563] In re Keller, 584 N.E.2d 1312, 1317 (Ohio App.1989). *See also* In re Estate of Pfoertner, 700 N.E.2d 438 (Ill.App.1998); Malachowski v. Bank One, 682 N.E.2d 530, 532 (Ind. 1997) (error

proved a breach of duty by trustees but unreasonably continued the litigation in a fruitless quest for large damages, the court only allowed part of their fees, saying their "folly . . . should not be rewarded."[564] Fees to attorneys for both sides in a will construction have been allowed on the theory that resolution of an ambiguity in the will benefited the estate.[565] The cases on attorney's fees are hard to reconcile, because trial courts have much discretion on the question.[566]

Attorney's fees are sometimes charged against persons who raise frivolous claims.[567] Fees of attorneys for beneficiaries who successfully sued a fiduciary have been charged to the fiduciary on the theory that they were a loss to the estate resulting from the fiduciary's breach.[568]

A body of case law has developed under the UTC which allows courts to award attorney's fees "to any party, to be paid by another party or from the trust . . . as justice and equity may require."[569] This provision was based on a comparable Massachusetts statute and "codifies the court's historic authority to award costs and fees, including reasonable attorney's fees, in judicial proceedings grounded in equity."[570] The Iowa Supreme Court, in construing a similar statute, specified the following non-exclusive list of factors in deciding what "justice and equity" requires in allocating fees: (1) reasonableness of the parties' claims, contentions, or defenses; (2) unnecessarily prolonging litigation; (3) relative ability to bear the financial burden; (4) result obtained in the litigation and prevailing party concepts; and (5) whether a party has acted in bad faith, vexatiously, wantonly, or oppressively.[571]

Although Section 1004 grants the court wide discretion in awarding fees, certain patterns have emerged. The court will award a trustee its attorney's fees from the trust for a successful defense against a claim,[572] may award a

---

to deny attorney's fees to beneficiaries who successfully sued to remove trustees). *But see* duPont v. Shackelford, 369 S.E.2d 673, 677 (Va.1988) (common fund rationale inapplicable when all beneficiaries had their own counsel).

[564] Leigh v. Engle, 858 F.2d 361, 370 (7th Cir.1988).

[565] Landmark Trust Co. v. Aitken, 587 N.E.2d 1076, 1086 (Ill.App.1992); Segal v. Levine, 489 So.2d 868 (Fla.App.1986); Matter of Will of Daniels, 799 P.2d 479, 485 (Kan.1990). *But see* In re Campbell's Trusts, 258 N.W.2d 856 (Minn.1977) (attorney's fees denied because trust was "not ambiguous"); In re Estate of Greatsinger, 492 N.E.2d 751 (N.Y.1986) (unsuccessful contender in will construction denied counsel fees because acting in own interest).

[566] Matter of Estate of Mathwig, 843 P.2d 1112, 1115 (Wash.App.1993) (statute allows court "in its discretion" to award attorney's fees); Diemer v. Diemer, 717 S.W.2d 160, 163 (Tex.App.1986); Rennacker v. Rennacker, 509 N.E.2d 798, 801 (Ill.App.1987).

[567] Matter of Estate of Barber, 779 P.2d 477, 489 (Mont.1989); In re Estate of Kerr, 949 P.2d 810 (Wash.1998) (attorney's fees against beneficiary who unsuccessfully sought executor's removal); Cal.Prob.Code § 11003 (bad faith contest of account by beneficiary or bad faith opposition to contest by personal representative); Estate of Ivey, 28 Cal. Rptr.2d 16, 19–20 (App.1994).

[568] In re Estate of Stowell, 595 A.2d 1022, 1026 (Me.1991). *See also* Lincoln National Bank v. Shriners Hospitals, 588 N.E.2d 597 (Ind. App. 1992); In re Estate of Dyniewicz, 648 N.E.2d 1076 (Ill.App.1995) (fees of GAL charged to guardian whose conduct make suit necessary); First Union National Bank v. Turney, 839 So.2d 774 (Fla.App. 2003) (based on a statute); *cf.* In re Niles, 823 A.2d 1 (N.J.2003) (plaintiffs' attorney's fees charged to defendants who had exercised undue influence over beneficiaries and embezzled money as trustee).

[569] UTC § 1004.

[570] UTC § 1004, cmt.

[571] In re Trust of Trimble, 826 N.W. 2d 474, 492–93 (Iowa 2013).

[572] *See, e.g.*, Brown v. Brown, 530 S.W.3d 35 (Mo.Ct.App. 2017).

trustee its fees if the breach of trust was unintentional,[573] but will deny an award to a trustee who violated a duty in bad faith.[574] A court has awarded a trustee its fees to be paid out of the shares of the petitioning and unsuccessful beneficiaries but not out of the share of the other beneficiary,[575] and has ordered a trustee to pay a beneficiary's attorney's fees even though the beneficiary did not suffer harm. By failing to keep the beneficiary informed, "the beneficiary had little choice but to file litigation to resolve any doubts about the trust's administration."[576] Finally, in a dispute between two charities over whether an amendment of the decedent's revocable trust was invalid on grounds of mental incapacity, the court awarded the unsuccessful plaintiff its attorney's fees to be paid from the trust because the action was brought in good faith and raised issues that only could be resolved by a judicial determination.[577]

Attorney as Executor or Trustee

Can an executor or trustee who is a lawyer receive compensation both as fiduciary and as attorney? Some courts allow dual compensation, citing the efficiencies involved in having the same individual act in both capacities.[578] "Usually money will be saved to an estate because . . . the fee . . . for dual services . . . will be smaller than the combined fee for a separate representative and attorney."[579] The UPC allows personal representatives to employ attorneys "even if they are associated with the personal representative."[580] The Third Restatement of Trusts uses more guarded language; trustees can be compensated for services to the trust as an attorney "when it is advantageous that the trustee rather than another perform those services."[581]

A similar problem arises when an estate or trust owns a company which employs the fiduciary. A will named Chambers as co-executor and trustee. Chambers, who was then serving as general counsel in a company owned by the estate thereafter became the president and received several salary increases, for which he was later surcharged. "Even attributing to Chambers an astute talent for business management one would be overly naive not to think that his position as . . . trustee did not assist him in ascending to the presidency. . . . A trustee, or one acting in a fiduciary capacity, is not permitted to place himself in such position that the interest of the beneficiaries and his

---

[573] In re Trust of Rosenberg, 727 N.W. 2d 430 (Neb. 2007).

[574] Shelton v. Tamposi, 62 A.3d 741 (N.H. 2013); Duke v. Simmons, 2009 WL 1175114 (Tenn. Ct. App., April 30, 2009); Fisher v. Fisher, 221 P.3d 845 (Utah Ct. App. 2009).

[575] O'Riley v. U.S. Bank, N.A., 412 S.W. 3d 400 (Mo. Ct. App. 2013).

[576] In re Estate of Forgey, 906 N.W.2d 618, 639 (Neb.2018).

[577] In re Gene Wild Revocable Trust, 299 S.W.3d 767 (Mo. Ct. App. 2009).

[578] In re Estate of Duffy, 774 N.E.2d 344 (Ohio App.2002). Not surprisingly, individuals do not commonly serve in both capacities in states where they are limited to a single fee. Stein & Fierstein, *The Role of the Attorney in Estate Administration*, 68 Minn.L.Rev.at 1169.

[579] In re Estate of Hackett, 366 N.E.2d 1103, 1106 (Ill.App.1977). *See also* In re Brown's Estate. 653 P.2d 928 (Okl.1982).

[580] UPC § 3–715(21). This language is borrowed from the Uniform Trustees' Powers Act § 3(c)(24).

[581] *Restatement (Third) of Trusts* § 38, cmt. d (2003). *See also* Lembo v. Casaly, 361 N.E.2d 1314, 1317 (Mass.App.1977).

own personal interest do or may conflict."[582] The Third Restatement, however, allows a trustee to receive a salary as an officer of a company controlled by the trust if the "salary is not greater than warranted by the services the trustee performs in the position with the enterprise."[583]

Multiple Fiduciaries

When a will or trust names more than one executor or trustee, does each collect a full fee or do they divide a single fee?[584] The answer varies in different states. In California, if there are two or more personal representatives, the compensation is apportioned among them "according to the services actually rendered by each."[585] In Missouri, on the other hand, the ordinary fee of the personal representative can be doubled if two or more serve, and in New York the fee can be tripled.[586] The Third Restatement of Trusts says that the aggregate fees for several trustees may reasonably exceed those of a single trustee because the "normal duty of each trustee to participate in all aspects of administration" may "result in some duplication of effort."[587]

When one fiduciary is an individual and the other is a corporation, the corporation usually gets a larger share.[588] In a case where an individual served as cotrustee with a bank, the testimony "overwhelmingly established that 'normal compensation' for a fully active individual cotrustee is, at most, 50 percent of the corporate cotrustee's fee."[589] A similar apportionment problem arises when a single fiduciary is unable to complete the job and a successor does so.[590]

Many people use revocable living trusts to avoid the cost of executor's fees based on the probate estate, but some trust companies impose a special charge "for services performed by the bank which are similar to those usually performed by an Executor."[591] Fees can often be saved by designating the same person as executor and trustee, because many corporate trustees do not charge a fee for accepting the trust if they also serve as executor.[592] The Third Restatement allows an executor-trustee "such compensation as is reasonable in view of all the duties performed."[593]

---

[582] Schmidt v. Chambers, 288 A.2d 356, 370–71 (Md.1972). *See also* Childs v. National Bank, 658 F.2d 487, 493 (7th Cir. 1981).

[583] *Restatement (Third) of Trusts* § 78, cmt. d(1) (2007); Ferber v. American Lamp Corp., 469 A.2d 1046 (Pa. 1983); Harper v. Harper, 491 So.2d 189 (Miss.1986) (salary "commensurate with prior amounts" paid); Bartlett v. Dumaine, 523 A.2d 1 (reasonable compensation).

[584] Sometimes an estate hires more than one attorney. In re Estate of Knott, 615 N.E.2d 357, 360 (Ill.App.1993) allowed an estate to hire a second attorney for litigation in this "age of specialization."

[585] Cal. Prob.Code § 10805. A similar rule applies to trustees. Cal.Prob.Code § 15683.

[586] Mo. Rev. Stat. § 473.153.2; N.Y.Surr.Ct.Proc.Act § 2307.5.

[587] *Restatement (Third) of Trusts* § 38, cmt. i (2003). *See also* UTC § 708, cmt.

[588] Jack, *Fiduciary Fees: Variations and Complexities,* 112 Tr. & Est. 622, 623 (1973).

[589] Fred Hutchinson Cancer Research Center v. Holman, 732 P.2d 974, 978–79 (Wash.1987).

[590] *Restatement (Third) of Trusts* § 38, cmt. j (2003); Ga.Code § 53–12–211(2) apportions the fee based on the relative time expended and denies compensation for the time spent in transferring the trust property and responsibility.

[591] Quoted in Bogert, *The Law of Trusts and Trustees* § 975, at 26 (2d rev. ed. 1983).

[592] Jack, *Fiduciary Fees: Variations and Complexities,* 112 Tr. & Est. at 623.

[593] *Restatement (Third) of Trusts* § 38, cmt. h (2003).

Court Review

In most states, prior court approval is required before fees can be paid to personal representatives or their attorneys. Lawyers have been disciplined for taking attorney's fees from an estate without prior court approval.[594] The UTC, on the other hand, allows trustees to pay themselves without court authorization,[595] and this is the prevailing practice for inter-vivos living trusts, which are freer of court supervision than decedent's estates.[596] The UPC follows this model even for decedent's estates, permitting personal representatives to "fix their own fees and those of estate attorneys." But "any interested person can get judicial review of fees," and one who has received "excessive compensation" may be ordered to refund it.[597] Courts have sometimes reduced fees *sua sponte*.[598] Lawyers who charge excessive fees for representing an estate are subject to discipline.[599]

§ 14.8 Remedies of Beneficiaries

This section discusses the remedies available to beneficiaries against fiduciaries for breach of their duties in administering an estate or trust. While the discussion principally focuses on personal representatives and trustees, many of these remedies also apply to custodians, conservators/guardians, and fiduciaries of pension plans under ERISA.

Jurisdiction

The court which appoints a fiduciary has primary although not necessarily exclusive jurisdiction over claims against the fiduciary. Beneficiaries of a will probated in Ohio were not allowed to sue the executor in federal court for "irregularities" in her administration, because federal courts have no probate jurisdiction and can entertain actions to redress wrongs in the administration of an estate only if the state allows such actions to be pursued in its courts of general jurisdiction which Ohio did not.[600] But another federal

---

594 State of ex rel. Oklahoma Bar Ass'n v. Besly, 136 P.3d 590 (Okl.2006) (lawyer suspended); In re Altstatt, 897 P.2d 1164, 1169 (Or.1995) (same). *See also* Murray v. State Bar, 709 P.2d 480 (Cal.1985); Office of Disciplinary Counsel v. Burkhart, 581 N.E.2d 540 (Ohio 1991); Harper v. Harper, 491 So.2d 189, 203 (Miss.1986) (executor removed, among other reasons, for paying attorney's fee without court approval).

595 UTC § 816(15). *See also* N.J.Stat. § 3B:18–17 (can take annual allowance without court action).

596 Section 10.4, note 112.

597 UPC § 3–721.

598 In re Estate of Santarelli, 74 P.3d 523 (Colo.App.2003).

599 Matter of Tuley, 907 P.2d 844 (Kan.1995) (lawyer censured for charging a fee amounting to 8% of estate where normal fee was 5%).

600 Bedo v. McGuire, 767 F.2d 305 (6th Cir.1985). The probate exception is truly limited to probate matters. "[T]he probate exception reserves to state probate courts the probate or annulment of a will and the administration of a decedent's estate; it also precludes federal courts from endeavoring to dispose of property that is in the custody of a state probate court. But it does not bar federal courts from adjudicating matters outside those confines and otherwise within federal jurisdiction." Marshall v. Marshall, 547 U.S. 293, 296 (2006). *Marshall* involved an action for tortious interference with an expectancy.

court upheld a similar suit arising in Illinois, because Illinois did *not* give its probate court exclusive jurisdiction over such cases.[601]

Furthermore, a Massachusetts court entertained a suit against an executor who had been appointed in Greece, saying "the fact that a fiduciary will be made to account for his administration in a court of probate jurisdiction does not deprive an equity court of jurisdiction." Its assumption of jurisdiction would not derogate from the authority of the domiciliary court, but rather assist it "by securing and preserving estate property."[602] However, a court that has jurisdiction may decline to proceed if another court offers a more convenient forum.[603]

The state in which a trust has its principal place of administration has jurisdiction over the trustee[604] and beneficiaries.[605] A state continues to have jurisdiction over fiduciaries who move to another state.[606] On the other hand, when the *beneficiaries* of a trust created in Ohio moved to Rhode Island, a Rhode Island court had no jurisdiction over the trustee whose only contact with the state had been sending accounts and distributions to the beneficiaries at their new residence.[607]

If the trust has property in a state other than in the principal place of administration, obtaining jurisdiction over the trustee in the court of that other state depends on the ordinary rules of civil practice. Where predecessor trustees of a Florida trust had sold contaminated property in New Hampshire without disclosing the environmental hazard, the New Hampshire court held that it did not have jurisdiction over the successor trustee who had not had any contact with the state.[608]

Form of Trial

Since historically trusts were enforced in equity, there is usually no right to trial by jury in a suit for breach of trust[609] or in a suit against a conservator or personal representative.[610] However. the historical distinction between

---

[601] Hamilton v. Nielsen, 678 F.2d 709 (7th Cir.1982). *See also* Beattie v. J.M. Tull Foundation, 941 F.Supp. 57 (D.S.C. 1996); Donato v. BankBoston, N.A., 110 F.Supp.2d 42,46 (D.R.I.2000).

[602] Kaltsas v. Kaltsas, 497 N.E.2d 26 (Mass.App.1986). *See also* Cocke v. Duke University, 131 S.E.2d 909 (N.C.1963) (N.C. has jurisdiction over trust created by resident of N.J.); Israel v. National Board of Y.M.C.A., 369 A.2d 646 (R.I.1977) (N.Y. judgment regarding Rhode Island testamentary trust is valid).

[603] Bartlett v. Dumaine, 523 A.2d 1, 15 (N.H.1986).

[604] UTC § 202(a): Acree v. Acree, 2012 WL 5873578 (Tenn. Ct. App., Nov. 20, 2012).

[605] UTC. § 202(a); Cundall v. U.S. Bank, N.A., 882 N.E. 2d 481 (Ohio Ct. App. 2007).

[606] Norton v. Bridges, 712 F.2d 1156, 1162 (7th Cir.1983). *See also Restatement (Second) of Conflict of Laws* § 361 (1971).

[607] Rose v. Firstar Bank, 819 A.2d 1247 (R.I.2003). *See also* Hanson v. Denckla, 357 U.S. 235 (1958). *But cf.* Guardianship and Conservatorship of Miles, 660 N.W.2d 233, 242 (S.D.2003) (California trustee had sufficient contacts with South Dakota to give court jurisdiction over him); Section 4.6, note 422 et seq.

[608] Fellows v. Colburn, 34 A.3d 552 (N.H. 2011).

[609] Matter of Trust Created by Hill, 499 N.W.2d 475, 490 (Minn.App.1993); Kann v. Kann, 690 A.2d 509 (Md.1997); Mest v. Dugan, 790 P.2d 38, 39 (Or.App.1990); *Restatement (Second) of Trusts* § 197 (1959); Cal.Prob.Code § 17006.

[610] Estate of Grove v. Selken, 820 P.2d 895, 900 (Or.App.1991); Kaitz v. District Court, 650 P.2d 553 (Colo.1982); Conservatorship of Estate of Coffey, 231 Cal.Rptr. 421, 427 (App.1986).

courts of law and equity does not bar states from extending jury trial to trust cases and some states have done so.[611]

Equitable Remedies

Traditional equitable remedies are often invoked against fiduciaries. Courts can enjoin fiduciaries from making an improper investment or sale or order them to sell property.[612] An improper sale that has already taken place can be vacated,[613] but not if the buyer was a bona fide purchaser.[614] A trustee who has wrongfully sold property to a bona fide purchaser can be compelled to buy a replacement if this is reasonably possible.[615]

The beneficiaries can also elect to affirm a wrongful purchase if the property later rises in value or may affirm an improper sale if the property declines in value after the sale.[616] This right of election allows beneficiaries to speculate at the fiduciary's expense, but if they delay too long, their remedy may be barred by laches.[617]

The UTC contains a list of equitable remedies, but the list is non-exclusive.[618]

Damages

Sometimes damages are the only appropriate remedy for the loss suffered by the trust.[619] If a sale was proper but the price was too low, damages are based on the value of the property when it was sold, *i.e.*, the difference between what the trustee received and what the buyer should have paid, with an adjustment for what that lost amount would have earned between the date of sale and the time of surcharge.[620] But when a trustee sells an asset which

---

[611] *See, e.g.*, In re Troy S. Poe Trust, 591 S.W.3d 168 (Tex. Ct. App. 2019) (jury trial available in trust modification action to determine disputed facts). First Union Nat'l Bank v. Turney, 839 So.2d 774, 776 (Fla.App.2003) (affirming jury award of damages in suit for breach of trust).

[612] Donovan v. Bierwirth, 680 F.2d 263 (2d Cir.1982) (injunction against trustees of pension fund); Matter of Estate of Rolczynski, 349 N.W.2d 394 (N.D.1984) (executor ordered to sell land); Lowell v. Bouchillon, 271 S.E.2d 498 (Ga.1980) (TRO against sale of land); In re Estate of Hughes, 515 A.2d 581 (Pa.Super.1986); *Restatement (Second) of Trusts* § 199 (1959); UTC § 1001(b).

[613] Matter of Estate of Ostrander, 910 P.2d 865 (Kan.App.1996) (unauthorized sale by administrator set aside); Smiley v. Johnson, 763 S.W.2d 1 (Tex.App.1988) (constructive trust imposed on buyers from agent); Walter E. Wilhite Revocable Living Trust v. Northwest Yearly Meeting Pension Fund, 916 P.2d 1264 (Idaho 1996) (transfer rescinded but transferee reimbursed for liens removed from property).

[614] Jarrett v. United States National Bank, 725 P.2d 384, 388 (Or.App.1986).

[615] Application of Kettle, 423 N.Y.S.2d 701 (App.Div.1979); *Restatement (Second) of Trusts* § 208, cmt. e (1959). For further discussion of bona fide purchasers, *see* Section 14.9, note 726 et seq.

[616] *Restatement (Third) of Trusts* § 100, cmt. a(1) (2012).

[617] For further discussion of laches, *see infra* note 738 et seq.

[618] UTC § 1001.

[619] "Damages in equity . . . for breach of trust are sometimes called 'surcharge' " because they represent a "charge on (*sur*) the account filed by the breaching trustee." Langbein, *What ERISA Means by "Equitable": The Supreme Court's Trail of Error in Russell, Mertens, and Great West*, 103 Colum. L. Rev. 1317, 1352–53 (2003).

[620] *Restatement (Third) of Trusts* § 100, cmt. b(1) (1992). *See also* Hatcher v. U.S. National Bank, 643 P.2d 359 (Or.App.1982); cf. In re Guardianship of Eisenberg, 719 P.2d 187, 192 (Wash.App.1986) (surcharge based on difference between fair rental value and rent received); Murphy v. Central Bank & Trust Co., 699 P.2d 13 (Colo.App.1985) (surcharge based on higher price received by buyers on resale).

should have been retained, the damages can be based on the increase in value at the time of trial, because the loss of appreciated value of the sold asset constitutes "an actual loss" to the trust.[621] Dividends paid on stock after it was improperly sold (reduced by interest received on the sales proceeds) are also awarded.[622]

Trustees may also be surcharged for failing to sell assets that are improper investments. An executor who unduly delayed selling stock while its value dropped was charged the value of the stock on the date it should have been sold less "the proceeds from the sale of the stock [when sold] or, if the stock is still retained, the value of the stock at the time" of trial.[623] The trial court also awarded the plaintiffs prejudgment interest at the legal rate, compounded from the date when the sale should have occurred. But the Third Restatement takes a different perspective, awarding damages based on what the portfolio would have been worth at the time of trial had the breach of trust not occurred.[624] This can be determined based on "the return experience (positive or negative) for other investments," or "portfolios . . . of other trusts having comparable objectives and circumstances."[625] A bank which invested solely for the benefit of the income beneficiaries without regard to the growth of corpus for the remaindermen had to pay damages based on the rate of appreciation realized by its common equity funds.[626] But, in another case, a court awarded prejudgment interest but not "investment potential" on estate funds wrongfully used by an executor, on the theory that "while a trustee has a duty to invest . . . , an executor has a duty to conserve estate assets."[627]

Courts refuse to impose a surcharge if they find no causal link between the breach of trust and the loss. A trustee which was authorized to invest in bonds with AAA or AA ratings bought some with only an A rating. They declined in value but the decline in higher rated bonds was even greater. The court refused to surcharge the trustee because the loss would have occurred in the absence of the breach.[628] But a trustee who buys an asset from himself

---

Conversely when a fiduciary pays too much for a proper investment, damages are based on the excess payment. *See* McCormick v. McCormick, 455 N.E.2d 103, 110 (Ill.App.1983) (trustees used a more expensive method of financing than necessary).

[621] Taylor v. Crocker National Bank, 252 Cal.Rptr. 388, 397 (App.1988) (not officially published). *See also Restatement (Third) of Trusts* § 100 (2012); Estate of Rothko, 372 N.E.2d 291, 297 (N.Y.1977) (executors). As to ERISA, *see* Langbein, 103 Colum.L.Rev., at 1337.

[622] Matter of Donald E. Bradford Trust, 538 So.2d 263, 268 (La.1989).

[623] Matter of Estate of Janes, 681 N.E.2d 332, 339 (N.Y.1997). *See also* Estate of Lindberg, 424 N.E.2d 1161 (Ill.App.1981). In In re Saxton, 712 N.Y.S.2d 225 (App.Div.2000), damages were similarly computed for a trustee which had retained an undiversified portfolio, but were reduced by capital gains taxes which a sale would have caused.

[624] *Restatement (Third) of Trusts* § 100 (2012). The leading case on "appreciation" damages is In re Rothko, 372 N.E.2d 291 (N.Y.1977).

[625] *Restatement (Third) of Trusts (Prudent Investor Rule)* § 100, cmt. b(1) (2012). *See also* Estate of Wilde, 708 A.2d 273, 275 (Me.1988) (damages based on the value of trust assets "had they been managed by a prudent trustee").

[626] Noggle v. Bank of America, 82 Cal.Rptr.2d 829, 836 (App.1999). *But see* Gillespie v. Seattle-First National Bank, 855 P.2d 680, 694 (Wash.App.1993).

[627] NC Illinois Trust v. First Illini Bancorp, 752 N.E.2d 1167, 1180 (Ill.App.2001). As to the differing duties of trustees and personal representatives in investing, *see* Section 14.2, note 54 et seq.

[628] Fort Myers Mem. Gardens v. Barnett Banks, 474 So.2d 1215, 1218 (Fla.App.1985).

which declines in value is surcharged even though the same decline would have occurred if he had bought the asset from someone else.[629] Perhaps the trustee would not have bought the asset at all without the conflict of interest, so there may in fact be a causal connection between the breach and the loss in this case.

Fiduciaries are not liable for losses to property in a trust or estate that occur without their fault. But the general duty of prudence and to preserve property may require them to take out insurance against such eventualities.[630] Should the fiduciary profit from the breach personally, the fiduciary is liable for the greater of the damages to the trust or the profit made by the trustee.[631] An example of a profit is when a trustee uses trust assets to secure a loan with which he made a profitable purchase for himself. In this case, the court awarded damages even though the trust suffered no loss. "Any benefit or profit inures to the trust estate, even though no injury was intended and none was in fact done to the trust estate."[632] The trustee is also liable for any profit that the trustee made from the trust even absent a breach.[633] Any profits claimed against a fiduciary must be shown with reasonable certainty. A bank that wrongfully invested trust funds in its own passbook accounts was not charged with its profits from use of the funds because they could not accurately be determined; instead, it had to pay interest at the legal rate on the amounts (less the interest already paid to the trust) as damages.[634]

Punishment

Traditionally, courts did not award punitive damages for breach of trust, because equity did not give punitive damages.[635] But some states do allow an award of punitive damages against trustees who have acted in "bad faith or conscious indifference to the rights of the beneficiaries."[636] Courts may also use contempt procedures against recalcitrant fiduciaries.[637] Beneficiaries of a trust have an advantage over ordinary creditors of a trustee who becomes insolvent; the beneficiaries "retain their equitable interests in the trust property if it can be identified, or in its product if it can be traced into the product."[638] If the trust

---

[629] Matter of Guardianship of Eisenberg, 719 P.2d 187, 191 (Wash.App.1986). For a further discussion of the duty of loyalty, *see* Section 14.1.

[630] *Restatement (Third) of Trusts* § 76, cmt. d (2007).

[631] UTC § 1002(a). *See* Joyce, *Trustee Liability for Breach of Trust—Loss or Profit, or Loss and Profit*, 45 ACTEC L.J. 43 (2019).

[632] Coster v. Crookham, 468 N.W.2d 802, 806–07 (Iowa 1991). For a more recent case involving self-dealing and application of the disgorgement remedy, *see* Miller v. Bank of America, N.A. 352 P.3d 1162 (2015). *See also Restatement (Third) of Trusts (Prudent Investor Rule)* § 205(a) (1992); 29 U.S.C. § 1109(a) (ERISA); UTC § 1002(a)(2).

[633] UTC § 1003(a).

[634] Stephan v. Equitable Savings and Loan Association, 522 P.2d 478, 492 (Or.1974). (Md.1991); *cf.* Maryland National Bank v. Cummins, 588 A.2d 1205, 1217 (Md.1991).

[635] Kohler v. Fletcher, 442 N.W.2d 169 (Minn.App.1989); Kaitz v. District Court, 650 P.2d 553 (Colo.1982); *cf.* Bank of America National Trust v. Superior Court, 226 Cal.Rptr. 685, 693 (App.1986) (guardian of the estate).

[636] Cartee v. Lesley, 350 S.E.2d 388, 390 (S.C.1986). *See also* Wells Fargo v. Militello, 2017 WL 2645430 (Tex. Ct. App., June 20, 2017) ($1 million in damages for mental anguish and $3,465,000 in exemplary damages); InterFirst Bank Dallas v. Risser, 739 S.W.2d 882 (Tex.App.1987) ($2.6 million in punitive damages awarded); NC Illinois Trust v. First Illini Bancorp, 752 N.E.2d 1167 (Ill.App.2001) ($1.3 million punitive damages against an executor).

[637] Matter of Elder, 763 P.2d 219, 221–22 (Alaska 1988).

[638] UTC § 507 & cmt.; *Restatement (Third) of Trusts* § 5, cmt. k (2003).

property can no longer be identified or traced, the trustee remains personally liable for damages. Claims arising out of "fraud or defalcation while acting in a fiduciary capacity" are not dischargeable in bankruptcy.[639]

Lawyers acting as fiduciaries who commit a breach of duty are subject to discipline under the rules of the profession, *e.g.*, attorneys have been disbarred for stealing money from a trust of which they were the trustee.[640]

Defenses: Standing

A suit may be dismissed for lack of standing. The key to determining standing often is whether the plaintiff will benefit financially from a favorable outcome. A beneficiary does not have standing to challenge actions that only affect other beneficiaries; thus, remaindermen under a trust were not permitted to question a loan made by the trustee at an interest below the market rate, because any increased income generated from the loan would not go to them but to the income beneficiary.[641] On the other hand, the fact that a trust beneficiary's interest is contingent does not deprive the beneficiary of standing to sue.[642]

Courts are liberal about standing when incapacitated persons are involved. An attorney had standing to challenge a conservator's accounts because "any person may petition the court as the next friend of the children to bring the conservator's conflict of interest to the court's attention."[643] The UPC allows "any person interested in the welfare" of a protected person to petition for relief against the conservator.[644]

Co-trustees have standing to sue fellow trustees,[645] and successor trustees can sue the predecessor (or the personal representative of the estate in the case of a testamentary trust) for breaches by the latter.[646] The state attorney general has standing with respect to charitable trusts.[647] Courts on their own motion may raise questions about a fiduciary's conduct.[648] A settlor who has

---

[639] 11 U.S.C. § 523(a)(4).

[640] In re Stern, 682 N.E.2d 867 (Mass. 1997); People v. Rouse, 817 P.2d 967 (Colo. 1991).

[641] Regan v. Uebelhor, 690 N.E.2d 1222, 1226 (Ind.App.1998). *See also* In re Trust of Strong, 734 N.Y.S.2d 668, 670 (App.Div.2001). *But see* Jarrett v. United States Nat'l Bank, 725 P.2d 384, 389 (Or.App.1986) (remaindermen damaged by failure to maximize income because it "would reduce the potential need to invade the corpus" to provide for needs of income beneficiary).

[642] Giagnorio v. Emmett C. Torkelson Trust, 686 N.E.2d 42, 45 (Ill.App.1997); Gaynor v. Payne, 804 A.2d 170, 176 (Conn.2002).

[643] Matter of Conservatorship of L.M.S., 755 P.2d 22, 25 (Kan.App.1988).

[644] UPC § 5–414.

[645] Cal.Prob.Code § 16013(b); UTC § 703(g). In Merrill Lynch Inc. v. Nora-Johnson, 797 A.2d 226 (N.J.Super., App.Div.2002), a co-trustee was allowed to sue a broker who had executed improper trades for the trust, even though her co-trustee refused to join in the suit.

[646] UTC § 812. A good faith determination by successor trustees not to pursue a possible claim against a former trustee bars the beneficiaries from doing so. Axelrod v. Giambalvo, 472 N.E.2d 840, 846 (Ill.App.1984).

[647] *Restatement (Third) of Trusts* § 94(2) (2012). As to charitable trusts, *see also* Section 10.10, note 614 et seq.

[648] Estate of Kerns v. Western Surety Co., 802 P.2d 1298 (Okl.App.1990); *Restatement (Third) of Trusts* § 94, cmt. a(1) (2012).

reserved no interest in the trust generally does not have standing.[649] However, the UTC grants the settlor standing to enforce a charitable trust,[650] and a settlor has standing to intervene in an action by the beneficiaries to modify or terminate a trust on account of lack of material purpose.[651]

Good Faith

Occasionally courts refuse to impose liability on a trustee who has committed a breach of trust in good faith, *e.g.*, sums disbursed "grounded on a good faith, albeit erroneous, interpretation of the hardship clause of the trust document."[652] California allows a court to excuse a trustee from liability for breach of trust if the trustee has acted honestly and reasonably and it would be equitable to do so.[653] But the Third Restatement takes the opposite view, stating that a trustee who makes a mistake in interpreting the law or the instrument is not immune from liability even if acting reasonably and in good faith. In doubtful cases the trustee can protect itself from risk by obtaining instruction from the court.[654]

Exculpatory Clauses

Clauses that exculpate a fiduciary from liability are sometimes given effect. When a trust provided that the trustee "shall not be liable if [the trust powers] are exercised in good faith," a judgment surcharging the trustee for imprudent transactions was reversed. The lower court had "incorrectly used the prudent man standard" whereas the "administration of the trust was fully consistent with the good faith standard which must be used to test her management of the trust."[655] However, a trustee was held liable for a wrongful distribution despite a clause holding the trustee harmless for actions taken "except in the case of fraud." Although the trustee's actions were not "wanton or malicious," it had "acted with reckless indifference" and hence was liable for compensatory damages.[656] A New York statute invalidates even clauses which exonerate an executor or testamentary trustee from liability for ordinary negligence.[657] The UTC is more forgiving, enforcing an exculpatory clause except to the extent it "relieves the trustee of liability for breach of trust

---

[649] *Restatement (Third) of Trusts* § 94(1) (2012). *But see* Section 10.10, note 593 et seq.; Langbein, *The Contractarian Basis of Trust Law*, 105 Yale L. J. 625 (1995) (criticizing traditional rule denying standing to the settlor).

[650] UTC § 405(c).

[651] UTC § 410(b).

[652] Griffin v. Griffin, 463 So.2d 569, 574 (Fla.App.1985).

[653] *See* Cal.Prob.Code § 16440(b).

[654] *Restatement (Third) of Trusts* § 93, cmt. c (2012). *See also* National Academy of Sciences v. Cambridge Trust Co., 346 N.E.2d 879, 885 (Mass.1976) (trustee liable for payment to beneficiary in ignorance of her remarriage, which by the terms of the trust disqualified her).

[655] Kerper v. Kerper, 780 P.2d 923, 930–31 (Wyo.1989). *See also* Jewish Hospital v. Boatmen's National Bank, 633 N.E.2d 1267, 1280 (Ill.App.1994); Texas Commerce Bank, N.A. v. Grizzle, 96 S.W.3d 240 (Tex.2002).

[656] Feibelman v. Worthen Nat'l Bank, N.A., 20 F.3d 835, 836 (8th Cir.1994), following *Restatement (Second) of Trusts* § 222(2) (1959). *See also* Cal.Prob.Code § 16461(b); Lincoln National Bank v. Shriners Hospital, 588 N.E.2d 597, 600 (Ind.App.1992).

[657] N.Y.EPTL § 11–1.7(a)(1). The statute does not apply to inter-vivos trusts. Price, *Contemporary Estate Planning* § 4.27.6 (2014 ed.). In In re Estate of Lubin, 539 N.Y.S.2d 695 (Surr.1989), a lawyer was criticized for inserting an exculpatory clause which because of its validity might mislead fiduciaries and beneficiaries.

committed in bad faith or with reckless indifference to the purposes of the trust or the interests of the beneficiaries."[658] The Third Restatement also adds that an exculpatory provision cannot immunize a trustee from accountability for profits derived from a breach of trust.[659] Care should be taken when drafting an exculpatory clause. A Kansas court refused to enforce an exculpatory clause making the trustee liable only for acts of "willful default," concluding that it was more protective of the trustee than was allowed under the UTC provision quoted above.[660]

Courts are particularly averse to exculpatory clauses when they are invoked by professional fiduciaries. One held that to give effect to an exculpatory clause "would violate public policy" if applied to defendants who had "held themselves out to be professional investment advisors."[661] Lawyers who attempt to limit their liability for malpractice by an exculpatory clause may violate the rules of professional conduct.[662]

An exculpatory clause will be disregarded if the trustee "improperly inserted" it in the instrument, *e.g.*, when a lawyer who drafted a trust in which he was named trustee failed to bring the clause to the settlor's attention and explain its implications, the settlor being 70 years old and "in questionable health."[663] However, another court upheld such a clause even though the trustee drew the instrument and suggested the clause. The drafter had discussed the clause with the testator who "was competent in financial matters" and thus there was no "abuse of [a] fiduciary relationship."[664]

Forfeiture Clauses

Forfeiture ("no contest") clauses are being used increasingly in trusts. Many of these clauses are not limited to a contest of the basic validity of the trust but also extend to a beneficiary's questioning of the trustee's administration. In addressing whether such clauses in trusts are valid, the courts are basing their decisions on the case law on the enforcement of forfeiture clauses in wills.[665]

---

[658] UTC § 1008(a)(1). For a discussion of the UTC exculpation provision in light of contract law's unconscionability doctrine, *see* Horton, *Unconscionability in the Law of Trusts*, 84 Notre Dame L. Rev. 1675, 1727–32 (2009).

[659] *Restatement (Third) of Trusts* § 96(1) (2012); *Restatement (Second) of Trusts* § 222(2) (1959). For a discussion of the exculpatory provisions of the UTC and Restatement with a comparison to the treatment of an exculpation provision under the UPC, *see* Hill, *Fiduciary Duties and Exculpatory Clauses: Clash of the Titans or Cozy Bedfellows?*, 45 U. Mich. J.L. Reform 829 (2012).

[660] Schwartz v. Barker, 2013 WL 189686 (Kan. Ct. App., Jan. 11, 2013).

[661] Erlich v. First Nat'l Bank, 505 A.2d 220, 233 (N.J.Super.L.1984). For a case where the court upheld the exculpatory clause itself but found that the trustee's conduct constituted gross negligence not protected by the clause, *see* Wells Fargo v. Militello, 2017 WL 2645430 (Tex. Ct. App., June 20, 2017).

[662] ABA Model Rules of Prof. Conduct 1.8(h).

[663] Rutanen v. Ballard, 678 N.E.2d 133, 141 (Mass.1997), citing *Restatement (Second) of Trusts* § 222, cmt. d (1959). *See also* UTC § 1008(a)(2); *Restatement (Third) of Trusts* § 96, cmt. d (2012).

[664] Marsman v. Nasca, 573 N.E.2d 1025, 1032–33 (Mass.App.1991).

[665] *See* Jacobs, *Forfeiting Trust*, 57 Wm. & Mary L. Rev. 455 (2015). For the enforceability of forfeiture clauses in wills, *see* Section 13.3, note 154 et seq.

Throwing the Blame on Others

Fiduciaries sometimes try to shift the responsibility for a breach to others. A court surcharged a personal representative for penalties incurred by the estate for a late tax return despite her claim that "she reasonably relied on the advice of her accountant who . . . reasonably informed her that the return had been timely filed." She was not justified in leaving "all tax matters to the accountant."[666] On the other hand, an executor who filed an improper estate tax return was exonerated because it had relied on the advice of the lawyer for the estate. "The Bank had a right to . . . rely on the attorney's advice, unless the Bank knowingly chose incompetent counsel or had some reason to know that the advice given was not sound."[667]

The Second Restatement of Trusts said that trustees had a duty "not to delegate to others the doing of acts which the trustee can reasonably be required to perform personally."[668] The Third Restatement reflects a more favorable attitude toward delegation; indeed trustees may now be deemed imprudent for *failure* to delegate in some situations.[669] The Uniform Prudent Investor Act "reverses the much-criticized rule that forbad trustees to delegate investment and management functions."[670] Trustees must exercise reasonable skill in selecting the agent and "periodically reviewing the agent's actions." If they do this, they are not liable for the agent's actions, but the *agent* has a duty to exercise reasonable care in carrying out the delegated duties.[671]

Multiple Fiduciaries and Advisors

A co-fiduciary may be held liable for a breach of duty committed by another co-fiduciary, a particular problem where one of the fiduciaries takes a leading role and the others sit on the sidelines. An attempt by a co-trustee to escape liability for the failure to sell a trust asset was rejected because "a cotrustee must participate in the administration of the trust and use reasonable care to prevent a co-trustee from committing a breach of trust."[672]

In such situations, each fiduciary is jointly liable for the whole loss, but has a right of contribution against the other(s) if the beneficiary sues only one

---

666 Gudschinsky v. Hartill, 815 P.2d 851, 855 (Alaska 1991).

667 Jewish Hospital v. Boatmen's Nat'l Bank, 633 N.E.2d 1267, 1281 (Ill.App.1994). *But see* NC Illinois Trust v. First Illini Bancorp, 752 N.E.2d 1167 (Ill.App.2001), in which the court found a bank was unreasonable in relying on the advice of counsel.

668 *Restatement (Second) of Trusts* § 171 (1959).

669 *Restatement (Third) of Trusts* § 80, cmt. d(1) (2007). *Compare Restatement (Third) of Trusts* § 80, cmt. c (2007) (condemning permanent "delegation of entire administration").

670 Unif. Prudent Investor Act § 9, cmt.

671 Unif. Prudent Investor Act § 9. *See also* UTC § 807; *Restatement (Third) of Trusts* § 80 (2007).

672 Rutanen v. Ballard, 678 N.E.2d 133, 140 (Mass.1997) (quoting *Restatement (Second) of Trusts* § 184 (1959)). *See also* Ramsey v. Boatmen's First National Bank, 914 S.W.2d 384, 388 (Mo.App.1996). The same principles apply to co-executors. Matter of Estate of Donner, 626 N.E.2d 922, 926 (N.Y.1993). The UTC excuses monitoring for minor misdeeds. The obligation to exercise reasonable care to prevent a co-trustee from committing a breach of trust applies only when the breach is "serious." UTC § 703(g). In Racetrac Petroleum v. Ahmed, 2012 WL 6093446 (Bankr. E. D. Va. Dec. 7, 2012), a co-trustee was liable for failing to monitor the actions of the other co-trustee who embezzled funds.

of them.[673] A fiduciary who is substantially more at fault than the other(s) is not entitled to contribution and the other fiduciaries can get full indemnity from the fiduciary primarily at fault.[674]

The more liberal attitude of the Third Restatement of Trusts toward delegation by trustees to agents also extends to delegation to a co-trustee. First, the co-trustees may divide among themselves what are essentially ministerial functions, such as custody of assets. Second, the co-trustees may delegate functions that it might be unreasonable for an individual co-trustee to perform personally, or where joint action might be inefficient or inconsistent with the settlor's expectation. For example, a delegation of investment authority to a professional co-trustee by a surviving spouse co-trustee might be justified on grounds of efficiency and settlor expectation, and it also might be a function for which the spouse, because of lack of skill, might not be able to perform personally.[675] The UTC is less detailed than the Restatement. The UTC prohibits a co-trustee from delegating functions which "the settlor reasonably expected the trustees to perform jointly."[676] Instead of relying on the underlying law, the better approach is to address delegation in the trust instrument, in which event the trust instrument, and not the underlying law, will control.[677]

Res Judicata

Fiduciaries frequently claim they are protected from liability by a prior judgment. A trustee who gets court instructions as to the propriety of an action should be protected for actions taken in compliance with them.[678] Even transactions involving a conflict of interest are allowed when they are "approved by the Court after notice to interested persons."[679] However, this protection does not apply if grounds exist under the general rules of civil procedure for setting aside the judgment and the time for bringing the relevant motion has not yet expired. A judgment approving fees was set aside for "excusable neglect" by a devisee who had "no prior experience with the probate system . . . and no idea what an estate attorney's fees should have been."[680] Nor does res judicata extend to questions not covered by the decree. An order approving a executor's sale of property at a specified price did not bar a later

---

[673] UTC § 1002(b); In re Estate of Chrisman, 746 S.W.2d 131, 134–35 (Mo.App.1988); Gbur v. Cohen, 155 Cal.Rptr. 507 (App.1979).

[674] *Restatement (Second) of Trusts* § 258 (1959); In re Mueller's Trust, 135 N.W.2d 854, 866 (Wis.1965) (contribution but not indemnity given). For a discussion of relevant factors in giving or denying contribution, *see* UTC § 1002, cmt.

[675] *Restatement (Third) of Trusts* § 81, cmt. c(1) (2007).

[676] UTC § 703(e). *Contrast* UTC § 807 as to delegation to agents. Uniform Prudent Investor Act § 9 only addresses delegation to agents.

[677] UTC § 105.

[678] Estate of Fales, 431 N.Y.S.2d 763, 765 (Sur.1980) (order approving sale "protects the trustee against even a claim of liability"); Harper v. Harper, 491 So.2d 189, 199 (Miss.1986) (challenge to action which court had approved rejected).

[679] UPC § 3–713. *See also Restatement (Third) of Trusts* § 71, cmt. b (2007); In re Scarborough Properties Corp., 255 N.E.2d 761 (N.Y.1969).

[680] Johnson v. Doris, 933 P.2d 1139, 1143 (Alaska 1997).

claim that the executor had "mishandled the business in such a manner that the value [of the property had] decreased significantly."[681]

The effect of court approval of a fiduciary's accounts is often litigated. After trustees filed annual accounts for several years, beneficiaries claimed that they had wrongfully retained an under-productive asset. A statute expressly made a trustee's *final* account conclusive, but no such language appeared in the provision requiring intermediate accounts. The court nevertheless gave summary judgment to the trustees. "[A] judicial settlement of a trustee's accounts, as to persons who receive notice and are subject to the court's jurisdiction, bars subsequent litigation seeking to raise defaults or defects with the matters shown or disclosed in the accountings. . . . The beneficiaries are barred from questioning later matters which are disclosed by the accounting, but *not* those *not* disclosed."[682]

Even approval of a final account may leave issues open. Courts have allowed the beneficiaries of a testamentary trust to surcharge the executor-trustees for actions during the administration of the probate estate even after the executor's final account had been approved on the theory that in its capacity as trustee the bank had improperly failed to question its own account as executor. Trustees have an obligation to pursue claims against a prior fiduciary, even if this requires them to question their own conduct.[683]

Sometimes court approval is not binding because the court was not informed of a relevant fact. The UPC protects personal representatives from claims not brought within 6 months after filing of a "closing statement," but not if there was "fraud, misrepresentation, or inadequate disclosure."[684] A conservator was held liable for allowing an insurance policy to lapse even though his final account had been approved because the account did not reveal the policy lapse.[685] When an administrator sold land to his step-daughter, a court approval of the sale without the court being aware of the relationship was later revoked.[686] Not all claims of "fraud" are sufficient to avoid res judicata, however. A claim that a bank "fraudulently misrepresented its skill" as an investor was not enough to allow an account to be reopened, because "it

---

[681] First of America Trust v. First Illini Bancorp, 685 N.E.2d 351, 358 (Ill.App.1997).

[682] Fraser v. Southeast First Bank, 417 So.2d 707, 710–12 (Fla.App.1982). *See also* In re Trust Created by Hill, 499 N.W.2d 475, 489 (Minn.App.1993); In re Conservatorship of Holman, 849 P.2d 140 (Kan.App.1993); *Restatement (Third) of Trusts* § 83, cmt. c (2007).

[683] Matter of Irrevocable Inter-Vivos Trust, 305 N.W.2d 755, 762 (Minn.1981). *See also* Pepper v. Zions First National Bank, 801 P.2d 144,151 (Utah 1990); *Restatement (Second) of Trusts* § 177, cmt. a (1959); Cal.Prob.Code § 16403 (successor trustee liable for failure to redress predecessor's breach that successor knew or should have known). *But cf.* In re Will of Scheele, 517 N.E.2d 418, 427 (Ind.App. 1987); UTC § 812 (duty only to redress "known" breach by former trustee).

[684] UPC § 3–1005.

[685] Conservatorship of Coffey, 231 Cal.Rptr. 421, 424 (App.1986). *See also* Altshuler v. Minkus-Whalen, 579 N.E.2d 1369 (Mass.App.1991) (approval of administrator's account revoked because she failed to disclose the existence of other heirs).

[686] Satti v. Rago, 441 A.2d 615 (Conn.1982). *See also* In re Guardianship of Eisenberg, 719 P.2d 187, 192 (Wash.App.1986).

had no effect on [the ward's] ability to attend the hearing of which she received notice and to litigate . . . her claims of wrongdoing by Bank."[687]

The court which renders a judgment must have jurisdiction in order for it to have res judicata effect. An Oklahoma court rejected a guardian's attempt to rely on a Michigan court's judgment approving withdrawals from an estate, because "the Michigan court never acquired jurisdiction over the guardianship assets."[688] An approved account can bind beneficiaries who live outside the jurisdiction of the court but only if they are given notice and an opportunity to appear. Notice by publication is sufficient for beneficiaries whose interests or addresses were unknown to the trustee, but as to those whose addresses were on the trustee's books "a serious effort to inform them personally of the accounting at least by ordinary mail to the record addresses" was constitutionally required.[689] Court-approved transactions can be set aside for failure to comply with statutory notice requirements.[690]

Requiring court approval of transactions may not be an adequate safeguard against abuses because often "the proceeding is not adversary, . . . there is no thorough investigation into the desirability of the transaction,"[691] and court scrutiny of fiduciary accounts tends to be superficial.[692] Therefore, the UPC allows personal representatives to dispense with it; they are protected from claims for breach of fiduciary duty 6 months after they file a closing statement which adequately discloses their handling of the estate.[693] But the 6 month limitation cannot be invoked if the disclosure in the fiduciary's final statement was incomplete, even if the beneficiary had reason to know this.[694]

Consent

Beneficiaries' consent may prevent them from challenging a fiduciary's action.[695] An attempt to surcharge trustees for "having pursued an aggressive, risky investment policy" failed because the beneficiaries had signed a form by which they "acknowledge the high degree of economic risk associated with these investments" and nevertheless approved them.[696] In this case, the

---

[687] Bank of America National Trust v. Superior Court, 226 Cal.Rptr. 685, 690 (App.1986). *See also* Herbert M. Dorsett Trust, 791 P.2d 398, 406 (Haw.App.1990) (claim of fraud is barred by res judicata); Hooks v. Bonner, 543 N.E.2d 953 (Ill.App.1989).

[688] In re Estate of LaRose, 1 P.3d 1018, 1023 (Okl.Civ.App.1999).

[689] Mullane v. Central Hanover Bank & Trust Co., 339 U.S. 306, 318 (1950).

[690] Hawkins v. Walker, 281 S.E.2d 311 (Ga.App.1981) (approval of sale vacated for failure publish notice); In re Trust of Strong, 734 N.Y.S.2d 668 (App.Div.2001) (trustee's approved accounts res judicata only for those where notice was served on beneficiary). *But see* Bohl v. Haney, 671 P.2d 991 (Colo.App.1983) (bona fide purchaser at court-approved sale protected despite failure to give notice).

[691] Fratcher, *Trustees' Powers Legislation*, 37 NYU L.Rev. 627, 662 (1962).

[692] Wellman, *Recent Developments in the Struggle for Probate Reform*, 79 Mich.L.Rev. 501, 516 (1981).

[693] UPC § 3–1005: Torvea v. Nolam, 875 P.2d 144, 148 (Ariz.App. 1993); Maryhew v. Gillingham, 893 P.2d 692 (Wash.App. 1995).

[694] Estate of K.H. v. Continental Ins. Co., 73 P.3d 588 (Alaska 2003).

[695] *Restatement (Third) of Trusts* § 97 (2012); UTC § 1009; Brent v. Smathers, 547 So.2d 683 (Fla.App.1989).

[696] Beyer v. First Nat'l Bank, 843 P.2d 53, 56 (Colo.App.1992). *See also* In re Estate of Gleeson, 655 N.W.2d 69, 74 (N.D.2002) (sale by executor at below market value not a breach when devisees consented).

approval was in writing but this is not necessary, although obviously advisable. The Second Restatement says that mere failure to object does not amount to consent, but there are many cases to the contrary, *e.g.*, a trustee had abused its discretion in making distributions, but "there had never been any objection" by the disfavored beneficiaries, whose "inaction for so many years acted as a ratification of SNB's conduct."[697] (The rules on consent before or at the time of an act are essentially the same as those for a later affirmance).[698] Consent and laches sometimes overlap. Beneficiaries who sought to upset an executor's sale of mineral interests were held to have "ratified" the sale by accepting checks arising therefrom.[699]

When one beneficiary has consented, but others have not, courts will give a remedy to the nonconsenting beneficiaries. The fact that the settlor's daughter, a beneficiary and co-trustee of a trust, had participated in making improper investments did not preclude her children from recovering from the other trustees.[700] The result might have been different had the trust provided (as some do) that children are bound by their parents' consent.[701]

A spendthrift trust beneficiary can effectively consent but not a beneficiary who lacks legal capacity[702] or who is of limited understanding," *e.g.*, "an elderly woman whose schooling had ended at age 10."[703] But a trustee who reasonably believed that a beneficiary was capable of consenting may be protected. When the settlor authorized withdrawals from a revocable trust, a claim that she was incompetent at the time was irrelevant if "the trustee did not know or have any reason to believe" this.[704]

Consent given by a beneficiary who did not know relevant facts is ineffective. A beneficiary who consented to a trustee buying land from the trust for $40,000 without knowing that the property had been appraised at $500,000 was allowed to have the sale vacated. Consent is binding only when "given voluntarily after full disclosure by the trustees of all the facts, . . . and the burden is on the fiduciary to show that the transaction was fair."[705] A

[697] In re Estate of Winograd, 582 N.E.2d 1047, 1050 (Ohio App.1989). *See also* In re Higgins' Trust Estate, 162 N.W.2d 768 (S.D.1968); In re Trusts Under Will of Dwan, 371 N.W.2d 641, 643 (Minn.App. 1985) (failure to object for years "constituted a waiver").

[698] *Restatement (Third) of Trusts* § 97 (2012); UTC § 1009; Cal.Prob.Code §§ 16463–16465.

[699] Jackson v. Braden, 717 S.W.2d 206 (Ark.1986).

[700] Gillespie v. Seymour, 823 P.2d 782, 790 (Kan.1991). *See also Restatement (Third) of Trusts* § 97, cmt. c (2012); Gaynor v. Payne, 804 A.2d 170, 176 (Conn. 2002) (release by income beneficiaries did not bar their children who had remainder interests). .

[701] Beyer v. First Nat'l Bank, 843 P.2d 53, 62 (Colo.App.1992); In re McGuire Marital Trust, 660 N.W.2d 308, 316 (Wis.App.2003) (trust provision making income beneficiaries' approval of accounts binding).

[702] *Restatement (Third) of Trusts* § 97, cmt. a (2012).

[703] Stephan v. Equitable Savings and Loan Ass'n, 522 P.2d 478, 489 (Or.1974).

[704] Cloud v. United States Nat'l Bank, 570 P.2d 350, 355 (Or.1977). Under *Restatement (Second) of Trusts* § 216(2) (1959) and Cal.Prob.Code § 16463(b), however, a trustee's reasonable belief is relevant as to the beneficiary's knowledge of material facts, but not as to the beneficiary's capacity. *Contrast* UTC § 1009, which omits the reference to the trustee's reasonable belief. *See also Restatement (Second) of Contracts* § 15(2) (1979), which protects persons who make contracts with a mental incompetent without knowledge of the mental condition.

[705] Ford City Bank v. Ford City Bank, 441 N.E.2d 1192, 1195 (Ill.App.1982). Some courts say that consent to a breach of trust by a beneficiary who does not have "full knowledge of legal rights" is not binding. In re Saxton, 712 N.Y.S.2d 225, 231 (App.Div.2000). Under UTC § 1009(2),

beneficiary's consent to a trustee's account was not binding when she had signed the consent without any *opportunity to review the account.*[706]

Representation and Settlements[707]

Court orders are not binding on legally incompetent beneficiaries unless they are adequately represented. An order authorizing a conservator to use assets of the estate to pay a claim was not binding because no guardian ad litem had been appointed.[708] Appointing a guardian ad litem for incompetent beneficiaries is costly because GALs are entitled to compensation and reimbursement of attorney's fees from the estate.[709] Commentators have argued that guardians ad litem should be appointed only when there is no other way to protect the incompetent. "Where a necessary party who is adult and competent has interests substantially identical to those of a . . . minor or incompetent, the court should be reluctant to burden the estate with the expenses of a guardian ad litem."[710]

Yet, without the appointment of a guardian ad litem, it may not be possible to obtain an order binding an incompetent beneficiary. Similar problems arise when the beneficiaries are seeking to approve a transaction by the trustee without having to go to court. No matter how much disclosure the trustee provides, an incompetent beneficiary is incapable of giving a valid consent, particularly if the trustee is aware of the incapacity.[711] To obtain a valid consent in such situation traditionally required the filing of a judicial action and the appointment of a GAL to consent on behalf of the incompetent beneficiary.

An alternative to consider in such situations is the concept of representation. When representation is applicable, a person other than the beneficiary can give a consent and otherwise act on behalf of beneficiaries unable to represent themselves due to minority or incapacity or because the beneficiaries cannot be ascertained or are potentially unborn. A fiduciary, such as a trustee, may also represent its own beneficiaries in connection with transactions affecting the beneficiaries, such as approval of an executor's account making distribution to the trust. The most comprehensive representation provisions are found in the UTC and UPC. The UPC makes

---

a consent is invalid if "the beneficiary did not know of the beneficiary's rights or of the material facts relating to the breach. For cases under this provision concluding that the beneficiary had been given adequate information, *see* Mendoza v. Gonzales, 204 P.3d 995 (Wyo. 2009); Schmidt v. Killmer, 201 P.3d 1121 (Wyo. 2009).

[706] In re Estate of Hunter, 739 N.Y.S.2d 916 (Sur.2002).

[707] Portions of the following discussion are based on English, *The Uniform Trust Code: Significant Provisions and Policy Issues*, 67 Mo. L. Rev. 143, 158–62 (2002).

[708] Matter of Conservatorship of L.M.S., 755 P.2d 22, 25 (Kan.App.1988). *See also* Matter of Estate of Bomareto, 757 P.2d 1135 (Colo.App.1988) (child not bound by order because he was not made a party in proceedings). *Compare* Matter of Estate of Nuyen, 443 N.E.2d 1099, 1104 (Ill.App.1982) (minor bound by order when he was represented by a GAL). Even when a guardian was appointed, the judgment may not be binding when the guardian "failed to . . . defend the action with due diligence." *Restatement (Second) of Judgments* § 72 (1982).

[709] Cal.Prob.Code § 1003(c); Matter of Estate of Trotalli, 366 N.W.2d 879 (Wis.1985).

[710] Martin, *Professional Responsibility and Probate Practices*, 1975 Wis. L.Rev. 911, 948.

[711] *See supra* notes 702–704.

representation available only in judicial proceedings.[712] The UTC provisions on representation apply to both judicial proceedings and nonjudicial settlements.[713]

Both Codes provide not only for representation by fiduciaries (guardians, conservators, personal representatives, trustees, or agents under a durable power of attorney),[714] but also for what is known as virtual representation, under which an otherwise unrepresented person (such as a child who may not yet be born) may be represented and bound by another beneficiary with a substantially identical interest with respect to the particular matter or dispute.[715] A common example where use of virtual representation would be appropriate is a trust providing for distribution to the settlor's children as a class, where an adult child would be able to "virtually" represent the interests of children who are either minors or unborn. In addition, both Codes authorize a holder of a general power of appointment, whether presently exercisable or testamentary, to represent and bind permissible appointees, takers in default, and others whose interests are subject to the power.[716] Finally, both Codes authorize a parent to represent and bind a minor child, and the UTC authorizes a parent to represent and bind an unborn child.[717]

Although the representation provisions provide legal practitioners with an added tool, they should not be used without thought. Notice to and the consent of a representative is not binding if there is a conflict of interest between the representative and those ostensibly represented.[718] If conflict of interest is a possibility, the practitioner should consider requesting the court to appoint a guardian ad litem (termed a "representative" under the UTC) to represent the otherwise unrepresented beneficiary. Under the UTC, the appointment of a representative is available whether the matter to be resolved is in or out of court. In making decisions, a representative may consider general family benefit accruing to living members of the individual's family.[719]

---

[712] UPC § 1–403.

[713] UTC § 111, Art. 3. For a critical examination of the UTC provisions on representation, *see* Begleiter, *Serve the Cheerleader—Serve the World: An Analysis of Representation in Estate and Trust Proceedings and Under the Uniform Trust Code and Other Modern Trust Codes*, 43 Real Prop. Prob. Tr. & Est. L. J. 311 (2008).

[714] UTC § 303; UPC § 1–403(2)(B). Representation by a guardian is allowed only if a conservator for the ward has not been appointed. The UPC does not mention agents under powers of attorney. Under the UTC, representation by an agent is permitted only if the agent has authority to act with respect to the particular matter or dispute. UTC § 303(3).

[715] UTC § 304; UPC § 1–403(2)(B). For an application of the UTC provision, *see* First Charter Bank v. American Children's Home, 692 S.E.2d 457 (N.C. Ct. App. 2010). Neither Code specifically requires that the representation be adequate. Under the Restatement of Property, representation is deemed sufficiently protective if it does not appear that the representative acted in hostility to the interest of the person represented. *Restatement (First) of Property* § 185 (1936).

[716] UTC §§ 302, 603; UPC §§ 1–108, 1–403(2).

[717] UTC § 303(6); UPC § 1–403(3). Under both provisions, a parent may act only if a guardian or conservator has not been appointed for the child.

[718] *See* UTC §§ 302–304; UPC § 1–403(2)(B).

[719] UTC § 305. This section authorizes the court to appoint a representative to receive notice, give consent, and otherwise represent, bind and act on behalf of otherwise unrepresented person or persons for whom the court concludes that the available representation is inadequate. A representative may be appointed either to represent a single individual or interest or several persons or interests.

The representation provisions of the UTC can be utilized to settle any dispute whether in or out of court. Section 111, the Code's nonjudicial settlement provision, is broad. The parties may enter into a nonjudicial settlement agreement with respect to any matter involving a trust.[720] The settlement agreement can contain any term or condition that a court *could* properly approve.[721] Under the UTC, among the issues that can be resolved by a nonjudicial settlement agreement are "the interpretation or construction of the terms of the trust; . . . approval of a trustee's report or accounting; . . . direction to a trustee to refrain from performing a particular act or to grant a trustee any necessary or desirable power; . . . resignation or appointment of a trustee and determination of a trustee's compensation; . . . transfer of a trust's principal place of administration; . . . and liability of a trustee for an action relating to the trust."[722] It has been held that a non-judicial settlement agreement cannot be used to remove a trustee[723] but can be used to eliminate a requirement that a trustee post bond.[724]

Because there are sometimes doubts about the enforceability of settlements made outside of court, the UTC provides that any interested person may request the court to approve the settlement, determine whether the representation was adequate, or determine whether the agreement contains terms and conditions the court could have approved.[725] This provision has been tested in several court decisions, with the court in each case favoring enforcement. In rejecting actions to set aside non-judicial settlements, courts have found that a co-trustee had authority to bind the other co-trustee to the settlement,[726] that an agreement to appoint a corporate trustee was not a material purpose of the trust negating the possibility of settlement,[727] and that the settlement of a trust contest would not be disturbed because a beneficiary, following the settlement, had found an additional amendment to the trust.[728]

Alternative Dispute Resolution

A nonjudicial settlement agreement is a type of alternative dispute resolution (ADR) under which parties settle their disputes outside of court. Other forms of ADR frequently used to resolve estate and trust disputes are

---

[720] UTC § 111(b).

[721] UTC § 111(c).

[722] UTC § 111(d). For a discussion of UTC § 111 and comparable statutes, *see* Mautner & Orr, *A Brave New World: Non-Judicial Dispute Resolution Procedures Under the Uniform Trust Code and Washington's and Idaho's Trust and Estate Dispute Resolution Acts*, 35 ACTEC J. 159 (2009). *See also* Warnick, *Nonjudicial Settlements Under the CUTC*, Colorado Lawyer, May 2020, at 42; Daniel, *Alternative Dispute Resolution and the Uniform Trust Code—Colorado's Approach*, 45 ACTEC L.J. 11 (2019); Kotis, *Nonjudicial Settlement Agreements*, Prob. & Prop., March/April 2017, at 42 (discussing Maryland statute).

[723] Trust Under Agreement of Taylor, 164 A.3d 1147 (Pa. 2017). *See* Ahrens, *Hitting Rewind: The Supreme Court of Pennsylvania in Trust Under Agreement of Taylor Signals a Move Away from Modern Developments of Trust Law by Requiring More Stringent Standards for Corporate Trustee Removal*, 63 Vill. L. Rev. 691 (2018). *Taylor* is consistent with Testamentary Trust of Conti, 2014 Phila. Ct. Com. Pl. LEXIS 289 (Pa. C.P., Sept. 17, 2014).

[724] In re Frank, 910 N.E. 2d 253 (Ohio Ct. App. 2009).

[725] UTC § 111(e).

[726] Adams v. French, 2010 WL 716161 (Del. Ch., Feb. 5, 2010) (applying Maine law).

[727] In re Estate of Isner, 2019 WL 856255 (W.Va., Feb. 22, 2019).

[728] In re Frank M. Lambrecht, Jr., Trust, 2018 WL 4574750 (Mich. Ct. App., Sept. 20, 2018).

mediation[729] and arbitration.[730] Increasingly, drafters are inserting provisions in trust documents that mandate arbitration of disputes between the trustee and beneficiaries.[731] Such provisions were traditionally unenforceable and are still unenforceable in many states unless the beneficiaries agree to arbitration. But the Texas Supreme Court has enforced a mandatory arbitration provision[732] and a number of states have enacted statutes approving mandatory arbitration provisions.[733] The UTC, which was approved in 2000, has not yet been amended to address whether a mandatory arbitration provision is enforceable.[734] None of the state statutes authorizing arbitration permit arbitration to be used to determine whether a trust was validly created in the first place and neither have the courts.[735] Instead, arbitration is typically used to resolve disputes over trust administration.

Trustees often delegate investment responsibility to investment advisors.[736] Contracts with investment advisors typically include mandatory arbitration provisions. Recognizing that it would be difficult to hire an advisor who would be willing to forego an arbitration provision, at least one court has held that such arbitration provisions are binding against a non-signing beneficiary.[737]

---

[729] Radford, *An Introduction to the Uses of Mediation and Other Forms of Dispute Resolution in Probate, Trust, and Guardianship Matters*, 34 Real. Prop. & Tr. J. 601 (2000).

[730] *See generally*, Strong, *Arbitration of Trust Disputes: Two Bodies of Law Collide*, 45 Vanderbilt J. Transnational Law (2012); Strong, ed., *Arbitration of Trust Disputes: Issues in National and International Law* (2016); Strong, *The European Succession Regulation and the Arbitration of Trust Disputes*, 103 Iowa L.Rev. 220 (2018).

[731] For drafting suggestions, *see* McCulloch & Rosenblatt, *Drafting & Enforcing Arbitration Clauses in Wills, Trusts & Settlement Agreements*, 12 Est. Plan. & Community Property L.J. 103(2019); Strong, *Empowering Settlors How Proper Language Can Increase the Enforceability of a Mandatory Arbitration Provision in a Trust*, 47 Real Prop. Prob. Tr. & Est. L. J. 275 (2012); Goldman, *ACTEC's Simplified Trial Resolution Option with Model Laws and Clauses*, in Strong, ed., *Arbitration of Trust Disputes: Issues in National and International Law* (2016).

[732] Rachal v. Reitz, 403 S.W.3d 840 (Tex. 2013); Tipton, *Can You Trust Your Trust?: Analyzing the Decision and Implications of Rachal v. Reitz on Arbitration Provisions in Trust Agreements*, 48 Akron L. Rev. 979 (2015). *See also* Baker, *Rachal v. Reitz and the Efficacy and Implementation of Mandatory Arbitration Provisions in Trusts*, 79 Est. Plan. & Community Prop. L.J. 191 (2018). *See also* Basassadegan v. Vernon, 588 S.W.3d 796 (Ark.Ct. App. 2019) (arbitration provision enforceable against successor trustees both as trustees and as beneficiaries).

[733] *See, e.g.*, Ariz. Rev. Stat. Ann. § 14–10205; Fla. Rev. Stat. § 731.401; Mo. Rev. Stat. § 456.2–205; N.H. Rev. Stat. § 564–B:1–111A; S.D. Codified Laws § 55–1–54.

[734] But assuming the mandatory arbitration provision is otherwise enforceable, the UTC, with its provisions on representation and nonjudicial settlements, facilitates the use of such provisions. English, *Arbitration and the United States Uniform Trust Code*, in Strong, ed., *Arbitration of Trust Disputes: Issues in National and International Law* (2016).

[735] *See* Gibbons v. Anderson, 575 S.W.3d 144 (Ark. Ct. App. 2019) (arbitration provision, if enforceable at all, cannot be enforced to preclude court from determining validity of trust instrument).

[736] For the law on delegation, see Section 14.4, note 285 et seq.

[737] Harvey ex rel. Gladden v. Cumberland Trust & Investment Co., 532 S.W.3d 243 (Tenn. 2017). *See* Rounds, *Arbitration Contracts Between Trustees and Their Investment Agents: A Warning Label*, 93 N.D.L.Rev. 263 (2018). *But see* Lincoln Fin'l Advisors Corp. v. Ards as next friend of Ards, 2019 WL 6907074 (Tex. Ct. App., Dec. 19, 2019) (beneficiary not bound by arbitration agreement between trustee and brokerage firm).

Laches and Statutes of Limitations

Laches is an equitable remedy that bars a claim if the claimant waited too long to bring the action. Whether laches will be applied depends on a variety of factors in addition to the mere lapse of time, such as the reason (if any) for the plaintiff's delay in bringing suit, and the extent of hardship to the defendant if relief were given despite the delay.[738] A complaint that a bank trustee committed a breach of trust in selling stock was held to be barred by laches when the trustee began selling the stock in 1958 but the beneficiary did not complain until 1977. The trustee's quarterly reports showed the sales, so the beneficiary "had or should have had knowledge . . . of the trustee's conduct for nearly nineteen years before filing suit."[739] Furthermore, "the trustee was prejudiced by the delay. . . . During the nineteen-year delay, . . . various records were misplaced or destroyed. . . . More importantly, the amount of potential damages increased greatly during this period and the ability of the trustee to reverse its actions by repurchasing the stock became more difficult."[740] On the other hand, a court rejected the laches defense asserted against two beneficiaries, one of whom was a minor. "Laches cannot be imputed to a person during his or her minority."[741] As to the other beneficiary, even though usually plaintiffs must be diligent in ascertaining the facts underlying a claim, "when a fiduciary has a duty to disclose certain facts to the plaintiff but fraudulently fails to do so, the plaintiff's failure to discover the facts is excused and the time begins to run when the fraud is actually discovered."[742]

Statutes of limitations provide a fixed period rather than leaving the question of whether a lawsuit was timely commenced to the court's discretion,[743] but the statutes raise a number of issues, including when the statute begins to run and whether the statute is tolled (suspended) on account of fraud or the complainant's minority or incapacity. A trustee invoked a two-year statute of limitations when sued for an allegedly improper sale of stock. The court rejected the defense on the basis of another statute which postponed commencement of the limitation period "when the defendant has concealed the existence of the cause of action from the plaintiff."[744] The UTC contains the

---

[738] *Restatement (Third) of Trusts* § 98, cmt. b (2012).

[739] Stevens v. National City Bank, 544 N.E.2d 612, 621 (Ohio 1989). *Cf.* Boston Safe Deposit & Trust Co. v. Wilbur, 728 N.E.2d 264, 272 (Mass.2000) (remand to determine when beneficiary learned of claim so as to pass on laches defense).

[740] Stevens v. National City Bank, 544 N.E.2d 612, 621 (Ohio 1989); *cf.* First Alabama Bank v. Martin, 425 So.2d 415, 424 (Ala.1982) (laches defense rejected because no showing of prejudice to the defendant); Murphy v. Emery, 629 S.W.2d 895, 898 (Tenn. 1981).

[741] Kurtz v. Solomon, 656 N.E.2d 184, 192 (Ill. App.1995). *Accord, Restatement (Third) of Trusts* § 98, cmt. b(1) (2012) (no laches while beneficiary is under legal incapacity).

[742] Kurtz v. Solomon, 656 N.E.2d 184, 192 (Ill. App.1995).

[743] *E.g.*, McDonald v. United States National Bank, 830 P.2d 618 (Or.App.1992) (trustee protected by 2-year statute); Beall v. Beall, 577 S.E.2d 356, 360 (N.C.App.2003) (custodian protected by three year statute); Vorholt v. One Valley Bank, 498 S.E.2d 241 (W.Va. 1997).

[744] Malachowski v. Bank One, Indianapolis, 590 N.E.2d 559, 563 (Ind.1992). *See also* Hagney v. Lopeman, 590 N.E.2d 46 (Ill. 1992); Goldston v. Bank of America Corp., 577 S.E.2d 864 (Ga.App.2003) (action allowed 30 years after trust ended). Attempts by a trustee to conceal facts until the statute of limitations has run may trigger the "crime-fraud exception to the attorney client privilege" when a lawyer is involved. First Union National Bank v. Turney, 824 So.2d 172, 191 (Fla.App. 2001).

most widely enacted statute of limitations.[745] Following the sending of a trustee's annual or other report, a beneficiary must commence an action for breach of trust within one year but only if the report "adequately disclosed the existence of a potential claim for breach of trust and informed the beneficiary of the time limit."[746] A report adequately discloses the existence of a potential claim for breach of trust if it provides sufficient information so that the beneficiary or representative knows of the potential claim or should have inquired into its existence.[747] With respect to the beneficiary's obligation to inquire into a potential claim, a mere "general feeling of suspicion" of how the trustee is handling the trust is not sufficient to trigger the obligation.[748] Should the trustee not report or inadequately disclose, the trustee must commence an action within five years after the first to occur of the termination of the trust, the termination of the beneficiary's interest, or the date the particular trustee complained of leaves office.[749] A number of states enacting the UTC have changed the five-year limit to conform with other limitations law in the particular state.[750] The courts have held that a trust "terminates" under this statute not when the terminating event, such as the death of a life beneficiary, occurs but when the trustee completely distributes the trust assets.[751]

§ 14.9 Relationships with Third Parties

Beneficiaries of an estate or trust may also have remedies against persons other than the fiduciary. Trust beneficiaries were allowed to sue accountants hired by the trustees. A beneficiary

> has the right that third persons shall not knowingly join with the trustee in a breach of trust. . . . Mere knowledge by a third person that a breach of trust is in process, coupled with a failure to notify the beneficiary or to interfere with the action of the trustee, does not amount to participation in a breach . . . On the other hand, if the third party by any act whatsoever assists the trustee in wrongfully transferring the benefits of the trust property to the trustee, [or] another person . . . liability can be [imposed].[752]

---

[745] *See generally* Newman, *You Don't Know What You've Got Till Its Gone: Time-Barred Claims Under the Uniform Trust Code*, 48 Real Prop. Tr. & Est. L.J. 459 (2014).

[746] UTC § 1005(a).

[747] UTC § 1005(b); Meyers v. First Tennessee Bank, N.A., 503 S.W.3d 365 (Tenn. Ct. App. 2016) (mass of letters, emails, faxes, and phone calls did not constitute a sufficient "report" to start statute to bar claims regarding condition of warehouse property); Parris v. Regions Bank, 2011 WL 3629218 (W.D. Tenn., Aug. 17, 2011) (letter sent by trustee did not adequately disclose details of proposed investment in order to trigger inquiry notice).

[748] *See, e.g.*, Deutsch v. Wolff, 994 S.W.2d 561, 572 (Mo.1999).

[749] UTC § 1005(c). The five-year statute is intended to provide some ultimate repose for actions against a trustee. It applies only if the trustee has failed to report, the report does not contain adequate disclosure, or the report fails to warn of the one-year time limit. UTC § 1005, cmt.

[750] *See., e.g.*, Billewicz v. Ransmeier, 13 A.3d 116 (N.H. 2010) (action dismissed for failure to bring action within three years following trustee's resignation).

[751] Meyers v. First Tennessee Bank, N.A., 503 S.W.3d 365 (Tenn. Ct. App. 2016); In re Lloyd Revocable Trust, 2017 WL 4682255 (Ariz. Ct. App., Oct. 19, 2017).

[752] Gillespie v. Seymour, 796 P.2d 1060, 1065 (Kan.App.1990) (quoting Bogert, *Trusts and Trustees* § 901). *See also Restatement (Third) of Trusts* § 108 (2012).

The Uniform Prudent Investor Act imposes on agents exercising a delegated function a duty of reasonable care to the trust.[753] In addition, a person who has power by the terms of a trust to control the trustee's actions may be deemed a fiduciary and be "liable for any loss resulting to the trust estate from a breach of his duty as fiduciary."[754]

Normally actions against third persons who injure trust property must be brought by the trustee, but a beneficiary can sue when "the beneficiary's interests are hostile to those of the trustee,"[755] *e.g.*, when the third party and trustee have participated in a breach of trust. Suit may also be brought by a co-fiduciary or a successor fiduciary.[756]

Attorneys for fiduciaries in certain circumstances have been held to owe duties not only to the fiduciary, their primary client, but also to the beneficiaries. In such cases, courts have held that the beneficiaries may sue the attorney for malpractice or for participating in a breach of trust even though the attorney and beneficiaries were not in privity of contract. A court upheld a claim against a lawyer who had established a guardianship without having the guardian post a bond as required by law, saying that the "attorney-client relationship between [the lawyer and the guardian] was established to benefit [the child]" and an "action for breach against the guardian is likely to be an empty remedy absent a bond."[757] But another court rejected a claim by beneficiaries of an estate against the attorney for the personal representative, saying that imposing duties on lawyers "to a nonclient creates a risk of divided loyalties because of a conflicting interest."[758]

Banks

Banks are often sued for participating in a breach of trust. According to the Restatement, a third party such as a bank is protected from liability for permitting a withdrawal of trust funds from an account if it had no knowledge or reason to know of the trustee's improper conduct.[759] A trustee stole thousands of dollars from a trust checking account by issuing checks to himself. The trustee was unable to reimburse the trust so the beneficiaries sued the bank, but their claim was rejected. The bank would be liable only if it knew that the withdrawals were a breach of fiduciary duty and there was no evidence of this.[760] In another case, where the bank arranged for the transfer of estate

---

[753] Unif. Prudent Investor Act § 9(b).

[754] *Restatement (Third) of Trusts* § 75, cmt. f (2012).

[755] Anderson v. Dean Witter Reynolds, Inc., 841 P.2d 742, 745 (Utah App.1992); *cf. Restatement (Second) of Trusts* § 282(2) (1959) (beneficiary can sue when trustee improperly neglects to sue).

[756] Hosselton v. K's Merchandise Mart, 617 N.E.2d 797 (Ill.App.1993) (suit against store which had accepted guardianship funds from plaintiff's predecessor); Matter of Estate of Ostrander, 910 P.2d 865 (Kan.App.1996) (suit to recover property sold by plaintiff's co-administrator).

[757] In re Guardianship of Karan, 38 P.3d 396, 400–01 (Wash.App.2002). As to bonds, *see* Section 14.6, note 404 et seq.

[758] Trask v. Butler, 872 P.2d 1080, 1085 (Wash.1994). *See also* Neal v. Baker, 551 N.E.2d 704 (Ill.App.1990).

[759] *Restatement (Third) of Trusts* § 108(1) (2012).

[760] Heilig Trust and Benef. v. First Interstate, 969 P.2d 1082, 1085 (Wash.App.1998). *See also* Hosselton v. First American Bank N.A., 608 N.E.2d 630 (Ill.App.1993) (bank not liable for

funds into the fiduciary's personal account at the same bank, the bank was held liable for the full amount withdrawn.[761]

Banks have been held liable for paying a depositor's money to an "agent" under a forged power of attorney.[762] In order to encourage banks to deal with agents under durable powers, many statutes, including the UPC and the more recent Uniform Power of Attorney Act, protect third persons who deal with an agent "in good faith" despite defects in the agent's power.[763] Such a statute was successfully invoked by a savings and loan association which had allowed an agent to withdraw over $135,000 from the principal's account. The principal's administrator claimed that the principal had been incompetent when she executed the power, but the court held that the defendant had no duty to investigate this absent "actual knowledge."[764]

The Second Restatement of Trusts imposed liability on corporations which registered transfers of securities "with notice" that they were in breach of trust, but added that "experience indicates" that this rule "has not been very effective" in preventing breaches of trust, and should be abolished.[765] This was accomplished by a widely adopted Uniform Act for the Simplification of Fiduciary Security Transfers, based on the idea that "the responsibility of corporations to inquire into the propriety of transfers of their shares is . . . anachronistic."[766] This Act has since been superseded by the 1994 revision of Article 8 of the Uniform Commercial Code.[767]

Bona Fide Purchase

When property of an estate or trust has been transferred to a bona fide purchaser for value, the latter is protected even if the fiduciary was acting improperly. A representative statute is Section § 3–714 of the UPC which protects persons who deal with a personal representative "in good faith for value."[768]

Persons claiming to be bona fide purchasers often flounder on the issue of good faith. One who knows *or should know* of the breach of trust does not

---

cashing check made out to guardian); Heffner v. Cahaba Bank & Trust Co., 523 So.2d 113 (Ala.1988) (bank not liable for checks drawn by embezzling executor); Wetherill v. Bank IV Kansas, N.A., 145 F.3d 1187 (10th Cir. 1998).

761 DeLaRosa v. Farmers State Bank S/B, 474 S.W.3d 240 (Mo. Ct. App. 2015).

762 In re Estate of Davis, 632 N.E.2d 64 (Ill. App.1994).

763 For discussion of the various approaches to this issue, *see* Whitton, *Durable Powers as an Alternative to Guardianship: Lessons We Have Learned*, 37 Stetson L. Rev. 7, 38–48 (2007).

764 Bank IV, Olathe v. Capitol Federal S & L, 828 P.2d 355, 357–58, 363 (Kan.1992). *See also* Johnson v. Edwardsville National Bank & Trust Co., 594 N.E.2d 342, 345 (Ill. App.1992) (bank protected where principal incompetent when power executed); *Restatement (Second) of Trusts* § 324, cmt. g (1959) (trustee making check to self from trust account does not create duty of inquiry on bank).

765 *Restatement (Second) of Trusts* § 325.

766 Unif. Simplification of Fiduciary Security Transfers Act Prefatory Note.

767 UCC § 8–602, cmt.

768 The same principle applies to persons dealing with other types of fiduciaries. *See also Restatement (Second) of Trusts* § 108(2) (2012); UTC § 1012(a); Unif. Transfers to Minors Act § 16; UPC § 5–424 (conservators).

qualify.[769] In a state which required a court order for all sales by personal representatives, a buyer at a sale without such an order was not a bona fide purchaser.[770] A lessee was not allowed to exercise an option in a lease because the trustees had no power to give it and "persons dealing with [a fiduciary] are bound to know the extent of his powers."[771]

Traditionally purchasers could rarely be in "good faith" if they knew they were dealing with a fiduciary.[772] Whether or not they knew this often depended on how title to the property was held. If land was conveyed "to *X*" without designating *X* as trustee in the deed, *X* might be treated as the outright owner as to persons "dealing with *[X]* in good faith and for a valuable consideration."[773] Transactions in securities could be facilitated if title was registered in a way that did not reveal that the registered owner was a trustee. At common law trustees were supposed "to see that trust property is designated or identifiable as property of the trust,"[774] but modern trust documents often expressly allow trustees to hold property in the name of a nominee rather than "as trustee."[775] The UTC and many state trust statutes also permit this.[776] The UPC has a similar provision for personal representatives and conservators.[777]

Historically, the liability of third parties was often needed to make the beneficiaries whole, because their remedies against a defaulting trustee were "apt to be of little value."[778] Today, fiduciaries are often solvent (or bonded), and so modern law tends to give purchasers more protection in order not to deter them from dealing with fiduciaries. In order to "facilitate prompt and economic administration of estates" third parties should "be able to deal with personal representatives without concern for [their] authority or duty to the beneficiaries . . . The beneficiaries' remedy is not to void the transaction but to seek damages for the personal representative's breach of his fiduciary duty."[779]

The Restatement Second imposed on purchasers from a trustee a duty "to inquire as to the terms of the trust,"[780] but the UPC relieves third parties who deal with personal representatives from any duty "to inquire into the existence

---

[769] *Restatement (Second) of Trusts* § 297 (1959); Nozik v. McDonald, 650 N.E.2d 923, 927 (Ohio App. 1994). As stated in *Restatement (Third) of Trusts* § 108 Rptr's Note to, cmt. c, the Restatement Third "does not undertake the laborious treatment of the 'bona fide purchaser' found in *Restatement Second, Trusts* §§ 284–320."

[770] Matter of Estate of Ostrander, 910 P.2d 865, 868 (Kan.App.1996).

[771] Adler v. Adler, 118 S.E.2d 456, 458 (Ga.1961).

[772] "Trust law purported to protect the bona fide purchaser of trust assets, but as a practical matter made it 'very difficult to qualify as a *bona fide* purchaser.' " Langbein, *The Contractarian Basis of Trust Law*, 105 Yale L. J. 625, 641 (1995).

[773] Applying Cal.Prob.Code § 18103.

[774] *Restatement (Third) of Trusts* § 84 (2007).

[775] *Restatement (Third) of Trusts* § 84, cmt. d(1).

[776] UTC § 816(7)(B); N.Y.EPTL § 11.1–1(b)(10).

[777] UPC §§ 3–715(14), 5–425(b)(17).

[778] Maitland, *Equity* 171 (1913).

[779] Wittick v. Miles, 545 P.2d 121, 126 (Or.1976). Even if the consideration for a purchase is below the value of the property, the buyer may still be a bona fide purchaser for value unless the consideration is insignificant. *Restatement (Second) of Trusts* § 298, cmt. i (1959).

[780] *Restatement (Second) of Trusts* § 297, cmt. f (1959).

of a power or the propriety of its exercise,"[781] and a similar provision appears in the UTC[782] and in the Restatement Third.[783] Under the Uniform Commercial Code, even if a security is registered in the name of a fiduciary, a purchaser has no duty of inquiry into the rightfulness of the transfer.[784] Thus "the modern trustee has been empowered to transact with trust assets on an equal footing with other market actors."[785] These provisions not only facilitate transfers, they protect the privacy of the trust beneficiaries. Under the UTC, third persons who do inquire into the terms of a trust must be content with a certification of the facts relevant to them, *e.g.*, the powers of the trustee, without seeing the dispositive terms of the trust.[786]

Creditors

Creditors of a trustee sometimes seek to reach trust property claiming they had no notice that it was held in trust. But a court rejected such a claim, finding that the creditors "had not relied on the debtor's apparent ownership of the property when they made the loan."[787]

Donees

A donee is not a bona fide purchaser for value even if he had no inkling that the transfer was improper.[788] This is not the case, however, if the donee has "so changed his position that it would be inequitable to compel him to restore" the property.[789] Similarly, when a fiduciary pays a beneficiary more than he is entitled to, the beneficiary must restore the money unless he "has so changed his position as to make it inequitable to enforce payment."[790]

Contracts

Traditionally, a personal representative who made a contract on behalf of the estate was personally liable on the contract.[791] Similarly, trustees were personally liable on contracts they make in administering a trust, even though in making the contract they were properly performing their duties.[792] Trustees and personal representatives could get reimbursement from the estate or trust

---

[781] UPC § 3–714.

[782] UTC § 1012(c). *See also* Cal.Prob.Code § 18100. The terms of a trust sometimes expressly protect third parties who deal with the trustee. ITT Commercial Finance v. Stockdale, 521 N.E.2d 417 (Mass. App. 1988).

[783] *Restatement (Third) of Trusts* § 108(3)(a) (2012). On the duty of inquiry by fiduciaries, *see* Wendel, *Evolution of Law of Trustee's Powers and Third Party Liability for Participating in Breach of Trust*, 35 Seton Hall L. Rev. 971 (2005).

[784] Unif. Commercial Code § 8–304. UTC § 1012(e) makes the "protective provisions of other laws relating to commercial transactions or transfer by fiduciaries" applicable to trusts.

[785] Langbein, *The Contractarian Basis of Trust Law*, 105 Yale L.J. 625, 642 (1995).

[786] UTC § 1013, based on Cal.Prob.Code § 18100.5. As to the use of trusts as a will substitute in order to protect privacy, *see* Section 10.4, note 104 et seq.

[787] Lagae v. Lackner, 996 P.2d 1281, 1286 (Colo.2000).

[788] Kampschroeder v. Kampschroeder, 887 P.2d 1152, 1158 (Kan.App.1995); *Restatement (Second) of Trusts* § 289 (1959).

[789] *Restatement (Second) of Trusts* § 292(1).

[790] Brent v. Smathers, 547 So.2d 683, 686 (Fla.App.1989). *See also Restatement (Second) of Trusts* § 254 (1959); UPC § 3–909.

[791] Sanni, Inc. v. Fiocchi, 443 N.E.2d 1108, 1111 (Ill.App.1982). *See also* Corpus Christi Bank & Trust v. Cross, 586 S.W.2d 664 (Tex. Civ.App.1979).

[792] *Restatement (Second) of Trusts* § 262 (1959).

for their liability if the contract was properly made, but only to the extent the estate was sufficient to cover the liability.[793]

Most states have enacted statutes overturning this restrictive rule and the Restatement Third of Trusts has joined this trend. These statutes treat trustees more like agents. Agents are normally not liable on contracts they make for a principal as long as they are acting within the scope of their authority.[794] Under the UPC, "a personal representative is not individually liable on a contract properly entered into in his fiduciary capacity . . . unless he fails to reveal his representative capacity and identify the estate in the contract."[795] This is restricted to "contracts properly entered;" under the Restatement Third of Trusts a trustee who makes an *unauthorized* contract may still incur personal liability.[796] Under the UTC, the trustee need disclose only the fiduciary capacity. The trustee need not disclose the name of the trust.[797] However, in some states simply signing the contract "as trustee" may not be enough.[798]

When creditors try to reach trust assets both they and the trustee have an incentive to argue that the contract was within the trustee's powers because this (a) allows the creditor to reach the trust assets, and (b) negates any personal liability of the trustee.[799] This creates a conflict of interest between the trustee and the beneficiaries, a problem the Uniform Probate Code addresses by allowing the beneficiaries to intervene in litigation against the trustee.[800]

Tort Claims

Traditionally, a trustee or personal representative was also "personally liable for torts committed by an agent or employee in the course of the administration of the trust."[801] This rule is harsh if the trust estate is insufficient to indemnify the trustee, but trustees can protect themselves by

---

[793] *Restatement (Second) of Trusts* § 246, cmt. a, § 262, cmt. b (1959).

[794] *Restatement (Third) of Agency* § 6.01, cmt. c (2006).

[795] UPC § 3–808(a). Similar protection is extended to conservators. UPC § 5–430(a).

[796] *Restatement (Third) of Trusts* § 106, cmt. b(1) (2012). But not when the other party had reason to know the trustee was exceeding his authority. Gerhardt Const. Co. v. Wachter Real Estate Trust, 306 N.W.2d 223 (N.D.1981).

[797] UTC § 1010(a) & cmt. *But see* In re Autoclub Body and Paint Services, Inc., 2011 WL 766972 (Bankr. S.D. Fla., Feb. 23, 2011) (interpreting identical statutory language, court holds that trustee was not protected because the contract did not disclose the name of the trust).

[798] *Restatement (Second) of Trusts* § 263 (1959). *But cf.* Church v. First Union Nat'l Bank, 304 S.E.2d 633, 635 (N.C.App.1983) (trustee not liable on note signed "in our fiduciary capacity but not individually").

[799] Johnston, *Developments in Contract Liability of Trusts and Trustees*, 41 N.Y.U.L.Rev. 483, 517 (1966).

[800] UPC § 3–706, cmt.

[801] *Restatement (Second) of Trusts* § 264 (1959); Evans v. Johnson, 347 N.W.2d 198 (Mich.App.1984) (executor). In McCarthy v. Poulsen, 219 Cal. Rptr. 375 (App.1985), a trust owned land which created a risk of substantial liability for mud slides. For fear of liability the trustee resigned and no one could be found who would agree to succeed him. The court ordered a receiver appointed instead because a receiver "is not personally liable for torts committed in the performance of his receivership duties."

buying liability insurance and paying the premiums from the trust.[802] Because they are in a better position than a tort victim to get insurance, they should arguably bear the "risk of insolvency of the trust estate."[803] Trust beneficiaries are usually not liable for torts committed by the trustee in administering the trust.[804]

The UTC, UPC, and Restatement Third of Trusts treat trustees and personal representatives as if they were agents of the trust or estate for purposes of tort as well as contractual liability. The personal representative or trustee is not liable for torts committed in the course of estate administration" unless the personal representative was "personally at fault."[805] Furthermore, if the tort was "committed in the course of administration of the estate," the tort victim may reach the estate or trust assets directly instead of first trying to collect the judgment from the fiduciary.[806]

A type of liability of great concern to fiduciaries today arises out of land ownership. When a bank as trustee succeeded to ownership of a landfill which it later sold to a city, the city sued the bank under CERCLA (Comprehensive Environmental Response, Compensation and Liability Act) to recover costs it had incurred in cleaning up hazardous substances deposited on the land while it was in the trust. The court held that if the trustee "had the power to control the use of the property at the time it was contaminated," it would be personally liable "regardless of the trust's ability to indemnify him."[807] Presumably the result would be the same under both the UTC and UPC, which impose personal liability on a trustee "for obligations arising out of the ownership or control of property of the trust estate . . . only if [the fiduciary] is personally at fault."[808] Fortunately, trustee concerns have been eased somewhat by later amendments made to CERCLA.[809]

---

[802] UTC § 816(11); Cal.Prob.Code § 16240. According to *Restatement (Second) of Trusts* § 247, cmt. e (1959), the trustee has a *duty* to obtain liability insurance and loses the right to exoneration if she fails to do so.

[803] Cook v. Holland, 575 S.W.2d 468, 472 (Ky.App.1978).

[804] *Restatement (Third) of Trusts* §§ 103, 104 (2012), which also extends to protection of the beneficiaries from contractual liability; Abraham Zion Corp. v. Lebow, 761 F.2d 93, 103 (2d Cir.1985), but not if the trustee acts under the control of the beneficiaries as their agent. Kessler, Merci, and Lochner, Inc. v. Pioneer Bank & Trust Co., 428 N.E.2d 608, 611 (Ill.App.1981).

[805] UTC § 1010(b); UPC § 3–808(b) (personal representatives), § 5–430(b) (conservators); *Restatement (Third) of Trusts* § 106(2) (2012). *See also* N.Y. EPTL § 11–4.7(b); Cal.Prob.Code § 18002.

[806] UTC § 1010(c), UPC § 3–808(c), 5–430(c); *Restatement (Third) of Trusts* § 106(2) (2012). *See also* N.Y. EPTL § 11–4.7(c) (estates); Vance v. Myers' Estate, 494 P.2d 816 (Alaska 1972).

[807] City of Phoenix v. Garbage Services Co., 827 F.Supp. 600, 604–5 (D.Ariz.1993) (citing *Restatement (Second) of Trusts* § 264 (1959)).

[808] UTC § 1010(b); UPC § 3–808(b) (personal representatives), § 5–403(b) (conservators). Further protection for trustees from environmental liability is provided by the powers conferred on them. *See* UTC § 816(13).

[809] 42 U.S.C. § 9607(n).

Chapter 15

OVERVIEW OF THE FEDERAL TAX LAWS RELATING TO ESTATES AND TRUSTS

Analysis

Sec.

15.1 Introduction.
15.2 Income Taxation of Gifts and Bequests and Basis of Gifted and Inherited Property.
15.3 Gift Tax.
15.4 The Estate Tax.
15.5 Generation Skipping Transfer Tax.
15.6 Income Taxation of Estates and Trusts.
15.7 Income Taxation of Grantor Trusts.

§ 15.1 Introduction

There are several federal taxes affecting an individual's transfer of property wealth both during life and at death. Originally enacted in 1916, the federal estate tax is a tax on the right to transfer property at death.[1] Because the federal estate tax could easily be evaded by lifetime transfers, Congress later enacted a gift tax, which is a tax on the right to transfer during lifetime.[2] Ordinarily, parents leave their estates to their children, who in turn leave their estates to their children and so on. But for those with significant wealth, such a simple strategy could result in the payment of federal estate tax at each generation. To avoid paying an estate tax at each generation, the very wealthy could leave their estates to their grandchildren and the children could leave their estates to their grandchildren. Using such a strategy, an estate tax would be payable only every other generation or even less. To close this gap, Congress enacted a tax on generation-skipping transfers, the current version of which dates to 1986.[3]

The federal estate, gift, and generation-skipping tax have little impact on the average client. No federal gift tax is payable until a donor's lifetime taxable gifts exceed $11,700,000 (2021 figure).[4] For individuals dying in 2011 or later, no federal estate tax is payable unless the combined total of the taxable estate and taxable gifts with certain adjustments exceeds $11,700,000 (2021 figure).[5]

---

1 *See* Section 15.4.

2 *See* Section 15.3.

3 *See* Section 15.5.

4 I.R.C. §§ 2010(c), 2505(a).

5 I.R.C. § 2010(c).

Similarly, the first $11,700,000 (2021 figure) of generation-skipping transfers are exempt from the GST tax.[6]

But income tax issues relating to property transfers affect nearly all individuals. The recipient of a lifetime gift is generally not taxed on the value of the gift.[7] The value of the property on the date of the gift may establish the recipient's income tax basis, however. Following an individual's death, the beneficiary's income tax basis in property received from a decedent is usually the property's fair market value at death.[8]

A probate estate and a trust are treated as separate income taxpayers. Following an individual's death or the date a trust is created, the income of the estate or trust is taxed to the estate or trust although a deduction is available for distributions to beneficiaries.[9] Trusts over which the settlor has retained certain powers may be classified as "grantor" trusts, in which event the trust income is taxed directly to the settlor regardless of whether distributions are made.[10]

Knowledge of these taxes is important for planning estates, particularly for those with significant wealth. Additionally, tax considerations often impact the language chosen in drafting wills and trusts, particularly in making certain the document qualifies for tax benefits such as the gift tax annual exclusion or marital or charitable deductions. Knowledge of these taxes is also important for preparing the relevant tax returns.

The federal gift, estate and generation-skipping tax apply to increasingly smaller portions of the population. Prior to 1977, the exemption from federal estate tax was limited to $60,000. Over the years, Congress repeatedly increased the amount exempt from the tax (termed "applicable exclusion") until it reached $675,000 for decedents dying in 2001. In 2001, Congress enacted even more dramatic increases.[11] The amount of the applicable exclusion was $1,000,000 for decedents dying in 2002–2003, $1,500,000 for decedents dying in 2004–2005, $2,000,000 for decedents dying in 2006–2008, and $3,500,000 for decedents dying in 2009.

The 2001 Congressional legislation that dramatically increased the estate and GST exclusion was effective for only ten years. The 2001 Act provided for the complete repeal of the estate and GST tax effective January 1, 2010. But this repeal was short lived. The estate and GST tax were reinstated effective 2011 but with a $5,000,000 applicable exclusion with adjustments for inflation after 2011.[12] The maximum tax rate was also dropped. From a top rate of 55% on taxable transfers, Congress in 2001 legislated an immediate reduction to

---

6 I.R.C. § 2631(c).

7 *See* Section 15.2.

8 *See* Section 15.2.

9 *See* Section 15.6.

10 *See* Section 15.7.

11 Economic Growth and Tax Reconciliation Relief Act of 2001, Tit. V, Pub. L. No. 107–16, § 521(a) (June 7, 2001).

12 Tax Relief, Unemployment Insurance Reauthorization, and Job Creation Act of 2010, Pub. L. No. 111–312, § 302(a)(1) (Dec. 17, 2010).

50% and then a gradual reduction to 45%.[13] For transfers in 2011–2012, the tax rate was fixed at 35%.[14] For transfers in 2013 or later, the tax rate is 40%.[15]

The legislation effective in 2011 also introduced the concept of "portability."[16] Where applicable, this allows a surviving spouse to apply any exclusion that was not used by the predeceased spouse, thereby potentially doubling the surviving spouse's exclusion from $5,000,000 to $10,000,000.

Finally, as part of the Tax Cuts and Jobs Act of 2017, the applicable exclusion was doubled from $5,000,000 to $10,000,000 but with adjustments for inflation occurring after 2011.[17] With portability, the combined exclusion of a married couple was effectively doubled from $10,000,000 to $20,000,000.

The result of the above changes is a massive decrease in the number of federal estate tax returns filed. During 2001, 109,600 federal estate tax returns were filed. For 2020, it is estimated that only 4,100 returns were filed. The amount of estate tax collected has also fallen, although not as dramatically. In 2001, $23.7 billion in estate tax was collected. For 2020, the figure is $16.0 billion.[18]

§ 15.2 Income Taxation of Gifts and Bequests and Basis of Gifted and Inherited Property

Section 102 of the Internal Revenue Code excludes from gross income for income tax purposes the value of property received by a donee by lifetime gift or by a beneficiary following a decedent's death from a bequest, devise, or inheritance.[19] This exclusion does not apply, however, to income earned on gifts after the date of the gift or on bequests after the date of death.[20]

Section 102 does not define the meaning of a gift or bequest. However, the Supreme Court has defined a "gift" as a transfer made from disinterested generosity.[21] A similar disinterested generosity concept has been applied to exclude from gross income property transferred at death.[22] But in most cases, the state law concept of gift or bequest will be dispositive. Transfers made within families where the donee is not required to make payment or provide services in return will be treated as excludable gifts; transfers made by will or intestate succession will ordinarily be treated as excludable bequests or inheritances. Problem areas include situations where a payment is not contractually required but is made in expectation of future services. Thus, a tip paid to a waitress or holiday packages delivered to business associates are

[13] Economic Growth and Tax Reconciliation Relief Act of 2001, Tit. V, Pub. L. No. 107–16, § 511 (June 7, 2001).

[14] Tax Relief, Unemployment Insurance Reauthorization, and Job Creation Act of 2010, Pub. L. No. 111–312, § 302(a)(2) (Dec. 17. 2010).

[15] American Taxpayer Relief Act of 2012, Pub. L. No. 112–240, § 101(c)(1) (Jan. 2, 2013).

[16] I.R.C. § 2010(c).

[17] Tax Cuts and Jobs Act, Pub. L. 115–97, § 11061(a) (Dec. 22, 2017).

[18] Tax Policy Center Briefing Book, available at https://taxpolicycenter.org.

[19] Likewise, Section 101 excludes from the beneficiary's gross income the proceeds of any life insurance payable by reason of an insured's death.

[20] I.R.C. § 102(b).

[21] Commissioner v. Duberstein, 363 U.S. 278 (1960).

[22] *See* Wolder v. Commissioner, 493 F.2d 608 (2d Cir. 1974).

not made out of disinterested generosity and are not eligible for the Section 102 exclusion.[23] Similarly, a devise made to a personal representative in lieu of statutory commissions was not made by the decedent from altruistic motives and is therefore not excludable.[24]

The Section 102 exclusion for transfers at death refers to "bequest, devise, or inheritance" but the exclusion is not limited to transfers made only by will or intestate succession. Rather, the exclusion applies to any transfer made at death, whether probate or nonprobate. While Section 102 could arguably apply to exclude life insurance proceeds from income taxation, there is no need to make this argument. Section 101 of the Code specifically excludes from gross income life insurance proceeds received by reason of the insured's death. But not excluded from gross income is interest earned on the policy proceeds between the date of the insured's death and the date of payment.[25]

For outright gifts or bequests the operation of Section 102 is straightforward. For example, if Oscar gives Sally 100 shares of X Corporation common stock, the value of the stock on the date of the gift is excluded from Sally's gross income. On the other hand, dividends paid by X Corporation to Sally after the date of the gift are included in Sally's gross income.

The receipt of a gift is not a taxable event for income tax purposes even if the property, on the date of the gift, is worth more than what the donor paid for it. Thus, if a donor gives appreciated stock to a donee, the donor realizes no capital gain as a result of the gift. Gain will be realized, if any, only at such time as the donee sells or otherwise disposes of the gifted property. In the case of gifts of appreciated property, the donee's basis is the donor's basis at the time of the gift increased by the gift tax paid, if any, with respect to the gift.[26] If no gift tax was paid with respect to the gift, which is the usual case, then the donee's basis equals the donor's basis.

This "carryover basis" rule means that any appreciation on gifted property is taxed in the donee's hands, not the donor's hands, but only when the donee disposes of the gifted property during the donee's lifetime. For example, suppose Anna gives John 100 shares of Y Corporation common stock having a value of $1,000 on the date of the gift. Suppose further that Anna paid $100 for this stock. Anna realizes no gain on this gift even though at the time of the gift the stock had appreciated by $900 over what Anna had paid for it. If two years later, John sells the stock for $1,500, John realizes a capital gain of $1,400. This amount is the difference between the amount he realized and the carryover basis of $100.

If the donor's basis in gifted property on the date of the gift is greater than the property's then fair market value, then for purposes of determining loss on a sale or exchange of the property, its basis equals its fair market value on the date of the gift.[27] For example, if Fred gives Herman a piece of real estate in

[23] Commissioner v. Duberstein, 363 U.S. 278 (1960).

[24] Wolder v. Commissioner, 493 F.2d 608 (2d Cir.1974).

[25] I.R.C. § 101(c)–(d).

[26] I.R.C. § 1015(a), (d).

[27] I.R.C. § 1015(a).

which Fred, at the time of the gift, had a basis of $100,000 but the property was worth only $50,000, the loss rule may operate. If Herman later sells the property for $30,000, Herman's basis will be $50,000 and Herman will realize a $20,000 loss on the sale. But if Herman later sells the property for $120,000, the loss rule cannot operate and carryover basis will then apply. Herman's basis will be $100,000 and Herman will realize a $20,000 gain on the sale. But should Herman sell the property for more than the $50,000 fair market value but for less than Fred's $100,000 basis, the statute cannot operate and Herman will realize no gain or loss on the sale.[28]

Lifetime transfers made between spouses or to an ex-spouse incident to a divorce are subject to a different rule. Regardless of whether the gifted property has appreciated or depreciated, the donor's basis always carries over to the donee.[29]

For property acquired by bequest, inheritance, or other transfer at death, the basis of the property in the beneficiary's hands is the property's estate tax value.[30] If the decedent's estate was not required to file an estate tax return, then the property's basis is its fair market value on the date of the decedent's death. The property's estate tax value is usually also its fair market value as of decedent's death although there are exceptions such as the alternate valuation election.[31] Because the basis of inherited property is "stepped up" to its estate tax value, increases in value during the decedent's lifetime will not be subject to income tax.[32] The "stepped up" basis rule provides a powerful incentive to hold property until death rather than sell or gift the property during lifetime. For example, Alice purchased Blackacre for $50,000 and held on to it. Blackacre was worth $450,000 when Alice dies. Under her will she devises Blackacre to Chris. Chris will acquire a basis in Blackacre equal to the property's date-of-death value of $450,000, Chris may sell the property without incurring any capital gain. On the other hand, had Alice gifted the property to Chris during lifetime, Chris would have succeeded to Alice's lifetime basis of $50,000. Had Chris later sold the property when it was worth $450,000, Chris would have had to pay capital gains tax on the $400,000 in appreciation.

The rule on the basis of property acquired from a decedent is not limited to transfers by wills or intestate succession. It also applies to property otherwise included in a decedent's gross estate. For example, if Bob transferred stock into a revocable trust which Bob acquired for $5,000, the basis of the stock in the trustee's hands is $5,000 under Section 1015. When Bob later dies, the trust assets will be included in Bob's gross estate and subject to the estate tax because of his retained power of revocation.[33] If, at Bob's death, the stock

---

28 *See* Treas. Reg. § 1.1015–1(a)(2).

29 I.R.C. § 1041.

30 I.R.C. § 1014.

31 *See* Section 15.4, note 147 et seq.

32 Decedent's basis immediately prior to death usually equals the cost of the asset in the decedent's hand. *See* I.R.C. § 1012.

33 I.R.C. § 2038. The step-up in basis is available even if Bob's estate is too small to warrant the filing of an estate tax return, although in such case the property tax basis will equal its fair market value on Bob's death, not its estate tax value. *See generally* I.R.C. § 1014.

is worth $50,000 and it then becomes distributable to Jim, Jim's basis in the property will be $50,000.

§ 15.3 Gift Tax

Federal law imposes a tax on the privilege of transferring property by gift, bequest or inheritance. This transfer tax takes the form of a gift tax in the case of completed lifetime taxable gifts[34] and an estate tax in the case of property includable in the decedent's gross estate, the gross estate includes the probate estate, certain lifetime transfers, annuities, joint tenancy property, property over which decedent had, exercised or released a general power of appointment, life insurance, and certain qualified terminable interest property.[35]

Generally, gifted property is not included in the donor's gross estate but this is not always the case. Where the transferor makes a gift but retains an interest in the retained property until death, the value of the property will sometimes also be subject to estate tax. However, the adjusted taxable gift concept[36] will prevent double counting in such cases. For example, suppose Helen makes a completed gift of property with a value of $500,000 to a trust and retains the income for life with a remainder to her children. This property is worth $750,000 when Helen dies and is included in her gross estate because of her retained life estate.[37] Because of the adjusted taxable gift concept, only a total of $750,000 will be subject to tax.

Gift and estate taxes are computed based on the unified rate table set forth in Section 2001 of the Internal Revenue Code. First, a tentative tax is computed based on the cumulative lifetime taxable gifts and death-time transfers. Second, a "unified credit" is applied that will assure that no gift or estate tax will be payable unless the cumulative transfers exceed the "applicable exclusion," which is $10,000,000 with adjustments for inflation after 2011.[38] The best way to learn the computation process is by studying examples. A sample gift tax computation is included later in this section, and a sample estate tax computation is included in Section 15.4.

The Meaning of Taxable Gift

A federal gift tax is imposed on the value of lifetime gifts. For gift tax purposes a gift is defined as the transfer of property for less than an adequate and full consideration in money or money's worth, other than a transfer in the "ordinary course of business."[39] Most transfers that meet the common law definition of a gift also are gifts for gift tax purposes. Certain lifetime transfers, however, may not be gifts for state property law purposes but nonetheless are

---

[34] *See infra* note 39 et seq.

[35] *See* Section 15.4.

[36] I.R.C. § 2001(b).

[37] I.R.C. § 2036(a).

[38] I.R.C. §§ 2010(c), 2505(a).

[39] Treas. Reg. § 25.2512–8. A transfer is in the "ordinary course of business" if it is a bona fide arms' length transaction free of any donative intent. For example, when a department store has a sale and sells goods at a price that is less than the marked price, no gift results because of the ordinary business transaction exception.

gifts for gift tax purposes. This is because the consideration necessary to support a contract under state law may not be sufficient to avoid a gift under federal tax law.

For gift tax purposes, consideration that cannot be valued in money or money's worth is ignored. For example, if John transfers Blackacre, valued at $100,000, to his daughter, Mary, for cash in the amount of $100,000, John receives adequate and full consideration in money or money's worth and no gift has been made. On the other hand, suppose John promises to pay Mary $20,000 if Mary does not smoke for a year. Mary stops smoking for one year and John pays her $20,000. John makes a gift to Mary of $20,000. While Mary's performance may be sufficient consideration under state law to support the enforcement of John's promise, it is not consideration in money or money's worth because it does not replenish the value of John's personal estate which has been depleted by $20,000.

A transfer in consideration for the donee's release of dower or curtesy or a statutory right in lieu thereof is also not consideration in money or money's worth.[40] On the other hand, a transfer to a spouse in consideration for the spouse's release of a support obligation is a transfer for adequate and full consideration in money or money's worth.[41]

The computation of the gift tax depends on the amount of the donor's "taxable gifts." To compute the donor's taxable gifts, one begins with the total transfers made during the year and then subtracts annual exclusions and charitable and marital deductions allowable under Sections 2522 and 2523.

The annual exclusion allows for the subtraction of up to $15,000 per donee for gifts made during a calendar year.[42] To illustrate, suppose Mary gave her friend, Alice, $100,000 in cash. Because of the annual exclusion, Alice's taxable gift will equal $85,000. On the other hand, suppose the gift had been made to Mary's husband, George. In this case, the taxable gift is $0. First, the annual exclusion would have reduced the otherwise taxable gift from $100,000 to $85,000 and the marital deduction would have eliminated the balance.[43]

The amount of a donor's taxable gift is also affected by the "split gift" rule,[44] under which a married donor's gifts can be treated for gift tax purposes as having been made half by the donor and half by the donor's spouse if the donor and the donor's spouse so elect on a gift tax return. Thus, if Mary gives Alice $30,000 and Mary and her husband, George, elect to split the gift for gift tax purposes, then for purposes of computing the taxable gifts of Mary and George, each of them is deemed to have given Alice $15,000. Because each of them is entitled to an annual exclusion for gifts up to $15,000 (for gifts made

---

[40] Treas. Reg. § 25.2512–8; Merrill v. Fahs, 324 U.S. 308 (1945); I.R.C. § 2043. *But see* I.R.C. § 2516 relating to divorce, infra note 103.

[41] *See, e.g.*, Glen v. Commissioner, 45 T.C. 323 (1966); Rev. Rul. 68–379, 1968–2 C.B. 414.

[42] *See infra* notes 83–84 (relating to present and future interests). The annual exclusion was formerly $10,000, but for gifts made after 1998, the amount of the $10,000 annual exclusion is subject to increase for an inflation adjustment in multiples of $1,000. *See* I.R.C. § 2503(b)(2).

[43] *See infra* note 116 et seq.

[44] I.R.C. § 2513. The split gift option is designed to equalize the treatment of gifts for married persons whether they live in common-law property states or community property states.

in 2021), each of them makes a taxable gift of $0 to Alice. The split gift rules permit electing married couples to double up on their annual exclusions and unified credits. Thus, between them they can make gifts of $30,000 annually to any donee without making a taxable gift, with gifts in excess of that amount shielded from transfer tax by the use of their unified credits.[45]

Valuation of Gifted Property

Gifted property is valued at its fair market value on the date of the gift.[46] Fair market value is the "price at which [gifted] . . . property would change hands between a willing buyer and a willing seller, neither being under any compulsion to buy or to sell, and both having reasonable knowledge of relevant facts."[47]

Where the gifted property is an annuity, life estate or remainder or reversion, the value of the property from which the annuity, life estate, remainder or reversion is carved must first be valued under the willing seller-willing buyer test. This value is then multiplied by the appropriate factor set forth in the Treasury regulations[48] taking account of the age of the relevant beneficiary or the term for which the interest is payable. To illustrate, suppose Mary transfers Blackacre to Alice for life, remainder to Bernie. In order to value the gifts to Alice and Bernie, Blackacre first must be valued. Assume that under the willing seller-willing buyer test, Blackacre is valued at $100,000. Suppose that Alice's interest, under the appropriate valuation table, is valued at $88,198, and Bernie's interest is valued at $11,934. In computing the amount of Mary's gift tax liability, Mary is deemed to have made a gift of $88,198 to Alice and a transfer of $11,934 to Bernie. However, the gift to Alice is a present interest[49] and qualifies for an annual exclusion but the gift to Bernie is a future interest[50] and does not qualify for the annual exclusion.

If the donor retains an interest in gifted property, then the value of the gift must be reduced by the value of the donor's retained interest. However, under Section 2702 in most cases where the donor transfers property into an irrevocable trust for the benefit of a family member and retains an interest in the trust, the value of the donor's retained interest will be deemed to be zero. This results in the transferred property's entire value being subject to the gift tax notwithstanding that under state law the donor has retained a life estate or other interest in the transferred property. Section 2702 does not apply to otherwise completed gifts if the donor's retained interest is in the form of a GRAT (grantor retained annuity trust), GRUT (grantor retained unitrust), or QPRT

---

[45] For a discussion of the unified credit and a computation example, *see* Section 15.4, notes 141–142.

[46] A gift is deemed made when the gift is complete. *See infra* notes 71 et seq. For discussion of the federal estate tax marital deduction, *see* Section 15.4, note 280 et seq.

[47] Treas.Reg. § 25.2512–1.

[48] Treas.Reg. § 25.2512–5.

[49] A present interest for gift tax purposes is an "unrestricted right to the immediate use, possession, or enjoyment of property or the income from property." Treas.Reg. § 25.2503–3(b).

[50] A future interest for gift tax purposes is "a legal term, and includes reversions, remainders, and other interests or estates, whether vested or contingent, and whether or not supported by a particular interest or estate, which are limited to commence in use, possession, or enjoyment at some future date or time." Treas.Reg. § 25.2503–3(a).

(qualified personal residence trust), which are advanced planning techniques beyond the scope of this chapter.

Even if Section 2702 is inapplicable, if the donor's retained interest cannot be valued by recognized actuarial methods, then its value is presumed to be zero.[51]

Calculation of Gift Tax and Payment of Tax

The amount of gift taxes payable on taxable gifts for the calendar year is determined by first calculating a tentative gift tax using current tax rates on the aggregate value of taxable gifts for the calendar year and all prior calendar years, and then reducing this tentative tax by a tax computed using current tax rates on the aggregate value of taxable gifts for all prior years.[52] The resulting tax is then reduced by the remaining amount of the taxpayer's unified credit.[53] The first $10,000,000 in the donor's lifetime taxable gifts (as adjusted for post-2011 inflation) will be shielded from payment of gift tax by use of the gift tax unified credit. But even if no gift tax is payable, performing the computation and filing the return is still important. To the extent the donor makes lifetime taxable gifts, such gifts will be part of the base for computing the federal estate tax at the donor's death. For this reason, a donor is required to file a Form 709 gift tax return whenever a donor makes a taxable gift.[54]

To illustrate, suppose Harry makes a gift of $14,000,000 to Andrea in 2021, when the gift tax exclusion as adjusted for inflation was $11,700,000. Harry's aggregate taxable gifts for years prior to 2021 equal $1,000,000. In computing the gift taxes thereon in prior years Harry used $345,800 of his unified credit. The amount of his 2021 gift tax liability is $1,320,000 determined as follows:

Harry's 2021 gift	$14,000,000
Harry's gifts in prior years	$1,000,00
Total taxable gifts	$15,000,000
Tentative tax on $15,000,000	$5,945,800
Tentative tax on $1,000,000	$345,800
Difference	$5,600,000
Unified gift tax credit	$4,625,800
Credit used prior years	$345,800
Remaining credit	$4,280,000
Gift tax due ($5,600,000 – $4,280,000)	$1,320,000

51 Robinette v. Helvering, 318 U.S. 184 (1943).

52 I.R.C. §§ 2502, 2001(g).

53 I.R.C. § 2505. *See also* Chart II at the end of the chapter.

54 I.R.C. § 6019.

The Form 709 gift tax return and any gift tax payable is due on or before April 15 following the close of the calendar year in which the taxable gifts were made.[55]

Identity of the Donee

Since the gift tax is imposed on the value of property transferred by a donor, rather than upon the value of property received by a donee, the identity of a donee often is not important to the assessment of the gift tax. In certain cases, however, the identity of the donee or the nature of the interest received will determine eligibility for a deduction or annual exclusion. For example, if the donee is a charity, gifts to the donee may qualify for a gift tax charitable deduction.[56] If the donee is the donor's spouse, the gift may qualify for a gift tax marital deduction.[57] If the interest passing to the donee is a "present interest," the value thereof qualifies for the annual exclusion. Lastly, if transfers are made in trust, the donee is the person or persons entitled to the beneficial interests in the trust, not the trustee. The gift must be allocated among the trust beneficiaries in accordance with the beneficiaries' actuarial interests as determined from the valuation tables published in the Treasury Regulations.[58] Only the value of beneficial interests qualifying as present interests will qualify for the annual exclusion.

The Annual Exclusion and Medical and Tuition Payment Exclusion

Section 2503(b) provides an annual exclusion not to exceed $15,000 (2021 figure) for gifts of a present interest to any donee in each calendar year. Gifts of a future interest do not qualify for the exclusion.[59] An unrestricted right to the use, possession or enjoyment of property or the income therefrom is a gift of a present interest.[60] Gifts of discretionary income interests, even if limited by a standard, do not qualify for the annual exclusion. Similarly, gifts of reversions and remainders do not qualify for the annual exclusion as they are gifts of a future interest.

Use of the annual exclusion to avoid gift taxes on annual transfers can result in a significant shift of wealth from one generation to another without any transfer tax cost. For example, if $15,000 is given annually to a child for 20 years, $300,000 of tax-free gifts can be made to that child over a 20-year period. For married couples utilizing the split gift rules, annual gifts to any donee of $30,000 can be made gift tax free. Gifts shielded from tax by the annual exclusion do not result in any further use of the donor's unified credit. For large families there are significant planning opportunities to shift wealth from one generation to another at little or no transfer tax cost using only the annual exclusion.

---

55 I.R.C. § 6075(b).

56 *See infra* notes 112 et seq.

57 *See infra* notes 116 et seq.

58 Treas.Reg. § 25.2512–5(d).

59 I.R.C. § 2503(b).

60 Treas.Reg. § 25.2503–3(b).

2503(c) Trust

A transfer to a minor that does not meet the ordinary definition of a present interest can qualify for the annual exclusion if the transfer qualifies as a present interest under Section 2503(c). Under Section 2503(c), no part of a gift is considered to be a gift of a future interest if the gift is made to a person under age 21 and if the gifted property and the income therefrom may be paid to, or applied towards the benefit of, the donee prior to the donee attaining age 21. Furthermore, such property and the income must pass to the donee when the donee attains age 21 or, if the donee dies prior to attaining age 21, the property and the income must be payable to either the donee's estate or as the donee may appoint pursuant to a general power of appointment.

This statute has led to the creation of so-called Section 2503(c) or annual exclusion trusts. Key issues when drafting such a trust include (1) do not overly restrict the trustee's discretion to make current distributions to the donee; (2) make certain that the donee has the right to receive the trust no later than age 21; and (3) make certain that if the donee dies prior to age 21 that the trust will pass to the donee's estate or, if not, that the donee was granted a general testamentary power of appointment. If the trustee's power to pay income to the donee is substantially restricted, the gift in trust will not qualify as a present interest under Section 2503(c).[61] A trustee's discretion is not substantially restricted if payments are limited to providing for the donee's "support," "care," or "education."[62] For donors concerned that the beneficiary not receive the trust funds at age 21, the annual exclusion is still available if the beneficiary is given a right, no later than age 21, to withdraw the beneficiary's trust share[63] and if the beneficiary is told of the right to withdraw.[64] If the beneficiary fails to exercise the withdrawal right, the trust instrument may provide that the property will be retained in trust until whatever age the donor wishes.

Uniform Transfers to Minors Act

Gifts to minors under Uniform Transfers to Minors Act also qualify for the annual exclusion under the Section 2503(c) exception.[65]

Crummey Withdrawal Power

In lieu of a Section 2503(c) trust, donors may qualify transfers in trust for the annual exclusion through the use of so-called "Crummey" powers.[66] A Crummey power is a provision added to an irrevocable trust that allows the donee to withdraw contributions made to the trust for a limited period. The amount of withdrawal is normally limited to the lesser of the annual exclusion amount or the contribution made. The hope of the donor to the trust is that the holder of the Crummey withdrawal power will permit the power to lapse, permitting the property to remain in trust. Because the donee has a general

---

[61] Treas.Reg. § 25.2503–4(b)(1).

[62] *See* Rev. Rul. 67–270, 1967–2 C.B. 349.

[63] Rev. Rul. 74–43, 1974–1 C.B. 285.

[64] Rev. Rul. 81–7, 1981–1 C.B. 474.

[65] Rev. Rul. 59–357, 1959–2 C.B. 212. For a discussion of this Act, *see* Section 10.5, notes 166 et seq.

[66] Crummey v. Commissioner, 397 F.2d 82 (9th Cir.1968).

power of appointment, although only for a limited period, the power qualifies as a present interest, and the property over which the power is exercisable qualifies for the annual exclusion. Crummey powers work so long as (1) the donee receives notice of the contribution and a reasonable opportunity to exercise the power,[67] and (2) in the Service's but not the courts' view, the holder of the power has either a current income interest or a vested remainder.[68]

Tuition/Medical Expense

Tuition payments made to an educational institution or for an individual's medical care are not taxable gifts. This exclusion is not available if the payments are made to the intended donee who then pays the tuition or medical expense.[69] To qualify for the exclusion, the payments must be made directly to the medical or educational provider.

529 Plans

A 529 plan, which is named after the section that authorized them, is a favored technique for saving for the college expenses of a child or grandchild. 529 plans may be sponsored either by a state or directly by an educational institution. A 529 plan may be created for a beneficiary of any age, and by any donor regardless of income level. Earnings withdrawn from the account and used to pay the beneficiary's qualified higher education expenses are income tax-free.[70] Contributions to 529 plans are subject to special annual exclusion rules. For 529 Plans (and no other asset), the owner of the account can contribute up to five years annual exclusion amounts (or $75,000), and carry over the balance and apply it to the annual exclusion for succeeding years.[71]

Complete and Incomplete Gifts

The gift tax is imposed only upon completed gifts. A transfer for less than adequate and full consideration in money or money's worth is a completed gift for gift tax purposes only if the enjoyment of the transferred property is placed beyond the donor's dominion and control. The dominion and control test is explained as follows:

> As to any property, or part thereof or interest therein, of which the donor has so parted with dominion and control as to leave in him no power to change its disposition, whether for his own benefit or for the benefit of another, the gift is complete. But if upon the transfer of property (whether in trust or otherwise) the donor reserves any power over its disposition, the gift may be partially complete and partially incomplete, depending upon all the facts in the particular case.[72]

---

[67] *See* Rev. Rul. 81–7, 1981–1 C.B. 474.

[68] *See* Tech. Adv. Mem. 96–28–004 (7/12/96). Crummey power granted to persons with no underlying interest in the trust are called "naked powers." The Tax Court rejects the Service's view. *See, e.g.*, Kohlsaat v. Commissioner, 73 T.C.M (CCH) ¶ 2732 (1997); Cristofani v. Commissioner, 97 T.C. 74 (1991).

[69] I.R.C. § 2503(e).

[70] I.R.C. § 529(c)(3).

[71] I.R.C. § 529(c)(2).

[72] Treas.Reg. § 25.2511–2(b).

If the donor transfers property outright and the donor can no longer change its disposition, whether for the donor's own benefit or the benefit of others, the gift is complete for gift tax purposes. Alternatively, if the donor retains any power to regain possession or ownership of the property or retains the power to determine who shall enjoy the benefits of the property, the gift is incomplete[73] and no taxable gift occurs until the donor's power of disposition terminates. In many cases, however, the gift will remain incomplete for the donor's entire lifetime. In this case, more likely than not, the property will be included in the donor's gross estate for estate tax purposes[74] and not be included in the donor's gift tax base. For example, if Mary transfers property into a revocable trust, no gift occurs when the trust is created because Mary retains the power to regain the transferred property. If two years later Mary releases the power of revocation, a gift occurs at that time because after the release Mary will no longer have a power to change its disposition.[75] If Mary fails to release the power during her life and dies in possession of the power, the property in the trust is included in Mary's gross estate.[76]

A gift is incomplete even if a retained power cannot be exercised for the donor's personal pecuniary benefit. For example, suppose Mary transfers property into an irrevocable trust but retains the power to pay the income to such of Alice, Bob and Charlie as Mary from time to time directs. Upon Mary's death the trust terminates and the principal is distributable to Alice, Bob and Charlie. In this case, Mary retains a power of disposition over the income interest but no power over the remainder interest. In measuring whether there is a completed gift, each interest in the trust is considered separately. Because of Mary's retained power to determine how the income is distributed, the gift of the income interest is incomplete. The gift of the remainder interest is complete because Mary has no authority to alter the shares. The trust property will also be included in Mary's gross estate under Section 2036 because Mary retained a power to control the beneficial enjoyment of the income interest. When the estate tax is computed on Mary's estate, however, appropriate credit will be allowed for any gift tax paid on the completed gift of the remainder interest.[77]

An incomplete gift may become complete for gift tax purposes when property subject to a donor's retained power is released to a beneficiary. For example, suppose John creates a revocable trust for the primary benefit of Alice and transfers $100,000 to the trustee. This transfer is not a completed gift because of John's power to revoke the transfer. The following year the trustee distributes the trust's entire income for that year to Alice. The income in Alice's

---

[73] An exception is found in Treas.Reg. § 25.2511–2(d), where it is provided that if the donor retains the power only to affect the time and manner of enjoyment of property, the gift is complete for gift tax purposes. For example, if the donor transfers property to T in trust to pay the income to A until A attains age 21 when the trust terminates and the principal is distributable to A, the gift is complete even though the donor retains the power to direct that trust income be accumulated until A attains age 21 and be distributed to A at that time.

[74] *See, e.g.*, the discussion of retained life estates at § 15.4, note 166 et seq.

[75] Treas.Reg. § 25.2511–2(f).

[76] I.R.C. § 2038.

[77] *See* I.R.C. § 2001(b).

hands is no longer subject to John's power of revocation. Consequently, the distribution of income to Alice constitutes a completed gift.[78]

Whether a gift is complete or incomplete for gift tax purposes does not determine whether the gifted property is included or excluded from the donor's gross estate. The taxability of any transfer is determined separately under rules governing each tax. In those cases where a gift is incomplete for gift tax purposes, the entire gift or some portion thereof will be included in the donor's gross estate. Less logically, however, gifts that are wholly complete for gift tax purposes may nonetheless also be included in the donor's gross estate. One example occurs when a donor retains a power over transferred property that is exercisable only with the consent of a person having a substantial adverse interest. Under the estate tax, the substantial adverse interest will be ignored, while under the gift tax, the gift of the transferred property is complete.[79]

A substantial adverse interest exists only if there is a substantial economic interest that could be prejudiced or destroyed if the power over the interest was exercised.[80] No adverse interest exists in a property interest in which the co-holder of power has no economic benefits. For example, suppose Mary creates a revocable trust under which income is payable to Allan and the remainder is distributable to Betty. Mary retains the power to revoke the trust but only with Allan's consent. In this case there is a completed gift only of the income interest. Allan has no economic interest in the remainder interest distributable to Betty when he dies.

While a transfer to an irrevocable trust is normally a completed gift, the gift is incomplete if the donor retains a power of disposition. Such cases often arise when the donor is also acting as trustee and, as trustee, has a power to make discretionary distributions. In that case, because the donor has not parted with control, the gift is deemed to be incomplete. But if the donor-trustee's discretion is limited by an ascertainable standard, the donor's control is now considered sufficiently hemmed in so that the transfer will be a completed gift.[81] For example, if Bob creates a trust to pay as much of the income to Pat and Jenny as they need for their support and upon the death of Bob to distribute the principal to Emily, the gift of the income interest is complete even though Bob is a trustee.[82] The ascertainable standard limitation is deemed to sufficiently restrict the donor so that the donor is not deemed to have retained dominion and control over how the transferred property is distributed.

Subject Matter of a Gift

The gift tax is assessed against transfers of property. Property includes real and personal property, tangible and intangible property.[83] The tax applies

---

78 Treas.Reg. § 25.2511–2(f).

79 Treas.Reg. § 25.2511–2(e).

80 *See* Camp v. Commissioner, 195 F.2d 999 (1st Cir. 1952); Commissioner v. Prouty, 115 F.2d 331 (1st Cor. 1940).

81 Treas.Reg. § 25.2511–2(g).

82 *See* the discussion of the ascertainable standard exception under the estate tax law, Section § 15.4, notes 177–178 & 240.

83 I.R.C. § 2511(a).

whether a legal or equitable interest in property is transferred.[84] A gift can be made of a present or a future interest, a vested or a contingent interest.[85] An income interest can be the subject of a gift.[86] Thus, if John creates a trust under which Alice is entitled to the income for life and subsequently Alice transfers her income interest to Bob, Alice makes a gift to Bob equal to the value of her income interest at the time of the transfer measured by reference to her life expectancy.

Because many annual exclusion gifts are made late in the year, attention must be paid to timing, particularly when it comes to payment by check. If a donor writes and delivers a check to a donee in Year 1 that does not clear the donor's bank account until Year 2, a rigid application of the completed gift test would suggest that the gift was not made until Year 2 because the donor, up until the time the check cleared the donor's account, could have stopped payment. But the U.S. Tax Court, applying the "relation back" doctrine, held that a check which clears in a subsequent year will be treated as a gift in the prior year if the check was both delivered and deposited in the prior year.[87] The Service has also adopted the "relation back" approach.[88]

Property applied towards the benefit of another rather than paid to him can constitute a gift. Thus, if Don owes Arnie $5,000 and Oscar pays Don's debt to Arnie, Oscar makes a gift to Don, not Arnie.

The forgiveness of a debt is a gift.[89] A gift can also occur when a lender fails to secure repayment of a debt within the statute of limitations on collection.[90]

Life insurance can be the subject matter of a gift although the value of the gift, if the insured is living, equals the current value of the policy and not the proceeds payable at the insured's death.[91] A gift of a life insurance policy can be made by its irrevocable assignment to another.[92] However, the designation of someone as the beneficiary of a life insurance policy is not a gift if the owner retains the right to change the beneficiary as is usually the case. The proceeds of gifted life insurance are included in the insured's gross estate if the insured dies within three years of the gift.[93]

The gift tax does not apply to a gift of personal services by the donor regardless of value.[94] But if the donor pays a third person to perform a personal

---

[84] Treas.Reg. § 25.2511–1(g)(1).

[85] Goodwin v. McGowan, 47 F.Supp. 798 (W.D.N.Y.1942).

[86] *See, e.g.*, Lockard v. Commissioner, 166 F.2d 409 (1st Cir.1948).

[87] Estate of Metzger v. Commissioner, 100 T.C. 204, 215 (1993), *aff'd*, 38 F.2d 118 (4th Cir. 1994).

[88] Rev. Rul. 96–56, 1996–2 C.B. 161.

[89] Treas.Reg. § 25.2511–1(a).

[90] Estate of Lang v. Commissioner, 613 F.2d 770 (9th Cir. 1980); Rev. Rul. 81–264, 1981–2 C.B. 185.

[91] *See* Treas.Reg. § 25.2512–6 for the valuation of gifted life insurance policies.

[92] Treas.Reg. § 25.2511–1(h)(8).

[93] I.R.C. § 2035. Gifts of life insurance can be an effective way to transfer significant wealth at little or no transfer tax cost. *See* Section 15.4, notes 257–258.

[94] *See generally* Commissioner v. Hogle, 165 F.2d 352 (10th Cir.1947); Rev. Rul. 64–225, 1964–2 C.B. 15, Rev. Rul. 66–167, 1966–1 C.B. 20, Rev. Rul. 70–237, 1970–1 C.B. 13.

service for another, the amount paid is a gift.[95] Thus, if Scott pays Nancy $15,000 to repair Tom's house, Scott makes a gift to Tom of $15,000.

Powers of Appointment

Section 2514 governs the gift taxation of property subject to a general power of appointment that has been exercised or released during the donee powerholder's lifetime.[96] For gift tax purposes, a general power of appointment is a power under which the donee can appoint to himself, "his estate, his creditors, or the creditors of his estate."[97] Under Section 2514, if a donee of a general power exercises or releases the power, the donee is deemed to have made a completed gift of the property subject to the power unless the donee, following the exercise or release, retains dominion or control of the property in some other capacity.

For example, suppose Olive transfers property in trust to pay the income to Cecil for life, remainder to Cecil's surviving descendants. Olive grants Cecil a general inter-vivos power to appoint the property to himself or anyone else. Two years later, Cecil exercises the power and appoints the entire trust principal to Jack. The exercise of the power results in a transfer of the trust property from Cecil to Jack. Since Cecil, following the exercise, retains no dominion and control over the transferred property, the exercise of the power also results in the making a completed gift.

If Cecil does not exercise the power but rather releases the power, Cecil also makes a transfer of the property subject to the power under Section 2514. Of course, because a person cannot make a gift to himself, this release/transfer results in a gift of the remainder interest only. This gift would not qualify for any annual exclusion because it is a gift of a future interest. Cecil's release of the general power does not result in the termination of his income interest.

The lapse of a general power of appointment is treated as a release of a power.[98] A lapse of a power occurs when the donee fails to exercise the power within the time limit specified in the instrument creating the power. Thus, if Oscar grants Felix a general inter-vivos power exercisable prior to January 1, 2022 and Felix fails to exercise the power by that date, on January 1, 2022, when the power lapses, Felix is deemed to have released the power and to have made a gift of the property subject to the power. But this "lapse equals a release" rule is tempered by a special exception. The lapse of a power during any calendar year is treated as a release of a power in that year "only to the extent that the property which could have been appointed by exercise of such lapsed powers exceeds in value the greater of '$5,000 or 5%' of the aggregate value of the assets out of which, or the proceeds of which, the exercise of the

[95] Regs. § 25.2511–1(h)(3).

[96] Section 2514 distinguishes between general powers created on or before October 21, 1942 (so-called "pre-42 powers") and powers created after October 21, 1942 (so-called "post-42 powers".) The discussion in the text is limited to post-42 powers. For a discussion of powers of appointment, *see* Section 11.5.

[97] I.R.C. § 2514(c). This broad definition of a general power is subject to several refinements. These are discussed in § 15.4. For the distinction between general and special powers of appointment for non-tax purposes, *see* Section 11.5, note 181 et seq.

[98] I.R.C. § 2514(e).

lapsed powers could be satisfied."[99] This so-called "5 and 5" rule has led to the development of an important estate planning tool.

Under the "5 and 5 rule," a donee may be granted a general power of appointment, exercisable annually, to withdraw from the principal of a trust an amount equal to the greater of $5,000 or 5% of trust principal valued annually. If the donee exercises the power, there is no gift because a person cannot make a gift to herself. If the donee permits the power to lapse, no release (and therefore no taxable gift) occurs because of the 5 and 5 rule. This type of power is attractive because it permits the donee to withdraw trust principal to the dollar limits of the power for any reason whatsoever and without the approval of any other person.[100] If a donee is given an annual withdrawal power measured by a fixed dollar amount which exceeds the 5 and 5 limits, the lapse of the power results in a taxable release of the power only to the extent of the excess.

Transfers Pursuant to a Property Settlement Agreement

Section 2516 sets forth special rules relating to the gift tax consequences of property transfers made pursuant to the terms of a property settlement agreement. If a married couple executes a written agreement relating to their marital and property rights and the parties are divorced within a three year period beginning on a date that is one year prior to when the agreement was made, transfers of property or interests in property pursuant to the terms of the agreement to either spouse in settlement of the spouse's marital or property rights or to provide a reasonable allowance for the support of the issue of the marriage during minority are deemed to be transfers for adequate and full consideration in money or money's worth and are therefore not transfers for gift tax purposes.[101] Section 2516 applies even though the agreement is not approved by the court.

Disclaimers

A disclaimer is a refusal to accept a gift of property, whether made during lifetime or at death. Following a disclaimer, the property interest disclaimed will pass as specified in the state's disclaimer statute. Normally, the property disclaimed will pass as if the disclaimant had predeceased the date on which the property interest was created, which is usually the date of the donor-decedent's death.[102] Disclaimers are frequent in estate and gift tax planning. They are most often used by spouses to adjust the amount of the marital deduction or by an estate beneficiary with an already large estate who would prefer that the estate property pass instead to the next generation.

If a person makes a qualified disclaimer that satisfies the provision of Section 2518(b), the estate or gift tax is to be computed as if the disclaimant never had a right to the disclaimed property.[103] For example, if T devises $100,000 to spouse S who disclaims the devise in accordance with the

---

[99] I.R.C. § 2514(e).

[100] *See also* Section 15.4, note 243 et seq.

[101] I.R.C. § 2516.

[102] For a detailed discussion of disclaimers, *see* Section 2.8.

[103] I.R.C. § 2518.

procedure in the state disclaimer statute, and by reason of the disclaimer the devise passes to friend F, the devise is treated as passing directly from T to F. Consequently, the disclaimed devise will not qualify for the estate tax marital deduction. Likewise, it would not be treated as a taxable gift from S to F. Alternatively, if T devises $100,000 to Child A who timely disclaims and, as a result of the disclaimer the property passes to T's spouse, the property is deemed to pass from T to the spouse and qualifies for the marital deduction.

Under Section 2518(b), a qualified disclaimer is an irrevocable and unqualified refusal by a disclaimant to accept an interest in property if:

1. The refusal is in writing;[104]

2. The writing is received by the transferor of the disclaimed interest, by the transferor's legal representative or by the holder of the legal title to the property from which the disclaimed interest is carved, not later than nine months after the day on which the transfer creating the interest is made.[105] However, in no event will the period for making the disclaimer expire until nine months after the day on which the disclaimant attains age twenty-one;[106]

3. The disclaimant has not accepted the interest or any of its benefits prior to the disclaimer;[107] and

4. The disclaimed interest will pass as a result of the disclaimer and without any direction on the part of the disclaimant to either the decedent's spouse or to a person other than the disclaimant.[108] Thus, a decedent's spouse may effectively disclaim an interest passing to the spouse under the decedent's will even though the disclaimed interest would then pass into a trust of which the spouse is the income beneficiary.

A disclaimer of an undivided portion of an interest is treated as a qualified disclaimer of the portion of the interest if the disclaimer otherwise satisfies the foregoing four requirements.[109]

Qualifying Income Interest for Life

If a person makes a gift of a qualifying income interest for life in any property, the transferor is deemed to have transferred the remainder interest as well.[110] A more thorough discussion of this provision is contained in the section on qualified terminable interest property.[111]

---

[104] I.R.C. 2518(b)(1).

[105] I.R.C. § 2518(b)(2)(A).

[106] I.R.C. § 2518(b)(2)(B).

[107] I.R.C. § 2518(b)(3).

[108] I.R.C. § 2518(b)(4). As to what happens to disclaimed property under state law, *see* Section 2.8, note 353 et seq.

[109] I.R.C. § 2518(c)(1).

[110] I.R.C. § 2519.

[111] *See* Section 15.4, paragraph following note 291.

Gifts to Charity or to the Donor's Spouse

Gifts to qualified[112] charitable organizations qualify for an unlimited charitable deduction.[113] Special rules apply when gifts are made in trust for the benefit of both charities and private individuals.[114] These special rules are more fully discussed in the section on the estate tax charitable deduction.[115]

A gift to the donor's spouse qualifies for an unlimited marital deduction[116] so long as the gift is not disqualified for the deduction under the nondeductible terminable interest rule.[117] The marital deduction rules are more fully discussed in the section on the estate tax marital deduction.[118]

§ 15.4 The Estate Tax

A federal estate tax is a tax on the right to transfer property at death.[119] The tax is measured against a tax base that includes not only the assets of decedent's probate estate[120] but also certain gifts by the decedent during life that are deemed to be the equivalent of testamentary transfers because the decedent retained either an interest in or power over the gift. Items included in a decedent's gross estate are reduced by various deductions to calculate decedent's taxable estate.

The gross estate is computed by adding the following:

1. Property owned at death.[121]
2. Certain property transferred within three years of death.[122]
3. Lifetime transfers in which decedent retained an interest for life.[123]
4. Certain lifetime transfers taking effect at the decedent's death.[124]
5. Revocable transfers.[125]
6. Annuities.[126]

---

[112] I.R.C. § 2522(a). The definition of "charitable" for tax purposes, while similar, is not identical to its definition for "trust law" purposes. *See* Section 10.10, note 570 et seq.; Section 15.4, note 271.

[113] I.R.C. § 2522.

[114] I.R.C. § 2522(c).

[115] Section 15.4, note 271 et seq.

[116] I.R.C. § 2523.

[117] I.R.C. § 2523(b).

[118] *See* Section 15.4, note 280 et seq.

[119] *See* Hodel v. Irving, 481 U.S. 704 (1987) (holding that the complete abolition of both the devise and descent of property can be an unconstitutional taking).

[120] Probate estate property is limited to property capable of passing by a decedent's will or under the laws of intestate succession. Thus, it excludes such property as joint tenancy property, life insurance and annuities payable to a named beneficiary. For possible, non-tax advantages to keeping property out of the probate estate, *see* Section 10.5.

[121] I.R.C. § 2033.

[122] I.R.C. § 2035.

[123] I.R.C. § 2036.

[124] I.R.C. § 2037.

[125] I.R.C. § 2038.

[126] I.R.C. § 2039.

7. Joint tenancy property.[127]
8. General powers of appointment.[128]
9. Life insurance.[129]
10. Qualified Terminable Interest Property.[130]

The deductions available to compute the decedent's taxable estate are:

1. Debts, expenses, and taxes.[131]
2. Losses.[132]
3. Charitable deduction.[133]
4. Marital deduction.[134]
5. State death taxes.[135]

To assure that cumulative lifetime and testamentary transfers are taxed in accordance with the progressive unified rate schedule, the estate tax base also includes the value of decedent's adjusted taxable gifts.[136] A tentative estate tax is then computed against this base which is then reduced by the gift taxes payable on the adjusted taxable gifts. The resulting tax is then reduced by the unified credit[137] and, if applicable, the credit for pre-1977 gift taxes,[138] the tax on prior transfers,[139] and the foreign death tax credit.[140]

The amount of the unified credit is set so that an estate tax base of $11,700,000 (2021 figure) will be excluded from tax, an amount that is adjusted for inflation after 2011.[141] The amount of the exclusion is increased by the amount of any exclusion unused by the decedent's predeceased spouse, or if more than one, the decedent's last predeceased spouse. This "portability" provision, which has major implications in planning for married couples, is discussed further later in this section.[142]

---

[127] I.R.C. § 2040.

[128] I.R.C. § 2041.

[129] I.R.C. § 2042.

[130] I.R.C. § 2044.

[131] I.R.C. § 2053.

[132] I.R.C. § 2054.

[133] I.R.C. § 2055.

[134] I.R.C. § 2056.

[135] I.R.C. § 2058.

[136] Adjusted taxable gifts are gifts made after December 31, 1976 that are not included in the decedent's gross estate. I.R.C. § 2001(b). To prevent double counting, taxable gifts that would be taxed again as part of the estate tax base are "adjusted" or netted out for purposes of the estate tax computation. While "adjusted taxable gifts" are added to the taxable estate to assure progressivity in the calculation of the estate tax, that should not suggest there is no benefit in making lifetime gifts. Once a lifetime gift is made subsequent appreciation on that gift and income earned is excluded from both the donor's gift and estate tax base.

[137] I.R.C. § 2010. *See also* Chart I at the end of the chapter.

[138] I.R.C. § 2012.

[139] I.R.C. § 2013.

[140] I.R.C. § 2014.

[141] I.R.C. § 2010(c).

[142] *See infra*, note 300.

To illustrate computation of the estate tax, suppose John dies in 2021 when the unified credit was $4,625,800, leaving a gross estate of $14,000,000, deductions of $1,000,000, and adjusted taxable gifts of $2,000,000. The estate tax on John's estate is $1,804,000, determined as follows:

Gross estate	$14,000,000
Less: Deductions	1,000,000
Taxable estate	$13,000,000
Adjusted taxable gifts	2,000,000
Estate tax base	$15,000,000
Tentative tax on base	$5,945,800
Gift tax payable on adjusted taxable gifts	-0-
Tentative tax less gift tax payable	$5,945,800
Unified Credit	4,625,800
Federal estate tax	$1,320,000

The above calculation assumes that the exclusion for John was not enlarged by the unused exclusion of a predeceased spouse. Had John's spouse predeceased and not used any of her exclusion, the amount of the spouse's unused exclusion would have been added to John's exclusion under portability, potentially eliminating the estate tax payable at John's death.

Valuation and Income Tax Basis; Due Date of the Return

Two separate questions must be kept clearly in mind when calculating the value of the gross estate. The first is whether a particular asset is included in the gross estate; the second is what is the included asset's value. An included asset's value is determined under one of three sections of the estate tax law.

Section 2031 provides that assets included in the gross estate are valued at the "fair market value" on the date of the decedent's death. Similar to the gift tax, fair market value is determined under the willing seller-willing buyer test.[143]

In lieu of the date of death valuation method, the personal representative may elect on the estate tax return to value all of the gross estate assets under the alternate valuation method.[144] This valuation method is available only if as a result of the election: (1) the value of the gross estate will be less than its value based upon date of death values and (2) the amount of the estate tax will be less than it would be if estate tax values were determined on decedent's date of death.[145] This provision prevents the use of the alternate valuation method merely for the purpose of obtaining higher estate tax values and therefor a

[143] Treas.Reg. § 20.2031–1(b).

[144] I.R.C. § 2032(a).

[145] I.R.C. § 2032(c)

higher income tax basis in cases where no estate tax is due. This might occur where the estate qualified for an unlimited marital deduction.

Under the alternate valuation method gross estate assets are valued on the sixth month anniversary of the decedent's date of death or, if any asset is sold, distributed, exchanged, or otherwise disposed of between the date of decedent's death and six months thereafter, on the date of its sale, distribution, exchange, or other disposition. To illustrate, if Harry owned Asset A valued at $100 at his death and $50 on the sixth month anniversary of his death, Asset A would be valued at $100 if date of death values were used or at $50 if the alternate valuation method is used. If between Harry's death and the sixth month anniversary thereof Asset A were sold for $65 and Harry's estate was valued under the alternate valuation method, Asset A would be valued at $65.

Under Section 2032A, certain qualifying real estate can be valued under the so-called "special use" valuation method.[146] Under this method, value is not determined by reference to the property's highest and best use but at its actual value taking account of its farming or business use. Section 2032A is exceptionally complicated by rules designed to assure that the statutory benefits are available only to committed, long-time farm and small-business owners.

The income tax basis of inherited property equals its estate tax value determined as of date of death or under the alternate or special use valuation methods.[147] Thus, decedent's income tax basis in the property is ignored in favor of a basis that is "stepped up" (or "stepped down") to the property's estate tax value. This rule applies even if the decedent's estate is too small to require the filing of an estate tax return. In such case, the property's fair market value on the date of decedent's death controls the determination of basis because the alternate valuation method is available only for estates for which an estate tax return must be filed.[148]

The effect of Section 1014 is to allow increases in the value of property between the time decedent acquired the property and the time the decedent dies to escape income tax. Similarly, losses in value between those dates go unrecognized.

The federal estate tax return, Form 706, and any estate tax payable thereon, is due nine months after the date of the decedent's death unless the time is extended.[149]

Property Owned at Death

Section 2033 subjects "property owned by the decedent" to inclusion in the decedent's gross estate. The meaning of the phrase "property owned by the decedent" is not obvious. Is it limited to assets passing by will or intestate succession? Or does it also include nonprobate assets such as joint tenancies in which the decedent immediately before death had a property interest? The

---

[146] I.R.C. § 2032A.

[147] I.R.C. § 1014; Section 15.2, note 30 et seq.

[148] *See* Rev. Rul. 56–60, 1956–1 C.B. 443; Treas.Reg. § 20.2032–1(b)(1).

[149] I.R.C. § 6075(a).

Supreme Court early on held that Section 2033 excludes nonprobate assets such as a joint tenancy or revocable trust that is includable in the gross estate under some other section.[150] Section 2033 is instead limited to probate estate assets, which would include personal property, whether tangible or intangible, over which the decedent had absolute ownership, and real property that the decedent owned in fee simple or as a tenant-in-common.

The categories of assets subject to Section 2033 is almost limitless. It includes real property, tangible and intangible personal property, such as stocks, bonds, notes and cash, and a variety of miscellaneous rights, including claims to tax refunds and the value at the date of death of lawsuits in which the decedent was a plaintiff. The decedent's property interest must have been a beneficial interest.[151] Thus, if decedent owned property merely as a trustee at the time of the decedent's death, the property is not included in the decedent's gross estate.[152] Decedent's property interest can be a future interest[153] but does not include interests that terminate at the decedent's death. Thus, a decedent's life estate that terminated at decedent's death is not included in the decedent's gross estate.[154]

Generally, whether decedent has a property interest is determined under state law,[155] but a state law characterization of an interest does not always control for federal estate tax purposes. This principle is well illustrated by the case of *Commissioner v. Bosch's Estate*.[156] After Mr. Bosch died his estate claimed a marital deduction for property passing to Mrs. Bosch under the terms of a revocable trust that was included in Mr. Bosch's gross estate. The availability of that deduction depended upon whether Mrs. Bosch possessed a general power of appointment over the trust.[157] While the case was pending in the Tax Court, the executor of Mr. Bosch's estate initiated a state court proceeding for the settlement of certain accounts. In that proceeding, to which the federal government was not a party, it was held that Mrs. Bosch had a general power of appointment. The Tax Court accepted the state court decision as controlling and a divided Court of Appeals affirmed. The Supreme Court reversed, holding that the federal courts, in interpreting a federal statute, are not bound by a state court decision unless that decision was issued by the state's highest court. Lower court decisions need receive only "proper regard."

Section 2034 clarifies that inclusion in the gross estate is not affected by the fact a property interest is subject to a surviving spouse's claim for dower, curtesy or a statutory right in lieu thereof.[158] Section 2034, however, applies only to marital property rights arising at the decedent's death. A surviving spouse's interest in community property, an interest that is created when the

---

[150] Helvering v. Safe Deposit & Trust Co. of Baltimore, 316 U.S. 56 (1942).

[151] *See, e.g.* Reed v. Commissioner, 36 F.2d 867 (5th Cir.1930).

[152] Reed, 36 F.2d 867.

[153] Arrington v. U.S., 34 Fed. Cl. 144 (1995).

[154] May v. Heiner, 281 U.S. 238 (1930).

[155] Blair v. Commissioner, 300 U.S. 5 (1937).

[156] 387 U.S. 456 (1967).

[157] I.R.C. § 2056(b)(5). *See also infra* note 234 et seq.

[158] I.R.C. § 2034.

asset was acquired, is not includable in the decedent's gross estate. The spouse's interest was at all times owned by the spouse.

Transfers Within Three Years of Death

Prior to 1977, Section 2035 included in the gross estate gifts made within three years of death that were made in contemplation of death. But the scope of this provision was significantly narrowed by the 1976 Tax Reform Act.[159] The provision was narrowed to include only lifetime transfers that would have been includable in the gross estate under Sections 2036, 2037, 2038, or 2042 had the gift not been made.[160] In addition and as explained below, also brought back into the gross estate is any gift tax paid on gifts by the decedent or the decedent's spouse that were made within three years of the decedent's death.[161] Significantly, Section 2035 does not apply to any transfers made during life from the decedent's individual assets. Consequently, there is a major incentive for individuals to make gifts, particularly annual exclusion gifts, shortly before death.

The gross estate includes the value of all life insurance policies transferred by the decedent within three years of the decedent's death for less than adequate and full consideration in money or money's worth.[162] For example, if Mary gratuitously transfers to Andy a life insurance policy having a cash value on the date of transfer of $5,000 and a face value of $100,000 and dies within three years of the transfer, $100,000 is included in Mary's gross estate. If, on the other hand, Andy paid Mary $5,000 for the transfer, the policy is excluded from Mary's gross estate because the lifetime transfer was for adequate and full consideration in money or money's worth.

The gross estate also includes the value of any interest in property transferred by the decedent within three years of death or the value of any property over which the decedent relinquished a power within three years of death if the value of such property would have been included in the decedent's gross estate under Section 2036 (relating to retained life estates), 2037 (relating to transfers taking effect at death) and 2038 (relating to revocable transfers) had the transfer or relinquishment not occurred.[163] However, an exception is created for the standard revocable trust that is intended to avoid probate. Such trusts are includable in the gross estate under Section 2038 because of the grantor's power of revocation. Consequently, without a special exception, distributions from such trusts made within three years of the grantor's death to beneficiaries other than the grantor would have been includable in the settlor's gross estate under Section 2035. The exception excludes from the three-year rule distributions from, or powers relinquished over, revocable trusts if the trust was revocable and the grantor was treated as owner of the trust for income tax purposes under the grantor trust rules.[164] For example, suppose Gary creates a revocable trust and two years before he

[159] Tax Reform Act of 1976, Pub. L. No. 94–455, § 2001(a)(5), (d)(1) (Oct. 4, 1876).

[160] I.R.C. § 2035(a).

[161] I.R.C. § 2035(b).

[162] I.R.C. § 2035(a)(2).

[163] I.R.C. § 2035(a)(2).

[164] I.R.C. § 2035(e). The applicable grantor trust provision is I.R.C. § 676.

died, he directs the trustee to distribute $15,000 of trust principal to Anita. In this case, the distribution is treated as if Gary made it directly from his individual funds. The $15,000 is not brought back into Gary's gross estate and the transfer will qualify for the gift tax annual exclusion.

Lastly, the gross estate also includes the amount of any gift taxes paid by the decedent or the decedent's estate on gifts made by the decedent or the decedent's spouse after December 31, 1976 and within the three years preceding the decedent's death.[165] This section prevents the making of substantial gifts within three years of death for the purposes (intended or not) of removing the gift tax thereon from the donor's estate tax base. The estate tax is a so-called "gross up" tax meaning that the estate tax base includes funds that will be used to pay the estate tax itself. The gift tax, on the other hand, is not grossed up. The gift tax is computed on the value of the gift, not the value of the gift increased by the amount of gift tax thereon.

Transfers with a Retained Life Estate

The gross estate includes the value of all property transferred by the decedent during life, in trust or otherwise, for less than adequate and full consideration in money or money's worth[166] and under which the decedent retained for one of three time periods (1) life, (2) any period not ascertainable without reference to decedent's death,[167] or (3) any period that does not in fact end before the decedent's death[168] either (1) the possession or enjoyment of, or the right to receive the income from, the transferred property, or (2) the right to designate the persons who shall enjoy the transferred property or the income therefrom.

The most common example of a retained life estate transfer that is included in the decedent's gross estate occurs when a decedent transferred property in trust and retained the income interest in the trust for life.[169] Similarly, if decedent transferred real property and retained a life estate in the property, express or implied, then at death the real estate will be included in the decedent's gross estate.[170]

---

165 I.R.C. § 2035(b).

166 If decedent received partial consideration for the transfer, then the amount that would otherwise be included in the decedent's gross estate under Section 2036 is reduced by the amount of the partial consideration received. *See generally* I.R.C. § 2043.

167 For example, if decedent retained the income for a period that ended on the last day of the month preceding the decedent's death, Section 2036 applies because the period of time for which decedent retained the income cannot be determined without reference to the date of the decedent's death.

168 For example, suppose decedent retained the income from the property transferred in trust for 10 years and decedent died three years after the transfer was made. Decedent retained an interest that did not in fact end before the decedent's death. If decedent outlived the 10 year period, Section 2036 is inapplicable.

169 I.R.C. § 2036(a)(1).

170 *See, e.g.*, Estate of Whitt v. Commissioner, 751 F.2d 1548 (11th Cir. 1985). *But see* Gutchess v. Commissioner, 46 T.C. 554 (1966), acq., 1967–1 C.B. 2 (Section 2036 inapplicable to case where husband transfers family home to wife and continues to live in home as incident of the marital relationship.).

A transfer with a retained life estate also occurs where the decedent retained the right to have the income used to discharge decedent's legal obligations, such as the support of the decedent's dependents.[171]

There has been much litigation focusing on whether decedent's right must be expressly retained or whether it is sufficient that decedent's right arises from an implied understanding. Where payments to the decedent are wholly discretionary and there has been no implied understanding to make payments to the decedent, Section 2036 may not apply. Where, however, payments to the decedent were to be wholly discretionary but there had been actual payments of income to the decedent during the decedent's life, receipt may give rise to an inference of an implied understanding.[172] It would appear that the more regularized the "discretionary" income payments are, the greater the inference.

A decedent is deemed to have retained the use or enjoyment or the right to income from transferred property if the decedent retained the right to vote shares of controlled corporation stock[173] even though decedent retained no right to the dividends paid on the stock.

Transfers with a retained life estate also include transfers in which decedent did not retain any economic benefits but retained the power, exercisable alone or in conjunction with any other person, to designate the persons who shall possess or enjoy the transferred property or the income therefrom.[174] Thus, if John creates a trust for the primary benefit of Alice, Bob and Charlie and retains the power to determine their respective shares of the income for his life, the trust is included in John's gross estate.

The statute also applies where there are one or more income beneficiaries and the decedent retained the power to direct that income be accumulated for ultimate distribution to the remainderman of the trust.[175] For example, if Mary

---

[171] *See* Commissioner v. Douglass' Estate, 143 F.2d 961 (3d Cir.1944), acq. 1971–1 C.B. 2; Estate of Chrysler v. Commissioner, 44 T.C. 55 (1965), *rev'd*, 361 F.2d 508 (2d Cir.1966), acq. in result only, 1970–2 C.B. xix; National Bank of Commerce in Memphis v. Henslee, 179 F.Supp. 346 (M.D.Tenn.1959); Exchange Bank of Fla. v. United States, 694 F.2d 1261, 82–2 USTC ¶ 13,505 (Fed.Cir.1982).

In those cases where decedent's right to income is limited to either decedent's support or the support of a dependent, it may be relevant for valuation purposes to consider the level of support due the decedent or decedent's dependent. *See* Pardee's Estate v. Commissioner, 49 T.C. 140, 148 (1967).

[172] *See* Skinner's Estate v. United States, 316 F.2d 517 (3d Cir.1963). *See also* McNichol's Estate v. Commissioner, 265 F.2d 667 (3d Cir.1959); Estate of German v. United States, 55 AFTR2d 85–1577 (Ct.Cl.1985). But *see* Estate of Uhl v. Commissioner, 25 T.C. 22 (1955), *rev'd*, 241 F.2d 867 (7th Cir.1957) (in dicta concluding that if under local law the creditors of the grantor of a wholly discretionary trust could reach the trust assets, trust included in gross estate because grantor could reach trust assets merely by incurring debt). *Cf.* Outwin v. Commissioner, 76 T.C. 153 (1981) (grantor of discretionary trust makes incomplete gift where, under state law, grantor's creditors could reach the trust assets to satisfy grantor's debts accruing after trust created.

[173] I.R.C. § 2036(b). A corporation is a controlled corporation if at any time after the transfer of the corporation's stock and within three years of the decedent's death the decedent owned (using family attribution rules under Section 318) or had the right to vote, alone or in conjunction with another, stock possessing 20% or more of the total combined voting power of all classes of the corporation's stock.

This statutory section legislatively overturns the holding in United States v. Byrum, 408 U.S. 125 (1972).

[174] I.R.C. § 2036(a)(2).

[175] *Cf.* United States v. O'Malley, 383 U.S. 627 (1966).

creates a trust to pay the income to John, remainder to John's children and retains the power to accumulate the income, the trust is included in Mary's gross estate because her retained power permits her to shift the enjoyment of the income from John to his children.

Section 2036(a)(2) is inapplicable if decedent retained only managerial powers over the transferred property, such as the power to allocate receipts and disbursements between income and principal or the power to make investments.[176] Furthermore, the statute is inapplicable if the power to designate is controlled by an ascertainable standard and the beneficiaries are not dependents of the decedent.[177] An ascertainable standard is a standard relating to health, education, or support. It does not include a power to pay for mere comfort or happiness.[178]

Section 2036(a)(2) applies even though decedent's power is exercisable only in conjunction with a person having a substantial adverse interest in its exercise.[179] Thus, even though the gift of the interest is complete for gift tax purposes,[180] the transferred property is still in the donor-decedent's gross estate. But, because under Section 2001 taxable gifts that are later included in the gross estate ("adjusted taxable gifts") are not counted in computing the federal estate tax, effectively only the value of the appreciation, if any, between the time of the gift and the donor-decedent's date of death is subject to estate tax.

Section 2036(a)(2) applies even if the decedent's power is exercisable only in a fiduciary capacity. Furthermore, even if the decedent did not retain the power directly but granted it exclusively to a third party trustee, Section 2036 applies if the decedent retained the power to fire the trustee and appoint a successor trustee, including himself.[181] The statute also applies if decedent could name himself trustee only if the independent trustee resigned, died or was removed from office.[182]

While the courts have imputed a trustee's powers to a settlor only if the settlor is able to place herself in the office of trustee, the Service has long sought to bring in trusts even if the settlor could only place someone else in office. In *Revenue Ruling 79–353*,[183] the Service included an irrevocable trust in the settlor's gross estate based solely on the settlor's power to remove a corporate trustee and to replace it with another corporate trustee. The

---

[176] *See, e.g.*, Old Colony Trust Co. v. United States, 423 F.2d 601 (1st Cir.1970).

[177] *See, e.g.*, Jennings v. Smith, 161 F.2d 74 (2d Cir.1947); Leopold v. United States, 510 F.2d 617 (9th Cir.1975).

[178] *See* Old Colony Trust Co. v. United States, 423 F.2d 601 (1st Cir.1970).

[179] Treas. Reg. § 20.2036–1(b)(3).

[180] Treas. Reg. § 25.2511–2(e). *See* Section 15.3, note 72 et seq.

[181] Treas.Reg. § 20.2036–1(b)(3).

[182] Estate of Farrel v. United States, 213 Ct.Cl. 622, 553 F.2d 637 (1977). The Service maintained at one time that the statute applies if the original trustee was a corporate trustee and decedent could fire the corporate trustee and appoint only another corporate trustee. *See* Rev. Rul. 79–353, 1979–2 C.B. 325. The Service later limited inclusion to situations where the replacement trustee is the settlor's spouse, other close family, or an employee. Rev. Rul. 95–58, 1995–2 C.B. 191. The Service's 1979 ruling was repudiated in Estate of Wall v. Commissioner, 101 T.C. 300 (1993), and the logic of that opinion suggest that the court would also reject the 1995 ruling.

[183] 1979–2 C.B. 325.

Service's position was later repudiated by the Tax Court.[184] Following this decision, the Service limited its prior ruling, concluding that a power to remove and replace a trustee with another person triggers inclusion of the trust in the gross estate only if the "another person" is the settlor's spouse, other close family, or an employee.[185]

The reciprocal trust doctrine can cause a trust to be includable under Section 2036 even though the decedent was not the formal creator of the trust. For example, suppose John creates a trust to pay the income to Mary for life, remainder to their children, and Mary creates a trust to pay the income to John for life, remainder to their children. Formally, neither John nor Mary is the creator of the trust of which he or she is the income beneficiary. Nonetheless, Section 2036 could apply causing the trust formally created by John of which Mary is the income beneficiary to be included in Mary's gross estate (and the trust formally created by Mary of which John is the income beneficiary to be included in John's gross estate) if a court concluded that the trusts were reciprocal.[186] The basic notion underlying the reciprocal trust doctrine, as originally formulated,[187] was that if two trusts were created in consideration of each other, the grantors of each trust would be switched for estate tax purposes with the result that each would be deemed to be the substantive grantor of the trust formally created by the other. This initial test was based upon subjective intent. But the Supreme Court later held that application of the reciprocal trust doctrine did not depend upon a finding that the trusts were created in consideration of each other.[188] Rather, "the application of the . . . doctrine requires only that the trusts be interrelated, and that the arrangement, to the extent of mutual value, leaves the settlor in approximately the same economic position as they would have been in had they created trusts naming themselves as life beneficiaries."[189]

If Section 2036 applies then the entire trust, not merely the value of the decedent's retained interest, generally is included in the decedent's gross estate.[190] However, if decedent retained only a portion of the income interest or the right to designate only a portion of the income, then only a like portion would be included in the decedent's gross estate under Section 2036. For example, if decedent created a trust and retained only one-half of the income, then only one-half of the trust would be included in the decedent's gross estate.[191]

---

184 Estate of Wall v. Commissioner, 101 T.C. 300 (1993).

185 Rev. Rul. 95–58, 1995–2 C.B. 191. The definition of the disqualified person is taken from I.R.C. § 672(c).

186 The reciprocal trust doctrine can also apply to Section 2037 and Section 2038 transfers.

187 *See* Lehman v. Commissioner, 109 F.2d 99 (2d Cir.1940).

188 United States v. Grace's Estate, 395 U.S. 316 (1969).

189 Grace's Estate, 395 U.S. at 324.

190 Treas.Reg. § 20.2036–1(a). *Cf.* I.R.C. § 2038, under which only interests subject to a power to revoke, alter, amend or terminate are included in the decedent's gross estate. This would also include any income accumulated as a result of the decedent's lifetime directions. *See* United States v. O'Malley, 383 U.S. 627 (1966).

191 Treas.Reg. § 20.2036–1(a). If the decedent retained the right to a specific dollar amount of income, then only such percentile of the trust necessary to produce that amount of income is

Also, if a decedent creates an interest in property that precedes the decedent's retained interest, the value of the preceding interest is excluded from the decedent's gross estate. For example, suppose George created a trust to pay the income to Ann for life, then to George for life, remainder to Barney, and George dies survived by Ann and Barney. The trust is includable in George's gross estate under Section 2036 because of George's retained life estate, but the value of Ann's preceding income interest would be excluded from the valuation.[192]

Transfers Taking Effect at Death

Section 2037 provides that the gross estate includes the value of all property transferred by the decedent during life for less than an adequate and full consideration in money or money's worth if (1) possession or enjoyment of the property transferred by the decedent can only be obtained by the transferee surviving the decedent *and* (2) immediately before the decedent's death, decedent had a reversionary interest retained at the time of transfer valued at more than 5% of the transferred property.[193] However, Section 2037 will not apply if possession or enjoyment could have been obtained by a beneficiary during the decedent's life through the exercise by that beneficiary of a general power of appointment that was exercisable immediately before the decedent's death.[194] The statute applies only if both the survivorship test and the reversionary interest test are satisfied. If the decedent has a reversion in the property but Section 2037 is inapplicable, the value of the reversion is included in decedent's gross estate under Section 2033.[195]

The survivorship test relates to whether a beneficiary can obtain possession or enjoyment of the transferred property *only* by surviving the decedent. If John transfers property to Amy for life, remainder to Amy's children who survive her, Section 2037 is inapplicable even though John has a reversionary interest because neither Amy nor her children must survive John to obtain possession or enjoyment of their interest. On the other hand, if John transfers property to Amy for life, remainder to such of Amy's children as survive John, Section 2037's survivorship test is met and, if the value of John's reversion exceeds 5% of the value of the trust immediately before John's death, the value of the remainder is included in John's gross estate.

Under the reversionary test, decedent must have retained a reversionary interest valued at more than 5% immediately before death using the appropriate valuation methods and tables. A reversionary interest includes any possibility that the transferred property will return to the decedent or to the decedent's estate or that the property will be subject to decedent's power of

---

included in the decedent's gross estate. *See* United States National Bank v. United States, 188 F.Supp. 332 (D.C.Or.1960). *Cf.*, Industrial Trust Co. v. Commissioner, 165 F.2d 142 (1st Cir.1947).

[192] *See* Marks v. Higgins, 213 F.2d 884 (2d Cir.1954). *See also* Treas.Reg. § 20.2036–1(a).

[193] If decedent received partial consideration for the transfer, then the amount otherwise included under Section 2037 is reduced by the amount of partial consideration received. *See* I.R.C. § 2043.

[194] I.R.C. § 2037(b).

[195] *See* Graham v. Commissioner, 46 T.C. 415 (1966).

disposition.[196] A power of disposition need not be a general power of appointment.[197] It is irrelevant whether the reversionary interest arises under the express terms of the governing instrument or by operation of law.[198]

The value of the reversionary interest must exceed 5%. In determining whether the more than 5% test is met, the reversionary interest is valued immediately before the decedent's death on the assumption that the estate assets are valued under the date of death valuation method only.[199] The value of the reversionary interest is compared to the value of the entire property not merely the value of the interest dependent upon survivorship.[200]

Even if both the reversionary interest and survivorship tests are met, Section 2037 is inapplicable if possession or enjoyment of the property could be obtained by a beneficiary during decedent's life through exercise by that beneficiary of a general power of appointment.[201] Suppose Sam creates a trust to pay the income to Betsy for life, remainder to her children who survive Sam. Sam grants Betsy a general inter-vivos power to appoint the property to anyone. In this case even though Sam's reversionary interest meets the more than 5% test, Section 2037 is inapplicable because Betsy has a general power of appointment.[202]

If Section 2037 applies, the amount included in the decedent's gross estate is the value of the interest whose possession or enjoyment is dependent upon surviving the decedent. Thus, if Section 2037 applies to John's transfer to Alice for life, remainder to Alice's children who survive John, only the children's interest is included in John's gross estate.

Revocable Transfers

The gross estate includes the value of all interests in property transferred by the decedent during life for less than adequate and full consideration in money or money's worth which at the time of the decedent's death are subject to a power, exercisable by the decedent alone or in conjunction with any other person, to alter, amend, revoke or terminate.[203] If the decedent had a power of

---

[196] A power of disposition does not include the possibility that the income from the property alone will be subject to the power. I.R.C. § 2037(b). If decedent had such a power either Section 2036 or 2038 would apply.

The possibility the decedent might receive back the property by inheritance through the estate of another person is not a reversionary interest. Treas.Reg. § 20.2037–1(c)(2).

[197] *See* Costin v. Cripe, 235 F.2d 162 (7th Cir.1956).

[198] *But see* Treas.Reg. § 20.2037–1(f).

[199] Treas.Reg. § 20.2037–1(c)(3). For Section 2037 purposes, the valuation tables should be used exclusively. The actual circumstances surrounding the decedent's death should be ignored. *See* Roy's Estate v. Commissioner, 54 T.C. 1317 (1970). *Contra,* Hall v. United States, 353 F.2d 500 (7th Cir.1965).

[200] Treas.Reg. § 20.2037–1(c)(4).

[201] I.R.C. § 2037(b).

[202] *See infra* note 234 et seq. for a discussion of powers of appointment.

[203] I.R.C. § 2038. If decedent received partial consideration for the transfer, the entire value less the amount of partial consideration received would be included in the gross estate. *See* I.R.C. § 2043. In most states, inter-vivos trusts are irrevocable unless the grantor expressly retains a power of revocation. However, in some states, the opposite rule applies. In those states it is essential to expressly provide in the trust instrument that the trust is irrevocable to avoid Section 2038.

revocation that was relinquished within three years of decedent's death, the property interest subject to such power also is included in the decedent's gross estate.[204]

In order for Section 2038 to apply the decedent must have possessed the power to alter, amend, revoke or terminate at the time of death or must have relinquished the power within three years of death. It is irrelevant whether the decedent's power was exercisable in a fiduciary capacity. If the power of revocation was only exercisable by someone other than the decedent, Section 2038 is inapplicable. However, if the decedent possessed the power to fire the trustee and hire himself as trustee, all the trustee's powers are attributable to the decedent, and, if the trustee possessed a power to alter, amend, revoke or terminate, the decedent will be deemed to possess that power as well.[205]

Section 2038 applies even though decedent had only a co-held power and even though the co-holder of the power has a substantial adverse interest in the exercise of the power.[206] Thus if Jim creates a trust to pay the income to Priscilla for life, remainder to Bonny, and Jim reserves a power exercisable only with Priscilla's consent to revoke the trust, the trust is included in Jim's gross estate even though Priscilla, who holds an adverse interest, must join in the exercise of the power. But suppose the trust provides that Jim can revoke the trust only with the consent of both Priscilla and Bonny. In *Helvering v. Helmholz*,[207] the Court held that a trust that could be revoked only with the consent of all beneficiaries of the trust was not includable in the grantor's gross estate because even in the absence of the revocation clause the settlor and beneficiaries could terminate the trust under state law.[208] Therefore, the clause did not add to rights the grantor already possessed.[209]

Section 2038 applies even though the deceased transferor did not retain the power at the time of the transfer. Under the statute, the key is whether the grantor held the power at death, and this is clarified by a statutory parenthetical stating that the source of the power is irrelevant. For example, suppose John creates a trust that a trustee is empowered to alter or amend and names Mary as trustee. Ten years later, Mary resigns and the court having jurisdiction of the trust appoints John as successor trustee. John dies in possession of the power to alter or amend. The trust is included in John's gross estate.

In order for Section 2038 to apply, the decedent must have possessed a power to "alter, amend, revoke or terminate." The power to revoke and power to terminate appear to be synonymous. Both appear to address a power permitting the decedent, through exercise of the power, to regain title or possession of the trust property. A power to alter or amend contemplates a power that affects the enjoyment of the trust property or some interest therein

---

[204] I.R.C. § 2038(a)(1). *See also* I.R.C. § 2035(d)(2).

[205] Treas.Reg. § 20.2038–1(a)(3). *See also supra* notes 181 et seq.

[206] Helvering v. City Bank Farmers Trust Co., 296 U.S. 85 (1935).

[207] 296 U.S. 93 (1935).

[208] For the ability of the settlor and beneficiaries to terminate an irrevocable trust, *see* Section 10.9 note 504 et seq.

[209] *Accord*, Treas.Reg. § 20.2038–1(a)(2).

without revoking or terminating the trust. It does not include powers to administer or manage the trust property, such as a power to control investments or allocate receipts between income and principal.[210] Examples of Section 2038 powers include situations where the grantor named himself trustee and, as trustee, had power to make discretionary distributions among a group of beneficiaries,[211] and even situations where the grantor merely held the right to determine when distributions would be made to a single beneficiary.[212] However, If the power is limited by an ascertainable standard relating to health, support, education or maintenance, it is not a power to alter or amend for purposes of Section 2038 unless the exercise of the power permitted the deceased transferor to enjoy the economic benefits of the trust.[213]

Section 2038 applies only if the deceased transferor possessed the power at death or the power was relinquished within three years of death.[214] If the decedent's power was subject to a contingency beyond the decedent's control such that it was not exercisable at the time of the decedent's death, then Section 2038 is inapplicable.[215] For example, if John transfers property subject to his power to name himself trustee in the event of a vacancy, the trust is not includable under Section 2038 unless the office of trustee was in fact vacant at John's death. On the other hand, such a contingent power may be taxable under Section 2036.[216] A power is deemed to be in existence when decedent dies even though the decedent prior to death was incompetent to exercise the power.[217]

If the exercise of the power is subject to a precedent giving of notice that was not given at the time of the decedent's death, the power is deemed to be in existence at the time of the decedent's death.[218] For example, suppose Ron creates a trust of which he is not a beneficiary that is revocable by Ron only upon the giving of one year's notice. Ron dies without having given such notice. The trust is included in Ron's gross estate although the amount included in the gross estate is reduced by the value of the year's income that Ron would not have received had he in fact decided to revoke the trust.

Only the value of the interest subject to the power is included in the gross estate under Section 2038. If decedent possessed the power to revoke the entire trust, then the value of the entire trust is included in the gross estate. If the

---

[210] *See supra* note 176.

[211] Old Colony Trust Co. v. United States, 423 F.2d 601 (1st Cir.1970).

[212] Lober v. United States, 346 U.S. 335 (1953).

[213] *See* Jennings v. Smith, 161 F.2d 74 (2d Cir.1947). There has been much litigation concerning whether the language attached to a power limiting its exercise causes the power to be limited by an ascertainable standard. *See generally,* Bittker & Lokken, *Federal Taxation of Income, Estates & Gifts* ¶ 126.6.4.

[214] *But see* I.R.C. § 2035(e) (three-year rule inapplicable to transfers from a revocable trust where grantor was the owner of the trust under I.R.C. § 676).

[215] Treas.Reg. § 20.2038–1(b). On the other hand, the contingent power may be taxable under Section 2036 if the power is a right to designate who shall possess or enjoy the property or the income therefrom. *See* Treas.Reg. § 20.2036–1(b)(3)(iii).

[216] *See* Estate of Farrel v. United States, 213 Ct.Cl. 622, 553 F.2d 637 (1977).

[217] Hurd v. Commissioner, 160 F.2d 610 (1st Cir.1947). As to whether a conservator can exercise a power to revoke when the settlor is incompetent, *see* Section 5.2, notes 80–81.

[218] I.R.C. § 2038(b).

decedent possessed only the power to revoke the principal interest, the entire trust is again includable because revocation of the principal would eliminate the income interest. But if the power to revoke affects only the income interest, then only the value of that interest is included in the gross estate under Section 2038. For example, suppose Ron creates a trust to pay the income to Nancy for life, remainder to Bob. If Ron reserves the power to direct payment of income to Sue rather than Nancy, then under Section 2038 the value of the income interest is included in Ron's gross estate although under Section 2036(a)(2) the entire trust is included in Ron's gross estate based on the power to control income alone. If Ron reserves no power over the income but reserves a special testamentary power to designate a remainderman other than Bob, then the value of the remainder interest only is included in Ron's gross estate under Section 2038 and Section 2036 is inapplicable.[219]

As indicated by the preceding discussion, there is significant overlap between Section 2038 and Section 2036(a)(2). Most transfers taxable under one of these provisions are also taxable under the other, but there are important exceptions. Furthermore, the amount that is included in the gross estate can differ depending on which of the statutes governs. For example, if decedent possesses at death a power to alter the interests of two or more beneficiaries in trust income and that power was created a retained at the time of the original transfer, both Section 2036 and Section 2038 apply. However, under Section 2036(a)(2) the entire trust is included in the gross estate, whereas under Section 2038 only the income interest subject to the power would be included in the gross estate. If decedent did not retain the power at the time of the transfer but acquired the power thereafter, Section 2036 does not apply but Section 2038 would apply. Contingent powers are taxable under Section 2036 but not under Section 2038. If an asset is includable in the gross estate under more than one section of the Code, the asset is not taxed twice, but is includable in the gross estate under the Code section that results in the greatest inclusion.

Annuities

Under Section 2039 annuities with survivorship benefits can be included in a decedent's gross estate. More particularly, Section 2039(a) provides that the value of decedent's gross estate includes the value of an annuity or other payment[220] (other than life insurance) that is receivable by any beneficiary by reason of surviving the decedent under the terms of a contract or agreement[221] if, under the terms of the same contract or agreement, an annuity or other payment had been payable to the decedent at the time of death or the decedent had the right to receive an annuity or other payment,[222] alone or in conjunction with another person, for one of three time periods (life, a period not

---

[219] *See, e.g.*, Commissioner v. Bridgeport City Trust Co., 124 F.2d 48 (2d Cir.1941).

[220] This phrase refers to one or more payments that extend over a period of time whether the payments are equal or unequal, conditional or unconditional, periodic or sporadic. Treas.Reg. § 20.2039–1(b)(1).

[221] A contract or agreement includes any arrangement, understanding or plan, or any combination thereof, written or oral. Treas.Reg. § 20.2039–1(b)(1).

[222] This language contemplates the case where decedent had a right to receive an annuity in the future without regard to whether decedent was receiving payments at the time of the decedent's death. Treas.Reg. § 20.2039–1(b)(1).

ascertainable without reference to decedent's death, or a period that did not in fact end before the decedent's death).

Section 2039 applies only when something of value passes to a survivor. Consequently, it does not apply to a single life annuity payable to the decedent that terminates at the decedent's death but it does apply to a common commercial annuity contract providing benefits to the decedent and then to another upon the decedent's death. Section 2039 also applies to individual annuity arrangements between employers and employees, such as deferred compensation agreements.

Most importantly, Section 2039 also applies to annuity arrangements between employers and employees, such as deferred compensation agreements, and to the many common qualified retirement plan arrangements and IRAs to which contributions during the decedent's life were deductible for income tax purposes. These tax deferred plans are not only included in the decedent's gross estate but are taxable for income tax purposes when distributed as income in respect of a decedent under Section 691. Income in respect of a decedent is previously untaxed income that was earned by the decedent prior to death but which is not payable until after death. Income in respect of a decedent, while an asset of the estate, has a zero basis and is not entitled to a step-up in basis at the decedent's death.[223] Consequently, the aggregate income and estate tax liabilities associated with retirement plan assets can be quite significant. The impact of assessing both an income and estate tax on income in respect of a decedent is reduced to some extent by allowing the person taxed on the income in respect of a decedent in the person's gross income to claim a deduction for the estate tax attributable to such income.[224]

Marital Joint Tenancies

If husband and wife own property as joint tenants with right of survivorship or as tenants by the entireties, then upon the death of the first of them to die, one-half of the property's estate tax value is included in the decedent's gross estate.[225] The entire value of the property is included in the survivor's estate under Section 2033 unless transferred or consumed during the survivor's lifetime. Section 2040 is inapplicable to tenancies in common. With respect to a tenancy in common, each co-tenants' undivided interest is included in the co-tenant's gross estate under Section 2033. Because only one-half of a marital joint tenancy is included in the gross estate of the first spouse to die, only that half receives a step-up in basis for income tax purposes. For example, John and Mary purchase Blackacre for $50,000 as joint tenants with right of survivorship. John dies ten years later when Blackacre is worth $150,000. One-half of Blackacre's value is included in John's gross estate such that in Mary's hands Blackacre has a basis of $100,000 ($75,000 attributable to the half included in John's gross estate and $25,000 attributable to Mary's one-half cost basis in the property).[226] If John and Mary owned Blackacre as

---

[223] I.R.C. § 1014(c).

[224] I.R.C. § 691(c).

[225] I.R.C. § 2040(b).

[226] *See* I.R.C. § 1014(b)(9).

community property, only one-half of its value would be included in John's gross estate but both John and Mary's community halves would get a step-up in basis by virtue of a special rule in section 1014 applicable to community property.[227]

Other Joint Tenancies

Under Section 2040(a), a decedent's gross estate includes the entire value of all non-marital joint tenancy property in which the decedent had an interest at the time of the decedent's death, except to the extent the surviving joint tenancy can prove that he contributed part of the property itself or the purchase price of the property. If the decedent and the survivor acquired the joint tenancy property by gift, bequest or inheritance, the value of the property included in the gross estate of the first joint tenant to die is determined by dividing that value by the number of joint tenants.

To illustrate, suppose Andrea and Becky own Blackacre as joint tenants. Andrea dies survived by Becky. Blackacre's entire value is included in Andrea's gross estate unless Becky can prove that she contributed towards the acquisition of Blackacre or that she and Andrea acquired Blackacre by gift, bequest or inheritance.

If Becky can establish that she contributed towards the acquisition of Blackacre, then a proportionate part of Blackacre's value is excluded from Andrea's gross estate. For example, suppose Becky and Andrea acquired Blackacre as joint tenants. Of the $5,000 purchase price, Andrea contributed $2,000 and Becky contributed $3,000. At Andrea's death, 40% of the value of Blackacre is includable in her gross estate; if Becky predeceases Andrea, then 60% of Blackacre's value is included in Becky's gross estate.[228] Section 2040(a) applies even though the joint tenants who make unequal contributions towards the acquisition and maintenance of the property have agreed to equal ownership.

If the survivor's contribution was originally gifted to the survivor from the decedent, then the contribution will be classified as coming from the decedent no matter how much time may have elapsed between the date of the gift and the date the joint tenancy property was acquired.[229] For example, suppose Andrea gives Blackacre to Becky. Thereafter Becky reconveys Blackacre to Andrea and herself as joint tenants. Andrea dies survived by Becky. The entire value of Blackacre is included in Andrea's gross estate.[230] The survivor's contribution towards the joint tenancy property can take the form of the assumption of liability on a mortgage. For example, in *Bremer v. Luff,*[231] Louis

---

[227] I.R.C. § 1014(b)(6).

[228] *But see* Peters' Estate v. Commissioner, 386 F.2d 404 (4th Cir.1967). In *Peters,* the surviving joint tenant did not contribute to the acquisition of joint tenancy property. Rather the survivor contributed towards an improvement to the property. The court held that the value of the joint tenancy property less the amount of the contribution towards the improvement was included in the decedent's estate. No appreciation in the value of the property subsequent to the improvement was credited to the survivor's contributions. *See also* Section 7.4, notes 241–242.

[229] Treas. Reg. § 20.2040–1(a)(2).

[230] Treas. Reg. § 20.2040–1(c) ex. 4. *See also* Dimock v. Corwin, 99 F.2d 799 (2d Cir. 1938), affirmed, U.S. v. Jacobs, 306 U.S. 363 (1939).

[231] 7 F.Supp. 148 (N.D.N.Y.1933).

and Emma acquired Blackacre as joint tenants. Each assumed joint and several liability on the purchase money mortgage. The court held that each was deemed to have contributed one half of the mortgage liability towards acquisition of the property.[232] Their percentage contributions remain unchanged if the mortgage is discharged with income from the joint tenancy property. However, if either Louis or Emma uses personal funds to discharge the mortgage debt, their respective contributions on account of the mortgage must be readjusted.[233]

Powers of Appointment

The gross estate includes the value of all property over which the decedent (1) possessed at the time of death a general power of appointment,[234] or (2) during life exercised or released a general power of appointment.[235] However, category (2) applies only if the disposition is of such a nature that had the powerholder been the original grantor, the property subject to the power would have been includable in the powerholder's gross estate under one or more of Sections 2035 to 2038.[236] For example, Ruth held a general power of appointment over the principal of a trust created by another and later exercised her general power by directing the trustee to hold the trust assets in a revocable trust for the primary benefit of Andy. This revocable trust, if unrevoked at Ruth's death, will be includable in Ruth's gross estate under Section 2041 because the trust would have been includable in Ruth's gross estate under Section 2038 had Ruth been the original grantor.[237] On the other hand, if during life Ruth exercised a general power by appointing the property outright to Andy and Ruth retained no interest in, or power over, the appointive assets following the exercise, then the property would not be included in her gross estate, although the exercise would be a transfer for gift tax purposes.[238]

A general power of appointment is a power that enables the donee of the power to appoint the assets subject to the power to the donee, the donee's estate, the donee's creditors *or* the creditors of the donee's estate.[239] It does not include a power to consume, invade or appropriate property for the donee if the donee's power is limited by an ascertainable standard relating to the donee's

---

232 *Accord,* Rev. Rul. 79–302, 1979–2 C.B. 328; Rev. Rul. 81–183, 1981–2 C.B. 180; Rev. Rul. 81–184, 1981–2 C.B. 181.

233 *See* Awrey v. Commissioner, 5 T.C. 222 (1945).

234 I.R.C. § 2041.

235 The textual discussion relates only to general powers created after October 21, 1942. Property subject to a general power created on or before that date is included in the decedent's gross estate only if the decedent exercised the power by will or in a disposition that if made by the decedent with the decedent's own property would cause that disposition to be included in the decedent's gross estate under Sections 2036, 2037 or 2038.

236 I.R.C. § 2041(a)(2).

237 *Cf.* I.R.C. § 2038.

238 I.R.C. § 2514; Section 15.3, note 96 et seq. Even if the decedent exercised or released the power in a manner that would cause the property to be included in the decedent's gross estate, decedent's exercise or release could result in a transfer for gift tax purposes. In such case, credit for gift taxes paid due to the exercise or release would be available in computing the estate tax on the decedent's estate.

239 I.R.C. § 2041(b)(1).

health, education, support or maintenance.[240] The power is not a general power if exercisable only with the consent of the creator of the power[241] or with the consent of another person with a substantial adverse interest in the property subject to the power.[242] For example, Alex's power is not a general power if Alex can exercise the power only with the consent of Mary, who is a beneficiary of the trust whose interest could be extinguished upon Alex's exercise of the power.

The lapse of a power is treated as the release of a power.[243] A lapse of a power occurs when the right to exercise the power terminates upon the passage of time or the happening of an event, other than the donee's death. Thus, if Jerry grants Betty a general power exercisable on or before January 1, 2022 and Betty fails to exercise the power by that date, then on that date the power lapses and Betty is deemed to have released the power. However, during any calendar year the lapse of a power is a release of a power "only to the extent that the property, which could have been appointed by exercise of such lapsed power, exceeded in value, at the time of such lapse, the greater of $5,000 or 5% of the aggregate value at the time of the lapse of the property, or the proceeds of the property, out of which the power could have been satisfied."[244] Thus, if the donee possessed an annual noncumulative power to draw down from the principal of a trust an amount limited to the greater of $5,000 or 5%, the annual lapse of the power would not result in a release. Even if the donee's power exceeded the 5 and 5 standard, only annual lapses valued in excess of the greater of $5,000 or 5% are taxable releases. For example, suppose Mary had the power to withdraw up to $25,000 annually from a $200,000 trust, a power she fails to exercise and lets lapse. In that case, there would be a taxable release of only $15,000, the difference between $25,000 and 5% of $200,000.

Where a lapse results in a taxable release, the amount that is included in the donee's gross estate because of the release is determined by computing the percentage of the trust the donee is deemed to own because of the release and then applying that percentage to the value of the trust as determined for estate tax purposes. In the preceding example Mary let her power lapse over $25,000, resulting in a taxable release of $15,000. This represents 3/40 of a $200,000 trust. Assuming no further releases, then 3/40 of the trust is included in Mary's gross estate valued at Mary's death. Should there be taxable releases in later years, the percentages would need to be recomputed.[245]

The 5 and 5 rule applies only to a calendar year in which the power lapsed and the donee survived. If the donee dies during any calendar year without having exercised the power and prior to the lapse of the power, the entire amount the donee could have withdrawn that year is included in the donee's

[240] I.R.C. § 2041(b)(1)(A).

[241] I.R.C. § 2041(b)(1)(C)(i).

[242] I.R.C. § 2041(b)(1)(C)(ii).

[243] I.R.C. § 2041(b)(2).

[244] I.R.C. § 2041(b)(2)(A) & (B).

[245] *See* Treas.Reg. § 20.2041–3(d)(5).

gross estate because with respect to such amounts the donee died possessing a general power.[246]

Life Insurance

The gross estate includes the value of all life insurance payable to the insured's probate estate.[247] This includes insurance not payable directly to the estate, but which is required to be used for estate-related expenses, including "taxes, debts, or other charges enforceable against the estate."[248]

The gross estate also includes the value of all life insurance on the decedent's life payable to a named beneficiary if, at the time of the insured's death, the insured possessed any incidents of ownership with respect to the life insurance exercisable by the insured either alone or in conjunction with any other person.[249]

The phrase "incidents of ownership" is not limited to ownership in the strict sense. Rather it refers to the ability of the insured to affect who shall enjoy any of the economic benefits of the policy. Thus, incidents of ownership include, among other things, the right to change the beneficiary, the right to cancel the policy or borrow against it, and the right to pledge the policy as security for a loan.[250] The term "incident of ownership" also includes certain reversionary interests the decedent might have in a life insurance policy.[251]

Under certain circumstances the incidents of ownership held by a corporation may be attributed to the insured, causing the proceeds to be fully includable in the insured's estate. If the policy proceeds are payable to the corporation, they are considered corporate assets for purposes of valuing the decedent's stock for estate tax purposes. If not payable to or for the benefit of the corporation, the corporation's incidents of ownership are attributable to the deceased insured if the insured was the sole or controlling shareholder.[252] The decedent is a controlling shareholder if decedent owned stock possessing more than 50% of the total combined voting power of the corporation.[253]

There has been much litigation concerning whether Section 2042 applies where the insured possessed incidents of ownership over policies on the insured's life that were exercisable by the insured only in a fiduciary capacity such as that of a trustee. Some courts hold the proceeds are subject to inclusion in the gross estate regardless of whether the incidents are exercisable only in a fiduciary capacity;[254] other courts hold that Section 2042 applies only if the insured fiduciary could exercise the incidents of ownership for the fiduciary's

246 Treas.Reg. § 20.2041–3(d)(3).

247 I.R.C. § 2042(1).

248 Treas. Reg. § 20.2042–1(b)(1).

249 I.R.C. § 2042(2).

250 Treas.Reg. § 20.2042–1(c)(2).

251 I.R.C. § 2042(2); Treas.Reg. § 20.2042–1(c)(3).

252 Treas.Reg. § 20.2042–1(c)(6).

253 Treas.Reg. § 20.2042–1(c)(6).

254 *See, e.g.*, Rose v. United States, 511 F.2d 259 (5th Cir.1975).

own personal economic benefit.[255] The Internal Revenue Service has adopted the latter position.[256]

In addition to life insurance payable to the insured's probate estate and insurance over which the decedent has incidents of ownership at death, insurance on the insured's life transferred by the insured within three years of death is included in the insured's gross estate.[257] But insurance transferred by the insured more than three years before death is excluded from the insured's gross estate if the insured retained no incidents of ownership and the proceeds are not payable to the insured's estate.

This combination of rules has led to the development of a number of planning techniques. First, it is rare that life insurance should ever be payable to the probate estate if tax savings is the goal. Second, estate tax can be avoided if a life insurance policy and all incidents of ownership are relinquished more than three years before death. Life insurance is often an excellent asset to gift. The current value, particularly of term insurance, is usually very low, meaning that gifts of life insurance can usually be structured to fit easily within the annual exclusion, whereas the reduction of the gross estate can be quite significant if the insured survives for three years. Contrast that with a gift of stock or cash where to eliminate $100,000 from the gross estate at death an individual must make a $100,000 gift during lifetime.

Estate reduction can be achieved by transferring life insurance directly to a spouse or child, but the creation of an irrevocable life insurance trust provides more control and can assure better coordination with other parts of the estate plan. For example, Abe transfers a $1,000,000 term life insurance policy to an irrevocable trust for the benefit of his wife, Mary, with the remainder to their children. At the time of this transfer the policy has little value. Annual exclusions for the value of the transfer can be assured by including Crummey withdrawal powers in the trust. If Abe dies within three years, the insurance is includable in his gross estate. If Abe survives three years, the policy is not included in his gross estate. In either case the proceeds are not included in Mary's gross estate and thus pass to the children transfer tax free at her death. If the proceeds are also excluded from Abe's gross estate, then ultimately the children have received $1,000,000 transfer tax free.

It is also possible to create a life insurance trust that is excluded from the gross estate even though the insurance proceeds payable to the trustee at the insured's death can be used for the payment of the debts, expenses, and taxes of the insured's estate. But this can occur only if the use of the insurance proceeds for such purposes is wholly discretionary with the trustee of the insurance trust. If the trustee is required to use the insurance proceeds for such purposes, then to that extent the proceeds are included in the insured's gross estate under Section 2033.[258]

[255] *See, e.g.*, Estate of Skifter v. Commissioner, 468 F.2d 699 (2d Cir.1972).

[256] *See* Rev. Rul. 84–179, 1984–2 C.B. 195.

[257] I.R.C. § 2035(a)(2).

[258] *See* Treas. Reg. § 20.2042–1(a)(2).

Qualified Terminable Interest Property

The gross estate includes the value of all property in which the decedent possessed a qualifying income interest for life. The rules relating to QTIP property, a major marital deduction planning technique, are discussed below.[259]

The Taxable Estate

The federal estate tax is computed against an estate tax base equal to the sum of the taxable estate and decedent's adjusted taxable gifts. Adjusted taxable gifts are taxable gifts[260] made by the decedent after December 31, 1976, other than gifts that are included in the decedent's gross estate. The taxable estate equals the value of the gross estate less the deductions allowed under Section 2053 for debts, expenses and taxes, Section 2054 for losses, Section 2055 for transfers to charity, Section 2056 for transfers to the surviving spouse, and Section 2058 for state death taxes.

Deductible Debts, Expenses and Taxes

In computing the value of the taxable estate, a deduction is allowed against the gross estate for decedent's funeral expenses, expenses incurred in the administration of the estate,[261] claims against the estate,[262] and unpaid mortgages and other indebtedness against property includable in the gross estate. But to be deductible, such expenses must be paid from the probate estate and be allowable under the laws of the state in which the estate is being administered.[263] If paid from nonprobate assets, claims and other expenses are either taken into account in valuing the asset or are allowable as expenses incurred in administering "property not subject to claims."[264] These expenses are deductible as if such property had been subject to claims but only if such expenses are paid before the running of the statute of limitations on the decedent's estate tax return.[265]

The deduction under Section 2053 for claims, unpaid mortgages or any other indebtedness founded upon a promise or agreement are limited to the extent that they were incurred bona fide and for an adequate and full consideration in money or money's worth.[266] Thus, if John promised to pay Mary $50,000 if she stopped smoking and John owed Mary this amount when

---

[259] *See infra* note 291 et seq.

[260] *See supra* note 136.

[261] This would include attorneys' fees and personal representative fees. *See* Treas.Reg. § 20.2053–3.

[262] Claims would include decedent's unpaid federal and state income, gift and property taxes. It would not include the federal estate tax payable on the decedent's estate. *See generally* Treas.Reg. § 20.2053–6.

[263] I.R.C. § 2053(a).

[264] This would include property transferred during the decedent's life that is included in the decedent's gross estate which under state law is immune from claims against the decedent's estate. *See* Treas.Reg. § 20.2053–8. *See also* Section 13.6 regarding the extent to which non-probate property is exempt from the claims of the decedent's creditors.

[265] I.R.C. § 2053(b).

[266] I.R.C. § 2053(c).

he died, no deduction is allowed for this claim because it was not a promise for an adequate and full consideration in money or money's worth.

State Death Taxes

A deduction is available for any death tax (broadly defined) payable on property included in the decedent's gross estate.[267] However, a deduction is allowed only if the state death tax is paid within the time limits specified in the statute.[268] Approximately a third of the states assess a tax on the transfer of property at death. These state taxes take a variety of forms, creating an incentive for individuals to change domicile to reduce state taxes payable at death.[269]

Losses

Losses incurred during the administration of the estate arising from fire, storm, shipwreck, or other casualty or from theft that are not compensated for by insurance or otherwise are deductible in computing the value of the taxable estate.[270]

Swing Deduction Rule

Section 642(g) provides that administration expenses and losses allowable as deductions in computing the value of decedent's taxable estate cannot also be allowed as a deduction for income tax purposes or as offsets for the purpose of computing gain or loss on sales for income tax purposes. If a decision is made to take such expenses, losses or offsets as income tax deduction, the taxpayer must waive the right to take these items as estate tax deductions. The election is not all or nothing. The taxpayer may elect to deduct some of these expenses on one return and the balance on the other.

Ordinarily the personal representative will claim such items as deductions (or offsets) on whichever return results in the greatest tax savings. For example, if the estate is in the marginal estate tax bracket of 40% but the marginal income tax bracket is 28%, it would ordinarily be most beneficial to claim these "swing deductions" as an estate tax deduction since overall estate and income taxes will be reduced by an additional 12%. Of course, if the estate is not subject to any estate tax liability, it would be advisable to claim swing deductions as an income tax deduction or offset.

Charitable Transfers

In computing the value of the decedent's taxable estate, Section 2055 allows an unlimited deduction for outright transfers to charity. If the decedent bequeaths the decedent's entire estate to charity, the decedent's taxable estate

---

[267] I.R.C. § 2058(a).

[268] I.R.C. § 2058(b).

[269] *See* Robert Yablon, *Defying Expectations: Assessing the Surprising Resilience of State Death Taxes*, 59 Tax Lawyer 251 (2005); Jeffrey A. Cooper, et al. *State Estate Taxes After EGTRRA: A Long Day's Journey into Night*, 17 Quinnipiac Prob. L.J. 317 (2004); Robert C. Pomeroy, et al., *Ramifications for Estate Planners of the Phase Out of the Federal State Death Tax Credit: Boom, Bust, or Unknown*, 38 Heckerling Inst. on Est. Plan. ¶ 1700 (2004); William P. Lapiana, *State Responses to the Repeal of the State Death Tax Credit*, 37 Heckerling Inst. On Est. Plan. ¶ 700 (2003).

[270] I.R.C. § 2054.

would be zero. For purposes of both the gift and estate tax laws, charities include the federal and state governments and subdivisions thereof and most organizations engaged in religious, charitable, scientific, literary, or educational activities.[271]

For purposes of Section 2055, transfers include property passing to charity as a result of a bequest, legacy, devise and inter-vivos dispositions that are included in the decedent's gross estate.[272] For example, if decedent created a revocable inter-vivos trust providing that upon the decedent's death the remainder would be paid to charity, the property passing to charity at decedent's death qualifies for the estate tax charitable deduction because the revocable trust is included in the decedent's gross estate. On the other hand, if George grants Martha a special testamentary power of appointment enabling Martha to appoint the trust property to her issue and to charity, property Martha appoints to charity does not qualify for the estate tax charitable deduction because it is not included in Martha's gross estate because she did not hold a general power of appointment.

To the extent that the property passing to charity is subject to the payment of any death tax, whether federal or state, the charitable deduction must be reduced by the amount of that tax.[273] A charitable deduction is allowable only for the net amount received by the charity.

If property passes in a form that benefits both individuals and charity, special and complex rules apply to the allowance of the charitable deduction for the charitable portion of the transfer. If the transfer is in the form of a trust in which the remainder interest passes to charity, no deduction is allowed for the charitable remainder interest unless the trust qualifies as either a charitable remainder annuity trust (CRAT) or a charitable remainder unitrust (CRUT).[274]

Generally, a charitable remainder annuity trust is a trust providing that an annuity in an amount equal to at least 5% of the initial value of the trust principal shall be paid to the individual beneficiary or beneficiaries for their lives or for a term of years not exceeding 20 years, from which no amount, other than the annuity, can be paid to the noncharitable beneficiaries, and upon the termination of which the remainder will pass to charity.[275]

A charitable remainder unitrust is a trust providing that a fixed percentage, not less than 5% of the value of the trust assets determined annually and no other amounts,[276] be paid to the noncharitable beneficiary for

---

[271] I.R.C. § 2055(a)(1)–(5).

[272] It has been held that property passing to a state because decedent died intestate does not qualify for the deduction because it does not pass to charity as the result of decedent's transfer. *See* Senft v. United States, 319 F.2d 642 (3d Cir.1963).

[273] Treas. Reg. § 20.2055–3(a).

[274] I.R.C. § 2055(e)(2)(A).

[275] *See* I.R.C. § 664(d)(1).

[276] Referred to as a NIMCRUT, a unitrust may in the alternative provide that the beneficiary will receive the lesser of the specified percentage or the trust's actual accounting income. *See* I.R.C. § 664(d)(3).

life or for a term of years not to exceed 20 years and that upon the termination of the trust the remainder shall pass to charity.[277]

Under the unitrust, the amount paid to the noncharitable beneficiary varies each year and rises or falls as the value of the trust principal rises or falls over the life of the trust. With an annuity trust, the annual amount the noncharitable beneficiary receives remains constant.

A charitable deduction is also available for so-called charitable "lead" trusts which provide for payment of an annuity or unitrust amount to charity for a term certain or a term measured by the life of an individual and a remainder to a noncharitable beneficiary.[278]

Similar rules concerning split-interest charitable trusts apply to the gift tax charitable deduction.[279]

Split-interest charitable trusts have become common estate and financial planning tools not only for their potential to avoid or reduce transfer taxes but also because of the potential income tax deduction under Section 170 of the Code.

Marital Deduction

An unlimited deduction is allowed in computing the value of the taxable estate for the value of all property included in the decedent's gross estate passing from the decedent to the decedent's surviving spouse.[280] This is the most important deduction available to married couples wishing to minimize transfer taxes on their property. This deduction reflects a strongly held policy that it is inappropriate to assess transfer taxes on transfers of property between spouses.

The marital deduction is available only for a deductible interest passing from the decedent to the surviving spouse. A deductible interest is a property interest passing to the spouse that is not made nondeductible by the "nondeductible terminable interest rule."[281] Under this rule, a property interest passing from the decedent to the surviving spouse is nondeductible if, upon the happening of an event or contingency or upon the lapse of time, the spouse's interest will terminate, and upon such termination the interest or the property from which the interest is carved will pass to someone other than the spouse for less than an adequate and full consideration in money or money's worth.[282] The rule is best illustrated by an example. John bequeaths $100,000 in trust to pay the income to Abigail for 20 years, remainder to John, Jr., Abigail's term interest is nondeductible because (1) it will terminate upon the lapse of 20 years, and (2) upon the termination of that interest the trust, which is the property out if which the spouse's interest is carved, will pass to John, Jr. for less than an adequate and full consideration in money or money's worth. On the other hand, if John bequeaths Abigail his remaining term interest in a

[277] I.R.C. § 664(d)(2).

[278] I.R.C. § 2055(e)(2)(B).

[279] *See* I.R.C. § 2522.

[280] I.R.C. § 2056(a).

[281] I.R.C. § 2056(b).

[282] I.R.C. § 2056(b)(1).

copyright, the interest passing to Abigail qualifies for the marital deduction. While Abigail's interest terminates at the end of the copyright term, upon the termination of her interest there is nothing left to pass to another person.

The nondeductible terminable interest rule essentially assures that property passing from one spouse to another qualifies for the marital deduction only if such property is transferred in a way that it will be included in the surviving spouse's gift or estate tax base unless consumed by the surviving spouse during the spouse's lifetime.

The nondeductible terminable interest rule is subject to several important exceptions, exceptions which form the basis for most marital deduction planning. First, a spouse's interest can be made subject to a survivorship condition of up to six months or a common accident or disaster clause. A marital deduction is allowed if the spouse in fact survives for the required period and does not die from a common disaster.[283]

Second, the decedent can create a general power of appointment trust. To qualify for the marital deduction, the trust must provide that (1) the spouse will receive all of the income[284] from the property, or a specific portion thereof,[285] for life payable at least annually, (2) the spouse will have a power to appoint the property either to herself or to the spouse's estate[286] which is exercisable alone and in all events,[287] and (3) no person, except the spouse, will have a power to appoint the property to any person other than the spouse.[288] To illustrate, suppose Dolly creates a $100,000 trust to pay the income to her husband, James, for life, remainder to such persons, including James's estate, as he appoints by will and in default of appointment to Allan. Dolly's estate is entitled to a marital deduction in the amount of $100,000. Likewise, the trust would qualify for a $100,000 marital deduction even if the trustee of the trust could invade the trust principal for James. However, if during Dolly's lifetime the trustee could invade the principal for the benefit of another person, the trust would not qualify for the marital deduction.

Property qualifying for the marital deduction under the general power of appointment trust exception is included in the surviving spouse's gross estate

---

[283] I.R.C. § 2056(b)(3). Assuming the spouse survives for the required period, this provision validates survivorship requirements of six months or less, whether in the governing instrument or state statute, including the 120-hour survivorship requirement under the UPC.

[284] Treas.Reg. § 20.2056(b)–5(f).

[285] The specific portion can be either a specific portion of the income from the entire trust, or all of the income from a specific portion of the trust. *See* Treas.Reg. § 20.2056(b)–5(a)(1).

[286] Treas.Reg. § 20.2056(b)–5(g). The terms of this general power are not coterminous with the definition of a general power in Section 2041. Under Section 2041, a general power includes a power to appoint to the donee, the donee's estate, the donee's creditors or the creditors of the donee's estate.

[287] Treas.Reg. § 20.2056(b)–5(g). Thus, co-held powers do not qualify for the Section 2056(b)(5) exception and a general power that is not exercisable from the date of the decedent's death until the date of the surviving spouse's death either as an inter-vivos power or a testamentary power does not qualify under Section 2056(b)(5).

[288] Treas.Reg. § 20.2056(b)–5(j)

if the spouse exercises or releases the general power during life[289] or if the spouse still possessed the general power at the surviving spouse's death.[290]

Third, the decedent can create a qualified terminable interest property (QTIP) trust or some other arrangement, such as a life estate in real property, that meets the Section 2056(b)(7) QTIP requirements. QTIP property is property in which (1) the spouse is entitled to all of the income for life payable at least annually, (2) no person, including the spouse, has the power to appoint any of the property to anyone other than the spouse during the spouse's lifetime[291] and (3) the decedent's personal representative has made an election that the property should qualify for the marital deduction. To illustrate, a transfer from Helen in trust to pay the income to William for life, remainder to Helen's descendants qualifies as QTIP if the personal representative for Helen's estate elects to treat the property as QTIP but only if no one can appoint the property to anyone other than William during William's lifetime. This type of devise is often used by spouses who have children from a prior marriage and who do not wish to risk the loss of property for their children by leaving their property to the spouse outright or by giving the spouse a general power of appointment.

Because the prohibition against granting a power of appointment disqualifies a QTIP for the marital deduction only if the power is exercisable during the spouse's lifetime,[292] the surviving spouse can be granted a special testamentary power of appointment without disqualifying the QTIP for the marital deduction.

Sections 2519 and Section 2044 were enacted to assure that the QTIP property is includable in the surviving spouse's transfer tax base either under the gift or the estate tax law. If the spouse makes a lifetime transfer of an income interest in a QTIP, Section 2519 provides that the gift also includes a gift of the corresponding remainder interest. For example, suppose Grace transfers $100,000 in trust to pay the income to her husband, Cal, for life, remainder to Jim. Grace elects to treat the $100,000 as QTIP and the transfer qualifies for the gift tax marital deduction. Five years later when Cal's life estate is worth $40,000, he transfers it to Bert who therefore acquires a life estate in the property measured by Cal's life. Cal will be deemed to have made a gift of $100,000 except to the extent Cal received adequate and full consideration for the transfer of the remainder.

When the spouse who possesses a qualifying income interest in QTIP dies, the QTIP is included in the spouse's gross estate under Section 2044 unless during the spouse's life a Section 2519 transfer occurred. Thus, in the preceding example, if Cal died never having transferred the income interest, the trust is included in his gross estate under Section 2044. If Cal made a Section 2519 disposition with respect to that trust, nothing would be included in his gross estate under Section 2044.

---

[289] I.R.C. §§ 2514, 2041.

[290] I.R.C. § 2041.

[291] *Contrast* I.R.C. § 2056(b)(5), discussed *supra* note 284 et seq.

[292] I.R.C. § 2056(b)(7)(B).

Fourth, Section 2056(b)(8) creates an additional exception to the nondeductible terminable interest rule for charitable remainder trusts[293] in which the surviving spouse has an annuity or unitrust interest. This exception is used rarely because similar tax consequences can be achieved through the use of a QTIP trust with a charitable remainder. A QTIP with a charitable remainder is a more flexible device than a charitable remainder annuity or unitrust. Unlike a charitable remainder annuity or unitrust, a QTIP can allow the trustee to invade the principal for the benefit of the spouse.

Section 2523 contains comparable provisions for the gift tax marital deduction, including a gift tax nondeductible terminable interest rule,[294] a life estate power of appointment[295] and a QTIP[296] exception to that rule and a special rule for gifts to a charitable remainder trust.[297]

Marital Deduction Planning

Basic Decisions

Marital deduction planning involves several steps. The first decision is to select the type of marital bequest. There are three principal choices; outright gift, general power of appointment trust,[298] and QTIP.[299] The decision on which to choose is primarily a non-tax matter. A trust is most appropriate if there are concerns about the spouse's management ability or concerns about how the surviving spouse might ultimately dispose of the property. If creating a trust, a decision must be made between a general power of appointment trust and a QTIP trust. The advantage of the QTIP is that the grantor can control who will receive the trust at the surviving spouse's death, a common concern in a multiple marriage situation.

The second decision is to decide on the amount of the marital deduction. There are options here as well. One option is to leave the entire estate to the spouse. This is often accompanied by a backup plan allowing for the amount of the marital deduction to be adjusted following the first death. The second major option is what might be termed the standard plan. Under the standard plan, an amount equal to the applicable exclusion ($11,700,000 in 2021) is left to a Bypass Trust or other beneficiaries, with the balance passing to the spouse in a form qualifying for the marital deduction.

Standard Plan

To make certain the correct amount is transferred to the Bypass Trust and marital deduction share, a marital deduction formula clause is used. Formula clauses are necessary because changes in the value and composition of the decedent's assets and the amount of the applicable exclusion will change between the time the estate planning documents are executed and the time the

---

293 *See supra* notes 281 et seq.

294 I.R.C. § 2523(b).

295 I.R.C. § 2523(e).

296 I.R.C. § 2523(f).

297 I.R.C. § 2523(g).

298 I.R.C. § 2056(b)(5).

299 I.R.C. § 2056(b)(7).

first spouse dies. Under a formula clause, the exact amount passing to or for the benefit of the surviving spouse is not determined until the first spouse's death when the precise value of the decedent's assets is known, as well as the amount of debts and expenses and the allowable unified credit. Formula provisions also make clear whether the spouse shares in appreciation and depreciation occurring on estate assets between the date of death and date of distribution.

Because the amount passing to the Bypass Trust will not exceed the decedent's applicable exclusion, no estate tax is payable at the first death. As its name suggests, the Bypass Trust will also not be subject to tax at the surviving spouse's death. Anyone can be named as a beneficiary of the Bypass Trust, but it is usual to name the spouse as at least one of the beneficiaries. Care must be taken in naming the trustee. If the spouse is named as trustee, the Bypass Trust will be includable in the spouse's gross estate if the spouse is given a Section 2041 general power of appointment. A discretionary power in a trustee to make distributions to the trustee as beneficiary is a general power of appointment. To avoid estate inclusion, the spouse/trustee/beneficiary's discretion must be limited by an ascertainable standard as defined in Section 2041(b)(1)(A). Reg. § 20.2041–1(c)(2) contains approved phrases that should be consulted when drafting.

Portability v. Standard Plan

Under portability, which became effective in 2011, the unused exclusion of the last predeceased spouse can be transferred to the surviving spouse.[300] Portability is a possible planning option no matter how large the estates, particularly if an outright marital bequest is chosen.

Portability Example:

> Sam and Clara were married. Sam has an estate of $20,000,000; Clara has no assets. If Sam leaves his estate 100% to Clara, Sam's gross estate will be $20,000,000, the marital deduction will be $20,000,000, and Sam's taxable estate will be zero. At Clara's subsequent death, Clara may use her own estate tax exclusion plus all of Sam's exclusion and avoid tax on the entire $20,000,000. If Clara dies first, because she has no assets, none of her estate tax exclusion will be used. At Sam's subsequent death, Sam could similarly avoid taxation by using both his own exclusion plus Clara's entire exclusion.

Portability has advantages over the standard plan. No trust is required so it is simpler for clients to understand and administer than a Bypass Trust and formula clause. Furthermore, at the second death, a full step-up in basis is available on the couple's combined assets.

But portability has potential disadvantages. If the surviving spouse remarries and the new spouse dies first, the portability election may be made only with respect to the unused exclusion of the last spouse to predecease. Second, even if the first spouse to die has no assets, an estate tax return must

[300] I.R.C. § 2010(c).

be timely filed for the first spouse in order for portability to be elected in the surviving spouse's estate. Furthermore, because the surviving spouse will receive the first decedent's entire estate, all of the appreciation on the couple's combined assets will be subject to estate tax at the survivor's death. In the case of a Bypass Trust, appreciation on the Bypass Trust assets between the first and second deaths will escape estate tax. Finally, portability does not apply to the tax on generation-skipping transfers, discussed in the next section.

Post-Mortem Flexibility

Sometimes a decision is made to adjust the amount of the marital deduction after the first death. This issue often arises when the decedent leaves the entire estate to the spouse and it is decided after the first death that it might have been better to have transferred the applicable exclusion amount to a Bypass Trust.

There are three techniques for adjusting the amount of the marital deduction after the first death: Disclaimer Trust; Partial QTIP; and Clayton Trust.

Disclaimer Trust

Section 2518 provides generally that a disclaimant cannot be a beneficiary of disclaimed property, but an exception is created for the spouse.[301] Under a Disclaimer Trust plan, the entire estate is initially left outright to the spouse. But following the first death, to the extent the spouse disclaims, the disclaimed property will drop into a Bypass Trust of which the spouse will usually although need not be a beneficiary.

Partial QTIP

The QTIP marital deduction is elective. In a typical QTIP trust plan, the governing document divides the estate into a QTIP marital trust and a Bypass Trust, with the Bypass Trust receiving the applicable exclusion amount. Under a partial QTIP plan, the decedent will leave the entire estate to a single trust under which the spouse is a life income beneficiary. The entire trust can therefore qualify for the QTIP marital deduction to the extent the personal representative elects. Following the death, the personal representative will then decide how much of the trust to qualify for the marital deduction, all, none, or a fraction.

Clayton Trust

This technique is named after the plan at issue in *Clayton v. Commissioner*,[302] although actual planning has been refined in practice. Under a Clayton Trust plan, two trusts are created, a Bypass Trust and a QTIP marital deduction trust, but the amount that will pass to each trust is not determined in advance. Rather, the personal representative is given authority to determine the fraction of the estate that will pass to the QTIP trust and qualify for the marital deduction. Whatever portion does not pass to the QTIP trust will pass to the Bypass Trust.

---

[301] I.R.C. § 2518(b)(4)(A).

[302] 976 F.2d 1486 (5th Cir. 1992).

§ 15.5 Generation Skipping Transfer Tax

The federal estate tax does not apply to property passing as the result of the termination of an interest of a beneficiary in a continuing trust unless the beneficiary whose interest terminated has a general power of appointment.[303] Federal estate and gift taxes on property passing into a trust providing benefits to beneficiaries of multiple generations generally are payable only when the trust is created. Persons of substantial wealth can avoid transfer taxes at each generational level by using generation-skipping trusts. To illustrate, suppose John devises his personal estate of $20,000,000 to daughter Carol who, in turn, devises her entire estate that she inherited from John to her daughter, June. Upon John's death in 2021, $3,320,000 of estate taxes were paid, and Carol received $16,680,000. Upon Carol's subsequent death, an additional $1,992,000 of estate taxes is payable (based on 2021 rates), and June receives $14,688,000. Thus, a total of $5,312,000 of estate taxes are paid as John's property wound its way down to June. On the other hand, if John had created a trust to pay the income to Carol for life, remainder to June, the $1,992,000 in estate taxes payable at Carol's death could have been avoided.

In 1976 Congress enacted Chapter 13, Tax on Generation-Skipping Transfers, for the purpose of minimizing the opportunities to avoid transfer taxes by use of generation-skipping trusts. The initial GST provisions, however, were retroactively repealed by the Internal Revenue Code of 1986 and replaced with the provisions discussed below.

Critical Definitions

Transferor

In the case of a transfer that is included in the transferor's gross estate under the federal estate tax, the transferor for GST purposes is ordinarily the decedent.[304] In the case of a transfer that is included in the transferor's gift tax base, the transferor for GST purposes is ordinarily the donor.[305] There are two special cases under the GST tax where the transferor is someone other than the decedent or donor. First, if one spouse makes a lifetime transfer to a donee other than the other spouse, and the spouses elect under Section 2513 to split this gift for gift tax purposes,[306] for GST purposes each spouse is deemed the transferor of one-half of the gift.[307] Second, if a donor spouse or a deceased spouse transfers property to the other spouse in a form that qualifies for the estate or gift tax marital deduction as qualified terminable interest property,[308] the transferee spouse is the transferor for GST purposes unless the donor spouse or donor spouse's estate elects otherwise.[309] If an election is made, then the deceased spouse or the donor spouse is treated as the transferor for GST purposes even though for gift or estate tax purposes the property will

[303] I.R.C. § 2041.

[304] I.R.C. § 2652(a)(1)(A).

[305] I.R.C. § 2652(a)(1)(B).

[306] For a discussion of split gifts, *see* Section 15.3, notes 44–45.

[307] I.R.C. § 2652(a)(2).

[308] I.R.C. §§ 2056(b)(7), 2523(f). *See also* Section 15.4, note 291 et seq.

[309] I.R.C. § 2652(a)(3).

later be taxed to the donee spouse.[310] This election may assist married couples in planning to take maximum advantage of GST deductions and exclusions.

Interest in Trust

Under the GST tax, it may be important at certain times to determine whether a person has an interest in a trust. Ordinarily, the time a determination is to be made is when some other person's interest has terminated.[311] A person has an interest in a trust if the person has a present right to receive the income or principal of the trust or is a permissible *current* recipient of either the income or principal of the trust.[312]

Skip Person and Non-Skip Person

A "skip person" is a person who is assigned to a generation that is at least two generations below the transferor's generation.[313] A trust can be a skip person if (1) all present interests in the trusts are held by skip persons or (2) no person currently holds a present interest in the trust and, after the transfer, no distribution, including terminating distributions, can be made to a non-skip person from the trust.[314] A non-skip person is a person who is *not* a skip person.[315] To illustrate, suppose Amy creates a trust to pay the income to her son, Bernie, for life, remainder to his children (grandchildren of Amy). This trust is *not* a skip person because Bernie, who is assigned to the first generation below Amy and who is not a skip person, has a present interest in the trust. Bernie's children, however, are skip persons.[316] But if Amy transfers property in trust to pay the income to her grandchildren for their lives remainder to her great-grandchildren, the trust is a skip person.[317] Suppose the trust provides that if none of Amy's great-grandchildren survived Amy's grandchildren, then upon the death of the survivor of them, the principal would be distributed to Amy's nieces and nephews. The nieces and nephew are in the first generation below the grantor's generation and thus are non-skip persons. But the trust is nonetheless a skip person because all present interests (which by definition excludes future interests)[318] are held by skip persons.

Assignment of Generations

Under the GST tax, there are detailed rules to determine a person's generation assignment.[319] These rules fall into three categories: rules relating

---

[310] No similar election is available for property qualifying the marital deduction under the life estate/power of appointment exceptions in I.R.C. §§ 2056(b)(5) and 2523(e).

[311] *See* I.R.C. § 2612(a).

[312] I.R.C. § 2652(c)(1)(A). For GST purposes, a trust is defined to also include a legal life estate followed by a remainder and similar trust equivalents. I.R.C. § 2652(b)(1).

[313] I.R.C. § 2613(a)(1). *See infra* note 332 et seq. for a discussion of the generation assignment rules.

[314] I.R.C. § 2613(a)(2). An example of this trust would be a transfer to T in trust to accumulate the income for 15 years and at the end of the term to distribute the principal and accumulated income to the grantor's then living grandchildren and more remote descendants.

[315] I.R.C. § 2613(b).

[316] The fact that a trust is not a skip person does not mean it or its beneficiaries are not subject to the generation skipping transfer tax.

[317] I.R.C. § 2613(a)(2).

[318] I.R.C. § 2652(c).

[319] I.R.C. § 2651.

to the generational assignments of blood or adopted descendants and other relatives of the transferor,[320] rules relating to the generational assignment of persons related to the transferor by marriage,[321] and rules relating to the generational assignment of persons who are not related to the transferor.[322] These rules are:

1. The transferor's children are assigned to the first generation below the transferor,[323] the transferor's grandchildren are assigned to the second generation below the transferor, the transferor's great-grandchildren are assigned to the third generation below the transferor and so forth. The transferor's siblings are assigned to the transferor's generation; nieces and nephews are assigned to the first generation below the transferor, grandnieces and grandnephews are assigned to the second generation below the transferor and so forth.

2. A lineal descendant of the grandparents of the transferor's spouse, other than the transferor's spouse who is always assigned to the same generation as the transferor,[324] is assigned to the generation resulting from comparing the number of generations between the lineal descendant and the grandparent and the number of generations between the grandparent and the transferor's spouse.[325]

3. In determining the generation assignments of lineal descendants of the grandparents of the transferor or the transferor's spouse, relationships created by adoption are treated as relationships by blood[326] and relationships by the half-blood are treated the same as relationships by the whole-blood.[327]

4. A person who at any time was married to the transferor is assigned to the transferor's generation.[328] A person who at any time was married to a lineal descendant of the grandparents of the transferor or the transferor's spouse is assigned to the same generation as that lineal descendant.[329]

5. If none of the foregoing rules apply, a person born no more than 12 1/2 years after the transferor is assigned to the transferor's generation, a person born more than 12 1/2 years after the birth of the transferor but not more than 37 1/2 years after the transferor is assigned to the first generation below the

---

[320] I.R.C. § 2651(b).

[321] I.R.C. § 2651(c).

[322] I.R.C. § 2651(d).

[323] I.R.C. § 2651(b)(1). Determined by subtracting the number of generations between the transferor and the transferor's grandparents (2) from the number of generations the transferor's children are removed from the transferor's grandparents (3).

[324] I.R.C. § 2651(c)(1).

[325] I.R.C. § 2651(b)(2).

[326] I.R.C. § 2651(b)(3)(A).

[327] I.R.C. § 2651(b)(3)(B). Half-blood, unlike whole-bloods relatives, are related to each other only through one common ancestor. For example, if H and W have Child A, and then H dies and W remarries H-2 with whom she has Child B, Child A and Child B are half-bloods. Only W is the parent they have in common. *See also* Section 2.2, note 75 et seq.

[328] I.R.C. § 2651(c)(1).

[329] I.R.C. § 2651(c)(2).

transferor and every person in the next successive 25-year period is assigned to the next younger generation.[330]

6. If, in applying the foregoing rules, a person could be assigned to more than one generation, such person shall be assigned to the youngest such generation.[331] For example, suppose Harry adopts his grandchild, Allan, who but for the adoption would be assigned to the second generation below Harry. Under the general rule relating to the generation assignment of adopted persons, Allan would be in the first generation below Harry. However, because Allan is also a grandchild, Allan is assigned to the younger of the two generations and he is therefore a skip person.

7. Under the predeceased ancestor exception, if the transferee is a lineal descendant of the parent of the transferor (or the transferor's spouse or former spouse), and the transferee's parent is dead at the time the transfer was subject to gift or estate tax, then the descendant's generation assignment shall be moved up, ordinarily by one, so that a grandchild will be treated the same as a child, a great-grandchild like a grandchild, and a child of a predeceased niece or nephew the same as a niece or nephew. Additional adjustments are made if more than one generation of ancestor is predeceased. For example, a great-grandchild would be moved up to the child generation if both the child's parent and grandparent (and transferor's descendant) predeceased.[332]

Because lineal descendants of the transferor's parents include brothers and sisters, nieces and nephews, and so on, the predeceased ancestor exception and the ability to move up a generation could potentially apply to collateral relatives, but the statute provides that collateral relatives are covered only if the transferor was not survived by any lineal descendants.[333]

8. If an entity[334] has an interest in property, every person having a beneficial interest in that entity is treated as having an interest in the property.[335] Each such person is then assigned to a generation under the foregoing rules.[336]

Generation Skipping Transfers

There are three types of generation skipping transfers: taxable terminations, taxable distributions, and direct skips.

Taxable Termination

A taxable termination means "the termination (by death, lapse of time, release of power, or otherwise) of an interest in property held in a trust *unless*:

---

[330] I.R.C. § 2651(d). This is identical to the provisions under prior law. Former I.R.C. § 2611(c)(5).

[331] I.R.C. § 2651(e)(1).

[332] I.R.C. § 2651(e)(1).

[333] I.R.C. § 2651(e)(2).

[334] An entity includes an estate, trust, partnership, corporation, or other entity. I.R.C. § 2651(f)(2).

[335] I.R.C. § 2651(f)(2).

[336] Organizations described in Section 511(a)(2) and charitable trusts described in Section 511(b)(2) are assigned to the transferor's generation. I.R.C. § 2651(f)(3).

1. immediately after such termination, a non-skip person has an interest in such property, or

2. at no time after such termination may a distribution (including distributions on termination) be made from such trust to a skip person."[337]

The amount taxed generally equals the value of property with respect to which the taxable termination has occurred.[338] The tax is payable by the trustee of the trust.[339]

For example, suppose Bess creates a trust to pay the income to her husband, Harry, for life, remainder to their surviving children, or to the survivors or survivor of them,[340] for their lives and upon the death of the survivor of the last child to distribute the principal equally to their then living grandchildren. Harry is assigned to Bess's generation and is a non-skip person; their children are assigned to the first generation below Bess. They are also non-skip persons. The grandchildren are assigned to the second generation below Bess and are skip persons. Harry dies survived by two children, Ann and Billy. No taxable termination then occurs, even though Harry's interest terminates because immediately after this termination non-skip persons, Ann and Billy, have interests in the trust. Likewise, if Ann dies survived by Billy, no taxable termination then occurs because Billy, who has the continuing present interest, is a non-skip person. When Billy dies survived by Bess's grandchildren, a taxable termination occurs.

Taxable Distribution

A taxable distribution is a distribution, including distributions of income from a trust, to a skip person (other than a taxable termination).[341] In the case of a taxable distribution, the taxable amount is generally the value of the property received by the transferee.[342] The tax on a taxable distribution is paid by the transferee.[343] A common example of a taxable distribution is where a transferor creates a trust where the children and grandchildren are beneficiaries and the trustee makes a discretionary distribution to a grandchild. No taxable termination has occurred because the children are still beneficiaries. Nor is it a direct skip (described below) because the distribution did not occur at the time of the initial transfer. Consequently, by process of elimination, the distribution is a taxable distribution. To illustrate, suppose Martha creates a trust to pay the income among her children and grandchildren and their spouses living at Martha's death in such shares as the trustee deems advisable. The children and their spouses are assigned to the first generation below Martha and are therefore non-skip persons. The grandchildren and their spouses and Martha's more remote descendants are assigned to the second and lower generations and are therefore skip persons.

---

337 I.R.C. § 2612(a).

338 I.R.C. § 2622.

339 I.R.C. § 2603(a)(2).

340 *See* Section 11.1, note 90 et seq. (discussion of cross remainders).

341 I.R.C. § 2612(b).

342 I.R.C. § 2621.

343 I.R.C. § 2603(a)(1).

Distributions of income or principal to Martha's children and their spouses are not taxable distributions because the children are non-skip persons. Distributions of income or principal to the grandchildren or their spouses are taxable distributions because they are skip persons.

Direct Skip

A "direct skip" is a transfer to a skip person that is subject to the estate or gift tax.[344] In the case of a direct skip the taxable amount is the value of the property received by the transferee.[345] In the case of a direct skip, other than a direct skip from a trust, the generation skipping tax is paid by the transferor.[346] In the case of a direct skip from a trust, the tax is paid by the trustee.[347]

Direct skips do not include transfers eligible for the gift tax annual exclusion or tuition or medical expense exclusion.[348] However, the annual exclusion for GST purposes is narrower than the annual exclusion for gift tax purposes. In order for a transfer in trust to qualify for the GST annual exclusion, during the life of the beneficiary for whom the gift was made, (1) no portion of the trust may be distributed to any other beneficiary, and (2) if the beneficiary for whom the gift was made dies prior to the termination of the trust, the assets of the trust must be includable in the beneficiary's gross estate.[349] Section 2503(c) trusts and Uniform Transfers to Minors Act accounts meet these requirements but careful drafting is required to qualify a trust with Crummey withdrawal rights for the GST annual exclusion.[350]

For purposes of determining whether a transfer is a direct skip, the generation assignment rules, including the predeceased ancestor exception, are applicable.[351] Consequently; under the predeceased ancestor exception, if the transfer is to the transferor's grandchild and the parent of such grandchild is not living, the grandchild is treated as if she was a child of the transferor or the transferor's spouse.

The GST Exemption

Every person is allowed an aggregate GST exemption equal to the applicable exclusion under the federal estate tax[352] ($11,700,000 in 2021). The exemption is allocated among generation-skipping transfers as the transferor or transferor's personal representative may elect on a timely filed gift or estate tax return.[353] Any available exemption not allocated by the transferor or personal representative is first automatically allocated to lifetime direct skips,

---

344 I.R.C. § 2612(c).

345 I.R.C. § 2623.

346 I.R.C. § 2603(a)(3).

347 I.R.C. § 2603(a)(2).

348 I.R.C. § 2642(c)(3).

349 I.R.C. § 2642(c)(2).

350 For the various annual exclusion planning techniques, *see* Section 15.3, notes 59 et seq.

351 *See supra* note 332 et seq.

352 I.R.C. § 2631(c).

353 I.R.C. § 2632(a).

with complex rules applying to the allocation of the remaining exemption.[354] Much GST planning involves how to best allocate the GST exemption. If the entire exemption is allocated to a single $11,700,000 transfer, then the entire transfer is exempt from the GST tax for all time even though at a later time the property has grown in value. For example, suppose Oscar transfers $11,700,000 in trust to pay the income to son, Sam, for life, remainder to grandchild, Eddie, for life, remainder to Eddie's surviving descendants. Oscar allocates his entire GST exemption to this transfer. When Sam dies the trust property is worth $20,000,000. It is worth $30,000,000 when Eddie dies. No generation skipping transfers occur upon the deaths of Sam or Eddie. On the other hand, if only 50% of Oscar's GST exemption had been allocated to the transfer, 50% of the property is exempt from the GST tax and upon the deaths of Sam and then Eddie, 50% of the trust's value at that time would be subject to the GST tax. It is often advisable to allocate the GST exemption to transferred assets that are expected to increase significantly in value, such as a life insurance trust or closely held corporate stock.

Computation of the Tax

The GST tax on a transfer equals the "taxable amount" multiplied by the "applicable rate."[355] The taxable amount in the case of taxable distribution is generally the value of property received by the transferee;[356] in the case of a taxable termination, it is generally the value of the property with respect to which a taxable termination occurs;[357] with respect to a direct skip it is the value of property received by the transferee.[358] Generally, values are determined at the time the generation skipping transfer occurs although the estate tax alternate valuation method is available for direct skips includable in the gross estate and taxable terminations occurring at the transferor's death.[359]

The "applicable rate" equals the maximum federal estate tax rate (40% after 2012) times the inclusion ratio.[360] The inclusion ratio equals 1 minus the "applicable fraction."[361] The applicable fraction is determined as follows: the numerator of the fraction is the amount of the GST exemption allocated to the trust or to the direct skip; the denominator is generally the value of the property transferred to the trust or involved in the direct skip.[362]

To illustrate, in 2017 suppose John transfers $5,000,000 in trust to pay the income to daughter, Sally, for life, remainder to Sally's daughter, Roz, for life, remainder to Roz's descendants. No portion of John's GST exemption is allocated to this trust. Therefore, the applicable fraction is zero and the

---

[354] I.R.C. § 2632(b).

[355] I.R.C. § 2602.

[356] I.R.C. § 2621.

[357] I.R.C. § 2622.

[358] I.R.C. § 2623.

[359] I.R.C. § 2624(b).

[360] I.R.C. § 2641.

[361] I.R.C. § 2642(a).

[362] I.R.C. § 2642(a)(2)(B). This value is reduced by the sum of federal and state death tax attributable to the property and recovered from the trust and any gift or estate tax charitable deduction with respect to the property.

inclusion ratio is 1 (1–0). With respect to the generation skipping transfers occurring at the death of Sally and then Roz, the applicable rate applied to the value of the property at the time the transfers occurred would be 40%. Thus, if the $5,000,000 value remains unchanged, then at Sally's death, the GST tax is $2,000,000; at Roz's death a tax of $1,200,000 would be payable on the $3,000,000 balance.

Suppose, however, that John allocated $2,500,000 of his GST exemption to this trust. In this case the applicable fraction for this trust is $2,500,000/$5,000,000 or 50%; the inclusion ratio is 50% and the applicable rate would be 20% (40% times 50%).[363] At the termination of the trust the amount of the generation skipping transfer is taxed at the rate of 20%.

Other Exemptions

The GST tax is inapplicable to transfers from a trust that, if made by an individual, would not be subject to gift tax because of the exclusion for payments of tuition or medical expenses.[364] For example, if Mary creates a trust to apply the income towards the medical expenses of children and grandchildren, these payments are not generation skipping transfers.

§ 15.6 Income Taxation of Estates and Trusts

The Subchapter J Estate

Both estates and trusts are separate entities for income tax purposes, just as corporations and partnerships are separate entities for income tax purposes. The income taxation of estates and trusts is governed by the provisions of Subchapter J of the Internal Revenue Code and particularly the provisions of Sections 641 through 664.

The Subchapter J estate (the property subject to taxation under Subchapter J) is not co-extensive with the property of a decedent subject to the federal estate tax. The estate tax reaches property in a decedent's probate estate as well as certain lifetime-transferred property, joint tenancy property and life insurance.[365] In the case of a decedent, however, the Subchapter J estate is limited to the decedent's probate estate. For income tax purposes, the Subchapter J estate terminates when the decedent's probate estate is closed.

With respect to lifetime or testamentary trusts, the Subchapter J estate includes the value of the trust property in the hands of the trustee and lasts until the trust terminates.

At one time there was a significant income tax advantage to creating a trust, not distributing all of the trust's income, and having undistributed income taxed at the trust level instead of to the trust beneficiaries. This advantage has disappeared because the current income tax rates for estates and trusts escalate from 10% for taxable income up to $2,650 (2021 figure) to

---

[363] *But see* I.R.C. § 2653(b), directing an adjustment of the inclusion ratio in the case of multiple skips.

[364] I.R.C. § 2611(b)(1). *See also* I.R.C. § 2503(e).

[365] *See* Section 15.4.

37% when taxable income reaches $13,050.[366] Under current law it is often advisable to have the income of the estate or trust taxed to the beneficiaries rather than at the trust level because the rate of tax on income distributed to the beneficiaries will be significantly lower.

The Purpose of Subchapter J

The primary purpose of Subchapter J is to provide a method for determining whether the estate or its beneficiaries, or a trust or its beneficiaries, is taxable on the income of the estate or trust for any taxable year. Subchapter J is designed to assure that either the entity or its beneficiaries, but not both, are taxed on the entity's income. Estates and trusts are taxed differently than corporations and partnerships. Net income of a corporation is taxed at both the corporate and shareholder level because the corporation is not entitled to any deduction for dividends paid to shareholders. Partnerships do not pay taxes; all partnership income is deemed distributed to the partners and taxed to them even if the income is actually retained by the partnership.

The Distributions Deduction and the Beneficiary Gross Income Inclusion

The starting point in the analysis is to determine the gross income of the estate or trust, which is determined in the same manner as for an individual. For most estates and trusts, typical items of gross income would include dividends, interests, rents, and capital gains. Estates and trusts are also entitled to certain deductions in calculating their taxable income. One of these deductions, unavailable to individuals, is the "distributions deduction."[367]

The distribution deduction equals the amount during the taxable year that is distributed to or set aside for the benefit of the beneficiaries. Amounts distributed include both cash and property distributed in kind, such as securities. If property in kind is distributed, it is valued, for purposes of computing the distributions deduction, at its fair market value on the date of distribution.[368] The flip side of this deduction is that the beneficiaries must include in their gross income amounts that the estate or trust claimed as a distribution deduction.[369]

It is the combination of the distribution deduction and the beneficiaries' gross income inclusion that assures that the income received by the estate or trust is taxed to the estate or trust or to the beneficiaries but not both. However, there are many nuances that complicate how the taxable income of an estate or trust and its beneficiaries is calculated.

---

366 I.R.C. § 1(e). For married couples filing jointly, the 37% rate does not kick in until taxable income reaches $622,050 (2021 figure).

367 I.R.C. §§ 651, 661.

368 Treas. Reg. § 1.661(a)–2(f). If property is distributed in kind to a residuary legatee or remainderman, no gain or loss is realized by the estate or trust because of the distribution even though the fair market value of the distributed property differs from the property's income tax basis. On the other hand, if property is distributed in kind in satisfaction of a right to receive a specific dollar amount, the estate or trust may recognize gain or loss on the distribution. Treas. Reg. § 1.661(a)–2(f).

369 I.R.C. §§ 652, 662.

Specific Bequest Rule

For estates, and to a limited extent for trusts, certain distributions can be made which do not generate either a distributions deduction for the estate or a gross income inclusion for the beneficiary. These distributions are described in Section 663 and generally are referred to as specific bequests. Specific bequests include both specific bequests as defined by state law[370] as well as general devises, typically of a specific sum of money. They do not include distributions to residuary legatees.

For example, if, in the year 2021 the estate has gross income of $20,000 and pays $5,000 to John in satisfaction of a general devise, the estate is not entitled to any deduction in computing its taxable income for the amount of the distribution to John and none of the $5,000 is included in John's gross income. On the other hand, if the $5,000 had been distributed to a residuary beneficiary, the estate would have been entitled to a distributions deduction of $5,000 and $5,000 would have been included in the gross income of the residuary beneficiary. Thus, of the estate's $20,000 of income, $15,000 would be taxed to the estate and $5,000 would be taxed to the residuary legatee.

Distributable Net Income

Unlike trusts, an estate is rarely required to make distributions to beneficiaries until it terminates. As a result, estate distributions, except in the year of the estate's termination, are essentially discretionary. Trusts, on the other hand, are often required to make distributions and trustees often are permitted to make discretionary distributions.[371] It is not uncommon, for example, for a trust to mandate required distributions of income and authorize discretionary distributions of principal. To illustrate, suppose Rhonda transfers property to Bank in trust. The trust instrument directs Bank to distribute the trust's income to Able and authorizes Bank to invade principal in its discretion for the benefit of Able and Able's children. Here, there are both required and possible discretionary distributions.

Under Subchapter J, all required and discretionary distributions, other than distributions in payment of a specific bequest, usually will generate a distributions deduction for the estate or trust as well as a gross income inclusion for the beneficiary. To sort out the possibilities, the concept of distributable net income (DNI) is used. There is no counterpart to DNI in the income taxation of corporations, partnerships, or individuals.

Quantitatively, DNI is the uppermost ceiling on the distributions deduction and the amount that can be included in a beneficiary's gross income because of a distribution. Amounts distributed to beneficiaries that exceed DNI do not qualify for a distributions deduction and are not included in the

---

[370] Typically, these are bequests of specific, identifiable property. The distinction discussed Section 6.2, note 15 et seq. between specific and general devises for ademption purposes is not determinative in interpreting Section 663.

[371] These distinctions are reflected in the fact the sections 651 and 652 apply exclusively to trusts required to distribute their income currently whereas sections 661 and 662 apply to all other trusts as well as estates.

beneficiary's gross income. They are effectively income-tax free gifts and inheritances.

Essentially, DNI[372] equals the gross income of the estate or trust plus tax exempt income,[373] if any, less net capital gains included in its gross income and deductions, other than the distributions deduction, and the deduction for the estate's or trust's personal exemption, which for an estate is $600 and for a trust either $100 or $300.[374] For example, assume the estate or trust has $20,000 of rents, $5,000 of capital gains, and $8,000 of tax-exempt municipal bond interest. It paid $4,000 in state income taxes last year. Its DNI equals $24,000, which includes the rents and the municipal bond interest less the state income taxes. DNI excludes the capital gains.[375]

DNI preserves the characterization of items included in DNI as either rents, dividends, interests, tax exempt income and, when applicable, capital gains. This assures that to the extent DNI is distributed, the beneficiary is taxed pro-rata on each of the items includable in DNI.

The Tier Structure

For purposes of Subchapter J, a distinction is made between distributions of income which by state law are required to be distributed in the current taxable year and all other distributions, whether discretionary income distributions or principal distributions. DNI is allocated first to trust beneficiaries to whom trust accounting income is required to be distributed,[376] and only secondarily to other beneficiaries.

For example, suppose a trustee is required to distribute $500 of income to A, and also makes a $4,000 distribution of principal to B. DNI equals $2,000 and is wholly characterized as rents. A includes $500 in A's gross income; B includes $1,500 in B's gross income (thus exhausting DNI) and B receives the balance income tax free. If the trustee had been required to distribute $2,000 of income to A, then $2,000 of income would be included in A's gross income and nothing would be included in B's gross income.

The tier structure places the beneficiaries of discretionary distributions in a favored position over beneficiaries of income required to be distributed. Beneficiaries of discretionary distributions only include amounts distributed to them in their gross income to the extent the beneficiaries of income required to be distributed have not exhausted DNI. For estates, however, this is of little consequence because for the years prior to the year the estate terminates there are rarely beneficiaries to whom income is required to be distributed, and for

---

[372] I.R.C. § 643(a).

[373] I.R.C. § 103 (tax-exempt interest is interest payable on state and municipal bonds).

[374] I.R.C. § 642(b).

[375] Capital gains are included in DNI if they are required to be distributed. I.R.C. § 643(a)(3). Usually this only occurs in the taxable year the entity terminates when all of its income is required to be distributed. Capital gains are not ordinarily treated as income for trust accounting purposes. *See* Section 10.6, note 234.

[376] Income required to be distributed is also called "state law income" and means that amount of income to which a beneficiary is entitled under state law. Typically, the amount of such income is determined by reference to the applicable Uniform Principal and Income Act. *See* Section 10.6.

the year the estate terminates, the estate's income will be carried out and taxed to the estate's residuary beneficiaries.

Terminating Distributions—Excess Deductions

In the year in which an estate or trust terminates, if the estate or trust has deductions, other than a distributions deduction and personal exemption, that exceed its gross income, the excess deduction is allowable as a deduction on the personal tax returns of the persons succeeding to the property of the estate or trust.[377] For example, Alice's estate is about to terminate. In the year of termination, it has gross income of $12,000 and pays a deductible attorney fee of $15,000. The $3,000 excess can be claimed as a deduction on the residuary legatee's personal income tax return. The deduction is allowable only as an itemized deduction, not as an adjustment to gross income, and, thus, is unavailable to beneficiaries claiming the standard deduction.[378]

Charitable Deduction for Entity

Estates and trusts, like individuals, are entitled to a charitable deduction but the deduction available to estates and trusts differs in two important respects from that available to an individual. First, the deduction is unlimited.[379] It is not subject to a percentage limitation as it is with individuals. Thus, if all of the gross income of the estate or trust is paid to charity, all of it qualifies for the charitable deduction. Second, only estate or trust income distributable to charity pursuant to the terms of the governing instrument qualify for the charitable deduction.[380]

§ 15.7 Income Taxation of Grantor Trusts

Sections 671 through 679 set forth a series of rules under which a grantor of an inter-vivos trust may be required to include in the grantor's gross income either the trust's ordinary income or capital gains or both. Classification as a "grantor" trust will also entitle the grantor to claim the trust's deductible items and tax credits. Generally, the grantor trust rules apply whenever the grantor has retained an economic interest or "too much power over" either the income interest or the remainder interest or both. The rules are similar to but not identical to the rules on inclusion of inter-vivos trusts in the grantor's gross estate for federal estate tax purposes. It is possible to create a trust excludable from the gross estate on which the grantor continues to be taxed on the income. Given the high income tax rates on the retained income of an estate or trust,[381] there is an incentive to create an intentionally defective grantor trust (IDGT) which is excludable from the gross estate but on which the grantor continues to be taxed on the income at a presumably lower tax rate.

The most important of the grantor trust provisions are as follows:

---

377 I.R.C. § 642(h).

378 Treas. Reg. § 1.642(h)–2(a).

379 I.R.C. § 642(c)(1).

380 I.R.C. § 642(c)(1).

381 37 % on taxable income above $13,050 (2021 figure).

Grantor Retains a Reversionary Interest

The grantor is treated as the owner of any portion of a trust (that is the income interest or the remainder) in which the grantor has a reversionary interest if the value of the grantor's reversionary interest as of the inception of the interest exceeds 5% of the value of such portion.[382] For example, Harry creates a trust to pay the income to Able for life, and when Able dies, to distribute the trust principal back to Harry. Harry owns the entire reversion in this trust. Thus all of the trust's capital gains are included in Harry's gross income under section 673 if the actuarial value of Harry's reversion at the time of the trust's creation exceeds 5% of the trust's value.

Power to Control Beneficiary Enjoyment or Retains Administrative Control

Sections 674 and 675 apply when the grantor (whether or not in the capacity of trustee) *or a nonadverse party* retains the power to control the beneficial enjoyment of the trust power or retains certain administrative powers over the trust. It should be emphasized that Sections 674 and 675 can apply even if the grantor has no retained power and the only "tainted" power is held by a nonadverse party.

Section 674 generally treats the grantor as the owner of the portion of any trust over which the grantor or a nonadverse party has a "power of disposition," exercisable without the approval of an adverse party. A power of disposition is a power "to dispose of the beneficial enjoyment of the corpus or income unless the power"[383] is specifically excepted under the provisions of Section 674(b), (c) or (d). The exceptions to the general rule of Section 674 relate to the following: (1) power to apply income to support a dependent, (2) power exercisable only after the occurrence of an event, (3) testamentary power, (4) power affecting charities, (5) power to distribute principal, (6) power to withhold income temporarily, (7) power to withhold income during the beneficiary's disability, (8) power to allocate between principal and income, (9) powers exercisable by certain independent trustees and (10) powers limited by an ascertainable standard.

Section 675 applies to powers held by the grantor or a nonadverse party without the consent of an adverse party (1) permitting the grantor or any other person to deal with the trust assets for less and adequate and full consideration, (2) enabling the grantor to borrow trust assets without adequate interest or security, (3) permitting the exercise of certain powers of administration.

Because the rules of Sections 674 and 675 are highly complex and not easily committed to memory, whenever an attorney prepares an inter-vivos trust in which the grantor has any retained power, the attorney is well-advised to carefully examine Sections 674 and 675 to assure that the power held by the grantor or a nonadverse party will result in the intended income tax result.

---

[382] I.R.C. § 673(a).

[383] Treas. Reg. § 1.674(a)–1(b).

Revocable Trust

Under Section 676, the grantor is treated as the owner of any portion of a trust where the title to the portion can be revested in the grantor by a power exercisable by the grantor or a nonadverse power. The typical trust to which Section 676 applies is the revocable trust. Thus, if Ralph transfers property into a revocable trust to pay the income to Sally for life, remainder to Don, and Ralph retains the power to revoke the trust, the trust is a grantor trust and all of the trust's ordinary income and capital gains will be included in Ralph's gross income.

Trust Whose Income Is Payable to Grantor

With some limited exceptions, the grantor is treated as the owner of any portion of a trust the income from which is, or may be, distributed to the grantor or the grantor's spouse or held or accumulated for future distribution to the grantor or the grantor's spouse.[384] In addition, the grantor is treated as the owner of any portion of a trust the income from which is, or may be applied, toward payment of premiums on life insurance policies on the grantor or grantor spouse's life.[385] A typical Section 677 trust is a trust where either the grantor or the grantor's spouse is entitled to the income for life.

Income Taxation of Beneficiary with an Inter-Vivos General Power of Appointment

Among the grantor trust provisions of the Code is a provision treating the holder of a general power of appointment exercisable during the donee's life (as distinguished from solely by the donee's will) as the owner of the portion of the trust over which the lifetime general power is exercisable.[386] Thus, suppose Patricia creates a trust to pay the income to Don for life, remainder to Alice. The trustee is granted the discretion to accumulate income rather than pay it to Don. However, Don is granted a lifetime general power of appointment to distribute the trust principal to himself. Under Section 678, all of the trust income and gains are included in Don's gross income the same as if Don was the grantor of a revocable trust.

---

[384] I.R.C. § 677(a)(1)–(2).

[385] I.R.C. § 677(a)(3).

[386] I.R.C. § 678(a).

CHART I

Computation of Federal Estate Tax

GROSS ESTATE	§ 2031(a) (valuation at date of death).
	§ 2032 (alternate valuation method).
	§ 2032A (special use valuation method).
	§ 2033 Property interests owned at death including under § 2034 the
MINUS	surviving spouse's dower or curtesy interest or an estate in lieu thereof.
	§ 2035 Transfers within 3 years of death.
	§ 2036 Transfers with retained life estates.
	§ 2037 Transfers conditioned on surviving decedent.
	§ 2038 Revocable Transfers.
	§ 2039 Annuities.
	§ 2040 Jointly-owned property.
	§ 2041 Property subject to general power of appointment.
	§ 2042 Life insurance on decedent's life.
	§ 2044 Qualified Terminable Interest Property.
DEDUCTIONS FROM GROSS ESTATE	§ 2053 Funeral, debts, expenses and taxes.
	§ 2054 Losses incurred during administration.
	§ 2055 Unlimited charitable deduction.
EQUALS	§ 2056 Unlimited marital deduction.
	§ 2058 State Death Taxes (for persons dying after 2004).
TAXABLE ESTATE	Defined § 2051.
PLUS	
ADJUSTED TAXABLE GIFTS	(post-1976 taxable gifts, other than those gifts includible in gross estate.)
EQUALS	
TAX BASE	
APPLY TAX RATES (§ 2001)	
TENTATIVE TAX BEFORE CREDITS	
MINUS	
GIFT TAX PAYABLE ON POST-1976 GIFTS	§ 2001(b)(2).
	§ 2010 Unified Credit.
MINUS	§ 2011 State death tax credit (for decedent's dying before 2005).
OTHER CREDITS	§ 2012 Gift tax credit on pre-1977 gifts.
	§ 2013 Credit for tax on prior transfers.
EQUALS	§ 2014 Foreign death tax credit.
	§ 2015 Credit for death tax on remainder.
FEDERAL ESTATE TAX DUE	

CHART II

Computation of Federal Gift Tax

GIFTS DURING CALENDAR YEAR	§ 2501 Defined generally.
	§ 2512 Valuation of gifts.
MINUS	§ 2513 Gifts attributable from spouse.
	§ 2514 Powers of appointment.
	§ 2516 Property settlement agreements.
	§ 2517 Annuities.
	§ 2518 Disclaimers.
	§ 2519 Qualifying income interest for life.
GIFTS ATTRIBUTABLE TO SPOUSE	§ 2513 Gift by husband or wife to third party.
EQUALS	
GIFTS DURING CALENDAR YEAR BEFORE DEDUCTIONS AND EXCLUSIONS	
MINUS	
DEDUCTIONS AND EXCLUSIONS	§ 2503(b) (c) & (e) Annual exclusion of $10,000 (plus inflation adjustment) per donee for present interests.
EQUALS	§ 2503(e), Gifts of certain educational and medical expenses.
	§ 2522 Unlimited charitable deduction.
	§ 2523 Unlimited marital deduction.
TAXABLE GIFTS FOR CALENDAR YEAR	§ 2503(a) Defined.
PLUS	
TAXABLE GIFTS FOR PRIOR YEARS	§ 2504 Defined.
APPLY TAX RATES (§ 2502)	
TAX ON TOTAL GIFTS	
MINUS	
TAX ON GIFTS FOR PRIOR PERIODS	
EQUALS	
TAX BEFORE UNIFIED CREDIT	
MINUS	
UNIFIED CREDIT	§ 2505 Defined.
EQUALS	
FEDERAL GIFT TAX DUE	

Table of Cases

1942 Gerald H. Lewis Trust, Matter of, 377
21 Merchants Row Corp. v. Merchants Row, 559
A. v. B., 244
AAM/US Bank LLC v. Lake Carroll Ass'n, 555
Abbett Elec. Corp. v. Storek, 356
Abbiss v. Burney, 520
Abbot, Matter of Estate of, 302
Abernathy v. Latham, 215, 216
Ablamis v. Roper, 363
Ablin v. Richard O'Brien Plastering Co., 75
Abney v. Western Res. Mut. Cas. Co., 155
Abo Petroleum Corp. v. Amstutz, 520
Abraham Zion Corp. v. Lebow, 686
Abram v. Wilson, 531, 534, 538
Abrams v. Templeton, 529, 543
Ackel v. Ackel, 362
Acord, Estate of v. Commissioner, 275
Acree v. Acree, 663
Adair v. Martin, 328
Adair, Matter of Will of, 285
Adams v. French, 677
Adams v. Jankouskas, 124, 358
Adams v. Link, 464
Adams v. Vidal, 490
Adkins v. Oppio, 179
Adler v. Adler, 683
Aetna Life Ins. Co. v. Boober, 360, 362
Aetna Life Ins. Co. v. Bunt, 121
Aetna Life Ins. Co. v. Primofiore, 89
Agans, In re Estate of, 333
Agostini's Estate, In re, 221
Aiello v. Clark, 164
Akerman v. Trosper, 226
Akers v. Hodel, 221
Akin v. Dahl, 643
Akron Bar Ass'n v. Parker, 244
Albinger v. Harris, 205
Albrecht v. Brais, 158
Albro v. Allen, 212
Alcorn, Matter of Estate of, 118
Aldridge v. Mims, 47
Alexander v. Alexander, 103
Alexander v. Georgia Baptist Foundation, Inc., 478
Alexander v. Harris, 452
Alexander v. Snell, 211
Alexander, In re Estate of, 123
Alexander, Matter of Estate of, 224, 241
Alfaro, In re Estate of, 143
Allard v. Pacific National Bank, 618, 637
Allemand v. Weaver, 271
Allen v. Amoco Production Co., 584
Allen v. Dalk, 132, 133
Allen v. Dutton's Estate, 237
Allen v. Estate of Allen, 651
Allen v. Hall, 232
Allen v. Maddock, 294
Allen v. Storer, 38, 41, 121
Allen v. Talley, 268
Allen v. Western Conference of Teamsters Pension Trust Fund, 119
Allen, Estate of, 94
Allen, In re Marriage of, 359
Allen, Matter of Estate of, 32, 118, 272, 510
Almeida v. Almeida, 206
Aloha Lumber Corp. v. University of Alaska, 637, 638
Alsenz v. Alsenz, 358
Alsup v. Montoya, 426
Altazan, Succession of, 196
Altshuler v. Minkus-Whalen, 643, 672
Altstatt, In re, 662
Ambrose Succession v. Ambrose, 326
American Cancer Soc. v. Hammerstein, 436
American National Bank and Trust v. Vinson, 312, 313
American National Bank v. Miller, 461
American Western Life Ins. Co. v. Hooker, 209
Amerige v. Attorney General, 30, 547
Ancell, In re Estate of, 176
Anderson v. Baker, 299
Anderson v. Brinkerhoff, 234, 303
Anderson v. Dean Witter Reynolds, Inc., 681
Anderson v. Dubel, 192
Anderson v. Ferris, 314
Anderson v. Gilliland, 359
Anderson v. Marquette National Bank, 414, 576
Anderson v. Meadowcroft, 233
Anderson, Estate of, 121, 285
Anderson, In re Conservatorship of v. Lasen, 230, 425
Anderson, In re Estate of, 121
Anderson, Matter of Estate of, 113, 264, 281, 526, 539, 588
Andrews v. Gorby, 654, 657
Andrews v. Hall, 557
Andrews v. Troy Bank & Trust Co., 155
Anello, Estate of v. McQueen, 213
Angier, In re Estate of, 288

Angleton v. Estate of Angleton, 83, 84, 86, 87
Annan v. Wilmington Trust Co., 49, 105
Antoinette, In re Estate of, 232
Anton, In re Estate of, 251
Antonopoulos, In re Estate of, 50, 122, 210, 345, 348, 349
Apple v. Kile, 623
Aragon v. Rio Costilla Cooperative Livestock Ass'n, 168
Aranda v. Camacho, 85
Araneo, Matter of, 289
Arch, Ltd. v. Yu, 363
Archer's Case, 520
Arens' Trust, In re, 43
Arman v. Bank of America, N.T. & S.A., 475
Armendaris Water Dev. Co. v. Rainwater, 314
Armijo, In re Estate of, 179, 287
Armstrong v. Armstrong, 588
Armstrong v. Bray, 88
Armstrong, In re Estate of, 86
Arrington v. United States, 709
Arrowsmith v. Mercantile-Safe Deposit, 538, 544, 546, 548
Artope, In re Will of, 290
Artz, Estate of v. Artz, 86
Ascherl, Matter of Estate of, 370
Ash v. Calvert, 567
Ashbaugh v. Ashbaugh, 312
Ashe, Matter of Estate of, 158
Ashman v. Pickens, 647
Ashton v. Ashton, 313
Atchison v. City of Englewood, 560
Atchison, In re, 93, 94
Atkins v. Atkins, 37
Atkins v. Marks, 448
Atkins, Petition of, 575
Atkinson v. Kish, 559
Attorney Grievance Comm'n v. Brooke, 242, 244
Atwater v. Nortel Networks, Inc., 85
Atwood v. Atwood, 605, 609, 610
Auburn, Estate of, 199, 201
Auen, Estate of, 242, 580
Augusta, City of v. Attorney General, 458
Ault, In re Estate of, 153
Aurora Nat. Bank v. Old Second Nat. Bank, 506
Ausley, Matter of Estate of, 192, 199
Austin v. City of Alexandria, 208
Austin v. Dobbins, 531
Austin v. United States Bank of Washington, 434
Austin, In re Estate of, 581
Austin, Succession of, 577
Autoclub Body and Paint Services, Inc., In re, 685
Awrey v. Commissioner, 722
Axelrod v. Giambalvo, 667
Ayala v. Martinez, 147, 641
Azcunce v. Estate of Azcunce, 336
Baars v. Campbell University, 577
Bach, Estate of, 366
Bachand's Estate, In re, 590
Bacot, Succession of, 146, 147, 285
Bader v. Digney, 154
Badger Bldg. Corp. v. Gregoric, 307
Baer's Estate, Matter of, 343
Baggerley's Estate, Matter of, 370, 372
Bahler v. Doenges, 594
Bailey v. Arlington Bank & Trust Co., 235
Bailey v. Cherokee County Appraisal Dist., 587
Bailey v. Kennedy, 201
Bailey v. Retirement Board of Policemen's Annuity and Ben. Fund, 84
Baizley v. Baizley, 306
Baker v. Leonard, 46, 299, 300
Baker v. Mohr, 181
Baker, Estate of, 234
Balanson, In re, 358
Balboni v. LaRocque, 196
Baldwin, Estate of, 615
Baldwin, In re, 448
Baldwin, In re Estate of, 581
Bales, Matter of, 243, 651, 657
Ball v. Curtis, 426
Ballard v. McCoy, 164
Ballenger v. Ballenger, 434
Balter, In re Estate of, 248
Bancker, In re Estate of, 193
Bank IV, Olathe v. Capitol Federal S & L, 682
Bank of America National Trust v. Superior Court, 666, 673
Bank of America v. Angel View, 44, 46
Bank of Delaware v. Buckson, 470
Bank of Kansas City v. District Director, 590
Bank of New England v. Strandlund, 453
Bank of New York v. Black, 511
Bank of New York, In re, 616
Bank One Ohio Trust Co., N.A. v. Hiram College, 45
Bank One Ohio Trust Co., N.A. v. United States, 453
BankAmerica Pension Plan v. McMath, 132, 210
BankBoston v. Marlow, 286
Banko, Matter of Estate of, 237
Banks, In re Estate of, 118
Barber, In re Estate of, 653, 659
Barboza v. McLeod, 178
Barcelo v. Elliott, 245
Barham v. Jones, 154, 155, 157
Barlow Soc. v. Commercial Sec. Bank, 156

Barlow v. Olguin, 418
Barnedt v. Wilder, 204
Barnett Banks Trust Co. v. Herr, 434, 438
Barnett v. Barnett, 328, 366
Barnette v. McNulty, 167, 208
Barrenger v. Barrenger, 418
Barrett's Estate, In re, 202
Barrie, In re Estate of, 32
Barrientos v. Nava, 166
Barron v. Puzo, 329
Bartell, Matter of Estate of, 341
Bartlett v. Commissioner, 186
Bartlett v. Dumaine, 661, 663
Bartlett, In re Estate of, 329
Bartlett, Matter of Estate of, 655
Basassadegan v. Vernon, 678
Basich, Estate of, 220, 236
Baskin v. Commerce Union Bank, 561
Bassett v. Bassett, 308, 310, 311
Batcheldor v. Boyd, 103
Batey v. Batey, 118, 119
Batton, Succession of v. Prince, 647
Baugh v. Baugh ex rel. Smith, 75
Baxter, Estate of, 375
Bayer v. Bayer, 358
Bayley Trust, In re, 462
Beacham v. Palmer, 585
Beal, Matter of Estate of, 190, 581
Beale, Estate of, 292
Beall v. Beall, 38, 679
Beals v. State St. Bank & Trust Co., 514
Bearbower, Matter of Estate of, 141
Beard, In re Estate of, 622
Beattie v. J.M. Tull Foundation, 663
Beatty v. Beatty, 372
Beauchamp v. Beauchamp, 35, 558, 560
Beaudoin v. Trudel, 366
Beauregard, In re Estate of, 196
Beck, Estate of v. Engene, 569
Becker v. Brozek-Robinson, 460
Bednar v. Bednar, 166
Bedo v. McGuire, 662
Bedree v. Bedree, 235
Beelman v. Beelman, 306, 307, 312
Beeruk's Estate, In re, 182, 184
Beesley, Matter of Estate of, 372, 373
Beglinger Trust, In re, 580
Beider, In re Estate of, 589
Belcher v. Conway, 475
Bell v. Estate of Bell, 340
Bell v. Forti, 105
Bell v. King, Phipps & Assoc., P.C., 584
Bell, Matter of Estate of, 332
Belleville National Bank v. Trauernicht, 520
Bellingham, Matter of Estate of, 360
Bellingroehr, In re, 421
Bemis v. Estate of Bemis, 166
Benjamin v. Woodring, 221
Bennett v. Allstate Ins. Co., 90
Bennett, Estate of, 93, 94
Bennett, Matter of Estate of, 4
Bennion v. Hansen, 157
Benson v. Benson, 330
Benson v. Patterson, 328
Benson, Estate of, 90
Benson, In re Estate of, 487, 488
Bentley, In re, 580
Berdrow, Estate of, 267
Berg, In re Estate of, 221, 590
Bergau, Matter of Estate of, 287
Bergen v. Travelers Ins. Co., 226
Berger v. United States, 305
Berger, In re Estate of, 624
Berke v. First Nat. Bank & Trust Co., 589
Bernard's Settlement, In re, 200
Bernstein v. Rosenthal, 87
Berry v. Trible, 146
Berry v. Union Nat. Bank, 528, 532, 542
Berry, In re Estate of, 289
Berry, Matter of, 19
Berry, Matter of Estate of, 228
Bert Bidwell Inv. v. LaSalle and Schiffer, 559
Berthot, In re Estate of, 653
Bertrand, In re Marriage of, 329
Besnilian v. Wilkinson, 335
Bessett v. Huson, 47, 156
Best, Matter of Estate of, 105
Bestwick, Estate of, 250
Betlem, In re, 100
Bettencourt v. Bettencourt, 179
Bettis' Estate, In re, 636
Betts By and Through Parker v. Parrish, 273
Betts v. Ginlickson, 638
Betty G. Weldon Revocable Trust, In re, 603
Beyer v. First Nat'l Bank, 673, 674
Bible Ministry Ass'n v. Merritt, 375
Bielat v. Bielat, 47
Bigej v. Boyer, 223, 226
Billewicz v. Ransmeier, 680
Billings v. Fowler, 50
Billings, In re Estate of, 658
Bilse, In re Estate of, 353
Biltmore Village v. Royal, Biltmore Village, 551
Bird v. Plunkett, 87
Bird's Estate, In re, 545
Birkeland's Estate, In re, 144
Bischof, Estate of, 167
Bishop v. Kenny, 222
Bixby v. California Trust Co., 502
Black v. Poole, 158
Black v. Unknown Creditors, 61
Black, Estate of v. Rombotis, 130, 146
Black's Estate, In re, 281

Blackmon v. Estate of Battcock, 183
Blair v. Commissioner, 709
Blair v. Ing, 245
Blaircom v. Hires, 299
Blake's Estate v. Benza, 148, 149, 191
Blalak v. Mid Valley Transp., Inc., 310
Blancett v. Blancett, 156
Blanchette v. Blanchette, 178
Bland v. Graves, 220
Blank, In re Estate of, 336
Blech v. Blech, 451
Bledsoe v. Hill, 303
Blettell, Estate of v. Snider, 153
Blissard v. White, 239
Block v. Edge, 273
Blocker v. State, 475
Blodgett, In re Estate of, 295
Blom, In re Estate of, 303
Blomdahl's Will, In re, 249
Blood v. Poindexter, 33
Bloom v. Selfon, 203, 273
Blough's Estate, Matter of, 491
Blouin, Estate of, 600, 637
Blue Valley Federal Savings and Loan Ass'n v. Burrus, 166, 167
Blumenthal, In re Estate of, 186
Bo, Matter of, 225
Boan v. Watson, 48
Board of Curators University of Missouri, State ex rel. v. Green, 638
Board of Education v. Browning, 111
Board of Education v. Miles, 44, 51, 551
Board of Regents v. Bates, 282
Board of Trustees of University of Alabama v. Calhoun, 192
Boatmen's Trust Co. v. Conklin, 49
Bob Jones University v. United States, 470
Bobeck, Matter of, 178
Boehm v. Allen, 233
Boerstler v. Andrews, 250, 257
Boggs v. Boggs, 363, 366
Bohac, In re Guardianship of, 228
Bohl v. Haney, 673
Bohnke v. Estate of Bohnke, 370
Bolinder, Matter of Estate of, 239
Bolinger, Matter of Estate of, 170
Bolton, In re Estate of, 156
Bomareto, Matter of Estate of, 675
Bonds, In re Marriage of, 368, 371
Bongaards v. Millen, 187, 208, 321, 348
Bonner, In re Will of, 196
Bonney v. Granger, 303
Bono v. Clark, 359
Bonta v. Burke, 442
Bookasta, Conservatorship of, 225, 578
Booker v. Lal, 57, 75, 76
Booker, Matter of, 563
Boone County State Bank v. Andrews, 228
Boone v. Grier, 304
Booth v. McKnight, 622
Boright, Matter of, 461
Borom, Matter of Estate of, 196
Bortolotti v. Hayden, 523, 555
Bosch, Estate of, Commissioner v., 460, 709
Bosone v. Bosone, 361, 362
Boston Safe Deposit & Trust Co. v. Goodwin, 61
Boston Safe Deposit & Trust Co. v. Wilbur, 45, 72, 286, 679
Bouchat, Matter of Estate of, 224
Bouquet, In re Marriage of, 48
Bouton v. Labiche, 110
Bowen v. Bowen, 210, 373
Bowers, Matter of Guardianship of, 585
Bowling v. Deaton, 273
Bowman, Matter of Estate of, 333, 643
Boyd, Estate of, 76
Boydstun v. Loveless, 205
Boyer v. Sparboe, 591
Boykin, Ex parte, 452
Boyle v. Schmitt, 182
Bracken v. Block, 437
Bradley v. Bradley, 90
Bradley v. Hill, 353
Braman, In re Estate of, 264
Brame v. Read, 168
Brammer v. Taylor, 141
Brandon v. Robinson, 449
Branigan, Matter of Estate of, 287, 459
Bratley v. Suburban Bank, 275
Bratton v. Owens, 237
Braun v. Braun, 329
Breckheimer v. Kraft, 280
Brecklein's Estate, Matter of, 256, 642
Breckner v. Prestwood, 256, 282
Breeden v. Stone, 220, 221
Breeden, Estate of, 469
Brees v. Cramer, 373
Bremer v. Luff, 721
Brenholdt v. Brenholdt, 365
Brenner, Estate of, 145, 166
Brent v. Smathers, 624, 673, 684
Brent v. State Cent. Collection Unit, 450
Brenzikofer, Estate of, 186
Brickhouse v. Brickhouse, 138, 143
Bridgeport City Trust Co., Commissioner v., 719
Briggs v. Crowley, 619
Briggs v. Liddell, 304
Briggs v. Wyoming Nat. Bank of Casper, 371, 582
Briley, Matter of Estate of, 176, 252
Brinkman, In re Estate of, 260
Brittin, In re Estate of, 106, 109

Brock v. Citizens Bank of Clovis, 598, 609
Brodbeck, Matter of Estate of, 236
Brodrick v. Moore, 80
Brody v. Bock, 181
Brook v. Warde, 575
Brookbank v. Gray, 75
Brookline v. Carey, 552
Brooks v. Kunz, 124
Brooks, Matter of Estate of, 136, 140
Brosamer v. Mark, 454
Brosseau, Matter of Estate of, 372
Brotman v. East Lake Creek Ranch, L.L.P., 163
Broughton, Matter of Estate of, 338, 486
Brouse v. Old Phoenix Nat. Bank, 511
Browder v. Hite, 308, 311
Brown v. American Fletcher Nat. Bank, 488, 524, 531
Brown v. Boeing Co., 362, 368
Brown v. Branch, 160
Brown v. Brown, 360, 617, 641, 659
Brown v. Carr, 118, 122
Brown v. Crawford, 338
Brown v. Eiguren, 591
Brown v. Fluharty, 131
Brown v. Labow, 249
Brown v. Leadley, 271
Brown v. Metz, 157
Brown v. Parry, 349
Brown v. Ryan, 30, 39, 548
Brown v. Sackville, 127
Brown v. Sammons, 349
Brown v. Trust Co., 49
Brown, Estate of, 149, 354, 369
Brown, Estate of v. Fulp, 225
Brown, In re Estate of, 458
Brown, Matter of Estate of, 36, 42, 249, 263, 282
Brown, Petition of, 121
Brown, Succession of, 101
Brown, Will of, 514
Brown's Estate, In re, 509, 660
Brown's Estate, Matter of, 234
Brownell v. Edmunds, 532
Browning v. Sacrison, 484, 489
Browning, In re Guardianship of, 395
Brownlee, In re Estate of, 154, 261, 282, 283
Bruce, Estate of, 348
Bruce, Matter of Estate of, 99
Brune's Estate, Matter of, 194
Bruner, Estate of, 292
Brunson v. Citizens Bank and Trust Co., 74, 282
Bryan v. Norton, 234, 236, 237
Bryan's Appeal, In re, 295
Bryant, Estate of, 98
Buchea v. United States, 41
Buchholz v. Storsve, 46
Buck Trust, In re, 511
Buck v. Banks, 554, 556
Buckley, Estate of, 35, 36
Buder v. Sartore, 607
Budin v. Levy, 464
Buehler v. Buehler, 47
Buffalo Seminary v. McCarthy, 523, 554
Buffi's Estate, Matter of, 150
Buhler, Matter of Estate of, 332
Bulger, In re Estate of, 267
Bunch, Estate of v. Heirs of Bunch, 470
Buol, In re Marriage of, 44, 52
Burch v. Dodge, 655
Burcham v. Burcham, 578
Burdette, Estate of, 136
Burford, Estate of v. Burford, 120
Burgess, Matter of Estate of, 510
Burke v. Kehr, 242
Burke, Matter of Estate of, 141
Burkett v. Mott, 210, 295
Burmeister, Estate of, 98
Burns v. Adamson, 131, 143
Burrough, In re Estate of, 536, 537, 540
Burruss, Matter of Estate of, 267
Burshiem, Matter of Estate of, 36
Burt v. Commercial Bank & Trust Co., 548
Burton v. Hicks, 538
Burton, Estate of v. Didricksen, 131
Butcher v. Pollard, 101, 105
Butler v. Dobbins, 249, 258
Butler v. Halstead, 76
Butterfield, Matter of Estate of, 431
Button by Curio v. Elmhurst Nat. Bank, 87
Button, In re Estate of, 266
Bybee, In re Will of, 267
Byke Const. Co., Inc. v. Miller, 554
Byrd v. Lanahan, 167
Byrne v. Laura, 123
Byrum, United States v., 712
C & L Lumber and Supply, Inc. v. Texas American Bank, 361
Cable Family Trust dated June 10, In re, 409
Cadell v. Palmer, 522
Caffoni, In re, 94
Caffrey, Matter of Estate of, 331, 332
Cahill, In re Estate of, 590
Calcutt, Estate of v. Calcutt, 349, 368, 373
Calden, Estate of, 73, 270
Calhoun v. Campbell, 49
Calhoun v. Higgins, 153
Calhoun, In re Will of, 580
Calhoun, Matter of Succession of, 139
Califano v. Boles, 123
Califano v. Jobst, 123
California-Western States Life Ins. Co. v. Sanford, 87

Caliman v. American General Fire & Cas. Co., 89
Callan v. Winters, 49
Callard v. Callard, 152
Callaway v. Callaway, 144
Camac, In re, 234
Came, In re Estate of, 337
Camerlo v. Howard Johnson Co., 555
Camilli v. Cemetery, 222
Camin, In re Estate of, 224
Camp v. Commissioner, 700
Campbell v. Black, 212, 226
Campbell, In re Estate of, 101
Campbell, Matter of, 502
Campbell, Matter of Estate of, 40, 581, 582
Campbell's Trusts, In the Matter of, 435, 659
Canal Nat. Bank v. Chapman, 296
Canoy v. Canoy, 489
Cantor v. Dep't of Income Maintenance, 30
Carano, Matter of Estate of, 239
Caraway, Succession of, 363
Cardwell v. Estate of Kirkendall, 589
Carey v. Jackson, 154
Carey v. Lincoln Loan Co., 559
Cargill, Matter of Will of, 52, 624
Carl J. Herzog Foundation v. University of Bridgeport, 474
Carlisle, In re Estate of, 120
Carlson v. Carlson, 366
Carlson, Estate of, 276
Carlton's Estate, In re, 190
Carma Developers (California), Inc. v. Marathon Development California, Inc., 557, 559
Carmedy, In re Estate of, 136
Carmer, Matter of Estate of, 256
Carmichael v. Lathrop, 82, 257
Carmichael v. Lively, 94
Carolina Production Credit Ass'n v. Rogers, 334, 349
Carpenter, Estate of v. Cosby, 200
Carper, Estate of, 292
Carr v. Carr, 120
Carrell v. Ellingwood, 576
Carroll v. Israelson, 203
Carroll, In re Estate of, 134, 144
Carroll, Matter of, 155
Carroll, Matter of Estate of, 203
Cartee v. Lesley, 666
Carter v. Berry, 534, 542
Carter v. Carter, 234, 313, 605
Carter v. First United Methodist Church, 199
Carter, In re Estate of, 510, 511, 569
Casey, Estate of v. Commissioner, 230, 389
Casey, In re Estate of, 182
Casey, Matter of Estate of, 155
Cason v. Taylor, 149, 190, 191, 198
Casselman, In re Estate of, 149
Cassiday v. Cassiday, 155
Cassity, Matter of Estate of, 658
Casson v. Swogell, 143
Cast v. National Bank, 557, 558
Castaneda, In re Estate of, 111
Castiglioni, Estate of, 88
Castruccio v. Estate of Castruccio, 135
Catanio, Matter of, 128
Catch v. Phillips, 132
Cates v. Fricker, 580
Cavalier, In re Estate of, 650
Cavenaugh, Estate of v. Commissioner, 355
Cavill's Estate, In re, 374
Cavin, In re Estate of, 609
Cayo, Matter of Estate of, 339
Cazares v. Cosby, 154
Celestin, In re Succession of, 74
Cent. Trust Co. of N. Ohio, N.A. v. Smith, 495
Center v. Hampton Affiliates, Inc., 154
Central Bank-Granite City v. Ziaee, 223, 226
Central Delaware County Authority v. Greyhound Corp., 551
Central Nat'l Bank v. Fitzwilliam, 594
Central Nat'l Bank v. United States Dept. of Treasury, 647
Central Trust Bank v. Stout, 58
Central Trust Co. of N. Ohio, N.A. v. Smith, 493
Certificates of Deposit, In re, 594
Certified Corp. v. GTE Products Corp., 554
Chaitlen, In re Estate of, 166
Chambers v. Warren, 270
Chandler v. Central Oil Corp., 118
Chandler v. Chandler, 170
Chandler v. Hale, 449
Chandler, United States v., 155
Chaney, Matter of Adoption of, 109
Chaney, Matter of Succession of, 317
Chapman v. Chapman, 252
Chapman v. Citizens and Southern Nat. Bank, 184, 313
Charles C. Wells Revocable Trust, In re, 644
Charleston Nat. Bank v. Thru the Bible, 146, 195
Chase v. Pevear, 608, 616, 657
Chastain, In re Estate of, 135
Chavez v. Carpenter, 76, 78
Chavin v. PNC Bank, 276
Chemical Bank, In re, 530
Cheney v. Jemmett, 559
Cheney, Will of, 562, 563
Chesnin v. Fischler, 364
Cheuvront v. Haley, 73, 499
Cheyanna M. v. A.C. Nielsen Co., 75
Chicago Police Sergeant's Association v. Pallohusky, 411

Chicago Title and Trust Co. v. Steinitz, 44, 45
Chichester Diocesan Fund v. Simpson, 471
Chiesi, Estate of v. First Citizens Bank, 90, 595
Childress v. Currie, 236
Childs v. First National Bank, 299
Childs v. National Bank, 661
Chipman v. Spitznagel, 269
Chlebos, In re Estate of, 223
Choman v. Epperley, 175
Choyce, Succession of, 118, 119
Chrisman, In re Estate of, 671
Chrisp, In re Estate of, 593
Christensen v. Britton, 226, 239
Christensen, Estate of, 285
Christensen, Estate of v. Christensen, 342
Chrysler, Estate of v. Commissioner, 712
Chudleigh's Case, 520
Chumbley, In re Marriage of, 359
Chun Quan Yee Hop's Estate, In re, 523, 542
Church v. First Union Nat'l Bank, 685
Church v. Morgan, 250
Church, Estate of v. Tubbs, 205
Church, Matter of Will of, 148
Churchill v. Allessio, 199, 200
Cickyj v. Skeltinska, 170
Cincinnati Bar Ass'n v. Lowery, 570
Cinnaminson Township v. First Camden Nat'l Bank & Trust Co., 479
Ciochon's Estate, Matter of, 183
CitiFinancial Inc. v. Balch, 18
Citizens Nat. Bank v. Stasell, 215
Citizens State Bank & Trust Co. v. Nolte, 227
City Bank & Trust Co. in Dixon v. Morrissey, 43, 502
City Bank of Farmers Trust Co., Helvering v., 717
City Nat. Bank of Birmingham v. Andrews, 502
Claflin v. Claflin, 462
Clairmont v. Larson, 460
Clark v. Campbell, 410
Clark v. Gale, 180
Clark v. Greenhalge, 293, 295
Clark v. Strother, 483
Clark v. Studenwalt, 134
Clark v. Unknown Heirs of Osborn, 573
Clark, Estate of, 31
Clark, Estate of v. Foster & Good, 581
Clark, Matter of, 255
Claveloux v. Bacotti, 578
Clay v. Woods, 347
Clayton v. Commissioner, 734
Cleary v. Cleary, 237, 241
Cleaveland v. United States, 97
Cleopatra Cameron Gift Trust, In re, 446
Clermont Cty. Bar Ass'n v. Bradford, 242
Cleveland, Estate of, 112
Cline v. Finney, 222
Clobberie's Case, 488
Clopton, Estate of, 470
Cloud v. United States Nat'l Bank, 624, 674
Clouse, In re Estate of, 158
Clymer v. Mayo, 113, 215, 281, 298
Cocke v. Duke University, 663
Coddington v. Stone, 485
Coe, Estate of, 43
Coffee v. William Marsh Rice University, 477
Coffey, Conservatorship of, 605, 663, 672
Coffman v. Woods, 185
Cohen v. City of Lynn, 163
Cohen v. Cronin, 589
Cohen, In re, 599
Cohen, Matter of Estate of, 181
Cohn v. Heymann, 32, 33, 39, 42
Cohn, In re, 38
Colby v. Colby, 553, 557, 560
Cole ex rel. Cole Revocable Trust v. Cole, 208
Cole v. Guy, 153
Cole v. Rivers, 181
Cole, Matter of Estate of, 344
Coleman, In re Estate of, 380
Coleman, Matter of Estate of, 340
Colgan v. Sisters of St. Joseph, 478
Collection Bureau of San Jose v. Rumsey, 575
Collier, Matter of, 160, 172
Collins, In re Estate of, 607
Colombo v. Stevenson, 268
Combee, In re Estate of, 301
Commerce Union Bank v. Warren County, 550
Committee on Professional Ethics v. Winkel, 626
Compton, In re, 469
Conduct of Carey, In re, 599
Conduct of Hedrick, In re, 190, 570
Congdon's Estate, Matter of, 87
Conn v. Trow, 213
Connecticut Bank & Trust Co. v. Brody, 43, 50, 529, 533, 534
Connecticut Bank & Trust Co. v. Coffin, 465
Connecticut Bank & Trust Co. v. Cyril and Julia C. Johnson Mem. Hosp., 470
Connecticut Gen. Life Ins. Co. v. Gulley, 209
Connecticut National Bank & Trust Co. v. Chadwick, 285

Connell v. Francisco, 124
Connin v. Bailey, 328
Connolly's Estate, In re, 475, 478
Conrad, In re Estate of, 354
Conradi v. Perkins, 153
Conroy, In re Matter of, 394
Constan, In re Estate of, 68
Consupak, Inc., In re, 655
Continental Bank, N.A. v. Herguth, 49
Conway v. Childress, 49
Cook v. Estate of Seeman, 375
Cook v. Holland, 686
Cook v. Loftus, 232
Cook v. Nale, 86
Cook, Matter of Estate of, 41
Cooke, In re Estate of, 337, 338
Cooley v. Williams, 9
Coomes v. Finegan, 97
Coomler v. Shell Oil Co., 555
Cooper v. Cooper, 361
Cooper v. Crabb, 299
Cooper v. Harris, 48
Cooper v. Jones, 612
Cooper v. Tosco Corp., Lion Oil Div., 568, 579
Cooper, Matter of Estate of, 609, 613
Corbet's Case, 519
Corlett v. Smith, 590
Cornelious, Estate of, 102
Cornelius, Matter of Estate of, 580
Cornell, In re, 94
Corning Bank v. Rice, 174
Corpus Christi Bank & Trust v. Cross, 684
Corrigan, In re Estate of, 270, 282
Corron v. Corron, 578
Costello v. Hall, 224
Coster v. Crookham, 666
Costin v. Cripe, 716
Cotham v. First Nat. Bank, 529
Cotten v. Cotten, 233
Cottingham v. McKee, 380
Coughlin, Estate of, 655
Council v. Owens, 449, 452
Courtenay C. & Lucy Patten Davis Foundation v. Colorado State University Research Foundation, 474
Courts v. Annie Penn Memorial Hospital, 206
Coussee v. Estate of Efston, 189, 577
Covert, In re Estates of, 87, 88, 90
Cowden v. Sovran Bank/Central South, 478
Cox v. Forristall, 486
Cox v. Whitten, 109
Crabtree, In re, 314
Crabtree, In re Will of, 475, 649
Craft, United States v., 594
Craig Living Trust, In re, 420
Craig, Matter of Estate of, 477
Crawford & Lewis v. Boatmen's Trust Co., 656
Crawford, Matter of Estate of, 370
Creech, In re Estate of, 202
Creekmore v. Creekmore, 156
Cregar, In re Estate of, 107
Crichton's Estate, In re, 35, 364
Crist, Matter of Estate of, 255
Cristofani v. Commissioner, 698
Crittell v. Bingo, 221, 224, 233, 238
Crockett, In re Estate of, 118
Crohn's Estate, In re, 47, 203
Crook v. Contreras, 207
Crosby v. Alton Ochsner Medical Foundation, 200
Cross v. Cross, 109, 512
Crossmore, Estate of, 222
Crossroads Shopping Center v. Montgomery Ward & Co., Inc., 554, 555
Crowden v. Aldridge, 100
Crowell v. Shelton, 380
Crowl, Matter of Estate of, 554
Crowther v. Mower, 210
Cruikshank, In re Estate of, 45, 485, 487
Crummey v. Commissioner, 697
Crump v. Moss, 235
Crumpton v. Mitchell, 50
Cruse, Matter of Estate of, 100
Cruzan v. Director, Missouri Department of Health, 390, 392
CS-Lakeview at Gwinnett, Inc. v. Simon Property Group, Inc., 555
Cudworth v. Cudworth, 599
Cummings, In re Estate of, 373
Cundall v. U.S. Bank, N.A., 663
Cunningham v. Hastings, 210
Cunningham, In re Estate of, 147
Curley v. Giltrop, 213
Currier Gallery of Art v. Packard, 149
Curry v. Williman, 66, 111
Cushman, Estate of, 255
Custick, Matter of Estate of, 190
CVR 1997 Irrevocable Trust, In re, 600
Dabney v. Thomas, 150
Dahl v. Dahl, 31
Dahlgren v. First National Bank, 147, 164
Daigle's Estate, In re, 590
Daily, Matter of Estate of, 569
Dale, In re, 180, 184
Dalton, In re Estate of, 121
Daly v. Hussey, 222
Dammann's Estate, In re, 272
Damskog, In re Estate of, 646
Danelczyk v. Tynek, 287
Daniel v. Brown, 512
Daniels v. Retirement Board, 118
Daniels, Matter of Will of, 297, 659
Dankbar, Matter of Estate of, 233, 241

Danz v. Danz, 482
Daoang, Matter of Trust Estate of, 208
Dauer v. Butera, 488
Dauray v. Mee, 190
Davenport v. Attorney General, 550
Davenport, Estate of v. Commissioner, 155, 157
David v. Russo, 306
Davis v. Miller, 368, 371, 372
Davis v. Secretary of Health and Human Services, 86
Davis v. U.S. Bank, N.A., 644
Davis v. Young, 412
Davis, In re Estate of, 215, 463, 533, 580, 682
Davis, In re Marriage of, 117
Davison v. Feuerherd, 290
Davisson v. Indiana Nat. Bank, 298
Dawson v. Yucus, 271
Day, Matter of Estate of, 197
De Avila v. Estate of DeHerrera, 591
De Domenico, In re Estate of, 96
De Laurentiis Entertainment Group, Inc., In re, 624
De Nicols v. Curlier, 365
De Prins v. Michaeles, 444
De Werthein v. Gotlib, 34, 349, 354
Deahl, In re Estate of, 160
Deal v. Huddleston, 441
Deardoff, In re Estate of, 651
Death of LaFuente, In re, 277
Decker v. Meriwether, 42, 105
Decker, Estate of v. Farm Credit Services, 591
DeCoste v. Superior Court, 336
Dees, In re Estate of, 533
Defilippis, In re Estate of, 347
Degner, In re Estate of, 331
deGraaf v. Owen, 191
Deida v. Murphy, 213
Deiss v. Deiss, 531
Del Buno, Succession of, 326
Delaney, In re Estate of, 39, 177, 351, 576, 577
Delaney, In re Marriage of, 210, 237
DeLaRosa v. Farmers State Bank S/B, 682
Delaware v. New York, 34
Della Sala, Estate of, 336
Dellinger, Estate of v. 1st Source Bank, 144
Delmege, In re Estate of, 268
Delorey, Matter of, 243
Deluca v. Jordan, 623, 624
Demaris' Estate, In re, 142
Dementas v. Estate of Tallas, 160, 182
Dempsey v. Dempsey, 497, 500
Dennis, Estate of, 341, 373
Deoneseus, In re Estate of, 342
DePaoli v. Commissioner, 92
Department of Human Resources, State ex rel. v. Payne, 590
Department of Income Maintenance v. Watts, 94
Department of Social Serv. v. Saunders, 43
Derman v. Dreznick, 303
DeSantis v. Prothero, 155
Detlefsen, In re, 94
Detroit Bank & Trust Co. v. Grout, 264
Deupree, In re Estate of, 303
Deutsch v. Wolff, 680
Deutsch's Estate, Matter of, 261
Devine v. Devine, 366
Devroy's Estate, In re, 651
DeWald, Estate of v. Whittenburg, 192, 199
Dewire v. Haveles, 61, 539
Dewitt, In re Estate of, 43, 44, 46
Di Siena, Matter of Estate of, 179
Diamond v. Trawick, 448, 449
Diana v. Bentsen, 636
Dickerson v. Union Nat. Bank, 530
Dickey, Matter of Last Will of, 223, 238
Dickie v. Dickie, 184, 186
Dickinson v. Wilmington Trust Co., 505
Dickson v. Renfro, 73
Dickson, In re Estate of, 192
Dieden v. Schmidt, 594
Diemer v. Diemer, 113, 659
Diep v. Rivas, 90
DiFilippo v. DiFilippo, 489
DiFilippo v. Reed, 595
Dillingham, Estate of v. Commissioner, 156
Dillon v. Phillips, 221
Dillow v. Wagner, 117
Dimock v. Corwin, 721
Dinwiddie, Succession of, 72
Disciplinary Counsel v. Bandy, 143
Disciplinary Counsel v. Coleman, 18
Disciplinary Counsel v. Galinas, 243
Disciplinary Proceeding Against Gillingham, Matter of, 242
DiSesa v. Hickey, 511
Disney, In re Estate of, 352
District of Columbia v. Estate of Parsons, 273, 287
Dittus, Matter of Estate of, 156, 158
Dixon v. Rivers, 555
Dobert, Matter of Estate of, 46
Dobler v. Arluk Medical Center Indus. Group, 594
Dobson, Matter of Estate of, 146
Dodge Testamentary Trust, Matter of, 49, 498, 499
Dodge v. Trustees of Randolph Macon Woman's College, 474
Dodge, Matter of Estate of, 333
Dodge's Trust, In re, 503
Dodson v. Walton, 194

Dollar Savings & Trust Co. v. First Nat. Bank, 513, 545, 547
Dombek v. Reiman, 312
Dompke, Estate of v. Dompke, 214
Donahue v. Shughart, Thomson & Kilroy, P.C., 156
Donald E. Bradford Trust, Matter of, 665
Donato v. BankBoston, N.A., 605, 610, 663
Donnelly, Estates of, 107
Donner, Matter of Estate of, 378, 604, 607, 670
Donovan v. Bierwirth, 664
Dooley v. Reimer Farms, Inc., 48
Dorfman v. Allen, 138, 273
Dorman, Re, 253
Dorrance, In re Estate of, 41
Dorrance's Estate, In re, 41
Dorsey, Matter of, 87
Dotterrer, In re Estate of, 169
Dougherty v. Cole, 86
Doughty v. Morris, 232, 235
Douglas v. Douglas, 361
Douglas v. Newell, 253
Douglass' Estate, Commissioner v., 712
Dow v. Atwood, 512
Downey, In re Estate of, 330
Doyle v. Schott, 224
Drabick, Conservatorship of, 392
Drahos v. Rens, 359
Draper v. Pauley, 135
Dreher v. Dreher, 346, 347
Drosos v. Drosos, 138
Drye v. United States, 94
Duberstein, Commissioner v., 689, 690
Ducey, Matter of Estate of, 354
Dudek, In re Marriage of, 214
Duemeland, Matter of Estate of, 281
Duffy v. Heffernan, 636
Duffy, In re Estate of, 660
Duggan v. Keto, 160, 164
Duke v. Simmons, 660
Duke, In re Marriage of, 203, 577
Duke, Matter of, 109
Dulles, Estate of, 48, 105
Dumaine, In re, 41, 105
Dumas' Estate, In re, 269, 271
Dunbar v. Board of Trustees, 470, 477
Duncan by Duncan v. Duncan, 301
Duncan v. Moore, 236
Duncan, Matter of Estate of, 120
Duncan's Estates, In re, 83
Dunkley v. Peoples Bank & Trust Co., 437, 624
Dunnewind v. Cook, 348
Dunnuck v. Mosser, 581
duPont v. Shackelford, 659
duPont v. Southern Nat'l Bank, 428
Duran v. Komyatte, 183
Durward v. Nelson, 309
Dutra De Amorim v. Norment, 104
Dwyer v. Allyn, 170, 171
Dye v. Battles, 266, 283
Dye, In re Estate of, 47
Dyer v. Eckols, 93
Dyniewicz, In re Estate of, 659
E.F. Hutton & Co., Inc. v. Wallace, 173
Earle v. International Paper Co., 535
Early v. Bowen, 268
East v. East, 122
East v. Estate of East, 255, 282
Eastman, In re Estate of, 194
Easton v. Hall, 535
Eckland v. Jankowski, 579
Eddy, Estate of, 514
Edgerly v. Barker, 541
Edinburg v. Cavers, 642
Edinburg v. Edinburg, 165
Edington, Matter of Estate of, 182
Edmonds v. Edmonds, 196
Edwards Irrevocable Trust, Matter of, 461
Edwards v. Edwards, 649
Edwards v. Shumate, 289
Edwards, In re Marriage of, 186
Edwards, Matter of Estate of, 38, 111
Effron, Estate of, 651, 653
Efird v. Efird, 349
Egelhoff v. Egelhoff ex rel. Breiner, 85, 214, 362
Eggebrecht, Matter of Estate of, 234
Eglee, Estate of, 192
Ehlers, In re Estate of, 644
Ehrlich, In re Estate of, 147
Eikel v. Burton, 583
Eisenberg, In re Guardianship of, 664, 666, 672
Eisenhart v. Lobb, 304, 311
Eisenhauer, Matter of, 243, 244
Elam v. Elam, 359
Elam, In re Estate of, 223, 224, 236
Elder, Matter of, 666
Elgar v. Elgar, 32, 370
Eliasen's Estate, Matter of, 87
Ellingrod v. Trombla, 504
Ellinwood, Matter of Marriage of, 182
Ellis v. Vespoint, 168, 308
Elmer, Estate of, 269
Elmhurst Nat. Bank v. Glos, 601
Elson, In re Estate of, 37
Elyachar v. Gerel Corp., 163
Emberson v. Hartley, 100
Emery, In re Estate of, 588
Emmert v. Hearn, 255
Emmert v. Old Nat'l Bank, 437
Enders v. Parker, 581
Engel v. Breske, 311
England, Estate of, 211, 215
Englund v. First Nat'l Bank, 428
Epstein, Matter of Estate of, 176
Equitable Life Assurance Society v. McKay, 38

Equitable Trust Co. v. Foulke, 512, 514
Erb v. Kohnke, 309
Erb v. Lee, 235
Erbach's Estate, In re, 294
Eredics v. Chase Manhattan Bank, 213, 215
Eresian v. Mattei, 589
Erickson v. Erickson, 341
Erickson v. Reinbold, 490
Erickson, Estate of, 124
Erickson, Matter of Estate of, 134, 147
Erlenbach v. Estate of Thompson, 267
Erlich v. First Nat'l Bank, 612, 669
Ernst v. Shaw, 98
Erny's Trust, In re, 203
Erwin & Erwin v. Bronson, 647
Eschler v. Eschler, 209, 213
Espey, In re Estate of, 184
Estate of Brown, In re, 463
Estate of Cooney, In re, 566
Estes Estate, In re, 477, 563
Estes' Estate, Matter of, 615
Evanco, Matter of Estate of, 175
Evans & Luptak v. Obolensky, 451
Evans v. Cass, 72
Evans v. Evans, 211
Evans v. Giles, 483
Evans v. Johnson, 685
Evans v. May, 193
Evans v. McCoy, 44, 52, 109
Evans' Estate, In re, 494
Eversole, Matter of Estate of, 45
Ewing v. Hladky Const., Inc., 206
Ewing v. Ruml, 436
Exchange Bank of Fla. V. United States, 712
Eychaner v. Gross, 164
Eyerman v. Mercantile Trust Co., N.A., 379, 412
Fabian, In re Estate of, 281
Faith v. Singleton, 141
Fajardo, In re Estate of, 122
Fales, Estate of, 671
Falk v. Vreeland Trading Corp., 263
Falk, In re Will of, 144
Farkas v. Williams, 166
Farley, In re Estate of, 568
Farm Credit Bank v. Brown, 43, 590
Farmers State Bank v. Harmon, 649
Farnsworth's Estate, In re, 646
Farone, Matter of Estate of, 255
Farr, In re Estate of, 138, 222, 236
Farrel, Estate of v. United States, 713, 718
Farrell v. McDonnell, 140
Farrell v. Porter, 121
Farris, Matter of Estate of, 267
Fay v. Smiley, 211
Federal Kemper Life Assur. v. Eichwedel, 87, 89
Federal Trade Commission v. Affordable Media, LLC, 445
Feibelman v. Worthen Nat'l Bank, N.A., 438, 668
Feinberg, In re Estate of, 317, 411
Fellows v. Colburn, 663
Felonenko v. Siomka, 304
Fennell v. Foskey, 552
Fenske, In re, 645
Fenton v. Walter, 311, 312
Fenwick, In re, 280
Fenzel v. Floyd, 281
Ferber v. American Lamp Corp., 661
Ferguson, In re Estate of, 368
Fernandez v. Fernandez, 363
Ferree, In re Will of, 130, 147
Ferrell-French v. Ferrell, 513
Ferri v. Powell-Ferri, 467
Ferris v. Faford, 196
Ferry's Estate, In re, 483, 486
Festing v. Allen, 520
Field, In re Estate of, 418
Fields v. Mersack, 237
Fields, In re Estate of, 172, 299
Fields, In re Will of, 577
Fifth Third Bank v. Crosley, 35, 39, 49
Fifth Third Bank v. Fifth Third Bank, 578
Finch, In re Estate of, 334
Fine v. Cohen, 281, 303
Finkelstein, In re Estate of, 177
Finnemore, Re, 200
Fiore, In re Estate of, 88
Fiori, In re, 392
Firestone Tire and Rubber Co. v. Bruch, 435
First Alabama Bank v. Adams, 532, 534
First Alabama Bank v. Martin, 679
First Alabama Bank v. Spragins, 601
First Charter Bank v. American Children's Home, 676
First Federal Sav. Bank v. Key Markets, 559
First Huntington National Bank v. Gideon-Broh Realty Co., 553
First Illini Bank v. Pritchard, 61
First Interstate Bank of Washington v. Lindberg, 203
First Interstate Bank v. First Wyo. Bank, 227
First Interstate Bank v. Haynes, 592
First Interstate Bank v. Young, 280
First Kentucky Trust Co. v. United States, 88
First Midwest Bank/Joliet v. Dempsey, 622
First Nat. Bank of Arizona v. First Nat. Bank of Birmingham, 513, 514
First National Bank v. Anthony, 264, 301
First National Bank v. Cooper, 597

First National Bank v. Daggett, 31, 32
First National Bank v. Department of Health, 436
First National Bank v. Ettlinger, 511, 515
First National Bank v. Gregory, 153
First National Bank v. King, 3, 44
First National Bank v. Union Hospital, 258
First National Bank, State ex rel. v. Skow, 643
First of America Trust v. First Illini Bancorp, 672
First Security Bank v. Geels, 156
First Union National Bank v. Cisa, 437
First Union National Bank v. Estate of Mizell, 201
First Union National Bank v. Ingold, 505, 510
First Union National Bank v. Turney, 659, 664, 679
First United Methodist Church v. Allen, 171
First Universalist Society v. Boland, 533
Fischer v. Kinzalow, 130
Fisher v. Fisher, 660
Fitch v. Maesch, 144
Fitch's Will, Matter of, 249
Fitts v. Stokes, 214
Fitzgerald, Matter of Estate of, 46
Flagle v. Martinelli, 142
Flannery v. McNamara, 285
Flasted, Matter of Estate of, 255
Flecken, In re Estate of, 300
Fleet National Bank v. Colt, 51, 530, 540
Fleet National Bank v. Marquis, 459
Fleisch v. First American Bank, 464
Fleming, Estate of v. Commissioner, 95
Fletcher v. Fletcher, 619
Fletcher v. Hurdle, 483
Fletcher, Estate of, 275
Flood v. Fidelity & Guar. Life Ins. Co., 89
Flowers, Matter of Estate of, 336
Floyd v. Hoover, 557
Flyer's Will, In re, 437
Foley v. Evans, 530, 542
Folkerds v. United States, 262
Fontaine v. Colt's Mfg. Co., Inc., 157
Foran, Matter of Marriage of, 373
Ford City Bank v. Ford City Bank, 674
Ford v. Ford, 86
Ford v. Peoples Trust & Savings Bank, 652
Ford v. Thomas, 490
Ford, In re Estate of, 111
Fordonski, In re Estate of, 144
Foreman, In re Estate of, 135
Forest Guardians v. Wells, 637
Forgey, In re Estate of, 620, 660
Forrest v. Forrest, 121
Forrest, Estate of, 73, 501, 502
Forrest, In re Estate of, 203
Forrester, Matter of Estate of, 52
Fort Myers Mem. Gardens v. Barnett Banks, 665
Fortune v. First Union Nat'l Bank, 615
Foster v. Foster, 141
Foster, Estate of, 562
Foster, In re Estate of, 581
Foulds v. First Nat. Bank, 183
Fowler v. Montgomery, 312
Fowler, Estate of v. Perry, 197
Fox v. Woods, 589
Foxley, In re Estate of, 190
Foxworth's Estate, In re, 294
Frailey, Estate of, 271
Frakes v. Nay, 460
Frances Slocum Bank and Trust Co. v. Martin, 93
Francis v. Marshall, 85, 90
Francis v. Piper, 245
Frank M. Lambrecht, Jr., Trust, In re, 677
Frank, In re, 546, 677
Frank, In re Estate of, 257
Fraser v. Southeast First Bank, 672
Fray, Matter of, 118
Fred Hutchinson Cancer Research Center v. Holman, 661
Freeman, Estate of, 562
French v. French, 164, 168, 313
French v. Wachovia Bank, 605
French, Estate of, 374
Friedberg v. Sunbank/Miami, N.A., 346
Friedman v. Hannan, 203
Friedman, In re, 143
Frietze, Matter of Estate of, 280, 281, 287
From the Heart Church Ministries, Inc. v. African Methodist Episcopal Zion Church, 206
Froman, Matter of Estate of, 347
Frost Nat'l Bank of San Antonio v. Newton, 463
Fuller, Matter of Estate of, 118
Fuller's Estate, In re, 196
Fulton, Estate of, 120
Fund for the Study and Economic Growth v. Internal Rev. Serv., 469
Funk v. Funk, 33, 252
Furia, Estate of, 111
Furr v. Hall, 598, 600
Furst, In re Estate of, 215
Gabel v. Manetto, 208
Gafford v. Kirby, 282
Gager v. Gager and Peterson, LLP, 1
Gagliardi, Matter of Estate of, 168

Gagnier, In re Estate of, 367, 371
Gagnon v. Coombs, 230
Gaines, In re Estate of, 569
Gala v. Magarinos, 238
Gallagher v. Evert, 12, 350, 353
Gallavan, In re Estate of, 219
Gallimore v. Washington, 88
Gallio, Estate of, 305
Galloway v. Cinello, 154
Gammarino v. Hamilton Cty. Bd. of Revision, 169
Gannon, Appeal of, 463
Garcia v. Marquez, 312
Garcia, Guardianship of v. Garcia, 228
Gardner v. Balboni, 135, 143
Gardner v. Cox, 610
Gardner v. Hancock, 111
Gardner, Estate of, 52
Gardner, In re Estate of, 95
Gardner, Matter of Estate of, 251
Gardner, Matter of the Estate of, 95
Garrett, Estate of, 234
Garrett, In re Estate of, 227, 238, 486
Gartin v. Taylor, 156
Gartley v. Ricketts, 553, 557, 559
Garver, Matter of Estate of, 37
Garwood, In re Estate of, 334
Garwood's Estate, Matter of, 598
Gary-Wheaton Bank v. Meyer, 314
Gasparovich's Estate, In re, 147
Gaspelin, In re Estate of, 342
Gautier's Will, In re, 486
Gaymon v. Gaymon, 262
Gaynor v. Payne, 667, 674
Gbur v. Cohen, 671
Geary, In re Estate of, 249
Gedgaudas, In re Marriage of, 595
Geduldig v. Posner, 235, 289, 577
Geer, Matter of Estate of, 368
Gehl's Estate, In re, 113
Geissel v. Galbraith, 304
Gellerstedt v. United Missouri Bank, 36
Gene Wild Revocable Trust, In re, 660
Gerard, Estate of v. Gerard, 243
Gerbing's Estate, In re, 378
Gerhardt Const. Co. v. Wachter Real Estate Trust, 685
Gerhardt, In re Estate of, 143
German, Estate of v. United States, 712
Gersbach, Matter of Estate of, 234
Gershaw v. Gershfield, 300
Getty v. Commissioner, 186
Getty v. Getty, 305, 642
Getty, Matter of Estate of, 581
Geyer, In re Estate of, 370, 372
Ghiglia's Estate, In re, 529, 534
Giagnorio v. Emmett C. Torkelson Trust, 667
Gibbons v. Anderson, 678
Gibbs, Matter of Estate of, 85, 87
Gibson v. Boling, 155
Gibson, Estate of, 368
Gibson, In re Estate of, 183, 185
Gibson's Estate, In re, 282
Giefer v. Swenton, 156
Giles v. Ingrum, 444
Gilford v. Wurster, 328, 329
Gill ex. rel. Grant, Estate of v. Clemson University Foundation, 82
Gillespie v. Davis, 170, 281
Gillespie v. Seattle-First National Bank, 665
Gillespie v. Seymour, 674, 680
Gillespie, Estate of, 29, 240, 280
Gillilan's Estate v. Gillilan's Estate, 373
Gilmore, Matter of Estate of, 37, 38
Gitto v. Gitto, 310
Glasco, In re, 122
Glass v. Adkins, 88
Gleeson, In re Estate of, 25, 225, 673
Glen v. Commissioner, 693
Glenn v. Mann, 142
Glenn's Estate, In re, 87
Glennie, In re Estate of, 199, 232
Gloege, In re Estate of, 215
Glogovsek, In re Estate of, 237
GME, Inc. v. Carter, 204
Goar, In re, 618, 621
Gobernatz, In re Conservatorship of, 252
Godfrey v. Chandley, 434, 563
Goff, Matter of, 450
Goforth v. Gee, 447
Goldberg, In re Marriage of, 118
Golden v. Golden, 302
Goldfarb v. Virginia State Bar, 653
Goldfarb, State v., 591
Goldman v. Goldman, 214
Goldman v. Rubin, 601
Goldstein v. Ancell, 263
Goldstick, In re, 608
Goldston v. Bank of America Corp., 679
Golini v. Bolton, 197
Golleher v. Horton, 165
Gonzales v. Oregon, 393
Gonzales, Matter of Estate of, 239
Gonzalez, Estate of, 582
Gonzalez, In re Estate of, 147
Gonzalez, Matter of, 476
Goodlett, In re Estate of, 351
Goodman v. Zimmerman, 221
Goodridge v. Department of Public Health, 125
Goodwin v. McGowan, 701
Goodwin, In re Estate of, 7, 61, 286
Goodwine State Bank v. Mullins, 482
Goodwine v. Goodwine, 428
Gordon v. Gordon, 302
Gordon v. Portland Trust Bank, 407
Gordon, Estate of, 276

Gordon, In re, 599
Gore v. Beren, 554
Gotthardt v. Candle, 300
Gottwig v. Blaine, 590
Goulding v. James, 462
Goytizolo v. Moore, 169, 206
Grace's Estate, United States v., 714
Grady v. Grady, 203
Graham v. Commissioner, 715
Graham v. Farmers New World Life Ins. Co., 209, 348
Graham, In re Succession of, 141
Graham's Estate, In re, 251
Granado v. Granado, 313
Grasseschi, Matter of Estate of, 350
Grassman, In re Estate of, 370
Grau v. Dooley, 160
Graves v. Hyer, 72
Graves v. Summit Bank, 300
Gray, Matter of Estate of, 332
Greatsinger, In re Estate of, 659
Green Charitable Trust, In re, 618
Green v. Higdon, 567
Green v. Lombard, 621
Green, Estate of, 342
Green's Will Trusts, In re, 468, 548
Greenberg's Estate, In re, 646
Greenfield, Matter of Estate of, 281
Greenheck, In re Estate of, 642
Greenwald v. Spring Hill Ford, Inc., 311
Greenwald, Matter of Estate of, 201
Greenwood's Will, In re, 531
Gregory v. Estate of Gregory, 184
Gregory v. Rice, 100
Greil Memorial Hospital v. First Alabama Bank, 475
Gresham, Succession of, 47
Griffin v. Baucom, 232
Griffin v. Gould, 256
Griffin v. Griffin, 286, 301, 668
Griffin, Matter of Estate of, 94
Griffith v. Adams, 258
Grigg, In re Estate of, 595
Grimes v. Commissioner, 186
Grimm, Matter of Estate of, 100, 579
Grimm, United States v., 453
Griswold, Estate of, 69
Griswold, Matter of Estate of, 110
Grobman's Estate, Matter of, 145
Groden v. Kelley, 312
Groesbeck, Matter of Estate of, 166, 214
Groffman, In re, 140, 144
Groh v. Ballard, 304
Gross v. Gross, 373
Gross v. Slye, 580
Grossen's Estate v. Vincent, 136
Grossman v. Selawacz, 590
Grove, Estate of, 529, 532, 542
Grove, Estate of v. Selken, 175, 663
Groves, Matter of Estate of, 340
Gruen v. Gruen, 151, 154
Grund, Estate of v. Grund, 88
Grunebaum, Matter of Will of, 546
Guaranty Bank & Trust Co., Ex parte, 458
Gudschinsky v. Hartill, 670
Guidotti, Estate of, 377
Guidry v. Hardy, 138
Gulack v. Gulack, 306
Gulbankian, State v., 197
Gulf Nat'l Bank v. Sturtevant, 435
Gunther v. Gunther, 417
Gushwa v. Hunt, 190, 194
Gustafson v. Svenson, 74
Gustafson, Matter of, 486, 489
Gustie, In re, 314
Gutchess v. Commissioner, 711
Guy v. Guy, 306
Guy v. Johnson, 76
Hackett, In re Estate of, 660
Hackmann v. Dawley, 590
Hafferman, Matter of Estate of, 254
Hafner, Estate of, 119
Hagaman v. Morgan, 109
Hagan v. Shore, 230
Hagemann v. National Bank and Trust Co., 528, 532, 537, 542
Hager v. Hager, 36
Haggerty, Matter of Estate of, 100
Hagney v. Lopeman, 679
Haines, In re Marriage of, 237
Hairelson v. Estate of Franks, 40
Hale v. Groce, 245
Hale, Matter of Estate of, 261
Haley v. Pickelsimer, 582
Hall v. Eaton, 378, 577
Hall v. McBride, 343
Hall v. United States, 716
Hall v. World Savings and Loan Ass'n, 169
Hall, Estate of, 95
Hall, In re Estate of, 122, 132, 137
Halmaghi, Matter of Estate of, 368, 370
Halpern, In re Will of, 144
Hamilton Living Trust, In re, 640
Hamilton Nat. Bank v. Hutcheson, 495
Hamilton v. Caplan, 158, 160
Hamilton v. Hamilton, 120, 321
Hamilton v. Needham, 288
Hamilton v. Nielsen, 604, 663
Hamilton, Estate of v. Morris, 232, 236, 237
Hamilton, In re, 86
Hamilton, Matter of Estate of, 331
Hamiter, Succession of, 235
Hammer v. Powers, 582
Hammer, Estate of, 642
Hanau, Estate of v. Hanau, 361, 365
Hancock v. Krause, 72
Hand, In re Estate of, 145

Haneberg, In re Estate of, 232, 270
Hanesworth v. Johnke, 43
Hankins v. Mathews, 557
Hanna v. Hanna, 254
Hannah v. Hannah, 350
Hannam v. Brown, 582
Hannan, In re Estate of, 33
Hanners v. Sistrunk, 196
Hansel v. Head, 194, 195, 198
Hansen v. Hansen, 122
Hansen v. Stroecker, 539
Hansen, Matter of Estate of, 373
Hanson v. Denckla, 663
Harbaugh's Estate, Matter of, 463
Hardenbergh v. Commissioner, 97
Hardman v. Feinstein, 474
Hardt v. Vitae Foundation, Inc., 474
Hargrove v. Taylor, 88
Harmon, In re Estate of, 233
Harmston v. Harmston, 305
Harper v. Harper, 592, 615, 661, 662, 671
Harper v. Prudential Ins. Co., 84
Harper v. Springfield, 502
Harper, Estate of, 297, 298, 350
Harper, Matter of Estate of, 184
Harrell, Appeal of, 456
Harrington, Matter of Estate of, 146, 295
Harris Testamentary Trust, In re, 286, 461
Harris Trust & Savings Bank v. Beach, 483, 486, 489, 503
Harris Trust & Savings Bank v. Donovan, 105
Harris v. Rock, 347
Harris' Estate, In re, 320
Harrison v. Bird, 197
Harrison v. Harrison, 375
Harrison v. Marcus, 546, 549, 551
Harrison, Matter of Estate of, 138, 348
Hart v. Connors, 437, 438
Hart, Conservatorship of, 228
Hart, Estate of, 110
Hart, In re Estate of, 348
Hart's Estate, In re, 89
Hartford National Bank and Trust Co. v. Birge, 485
Hartman v. Hartle, 599
Hartnett v. Jones, 561
Harvard College v. Amory, 606
Harvey ex rel. Gladden v. Cumberland Trust & Investment Co., 678
Harvey, Succession of, 138
Hasso v. Hasso, 430
Hastings v. Bridge, 294
Hatcher v. Hatcher, 355, 360
Hatcher v. U.S. National Bank, 664
Hatfield, Matter of Estate of, 256
Hatton v. Meade, 163
Hauck v. Seright, 223, 224
Haugk's Estate, In re, 193
Hauseman v. Koski, 208
Hawaiian Trust Co., Ltd. v. Hogan, 651
Hawes v. Hawes, 175
Hawes, State v., 444
Hawkins v. Walker, 673
Hawkins' Estate, In re, 88
Hayes v. Apperson, 233
Hayes v. Hammond, 490
Haynes v. Williams, 269
Head, In re Estate of, 408
Hearn, Estate of v. Hearn, 180, 181
Heater, In re Estate of, 96
Heath by Heath v. Heath, 302
Heck v. Archer, 236, 307
Hedke, In re Estate of, 412, 621, 626
Heffernan v. Wollaston Credit Union, 594
Heffner v. Cahaba Bank & Trust Co., 682
Hegel, In re Estate of, 252
Heggstad, Estate of, 162, 408
Heidenreich's Will, In re, 601
Heilig Trust and Benef. v. First Interstate, 681
Heim, Estate of v. Commissioner, 286
Heiman v. Parrish, 205
Heimbach, Matter of Estate of, 334
Hein v. Hein, 461
Heinzman v. Mason, 90
Heirs of Ellis v. Estate of Ellis, 275
Heirship of McLeod, Matter of, 47
Helgason v. Merriman, 643
Heller, Estate of, 626, 655
Heller, In re Estate of, 379
Helmer v. Voss, 270
Helmholz, Helvering v., 717
Helton v. Helton, 210
Henderson v. Collins, 449
Henderson v. Millis, 51
Henderson v. Parker, 271
Henderson, Matter of, 243
Hendricks v. Hendricks, 329
Hendrickson, Matter of Estate of, 118
Hendrix, In re Estate of, 576
Hengst v. Hengst, 157
Henkle v. Henkle, 304
Henley v. Henley, 214
Hensley, Matter of Estate of, 601
Herbert M. Dorsett Trust, Matter of, 673
Herbert, In re Estate of, 234, 280
Herbst, In re, 207
Herceg, In re Estate of, 283
Hering's Estate, Matter of, 202
Herman v. Herman, 173
Hermanson v. Hermanson, 47
Hermon, Estate of, 203
Herron v. Underwood, 158
Hertel ex rel. Hertel v. Nationsbank N.A., 434, 438
Hess v. Proffer, 498

Hess v. Whitsitt, 102
Hessenflow, Matter of Estate of, 351, 368
Hetherington, In re, 470
Hettinga v. Sybrandy, 4
Heyer v. Flaig, 343
Heyn, In re Estate of, 156
Hickman v. Trust of Heath, House & Boyles, 169
Hickox v. Wilson, 135
Hicks v. Boshears, 88
Hiddleston v. Nebraska Jewish Education Society, 44, 51, 551
Hieber v. Uptown Nat. Bank, 155
Hiers v. Estate of Hiers, 333
Higgins' Trust Estate, In re, 674
Higgs v. Estate of Higgs, 19, 236, 239
Highgate, Matter of Estate of, 204
Hilbert v. Benson, 226
Hilgendorf v. Estate of Coleman, 417
Hilgers, In re, 451
Hill v. Nakai, 112
Hill, In re Estate of, 176, 299
Hilliard v. Hilliard, 308, 310, 311, 312
Hillman v. Hillman, 505
Hillman, Matter of Estate of, 266, 273
Hilt, In re Marriage of, 124, 360
Hilterbrand v. Carter, 212
Hilton, Estate of, 43
Hilton, Matter of Estate of, 337
Himes, In re Marriage of, 120
Hinchee v. Security Nat. Bank, 594
Hinderliter, Matter of Estate of, 47
Hinders v. Hinders, 202
Hinds v. McNair, 488
Hinson v. Hinson, 313
Hintze v. Black, 276
Hisquierdo v. Hisquierdo, 366
Hjersted, In re Estate of, 316, 344
Hock, Matter of Estate of, 310, 311
Hockman v. Estate of Lowe, 61
Hodel v. Irving, 12, 326, 705
Hodge, Matter of Marriage of, 102
Hodges v. Callaway, 179
Hodges v. Genzone, 224
Hoeppner's Estate, In re, 187
Hoesly v. State, Dept. of Social Services, 94
Hoffas, Matter of Estate of, 622
Hofferkamp v. Brehm, 308, 309, 310
Hoffman v. First Virginia Bank, 605
Hoffman, In re Estate of, 211, 585
Hoffman, Matter of Estate of, 191
Hoffman's Estate, In re, 173
Hofing v. Willis, 485
Hogan v. Hermann, 47
Hogle, Commissioner v., 701
Hoisington Living Trust, In re, 418
Holcomb, In re Estate of, 233, 238, 239
Holdfast v. Dowsing, 137
Holien v. Trydahl, 560
Holley v. Holley, 329
Holley v. Marks, 426
Holliday v. McMullen, 87
Hollister, In re Estate of, 43
Holloway, Succession of, 146
Holm v. Superior Court, 222
Holman, Matter of Conservatorship of, 600, 672
Holmes, Matter of Estate of, 257
Holst v. Purdy, 642
Holt v. College of Osteopathic Physicians & Surgeons, 475
Holt, Matter of Estate of, 540
Holtz v. Diesz, 249, 252, 253
Homanich v. Miller, 88
Home for Incurables v. University of Maryland Medical System Corp., 477, 478
Honigman, In re, 407
Honnas v. Honnas, 359
Hood v. Todd, 3
Hood v. Vandevender, 86
Hooks v. Bonner, 673
Hooks v. Owen, 78
Hoopingarner v. Stenzel, 209
Hoover v. Smith, 176
Hoover, In re Estate of, 233
Hopper v. Rech, 303
Horn v. Horn, 310
Horne v. Title Ins. & Trust Co., 513
Horowitz, Matter of Estate of, 96
Hosselton v. First American Bank N.A., 681
Hosselton v. K's Merchandise Mart, 681
Hotarek v. Benson, 91
Hotz v. Minyard, 239
Houska, State ex rel. v. Dickhaner, 588
Housley, Estate of, 181
Howard Hughes Medical Institute v. Gavin, 198
Howard Savings Inst. v. Peep, 477, 479
Howard v. Himmelrick, 154
Howard v. Howard, 331
Howard v. Reynolds, 32, 35
Howard v. Spragins, 452
Howard, In re Estate of, 257
Howe v. Johnston, 226, 227
Howser, In re Estate of, 242
Howson v. Crombie St. Congregational Church, 550, 552
Hoyle, Matter of Estate of, 156
Hrnicek, In re, 405
HSBC Bank, USA, In re, 609, 610
Hubbard, In re Succession of, 364, 365
Huff v. Union Fidelity Life Ins. Co., 86
Hughes v. Hughes, 237, 333
Hughes, In re Estate of, 599, 637, 664
Hughlett, In re Matter of Estate of, 499
Huie v. DeShazo, 617

Hulett v. First Nat. Bank and Trust Co., 90
Hull, Estate of v. Williams, 22, 361, 362
Hume, In re Estate of, 248, 251
Hund v. Holmes, 515
Hunt v. United States, 98
Hunter v. Clark, 373
Hunter v. Newsom, 579
Hunter, In re Estate of, 675
Huntington Nat'l Bank v. Toland, 225, 227
Huntington Nat'l Bank v. Wolfe, 601, 636
Hurd v. Commissioner, 718
Hurley v. Hurley, 452
Hurst, Estate of v. Hurst, 176, 288, 304, 305, 497
Hurt v. Noble, 110
Hurt v. Smith, 262
Huskins v. Huskins, 158, 255
Huston, Estate of, 231
Hutton v. Rygalski, 351
Iglehart v. Phillips, 560
Ike v. Doolittle, 206, 287
Ike, In re Estate of, 147, 149
Ikuta's Estate, Matter of, 214, 285, 582, 647
Imerys Marble Co. v. J.M. Huber Corp., 558
Independent Congregational Society v. Davenport, 476
Indiana Department of State Revenue v. Estate of Puschel, 33
Industrial Nat. Bank v. Barrett, 545
Industrial Trust Co. v. Commissioner, 715
Ingram, Matter of Estate of, 215, 216
Inlow, In re Estate of, 658
InterFirst State Bank Dallas, N.A. v. Risser, 598, 666
Ioupe, Estate of, 225
Iozapavichus v. Fournier, 271
Irish v. Profitt, 492
Irrevocable Inter-Vivos Trust, Matter of, 672
Isaak v. Smith, 153
Isbell v. Williams, 299
Isner, In re Estate of, 677
Israel v. National Board of YMCA, 473, 663
ITT Commercial Finance v. Stockdale, 684
Ivancovich, Matter of Estate of, 341
Ives, In re Estate of, 432
Ivey, Estate of, 659
J.C. Vereen & Sons, Inc. v. City of Miami, 551
J.P. Morgan Chase Bank, N.A. v. Longmeyer, 617
Jackson v. Braden, 674
Jackson v. Breton, 426
Jackson v. Phillips, 478
Jackson v. Schultz, 269
Jackson, In re Estate of, 375
Jacobs-Zorne v. Superior Court (Swonetz), 582
Jaekel's Estate, In re, 511
James v. Elder, 299, 302
James, Estate of, 563
Jamieson, In re Estate of, 498
Janes v. Commerce Federal Savings & Loan Ass'n, 573
Janes, Matter of Estate of, 604, 609, 665
Janney, In re Estate of, 33
Janus v. Tarasewicz, 275
Janussek, In re Estate of, 41
Jarrett v. United States National Bank, 664, 667
Jarvis v. Jarvis, 370
Jefferson's Will, Matter of, 142
Jenkins, Estate of, 275
Jenkins, Matter of Estate of, 49, 111, 486
Jennings v. Smith, 713, 718
Jensen v. Jensen, 360
Jeruzal's Estate v. Jeruzal, 42
Jeschke v. United States, 100, 299
Jessman, In re Estate of, 237
Jetter, Matter of Estate of, 376
Jewish Community Ass'n v. Community First Nat. Bank, 164
Jewish Hospital v. Boatmen's National Bank, 668, 670
Jeziorski, In re Estate of, 577
Jiles v. Flegel, 377
Jobes, In re, 394
Joffe, Matter of Estate of, 580
Johannes Trust, In re, 447
John Deere Indus. Equipment Co. v. Gentile, 314
Johnson by and Through Lackey v. Schick, 161
Johnson v. Adams, 102
Johnson v. Doris, 671
Johnson v. Edwardsville National Bank & Trust Co., 682
Johnson v. Farmers & Merchants Bank, 346
Johnson v. First Nat'l Bank, 461
Johnson v. Girtman, 184
Johnson v. Johnson, 61, 213, 294
Johnson v. Kotyck, 617
Johnson v. Ramsey, 156
Johnson v. Sandler, Balkin, Hellman & Weinstein, P.C., 346
Johnson, In re Estate of, 130, 148, 182, 575
Johnson, Matter of Estate of, 144, 276
Johnson's Will, In re, 72, 499
Johnston v. Estate of Wheeler, 250, 251, 253
Jolley v. Corry, 594

Jolliff, In re Estate of, 69
Jones v. Bransford, 274
Jones v. Equitable Life Assur. Soc., 119
Jones v. Heritage Pullman Bank & Trust Co., 563
Jones v. Jones, 76
Jones v. LaFargue, 222
Jones v. Peacock, 352
Jones v. Sun Bank/Miami, N.A., 588
Jones, Estate of v. Howell, 37, 75, 111
Jones, Estate of v. Jones, 236, 337
Jones, In re, 109
Jones, In re Estate of, 203
Jones, Matter of, 227
Jones, Matter of Estate of, 658
Jones' Estate, In re, 200
Jordan v. Exxon Corp., 169
Joseph, Estate of, 112
Josephsons' Estates, Matter of, 86
Joslyn, Estate of, 109
Jost v. Burr, 638
Jud, Matter of Estate of, 425
Judson Post Estate v. Commonwealth Bank and Trust Co., 160
Julian v. Petersen, 152, 156
Juliano & Sons v. Chevron, U.S.A., 51, 556
Jung, In re Estate of, 143
Junot v. Estate of Gilliam, 47, 179
Jurek, Matter of Estate of, 67
Jurgensen v. Haslinger, 576
Justesen, Estate of, 276
K.H., Estate of v. Continental Ins. Co., 673
K.I., In re, 394
Kahn v. First Nat. Bank, 181
Kaila, Estate of, 283, 288
Kaitz v. District Court, 663, 666
Kalk v. Security Pacific Bank Washington, 594
Kalouse's Estate, Matter of, 269, 271, 279, 284
Kaltsas v. Kaltsas, 663
Kalwitz, Estates of v. Kalwitz, 306, 307, 312, 313
Kamberos v. Magnuson, 291
Kampschroeder v. Kampschroeder, 684
Kane v. Locklin, 421
Kania v. Chatham, 474
Kann v. Kann, 663
Kaplan, In re Estate of, 179
Kapur v. Scientific Gas Products, Inc., 637
Karan, In re Guardianship of, 681
Karmey, In re Estate of, 234, 237, 238
Karnen, In re Estate of, 345, 350
Kaskel, Matter of Will of, 459
Kasper, Matter of Estate of, 196
Kassahn v. Kassahn, 185
Katleman, Estate of, 342
Katz, In re Estate of, 375
Katze-Miller, Matter of Estate of, 100
Kauffman-Harmon v. Kauffman, 312, 313
Kaufhold v. McIver, 286
Kaufman's Estate, In re, 200
Kauzlarich v. Landrum, 290
Kavanaugh v. Dobrowolski's Estate, 165
Kay v. Sandler, 150
Keenan, Matter of Estate of, 542
Keeney, Matter of Estate of, 232, 233, 235
Keeven, Matter of Estate of, 342
Keffalas' Estate, In re, 377, 378
Kehler, Estate of, 271
Keith Estate v. Keith, 426
Keith, State v., 302
Keller v. Department of Revenue, 121, 355
Keller, In re, 658
Keller, In re Estate of, 276, 286
Kelley v. First State Bank of Princeton, 408
Kelley v. Johns, 234
Kelley v. Kelley, 307
Kelley v. Neilson, 251
Kelley v. Yadon, 4
Kelly v. Estate of Johnson, 283
Kelly v. Foster, 599
Kelly v. Lansford, 426
Kelly v. McNeel, 224
Kelly, Estate of, 559, 560
Kelly, Estate of v. Stambaugh, 203
Kelly, In re Estate of, 157
Kelson v. Salt Lake County, 75
Kenly, Estate of, 361
Kennedy v. Plan Adm'r for DuPont Sav. and Inv. Plan, 210, 213, 214
Kenney v. Morgan, 557
Kenney, In re Estate of, 609
Kenworthy, In re Estate of, 155
Kerley v. Nu-West, Inc., 553, 557
Kern, Matter of Estate of, 243
Kerns, Estate of v. Western Surety Co., 667
Kerper v. Kerper, 184, 642, 668
Kerr, In re Estate of, 203, 659
Kerr, Matter of Estate of, 47, 183
Kesler, Matter of Estate of, 222, 225
Kessler, Merci, and Lochner, Inc. v. Pioneer Bank & Trust Co., 686
Kesterson v. Cronan, 158
Kettle, Application of, 664
Keville v. McKeever, 227
Key v. Key, 312, 313
Keybank, N.A. v. Thalman, 459
Kidd v. Gunter, 134
Kiejliches, In re Estate of, 86
Kiken v. Kiken, 328
Kilcoyne v. Reilly, 260
Killen, Matter of Estate of, 221, 581

Killian, Matter of Trust of, 117, 203
Kilpatrick v. Snow Mountain Pine Co., 552
Kiltz v. Kiltz, 330
Kimbrough v. Estate of Kimbrough, 235
Kinder Morgan, Inc. v. Crout, 577
King v. Beck, 501
King v. Cancienne, 119
King v. Commonwealth, 101
King v. King, 350, 446
King v. Smith, 138, 139
King v. Talbot, 606
King v. Travis, 179
King v. Trustees of Boston University, 160
King v. William M. King Family Ent., Inc., 270
King, In re Estate of, 194, 195, 197, 202, 277
Kinnamon, Matter of Estate of, 268
Kinne v. Kinne, 184
Kinney v. Ewing, 212
Kinney v. Shinholser, 93
Kinsella v. Landa, 580
Kintzinger v. Millin, 155
Kipnis Section 3.4 Trust, In re, 617
Kirk, Matter of Estate of, 375, 548
Kirkeby v. Covenant House, 131, 140, 353
Kissinger, Estate of v. Hoge, 86
Kitchen v. Estate of Blue, 183
Klamath Falls, City of v. Bell, 533, 550
Klassen v. Klassen, 471
Klein v. Shaw, 306
Klein, Matter of Estate of, 288
Kleinman, In re Estate of, 146, 147
Kline, In re Estate of, 19
Klugh v. United States, 522
Knickerbocker, In re Estate of, 209
Knight v. Knight, 35
Knott v. Garriott, 340
Knott, In re Estate of, 661
Knupp v. District of Columbia, 280
Koch v. James, 261, 636
Koch, In re Estate of, 309, 311
Koch, Matter of Estate of, 239
Koeninger v. Toledo Trust Co., 296
Koester, In re Estate of v. First Mid-Illinois Bank & Trust, N.A., 196
Kohler v. Fletcher, 666
Kohlsaat v. Commissioner, 698
Kokjohn, Matter of Estate of, 215, 216
Kolacy, In re Estate of, 495
Kolbinger, In re Estate of, 252, 590
Kolodney v. Kolodney, 434, 435, 436
Konopka, In re Estate of, 654, 657
Koors, Matter of Guardianship of, 339
Korten v. Chicago City Bank and Trust Co., 465
Kosak v. MacKechnie, 120
Kostelnik v. Roberts, 312, 313, 333
Kostick, In re Estate of, 320
Kotowski, In re Estate of, 588
Kottke, In re Estate of, 221, 236
Kotz, Estate of, 349
Kradwell's Estate, In re, 441
Kraft v. Commissioner, 453
Kraft, In re Estate of, 262
Kraft, In re Marriage of, 366
Kramer v. Freedman, 290, 512
Kramer, Matter of Guardianship of, 98
Kramme, Estate of, 84
Krebs v. Krebs, 237
Krebs, In re Estate of, 563
Kreitman's Estate, In re, 82
Kremer, In re Estate of, 154, 158, 590
Kresser v. Peterson, 158, 175
Kreuzer, Matter of Estate of, 541
Krischbaum v. Dillon, 241
Kritchman v. Wolk, 629
Krokowsky, Matter of Estate of, 19, 375
Kroll v. Nehmer, 192, 199
Kroll, In re, 467
Kronauge v. Stoecklein, 192
Krooss, In re, 484
Kroslack v. Estate of Kroslack, 333
Krotz, In re Estate of, 171
Kruegel, In re Estate of, 351
Krueger, Matter of Estate of, 146
Kryder v. Kryder, 462
Kubiczky v. Wesbanco Bank Wheeling, 268
Kueber, Matter of Estate of, 121
Kuehn, Matter of, 429
Kugler, In re Estate of, 272
Kujawinski v. Kujawinski, 329
Kulawik v. ERA Jet Alaska, 77
Kully v. Goldman, 165
Kummer v. Donak, 109
Kumstar, Matter of Estate of, 220
Kunewa v. Joshua, 230
Kunzler, In re Estate of, 636
Kupec v. Cooper, 110
Kuralt, In re Estate of, 147, 148, 261, 585
Kurkowski's Estate, In re, 615
Kurtz v. Solomon, 170, 679
Kuruzovich, In re Estate of, 268, 287
Kuster v. Schaumburg, 242
L.G. v. F.G.H., 590
L.M.S., Matter of Conservatorship of, 667, 675
L.W.K. v. E.R.C., 328, 329
L'Argent v. Barnett Bank, N.A., 207
Lacer v. Navajo County, 555
Lagae v. Lackner, 684
Lagreca, Matter of Estate of, 201
Lah v. Rogers, 226, 241
Lahey, Estate of, 120, 204
Lahren, Matter of Estate of, 173
Lake, Will of, 202

Lamb v. NationsBank, N.A., 484, 486, 492
Lamb's Estate, Matter of, 41, 124
Lambert, In re Estate of, 147, 302
Lamfrom's Estate, In re, 111
Lamplaugh, In re Estate of, 156
Lamson, In re Estate of, 96
Lanasa, In re Succession of, 141
Lancaster v. Merchants Nat'l Bank, 471
Lande, Matter of Estate of, 76
Landi v. Arkules, 101
Landmark First Nat'l Bank of Fort Lauderdale v. Haves, 447
Landmark Trust Co. v. Aitken, 659
Lane, Estate of, 232
Lane, In re Estate of, 333
Lang, Estate of v. Commissioner, 701
Langley, Matter of Estate of, 177
Langston v. Hunt, 170
Lanier v. Lanier, 531
Laning, In re Estate of, 377
Lankford v. Wright, 111
Lansburgh v. Lansburgh, 73
Larabee v. Booth, 161
Larison v. Record, 270
LaRocca's Trust Estate, In re, 311
Larocque v. O'Connor, 232
LaRose, In re Estate of, 673
Larrick v. Larrick, 201
Larson v. Naslund, 582
Larson, Matter of Estate of, 655, 658
Laspy's Estate, In re, 87
Last Will and Testament of Lawson v. Lambert, 255, 283
Last Will and Testament of Tamplin, In re, 43
Last Will and Testament of Welch v. Welch, 579, 580
Latham v. Father Divine, 290
Lauerman v. Destocki, 156
Lauga, Succession of, 327
Lauper v. Harold, 124
Laura, In re Estate of, 190, 338
Laurin's Estate, In re, 148
Lavender v. Cooper, 250
Lawrence v. Ashba, 186
Lawrence v. First Nat. Bank, 223
Lawson v. Atwood, 111
Lawson v. Redmoor Corp., 554
Lawver v. Lawvor, 578
Layton's Estate, In re, 181, 186
Le Cren Clarke, Re, 469
Leahy v. Leahy-Schuett, 213
Leake v. Robinson, 534
Leake's Estate, In re, 72
Leak-Gilbert v. Fahle, 340
Lealaimatafao v. Woodward-Clyde, Consl., 76
Leathers, Matter of Estate of, 100
Leathers, Matter of Marriage of, 371
Leatherwood v. Meisch, 338
Leavitt, In re Estate of, 186
Leavy's Estate, In re, 272
Lebitz-Freeman v. Lebitz, 213
LeCraw v. LeCraw, 230
Lee, In re Guardianship of, 228
Lee, In re Succession of, 191, 257
Leeks v. Leeks, 313
Lefkowitz, In re, 348
Legare v. Legare, 281, 285
Leggett v. Church of St. Pius, 584
Lehman v. Commissioner, 714
Lehmann v. Bank of America, N.A., 653
Leicht v. Quirin, 310
Leigh v. Engle, 658, 659
Leisch, In re Will of, 231
Lelux v. Chernick, 213
Lembach's Estate, Matter of, 290
Lembo v. Casaly, 660
Lemmons v. Lawson, 489
Lenhart v. Desmond, 157
Lennon, Estate of v. Lennon, 160, 212, 230
Leonard v. Counts, 309
Leonard v. Occidental Life Ins. Co., 362
Leone Hall Price Foundation v. Baker, 581
Leone, Matter of Estate of, 213, 229
Leopold v. United States, 713
Leslie, Estate of, 119
Lettengarver, Matter of Estate of, 309, 331, 332
Levie's Estate, In re, 117
Levin v. Fisch, 170
Levin v. Smith, 311
Levine, Estate of, 305
Levine, In re Estate of, 592
Levis v. Hammond, 183
Levy v. Crawford, 43
Lewis v. Burke, 152, 154
Lewis v. Steinreich, 39, 178, 590
Lewis v. Tanner, 185
Lewis, Matter of Estate of, 149, 302
Lewis, Matter of Will of, 516
Liberman, In re, 377
Life & Cas. Ins. Co. v. Webb, 85
Liginger, In re Estate of, 292
Liles, Estate of, 203
Lilienthal, Matter of Estate of, 182
Limb v. Aldridge, 349
Linck v. Barokas & Martin, 93
Lincoln Fin'l Advisors Corp. v. Ards as next friend of Ards, 678
Lincoln Life and Annuity Co. of New York v. Caswell, 209
Lincoln National Bank v. Shriners Hospitals, 598, 659, 668
Lind, Estate of, 243
Lindberg, Estate of, 625, 665
Lindemann v. Lindemann, 360

Lindgren, Matter of Estate of, 434, 436
Lindner, Estate of, 7
Lindsay, Matter of Estate of, 140, 373
Lindsey v. Burkemper, 268
Lindsey v. Wilcox, 112
Lindsey, Estate of v. Taylor, 254
Linger v. Rohr, 308
Link, Matter of Will of, 453
Linkins v. Protestant Episcopal Cathedral Foundation, 200
Lint, Matter of Estate of, 118, 289
Lipe v. Lipe, 329
Little City Foundation v. Capsonic Group, 158
Little Red Schoolhouse for Special Children, Inc. v. Citizens & Southern Nat. Bank, 511
Little, Matter of Estate of, 66
Littwin v. Littwin, 493
Livingston, In re Estate of, 138, 144
Lloyd Revocable Ttust, In re, 680
Lober v. United States, 718
Loberg v. Alford, 623
Lockard v. Commissioner, 701
Locken v. Locken, 312
Lockwood v. Killian, 470
Loeser v. Talbot, 286, 301
Logotheti v. Gordon, 245
Lohr, Matter of Estate of, 288
Lonergan v. Estate of Budahazi, 196
Lones v. Winzer, 490
Long v. Buehler, 183
Long v. Waggoner, 179
Long, Estate of, 236
Long, In re Estate of, 276, 483
Longaker v. Evans, 255
Longeway, In re Estate of, 394
Longstreet v. Decker, 157
Lopez, Matter of, 492
Lord Dacre, Re, 324
Lord, In re Estate of, 288
Lorentzen v. Smith, 560
Loring v. Karri-Davies, 513
Loring v. Marshall, 473, 514
Los Angeles County Pioneer Soc'y, In re, 473
Lotz v. Atamaniuk, 35, 42
Loughmiller, Estate of, 40, 117
Lourdes College v. Bishop, 208
Lovett v. Peavy, 642
Low v. Spellman, 50, 553, 554, 557, 560
Lowe, In re Estate of, 191
Lowell v. Bouchillon, 636, 664
Lowery v. Evonuk, 655
Lowrance v. Whitfield, 559
Lowry v. Norris Lake Shores Development Corp., 555
Lowry's Estate, Matter of, 171
Lowy v. Kessler, 656
Lubbe's Estate, In re, 138
Lubin, In re Estate of, 668
Lubins, Matter of, 180
Lucas v. Hamm, 245, 530
Lucas v. Mannering, 658
Lucero v. Lucero, 222
Luger, Matter of Estate of, 224
Luider v. Skaggs, 76
Luken, Matter of Estate of, 349
Lum, In re Estate of, 141
Lund, In re Estate of, 192
Lundgren v. Gaudiane, 587
Lundgren v. Hoglund, 453
Lung, In re Estate of, 250
Lunsford v. Western States Life Ins., 91
Lutz v. Fortune, 49, 107
Lutz v. Lemon, 176
Lux v. Lux, 494
Lyles, Estate of, 200
Lynch v. Lynch, 121, 360
Lynch's Estate, In re, 142
Lyons ex rel. Lawing v. Holder, 655
Mabry v. McAfee, 47, 181
Mabry, In re Guardianship of, 230, 636
Macaulay v. Wachovia Bank of SC, N.A., 223
MacCallum v. Seymour, 107
MacDonald, In re Estate of, 363, 369
Mache v. Mache, 233
Mack v. Carmack, 74, 75
Mack v. Evans, 205
Mack v. Mack, 391, 394
Mackaben's Estate, Matter of, 143
MacLean v. Citizens Fidelity Bank & Trust Co., 511
Mader, Estate of, 372
Maestas v. Martinez, 82
Magoon v. Magoon, 120
Maheras, Matter of Estate of, 235, 236
Mahoney v. Grainger, 72
Mahoney v. Leddy, 163
Mahoney, In re Estate of, 84, 566
Mahrenholz v. County Board of School Trustees, 303
Maier v. Henning, 636
Maimonides School v. Coles, 408
Maines v. Davis, 138, 147
Malachowski v. Bank One, Indianapolis, 301, 607, 658, 679
Malasky, In re, 617, 621
Malbrough, In re Estate of, 86
Malcolm, Estate of, 580
Malek v. Patten, 175
Malleiro v. Mori, 132
Mallory v. Mallory, 148
Malloy, Matter of Estate of, 194
Malmquist v. Malmquist, 359
Malone v. Guynes, 555
Malone, In re Estate of, 588
Mangel, In re Estate of, 270
Mannara, In re, 409

Manning v. Glens Falls National Bank, 226, 645
Manning v. Snyder, 407
Manon v. Orr, 417
Mansell v. Mansell, 366
Mantalis, In re Estate of, 190
Mapes, In re Estate of, 241
March v. Gerstenschlager, 306
Marcos, Matter of Estate of, 36
Marcotte, Matter of Conservatorship of, 225
Marcus, Matter of Will of, 297
Marcus, Probate of, 228
Marcy v. Markiewicz, 554
Marine v. Johnson, 580
Marinelli, In re Estate of, 76
Marinus, Matter of Will of, 341
Marion v. Davis, 378
Mark K. Eggebrecht Irrevocable Trust, In re, 463
Marks v. Higgins, 715
Marks v. Lyerla, 85
Marks, In re Estate of, 241
Marr v. Hendrix, 568
Marsh, In re Estate of, 232
Marshall v. Grauberger, 163
Marshall v. Marshall, 577, 662
Marshall, Estate of, 338
Marsman v. Nasca, 434, 436, 669
Martel v. Stafford, 586
Martelle, In re Estate of, 333, 334
Martin v. Dennett, 587
Martin v. Harris, 119
Martin v. Johnson, 262
Martin v. Kenworthy, 577
Martin v. Martin, 335, 577, 579
Martin v. Palmer, 113, 285
Martin v. Prairie Rod and Gun Club, 556
Martin, In re Estate of, 149, 334, 598
Martin, Matter of Estate of, 301
Martinez, In re Estate of, 189, 190
Martinez' Estate, Matter of, 79, 80, 149
Martinson v. Holso, 173, 178
Martone v. Martone, 580
Maruccia, Matter of Estate of, 204
Marvin v. Marvin, 123
Maryhew v. Gillingham, 673
Maryland Nat'l Bank v. Cummins, 601, 612, 655, 666
Mashburn v. Wright, 154
Masino v. Sechrest, 306
Mask, In re Estate of, 225
Massey, In re Estate of, 267
Massie, In re Estate of, 590
Masterson v. Department Social Services, 443
Matelich, Estate of v. Matelich, 177
Mathwig, Matter of Estate of, 655, 659
Mattes v. Olearain, 307
Matthews v. Matthews, 250
Maud v. Catherwood, 60
Maui Land & Pineapple Co. v. Naiapaakai Heirs of Makeelani, 112
Maxedon, Matter of Estate of, 609
May v. Estate of McCormick, 202
May v. Heiner, 709
May v. Hunt, 524
May v. Walter, 255
Mayberry, Estate of v. Mayberry, 250
Mayer, In re Estate of, 212
Mayfield, In re Estate of, 592
Mayo v. White, 97
McAbee v. Edwards, 343
McBride v. Jones, 196
McCaffrey v. Laursen, 169
McCart, Matter of Estate of, 434, 435, 437
McCarthy v. Aetna Life Ins. Co., 210, 216
McCarthy v. Poulsen, 650, 685
McCarton v. Estate of Watson, 157
McCarty v. McCarty, 366
McCarty v. State Bank, 173, 349
McCauley, In re Will of, 136, 190, 198, 201
McClain v. Hardy, 375
McClellan's Estate, In re, 150
McClenahan, Estate of v. Biberstein, 653, 654
McClintock v. Scahill, 97
McClinton v. Sullivan, 120, 643
McClinton, In re Succession of, 219
McClure v. Noble, 106
McCool, In re Estate of, 655
McCormick v. Brevig, 152, 164
McCormick v. Jeffers, 142
McCormick v. McCormick, 657, 665
McCormick, In re Estate of, 311
McCoy, Matter of, 217
McCoy, Matter of Estate of, 19, 238
McCrary, Estate of, 61
McCurdy v. McCurdy, 360
McDaniel v. McDaniel, 235
McDaniel, Matter of Estate of, 580
McDevitt, In re Estate of, 142
McDonald v. Moore, 560
McDonald v. Petty, 149
McDonald v. United States National Bank, 679
McElroy v. Taylor, 353
McEwen v. McEwen, 186
McFayden, In re Estate of, 82
McGahee, In re Estate of, 293
McGarvey v. McGarvey, 136
McGarvey v. State, 111
McGill v. Biggs, 307, 311
McGill v. Johnson, 271
McGill v. Lazzaro, 572
McGinley v. Bank of America, N.A., 629
McGlone, In re Estate of, 203
McGovern v. Attorney-General, 469

McGrew, Matter of Estate of, 143, 579
McGuigan, Estate of, 67, 623
McGuire Marital Trust, In re, 674
McGurrin, Matter of Estate of, 142
McHenry v. McHenry, 619
McInnis v. McInnis, 98
McIntosh, In re Estate of, 154
McKee v. Stoddard, 232
McKee, Estate of, 254
McKellar's Estate, Matter of, 140
McKelvy v. Terry, 510, 511
McKenzie v. Francis, 193
McKenzie v. Vanderpoel, 432
McKim, Matter of Estate of, 306
McKinney, In re, 643
McKnight v. McKnight, 342
McKusick, Estate of, 185
McLendon v. McLendon, 582
McLendon v. Priest, 441
McMahon v. McMahon, 313
McMillen v. McMillen, 255, 284, 286
McNeil v. McNeil, 618, 619, 644
McNeill, Estate of, 136, 509
McNeill's Estate, In re, 470
McNichol's Estate v. Commissioner, 712
McNicholas, Estate of v. State, 100
McPeak v. McPeak, 232, 237
McPeek v. McCardle, 41
McPherson v. Dauenhauer, 601
McRae, Estate of, 236
Mearns v. Scharbach, 46, 214
Mecello, In re Estate of, 3, 197, 198
Meckstroth v. Robinson, 265
Meek, In re Marriage of, 329, 332
Meeks v. Successor Trustees of Marital Trust, 655
Meinhard v. Salmon, 597, 600
Mellor v. O'Connor, 263
Melson, In re Last Will of, 237, 241
Melton, In re Estate of, 190
Mendelson, In re Estate of, 267
Mendez-Bellido v. Board of Trustees, 85
Mendoza v. Gonzales, 675
Mercantile Trust Co. Nat. Ass'n v. Shriners' Hosp., 563
Merchants Nat. Bank v. Curtis, 539
Mercury Bay Boating v. San Diego Yacht, 301
Merkel, Matter of Estate of, 334
Merrill Lynch Inc. v. Nora-Johnson, 667
Merrill v. Fahs, 693
Merrill v. Wimmer, 528, 533
Meskell v. Meskell, 306
Messer Trust, In re, 20
Mest v. Dugan, 600, 637, 663
Metropolitan Life Ins. Co. v. White, 85, 87
Metropolitan Transp. Auth. v. Bruken Realty Corp., 561
Metzger, Estate of v. Commissioner, 701
Meyer v. Mitnick, 205
Meyer, In re, 509
Meyer, In re Estate of, 625, 658
Meyer, Matter of Estate of, 254
Meyers v. First Tennessee Bank, N.A., 621, 680
Micheel, Matter of Estate of, 46, 265
Mieras v. DeBona, 245
Mildrexter, In re Estate of, 256
Miles v. Miles, 342
Miles, Guardianship and Conservatorship of, 663
Miller v. Allstate Ins. Co., 76
Miller v. Bank of America, N.A., 666
Miller v. Estate of Baer, 588
Miller v. Kramarczyk, 86
Miller v. SRS, 284, 353
Miller v. Todd, 580
Miller, Estate of v. Miller, 320, 586
Miller, In re Estate of, 89, 143, 233, 236, 254, 655
Milliken v. First Nat. Bank, 172
Millikin Trust Co. v. Jarvis, 364
Mills v. Habluetzel, 103
Milner v. Colonial Trust Co., 154
Miltenberger Estate, In re, 343
Milton H. Greene Archives, Inc. v. CMG Worldwide, Inc., 37
Milward, In re Estate of, 135, 184, 581
Mincey v. Deckle, 199
Minnesota Mutual Life Ins. Co. v. Ensley, 214
Minonk State Bank v. Grassman, 211
Minton v. Sackett, 577
Misenheimer v. Misenheimer, 90
Mitchell v. Cloyes, 579
Mitchell v. Diangelo, 120
Mitchell v. Mitchell, 191
Mitchell, Matter of Estate of, 4, 255
Mitchem v. First Interstate Bank, 84
Mittleman's Estate v. Comm'r of Internal Revenue, 505
Mizell v. Greensboro Jaycees, 553
Mlynarczyk Living Trust, In re, 643
Mocny, In re Estate of, 347, 348
Moffett v. Howard, 271, 273
Moi, In re Estate of, 342
Mongold v. Mayle, 316, 342
Monroe, Estate of v. Commissioner, 94
Montgomery v. Estate of Montgomery, 318, 343
Montgomery v. Michaels, 347
Montgomery, In re Estate of, 320
Montgomery, Matter of Estate of, 237
Montoya v. New Mexico Human Services Dept., 153
Montoya v. Torres, 233, 235
Montrone v. Valley Bank and Trust Co., 617
Mooney, In re Estate of, 265

Moore and Ferrie, In re Marriage of, 121, 365
Moore v. Anderson Zeigler, 245
Moore v. Harvey, 187
Moore v. Healy, 586
Moore v. Livingston, 33
Moore v. Moore, 89
Moore v. Phillips, 425
Moore v. Smith, 235
Moore, In re, 537, 545
Moore, Matter of, 513, 515
Moran, In re Conservatorship of, 160
Morgan Guaranty Trust Co., In re, 547
Morgan's Estate, In re, 96
Morone v. Morone, 123
Morris v. Cullipher, 35, 178
Morris v. Morris, 193
Morris v. William L. Dawson Nursing Center, 75
Morris, In re Estate of, 658
Morrison v. Doyle, 448
Morrison v. Morrison, 194
Morrison v. Piper, 554
Morrison v. Watkins, 658
Morrissey, Matter of, 253
Morse v. Kraft, 466, 467
Morse v. Volz, 222, 223, 237, 238
Morton v. McComb, 270
Morton v. Potts, 471
Morton's Estate, In re, 535
Moses' Estate, In re, 89
Mosher, In re Marriage of, 122
Motes/Henes Trust v. Motes, 511
Mothershed v. Schrimsher, 89
Mott v. Duncan Petroleum Trans., 41, 122
Mountain Brow Lodge No. 82 v. Toscano, 558
Mowdy, In re Estate of, 140, 234
Mowrer, In re Guardianship of, 232, 233
Muder, Matter of Estate of, 147
Mueggenborg v. Walling, 122
Mueller v. Forsyth, 489, 492
Mueller, In re Estate of, 90, 207
Mueller's Trust, In re, 671
Muhlbauer v. Muhlbauer, 133
Mulholland's Estate, Matter of, 489
Mullane v. Central Hanover Bank & Trust Co., 673
Mumby, In re Estate of, 582
Mundell v. Stellmon, 362
Mundell, Matter of Estate of, 361
Munford v. Maclellan, 646
Munger, In re Estate of, 607
Munoz, State ex rel. v. Bravo, 102
Murphy v. Central Bank and Trust Co., 637, 664
Murphy v. Emery, 679
Murphy v. Glenn, 181, 183, 186
Murphy, In re Estate of, 352
Murray v. State Bar, 662
Murray, Matter of, 228
Musselman v. Mitchell, 184
Mydland, Succession of, 249
Myers v. Maxey, 225
Myers v. Myers, 212
Myers v. Weems, 303
Myers, In re Estate of, 44, 350
Nable v. Godfrey's Estate, 84, 85
Nagel, Matter of Estate of, 593
Nahar v. Nahar, 37, 327
Nale v. Ford Motor Co., 85
Napier v. Compton, 236
Nash, In re Estate of, 204
Nathan Trust, In re, 636
National Academy of Sciences v. Cambridge Trust Co., 623, 668
National City Bank of Cleveland v. Ford, 499
National City Bank v. Beyer, 481, 482, 484
National Geographic Society v. Williams, 44
National Home Life Assur. Co. v. Patterson, 112
National Shawmut Bank v. Cumming, 31, 354
National Wildlife Federation v. Foster, 658
NationsBank of Virginia v. Estate of Grandy, 435
Naumoff, In re Estate of, 230
Naylor v. Koeppe, 270
NC Illinois Trust v. First Illini Bancorp, 665, 666, 670
Neal v. Baker, 681
Nease v. Clark, 234
Neff, Estate of, 230
Neff, Succession of, 282
Neisewander, In re Estate of, 603
Nelsen v. Nelsen, 602, 621
Nelson v. Kring, 549, 550, 552
Nelson v. Maiorana, 638
Nelson v. McGoldrick, 100
Nelson v. Nelson, 117
Nelson, In re Estate of, 506
Nelson, Matter of Estate of, 19, 296
Neshem, Matter of Estate of, 113
Nessralla v. Peck, 306
Neto v. Thorner, 34
Neu, Matter of Estate of, 236
Neuhauser, Succession of, 93
Neumann v. McMillan, 321
Neumann v. Rogstad, 124
Neville, In re, 223
Nevitt v. Rotham, 407
New England Merchants Nat'l Bank v. Kann, 455
New England Merchants Nat'l Bank v. Morin, 433
New Mexico Boys Ranch, Inc. v. Hanvey, 270

New Orleans Elec. Pension Fund v. DeRocha, 84, 85
New York Life Ins. Co. v. Cawthorne, 89
Newhoff's Will, Matter of, 608
Newick v. Mason, 441, 471, 529
Newman v. Dore, 347
Newman v. Wells Fargo Bank, N.A., 49
Newton v. Palmour, 142
Newton, In re Estate of, 121
Nicholas v. Nicholas, 214
Nichols Hills Bank v. McCool, 356
Nichols v. Eaton, 450
Nichols, Matter of Estate of, 186
Nicholson, Estate of, 286
Nicholson, In re Estate of, 221
Nicosia v. Turzyn, 206
Niehenke, Matter of Estate of, 254
Niemann v. Vaughn Community Church, 558
Nile v. Nile, 39, 183
Niles, In re, 659
Noble v. McNerney, 341, 654
Noell, Estate of v. Norwest Bank Wyo., N.A., 208
Noggle v. Bank of America, 43, 665
Noll v. Garber, 270
Nora v. Nora, 36
Norem, In re Estate of, 298
North Carolina Nat. Bank v. Apple, 272
North Carolina Nat. Bank v. Norris, 534
Northwestern University v. McLoraine, 208
Norton v. Bridges, 663
Norton v. Georgia R.R. Bank & Trust, Co., 522, 536
Norton v. Hinson, 132, 136
Norton, Matter of Estate of, 141, 293
Norton, Succession of, 195
Norwood v. Sellers, 143
Norwood, Estate of, 216, 250, 338
Novetzke, Estate of, 155
Novitt's Estate, Matter of, 354
Novotny, Guardianship & Conservatorship of, 455
Nozik v. McDonald, 683
Nunn's Estate, In re, 95
Nunnally v. Trust Co. Bank, 107
Nutis v. Schottenstein Trustees, 555
Nuyen, Matter of Estate of, 675
Nwabara v. Willacy, 102
O'Brien v. Dudenhoeffer, 225
O'Brien v. O'Brien, 79, 81
O'Brien, Estate of v. Robinson, 157
O'Connor v. Immele, 184
O'Connor-Sherrets, In re Marriage of, 122
O'Donnell, In re Trust of, 460
O'Hara v. State ex rel. Public Employees Retirement Board, 362
O'Keefe v. State, Department of Revenue, 34
O'Keefe, Matter of Estate of, 92
O'Loughlin's Estate, In re, 232
O'Malley, Matter of Will of, 238
O'Malley, United States v., 712, 714
O'Neal v. Wilkes, 111
O'Neill, In re Estate of, 331
O'Riley v. U.S. Bank, N.A., 660
O'Shaugnessy, United States v., 447
O'Steen v. Wineberg's Estate, 590
Oak Park Trust & Savings Bank v. Baumann, 492
Oak's Oil Serv. v. Massachusetts Bay Transp. Auth., 551, 553
Obergefell v. Hodges, 41, 125
Oberly v. Kirby, 480, 598
Obermeyer v. Bank of America, N.A., 476, 479
Oberstar, In re Estate of, 259, 262
Oelberg, Matter of Estate of, 580, 646
Offerman v. Rosile, 215
Office of Disciplinary Counsel v. Burkhart, 662
Office of Disciplinary Counsel v. Kurtz, 599
Offret v. DiDomenico, 300
Ogan v. Ogan, 263
Ohio Citizens Bank v. Mills, 49
Ohio Dept. of Human Services v. Eastman, 590
Ohio Society for Crippled Children & Adults, Inc. v. McElroy, 560
Ohrt, In re Estate of, 261
Oklahoma Bar Ass'n, State of ex rel. v. Besly, 662
Old Colony Trust Co. v. Cleveland, 296
Old Colony Trust Co. v. Rodd, 437
Old Colony Trust Co. v. Stephens, 61
Old Colony Trust Co. v. United States, 713, 718
Olesen v. Manty, 181
Olive v. Biggs, 184
Oliver v. Estate of Oliver, 120, 251
Oliver, Matter of Estate of, 225
Olliffe v. Wells, 413
Olson v. Toy, 226
OnBank & Trust Co., Matter of, 43
One Valley Bank, Nat. Ass'n v. Hunt, 215
Ongaro, In re Estate of, 591
Opatz, Matter of Estate of, 93
Opinion of the Justices, 51
Opperman v. Anderson, 251
Oravec v. Phillips, 179
Oregon Bank v. Hendricksen, 650
Orlando, In re Marriage of, 213
Oroke, In re Estate of, 579
Orozco v. Orozco, 133
Orpheus Trust, 432

Orr, In re Estate of, 180
Orrell v. Cochran, 135, 137
Ortmeyer v. Bruemmer, 153
Osborn v. Osborn, 166
Osborn, Estate of, 236
Osborne v. Boatmen's Nat. Bank, 124
Osborne v. Osborne, 373
Oshkosh Foundation, In re, 478
Osman v. Osman, 86
Osswald v. Anderson, 169
Ostrander, Matter of Estate of, 637, 664, 681, 683
Ouellette v. State Farm, 75
Outwin v. Commissioner, 712
Overmire, Estate of v. American Nat. Red Cross, 334
Overt, Estate of, 143
Owens, In re Estate of, 352, 567
Oxendine v. Overturf, 76
Ozee v. American Council on Gift Annuities, 647
Ozuna v. Wells Fargo Bank, 336, 338
Padilla v. Roller, 321
Page v. Buchfinck, 171
Paigo, In re Estate of, 220
Palizzi, Matter of Estate of, 285
Palmer v. Palmer, 329
Palmer v. White, 97
Panek, Matter of, 233
Papale-Keefe v. Altomare, 164
Papiernik v. Papiernik, 637
Parada v. Parada, 121
Parant's Will, In re, 504
Pardee's Estate v. Commissioner, 712
Parham, In re Succession of, 241
Parisi, In re Estate of, 275
Parker v. Hall, 340
Parker v. Kokot, 213, 303
Parker v. Marshall, 241
Parker, Guardianship of, 36
Parker, In re Estate of, 255
Parker's Estate, In re, 198
Parkhill, Matter of Estate of, 331
Parks v. Dumas, 83
Parks v. Zions First National Bank, 311, 358
Parris v. Regions Bank, 680
Parson v. Parson, 333
Parson v. United States, 155
Parson v. Wolfe, 54
Parsons v. Tickner, 573
Parsons, Estate of, 139
Pascale v. Pascale, 233, 239, 241
Pascucci v. Alsop, 335
Passarelli Family Trust, In re, 412
Passero v. Fitzsimmons, 627
Passoff, In re Estate of, 258, 259, 261
Pate v. Ford, 99, 495
Patrick v. Patrick, 195
Patterson v. Blanton, 205
Patterson v. Shumate, 445
Patterson-Fowlkes v. Chancey, 223
Patton, In re Estate of, 364
Paul F. Suhr Trust, In re, 461
Paul v. Constance, 163, 169
Pavlinko's Estate, In re, 284
Pay Less Drug Stores v. Bechdolt, 590
Pazzi v. Taylor, 47
Pearce v. Meek, 179
Pearson, In re Estate of, 580
Pechin v. Medd, 489
Pedersen v. Bibioff, 304, 313
Pedrick, In re Estate of, 235
Pedro v. January, 426
Peeples, Matter of, 242
Peffley-Warner v. Bowen, 124
Peirce v. Peirce, 183, 186
Pekol v. Estate of Pekol, 203
Pells v. Brown, 520
Peltomaa's Estate, Matter of, 122
Pena v. Dey, 418
Pendleton, In re Estate of, 52, 352, 354
Penn Mutual Life Ins. Co. v. Abramson, 209, 339, 497
Pennsylvania, Commonwealth of v. Board of Directors, 470
Pense v. Lindsey, 233
Pepper v. Zions First National Bank, 672
Peppler, In re Estate of, 582
Peralta v. Peralta, 577
Perez v. Gilbert, 196
Perfect Union Lodge v. Interfirst Bank, 427, 612
Pericles, In re Estate of, 353
Perino v. Eldert, 185
Perl v. Howell, 185
Perlberg v. Perlberg, 349
Perrenoud v. Harman, 187, 207
Perry v. Twentieth Street Bank, 472
Perry, Estate of, 263
Perry, In re Estate of, 196
Perry, In re Estates of, 275
Perry, In re Marriage of, 328
Perry, Marriage of, 329, 330
Pessein v. Pessein, 329
Peters v. Columbus Steel Castings Co., 77
Peters, In re Estate of, 57, 580
Peters' Estate v. Commissioner, 721
Peterson v. Kabrich, 310
Peterson v. Tremain, 554
Peterson, In re Estate of, 223, 354
Petesch, In re Estate of, 658
Petty's Estate, Matter of, 642
Pezza v. Pezza, 346
Pfahler, In re Estate of, 641
Pfannenstiehl v. Pfannenstiehl, 452
Pfau v. Moseley, 33
Pfoertner, In re Estate of, 658
Philip, In re, 293
Phillips v. Lowe, 461
Phillips v. Wellborn, 360
Phillips, In re Estate of, 219

Phipps v. Barbera, 283, 284
Phipps v. Palm Beach Trust Co., 466
Phoenix, City of v. Garbage Services Co., 686
Picillo, In re Estate of, 12
Pickett v. Brown, 103
Pickrell, Matter of Estate of, 261
Pike Family Trusts, In re, 463
Pilafas, Matter of Estate of, 208
Pilard, State ex rel. v. Berninger, 176
Pio v. Ramsier, 222
Pirie, Matter of Estate of, 604
Pittman, Estate of, 582
Pizel v. Pizel, 164
Pizel v. Whalen, 165
Platt v. Romesburg, 497
Platt, In re Estate of, 652
PNC Bank, Ohio, N.A. v. Stanton, 12, 72
Poach, In re Estate of, 249, 251
Pogue v. Pogue, 76
Polen v. Baker, 267
Poleson v. Wills, 589
Poling v. Northup, 158, 165
Politowicz' Estate, In re, 142
Polson v. Craig, 257
Poltz v. Tyree, 208
Pontius v. Nadolske, 302
Pontrello v. Estate of Kepler, 642
Pool v. Estate of Shelby, 143
Portales Nat. Bank v. Bellin, 266
Porter v. Porter, 185, 203, 273, 342, 360
Portillo v. Shappie, 359
Portnoy, In re, 38
Posey, In re Estate of, 641
Potucek v. Potucek, 307
Pouliot v. Cloutier, 365
Poullette v. Silverstein, 165
Pound v. Shorter, 530, 532, 539
Pouser, In re Estate of, 45, 288
Powell v. American Charter Fed. S. & L., 183
Powell v. City Nat. Bank & Trust Co., 173
Powell v. Powell, 86
Powell v. Thorsen, 600
Powell's Will, In re, 134
Power v. Scott, 580
Powers v. Steele, 32, 41
Powers v. Wilkinson, 46, 49
Premier Property Management, Inc. v. Chavez, 43
Presbytery of Southeast Iowa v. Harris, 51, 52, 552
Prescott, In re Estate of, 225
Price, In re Estate of, 277
Prichard v. Dep't of Revenue, 500
Prime v. Hyne, 530
Prince v. Prince, 492
Pringle v. Pringle, 359
Pritchett v. Turner, 558
Probate of Will and Codicil of Macool, In re, 147
Proctor on Behalf of Proctor v. Insurance Co. of North America, 118
Prouty, Commissioner v., 700
Prudential Ins. Co. of America v. Glass, 209
Puckett, Estate of, 477, 563
Purce v. Patterson, 319
Pyle by Straub v. United States, 183
Quarterman v. Quarterman, 222, 223
Quick v. United Benefit Life Ins. Co., 84
Quinlan's Estate, In re, 643
Quinn, In re Estate of, 655
Raak v. Raak, 620
Racetrac Petroleum v. Ahmed, 670
Rachal v. Reitz, 678
Radel, Estate of, 332
Rafert v. Meyer, 406
Raggio Family Trust, In re, 438
Ragsdale, Matter of Estate of, 588
Raichel v. Raichel, 177
Raiford, Succession of, 146
Rajanna v. KRR Investments, Inc., 306, 312
Rakhman v. Zusstone, 310
Ralston, In re Estate of, 47
Ramage v. Central Ohio Emergency Serv. Inc., 76
Ramage v. Ramage, 169
Ramirez, Matter of Estate of, 147
Ramsey v. Boatmen's First National Bank, 670
Rand, State v., 172, 550
Randeris, Estate of v. Randeris, 624
Randolph v. Reisig, 555
Raney, Matter of Estate of, 221
Ranney, Matter of Will of, 130, 131, 144
Ransom's Estate, In re, 465
Rape v. Lyerly, 264
Rapp, Estate of, 286
Rasmussen v. LaMagdelaine, 302
Ratchin v. Ratchin, 287
Rathblott v. Levin, 245
Ray Ellison Grandchildren Trust, In re, 285
Ray v. American Nat. Bank & Trust Co., 335
Ray v. Tate, 274
Raymond Estate, In re, 47
Raymond, In re Estate of, 268
Razzaghe-Ashrafi v. Razzaghe-Ashrafi, 38
Read, Estate of, 568
Reap, Estate of v. Malloy, 202
Record, Estate of, 224
Reddick, In re Estate of, 333
Redditt v. McDonald's Restaurant, 120
Redfearn v. Ford, 322
Reece, State v., 555

Reed v. Campbell, 48
Reed v. Commissioner, 709
Reed v. Reed, 582
Reed, Matter of Estate of, 133
Reed's Estate, In re, 568, 581
Reed's Estate, Matter of, 93, 129, 133, 134
Reed's, In re Estate of, 343
Reese v. Reese, 589
Reeves, Estate of, 203
Regan v. Uebelhor, 667
Regions Bank v. Lowery, 609
Regions Bank v. Lowrey, 627
Register of Wills v. Cook, 469
Register v. Coleman, 211
Reid, In re, 208
Reid, In re Estate of, 110, 232
Reif v. Reif, 32
Reilly, Matter of Will of, 47
Reiman's Estate, Matter of, 292
Reinwald, Matter of Estate of, 252
Renard, Matter of Estate of, 31, 327
Rennacker v. Rennacker, 643, 659
Renner, Estate of, 268
Reno v. Reno, 508
Renshaw v. Heckler, 41
Republic National Bank & Trust Co. v. Bruce, 650
Republic National Bank v. Araujo, 610
Retseck v. Fowler State Bank, 497
Revocable Trust of Moeder, In re, 456
Reynette-James, In re, 280, 287
Reynolds v. City of Los Angeles, 111
Reynolds v. Russell, 45
Reynolds, In re Estate of, 43, 588
Reynolds, Matter of, 508
Reznor's Estate, In re, 51
Rhoades, Matter of Estate of, 35, 353
Riccelli v. Forcinito, 211
Rice v. Stanley, 549
Richards v. Midkiff, 475
Richards v. Worthen Bank & Trust Co., 347
Richardson, In re Estate of, 294, 298, 335, 336
Richey v. Hurst, 99
Ricketts, In re Estate of, 144
Riconda, Matter of, 329
Riddell v. Edwards, 118, 223, 237, 575
Riddell, In re, 457
Riddle v. Harmon, 211
Ridenour, Estate of v. Commissioner, 43, 230
Rieck v. Rieck, 181
Rienhardt v. Kelly, 580
Riggs v. Riggs, 255
Rigsby, Matter of Estate of, 135
Riley, In re Estate of, 579
Rininger, Matter of Conservatorship of, 226, 229
Ripley, Estate of v. Mortgage One Corp., 591
Rishel v. Estate of Rishel ex rel. Gilbert, 213
Ritter, United States v., 507
Robak, Matter of, 351
Robbin, In re Estate of, 643
Robbins, In re, 444
Robbins, Matter of Estate of, 112
Roberg's Estate, In re, 568
Robert Paul, Matter of Adoption of, 109
Roberts v. Baker, 222
Roberts v. Fisher, 194
Roberts v. Roberts, 167, 483
Roberts, Matter of Estate of, 624
Roberts' Estate, In re, 268
Roberts-Douglas v. Meares, 236
Robertson v. Central Jersey Bank & Trust Co., 602
Robertson v. Robertson, 227
Robinette v. Helvering, 695
Robinson ex rel. Snell, In re, 587
Robinson v. Benton, 193
Robinson v. Delfino, 176, 299, 421
Robinson v. Mays, 338
Robinson, In re Estate of, 301
Robinson's Estate, In re, 488
Robison v. Graham, 183, 184
Robson v. Electrical Contractors Ass'n, 213
Roccamonte, In re Estate of, 47
Rock Springs Land and Timber, Inc. v. Lore, 637
Roddy, Matter of Estate of, 255
Rodriguez v. Gavette, 582
Roeske v. First Nat. Bank, 203
Rogers v. Helmes, 138
Rogers v. Rogers, 154, 160, 581
Rogers, Matter of, 147
Rogerson v. Wheeling Dollar Sav. & Trust Co., 563
Rohn, In re Estate of, 98
Rohrer, Matter of Estate of, 156, 175
Rolczynski, Matter of Estate of, 664
Rolf H. Brennemann Testamentary Trust, In re, 618, 621
Romanowski, In re Estate of, 230
Romero, Matter of Estate of, 376, 378
Rood v. Newberg, 234, 289, 300
Rood, In re Estate of, 478
Roots v. Uppole, 305
Rose v. Firstar Bank, 647, 663
Rose v. United States, 724
Rose, Estate of v. Loucks, 298
Rosen v. Rosen, 302
Rosen, In re, 144, 235
Rosen, In re Estate of, 222
Rosenberg v. Lipnick, 42
Rosenberger, Estate of, 332
Rosenbloom v. Kokofsky, 138
Rosenblum v. Gibbons, 166
Ross v. Caunters, 140
Ross, Matter of Estate of, 265

Rothko, In re, 597, 665
Rothko, In re Estate of, 255
Rouner v. Wise, 418
Rouse, People v., 667
Routh, Matter of Estate of, 261
Rowe v. Rowe, 265, 268
Rowell v. Plymouth-Home Nat. Bank, 182
Rowell, Matter of Estate of, 134
Rowett v. McFarland, 491, 499
Rowland v. Rowland, 371
Roy's Estate v. Commissioner, 716
Royal, Matter of Estate of, 143
Royce v. Estate of Denby, 37, 39, 339
Rubenstein v. Mueller, 184
Rubenstein v. Sela, 160, 235, 303
Rubert, In re Estate of, 32, 33, 35, 37
Rubinson v. Rubinson, 649
Ruby G. Owen Trust, In re, 457
Rucker, Ex parte, 158
Rudolph, Estate of, 146
Rudow v. Fogel, 306
Rudy v. Wagner, 488
Ruehl, Estate of v. Ruehl, 590
Ruhland, Matter of Estate of, 487
Rumlin v. Lewis, 102
Runser v. Lippi, 469
Rupert, In re Estate of, 37
Ruscilli v. Ruscilli, 102
Rush University Medical Center v. Sessions, 445
Rushing v. Mann, 483
Russell v. Hall, 333
Russell v. Russell, 500
Russell v. Wachovia Bank, N.A., 31, 39
Russell v. Walz, 348
Russell, Estate of, 257
Russell, In re Estate of, 273
Rutanen v. Ballard, 610, 612, 656, 657, 669, 670
Ruth v. First Nat. Bank, 489
Ruther, Matter of Estate of, 575
Ryan v. Ryan, 4
Ryan v. Ward, 527, 532
Ryan, Matter of Estate of, 47
Ryland Group, Inc. v. Wills, 554
Rynn v. Owens, 178
S.M.V. v. Littlepage, 103
Safe Deposit & Trust Co. of Baltimore, Helvering v., 709
Safran's Estate, Matter of, 86
Salathe, In re Estate of, 32, 36, 120, 145
Sale Guaranty Corp., In re, 314
Salisbury, Estate of, 268
Salus, In re Estate of, 654, 657
Salzman v. Bachrach, 123
Samaritan Health System v. Caldwell, 356
Samuel v. King, 162
Samuelson v. Ingraham, 313
San Antonio Area Foundation v. Lang, 18, 285
Sanchez v. Sanchez De Davila, 34, 167, 327
Sander, Matter of Estate of, 214
Sanders v. Brooks, 222
Sanders v. Pierce, 333
Sanders, Estate of, 576
Sanders, Matter of Estate of, 215
Sanni, Inc. v. Fiocchi, 684
Santarelli, In re Estate of, 662
Sarabia, Estate of, 237
Sarbacher v. McNamara, 36, 263, 353
Sasarak v. Sasarak, 370
Satterfield v. Bonyhady, 109
Satti v. Rago, 672
Sauer, In re Estate of, 426
Saueressig, In re Estate of, 143
Saunders v. AMG National Trust Bank, 463, 464
Saunders v. Callaway, 170
Sauter's Estate, In re, 642
Savage, Matter of Estate of, 299, 300, 303
Savage's Estate, Matter of, 353, 594
Sawyer v. Lancaster, 302
Sawyer v. Lebanon Citizens Natl. Bank, 70
Sax, In re Estate of, 119
Saxton, In re, 610, 655, 665, 674
Sayre, Will of, 353
Scarborough Properties Corp., In re, 671
Scatterwood v. Edge, 521, 522
Schaefer v. Schuhman, 184
Schafer v. Deszcz, 555
Schaffer, In re Estate of, 655
Schafroth, In re Estate of, 579
Schaneman v. Wright, 169, 307
Scheele, In re Will of, 672
Scheiner, Matter of Estate of, 349
Scherer, In re Estate of, 112
Schildberg v. Schildberg, 642
Schimke v. Karlstad, 211
Schlenker, In re Estate of, 580
Schloendorff v. Society of New York Hospital, 390
Schlosser v. Schlosser, 578
Schlueter, In re Estate of, 221, 222
Schmanski v. Schmanski, 213, 361
Schmidt v. Chambers, 661
Schmidt v. Killmer, 675
Schmidt, Estate of, 293
Schock, Matter of Estate of, 96
Schoppe, In re Estate of, 233
Schreiber v. Kellogg, 287, 451
Schreiber, In re Estate of, 1
Schreiner v. Scoville, 245
Schriver, In re Estate of, 352
Schroeder v. Herbert C. Coe Trust, 514
Schubert v. Reynolds, 230

Schuldt, In re Estate of, 656
Schultz v. Schultz, 213
Schulz v. Miller, 305
Schwartz v. Barker, 669
Scott v. Bank One Trust Co., 449
Scott v. Brunson, 482
Scott v. First Nat. Bank, 161
Scott v. Scott, 590
Scott, In Matter of Estate of, 589
Scott, In re Estate of, 509
Scott, Matter of Guardianship of, 352
Scott's Estate, In re, 80
Scribner v. Berry, 47, 49
Scribner v. Gibbs, 144
Seader, In re Estate of, 111
Seaman, Matter of Estate of, 66
Searight's Estate, In re, 472
Searl, In re Estate of, 46
Sears v. Coolidge, 546
Seaton, In re Estate of, 286
Second Bank-State Street Trust Co. v. Pinion, 296
Second Bank-State Street Trust Co. v. Second Bank-State Street Trust Co., 528, 534
Second Nat. Bank v. Harris Trust and Savings Bank, 545, 546
Secoy, In re Estate of, 653
Secrest v. Citizens National Bank, 591
Secretary of SRS, State ex rel. v. Jackson, 447
Security S & L v. Estate of Kite, 589
Seegers, Matter of Estate of, 238
Segal v. Himelfarb, 265
Segal v. Levine, 659
Sehota, Re, 118
Seidl v. Estate of Michelsen, 299
Seidman, Matter of Estate of, 437
Seifert v. Sanders, 147
Seifert v. Southern Nat. Bank, 346
Seifert's Estate, In re, 344
Seizer v. Sessions, 121, 360, 365
Sekanic, Estate of, 103
Selby, Estate of v. United States, 95
Sen v. Headley, 153
Senft v. United States, 728
Senter v. Furman, 312
Seven G Ranching Co. v. Stewart Title, 637
Sewart, Estate of, 277
Seymour's Estate, Matter of, 203
Seyse, In re, 36, 568
Shaffer v. Reed, 554
Shah, In re, 228
Shannon, Estate of, 341
Shannon, Matter of Will of, 265
Shapira v. Union Nat. Bank, 317, 377
Sharington v. Strotton, 152
Shaw v. Shaw, 345
Shaw v. Stutchman, 583
Shaw, Matter of Estate of, 196
Shear v. Gabovitch, 612, 637, 642, 655
Shearer v. Pla-Boy Inc., 591
Sheats v. Johnson, 528, 529
Shedrick, Matter of Estate of, 156
Sheldon v. Sheldon, 185
Sheldon, Estate of, 368
Sheldone v. Marino, 580
Shelley v. Kraemer, 558
Shelton v. Tamposi, 629, 660
Shenandoah Valley Nat'l Bank v. Taylor, 469
Shenkman, In re, 510
Shepherd v. Mazzetti, 181, 658
Shepley's Estate, In re, 590
Sheppard v. Junes, 66
Sheppard, In re Last Will and Testament of, 329
Sheridan v. Blume, 494
Sheridan v. Harbison, 198
Sherry, Matter of Estate of, 185
Shields, Matter of, 486
Shiflett, Petition of, 320
Shim v. Rutgers, 36
Shimp v. Huff, 185
Shimun, Estate of, 338
Shinkle, Estate of, 238, 241
Shippy, In re Estate of, 41, 118
Shire v. Unknown/Undiscovered Heirs, 455
Shoaf, In re Estate of, 263
Shoemaker v. Estate of Freeman, 305
Shortridge v. Sherman, 46
Shriners Hospital for Crippled Children v. Coltrane, 257
Shriners Hospitals v. Gardiner, 642
Shriners Hospitals v. Robbins, 626
Shriners Hospitals v. Zrillic, 374
Shriners' Hospital for Crippled Children v. Hester, 374
Shumway, In re Estate of, 233, 582
Shuraleff v. Donnelly, 124
Shurley, Matter of, 445, 449
Shwachman v. Meagher, 211
Sibley's Trusts, In re, 269
Siedel v. Snider, 572
Siegel Mobile Home Group, Inc. v. Bowen, 153
Siegel, In re, 613
Siegemund v. Shapland, 36
Sieh v. Sieh, 346
Sieh, In re Estate of, 333
Sikora v. Sikora, 83
Silberman's Will, In re, 494, 496
Silver, In re Estate of, 177, 299
Simches v. Simches, 286
Simeone v. Simeone, 370
Simmons v. Smith, 310
Simon v. Grayson, 293, 295
Simpson, In re Estate of, 582
Simpson, Matter of, 94
Simpson, Matter of Estate of, 268
Sims v. Cox, 335
Sims v. Heath, 637

Sims, Matter of Estate of, 77
Sinclair v. Fleischman, 156
Skifter, Estate of v. Commissioner, 725
Skiles v. Skiles, 36
Skinner v. Moore, 287
Skinner's Estate v. United States, 712
Skubitz, In re, 448
Slack v. Truitt, 140, 144
Sladoje, State ex rel. v. Belskis, 20
Slawsby v. Slawsby, 180
Sligh v. First Nat'l Bank of Holmes County, 452
Sligh v. Plair, 500
Smail v. Hutchins, 353
Small's Estate, In re, 138
Smart, Estate of v. Smart, 41, 118, 122
Smelser, Matter of Estate of, 280
Smid, In re Estate of, 367
Smiley v. Johnson, 664
Smith v. Estate of Peters, 250
Smith v. McCall, 348
Smith v. Shafer, 160, 236
Smith v. Smith, 142, 360, 364, 447
Smith v. Turner, 179, 181
Smith v. Underwood, 643
Smith v. United States, 191
Smith v. Weitzel, 293
Smith, Estate of, 280
Smith, Guardianship of, 641
Smith, In re Estate of, 48, 148, 194, 202, 223, 243, 280
Smith, In re Marriage of, 357
Smith, In re Succession of, 141
Smith, Matter of Will of, 147, 148
Smith, Will of, 147, 148
Smith's Estate, Matter of, 510
Smithers v. St. Luke's-Roosevelt Hosp. Center, 474
Smolen for Smolen v. Smolen, 211
Sneed, Matter of Estate of, 293
Snide, Matter of, 284
Snider v. Wood, 170
Snodgrass, In re Estate of, 282
Snuggs v. Snuggs, 169
Snyder v. Davis, 12, 333
Snyder v. Peterson, 305
Society Nat. Bank v. Jacobson, 43, 501, 502
Sogg v. Nevada State Bank, 370
Sola v. Clostermann, 50
Sola, Estate of, 190
Soles, In re Estate of, 250
Sollid, In re, 49
Solomon v. Central Trust Co., 109
Soltis v. First of America Bank of Muskegon, 346
Somers, In re Estate of, 405, 456
South Carolina Nat. Bank of Charleston v. Copeland, 296
South Carolina Nat. Bank v. Johnson, 493, 494
South Shore Nat. Bank v. Berman, 268
South Side T. & S. Bank v. South Side T. & S. Bank, 427
Southern Bank & Trust Co. v. Brown, 529, 532
SouthTrust Bank v. Winter, 192
Southworth, Estate of, 147, 148
Sparacio's Estate, Matter of, 171
Spaugh v. Ferguson, 499
Spear, Matter of Estates of, 88
Spearman v. Estate of Spearman, 170
Speelman v. Pascal, 161
Spencer v. Childs, 170
Spencer v. Williams, 353
Spencer, In re Estate of, 466, 514
Spetz v. New York State Dep't of Health, 444
Spicer v. Estate of Spicer, 580
Spindle, Matter of Conservatorship of, 225
Sprenkle-Hill, In re Estate of, 342
Sprinchorn, Matter of Estate of, 483, 485, 491
Spruance v. Northway, 221
Spurgeon, Matter of Estate of, 349
Squire, In re Estate of, 234, 238
Squires, Succession of, 133
Srubar, Matter of Estate of, 255
St. John's-St. Luke Evangelical Church v. National Bank of Detroit, 475
St. Regis Paper Co. v. Brown, 555
Stallworth v. Hicks, 48
Stalnaker, Estate of, 215
Standard Knitting Mills, Inc. v. Allen, 550
Stanley v. Brietz, 490
Stanley v. Potter, 248
Stanley, Estate of v. Sandiford, 302
Stanton v. Sayre, 637
Starkey, Estate of v. United States, 285, 471
Starr v. Rousselet, 176
Starratt v. Morse, 191
Stasis, In re Estate of, 134
State Employees' Retirement System v. Taylor, 210
State Farm Life Ins. Co. v. Pearce, 90
State Farm Life Ins. Co. v. Smith, 86
State Street Bank v. Reiser, 593
Stauffer v. Henderson, 176
Steckler, Succession of, 315, 326
Steele v. Steele, 373
Steen and Berg Co., v. Berg, 186
Steffes' Estate, Matter of, 124
Stegemeier v. Magness, 598
Stein v. Brown, 93
Stein, In re Estate of, 568
Steiner v. Hawaiian Trust Co., 598
Steinhauser v. Repko, 177
Steinke v. Novak, 286

Stellwag, Estate of v. Kennedy, 36, 592
Stenkamp v. Stenkamp, 250
Stenke v. Masland Development Co., Inc., 555
Stephan v. Equitable Savings and Loan Association, 666, 674
Stephens v. McPherson, 148, 170
Stephens v. Stephens, 522
Stephens, Estate of, 152, 238
Stephenson v. Rowe, 256
Sterling v. Wilson, 344
Stern, In re, 667
Stern, In re Estate of, 298
Stern, Matter of, 583
Stevens v. Casdorph, 131, 140
Stevens v. National City Bank, 679
Stevenson v. United States National Bank, 341
Stevenson, Estate of, 112
Stewart v. RepublicBank, Dallas, N.A., 378
Stewart, In re Estate of, 184
Stiles v. Brown, 194
Stilwell v. Estate of Crosby, 642
Stockert v. Council on World Service, 477
Stockwell v. Stockwell, 232
Stokes v. Stokes, 343
Stokes, Matter of Estate of, 167
Stone v. McCarthy, 310
Stone, Estate of, 653, 654
Stormont, In re Estate of, 202
Stowell, In re Estate of, 598, 658, 659
Strand's Estate, In re, 257
Stratman v. Sheetz, 554
Stratton, In re Estate of, 267
Straube, Estate of v. Barber, 269, 271, 272, 282, 499
Strauss v. Teachers Ins. & Annuity Ass'n, 209
Street v. Skipper, 363
Stroh, Matter of Estate of, 330, 346
Strong v. Holden, 222
Strulowitz v. Cadle Company, II, Inc., 588
Stuart Kingston, Inc. v. Robinson, 553, 555
Sturgis v. Stinson, 612
Sturm, Estate of, 592
Substitute Indenture of Trust, In re, 286
Sugden v. Lord St. Leonards, 198
Suggs v. Norris, 124
Sullivan v. Burkin, 42, 354
Sullivan v. Kodsi, 20
Sullivan v. Rooney, 123
Sullivan v. Sullivan, 271
Sullivan, In re Estate of, 192
Summerlin, United States v., 590
Summers v. Summers, 483, 485
Sun Bank/Miami, N.A. v. Hogarth, 232, 298
Sundin v. Klein, 84, 88, 89
Sundquist v. Sundquist, 166
SunMicrosystems, Inc. v. Lema, 132
Superintendent of Belchertown State School v. Saikewicz, 393
Sussman v. Sussman, 164
Sutherland, Matter of Estate of, 588
Svenson v. First Nat. Bank of Boston, 493
Swain v. Estate of Tyre, 90
Swanson v. Swanson, 489, 491
Swanson, Adoption of, 109
Swanson, In re Estates of, 87
Sweet, Estate of, 293, 295
Switzer, In re Estate of, 349
Swope v. Swope, 358
Swoyer, Matter of Estate of, 251
Symmons v. O'Keeffe, 617, 642
Symphony Space v. Pergola Properties, 553, 554, 556
Synovus Trust Co., N.A., Ex parte, 417
Syracuse University, Application of, 479
Taboni ex rel. Taboni v. Estate of Longo, 572
Taff's Estate, Matter of, 74
Taggart, Matter of Estate of, 341
Tait, In re, 445, 446
Takabuki v. Ching, 475
Taliaferro v. Taliaferro, 162, 281, 348, 408
Talley v. Succession of Stuckey, 338
Tamplin, In re Last Will and Testament of, 216
Tanner v. Robinson, 155
Tannler v. DHSS, 353
Tarkington v. Tarkington, 309
Tate v. Kennedy, 498
Tatum v. Tatum, 119
Taylor v. Abernethy, 186
Taylor v. Crocker National Bank, 665
Taylor v. Estate of Taylor, 142, 580
Taylor v. Hutchinson, 456
Taylor v. Johnson, 181
Taylor v. Koslosky, 224
Taylor v. Maness, 335
Taylor v. Nationsbank Corp., 619
Taylor v. Rapp, 377
Taylor, Ex parte, 75
Taylor, Matter of, 371
Taylor, Matter of Estate of, 576
Taylor, State v., 473
Temple Beth Israel v. Feiss, 483, 485, 488
Tennant, Matter of Guardianship & Conservatorship of Estate of, 224
Tensfeldt, In re Estate of, 185, 186, 351
Terner v. Rand, 207

Territorial Sav. & Loan Ass'n v. Baird, 444
Testa v. Roberts, 230
Testamentary Trust of Hasch, In re, 464, 493
Teubert's Estate, In re, 149, 471
Texas Commerce Bank, N.A. v. Grizzle, 668
Thellusson v. Woodford, 521, 561
Theodore Short Trust v. Fuller, 489
Theopold v. Sears, 58
Thies, Matter of Estate of, 370
Third Nat'l Bank v. Brown, 434
Thomann, In re Estate of, 83
Thomas v. Copenhaver, 147
Thomas v. Harper, 579
Thomas v. Reid, 305
Thomas v. Sullivan, 123
Thomas v. Thomas, 80, 196, 490
Thomas, In re, 376
Thomas, In re Estate of, 430
Thomas, Matter of Estate of, 43
Thomas, Matter of Marriage of, 124
Thomasi v. Koch, 306, 311, 312
Thompson v. Nesheim, 307, 311
Thompson v. Royall, 192
Thompson v. Thompson, 186
Thompson, In re Estate of, 476, 579, 588
Thompson, Matter of Estate of, 353
Thompson's Estate, In re, 266
Thor v. McDearmid, 309
Thornhill v. Riegg, 531
Thornton, In re, 77
Thornton, In re Estate of, 235
Thurston v. Thurston, 50
Tierce v. Macedonia United Methodist Church, 157, 165, 173, 294, 297
Timothy C. Wirt, M.D., P.C. v. Prout, 332
Tindol v. McCoy, 104
Tintocalis v. Tintocalis, 330
Tkachuk, Estate of, 138
Tobin, Matter of, 654
Todd v. Cartwright, 180
Tolbert v. Maner, 75
Toledo Trust Co. v. National Bank of Detroit, 354
Toledo Trust Co. v. Santa Barbara Foundation, 515
Toler v. Harbour, 43, 501
Tolin, In re Estate of, 193
Tollison, In re Estate of, 589
Tolson, In re Estate of, 37
Tomaso, Estate of v. Tomaso, 349
Tomlinson v. Tomlinson, 168, 169
Tomlinson's Estate, In re, 478
Toms v. Davies, 140
Toni 1 Trust, by Tangwall v. Wacker, 446
Tooahnippah v. Hickel, 321
Toombs v. Daniels, 623
Toon v. Gerth, 581
Tootle v. Tootle, 497
Torvea v. Nolam, 673
Tosh, In re Estate of, 208
Totten, In re, 24, 167
Townsend v. United States, 230
Townsend, In re Estate of, 643
Trabits v. First Nat'l Bank, 463
Trackman v. Ringer, 481, 485
Trammell v. Elliott, 470
Transamerica Occidental Life Ins. Co. v. Burke, 113, 285, 286
Trask v. Butler, 681
Travelers Ins. Co. v. Thompson, 87
Trbovich's Estate, In re, 169
Treloar, In re Estate of, 337, 338
Treschak v. Yorkville Nat. Bank, 310, 314
Tressel, Estate of v. Tressel, 178
Trim v. Daniels, 133, 147
Trobaugh, In re Estate of, 182
Trotalli, Matter of Estate of, 675
Trout v. Parker, 206
Troy S. Poe Trust, In re, 664
Troy v. Hart, 94
Trugman v. Klein, 488
Truhn, In re Estate of, 579
Trust Agreement of Westervelt v. First Interstate Bank, 492, 539
Trust Created by Belgard, Matter of, 109
Trust Created by Hill, Matter of, 643, 658, 663, 672
Trust Created Under Agreement with Lane, In re, 110
Trust Created Under Mitchell, In re, 658
Trust Estate of Daoang, In re, 563
Trust Estate of Dwight, Matter of, 61
Trust of Criss, In re, 531
Trust of Grover, Matter of, 655, 658
Trust of Lane, In re, 485
Trust of McManus v. McManus, 176
Trust of Rosenberg, In re, 660
Trust of Socha, In re, 644
Trust of Strong, In re, 667, 673
Trust of Trimble, In re, 659
Trust of VanderPoel, In re, 112
Trust of Walker, In re, 484, 485, 488
Trust of Woodworth, In re, 61
Trust Under Agreement of Taylor, 677
Trust under Deed of Kulig, In re, 420
Trust Under Will of Holt, In re, 485
Trustees of Baker Univ. v. Trustees of End. Ass'n of Kansas State College of Pittsburg, 82
Trustees of Presbytery v. Hammer, 169
Trustees of Schools of Township No. 1 v. Batdorf, 551
Trustees of University of Delaware v. Gebelein, 471

Trustees of Wheaton College v. Peters, 281
Trusts Created by Hormel, Matter of, 607, 609
Trusts of Holdeen, 563
Trusts Under Will of Dwan, Matter of, 653, 654, 674
Trynin, In re Estate of, 658
Tseng v. Tseng, 417
Tsilidis v. Pedakis, 110
Tuck's Settlement Trusts, In re, 377
Tucker v. Bradford, 441
Tucker v. Stacy, 196
Tudor v. Bradford, 198
Tuley, Matter of, 662
Tulsa Professional Collection Services, Inc. v. Pope, 42, 569, 587
Turkington, Estate of, 336, 338
Turley v. Adams, 186
Turner v. Estate of Turner, 86, 87
Turner v. Lo Shee Pang's Estate, 590
Turner v. Nesby, 48
Turner v. Reed, 256
Turner, In re Estate of, 196
Tuttle v. Simpson, 284
Tyler v. Suburban Trust Co., 178
Tyler, In re Estate of, 348
Tyson v. Henry, 297
U.S. Trust Co. v. Haig, 588
Uhl, Estate of, 200
Uhl, Estate of v. Commissioner, 712
Ulrikson, In re Estate of, 268
Unanue, Matter of, 365
Underwood v. Bank of Huntsville, 163, 207
Underwood v. MacKendree, 529
Union Nat. Bank v. Ornelas-Gutierrez, 174
United Cal. Bank v. Bottler, 511, 545, 546, 547
United States National Bank v. United States, 715
University National Bank v. Rhoadarmer, 448
University of Louisville v. Isert, 542
Unke, Matter of Estate of, 241
Unsel v. Meier, 107
Unthank v. Rippstein, 160
Upman v. Clarke, 236, 237, 408
Urquhart v. Teller, 560
Utterback, Estate of, 285
V-1 Oil Co. v. Ranck, 585
Vacco v. Quill, 393
Vaden, Matter of Estate of, 254
Vadney, Matter of Estate of, 176, 304
Vail, Estate of v. First of America Trust, 602, 626
Valladee v. Valladee, 310
Vallerius, In re Estate of, 85
Vallery, Matter of Estate of, 477
Valma M. Hanson Revocable Trust, In re, 261
Van Der Veen, Matter of Estate of, 90
Van Schaack v. American South Bank, N.A., 625
Vance v. Myers' Estate, 686
Vandenhook, Matter of Estate of, 122
Varns v. Varns, 73
Varnum v. Brien, 125
Varoz v. Estate of Shepard, 121
Vaughn v. Bernhardt, 212
Vaughn v. Hufnagel, 41
Vaupel v. Barr, 243
Velasquez, In re Marriage of, 213
Venables v. Seattle-First Nat'l Bank, 44, 428
Vento v. Colorado National Bank-Pueblo, 607
Ventura County Humane Society v. Holloway, 282
Venturi v. Taylor, 588
Verdi by Verdi, Estate of v. Toland, 222, 225, 236
Vertin, Matter of Estate of, 592
Vetter v. Hampton, 175
Via v. Putnam, 185
Vick, Matter of Estate of, 289
Viera v. Estate of Cantu, 569
Vigil v. Sandoval, 158
Villar, In re, 537
Villegas v. McBride, 588
Villwock, Matter of Estate of, 276
Vincent J. Fumo Irrevocable Children's Trust, In re, 643
Vincent v. Sutherland, 105
Vincent v. Torrey, 206
Virginia National Bank v. Harris, 173
Vissering, Estate of v. Commissioner, 437
Vittands v. Sudduth, 162, 165
Vittorio, In re Estate of, 300
Vogel, Estate of, 212
Volvo Commerical Finance LLC the Americas v. McClellan, 573
von der Nuell, In re Marriage of, 121, 360
Von Wendesse, Estate of, 181
Vorholt v. One Valley Bank, 679
Voss v. Brooks, 176
Vukmir v. Vukmir, 263
Wachovia Bank and Trust Co. v. Johnston, 600
Wachter v. Wachter, 309
Wagley, Matter of Estate of, 333, 341
Wagner, In re Estate of, 223, 225
Wahby, Matter of Estate of, 100
Waitkevich, In re Estate of, 174
Waitman v. Waitman, 172
Waitzman, Estate of, 568
Wakefield, In re Marriage of, 359
Waldrep v. Goodwin, 130, 143
Wales, Estate of, 250, 259
Walker v. Lawson, 245
Walker v. Roberds, 233

Walker v. Walker, 133
Walker, In re Estate of, 85
Walker's Will, In re, 523
Wall v. Pfanschmidt, 83
Wall, Estate of v. Commissioner, 713, 714
Wallace v. Comprehensive Personal Care Services, Inc., 645
Walpole v. Lewis, 195
Walsh v. Walsh, 306
Walter E. Wilhite Revocable Living Trust v. Northwest Yearly Meeting Pension Fund, 649, 664
Walton v. City of Red Bluff, 51, 172, 552
Walton v. Davy, 351
Walton v. Walton, 182, 186
Ward v. Fogel, 412
Ward v. Grant, 314
Ward v. Van der Loeff, 529
Ward v. Ward, 85
Ware v. Green, 426
Warman, In re Estate of, 248
Warner v. Warner, 38, 234
Warner v. Whitman, 43, 51
Warner, Matter of Estate of, 120, 568
Warren Boynton State Bank v. Wallbaum, 491
Warren Gen. Hosp. v. Brink, 47
Warren v. Albrecht, 483
Warren v. Compton, 347
Warren, Matter of Estate of, 251
Warren-Boynton State Bank v. Wallbaum, 492
Washburn, In re Estate of, 221, 224
Washington Hospital v. Riggs Nat'l Bank, 478
Washington State Grange v. Brandt, 527, 533
Washington v. Glucksberg, 393
Wasniewski v. Quick and Reilly, Inc., 150, 158
Wasserman v. Cohen, 42, 248
Wasson, Matter of Will of, 241
Waters, Matter of Estate of, 238
Watkins v. Watkins, 310
Watlack, Matter of Estate of, 221
Watson v. Santalucia, 257
Watson v. Warren, 237
Watson, In re, 241, 242
Watson's Estate, In re, 154
Watts' Estate, Matter of, 138
Wax, In re, 214
Wayne, In re Estate of, 197
Weaver v. Keen, 214
Weaver, In re Estate of, 51, 534
Webb v. Underhill, 482, 487
Webb v. Webb, 98
Webb, Matter of Estate of, 233
Weber v. Aetna Casualty & Surety Co., 101
Webster v. Mauz, 594
Webster, Estate of, 100
Webster, Matter of Estate of, 138, 271
Wedeberg, Matter of Estate of, 134
Weeks v. Cessna Aircraft Co., 75
Weeks, Estate of, 45, 465
Wehrheim v. Golden Pond Assisted Living Facility, 580
Weill, In re Estate of, 94
Weinberger's Trust, In re, 647
Weinen, In re Estate of, 418
Weingart, Estate of, 610
Weinstock's Estate, Matter of, 243
Weitzman, In re Estate of, 347
Welch v. Wilson, 111
Welder v. Hitchcock, 98
Weller v. Tagge, 286
Wells Fargo Bank v. Marshall, 203
Wells Fargo v. Militello, 666, 669
Wells, In re Estate of, 146, 341
Welton v. Gallagher, 204
Wendell v. AmeriTrust Co., N.A., 374
Wentworth, In re Estate of, 331, 334, 352
Wenzel-Mosset by Gaukler, Estate of v. Nickels, 232
Wernet's Estate, Matter of, 261
Wernher's Settlement Trusts, In re, 496
Wesley United Methodist Church v. Harvard College, 471
Wessels, Matter of Estate of, 239
West One Trust Co. v. Morrison, 304
West v. Francioni, 262
West v. White, 568
West, Matter of Estate of, 23
Westbrook v. Superior Court, 183
Westerfeld v. Huckaby, 168
Western States Construction v. Michoff, 124
Westpfal, Matter of Estate of, 646
Wetherill v. Bank IV Kansas, N.A., 682
Wetherill v. Basham, 511
Wetmore's Estate, Matter of, 160
Wetsel, Matter of Estate of, 268
Wetzel v. Watson, 179
Wharton, Matter of Marriage of, 41
Wheadon, Matter of Estate of, 198
Wheat, Matter of Estate of, 331
Wheeler v. Mann, 598
Wheeling Dollar Sav. & Trust Co. v. Singer, 111
Whicher v. Abbott, 172
Whirlpool Corp. v. Ritter, 37, 39, 44, 46
Whisnant v. Whisnant, 157
Whitacre v. Crowe, 142
Whitaker v. Estate of Whitaker, 612
Whitbread, Ex parte, 228
Whitchurch v. Perry, 111
White v. Fleet Bank of Maine, 532, 540, 562

White v. Flood, 190
White v. Jones, 148
White v. National Bank & Trust Co., 530
White v. United States, 515
White v. White, 252, 557
White v. Wilbanks, 202
White, Estate of, 646
White, In re, 650
White, In re Estate of, 180, 181, 344
White, In re Succession of, 191
White, Re, 195
White's Estate, In re, 499
Whitenhill v. Kaiser Permanente, 75
Whitlatch, Estate of v. Richardson, 136
Whitney v. Seattle-First Nat. Bank, 373
Whitt, Estate of v. Commissioner, 711
Whittaker v. Stables, 208
Whyte, Estate of v. Whyte, 119
Wiarda, Matter of Estate of, 196
Wich v. Fleming, 144
Wickersham, Appeal of, 653
Wickman's Will, In re, 622
Widmeyer, In re Estate of, 583
Wiedenmeyer v. Johnson, 466
Wigglesworth v. Cowles, 479
Wilbur v. Campbell, 377
Wilcox v. Gentry, 447
Wilcox v. Waldman, 623
Wild's Case, 503
Wilde, Estate of, 665
Wildenstein & Co., Inc. v. Wallis, 560
Wilhelm v. Zepp, 508
Wilhelm, Matter of Estate of, 332
Wilkerson v. McClary, 167
Wilkes v. Wilkes, 485
Wilkin v. Wilkin, 206
Wilkins v. Garza, 272
Wilkins v. Wilkins, 122, 295
Wilkinson v. Brune, 260
Wilkison v. Wiederkehr, 186
Willcox v. Penn Mutual Life Ins. Co., 44
William Dankworth Trust, In re, 653
Williams v. Estate of Pender, 4, 111
Williams v. Faucett, 261
Williams v. Fireman's Fund Ins. Co., 119
Williams v. Harrington, 625
Williams v. Kimes, 500
Williams v. Mason, 180
Williams v. Overton, 133
Williams v. Springfield Marine Bank, 148, 149
Williams v. Studstill, 212
Williams v. Williams, 173, 558, 559
Williams, In re Estate of, 133
Williams, Matter of Estate of, 156
Williamson v. Williamson, 215
Willingham v. Matthews, 90
Wilmington Trust Co. v. Annan, 32
Wilson v. Flowers, 471
Wilson v. Fritchy, 577
Wilson v. Wilson, 620
Wilson, Matter of Estate of, 198, 569
Windholz, Matter of, 572
Windsor v. Leonard, 347
Windsor, United States v., 125
Winebrenner v. Dorten, 203
Wing v. Wachovia Bank & Trust Co., 492
Wingader, In re Marriage of, 210
Winkelfoos v. Mann, 346
Winograd, In re Estate of, 674
Winslow, Matter of Estate of, 272
Winslow's Estate, Matter of, 603
Winsor v. Powell, 300
Winstead, Matter of Estate of, 263
Winters National Bank & Trust Co. v. Riffe, 260
Winterton v. Kaufmann, 175
Wires, Estate of, 122
Wise v. Poston, 558
Wise, Matter of Estate of, 581
Wisely v. United States, 286
Wisner v. Wisner, 366
Wissner v. Wissner, 366
Witmer v. Blair, 607
Witt v. Rosen, 288
Witt v. Ward, 174, 226, 252
Wittick v. Miles, 683
Wittman, In re Estate of, 233
Wittmond, In re Estate of, 164, 205
Wojtalewicz, Estate of, 582
Wolder v. Commissioner, 689, 690
Wolf v. Boren, 76
Wolfe v. Wolfe, 148, 149
Wolfe v. Young, 641
Wolfe, In re Estate of, 75
Wolfe, In re Marriage of, 359
Wolfsohn, Application of, 535
Wood v. Am. Sec. & Trust Co., 510
Wood v. Bettis, 219, 225
Wood v. Smith, 195, 220
Wood v. U.S. Bank, N.A., 610
Wood, Matter of Estate of, 579
Wood's Estate, In re, 508, 509
Woodward School for Girls v. City of Quincy, 606
Woodward v. Commissioner of Social Security, 103, 495
Woodward, Matter of Estate of, 336, 338
Woodward's Estate, In re, 101
Woodworth, Estate of v. Regents of the Univ. of Cal., 498
Workman v. Douglas, 310, 311
World of Sleep, Inc. v. Seidenfeld, 279
Worrell's Estate, In re, 589
Worsham, Matter of Estate of, 266, 577
Wortman v. Hutaff, 650

Wright v. Blevins, 304
Wright v. Bloom, 299
Wright v. Brandon, 73
Wright v. Greenberg, 510
Wright v. Union Nat. Bank, 160, 177
Wright v. Wright, 84
Wright, Matter of Estate of, 31, 327
WYHY Federal Credit Union v. Burchell, 591
Wyinegar, Estate of, 353
Wylie's Estate, In re, 506
Wyrick v. Wyrick, 186
Yager, Matter of Marriage of, 371
Yano v. Yano, 304
Yates v. Taylor, 309, 310
Yeager v. Lucy, 335
Yett's Estate, Matter of, 221
Yiatchos v. Yiatchos, 366
Yohe v. Yohe, 304, 305
York v. Nunley, 112, 580
York, In re Estate of, 98
Young v. Thompson, 576
Young v. Wheeler., 590
Young v. Young, 143, 156, 183, 264
Young, Estate of, 357
Young, In re Estate of, 288
Young, Matter of Estates of, 87
Young, Succession of, 158, 160
Younker, Matter of Estate of, 657
Zabolotny v. Fedorenko, 305
Zachary v. Mills, 242
Zahn, Matter of Estate of, 263
Zarrow, Matter of Estate of, 582
Zelikovitz, Matter of Estate of, 40, 143
Zimbleman, In re Estate of, 636
Zimmerman v. First Nat. Bank, 49
Zimmerman v. Mutual Life Ins. Co., 173
Zimmerman, Matter of Estate of, 120, 373
Zins by Kelsch, Estate of v. Zins, 300
Zobel by Hancox v. Fenendael, 225
Zonas, In re Estate of, 581
Zuckerman v. Alter, 166
Zukerman, In re Estate of, 166, 168, 264

Table of Uniform Probate Code Sections

§ 1–103 .... 91, 369
§ 1–106 576
§ 1–106, cmt. 10
§ 1–107(1) 277
§ 1–107(2) 277
§ 1–107(5) 277
§ 1–108 676
§ 1–109 .... 56, 332, 333
§ 1–201 566
§ 1–201(5) 112, 265
§ 1–201(9) 57
§ 1–201(10) 7
§ 1–201(11) 7
§ 1–201(15) 95
§ 1–201(18) 104, 214
§ 1–201(20) 72
§ 1–201(24) 7, 57
§ 1–201(35) 9
§ 1–201(57) 4, 10, 12, 13, 16, 18, 24, 189
§ 1–306(b) 575
§ 1–307 575
§ 1–309 575
§ 1–403 676
§ 1–403(2) 578, 676
§ 1–403(2)(B) 676
§ 1–403(3) 676
§ 1–403(4) 621
§ 1–403(5) 11
§ 2–101(b) 375
§ 2–102 .... 54, 117
§ 2–102(1)(A) 55
§ 2–102(1)(B) 55
§ 2–102(2) 56
§ 2–102(3) 55, 56
§ 2–102(4) 55, 56
§ 2–102A 355
§ 2–102A(b) 55
§ 2–103 58
§ 2–103(a)(2) 62, 63, 65
§ 2–103(c) 59, 65
§ 2–103(d) 56, 63
§ 2–103(d)–(f) 65
§ 2–103(e)(1) 63
§ 2–103(g)–(i) 65
§ 2–103(i) 65, 66
§ 2–103(j) 65, 66, 67, 112
§ 2–104 .... 27, 57, 116
§ 2–104(b)(2) 495
§ 2–104(b)(3) 116
§ 2–104, cmt. 276
§ 2–104, Ex. 2 116
§ 2–105 67
§ 2–106 .... 58, 60, 61, 98
§ 2–106(b) 59, 60
§ 2–107 66
§ 2–109 78
§ 2–109(a) 78, 79
§ 2–109(b) 81
§ 2–109(c) 81
§ 2–109, cmt. 79, 80, 81
§ 2–110 78
§ 2–112 344
§ 2–113 107
§ 2–114 104
§ 2–114(a) 91
§ 2–114(a)(2) 103
§ 2–115(1) 109
§ 2–117 .... 101, 104, 105
§ 2–118 106
§ 2–118(a) 106
§ 2–118(b) 108
§ 2–119(b) 107
§ 2–119(c) 91, 109
§ 2–120 115
§ 2–120, cmt. 116
§ 2–121 115
§ 2–201(35) 2
§ 2–202 .... 117, 586
§ 2–202(1) 348, 349
§ 2–202(a) 345
§ 2–202(b) 357
§ 2–202(d) 35, 40, 354
§ 2–203 .... 345, 352
§ 2–204 346
§ 2–205 508
§ 2–205(1) 349
§ 2–205(1)(B) 348
§ 2–205(1)(D) 348
§ 2–205(2) 348
§ 2–205(3) 348
§ 2–205, cmt. 348
§ 2–205, Ex. 4 348
§ 2–205, Exs. 6–7 348
§ 2–206 349
§ 2–207 .... 260, 350
§ 2–207(b) 260
§ 2–207, cmt. 350
§ 2–208(a) 321, 362, 369
§ 2–208(a)(1) 349
§ 2–209(a) 350, 364
§ 2–209(a)(1) 343
§ 2–209(a)(2) 350
§ 2–209, cmt. 350
§ 2–210(a) 349, 352
§ 2–211 351
§ 2–212 407
§ 2–212(a) 352, 353

§ 2–212(b) 162
§ 2–213 .... 368, 369
§ 2–213(d) 204
§ 2–213(h) 373
§ 2–301 .... 341, 342
§ 2–301(a)(1) 341
§ 2–301(a)(2) 342
§ 2–301(a)(3) 341
§ 2–301(b) 260
§ 2–301, cmt. 342
§ 2–302 .... 19, 335, 336, 341
§ 2–302(a)(1) 337
§ 2–302(a)(2) 339
§ 2–302(b) 337
§ 2–302(b)(1) 342
§ 2–302(b)(2) 341
§ 2–302(c) 288, 336, 341
§ 2–302(d) 260
§ 2–402 .... 13, 333, 334, 349
§ 2–402, cmt. 333
§ 2–402A 334
§ 2–403 .... 333, 334
§ 2–404 .... 117, 331, 332
§ 2–404(a) 332
§ 2–404(b) 332, 333, 349
§ 2–404, cmt. 331
§ 2–405 332
§ 2–405, cmt. 332
§ 2–501 219
§ 2–502 .... 130, 133, 134, 136, 140, 142, 145
§ 2–502(a) 137
§ 2–502(a)(2) 142
§ 2–502(a)(3) 140, 143
§ 2–502(a)(3)(B) 128, 130, 137
§ 2–502(b) 145, 146
§ 2–502(c) 135, 148
§ 2–502, cmt. 133
§ 2–503 .... 4, 130, 132, 160
§ 2–503, cmt. 132
§ 2–504(c) 135, 144
§ 2–505(a) 136
§ 2–505(b) 139
§ 2–505, cmt. 139
§ 2–506 .... 40, 46, 47, 150
§ 2–506, cmt. 40
§ 2–507 192
§ 2–507(a)(1) 189
§ 2–507(a)(2) 192, 193, 199
§ 2–507(c) 191
§ 2–507(d) 191
§ 2–507, cmt. 193
§ 2–509(a) 201
§ 2–509(b) 202
§ 2–509(c) 201
§ 2–510, cmt. 295
§ 2–511 .... 28, 297
§ 2–511(a) 297
§ 2–511(b) 298
§ 2–511(c) 298
§ 2–512 296
§ 2–513 295
§ 2–514 .... 179, 180
§ 2–514, cmt. 180
§ 2–515 197
§ 2–601 283
§ 2–601, cmt. 337
§ 2–602 264
§ 2–603 .... 264, 266
§ 2–603(a)(2) 269
§ 2–603(a)(4) 269
§ 2–603(b)(3) 267
§ 2–603(b)(5) 512
§ 2–604 272
§ 2–604(a) 272
§ 2–604(b) 272
§ 2–604, cmt. 272
§ 2–605 250
§ 2–605(a)(3) 258
§ 2–605(b) 251
§ 2–605, cmt. 257
§ 2–606 .... 251, 252
§ 2–606(a)(1) 251
§ 2–606(a)(5) 249
§ 2–606(a)(6) 252
§ 2–606(b) 251, 252
§ 2–606(d) 251
§ 2–606(e) 252
§ 2–608 263
§ 2–609 .... 82, 248, 257, 263
§ 2–610 510
§ 2–701 .... 104, 214, 339, 483
§ 2–702 .... 27, 275, 420
§ 2–702(b) 275
§ 2–702(c) 275
§ 2–703 .... 30, 31, 32
§ 2–704 .... 420, 510
§ 2–705 .... 116, 420
§ 2–705(b) 66, 104, 110, 126
§ 2–705(c) 113
§ 2–705(e)(1) 116
§ 2–705(e)(2) 116
§ 2–705(f) 110
§ 2–705, cmt. 113
§ 2–705, Ex. 13 117
§ 2–706 267
§ 2–706(b)(3) 267
§ 2–707 .... 44, 99, 420, 483, 487
§ 2–707(b) 266, 483
§ 2–707(b)(2) 486
§ 2–707(b)(3) 267, 489
§ 2–707, cmt. 485, 489
§ 2–708 .... 58, 61, 420
§ 2–709 .... 62, 420
§ 2–709(b) 62
§ 2–709(c) 62
§ 2–710 .... 420, 503
§ 2–711 .... 50, 61, 71, 72, 73, 74, 420, 441, 498
§ 2–802 .... 121, 345
§ 2–802, cmt. 120
§ 2–803 89
§ 2–803(b) 86
§ 2–803(c)(1) 643

§ 2–803(c)(2) 88
§ 2–803(d) 84
§ 2–803(e) 274
§ 2–803(f) 84
§ 2–803(g) 87
§ 2–803(h) 216
§ 2–803(h)(1) 91
§ 2–803(i)(1) 90
§ 2–803, cmt. 85, 88
§ 2–804 202
§ 2–804(a)(2) 204
§ 2–804(b) 203, 214, 643
§ 2–804(b)(1)(A) 202
§ 2–804(d) 204, 274
§ 2–804(e) 203
§ 2–804(f) 204
§ 2–804(g) 216
§ 2–804, cmt. 85
§ 2–805 21, 288, 289
§ 2–806 21, 286
§§ 2–901 et seq. 27
§ 2–907 472
§ 2–907(c)(4) 472
§ 2–907(c)(6) 472
§ 2–1003 133, 137
§ 2–1003(b) 141
§ 2–1003(e) 142
§ 2–1004(a) 135
§ 2–1009 137
§ 2–1101 93
§§ 2–1101 et seq. 27, 93
§ 2–1102(4) 96
§ 2–1104(b) 94
§ 2–1105 453
§ 2–1105(a) 97
§ 2–1105(b) 95, 96, 97
§ 2–1105(c) 94, 97
§ 2–1105(e) 94
§ 2–1106(b)(2) 99
§ 2–1106(b)(3)(A) 89
§ 2–1106(b)(3)(B) 98, 375
§ 2–1106(b)(3)(C) 98
§ 2–1106(b)(4) 99
§ 2–1107 97
§ 2–1108 97
§ 2–1112 94
§ 2–1112(c)(1) 97
§ 2–1112(d) 97
§ 2–1113 95
§ 2–1113(b)(3) 93
§ 2–1114 93
§ 3–103 640
§ 3–105 623
§ 3–108 419, 579
§ 3–108(a)(3) 569
§ 3–201 7, 23, 34
§ 3–201(a) 567
§ 3–201(d) 34, 568, 585
§ 3–202 37
§ 3–203 566
§ 3–203(a) 117, 641
§ 3–203(b) 641
§ 3–203(g) 585
§ 3–301 569, 575
§ 3–301, cmt. 570
§ 3–304 569
§§ 3–312 to 3–322 572
§ 3–401 570
§ 3–406(a) 136
§ 3–406(b) 144
§ 3–407 195, 231
§ 3–408 568
§ 3–408, cmt. 568
§ 3–409 575
§ 3–412 569
§ 3–412(1) 577
§ 3–412(3)(A) 580
§ 3–504 15, 622
§ 3–505 622
§ 3–602 646
§ 3–603, cmt. 646
§ 3–606 645
§ 3–610(c) 650
§ 3–611(b) 585
§ 3–703 607, 623
§ 3–703(c) 583, 586
§ 3–704 622, 638
§ 3–705 569
§ 3–706, cmt. 685
§ 3–709 96
§ 3–713 671
§ 3–714 682, 684
§ 3–715 632
§ 3–715(4) 592
§ 3–715(6) 635
§ 3–715(9) 638
§ 3–715(11) 96
§ 3–715(14) 683
§ 3–715(21) 602, 660
§ 3–715(23) 636, 638
§ 3–715(24) 605, 615
§ 3–716 650
§ 3–717 649
§ 3–718 649
§ 3–719 652, 656
§ 3–720 581, 658
§ 3–720, cmt. 581
§ 3–721 662
§ 3–801(a) 587
§ 3–801, cmt. 588
§ 3–802 591
§ 3–802(a) 591
§ 3–803(a) 587, 588, 589
§ 3–803(b) 589
§ 3–803(c)(1) 591
§ 3–804 588
§ 3–804(2) 589
§ 3–805 586
§ 3–805(b) 587
§ 3–806 586, 592
§ 3–807(b) 587, 592
§ 3–808(a) 685
§ 3–808(b) 686
§ 3–808(c) 686

§ 3–809 587
§ 3–810(b) 589
§ 3–812 587
§ 3–813 592
§ 3–816 586
§ 3–902 .... 258, 262
§ 3–902(a) 258, 259
§ 3–902(b) 261
§ 3–903 624
§ 3–904 254
§ 3–905 582
§ 3–906 .... 625, 636
§ 3–906(a)(2)(B) 625
§ 3–906(b) 625
§ 3–906, cmt. 625
§ 3–909 .... 48, 593, 624, 684
§ 3–912 100
§ 3–916(b) 260
§ 3–1001 620
§ 3–1003(a) 620
§ 3–1005 .... 672, 673
§ 3–1005, cmt. 620
§ 3–1101 .... 464, 579
§ 3–1102 579
§ 3–1102(3) 579
§ 3–1201 573
§ 3–1201(a)(1) 573
§ 3–1201, cmt. 574
§ 3–1202 573
§ 3–1203 574
§ 4–201 584
§ 4–204 583
§ 4–301 583
§ 4–401 585
§ 5–102(1) 5, 69
§ 5–102(3) 69
§ 5–104 624
§ 5–104, cmt. 624
§ 5–202 422
§ 5–209 422
§ 5–401 640
§ 5–401(2) 224
§ 5–411(a)(3) 508
§ 5–411(a)(4) 228
§ 5–411(a)(7) 227, 509
§ 5–411(c) 95
§ 5–413 .... 641, 652
§ 5–413(a)(2) 641
§ 5–414 667
§ 5–415 646
§§ 5–421 to 5–422 225
§ 5–424 682
§ 5–425 632
§ 5–425(a) 422
§ 5–425(b)(5) 605
§ 5–425(b)(6) 601
§ 5–425(b)(7) 635
§ 5–425(b)(17) 683
§ 5–426 252
§ 5–430(a) 685
§ 5–430(b) 686
§ 5–430(c) 686
§ 5–431(a) 422
§ 5–501 229
§§ 5–501 et seq. 229
§ 5B–110(a)(1) 425
§ 6–101 .... 159, 166, 167, 174
§ 6–102 .... 333, 334, 592, 593, 594
§ 6–102, cmt. 593
§ 6–102(b) 593
§ 6–102(h) 593
§ 6–104(a) 300
§ 6–201 .... 173, 177
§ 6–201(8) 167, 176
§ 6–204 .... 177, 178
§ 6–205 229
§ 6–211(b) 88, 212
§ 6–212 176
§ 6–212(a) 176, 177, 300
§ 6–212(b) 172
§ 6–212(b)(2) 270, 273
§ 6–212, cmt. 300
§ 6–213 .... 174, 178, 207, 212
§ 6–213(b) 216
§ 6–214 172
§ 6–215 594
§§ 6–221 to 6–227 216
§ 6–226 303
§ 6–305, cmt. 174
§ 6–307 273
§ 8–101(b) 46, 48
§ 8–101(b)(2) 47, 52

Table of Uniform Trust Code Sections

§ 102 407
§ 102, cmt. 401
§ 103 418
§ 103(2) 448
§ 103(5) 5
§ 103(7) 11
§ 103(13) 617, 640
§ 103(15) 445, 446
§ 103(17) 409
§ 103, cmt. 409
§ 105 .... 406, 631, 633, 671
§ 105(b) 435
§ 105(b)(1) 406
§ 105(b)(2) 439, 627
§ 105(b)(2)–(3) 406
§ 105(b)(4) 406
§ 105(b)(8) 619
§ 105(b)(8)–(9) 406, 619
§ 105(b)(9) 619
§ 105(b)(11) 406
§ 105(b)(13) 406
§ 105, cmt. 619
§ 106 405
§ 106, cmt. 405
§ 107(1) 30, 31, 39
§ 108(a) 639
§ 108(b)–(e) 639
§ 108(c) 633
§ 108(f) 639
§ 110(d) 473
§ 110, cmt. 473
§ 111 .... 676, 677
§ 111(b) 677
§ 111(c) 677
§ 111(d) 677
§ 111(e) 677
§ 112 420
§ 112, cmt. 339, 419
§ 201(b) 415, 605, 620, 621
§ 202(a) 638, 647, 663
§ 204 638
§ 302 676
§§ 302–304 676
§ 303 .... 465, 676
§ 303(2) 465
§ 303(3) 465, 676
§ 303(6) 676
§ 304 .... 466, 676
§ 305 676
§ 305(c) 465
§ 401 .... 162, 164, 406
§ 401, cmt. 162, 164, 406, 408
§ 402(a)(1) 408
§ 402(a)(2) 409
§ 402(a)(3) 410
§ 402(a)(5) 410
§ 402(b) 410
§ 402(c) 410, 442
§ 403 40
§ 404 .... 379, 411, 458
§ 405(a) 469
§ 405(c) 474, 668
§ 406 412
§ 407 .... 170, 413
§ 408 .... 403, 410, 472
§§ 408–409 406
§ 408(b) 472
§ 408(c) 472
§ 409 .... 403, 410, 472
§ 409(1) 549
§ 409(2) 472
§ 409(3) 472
§ 410 462
§ 410(a) 455
§ 410(b) 461, 462, 668
§ 411(a) 461
§ 411(a)–(b) 461
§ 411(b) 461
§ 411(b)(1) 462
§ 411(c) 463, 464
§ 411(d) 462
§ 411(e) 461
§ 412(a) 456
§ 412(b) 457
§ 412(c) 456
§ 412, cmt. 456
§ 413(a) 457, 476, 478
§ 413(b) 477
§ 414(a) 458, 633
§ 414(b) 458
§ 414(c) 458
§ 415 .... 283, 284, 286, 301, 459, 460
§ 416 .... 460, 461
§ 417 .... 459, 633
§ 501 446
§ 502(a) 448, 453
§ 502(b) 449
§ 503 451
§ 503(a)(3) 453
§ 503(b)(1) 452
§ 503, cmt. 451, 452
§ 504(c)(2) 448
§ 504(e) 448
§ 504, cmt. 448
§ 505(a)(1) 444, 507
§ 505(a)(2) 444, 453
§ 505(a)(3) 593
§ 505(b)(1) 507
§ 505, cmt. 507
§ 506 451
§ 507 .... 643, 666
§ 507, cmt. 666
§ 601 .... 226, 408, 416

§ 602 206
§ 602(a) 43, 46, 416
§ 602(b) 207, 421
§ 602(c) 216, 418
§ 602(c)(1) 208
§ 602(c)(2)(A) 208, 418
§ 602(c)(2)(B) 208, 209
§ 602(e) 418
§ 602(f) 418
§ 602(g) 208, 216, 418
§ 602, cmt. 187, 207
§ 603 .... 417, 617, 676
§ 603(a) 416, 630
§ 603(b) 417
§ 604 414
§ 604(a) 419
§ 604(a)(2) 576
§ 604(b) 623
§ 604(c) 624
§ 604, cmt. 419
§ 701 .... 565, 618, 640
§ 701(a) 164
§ 701(b) 164, 650
§ 702(a) 646
§ 702(c) 645
§ 703(a) 475, 649
§ 703(b) 649
§ 703(e) 633, 649, 671
§ 703(g) 649, 667, 670
§ 704(c) 640
§ 704(e) 649
§ 705 650
§ 705(a)(1) 650
§ 706(b)(2) 644
§ 706(b)(3) 644
§ 706(b)(4) 643
§ 706, cmt. 643, 644
§ 707 650
§ 708 652
§ 708(a) 618
§ 708(b) 656
§ 708, cmt. 653, 661
§ 709(b)(2) 656
§ 801 .... 416, 439, 627
§ 802(a) 597
§ 802(b) 598, 600
§ 802(b)(1) 600, 601
§ 802(b)(3) 598
§ 802(c) 599
§ 802(c)(4) 598
§ 802(d) 604
§ 802(f) 602
§ 802(h) 633
§ 802(h)(1) 657
§ 802(h)(3) 603
§ 802(h)(4) 601
§ 802, cmt. 598, 599, 602
§ 803 .... 439, 613
§ 803, cmt. 439
§ 804 .... 21, 607, 627
§ 805 .... 611, 628
§ 805, cmt. 628
§ 806 .... 607, 627
§ 807 .... 611, 628, 633, 670, 671
§ 807(a) 628
§ 807(a)(1)–(3) 629
§ 807(b) 629
§ 807(c) 629
§ 808 629
§ 808(a) 629, 630
§ 808(b) 629, 630
§ 808(b)–(c) 630
§ 808(c) 630
§ 809 630
§ 809, cmt. 630
§ 810(a) 621
§ 810(c) 631, 632
§ 810(d) 633
§ 810, cmt. 631
§ 811 631
§ 811, cmt. 592, 631
§ 812 .... 631, 667, 672
§ 812, cmt. 631
§ 813 .... 617, 621
§ 813(a) 618, 619
§ 813(b) 618
§ 813(b)(1) 619
§ 813(b)(4) 618
§ 813(c) 618
§ 813(d) 618
§ 813, cmt. 618, 619, 621, 637
§ 814(a) 435, 436, 439
§ 814(b) 438, 642
§ 814, cmt. 439
§ 815 633
§§ 815–816 425
§ 815(a) 633
§ 815(b) 633
§ 815, cmt. 632, 633
§ 816 634
§ 816(2) 635, 636
§ 816(6) 615
§ 816(7)(B) 683
§ 816(9) 638
§ 816(11) 686
§ 816(12) 637
§ 816(13) 637, 686
§ 816(14) 592
§ 816(15) 662
§ 816(21) 625
§ 816(21)(D) 625
§ 816(22) 625
§ 816(26) 636
§ 817(a) 625
§ 817(b) 626
§ 1001 664
§ 1001(b) 664
§ 1001(b)(8) 655
§ 1002(a) 666
§ 1002(a)(2) 666
§ 1002(b) 671
§ 1002, cmt. 671
§ 1003(a) 666
§ 1004 659

§ 1004, cmt. 659
§ 1005(a).. 680
§ 1005(b).. 680
§ 1005(c) 680
§ 1005, cmt. 680
§ 1006 313
§ 1007 623
§ 1008(a)(1) 627, 669
§ 1008(a)(2) 669
§ 1009 ....602, 631, 673, 674
§ 1009(2).. 674
§ 1010(a).. 685
§ 1010(a), cmt................................ 685
§ 1010(b).. 686
§ 1010(c) 686
§ 1012(a).. 682
§ 1012(c) 684
§ 1012(e).. 684
§ 1013 684
§ 1105 28
§ 1106 52
§ 1106(a)(3) 52
§ 1106, cmt. 44

Table of Restatement References

Restatement (First) of Property § 118 ... 426
Restatement (First) of Property § 124 ... 426
Restatement (First) of Property § 124, cmt. i ... 426
Restatement (First) of Property § 185 ... 676
Restatement (First) of Property § 370, cmt. i ... 523
Restatement (First) of Property § 370, cmt. p ... 523
Restatement (First) of Property § 371(1)(b) ... 531
Restatement (First) of Property § 377, illus. 3 ... 535
Restatement (First) of Property § 378 ... 524
Restatement (First) of Property § 383 ... 531
Restatement (First) of Property § 384, illus. 3 ... 529
Restatement (First) of Property § 386, illus. 5 ... 533
Restatement (First) of Property § 399 ... 555
Restatement (First) of Property § 402, illus. 3 ... 533
Restatement (First) of Property § 403, illus. 2 ... 552
Restatement (First) of Property § 442, cmt. a ... 563
Restatement (First) of Restitution § 187 ... 83
Restatement (First) of Restitution § 187, cmt. a ... 83
Restatement (First) of Restitution § 187, cmt. f ... 87
Restatement (First) of Restitution § 188, cmt. b ... 88
Restatement (First) of Restitution § 188, cmt. c ... 89
Restatement (Second) of Agency § 120 ... 229
Restatement (Second) of Agency § 122 ... 229, 424
Restatement (Second) of Conflict of Laws § 23, cmt. b ... 37
Restatement (Second) of Conflict of Laws § 122 ... 38
Restatement (Second) of Conflict of Laws § 122, cmt. a ... 38
Restatement (Second) of Conflict of Laws §§ 133–134 ... 38
Restatement (Second) of Conflict of Laws § 136, cmt. f ... 38
Restatement (Second) of Conflict of Laws § 138 ... 38
Restatement (Second) of Conflict of Laws § 187 ... 32
Restatement (Second) of Conflict of Laws § 223 ... 32
Restatement (Second) of Conflict of Laws § 223, cmt. b ... 33
Restatement (Second) of Conflict of Laws § 223, cmt. e ... 40
Restatement (Second) of Conflict of Laws § 224(1) ... 30
Restatement (Second) of Conflict of Laws § 224(1), illus. 1 ... 35
Restatement (Second) of Conflict of Laws § 224, cmt. e ... 31
Restatement (Second) of Conflict of Laws § 225 ... 33
Restatement (Second) of Conflict of Laws § 239 ... 31
Restatement (Second) of Conflict of Laws § 258 ... 365
Restatement (Second) of Conflict of Laws § 258, cmt. c ... 365
Restatement (Second) of Conflict of Laws § 259 ... 365
Restatement (Second) of Conflict of Laws § 260 ... 34, 37
Restatement (Second) of Conflict of Laws § 263 ... 31, 34, 37
Restatement (Second) of Conflict of Laws § 263, cmt. c ... 40
Restatement (Second) of Conflict of Laws § 264 ... 34, 37
Restatement (Second) of Conflict of Laws § 264(1) ... 30
Restatement (Second) of Conflict of Laws § 264, cmt. e ... 31
Restatement (Second) of Conflict of Laws § 264, cmt. f ... 36
Restatement (Second) of Conflict of Laws § 265 ... 34, 35
Restatement (Second) of Conflict of Laws § 268(1) ... 30
Restatement (Second) of Conflict of Laws § 268(2) ... 39
Restatement (Second) of Conflict of Laws § 268, cmt. b ... 31
Restatement (Second) of Conflict of Laws § 269 ... 31
Restatement (Second) of Conflict of Laws § 270 ... 31
Restatement (Second) of Conflict of Laws § 270(2) ... 39
Restatement (Second) of Conflict of Laws § 270, cmt. b ... 31

Restatement (Second) of Conflict of Laws § 270, cmt. c 39
Restatement (Second) of Conflict of Laws § 275, cmt. c 515
Restatement (Second) of Conflict of Laws §§ 277–278 32
Restatement (Second) of Conflict of Laws § 278, cmt. a 32
Restatement (Second) of Conflict of Laws § 278, cmt. e 33
Restatement (Second) of Conflict of Laws § 283(2) 40
Restatement (Second) of Conflict of Laws § 283, cmt. h 40
Restatement (Second) of Conflict of Laws § 283, cmt. i 41
Restatement (Second) of Conflict of Laws § 287, cmt. d 41
Restatement (Second) of Conflict of Laws § 290 110
Restatement (Second) of Conflict of Laws § 314 .... 34, 567
Restatement (Second) of Conflict of Laws § 317 .... 37, 568
Restatement (Second) of Conflict of Laws § 324, cmt. c 584
Restatement (Second) of Conflict of Laws § 329 584
Restatement (Second) of Conflict of Laws § 330 584
Restatement (Second) of Conflict of Laws § 354, cmt. a 583
Restatement (Second) of Conflict of Laws § 356, cmt. b 585
Restatement (Second) of Conflict of Laws § 358, cmt. g 583
Restatement (Second) of Conflict of Laws § 361 663
Restatement (Second) of Contracts §§ 14–15 624
Restatement (Second) of Contracts § 15(2) 227, 674
Restatement (Second) of Contracts § 17 151
Restatement (Second) of Contracts § 27 147
Restatement (Second) of Contracts § 69 290
Restatement (Second) of Contracts § 86 182
Restatement (Second) of Contracts § 90 160
Restatement (Second) of Contracts § 90(2) 160
Restatement (Second) of Contracts § 95 160
Restatement (Second) of Contracts § 110 153
Restatement (Second) of Contracts § 124, illus. 3 368
Restatement (Second) of Contracts §§ 125 et seq. 153
Restatement (Second) of Contracts § 129, illus. 4 153
Restatement (Second) of Contracts § 129, illus. 5 153
Restatement (Second) of Contracts § 129, illus. 10 181
Restatement (Second) of Contracts § 133, cmt. c 100
Restatement (Second) of Contracts § 137 .... 153, 181
Restatement (Second) of Contracts § 152, illus. 12 288
Restatement (Second) of Contracts § 155 .... 279, 301, 304, 313
Restatement (Second) of Contracts § 155, cmt. a 304
Restatement (Second) of Contracts § 155, cmt. b 305
Restatement (Second) of Contracts § 155, cmt. c 301, 311
Restatement (Second) of Contracts § 155, cmt. d 305
Restatement (Second) of Contracts § 155, cmt. f 303
Restatement (Second) of Contracts § 156 279
Restatement (Second) of Contracts § 163 304
Restatement (Second) of Contracts § 163, cmt. c 313
Restatement (Second) of Contracts § 177 .... 234, 236
Restatement (Second) of Contracts § 177(3) 235
Restatement (Second) of Contracts § 214, cmt. d 163
Restatement (Second) of Contracts § 253 186
Restatement (Second) of Contracts § 311 181
Restatement (Second) of Contracts § 311, cmt. c 209
Restatement (Second) of Contracts § 321(2) 161
Restatement (Second) of Contracts § 330 161
Restatement (Second) of Contracts § 332(1) 156, 204
Restatement (Second) of Contracts § 332, cmt. b 154, 161
Restatement (Second) of Contracts § 332, cmt. e 157, 158
Restatement (Second) of Contracts § 332, illus. 3 155
Restatement (Second) of Contracts § 332, illus. 4 155
Restatement (Second) of Contracts § 332, illus. 9 156
Restatement (Second) of Contracts § 364 182
Restatement (Second) of Contracts § 372, illus. 3 206

Restatement (Second) of Contracts § 373 180
Restatement (Second) of Contracts § 375 180
Restatement (Second) of Judgments § 72 675
Restatement (Second) of Property (Donative Transfers) § 1.1, cmt. a 522
Restatement (Second) of Property (Donative Transfers) § 1.2 527
Restatement (Second) of Property (Donative Transfers) § 1.2, cmt. d 545
Restatement (Second) of Property (Donative Transfers) § 1.2, illus. 11 545
Restatement (Second) of Property (Donative Transfers) § 1.3, cmt. a 537
Restatement (Second) of Property (Donative Transfers) § 1.4, cmt. c 550, 551
Restatement (Second) of Property (Donative Transfers) § 1.4, cmt. *l* 546
Restatement (Second) of Property (Donative Transfers) § 1.4, cmt. *o* 535
Restatement (Second) of Property (Donative Transfers) § 1.5, cmt. b 550
Restatement (Second) of Property (Donative Transfers) § 1.5, cmt. g 535
Restatement (Second) of Property (Donative Transfers) § 1.6 .... 548, 549
Restatement (Second) of Property (Donative Transfers) § 1.6, cmt. c 549
Restatement (Second) of Property (Donative Transfers) § 2.2(1) 562
Restatement (Second) of Property (Donative Transfers) § 2.2(2) 563
Restatement (Second) of Property (Donative Transfers) § 2.2(3) 562
Restatement (Second) of Property (Donative Transfers) § 2.2, cmt. e 561
Restatement (Second) of Property (Donative Transfers) § 3.4 558
Restatement (Second) of Property (Donative Transfers) § 3.4, illus. 4 558
Restatement (Second) of Property (Donative Transfers) § 4.1 559
Restatement (Second) of Property (Donative Transfers) § 4.1, cmt. a 559
Restatement (Second) of Property (Donative Transfers) § 4.1, illus. 3 558
Restatement (Second) of Property (Donative Transfers) § 4.1, illus. 11 560
Restatement (Second) of Property (Donative Transfers) § 4.2 559
Restatement (Second) of Property (Donative Transfers) § 4.2(3) 557
Restatement (Second) of Property (Donative Transfers) § 4.2, cmt. c 558
Restatement (Second) of Property (Donative Transfers) § 4.2, cmt. p 560
Restatement (Second) of Property (Donative Transfers) § 4.2, cmt. r 558
Restatement (Second) of Property (Donative Transfers) § 4.2, cmt. u 559
Restatement (Second) of Property (Donative Transfers) § 4.2, illus. 3 558
Restatement (Second) of Property (Donative Transfers) § 4.2, illus. 14 558
Restatement (Second) of Property (Donative Transfers) § 4.4 560
Restatement (Second) of Property (Donative Transfers) § 4.4, illus. 4 560
Restatement (Second) of Property (Donative Transfers) § 6.1 376
Restatement (Second) of Property (Donative Transfers) § 6.1, cmt. c 379
Restatement (Second) of Property (Donative Transfers) § 6.1, cmt. e 376
Restatement (Second) of Property (Donative Transfers) § 6.2, cmt. e 377
Restatement (Second) of Property (Donative Transfers) § 6.2, illus. 1 377
Restatement (Second) of Property (Donative Transfers) § 6.2, illus. 4 377
Restatement (Second) of Property (Donative Transfers) § 6.3 377
Restatement (Second) of Property (Donative Transfers) § 6.3, cmt. c 377
Restatement (Second) of Property (Donative Transfers) § 6.3, cmt. e 377
Restatement (Second) of Property (Donative Transfers) § 6.3, Statutory Note 377

Restatement (Second) of Property (Donative Transfers) § 7.1 378
Restatement (Second) of Property (Donative Transfers) § 7.1, cmt. b 378
Restatement (Second) of Property (Donative Transfers) § 7.2, cmt. e 377
Restatement (Second) of Property (Donative Transfers) §§ 8.1–8.3 379
Restatement (Second) of Property (Donative Transfers) § 8.1, cmt. e 379
Restatement (Second) of Property (Donative Transfers) § 8.2, illus. 4 379
Restatement (Second) of Property (Donative Transfers) § 11.1, cmt. c 504
Restatement (Second) of Property (Donative Transfers) § 13.2 507
Restatement (Second) of Property (Donative Transfers) § 13.2, Statutory Note 507
Restatement (Second) of Property (Donative Transfers) § 13.4 507
Restatement (Second) of Property (Donative Transfers) § 14.1, cmt. a 510
Restatement (Second) of Property (Donative Transfers) § 16.2, cmt. a 510
Restatement (Second) of Property (Donative Transfers) § 17.3, Statutory Note 510
Restatement (Second) of Property (Donative Transfers) § 18.1, illus. 1 252
Restatement (Second) of Property (Donative Transfers) § 18.3 .... 131, 509
Restatement (Second) of Property (Donative Transfers) § 18.6 512
Restatement (Second) of Property (Donative Transfers) § 19.3 466
Restatement (Second) of Property (Donative Transfers) § 20.1, illus. 4 512
Restatement (Second) of Property (Donative Transfers) § 22.1 548
Restatement (Second) of Property (Donative Transfers) § 23.2 547
Restatement (Second) of Property (Donative Transfers) § 24.1 514
Restatement (Second) of Property (Donative Transfers) § 24.2, cmt. d 512
Restatement (Second) of Property (Donative Transfers) § 25.1, cmt. a 486
Restatement (Second) of Property (Donative Transfers) § 25.2, cmt. a 105
Restatement (Second) of Property (Donative Transfers) § 25.2, illus. 1 105
Restatement (Second) of Property (Donative Transfers) § 25.8 486
Restatement (Second) of Property (Donative Transfers) § 26.1 496
Restatement (Second) of Property (Donative Transfers) § 26.1(2) 496
Restatement (Second) of Property (Donative Transfers) § 26.1, cmt. a 494
Restatement (Second) of Property (Donative Transfers) § 26.1, cmt. c 495
Restatement (Second) of Property (Donative Transfers) § 26.1, cmt. f 495
Restatement (Second) of Property (Donative Transfers) § 26.1, cmt. j 495
Restatement (Second) of Property (Donative Transfers) § 26.1, illus. 22–23 496
Restatement (Second) of Property (Donative Transfers) § 26.2(2) 496
Restatement (Second) of Property (Donative Transfers) § 26.2, cmt. m 494
Restatement (Second) of Property (Donative Transfers) § 26.2, cmt. *o* 494, 495
Restatement (Second) of Property (Donative Transfers) § 27.1, cmt. e 265
Restatement (Second) of Property (Donative Transfers) § 27.3, cmt. e 491
Restatement (Second) of Property (Donative Transfers) § 27.3, cmt. f 488
Restatement (Second) of Property (Donative Transfers) § 28.1, cmt. i 486
Restatement (Second) of Property (Donative Transfers) § 28.2 487
Restatement (Second) of Property (Donative Transfers) § 28.3 504
Restatement (Second) of Property (Donative Transfers) § 29.1 105
Restatement (Second) of Property (Donative Transfers) § 29.1, cmt. e 73
Restatement (Second) of Property (Donative Transfers) § 29.1, cmt. j 73
Restatement (Second) of Property (Donative Transfers) § 29.3 499

Restatement (Second) of Property (Donative Transfers) § 29.3, cmt. d 49
Restatement (Second) of Property (Donative Transfers) § 29.4, cmt. c 498
Restatement (Second) of Property (Donative Transfers) § 29.4, cmt. g 498
Restatement (Second) of Property (Donative Transfers) § 29.7, cmt. a 499
Restatement (Second) of Property (Donative Transfers) § 30.1(3) 502
Restatement (Second) of Property (Donative Transfers) § 30.1, cmt. a 501
Restatement (Second) of Property (Donative Transfers) § 30.1, Statutory Note 500
Restatement (Second) of Property (Donative Transfers) § 30.2, cmt. a 502
Restatement (Second) of Property (Donative Transfers) § 30.2, cmt. j 502
Restatement (Second) of Property (Donative Transfers) § 30.2, illus. 1 503
Restatement (Second) of Property (Donative Transfers) § 31.1 .... 154, 158, 159
Restatement (Second) of Property (Donative Transfers) § 31.1, cmt. a 155
Restatement (Second) of Property (Donative Transfers) § 31.1, cmt. b 155, 157
Restatement (Second) of Property (Donative Transfers) § 31.1, cmt. k 157
Restatement (Second) of Property (Donative Transfers) § 31.1, illus. 1 158
Restatement (Second) of Property (Donative Transfers) § 31.2, illus. 5–8 205
Restatement (Second) of Property (Donative Transfers) § 31.1, illus. 12 157
Restatement (Second) of Property (Donative Transfers) § 31.1, illus. 16 210
Restatement (Second) of Property (Donative Transfers) § 31.2, illus. 12 157
Restatement (Second) of Property (Donative Transfers) § 31.3 205
Restatement (Second) of Property (Donative Transfers) § 31.4, cmt. a 153
Restatement (Second) of Property (Donative Transfers) § 31.4, cmt. e 153
Restatement (Second) of Property (Donative Transfers) § 31.4, cmt. f 153
Restatement (Second) of Property (Donative Transfers) § 32.1 152
Restatement (Second) of Property (Donative Transfers) §§ 32.1–32.2 154
Restatement (Second) of Property (Donative Transfers) § 32.1, cmt. b 129
Restatement (Second) of Property (Donative Transfers) § 32.1, illus. 4 161
Restatement (Second) of Property (Donative Transfers) § 32.2, illus. 4 155
Restatement (Second) of Property (Donative Transfers) § 32.3 159
Restatement (Second) of Property (Donative Transfers) § 32.3, cmt. a 159
Restatement (Second) of Property (Donative Transfers) § 32.3, cmt. e 94
Restatement (Second) of Property (Donative Transfers) § 32.4 159
Restatement (Second) of Property (Donative Transfers) § 33.1, cmt. 135
Restatement (Second) of Property (Donative Transfers) § 33.1, cmt. c 132, 136, 141
Restatement (Second) of Property (Donative Transfers) § 33.1, cmt. g 129, 131
Restatement (Second) of Property (Donative Transfers) § 33.2, cmt. b 191
Restatement (Second) of Property (Donative Transfers) § 34.3(3) 593
Restatement (Second) of Property (Donative Transfers) § 34.3, Statutory Note 444
Restatement (Second) of Property (Donative Transfers) § 34.4, cmt. a 219
Restatement (Second) of Property (Donative Transfers) § 34.4, cmt. b 219
Restatement (Second) of Property (Donative Transfers) § 34.5, cmt. b 227
Restatement (Second) of Property (Donative Transfers) § 34.5, illus. 5 228
Restatement (Second) of Property (Donative Transfers) § 34.7, cmt. a 235

Restatement (Second) of Property (Donative Transfers) § 34.7, cmt. c 289
Restatement (Second) of Property (Donative Transfers) § 34.7, cmt. d 283
Restatement (Second) of Property (Donative Transfers) § 34.7, illus. 4 235
Restatement (Second) of Property (Donative Transfers) § 34.9 154
Restatement (Second) of Property (Landlord and Tenant) § 15.2(2) 559
Restatement (Second) of Torts § 774B 232, 290
Restatement (Second) of Torts § 774B, cmt. c 234
Restatement (Second) of Trusts § 1, cmt. b 24
Restatement (Second) of Trusts § 2, cmt. b 237
Restatement (Second) of Trusts § 17, cmt. i 407
Restatement (Second) of Trusts § 44(1)(a) 306
Restatement (Second) of Trusts § 44(1)(b) 306
Restatement (Second) of Trusts § 45(1)(a) 306
Restatement (Second) of Trusts § 45(1)(b) 306
Restatement (Second) of Trusts § 54, cmt. k 298
Restatement (Second) of Trusts § 54, illus. 5 296
Restatement (Second) of Trusts § 55 413
Restatement (Second) of Trusts § 57 166
Restatement (Second) of Trusts § 57, cmt. b 158
Restatement (Second) of Trusts § 62, cmt. e 467
Restatement (Second) of Trusts § 62, cmt. *o* 462
Restatement (Second) of Trusts § 62, cmt. q 538
Restatement (Second) of Trusts § 108(2) 682
Restatement (Second) of Trusts § 154 447
Restatement (Second) of Trusts § 155 447
Restatement (Second) of Trusts § 156 444
Restatement (Second) of Trusts § 157 447
Restatement (Second) of Trusts § 167 457
Restatement (Second) of Trusts § 170(2) 603
Restatement (Second) of Trusts § 170, cmt. m 601
Restatement (Second) of Trusts § 171 .... 628, 670
Restatement (Second) of Trusts § 171, cmt. d 628
Restatement (Second) of Trusts § 171, cmt. h 628
Restatement (Second) of Trusts § 173, cmt. c 620
Restatement (Second) of Trusts § 174 627
Restatement (Second) of Trusts § 174, cmt. a 627
Restatement (Second) of Trusts § 176, cmt. b 426
Restatement (Second) of Trusts § 177, cmt. a 672
Restatement (Second) of Trusts § 179 631
Restatement (Second) of Trusts § 184 670
Restatement (Second) of Trusts § 187, cmt. d 435
Restatement (Second) of Trusts § 189, cmt. c 638
Restatement (Second) of Trusts § 189, cmt. d 638
Restatement (Second) of Trusts § 194, cmt. a 649
Restatement (Second) of Trusts § 197 663
Restatement (Second) of Trusts § 199 664
Restatement (Second) of Trusts § 208, cmt. e 664
Restatement (Second) of Trusts § 216(2) 674
Restatement (Second) of Trusts § 222(2) 668, 669
Restatement (Second) of Trusts § 222, cmt. d 669
Restatement (Second) of Trusts § 223 631
Restatement (Second) of Trusts § 223(2)(a) 631
Restatement (Second) of Trusts § 226A 623
Restatement (Second) of Trusts § 227 612
Restatement (Second) of Trusts § 227(a) 606
Restatement (Second) of Trusts § 227, cmt. f 607, 608
Restatement (Second) of Trusts § 227, cmt. h 607
Restatement (Second) of Trusts § 227, cmt. m 608, 612
Restatement (Second) of Trusts § 227, cmt. p 51, 606
Restatement (Second) of Trusts § 228 609

Restatement (Second) of Trusts § 230, cmt. j 610
Restatement (Second) of Trusts § 246, cmt. a 685
Restatement (Second) of Trusts § 247, cmt. e 686
Restatement (Second) of Trusts § 254 684
Restatement (Second) of Trusts § 258 671
Restatement (Second) of Trusts § 262 684
Restatement (Second) of Trusts § 262, cmt. b 685
Restatement (Second) of Trusts § 263 685
Restatement (Second) of Trusts § 264 .... 685, 686
Restatement (Second) of Trusts § 282(2) 681
Restatement (Second) of Trusts §§ 284–320 683
Restatement (Second) of Trusts § 289 684
Restatement (Second) of Trusts § 292(1) 684
Restatement (Second) of Trusts § 297 683
Restatement (Second) of Trusts § 297, cmt. f 683
Restatement (Second) of Trusts § 298, cmt. i 683
Restatement (Second) of Trusts § 324, cmt. g 682
Restatement (Second) of Trusts § 325 682
Restatement (Second) of Trusts § 330 206
Restatement (Second) of Trusts § 330, cmt. j 208
Restatement (Second) of Trusts § 337 461
Restatement (Second) of Trusts § 337(1) 465
Restatement (Second) of Trusts § 337(2) 462
Restatement (Second) of Trusts § 337, cmt. e 463
Restatement (Second) of Trusts § 337, cmt. h 464
Restatement (Second) of Trusts § 338(2) 461
Restatement (Second) of Trusts § 340(2) 461
Restatement (Second) of Trusts § 340, cmt. e 465
Restatement (Second) of Trusts § 346 625
Restatement (Second) of Trusts § 348, cmt. f 475
Restatement (Second) of Trusts § 358, cmt. e 292
Restatement (Second) of Trusts § 362 374
Restatement (Second) of Trusts § 374, cmt. h 470
Restatement (Second) of Trusts § 381 479
Restatement (Second) of Trusts § 383 649
Restatement (Second) of Trusts § 389(2) 471
Restatement (Second) of Trusts § 391 .... 462, 475
Restatement (Second) of Trusts § 391, cmt. e 474
Restatement (Second) of Trusts § 399 .... 476, 479
Restatement (Second) of Trusts § 399, cmt. b 468
Restatement (Second) of Trusts § 399, cmt. c 478
Restatement (Second) of Trusts § 399, cmt. e 479
Restatement (Second) of Trusts § 401, cmt. d 550
Restatement (Second) of Trusts § 401, cmt. j 549
Restatement (Second) of Trusts § 401, illus. 3 549
Restatement (Second) of Trusts § 442 309
Restatement (Third) of Agency § 3.07 387
Restatement (Third) of Agency § 3.08 386
Restatement (Third) of Agency § 6.01, cmt. c 685
Restatement (Third) of Law Governing Lawyers § 51, illus. 4 245
Restatement (Third) of Law Governing Lawyers § 112, cmt. *l* 244
Restatement (Third) of Law Governing Lawyers § 127 241
Restatement (Third) of Law Governing Lawyers § 127(1) 242
Restatement (Third) of Law Governing Lawyers § 127(1), cmt. e 242
Restatement (Third) of Law Governing Lawyers § 127(2)(c) 243
Restatement (Third) of Law Governing Lawyers § 127, cmt. a 244
Restatement (Third) of Law Governing Lawyers § 127, cmt. d 242
Restatement (Third) of Property (Servitudes) § 3.3, cmt. a 523, 555
Restatement (Third) of Property (Wills and Other Donative Transfers), Introductory Note 524
Restatement (Third) of Property (Wills and Other Donative Transfers) Division 5, Scope Note 339

Restatement (Third) of Property (Wills and Other Donative Transfers) § 1.1 20
Restatement (Third) of Property (Wills and Other Donative Transfers) § 1.1, cmt. f 258, 259
Restatement (Third) of Property (Wills and Other Donative Transfers) § 1.1, cmt. j 334
Restatement (Third) of Property (Wills and Other Donative Transfers) § 1.1, illus. 20 77
Restatement (Third) of Property (Wills and Other Donative Transfers) § 1.2 263
Restatement (Third) of Property (Wills and Other Donative Transfers) § 1.2, cmt. e 276
Restatement (Third) of Property (Wills and Other Donative Transfers) § 1.3 68
Restatement (Third) of Property (Wills and Other Donative Transfers) § 2.1, Introductory Note 53
Restatement (Third) of Property (Wills and Other Donative Transfers) § 2.2, cmt. e 119
Restatement (Third) of Property (Wills and Other Donative Transfers) § 2.2, cmt. g 122
Restatement (Third) of Property (Wills and Other Donative Transfers) § 2.3, cmt. b 57
Restatement (Third) of Property (Wills and Other Donative Transfers) § 2.3, cmt. d 61
Restatement (Third) of Property (Wills and Other Donative Transfers) § 2.4, cmt. d 65
Restatement (Third) of Property (Wills and Other Donative Transfers) § 2.4, cmt. i 66
Restatement (Third) of Property (Wills and Other Donative Transfers) § 2.4, illus. 1 65
Restatement (Third) of Property (Wills and Other Donative Transfers) § 2.5 .... 101, 104
Restatement (Third) of Property (Wills and Other Donative Transfers) § 2.5(2) 106
Restatement (Third) of Property (Wills and Other Donative Transfers) § 2.5(5) 91, 103
Restatement (Third) of Property (Wills and Other Donative Transfers) § 2.5, cmt. i 107
Restatement (Third) of Property (Wills and Other Donative Transfers) § 2.5, cmt. j 112
Restatement (Third) of Property (Wills and Other Donative Transfers) § 2.5, cmt. k 111
Restatement (Third) of Property (Wills and Other Donative Transfers) § 2.5, cmt. *l* 103
Restatement (Third) of Property (Wills and Other Donative Transfers) § 2.6 78
Restatement (Third) of Property (Wills and Other Donative Transfers) § 2.6, cmt. c 78, 79
Restatement (Third) of Property (Wills and Other Donative Transfers) § 2.6, cmt. d 81
Restatement (Third) of Property (Wills and Other Donative Transfers) § 2.6, cmt. f 80
Restatement (Third) of Property (Wills and Other Donative Transfers) § 2.6, cmt. h 81, 82
Restatement (Third) of Property (Wills and Other Donative Transfers) § 2.6, cmt. j 161
Restatement (Third) of Property (Wills and Other Donative Transfers) § 2.6, illus. 1 80
Restatement (Third) of Property (Wills and Other Donative Transfers) § 2.7 375
Restatement (Third) of Property (Wills and Other Donative Transfers) § 2.7, cmt. c 375
Restatement (Third) of Property (Wills and Other Donative Transfers) § 3.1, cmt. e 40
Restatement (Third) of Property (Wills and Other Donative Transfers) § 3.1, cmt. g 281
Restatement (Third) of Property (Wills and Other Donative Transfers) § 3.1, cmt. h 141
Restatement (Third) of Property (Wills and Other Donative Transfers) § 3.1, cmt. k 134
Restatement (Third) of Property (Wills and Other Donative Transfers) § 3.1, cmt. *l* 135
Restatement (Third) of Property (Wills and Other Donative Transfers) § 3.1, cmt. m 143
Restatement (Third) of Property (Wills and Other Donative Transfers) § 3.1, cmt. n 133
Restatement (Third) of Property (Wills and Other Donative Transfers) § 3.1, cmt. *o* 138
Restatement (Third) of Property (Wills and Other Donative Transfers) § 3.1, cmt. *o* 136

Restatement (Third) of Property (Wills and Other Donative Transfers) § 3.1, cmt. p 142
Restatement (Third) of Property (Wills and Other Donative Transfers) § 3.1, cmt. q 144
Restatement (Third) of Property (Wills and Other Donative Transfers) § 3.1, illus. 2 135
Restatement (Third) of Property (Wills and Other Donative Transfers) § 3.2, cmt. b 146
Restatement (Third) of Property (Wills and Other Donative Transfers) § 3.2, cmt. c 148
Restatement (Third) of Property (Wills and Other Donative Transfers) § 3.2, cmt. e 146
Restatement (Third) of Property (Wills and Other Donative Transfers) § 3.2, illus. 4 147
Restatement (Third) of Property (Wills and Other Donative Transfers) § 3.3 131
Restatement (Third) of Property (Wills and Other Donative Transfers) § 3.3, cmt. b 132
Restatement (Third) of Property (Wills and Other Donative Transfers) § 3.4, illus. 3 336
Restatement (Third) of Property (Wills and Other Donative Transfers) § 3.5 .... 292, 295
Restatement (Third) of Property (Wills and Other Donative Transfers) § 3.5, cmt. b 135
Restatement (Third) of Property (Wills and Other Donative Transfers) § 3.5, cmt. c 135, 293
Restatement (Third) of Property (Wills and Other Donative Transfers) § 3.6, cmt. a 295
Restatement (Third) of Property (Wills and Other Donative Transfers) § 3.6, cmt. b 294
Restatement (Third) of Property (Wills and Other Donative Transfers) § 3.6, cmt. d 294
Restatement (Third) of Property (Wills and Other Donative Transfers) § 3.6, cmt. f 294
Restatement (Third) of Property (Wills and Other Donative Transfers) § 3.6, cmt. h 293
Restatement (Third) of Property (Wills and Other Donative Transfers) § 3.7, cmt. c 296
Restatement (Third) of Property (Wills and Other Donative Transfers) § 3.7, cmt. e 296
Restatement (Third) of Property (Wills and Other Donative Transfers) § 3.8, cmt. d 296
Restatement (Third) of Property (Wills and Other Donative Transfers) § 3.8, cmt. e 298
Restatement (Third) of Property (Wills and Other Donative Transfers) § 3.8, cmt. f 298
Restatement (Third) of Property (Wills and Other Donative Transfers) § 3.8, illus. 1 297
Restatement (Third) of Property (Wills and Other Donative Transfers) § 3.9, cmt. b 295
Restatement (Third) of Property (Wills and Other Donative Transfers) § 3.9, cmt. c 295
Restatement (Third) of Property (Wills and Other Donative Transfers) § 4.1 196
Restatement (Third) of Property (Wills and Other Donative Transfers) § 4.1, cmt. d 191
Restatement (Third) of Property (Wills and Other Donative Transfers) § 4.1, cmt. f 194, 290
Restatement (Third) of Property (Wills and Other Donative Transfers) § 4.1, cmt. g 192
Restatement (Third) of Property (Wills and Other Donative Transfers) § 4.1, cmt. i 194
Restatement (Third) of Property (Wills and Other Donative Transfers) § 4.1, cmt. j 196
Restatement (Third) of Property (Wills and Other Donative Transfers) § 4.1, cmt. k 198
Restatement (Third) of Property (Wills and Other Donative Transfers) § 4.1, cmt. n 202
Restatement (Third) of Property (Wills and Other Donative Transfers) § 4.1, illus. 9 193
Restatement (Third) of Property (Wills and Other Donative Transfers) § 4.1, illus. 12 204
Restatement (Third) of Property (Wills and Other Donative Transfers) § 4.2, cmt. i 202
Restatement (Third) of Property (Wills and Other Donative Transfers) § 4.3 199
Restatement (Third) of Property (Wills and Other Donative Transfers) § 4.3, cmt. b 201
Restatement (Third) of Property (Wills and Other Donative Transfers) § 4.3, cmt. c 199

Restatement (Third) of Property (Wills and Other Donative Transfers) § 4.3, illus. 7 200
Restatement (Third) of Property (Wills and Other Donative Transfers) § 4.3, illus. 14 200
Restatement (Third) of Property (Wills and Other Donative Transfers) § 4.3, illus. 17 200
Restatement (Third) of Property (Wills and Other Donative Transfers) § 5.1 247
Restatement (Third) of Property (Wills and Other Donative Transfers) § 5.1, cmt. c 247
Restatement (Third) of Property (Wills and Other Donative Transfers) § 5.1, cmt. d 247
Restatement (Third) of Property (Wills and Other Donative Transfers) § 5.2, cmt. b 249
Restatement (Third) of Property (Wills and Other Donative Transfers) § 5.2, cmt. c 249
Restatement (Third) of Property (Wills and Other Donative Transfers) § 5.2, cmt. d 250, 251
Restatement (Third) of Property (Wills and Other Donative Transfers) § 5.2, cmt. e 249, 257
Restatement (Third) of Property (Wills and Other Donative Transfers) § 5.2, cmt. i 251
Restatement (Third) of Property (Wills and Other Donative Transfers) § 5.2, illus. 4–6 253
Restatement (Third) of Property (Wills and Other Donative Transfers) § 5.3 258
Restatement (Third) of Property (Wills and Other Donative Transfers) § 5.3, cmt. f 257
Restatement (Third) of Property (Wills and Other Donative Transfers) § 5.4 .... 82, 248
Restatement (Third) of Property (Wills and Other Donative Transfers) § 5.4, cmt. h 257
Restatement (Third) of Property (Wills and Other Donative Transfers) § 5.5 264
Restatement (Third) of Property (Wills and Other Donative Transfers) § 5.5, cmt. b 265
Restatement (Third) of Property (Wills and Other Donative Transfers) § 5.5, cmt. g 267
Restatement (Third) of Property (Wills and Other Donative Transfers) § 5.5, cmt. h 267
Restatement (Third) of Property (Wills and Other Donative Transfers) § 5.5, cmt. j 269
Restatement (Third) of Property (Wills and Other Donative Transfers) § 5.5, cmt. *o* 272
Restatement (Third) of Property (Wills and Other Donative Transfers) § 5.5, cmt. p 266
Restatement (Third) of Property (Wills and Other Donative Transfers) § 5.5, illus. 4 267
Restatement (Third) of Property (Wills and Other Donative Transfers) § 5.5, illus. 7 268
Restatement (Third) of Property (Wills and Other Donative Transfers) § 5.5, illus. 15 272
Restatement (Third) of Property (Wills and Other Donative Transfers) § 6.1, cmt. f 364
Restatement (Third) of Property (Wills and Other Donative Transfers) § 6.2 154
Restatement (Third) of Property (Wills and Other Donative Transfers) § 6.2, cmt. b 157
Restatement (Third) of Property (Wills and Other Donative Transfers) § 6.2, cmt. d 158
Restatement (Third) of Property (Wills and Other Donative Transfers) § 6.2, cmt. e 158
Restatement (Third) of Property (Wills and Other Donative Transfers) § 6.2, cmt. g 157
Restatement (Third) of Property (Wills and Other Donative Transfers) § 6.2, cmt. h 155
Restatement (Third) of Property (Wills and Other Donative Transfers) § 6.2, cmt. i 155
Restatement (Third) of Property (Wills and Other Donative Transfers) § 6.2, cmt. k 158
Restatement (Third) of Property (Wills and Other Donative Transfers) § 6.2, cmt. *l* 205
Restatement (Third) of Property (Wills and Other Donative Transfers) § 6.2, cmt. m 205
Restatement (Third) of Property (Wills and Other Donative Transfers) § 6.2, cmt. n 156
Restatement (Third) of Property (Wills and Other Donative Transfers) § 6.2, cmt. p 155
Restatement (Third) of Property (Wills and Other Donative Transfers) § 6.2, cmt. t 154

Restatement (Third) of Property (Wills and Other Donative Transfers) § 6.2, cmt. yy 157
Restatement (Third) of Property (Wills and Other Donative Transfers) § 6.2, cmt. zz 205
Restatement (Third) of Property (Wills and Other Donative Transfers) § 6.3 152
Restatement (Third) of Property (Wills and Other Donative Transfers) § 6.3, cmt. c 152
Restatement (Third) of Property (Wills and Other Donative Transfers) § 6.3, cmt. e 156
Restatement (Third) of Property (Wills and Other Donative Transfers) § 6.3, cmt. n 153
Restatement (Third) of Property (Wills and Other Donative Transfers) § 7.1, cmt. 3 129
Restatement (Third) of Property (Wills and Other Donative Transfers) § 7.2, cmt. e 216
Restatement (Third) of Property (Wills and Other Donative Transfers) § 8.1 408
Restatement (Third) of Property (Wills and Other Donative Transfers) § 8.1(c) 226
Restatement (Third) of Property (Wills and Other Donative Transfers) § 8.1, cmt. c 219
Restatement (Third) of Property (Wills and Other Donative Transfers) § 8.1, cmt. g 226
Restatement (Third) of Property (Wills and Other Donative Transfers) § 8.1, cmt. h 225
Restatement (Third) of Property (Wills and Other Donative Transfers) § 8.2, cmt. d 219
Restatement (Third) of Property (Wills and Other Donative Transfers) § 8.3 412
Restatement (Third) of Property (Wills and Other Donative Transfers) § 8.3(a) 304
Restatement (Third) of Property (Wills and Other Donative Transfers) § 8.3, cmt. b 231
Restatement (Third) of Property (Wills and Other Donative Transfers) § 8.3, cmt. d 232
Restatement (Third) of Property (Wills and Other Donative Transfers) § 8.3, cmt. e 231
Restatement (Third) of Property (Wills and Other Donative Transfers) § 8.3, cmt. h 236
Restatement (Third) of Property (Wills and Other Donative Transfers) § 8.3, cmt. i 235
Restatement (Third) of Property (Wills and Other Donative Transfers) § 8.3, cmt. j 289
Restatement (Third) of Property (Wills and Other Donative Transfers) § 8.3, cmt. k 304
Restatement (Third) of Property (Wills and Other Donative Transfers) § 8.3, cmt. *l* 193, 290
Restatement (Third) of Property (Wills and Other Donative Transfers) § 8.4 84
Restatement (Third) of Property (Wills and Other Donative Transfers) § 8.4, cmt. j 89
Restatement (Third) of Property (Wills and Other Donative Transfers) § 8.4, cmt. k 89
Restatement (Third) of Property (Wills and Other Donative Transfers) § 8.4, cmt. m 85
Restatement (Third) of Property (Wills and Other Donative Transfers) § 8.5 582
Restatement (Third) of Property (Wills and Other Donative Transfers) § 8.5, cmt. d 582
Restatement (Third) of Property (Wills and Other Donative Transfers) § 8.5, cmt. e 582
Restatement (Third) of Property (Wills and Other Donative Transfers) § 9.1(c) 348
Restatement (Third) of Property (Wills and Other Donative Transfers) § 9.1, cmt. i 347
Restatement (Third) of Property (Wills and Other Donative Transfers) § 9.1, cmt. *l* 260
Restatement (Third) of Property (Wills and Other Donative Transfers) § 9.4(a) 368
Restatement (Third) of Property (Wills and Other Donative Transfers) § 9.4, cmt. k 370
Restatement (Third) of Property (Wills and Other Donative Transfers) § 9.5, cmt. f 260
Restatement (Third) of Property (Wills and Other Donative Transfers) § 9.6, cmt. b 260
Restatement (Third) of Property (Wills and Other Donative Transfers) § 9.6, Reporter's Note 335
Restatement (Third) of Property (Wills and Other Donative Transfers) § 11.2, cmt. r 286

Restatement (Third) of Property (Wills and Other Donative Transfers) § 11.3, cmt. i 485
Restatement (Third) of Property (Wills and Other Donative Transfers) § 12.1 ....284, 289, 305, 309, 459, 460
Restatement (Third) of Property (Wills and Other Donative Transfers) § 12.1, cmt. d 460
Restatement (Third) of Property (Wills and Other Donative Transfers) § 12.1, cmt. e 459
Restatement (Third) of Property (Wills and Other Donative Transfers) § 12.1, cmt. i 459
Restatement (Third) of Property (Wills and Other Donative Transfers) § 12.1, Reporter's Note 460
Restatement (Third) of Property (Wills and Other Donative Transfers) § 12.2 .... 286, 460
Restatement (Third) of Property (Wills and Other Donative Transfers) § 13.2(b)(2) 271
Restatement (Third) of Property (Wills and Other Donative Transfers) § 13.2, cmt. d 272
Restatement (Third) of Property (Wills and Other Donative Transfers) § 14.1(1) 486
Restatement (Third) of Property (Wills and Other Donative Transfers) § 14.1, cmt. g(1) 486
Restatement (Third) of Property (Wills and Other Donative Transfers) § 14.1, cmt. k 112
Restatement (Third) of Property (Wills and Other Donative Transfers) § 14.1, cmt. *l* 486
Restatement (Third) of Property (Wills and Other Donative Transfers) § 14.1, illus. 7 113
Restatement (Third) of Property (Wills and Other Donative Transfers) § 14.2 61
Restatement (Third) of Property (Wills and Other Donative Transfers) § 14.2, cmt. b 66
Restatement (Third) of Property (Wills and Other Donative Transfers) § 14.2, cmt. d 61
Restatement (Third) of Property (Wills and Other Donative Transfers) § 14.2, cmt. f 504
Restatement (Third) of Property (Wills and Other Donative Transfers) § 14.3 486
Restatement (Third) of Property (Wills and Other Donative Transfers) § 14.4 58
Restatement (Third) of Property (Wills and Other Donative Transfers) § 14.5 61
Restatement (Third) of Property (Wills and Other Donative Transfers) § 14.5, cmt. e 61
Restatement (Third) of Property (Wills and Other Donative Transfers) § 14.7, cmt. e 105
Restatement (Third) of Property (Wills and Other Donative Transfers) § 14.8, cmt. n 103
Restatement (Third) of Property (Wills and Other Donative Transfers) § 15.1 .... 493, 496
Restatement (Third) of Property (Wills and Other Donative Transfers) § 15.1, cmt. d 494
Restatement (Third) of Property (Wills and Other Donative Transfers) § 15.1, cmt. f 493, 494
Restatement (Third) of Property (Wills and Other Donative Transfers) § 15.1, cmt. h 495
Restatement (Third) of Property (Wills and Other Donative Transfers) § 15.1, cmt. j 496
Restatement (Third) of Property (Wills and Other Donative Transfers) § 15.1, cmt. k 496
Restatement (Third) of Property (Wills and Other Donative Transfers) § 15.1, cmt. *o* 494
Restatement (Third) of Property (Wills and Other Donative Transfers) § 15.1, cmt. p 495
Restatement (Third) of Property (Wills and Other Donative Transfers) § 15.1, illus. 4 495
Restatement (Third) of Property (Wills and Other Donative Transfers) § 15.2, cmt. a 269
Restatement (Third) of Property (Wills and Other Donative Transfers) § 15.2, cmt. b 270
Restatement (Third) of Property (Wills and Other Donative Transfers) § 15.2, Reporter's Note 269
Restatement (Third) of Property (Wills and Other Donative Transfers) § 15.3, cmt. b 487
Restatement (Third) of Property (Wills and Other Donative Transfers) § 15.4 .... 485, 486
Restatement (Third) of Property (Wills and Other Donative Transfers) § 15.4, cmt. e 486
Restatement (Third) of Property (Wills and Other Donative Transfers) § 15.4, cmt. i 486

Restatement (Third) of Property (Wills and Other Donative Transfers) § 16.1 ....71, 73, 105, 498
Restatement (Third) of Property (Wills and Other Donative Transfers) § 16.1, cmt. a 499
Restatement (Third) of Property (Wills and Other Donative Transfers) § 16.1, cmt. b 72
Restatement (Third) of Property (Wills and Other Donative Transfers) § 16.1, cmt. g 73, 499
Restatement (Third) of Property (Wills and Other Donative Transfers) § 16.1, cmt. h 73
Restatement (Third) of Property (Wills and Other Donative Transfers) § 16.1, cmt. i 74
Restatement (Third) of Property (Wills and Other Donative Transfers) § 16.1, cmt. *l* 499
Restatement (Third) of Property (Wills and Other Donative Transfers) § 16.1, illus. 2 498
Restatement (Third) of Property (Wills and Other Donative Transfers) § 16.1, illus. 3 498
Restatement (Third) of Property (Wills and Other Donative Transfers) § 16.2 502
Restatement (Third) of Property (Wills and Other Donative Transfers) § 16.2, cmt. a 502
Restatement (Third) of Property (Wills and Other Donative Transfers) § 16.2, cmt. b 501
Restatement (Third) of Property (Wills and Other Donative Transfers) § 16.2, Reporter's Note 500
Restatement (Third) of Property (Wills and Other Donative Transfers) § 16.3 503
Restatement (Third) of Property (Wills and Other Donative Transfers) § 16.3, cmt. a 503
Restatement (Third) of Property (Wills and Other Donative Transfers) § 17.1, cmt. a 505
Restatement (Third) of Property (Wills and Other Donative Transfers) § 17.1, cmt. e 504
Restatement (Third) of Property (Wills and Other Donative Transfers) § 17.1, cmt. g 505
Restatement (Third) of Property (Wills and Other Donative Transfers) § 17.3 505
Restatement (Third) of Property (Wills and Other Donative Transfers) § 17.4, cmt. e 505
Restatement (Third) of Property (Wills and Other Donative Transfers) § 17.4, cmt. f(2) 506
Restatement (Third) of Property (Wills and Other Donative Transfers) § 17.5 513
Restatement (Third) of Property (Wills and Other Donative Transfers) § 19.1, cmt. e 515
Restatement (Third) of Property (Wills and Other Donative Transfers) § 19.3 511
Restatement (Third) of Property (Wills and Other Donative Transfers) § 19.5, cmt. a 511
Restatement (Third) of Property (Wills and Other Donative Transfers) § 19.5, cmt. b 511
Restatement (Third) of Property (Wills and Other Donative Transfers) § 19.6 511
Restatement (Third) of Property (Wills and Other Donative Transfers) § 19.8(a) 508
Restatement (Third) of Property (Wills and Other Donative Transfers) § 19.8, cmt. f 508
Restatement (Third) of Property (Wills and Other Donative Transfers) § 19.9 509
Restatement (Third) of Property (Wills and Other Donative Transfers) § 19.10 509
Restatement (Third) of Property (Wills and Other Donative Transfers) § 19.10, cmt. b 509
Restatement (Third) of Property (Wills and Other Donative Transfers) § 19.10, cmt. c 509
Restatement (Third) of Property (Wills and Other Donative Transfers) § 19.10, illus. 4 509
Restatement (Third) of Property (Wills and Other Donative Transfers) § 19.12 512
Restatement (Third) of Property (Wills and Other Donative Transfers) § 19.14 466
Restatement (Third) of Property (Wills and Other Donative Transfers) § 19.14, cmt. a 513
Restatement (Third) of Property (Wills and Other Donative Transfers) § 19.16 513
Restatement (Third) of Property (Wills and Other Donative Transfers) § 19.19 513
Restatement (Third) of Property (Wills and Other Donative Transfers) § 19.20 514

Restatement (Third) of Property (Wills and Other Donative Transfers) § 19.20, cmt. b 514
Restatement (Third) of Property (Wills and Other Donative Transfers) § 19.21 514
Restatement (Third) of Property (Wills and Other Donative Transfers) § 19.22 514
Restatement (Third) of Property (Wills and Other Donative Transfers) § 19.23 514
Restatement (Third) of Property (Wills and Other Donative Transfers) § 19.23, cmt. c 514
Restatement (Third) of Property (Wills and Other Donative Transfers) § 20.1 510
Restatement (Third) of Property (Wills and Other Donative Transfers) § 21.2, cmt. a 509
Restatement (Third) of Property (Wills and Other Donative Transfers) § 22.1 507
Restatement (Third) of Property (Wills and Other Donative Transfers) § 22.2 507
Restatement (Third) of Property (Wills and Other Donative Transfers) § 22.3(a) 507
Restatement (Third) of Property (Wills and Other Donative Transfers) § 22.3(b) 508
Restatement (Third) of Property (Wills and Other Donative Transfers) § 23.1(1) 508
Restatement (Third) of Property (Wills and Other Donative Transfers) § 26.3, cmt. f 492
Restatement (Third) of Property (Wills and Other Donative Transfers) § 26.4 484
Restatement (Third) of Property (Wills and Other Donative Transfers) § 26.5 491
Restatement (Third) of Property (Wills and Other Donative Transfers) § 26.5, cmt. c 491
Restatement (Third) of Property (Wills and Other Donative Transfers) § 26.5, illus. 3 491
Restatement (Third) of Property (Wills and Other Donative Transfers) § 26.5, Reporter's Note 491
Restatement (Third) of Property (Wills and Other Donative Transfers) § 26.6, cmt. e 488
Restatement (Third) of Property (Wills and Other Donative Transfers) § 26.8 490
Restatement (Third) of Property (Wills and Other Donative Transfers) § 26.8, illus. 1 490
Restatement (Third) of Property (Wills and Other Donative Transfers) § 26.9, cmt. b 490
Restatement (Third) of Property (Wills and Other Donative Transfers) § 26.9, cmt. e(1) 493
Restatement (Third) of Property (Wills and Other Donative Transfers) Ch. 27, Introductory Note 543
Restatement (Third) of Property (Wills and Other Donative Transfers) § 27 499
Restatement (Third) of Property (Wills and Other Donative Transfers) § 27.1(a) 544
Restatement (Third) of Property (Wills and Other Donative Transfers) § 27.1(b)(1) 544
Restatement (Third) of Property (Wills and Other Donative Transfers) § 27.1, cmt. f 544
Restatement (Third) of Property (Wills and Other Donative Transfers) § 27.2 544
Restatement (Third) of Property (Wills and Other Donative Transfers) § 27.3 544
Restatement (Third) of Property (Wills and Other Donative Transfers) § 31.1 158
Restatement (Third) of Property (Wills and Other Donative Transfers) §§ 159–160 552
Restatement (Third) of Property (Wills and Other Donative Transfers) § 160, cmt. a 553
Restatement (Third) of Property (Wills and Other Donative Transfers) § 160, cmt. d 553
Restatement (Third) of Property (Wills and Other Donative Transfers) § 242, cmt. d 286
Restatement (Third) of Property (Wills and Other Donative Transfers) § 242, cmt. f 286
Restatement (Third) of Property (Wills and Other Donative Transfers) § 243, illus. 3 490
Restatement (Third) of Property (Wills and Other Donative Transfers) § 250, illus. 4 492
Restatement (Third) of Property (Wills and Other Donative Transfers) § 252 491
Restatement (Third) of Property (Wills and Other Donative Transfers) § 252, cmt. f 492

Restatement (Third) of Property (Wills and Other Donative Transfers) § 253, illus. 1 482
Restatement (Third) of Property (Wills and Other Donative Transfers) § 254 491
Restatement (Third) of Property (Wills and Other Donative Transfers) § 255 485
Restatement (Third) of Property (Wills and Other Donative Transfers) § 261 483
Restatement (Third) of Property (Wills and Other Donative Transfers) § 264 489
Restatement (Third) of Property (Wills and Other Donative Transfers) § 266 490
Restatement (Third) of Property (Wills and Other Donative Transfers) § 269 490
Restatement (Third) of Property (Wills and Other Donative Transfers) § 272 490
Restatement (Third) of Property (Wills and Other Donative Transfers) § 278, illus. 1 482
Restatement (Third) of Property (Wills and Other Donative Transfers) § 286 104
Restatement (Third) of Property (Wills and Other Donative Transfers) § 286(1)(a) 104
Restatement (Third) of Property (Wills and Other Donative Transfers) § 286(2)(c) 105
Restatement (Third) of Property (Wills and Other Donative Transfers) § 316 81
Restatement (Third) of Property (Wills and Other Donative Transfers) § 328, cmt. a 507
Restatement (Third) of Property (Wills and Other Donative Transfers) § 370, cmt. k 528
Restatement (Third) of Property (Wills and Other Donative Transfers) § 371, cmt. a 534
Restatement (Third) of Property (Wills and Other Donative Transfers) § 374, cmt. j 529
Restatement (Third) of Property (Wills and Other Donative Transfers) § 374, cmt. *o* 522
Restatement (Third) of Property (Wills and Other Donative Transfers) § 375 532
Restatement (Third) of Property (Wills and Other Donative Transfers) § 375, cmt. b 532
Restatement (Third) of Property (Wills and Other Donative Transfers) § 376, illus. 2 534
Restatement (Third) of Property (Wills and Other Donative Transfers) § 377, illus. 3 529
Restatement (Third) of Property (Wills and Other Donative Transfers) § 377, illus. 4 529
Restatement (Third) of Property (Wills and Other Donative Transfers) § 389, cmt. a 534
Restatement (Third) of Property (Wills and Other Donative Transfers) § 389, cmt. g 534
Restatement (Third) of Property (Wills and Other Donative Transfers) § 395 555
Restatement (Third) of Property (Wills and Other Donative Transfers) § 399, cmt. d 555
Restatement (Third) of Property (Wills and Other Donative Transfers) § 403, cmt. c 532
Restatement (Third) of Property (Wills and Other Donative Transfers) § 406, cmt. p 557
Restatement (Third) of Property (Wills and Other Donative Transfers) § 406, illus. 1 559
Restatement (Third) of Property (Wills and Other Donative Transfers) § 419 559
Restatement (Third) of Property (Wills and Other Donative Transfers) § 442, cmt. a 563
Restatement (Third) of Trusts § 1, cmt. b 401
Restatement (Third) of Trusts § 1, cmt. e 5
Restatement (Third) of Trusts § 2, cmt. a 9
Restatement (Third) of Trusts § 2, cmt. b 10
Restatement (Third) of Trusts § 2, illus. 3 24
Restatement (Third) of Trusts § 2, illus. 5 24
Restatement (Third) of Trusts § 3, cmt. a 23
Restatement (Third) of Trusts § 3, cmt. b 21
Restatement (Third) of Trusts § 5, cmt. a 163
Restatement (Third) of Trusts § 5, cmt. a(1) 423
Restatement (Third) of Trusts § 5, cmt. b 425, 427
Restatement (Third) of Trusts § 5, cmt. c 604
Restatement (Third) of Trusts § 5, cmt. e 164

Restatement (Third) of Trusts § 5, cmt. h 171, 172
Restatement (Third) of Trusts § 5, cmt. k 666
Restatement (Third) of Trusts § 6 410
Restatement (Third) of Trusts §§ 7–8 22
Restatement (Third) of Trusts §§ 7–9 403
Restatement (Third) of Trusts § 7, illus. 1 482
Restatement (Third) of Trusts § 8 308
Restatement (Third) of Trusts § 8, cmt. a 266, 273
Restatement (Third) of Trusts § 9 .... 308, 309
Restatement (Third) of Trusts § 9(1)(a) 309
Restatement (Third) of Trusts § 9(1)(b) 313
Restatement (Third) of Trusts § 9(2) 309
Restatement (Third) of Trusts § 9, cmt. a 309
Restatement (Third) of Trusts § 9, cmt. c 310, 312
Restatement (Third) of Trusts § 9, cmt. d 310
Restatement (Third) of Trusts § 9, cmt. e 310
Restatement (Third) of Trusts § 9, cmt. f 311, 314
Restatement (Third) of Trusts § 9, cmt. g 312, 313
Restatement (Third) of Trusts § 10 .... 162, 406
Restatement (Third) of Trusts § 10, cmt. e 162
Restatement (Third) of Trusts § 11(1) 416
Restatement (Third) of Trusts § 11(2) 408
Restatement (Third) of Trusts § 11, cmt. b 226
Restatement (Third) of Trusts § 11, cmt. c 226, 408
Restatement (Third) of Trusts § 11, cmt. d 408
Restatement (Third) of Trusts § 11, cmt. e 409
Restatement (Third) of Trusts § 11, cmt. f 227
Restatement (Third) of Trusts § 11, illus. 3 228
Restatement (Third) of Trusts § 12 412
Restatement (Third) of Trusts § 13 409
Restatement (Third) of Trusts § 13, cmt. a 409
Restatement (Third) of Trusts § 13, cmt. d 170
Restatement (Third) of Trusts § 13, illus. 5–7 170
Restatement (Third) of Trusts § 13, illus. 8 171
Restatement (Third) of Trusts § 14, cmt. b 295, 296
Restatement (Third) of Trusts § 14, cmt. d 164
Restatement (Third) of Trusts § 15 162
Restatement (Third) of Trusts § 15, cmt. b 165
Restatement (Third) of Trusts § 16, cmt. b 165
Restatement (Third) of Trusts § 17 165
Restatement (Third) of Trusts § 17, cmt. a 166
Restatement (Third) of Trusts § 18 413
Restatement (Third) of Trusts § 18(2) 290
Restatement (Third) of Trusts § 18, cmt. a 292
Restatement (Third) of Trusts § 18, cmt. b 291
Restatement (Third) of Trusts § 18, cmt. c 292
Restatement (Third) of Trusts § 18, cmt. d 290
Restatement (Third) of Trusts § 18, cmt. f 291
Restatement (Third) of Trusts § 18, cmt. e 292
Restatement (Third) of Trusts § 18, cmt. h 291, 292
Restatement (Third) of Trusts § 19, cmt. a(2) 298
Restatement (Third) of Trusts § 19, cmt. f 298
Restatement (Third) of Trusts § 19, cmt. h 297
Restatement (Third) of Trusts § 20 413
Restatement (Third) of Trusts § 20, cmt. a 168
Restatement (Third) of Trusts § 20, Reporter's Notes 413
Restatement (Third) of Trusts § 21 307
Restatement (Third) of Trusts § 22(1) 169
Restatement (Third) of Trusts § 22, cmt. a 308
Restatement (Third) of Trusts § 22, cmt. b 169
Restatement (Third) of Trusts § 22, cmt. c 169
Restatement (Third) of Trusts § 23(1) 169

Restatement (Third) of Trusts § 23(2)(b) 169
Restatement (Third) of Trusts § 24 309
Restatement (Third) of Trusts § 24(2)(a) 306
Restatement (Third) of Trusts § 24(2)(b) 306
Restatement (Third) of Trusts § 24, cmt. c 168, 307
Restatement (Third) of Trusts § 24, cmt. d 306
Restatement (Third) of Trusts § 24, cmt. e 306
Restatement (Third) of Trusts § 24, cmt. f 306
Restatement (Third) of Trusts § 24, cmt. h 308
Restatement (Third) of Trusts § 24, cmt. h(1) 311
Restatement (Third) of Trusts § 25 166
Restatement (Third) of Trusts § 25, cmt. a 168
Restatement (Third) of Trusts § 25, cmt. d 347, 375
Restatement (Third) of Trusts § 25, cmt. e 266, 444, 593
Restatement (Third) of Trusts § 25, illus. 11 215
Restatement (Third) of Trusts § 26 .... 167, 207
Restatement (Third) of Trusts § 26, cmt. a 301
Restatement (Third) of Trusts § 26, cmt. c 215
Restatement (Third) of Trusts § 26, cmt. d 259
Restatement (Third) of Trusts § 26, illus. 7 215
Restatement (Third) of Trusts §§ 27–30 411
Restatement (Third) of Trusts § 27(2) 458
Restatement (Third) of Trusts § 27, cmt. b(1) 402
Restatement (Third) of Trusts § 28 469
Restatement (Third) of Trusts § 28, cmt. a 468, 469, 471
Restatement (Third) of Trusts § 28, cmt. a(1) 469
Restatement (Third) of Trusts § 28, cmt. c 468
Restatement (Third) of Trusts § 28, cmt. d 468
Restatement (Third) of Trusts § 28, cmt. e 471
Restatement (Third) of Trusts § 28, cmt. f 470, 471
Restatement (Third) of Trusts § 28, cmt. g 469
Restatement (Third) of Trusts § 28, cmt. h 469
Restatement (Third) of Trusts § 28, cmt. i 470
Restatement (Third) of Trusts § 28, cmt. *l* 469, 470, 472
Restatement (Third) of Trusts § 28, illus. 3 471
Restatement (Third) of Trusts § 28, illus. 5 469
Restatement (Third) of Trusts § 28, Reporter's Note to cmt. *l* 469
Restatement (Third) of Trusts § 29, cmts. d–f 411
Restatement (Third) of Trusts § 29, cmt. h 538
Restatement (Third) of Trusts § 29, cmt. h(1) 462, 524
Restatement (Third) of Trusts § 29, cmt. i(2) 379
Restatement (Third) of Trusts § 29, cmt. j 376, 377, 378
Restatement (Third) of Trusts § 29, cmt. m 380
Restatement (Third) of Trusts § 29, illus. 1 377
Restatement (Third) of Trusts § 29, illus. 3 377
Restatement (Third) of Trusts § 31 .... 165, 412, 640
Restatement (Third) of Trusts § 32, cmt. a 138
Restatement (Third) of Trusts § 32, cmt. b 162
Restatement (Third) of Trusts § 32, cmt. d 646
Restatement (Third) of Trusts § 34(1) 640
Restatement (Third) of Trusts § 34(3) 646
Restatement (Third) of Trusts § 34, cmt. c(1) 640
Restatement (Third) of Trusts § 34, cmt. d 649
Restatement (Third) of Trusts § 34, cmt. f(1) 640
Restatement (Third) of Trusts § 35(1) 650
Restatement (Third) of Trusts § 35(2) 650
Restatement (Third) of Trusts § 35, cmt. b 650
Restatement (Third) of Trusts § 36 650
Restatement (Third) of Trusts § 37, cmt. c 644
Restatement (Third) of Trusts § 37, cmt. e 616, 643, 644, 645, 647
Restatement (Third) of Trusts § 37, cmt. e(1) 642
Restatement (Third) of Trusts § 37, cmt. f 642

Restatement (Third) of Trusts § 37, cmt. f(1) 642
Restatement (Third) of Trusts § 37, cmt. g 642
Restatement (Third) of Trusts § 38 652
Restatement (Third) of Trusts § 38, cmt. b 657
Restatement (Third) of Trusts § 38, cmt. c(1) 653, 654, 655
Restatement (Third) of Trusts § 38, cmt. d 602, 660
Restatement (Third) of Trusts § 38, cmt. e 656, 657
Restatement (Third) of Trusts § 38, cmt. f 657
Restatement (Third) of Trusts § 38, cmt. g 657
Restatement (Third) of Trusts § 38, cmt. h 661
Restatement (Third) of Trusts § 38, cmt. i 661
Restatement (Third) of Trusts § 38, cmt. j 661
Restatement (Third) of Trusts § 38, illus. 1 657
Restatement (Third) of Trusts § 39 .... 475, 649
Restatement (Third) of Trusts § 39, cmt. e 649
Restatement (Third) of Trusts § 40 407
Restatement (Third) of Trusts § 40, cmt. d 165
Restatement (Third) of Trusts § 40, cmt. e 407, 408
Restatement (Third) of Trusts § 41 165
Restatement (Third) of Trusts § 41, cmt. a 482, 484
Restatement (Third) of Trusts § 45 441
Restatement (Third) of Trusts § 45, cmt. d 441
Restatement (Third) of Trusts § 46 442
Restatement (Third) of Trusts § 46, cmt. g 442
Restatement (Third) of Trusts § 47 .... 403, 472
Restatement (Third) of Trusts § 48 473
Restatement (Third) of Trusts § 49, cmt. a 502
Restatement (Third) of Trusts § 49, cmt. c(2) 625
Restatement (Third) of Trusts § 49, cmt. c(3) 493
Restatement (Third) of Trusts § 50, cmt. b 434, 435
Restatement (Third) of Trusts § 50, cmt. c 435, 436
Restatement (Third) of Trusts § 50, cmt. d 433, 436
Restatement (Third) of Trusts § 50, cmt. e 434, 436, 438, 440
Restatement (Third) of Trusts § 50, cmt. f 433, 437
Restatement (Third) of Trusts § 50, illus. 1 437
Restatement (Third) of Trusts § 51 481
Restatement (Third) of Trusts § 53, cmt. a 169
Restatement (Third) of Trusts § 56 449
Restatement (Third) of Trusts § 56, cmt. b 507
Restatement (Third) of Trusts § 56, cmt. e 446
Restatement (Third) of Trusts § 57 451
Restatement (Third) of Trusts § 58 .... 449, 488
Restatement (Third) of Trusts § 58(2) 444
Restatement (Third) of Trusts § 58, cmt. b 449, 453
Restatement (Third) of Trusts § 58, cmt. c 453, 510
Restatement (Third) of Trusts § 58, cmt. d 450
Restatement (Third) of Trusts § 58, cmt. d(1) 453
Restatement (Third) of Trusts § 58, cmt. f 445
Restatement (Third) of Trusts § 58, cmt. g 488
Restatement (Third) of Trusts § 59(a) 452
Restatement (Third) of Trusts § 59(b) 451
Restatement (Third) of Trusts § 59, cmt. a(1) 453
Restatement (Third) of Trusts § 59, cmt. a(2) 453
Restatement (Third) of Trusts § 59, cmt. b 452
Restatement (Third) of Trusts § 59, Reporter's Note 452
Restatement (Third) of Trusts § 60, cmt. c 447
Restatement (Third) of Trusts § 60, cmt. e 447, 448
Restatement (Third) of Trusts § 60, cmt. f 444
Restatement (Third) of Trusts § 60, cmt. g 448
Restatement (Third) of Trusts § 62 .... 283, 301
Restatement (Third) of Trusts § 62, cmt. a 305
Restatement (Third) of Trusts § 63, cmt. c 206, 416

Restatement (Third) of Trusts § 63, cmt. h 208
Restatement (Third) of Trusts § 63, cmt. i 208
Restatement (Third) of Trusts § 63, cmt. j 207
Restatement (Third) of Trusts § 63, cmt. k 207
Restatement (Third) of Trusts § 63, cmt. *l* 207, 418
Restatement (Third) of Trusts § 63, Reporter's Notes to cmts. h–j 417
Restatement (Third) of Trusts § 65 463
Restatement (Third) of Trusts § 65(2) 461, 462
Restatement (Third) of Trusts § 65, cmt. b 465
Restatement (Third) of Trusts § 65, cmt. c 461
Restatement (Third) of Trusts § 65, cmt. d 463
Restatement (Third) of Trusts § 65, cmt. e 464
Restatement (Third) of Trusts § 65, cmt. h 464
Restatement (Third) of Trusts § 65, illus. 5 463
Restatement (Third) of Trusts § 66 .... 457, 560
Restatement (Third) of Trusts § 66(1) 456
Restatement (Third) of Trusts § 66, cmt. b 456
Restatement (Third) of Trusts § 66, illus. 6 487
Restatement (Third) of Trusts § 67 478
Restatement (Third) of Trusts § 67, cmt. b 476, 478
Restatement (Third) of Trusts § 67, cmt. c 477
Restatement (Third) of Trusts § 67, cmt. d 468, 477, 479
Restatement (Third) of Trusts § 67, cmt. e 478, 480
Restatement (Third) of Trusts § 67, cmt. f 476, 479
Restatement (Third) of Trusts § 68, Reporter's Note 459
Restatement (Third) of Trusts § 69 411
Restatement (Third) of Trusts § 70, cmt. d(1) 627
Restatement (Third) of Trusts § 71 .... 606, 622
Restatement (Third) of Trusts § 71, cmt. b 671
Restatement (Third) of Trusts § 71, cmt. d 434, 606
Restatement (Third) of Trusts § 74(a)(ii) 208
Restatement (Third) of Trusts § 74, cmt. e 617
Restatement (Third) of Trusts § 75, cmt. f 681
Restatement (Third) of Trusts § 76(1) 627
Restatement (Third) of Trusts § 76(2)(b) 630
Restatement (Third) of Trusts § 76, cmt. a 628
Restatement (Third) of Trusts § 76, cmt. d 426, 631, 666
Restatement (Third) of Trusts § 76, cmt. f 623
Restatement (Third) of Trusts § 77(1) 627
Restatement (Third) of Trusts § 77(3) 627
Restatement (Third) of Trusts § 77, cmt. b 607
Restatement (Third) of Trusts § 78(1) 597
Restatement (Third) of Trusts § 78(3) 603
Restatement (Third) of Trusts § 78, cmt. b 600
Restatement (Third) of Trusts § 78, cmt. c 600
Restatement (Third) of Trusts § 78, cmt. c(2) 600
Restatement (Third) of Trusts § 78, cmt. c(6) 601
Restatement (Third) of Trusts § 78, cmt. c(7) 603
Restatement (Third) of Trusts § 78, cmt. c(8) 602
Restatement (Third) of Trusts § 78, cmt. d 592, 597
Restatement (Third) of Trusts § 78, cmt. d(1) 661
Restatement (Third) of Trusts § 78, cmt. e 599
Restatement (Third) of Trusts § 78, cmt. e(2) 601
Restatement (Third) of Trusts § 78, cmt. g 603
Restatement (Third) of Trusts § 79(2) 612
Restatement (Third) of Trusts § 79, cmt. c 435
Restatement (Third) of Trusts § 79, cmt. d 434
Restatement (Third) of Trusts § 80 .... 628, 670
Restatement (Third) of Trusts § 80, cmt. c 670
Restatement (Third) of Trusts § 80, cmt. d(1) 670
Restatement (Third) of Trusts § 81(2) 649
Restatement (Third) of Trusts § 81, cmt. c(1) 671

Restatement (Third) of Trusts § 82 426
Restatement (Third) of Trusts § 82(a)(1) 617
Restatement (Third) of Trusts § 82(a)(2) 621
Restatement (Third) of Trusts § 82, cmt. a(2) 620
Restatement (Third) of Trusts § 82, cmt. f 617
Restatement (Third) of Trusts § 83 621
Restatement (Third) of Trusts § 83, cmt. c 672
Restatement (Third) of Trusts § 83, cmt. d 621
Restatement (Third) of Trusts § 84 .... 631, 683
Restatement (Third) of Trusts § 84, cmt. d(1) 683
Restatement (Third) of Trusts § 85 633
Restatement (Third) of Trusts § 85(2) 633
Restatement (Third) of Trusts § 85, cmt. a 632
Restatement (Third) of Trusts § 85, cmt. d 650
Restatement (Third) of Trusts § 85, Reporter's Note to, cmt. a 632
Restatement (Third) of Trusts § 86 633
Restatement (Third) of Trusts § 86, cmt. c 560
Restatement (Third) of Trusts § 86, cmt. c(1) 638
Restatement (Third) of Trusts § 86, cmt. f 637
Restatement (Third) of Trusts § 88 628
Restatement (Third) of Trusts § 89 636
Restatement (Third) of Trusts § 90 626
Restatement (Third) of Trusts § 90(a) 616
Restatement (Third) of Trusts § 90(b) 609
Restatement (Third) of Trusts § 90, cmt. b 616
Restatement (Third) of Trusts § 90, cmt. c 613, 614
Restatement (Third) of Trusts § 90, cmt. d 607
Restatement (Third) of Trusts § 90, cmt. e 608, 613
Restatement (Third) of Trusts § 90, cmt. h 610, 611
Restatement (Third) of Trusts § 90, cmt. i 612
Restatement (Third) of Trusts § 90, cmt. j 611
Restatement (Third) of Trusts § 90, illus. 14 610
Restatement (Third) of Trusts § 91(b) 604
Restatement (Third) of Trusts § 91, cmt. e 604
Restatement (Third) of Trusts § 92, cmt. a 609
Restatement (Third) of Trusts § 92, cmt. d 610
Restatement (Third) of Trusts § 92, cmt. e 615
Restatement (Third) of Trusts § 93, cmt. c 668
Restatement (Third) of Trusts § 94 .... 473, 474
Restatement (Third) of Trusts § 94(2) 667, 668
Restatement (Third) of Trusts § 94, cmt. a(1) 667
Restatement (Third) of Trusts § 94, cmt. e 475
Restatement (Third) of Trusts § 96(1) 627, 669
Restatement (Third) of Trusts § 96, cmt. d 669
Restatement (Third) of Trusts § 97 .... 673, 674
Restatement (Third) of Trusts § 97, cmt. a 674
Restatement (Third) of Trusts § 97, cmt. c 674
Restatement (Third) of Trusts § 98, cmt. b 312, 679
Restatement (Third) of Trusts § 98, cmt. b(1) 679
Restatement (Third) of Trusts § 100 665
Restatement (Third) of Trusts § 100, cmt. a(1) 664
Restatement (Third) of Trusts § 100, cmt. b(1) 664
Restatement (Third) of Trusts § 103 686
Restatement (Third) of Trusts § 104 686
Restatement (Third) of Trusts § 104, cmt. g(3) 624
Restatement (Third) of Trusts § 106(2) 686
Restatement (Third) of Trusts § 106, cmt. b(1) 685
Restatement (Third) of Trusts § 107 426
Restatement (Third) of Trusts § 108 680
Restatement (Third) of Trusts § 108(1) 681
Restatement (Third) of Trusts § 108(3)(a) 684
Restatement (Third) of Trusts § 108, cmt. c 313

Restatement (Third) of Trusts § 108, Reporter's Note to, cmt. c 683
Restatement (Third) of Trusts § 109 427
Restatement (Third) of Trusts § 110 427
Restatement (Third) of Trusts § 111 427
Restatement (Third) of Trusts (Prudent Investor Rule) § 100, cmt. b(1) 665
Restatement (Third) of Trusts (Prudent Investor Rule) § 190 635
Restatement (Third) of Trusts (Prudent Investor Rule) § 205(a) 666
Restatement (Third) of Trusts (Prudent Investor Rule) § 227, cmt. j 628

Index

References are to Pages

ABATEMENT
Generally, 258
Apportionment, 260
Classification of devises, 261
Contrary intent, 261
Defined, 1
Hierarchy of devises, 258

ACCELERATION OF REMAINDERS
See Modification and Termination of Trusts

ACCOUNTS
See also Duty to Inform
Approval by beneficiary designated in trust instrument, 621
Approval by court, 672
Blind trust, 617
Closing statement in lieu of court approval, 673
Court accounting, 620
Final account, 672
Incompetent beneficiaries, 675
Intermediate accounts, 672
Jurisdiction to approve, 673
Misrepresentation, 673
Notice, 673
Personal representatives, 620
Recordkeeping, 621
Representation, 675
Trustees, 620
Waiver by beneficiary, 621

ACCUMULATIONS
Charitable trusts, 563
Limitations on, 561
Presumption against, 562

ADEMPTION
By extinction, 248
By satisfaction, 256
Change in form, 250
Defined, 1
Involuntary transfers, 251

ADMINISTRATION
See also Ancillary Administration, Probate
Civil law system, 571
Collection by affidavit, 573
Difference from probate, 570
Heirs as universal successors, 572
History, 570
Income and appreciation during, 253
Right of heirs to collect assets, 572
Small estates, 573
Summary distribution, 574

ADMINISTRATOR
See Fiduciary

ADOPTION
Adult adoption, 109
Child's intestate share,
From adoptive family, 106
From prior family, 106
Class gift, taking under, 107
Equitable adoption, 110
History, 106

ADVANCE HEALTH-CARE DIRECTIVE
See End-of-Life Decisionmaking, Guardianship

ADVANCEMENTS
Application, 78
Computation of shares, 80
Defined, 2
Hotchpot, defined, 13
Proof of intent, 78
Satisfaction of devises, compared, 81

ALIENS
Intestate share of, 68

ALIMONY
Spendthrift provisions, 452

ALTERNATIVE DISPUTE RESOLUTION
Generally, 677
Arbitration statutes, 678
Investment advisor contracts, 678
Mandatory arbitration provisions, 678
Nonjudicial settlement agreements, 677

ANATOMICAL GIFT
Generally, 398

ANCILLARY ADMINISTRATION
See also Administration
Bank accounts, 584
Claims against decedent, 585
Defined, 2
Distribution of ancillary assets, 586
Identity of ancillary administrator, 585
Land, 584
Planning, 586
Rationale, 583
Stock, 584
Suit against foreign representative, 585
Tort claims, 584
Uniform Probate Code, 583

ANNUITY
See Principal and Income

APPORTIONMENT
See Abatement

ASSISTED REPRODUCTION
Generally, 113
Class gift, taking under, 116
Non-surrogacy, 114
Parent-child status, 113
Posthumous parentage, 116

Surrogacy, 115

ATTESTATION CLAUSE
See Wills

ATTORNEYS FEES
See also Legal Profession
Award to beneficiaries, 658
Bar fee schedules, 653
Common fund theory, 658
Estate planning services, 654
Fiduciary-attorney, 660
Frivolous claims, 659
Litigation over fees, 658
Nonprobate assets, 657
Reimbursement of fiduciaries for, 658
Time spent, 654
UTC, 659, 660

BANKS
Liability for dealing with agent, 682
Participating in breach of trust, 681
Self-deposit, 601

BASIS
Gifts, 690
Inherited property, 691
Stepped-up basis, 691

BEQUEST
See Devise

BONA FIDE PURCHASER
See also Sales by Fiduciaries
Certification of trust, 684
Donees of gifts, 684
Duty to inquire, 683
Good faith requirement, 682
Improper action by fiduciary, 682
Registration of title, 683

BOND
Personal representatives, 645
Trustees, 646
Waiver, 645

CAPACITY
See also Wills
Creation of trusts, 408, 416
Guardianship, 383
Incapacity of settlor of revocable trust, 416
Powers of appointment, 508

CHANGE IN THE LAW
Generally, 42
Date of death, 47
Determination of heirs, 498
Execution of an Instrument, 45
Fiduciary administration, 51
Future interest, applied to, 49
Life insurance, 46
Marital deduction, 45
Powers of appointment, 515
Rule against perpetuities, 50, 543
Unconstitutional Laws, 48

CHARITABLE TRUSTS
See also Cy Pres
Accumulations, 563
Attorney general, 473
Benevolent purposes, 471
Cemetery plots, 470, 472
Comparison with corporations, 479
Construction of restrictions, 475
Cotrustees, 475
Definition of charitable, 3, 468
Distinctive characteristics of, 467
Education expenditures 468
Gender restrictions, 471
Honorary trusts, 403, 472
Mixed charitable and non-charitable purposes, 471
Narrow group of recipients, 469
Persons with special interests, 474
Planning, 479
Promoting change in the law, 469
Racial restrictions, 470
Religious restrictions, 471
Restricted gift to charitable entity, 475
Settlor's right to enforce, 474
Social investing, 614
Standing to enforce, 473
Statute of Charitable Uses, 468
Stewardship trust, 473
Tax definition, 469, 728
Uniform Supervision of Trustees for Charitable Purposes Act, 473

CHILDREN
See also Adoption, Assisted Reproduction, Class Gifts, Defacto Parentage, Future Interests, Nonmarital Children, Rule of Convenience
Adopted children, 106
ART children, 113
Child, defined, 3
Defacto parentage, 107
Nonmarital children, 101
Pretermitted heirs, 335
Support, right to post-death, 327
Stepchildren, 112

CIVIL LAW
Defined, 3
Forced share for children, 318
Method of consanguinity, 64

CLAIMS AGAINST ESTATE
Arising after death, 589
Contingent, 589
Court approval of payment, 592
Covered by insurance, 590
Debts and expense provision, 590
Duty to pay, 586
Estoppel, 591
Governmental, 589
Liability of fiduciary, 592
Liability of heirs and personal representative, 587
Non-claim statute, 17, 587
Notice to creditors, 587
Priorities, 586
Property, 590
Recoupment, 590
Statutes of limitation, 591

Suit pending, 589
Tulsa decision, 569, 587

CLASS GIFT
See also Adoption, Assisted Reproduction, Children, Nonmarital Children, Rule Against Perpetuities, Rule of Convenience
Defined, 3

CLEAR AND CONVINCING EVIDENCE
Contracts to Make Will, 179
Defined, 3
Gift made before death, 160
Reformation, 459

CODE OF PROFESSIONAL RESPONSIBILITY
See Legal Profession
Defined, 16

CODICIL
See also Wills
Defined, 4
Republication by, 294

COLLATERAL RELATIVES
Defined, 4

COMMUNITY PROPERTY
Choice of law, 364
Classification of property, 358
Compared to elective share, 363
Defined, 4
History, 356
Justification for, 357
Non-probate transfers, 361
Powers of appointment, effect on, 508
Quasi-community Property, defined, 21
Separate property, 23, 358
Significance of, 354

CONDITIONS
See also Charitable Trusts, Cy Pres, Gifts
Charitable gifts, 475, 548–49

CONFIDENTIAL RELATIONSHIP
See Constructive Trust, Undue Influence
Defined, 5

CONFLICT OF LAWS
See also Domicile
Designation by transferor, 30
Domicile, 34
Drafting, 41
Favoring validity, 40
Forum, 38
Importance, 30
Interests, 39
Mobilia sequuntur personam, defined, 16
Powers of appointment, 514
Separate property, 358
Situs, 32

CONSANGUINITY
Chart, 61

CONSENT
Contract between fiduciary and beneficiary, 603
Defense to breach of trust, 673
Incapacitated beneficiary, 675
Knowledge of facts, 674
Nonjudicial settlement agreements, 677
One of several beneficiaries, 674
Representation, 675

CONSERVATOR
See also Guardianship
Defined, 5
Power to claim elective share, 352
Standing to challenge acts of, 667
Substituted judgement, defined, 24
Transfers by, 227, 335

CONSTRUCTIVE TRUST
Confidential relationship, 5, 306
Defined, 5
Elements, 305, 385
Mistakes, 288–89
Oral gifts of land, 157
Oral trust of land, 306
Secret and semi-secret trusts, 292, 394

CONTRACTS TO MAKE WILL
See also Joint Will
Generally, 179
Clear and convincing evidence, 181
Consideration, 182
Executory contracts, 181
Fairness, 182
Part performance, 182
Planning, 186
Remedies, 185
Repudiation, 181
Statute of Frauds, 180
Third party enforcement, 184
Will changes, 183

CORPORATIONS
Liability for participating in breach of trust, 680
Liability for transfer of securities, 682
Trustee holding own stock, 601

COTRUSTEES
Contribution and indemnification, 670
Delegation among, 649
Disagreement between, 649
Duty to participate, 670
Standing to sue, 475, 667

CREDITORS
See also Claims Against Estate, Spendthrift Trusts
Determining who the settlor was, 445, 446
Discretionary trusts, 447
Fraudulent conveyance, 10, 444
Joint tenancy, 594
Life insurance, 595
Multiple-Person Bank Accounts, 594
Non-claim statute, defined, 17
Nonprobate transfers, 592
Of holder of power of appointment, 507
Of settlor of irrevocable trust, 444
Of settlor of revocable trust, 444, 593
Of trust beneficiaries, 446
Power of beneficiary to reach trust assets, 447

Several settlors, 446
Support trusts, 447
Tenancy by the entirety, 594
Without notice property held in trust, 684

CUSTODIANSHIP
See Uniform Custodial Trust Act, Uniform Transfers to Minors Act
Custodian, defined, 6

CY PRES
See also Charitable Trusts
Defined, 6
Deviations in administrative provisions, 479
Effect of substitutional gift, 478
Entity goes out of existence, 478
Excess or inadequate funds, 477
Extrinsic evidence, 479
General charitable intent, 476
Judicial restraint in use of power, 478
Racial restrictions, 477
Removing restrictions in charitable trusts, 476
Scholarships, 477
Violations of Rule Against Perpetuities, 541

DATE OF DEATH
See also Change in the Law
Governing law, 47
Unconstitutional laws, effect, 48

DEAD MAN STATUTE
Defined, 6

DEATH TAXES
See also Estate Tax
2001 Tax Act, 688
2010 Tax Act, 688
2017 Tax Act, 689
Defined, 6
Types of, 687
Why important, 688

DEEDS
Clean hands, 312
Constructive trusts, 305
Deed, defined, 6
Execute, defined, 9
Fraud, 314
Nature of proof, 311
Reformation of, 304
Resulting trust, 307
Third parties, protection of, 313

DEFACTO PARENTAGE
Generally, 107

DELEGATION
See Remedies Against Fiduciaries

DEPENDENT RELATIVE REVOCATION
See also Revocation of Will
Described, 198

DESCENDANT
See Class Gift, Intestate Succession
Descendant, defined, 7

DESTRUCTIBILITY OF CONTINGENT REMAINDERS
See Rule Against Perpetuities

DESTRUCTION OF PROPERTY
Validity of direction to destroy, 379

DETERMINATION OF DEATH
Definition of death, 277
Disappearance, 277
Simultaneous death, 274

DEVISE
Bequest, defined, 2
Classification of devises, 247, 249
Construction problems, 255
Demonstrative devises, 247, 250
Devise, defined, 7
General devise,
Generally, 247
Defined, 11
Income, entitlement to, 253
Residuary devise, defined, 22
Specific devise,
Generally, 247
Defined, 23
Increases, 257

DIGITAL ASSETS
Generally, 634
Revised Uniform Fiduciary Access to Digital Assets Act, 634

DISCLAIMERS
Generally, 92
Creditors' rights, 93
Defined, 7
Effect of disclaimer, 98
Fiduciary disclaimer, 95
Formalities, 97
Interests disclaimable, 97
Partial disclaimer, 97
Requirements, 94
Tax consequences, 94, 703

DISCRETIONARY TRUSTS
Comparison with spendthrift trusts, 454
Conflict of interest, 437
Creditors' rights, 444, 446
Drafting, 439
Duty of support of parent or spouse, 438
Factors other than need, 440
Incentive trusts, 440
Income and principal, 437
Interpretation of, 435
Judicial review of trustee discretion, 434
Medicaid eligibility, 442
First-party trusts, 443
Revocable trusts, 442
Third-party trusts, 442
Trusts for spouse, 443
Other resources of beneficiary, 438
Preferred beneficiaries, 437
Reasons for, 433
Single v. separate trusts, 440
Support, 436

DISTRIBUTION
Decree of, 622
Delay in, 626
Effect of decree, 622
Facility of payment statutes, 624
In kind, 625
Liability of fiduciary for improper, 623
Liability of recipient for, 623
Non-prorata, 625
Retainer, 624
To incompetents, 624

DIVIDENDS
See Principal and Income

DIVORCE
Designation of spouse as fiduciary, 643
Divorce, claim for division of trust upon, 452
Revocation of nonprobate transfers, 214
Revocation of will, 202

DOCTRINE OF WORTHIER TITLE
See Future Interests, Heir
Defined, 29

DOMICILE
Basis of probate jurisdiction, 567
Conflict of laws, 28
Defined, 7
Determination of, 568

DOWER
See also Elective Share
Generally, 342
Curtesy, defined, 6
Dower, defined, 8

DURABLE HEALTH CARE POWERS OF ATTORNEY
See Durable Powers of Attorney, End-of-Life Decisionmaking, Guardianship

DURABLE POWERS OF ATTORNEY
Generally, 229
Abuse by agent, 390
Acceptance by agent, 388
Common law background, 386
Comparison with trust, 425
Death of principal, 425
Defined, 8
Execution requirements, 387
Gifts, agent's authority to make, 389
Immediately effective vs. springing powers, 387
Living trust funding, 388
Nominating agent as guardian, 389
Protection of third persons, 682
Required language, 387
Statutory form, 388
Successor agents, 389

DUTIES OF FIDUCIARIES
See also Accounts, Cotrustees, Discretionary Trusts, Duty to Inform, Duty of Loyalty, Fiduciary, Remedies Against Fiduciaries
Administer trust, 627
Collect trust property, 639
Control trust property, 630
Costs of administration, 628
Delegation, 628
Effect of compensation, 627
Enforce claims, 630
Identification of property, 631
Impartiality, 434, 467, 613
Power to direct, 629
Predecessor fiduciaries, 631
Professional fiduciaries, 627
Protect trust property, 630
Prudence, 626
Resigning trustee, 650
Trust directors, 629
Trust protectors, 629

DUTY OF LOYALTY
See also Remedies Against Fiduciaries
Acting in two fiduciary capacities, 602
Authorization of self-dealing in instrument, 600
Closely-held business, 603
Contract between fiduciary and beneficiary, 603
Corporate directors, 598
Corporate ties, 598
Court approval, 599
Duty of, 597
Lawyers, 599
No further inquiry, 597
Proprietary mutual funds, 602
Relatives of fiduciary, 599
Self-deposit, 601
Self-dealing, 597
Self-hiring, 602, 660
Stock of trustee, 601

DUTY TO INFORM
See also Accounts
Beneficiary entitled to information, 617
Copy of trust instrument, 619
General obligation, 617
Purpose, 616
Revocable trusts, 617
Special circumstances, 618
Specific requirements, 618
Trustee's report, 621
Uniform Trust Code, 617
Waiver by settlor, 619

ELECTIVE SHARE
See also Community Property
Compared to community property, 363
Compared to dower, 344
Choice of law rules, 353
Effect of other benefits, 349
Election by conservator, 352
Fixed-share v. discretionary restraints, 318
History, 343
Making the election, 351
Non-probate assets, 346
Power of appointment, 508
Purpose, 344
Size, 344
Waiver,
Generally, 367
Construction, 373
Disclosure, 369
Fairness, 371

Formal requirements, 368
Time of, 367

END-OF-LIFE DECISIONMAKING
Anatomical gifts, 398
Best interest test, 393
Competent patient, 390
Conroy case, 394
Cruzan case, 390, 392
Durable health care powers of attorney, 396, 400
Expressed wishes test, 393
Family consent laws, 397
Jobes case, 394
Living wills, 395, 400
Patient Self-Determination Act, 397
Physician-assisted suicide, 393
Physician's Order for Life-Sustaining Treatment (POLST), 397
Quinlan case, 391
Right to refuse medical treatment, 390
Schiavo case, 395
Substituted judgement, 23, 392
Uniform Health-Care Decisions Act, 396
Uniform Rights of the Terminally Ill Act, 395

ENTIRETIES
See also Joint Tenancy
Creditor claims, 594
Defined, 8

EQUITABLE CONVERSION
Defined, 8

ERISA
Defined, 8
Diversification in investments, 609
Prudence in investments, 607
Social investing, 614
Unassignability of benefits, 454

ESCHEAT
See Intestate Succession
Defined, 8

ESTATE TAX
See also Generation Skipping Transfer Tax, Gift Tax
Alternate valuation method, 708
Bypass trust, defined, 2
Calculation of tax, 706
Deductions,
Charitable, 727
Debts and expenses, 726
Items included, 705
Losses, 727
Marital deduction, 729
State death taxes, 727
Swing (or double) deduction rule, 727
Disclaimers, 703
Grantor as trustee, 713
Gross estate, items included, 705
Individual retirement accounts, 720
Joint tenancies,
Marital, 720
Non-marital, 721
Life insurance, 724
Marital deduction,
Generally, 729
Clayton Trust, 734
General power of appointment trust, 730
Marital deduction planning, 732
Nondeductible terminable interest, 729
Qualifying terminable income property (QTIP), 731, 734
Overlap between 2036 and 2038, 719
Portability, 689, 733
Power to remove and/or replace trustee, 713
Powers of appointment, 722
Property owned at death, 708
Qualified retirement plans, 720
Qualified terminable interest property (QTIP), 726, 731, 734
Reciprocal trusts, 714
Retained life estate, transfers with, 711
Returns, due date, 708
Reversionary interest, more than 5%, 715
Revocable transfers, 716
Special use valuation, 708
Split-interest trusts, 728
Swing (or double) deduction rule, 727
Three years, transfers within, 710
Valuation, 707

EXCULPATORY CLAUSES
See Remedies Against Fiduciaries

EXECUTORS
See Fiduciary
Defined, 9

EXECUTORY INTERESTS
See Rule Against Perpetuities
Defined, 9

EXEMPT PROPERTY
See Statutory Allowances

EXONERATION
Described, 262

EXPECTANCY
Defined, 9

EXPRESS TRUST
See Trusts
Defined, 9

EXTRINSIC EVIDENCE
See also Mistake
Latent ambiguity, 281
Patent ambiguity, 282
Protection of third parties, 303
Types of evidence, 301
Will substitutes, 299

FACTS OF INDEPENDENT SIGNIFICANCE
Described, 295
Pour-over wills, application to, 296

FAMILY ALLOWANCE
See Statutory Allowances

FAMILY CONSENT LAWS
See End-of-Life Decisionmaking

FEE TAIL
See Heir, Rule Against Perpetuities

FEES OF FIDUCIARIES
See also Attorneys Fees
Attorney as executor-trustee, 660
Compensation of agents, 657
Conflict of interest, 656
Contract, 656
Court approval, 662
Custom, 653
Family members, 655
Individual v. corporate, 647
Multiple, 661
Percentage compensation, 652
Poor performance, 655
Provision in instrument, 656
Reasonable compensation, 652, 653
Size of trust, 653
Skill and experience of fiduciary, 655
Termination fee, 653
Time spent, 654

FIDUCIARY
See also Duties of Fiduciaries, Fees of Fiduciaries, Remedies Against Fiduciaries
Administrators, 1, 641
Attorneys' role, 651
Bond, 645
CERCLA liability, 687
Change of circumstances, 643
Conflict of interest, 641
Contract liability, 684
Corporate, 647
Court appointment, 640
Defined, 10
Designation by beneficiaries, 640
Disagreement between, 649
Executors, 641
Exoneration right, 685
Hostility with beneficiaries, 642
Incompetence, 645
Insolvency, 643
Multiple, 648
Nonresident, 646
Powers of successor, 650
Removal, generally, 642
Removal by beneficiaries, 644
Removal for misconduct, 643
Removal under UTC, 643, 644
Resignation, 650
Selection of, 639
Standing to contest will, 580
Tax considerations in selecting, 642
Trustees, selection of, 412

FORCED SHARE FOR SPOUSE
See Elective Share

FORFEITURE CLAUSE
See Probate

FORMAL REQUIREMENTS
See Gifts, Holographic Wills, Powers of Appointment, Wills

FORMALITIES OF WILL EXECUTION
See Wills

FRAUD
Accounts, 672
Defined, 10
Extrinsic fraud, 576, 623
Fraudulent conveyance, 10, 422

FREEDOM OF TESTATION
See also Wills
Issue described, 315
Pro and con, 317

FUTURE INTERESTS
See also Heir, Rule Against Perpetuities, Rule of Convenience
Alienability, 484
Avoiding intestacy, 485
Conditions of survival, 481
Contingent remainder, defined, 5, 482
Defined, 10
Destructibility of contingent remainders, 519
Doctrine of worthier title, 502
Drafting errors, 487
Extending anti-lapse statutes to, 486
Fee tail, 10, 500, 519
Gift on "death without issue," 489
Gifts to "children," 486
Gifts to "issue," 486, 503
Implied gift to issue, 490
Implied survivorship contingency, 259
Income interests, 492
Indefinite failure of issue construction, 490
Keeping property in the bloodline, 484
Planning, 492
Preference for early vesting, 483
Protecting remoter issue, 486
Reversion, defined, 22
Rule in Shelley's Case, 501
Rule in Wild's Case, 503
Spendthrift provision, 488
"Surviving," 489
"To A at age," 488
"To A or his children (heirs)," 490
Vested and contingent remainders, 482

GENERAL DEVISE
See Devise

GENERATION SKIPPING TRANSFER TAX
Computation, 741
Exemption, 740
Generation assignment, 736
Non-skip person, 736
Skip person, 736
Generation skipping transfer,
Direct skip, 740
Taxable distribution, 739
Taxable termination, 738
Transferor, 735
Tuition and medical expense exclusion, 742

GIFT TAX
See also Estate Tax
Annual exclusion amount, 696
Ascertainable standard, 700

Calculation of gift tax, 695
Charitable deduction, 705
Checks, gift by, 701
Completed gifts, 698
Consideration in money or money's worth, 692
Crummey power, 697
Debt forgiveness, 701
Disclaimers, 703
Donee, identity of, 696
Dower and curtesy, release as consideration, 693
Future interests restriction, 696
Gift, defined, 692
Incomplete gifts, 698
Life insurance, gifts of, 701
Marital deduction, 705
Medical payments, 698
Minors,
    529 plans, 698
    Gifts (or Transfers) to Minors Act, 697
    Section 2503(c) trust, 697
Personal services not a gift, 701
Powers of appointment, 702
Property settlements, 703
Qualifying income interest for life (QTIP), 704
Retained powers, 699
Split gifts for married persons, 693
Subject matter of gift, 700
Substantial adverse interest, 700
Tuition payments, 698
Valuation of gifts,
        Generally, 694
    Retained interest of donor, 694

GIFTS
    See also Gift Tax
Anatomical gift, 398
Causa mortis, 11, 204
Conditions, charitable gifts, 450
Deed, effect of, 156–57
Delivery, 151, 156
Delivery excused, 157
Delivery to third party, 158
Donee, defined, 8
Formalities, 150
Gifts vs. promises, 160
History, 151
Intangibles, gifts of, 154
Personal property, gifts of, 154
Presumption of intent, 156
Power to revoke, 204
Recording statutes, 153
Substituted judgment, defined, 23
Tangibles, gifts of, 154
When testamentary, 158
Writing, when required, 152

GRANTOR
    See Deeds, Grantor Trusts, Trusts
Defined, 11

GRANTOR TRUSTS
General power of appointment, beneficiary with, 748
Grantor, defined, 11
Income payable to grantor, 748
Power to control beneficial enjoyment, 747
Reversionary interest retained, 747
Revocable trusts, 748

GUARDIAN AD LITEM
    See also Representation
Consent to trust modification or termination, 465
Defined, 11
Inadequate representation by, 622
Payment of claim, 675

GUARDIANSHIP
    See also Conservator, End-of-Life Decisionmaking
Definition of incapacity, 383
Guardian, defined, 11
Jurisdiction disputes, 385
Least restrictive alternative, 384
Need for, 383
Procedure for appointment, 384
Supported decision-making, 385
Types, 382
Ward, defined, 27

HALF-BLOODS
See Intestate Succession

HEIR
Change in the law, 498
Choice of law, 73
Defined, 12
Doctrine of Worthier Title, 502
Equivalent words, 71
Fee tail, 10, 500
Gift to heirs in will, 72
Immediate devise to heirs of "A," 498
Meaning of word, 71
Private agreements among, 99
Rule in Shelley's Case, 501
Spouse as heir, 73
Time of determination, 498
Use of word in drafting, 497
Word of limitation, 499

HOLOGRAPHIC WILLS
    Generally, 145
Date, 145
Defined, 12
Desirability, 149
Printed matter, effect of, 146
Testamentary intent, 147

HOMESTEAD
See Statutory Allowances

HOMICIDE
Alternate takers, 89
Avoiding forfeiture, 87
Degree of crime, 85
Effect on inheritance, 83
History, 83
Proof, 86
Protection of third parties, 90
Statutes, 84

HONORARY TRUSTS
    See Charitable Trusts
Defined, 13

HOTCHPOT
See Advancements
Defined, 13

ILLEGITIMATE
See Nonmarital Children
Defined, 13

IMMOVABLE PROPERTY
Defined, 13
Mobilia sequuntur personam, defined, 16

IN TERROREM
See Probate, Trust
Defined, 14

INCOME
See Principal and Income

INCOME TAX
See also Basis, Grantor Trusts
Beneficiary gross income inclusion on distributions, 743
Charitable deduction for estate or trust, 746
Distributable net income (DNI), 744
Distributions deduction, 743
Exclusion of gifts from gross income, 689
Specific bequest rule, 744
Subchapter J estate, 742
Terminating distributions, 746
Tier structure, 745

INCORPORATION BY REFERENCE
Generally, 292, 293
List of tangibles, 295

INCREASES
Shares of stock, 257

INSTRUMENT
Defined, 13

INTANGIBLE
Defined, 13

INTEGRATION
See Wills

INTER VIVOS
Defined, 14

INTEREST
See Principal and Interest

INTERESTED WITNESS
See Wills

INTERNATIONAL WILLS
Defined, 13

INTESTATE
See Intestate Succession
Defined, 14

INTESTATE SUCCESSION
See also Adoption. Advancements, Assisted Reproduction, Children, Defacto Parentage, Disclaimers, Homicide, Nonmarital Children, Wrongful Death
Adopted children, 105
Advancements, 78
After-born child share, 335
Aliens, 68
Ancestral property, 65
ART children, 113
Children, generally, 54
Computation of shares among descendants, 58
Consanguinity, table of, 64
Defacto parentage, 107
Descendants, share of, 57
Disclaimers, 92
Empirical studies, 68
Escheat, 66
Half-bloods relatives, 65
Homicide, 83
Laughing heirs, 66
Misconduct, effect of, 91
Nonmarital children, 101
Parents and their descendants, 62
Representation, 57
Remote relatives, 63
Stepchildren, 112
Surviving spouse share of, 53
Why not to die intestate, 69

INVESTMENTS
See also Remedies Against Fiduciaries
Circumstances of beneficiaries, 611
Common trust funds, 4, 611
Court approval, 600
Differences between types of fiduciary, 604
Diversification, 608
Evaluating performance, 615
Failure to invest, 612
Family business, 615
Following the crowd, 608
Impartiality, 613
Income production, 612
Legal lists, 606
Mutual funds, 611
Professional fiduciaries, 607
Proprietary mutual funds, 611
Prudent man rule, 606
Removal of restrictions, 458
Retention of investments, 609
Social investing, 613
Speculation, 607
Tax consequences, 613
Terms of instrument, 604
Total portfolio approach, 612
Uniform Prudent Investor Act, 608

ISSUE
See Class Gifts, Future Interests, Intestate Succession
Defined, 14

JOINT TENANCY
See also Entireties, Will Substitutes
Generally, 174
Creditors' rights on death, 594
Defined, 14
Disadvantages of, 421
Divorce, effect on, 214
Land, 210
Modern joint tenancy, 175

Multiparty bank accounts, 176
Payable on death transfers, comparison with, 172, 421
Revocation, 210, 212
Safe deposit box, 177
Severance, 210–12
Tenancy by the entirety, 594
Validity, 178
Will, revocation by, 215

JOINT WILL
See also Contracts to Make Will
Defined, 14
Contractual joint and mutual will, 179

JURY TRIAL
Suits against fiduciaries, 663
Will contests, 575

LACHES
Defense for fiduciary, 679
Defined, 14
Prejudice to defendant, 679
Reason for delay, 679

LAPSE
See also Powers of Appointment
Generally, 263
Antilapse statutes, 264
Class gifts, 268
Contrary intent, 267
Defined, 15
Implied survivorship condition, 266
Intestacy resulting from, 273
No residue of a residue, 272
Scope of statutes, 257
Substitute gifts, 269

LATENT AMBIGUITY
See Extrinsic Evidence
Defined, 15

LAUGHING HEIRS
See Intestate Succession
Defined, 15

LEGACY
See Devise

LEGAL INTEREST
Defined, 15

LEGAL LIFE ESTATES
Construction as a trust, 427
Disadvantages as compared with trusts, 425
Remedies of remainderman, 426
Sale by life tenant, 427

LEGAL LIST
See Investments
Defined, 15

LEGAL PROFESSION
See also Attorney Fees, Duty of Loyalty, Malpractice
Abuse of ex parte probate, 570
Conflict of interest, 599
Rules of the profession, 240

LEGITIMATE
See Children
Defined, 15

LETTERS
See Probate
Defined, 15

LIFE INSURANCE
Change of beneficiary, 209
Collecting at death, 565
Exemption from creditors, 595
Putting proceeds in trust, 421
Tax planning, 725

LINEAL DESCENDANTS
See Class Gifts, Intestate Succession
Defined, 16

LISTS OF TANGIBLE PERSONAL PROPERTY
See also Facts of Independent Significance, Incorporation by Reference
Validity of, 292

LIVING WILL
See End-of-Life Decisonmaking
Defined, 16

LOST WILLS
See Wills

MALPRACTICE
Attorney's duty to beneficiaries, 681
In relation to capacity, 244

MARITAL DEDUCTION
See Estate Tax, Gift Tax
Defined, 16

MARITAL PROPERTY
Defined, 16

MEDICAID TRUST
See Discretionary Trusts
Defined, 16

MISCONDUCT
See also Intestate Succession
Effect of, 87

MISTAKE
See also Deeds, Reformation
Admission of extrinsic evidence, 280
Ambiguity, 281
Circumstantial evidence, 286
Constructive trust, 289
Defined, 16
Devise of unowned property, 281
Latent ambiguity, 281
Malpractice, 288
Mistake of fact or law, 459
Nature of evidence, 274
Patent ambiguity, 282
Reformation of trusts, 459
Wills, correcting for, 279

MODIFICATION AND TERMINATION OF TRUSTS
Achievement or failure of purpose, 455

Administrative provisions, 456, 479
Cases of refusal to modify, 455
Claflin rule, 462
Complete distribution of assets, 680
Consent of beneficiaries, 461
Consolidation and division of trusts, 458
Decanting, 466
Guardian ad litem, 465
Interest in "heirs", 464
Material purposes of trust, 462
Partial termination, 461
Planning, 467
Possibility of further children, 465
Reasons for, 454
Reformation for mistake, 459
Removal of restrictions, 456
Representation of beneficiaries, 465
Settlement of will contests, 464
Settlor consent, 461
Special needs trust, 457
Spendthrift provision, 464
Tax modifications, 460
Unanticipated circumstances, 455
Uneconomic trusts, 458

MORTMAIN
Decline of, 358
Defined, 16

MOVABLE PROPERTY
See Immovable Property

MULTIPARTY ACCOUNTS
See Joint Tenancy

MUTUAL WILLS
See Wills, Contracts to Make Will
Defined, 17

NEGATIVE WILL
Validity of, 375

NEXT OF KIN
See Heir

NO CONTEST CLAUSE
See Probate, Trust

NON-CLAIM STATUTE
See Claims Against Estate
Defined, 17

NONMARITAL CHILDREN
See also Assisted Reproduction, Children
Generally, 101
History, 101
Inheritance from, 104
Paternity, proof of, 102
Planning for, 105
Policy, 101
Presumptions about, 103
Wills, taking under, 104

NOTARY PUBLIC
Defined, 17

NUNCUPATIVE WILL
Generally, 150
Defined, 17

OMITTED CHILDREN
See Children, Pretermitted Heir

OMITTED SPOUSE
See Spouse

ORAL WILLS
See Nuncupative Will

PARENTAGE
See Children

PATENT AMBIGUITY
See Extrinsic Evidence

PAYABLE ON DEATH TRANSFERS
See Will Substitutes

PENSIONS
See ERISA

PER CAPITA
See Representation
Defined, 17

PER STIRPES
See Representation
Defined, 17

PERSONAL PROPERTY
Defined, 18

PERSONAL REPRESENTATIVE
See Fiduciary, Probate
Defined, 17

PLANNING FOR INCAPACITY
See also Durable Powers of Attorney, End-of-Life Decisionmaking, Guardianship
Need for, 381
Types of planning documents, 381

POSSIBILITY OF REVERTER
See Rule Against Perpetuities
Defined, 18

POUR-OVER
Generally, 284
Defined, 18

POWER
See Powers of Fiduciary, Sales by Fiduciary
Defined, 18

POWER OF ATTORNEY
See Durable Powers of Attorney
Defined, 18

POWERS OF APPOINTMENT
See also Rule Against Perpetuities
Appointment in trust, 512
Capacity, 508
Capture, 514
Choice of law, 514
Contract to exercise power, 509
Creditors' rights, 507
Defined, generally, 18
Definitions of specific terms, 504
Exercising, 517

Extrinsic evidence of intent, 511
Failure to exercise, 514
Formalities, 509
Fraud on power, 513
Intent to exercise, 510
Lapse, 512
Marshalling, 513
Non-exclusive powers, 513
Nongeneral powers, 512
Powerholder, defined, 504
Relation back, 506
Release of power, 509
Requirement of specific reference, 510
Spouse's rights, 508
Taxes, 506
Unknown powers, 518
Use of powers in planning, 515

POWERS OF FIDUCIARY
See also Digital Assets, Distribution, Fiduciary, Investments, Principal Place of Administration, Sales by Fiduciaries
Distinction from duty, 632
Uniform Trustees' Powers Act, 632

PRECATORY
See Trusts
Defined, 19

PRESUMPTION
Defined, 19

PRETERMITTED HEIRS
Generally, 335
Defined, 19

PRINCIPAL
See Durable Powers of Attorney, Principal and Income
Defined, 20

PRINCIPAL AND INCOME
Annuity, 2
Corporate distributions, 430
Corpus, defined, 5
Effect on investment decisions, 431
General principles, 428
Intent controls, 428
Interest on bonds, 431
Planning, 431
Power to adjust, 432
Proceeds of sale, 430
Purpose of Principal and Income Acts, 428
Reserve for depreciation, 431
Steady stream of income, 429
Tax accounting, 429
Trustee discretion, 430
Under-productive property, 430
Uniform Principal and Income Act, 427, 428
Unitrusts, 432, 433
Wasting assets, 431

PRINCIPAL PLACE OF ADMINISTRATION
Determining, why important, 638
Relationship to jurisdiction, 663
Transfer, 639, 647
Uniform Trust Code provision, 639

PRIVATE TRUST
See Trusts
Defined, 20

PROBATE
See also Ancillary Administration, Claims Against Estate, Wills
Ante-mortem, 578
Attorneys fees in will contests, 581
Avoiding, 572
Bona fide purchasers, 579
Common and solemn, 569
Consequences of, 569
Coordination of probate and non-probate transfers, 415
Cost, 414
Creditors, 415
Defined, 20
Delay, 415
Domicile determination, 568
Federal court jurisdiction, 577
Forfeiture clauses, 581
In terrorem clause, 581
Jury trial, 575
Later discovered will, 577
Location of property, 567
Multi-state, 567
Necessity of, 565
No contest clause, 581
Notice of, 569
Persons under legal disability, 578
Publicity, 414
Standing to contest will, 580
Time limits on contest, 576
Time limits on probate, 579
Ways to avoid, 413, 421
Will contests, 29, 575

PROBATE COURT
Determination of title, 623
Organization of courts, 566
Qualification of judges, 575
Unification of courts, 566

PRUDENT PERSON RULE
See Investments
Defined, 20

PUBLICATION
See Wills
Defined, 21

PUTATIVE SPOUSE
Defined, 21

QTIP TRUST
See Estate Tax, Gift Tax
Defined, 21

QUASI-COMMUNITY PROPERTY
See Community Property
Defined, 21

REFORMATION
See also Mistake
Generally, 21, 459
Clear and convincing proof required, 459
Defined, 21, 459

Trusts, 459

RELATIVES
Devise to, 441

RELEASE
See Powers of Appointment, Spendthrift Trusts

REMAINDERS
See Future Interests

REMEDIES AGAINST FIDUCIARIES
See also Account, Consent, Laches, Statutes of Limitation
Against third persons, 680
Alternative dispute resolution,
Generally, 677
Mandatory arbitration provision, 678
Appreciation damages, 665
Beneficiary consent, 673
Causation, 665
Co-fiduciaries, 661
Contempt, 666
Damages, 664
Delegation, 670
Election to affirm, 664
Equitable remedies, 664
Exculpatory clauses, 668
Fault of others, 670
Forum non conveniens, 663
Good faith defense, 668
Indemnification of fiduciary, 671
Insolvency of trustee, 666
Interest, 665
Jurisdiction of courts, 662, 673
Jurisdiction over nonresidents, 663
Jury trial, 663
Laches, 664, 679
Loss to estate, 664
Participation in breach, 680
Profits of fiduciary, 666
Punitive damages, 666
Res judicata, 671
Standing, 667
Statutes of limitation, 679

REPRESENTATION
See also Intestate Succession
Ante-mortem probate, 578
Defined, 21
Judicial and nonjudicial settlements, 675
Modification and termination of trusts, 465
Per capita, defined, 17
Per stirpes, defined, 17

RES
See Trusts
Defined, 21

RESIDUE OR RESIDUARY ESTATE
See Devise
Defined, 22

RESTATEMENT(S)
Defined, 22

RESTRAINTS ON ALIENATION
Contracts to sell and leases, 559
Defined, 22
Forfeiture and disabling restraints, 558
Future interests, 559
History and rationale, 556
Life estates, 558
Partial restraints, 558
Planning, 561
Preemptive rights, 560
Reasonableness, 557
Restraints on use, 558
Transfer with consent, 559
Trusts, 560

RESULTING TRUST
Defined, 22
Elements, 371

REVERSION
See Future Interests
Defined, 22

REVIVAL
See Revocation of Wills
Defined, 23

REVOCABLE TRUSTS
See also Creditors, Duty to Inform, Trusts
Administration at settlor's death, 565
Contest of, 419
Disclosure to beneficiaries, 416, 617
Joint trust, 420
Medicaid eligibility, 442
Method of revocation, 418
Presumption of revocability, 416
Rights of settlor, 416
Rules of construction, 419
Tax treatment, 415, 716

REVOCATION OF WILL
Consequence of partial revocation, 194
Dependent relative revocation, 199
Divorce, 202, 213
Inconsistency, 191
Intent required, 191
Lost wills, 197
Partial revocation, 194
Physical act, 192
Presumption of revocation, 195
Revival, 200
Subsequent instrument, 189

RULE AGAINST PERPETUITIES
See also Future Interests, Restraints on Alienation
Administrative contingencies, 530
Age contingencies, 528
Alienability, 522
Alternative contingencies, 535
Applicability to trusts, 523
Changes in the law, 44
Charitable gifts, 548
Choice of law, 547
Class closing, 531
Commercial transactions, 553
Covenants, 555
Cy pres, 541
Defined, 23

Destructibility of contingent remainders, 519
Duke of Norfolk's Case, 521
Duration of trusts, 538
Effect of rule on construction, 531
Effect of rule violation, 532, 549
Executory interests, 520
Executory interests following charitable gifts, 549
Fair balance between generations, 526
Fee tail, 519
Impact on estate taxes, 524
Impact on wealth concentration, 524
Infectious invalidity, 533
Leases, 555
Lives in being plus years, 521
Operation, 527
Options, 553
Period in gross, 528
Planning to avoid Rule, 535, 547
Possibilities of reverter, 550
Possibility of trust extending beyond rule period, 528
Powers of appointment,
    Capture, 546
    Choice of law, 547
    Planning for exercise, 547
    Second look, 546
    When Rule begins to run, 527
Precision of Rule, 526
Repeal of, 543
Restatement (Third) of Property reforms, 543
Reverter statutes, 551
Rights of first refusal, 555
Rule of convenience, 531
Savings clauses, 536
Separability of class gifts, 535
Suspension of the power of alienation, 522
Time of decision, 539
Transfers of possibilities and rights of entry, 552
Two-generation trust, 529
Unborn spouse, 530
Uniform Statutory Rule, 540, 556
Vested interests, 530, 548
Wait and see, 538
Who are the measuring lives, 539

RULE IN SHELLEY'S CASE
    See Future Interests, Heir
Defined, 23

RULE OF CONVENIENCE
    See also Class Gift
Contrary intent, 496
Income interests, 495
Intent to limit class, 496
No class member in being, 496
Operation, 494
Planning, 497
Posthumous and adopted children, 495
Rule Against Perpetuities, 531
Time of distribution, 494

SALES BY FIDUCIARIES
    See also Powers of Fiduciary, Remedies Against Fiduciaries
Abandonment of property, 637
Consent of beneficiary, 637
Court confirmation, 637
Grant of option, 638
Implied power, 635
Leases, 638
Power of sale, 635
Price, 637
Prohibition on, 636
Specifically devised property, 636

SAME SEX MARRIAGE
See Spouse

SATISFACTION
See Advancements

SECRET AND SEMI-SECRET TRUSTS
See Constructive Trusts, Trusts

SEPARATE PROPERTY
    See Community Property
Defined, 23

SETTLOR
    See Trusts
Defined, 23

SEVER, SEVERANCE
    See Joint Tenancy
Defined, 23

SIMULTANEOUS DEATH
    See Determination of Death
Generally, 274

SITUS
Basis of probate jurisdiction, 567
Conflict of laws, 30
Defined, 23
Determining, 568

SLAYERS
See Homicide

SPENDTHRIFT TRUSTS
After distribution, 450
Alimony and child support, 452
Beneficiary's need for protection, 450
Contrast with exemption laws, 449
Defined, 23
Determining who the settlor was, 445
Divorce, claim of spouse for division upon, 452
Domestic asset protection trust, 445
Effect on construction of future interests, 488
Effect on trust termination, 463
Exception creditors, 451
Necessaries, 451
Offshore trusts, 445
Pensions, 454
Planning, 453
Protective trusts, 451
Releases, 453
Self-settled trusts, 444
Settlement of will contests, 464
Special needs trust, 452
Statutory, 449
Tort claims, 452
Validity of, 448
Voluntary transfers, 453
Words needed to create, 449

SPOUSE
See also Elective Share, Intestate Succession
Alimony, 329
Bigamy, 118
Common law marriage, 122
Divorce, effect on estate of, 120, 202, 213
Divorce, claim for division of trust upon, 452
Elective share, 318
Family maintenance, 319
Marriage, effect on prior will, 342
Omitted from will, 340
Protection against disinheritance, 315
Putative spouse, 21, 119
Restraints on marriage, 376
Rights of, 117
Same-sex marriage, 125
Separation, effect of, 120
Unmarried cohabitants, 122

STATUTE OF FRAUDS
Contracts to make wills, 180
Defined, 24
Trusts, 402, 412

STATUTE OF USES
Historical origin of trusts, 402

STATUTES OF LIMITATIONS
Comparison with non-claim statutes, 591
Defense for fiduciary, 679
Effect of debtor's death, 591

STATUTORY ALLOWANCES
Exempt property, 333
Family allowance, 330
Homestead, 13, 333

STATUTORY WILLS
Generally, 70
California, 71
Uniform Act, 71

STEWARDSHIP TRUST
See Charitable Trusts

SUBSTANTIAL COMPLIANCE
Execution of wills, 130
Exercising powers, 510
Revocation of trusts, 417

SUBSTITUTED JUDGEMENT
See Conservator, End-of-Life Decisionmaking
Defined, 24

SUPPORT
See Discretionary Trusts, Spendthrift Trusts

SURVIVAL
See Future Interests, Lapse

SURVIVAL OF CLAIMS
See Wrongful Death

SUSPENSION OF THE POWER OF ALIENATION
See Rule Against Perpetuities

TORT
Claims against fiduciaries, 685
Relationship to will contest, 576
Spendthrift trusts, 452

TOTTEN TRUST
See Will Substitutes

TRUSTOR
See Trusts
Defined, 24

TRUSTS
See also Charitable Trusts, Discretionary Trusts, Modification and Termination of Trusts, Revocable Trusts, Spendthrift Trusts
Advantages over guardianship, 422
Avoiding publicity, 414
Comparison with legal life estate, 425
Contest of, 412, 414, 419
Court Supervision, 415
Creation, requirements for,
- Active duties, 409
- Capacity, 408, 416
- Definite beneficiary, 410
- Intention, 409
- Property, 407

Declaration of trust, 407
Defined, 24
Doctrine of merger, 410
Domestic Asset Protection Trust, 445
Duration of, 538
Elements, 402
Forfeiture clause, 669
Formalities, 162
- Consideration, 162
- Charge and condition, 171
- Delivery, 162
- Precatory language, 170
- Transfer of property to trustee, 164
- Words of futurity; expectancies, 165

Historical background, 402
Honorary trusts, 13, 406, 472
In terrorem clause, 669
Insurance, 421
Method of revocation, 417
Need for management, 422
No contest clause, 669
Purposes of, 411
Reasons for using, 402
Res, defined, 21
Revocation of, 206, 417
Secret trusts, 413
Semi-secret trusts, 413
Statute of Uses, 402
Tax savings, 415
Testamentary, 24, 166, 406
Time limits on contest of, 419, 576
Transfer of property to trustee, 164, 407
Transfer of trust situs, 639, 647
Ways to create, 406
Writing requirement, 168, 412

UN CONVENTION
Rights of Persons With Disabilities, 386

UNDUE INFLUENCE
See Wills

UNIFORM ACTS
Generally, 24
Specific Acts,
Adoption, 25
Adult Guardianship and Protective Proceedings Jurisdiction, 385
Anatomical Gift, 398
Common Trust Fund, 25
Custodial Trust, 25, 404, 424
Directed Trust, 25, 630
Disclaimer of Property Interests, 25
Disposition of Community Property Rights at Death, 25
Durable Power of Attorney, 386
Electronic Wills, 25
Estate Tax Apportionment, 27
Fiduciaries, 25–26
Fiduciary Income and Principal Act, 26, 427
Guardianship and Protective Proceedings, 26, 382
Guardianship, Conservatorship and Other Protective Arrangements Act, 26, 385
Health-Care Decisions, 396
Management of Institutional Funds, 26
Marriage and Divorce, 26
Parentage, 26
Power of Attorney, 26, 387
Powers of Appointment, 26, 505
Premarital and Marital Agreements, 367
Principal and Income, 26, 427
Probate Code, 27,
Prudent Investor, 27, 608
Prudent Management of Institutional Funds, 28
Revised Fiduciary Access to Digital Assets Act, 25, 634
Rights of the Terminally Ill, 395
Simultaneous Death, 26
Statutory Rule Against Perpetuities, 27
Statutory Will, 28
Supervision of Trustees for Charitable Purposes, 28, 473
Testamentary Additions to Trusts, 28
Transfers to Minors, 28, 423
Trust Code, 28, 403, 406, 439, 617, 639
Trust Decanting, 28, 466
Trustees' Powers, 28, 632
Trusts Act, 28

UNITRUST
See Principal and Income

VESTED REMAINDER
See Future Interests, Rule Against Perpetuities
Defined, 29

WAIT-AND-SEE
See Rule Against Perpetuities
Defined, 29

WARD
Defined, 29

WASTE
See also Legal Life Estates
Defined, 29
Destruction by executor, 363

WILL CONTESTS
See Probate

WILL SUBSTITUTES
See also Entireties, Joint Tenancy
Defined, 29
Effect of will on, 215
Multiple-party bank accounts, 176
Payable-on-death transfers,
Generally, 172
Joint tenancy, comparison with, 421
Securities registration, 421
Totten trusts,
Generally, 167
Defined, 24

WILLS
See also Abatement, Ademption, Holographic Will, Joint Will, Lapse, Revocation
Ademption, 242
Attest, defined, 2
Classification of devises, 247, 249
Codicil,
Defined, 4
Republication by, 294
Conditions on behavior, 376
Contracts to make will, 179
Defined, 29
Execute, defined, 9
Exoneration, 262
Facts of independent significance, 295
Formalities,
Affidavits, self proving, 143
Attestation clause, 143
Function of, 128
Liberalization, 129
Number of witnesses, 136
Presence requirement, 140, 141
Publication, 140
Request, 140
Sign in testator's presence, 141
Signature, 133
Substantial compliance, 130
Witnessing, 136
Freedom of testation, 315, 317
General mental incapacity,
Generally, 219, 221
Medical evidence, 222
Naturalness of will, 223
Test of, 220
Testimony of witnesses, 223
History, 127
Holographic will, 145
Incorporation by reference, 292
Insane delusion, 220
Integration, 292
Interested witness, 137–40
International will, defined, 14
Lawyer as a witness, 238
Lost wills, 190, 197

Mutual wills, 17, 179
Negative will, validity of, 375
Pour-over will, 296
Self-proved, 135
Simultaneous death, 274
Statute of wills, 128, 173
Statutory wills, 68, 70
Tangibles, list of, 295
Testamentary capacity, 219
Undue influence,
        Generally, 231
    Combined with lack of capacity, 233
    Confidential relationship, defined, 4
    Duress, 234
    Lawyers, 239
    Portion of will affected, 232
    Presumptions, 235
    Test of, 231

WORKERS' COMPENSATION
Defined, 29

WRONGFUL DEATH
Defined, 29
Recovery, entitlement to, 75
Survival claims, contrast, 77